The Correspondence
of John Bartram

The Botanist. From Howard Pyle, "Bartram and his garden," *Harper's New Monthly Magazine* 60 (February 1880): 321–30.

The Correspondence of

JOHN BARTRAM

1734–1777

Edited by
Edmund Berkeley and Dorothy Smith Berkeley

University Press of Florida
Gainesville Tallahassee Tampa Boca Raton
Pensacola Orlando Miami Jacksonville

Copyright © 1992 by the Board of Regents
of the State of Florida
Printed in the U.S.A. on acid-free paper

Library of Congress Cataloging-in-Publication Data
Bartram, John, 1699–1777.
[Correspondence]
The correspondence of John Bartram, 1734–1777
/edited by Edmund Berkeley and Dorothy Smith
Berkeley.
p.   cm.
Includes bibliographical references and index.
ISBN 0-8130-1123-X
1. Bartram, John, 1699–1777—Correspondence.
2. Botanists—United States—Correspondence.
3. Naturalists—United States—Correspondence.
I. Berkeley, Edmund.   II. Berkeley, Dorothy
Smith.   III. Title.
QK31.B3A4   1992
508.73—dc20   91-36371

The University Press of Florida is the scholarly
publishing agency of the State University System
of Florida, comprised of Florida A&M University,
Florida Atlantic University, Florida International
University, Florida State University, University
of Central Florida, University of Florida,
University of North Florida, University of South
Florida, University of West Florida.

Orders for books should be addressed to University
Press of Florida, 15 NW 15th Street, Gainesville, FL
32611.

This work is dedicated to Nesta and Joseph Ewan, whose lifelong dedication to the study of the history of American botany, and whose generous assistance to others so engaged, has been an inspiration to many.

CONTENTS

List of Illustrations viii

Acknowledgments ix

Editors' Introduction xi

The Correspondence 1

*Appendix I. Bartram's descriptions
of North American forest trees
and shrubs 777*

*Appendix II. Bartram's notes
in the Medicina Britannica 780*

Glossary of Names 784

Bibliography 792

Index 798

ILLUSTRATIONS

frontispiece *The Botanist*
page 5 Peter Collinson
  15 Joseph Breintnall's snakeroot
  32 James Logan
  39 Rattlesnake charming a rabbit
  69 Bartram's house
  98 William Byrd II
100 John Custis
161 George Whitfield
203 Cadwallader Colden
227 J. F. Gronovius
231 John Fothergill
294 Carolus Linnaeus
314 The Delaware Water Gap
326 Moses Bartram
326 Young Billy Bartram
426 Benjamin Franklin
464 Bartram's house and garden
502 Bartram coat of arms
526 Bartram's letter to Peter Templeman
542 Henry Bouquet
569 Mastodon
602 Indians talk with Colonel Bouquet
660 Picolata
671 Henry Laurens
690 Benjamin Rush

ACKNOWLEDGMENTS

PERMISSION TO PUBLISH the following here included was graciously given by a number of institutions through their librarians or others charged with the care of their manuscript collections. We wish to express our appreciation of this courtesy, and our indebtedness both to the institutions for granting permission and to their representatives for their very helpful assistance and encouragement. Our most sincere thanks go to each and all of the following: Academy of Natural Sciences of Philadelphia, Karen D. Stevens, manuscripts/archives Librarian; American Philosophical Society, Beth Carroll-Horrocks, Manuscripts Librarian; Beinecke Rare Book and Manuscript Library, Yale University, Vincent Giroud, curator of Modern Books and Manuscripts; Boston Public Library, Laura V. Monti, Keeper of Rare Books and Manuscripts; British Library, Ann Payne, curator, The Manuscript Collections; Chicago Historical Society, Corey Seeman, assistant curator; College of Physicians of Philadelphia, Thomas A. Horrocks, director of the library; Friends Historical Library of Swarthmore College, J. William Frost, director; Gray Herbarium Archives, Harvard University, Jean R. Boise, reference and archives librarian; Haverford College, Diana F. Peterson, manuscripts cataloger; Historical Society of Pennsylvania, Maria A. Hall, collections manager, and Louise T. Jones, assistant curator, Manuscripts and Archives; Hunt Institute for Botanical Documentation, Carnegie-Mellon University, Anita L. Karg, archivist; Laboratoire de Phanérogamie, Muséum National d'Histoire Naturelle, Paris, G. G. Aymonin, sous-directeur; Library Company of Philadelphia, John C. Van Horne, librarian; Linnean Society of

London, Gina Douglas, librarian and archivist; Natural History Museum, London, Rex E. R. Banks, head of Library Services; New York Historical Society, Jean Ashton, acting librarian; New York Public Library, Wayne Furman, Office of Special Collections; Royal Society, London, K. Moore, archivist; Royal Society for the Encouragement of Arts, Manufactures, and Commerce, London, Jacqueline Judge, library and records administrator; Royal Swedish Academy of Sciences, Stockholm, Christer Wijkström, librarian, Department of Manuscripts; City of Salford Arts and Leisure Department, Salford, England, T. Ashworth, local history librarian; Smith College, Alison M. Scott, assistant curator of rare books; Universitetsbiblioteket, Uppsala, Sweden, Carl-Otto von Sydow, keeper of manuscripts; Yale University Press, Ann S. Bujalski, rights and permissions.

In addition to the above institutions and individuals we wish to express our special thanks to Pauline M. Page, microphotographer at the Alderman Library, University of Virginia, for all that she did to help us with the illustrations that we have used.

It was obvious to us that whoever was given the assignment of preparing this manuscript for a printer, and whoever had to do the printing, would be faced with very serious problems. The lack of punctuation (requiring very careful spacing), the many oddities of spelling and capitalization, and other peculiarities of the letters would present serious difficulties. We are pleased to express our indebtedness to Deidre Bryan, our editor at the University Press of Florida, and Peirce Graphics in Stuart, Florida, who did the typesetting, for what we feel has been a superb job. It has been a real pleasure to work with Miss Bryan on our 1,089 pages of typescript. Her patience and unfailing good humor have been a delight. If any errors have crept in they are not to be blamed on her.

E.B. and D.S.B.

EDITORS' INTRODUCTION

*T*HE BOTANIST JOHN BARTRAM is a familiar figure to those who study the history of American science in the eighteenth century. Readers of these letters may, however, find a short account of his early life and family background helpful in understanding and appreciating them.

He was born at Darby, Pennsylvania, near Philadelphia. His grandparents John and Elizabeth Bartram were among the many English Quakers who followed William Penn to Pennsylvania from England to avoid persecution. They came from the parish of Ashbourne, Derbyshire, in 1683, with their three sons, John, Isaac, and William, and a daughter, Mary. A second daughter, Elizabeth, was born at Darby. William married Elizah Hunt in 1696. Her parents had emigrated from Kent and acquired land in a region which earlier Swedish settlers had called Kingsessing, southwest of Philadelphia on the west bank of the Schuylkill River.

The future botanist was born to Elizah and William Bartram on May 23, 1699. A second son, James, was born in 1701. Since Elizah died soon after the birth of James, her sons lived with their father, grandmother, aunt Elizabeth, and uncle Isaac. Their grandfather had died in 1696. William remarried in 1707, his bride being Elizabeth Smith, daughter of a neighbor. William had acquired 100 acres of land from his father and had purchased an additional 350 acres. The remaining 200 acres of the family farm had been deeded by their father to William's brother, Isaac. The latter died unmarried in 1708, leaving the family farm to his mother for her lifetime and to William's son John upon her death.

William Bartram did not long devote himself to farming either his own land or the family farm after his remarriage. Instead, he left his wife and their small daughter, Elizabeth, and went to North Carolina in search of more land. There he acquired two tracts on Bogue Sound, Bath County (now Carteret), in December 1709. Soon afterward he returned to Pennsylvania to conduct his wife and daughter to their new home. While in Pennsylvania he made a will directing the sale of his land there, with the money from the sale to be divided between his sons, John and James. A third son, William, was born in North Carolina in 1711. Very soon after the birth of William, his father was one of many people killed when settlers were attacked by Tuscarora Indians. Elizabeth and her two children were among those made captives. They were later rescued and returned to Pennsylvania.

By his own later accounts, John Bartram was a delicate child, inclined to be timid and particularly fearful of thunderstorms. With other children of the neighborhood he attended a small Quaker school not far from his home. His only formal education was obtained there; little is known about it, but there is no doubt that it was thorough as far as it went. He later commented that he had an early interest in physic, particularly its botanical aspects. He became an avid reader but had little access to scientific works.

On April 25, 1723, John married Mary Maris, whose family had come from Worcestershire to Pennsylvania in 1683. Shortly after their marriage, John's grandmother died. He then acquired title to the family farm which he had long helped to run. Until he reached the age of twenty-one his financial affairs had been under the jurisdiction of the Orphans Court. He was now twenty-four, an experienced farmer and the owner of substantial property for a young man. A son, Richard, was born on March 24, 1724, and a second son, Isaac, in November 1725. Mary died in 1727 and their son Richard soon afterward, leaving John with his three-year-old son Isaac.

Perhaps because of these tragedies, John bought land at Kingsessing on which there was a small house. He enlarged the house, quarrying the stone for the construction and doing the work himself, and it is still standing today. He later purchased additional land and, in his lifetime, built five stone houses. In 1729 he married again; his bride was Ann Mendenhall, whose parents had come from Suffolk in 1686. John and Ann made their home at Kingsessing, leasing the old home place. It was well that John had enlarged the house, because soon little Isaac was joined by James (1730), Moses (1732), Elizabeth (1734, died in infancy), Mary (1736), twins, Elizabeth and William (1739), Ann (1741), John (1743), and Benjamin (1748). John had very definite ideas about the rearing of children, as will appear in his letters to them.

A variety of family affairs required that John go to Philadelphia from time to time. Even as a young man he became well known in the city, particularly among the merchants. One of the latter was Joseph Breintnall, whose family, like John's, had come from Derbyshire. They shared an interest in plants. In 1733 Breintnall was absorbed in the ancient hobby of making leaf impressions. John, having an extensive acquaintance with local plants, was able to assist him in collecting and identifying them. Friends of Breintnall brought visitors to see his collection of impressions. Among these was Dr. Samuel Chew (1693–1743), who had moved to Philadelphia from Maryland in 1732. They had a mutual friend in London, Peter Collinson, to whom Breintnall sent some of his impressions.

Collinson was a woolen draper who conducted a great deal of business with the colonists and had a number of correspondents in Philadelphia. He was an avid gardener, obsessed with introducing foreign plants to his garden at Peckham, in Surrey. His shipping of goods necessitated that he have an extensive acquaintance with ship captains, many of whom tried to assist him with his hobby. He made use of all contacts in his effort to obtain new plants. Both his business contacts and his membership in the prestigious Royal Society of London provided him with many contacts with prominent people. The introduction of new plants not only provided him with interesting items to report to the Royal Society, but proved also to be a social asset. Gardening was becoming popular in England among those who could afford large and impressive gardens.

Collinson knew that there were vast numbers of interesting plants in North America unknown in England. Numerous friends promised to send him seeds or plants, and some did so, but he was frustrated in his attempts to obtain an impressive number. By 1733 he had become convinced that he needed to find a man in the colonies with some knowledge of plants, who could be persuaded to make collections for him on a mutually beneficial basis. He sought help from Dr. Samuel Chew, whom he had apparently known in London. Chew unhesitatingly recommended John Bartram, and Collinson wrote to him. Their 1733 correspondence has not survived, but a surprising amount of that which followed has done so, and forms the basis for this volume.

The importance of Bartram's correspondence as a commentary on eighteenth-century American history was first recognized by William Darlington (1782–1863), physician and botanist. It had been placed in his hands by Bartram's granddaughter Ann, daughter of his son John, and her husband, Colonel Robert Carr, who had inherited Bartram's house and garden when Ann's father died in 1812. Darlington had previously obtained the correspondence of Bartram's kinsman Humphry Marshall. In 1849 he published *Memorials of John Bartram and Humphry Marshall,* a compilation of much of the correspondence of both men. In his "Advertisement," or introduction, he explained how he came to obtain the correspondence, commenting about the Bartram papers: "These ancient manuscripts were not only jumbled together in a chaotic mass, but were generally much injured by time, and many of them scarcely legible; so that it required no little care and patient perseverance to decipher and arrange them." He welcomed the opportunity to help preserve part of this correspondence and hoped that the originals might eventually "pass into the safekeeping of the Pennsylvania Historical Society, and thus be handed down to a curious and grateful posterity." What he hoped came to pass. The letters are today preserved with care by the society, and thus were available for this study. In the years since Darlington wrote, there has been some loss of legibility. It is, however, remarkable that most of the letters can still be read and could be reproduced here to a great extent intact. In fact, it has been possible to include, in a great many cases, portions of letters which Darlington omitted.

Darlington dealt only with those letters which the family had given him. He was able to transcribe approximately 298 of them in his book. Few, if any, publications have been as widely used by students of the history of botany in the United States, and their commentary on many other subjects has been of the greatest interest to others. These were, however, only a part of Bartram's correspondence. A number of libraries in the United States and elsewhere have preserved other parts of it; perhaps Darlington's work has been partly responsible for this. In any event, we were able to assemble from twenty-five libraries more than 300 additional letters to and from Bartram, in the course of our research for his biography, *The Life and Travels of John Bartram* (1982). Sharing Darlington's conviction that the correspondence should be enjoyed by posterity, we felt impelled to integrate all of these additional letters with those he published and make them available.

Before undertaking the editing of Bartram's correspondence we had devoted many years to the research required in writing not only his biography but, earlier, those of his friends John Clayton, Alexander Garden, and John Mitchell. We had, of course, obtained copies of as many of their letters as we were able to locate in numerous libraries in this country, and a number elsewhere during three summers spent abroad. Far more of Bartram's correspondence has survived than has that of the other three men. Although these letters provided us with much of the information required for biography, we became convinced that others would enjoy, as we had done, the letters themselves. In addition to Darlington's 1849 book, Edward E. Wildman had prepared an extensive, unpublished manuscript of many of the letters in the 1930s which is now deposited in the library of the American Philosophical Society. But the complete correspondence had never been published.

After much thought we convinced ourselves that we had some obligation to undertake what we knew would involve a great deal of hard, but enjoyable, work. It has taken eight years, with numerous interruptions. We wanted to present the letters chronologically and as nearly as possible exactly as they had been written, without alteration of spelling, capitalization, punctuation, or other aspects characteristic of the author's writing, and we have attempted to do so.

Bartram's writing, as he sometimes commented, was often done by candlelight after a hard day's work. Let those of us who find letter writing a chore reflect upon his problems. He wrote each letter twice, keeping the first draft and mailing the second. It must be kept in mind that letters received by Bartram will be presented as they were received by him, whereas most of his to others are derived from the copies which he retained. He kept his copies apparently because many months might elapse before he received a reply. In some cases it has been possible to compare his first draft with the letter he actually sent; naturally, the latter is more polished. The reader will note that the copy sometimes lacks a signature.

As noted in our introduction, Darlington found that some of the letters made available to him were badly faded or eroded. Some of these are probably more so today, but the remarkable fact is that a large percentage of them are still reasonably legible. There were, of course, some that we were unable to read, or which we could only read in part. In those cases we have used the rendition of Darlington or Wildman, if they had been more successful. Faded portions of some letters, which neither they nor we succeeded in reading, required that illegibility be indicated in our rendition. The frequent lack of punctuation at the end of a sentence, and the failure to capitalize the initial word of the following sentence, required that we leave an additional space to provide a break in continuity. Peculiarities of capitalization, spelling, and punctuation were by no means limited to Bartram's letters; many of his correspondents were also erratic. Italics in the body of a letter indicates underlining by the letter writer.

We have used several abbreviations: BP indicates the Bartram Papers of the Historical Society of Pennsylvania; D. denotes the page, or pages, in Darlington's *Memorials*; and LPCC, the *Letters and Papers of Cadwallader Colden*.

An attempt has been made to identify the many persons mentioned in the letters, other than ship captains. When we were successful we included these persons in the glossary of names at the end of the book, or in a footnote. In general, the names in the glossary are those that appear frequently in the letters.

Some readers may wish that we had attempted to identify the many plants mentioned. To them we say that botanists who wish to identify a plant with any degree of accuracy and confidence want a specimen typical of the plant to examine. To attempt to identify one from sketchy comments in old letters is highly speculative. We have chosen not to do so.

E.B. and D.S.B.

THE CORRESPONDENCE

To PETER COLLINSON[1]

Philadelphia, July 17, 17[33/]34

Mr. Collinson,

Near *German Town,* about six miles from this City, we found a *Rattle Snake,* which is now become a Rarity so near our Settlements. I took it home and dissected it. In the head I met with what has not been observed before by any, that I remember: that is a Cluster of Teeth on each side of the upper Jaw, at the root of the great Fangs, thro' which the Poison is ejected — I observed in the same case, that the two main Teeth were Sheath'd, in which lay four others at the root of each Tooth in a cluster together, of the same Shape and Figure with the great ones; and I am apt to think for the same use and purposes: if by accident the main Teeth happen to be broken; as was the fellow to this that I send you. May not these Clusters of Teeth be placed to supply such a defect successively, for the support and defence of this Creature?

I am not certain whether this is an uncommon case:[2] Perhaps others have not dissected the head of this Animal with the same care that I have done. I wish you would make Inquiry about it, which will oblige yours

John Bartram

Royal Society of London Archives, LBC 22.94. Printed in their *Philosophical Transactions* 41 (1740):358–59.
1. There are two copies of this letter, the first being the secretary's copy in a bound volume in which Bartram was spelled "Bertram." The second, in another bound volume, had variations which seem to be more as Bartram would have written it; we have used the second, since Bartram's original is missing.
2. All snakes have reserve fangs to replace the functional pair if lost.

From COLLINSON

Londn – January 24, 1734/35[1]

My Good Frd
John Bartram

I am very much oblig'd to thee for thy Two Choice Cargos of plants which Came very Safe & in good Condition, & are very Curious & Rare & Well worth my Acceptance. I am very sensible of the great pains & many Tiresome Trips to Collect so many Rare plants scattered att a distance. I shall not forget It: but in some measure to show my Gratitude, tho' not In proportion to thy Trouble I have sent thee a small token a Callico gown for thy wife & some odd Little things that may be of use amongst the Children & family [illegible] they come in a box of Books to my Worthy frd. Jos Breintnall with another parcel of Waste paper which will serve to wrap up seeds &c and there is Two Quires of Brown & one of whited Brown paper, which I propose for this use & purpose & will save thee a great deal of Trouble in writeing — That Is when thee Observes a curious plant in

Flower, or when the gathers seed of a plant thee has an Intention to Convey Mee a Description of on both these Occasions thee has nothing More to do than to gather branches or spriggs of the plants, then in Flower with their Flowers on and with their Seed Vessels fully Form'd for by these Two charistics the genus is known that they belong too.

Then Take these and spread them between the sheets of Brown paper Laying the Stems Straight & Leaves Smooth & Regular & when this is Done, putt a Moderate weight on a Board the size of the paper — in Two Days Remove the specimens into the other Quire of brown paper, keeping the Weight on & then In a week or Two, being pretty well Dryed —

Convey them thence into the Quire of Whited Brown paper: Thus when now & then thee observes a Curious odd plant, thee may Treat it in this manner by which thee will convey a more Lively idea than the best Description, & when thee Gathers Seeds Mark the same Number on the Seeds, as thee marks It in the Sheet, where the Specimen Is, — only writeing under it, the Country Name. So once a year, Return Mee the Quire of Whited Brown paper with the dryd Specimens Tied Fast between Two Broad Boards — & then I will send some more in their Roome. When the sheet of paper will hold it, putt one, Two or Three Specimens, of the same plant in the same sheet, so they will but Lay Smooth by each other —

Besides what I have further to propose per this Methode is thy own Improvement in the knowledge of plants, for thou shall send mee another Quire of Duplicates of the Same Specimens. I will gett them nam'd by our most knowing Botanists & then Returne them again — which will Improve thee more then Books for it is impossible for any one Author to give a General History of plants. Lett the Specimens be the Length of the Paper

Thee cans't not think how well the Little Case of plants came, being putt under the Captains Bed & Saw not the Light till I sent for it, but then Capt. Wright had a very Quick passage — & it was putt on board In a Right Month for when plants are down in the Ground & in the Mid-Winter Months they may be Stow'd any where but it must not be attempted any Time this side Xmas — the Warmth of the ship & Want of Air had Occasion'd the Skunk Weed to putt Forth Two fine Blossoms, very beautiful it is of the Arum Genus, the Cedum is a very rare pretty plant, the Leaves finely Vein'd   it came very fresh & green   thy Herb Two pence was very Acceptable   I have had it formerly — but I lost It, it is a pretty plant —

the Cane Wood is pretty common in our Gardens   It goes Here by the name of the Virginian Guelder Rose.   the Two Laurells was very Fresh & lively & the shrub Honesuckles, which I have had formerly from So Caroliny   flower very fine but in Two or Three years went off, neither our soil or Climate agreed with It but yours phaps from the Northward may do better —

the Laurell & shrub Honesuckle are plants I much Value, I wish att a proper season Thee would procure a strong Box 2 feet square & about 15 or 18 inches Deep — but a foot Deep in Mould will be Enough — Then Collect half a Dozen Laurells & half a Dozen shrub Honesuckles, & plant in this Box but be sure to make the bottome of the Box full of Large Holes, & cover the Holes with Tiles or oyster shells to Lett the Water draine better off, then Lett this box stand in a proper place in thy Garden for Two or Three years till the plants have taken good Root & made Good Shoots — but thee must be Care full to Water it in Dry Weather

I wish that thee would not fail to putt 3 or 4 Specimens of the sprigs of the Laurell with the flowers fully Blown (for I Long to see it) in the paper Transferring them from one to another as I have Directed — as my Designe is not to give thee More Trouble so a few Specimens will Content Mee. I have Further to Request thee to putt up a Little Box of plants (yearly) In Earth, Such as thou finds in the Woods that are odd & uncommon

Peter Collinson (1694–1768). Courtesy of the Linnean Society of London.

What Thee Observes of the Frost, to be sure, had the Effect thee Discribes, I once Remember one like it in England but the Effects was not so Severe — I hope next year thee will be Able to make some Collections that may make thee some Returns —

The White Flowering Bay is a plant that grows in Moist places — the Leaves are Long of a 'Bay' shape and of a Silver Colour on the back of the Leaves. It bears a fine Large white flower like the Water Lillie of a Fine perfum'd Smell which is succeeded with a Seed Vessel of a Cone-like Figure, I have a plant that Flowers finely in my Garden   It is in abundance of places in Maryland but weither it is found more northward I can't say, It is a fine plant to adorn thy own Garden but give thy self no trouble about It and as the Firr and Cypress cones are not found near thee, we will wait for some more favourable opportunity to Collect them, Send First Those Seeds that are near thee —

The Box of seeds came very safe & in Good Order. thy Remarks on them are very Curious but I think take up to much of thy Time & Thought — I would not make my Correspondence Burdensome but must Desire thee to continue the same Collections over again — & to prevent Trouble only number the papers & give the Country Name or any name thee may know it by   Again, then keep a List of them by thee with ye number to the Names — & when they come Here those that do not come up, Wee have only to write to Thee for the same seed to such a number to send over again as I Design to make a present of part of these seeds to a very curious p'son[2]   I hope to procure thee some present for thy trouble of Collecting. I am thy very sincere friend,

P. Collinson

Historical Society of Pennsylvania Library, Bartram Papers, 2:9 (hereafter, BP); William Darlington, *Memorials of John Bartram and Humphry Marshall* (Philadelphia, 1849; facs. ed., New York: Hafner, 1967), 63–65 (hereafter, D.).
1. The year is not now legible in the date of this letter. We believe it to have been 1734/35, and the oldest surviving letter from Collinson to Bartram.
2. Lord Petre.

From COLLINSON

February 12, 1734/5

To Observe   Never to take any of the Butterflie kinde, but with the (Rackit Netts) & when you have taken them between the netts, press your forefinger naile against the brast of the flie, softer or harder as Ocasion, which will imeadiatly stop the flie from fluttering, but must be prest so hard – till you perceave the bones crack, & shee will soone die, then put a pin through her by wich you may move her where you please, but allways be carefull not to touch her with nothing but the nets for in so doing you take of those fine particles of maile or Downe which make her Beautifull, further be shure allways to make use of as Small a pin as the Size of the flie does require by reason a large pin takes of part of the sight, by wch a part of the Beauty of the flie is lost, another thing to be observ'd, allways Stick a Butterflie with her underside Upermost, for if shee is pin'd thro the out side, shee in dying will Close her wings that you can't take hold of the pin to move her   As for the Beetles or Scaly flie kinde, the method here is to put them into any Sort of Spirit which will soon kill them, but be shure allways to preserve Every Leg and horn of these as well as the flies above

As for moths which are flies with large pulpy Bodys and generally fly in the night, it is very difficult to take any of them perfect, but if you meet with any the method is, Stick your pin thro them as they stand proper, by which You may take them up & to kill take hold of their Chest, or brest, with your thumb & fore finger Naile, & pinch them hard & Close holding them for the Space of 2 or 3 Minnets, which will make them Sick & take their Strength away, but they will be much longer dying than the Butterflie kinde, if you have an Opertunity heat the End of a fine wire red hot, & push it into the brest Slantways towards the head, which is A much Quicker way of Killing them, but the only way to have these moths as well as Butterflies in perfection, is to seek for Catterpillers & keep them feeding on the Leaves or whatever they are found feeding upon till they Change to a Chrysalis, or Dormant State, which all flies ly in for some time (between the Catterpiller & the flie) & then you will take them in perfection haveing not flown to shake of any of those particles, of which their Beauty consists, when you have taken any flies or Beetles of any kinde after thay are dead cure them well before a Moderate fire, otherwise they are liable to be Eaten by a Small insect (hardly perceavible) that preys on the Carcases of all pulpy body'd flies, a Small Quantatiy of Camphore put into the box with the flies is a good Antidote, against those devouring Insects.

Your Seasons being so different from ours, otherwise I could give you some instructions for the finding of the Chrysalis, both of the Butterflies & Moths (first) when you find Catterpillers have don feeding, and are not seen on the trees plants &c: by the help of a Trowell or such like instrument digg round the foot of the trees, such as willow, poplar, Elm or any other trees you think most likely for Catterpillers to feed on, about 2 or 3 inches deep & half a foot in circumferemce where you will finde, the Chrysalis of the Catterpillers that fed on the same, take them home put them in Mould, covering them that they don't fly away, when they come out of the Shell, & by this means You will have them in the utmost perfection, this instruction is chiefly for the moth kinde, the Butterflie Catterpillers go into Chrysalis, but thay generally tye themselves up under the Copeings of walls, or sides of pales, houses or under leaves &c but never are to be found in the Ground as the Moth Chrysalis are — if you send any flies beetles &c into England take Care to Stick them very Secure, for if one Should Chance to be loose, in Shakeing, he would Spoile the whole box, another thing I must advise, to Endevour to take or breed, Severall of a Sort, by which means there may be some very good & perfect[1]

The Methode of Takeing a Fly with the Netts is to Observe when Shee settles on a Leafe, flower or Twigg & then go Gently with a nett in Each Hand Claping one under the Leafe & the other over so press them Close, then without moveing from the place Squeeze or press the Fly as Direct'd & thrust the pin through Her & then she is taken to pin her in a box.

Good Friend

The Intention of these Directions are not to Engage thee in the pursuits of this affair on purpose or to take thee from thy Business – Butt as it Occationally happens, when Thee goes abroad Into the Woods & Fields or any Journey or other Business – [illegible]   It is but to take the Netts which are Light in a Bagg & hang by thy Girdle or Cross thy shoulder under thy upper Coat & take a few pins & a Box in thy pockett & if any thing presents take it, & pin it fast in the Box & so thee may Carry it Miles with Safety & when thee comes Home Dispose it in a Larger Box as my Friend Directs, to give thee a Little Idea of the Matter I have sent thee 2 Moths & 5 Flys of our English sort — a Collection is very fine and it is amazeing to see the wonderfull works of the Almighty Creator in these Lower Class of Being — the Black & Gold Fly Thee sent is a Most Elegant Creature   pray if thee can procure 1 – 2 or 3 or 4 as just it Happens I think thee has but one from [illegible]   If thee has any Little Boyes or Girls teach them this Work & Wee will well Reward them   Wee have some in England very Dextrous

BP 2:80.
1. The first part of the letter is not in Collinson's handwriting. His begins at this point.

From COLLINSON

Lond: March 1, 1734/35[1]

Kind Friend
John Bartram

I am Just Returned to Town from paying a Visit to a Noble Lord my most Valuable & Intimate Friend,[2]   One of my proposals I sent thee last year to Collect the Seeds of your Forest Trees was for Him, as He is a universal Lover of plants. I presented him with a share of the seeds thou sent Last Year wch was very Acceptable as he is a Man of a Noble & Generous spirit, He very Rationally considered thy pains & Trouble in Collecting them & Desired to make thee Some Returns, & left it to Mee, I thought a good Suite of Cloths for thy own Wear might be as Acceptable as anything So have sent thee One with all appurtenances necessary for its makeing up — which I hope will Meet with thy approbation & help in some Measure to Compensate for thy Loss of Time —

My Noble Friend Desires thee to Continue the Same Collections — Send the Same Sorts Over Again & what new ones happens in thy Way & sent att the same time a year & in the same Manner — will do very Well — please to look in my other Letter for my further remarks on this head   all the seeds was in good order Except the All Spice Seed which was musty, phaps that was owing to the Dampness of the Roots put up for Sr Hans Sloane, for the future putt up no Moist thing with the seeds but send them in a Little Box by themselves.

If thee can compass to send 30 or 40 sorts of your Herbaceous Seeds every year it will be sufficient, as to Invoice of Forest Tree seeds their Quantity & price is fix'd so thee knows what thee does — thee has had great Luck heitherto In sending the seeds in Good Order — I hope the like will attend thee in Forest Tree Seeds, I Refer thee to My Letters on that Head sent with ye Catalogue.

As Our Noble Friend will be always Gratefull I hope it will Encourage thee to go on — but yett I would have thee so proceed as not to Interfere with thy publick Business, Indeed the Forest Tree Seeds I hope will bring Money into thy pocket so the time spent in makeing ye Collection cannot be Said to be Lost or Misspent.

There is Inclosed 3 Sorts of Seeds which happened to be Mislaid, but if they fail I will Endeavour to Recruite ano'r year.

I hope thee hath mine per Capt Richmond with a pcell in the Library Companys Trunk & a Box of seeds in sand per Richmond —

I heartily wish thee & thine Health & Prosperity & am thy Real frd

P Collinson

Pray give no body a hint how thee or thy wife cam by the suit of Clothes. There may be some with you may think they deserve something of that nature.

The Druget[3] is pack up in Brown paper Directed for thee to the Care of Jos Breintnall in a Case of Goods of Capt. Wrights

If thee Observes any curious Insects, Beetles, Butterflies &c they are Easily preserved being pin'd through the body to the Inside of a Little Box when it is full send it nail'd up & put nothing within it & they will Come very Safe   Display the Wings of the Butterflies with pins & rub off the Down as Little as possible   when thee goes abroad putt a little Box in thy pocket and as thee meets with the Insects putt them in and then stick them in the other Box when thee gets home

I want a Terapin or Two   Putt them in a box with Earth & they will come safe   They will live a long while without food

BP 2:12; D. 69–70.
1. The date of this letter on the original is no longer legible; it was dated by Darlington.
2. Lord Petre.
3. A coarse cloth usually made of a mixture of wool and linen.

From COLLINSON

March 31, 1735

Dr. John —

I hope before this Comes to hand that thee has Recd the Drugett suite which Capt Wright pack'd up in his pcell & was Directed for thee (My Noble Friend) that sent It Desires thee to go gently on & he will not Forgett thee   I refer thee to my Former Letters   thee knowest what will please Mee   I am afraid it will be too Late   however I will Venter to send the Inclosed seeds; they are but lately arrived so could not come sooner I heartily wish thee Health & prosperity & am thy Real frd

P Collinson

I question wether the Cypress will be without shelter [until] after the first year for which reason it may be best to putt some in a Box or Tub to be removed in Doors in cold weather & sow some in a Warm South Border If thee have a Mind may Venter to sow the [illegible] & Onions but it will be to Late for the Radish   Make much of the Green & Brown Cole   sow half this spring & half next spring   it is a very hardy Winter Green comes from Germany — when the Flower appears in a bud in the Middle it is Fitt to eat   Lett some run to Seed

BP 2:14.

From COLLINSON

LONdn June 19th: 1735

Dr Friend
J:Bartram

I was well pleased with thine of March 2d & am glad to heare that Some of the Seeds was Acceptable   I shall Endeavour to Send what I can in thy List but as they grow very Wide from London I can't propose to Send all but when I make Excursions into the Country shall Endeavour to be Mindfull as they fall in my way.

This year Better Luck attends thy seeds   a great many are Come up and are very Curious but thee art not to wonder if Some Fail which is principally for want of your Heat tho' Wee Endeavour to supply that Defect with Hott beds — which are precarious without manag'd with Great Skill, to be sure the natural Heat & Soil is most suitable for Vegitation   If with Care a 3d part Grows it is Well —

please to Go On Collecting as Seeds happens to be in thy Way, only Observe to Number them as I before observed & make a Name to that Number that thee may know them by & then Wee shall only write for those that Miscarry, but this is the further to be Observed that Some Seed Come not up the first year, as Several of those thee first sent Mee are Come up this Spring   thee Observes you have a Linaria & Mullen grows wild with you, if you have variety of Sorts pray Send Some of Each   Phaps it may be Different   Now my Kind Frd I come to give thee some Account of the Tub of plants p Captain Wright, which being sent in a right Season Succeeded well & gives Mee great pleasure. I have Six Sorts of the Ferns &c grows Some are very different from ours   I admire them much   I have the Cluster and thorough Leafd Solomon's Seal   grows Well   So doth both Sorts of Hellebore, the small kind is new & very Curious as also the Dittany and Golden Rod, the Dragon & Indian Turnip   both grows & are fine plants   the Skunk Weed putt forth 2 fine Blossoms   The Laurells, Dwarfe Service & HoneSuckle thrive Well and are fine plants   pray Send Mee 2 or 3 HoneSuckles   there is Different Colours   Some are Deep Red & Pale Red Flowers but the Sedum so finely Vein'd in the Leaves is a very Ticklish plant, will neither grow in the Shade or in Our Sun — it is a very pretty plant which I much admire & yett I am afraid Our Climate Will not Suite It when thee Sends Seeds Next send 2 or 3 plants & I will try different Ways the penny Wort I hope will Do — In so fine a Collection only Pocoons which I have but I want that with Double Flowers and the Devils Bitt or Blazeing Star which has faild & Smooth Leafe & Rough Leafe Solomons Seal — I shall only Observe when thee Sends another Tub of plants thee Make Holes in the bottome an Inch Diameter & Cover with Shells to Draine the Water — The Tub thee Sent was very Wett, & if the plants had Lain Long or had had Much Wett would be Rotted for Want of Larger Vents — please to Remember Red Lillie   Pray has thee again Mett with the Hermaphrodite Flower   I have Read of It p those that Describe North America — Should be glad to See the flower, but if that can't be please to Send Mee a Dry'd Specimen In paper as I formerly directed & the Flower of that pretty Wood Cedum — before Mentioned —

Any plants thee wants to know their Names Send over the Specimens & I will Return them nam'd —

I hope the Calamanco[1] & Druggett are Come to Hand & prove Acceptable — the First I sent to thee Care or Jos Breintnall & the Drugt in Capt Wrights Goods p Capt Reves —

Inclosed is a paper relateing to the Bite of the Rattle Snake   please to give Mee thy opinion of It —

There is no Doubt but Spruce, Firr & Pine Cones & their Variety, will be very acceptable & Do Well   I hope that this will prove a Good Seed Year

If any pretty Insects remember Mee   In a Box p Capt Wright is the following Roots   2 Cyclamens with Seed to them   Sow it Carefully   2 Squills   2 Male Peonys   Double pilewort   white Melody Gladiolus   double white Sarsfrage   Double Snow Drop   1 great Colchicum Hyacinths   Wood Anemones   Some Small bulbs of the Fiery Red Lillie & Divers Sorts of Seeds in the Sand   4 Hyacinths of Peru Lay uppermost in the Box   Variety of offsetts of Tulips   I have heard that your Severe Winters have killd the Cyclamins & Hyacinths of Peru   it may be Safest to plant in potts or tubs & house them in the Winter but if they are planted in the Ground It must be in the Warmest place, & pretty Deep & in the Winter Cover them Well with Pea Straw which I find better than any   the Squills come from a Warm Country   will not Endure Severe Cold but ought to [be] planted in Potts to be Housed the Winter or Else great Care of them the[y] Love to Grow in the Sea Sand with a Mixture of Light Rich Mould —

BP 2:16.
1. Calamanco, a shiny wool material with a checked or striped design woven in it.

From COLLINSON

June 28 1735

Frd Bartram

I had besides putt in the Box 2 doz ½ Ranunculas   In Severe Weather the beds should be Cover'd with a Good Heap of pea Straw but taken off in the Day if the Sun Shines to give them air   plant them in a South Shelter'd aspect, they must be taken up Ev'ry Year when the Leaves dries Away & planted again Early in the Spring — but these if there is the Least appearance of buding — must be presently planted — but if not putt them in a paper bag or box & keep them very Dry & Look often att them to see they don't Mould for that kills them and then plant them When the Severest of your Weather is Over —

Thine
P Collinson

BP 2:17.

From COLLINSON

Lond August 16th 1735

Kind Friend
John Bartram —

I had the pleasure of thine of June 13: & am pleased the things was Acceptable   I have sent the little Box of seeds to our Noble Friend, what he Raises I have always share of — The Large Invoice that I sent thee was for Him   I hope this will prove a good Seed Year that Thee may be able to send a Cargo — wch will produce thee some Money Here —

The Water Beach or Buttonwood Is known Here as the Western Plane & is in great plenty Here & makes a noble Tree   thee need not send any, for it is raised plentifully by Cuttings —

Butt as for the Linden or Lime Tree for aught I know may be a stranger so pray send some Seed —

There is two Captains, Richmond & Wright, whom I love & Esteem & will take Care of any thing for Mee   if it is a Suitable Time send what thee Canst per them — What is in Casks or Boxes tell them I will pay Freight for — but little Matters they are so kind to bring Free

I am Mightily pleased with thy Account of the Sugar tree — pray send Mee a Little Sprig with Two or Three leaves dried between a sheet of paper & if thee Canst the Blossom — Wee imagine Here It is a Poplar or Maple but when Wee see the Flower or Seed Vessel Wee shall soon Determine. The Red Shrub Honesuckle I have had from So Carolina   It flowered & throve well for 3 years & then went off   these are Ticklish plants & will not do unless they are Removed & Stand to be well Rooted before Wee have them — I never saw so Milk a white before — please to procure some of Each & plant them for Mee   Thou will have recourse to my former Letter   it is

Indeed an Instance on thy part of great Respect to keep them, that are much fitter for another Use   However I Except thy Love & Value thy Friendship

My valuable Friend John White[1] who is Curious in Our Way — Carried over the Best Collection of Pears that I believe ever came from England, if they come safe & thrive att my Desire He will oblige thee with Buds or scions att proper seasons   pray wait on Him with my Respects — & ask the favour —

As for Plums, Nectarines & apricots I may send thee some grafts in the Spring, but it is my Firme opinion if they was buded or grafted on Peach or Almonds which are Stocks that produce the juices freer than Any Other they would succeed much better   I should be glad thee'd Try that I may know the Event

If the Frost has such an Effect on yr Vines which I could scarcely Believe in so south a Latitude to us — you must do as they do in Germany   when the Frosts Sett in Dig Holes round the Vines & Lay the Last years shoots in & Cover them with Earth to preserve from the frosts & att Spring take them up again & then prune them for bearing — I am glad to Hear that the Medlar Grows   it is the Large Neapolitan Sort which produces a Large Fruite, Doc Witt att German Town wants it much. I sent Him some att the same time but whether he has any Luck I can't tell

I shall be Carefull to send the seeds thee Mentions & what others I can Collect.

My kind Friend, I heartily Wish thee & thy Good Wife Health & prosperity — I am thy Real frd

P Collinson

I have not Seen my Garden for Near Two Months haveing been a Long Journey In to Cornwall & Devonshire so that what Condition thy fine plants are I can't say

BP 2:16; D. 70–71.
1. Unidentified.

From COLLINSON

Sep 3d:1735

Frd Bartram

I have little to Say but to advise thee of my Welfare & Inclose some seed of the White Foxglove a Delicate fine plant & Rare   as soone as thou has the Seed, Scatter Some on the Ground without Covering, & very Lightly Cover Some of the Seed, it Loves an open Dry Soil — if thou have any thing to Send if it is suitable Lett it come p my good frd Capt Wright

I wish thee Health & am thine

P Collinson

I hope thou have the box p Wright   He or Capt Nath Coman & Capt Richmond will take Care of any thing for Mee

By any of the Above Captains please to send Mee a Terapin or Two the Largest the happens to Meet With   when it is a proper Season if they are putt in a Large Open half barrel with a Little Sand in the bottome, & a few Carrots or Turnip Roots to Live on I fancy they will Come safe   make holes in the bottome of the Barrel in Case of Sea Water or Rain that it may Dreine off

BP 2:19.

From COLLINSON

Londn Jany 1735/36

My Good frd.
John Bartram

I now do my Self a further pleasure to Consider thy Curious Entertaining Letters of [?]nber 6. I am only afraid In doing Mee a pleasure so much Time was loss'd which would turn to a more profitable account in thy own affairs.

Thee writes for some Botanical books and Indeed I am att a Loss which to recommend, for as I have observed a Compleat History of plants is not to be found in any author – for the present, I am pswaded the Gentle Men of the Library Company, att my Request will Indulge thee the liberty, when thee comes to Town to peruse their Botanical Books   there is Miller's Dicy[1] & some others

please to Remember those Solomons Seals, that Escaped thee Last year

The Great & Small Hellebore are great Rarities here so pray send a Root or Two of Each next year. please to Remember all your sort of Lillies as they happen in thy Way & your spotted Martigons will be very acceptable. the Divils Bitt or Blazeing Star pray send a Root or Two and any of the Lady Slippers.

My Dr. frd, I only mention these plants – but I beg of thee not to neglect thy more Material affairs to oblige Mee   a Great Many may be put in a Box 20 inches or Two feet square & 15 or 16 inches High: — and a foot in Earth is enough. this may be putt under the Capts bed or sett in the cabin, if it is sent in Octobr or Novembr. nail a few small Narrow Laths cross it to keep the Catts from Scratching It.

If thee could procure Some Layers of the Woody Vine, with Variegated Leaves it would be acceptable, also a Root of the Aristolochia which is of such sovereign Remedy for sore Breasts would be well worth haveing —

I hope Thee had Mine per Capt' Davis with a Box with seeds in sand, & 2 parcels of seeds per my Good Friend Isaac Norris, Jr.   one parcel I sent after Him to the Downs[2] but whether he was sail'd, or no, before it came to hand, I can say but by the List Inclosed, thee will know if they are Come to hand, or if He had them.

pray what is your Sarsaparilla   The May Apple is a pretty plant   is what I have had for some years sent Mee per Doctr. Witt. It Flowers well with us, but our summers are not Hot Enough to perfect its Fruite.

The pretty Humble Beautifull plant with a Spike of yellow Flowers I take to be a Species of Orchis or Satyrion, what sort of Root it has thee hath not mentioned. If it is taken up with the Earth about the Roots it will certainly flower the first if not the second year   I wish thee'd send Mee two or Three Roots if it is plenty —

The Ground Cypress is a singular pretty plant, if it bears berries or seeds pray send some — and if it bears flowers or seeds, pray send some specimens in both states.

pray send Mee a good specimen or Two of the shrub 3 foot High that grows by the Water Courses.

The Shrub that grows out of ye sides of Rocks sometime 5 or 6 foot high bearing Red Berries hanging by the Husks is Call'd Euonymus Spindle Tree

Joseph Breintnall's snakeroot. Courtesy of the Library Company of Philadelphia.

or Prick Wood   Wee have the same plant with a small Difference   Grows plenty in England.

Your wild Senna with yellow flowers is a pretty plant   Send seeds of both this & Mountain Goat's Rue.

Thee need not Collect any more of the White Thorn Berries that has prodigious long sharp Thorns. it is what Wee call the Cock spur Thorn. I had a Tree last year that had att least a Bushel of berries but Haws of any other sort of Thorns will be very acceptable.

pray send Mee a Root or Two of Cluster bearing Solomons Seal   it is in all appearance a very Rare plant as is the panax.

pray a Root or Two of Joseph Breintnal's Snake Root.

pray send a Root of the Grasse leaves that bears pretty little blew flowers that is good against obstructions of the bowells.

when it happens in thy Way send Mee a Root or Two of the Little Tuberous Root Call'd Divils bitt which produces one or Two Leaves Yearly

I only bearly Mention these plants — not that I Expect thee to send them. I don't Expect or Desire them, but as they happen to be found accidentally & what is not to be meet with one year, may be anor.

It happens that your Late Ships in the Autumn come away before a great many of our Seeds are Ripe & the spring I dont aprove as the best season to send them, but as it rarely happens otherwise, I have taken a Methode to send some in paper & some in sand   after thee has pick'd out the Largest which must be instantly sett for very probably they was Chilled comeing over, when It is my Case as it often happens takeing the following Methode I have raised a great many pretty plants out of your Earth — I lay out a bed 5 or 6 feet long by 3 feet Wide   then I pare off the Earth an Inch or two Deep   Then I Loosen the bottom and lay it very smooth again and thereon (if I may use the Term) I sow the sand and seed together as thin as I can — then I sift some good Earth over it about half an Inch thick — This bed ought to be In some place that It may not be Disturbed & kep'd very Clear from Weeds — for several seeds come not up till ye second year. I have put some Hard Shelled almonds of my own growth & some Soft Shell'd from Portugal: they are Easily distinguished   the almond Makes a fine pie taken whilst a pin can be run through them, for you eat Husk shell & kernel altogether — they must be first Codled over a gentle Fire & then putt in a Crust — I query whether your peaches wou'd be as good before the shell is hard.

I have putt in the sand some Vine Cuttings and some of the great Neapolitan Medlar which Wee always graft on White Thorns & so must you — as Soone as these Cuttings come to hand Soake them all over in Water for 24 hours & then plant the Vines (the Earth being well Loosen'd) as Deep as only the uppermost bud of the Cutting may be Level with the Earth. Water them in Dry Weather   these seldom fail growing. the Grafts after soaking may be laid in the Earth or in a Moist place Till grafted wch should be soone — I hope thee will take these Two Long Rambling Epistles in good part they are writt a bitt now & then, as business will permit. Lett Mee hear from thee att thy Leisure, which will much oblige thy Real frd

P Collinson

Sent to I Norris in the Downs
- pimpernella saxifraga
- galeaga Goats Rue
- Calamentha
- Caryophelata Avens

Pigellium Flea wood
Gordium
Imperatoria
Eryngium
Ferula galbanifera

Send a quantity of seed of the Birch or Black Beech; it seems to be new. Send Mee a good root of the Swallow-wort, or Apocinon, with narrow

Leaves & orange Coloured flowers, & of the pretty shrub call'd Red Root, and of the Cotton-weed or Life Everlasting & some more seed of the perannual Pea, that grows by rivers; this year, or next, or next after, as it happens. pray send Mee a walking-cane of the Cane-wood.

BP 2:8; D. 59–63.
1. Philip Miller's *Gardener's Dictionary.*
2. South-southeast coast of England.

From COLLINSON

Londn February 3d 1735/36

Dear Friend
John Bartram

I am vastly Obliged to thee for thy many kind Favours — which I shall answer in Course — but if it is Irregular, I can't help taking Notice of thine of the 18 9ber In which thee thinks I have neglected to take notice of thy Favour by young Israel Pemberton — which thee Certainly must misapprehend or Else my two Letters (in answer to that), per Capt Cox Augst 16 & per Capt Green are not come to hand for I keep a regular Account of Letters & by whom answered — so can't mistake. Thee should not suspect thy Friend but suspend thy Resentment till thee art Certainly informed how things happened. Thee may assure thyself thee shall not fail of Suitable and grateful returns from me. Phaps I may be slow but I am sure.

The Box of seeds by Israel came safe & was very acceptable to thy Noble Friend — The terrapins which I designed for him had bad luck. Some died others the sailors stole but Israel made all the amends he could & gave me one that he had. He is a very ingenious, kind, good-natured Lad —

I was pleased to hear the few things proved worth your acceptance   I hope this year to send thee something as a reward for thy trouble which is more than I can imagine but thee may felicitate thyself that the pains thee has taken is not for those who are insensible of it & who will make suitable returns, though not equal to thy deserts.

Thee writes for Cions of pears. If my good Friend John Whites Collection Came safe He has the best we have in England   no doubt for my sake he will Oblige thee with some Cions.

I never heard it was Insects that annoyed your plums Apricots & Nectarines   If they are att the Root, Water that has tobacco Leaves soaked in it will kill them by making a Bason round the tree & watering it frequently with this water.

I was amazed to hear that the Frost in your Latitude kills the vines in the Winter   You must use the German Method   Dig a Trench or hole close to your vine & therein Lay the young shoots & then cover them with Earth, wch protects them from the Frosts & when they are over, take them up again & prune them.

Pray how fares it with your wild Country vines — I am strongly of Opinion they will be best to make a vineyard because they are habituated to your seasons but then it will much Depend on the skill of the pson that chooses the Vines to propagate — When they are ripe a knowing pson in grapes should ride the woods where they grow & select out those that have good qualities as good bearers   best-flavoured fruit, large berries, close bunches, early ripeners & mark the trees so as to know them again & from these take cuttings for a vineyard — In all wild fruite there is a remarkable Difference — when these come to be cultivated (as all Fruites were once Wild & have been improved by culture) who knows but you may make as pretty a wine fit for your own drinking & to serve your West India neighbours — as Madeira or any other peticular country wine

I am pleased to hear the Medlar Grew. It is the great sort from Naples.

Please to remember as I formerly desired to get some strong plants of your Ivy or Bay that thee sent me some Specimens of & plant in a Box to Stand a year or two or three till it Flowers in the box, and some of your shrub White & Red Honesuckles — these are ticklish plants to keep Here —

I now come to answer thy kind letter of September 9th per Budget   I am pleased to hear thee art acquainted with Dr. Witt an old Correspondent of mine and has sent Mee Many a Valuable Curious plant but I am afraid the old Gentleman has been too cunning for thee. those fine Lady's Slippers which makes my mouth Water have slipped beside it. The Docr says He would have sent them Mee but that He was afraid they were spoiled in bringing home for want of proper Care to wet the roots by the way.

This accident brings to my mind a very pretty Method by which plants will keep fresh 3 or 4 days on a Journey – take 3 or 4 largest ox Bladders Cut off the Neck high & when a plant is found take it up with Little Earth to the roots, put this into the Bladder   then put water in the Bladder to Cover the Roots then tie up the neck of the bladder close round the stalk of the plant, leaving the Leaves, Flowers, &c without   Large plants won't do so well but several small plants may be put in a Bladder   When tied hang it to the pummel or skirts of the saddle or any other convenient way thee may choose   if the water wastes add more. Thus plants with little trouble may be kept a long while fresh. It is always best if water can be had to add it immediately at taking up the plants.

But these fine Lady's Slippers, don't let Escape, for they are my favourite plants. I have your yellow one that thrives well in my Garden but I much want the other sorts. pray show the Docr no More but I find thee has taken the hint thyself, don't say any thing I have writ   neither shall I take any notice of thine.

It is with pleasure when we read thy Excursions (& wish to bear thee Company) but then it is with concern that we reflect on the Fatigue the undergoes the great risks of thy Health in Heats & Colds but above all the Danger of Rattlesnakes. this would so curb my Ardent Desires to see vegitable Curiosities that I should be afraid to venter in your woods unless on Horseback & so Good a guide as thee art by my side.

Thy Expedition for the Curious Tree, in the Jerseys, Truly shows an Indefatigable Disposition in thee to oblige us here   I hope thee will not fail to find some Gratitude in us —

the seed is exceeding Fresh but such as I never saw before   of a pleasant tast some thing like Juniper berries — I wish thee had Discribed the Tree to us, but what would have saved thee that pains would have been to send us two or three Specimens of the Leaves or Branches of a size proper to Inclose between a sheet of paper & then have told us wether it sheds its Leaves or is an Evergreen & what blossoms it has. do not go on purpose but when ever thee goes that way pray procure some —

The Leaves of the Sugar Tree are very Informing and are a great Curiosity but Wee Wish thee had gather'd Little Branches with the flowers on them & some Little Branches with the keys on them. the seeds of this Tree which by the Leaves & keys is a Real Mapple   I cracked a many of them & not one has a kernel in them which I am surprised   whether they were not fully ripe, thee canst best Judge — but so it is — Wee must Desire thee next year to make another Attempt & Send us some Specimens — Its bearing white Blossoms is an Elegance above any other of this Tribe that I know off — for Wee have two sorts in England – a Major which is Comminly Here call'd the Sycamore and the other is a Minor less every way & both bear bunches of greenish Blossoms succeeded by keys like those thee sent.

From thy assured friend,
P. Collinson

BP 2:33; D. 85–88.

From COLLINSON

London, Feb. 12, 1735/36

Dear Frd:
John Bartram

Tho I am vastly Hurried in Business and no Leisure yett the many Instances or thy regard for us oblige Mee to steal Time to say something further to thy kind Letters

I am glad the Roots in a box per Capt Wright came to hand & was acceptable   I Received the Box of Berries Fresh & in good order   the Sarsafras was a fine parcel & the Cherry Stones & several others are what Wee had not before. I sent them to our noble Friend.

The Leaves of that Golden Rod are finely scented   pray have Wee any of the seed   now Dear Friend I have done with thine of the 9th of Sept.

And now I shall only tell thee I have rec'd thine of November 18th, December lst & the 9th & thine of the 10th, with the Invoices.

Capt Savage has been Exceedingly kind & obliging   pray when thee sees Docr Flexner[1] give my Respects to Him & thank Him also

I have gott all the Boxes on Shore but No 3 & 4 which are the Large

Boxes   the Seeds in No 2 was nicely pack'd & came in good order – but the 12 pticular sorts in that Box are mostly new & Curious

the Box of Specimens with the Seeds came very Dry   Safe & Well. I think thee has Discharged that affair very Elegantly & gives us great pleasure & Conveys to us stronger Ideas of your plants than can be Discribed & saves a great Deal of writing. I shall att my first Leisure send thee their True Botanical Names & I shall send thee more paper but one Quire a year will be sufficient. the Box of Insects was very prettyly done & nicely putt up & Discribed but pray Chain up that unruly Creature, the smith that he may do us no more Damage, next time. I shall have some Fresh Requests to make as to Insects which by enclosed instructions thee may Learn thy little Boys to catch & I will reward them.

Thee will hear att Large from Mee when I have oppertunity to Discourse with thy noble patron.

All the things thee wrote for, I shall send the small things by Israel Pemberton & the Box of Nails by Capt. Savage or some other ship, which I am not yett Determined but I shall acquaint thee with It –

Butt I almost Forgot thy Noble present of plants which came very safe & well to all appearance — & Contains a many Curious plants.

This year pray rest a Little from thy Labours — I shall only ask thee one Sett of plants & that is all the sorts of Ladies Slippers thee happens to meet with if not far to Fetch for I expect none from the Docr. He has indeed sent Mee a few seeds but they are fine sorts — the large Jacea or Blazing Star & 2 sorts of seeds of Martigons & Clinopodium, a fine plant.

I have got a Box of Chestnuts in sand & some Spanish nutts & some of our Katherine peach stones   it is the last & a large peach that ripens with us in October but will sooner with you. It is a hard sound well flavoured peach none better & Clings to the stone 17 & as many apricot stones & in the Little Box that the Insects came in are some seeds   the China Aster is the Noblest & finest plant thee Ever saw of that Tribe. it was sent per the Jesuits from China to France & from thence to us   it is an Annuall   sow it in rich mould immediately & when it has half a Dozen Leaves transplant to the Borders   it makes a Glorious autumn flower. There is white and purple in the seeds.

The Lebanon Cone, with a knife carefully pick out the seeds   sow in box   put large holes in the bottom & cover with shells in sandy Light mould. Lett it only have the morning sun

I sent 2 parcels of the Aster for fear, by sowing Late it should not ripen seed   I have sent the Docr Some —

I am my Dear friend with Hearty acknowledgments for all thy pains & Trouble & thy many favours,

In haste, thine sincerely,
P. Collinson

The Spanish chestnuts &c., come in a Little Box in sand committed to the care of Israel Pemberton.

We have been largely supplyd with Chinquapins from Virginia but I Design thee shall have the credit and profit of them, for our noble friend knows nothing but that they come from thee. I can Easily be supplyd from that country so give thyself no further trouble about them for I know they grow not near you to the perfection they do in that country.

Butt one Thing Dear John I must request of Thee our curious Bottanists are sadly perplexed about the Difference between the Red & White Cedars. pray be so kind to gather 3 or 4 specimens of Each sort of the size of the paper, Branches with their Leaves and when Dryd by First opertunity, the size & height of each sort & their uses & a few Berries of Each sort by way of sample, the Red we have but want seeds of the White Cedar one of my Curious Friends is writing a Book & wants to Insert the Cedars Red & White & show their Differences which is not perticularly Described by any author. so pray be exact & the'll much oblige thine,

P. C.

BP 2:10; D. 66–68.
1. Unidentified.

From COLLINSON

Lond February 20th <u>1735</u>
1736

Resp Frd
Jo Bartram –

I have sent the goods as under which I hope will meet with thy approbation and as there was no Direction Either to Quality or Quantity I have done to the best of my Judgmt — When I have settled with our Noble Friend who takes all the Cargo to his own Acct I will Advise thee of the ballance.

Young Israel Pemberton to whom thou art much Obliged at my request has pack'd up thy goods with His — which consists of 5 pcells

    viz: 1 pcell with Quality Silk, Combs & Girdles with some other things
         1 pcell with the Garlick[1] & Cambrick
         1 pcell being a fine Sagathie[2] for Lineings for a Summer Coat & Breeches for thy Self
         1 pcell being a summer Gown & Hood for thy Wife &c
         1 pcell being Camletes[3] &c for Coats for thy Children or Wast-coats for thy Self

Whatever thou finds is not charged in thy bill of pcells is presents for thy Self Wife & Children — Receive it in Love as it was sent I shall write thee fuller on all matters the first Leisure.

I have procured from my knowing Friend Philip Miller gardener to the

Physick Garden att Chelsea belonging to the Company of Apothecarys 69 sorts of Curious seeds and some others of my own Collecting — this I hope will Convince thee I do what I can and if I lived as thou does always in the Country I should do More But in my Situation it is Impossible. Besides most of the plants thee writes for are not to be found in gardens but growing Spontaneously Many Miles off and a Many Miles from one another — It is not to be Expected I can do as thou does, my inclination's good, but I have affairs of greater Consequence to Mind

and as I have Observed to thee before affairs of this Nature should not Interfere with Business & I do request thee not to suffer anything thee does for us to interfere with thine. Indeed for the Cargo thou sent, there was some Reason for thy making it thy Business because thee will have some gratification but in thy other Curious Collections which is done purely to oblige us pray give thy Business the preference but if in the Course of that without neglecting It, thou can pick up what thou thinks will be acceptable we shall be obliged to thee & study some Requital.

So for the Future no more Censure me for not sending the one Sixth part thee wrote for the reasons above.

But yett transmit Mee yearly what thou wants & anything in my power or my friend Miller's will be always at thy service & if I send thee the same thing 2 or 3 times over thee must Excuse it & place it to the Multiplicity of affairs that Fill my thoughts & not suspect my care and then thee will Deal kindly & Friendly & Lovingly wth thy

Frd P. Collinson

All these seeds come in Joseph Breintnall's packet.

P. Collinson Dr.	s	d	£
240 yd finest Quality binding @	1	4	
2 # belladene Silk	19		: 9 : 6
5 Flowerd Girdles		4	: 1 : 8
1 doz ½ Lt Coloured Ditto		7	: 10 : 6
1 doz ½ Cloth Coloured Do		7	: 10 : 6
1 doz [pub?] Ditto			: 8 : –
4 Ell Long Ditto		12	: 4 : –
3 Gross Finest Cotton for Wastcoats		1	: 3 : –
1 Pcl Cambrick			1: 5 : –
1 Pc Garlix			1: 10 : –
3 Combs		4	: 1 : –
3 Ditto		5	: 1 : 3
3 Do		6	: 1 : 6
3 Dandruffe Do		6	: 1 : 6
3 fine Ditto		7	: 1 : 9

I presume what is More than for thy own use thee will trade amongst thy neighbors. I have not forgott the Cask of Nails but I managed to send it per Capt Savage which in Gratitude I ought to do for his great Civility but if he does not speedily return I shall then alter my Regard.

Please to wait on Jos Breintnall for Seeds thay come in Library Company pcell. [Last sentence illegible].

BP 2:11; D. 68–69.
1. Unidentified.
2. A fine twilled woolen resembling serge.
3. Camlet, plain woven woolen, often dyed red.

From COLLINSON

London, March 12th 1735/6

Dear Friend

On the other side thou will see thy Account Drawn out with as much Exactness as I could Collect it From thy Invoices — I have endeavour'd to do Justice between thee & thy Noble Employer — I have shown it to him, and he approves of It, and has ordered Mee to give thee Credit for £18 13s. 3d: part of it has been sent to thy order and for the ballance thou may draw a bill on Mee or order it in goods, which suits thee best — His Lordship paid freight and all charges on the seeds being willing to give thee all the advantage for thy Encouragement.

The things for thine & thy wife's wear are a Joynt present from Mee & His Lordship for thy other seeds, and plants & specimens &c —

As Lord petre desired to see thy Letters they are all there He admires thy natural way of writing and thy observations & Discriptions of several plants — for want of them I shall only take notice of thy proposal in one of them, for an annual allowance to Encourage & Enable thee to prosecute further discoveries, Lord petre is very willing to contribute handsomely towards it He will be Ten guineas and we are in Hope to Raise Ten more

This Wee think will Enable thee to sett a part a Month, Two, or Three to Make an Excursion on the Banks of the Schuylkill to trace it to its Fountain — But as so great an undertaking may require Two or Three years and as many Journeys to Effect it, so we must leave that wholely to thee; But Wee do expect that after Harvest & when the season is that all the seeds of trees and shrubs are Ripe thou will sett out & them that happen not to be ripe when thou goes, they may have attained to maturity when thou comes back Wee shall send thee paper for Specimens and writing and a pocket Compass, Expect thee'l keep a regular journal of what occurs every Day and an exact observation of the course of the river which with a Compass thee may easily Do.

It will we apprehend be necessary to take a servant with thee and two horses for yourselves, and a spare one to carry linen, provisions and other necessaries. If the spare horse, and the man's horse, had two panniers or large baskets on each side, they will be very convenient to carry paper, to take specimens by the way, and to bring back the seeds; thee may make a good many little, middling, and large paper bags to put the seeds in; and be sure have some good covering of skins over the baskets, to keep out the rain, &c, Take some boxes for insects of all sorts, with the nets; and on thy return, some particular plants, that thee most fancies, may be brought in the baskets, if there is room.[1]

Thee need not collect any more Tulip cones   Swamp Laurel cones, Hickory, Black Walnut   Sassafras, nor Dogwood, Sweet Gum, White Oak acorns, Swamp Spanish Oak, nor Red Cedar berries — but all other sorts of acorns, Firs, Pines, Black Gum, or Black Haw, Judas Tree, Persimmon, Cherries, Plums, Services, Hop Tree, Benjamin, or allspice   all the sorts of Ash   Sugar Tree, Wild Roses, Black Beech, or Hornbeam; all sorts of flowering and berry-bearing shrubs, Honey Locust, Lime tree, Arrow-wood, a particular Locust, Guelder Rose; not anything can come amiss to thy friends, and in particular to thy True Friend,

P. Collinson

Lord Petre   Dr to John Bartram

			£	s	d
No 1 Box	250 Hickery	1		2	6
	30 Long Walnutts	5	–	2	6
	1 peck Sarsifrax		– :	5 :	–
No 2	550 Common Hickery	1	– :	5 :	6
	¾ qrs peck Dogwood	5	– :	3 :	9
	2 peck Red Cedar	5	–	10 :	–
	500 Sweet Gum Cones	5	1 :	5 :	–
	500 Swamp Laurell Cones	5	1 :	5 :	–
	100 Spruce Cones		– :	5 :	–
	200 Chesnutt Acorns &c		– :	2 :	–
	1 peck Dogwood Berries		– :	5 :	–
	500 Swamp Laurell Cones	5	1 :	5 :	–
	1000 Spruce Cones	5	2 :	10 :	–
	500 Gum Burrs	5	1 :	5 :	–
	1500 White oke Acorns	1	– :	15 :	–
	700 White Hickery	1	– :	7 :	–
	600 Sweet Hickery	1	– :	6 :	–
	2000 Swamp Spanish Acorns	1	1 :	– :	–
	2000 Black Walnutts	1	1 :	– :	–
	1000 White oake Acorns	1	– :	10 :	–
	400 White Hickery	1	– :	4 :	–
	1200 Swamp Spanish oke	1	– :	12 :	–
	300 Sweet Hickery	1	– :	– :	–
	1500 Tulip Tree Cones	5	3 :	15 :	–
	500 White & Black Walnutts	1	– :	10 :	–
			£18:	13 :	3

By Haberdashery Linnen &c p Bill	6 : 9 : 2	
By Cask of Nails	5 : 1 : 7	
	11 : 10 : 9	
Due to thee	11 : 10 : 9	
	7 : 2 : 6	

The Cask of Nails is shipped by the St. George Capt Lindsay   I shall write thee by Him and Inclose Bill Loading & pay the Freight which must be paid out of the Bill 7:2:6

BP 2:13; D. 72–73.
1. Because this paragraph and the following one are almost illegible, much of it was taken from Darlington, who omitted the list.

From COLLINSON[1]

Dr Frd

— as thee has given Mee Many Instances of thy Curious Speculative Disposition it has put me on Enlarging thy Knowledge in Natural Inquiries, as the Earth is filled with wonders, & Everywhere is to be seen the Marks & Effects of Almighty power — Most things were made for the use & pleasure of mankind, others to Raise our Admiration and astonishment, as in particular what are called Fossils — being stones found all the World over — that have either the impressions, or else the regular form of shells leaves, fishes, fungi, teeth, sea-eggs, and many other productions. That thee may better apprehend what I mean, I have sent thee some specimens, in a packet of paper for specimens of plants for Lord Petre, with some seeds, and a pocket compass. Captain Savage has promised to take care of the parcel. In the course of thy travels, or in digging the earth, or in thy quarries, possibly some sorts of figured stones may be found, mixed or compounded with earth, sand, or stone and chalk. What use the learned make of them, is, that they are evidences of the Deluge, of which thee may Hear more when [illegible]   I hope Israel Pemberton is safe arrived, and the little box with chestnuts, and all the other parcels, with my letters, and the box of insects, are come safe. Pray don't forget, as soon as possible, the specimens of Red and White Cedar, and a few white cedar berries.

BP 2:13; D. 73.
1. This appears to have been a sort of postscript to his letter of March 12, 1735–36. See his letter of March 20, in which he wrote: "I hope mine of the 12th instant with the paper pcells with seeds & pocket Compass enclosed per Capt Savage are come to hand. . . ."

From COLLINSON[1]

London, March 20th, 1736

Dear Frd –

I hope Mine of the 12th instant with the paper pcells with seeds & pocket Compass enclosed per Capt Savage are come to hand as well as the sundry parcels & letters per Israel Pemberton . . . I further took notice of thine of November 3rd, in which thee modestly proposed to be allowed for thy pains and trouble in collecting seeds, and to enable thee to penetrate to the original of Schuylkill. His lordship is both ready and willing to encourage so laudable a design, and will endeavour to engage others to join with him. He proposes to be, himself, ten guineas, and to engage some others to be ten more. This, he is in hopes, will enable thee to set apart one, two, or three months after harvest – or as near as thee guesses when all sorts of mast & seeds are Ripe.

Thee talks of the Spring, which is no suitable time to sett out on such an Expedition, for the Interest of the Gentlemen concerned — for what they propose is that thou may be able to Furnish them with sorts of seeds &c that they had not before and so Desire thou will make some essay in the autumn & make some progress on the Schuylkill for such an Expedition may require 2 or 3 Journeys to make the Discoveries thou Intends   Every uncommon thing thou finds in any branch of Nature, will be acceptable.

Butt next time after thee has Covered the Holes with Shell then putt two or 3 Inches of Light sandy Mould and then Putt in the plants and Cover them with the same as they may require   the Dwarf Cypress as I called it & the pretty Wood Cedum & some others was Totally Rotted but as thee observes these are plants that Grow in a Singular manner so I will not ask thee to Trouble thy Self Further about them but send us Some good Specimens when they are in Flower & ye Seed Vessels, & this Shall Content Mee

With the pockett Compass, observe 2 or 3 Times of the Day the course of the River & set it down in thy journal in wch Every day, write in short thy observations of that day. There is a dial to it, besides, which will be convenient to know the hour of the day . . .

Thy Account of the Effects of the Poison stick in thine of the 9th december is very Extraordinary   pray send us a Specimen of the plant & make further inquiries about it. Give Mee a List per first ship what seeds thou wants. I have the Gardener of the Physic Garden att Oxford will assist me. Be mindful of Insects of all kinds & Fossils, any Birds nest that is uncommon in its Structure of materials   I have 2 or 3 humming-birds already; however, if any More happens to fall in thy way I'll not refuse them. I have heard say, your swallow's nest, and your bee's, wasp, or hornet's nest that hangs on the boughs of trees, is very curious.

My dear friend, I wish thee health and increase of thy store, and be assured that I am thy real loving friend. In haste

P. Collinson

BP 2:23; D. 73–74; American Philosophical Society Library, Wildman transcript.
1. Most of this letter is illegible in the original, so much of it was taken from Wildman and Darlington. A small section has been omitted.

From COLLINSON

London
April 21, 1736

Dear Friend
J. Bartram

I have now the pleasure to tell thee that I have Gott subscribed Twenty Guineas to Encourage thee to undertake thy Intended Expedition and as our Gentlemen find Encouragement it will be Continued Annually, this is a pretty Sum in Sterling Money which I hope will Enable thee to supply thyself with Necessaries from Hence or if more for thy profit thou may Draw for it when we have received thy Cargoes —

this I believe thee will think reasonable that the gentlemen should first see what they have for their Money — This I can assure thee that thee has to do with people that are not unreasonable in their Expectations —

I hope the Goods p Israel pemberton are Come Safe & the pcels of seeds &c In my Good Friend Breintnalls pcell are Come Safe to Hand

I writt thee also per Capt Lindsay & Inclosed Bill of Lading for the Nails & thy acc't Currant & 6:15:6 is the Ballance Remaining in My Hands —

pray remember 2 or 3 Specimens of the White and Red Cedars & if possible pray send the Berries or seed vessel of each in particular the White Cedar for the Seeds of This I am a Stranger too, half a Dozen, per way of Specimen, will be sufficient — for tho you call it the White Cedar yett Wee are in Doubt what Class it belongs too till wee see its seed Vessels — Thy subscription keep to thy Self — Remember the Calceolus Marianus or Ladies slippers & Gentians. I refer thee to my Former Letters for I have nothing More to Add but my Sincere Wishes for thy Health & Safety, and am thy affectionate Frd,

P. Collinson

Specimens of the Sugar Tree blossom & more seed   Remember all sorts of Firr & pine Cones & more Spruce   I am informed that the Jersies is noted for producing abundance of Firrs & pines — I wish thee could procure some specimens of the Curious Tree in the Jersies either the Leaves or Blossoms or both together would be better —

I am Highly delighted with reading thine of the 3d November with the pleasing account of thy Expedition to the Mountains and the many Valuable plants thee observed there — I hope thee will make an Early Expedition into those parts — The Thorn that thee tells Mee of must be very Curious   it is a pitty but it should be propagated   it will take Easily if Grafted on other Thorns in the Spring; which would be the most sure way, for seed does not always keep strictly to the Mother plant —

I have sent the paper so pray Continue thy Specimens of all Rare plants — One of the plants that is not Named that bears spikes of White flowers & the leaves sett in the Joynts Like a star four at a Joynt, is Call'd Veronica or Speedwell.

If thee can procure some Terrapins for Lord Petre putt them in a Box of Earth & nail Cross bars on the top & if thee knows what they feed on put in some food, I know they eat apples cut in slices.

BP 2:25; D. 75–76.

From COLLINSON

London June 1:1736

Dear Frd
John Bartram —
Capt Richmond being a Friend of thine could not let him sail without a Line, tho' I have nothing to add to my former Butt to Enquire after thy Wellfare — for fear my former of March 12th/ and 20th & Aprill 21st shou'd any Miscarrie; I will now repeat what I then told thee that I have 20 Guineas subscribed to Encourage thy Expedition so I hope thou will proceed — a great Many of thy seeds are come up but I am afraid the Tulip Tree Cones was not well pfected for none is yett Come up — I indeed open'd several and found them Imperfect, as well as the Sugar Tree. Must in pticular Desire thee to Recruit these Two Sorts next year   I am afraid the Acorns will Also Fail — so pray send a Collection of all Sorts Especially the Narrow Leafed Okes — the seeds of the Jersie Tree are Come up — by present appearance it seems to be a Lotus or Nettle Leafed Tree which grows Common in Italy & other pts of Europe   Per my next, I may Give a more pticular [account]

The wetness of the Mould in the Box of plants Rotted several things, I have but one Martigon & I am afraid it is not ye marsh one — not one Lillie, pray be so kind to Recruit thee with some of the fine Large Slippers thou showed Dr Witt and pray send some More of that pritty plant thou calls the Rock Blood Wort, it was rotted by over Wett — I take it to be a Cistus by its flower   Divils Bit or Blazeing Starr Lost — if the pretty Cedum Grows near thee I would be glad of one Tryal More —

all the White and Red Shrub hone Suckle failed   this is a ticklish plant One of the Laurell stands —

Pray Send a Root or Two of the White Minor Hellebore   I have Two fine plants of the Cluster bearing Solos. Seal; but the other sorts failed —

pray make Large Holes in next Box and Lett it be Light Mould and not Clay for that retains the Wett

Please to send over some Good Specimens with the Flowers to them, of the 5 Humble Ever Green plants that grows in the Woods — for I despair to have them in the Garden   they are So nice and Difficult in their Culture —

I am oblig'd to thee for the Canes. I have putt a Neat head on one of them

& use it dayly for thy sake — Whatever seeds thou sends for the Future, Send to Mee & I shall divide them in proportion to my Three Contributors, Lord Petre is ten Guineas, & the Duke of Richmond Five, & Philip Miller the other Five —

I shall now conclude referring thee to my other Letters for what former Requests & Instruction I have made & hope thee will Excuse them,

from thy Loving friend.
P. Collinson

pray send Root or seed of that sweet scented Golden Rod thou sent the leaves off

pray Remember the White Cedar to send 2 or 3 good Specimens — and ½ doz. of its Cones or seed vessels & pray sent Mee for a Specimen a Little Board about 2 foot Long of Each Sort of Cedar for a Specimen. I have Large trees of Cedars raised from Berries in my Garden, which I call Red Cedar but I never was sure which was Either white or red & wherein the difference lay.

I have a Tree of Your Acacia or Sweet White Flowering Locust finely in Blossom – has an agreeable Scent

Friend John, this is only a hint, by the way — Lord Petre is a great admirer of your Foreign Wild Water Fowl, if att any Time an oppertunity offers, send him some   Thou will Lose nothing by it

Butt this He Desired Mee to tell thee that He Desires thy Children will Bring Him up some Red Birds Cocks & Hens, for He has an Intention to Naturalize them to our Climate and I doubt not of Success

These things I barely Mention, for thy Notice, and am thine,

P. C.

BP 2:26; D. 76–77.

From COLLINSON

Lond June 6 1736

Frd John —

By the Curious Impressions Sent per J. Breintnall I Find I have the Snake Root of Peter Sonmans[1] from Albany being the same recommended per Doc Witt who sent Mee a plant 2 or 3 years agone but I dont find by another impression taken 18 August 1734 that I have what my Friend Breintnall Calls thy Snake Root — as it is Difficult keeping thy marks Regular to the plant the Designs them so I have some plants in thriving order that I can't tell what they are — to Informe Mee please to send a Specimen of Aristolochia No. 3

    a Specmn —— of Panax —— 5
    Ditto —— of Breintnalls Snake Root 6
    and a Good Specimen of the Minor Hellebore —— in flower

Ditto Cotton Weed —— 17
Sarsaparella I don't see any 20

the Woody Vine has not yett Shott   it is by the Berries a Euonymous or prick or Skure wood, used by the Butchers

The Apocinon, or Swallowwort with Orange flowers thrives well   one of the Dwarfe Laurell Grows well   the climbing Apocinon that thee sent — the pods fill'd with silk   the seeds are Come up — there is a great variety of plants, on ye Continent, that bear Seed vessels of the same figure & Consistence, these are all Apocinons & have pticular Distinctions from the Colour of the Flower. shape of the Leafe or pticular growth of the plant — One would Conceive from the Great provision Made (by our all wise Creator) for the spreading this plant it was Design'd for pticular uses to Mankind for Every Seed has a silken Thrum[2] fix'd to it sufficient to keep it floating in the Air & when the pod bursts then the Wind Conveys the seed to all Quarters   if thee'll Excuse my bitts & Scraps of Letter which I write as oppertunity offers, thee'l oblige thyne

P. Collinson

BP 2:27; D. 78.
1. Unidentified.
2. Plant fiber or hair resembling a thrum (warp threads remaining on a loom when the cloth has been removed).

From COLLINSON

June 7 1736

Frd John

I have now a very Curious Account before Mee sent by Paul Dudley from his House in Roxbury New England, October 24:1735 — who very Ingeniously Describes the Evergreens of New England in two sheets of paper.

This is his Catalogue —

White Pine ——
Pitch Pine ——
Saplin or Pople pine
Apple pine ——
Hemlock   a small Firr
Balm of Gilead Firr
Spruce Tree { Distinguished into white Black & Red from the Colour of the Bark & Leafe
White Cedar ——
Red Cedar ——
Savin ——
Juniper ——

Holly ———
Ivy & Shrub ———
Box ———

My kind Frd, Docr Witt sent Mee some years agone several small plants that he call'd spruce but by the very pticular Discription of P. Dudley they prove to be the Hemlock for I have 2 fine plants in my Garden which agree Exactly with his Discription of the Hemlock & confirm Mee that P. Dudley is right   I had this year come from Newfound Land Two fine Spruce Trees which both grow and prove very different plants from what the Doctor sent Mee but agree exactly with P. Dudley's description of the Spruce.

This I send by way of Information & To put thee on Observing what you have of these kinds growing near you —

Very probably in process of Time thy Noble Employers may send thee to visit New England, on One Side & Maryland & Virginia on the other — but this by the by.

But be it how it may, thee may be assured of the Friendship of

Thine
P. Collinson

If thee observes any sort of Fresh Water or River shell fish pray send Mee 2 or 3 of Each Sort of Shells as Specimens or any sort of Land Snails &c Send Mee 2 or 3 shells of a sort for a Specimen — my Inclination and fondness to natural productions of all kinds is agreeable to the Old proverb (Like the parson's barn – refuses nothing)

BP 2:28; D. 79–80.

From JAMES LOGAN

Stenton, 19th June 1736

Friend J. Bartram: –

Last night, in the twilight, I received the inclosed, and opened it by mistake. Last year Peter sent me some tables, which I never examined till since I last saw thee. They are six very large sheets, in which the author digests all the productions of Nature in classes.[1] Two of them he bestows on the inanimate, as Stones, Minerals, Earths; two more on Vegetables, and the other two on animals. His method in the Vegetables is altogether new, for he takes all his distinction from the *stamina* and the *styles,* the first of which he calls husbands, and the other wives, He ranges them, therefore, under those of 1 husband, 2, 3, 4, 5, 6, 7, 8, 9, 10, 12, 20, and then of many husbands. He further distinguishes by the styles, and has many heads, under which he reduces all known plants.

The performance is very curious, and at this time worth thy notice. I would send it to thee, but being in Latin, it will want some explanation,

James Logan (1674–1751). *Harper's New Monthly Magazine* 52 (1876):713.

which, after I have given thee, thou wilt, I believe, be fully able to deal with it thyself, since thou generally knows the plants' names. If thou will step to town to-morrow, thou wilt find me there with them, at E. Shippen's,[2] or I. Pemberton's, from 12 to 3. I want also to say something further to thee, on microscopical observations.

Thy real friend,
J. Logan

D. 307–8.
1. Carolus Linnaeus's *Systema Naturae*.
2. Edward Shippen, member of the Governor's Council.

To COLLINSON[1]

I engag'd an owner of part of a Cedar swamp for my Guide without whom I could hardly have found It. Wee travel'd about Twelve Miles beyond the inhabitants over Desarts of sand & such deep mirery Swamps that sometimes both Wee and our Horses had much ado to gett out. The Sand lies in Ridges 40 or 50 or 60 poles over & the swamps lie between which are the heads of Rivers & Brooks but so thick sett with shrubs and Bushes about 10 poles Wide yt wee had great Difficulty in passing these swamps   att Last wee came to the Head of (Egharbour River) where the great Cedar Swamp Began containing many hundred Acres Chiefly produceing White Cedar but in some dryer places, Silver Laurell or Bay Maple, Holley, & Sassafras & about the Ridges Some pines, but I observed no Red Cedar. The White grows only in wett places often knee deep in Water in wett seasons — they grow near together   the small ones within a foot or Two of one another a white Cedar of Two inches Diameter will be 20 feet high, the larger Trees grows all at 10 or 20 feet Distance which makes them grow very tall, a Tree of Two feet diamr att the Stump, will be 80 or 100 feet in highth and 30 or 40 feet without a Limb, the soil where they grow I take to be Clay but the surface is a matt of Roots all interlac'd one with another which intangles the Leaves and Rubish & makes a Bogg   the Bark of the Root is Red which gives a tincture to the Waters that runs from them but the Tast is good & sweet. Our Ceterach & Sarsaparilla grows at the Roots where the sun is rarely seen so thick is the shade above, the Leaves is not near so long & prickly as the Red Cedar, the Fruite is Coniferous & seed very small — to satisfie your Immediate Curiosity I inclose a small specimen, but this second of Last June I cutt down a Large Tree for to send you Larger specimens which I shall send by first oppertunity.

Oxford University, Department of Botany, Sherardian Collection.
1. This portion of a Bartram letter was quoted by Collinson in a letter to Johann Jacob Dillenius, July 31, 1736. It was printed in the Royal Society of London's *Notes and Records* 81 (1857):186–88.

From COLLINSON

Lond Augt 28:1736

Dr. Frd.
John Bartram

I Reced thy Entertaining Letter & the Acct of thy Expedition to the Rattlesnake Mountains — which his Lordship now has so can't In pticular Answer it —

It was very well thought to putt the small Specimen of Cedar with the little Cones in the letter   my Friend says it is a True Cypress haveing both the figure and properties of the Common Cypress but the Cones Exceedingly Less   the plant the gathered last Year near the Mountains hath the appearance In Leaves & Flower of Mallows, but by the pticular Figure of the seed Vessel it is call'd an Abutilon — There is another species that much Resemble Mallows, but the Seed Vessel being Like a pod — its call'd Ketmie

I did not send thy Goods by this ship because I am in hopes by the next which sails in 2 or 3 Weeks to save the Freight — pray send some Acorns of the Narrow Leaved Okes Cones of Tulip Tree, a Specimen in Flower of the

Sugar Maple, and the seed, Flowering bay Cones & what ever Else thou thinks well of – of Timber Trees & Shrubs &c

Inclosed is some Fresh Seed of your True Cowslip   Scatter the Seed on the Ground in a half Sandy place but don't Cover

I am thy real frd,

P. Collinson

Send More, Black Walnuts, Long Walnuts, and both sorts of Hickory, Acorns of all sorts, Sweet Gum, Dog Wood, Red Cedar Berries, Allspice, Sassafras these will be acceptable to the Duke of Richmond — & Lord Petre will Like some More   pack all the Seed the same way as last year for they succeed very well a few Excepted. The Acorns & Sweet Gum and indeed Most of all the other seeds are finely Come up — the greatest Deficiency is in the poplar or Tulip Cones — & the Sugar Tree, not one of the Sassafras nor Cedar Berries appear but I presume they lie two years —

Thy kind neighr James Logan is so Good as to order Mee to Buy thee Parkinson's Herbal if I can have it for 25 shillings — He has shown a very Tender Regard for thee In his letter to Mee — it may Look Gratefull every now & then to Call and Inquire after thy Good Frd Logan's Welfare   He is a Great Man in every Capacity & for whome I have the Highest Value

Dr. frd. I thought when I began, to write but 2 or 3 lines — but I go on scribbling till the paper Confines Mee —

Thine,
P C

BP 2:29; D. 80–81.

From COLLINSON

Lond Sept 20 1736

Frd John

I writt thee per Capt Pearce and I have not much to add, but to Acquaint thee that I have sent a Case of Glass as per bill Inclosed. I could not gett the quality binding to my Mind to Come by this Ship it being a Narrower Sort then is Sold Here — I was obliged to gett it made on purpose & one man made it so Ordinary that I was obliged to returne them & then I had to find a man to begin again   att Last I Meet with one to undertake it   I hope He will Do it to my Mind   I will Send it by first oppertunity & then will Close the Accot —

I have after Some Inquiry Mett with Parkinsons Herbal which I have bought p 25s by the Directions of My Good Friend J:Logan — He Designs it as a present to Thee   It may not be amiss att a suitable Time to Wait on Him but take not the Least Notice that I gave thee this Hint unless He should ask thee & then tell him freely —

I have the pleasure to tell thee that the noble Marsh Martagon flowered with me which thou sent this spring   It is a Delicate flower —

I have sent in a Trunk to J. Breintnall a paper parcel for thee, being Apricot   Nectarines & some fine Peaches & Plum stones of the best sorts   these Fruites I apprehend will succeed better than by grafting unless on Peach stocks   Sow them in a proper place   if where they are always to stand, it may be better — but if they are removed I apprehend if Apricots, Plums & Nectarines was planted on the Margin of a River or on the side of a feeding Spring where they may be Always supply'd with Moisture to their Fibres thay would not be so apt to shrivel & Drop their Fruite in the very hot weather —

I have further to request of thee, as thee on thy Own affairs art oblig'd to traverse the Woods, to take all oppertunities to make observations on the Rattle Snake or indeed any other snake, That Birds, squirrels &c are found in their Bellies is notoriously known, but the Question is how they came there — whether the Snake lying Perdue[1] on a sudden darts on her prey & Bites it & then Lays on the spot Expecting the Effect of her poisonous Bite will at last bring the Little animal down Dead to her Devouring Jaws — Sir Hans Sloane and a great many others are of this Opinion and by an Ingenious Letter from a Curious person in your City their opinion is very Much Confirm'd

But on the other Side of the Question I have Rec'd from my Ingenious frds. J. Breintnall & Docr Witt very pticular accts of the power it has over Creatures by Charming them Into its very Jaws — possibly some accidental discovery may be made when it is Least thought on   it will require a nice & Exact observation to Determine this Matter, if thee knows any thing of thy own knowledge, please to Communicate it   The hear say of Others, can't be Depended on. The Common & long Received opinion of Charming is so Riveted in people's Imagination that unless they will Divest themselves of It they may not easly Distinguish to the Contrary

pray has thee heard or Observed that a Certain Species of Locust returns Every fifteenth year — I have been Inform'd of such a thing from New England.

I want very much to be satisfied about the Sugar Maple, as to its Flowers, if they are White as thee has Informed me before. please in the Spring to gather some Specimens when in Flower and send Mee & be very pticular in thy remarks on it.

We have Raised a pretty many fine plants from the tree in the Jerseys. It is a real Lotus or Nettle Tree and is a native of your part of the World: is found in virginia and in other parts, parkinson knew only of one sort which is the European, with Black Fruite but we have in the gardens Two sorts from your part of the World Distinguished by the Colour of their Fruite

Inclosed is the Bill   pCells for the Glass and the Receipt for it on Board   I got Lawrence Williams[2] to Enter it with his goods to save thee Expence of Shipping Charges   I have been Twice with the Capt to pay

Freight but being a small Box his Mate had not given him a Memorandum of it, So I hope if He takes any thing It will be but a small Matter

So that thee has nothing More to Do Either to go thy Self or Gett thy Frd. Breintnall to Carry the Receipt & Ask for the Box Marked a p the Inclosed paper which was my Direction for Shipping it

Dear frd. John, I am thy real fr.

P. Collinson

BP 2:30; D. 81–82.
1. Concealed.
2. Ship captain.

From COLLINSON[1]

Frd. John

I have put some Roots of Madder in a Box of Sand — it is scarse with us — Loves a Deep Fatt Soil   the Duch makes a great proffit by It. I think Wee might do the Same, I have putt some of our Sloes or Black Thorn it is a pretty Fruit when Bitten by the Frost & Flowers Early — and I have thrown in some Seed of Meadow Sweet   Sure if this Comes Safe thou will Raise it by one Means or Another — I have sent some in yr parcell — Eye bright grows so Remote on wild uncultivated places that I dispair of getting any, I shall not forgett Evergreen Seeds — the Laurell Berries sent in J. Breintnals parcel are very Scarse to be gott   the birds run away with them — this Box comes by the Care of Elias Bland pack'd in his parcell

I am thine
P. Collinson

Docr. Gronovius forgetting to send the Names to the Last Specimens — Desires Mee to send them over again to Him but when an oppertunity will offer I know not   besides making Double Trouble & Expence. What Cant be Cured must be endured   the Box is Tied up in Brown paper Directed for thee   black thorn comes not up I think till 2d year

Historical Society of Pennsylvania Library.
1. This letter was probably written early in 1737. In his letter of December 20, 1737, Collinson expresses surprise that Bartram already has "Slow Trees Enough."

From COLLINSON

Lond Feby 1 1736/37

Fr John

I have a Strong Opinion that our Mistletoe may be propagated with you In a Manner I have often try'd with Success and then again yours may be with Us. I have Sent Some Berries in a Box

My Methode Is to Choose the Smoothest part of Some Branch of an apple Tree & thereon I bruize the Berry but not the Seed by Vertue of the Glutinous Matter about it, it will Stick in the Bark   the north Side of the branch is Best — if it Sticks but Loosely att First, yett in a few Days there is a Mutual Attraction on both Sides and the Seed will be found Closely Stuck to the Bark, It is very prety to see the progress of Vegitation and how the seed pushes forth Two Roots which Insenuate themselves into the Bark — Its natural way of propagation Is by a Thrush that is fond of the Berries and Lives mostly on them whilst they Last. In Dunging it is Squirted out on Branches of Trees where they happen to Sett   It is Surprizing to think the Seed should preserve Its Vegitative Quality through the Heat of the Intestines of the Bird, & the Glutinous part with It   thus where ever It Lights it Sticks Fast, but such is the Order of providence and an Evidence of the Great Wisdome & power of the Creator — to whome all things are possible   pray Send Mee Some of your Berries for no Doubt your Mistletoe Differs from ours & please to Send a Specimen of what Sorts you have Wee have but one with Us, but with this Difference   Some are Male & some Female which bear Berries   Others none but the Farina to Impregnate the Female Blossomes   I have a Deal on Sundry Trees in my Garden for I try all Sorts by the Methode prescribed   being an Ever Green it makes a pretty Show in Winter   as this is a Secret thee make it so, for few believe It but it is a fact

the Two or Three Remts may make the Little Boys Some Cloths — The Two Boxes of Fossills I shall take Notice of   I am much obliged to thee & the Gentleman for Sending them   the Tulip Tree Seed seems very Good It is [a] noble Cargo   I think thee has not Mention'd what Sort of pine Cones those was in the partition in the Large Case and thee has Omitted to Name the Seeds to Number Eleven & Number 11 In the Growing plants but it is to Easily Looked over when thee has thought of so much — I am thine
P Collinson

BP 2:46; D. 84.

From COLLINSON

Lond fby 26 1736/7

Dr fd John

Thou omitted to tell us how many Miles thou travell'd from Home — pray by the first ship lett Mee know to what part of the Country thy Inclination Leads thee next Fall, by very first Ship —

I believe it will be Acceptable to all thy Friends to make a general Collection of all the pines & Firrs your part affords   I am apt to think the Jerseys may afford all the pines & Firrs mentioned by Dudley & save a further Journey —Wee are very poorly furnished with this Tribe, the few seeds & specimen No. 113 of the white pine is a Sort Wee very much want, the Difference between pines & Firrs is that all pines have their Leaves sett by pairs and in all Firrs the Leaves are sett singly on the Branch — It is a noble Collection of Spruce Cones that thee has sent, but we are att a Loss to know the plant it belongs to for want of specimens, pray send some by first [opportunity] for there is severall sorts of Firrs that bears small Cones — it is a fine pcel of White Cedar that thee has sent, I wish we may be so fortunate to raise some   it is a plant that Wee have not In England. I wish thee would Collect a few young Seedlings a foot or Two high & plant in thy Garden till they have stood a year & taken root & then send them or what would be better is to plant 6 or 8 in a Box about 2 foot square & if they grow they may be sent without Danger of removing & pray send more seed next year.

pray some more white Cedar, what does thee make of those substances with the spriggs growing through them   I take them to be Excrescences, tho they have some small resemblance of the Cypress cone.

But of the Great Variety of new & Curious plants in the 4 quires of Specimens, none Strikes Mee so much as the Laurell No. 102, what class our Botanists will rank it in, I can't say   had we but the flowers, it could then be Easily determined, but it has all the appearance of a Noble plant and will be undoubtedly a great ornament to Our Gardens, by all means Either send seeds or plants, I hope some may be Discovered nearer Home then go so far, all those specimens that have neither flower nor seed-vessel, it will be Difficult to Determine what Class they beelong too   This I must observe to thee that I really think no pains has been wanting to Oblige us with a prodigious Variety in Every Kind, as to thy pticular regard to Mee, I am truly sensible of It, & that I may not be behind in gratitude, I have really taken a task on me, which takes up so much of my Time and is so much Trouble, that for thy sake only, I undertake It, in hopes 20 guineas a year may be of some service — but thee art not sensible the Time & trouble it takes up, to gett these things from on board and from the Custom House and had I not good friends amongst the Commissioners, I should have a great deal more and pay a Duty besides, and what is yett a Greater Difficulty on Mee it happens [illegible] As to thy objection, as to the size of your Cypress cone, it is none; for the same is to be observed in other seeds. There are very small acorns, and very large ones, and yet one as much an oak as the other. The cone of the Cypress that sheds the leaves, very much resembles the Italian, for size and figure. Of this we have raised abundance, from Virginia and Carolina. It is a fine tree, and thrives mightily with us. pray Some More White Cedar

BP 2:21; D. 90–91.

To COLLINSON

Pensilvania Feby 27:1727[1]

What I have heard and remarked of the Rattle-Snake's Power of Charming is surprising to me: for I have received many particular Relations from very

Rattlesnake charming a rabbit. *Harper's New Monthly Magazine* 10 (1854–55):474.

judicious Persons, who have told me the whole Process: who have stood and observed the Snake exerting his Power, and seen the poor deluded Creature, either Bird or Squirrel draw nearer and nearer to the Snake, & Just ready to run into it's mouth; nay some that have been half their length ingorged, and yet by either interposing between the Creature and the Snake, or striking the Snake, the Charm has been interrupted, or the Creature disgorged, and then have made their Escapes, to all appearance unhurt. But had they been bit before, in order the easier to captivate them, as is Sir Hans Sloan's opinion, they could not have made their Retreat so briskly.

It is possible, the Rattle-Snake may be endued with such Sagacity as to bite those Creatures at unawares, that may be too large and too strong to swallow alive: but this I doubt, because I have had accounts from several persons of undoubted Credit, who have affirmed to me that there is a surprizing Fascination in the looks of this Snake. For they were so overcome when the Snake fixed his Eyes upon them, that they were presently seized with such a feebleness & Languor all over them, that they were ready to drop down. This confirms to me, that there proceeds such subtle Emanations from the Eyes of this Creature beyond what we can comprehend.

And yet it may be possible many Creatures may come within their reach, as she lies coil'd up, and motionless either in Rage or Anger, against their common Enemy, or else in Surprize or Admiration at the Shape and different Colours of this subtil Serpent, who by the power of muscular motion can appear or change to various Shades of Colours, to allure Squirrels or Bird to come within its reach: the Snake lying so still they apprehend no danger.

As the Bite of this Creature proves frequently so fatal to Man and Beast, yet with us it is not so mortal as in the Provinces to the Southward of us. For if a Person is bit in Maryland or Virginia in the highth of the Summer, & is not within a half an hour's Ride or Walk for help; he may as well sit down & dye on the Spot as attempt a relief at a greater distance. Yet we may justly admire the goodness of Providence in giveing this noxious Animal a Rattle in his Tail to give notice where he is – when in motion: for it happens that most that are bit is by accident, by treading on them at unawares as they lie coil'd up, or asleep. And we may further admire that not withstanding they are great Increassors, breeding of sixty at a time (the striped Snake more, and the black Snake lays twenty and thirty Eggs) yet the wisdom of Providence is great in preserving a Ballance, by Preventing their Increase, by providing Animals to destroy them. Our Eagles and Buzzards cunningly dart down and strike their Claws into them, kill and eat abundance of them: and our Hunters affirm that the Deer have a natural Antipathy against them, and destroy them by jumping on their Heads with their fore-feet, so bruise and kill them: and not a few fall by the Indians as well as the European Inhabitants.

If these Remarks, which are oddly huddled together, will be any ways acceptable, it will be a pleasure to thy sincere friend

John Bartram

P.S. What is further observable of Snakes is, that they will prey on one another (as some sort of Fish is known to do) My wife observed two Snakes pretty near together in my Yard, the one a large black Snake, which is the most domestick of all others: as their Bite is not dangerous, they are permitted to harbour about the House to destroy Ratts, Mice, Froggs &c. The other was a middle sized striped Snake. The black Snake lay still with his eyes fixed on the striped one, which crept directly into the black Snake's mouth. My wife seeing this fetch'd the Tongs & pulled very hard to get him out of the black Snake's mouth for he was near half swallowed down. But the black Snake, far from being scared at such usage, crept about as in search of his Prey, that he had been robbed of, and would not go of the Premises, till a Stick made him run away.

Royal Society of London Archives, LB 25.118.
1. This date was written in error, for it must have been 1736/37. See Collinson to Bartram,

September 20, 1736, and December 10, 1737 (read to the Society on December 21, 1738, edited by Collinson or the society's secretary).

From COLLINSON

Londn: March 14 1736/7

Fr John

    I am just now returned from paying Our Noble Friend a Visit, where I have been Viewing his plantations, & Concerting Measures for another progress if thee thinks proper to Undertake One. He thinks with Mee that to take a Turn through Your three lower Counties & then a long the Sea Coasts of the Eastern Shore to the Capes & then returne round the Bay home Leaving the Western Shore of Maryland & Virginia for another Time and the going northward in Search of Firrs & pines, may be for the present Deferred — Besides the Sorts I mentioned before that a few of Each would be sufficient for our Two Correspondents that did not share in the first Cargo   I have Here added a list of what sorts will be acceptable to the general. butt this I have to Observe to thee — if these seeds can be Gott nearer home, then there is no Occation to go far for them; for the Time spent in Journeying, may be spent nearer in gathering — Butt this we shall leave to thee, being persuaded all thee does will be for the Best — Butt if thee should think fitt to visit the Eastern Shore, I have some pticular friends there, to whom I shall give thee Letters, who no doubt will give thee Hospitable Entertainment.

    March the 20th   thy Collumbine is in flower which is Earlier then any Wee have, by 2 months   it is a pretty plant & more so, for its Earliness. Wee thought Wee should have had but a small crop of the Wild Cherries for some came up the first year & kept their Leaves all winter like an Evergreen but to our surprise they are now comeing up in abundance as well as the Red Cedar, the Sassafras does not stir yett   There is thousands of Sweet Gum some kept their green leaves all Winter –

    Inclosed are some berries of the Butcher's Broom and Juniper which grows wild in his Lordships Woods & which He gathered with his own hands March 10th so must be full ripe, but will not appear till the Second year, Where they are sown, be sure keep the bed Clear from Weeds.

    pray be so kind to mention if those nests are Wasps — Bee's or Hornet's, & send Mee 2 or 3 of the Creatures that build them   they are very Curious   one I gave to Sir Hans Sloane.

    His Lordship was mightily pleased with thy Journal but Wants to know the Length of the Cave & how far you went from Home — He very much desires some seed of that fine Laurel thee Discovered beyond the Blue Mountains & some specimens of it when in flower — if this can be Obtained without Difficulty — There is another plant that we want seed & specimens of — that is the Papaw. His Lordship has one plant of it but they tell us such stories of its fruite that we would be glad to see it, which may be Easily done by gathering two or three bunches of its Fruite full ripe & putting them into strong Rum in a Jar or pot & corking it up Close, will keep very well Here — Specimens of it in Flower will be Acceptable.

pray how long does thou think is the course of the Schuylkill?

pray remember Specimens of sugar Maple in flower — The Berry Tree in the Jerseys are come up freely   is real Lotus.

I believe thee Forgot to send the large Specimens of White Cedar with the cones on them   I take it, your Spruce is certainly Dudley's Hemlock Firr, which is called here the Yew leafed Firr. I believe that tree in the Jerseys by thy Account of it must be the Carolina Cypress, is a Noble quick growing Tree, and thrives well here.

In thine of 7 mo 4 D thee gives a very pticular Acct how your plums are Destroyed by an Insect, pray Change the Stock & graft plums & Nectarines on peach Stocks, which being a vigorous free stock and not Liable to these Insects may Succeed better   pray Try I have a great Opinion of Its Succeeding

What Thou Observes on the Vines and their Culture, Ought not to Discourage (nor will not) the Indefatigable Man, patience & perseverance overcomes the Hardest things   In time no doubt but a Vineyard may be Raised of the Select Sorts of your Country Grapes, from one Vine the branches may be Laid down on Every Side & in a few years a Large Spott may be run Over ¼ of an acre or half an acre with us will yield 5 and 10 hogsheads per year which is Enough to make the Experiment, but the great art, besides planting is pruning. A person well skilled will never want Fruite if the seasons permit.

Some of the Living creatures thou mentions — in pticular the Large Squirrels to turn loose in his Lordship's woods — but this we must leave till Wee can find a Captain that will take Care of them. If our friend Charles Reed's son Charles should have a ship we might have some hopes but to send red birds or anything else till Wee have a proper conveyance is great time and Trouble Lost. But this I think may be easily done to send Terrapins, but put them into a Cask with Earth att Bottom and Holes all round but this must be in the Autumn after they have had their summers feed. And your water turtles no doubt may be sent the same way & att the Same Time of year, being taken before they hide themselves in the Ground & then they will live without food and have a Chance of Coming safe to us, for the Last were all washed overboard.

Dr Fred. thy Entertaining Letters of June 5th & 15th I should have taken notice of Sooner but they have been out of my hands att his Lordships — thy Account of the White Cedar is very Satisfactory. It is a very odd Whim in yr people to think that the Barbery blasteth Corn.[1] — Thy Journey to the Blew Mountains Shows thee art not to be Daunted by faint hearted Fellows but yet where there is a Mortal Enemy Near it Requires prudence & Caution in Every Step that is Taken. If thee apprehend any of the Specimens is not Exactly Named, it is but sending Mee the Same over again with thy Remarks. Thee forgot a Specimen of the Leather Wood, it seems to be Bacciferous or Berry bearing, Send more Seed.*

I hope by Robert Grace thee Will receive 3 Small Boxes, 1 Long Brown paper parcel, 1 brown paper parcel & 1 Bundle of paper for Specimens with Letters in one of the parcels or boxes. The Last Specimens was very Good only some the wrong Side outwards.

Thy Letter came too Late for Briony Seeds, but I will send some next year, & some of those other Seeds thou mentions, but as they are plants that are but few of them cultivated in gardens, but grow wild up and down the country that makes the difficulty to procure them.

Thee Need Send no Tulip Tree or bla Walnut   any in this Catalogue will be Acceptable & some few as I hinted before

Now I Shall take my Leave of thee wishing thee & thy Good Woman & Children Health & Prosperity   I am thy Sincere frd

P Collinson

I wonder thou did not Send thy Invoice for Goods to the Value of 21 pounds — had them by these last Ships —

*All the Specimens are gone to Oxford   when they are sent back with their names, thee shall hear from Mee.

BP 2:22; D. 91–94.
1. Darlington apparently agreed with Collinson. The "Corn" to which Collinson referred was probably wheat, which was commonly called corn in England. It is interesting to note that the colonists had apparently recognized, as Darlington had not, that wheat is injured by the heteroecious rust, *Puccinia graminis,* which requires both wheat and the common barberry to complete its parasitic life cycle.

From COLLINSON

Londn March 22 1736/37

Dear Frd John Bartram

att the receipt of this go to Mr. Shippen who is partner with our Worthy Friend J: Logan, and ask for a pcell Directed for thee, In it thou will find a Box of seeds, as per Catalogue thou will find Inclosed, with Two Letters for thee & two More to Gentlemen my pticular Friends, on the Eastern Shore of Maryland. Seal them if they will be any use to thee. James Holladay Esq. lives on Chester River & George Robins, Esq. on Choptank River, these Directions (being in a hurry) I forgot to set down   there is one for Docr. Hill of London Town but as that is on the Western Shore lay it by till thou visits that Quarter where I have many Friends & some of the first rank in Virginia. if Letters will be any service to thee, thou shall not want them — Inclosed is some seed of a Noble Annual, grows 6 or 7 feet high & makes a beautifull show with its long bunches of red flowers, but I am afraid it will [be] to Late to venture it this year, However, sow half & keep the other till next year, it is called the great Oriental Persicaria. I am with Love thy sincere Friend

P. Collinson

take Care Some Seeds in the Letter

pray does the Marsh Trefoil or Buck Bean Increase that was sent to our friend Charles Reed — it grows wonderfully in very moist, shallow, watery places.

I find I had none of the plants of the first Cargo grow, as under, if it happens in thy way to supply them pray do —

Smooth Leaved Solomons Seal
Rough Leaved Solomons Seal
Blew Berried Solomons Seal grows 4 feet high something Like our
   English
the Berry Bearing and ⎫ both grow and are rarities
the rough Leaved ⎭ but the Berry bearing sort
is Recon'd a Smilax with Solomon Seal Leaves
Dittany good against the bite of snake   did not grow
Small white Hellebore, if there is not some in the Cargo pray send a root
   or Two of the same
Devils Bitt or Blazing Star   send a Root or Two – this failed.

pray has thee happened to be that way when the wild Lupin was in seed   It flowers in the Spring & Grows in sand as thee observes. The root is long & stringy; so must be raised from seed being very difficult to transplant.

pray have I that plant lately discovered of such wonderful Efficacy to Cure sore breasts   A sort of Colts foot   by the Palatines[1] called Aristolochia. Pray send the method of cure, and some seed

pray what are the Vertues of the plant sent Mee by the name of the panax? it grows well, and is Called by Tournfort, Aralia Canadensis

Thee has twice sent me a Catalogue of divers plants thou Desires, I have sent it to P. Miller & Desired him to plant what He has of them in a Case, to be ready to be sent by the Last Ship in the Autumn.

I consider Double postage to have putt ½ doz seeds in this Letter

BP 2:24; D. 94–95.
1. German settlers.

To COLLINSON[1]

Pensilvania: April 26:1737

I have observed for many years past the annual Progress of a certain Species of Caterpillers. Their Course is from West to East, about ten, twenty or thirty miles a year, and so they proceed Eastward towards the Sea, where it is concluded when they come into their flying state, they are blown off the Land, and perish in the Sea.

Once in twenty Years this sort of Caterpiller appears in prodigious numbers: twice we have observed since this Province was settled by the English; and the Swedes observed them once in their time.

When they are in such Swarms, they devour whole Woods before them, especially Oaks of all kinds, leaving not a green Leaf, that in June the woods appear like mid Winter: which is the destruction of abundance of Trees. For this happens in the heighth of Vegetation, and then the Sap receives such a Check for want of Leaves and Shoots to divert it, that it never circulates again. This is very surprizing to behold such noble stately oaks killed by so small an Insect: but this happens not only with us but in our neighboring Provinces.

These Caterpillers are very hairy, and two Inches long: When they come to maturity they creep or fall from the great Trees and creep up the Bushes, and weave themselves up in a Case or Webb like a Silk worm, coming out a Fly. They then copulate and lay their Eggs in Clusters in an enamell'd Ring round the Twiggs of Bushes: which by some glutinous matter sticks very fast during the Winter, but hatch in the Spring[2]

This leads me to remember, about twelve or fourteen years agon there came a great number of Bears amongst our Inhabitants in the Fall of the year. This was reasonably concluded was owing to want of Acorns, their autumn food, a very great way Westward, which might be occasioned by the Caterpillers devouring the leaves and so disabling the Trees from bearing Acorns.[3]

About ten years past there came incredible numbers of Pigeons from the West and directed their Course Eastward. They came in great Flocks a mile or more long and half a mile broad in a Flock, continuing several days from morning to night, and when they settled to roost, they sat so close, and were so numerous that they broke down Limbs from Trees. Our people used to go in the night and shoot among them killing as many as they could carry home.

I conclude their coming in such numbers might be for want of Food, a scarcity of Acorns and other Mast, several hundred Miles to the Westward and with us we had a very great quantity, till the Pigeons came, and clear'd all before them.

In the Spring they return flying West towards their own Country, making little Stay by the way: but not near so many went back as came out.

I shall now beg leave to make some Remarks on these Observations, as first the wonderfull order and Ballance that is maintain'd between ye vegetable and Animal Oeconomy, that the Animal should not be too numerous to be supported by the Vegetable: nor the Vegetable Production be lost for want of gathering by the animal.

Secondly, the surprizing Instinct these Creatures are endowed with, that leave their natural Habitations to travel such a long Way after their Food, and return back again to breed.

Thirdly it persuades me to think that there must be very great Forests and a fertil Country to the Westward, that can maintain & support so many Millions of Pigeons (besides other animals). For it is observed the Pigeons always frequent the most fruitfull part of the Country: there being the greatest variety of Vegetables produced for their support.

Royal Society of London Archives, LBC 25.148–50 (read February 8, 1738).
1. Copy of part of Bartram's letter, organized into three sections by Collinson.
2. Here ends the first section.
3. Here ends the second section.

To COLLINSON

Pensilvania April 26, 1737[1]

Kind Friend,

What Mr. Paul Dudley remarks of the periodical appearance of a particular Species of Locust, I have remarked twice in my memory with us in Pensilvania that every fifteenth year they are seen in prodigious Swarms. It is now about five years since the last time, but we have a very few every year. In my journey to ye Country North West from Philadelphia I was surprized to see the curious manner in which these Locusts make their Nests. There is Male and Female. The latter is furnished with a Dart half an inch long between her Breast and Belly and reaches to the end of her Tail. She sheaths it up when she does not use it, as you may see by that which I send you. It is very wonderful to observe the use she make of her Dart to pierce the small branches of Trees, Forest as well as Fruit Trees, and therein she deposits her Eggs. Specimens of Twigs so darted I here inclose, that you may observe ye laborious dexterity of these Insects, in providing a proper nidus for their Eggs. They are undoubtedly hatched, and supported by the Pith and Juices of the Trees, but how long this is in operation I know not, nor how they get into the ground.

But this I know that they begin to come out of the ground in June and continue so for about a month, but I believe it is in the night for I never could see them break the Ground tho' in some places it is so full of holes it is like an Honey Comb. I have digged them up two feet deep in the Earth, but the common opinion is, they go down much deeper.

When they first creep out of the Ground they have not the appearance of a Locust, but an odd shappen Grub with Leggs. They crawl up on green Wood or dry Wood, or on the Bark of Trees & thereon fix themselves fast with their Claws. Being in this Posture a little while, the Skin or Shell of their Back opens, and out creeps the Locust, leaving the Husk or Chrysalis in the exact form & size it was in which it crept out of the Earth. (The Dragon Fly or Horse Stinger is produced after ye same manner, but that their Chrysalis creeps out of the water).

In a Day's time the Locust with the Wings & Body is at full growth but tender and not of so dark a Colour as when a few Days older.

Then they proceed to Copulation, and darting their Eggs. The Male is almost continually making such a noise flying from Tree to Tree, that when we are in the woods, we can scarcely hear anything else.

46

What is further remarkable notwithstanding their prodigious Swarms, we can scarcely perceive yet they devour little or nothing: whereas Swarms of Locusts in other Countries are reported to eat up every Green thing, and become a Plague to the Inhabitants; they are rather a Benefit than Distress to us for they are food for most kind of Fowl, and many Beasts, and our Indians will pluck off their Wings, boil and eat them.

After their time of their coming out is over, they soon disappear, being the Prey of so many Animals

John Bartram

Royal Society of London Archives, LBC 25.112–16 (read December 14, 1738).
1. Although dated April 26, 1737, there is reason to believe that this letter was written on part of a February 27 letter. See Collinson's letter of December 10, 1737, commenting on it. Bartram did write a letter on April 26; see Collinson's reply of December 14, 1737.

From JOHANN JACOB DILLENIUS

Oxford. April 26, 1737

Honest Mr. Bartram:
I have received ye quire of plants you sent me by ye hands of Mr. Collinson. I am obliged to you for them. I am glad to hear Miller's Dictionary was acceptable to you.

Your great Laurel must be a fine plant. I should be glad to have some account of it, viz. to what size it grows, when it bears its flowers &c & if opportunity offers, send me a specimen with seed vessels & another or two with flowers. If you will clap some flowers separately into a pocket Book they will dry & show ye thing better   Dr. Plukenet makes mention of a Cornelian Cherry with a Bay Leaf, growing in Virginia, which I have no specimen of, nor do I know ye Plant. If it should be known by that Name in your Country, pray send me a Specimen & some Seeds if you can.

I have not had Time yet to examine Mr. Collinsons two Quires of plants & to marque, which I want. I believe it will be less trouble for the future both to you & me, if you will send at once a couple of Specimens, so if I want it, I may have it without having to wait two or more years for it & it will save you trouble to look it out or perhaps be obliged to gather it.

If you should have duplicates of ye Yappon or Casena, send me a Specimen, with flower or fruit if you have it so.

Of your white long coned Pine, as you call it, I have had formerly Specimens from N. Engl. whence it seems to be more common, than with you, but if you meet with it again, search between ye Scales & you will find at ye end of ye wings, which lie between ye Scales, a small Seed, in shape like a crab or Apple Seed, which is ye true Seed. The thing is to know ye time, when ye cone is ripe & begins to open, & if these seeds are apt to drop out, they may perhaps be found under ye Trees. The cone you sent of it, had still his wings, two at each scale as usual, but ye Seeds at ye end of them were not ripe. I find Paper is scarce in your Parts & that you with Difficulty write upon ye crse paper on which ye plants are fastened, therefore have desired Mr. Collinson to send you a Crowns worth of writing Paper.

I am your obliged friend & Servant

J J Dillenius

I should be glad of some more Seeds of Whych Hasel. I want likewise Sassafras Seeds; take some of each & put them single up in Bees wax, which will keep them fresh & exclude ye air that dryes them up.

As to other seeds, I cannot direct you, the Authors varies so much in Names & so they do in your Parts that one hardly understands one another. Any thing that comes in your way will be acceptable to me.

Pray send me a Specimen of your Common Pine numb. 2, with ye Cones being on it to see whether they hang or grow upon it. Seeds of ye common Candle berry Tree are wanted.

Historical Society of Pennsylvania Library.

From COLLINSON

Lond May 20th 1737

Friend John

I Here Inclose thee, the Names of the plants or Specimens Last Sent as I had them from Docr Delenius professor of Botany att Oxford, to whome I have yearly Imparted of thy Seeds, He is Willing to make thee Some Acknowledgmt, for thy Trouble of Collecting, I could not think of any thing I thought would be more acceptable then Philip Millers Dictionary as it Contains the whole System of Gardening & Botany — by the Assistance of that Book & Parkinson thou will be Enabl'd by their Indexes to find out any plant with a Lattin Name that may be Mention'd in the Inclosed Catalogue

As I have taken a pretty deal of pains In the Catalogue I have the Less to write Here there is Seeds & Specimens Mention'd of Several plants but it is not expected thee Canst Comply with them all

By what I can Observe of the fine Laurells No 102 & 108 or Chamaerhododendron their Seeds Seems to be Light & Chaffey which is the worst Sort of Seed to Send Over for Keeping that I don't Expect Wee shall Ever raise them Here but Must Depend on plants — So prethee go att a proper Season to the nearest place and Load a pair of panniers or Basketts with young plants — and Sett Some in thy Garden to take Root & Send ½ dozen over att a Time for this Seems to Mee to be the Most Elegant Tree that has been Discovered in your province Indeed in South Carolina there Is the Magnolia Great Laurell Leafed Tulip Tree, which is an Ever Green grows 60 feet High — its Leaves are as Long again as yours & the flowers White of a Rose or water lillie Figure, but as Large as the Crown of Ones Hatt, There is one in England that Flowers Every year finely and I have Several plants in my Garden — Another pticular thing I must Request Is to gett a Handfull or Two of white Cedar Cones for Philip Miller for in Separating the Seeds by Accident He had none of the White Cedar Cones

But what I admire Is that thee doth not tell Mee how thee would have Returns Made for the Twenty Guineas   thou looses Time in Makeing Money & an oppertunity to have sent Goods freight Free p Capt Richmond or Capt Savage   It is Surprizing to Mee thou did not Send the Order with the Seeds & Left it to my Discretion to Send thy Returns, Now as Soone as thou can It will be near Twelve Month before thou will see any thing for thy Trouble and att Last be Obliged to pay freight if a strange Captain or Else not Send the Goods So that be as it will thee art like to Suffere by thy own Neglect —

Another thing I would Gently touch On & that Is, to be as Close & Compact in thy packing of the Seeds as possible, for the freight & Charges Comes to a great Deal   the Last Cargo came to £2:12s:6d, had thee a thought on this thee would have packed Some things Closer   To Give thee an Idea of the Charges I shall inclose a Freight Bill In which the Captain has Charged priage to Every pcell wch is not Customary but that Depends on an Agreement made in the Bill of Loading, Next Cargo I shall beg the assistance of our Frd Israel pemberton or Joseph Breintnall to make the Agreement in the Bill of Loading —

If another Time thee Sends any Growing plant a Great many may be pack'd Close together in a Case Two feet square or Two feet Wide & three long — as to thy Care of the Names, it does not much Signifie for when I see them grow or flower can soone Distinguish them, I hope thee will take these Friendly Hints in good part as it is Intended   I am with much Love thy Sincere friend

P Collinson

the pretty flower Cal'd the Dutch Twins has flowered but it is plain to Mee a Calceolus Maria or Species of the Leafe or Heleborine   the fine white Ladies Slipers have not yett flower'd   Wee have had an unkindly Spring which has kept the plants back, but Most if not all seem Alive Except the flowering Shrub, I must say I never saw plants taken up with more Judgment & Come better, but great allowance must be made for Difference in Climate Soil & Season, Wee want a Little More of your Heat att this Season of the year for your Country plants & yett Some Sorts grow & thrive well as in their own Country   the Marsh Martigon is going to flower very Strongly — pray Look out for 2 or 3 Roots of Yellow flowering Ladies Slippers, Mine begin to Decline — I presume thee Continues thy Resolve for thy Intended progress through the Lower Countys to the Capes & then round the Eastern Shore of Maryland Home — but if thee thinks thee Can do better nearer Home, then save thy Self that trouble   Variety of acorns are Wanting — I refer thee to my other Letters as to other pticulars   I hope thou have Mine & the things by our Friend Robt Grace — who has taken some pains to make himself Master of fluxing Mettles, He will be able to give our friend Wolley Some Satisfaction as to the Richness & Quallity of His Ores, I have shown them to a Knowing Man who has given

Mee his Opinion of them as farr as he could Guess without Smelting which att my Leisure I shall Communicate

I have Sent the Catalogue of what Seeds thee wants to Oxford & to Phillip Millar who has promised Mee Seeds & plants so I hope thee will have Some Chance of Some next Season

Dear John I shall only now Acknowledge the Receipt of thine by Capt Steadman — It contains many Curious remarks & Observations In Nature and very pertinently and Well Expressed   needs no apology for thy Natural Way of Expressing thy self   is more Acceptable Clear & Intelligent, then a fine Sett of Words & Phrases — I take it very kind att thy Hands   the Variety of Matter it Contains a great pleasure

to thy Loveing frd
P Collinson

our Friend Capt Richmond often talks of thee and of a fine Ivy or Bay that grows on a Bank going down to the River   pray Send Mee a good Specimen or Two in full Flower, for I have not a good one but I have Two or 3 plants grow Well that I hope to See flower

> No 1—This used to be called Clenopodium but Tournefort refers it to the Leonurus and names it Leonurus Canadensis organi folio
> 2—a sort of Germander   Tournefort calls it Chamadrys Canadensis urtica folio
> 3—Vervain with a Nettle Leafe   Verbena Urtica folio Canadensis of Tournefort
> 4—Hedysarum a sort of French Honysuckle if not a Sensitive   Wee have it not   pray send some specimens & Seeds for the Oxford Garden
> 5—Gratiola a sort of Fox Glove   Wee have it not   Send another for the Oxford Garden
> 6—Flor Clitorius
> 7—a Crysanthemum or Sunflower
> 8—Plucknett calls these sorts of plants Serpentaria but Plumier more properly calls it Saururus or Lizard Taile
> 9—Sweet sented Golden Rod
> 10—This Genus is not known   it goes for a Ornithogalum or hyacinth   if it has bulbous Roots may be Easily Sent   the Seed so Chafey I am afraid Wee shant Raise   pray send a specimen of the female Blossome
> 11—Origanum   a sort of Wild Marjorum
> 12—Enchanters Night Shade   Described by Tournefort
> 13—Chamacrista   a sort of Wild Senna
> 14—Sium   a sort of Water Parsnep   is not in our Collection att Oxford   Send Seeds and specimens for them
> 15—Not well known   I believe it to be an Adhakoda   Send specimens & Seeds for Oxford
> 16—Persicaria Frutescens   Parkinson 857   A sort of Aromart

17—Cynoglossum Virginianum   a sort of Hounds Tongue
18—Plucknett calls this Anagalis or yellow pimpernell
19—Lychnis or Campion   figured by Plucknett
20—Wild Senna
21—Call'd by Plumier Dioscorea from Dioscorides   I believe it male & Female with you by the specimens
22—An Aster or Starr flower I have not seen before   Send Specimen & Seed for Oxford
23—Chondrilla   a species of Succory, a very pretty plant   I have a plenty in my Garden   Docr Witt has Just Sent Mee His receipt for using the Root & account of Its curing Some bitt by the Rattle Snake
24—Blew Cardinal flower   Send more Seed
25—Elichrysum of Tournefort   a sort of Everlasting flower
26—a new Aster or Starr flower not yett Described   Send Seed & specimen for Oxford
27—Ambrosia Canadensis platanifolio, Tournefort
28—Lysimachia Canadensis Lates flore   yellow Willow Herb by Borehave
29—Crysanthemum or Bidens with peach like Leaves
30—A Sort of Galeopsis   Dead Nettle or Horehound which is not in the Oxford Collection   Send specimens & Seeds
31—Digitalis or Foxglove with broad leaves   the Colours of the flower Wee can't Judge by the Specimen
32—another Digitalis or Fox Glove with Narrow Leaves but Can't Judge of the Colour of the flower   I wish Wee could gett these plants in our Gardens
33—Satureja Virginiana   a pretty plant   Send Seed and Specimen Species of Savery
34—Apocinon or Dogs Bane with Rosemary Leaves (New)
35—A Species of Gentian   is not in the Oxford Collection   Send specimen & Seed
36—a New Sort of Cleaver
37—Four leafed Madder Rubia   Tetraphyllos Virgineanas of Plucknett
38—a New sort of Aster   Send specimen & seed for Oxford
39—Digitalis Mariana Filipendula Folio of Petiver
40—Eupatorium americanum (Scandens of Valiant)   Hemp Agrimony
41—a new sort of Orach, or Chenopodium   Send Seed & specimens for Oxford
42—Gentiana Virginiana Saponaria folio flore Ceruleo Longiore
43—a new Cardinal flower   Send Specimen and seed for Oxford
44—the Genus of this is not yett known   if the seed grows Wee shall find it but I am afraid the seed is not full ripe   Send more
45—Breintnals Snake Root   Sanicula canadensis amplissima folio Lacinata (of Tournefort)
46—Elichrysyma   species of Everlasting flower
47—anemony
48—Yellow Milkwort   polygala   better or more seed for Oxford

49—a Remarkable Convolvulus   More Seed & Specimen
50—A new Aster   send Specimen & Seed for Oxford
51—Centary, Centaurium Virginianum, send seed
52—Balsamine Lutea, the Huming Bird plant of Josselyn
53—Three Leafed Hedysarum (of Cornutus)
54—Golden Rod, Virga aurea
55—Panax, or Aralia Canadensis of Tournefort
56—Golden Rod, all of this Class are distinguished by their Different Leaves
57—Aster or Starr flower, these are Distinguished by their Different Leaves
59[1]—Shrub Trefoil, or perhaps a Barba Jovis – Seed for Oxford
60—Vaillant call it Aralia, Plucknett names it Christophoriana but it want of Flowers or Seed in the Specimen, can't determine
61—Virga Aurea, Golden Rod
62—This seems to be a Sium or Water parsnep, Docr Delenius professor of Botany att Oxford says He should be Glad to have good specimens of all the plants of this Class that bears their Flowers in umbels & Ripe Seed, for Ours are not perfect, nor have Wee many of them –
63—a Species of Lysimachia Silaquota or Padded Willow Herb, Seed
64—Abrotonum, Southern Wood
65—Apocynum flore Rubro
66—Very like our Pyrola folio Mucrinato Senato (of Casper Bauhinus) of Winter Green, I want a Specimen (for Oxford, & berries)
67—Virga Aurea
68—True Love or Ope Berries, Herba Paris, Call'd Solanum Millar? Triphillum Canadensis, there is one with a yellow & one with Red Flower, as this root is bulbous may be Easily sent –
69—Perhaps a Campanulla, but the flower is so very small Can't determine
70—Apocinon with orange Colour flowers, (a fine plant), seed
71—perhaps a Cacalia, but cant say for want of flower or seed Vessell
72—Virga Aurea Nova Anglia, See Parkinson page 243
73—Senchus or Sow thistle Like our Smooth Broad Leafed
74—Apocinon Minus Canadensis
75—a New Lychnides, if thou Ever goes to the blew Mountains bring down some plants for the Garden, from thence Wee can have Seed & Specimens for all our Friends, I presume this has white flowers
76—Capsida or Scutellaria
77—a Very pretty Grass
78—a Remarkable Water plant (Intirely New) if thou goes into New Castle County again see in what state it is, bring Specimens & plants for to be sett by the River or some pond side
79—Plucknett, & Ray, make this an Ornithogalum, I had it formerly in my Garden raised from Seed Docr Witt sent Mee, I could be glad to have it again, it is a pretty plant, I believe it is Chelcea
80—Plucknett, makes this a Species of Eupatorium

81—aster, Nova Anglia, altissimus, floribus Amplissimus (Parkinson)
82—a pretty Apocinon
83—Christophoriana or Herb Christopher. I have it in my Garden
84—Gallium or Ladys Bed Straw
85—Spear Head, or Sagittaria affinis, planta palustris, (Plucknett)
86—Our Lagopus or Haresfoot Trefoil
87—a Sort of Digitalis. Figur's in Oxford History, send seed
88—Onagra Angusta folio flore minor – Tournfort
89—Calceolis Maria vel Heleborina flore Albo Macculato
90—another Species of Cassida, vel Scutellaria
91—Satureija, a New Species, I have it in my Garden from thy first seed   it has a strong penny royal smell   I take it to be Different from Number 33 – which Wee have not
92—Hydrophyllon, Tournefort, or Water Leafe, send seed
93—Barba Jovis or rather a Spartium, I fancy Indigo may be made from this plant, its leaves appear so blewish when dry –
94—this I cant guess att for want of flower or seed vessell   I should be glad to see fair Specimens & seed
95—Serratula Virginia (Saw Wort), I have it in my Garden
96—a pretty polypody –
97—a Hemionitis
98—a Species of Hieracium or Hawkwood
99—this Curious umbelliferous plant, I can't say any thing for Want of the Seed Vessell, pray send Specimens and Seed for Oxford
100—*a perticular & fine sort of Hieracium,* or Hawkwood, seed & Specimens I Observe a Many rare plants from the Blew Mountains which if Thee has not taken care to bring plants for thy Garden – I am afraid Wee shall never see them Here, for it is not worth while to go on purpose, In my travells all over England, I have preserved Wild plants fresh for my Garden – by this Methode, first, Lett them be in what state soever I took them up, with some Earth to the Roots, then I always provided green moss, in this wrap'd the Roots & branches -- & tied It round In paper, & putt Into bags hanging by my Horses Side under my Close to keep from the sun, att Night, I unloosen'd the Branches & Leaves but not the Roots, & then Sett only the Roots with the Moss tied round it, in a Bason of Water Exposed to the Air & Dews, I used to putt 2–4 or 6 plants in one Bundle, short ones & Long Ones each by themselves   by this Methode I could Carry & Keep plants fresh & in Health for 2 or 3 weeks   att planting be sure Water, & Keep Waterd & shaded on Days for some time
101—a fine Species of poplar, There is one like it in South Carolina which Wee have Here in Our Gardens
102—This Species of Laurell is found growing on the Black sea   is a most beautifull plant, and very nearly agrees with Yours from pensilvania Tournfort gives it a hard Name, Chamarhododendron with a Laurel Leafe, bearing Tufts of Blew Flowers, Inclining to purple, it must be a noble Ornament for a Garden

103—Wee want both Flower & Seed Vessell

104—This is call Poison Wood Tree; our Poison Sumach by the Imperceptible Flying off of Its Efluvia it chiefly Affects the Eyes; of this plant the True Japan Varnish is made, it is named, Toxicodendron foliis Alatis fructu Rhomoide –

105—Wants Flowers & seed Vessells

106—but is [sic] Fruite   it is a sort of Water Elder, called by Tournft. Opulus

107—Black Haw, plucknett call this a Mispilas, Banister makes it a Rhamnus (send seed)

108—This is Quite New, think it a Species of Chamarhododendron pray send more Specimens, with the flowers & Seed Vessells   seems to be a very Curious plant

109—Can say nothing for want of Materials

110—Rhus or Sumach, this I have in my garden

111—Is a real Cypress – by you Call'd white Cedar

112—Candle Berry Myrtle, I have both kinds in my garden

113—This Pine I do not find Mention'd by any Author, this has 4 & 5 Leaves in one Sheath, pray send 2 or 3 more specimens & Cones, but pray Mention what Specimens the Cones belong to, thee forgot the Last.

114—This is a New Betula or Birch, pray send 2 or 3 better Specimens & Seed

115—Plucknett calls this Alnifolia, a sort of Spierica Frutex

116—a Sort of Cornus or Dogwood

117—Witch Hazel may be as proper name till we find a better

118—Cant Determine for want of proper Materials

119—this is Calld in Latin Carpinus, in Greek Ostrya, but the Hop bearing Tree is a good Significant Name

120—Red Cedar or Rather Juniper

121—Spirea Opule Folio, by Turnefort, Spirea with Water Elder Leafe

122—Can't Determine, wants materials

123—This is Call'd Viburnum, but for my part I am & shall be Dubious about its Genus till I see it Growing, it is not Described by any body, Thee may take this for one General Rule without my being perticular, that plants or Seeds will be always very acceptable If New & undescribed plants send

124—Crategus folio Arbutus, Tournfort

125—Acer Sacchariferum, Seeds & Specimens of its Flower on the Branches

126—Smilax, Bindweed or Sarsiparella

127—pray Send Specimens of Berries & Flowers in particular and then shall be able to Rank it

128—a new Species of Mezereon or Thymelea, has the Seed but want to see the Flower, pray send Specimens of It

129—Must have the Fruite or Seed to find out – it is pretty odd plant not known
130—the Blossoms of this ash Joyn'd with the Leaves and the Keys hanging on would make right Specimen but this is not always to be Expected   the Length of the Way & Time will not allow it (so must be Content)
131—Bullion Wood, plucknett calls this, scabiosa dendroides   Valliant calls it Platanecephalus, – seed –
132—Common Jersey pine, It is New to Mee, and has this Singular Difference from 113, for that has 4 & 5 leaves to a Sheath & this has but Two, pray send us 3 or 4 More Specimens, & Cones –
133—Sumach, Rhus Virginianum panicula Sparsa ramis patulis Glabris
134—If this Spirea grows wild it may Differ from our Garden Sort, but it looks very like it, pray Lett Mee Know
134—Burnett[2] leafed Rose, is this Wild with you
135—Eupatorium folio Oblongo, this is the Long Leafed purple Stalked Water Hemp
136—Sagitta   arrow Head
138—a Sort of Chickweed – call'd Samolus with broader Leaves then our Common
139—Pentaphilloides, Fragaria Folio –
140—a pretty Species of Aster not well known, seed & Specimen
141—this Seems to be a New Sort of Spirea, pray Seeds of It & Specimen
142—Polygala, Milkwort, with Red flower
143—Turritis –
144—Cardinal flower, which I think as before   is 1st or 2d Quire
145—Send but Seed Vessell & it will Clear this
146—this is very like Alsine Sparia, growing in Devonshire & Cornwall
147—belongs to the Lingus Cervina or Harts Tongue
148—Nymphea, Water Lillie   something like ours   (Observation) that all Coniferus or Conebearing Trees Ripens towards the Spring & Should then be Gathered
149—A Species of Amaranthus
150—a very pretty Helleborine, it seems to be Red or purple, when thee meets with it again collect a Root or Two
151—Seems to be a True Hellebore
151[3]—pedicularis Lousewort or Cristagalli   Rattle Grass
152—Orchis Satyrion or Dogs Stone
153—the same with yellow flowers
154—the same with white flowers

{ The plants may be taken while in flower with Earth to their Roots and so come to thy garden   the Yellow one would be a great Rarity I have a many times taken them up in flower & they never fail to blow again next year, – I never heard or saw a yellow one but the purple or the white will be acceptable

155—Virga Aurea ⎫ Distinguished only by the Likeness of their
156—Virga Aurea ⎪ Leaves to other plants   you have a great
157—Virga Aurea ⎬ Variety of this Tribe   must make a fine
158—Virga Aurea ⎪ show Collected together in a Row in One
159—Virga Aurea ⎪ Bed, then they'd show themselves to a
160—a pretty Fumetory ⎭ pleasant advantage
161—Virga Aurea
162—Chrysanthamum
163—This plant from the Island up Shulkil can't dtermine for want of Flowers or Seed Vessells
164—and Wee are as much att a Loss for this plant for same Reason
165—Prunella – Self Heale
166—Thlaspi:Virginiana foliis serratis, per Tournefort
167—A new Helleborine (send Specimens) for Oxford, I take this to be the plant with fine Vein'd Leaves which thee called a Cedum, there was a plant or Two in the last Cargo which I hope will grow
168—Quite New, there is a season no doubt but it bears some flowers and for want of them can't name it, pray send a Specimen or Two for Oxford
169—A Moss call'd Selago, not Differing from our English, but that the Leaves are bent Downward, Discrib'd by Ray.
170—Lycopodium, a Sort of Club Moss – perhaps 168 is the same Species
171—Plucknett, call this Echinophera Indica, pray send seed of It
172—Quite New, perhaps a Pedicularis or Crista Galli, send Specimen & Seed for Oxford
173—Aster Americanus frutescens Satureja foliis (plucknett)
174—Aster Americanus albus, white Flowering branch'd aster, Plucknett
175—Alsine, Spergula Mariana, of Plucknett
176—Eupatorium Mariano, plucknett, Water Hemp with Hawkweed Leaves
177—Imperatoria of Tournefort, a Species of Mather wort, this is one of the umbelliferous plants, that specimens & seed will be acceptable to Oxford but the seed of this seems fresh & good so hope will grow
178—pray send when oppertunity offers more perfect specimens
179—pray send the same, for by those sent cant say what tribe they be
180—Scutellaria or a Species of Cassida
181—I have this Beautifull Lychnides in my Garden in plenty, it came from So. Carolina
182—this Rare plant I have in my Garden, it bears pale blewish Flowers, but haveing not seen the seed Vessell, Wee can only Judge it to be an Apocinonides, it was a great pitty thee had not brought it from the Mountains –
183—a Sort of Bugloss –
184—Campanula perfoliata, send a better specimen
185—Anemonie Virginiana. See Parkinson –

186—must have a more perfect Specimen to Determine
187—Lysimachia Siliquosa, poded Willow Herb
188—Calaminta Mariana, plucknett, a pretty Mint
189—Virga Aurea Americana
190—a Pretty Aster or Starr Wort or Starr flower   Send
191—a pretty aster   pray some seed
192—Convolvulus – seems a Dwarfe Kind, seed
193—Call'd by the Virginians Side Sadle Flower, it is a singular odd flower & the Leafe as remarkable, I had it sent Mee from Virginia   it Lived a Summer but for want of a Bog, went off, the Leaves of the Virginia sort are foot & half Long & the Flowers proportionately Larger
194—Doc Delenius names this a Martigon, but as the flower Leaves are upright and turn not Inwards as the Martigons Do, I think it rather a Red Lillie, Docr Witt once sent Mee one of the Roots, which bore only one flower as this Seems to do whereas the Martigon has Many, if thee Meets with any of these Lillie Roots send Mee one or Two —
195—Send a better Specimen
196—a New Cardinal flower, pray Specimen & Seeds for Oxford
197—Althea Magna, a Noble plant, seeds are much Desir'd for us all
198—a Better Specimen ⎫
199—a Better Specimen ⎬ to Determine their Class
200—a New Sort of Lycopodium
201—Urtica or Nettle
202—Dr. Delenius, Declares this to be an Osmond Royal by its flowers & Seeds, but it differs from the common sort, in the way of its growth & place where its found
203 & 204—are both Lunaria, or Moon wort, with Divided thick Leaves (Plucknett)
205—A New Helleborine, should be glad to see the flower & Have a Root
206—Winter Green, Pyrola Fructesens, arbutus Flore, of Caspar Bauhins
207—Winter Green, Pyrola rotunda folia Niger, black round leafed Wintergreen
208—Winter Green, Pyrola figur'd in Plucknett, this I take to be thy Rock boot wax?

BP 2:48; D. 95–98 (plant list was omitted).
1. No. 58 missing.
2. Brown; there are two no. 134s; no. 137 is missing.
3. There are two no. 151s.

From COLLINSON

Lond August 12, 1737

Dear frd John

I am now to thank thee for thine By Linsay which contains many Curious things that Deserve My Notice & pticular remarks but at this Time a year I am so unsettled between town and Country that I have not really time to consider thy last Two Curious Letters, for this Reason don't think I slight them because I am for the present silent about them   I assure thee thou canst not do Mee a greater pleasure than to Entertain Mee with any History of Nature but this I must tell thee as a friend I am afraid thou takes up too much of thy Time to oblige me   I am so much thy Friend that I entreat thee not to let any of thy affairs suffer on my account

Indeed when Thou art Collecting thou art paid for It   I hope this year will prove kindly that Wee May have a Collection of Okes   Send but a few of the White Oke & Swamp Spanish Oke   I believe most thou sent are come up and thrive finely   Wee have a great Quantity of the Cherry up it is a fine plant   Red Cedar comes up very strong but I don't yet see the Sassafras — Tulip Poplar in great abundance   This with most other of your Country seeds will some come up the first, but more the second year, send no more Tulip Poplar   Some of your Swamp Laurel or Bay is come up & thrives well but we want a great Deal more of its Cones   It is a fine plant & when the Wind turns up the silver side of its Leaves it has a pretty Effect   as to the Bay Laurel Called Ivy it is in vain to send any of its seed (unless soon as gathered sown in a box of mould) for it is so small & Chaffy it will not keep. I have had a great deal from Virginia but none Grows [There] is no way so good as plants   I have sufficient for my self but Lord Petre may want Some but a year or Two hence may do   I am afraid a Like fate will attend the seed of that noble Laurel thou Discovered near the blew mountains   A Cargo of Growing plants will be a Rarity worth accepting Next Time thou must try what thou Canst Do, first gett a strong Cargo of young plants into thy Garden   pray make it thy Business this fall, & when they have stood a year & drawn Root they may with more safety be sent as Oppertunity offers

I Reced very Safe thy Two Boxes by Capt Lindsay   the Bulbous Roots came all in very Good Order   seem singular odd plants   I shall give thee Docr Delanius Opinion of them when he has seen Them — I am much obliged to thee for them —

I have not yett had time to Examine thy map up Skulkill and all the other Curious things in that Box but I shall do it first opertunity   nothing that thou sends is Lost or Forgot with Mee

But one thing I must tell thee while I think on it, that I admire thou has not given me Directions In what nature thou would have the twenty guineas Remitted, for the last Cargo   Thou Loses time, Certainly the Money's worth, would be very useful to thee — If to Draw on me for it, in money will be most advantageous to thee, do it, for it is entirely equal to Mee in what manner thee art paid.

As I have been up and down in the Country, I could not forgett my friend John but have Collected a variety of Seeds   possibly some will be acceptable they will have this use to help thee to know our wild plants   I would Advise thee to sow them all as soon as thou receives them, prepare a fresh bed of good Mould   Lay it out regular and sow the seeds in rows, at a foot or more Distant, mark each row with a Number & to that Number in thy book write the name. Keep the Bed Nicely Clean from weeds for suffering them to grow is the reason that many small seeds are Choked & lost & Observe never to Disturb a bed till after the Second Spring for some seeds Lie Two Seasons — I have sent thee two sorts of pines   the Silesia Pine & the Great Stone Pine with the Large Cone   this grows on the Alps   the seeds are large and sweet and much eaten in Italy   Sow these where they may not be Drip'd on by any Trees & where they may have only the Rising or Setting Sun, the Stone Pine is to be sown where it is to stand for they are Difficult to Remove —

pray does thou take a trip to the Eastern Shore in the Fall   I am glad to hear Clay[1] is arrived   I hope thou has mine by Richmond, I sent thee a Magnifying Glass for thy pockett & now send thee Ellis's book.[2] I am, dear John, thy

Sincere frd
P. Collinson

In the Earth is the small yellow Root a species of Ladys Slipper   The one small Ragged Root is Double Blossome Bellwort   The brown protuberant Root is the first showy flower   being the Spring acconite generally flowering att the end of December and all January with us [illegible] planted with it [illegible] Large white Root is small Starr Bethlehem [illegible] together Small Bulbs of Fiery Lillie   this is an odd plant all in [illegible]

Root of Little Narcissus will not flower freely with us because it is not hott enough   plant at once as close as can be to the South side of the House or Wall & cover with Pea straw in Winter   I doubt not but it will flower freely with you   it is a fine flower.

I hope the Cargo by Richmond is come safe, Lett Mee know what Luck pray Remember to send Mee the Blossome & fruite of the Papaw in a Little Jar of Rum   Wee never yet had a specimen of this tree in flower & I want much to See the Fruite which will keep fresh in Rum. pray send more White Cedar Cones for I don't see any

Black Haw & pine cones of all Sorts
Swamp Laurell Large
Chesnut Oke and all trees that we have not had
Sugar Tree Keys

and what Sorts I have listed in the names of the Specimens that can be conveniently procur'd without much trouble or Loss of Time — Three Roots of the Gentian grow, & 4 Roots of the Flower wch are great Rarities, and the pretty variegated Leafed Liverwort but the Rock Budwort with pointed Leaves is gone off as is the Swamp or pretty flowering Shrub that bears Spikes of Flowers, not one Calceolus or Ladies Slipper with white Flowers came up wch I wonder att

List of Seeds
Lysimachia —
Yorkshire Campanulla —
Spurting Cucumber —

Colour'd Cowslips —
Field Jacea —
Large Asphodel —
Marsh Ranunculas —
Virgin Thistle —
Marsh Valerian —
Silesia Pitch Pine —
Cristo galli R — Grass
Red Geranium —
Mercurialis —
Blew Bohemian Cranes Bill —
Our Sanicle —
Siberian Rhubarbe —
White Lychnis —
Blew flowering Geranium —
Small white Asphodel —
Cyanus —
Rapunculus —
Hyeraceum —
Niple Wort —
Yellow flowd Archangel —
Stone Pine   at Trunk in
   Large Clusters 6-9-12 in
   a bunch
Venus Navel Wort

aconite
purple Geranium
Monk's Hood, acconitarum   helmet
   flower
Shrub —

White flowering C —— bell
Wild Parsnip
pretty Clary
perannual Geranium
Wild Endive
White Briony
Creeping perannual —
Galeopsis
yellow flowering Vetch
White Primrose
Herb Paris
Valerian
Hieracium
fine Red Spanish Scrophularia
True Germander —
Conyza
Coletea Cretica
Species Galeopsis
Enchanters Nightshade

Flowery white pollen Cones

[in margin:] Some plants are Twice over because att different gatherings. I hope this Cargo and that per Capt Richmond will show thee I am no slothful forgetful fellow.

pray my Love & Respects to our Friend Joseph Breintnall
pray send or Carry the Inclosed Letter to Dr. Kearsley.

I have given Lord Petre the Humming-bird's nest & eggs so pray look out for another.

BP 2:37; D. 98–100.
1. Unidentified.
2. William Ellis (d. 1758), writer on various agricultural subjects and author of *The Modern Husbandman,* 8 vols. (London, 1750).

To LOGAN

August ye 19th 1737

Kind Friend

I here give thee some account of ye farina as I observed it at ye time when ye Apices opened & discharged it[1]   I observed all these flowers at several states of perfection with what judgment & ingenuity I was capable of   I believe it is near right but if thee sees mistakes I hope thee will consider that I am at ye best but A learning   pray excuse my freedom   So in Consideration of thy many favours & ye kind instructions I remain thy sincere friend

John Bartram

Abutilon	A kind of mallow ye Apices soround ye stiles of ye farina equal length
thorny malow	ye Apices encompas ye stiles of equal length
Ketmia Visicaria	Another kind of mallow ye Apices & stiles of equal hight
Malva perenis	ye Apices embrace ye top of ye stiles at ye discharge of ye farina alltho ye stiles grow longer soon after
Malva purpurea	ye tops of ye stiles curls down to tops of ye Apices
squash	is a little transparent yelowish ye male hath three stamina & ye female three stiles both divided near ye petals but at ye top united
Convolvolus major	hath four apices of different hights ye highest of which toucheth ye top of ye stile at ye discharge of ye farina
Convolvolus minor	hath ye same form & order in proportion
Germander blew flowered	hath one forked stile & four apices which touch ye top of ye stile at ye discharge of ye farina
Succory	is a double flower compounded of many small petals ye bottom of which incloseth 4 stamina & apices which closely embraceth one forked stile which riseth higher then ye apices

blew hawkweed	hath near ye same form & order in leser proportion
scrophulary	is limpid smooth & oval one stile & four stamina
white Campion	is limpid round with three stiles
red Cardinal	is limpid smooth ye apices Closely embrace ye top of ye stile & never seperates until they dry
ye male hamp	hath four apices which opens & discharges its farina in fine dust which is atracted by ye stile of ye female
ye male water blite	hath four apices which opens ye volatil farina is caryed away with ye wind like smoak & is atracted at A distance by ye female which hath A forked stile

here follows some plants whose male & female parts are seperate one from another so that ye farina must float in ye air to reach ye female part tho in ye same plant

our reed	ye male parts with ye apices is near half A foot below ye female stile which is finely feathered to intangle ye farina
great wild nettle	limpid smooth of several forms ye parts with ye apices is half A foot below ye female with ye stile so ye farina must ascend to be united
Ambrosia	this farina falls from A long spike of pendulous mossy flowers Containing ye apices & farina ye female parts with ye stile arises below from ye bosom of ye Cup upon ye branches so that here ye farina descends these three last plants Affords a Curious speculation I should be glad of an opertunity to shew thee ye plants in season that thee might observe them thy self
Amarathoides	very small roundish A little unequal the stile is forked & shorter then ye top of ye apices.
Blew spiked arrow head	long limpid with Six stamina & one stile
white arrow head	is limpid
marsh Crysanthemum	hath one forked stile which four Apices closely embraces this is A compound flower
sweet basil	is uneven darkish with one forked stile even with two apices ye other two shorter

mother wort	oval limpid one forked stile even with two apices ye other two shorter
Echium	large round darkish with one forked stile & five apices reaching to ye midle of ye fork of ye stile
Poylium of several forms	four apices which hang pendulous & touch ye top of a short stile
Cole	Limpid smooth oval one stile & six Apices four long Apices soround ye top of ye stile
Jacea	limpid burry & oval with four Apices which closely embraces ye forked stile

Historical Society of Pennsylvania Library, Logan Papers, 10:67.

1. The apices are the anthers of stamens in which farina (pollen) is produced. Bartram did not use the modern term filament (of stamen) or stigma (of the style). He made rough sketches of the pollen grains as they "appeared magnified by ye fourth magnifier."

From COLLINSON[1]

Dear John

This day I rec'd thy Letter per Wright [on the] Bristol & Lindsay sails to Morrow   Knowing that I have Gather'd my Stumps to send you Shalloons & Buttons & Gulix per him for it Maybe a pretty while before another opertunity offers, & I was very Desirous thee might have Something to turn in Money, indeed it is a pitty thee has been so Long without it

I have done the best I could for thee considering I had but 2 or 3 Hours to do it In. This Comes in a trunk marked, JB Brand – thy name att Length – with a Little Deck Box with Seeds Directed for thee –

Thee will heare further by first Oppertunity from thy Old friend

P Collinson

Goods per Lindsay

Pc Gulix		1 : 0 : –
3 pc fine Cloth yellow Shalloon	28	4 : 4 : –
1 pc Sky blew Do		1 : 9 : –
1 pc fine Green Do		1 : 10 : –
1 pc Olive Do		1 : 10 : –
9 Bags of fine fashble Buttons	6	2 : – : –
2 lls ¼ fine mohair	10	4 : 2 : –
Freight & shipping charges	1	
Due thee		7 :
		21 :

Pray Give my Love to J. Breintnall – I Rec'd his Letter & the Bill – PC   I Designed to have given our Friend Wolley what I had Learn'd about his Fossils, but I take it my Friend's Account is not to be Intirely depended on

— But Now, You have a more Certain Methode to know what Ore is Contain In each sort, per the means of my Ingenious Friend Robt Grace who has taken some pains to Quallifie himself Here for that Work & who is of Such an Obligeing Disposition that there is no Doubt but He will give you all the satisfaction in his power —

BP 2:38.
1. The date is indecipherable but this letter was written in the summer of 1737, as reference to this shipment is in Collinson's letter of September 8, 1737.

From COLLINSON

Londn. Sep. 8 1737

Dr: frd John —

I can now only tell thee that I have sent a pcell of seeds In a pcell to your proprietor, Thomas Penn —

Dress thy self Neatly in thy Best Habits & wait on him for them for I have in a pticular manner Recommended thee to Him —

I have Desired Him to show thee the Natural History of South Carolina in Eight Books, finely Colour'd to the Life so forget not to Ask that favour — first inquire his most Leisure Time & then wait on Him —

I hope the Goods & Box [of] seeds per Capt Lindsay with these now sent will let thee see I have not been idle this Summer   Some may be acceptable. What thee does not like throw away

pray think of the fine new Laurell — Wee sadly want a Specimen of it in flower with its Description.

pray Remember without fail if thou'll oblige Mee to send the papaw fruite full ripe Sent in a Bottle or Little Jar of Rum & 2 or 3 specimens of It, in flower, with a Description of the Colour of the flower for I want to have it engraved & painted —

I am three letters in thy Debt, but no Leisure yett   I am just going out of town for Some Time, so must bid thee

farewell
P. Collinson

Thee will see Docr Delanius's Seeds by his hand writing

BP 2:39; D. 100–101.

To COLLINSON[1]

ye 1st of november 1737

I have been this fall down to ye capes of chesapeake bay by land   ye people are in general very Cyvil   in this journey I have discovered more than I have done in any one journey that I undertooke before   specimens most of all but some that I observed in virginia I accidentally lost or some that I saw in one spot I expected to have found again & could not & so mist of them as with one of periploca   which rambles upon bushes winding about them it produced a then thick wire   the vines are strong & hard ye seed was not ripe   another I saw something like ye horned popy but A very strong peranual plant & a different   I observed but mist of A specimen & A diferent kind of swamp oak but I could find A very fine long leave & large coned pine which was realy different from ours   cones was green   also A thorn leaved like ye english but of ye cock spur kind   1 or 2 others of less note but If I go down ye western shore next year I hope [illegible] & if you think it Convenient for me to go I have nothing against it if [illegible] prosperity be for going down amongst & beyond ye back inhabitants & return along ye [illegible] later than this year whereby I should find most seeds in perfection then   I wrote to Paul dudley this summer but have received no answer   I have received that noble present of doctor delinius which was Philip millers dictionary which affords [illegible] as well as diversion & instruction   it being of general use for me I am much obliged to my good friend peter informing him what would be so very agreeable   I am well pleased with ye report on ye plants which I sent last year   I believe ye doctor hath performed his part with sincerity & been very industrous to name ye seeds & specimens hee desired which I could [illegible] ye catalogue came so late this year that many of ye seeds was ripe & lost that you wanted but I hope I may send ye remaining next year   I also received ye Cask but alas I believe there is nothing there but what wee had in plenty before except [illegible] and I have received ye goods thee sent me by [illegible] with thy present of gartering & ellis book of husbandry such things are acceptable   I shall no ways despise them tho they be sullied but indeed thee hath [illegible] with a great vairiety of rare seed   those by Lynsey & those by [illegible] are most of them rairitys & allso several of ye roots or specimens of these are not ripe when gathered   stone pine I have no hopes of ye seed was not ripe   dear friend I am very thankfull for this fine cargo of seeds   I hope now I shall show my friends that they never saw before   I have sown one half of ye peranual sort & saved ye other half of each sort of seeds to sow early in ye spring   ye rose laurel I mist tho I observed them ye week before thay shed thair seed when thay was close & [illegible] to gather them & there was hardly a perfect one left   these like other cones cast their [seed] dry but next year   I design to watch them daly but I will catch them in perfection [torn] direction to our proprietor but I have had no opertunity to ask for ye sight of [illegible] for as soon as I was sate down he sent for them to show me   I did not ask for them which he readily granted for A month & gave me leave to take them   I said that if he pleased it would suit me better to have them 2 or 3 weeks [illegible] in providing seeds & plants to send to london & had not time to [illegible] he was so free as to ask when ever I heard that [illegible]

BP 1:38:2; American Philosophical Society Library, Wildman transcript.
1. Wildman comments: "This is one of the first drafts retained by John Bartram. It is poorly preserved." Today the margins are eroded and torn.

To COLLINSON[1]

ye combe of a hornet nest for you to observe   ye iner part of ye cells with a Microscope [illegible] that he questions whether ye virginia crab [illegible] in england as is reported that thay do there   they may smell in your gardens but this I am [illegible] that this tree bears that produced this fruit which [illegible] oderiferous of all flowers I know produced by [illegible] ye air for 50 yards round & sometimes [illegible] ye spirea ye questioned whether it groweth wild

asure thy selfe whatever I send to you is not [illegible] but wholy a native of ye countrey except I remark it   now sent thee orders what sort of goods I shall want [illegible] as thee can conveniently for our stores is very full of goods so that our shopkeepers will chuse none but ye [illegible] can have it very cheap my customer writ by mee to thee [illegible] hair buttons with silk & hair twist but instead of that [illegible] ye shalum except one or two bags of them was bristol & not London shalums [illegible] high that I could hardly make as much more of them [illegible] to mee & obliged to stay half a year for my money   pray [illegible] amiss   I believe thee thy best & I know that it is to [illegible] of our towns people is very curious to have that which [illegible] frequent uses silk for summer wear as being very [illegible] is creeping into ye countrey too for wee can hardly find [illegible] opertunity now by Captain Stedman I venture to send thee [illegible] having no perticular business to write about [illegible] I think [illegible] letters which I received last summer as to thy perticular [illegible] what seeds or roots thee desired me to send which [illegible] some pains & care   I sent a large Colection of [illegible] carefully according to ye best method I could then think of   Captain wright who promised to take perticular care of them & [illegible] thy several kindnesses   I allso sent an order to thee what is due mee laid out upon believing thee would [illegible] more now I have an opertunity I must [illegible] thy opinion therein   I believe it might be most ingenious & Curious men that wee [illegible] study of natural secrets   arts & syences would [illegible] [acad]emy or society & have a house for to meet in to Communicate [illegible] discoveries freely   this I believe would [illegible]

BP 1:38; American Philosophical Society Library, Wildman transcript.
1. Wildman writes: "This draft is badly faded and was severely trimmed when mounted so that many words are lacking." It is now almost completely illegible. The letter must have been written from Maryland in the fall of 1737. Collinson thanked Bartram for it on January 27, 1737/8. He corrected Bartram's friend concerning the "shalums" but did not comment about the proposed scientific society until July 10, 1738.

From COLLINSON

Londn Dec. 10 1737

Dr John

    a Little Leisure invites me to peruse thy several Entertaining Letters   I shall proceed in order and begin with thine of feby 27th —

    Thy account of the Locusts is very Curious and very Entertaining to Mee & my Friends & shows that nothing escapes thy Notice   their Surprising method of darting the sticks is admirable   pray watch as it happens in thy way what shape they take as Soon as they are hatched   pray have they Wings when they creep out of the Ground   procure Mee one if thee Canst, in their first state of coming out of the Ground & when the back opens   is it a Real Grasshopper? for I take it all Grasshoppers are Locusts   Sett me right if I am wrong — pin some of Each sort in a Box with a number to Each for I am In Some Doubts if they have not three or four Different apearances   first from the Egg they are a worm or Caterpillar, then they go into the Ground and change when they come out of the Ground   their back opens & produces a Monstrous Large Fly   then I apprehend they Turn to a Grasshopper or Locust

    As to that Caterpiller that comes in such numbers Wee have something like it in England   they will eat the Okes & Hedges bare but never kill them which I take to be Owing that, as we have not the Sun's heat so strong with us, so our vegitation is weaker so the Tree by degrees recovers its verdure again but with you the Heat so rarifies the sap or Juices in Trees and puts it in such Vigorous Action and for want of young shoots & Leaves to Divert it by growth & perspiration the Vessels Burst, or the Circulation stop'd for Want of Vent, that the Tree soon Dies   if thee was to observe all these Caterpillars that Spin up Like silk worms produce a Large Moth & all Crysales that thee finds Hanging Naked produce Butter Flies or Day Flies —

    if thee was to take the Cluster of Eggs round the Twigs & keep them till time of Hatching & feed them with the Leaves of the Tree they was found on thee might see the whole process, or If I could have some sent time Enough with an account of what Tree they was found on, Wee have people would think it worth their while to Hatch them   this would be a pretty amusement for thy Children – They would soon learn, if a Little Instructed

    I have heard frequent accounts of the prodigious Flocks of pigeons but thy Remarks on the wonderful provision made by Our allwise Creator for the support of the Creation is well worth Notice   The ballance kept between the Vegitable & Animal productions is really a fine Thought & what I never met with before, but it is more remarkable with you than with us for you have Wild animals & mast in greater plenty than Wee have —

    I can't help but being of thy mind with regard to the Rattle Snake for if Creatures were Bitt by him first, I can't Imagine they could be able to run away   pray compare notes with Docr. Kearsley, who is of the Contrary opinion & supports it very Ingeniously — I wish it may be thy Lott without harm to Meet with this Creature to observe his Motions, but I am confirmed of his power over men, In the manner thou Mentions by a very Curious Friend of mine & a great Philosopher Colonel Byrd of Virginia who says you must not think Mee fanciful when I assure you, I have Ogled a Rattle Snake so Long till I have pceived a sickness in my stomach —

Now Dear John I have made some running Remarks on thy Curious Letter, which contained so many fine Remarks, that it Deserved to be read before the Royal Society & thee has their thanks for It, Desiring thee to Continue thy observations & Communicate them, pray make no apology, thy style is much beyond what one might expect from a Man of thy Education   The Facts are well described & very Intelligible.   I am with Love thy sincere friend,

BP 2:40; D. 101–2.

From COLLINSON

Lond Decem 14, 1737

Dear Frd

I now come to take notice of thine of the 26 of Aprill   Wee are much oblig'd to thee for thy Excursion to Conestogo, but it is a pity thee should have double Trouble for Laying of pea-straw   Litter or ashes or moss or straw thick about the Roots of Vegitables new planted will very much secure them against the effects of the frosts

The Gooseberry thou mentions must be a Curiosity, [illegible]

Thy observations on the Locust are Curious, but the sticks are much more so   It shows how Indefatigable thee art after Truth & the processes of nature. It may be very providential that they spread not over the Country elsewhere   This is undoubtedly to preserve the balance, that more is not produced than is necessary for food and to propagate the species.

The Book mentioned by Switzers I have sent thee which I hope is come to hand.

I have heard of thy House & thy great art & Industry in building it   it makes me long to see it & the builder.

I believe I gave thee a Hint that the Bays and the Cypress must be protected but I will send more seed & if I can a Cedar of Lebanon Cone which is very hardy & grows in the midst of snow so will endure in your Climate but the Cones are rare to get.

I commend thy caution not to Leave thy Home but on the most necessary occasions tho it was a tempting Expedition to go with Friend Wolley.

Thy Caution relating to the Docr is very good, As to what he may say of Mee I mind it not   I can readily overlook his weaknesses imputing them more to his natural Disposition which I take to be peevish & froward[1] than to his mind for he has many good qualities   I Despair doing any thing from the seed of the Laurell and Shrub Honesuckles   the seed is so small &

John Bartram's house, built by him in 1730. From William Darlington, *Memorials of John Bartram and Humphry Marshall* (Philadelphia, 1849).

chaffy – If there is any likelihood of success it must be from their being imediately when Ripe sown in a Box of mould & so sent nailed up only leaving some Holes for Circulation of air.

Thy thought of Collecting the bulbous roots was Exceeding kind they came in pfect good order so hope to see their appearance in the Spring there is one flower amongst the Specimens which is a very Double white flower with small Leaves something like Columbine this we call the small mountain Ranunculus as it really is I had it formerly sent Mee by Docr Witt but I should be glad of a few roots more, It is a pretty plant & keeps a long while in flower — I hope to send the names of the Rest —

Thy mapp of Skulkill is very prettily done and very Informing for now I can Read & Travel at the same Time Ld Petre has seen it & is much pleased with that & thy Journal for one helps to Illustrate the other I intend to communicate it to a Curious Map Maker it may be of use to him in laying down that part of the River Skulkill undescribed —

is there any account of the panthers do they attack man or cattle to see a live one I presume is not very Common to Europeans the other curiositys I have made some remarks on in my General Observations I hope nothing has escaped Mee

Thy next In course is July 6 —

I shall first take notice of thy Request to buy Tournfort I have inquired and there are so many books or parts done as come to 50 shillings, the first part may be gott phaps second hand but the others are not yett to be Expected now, I shall be so friendly to tell thee I think this is too much to Lay out besides now thee has got parkinson & Millar, I would not have thee puzle wth others for they contain the Ancient & Modern knowledge of Botany, Remember Solomons advice, in Reading of Books there is no End —

Far be It from Mee that I designed any reflection or to find fault when I required some information in Certain pticulars which escaped Thee I full well know thy many avocations and hoped thee would not take it in that Light to draw an Apology from thee, that I should overlook them considering thy affairs. Yes, all this could I redily do, and would have done if I thought thee had taken it in a sence I did not Intend, So I hope for the future thee will never take any thing from Mee in a lessening way or as if I Expected more pfect matters then the nature of things will allow of, I only beg to be Informed & thee has done it & I am obliged to thee for It

Some Wild Crab seed will be Very acceptable but I believe it will keep better without the apple for Too Much Moisture may rot them

The Manner in which the Hornets make their Nests is well worth knowing, ours in England Make a Nest as Large but More beautifully colour'd & Clouded with Light & Dark Brown, the[y] build in hollow Trees & hang them up to uper Corner of a Barn, Close to the Ridge —

Dear frd I am pleased to heare thee has been in the Jerseys & Kent County & that thee has Discovered the pitch or Red pine, which is a sort Wee want All sorts of pines & Firrs & white Cedar & Spruce are plants

Wee want — yett as they Live so Remote from each other, Content thy self with sending one sort a year unless any other sort is near at Hand, Wee Expect no unreasonable & hard things and will not have thee Exert thy self out of Reason to serve us — thy Accurate Observation & pfect knowledge In the Times of Gathering these sort of Trees must be thy Director In these Matters, but though thy Excursions are attended with Difficultys and great Fatigue yett the secret pleasure that Accrues & the New Discoveries and the Many Observations both Informing & Entertaining which tend to Enrich thy Mind with Natural knowledge and fill it with Exalted Ideas of the wonderfull Hand that made all these things, must yield thee such a secret pleasure as will fully Compensate for & Counterbalance all the other —

I have some pretty young plants from the Spruce Cones which is certainly Dudley's Hemlock.

I hope the Buck bean is not Intirely Dead   pray look next year again the place it was planted in seems very suitable   it bears a Curious Elegant flower & has great Virtues

I shall Endeavour to supply the Squills & G. Lilies   the frosts in your Country are surprising   It requires in a gardener Great Care & Diligence to secure & protect his plants against these Injurious Insults of the weather.

If thee will please to Inquire of our worthy & Learned friend James Logan who is well versed in opticks He will tell thee, that there is no making a glass to Magnify to such a Degree as thee wants   In such large Dimensions as thee Requires — for the Larger the Magnifier the smaller the glass   that Instead of taking Objects altogether they must be taken in parts   the greatest Discoverers in Nature have been obliged to this Method —

My friend Logan tells me thee are very dexterous in Dissecting Flowers, which requires in some of them both good eyes & good glasses to Discover their very minute parts   this is a very Curious study & full of wonders but must take up a great deal of time to be Exact & is a pretty amusement for those that have it hang upon their hands, but for thee and Mee I think we can't allow it, without prejudice to our other Weighty Affairs   Yett I would not Discourage thee, if Thy Circumstances will permit it

Dear frd thine of the 19th July is before Mee   I hope the pcell Shaloons &c Come Safely to hand — Lett Mee know what thee would have the remainder Ship'd In and it shall be done first ship   for the future when thou Sends the Seeds Send the Order with them

It is with great Concern I see so many Curious insects spoild   pray keep the Butterflies by themselves and then no Danger can happen   Some of the Last are Extravagantly fine   the white long-tail'd Moth is amazing — now & then, when a fine one happens in thy Way take him, being always provided with a Box in thy pocket when thee Walks abroad for these insects are seen accidentally, if thee was to go on purpose it is a query if thee finds one, there are some new ones amongst these Last, that I never saw before, and one that I think is in all parts exactly the same as Here.

The Curious Thorn thee mentions, I wish thee was to see in flower for I suspect the owner magnifies its beauties   Get it into thy own Garden & see for thy self & then if it proves what he says it will be a present worth sending & our accepting.

John White is now Here & gives thee great Commendations   I am sorry so fine a Collection of Pears is so Little Regarded —

I am Heartily glad thee has so good a friend as James Logan being a man of great Compassion & Humanity   He writt to Mee some time agon In thy Behalf, fearing Wee had no Consideration for thy Collections[2] — this I think was an instance of his great Regard for thee   no doubt but he considers thee for any Time taken up from thy own Affairs — (if thee psues the study of plants) in order to satisfy his Enquiries — whose surprising genius has enabl'd him to write very skilfull & knowing in this branch of Natural History as I think I may safely say in all others.

The Systema Naturae is a Curious pformance for a young man but His Coining a set of new names for plants tends but to Embarrass & perplex the study of Botany as to his system on which they are founded, Botanists are not agreed about It   very few like it, be that as it will He is certainly a very Ingenious Man & a great naturalist — As these were not in our Mother Tongue was the only reason I did not send them to thee   I hope not to be forgetful for the future. I am thy loving frd

P. Collinson

BP 2:41; D. 103–7.
1. Perverse.
2. Logan had called Collinson's attention to the fact that Bartram had a family to support, and that Collinson and Lord Petre were robbing him if they did not give him a "proper compensation." It is not clear whether Logan was unaware of Bartram's compensation or thought it was insufficient. See Logan to Collinson, June 8, 1736, Deborah Logan Papers, quoted in *The Friend* 11 (Philadelphia, August 4, 1838):347.

From COLLINSON

Lond December 20 1737

Dear Frd —

I shall now Consider the Remaining part of thine of July 19: —

The Magic Lanthorn is a Contrivance to make sport with Ignorant people — there is nothing Extraordinary in It — so not worth thy further Enquiry —

Thee art still Desirous of a magnifier for Flowers — pray make this complaint to J. Logan & try his thoughts — as thy Inquiries in some Measure to be owing to Him & thee art his pupil (which no Man Need be ashamed of) no doubt but He will furnish thee with Suitable Instruments for that purpose in order to render thy Discoveries more pfect, so undoubtedly more to his satisfaction

What I hinted as to thy Cargo coming when I am so much Engaged is not to have the Season altered but to show thee that as thee strains a point to serve Mee So I Strain a point to serve thee — pray pursue the same successful Track & Method thee has always done but this I tell thee what I do, I would do for none but thee — & yett by the Sequel of thy Letter thee thinks thy self not amply Rewarded — pray Frd John Consider twenty-one pounds p annum Sterling Returned In Goods or Money is a Hard Case [if it] will not make near or Quite or More than Forty pounds a year your Currency — this I think will pay for 5 or 6 Weeks spent annually In thy Collection & Hireing a man and other expences   Supposing thee art in Expense in this affair Tenn pounds your Currency p annum which I dont think, why to have Thirty Pounds yr Currency in Circulation In thy affairs, must certainly be a fine thing & sufficient to Content any Reasonable pson — I know thee art a man of More Equity than to Desire the subscribers Money for Little Matters, and on the other hand thee art so Honest to send the Most thee can afford to procure for them — more, they don't Desire — then what reason is there for thee to be uneasie   pray lett Mee hear no more of It, if thee canst not afford to go on with this business — tell us so — and it will be at an End —

Now Frd John I shall turn over and never think of the Last Mentioned matter unless thee revives it.

I wonder thou should be Sorry to see such a Bundle of White & Blew Lilacs, that wonder might have soon Ceased by throwing them away if you had them already — But as your neigbours of Virginia, In pticular Colo Custis att Williamsburgh, who has undoubtedly the best Collection In that Country, He Desired Some & then I thought possibly you might want them, for I never was over to see — however, this shall be a Caution to send nothing but what you write for — But Does thee know that there is both, Blew & purple Lilacs — I like thy project of Enarching the white and Blew together — I have the five Colours of the Althea Inarched on one Stock which looks very pretty when In Flower —

That you have Slow Trees Enough when James Logan writt to Mee for some, is very Surprising   I see I must Venter to send nothing without orders for fear you have it already

that you have neither Horse, or Spanish Chestnuts, nor French Walnutts, is not I see to be help'd for the Last Ships go before they are Ripe and the first in the spring when they are Rotten   I have kept them till near Xmas, & then putt them in a Box of Sand & yett they are lost by over Wett or over Drouth — However as thee art a great judge in these Matters prescribe a Way & I will Endeavour to follow it —

I am glad the Junipers Grow, pray does the English Broom Grow, this may be hardier and Endure your Climate better than the Spanish —

It is Surprising yr Winters kills Wood Sage for it grows on our High Hills & never suffers — plant it in Cases and House it, or Else cover it well with Pea Straw att the approach of Winter, removing it off in Mild Days and Covering at Nights — I hope the seed will come this year acceptable for I think I gather'd it pretty Ripe.

Dear frd John, I have thine of August 12, which gives me both pleasure & pain — I dreaded to go on board to see the Disaster & so much Labour

& pains thrown away by such a Swarm of Pestilent Beetles — as Wee say by a fine old Woman Ther's the Ruins of a fine Face, so I may say There's the Ruins of fine Flies, which as I never saw before, pray next time divide the precious from the Vile, I will send thee Boxes Enough, keep the Butter Flies or Day Flies by them selves, the Moths by them selves and these Devouring Beetles by them selves — but Drown them in Rum or Heat them in a Gentle oven will stop all their further progress — Moths are sometimes subject to breed Insects which will eat up their Bodies, but the Heat of a Very slack oven kills all — Butterflies are not Liable to these Accidents — but at the proper Time of Sending they may be Collected all in one Box & Desire the Capt to Sett in any Dry place In the Cabin, for the Last being putt in the Lazaretto under the Cabin Narrowly Escaped all being spoilt by a bag or Barrel of Salt being putt over them, which came through the Box, Capt Savage is a wonderfull goodnatured & obliging Man & can't prevent the Carelessness of his Servants   as thee Intends to repair that loss, which is very obligeing I only Just give this hint, that I prefer Butterflies & Moths before Beetles — and reason good, for there is Ten Times the Beauty & Variety In One as the Other — — —

I shall now tell the some thing which very much pleased Mee & will surprise thee — the Box of Turtle Eggs (which was an Ingenious thought of thine to send) on the Day I brought it from on Board ship being the 20 of October I took off the Lid haveing a Mind to see the Eggs & on peeping about I saw a Little Head just above the ground & while I was looking, I saw the ground Move In a place or Two More, In short in the space of 3 or 4 Hours, Eight Tortoises were hatch'd, it was very well worth observing how artfully they Disengaged themselves from the shell & then with their fore feet scratch their Eyes Open, they have had many Visitors   such a thing never happening I dare say In England before — They seem to be all one sort, but thee mentions two   I tryed if they would Eat with Lettuce leaves &c or if they would drink But they regarded neither; but after they had been Crawling about 3 or 4 days, they buried themselves in the Earth in the Box, where they Continue   Early in the Spring I Design to Turn them out at Ld Petre's who has Large ponds, if they are water-Turtles — I believe it was providential, that this Box was put in the Lazaretto, for the warmth of the ship supply'd the suns Heat & brought them to perfection, but the luckiness of the thing was their Hatching the Day they were brought home   I have the Specimens Dry'd of 4 sorts of ye American turtles but these seem Different from them all, by the length of their Tail & Figure of their shell — as for their not Eating & Burying themselves, In a State of Sleep, the Air supplies the Vital Flame, — and as Chickens are for some Time supported by some part of the youlk in their Stomachs, In order to Sustain them while the remainder of the Brood is Hatching, for if the Hen was to Leave her Charge to go & provide food for thos first Hatch, what must become of the remaining Eggs — So I conclude as these are Oviparous or produced from Eggs something of the same provision is prepaird to Support them till next Spring if they was to be all the While in Motion & Action it would not be

Sufficient; but as they soone Enter into a Dormant state it may be sufficient to preserve Life — I could be glad to see a Larger One of this sort of Land Turtle Dry'd, to compare with those I have by Mee —

all the other pretty Curiosities was very Acceptable   as for thy kind offer of Squirrel Skins, I would be farr from Rejecting It — if it would cost thee nothing but to give any thing, I am no ways free for thee to Do it for I presume it is more Matter of Curiosity, then really better to use than other Skins — the shells with the Likeness of Large Snails are peculiar to your pt of the World but the small Scallop found on East Jersey are found at New & Old England — but the present is not the less Esteemed because it shows the produce of yr shores —

I am persuaded not one of the Red Bellied Turtles is hatch'd   I should be glad to see one of these Dry. The Panax is a Choice plant.

I am thine,

P. Collinson

BP 2:42; D. 107–10.

To COLLINSON[1]

I saw several of these Wasps flying about a heap of Sandy loame, they setled on it and very nimbly scratched away the sand with their fore feet to find their nests, whilst they held a large fly under their Wings with one of their other feet, they crept with it, into the Hole that lead to the Nest & staid there three or four Minutes   when they came out with their hind legs the sand was so dexterously thrown Over the Hole, I could not discover It. then takeing flight soone returned with more Flies – settled down, uncovered the Hole & Entered in with their prey.

This raised my Curiosity to try to find the Entrance, but the sand fell in so fast I was prevented untill by repeated Essays I was lucky to find one   it was Six Inches in the Ground and at the farther End lay a large Magot near an Inch long & thick as a small goose Quill, with several Flies near It and the remains of many more, These Flies are provided for the Magot to feed on before it Changes Into the Nymph State   then it eats no more until it attains to a perfect Wasp –

The Order of Providence is very remarkable in prescribing the different Wayes & Means for this Noxious Tribe of Insects to perpetuate their several Species, no doubt for such good Ends & purposes with which Wee may not be well acquainted but most likely for the Prey & food of other animals.

One kind of a Wasp fabricates an Oblong nest of paperlike composition full of Cells for the harbour of its Young, and Hangs it on a branch of a Tree –

Some build Clay nests & feed their young with spiders, – Others sustain them with large Green Grasshoppers, – then there is those that build their combs in the ground like ours in England to nourish a numerous Brood –

But these Yellowish Wasps take a different Methode with great pains digs a Hole in the Ground & Lays its Egg which soone turns to a Magot – then Catches Flies to support it untill it comes to Maturity

The Wisdome of Providence is Admirable by giving annually a Check to this prolific Brood of Noxious Insects in suffering all the Males to Die, which are the most numerous in the Family and only reserving a few empregnated Females of Each Species, to continue their Race unto another year –

Whereas Bees whose Labours are so Beneficial to Mankind are permitted to Survive the Winter to raise New Colonies,[2]

Linnean Society of London Archives, Ms. 323, Collinson's Common Place Book, pp. 250–52.
1. This undated letter was written around January 1737/38, as there is a mention of it in Collinson's letter to Bartram of April 6, 1738.
2. This letter was read to the Royal Society on February 24, 1763, and published in their *Transactions* 53 (1763):37–38, under the title of "Observations made by Mr. John Bartram, at Pensilvania, *on the Yellowish Wasp of that Country: In a Letter to Mr.* Peter Collinson, F.R.S." Comparing the published version with the original, it is obvious that Collinson edited quite a bit. He introduced the second paragraph with a phrase of his own: "Extraordinary Operation."

From COLLINSON[1]

Lond Jany: 20: 1737/38

Dear frd John

I cant enough admire thy Industry and Curiosity in Descending to so many Minute Rarities that Came in the Box by Savage which are things very Acceptable but what commonly Escape the Observation of Most but such a prying Eye as Thine, they in as abundant manner Deserve my Thanks –

It is True, in doing this thou hast very Much Obliged Mee, but I suspect thee has Intailed on thy self more Trouble   the Eight of these glorious large flys thou sent has not abated but Inflam'd my Curiosity to ask the same over Again or any others thou can Add, for as some of these notwithstanding thy Care are a Little Torn   I hope in Time, with a little practice we shall have them perfect In all their parts, the Horns, part of the wings & bodies being deficient for I must tell thee I Designe to bestow some expense on them, and Enshrine them between Two [plates of] glass that Wee may see both Sides I know they are Ticklish Ware to Meddle with and the very touch of ones Fingers robs them of their Beauty — I will a Little revive thy memory with our Manner of Catching them   Wee putt sticks into the handle of the Netts 2: 3: or 4 foot long, for some Flyes are shier than others, and will not suffer us to come near them, Wee always watch till they settle on a Leafe &c then Wee apply both netts together   the one close under the Leafe with agility clap the other over the Fly   Thus she is Caught between the netts   The next thing is to gently disengage the netts from the Leafe or Twigg by gently drawing them but be sure keep them close together Least she Escape in this action, having Disengaged the Netts — wee lay them on the next smooth ground, and whilst the Fly is between the Netts wee turn it on its wrong side and give the body a pretty smart Squeeze between the fingers & Thumb, then till Wee hear the Ribs Crack, this prevents further strugling or beating their Wings to rub off the fine Down, then with a pin run It through the body and having a Box Large Enough Wee stick It in with his right side to the Box, when Wee come home Wee Display the Wings with pins run thro pieces of Cork which keep them regular and free from Fluttering as thee will find one In a Box, for a patron

The Two Moths are very surprising   the greenish one Especially   Our virtuosi cannot enough admire It, for the singularity of its shape uncommon to Moths, These I know are more Difficult to find, being Flies of the night Our virtuoso Either breed them from Caterpillars or Else Digg for the Crysalis in the ground and keep them in Earth till they Change into flies, and then in an hour or Two kill them with a hott knitting needle run into their bodies (for they are much harder than Flies to kill) and then they stick them up, as above mentioned   if thee has a fancy to Breed them Lett me know and Wee will Inform thee In a more pticular manner   it is a most Entertaining & surprising thing to observe their changing from the Caterpillar to the Crysalis   Every fly has a Different proceeding   Some spin themselves up in Balls of Silk others Tie themselves fast by the Tail & Cross the body — others with a glutinous Matter make them nests with Dry Leaves &c   all Moths when in Caterpillar when Done Feeding, go into the Earth & Change into Crysallus, their Duration in this State is very Remarkable Some Continue but a Month or Six Weeks and breed Twice a year, others stay, 2, 3, 6, or 9 Months   some Two years before they come forth a Fly and then How Entertaining it is to see from a Long black Grub, without head, Tail, wings or Leggs (as is the Crysalis) when the Time is come what Efforts the Imprison'd Embrio makes to Break the Shell and then what a Glorious Creature appears and what is prettyer still is to see the Wings grow whilst gazeing on It, for some Minutes, to their full Extent for att their first Comeing Forth, there is only the Appearance of the Rudiments of the Wings; for it would be Impossible that the narrow Limits of the Case In which they are Enshrined, could Contain their Wings att full Length; Oh How very wonderfull are the Works of the Almighty Author of all Things, Scarcely anything Displays it More then the Surpriseing Generation of this lowest Class of Animals, the More thou Dips Into It, the More will thy attention and Admiration be Raised to see the Industry and Art of the Contemptible Creature the Caterpillar to go through the several changes assign'd her p the Great Creator —

prithee Dear John whatever thou sends give but the Least hint where it was found, or how and what thou knows of It, It is a great help to Natural History as I know time is precious wee [know] so the shortest account is best, The Three sorts of shell thee sent Mee, shows nothing can Escape thee — they are very acceptable, but I am att a loss to know whether Lake, River or Sea Shells, I see I best not advise thee to lett not anything Escape thee when I see the Variety of Insects, thou has Collected (there is not above 3 or

4 like what we have) thy method to send them was well Contrived   They all came well & safe   I now plainly see that nothing of thine comes amiss, all are acceptable and well taken care of which I hope is Encouragement for thee to work and prosper — In Token of Gratitude, I Desire thy acceptance of a Magnifying Glass for thy pockett which I hope is what will please thee and Answer thy Question   pray Examine your Fine Flys and thou will be astonished att their Beauty — to see all the Colours of the Rainbow so Richly Enameled & blended together, our English Flys are pretty and neatly spotted and Wee have a great Variety but all small   Indeed all Bawbles & Trifles which makes them very Desirable but yett my Wishes are moderate and so they ought to be, when I consider, My Friend's Time is short, which all belonging to his Family

The Cotton stone or Asbestos, that thou sent Mee growing in the Cleft of the Rocks, is Indeed a Curiosity, but it is from the other Sort thou Sent Mee that paper & Cloth is made for it is more Spongey and pliable & has a Long Staple fitt for spinning, but that art is lost, being more matter of Curiosity then any Real use — but paper can be made from it now but then that is only Curiosity too, It makes only a Course Sort — & not fitt for Use — but I am oblig'd to thee for the Specimens

Unless thee had sent the Sticks it was Impossible to Conceive in what Manner they was Darted by the Locusts, it is a most surprising Method of Generation, for now I see them, I scarsly know how to understand it — for all along the Fissure or Crevice, there seems to be Tufts of thready Matter att Equall Distance & stuffed in as by art, what the Deesigne of it is I can't apprehend and weather it is produced from the Insect or the Tree, phaps it may be the small Vessells or Fibres of the Tree lacerated by the Teeth of the Insect, if I take it Right their Eggs are Laid att the Bottom of those Tufts, — pray sett Mee Right in this matter   thee Sayes they was Darted in June, pray how Long does the Eggs lay before they are Hatch'd

Wee have something like the caterpillars Eggs thee sent wrapp'd round a Twig of the apple Tree — only with this difference the Enameled side with us is outwards where as yours is Inwards & cover'd with a Downeyness backwards, which is Wisely provided to protect from the Severe Cold — when I find one of ours I think to send it to thee

I now Come to thank thee for the Two fine Large Crysalis's that are Cover'd with silk & Nicely Twisted or Woven to the Twigs of the Tree   by their Size they must produce a Large Fly

It is to be observed that [illegible] Spike a Ball of Silk round [illegible] is Design'd to protect from Weather [illegible] These always produce what is call'd [illegible] or Moths & if thee should be so Lucky [illegible] these Crysalis, before the Fly has Eat his way out [illegible] Cutt them off with the Twigg, Carry them inside & [illegible] putt them in a Box, & Cover the Top with a [illegible] Cloth being tied to Lett in the Air, & then thou will see the wonderfull production Brought Forth   See the Creature come forth Naked, & see them from the smallest appearance grow to their full size in 2 or 3 Minutes, wch is Exceedingly Curious, for the Wings could not be

Enclosed in so Narrow a Space without being rinckled & [illegible] but their Immediate Growth is no less wonderfull & Necessary in order for Conveying the Insect to places where both sexes may Meet, & properly be found — Our Virtuosi, when they go Observe & find Caterpillars, they bring them Home putt them in Large Boxes, & feed them with the Leaves of the plant they find them on, & wait their going into Crysalis, those that spin up in Silk stay but a short time in Crysalis phaps a month or Two Haveing Generally Two Broods a year — Look on these Crysalis opening so take the fly as soon as she is perfected which is within an Hour or Two, take it by the Belly — & give a Hard squeeze untill thee hears its ribs Crack which will prevent its fluttering & then Display it, a fly thus taken is in its highest pfection & beyond any that can be taken abroad

Butt the other sorts of Caterpillars that don't spin up, Butt go into the Earth & Rotten Trees to Change in Crysalis, for which Reason Our Virtuosi, Putt 6 or 8 Inches Deep of Mould in their Breeding & Feeding Boxes for them to go & Change In, those Leave only a Large^2
att a Time of year when Wee are in the greatest hurry of Business, Shiping Goods for the plantations & then I have Something to do to Divide the Cargo to three Subscribers, wch is much more trouble than to one, but yett all this & much more I should gladly undertake if it will butt be of any real Service to thee — for I must tell thee my Real sentiments, I never mett any pson Deserved It More,

But yett I have some Concern of Mind, wch I will freely Impart to thee, I am Jealous thy gratified Disposition may carry thee to farr to the Neglect of thy family affairs and yett when I think again that thee has some Compensation (tho phaps not Equall to thy pain & Trouble) I yett have hopes that thee will not suffer much by the bargain

My pticular Friend Robert Grace has promised to take Care of 3 small boxes and a peice of stuff for Summer Ware which thee may Ware or Sell, one of the boxes contains some of our Large Tree Walnuts & English weather you have these or no I can't Tell the Others has some seeds and the other Box has some odd things.

Thee takes not the Least notice of the Case of Glass is come to hand, or the Quallity bindgs which settled thy last years Acct

To answer all thy Curious Remarks & to Make Mine will take up more Time & paper than I can att present spare However I hope att my Leisure to Lett thee hear further I must confess I have been very remiss this year In the seeds thee Desir'd, I could not well keep It, being not setled Long in a place but paying Visits from one friend to another I rely on thy good nature to Excuse It, I hope to be better this year —

All the plants in the Case came Extremely Well but the Shrub Cactus, and are very acceptable In pticular the Ladys slippers the Red Lillie and Indeed all the rest they being skillfully taken up with a Sod About them, I have no doubt of their growing — I am vastly Oblig'd to thee for that Glorious Gentian 42 — but pray try what thee canst go for that other Gentian No. 55 —

My other Letters thee will find In the brown paper bundle   Some things I believe I have hinted att Twice over but that thee must attribute for want of Time to read what I have Writt, I being oblig'd to take opportunities to write a Little now & then, I hope Friend Logan has given thee Parkinsons Two books   He told Mee he desired them a present for thee — I have Little more to add but my best wishes for thy Health & prosperity.

> am thy True friend
> P Collinson

Pray what Length was the Rattle Snake   the Rattles are the narrowest I ever saw   Thou need send no more black Walnutts but some Sweet Gum for thy two other correspondents for Lord Petre has raised abundance from thy seed but send some Dogwood   Sassafras   Hickery   Red Cedar   Silver Laurel   black gum   ash for thy other two correspondents   no great quantity of each   Ld Petre has these the year before – but send some Sugar Tree for all parties and send Okes of all sorts if a good yeare, but in pticular the Willow Leaved Oakes as Ld Petre raised abundance from this seed but send a few others for the other two Correspondents who had none before and some long Walnutts   your Red Cedar is rather a Juniper   both are Baciferous or bear Berries   Some Junipers grows High & Bulky at the straights in the South parts of France & Spain   there is the Red Berried Juniper grows very large in the Island of Formentara Voica the Savin I never saw bear berries In England   It is all Increased by Slips

BP 2:20, 3:30–32; D. 82–84.
1. We have not been able to determine with certainty whether the following was a single letter or parts of two letters; we have chosen to treat it as the former. The date is somewhat faded. Darlington considered it to be 1736/37. We have dated it 1737/38 because of Collinson's comments in it on several things mentioned by Bartram in his letters of February 27, 1736/37 and April 26, 1737.
2. If what follows is part of this letter, at least one page of the original is missing.

From COLLINSON

January 27 1737/8

Dear Frd

I had the pleasure of thine from Maryland   I am glad My Friends were kind to thee and that Thee found Fresh Matter of Entertainment   I can't Enlarge now but to Tell thee that all the 2 Boxes of seeds, 2 Boxes of plants, 1 box of Specimens   1 box wasps nest came all safe and in perfect good order which is very pleasing — & for which I shall Make the some Returns per Capt Wright — with all the Goods Thee Mentioned Except the sewing silk, which is advanced to Two shillings a pound — It is expected to be cheaper and unless it is, neither thee nor I shall have any Credit In Sending It, so I would rather have the Remainder of thy Money ordered in other Goods. But one thing I must Desire of thee & that Is that the psons that gave Thee Their Orders, will afix their price to Every Thing, for we have the same sorts of Goods as they vary In Quality & goodness — a great Variety of prices — and that sort which is suitable for one Man's sale is not for another   with this Guide I hope to give Content, Thy Friend was wrong In His Conjectures, for those shalloons was from Yorkshire & not from Bristol so he may see every Like is not the same — for I never ordered a Quire of Shalloons from Bristol in my Life

I hope to send thee Letters to Maryland and Virginia. I have wrote already to several of my friends in Virginia.

If thy friend had sett a price to the Shalloons he would have had them send [what] he wanted   so for the future Lett thee have no goods without a price to them.

I am, dear frd Thy Sincere frd in haste

P. Collinson

Lord Petre has ordred Mee to give thee Two Guineas for thy Extraordinary Trouble about the Specimens.

all I shall now Send p our Worthy frd John White will be the Two peices Doulas which he was so good to Lett be pack'd up in his pcell Directed to thee — with Box seeds   the reason I Desire it to come p Capt Wright is to save thee freight for

The Laurells are pfectly fine   that and the White Cedar are Very Acceptable   Thee shall not Loose thy Reward.

Dear friend I must beg the Favour of thee to remember what I have formerly Requested In behalf of a Curious Naturalist[1] — who to Ingage thy memory sends thee a Specimen of his pformance — He neglected when in Virginia to Draw the Papaw, and as this is a Curious plant, In Flower & Fruite and not Figur'd by any Body   Now there is no Ways to Convey to us perfect Ideas of this plant but by gathering the Blossoms & Leaves & drying them between paper, but as the Colour & figure of the Flower is Liable to Change, then he begs a short Discription of its Colour

or Else to prevent further Trouble If some of the Flowers growing on a small Twig was putt into some Rum, one small Twig would be Enough, but thee may putt several Loose Flowers In the Jar of Spirits, & then a Couple of Fruite Full Ripe — and if it was not too remote, a Couple half Ripe — for I am informed they grow in Couples Like a Rams Testicles — It is observable that spirits does very Little alter the Colour of Fruits, if it does before thee sends It, pray give a Little Discription of Its Colour — now by these Helps my Ingenious Friend Will be enabled to Delineate the plant & fruite & if thee will further assist Him in the Height of Its Growth, & the Size of its Stem and what soil & place is most natural to It, – we shall be all Much obliged to Thee   pray Fail not — and thee will oblige thine,

PC

if it has any vertues, pray mention Them

BP 2:31; D. 110–11.
1. Mark Catesby.

From COLLINSON

Lond Feby lst: 1737/38

Dear Frd

As Capt Wright was to Sail So near Capt Savage & phaps as Soone and as he is thy very Good friend & will bring any thing for thee Freight Free —So I shall Send all thy things by Him Except the Two pieces of Linnen Cloth which my Worthy Friend John White will Deliver these being packed up in His pcell with a Box of Seeds   In it there are my Letters – to them I Shall Refer thee and am thy

Sincere frd
P Collinson

John White has a small Box of Seeds for thee

BP 2:35.

From COLLINSON

Lond feby 2d 1737/8

Frd John

I am not willing my Good Frd John White should come Empty handed so have Desir'd him to take Care of a Box for Thee of Seeds &c and He had 2 pieces of Garlix besides, the others had been sent but that I found thee must pay Freight — so Defer'd it till White Sails, who is so Much thy Friend that He will not take any thing   there is some Spanish & Hors Chestnutts In Sand and Some out of Sand   I hope Some of them will take   if as soon as the Receives them & before the plants them if they was Soak a Night In Water to plump them & fitt them for Vegitation. Try Some one Way Some another

The Proprietor has a Large Cargo of plants, I wish them safe to Hand I am thy Dear frd

P Collinson

In the Box thou'l find Some Long tedious Letters — thou may think I wanted business to Spare so much Time but I will assure thee I did not — but to Show thee I make no slight of thy pformances

Seeds In the Box
Arbutus or Strawberry Tree
Horse Chestnutts   these are Rougher Coated
Spanish Chesnutts   these are Smoother Coated
Larix Cones – Hardy Tree
Redish purple Lilac
Quick Beam ⎫
Bird Cherry ⎭ these I hope are Riper then last

St Johns Wort from Canaries   tender
Holly Berries – 2d year comes up
Flowering Shrub
Euonymus   Different from yrs
Opulus
Travellers Joy
Laurell Berries
Aria Theophartus or White Beam
Red Provence Rose
Mixt Rose Seeds
English Stinking Gladiolus
True Service
Scotch Thistle
Bay Berries
From Doc Delanius
Acanthus
Bestosta
Montpelier Cibestus
Phylleum Flea Wort
Jonynuum Alexander
Polyanthus

Consult Millar on all these   The Arbutus Seed is the finest & Best Ripened I ever Saw   Believe worth a Guinea an ounce   Sow that & Bays in A Case to protect them   within Doors the first approach of Sever frost — I putt the Bay Berries Last being thin I apprehend Least Subject to Mould

BP 2:32.

From COLLINSON

Lond febry 17 1737/38

Dear frd.
    I have sent in a Large Deal Box of Capt Wrights marked E W – No 5 the Goods thou wrote for which I wish safe to hand — I hope thou has the Two pcs of Garlix In John Whites pcell   The Bill of pcells of these Goods are Inclosed with them In the Box with thy Account   as Sewing Silk and all Silk is much advanced I did not Venter to Send the remainder of thy Acc't in that Comodity, but I have Sent Two pound for a Tryall – if the price & Silk is Liked more of the same may be had att that price unless there should be an Advance – as I have before hinted I now request again Send for no Goods without a price   if thee hast thy Instructions from any Dealer He must know It & According to the price I will Endeavour to Send the Best —
    As I know it was with great fatigue & pains that those Laurells was procured from the Mountains, so I would not willingly be behind hand In

Making Some Acknowledgment — I have Sent the Drugett for Coat & breeches & 2 lamb cotts[1] Wastcoats & 1 Calico & 1 prunella[2] Gown for thy Wife   Linings for thine & woods Cloths with sundry other odd things which I hope will prove acceptable

As thee designs for Virginia in the Fall I have sent thee Circular Letters to all my friends which letters come to J. Logan to save thee postage — I think it would be better to proceed along the bay of the Western Shore of Maryland first, & so to Williamsburgh & then up into the Country & so back as thou proposed and my Reason Is Little new or Curious is to be met with along the Western Shore or in the Lower settlements of Virginia. the Rare & Valuable things are to be found above, In the unsettled places & then thou will proceed Directly Home with what seeds thou has Gott whereas if thou goes the upper Way first thou will have to bring what thou has Collected down Virginia and over to Maryland, which will be very troublesome and fatiguing, and a Long Way About —

I have sent my Letters open that thou may make Memorandums from some pticular Contents therein mentioned & then seal them up – of all my Friends In Maryland I know none that are Curious in our branch of knowledge so that unless it is in the Course of Thy Travels it is not worth thy while to go out of thy Way on purpose to see them   I would have thee go if thee can to see Robt. Gover[3] to see the place where some surprisingly fashioned angular stones are found — as to the Rest take them as it suits thee — Butt in Virginia there is Colo Custis & Colo Byrd are both Curious Men   pray take down what I have remarked for thee to Inquire after, the Umbrella Trees at the first & the Ginseng at the last.

Then when thee proceeds Home I know no person will make thee more Welcome than Isham Randolph   He lives 30 or 40 Miles above the falls of James River in Goochland above the other settlements   now I take his House to be a very suitable place to make a settlement att for to take several Days' Excursions all Round, and to return to his House at Night — I think William Manduet[4] Lives in the upper Settlements of Maryland

One thing I must Desire of thee and do Insist that thee oblige Mee therein that thou make up that Druggett Clothes, to go to Virginia In and not appear to Disgrace thyself or Mee for tho I would not Esteem thee the less to come to Mee in what Dress thou Will, yet these Virginians are a very gentle, Well Dress'd people, & look phaps More at a Man's Outside than his Inside, for these and other Reasons pray go very Clean, neat & handsomely Dressed to Virginia   Never Mind thy Clothes I will send thee more another year —

I a Little wonder that the Eastern sea shore nor the Island, afforded no shells, that there was none I am persuaded for had they been there they would not have Escap'd thee — pray observe if there are no Land or River shells different from what thee has sent Mee   I want a fair specimen of your oysters; an uper and an under shell both belonging to one another will be acceptable, but no more Sassafras berries, the Cones of the Swamp Rose bay or Laurell are much wanted, and Acorns of Willow Leafed Oke   Thy last cargo is a fine Collection, & came in fine order   Tulip Poplar or Sweet Gum are not wanting   I thank thee for the Sweet Gum but I want some of the black gum   pignuts will be acceptable   they are a very small Species of hickery   Send more Acorns & Cones or Seeds of all the Evergreen Tribe will be Acceptable & some more Allspice or Benjamin & any other Forest Trees Sugar Maple, Birch, Horn Beam, Ash, beach & what thou Canst pick up   Red & White Cedar pine   firrs &c the specimens of the flower of ye Chamaerhododendron was very obligeing   I have much to say to thy Long Entertaining Letter with the Seeds & plants but must Defer till more Leisure I sent thee a Case of Boxes which are very hard and will save the Trouble of making   thee may cut down the Rims and accomodate them to thy pockett, pray take one or Two with the fly netts in a bag by thy side & some pins, phaps thee may meet with something Curious & may want Conveniency to Catch & Carry it   if the netts are Torn or worn out send them back to be repaired.

My wishes are for thy Health & Safety – I am truly thine,

P. Collinson

Pray give my love to Joseph Breintnall   hope he had mine by Savage   In thy packett to J:Logan I inclose a Letter to Ben Eastbourne[5] which please Deliver   In the Letter in J:Logans packett I send thee a Twig of a pear Tree with an Enamelled Ring of Caterpillars around it   they are not yett Come Out   if not Come out when thee Receives them putt them on a pear or apple & thee will see the produce   More Wild Crabs & Black Haw or Sheep Turds   it is a fine Eating Fruite, the Last specimens of pines was something Like   there was sufficient for myself & to spare a friend a slip I never saw any thorns to the size thee mentions   pray send a specimen of your black & white Thorn & a good specimen   of Sheep Turds in Flower if this can be done with Conveniency

As thee mentions the noble stone pine seed was bad I have sent in the Box some Seeds & some More Spanish Chestnutts   the Wasps & Nests are all very Curious & acceptable.

the Crysalis that is naked that thee sent Mee is alive as it is not spun up or taken out of the ground   it will prove a Butterfly for all that tribe Change in that manner but they Conceale themselves under the Leaves and against Trees & buildings that it is hard to find them

Docr Hill att London Town in Maryland is the only person that is Curious in Vegitables, He has Sent Some Account of their Vertues to the Royal Society   pray Call on Him   thee hast my Letter of Last year   Alter the Date of the Year and it will [Serve] Well Enough   the need Send no Cock Spur or white thorn   pray Send Some Seed of your Black thorn   I never heard you had any Except you call the Black Haw or Sheep Turd

---

BP 2:34; D. 88–90.
1. Matted or felted wool.
2. Silk or woolen cloth.
3. Quaker farmer.
4. Unidentified.
5. Surveyor-general of Pennsylvania.

From COLLINSON

Londn April 6:1738

Dear Frd John

The First thing I have to desire of thee is to send 3 or 4 or 6 Specimens of the Sweet Gum in Blossom   this being a very Extraordinary plant and some Curious Botanists in Holland beg this Favour In order to Settle its Botanical Character. I desire Specimens of these others 2 or 3 of a sort – Black Gum & Black Haw, these we desire in Blossom & in Fruite & Leaf as it happens — Sugar Birch, Black Thorn & sorts of White Thorn in Blossom & Fruite   I have recvd three sorts of Jaceas from Docr Witt. He Distinguishes them by Early Jacea, Elegant Jacea and Gigantic Jacea — I wish thee Could find them out to send Specimens of them as they grow in your Country   pray look out for a plant or two of White Cedar; for I am afraid that last sent Mee will go off, though it has a clod of its own earth about it — the smell of the Leaves a little dried smells like to Cinnamon. It is a fine plant. If mine stands it will be the only one in England though I have hopes to raise it from seed, this year. Set half a dozen young plants in a box & let them stand a year or two to strike root before they are sent.

Renew thy Collecting of Acorns and if Thee can send specimens to each which is a great Curiosity   Get what Sassafras berries thee can — and send as Many Red Cedar berries in a Little Box by themselves as Thee can afford for half a guinea being for a particular pson — and send some More what Thee can for thy Three Correspondents   Send more Sugar Maple seed — & Rose Laurell Cones; and send a specimen or two of the upland Rose and the Marsh Rose   Try what thee canst do to send us some Cones of the Long Cone White Pine, it is a very remarkable pine haveing 5 Leaves in a Sheath and the other from Jersey has but two leaves. I have great hopes most of the plants will grow   They promise well but I shall Defer giving thee an Account till next opportunity.

The Terrapins came very safe and well but I have Lost all the young ones from the eggs, which was 15 which is a great loss. If I ever have any More I will take another Method with them. But the Curiosity was great and admired by Many and it was very lucky that the first peeped its head out of the Earth the very day I brought the Box from on Board which I think was the 21st October. if I had sent them then directly into the country I had saved them but I thought keeping them in town I could better secure them from the Cold & so I lost them all which I was sorry for being I am persuaded the first that ever hatched in England   But I take it the warmth of the ship contributed much to it and supplyed the want of your sun's Heat.

The terrapins I gave to Ld Petre and He thanks Thee for them — Docr Delanius thanks thee for the seeds & Specimens   Thy observation on your Pines is remarkable, the Stone pine and the Long Coned pine don't open Like yours but I think all the Rest do

Thee has obliged Mee much with so fine a Collection of Wasps with their

Natural History which is very Entertaining & surprising In pticular the Clay Nests, their Fabrication & their provision for their Young with all the Rest are Evidences of the unlimited power & Wisdom of the Great Author of all things but that these Creatures wch are a Common Pest to mankind should have such wonderful Instincts bestowed on them for securing themselves & their Species, Exceeds our Comprehension but raises our Admiration   it may serve to abate Our pride & Conceit when Wee see so much bestowed on these Lower Classes of Being which is not unworthy of our Notice and it is owing to thy Indefatigable Industry that these things are brought to Light   Great is thy pleasure that at the same time thee art obliging thy Friend   thee are improving thyself in the Knowledge of Nature —

pray look out sharp next year and be beforehand with that saucy Raccoon that I may see that pretty nest built in the bush and send the Wasp and a better specimen of the clay Wasp for the last wanted its Head   Such a variety of these Creatures must be very troublesome   We have but one and that is bad enough that builds its nest in Dry Banks   two sorts of Bees   the Honey Bee and a large Humming Bee that builds in dry banks; and one sort of Hornet; and three sorts of Ants. But I am like to introduce a fourth for I found in the Earth that the plants came in the outer husk of a Chestnut and in it a colony of very small Ants. These I have carried into the country to see how they will thrive in our Climate.

Thee will continue thy observation on the Yellow Wasp   No. 1 and No. 2 may deserve thy notice for I find their building & increase is unknown to thee   If another insect with those surprising long hairs or Horn happens in thy way, pray secure it for it is very Extraordinary in its kind   The beautifull Sea Fly is a great Beauty could its wings be displayed. Pray never go without a box & pins in thy pockett   The Insect with what thee Esteems a long Horn is no other than a proboscis which He used to suck out the sweets of Flowers, for he has Two small Horns on each Side —

I am glad thee Meet with such Civil Treatment in thy Expedition through the Eastern Shore and that Thee found such Variety of plants   I am sorry Thee mist some plants that thee observed   I wish Thee had Collected specimens of that periploca and that other with Horned poppy Leaves and the Hypericon & the Long Leafed Large Cone pine & a Different Swamp Oke   pray never fail Getting Specimens, if thee Canst not gett plants or Seeds provide Two Flat Boards, the size of the paper thee Intends for the specimens — between these, putt thy paper and specimens in it & tie them fast   Thus these may be Carried any Ways, as it suits thy Convenience & with safety, Too —

I can't Conceive what your Black Thorn is — pray send a Specimen — Wee have but One sort that is that that bears Sloes & but one Sort of White Thorn — but I am surprised at their size with you, I question if Ever I Saw one above a foot diameter   that very Rare   I never saw our Black thorn above the size of the small of a Common Sized leg that but Rare for they are so useful in makeing Fences that they are rarely suffered to grow any size — The Great Laurell or Chamaerhododendron plants promise well which gives Mee great Joye   I am extremely obliged to thee for them and am with Love & Respect

> Thy assured friend,
> P. Collinson

I hope all things came safe by Capt. Wright

BP 2:36; D. 115–17.

To COLLINSON

May 1738

have received the two peices of garlicks but not opened them   thay seem to be very fine but cant yet know how they are charged   ye box of seeds & chestnuts was A rare present of curiosities & such as I wanted except ye lilium scotch thistle   canary St. John's wort & travelers joy which I had before both sorts of chestnuts was either mouldy or rotten & never a sound one   ye box was stowed in ye lazareto[1] & very damp   it was a pity such a Curious colection should not have been set in a dry place in ye cabin but dear Peter what Can we do in such a Case but exercise patience. I observed thy directions was to set it in ye cabin which if it had doubtless they had been preserved   ye box of insects I sent last by Savage   I delivered it into his own hands & desired him to set it in a safe place in ye cabin   he promised me it should & yet as thee saith it was cramed into ye Lazareto which I take to be as bad or worse then ye upermost Course in ye hould   I am exceed[ing]ly pleased with thy long letters as thee calls them but I wish they had been as long again. I shall make my observations on them, as follows; december ye 10th, – I am almost overjoyed in reading ye contents of this letter, – wherein thee acknowledges thy satisfaction of my remarks on ye locusts, caterpillars, pidgeons, and snakes   I am very thankful to thee, and the Royal Society, for taking so much notice of my poor performances   it is A great encouragement for me to continue my observations of natural phenomena and if I see any Locusts this year I shall be very perticular in my remarks as also ye Papaw to gratifie thy curious friend which the saith will send mee a specimen of his performances which will be very acceptable   december ye 14th – I am glad my map of Skullkil pleases thee & Lord Peter; The panthers have not seized any of our people that I have heard but many hath been sadly frightened with them   they have pursued several men both on horseback and on foot   many have shot them down & others have escaped by runing away but I believe as A Panther doth not much fear A single man so he hath no great desire to seize him for if he had runing from him would be A poor means to escape   such A nimble strong creature will leap above 20 foot at one leape   I knowed A man that was riding home when A panther met him sometimes leaping before and sometimes behind ye man & shaking his tail   when ye man shouted for help ye panther was so inraged ye man thought he should be tore of his horse   at length taking A leap behind, ye man whiped his horse & escaped being frightened almost to death; I take thy advice about books very kindly – altho I love reading such dearly and I believe if solomon had loved women less & books more he would have been a wiser & happier man then he was; in thy letter of december ye 20th thee supposed me to spend 5 or 6 weeks in colections for you & that ten pounds will defray all my anual expenses but I assure thee I spend more than twice that time anualy & ten pounds will not, at A moderate expense defray my charges Abroad beside my neglect of business at home in fallowing harvest and seed time. Indeed, I was more then two weeks time in gathering ye small acorns of the Willow leafed Oak, which are very scarce & faling with the leaves so that daily I had to rake up the leaves and reconed it good luck if I could gather 20 under one tree & hardly one in twenty bore any   yet I dont begrudge my labour but would do anything reasonable to serve you but by the sequel of thy letter, you are not sensible of the fourth part of ye pains I take to oblige you; thee seems to be surprised that I should write that we have sloe trees enough – and James Logan rote to thee for some but, my good friend, I assure thee, I assert nothing to thee but what is real fact   the first I observed sloe trees was at a plantation whose owner came two years into this country before A house was builded in Philadelphia   I brought some from there when I settled on my plantation   I saw another tree near Philadelphia as thick as my thigh & last year I showed James Logan English thorns, Bullises & sloes growing in A hedge which he rides close by from his house to town which I believe hath been planted 20 year & many others grow in several distant places in the country but are liable to be bit with ye same insects that the rest of our stone fruits except peaches and cherries is & are increased by plenty of suckers; in fact James Logan is posesed of a large field of learning & knowledge beyond any in our province or perhaps our neibors yet he hath but A measure of it & sometimes I can see as far into A milstone as he unless he puts on his spectacles   I design to be very mindfull of butterflies this year but dear friend thee can hardly think how pleased I am at thy account of ye turtle eggs   I design this summer to send another cargo of other sorts of egs   pray let mee know how these succeeds; thine of January ye 20th   I observe thy perticular care for my interest in endeavouring to send ye goods by freight free for which I am heartily thankfull but if thee cant always do this I shall be very well contented   its A great kindness in thee to send them allways   it is very well thee doth not send ye sewing silk if it be so dear   it is very plenty in our stores at present   I cant yet determine what goods to send for not knowing how much will be left behind nor how those will answer which is to come by White but thee may expect to hear further from mee by first opertunity   I observed thy advice to preserve plants from being heaved out or destroyed by our severe frost   I have tryed this method several years but it doth not succed so well here as it may with you by reason of ye diference of our winters being sometimes very warm & then in A few hours most cold   its frequent in ye midle of our hard winters to have 2 or 3 days or A week of very warm weather which if thay be covered will rot & if uncovered & warm when we go to bed A cold wind may rise before morning & freeze teribly moreover our moles & ground mice will sport here   now, my kind & generous friend I shall return thee my hearty thanks for thy care & pains which thee hath taken & ye many good services thee hath done for me & further if the finds any expressions in my letter A little out of ye way thee will not take it in ye wrong sence   I assure thee, I bear the A great deal of good will or if thee thinks I am too short and imperfect in explaining any subject which I give thee any account of pray let me know & I will satisfie thee according to ye best of my knowledge for I love plain dealing

BP 1:14:2; D. 119–20.
1. Lazaretto: ship's store-room.

From COLLINSON[1]

London, May 2, 1738

Dear Friend: –

I have sent thee, in a little jar, some of our *Dens Canis*. There are white and red flowers. This is in return for those with yellow flowers thee sent me, though thy did not flower this year. If thee meets with any more, pray get them.

It is a great advantage, to send plants with a sod of earth about them; for, many times there comes up odd plants – as it has happened this year; for in the sods of Herb Twopence, is come up two sorts of vegetables, the one I don't know, but one appears to be a sort of *Hepatica*, very like ours, but that the stalks of yours are very hoary, and not naked, as the footstalks of the leaves of ours are.

I also send thee one of our Humming Bees, from the sound it makes. These reside in dry banks; but whether they make combs, as others do, I doubt, – for this year I caught one in March, and whilst I looked on it, I perceived from round the neck a great many young ones creep out. Now, the combs I take to be repositories, both for food and to lay their eggs in; but, the way that these breed, and nurse their young up by the heat of their bodies, I take it there is no need of repositories for their young. Our Black Beetles, breed theirs the same way.

The Jar I have tied in a parcel, with my letter, and one from Doctor Dillenius, and directed to our worthy friend, James Logan, for thee.

Pray, next year, look out for the flower of the Sweet Gum, and the Papaw. Send a few in a little bottle or phial of spirits; and send some dried, in paper. Our friend Linnaeus, wants them much, as thee will see by Doctor Gronovius's letter, that I have sent to J. Logan. Pray desire him to show it thee. Pray my love to Joseph Breintnall   I am thine,

P. Collinson

Pray describe the colours of the flowers of the Papaw, and the Sweet Gum; for they may fade so in paper, and change so in spirits, that we may be at a loss to discern them; and send the seasons of their flowering – send two or three of the fairest Gum burs thee can get. Pray forget not a specimen of the Black Gum, in flower and leaf; for we are at a loss to know what it is; and a specimen or Black Haw, in flower and leaf, for this we know not

BP 2:15; D. 117–18.
1. This letter was addressed to "Joseph Breintnall, Mercht." We took it directly from Darlington, since the original was not legible.

To COLLINSON[1]

[illegible] & likewise ye valuable presents sent to mee my wife & children for which we are very thankful   thay are very prety necessary presents & we will use them as being more of thy friendship   as such we take great care of them so demonstrative of our friend & noble benefactor   I have received thy letters of Recommendation to maryland & virginia which I hope may assist me in my Journey thither which I design to take next fall I am obliged to my friend Catesby for the fine draughts   I have provided ye flowers of papaw for him & shall endeavor to procure ye fruite   I have had an excursion ye later end of May over Susquehana where I observed several curious plants & espetialy ye gin sang exactly agreable acording to ye best discription & ye famous root for ye cure of ye pleurisie   one day as I was Asearching ye woods over ye river my guide had like to run over A large rattle snake   I being just behind went round ye snake   he drew up in a quoil & rattled   then I stood staring at him to observe whether he would have any way afected mee by his looks but found no alteration   then I got a green stick & put it towards his mouth for him to bite it that I might have seen ye venum run up ye pores thereof as some relates but he would not ofer to bite altho provoked by gently striking & turning him over; as I came over ye river bank a man came over with one which [he] said he had that day kiled a rattle snake with 15 rattles, it had in its bely two chickens – one duck & 13 young snakes most of them from 6 to 10 inches long   ye next day after I came to a house a good while before night where I intended to lodge   I asked them how far it was to ye river   thay said two miles   I turned out my mare to pasture   I had in mind to go there to looke what kind of plants growed that way but ye man of ye house not being at home I had no guide but my pocket compas thee sent mee which is my constant companion in my distant travails & ye way being very uneven & hilly I steered directly toward ye river without either coat jacket or hat on   it was exceeding hot but ye way full of trees & shady   when I had travailed about half way I saw a thunder gust coming so fast after me that I could not get back to ye house before it rained   I had no way to help myself but by making hast to ye river before it overtook mee in hopes of finding some cave or Clift in ye rocks for shelter by ye riverside which seldom fails in such places   I reached ye river just before it began to rain but it thundered & lightened sharp all along; I happened to come to ye river where there was very high rocks & steep close to it where I spied a little cave about a hundred & fifty foot high in ye rock   I hastened up to it where I sate while it rained but loosing my foothold upon ye rock that gave way with me & I came to ye bottom & had unhospitable salutations & churlish compliments   by way of ye north wind blowing it soon cooled ye air so that I wanted my coat   haveing no other ways to help myself I puled off my trousers from of my breeches & put one arm in one leging & ye other arm in ye other so ye back part of my trousers hung down my back & I kept reasonably warm during ye shower; but if A Mohamatan had spied me there he might have taken mee for a hermit or pagan superstition might have thought I had been one of ye Silvan gods   however from this precipice I had A fine prospect of Susquehana being near enough to kick a stone into it but high above it that I could hardly see which way ye stream run although it run very swift between ye rocks which seemed to be dispersed all over ye bredth of ye river so that one could wonder how so much could pass between them for ye bank seemed scarcely to exceed A mile distance whereas where I left ye river about seven miles higher it was two mile wide & clear of rocks most of ye way over   This day I observed I believe a hundred papaw trees of diferent magnitudes   some near 30 foot high & 6 inches diameter but I could not see one fruite but abundance of dried blossoms that was not dropt of; these growed in such extravagant rich ground upon ye hill sides that I can hardly believe richer Champian soil[2] can be tho some say it is richer on potomick   here I observed a diferent kind of sumach of prodigious sizes near 25 foot high & 8 to 10 unches diameter   in 2 years shoots it will grow 15 foot high   ye first shoots is covered with redish down very like a bucks horn while it is tender but these sumachs are very much hindered of late by luxurious growth & shade of ye locust plane tree linden mulbery & a tree they call white ash   ye leaves are very Like ye lotus   these trees are naturaly of A very large growth to what ye papaws are & which cause ye decay of ye sumach which if it deprived of ye sun & air soon dies   indeed ye papaw will bear ye shade as well as most yet I believe overmuch shade may cause sterility & now to be more inteligible I shall inform you that this rich soil on both sides of ye river was formerly Indian fields & when ye indians was destroyed by marylanders ye sumach & papaw being of very swift growth took posesion first & held out on to ye course of ye luxuriant flowing of thair juices very much by thair roots running under ground & shooting at several distances but by degrees these other trees of slower but more permanent growth advances above & overcomes them like many human monarchs[3]

   I am just returned from jersey where I went to search for evergreens having heard of Curious trees which growed in A perticular place where I had not been before they proved to be ye long coned white pine I believe there is 20 of them amongst all of which I saw but one cone that would bear seed this year being 3 or 4 inches long but there is many young ones for next year these cones requiring one year & half for thair perfection so that I hope next year to procure some seeds from these trees for you

BP 1:14:5.
1. No date but probably June 13, 1738. The first several lines of this letter are illegible.
2. A level expanse of country.
3. Bartram had a good grasp of the essentials of plant succession.

From COLLINSON

London, July 10, 1738

Dear Frd –

I am obliged to thee for thine per Steadman, and have the pleasure to tell thee that Most of the plants in the Last Cargo thrive finely I never had such Luck Before. that Stately Martagon thee sent found on a bank near Schuylkill — is now Near flowering it is 5 foot ½ high & will I believe have 15 flowers which is prodigious, it Differs from the great Marsh Martagon for that will not flower till Midle of August and another sort I had formerly from Docr Witt but that was a smaller sort & never has but 4 or 5 flowers on a stalk I had 3 of your Red Lillies that flowered this year that came in the Last Cargo: they had but one flower on Each Root — pray have they no more with you — The Laurells all Grow, or Chamaerhododendrons the 2 Shrub Honeysuckles and a Very pretty plant, a Species of Hurtleberry a Vitis idaea — has been finely in blossoms The Gooseberry from Conestogo Grows Well, and above all the White Cedar thrives finely & the pine, which is what we Call Lord Weymouth's and a many other pretty plants which come out of the sods of mould taken up with the plants, 2 or 3 sorts of Helleborine as they seem to bee which shows that your Woods are sowed thick with Rare and odd plants — there is several other odd plants that I can't yett Discover what they are for all these I am much obliged to thee and Hope the things per Capt Wright are come Safe to hand and I hope will make some pt of amends for thy Great Care & Trouble —

I am much obliged to thee for thy kind offers of Service, I shall ask nothing that I have done sufficiently already It's fit thee should take breath a Little

As to the Society that thee Hints att, Had you a Sett of Learned Well Qualified Members to Sett out with It might Draw your Neighbours to correspond with you, Your Library Company I take to be an Essay towards such a Society but to draw Learned strangers to you to teach Sciences[1] requires Salaries & good Encouragement — and this will require publick as well as proprietary assistance — which can't be att present complyed with Considering the Infancy of your Colony —

I have sent a few Double Tulips, to ornament thy Garden and a few seeds — & some offsetts of best breeding Tulips which are Endowed with a wonderfull faculty to Diversifie into Variety of Colours consult Millar on their culture. they are (Duch Badges Primors)

The Ranunculuses will not bear yr severe frosts without great Tendance & Covering so I would advice them to be putt into the ground when their Severity is over

The pretty Spirea that thee sent Mee a Specimen of in the quire before Last that I Doubted if it was of your Natural Growth I have now a plant in flower, that Docr Witt sent Mee which shows that it is.

I have Little more to Add but my Love & Respects. I am thy sincere friend,

P. Collinson

BP 3:9; D. 131–33.
1. Bartram had not suggested teaching but rather a society for the mutual exchange of ideas and information. He continued to promote the idea with Franklin until the two founded the American Philosophical Society in 1743. See Bartram to Collinson, fall of 1737, p. 66.

To COLLINSON[1]

I designed afore this time to have gone into ye jerseys but my wife & children have been very sick of ye measles I have provided a fine colection of insects which I design to send by first opertunity which I hope will be within 2 weeks however dear friend I should not have sent by ye way of bristol but that if I stay two weeks longer thee can hardly answer my desire this fall to make ye returns of ye remainder of what is due to Mee altho I can hardly know what to send for I can't yet dispose of one half of what thee sent this spring so that if thee thinks thee can send ye remainder in coper half pence which does with us for pence which is double & will answer as well as goods (for which I must stay at least half year for my pay) if thee can send them safely I wish thee would send them by first opertunity but if thee cant conveniently pray send ye returns in beaten brass kettles without being bound with iron pray send one which will hould half a barrel & so lesser in several sises to one galland but I had rather have it come in pence dear friend I don't question but thee will do ye best thee can for me.

BP 1:14:5.
1. This letter is incomplete. It was probably written in the summer of 1738, as Collinson sent £10 in halfpence on February 7, 1739.

To COLLINSON[1]

I have delivered to ye care of my valuable friend Doctor bond[2] (a man who by his inocent conduct hath gained ye general respect of his acquain-

tances) 2 boxes one with earth wherein I have put severall sorts of turtle egs as ye great [illegible] belied & I believe ye [illegible] with 2 little snake egs I suppose may be our little black snake with a red bely & a white ring about his neck above 8 or 10 inches long thay mostly keep under or between loose stones I much [illegible] that ye ingenious Mr Catesby omited drawing this remarkable snake in that glorious performance which our Proprietor lent me last winter but that I suppose he was never subject to that hard fortune which I am to be so often grabing in ye earth & amongst ye rocks for these snakes are seldom seen abroad I have allso planted round ye side of ye box about half a score kinds of roots which hath near finished thair course of vegitation for this season so I hope thay will come alive in 2 corners I have planted several of ye ranunculus nemorosus
the other box contains variety of insects which I have been diligent in colecting in ye greatest perfection my capacity & circumstance would aford but let mee do what I could one insect or other would bite of ye horn or legs altho I set them in ye oven once A week or two; sometimes little spiders not much biger than A pins head would get in & bite them nay thay are so tender that A little shake will break of a horn or leg what thee asks about ye locusts I cant say much more yet haveing had no opertunity this year but when I was over susquehana I enquired of a man of good sence who observed them as he said very acurately last time of thair being out his opinion was that ye locust darted ye twigs always to ye pith & there layed thair egs which hatching thay descended down ye pith & out of ye extremities of ye roots into ye earth & there received thair growth & nourishment; this seems rather too Crude for my digestion & yet at present I cant give A more reasonable account for its certain ye locust darts ye twig to ye pith & ye fibers thee mentions is part of ye lacerated twig; If I should have an opertunity I think I should spend some time very frely to be more satisfied; as to ye duplycates thee mentions that is wanting to Ld Peters specimens I know not how to procure them for I have no coppy of ye remarks I made upon thine but as I fastened ye specimen & numbered it so I wrote what ocured to my memory by ye observation I had made of it & what I thought might be of service to inform you of ye manner of its growth but for ye future I shall be mindfull of them indeed I keep a Copy of ye letters which I send thee because I expect an answer for ye perticulars mentioned therein, as thee desires specimens of our dryed turtles I wish thee had instructed me how I should dry them for thay being so fleshy I believe thay will stink untolerably but if thee wants thair shells I could send thee enough of several kinds I have received thy letter with Doctor dillenius ye jar of roots & ye huming bee all which is acceptable but I cannot as yet be of thy opinion about thair manner of breeding this I am sure ours breeds in combs & as I remember many years ago an ould englandman mowed over a humble bee nest in my medow & he looked in ye comb for honey saying he used to find honey in thair combs in England [illegible] several of our large kinds of beetles I suppose thay lay an egg in its proper cel where it becomes a grub & makes its way out after which

it becomes a beetle after its kind   I have been this 2 years a learning ye natural generation of some of our beetles but yet cant be well enough satisfied to communicate my conclusions to you   sometimes by ranging many of my observations up together thay seem to Gingle prety well when another narow inquiry will pull all to peices again but perhaps by all I may fasten [illegible] both together but however I have often observed several insects runing very briskly about ye neck of ye beetles & huming bees which I am satisfied is realy lice   lst for thair scituation on ye neck where ye beetle cant disingage them from him   2ndly keeping where it is clear from hair that thay ye better feed upon them   3rd thair nimbleness & organical perfection tho so very small   I am glad thee sent me yt good remnant of druget to go to virginia with or els I would have gone in that fine Sagithee coat which thee sent mee 2 year ago & there was an ould hat thee sent my by Captain Wright   I desighn to have it drest up which was acceptable there was an ould fine velvet cap put into ye hat which was so rotten that I never brought it home   had this been whole I should endeavoured to have worn it at particular times for thy sake many years   I have put into A glass jar with rum several papaw flowers which are of a dirty brown Color blowing in ye latter end of April   allso single & double papaws ⅔ of thair full growth   thay sometimes grow 3 together

BP 1:42.
1. The first few lines are so faded that they cannot be read. This letter was probably written in the late summer of 1738 (see Bond to Bartram, February 20, 1738/39).
2. Dr. Thomas Bond.

To DILLENIUS

August ye lst 1738

Respected friend Doctor Dillenius
　　I am very thankfull to thee for thy kind letters & if thee thinks me worthy of thy friendship & that I can oblige thee with any of my performances pray write often to mee & let me know wherein I can serve thee which I shall readily do as it lyeth in my power   I never saw our great laurel grow any whear but near skulkill tho I have been tould it grows beyond ye mountains up Delaware river   it grows near ye water upon steep banks sides on poor dry soil some times on ye flats high up ye river where it is dry poor & sandy here it grows 2 foot high   it will bear flowers plentifully at 5 foot high in great white bunches   thee mentions ye cornelian chery with a bay leafe growing in Virginia mentioned by Dr. Plukenet   I do not at present know what tree he means nor how he described it never yet haveing a opertunity of reading that valuable author tho often desired it   I believe it neither is nor was ever in Pensilvania alltho I have observed 5 or 6 species of ye Cornus with us   the yapon grows with us then about ye capes of virginia so it is difficult at present for me to procure either flowers or fruits   as thee observes ye cones which I sent ye seeds at ye end of ye wing was not ripe

ye ripe seeds drops out & is blown away with ye wings two far of [illegible] found under ye tree before ye cone falls which is presently after ye discharge of ye ripe seed which is contrary to our common pine & hemlock spruce which hangs on ye tree 2 or 3 years after thay have discharged thair seeds; this white pine is a very poor bearer   I never saw any ripe seeds on this side ye blew mountains   on ye other side I fel a tree about 10 inches diameter & 60 foot high for ye seed & found 8 or 9 perfect seeds but most of them was dropt out   onely such imperfect ones as thee observed stay in untill ye cones drops out   I seldom see any trees less than a foot diameter & 50 foot high bear cones & but few at best & these but a few in a cone that is perfect but our common pines bear cones when they are 10 foot high & some of ye cones hang with a foot of ye ground & continues bearing when it is 3 or 4 foot diameter & near 150 foot high but ye white pine is more ornamental growing as straight as an arrow & a fine piramidel form

I am thy real friend

JB

our common pine cones shoot out sometimes on ye uper some under or of either side of ye twig but as they grow ye small end of ye cone inclines downward but some uper continue right up

BP 1:14.

From DILLENIUS[1]

Oxford, Sept 11 1738

& I found them more different than any other Seeds from abroad, & this not only by yours, but other Seeds I have had from several Persons in Virginia & Carolina.

I have sent you with this a few seeds, most of which are handsome garden plants. You will find three sorts of snails of Medica in one paper which are annuals, & which you may try whether they will serve for Cattle. You will likewise find a paper, named Medica legitima Clusi or Burgundy Trefoil which is still a better sort: for it is Perennial   will stand 15 or more years, runs much in herb & our cattle is greedy of it. This may prove a great improvement, not only to your self, but ye whole Country, which I have often heard wants Pasture. I am your obliged Friend

J J Dillenius

P.S. Sow ye Burgundy Trefoil very thin, for it spreads much.

BP 3:98; D. 309.
1. A large section of this letter has been torn away.

William Byrd II (1674–1744). Portrait by Kneller. From *The Writings of Colonel William Byrd, of Westover in Virginia, Esqr.*, ed. John Spencer Bassett (New York: Doubleday, Page & Co., 1901).

To WILLIAM BYRD II[1]

    I am safe returned home to my family in health as I have allso had ever since I saw thee for which [illegible] I am [illegible] gratitude to return sincere & hearty thanks to allmighty power whose merciful [illegible] is over all his works   soon after I came home I went to town & inquired for Michael Smith but could not meet with any one that could give me any account of him   I despaired of finding him until at last one informed me that he saw him in town but he keeps low for fear of being troubled for debt   he bears ye character of being a miserable fiendish deceitfull Cheating wretch as most inform   I am sory thee had any acquaintance with him for he is not to be depended upon: I shewed thy paper which describes thy land upon Roan oak to several as I came home & in town my friend Casper Wister to whom many of ye Palatines resorts both for advice &

assistance   he inquired of thy Character & I gave it him very much in thy favour   now dear friend I hope thee may not take it amis if I acquaint thee of ye success I met with after I parted from thee; my friend Isham Randolph rode with me over james river to shew me a tree which some caled juniper which proved to be that which is called in europe arbor vita which if thee could procure would be fine ornament to thy garden   allso as we went to ye mountain by adams mill there grows several trees caled silver fir or hemlock spruice which is much esteemed in ye english gardens & when I was upon betwen & beyond ye blew mountains upon a branch of Potomack I observed abundance of remarkable & vertuous plants & roots which if thair vertues were known might be a great benefit to mankind in ye hands of a juditious person that knowed how & when to apply them for it is my opinion that ye improper aplication hath put many a vertuous root out of credit   it was with some concern that I Observed that great variety & what little encouragement is given to any one to [illegible] into ye excelent vertues which if rightly understood might procure such great relief to many innocent people whose lives is rendered miserable by pain & what great gifts is bestowed upon many pretended infirmities & Lazy Cheats [illegible] to labour for thair Living

BP 1:14:10.
1. This letter is badly faded and incomplete, with no date. It was probably written in early November 1738, as Bartram reached home October 26.

To JOHN CUSTIS

19th November 1738

Dear friend Coll Custice
   I am safely returned home to my family which I found in good health as I have been ever since I left thee for which I am thankfull to divine providence whose powerfull regard is to all his creation [illegible] Now dear friend, I can't forget thy kind entertainment & it is with A great satisfaction & pleasure that I think upon ye agreeable hours I spent in thy Conversation, as well as thy kind expresions at parting which hath ingaged my respect after a perticular manner; I had a successfull journey up to, upon & beyond ye blew Mountains where I colected A fine variety of curious plants — there grows on ye other side of James river A little above Isham Randolphs, A tree ye kind of which is known in Europ by ye names of thuja or arbor vitae, which if thee could procure some seed thereof if it growed would be A curious ornament in thy garden; I doubt not if thee was to write or speak to Isham, he would procure thee some   he was very kind to me during ye time I stayed with him & sent his man with mee to ye mountains, which was kind indeed; if it lieth in thy way pray give my love to him   there is ye umbrella tree Cones near thee & ye rip berries of yapon & ye acrons of ye

John Custis (1678–1749). *Harper's New Monthly Magazine* 7 (1853):439.

live oak growing near Captain Caswells[1] would be very acceptable to me but I know not how to get them to Philadelphia   pray give my kind respect to John Blair who used severall endeavours to oblige mee

BP 1:23:1; D. 312.
1. Unidentified.

From BYRD

                        Virginia, the 30th November 1738

Sir

    No sooner than yesterday did I receive your kind letter which was twice as long in travelling From Philadelphia as the writer was when he favoured me with his company here. I am glad you met with so many Curiosities, as to recompense the fatigue of a long Journey, and it is with particular satisfaction that I hear of your having got safe home to your Family, and that you Found them in perfect Health. It is always a pleasure to look back upon

Labour past, especially when it procured an Improvement of Knowledge that continues to the end of the chapter.

I am surprised to understand that Michael Smith turns out a Knave because he had the appearance of a plain honest man. But no Faith is to given to outward appearances, since we are told that the Devil himself puts on the cloathing of an Angel of Light. However I have learnt by long Experience, to be upon my Guard against all strangers not well recommended, so that they can cheat me of nothing but my Civility, to which all mankind are welcome.

I expect every day the arrival of a little ship with Switzers and Germans to settle upon part of my Land at Roanoke. But they have been now 13 weeks at Sea so that I am under great apprehensions for them. They have purchased 33000 acres only in one body; so that there are 72000 stil remaining, to which your friend, Caspar Wistar, is very welcome, if He or any of his Countrymen are so inclined. I am greatly obliged to you for your good character and by the Grace of God shall endeavour never to forfeit it upon any Temptation of advantage. The Land is really very good for so large a Quantity, the clymate moderate and wholesome: the River navigable to the Great Falls, and the Road to James River very dry and level. Besides I have now a Bill depending before our assembly, to make all Foreigners that shall seat upon our Frontiers, free from Taxes for seven years, which I have Reason to believe will pass.

If these, and many other advantages which I have not room to mention will tempt any of Your Germans to remove hither I shall be very glad, upon the easy Terms mentioned in my Paper, And if you will be so good to employ your Interest and kind offices with them for that Purpose, it will be an obligation ever to be acknowledged by him who wishes every thing that is good to you and your Household, and is, without Guile, Sir

Your Hearty Friend and
Humble Servant,
W. Byrd

BP 1:94; D. 312–14; William Byrd, *The Correspondence of the Three William Byrds*, ed. Marion Tinling (Charlottesville, 1977), 2:529–30.

JOURNAL OF A TRIP TO MARYLAND AND VIRGINIA[1]

ye 25 of September I set out for maryland it raining very fast & crosed Susquehana near ye bay   then crosed gunpowder fery & Patapsico & came to Philip thomas[2] where I stayed all night & was kindly entertained   next night I lodged at richard halls[3] who entertained mee very kindly   next day I set out from there & tho it rained prodigiously he sent his negro with me to one dr hamiltons[4] where I stayed all night   next morning it cleared up this was ye first fair day I had since I set out from home & such a time for grevous rain I never knowed without one days fair weather   this day having crosed Patuxant I reached William Mauaits[5] near ye north branch of Potomeck being ye 2d of october   next morning set out & rode up to another branch then steered directly to ye river & crosed it into virginia 4 mile below ye falls then traveled down ye river to a house where I lodged then went to Rapahanack & crosed it a mile below ye fals   then traveled down ye river about a hundred mile   then crosing Panketank rode down to John Clatons where ye river was prety wide   here I had ye misfortune of a grevous disapointment for Claton was gone toward ye mountains to look after some land   I staid here all night with great uneasiness   next morning I set out for Williamsburg being 40 mile of where I got about sunset at Col Custises who received mee very kindly for thy sake   next day I went to wait upon ye governor[6] & deliver him a letter of recommendation from our Governor   he was very kind & civil to me & invited me to dine with him next day & ofered to recommend me to some of his acquaintance   I stayed about an hour with him & then went to Col Custise   this was ye first day of rest since I left home where I stayed all night   next morning being ye 11th of october I left my dear friend Col Custice who entertained mee all ye while with him with extraordinary Civility & respect beyond what ever I met with in all my travels before from a stranger   at night I reached to Col byrds who received me very kindly & next day shewed mee many of his Curiosities which indeed was very entertaining ye rest of ye day was spent in walking about his plantation in observing several curious plants   next morning set out & by night came to William Randolphs[7] where Col byrd recommended me   I set out for Isham Randolphs who received me with all ye expressions of kindness & Civility   next day after breakfast went to view the cavern in ye north side of James river which is distant from ye cavern about 100 yeards   ye cavern runs horizontaly north in between ye rocks 90 foot in length & in breadth 5 foot wide & 4 foot high & towards ye farther end it was so narrow that I could creep no further   I got a stick 5 foot long with which I could reach to ye far end   some said formerly thay could push stones further along & thay would drop down into water but I am sure that pasage is now stopt up   I suppose this cavern is 16 foot higher then I wrote in ye record under this cavern there is another into which I went about 12 foot but I believe foxes & hairs might go a great deal farther & it is posible these two may have communication together for ye rocks seems to have a many little cavities for little creatures to creep into in ye afternoon we walked about his plantation to look for plants   at night it rained then cleared up next morning   we breakfasted early   then he lent me one of his horses & we crossed james river over which we spent a good part of this day searching ye woods for plants & found two that was curious   then returned home before night   next morning I set out to go toward ye mountains my friend Isham went with me 12 milles on my way & sent his man along with me to ye mountains & gave us bread & [illegible] with us   we travailed all this day up ye north branch of james river & lodged at night in ye forks of ye river then set out soon in ye morning continuing up ye branch over hils &

vales & at night came to a Gentlemans house where my good friend Isham recommended me to at ye foot of ye mountain who entertained us civily I rose early this morning a little before day with a design to go up to ye top of ye mountain (which is allways my constant practice in all my travails after plants to rise as soon as it light & search all about before breakfast for I cant aford to loos any time) it being about one mile & half & light moon shine I got up to ye top just before ye sun rose where I had ye fines prospect of ye largest Landskip that ever my eyes beheld   A grand view from ye east to ye south & south west   all ye land of virginia as far as sight could reach   all seemed as even as ye sea   I seemed to bid adieu to all ye pleasant entertainments of virginia & conversations after I had observed ye sun to rise upon this wide horizon I descended down ye mountain & got my breakfast & parted with my host & set forward by myself into ye desert it being [illegible] & about noon crossed over   here I began to find some curious plants & before night crosed over ye ridge dividing james river & rapahanack & lodge between ye first & second ridge of mountains   next day I crosed[8] ye second ridge & lodged between ye second & third ridges these two days rising into very stony & hilly   next morning I set out early in the morning being 22 of ye month & first day of ye week   I set out & by noon travailed over ye mountain   from ye top of this I had a fine prospect of a spacous vail & ye next great ridge northward which is ye same which we in pensilvania call ye blew mountain which runs as I suppose thorow ye whole countrey   in this vail I travailed between 2 & 3 hundred miles & found great variety of plants & seeds   it is in some places [illegible] miles & in other 20 miles wide   in it runs many great branches of Potomack Susquehana skulkil & delaware rivers but ye main branchs of all these mentioned rivers runs thorow ye northern great blew ridge which runs east & west where delaware skoolkil & Susquehana runs thorow but farther westward it turns to ye south   after I descended down into this vail I crosed over Shonondore which was 22 pearch[9] wide & came to a house in ye forks of ye river   then I crosed another branch 14 pearch wide from whence I had 15 mile to a house where I lodged   next day I lodged upon a branch of Opecien & ye 24th crosed Potomock   it was not above one hundred & fifty yards over but two deep to ride over   I lodged at George parkers[10] 10 miles this side of Potomack & next day reached to a branch of Susquehanah having travailed about [illegible] miles along a very stumpy road   next day I reached within 10 miles of Susquehanah where I lodged having travailed about 40 miles   next morning I crosed Susquehanah & traveled to petapehela where I lodged   next morning I set out & crosed several ridges of mountains a very stony way for 5 miles   here I lost sight of ye great blew ridge & travailed to a branch of Conestoga where I lodged about 50 miles from home   next day I reached & past ye night [illegible] I reached home being ye 26 of October

BP 1:14:7, 1:14:6; American Philosophical Society Library, Wildman transcript.
  1. Most of this is taken from Wildman because the original has faded badly. It was

probably written in late fall, after the trip to Maryland and Virginia, and enclosed in a letter to Collinson.
2. Unidentified.
3. Unidentified.
4. Unidentified.
5. Unidentified.
6. Lieutenant-governor William Gooch.
7. William Randolph (1681–1742), of Tuckahoe.
8. BP 1:14:6 starts at this point.
9. One rod, or 16½ feet.
10. Unidentified.

To COLLINSON

10 December 1738

dear friend:
– I having performed my journey thorow maryland & virginia as far as Williams burgh so up james river to ye mountains so over & between ye mountains in many very crooked turnings & windings in which according to ye nearest computation I can make betwixt my setting out & returning home I traveled 1100 miles in 5 weeks time, haveing rested but one day in all that time & that was at Williamsburghe. I happened to go in the only time for gathering of seeds – the autumnal both in maryland and virginia & the exceeding mild fall favoured ye opertunity upon & between ye mountains whereby I gathered abundance of kinds of seeds in perfection which had not ripened for several years because of ye surly frosts which came A month or 6 weeks sooner than they did this year   indeed, beyond ye mountains in virginia & pensylvania there is a great variety that I saw & ye inhabitants say ye ground is covered with dilicate beautiful flowers in ye spring which is not to be found after hot weather comes on   when I first began to find many curious seeds I wraped them up in paper separately & put them in my leather bags but in riding & shaking thay freted ye paper & mixed together so after I gathered all together, as I found them which I send to you all mixed & as thay are most of them peranual I suppose they will do well enough sown together   I sent by friend thomas bond A box of turtle eggs & several roots packed up carefully but the captain was so long before he sailed after he talked of sailing within 2 or 3 days that I am afraid thay were damnified   I sent a box of insects & a jar of papaw flowers & fruite which I hope is come safe to hand   this hath been but a scarce year for several kinds of forrest seeds so could not procure several which thee sent for but I have made it up in A great variety of seeds of curious plants which grow betwen & upon ye mountains   next year there may be more plenty of several kind which you want so pleas to let mee know what sort may be acceptable & if you pleas to order me to new england next fall I am not much against it haveing health & prosperity   allso I should be glad to have letters of recommendation to thy friends there   I received thy letter of july ye 10th with ye names of ye plants I sent last year with ye seeds & tulip roots

all which I am obliged to thee for   I wish there may be some, difering from what we have already for we have great variety obtained from ye breeders which we have had these many years   ye red lyly seldom produces above one flower upon one stalk   this year ye Medlar bore which thee sent me for ye Neapoliton but I believe it is ye english manured kind.[1] However one of our Persimmons is worth A dozen of them for goodness in eating and as big but we have great variety of them, some are ripe in the middle of September, others not till Crismas   thay are extreme disagreeable to eat untill thay are thorough ripe & will fall with shaking ye tree then thair pulp is very Delicious but thair skin which is as thin as ye finest paper, still retains an astringent bitterness but many of our countrey people are so greedy of them that thay swallow down skin pulp & seeds all together   I admire thay are not cultivated with great care in europe in stead of many other kinds of fruite which are much inferior in goodness   thay make an excellent liquor or wine for pleasant drinking

Our friend, Isham Randolph (A generous good natured gentleman & well respected by most that is acquainted with him) hath agreed with me to have A correspondence together but cant tell well which way to carry it on whether back of ye mountains by way of Shenandore or below ye mountains, we can't yet tell   I think to be diligent in my observation on ye flower of our sweet gum to gratifie thee & thy curious friends   it seems strange that some accurate botanist hath not allready taken notice of it but I suppose ye difficulty of procuring ye flowers hath been some reason of ye neglect for ye tree generaly groweth straight & tall & seldom bears seed before ye tree is 40 or 50 feet high   When I was down in virginia my wife sent A box of all spice berries which I had with some expense of time Colected being most of what I could find about where I live, and for 20 miles distance. I obtained ye sight of ye coppy of Doctor gronovius letter which thee sent to James logan just before I set out for maryland which A gentleman had copied before logan sent it back which was soon after he received it   If I can any ways, without much loss of time oblige lineus or gronovius at thine or thair request I am willing to do it I perceive thay are curious & ingenious botanists.   I have put severall sweet gum burs in ye box of seeds. I observed diligently this fall if I could see any of ye prodigious large sumach which I found by susquehana last spring but I could find none neither upon potomock nor susquehana where I crosed it which was 30 or 40 miles below & above where I crosed it in ye spring   I cant hear of it growing any where else

BP 1:23:2, 1:17:3; D. 120–22.
1. BP 1:17:3 begins here.

To PAUL DUDLEY [?][1]

having by ye orders of several of ye members of ye Royal Society travailed eleven hundred miles in about five weeks time   travailing along ye western

shore of maryland   sometimes near ye falls of ye rivers of potomack &
rapahanack   then down Susquehana   then crosing york river near ye
bay   thence to Williamsburg up James river & crosing it 40 mille above ye
falls & searching ye woods for plants   then on to ye blew mountains
then travailling up ye northern branch of james river to ye mountains from
ye top of which I had a fair prospect of a great vail eastward thorow
pensylvania & in breadth 20 mile bounded on ye northwest by mountains which runs many hundred miles   in this vail runs a great branch of
potomach called opecon   allso a southern & northern branch of Susquehana & several branches of skulkill & delaware   I searched for plants
at several seasons of ye year & Colected specimens for ye observation
—— when I returned I went to Philadelphia to pay my respects to some of
my friends there   B franklin was one who presented me with ye boston
Gazette num 975 wherein I observed remarks [on] ye stramonium by ye
Medical Society of Boston with thair observations on ye qualities of it which
is very agreeable to ye frequent informations I have met with it is another
herb growing plentifuly with us ye root of which is more pernicious if taken
inwardly then any   thay can poison one to death in as short or long a
time as thay please with this root   I also expressed your desire of being
informed of ye maner of growth or a botanical description — mentioned in
ye newspapers of Philadelphia ye 27th July which is so exactly agreeable to
ye Chinese Gensang that no other description can at present be given
onely   I may inform you of ye place in which I found it growing which was
on ye western bank of ye river Susquehana   degrees no latitude about 200
yards from ye river upon a very rich hillside on a heape of rocks which was
surrounded with high trees by which thicket it growed   I spent most of ye
day over ye river in searching both high land & low for this plant   ye two
next days I spent in search for it on our side of ye river but found none; I
have in all ye mountain journeys made diligent inquiries but could not hear
of any growing but onely near ye Susquehana where it growed in ye rich
bottoms as well as on ye hills but in little quantities in either places but I
observed for ye space of 300 miles travail over & between ye mountains
several very likely [plants] for seeds but I was a month too late for it falls in
september & was covered with leaves & weeds   very early in ye spring it
was near its full growth by ye 20 of may at which time I discovered it
blooming   I brought 4 specimens home   one I sent to france   2 I design
for London   one to keep myself   I send these to you hopeing it may be
acceptable & be more informing [illegible] can give   I allso then observed
ye famous root which dr tenet[2] sets forth for ye cure of pleurisy &
pupneumonic fevers   a specimen of which I send   I allso send a specimen
of a plant which ye inhabitants of ye mountains   james river & rapahanack
calls angelika   it realy is a soverain remedy for ye flatulous [illegible] as to
your queries whether this may not be a kin to ye aralias I shall not [illegible]
am satisfied   it exactly resembles in form ye Chinese gensang tho I believe
it [illegible] as Chinese ascribed to one kind of thair aralias growing to
[illegible] 8 degrees no lat [illegible] it is caled aralia arborescens spinosa

Vaill. [illegible] which was 2 inches diameter   very prickly on ye stalk of ye leaves & branches

BP 1:38.
1. This letter appears to have been written late in 1738 to an unidentified individual, possibly Paul Dudley.
2. Dr. John Tennent.

To DILLENIUS[1]

Respected friend Doctor Dillenius

I have sent thee one quire of specimens which I hope may be acceptable but I thought it needless to make any remarks on ye perticulars having done it to those I send my friend Collinson (& think most of them the same) who I suppose will send his to thee to know thy oppinion of them   I also send severall kinds of seeds wraped up in perticular papers besides A share of that Large Colection I gathered in maryland virginia & ye farther parts of Pensilvania between ye branches of Potomak & Susquehana   I made inquirey in virginia about ye cornelian Chery with A big leaf but cant meet with any information about it   neither can I imagin what it should be unless it be our sour or black gum   thee signified how thee had ordered A crown worth of writing paper for me but I hear nothing of it   I hope thee hath received my letter dated last August[2]

No more at present but ye sincere good will of thy friend

BP 1:23:5.
1. This letter must have been written in late 1738 or early 1739, because Bartram is sending seeds collected in Virginia in the fall of 1738.
2. See Bartram to Dillenius, August 1, 1738.

From COLLINSON

Lond January 26 1738/9

Dear John

I am much obliged to thy good Wife for her kind Letter In thy Absence, & next I must tell thee I was pleased with thine to heare of Thy safe Returne from thy Virginia Expedition but am very Angry with that Sorry Man Ashton[1] for not takeing in thy Cargo [of] seeds — He was under Obligation to Mee — I did not treat him so but Trusted him Two pounds worth of goods, but was 3 or four years getting it, nay had it not been for Charles Read deceased who gott the Money I much Question if he would have had Honesty or Honour Enough to have paid it, to this Day — for During the time he owed Mee the Money, He came to England & promised to pay Mee   I thought him to be a Man of Honour but in short he Slunk away & Never paid Mee, and after that gave Ch Read much Trouble to gett it, and paid no Interest so I was a Looser for I sold the goods for Ready Money, and because Cash fell Short, took his Note and thus he has served Mee for my Civility — I shall remember Him —

I am att psent greatly Hurryed in business so must be very Short and only tell that I have sent thee a Box of Seeds under Cover to Tho Penn yr proprietor, for I was willing to take the advantage of the first ship because the Season Slips away for sowing

There is a small packett for Docr Witt   pray Some How or other convey it to Him —

Some Fine Mellon seed for Thos Penn — Some Burgundy Trefoil for J. Logan — and pray where there is sufficient Lett him have a share of the other Seeds — The Scorpiodes are a surprising Phenomenon in Nature, that the Seed of Fruits or podd of a plant should be so like an Annimall for when these are Green and pretty near full grown gather one and picc it Artfully on thy Neckcloth and there is not one In a great Many will Distinguish it from a smooth Green Caterpillar — beside this pretty Curiosity this Class of plants are of great Service in Hot dry Countries for Green fodder for their Milch Cattle in the Summer Months, please to Impart this to friend Logan with Some Seed of Each —

I have before Said Sufficient of the Burgundy Trefoil, but lest that sent in the Autumn should not be pfectly Ripe, I have sent some More   Docr Delenius is of strong Opinion, that it will prove the best, most productive of Herbage & Durable of any Grass — it requires some Care at first setting out so let it be sown Carefully in yr Gardens in Order to Raise seed for greater Crops abroad —

please to ask Friend Logan to Lett thee peruse the Philosophical Transactions that I send Him by Capt Wright — in It, thee will Find a Desertation on the Deer & Moose of yr Continent — we have but an Imperfect Idea of your male or Buck of your Fallow Deer as thee will pceive by the print or Figures annexed — I could be glad to have the Scalp of one of your Bucks with its horns full grown on it — phaps this may be attainable by thy own procurement or Some of Thy Friends — and if thee canst Informe Us further or better in Relation to those Animals, the Deer & Moose thee will Much oblige

thy sincere frd.
P. Collinson

pray Look out this year for Seed or ye Small Cones of yr Swamp Bay   its flowers are not unlike the Water Lillie   these Seeds will not keep out of Earth & must be Sent before the Rest   thee will heare further by Capt Wright   I hope to Send 10 pounds worth of Half pence by Him for I know not when I shall have such an other oppertunity to send them

Pray remember for Frd Catesby Flowers of the Papaw. He thanks thee very kindly for the Fruite and come they Either Dry or in spirits they will lose their Colour — so pray Describe It as well as thee Can, that he may be qualified to paint It & what colour is the Fruite when Ripe and its Time of Flowering & Time when the Fruite is Ripe.

Possibly some of yr Indian Traders may procure a Deer or Staggs scalp, with the Horns on.

att the Bottome of the Box are Horse Chestnutts — then they are Covered with Laris or Larch Cones   Sow in Shade but under no Drip   then uppon them are Spanish Eating Chestnutts   In the Brown paper are pines & Firr Seeds from Muscovy   this Requires to be Sown in the Shade but not to be Driped on by other Seeds — thee will find Docr Delenius pcell   pray gett Some Mosses for Him. He is now Engraving his Collection of Mosses in order to publish them   the Arbutus is Ld Petrees Saveing from his Seed Last year   the Same I Sent thee   He had Raised Some thousands   Sow it in the Shade for the Sun is apt to Scorch them when in Tender leafe —Sow Some in ye Ground but protect them the first Winter & Some in a Case to be Housed on approach of first Frosts

Sow pear kernells Carefully   they are fine Sorts & may produce Some good fruite   Suffer not the Weeds to Choake them which if not Carefully Looked after are the Bane of all Seeds by Choaking them but when thee finds these pears produced from Seed will neither Eat nor Bake they will make good Stocks to Graft on   please to give my Respects to Jo Breintnall & Inform Him C:Wright will Sail in a few Days   by Him shall Send the pamphlets &c

BP 2:43; D. 123–24.
1. A ship captain.

From COLLINSON

Lond February 1, 1738/9

Dr frd

I forgott in my Former to give thee Some account of the Success of the Turtle Eggs — Unluckky for thee and for Mee the Capt Sett the Box in the Forecastle of the Ship – where it was Cold & Wett and notwithstanding thy Care in pitching part of It – Some water gott to It and the Earth being Cold, Chiled the Eggs and I am afraid the box was Tumbled up and Down which might Bruise the Eggs and I think the Eggs was putt in too Large a Quantity of Heavy Earth — I carried them in the Mould & sett In a warm Bake house where they bake constantly Every Day but yet not one came to good —

Now before they was packed in Light Dry Mould in a smaller Box & Less Earth and Sett under the Cabin which is a very Close Warm place, and by that Genial Heat which penetrated Easily through the Earth Supplied the place of the Sun and Carried them on to Maturity —

but tho our Success was Indifferent in One, the Good state of the plants, that Came in the Mould made ample amends — I take Them very kindly att thy Hands — I shall soone Expect their appearance   I have Little to Wish but for Dens Canis with the yellow flower. I hope those Thou Sent will Flower this year tho I suspect It for I think they are not strong Enough —

The box of Insects came in pfect order are Extremely fine, and a great Variety and nicely Cured & displayed — I desire thy Acceptance of a peice of Sagathy in acknowledgment for them

It was very Lucky to find the Crysalis of that Noble fine Moth but it would have been More so to have had them Copulate for the Female presently after Copulation Layes her Eggs So should have been confined in a Small Box & the Eggs Immediately Sent Over for some kinds Hatch Soone   Others are Longer   Some not till the year after   it is very wonderfull to think of the Infinite Smallness & Divisibility of Matter   it is past our Conceiving the Subtility of those Steames or Effluvia Emitted by the Female Moth and the fineness of the Sence of the Male to be awaken'd att a distance   View the Organs of these Creatures how Minute they are past our Distinguishing without the best Glasses   how much More is their Emanations —

If ever a Female Moth happens in thy possession again, pinn her fast down In a Box and go into the Fields, and See if the Males Come not to Impregnate Her — Our Virtuoso Here have great Diversity this way they carry the hen Moth into the Fields and Sett down by Her, and they have taken a Dozen or More att a Time that come to Copulate — So Strong is their Excitement they regard no pson so they can but Embrace the Female and att that Time are very Easily taken.

I am much In a Hurry, So Cannot but add I am thy Real frd
P. Collinson

I Long the arrival of the Ship with the Seeds   I wish they are not much spoilt and I Desire as much to hear of thy Expedition into Virginia and what thee found and observed there

I wish Capt Wright may be able to gett thee Some Half pence   He has Several Times promised Mee, but how it will be I can't Say for He is in a hurry and I am in a Hurry for now is the Time that Ships for all the Colonies are going and every one are pressing for their Goods — and Wee have a great Deal to Do that way

I dare not Look into thy Letters for I know there are many things that require my Notice but I cant yett do it

I sent some Ginseng roots to China   If they sell well a good profitable trade may be Carried on, In the mean time sow the Seed & raise a Stock to furnish my friend when he returns   I intend the Benefit for thyself, Keep that a Secret & raise what thee canst for I have an opinion it will turn to account if my friend manages it rightly

Lord Petre Desires thee to procure a Bushel of Red Cedar Berries which thee shall be paid for Separately — I would be glad to see a Fair Specimen or Two of the Ginseng in Leafe, Flower, & Fruite, your proprietor Sent Mee one but it Wanted Seed Vessells and Flowers — I hope Next year thee'l Send Mee a Root or Two in Mould

BP 2:46; D. 125.

From COLLINSON

London, February 7, 1738/9

Dear Friend John: –

Notwithstanding thy cargo of seeds is not arrived, yett, as I know thy probity, and the service a Remittance may be to thee, and as such another oppertunity may not offer this year, to send Halfpence, because there is some Difficulty attends it, unless the Captain is in our Interest; for this Reason, our Right Trusty & welbeloved Capt Wright has procured for thee Ten pound worth of halfpence for which I this Day took his Recept, and paid Him the money for them. I wish ym safe to thy Hand and am thy Real friend,

P. Collinson

I would have sent Capt. Wright's Reccept but that it is my Voucher that I paid him the Tenn pounds for the Halfpence

[London, February 7, 1738–9

Captain Edward Wright: –

Pray deliver to John Bartram's own hand, ten pounds' worth of halfpence, for which I have your receipt; and my friend John's receipt shall be a sufficient discharge for so doing. I am your sincere friend,

P. Collinson

Captain Wright has also a brown paper parcel for thee][1]

Pray remember seed of the Red Cedar, for a friend of Lord Petre, for which thou shall be paid thy price, separately – a bushel or two: and a large quantity small cones of Swamp Laurel, or White Tulip Tree.

I hope thy box of seeds, from your proprietor has safe come to hand.

I hope for next ship, to hear of thy Virginia expedition.

I fancy, now the has made what Discoveries thee for the present Intends, thee will Lay still, and Lett thy Correspondent Reap the Benefit of them; for I know in rambling to and Fro, not many seeds can be gathered, or att least, but a few sorts but, when the knows where to go for a pticular plant, and the season of its ripening seed, is a Certainty, it is much securer then going on Discoveries. However, thee will heare more by next ship.

Frd John, pray call at J. Logan's. I have sent thee a print of the great Magnolia; and with it, thee will see a Catalogue of our American plants.

Linnean Society of London, James Collection, Ms. 298; BP 2:44; D. 126–27.
1. This bracketed section is not in the letter at the Linnean Society.

From THOMAS BOND

Paris, February 20, 1738–39

My good Friend: –

As I am writing to my American friends, I cannot forget my good friend Bartram, and send you my best respects, and hearty desire for your and family's health and happiness, than which nothing is more my wish.

I expected to have given you more pleasure in this letter than I find I shall; for by the assistance of that good man, our friend Collinson, I have a particular acquaintance with Monsieur Jussieu, Professor of Botany at the King's Garden, who is supposed to be one of the greatest men in that way in Europe. He promised to inform me what were the species of those plants you called Incognita, and in others where he thought you were mistaken.

I gave him all the dry specimens; five of which were new, and pleased him exceedingly, particularly the Seneka Root, which he then took to be a *Polygala*. But I could not meet him anywhere this week: for which reason, I must put it off to the next opportunity. He told me the Virginia Seneka Root was sent him with a recommendation and method of use in pleurisies, and repeatedly tried with surprising success, and is in the highest esteem with him, and many other physicians; but that another here, of the same species, was tried for the want of it, with equal advantage.

The Ginseng is now here common, but in no esteem. It was brought from Canada, and is exactly the same with what you discovered.

I have now spent three months in Paris, the most diligently I ever did any in my life, and, I fear, to the prejudice of my tender constitution; but if I was almost sure 'twould kill me, I could not avoid tending the curious courses of Anatomy, Surgery, Physiology, &c. And, in short 'tis impossible there can be better, if so good schools in the world.

My friend Jussieu tells me, that I shall believe myself at home, by being amongst so many of my native plants, as brought from America by himself; in quest whereof, he was sent by the King.

If I am not otherways too busy, I propose by his assistance, to improve myself in that science, at the King's Garden, which is a most beautiful place.

Pray do me the favour to recommend my best respects to your good spouse, and assure yourself I am with great esteem,

Your real friend,
Th. Bond

College of Physicians of Philadelphia, Historical Collections of the Library; D. 316–17.

From COLLINSON

Lond February 24, 1738/9
Pensilvania Coffee House

Frd John

To Morrow Capt Wright sails, So that I have only Time to Acquaint Thee that no Ship is yett arrived that makes Mee In pain for the Cargo of Seeds for this year

He has been so good to procure for thy Use Tenn pounds worth of halfpence — I paid him 4s. 6d. for procuring & Carrying on board — he has also a piece or Sagathe for thy own Wear   Capt Breame is nott yett gott Clear off the Channel   He has been stayed Some Weeks so that Wright may have a Chance of getting as soon as Him   I think I never remember the Like   Wee have had South West Winds with very short Intervals of E:NE which was so Variable that no Ship has got Clear of the Channel Since the 13th December   Some ships has had a Terrible Time on't. Lying So Long in the Downs, this wind has brought us Exceeding temperate Weather   our Almond Trees was in Blossom by the Latter End of January and all Vegitables in proportion   no frost since the 5 January & but very Slight ones Before —

I have writt by Capt Breame & sent a box of Seeds under Cover to Thos Penn and a pcell to J. Logan per Wright   But the principal Reason of my writeing now is to Desire thee to procure what plants thee canst of Genseng & plant in thy Garden & Raise what thee Canst from Seed   I am well assured it will prove a very profitable Comodity to China who Value it above any thing   I have Compared yours with the Chinese and find them in all Respects the same   Your proprietor was so kind to send Mee a Considerable pcell & I have Trusted a pticular Friend with it to Carry to China, to see how they approve of It and to find what price it bears — but my friend is under promise not to Discover that it is American for if they know that, they are so fancifull it may not be so good as their own —

So gett a stock by thee as soon as thee can, & be sure Conceal thy Intention from every one — In 24 months my Friend will be here again from China & then shall give thee Notice — pray send Mee a Root or Two In Mould for my Garden —

It is now very late so must Conclude

Thy real frd
P. Collinson

BP 2:45; D. 127–28.

From COLLINSON[1]

Frd John

I now come to take Notice of thy journal   I wish thee had been more pticular but possibly Time did not admitt   It was very agreeable to Mee to hear that my Friends was kind to thee   I shall not fail to Acknowledge it, but I should have been glad to have had thy pticular observations on them & their Familys and their Dwellings and their tasts in Life, but this is exacting to much from a Man of thy Active Genius so pray think no more About It —

I am concerned Robert Gover is Dead, but I think his son or his Family are in being, I wish Thee had gone and seen the Cliff from whence the angular Stones was taken which are so curiously formed in squares, that far exceed the Lapidarys art, no doubt but Some belonging to him could have shown it thee but as is Matter of Curiosity and only proposed for thy Sake another time may do as Well

I am sorry our brother Clayton was nott att Home   it was no doubt a great Disappointment that you could not open your Budgetts & Compare Notes —

I am informed my Frd Custis is a very Curious Man, pray what didst thee see New in his Garden   Butt I am told Colo Byrd has the best Garden in Virginia and a pretty Greenhouse well furnish'd with Orange Trees — I knew him well when in England and he was recon'd a very polite Ingenious Man   as for my frd Isham who I am also personally known to I did not doubt His Civility to thee   I only wish to have been there and shared it with thee —

Thee does not mention any Animals in this voyage; and yett I don't suppose the Country Destitute   pray Has thee Observed Two sorts of Fallow or small Deer whose principal Distinction I think Lies in their Horns — there is besides the smaller Elk or Stagg a pair of them I saw Lately with a pair of Buffaloes — that was brought to England   Butt there is ye Great Elk or Moose which I think Frequents more to the Northward — pray what Highth & Bulk was those Fine Pines with 3 Leaves that thee Discoverd in the Great Vail — but as to plants I shall make my Remarks when I Returne them nam'd —

Thy map was very Informing and gave a pretty Idea of thy Journey — pray what Inhabitants didst thee find in the Great Vale – wether Indians or English —

As this Journey has proved very Fatiguing and Troublesome to thee I can't advise another if it is possible to gratify thy Correspondents without It

It was very Curious of thee to Collect the Two Noble crysalises, Wee wait with impatience their new birth, I wish the Heat of our Climate is able to perfect them — for the ring of Eggs that thee Collected from the apple trees Hatch the very next Day I had them from on Board it being very warm wether but In a Day or Two it Changed to very Cold for the season and I am afraid has kill'd them all notwithstanding they was kept in the House and fed with young Leaves & blossoms of apple Tree   if Ever thee meets with any More I will keep the ring of Eggs in a Cold place till May and then I don't doubt but to Raise them & Carry them through their Changes — which will be a great Curiosity and is Frequently done Here by those that would raise a quantity of Rare & scarce Flies —

The Two Muscle Shells are great Curiosity & what I never saw before — but I apprehend with you as Well as with us there is great variety of Fresh Water and Land shells small & great but these Require Eyes like thine & Mine to find them out

If thee happens on such another Wasps nest that the Possum Destroyed in the Bush pray think of Mee — the possum is a most surprising Creature   the Great Query is if the young is really Form'd from the Seed of the

Male att the Teat or Received their Figure In the Womb in the Animalistic State and in that Minute State are Conveyed by proper Vessells from the Womb to the Teat   How is it the Great Author of their Being only knows, Wee poor Mortals see but a part   admire & wonder att the great Variety In the Creation, But know Little I may say Nothing in Comparison of what is to be known and which Wee on Every Occation want to know

I have Inclosed in my friend T. Penn's pcell Two Cones & some Seed of the Stone pine – please go to him for them

I am my good friend Thine very Truly

P. Collinson

One thing I forgot to Mention before and what very much surprises Mee to Find thee who art a philosopher prouder than I am, My Cap it's True, had a small Hole or Two on ye Border but the Lining was New   Instead of giving it away I wish thee had sent it Mee back again   It would have served Mee Two or Three Years to have worn in the Country in Rainy weather

BP 3:10; D. 112–14.
1. Undated, but probably around March 1738/39 (see Collinson to Bartram, February 7, 1738/9, in which he is expecting an account of Bartram's Virginia expedition on the next ship.

From BYRD

Westover the 23d of March 1738/9

Sir: –

I sent an answer to your kind letter by the Post, several months ago and congratulated your safe return to your family. This kisses your hand by my Friend, Dr. Tscheffely a Swiss gentleman, who is bound to Philadelphia to try if he can prevail with any of his Countrymen to come and settle upon my land at Roanoke and if you will be so kind as to lend a helping hand towards it, I shall ever acknowledge the obligation. The land is exceedingly good, with a fine River running through the whole length of it more than a quarter of a mile wide; Full of Wild Fowl in winter, and alive with fish all the Year. Very many Rivulets and Creeks run into it on both Sides, which help to fertilize the Soil, and will afford all manner of convenience for mills of every kind. The situation is high and the air very wholsome, Free from thos aguish vapours which infect the lower part of the Country. And as the Land lyes 40 miles on this side the mountains, the Indians have no manner of Claim or pretence to it, by the last Peace we made with them. The Price I sell this land for, you know, is very easy, being no more than £3 of our currencey for every Hundred acres. The quitrent is but 2 shillings a year, and since I saw you, I have prevailed with our assembly, to make all Foreign Protestants Free from Taxes for Ten years, that shall come and inhabit that part of the country. These, I think, are such Temptations and Encouragements, as are not to be met with elsewhere. Nor will the Distance exceed seventy miles to a ship landing, and the Road will be very good, and very level all the way, when we have cleared the Ridge that we intend; so that there will be little Difficulty in bringing the Fruits of their industry to market. We have had the misfortune lately to lose a ship, either by the villainy or Stupidity of the master, which had 250 Switzers and Germans on board, with effects to a considerable value. These were to seat on part of my land under the conduct of several Gentlemen of Fortune, who came along with them. But these Gentlemen perished and most of the People, and very little of their Effects is saved. Some few of these unhappy wretches are gone upon my Land to make a Beginning, and will soon be followed by more.

The bearer is a man of skill in his Profession, has been a great Traveller, and has great knowledge in Chymistry and Surgery. Thus as a virtuoso I recommend him to You, and likewise as a Friend of
Sr Your most humble servant,
W. Byrd.

Mrs. Byrd joins her best wishes with mine for the happiness of yourself and your Family.

BP 1:95; D. 314–15; Byrd, *Correspondence of the Byrds,* 2:530–31.

To COLLINSON[1]

Dear friend peter Collinson

I have received thy kind letter of September ye 26 wherein thee informed me of ye Cash thee had shipped for mee which if it Comes safe it will help me finely   I shall be glad if ye medicas be what I have not yet had   I have lately received 3 or 4 sorts of comical medicas like acorns from Germany with a great Collection of other kinds of seeds   I have had this several years 2 sorts of lucern which grows exceedingly rank if it be kept clean from weeds or ye natural grass   otherwise it dwindles away & comes to nothing so that ye common red & white clover seems to be more profit to us for thay will scuffle with ye weeds & natural grass & produce as large A crop a year with onely dunging as ye other will with howing weeding & dung; but I admire that medicas will not grow to be worth anything with us by any way or art bestowed upon it & yet it is said to be so profitable in europe   ye white briony I Cant raise to maturity neither in ye shade nor sunshin   ye larch came up wel but perished toward ye latter of summer   all but one which comes out bravely now to my great joy but I despair of raising ye hors chestnut   not one comes up but I saw one in Col Custis garden A foot high   ye gors will not live over winter with mee   ye cytisus is killed to ye roots & ye monpelior both root & branch   ye wood & tree sage branches is killed but ye roots is yet alive   I have A fine root of Angelica & Galeopsis yet Alive which I am well pleased with   the rose seed thee sent mee proves to be ye common single red rose & that thee sent for ye double blossomes was our common single sort   we have plenty of ye damask provence white cinamon & double & single red rose but I never saw ye yelow rose yet   ye larch   juniper   barcelona nuts   siberian rhubarb   wood sage wild anemone & [illegible] grow finely with many others which ye sent me & most of ye bulbous roots ye sent me at several times but ye ranunculus I see no appearance of

I am obliged to thee for the kindness about ye glas vesuls   I did not like sending for it myself nor my friends project but hee was so desirous of them & I believe would have paid money for them either whole or broken   I got A couple of hands & a cano & went a long way up skulkill against ye stream & fetched A parcel of ye great chamaerhododendron with A good sod of earth to each root & planted it in my garden to oblige thy friend Catesby with one or two

thine of october ye 19th I read with great satisfaction   I am glad my letters & insects was acceptable   I rejoyce that many of ye plants I send prosper with thee   ye Cash I received   ye pence & [illegible] thee mentions nothing of receiving ye glas jar of papaw flowers & fruit in rum for my friend Catesby which I gave in charge of my friend bond to deliver safe to thy hands I fear miscaried; I thank Lady Peter for ye pear kernels & am often thinking what to send her for A requitall

BP 1:14:6; American Philosophical Society Library, Wildman transcript.
1. Only two small sections of this letter have been found, so most of it is taken from Wildman. Although undated, it was written April 1, 1739 (see Collinson to Bartram, September 22, 1739).

From COLLINSON

Lond April 12 1739

Dear Friend

I hope thou has mine p Capt Wright with the Tenn pounds in Halfpence & a piece of Sagathy.

And now I shall take notice of Thine of December 9 — which came very oppertunely and In pretty good season for the Seeds, for it was March the 9th I recd thy Letter and in About a Weeks time I gott the Seeds from on Board   all seemed in good Order but 2 pcells of acorns that had spired[1] and was good for nothing – had been better Left behind than sent — These I have distributed as formerly — We think this year thee had better rest from thy Labours, for I find Travelling Furnishes little but Herbaceous Seeds & Specimens   what thy Employers most want are shrubs & Trees and I find nothing New of these that thee has sent seeds of but the fine pine which thou Found in the Vale, which seems new to us and if thou could go att a proper season and Bring a Horse Load of cones, it would be a very Acceptable Cargo   this sort I observe has 3 Leaves in a Sheath, and the White Pine of which thee sent a plant which thrives finely is call'd here, as thee will find by Millars Dictionary, Lord Weymouths pine — This sort is scarce

& Rare with us   now a Cargo of this will be very Acceptable and what thee must Indeavour to Collect, and a Quantity of the common Red or Jersey pine which has only 2 Leaves in a Sheath   more White & Red Cedar Rose Laurel Cones, this was the most valuable in the last Cargo — Papaw Sugar Maple   Black Haw or Indian Sweet Meat — Spruce cones and all sorts of Firrs — Phaps thee'l say these are only or chiefly to be had in New England or New found land   I should not be against going thither for them att a proper Time, but First letts get the seeds that are nearer Home for by thy several Expeditions thee art now fully informed where there is the Greatest Quantity of the kinds Wee want growing and if thee should go to New England and bring Home but Little I think it hardly Quits the Cost —In that Country I know no Body — after all that I have said It must be Left to thee but I think it had better be Defer'd, and only Ransack the Jerseys and the Country about, if it will afford the seeds Wee want — and to Encourage thee to proceed with Spirit I have gott another pson who Desires the Value of Tenn pounds sterling of Cones of all sorts of pines thee can gett, It is Left to thee, of the Jersey pine I take it there is no great Difficulty to get sufficient, and what thou can of the other sorts. Thee has not to do with unreasonable people.

The Tenn pound cargo putt in a Case by it self for I will have no more Trouble of Dividing and it would save Mee a great Deal of Trouble as Lord Petre has half, if his was putt in a Case by it Self   As to the other ½ I may make a shift to Divide that.

In my last I acquainted thee with the Fate of the Turtle Eggs — Some of the roots are alive that came with them   in pticular the Dwarf Double Mountain Ranunculus and there is another with Narcissus leaves which seems to me what I have had by the name of Attamasco Lilio Narcissus — a pretty flower — None of the yellow Flowering Dens Canis flowered this year   phaps the Roots are not of sufficient maturity — Butt the Box of Insects came safe and are very fine   in pticular that Noble Moth   The jar with the Papaws came safe and my Frd Catesby thanks thee very much —

Now, dear Frd John I come to thank thee for thy Curious Collection of living plants for my Self But oh! sad story for to tell, not the Least Glimpse of one was to be seen, if the unworthy Captain had sett that Case only in his Cabbin, all had been Safe, But it was stowed on the Deck above the Hold and Cover'd with pipe Staves; But all this might have been tolerable; if that Mischievous and unruly Vermin the Ratts, had not fell on board it, for so it was, when I came to gett it out of the Ship, Lo behold Two Nests of young Callow[2] Ratts were kindled[3] there; and I take it what with their Trampling, &c   Every thing above ground was totally Destroyed; and I am afraid by their Excretions have Effected the Roots, for only one appeared to have Life. It grieved me to the Heart to see so many Curious things and so much Labour & pains like to be Destroyed by these nasty Creatures and the neglect of the Captain. But for the future I must Desire thee to put the Living things in a Less Case which takes up so much roome that unless it is a Large ship there is not roome for It, for all the sodds of plants, might have been packed in half the Roome which would save a great Deal of Freight for thee knows the Earth about them is only Intended to keep them Moist till they come Here and then they are soon transplanted — so that the sods may be thrust as close as possible to one another 2 Inches of Earth below & covered 2 Inches may be sufficient to convey them Hither — be sure to make the Bottome full of Large Holes — and Rather make Two small Cases, which are more manageable and more convenient to be Stowed than such a Large one as the Last which I believe 2 or 3 hundred-weight and as much as Two men could Carry —

I have very carefully planted all I could find of the Roots and please myself with hopes; for I have had a many pretty plants come out of the Earth beside those Intended   the White Lychnis I most regret but pray don't part with it till thee has made sufficient Increase, — The Cluster Cherrys thee Formerly sent us are grown fine plants, but what is admirable they Hold their Leaves all Winter, that P Miller takes them for an Evergreen — & so do several of your Shrubs   The Mountain Laurells seem to Bud Strong this year, the Goose berry & Cedar and sundry others — which gives Mee great Entertainment   the Spiraea with spikes of white Flowers holds its Leaves all winter   is a pretty plant, and an Opulus as it seems to be   grows strongly and out of the mould is come your Hepatica   but what is surprising your Herb Two pence scarcely shoots 2 new leaves a year and I have tried it various Wayes   most of the Ferns thee formerly sent Mee grow finely   I have Hopes of these in sods. I shall Conclude with observing what seeds will be acceptable next spring

and am truly thine,
P Collinson

BP 2:47; D. 128–30 (plant list omitted).
1. Germinated.
2. Naked or hairless.
3. Born.

From ISHAM RANDOLPH

Virginia May 24, 1739

dear Sir

According to the method we proposed to correspond, this is the first oppertunity that has offer'd, Since I had the pleasure of Seeing you; it is by my friend and acquaintance Doctor Tschiffelley: who I believe to be a proficient in the art of chimistry. I take him to be a very honest gentleman, he hath a mind to See Philadelphia out of curiosity; and therefore I recommend him to your friendship

I am to acknowledge the letter you wrote by my man Cornelius wch is all that I have recd. I have lately had a letter from my friend P. Collinson; he makes no mention of my letter via Philadelphia, so I conclude you did not have the opportunity by your latter Ships to Great Britain. I wish I cou'd entertain you with an acct. of Some new discovery Since your progress here; but for the want of a penetrating genius in the curious beauties of Nature, I must make it good in assuring you that I am with great sincerity of heart,

Yor. affect. friend
and hum: servant
Isham Randolph

If you see any of my acquaintance make me acceptable to'em, My wife & family join in their best respects to you & Mrs. Bartram.

BP 4:100; D. 317–18.

To BYRD[1]

Dear Friend Colonel Byrd:

I received thy kind letter by ye post last winter & another dated March 23d which I received by ye hand of thy friend Doctor Tschiffely whom I received very kindly & made as welcome as my present circumstances would afford, for thy sake – having no other acquaintance than thine & another recommendation. I have this spring made severall microscopical observations upon ye malle & femalle parts in vegitables to oblige some ingenious botanists in Leyden who requested that favour of me which I hope I have performed to their satisfaction & as A mechanical demonstration of ye certainty of this hypothesis of ye different sex in all plants that have come under my notice
I cant find that any vegitable hath power to produce perfect seed & able to propagate without ye conjunction of ye malle seed any more than animals & by A good microscope ye malle & femalle organs was plainly discovered   I have made severall successful experiments of joining several species of ye same genus whereby I have obtained curious mixed colours in flowers never known before but this requires an accurate observation & judgment to know ye precise time when ye femalle organs is disposed to receive ye masculine seed & likewise when it is by ye masculine organs fully perfected for ejection   I hope by these practical observations to open A gate into A very bare field of experimental knowledge which if Judiciously improved may be A Considerable Addition to ye beauty of ye florists gardens

BP 1:17:4; D. 315; Byrd, *Correspondence of the Byrds,* 2:536–37.
1. Undated; probably summer of 1739, since Bartram is answering Byrd's letter of March 23, 1739.

To COLLINSON

July 1739

Friend Peter Collinson

I have received thy kind letters by Wright, which were very acceptable, as also ye cash which came in the very nick of time, when I wanted to pay the mortgage interest. It was A help in time of need & A demonstration of thy regard for my welfare & readiness to oblige me which lays me under an obligation to watch & improve all opertunities wherein I can gratifie [illegible] very good & acceptable[1] I could get nothing of what thee mentioned thee sent by captain bream but a letter by ye post & ye print of ye Magnolia which James Logan thought had been sent for him I went to our Proprietor & to Capt Bream, to inquire for ye box of seeds thee mentioned but they affirmed they knew nothing of such A box

BP 1:17:1; D. 122–23.
1. Part of this sentence is no longer legible. It was probably the contents of the "brown paper parcel" Collinson had sent by Captain Wright which Bartram found "good and acceptable."

To COLLINSON[1]

July 18 [1739]

This day I received ye parcel with thy two letters by [Thomas Penn] our proprietor which I was glad of as allso ye two books & letter [for] Wooley which gave him great satisfaction thee seems to think [illegible] my account of maryland & virginia but indeed there is little in ye lower parts but ould worn out fields without fences — naked fields of indian corn & tobaco which impoverishes ye land miserable poor houses ready to tumble down & ye countrey in general short of grass of sufficient food for Cattle yet notwithstanding there is some [good] livers in both provinces which hath large tracts of land with a many slaves that maintains thair masters to an exceeding [illegible] & luxuriant [illegible] but thair gardens is poorly furnished with Curiosities John Clatons & Col Byrds is ye best furnished with A variety of plants but falls short of our in pensilvania which is supplied from england france holland & Germany Col Byrd is very prodigal in Gates roads walks hedges & seeders [cedars] trimed finely & A little green house with 2 or 3 [orange] trees with ye fruit on but I saw very few that had a good notion of either good husbandry or house wifery ye great vail as well as ye mountains is very thinly inhabited with [illegible] that is lately settled there & lives A lazy life & subsists by hunting which hath driven ye elks & bufalos further back I did not see an Indian in all that Journey but thay have been very mischievous there about A little before I came which disturbed ye [settlers] grevously I should have inlarged much more but I suppose thee hath work that will turn to more account then perusing my letters or as thee often expresseth hath not ye leisure to read them so that I often write so short as hardly makes good sence I am very thankfull to thee for ye parcel directed to our proprietor for mee ye snaills are wonderfull & surpases any of our kinds we have not near ye variety of shels that you have ye pine seeds is mouldy & good for nothing ye paper thay was laped in was rotten I am very sory my cargo miscaried so much I tooke great care & pains to dispose each perticular in good order if ye ship had got out in ye fall I believe thay would have done well as for ye box of plants in earth it was not so large as thy directions which was 2 foot high & a foot long & I am sure I packed them close   nay there was two course of plants [illegible] for some roots will keep all winter half A foot or more under ground   as for ye [illegible] & white oak acrons I know not how to keep them from sprouting without I dry them in an oven   I watched them daly to gather them as soon as thay fell & caried them up & spread them on my chamber floor & turned them often where thay lay till thay [illegible] I hope this will be a prety good mast year   I desighn to procure A fair portion of forest seeds but dear Peter I am sory thee apeared rather too rash [illegible] velvet cap which was rotten mouldy & eat full of holes   I never did believe it was thine not having mentioned it in thy letter but one that ye box for me   I thought some sory felow had thrown it   what aileth ye doctor to return so many of my specimens I understood if I could send some [illegible] because he is weary of ye trouble or would not or could not [illegible] if ye latter if you will allow me ye honour of sending something new   if ye first pray let me have A book or two of botany & I will search for myself & return ye books again as I received them   ye danger of ye sea excepted — I believe it is next to impossible to procure such A quantity as you want of white pine seeds for tho A tree may appear as full as it can hold to ye inocent there is seldom one handfull of good seed amongst them   onely one in a thousand bears fruite to perfection   ye rose laurel groweth onely near ye mountains as I have observed it   I could not see one in all my travails from James [River]   neither is there one I believe from my land to ye head of Skulkill & [illegible] it is common in all our swamps, [illegible] thee seems to have A mighty opinion of Ginseng   more then it deserves   I esteem it no more then A common root   it will admit of no cultivation so as to raise any quantity of it   doth thee not believe that if it could be Cultivated in ye cleared fields here else ye Chinese who value it so much would not find out some method to grow great quantities of it   Col byrd had it in his garden but it dwindled away   several about us planted it but it is all perishing   but it is Comical to see what a bluster some of our gentlemen made this spring with sowing many acres with lucern seed & distributing it to all about ye countrey but Alas ye poor withered apearance it now makes discourageth them   but ye small trefoil which I sowed growed stoutly & so thick that it roted befor it was ripe yet was not so good A crop as our common red & white clover was without any pains bestowed upon it   I saw in friend Custice garden some fine yew trees & two little hors chestnuts & a statice which was new to me

BP 1:19:3.
1. Top right corner and lower left edge torn, and many parts illegible.

To ALEXANDER COLHOUN[1]

July ye 26 1739

My hopes was disapointed of enjoying thy good Company ye folowing day after thee favoured me with a visit which I should have been very glad to have had ye opertunity of; I have since I saw thee received orders from London to search for all sorts of Curiosities of ye vegitable kingdom that I Can discover in ye jerseys & for ye accomplishment of which I design in ye fall to visit your City of New York & in perticular to pay my respects to thee & then to travail towards Albany where I hope to meet with several species of ye several genus of plants shrubs or trees that I have not met with yet in my southward travels & as I am A stranger to those parts I desire that thee would please to inform me by A letter of ye distants [illegible] way from York to Albany & what kind of traveling or how far [illegible] people is setled up ye river that I may better be enabled to judge [illegible] ye time & expence I shall be at in ye performance of this Journey which I desighn to undertake in ye midle or latter end of next september & if I can do thee any service here please to mention it   any information will be joyfuly received & gratefuly acknowledged by thy friend

John Bartram

BP 1:19:3.
1. Surgeon of the British garrison at New York.

From COLHOUN

New York, August 18th 1739

Sr.

I was favoured with yours of the 27th of last month. I assure you, was sorry I had not the pleasure of visiting you a second time; being obliged to sett out for this place. I am heartily glad to hear you intend next month to be in the Jerseys & from thence to proceed to this Town; where I shall be very glad to see you. There are a great variety of Plants, &c., upon this Island.

But as you express a desire to know the distance between New York & Albany, how far this Province is peopled backwards, &c. We are distant from Albany 150 miles. It is situate on the West side of Hudson's River. I went there by water, with our Late Governor & from thence travelled beyond the farthest Palatine Settlement, belonging to this Province, Northwest from Albany, about 150 or 160 miles, near half way to our Garrison of Oswego, on the great Lake of Cataraqui. Several people travell from hence to Albany by land (& I believe it is much the same distance as by water.) From what I hear, there is good accomodation on the road

Two of Our Officers went up in a Sledge last winter; as severall people do from hence as well as on horse back in the Summer time; but more of this, &c., at meeting.

From, Sr. your sincere friend
& humble Servt,
Alexander Colhoun

P.S. I shall esteem myself very much obliged if you can procure for me some Ginseng Root.

BP 2:6; D. 318.

From COLLINSON

Londn Sept 22, 1739

Dear Friend John

In thine of Last 10br thee Seems to doubt if the Medlar is the Neapolitan, but I do not doubt It, phaps the stock, or soile does not suit It for they grow Here as Large as the bottom of a Common Wine glass, but thy dislike of the Fruite may proceed from not knowing when they are ripe   Wee have a Course Saying that a Medlar is not worth a Fart till it is as rotten as a Turd.

The Persimmon that thee so much Commends is what I never mett with from others but there may be different sorts, that which is ripe in September is fittest for us who lie Twelve degrees more to the North than you do —

I have in my Garden the Tallest Tree I Ever yett saw sent Mee some years agone by Docr Witt   It thrives and grows vigorously and bears blossoms but no Fruite, but I have seen fruite ripe in England but it has but little reputation here — phaps for the same Reason that I assign'd for the Medlar — Wee have now plenty of this Tree in some Gardens which is much admired for its beautiful green Leaves —

In thine of April the 1st thee observes what Difficulty there is to raise the white Bryony which with us is a weed that we can't well gett rid off however I Intend to Send more Seed for Further Trial — with us it delights to grow on Dry banks that have stunted shrubs growing on them, These it covers & makes a pretty show when the Berries are Ripe —

I hope Thee has better success with the Larch Cones sent this year   I have some fine Trees of this kind sent Mee from Newfoundland. I am surprised the Gorse should be killed with your Cold — when they grow in the North of England where the weather is much more severe than in the south, if this was sown on some dry banks in your woods, I can't think it would Succeed better for thick woods and the Falling Leaves keep off the Severe Cold — I conceive it would be a Good protection to any woody plant if Heaps of Dry leaves were heaped up about it, in Sharp Weather it would keep the Cold from penetrating from above & below as for Instance if the Tree Sage was protected in this Manner — as for the Wood Sage that goes down every year   I am glad that thee has the Archangel and Galeopsis they will Endure —

I do not wonder that neither Rose nor Sweetbriar comes Double Like their original, thee hadst a Chance for It But if thee considers no full Double Flowers are apt to produce seed some few excepted but seed is generally produced from what we Call semi Double Flowers and these are the more Liable to go single   I am pleased to Here of More Success   that the

Juniper   Spanish Nutts   Philberts   Siberian Rhubarb   Wood anemone   Flags & Fox Gloves   I wish Wee could raise Some of yours but those mischievous Ratts spoilt the Last Cargo Else there might have been hopes   from the Root thee Sent of your perennial Fox Glove   of this Cargo I can give but a poor account tho great Care was taken and the Sods all whole but no Doubt Poison'd   there is Two pretty Ferns and some Worts & Hurtle berries Come up well   the pretty Shrub with White Flowers which is a Spirea   Little Else appears that I can make any thing off — of the Other Cargo, the Chamerhododendron Grows but Slowly   Jersey Tea grows, Calceolus Maria with yellow Flowers   2 sorts of Martagons Flower Finely The Tall Early Jacea is now Strongly in Bloome   Lord Weymouth or the five leafed pine & the white Cedar thrive finely   the Dwarf or Shrub Honesuckel Blooms finely, and the Large [illegible] Bloome well but no Fruites   a variety is Come up from the Seed thee Collected in thy Bogg in the Clump of Earth that Came round the White Cedar was a white Orchis with a fringed Labiate Flower a great Rarity   I have this Day Received a letter from Petersburgh and am assured per Docr Amman professor of Botany there that the Siberian Rhubarb is the true sort — I wish a Quantity was produced with you to try the Experiment   both this and the Rhapontick make excellent tarts before most other Fruits fitt for that purpose are ripe   all you have to Do is to take the stalks from the Root & from the Leaves, peel off the Rind and cutt them in Two or Three pieces and putt them in Crust with sugar & a little Cinnamon, then Bake the Pye or Tarts   Eats Best Cold, it is much admired here, and has none of the Effects that the Roots Have, it eats most like Gooseberry Pye —Our friend Catesby gives thee many thanks for thy remembrance of Him and for the Papaw Blossoms & Fruite

an Acceptable present to Lady Petre I believe would be a Humming-bird's nest with eggs   I am obliged to thee for thy Care of the Sugar Birch (pray send me a good specimen of it) and for the Laurustinus thee intends me pray let it be well grown and a flowering plant   I am not in Hast — The root of the oke shows what a Rich depth of soil you have   I think I informed thee of the Two fine Flies produced from the Two Crysalis   the one the Same that thee hatched in the House that the Cock Came in and paid a Vissit to   the other a very Curious Moth very Different from any Sent which makes it the More Valuable

If I write the same things over again Thee must Excuse it for multitude of affairs divert my Memory & my Letters are not worth copying being mostly writ behind the Counter — I have procured the other things mentioned in thy order which I have committed to the care of Lawrence Williams[1] they are all in a Box marked J.B. No 1 and thy name in length on the side   at the bottom of the Box is a specimen of what our Botanists have dubbed Collinsonia but I think it should be Bartramia for I had it In the very first seeds thee sent me   Miller is mistaken in making it come from Maryland — pray fail not Next year to send Mee some seed of it for it flowers so late it will not Ripen Here —

I have now Two fine Jaceas in flower, Raised from Seed Sent Mee by Docr

Witt   these He calls the Early and the Elegant Jaceas   I have another that He calls the Gigantick Jacea that does not flower this year   a very pretty class of plants — I have Sent thee in the Box Some Horse Chestnutts   Sett them Soone and some Narcis polyantris   Sett them in a Warm place and protect from your Severe Cold — Cover them over very High with Dryed leaves   Docr Witt Loss't his by your Cold Weather so take Care and give them Every protection for they are Choice flowers   the Jersey Tea plant is now in flower   it seems by the flower to be a Vitis Idea — its flower is much Like the Arbutus

Lord Petre has sent thee a present of Philip Miller's second part of his Dictionary in return for the specimens sent him   Thou will see a cut in P. M.'s Dictionary of a Polygala which is a reputed specific for a pleurisy.

BP 2:51; D. 133–35.
1. A ship captain.

To RANDOLPH[1]

Dear friend Isham Randolph

I have not received any letters from thee since Doctor Tschiffely brought me one which I answered by him at his return back to virginia   he promised me to deliver it safe to thee & to write to me & give me an account of his proceedings as soon as he could but I never Could hear any account of him since which I think was very ungrateful being I kept his hors in very Good pasturage all ye time he stayed in our parts, beside he was welcome any time to my house & charged not A farthing which was Considerable with us so near Philadelphia where all things of this nature is in cash   beside he did not so much as come to take his hors but sent A man for it ye day before he set of for virginia   but dear Isham I am obliged to thee for thy kind remembrance of me twice by our good friend Peter Collinson   I wish we could hear oftener one from Another   I long to hear of thy welfare & how thy dear Lady & children do   my family is in good health & I am just A setting out for albany to oblige my Corespondents in europ   pray as the hath an opertunity give my love to dear Col Custis & Col byrd which will oblige thy Sincear friend who wishes the & thine health & prosperity & remains without guile thy friend

BP 1:20:2.
1. The date of this letter is probably September 1739, because of Bartram's reference to Tschiffely's Philadelphia visit.

To COLLINSON[1]

november 1739

towards ye latter end of August I went into Jersey to [illegible] laurel Cones & I thought I would observe ye long coned or white pine I observed last year in July about 20 trees of this sort with A very few half grown green cones & which I thought would not be ripe before September   I then observed a prety many young ones which was set for this year which I went to looke at now which to my surprise was opening & upon A little shaking ye seeds would shake out & fall into ye water   for all that was of this kind that I observed in ye Jersey grow upon ye bank close by ye water & most hangs over but beyond ye blew mountains thay grow sometimes near a quarter of A mile from ye river but mostly near ye water   some trees had shed but few seeds   these I gathered carefully & held my hat under ye cones to catch ye seed that shooke out with breaking ye cone of which I put directly in A bag which I tooke up ye tree with me; being thus disapointed in some measure I resolved to take A Journey up delaware beyond ye blew mountains where I was informed A many grows which being near north from us I thought would not be so forward as southward   besides I expected to find many other curiosities either on our side or jersey for I intended to have crost ye river A great way up but I was grevously disapointed in this design for ye night before I intended to have crosed ye mountains my mare was stolen from mee & three days search by 3 white people & 2 indians & could not hear nor see anything of her   I was obliged to hire a cretur to ride home on   this was a miserable disapointment both as to observing many Curious plants which grow in that part of ye countrey & ye loss of A beast which I brought up for this — which was hardly to be equaled both for easiness in going [illegible] out A journey for I have rode her near 70 mile & carried a heavy load of plants & roots on her which I gathered ye same days in ye woods as I traveled   yet notwithstanding this misfortune I found severall plants near ye river which I little thought of finding specimens of which I send to thee with remarks where I found them   in perticular ye ginseng I found on ye northeast side of A very steep shady hill which contained such prodigious steep perpendicular rocks which my guide said was measured & was 40 pearch high perpendicular from ye river which was so near that I saw my guide [illegible] into ye water & what seemed remarkable we could [illegible] of this precipice see ye fish playing in ye river   there was in this precipice A opening between ye rocks from ye top to ye bottom but so very steep that we could hardly scramble up & about 2 or 3 rod wide   in this dark shady place ye gin seng growed   as for ye seneca snake root so profligate it grows in poor sandy ground   sometimes in poor moist & sometimes in rich champion ground & yet one may ride 50 or 100 miles in several parts of ye countrey & over these different soils & not see A plant ye nearest that I observed it from Philadelphia is near 50 mile altho it groweth north south & westward of it but I never could see any in west jersey   neither this afore mentioned misfortune come A lone for about ye midle of september when I was about provideing for A journey thorow east jersey (wher I did not doubt of finding many curiosities & intended to have taken ye lakes upon a branch of delaware where our friend wooley found that fine sweet scented tree which I sent thee a sprig of about a year ago) I unfortunately cut my foot which confined me to my bed for a month neither do I expect it will be well this fall by this confinement I have mised gathering of white & red ceder seeds & sugar maple & many more which I should have gathered I hired several men & boys to gather these but thay could make no hand of it thay said thay had not patience for thay could not gather A peck in A weeks time; but since I have been able to go with crutches or ride or sit in A cano or boat I have been 3 times in jersey & took 4 hands with me at a time to climb ye trees & cut ye cones whereby I have colected 2 sorts of pine cones & should have gathered A fine parcel of ye right 3 leaved pine whose cones I think do not shed thair seed in ye fall as all our other kinds do; if I could hold out to ye desert where I saw them grow these pines grow very straight & tall as ye other kinds do

BP 1:19:4.
1. The second page is almost illegible.

From COLHOUN

New York Novr. 5. 1739

Sr.

I receiv'd yours of October 23d & assure you am heartily sorry for your misfortune wch prevented me of having the pleasure of seeing you this fall: but I hope may not be disappointed in next Spring you've been pleas'd to offer me some Genseng & Seneca Snake root for wc. I esteem my self very much oblig'd & when you come here I hope I may be able [illegible] of gratifying you in the like, or in some other manner.

If you please to send them (to Mr. Levies Mercht in Front Street near the Coffee houses) directed for me, he will forward them by first sure hand.

Your compliance wt the above request will exceedingly oblige

Sr your most humble Servt
Alexander Colhoun

BP 2:7.

To DILLENIUS

December ye 5th 1739

Respected friend
Doctor dilenius

I received thy kind letter dated december which was very acceptable as allso ye specimens of mosses & seeds tho I believe ye seeds is good for nothing but I am obliged to thee for thy care in sending them the scorpoides I never had growing so is rare ye others I had before but alas I did not receive ye box till this latter end of october it was brought here in ye spring & taken back again to europe before it was found then brought back to philadelphia when I received it if I had received ye specimens & letter in ye spring I should have endeavoured to colect A fine variety of mosses for thee but I haveing received no answer neither to my letter sent last summer nor that sent last winter with a variety of seeds made me more careless for I thought thee had forgot me but as since I have received thy letter I have endeavoured to procure what I could for thee & much as my decripid capacity would permit & its likely if I am able this winter I may make further observations tho it is A by path from my common road yet it is not unpleasant but my fancy runs all upon herbs & trees   as for ye draughts of ye carnelian chery thay seem neatly done but thay give me but little information without a description of ye bigness of ye tree   ye size & time of blosoming & whether ye seed is included in A stone or only scin or pulp & ye color when ripe & ye amomum   whether it is an herb or shrub   ye bigness & time of flowering & perfecting its seed & whether it is included in pulp or blader   all these are necessary to be described before I can judge rightly upon it for I suppose Plucknet hath described them in all thair degrees of perfection

BP 1:19:6.

To COLLINSON

december ye 6th 1739

I have received thy kind letter of Sepr ye 3d wherein thee informed me of thy shiping a box of sundry goods with A book being A present from Lord Petre which will be A very acceptable present for I love such kind of bookes that treats of any branch of botany   I am very thankfull to my good friend for it & I long to see it   haveing seen thy present to the lybrary company I was talking to my friend Breintnall of hiring it for a week who said I must leave ye value of ye booke in security besides six pence for ye hire   just then I read in my letter that I had one of ye same impression sent me which pleased me wonderfully   I received ye box of cutlery by Stevenson but I have yet no invoice for its perticular account   I went yesterday aboard ye last vesail from london to looke after ye box but it could not be found   israel pemberton thinks it was put on board of stedman or brown who is not yet arived   I have sent A fine cargo of pine cones & two boxes of plants by Whright with directions how I would have ye returns   I have not yet been at dr wits since my [accident] so cant satisfie thee yet so well as I would Concerning ye plants he mentioned wch amused thee with in his two letters but I believe thay wont turn out very extraordinary   ye doctor is easily imposed upon by odd information   ye seneca snake root is scarce about us & very little used so cant well inform thee of ye dose but tenent is I hope at london before now who can inform thee exactly   I believe still ye medlar thee sent me is not ye neapolitan kind by its leaves and growth which agrees exactly with ye [illegible] according to all ye descriptions I have met with

I alow ye Clymate & stock may alltter ye tast magnitude of ye fruite   I am much obliged to thee for thy Care in sending ye goods mentioned in thy letter but it is too much care for thee to send more then is my due but it shows thy exceeding kindness & good will which layeth me under an obligation

BP 2:7.

To COLLINSON[1]

I have received ye second part of phillip millers dictionary being that present of my good friend Lord Peters   pray return my hearty thanks for his good will in sending it to me ye reading of which afords me A prety deal of satisfaction   but in reading millers account of ye Colinsonia I think he has neither done me nor my province Justice for this plant hath been observed by mee this 20 years for when I was a little boy I used to pluck ye flowers to smell at them thinking thay smeled something like hops & as I was ye first that ever sent it into Europe & I think he ought to have taken care to mention ye word ye true place where it was sent from & who sent it seeing he hath so very often mentioned ye names of Robert [Millar] & doctor Houston   this plant is very rare in ye lower parts of maryland & virginia but in ye back & mountainous parts I have observed it   it grows often upon ye sides of steep Hills & ye roots is as thick as ones arm with many uneven knobs contrary to his description

I am certainly pleased with doctor gronovius present whereby I have been informed what kind of plants my brother Claton hath discovered & how far to ye northward mountains he hath travailed as well as my friends ingenious observations upon them & ye good order which he hath digested them in   pray return my hearty thanks to him & desire him from me to use much freedom with me as to let me know what he desires wherein I can oblige him

BP 1:20:3.
1. This letter is extremely faded. The date was probably late December 1739; Collinson sent Miller's *Dictionary* on September 20, 1739.

To J. SLINGSBY CRESSY[1]

I received thy kind letter specimens & seeds by ye hands of my friend Graham which was very acceptable   I am exceedingly pleased to have A Correspondent of such A curious tast in your southward Islands for botany which is my darling study altho I am very much hindered in ye pursuite of it having to labour for ye maintenance of my family but whenever I can steal A little time I miss no opertunity of making all ye observations & discoveries that comes under my notice acording to the best of my capacity in any branch of nature in ye vegitable & animal kingdom: tho often my domestick affairs sufers for no institution of our province alows heavy support for any Curious enquiries; yet notwithstanding this confinement I have travailed several hundreds of miles in Searching ye woods for plants with ye success of having discovered many Hundreds of remarkable vegitables many of which was never before I sent them seen in europ nor mentioned in any bookes of botany & extra specimens I keep for my winters amusement now as to ye specimens which thee was pleased to present me   ye ricinus Gold I have growing in my garden four foot high   ye Papaver spinosum or Orgemone grows with us to perfection   I have read ye Gutta gambo is made of this plant   stramonium we have in abundance about dung hills long cucumbers I have seen grow well   ye blew anual cononbo this I have flowering in august & continuith til frost kills it   by these the guess what will come to perfection with us but if it will not produce flowers or seed in 5 or 6 months from ye planting it will not signify any thing to us   ye frost will kill it before we can enjoy ye beauty of it so that whatever plants you have that arives to its perfection within this time ye seed of them will be acceptable of what kind whatsoever whether great or small   ugly or handsom   sweet or stinking as is commonly reputed   but every thing in ye universe in thair own nature apears beautifull to mee   thy daphnoides florida a name belonging to ye species of ye thymelea which bears berries but this seems to me by ye flowers & leaves to be one of ye oleanders which bears pods with a pertition Containing many seeds   I have sent by Captain Coultis A few specimens as A token of my friendship   I intend to provide more for thee & some seeds of our native plants but it hath rained every day since I saw thy letter or heard any thing of thee & I knew nothing of Captain Coultice going to antigua till today & he saills tomorow so that I have been hurried to provide this imperfect present as it is

BP 1:23:4.
1. Undated, but probably March or April 1740; Cressy replied on May 26, 1740.

To COLLINSON[1]

[illegible] have had for 3 year lychnis which produced flesh coloured flowers male & female upon several plants   one large plant which produced male flowers flowered most part of summer but produced no seed which engaged my perticular notice & I observed that those seed which thee sent me is produced male & female plants; A year after I had sent from england some of ye seed of ye white lychnis which produced male & female flowers distinct upon different plants   It hapened that one female plant flowered neare two weeks before any male flowered which I observed daly & observed that tho there was no stamina or anthers in ye flower yet ye capsula was filed with perfect seed which I sowed as soon as it was ripe which came up very well in a few days but by that time that the capsula of this first flowering white lychnis was near full grown   there were several malle plants flowered in ye same bed   I then puled of all ye capsules that was set before that I might observe what diference there would be between seed that was produced of that plant before any of these male flowers of ye white Lychnis appeared & that which was produced after ye male blossoms opened & shed thair farina; for I concluded that either that this female white lychnis must be impregnated by ye male red lychnis which grew 10 yards off   if so then it must pertake of ye nature & color of ye red one else we should be pusled to reconcile ye hypothesis of receiving of male & female parts; agreeable it happened acording to my expectation for it produced flowers a great deal paler than ye red & as much higher coloured then ye white but ye seed of ye white lychnis that was produced after ye male plant flowered produced plants which bore flowers as white as thair original moreover I gave doc witt one plant of ye female lychnis which flowered plentifuly with him & produced ye capsule but containing onely ye husks of ye seed but no vegitative life in them. by which it appears that ye male parts of vegitable is realy as necessary to vegitation

BP 1:18.
1. Incomplete and undated, but undoubtedly written April 29, 1740 (see Collinson to Bartram, July 22, 1740).

From MARK CATESBY

London, May 20, 1740

Mr. Bartram: –

Your kind remembrance of me, in the three plants you sent me with those of Mr. Collinson, encourages me to give you further trouble, though not without an intention of retaliation.

As I have the pleasure of reading your letters, I see your time is well employed; therefore, in what I propose, I shall be cautious of desiring anything that may much obstruct your other affairs. But, as you send yearly to our good friend Mr. P. Collinson, the same conveyance may supply me; which I shall confine to as narrow a compass as may be, for I find my taste is agreeable with yours, which is, that I regard most, those plants that are specious in their appearance, or use in physic, or otherwise. The return that I propose to make you, is my book; but it will be first necessary to give you some account of it. The whole book, when finished, will be in two folio volumes, each volume consisting of an hundred plates of Animals and Vegetables.[1]

This laborious work has been some years in agitation; and as the whole, when finished, amounts to twenty guineas, a sum too great, probably, to dispose of many, I chose to publish it in parts: viz., twenty plates with their descriptions, at a time, at two guineas. By this easy method, I disposed of many more than I otherwise should. Though I shall set a due value on your labours, the whole book would be too considerable to send you at once;

Therefore, I propose to send you, annually, a Part (i.e. twenty plates with their descriptions), for what you send me.

I, having already told you what plants I most affect, shall, in general leave it to you what plants to send me, though the specimens you send Mr. Collinson will somewhat direct me.

My method has been to set down a greater number of things than I could expect to be complied with, to be sent at one time; because, as all things are not at all times to be had, others may offer. Thus far, is a duplicate of my first letter to you

D. 319–20.
1. *Natural History of Carolina, Florida and the Bahama Islands*, completed in 1748.

From CRESSY

Antigua
May 26th 1740

Sir

I wrote by Capt Bowers to Mr Grayham who desires my Respects to you with acknowlegmts. of your favours   Parson Byam[1] returns his thanks for the beautiful Amaramthus you Sent him, He as well as my self have tryed those Seeds you was so kind as to send, but none have come up except the Buckthorn Berries, and they grow very Slowly

By this Opportunity I send You about 36 Specimens of Plants & some Seeds, I wish you may get the Sand Box Seed to grow, it is a most beautifull & Shadey Tree & of quick growth here

Your kind offer of favouring Me with things in your Country, encourages me to beg you to send Me some of the Cotton Stone wch I hear is found in your parts of Philadelphia, I am told that our Officinal[2] white Poppy grows with You (if so) pray send Me some fresh with the Seed & the pod too if you have it: and some Marshmallow Seed   you seem to be so well furnisht with the Vegitable Kind that I fear I shall not be able to oblige You with any thing New, however till you tell me so, I shall not omit any convenient Opportunity of remitting You whatever I think may be pleasing

I most heartily wish you health and Prosperity and beg you to rank Me in the Number of your Friends and permit me to Subscribe my Self
Sir   Your Affectionate Humble Servant
S. Cressy

I would have sent you & our friend Grayham some Limes but none of our Islands has afforded any these three Months worth acceptance   Capt Bowers arrived here again a Few Days ago

BP 3:91.
1. Francis Byam of Antigua, who studied rainfall there, sent his observations (and also

fossilized fish) to the Royal Society of London, where his article was published in their *Transactions*.
2. Medicinal.

To COLLINSON[1]

I received thy letter of 2 March 1739/40 & ye ten pound of half pence & peper in ye library Company chest which was very acceptable & came in A good time to relieve my necessity but I am sadly afraid ye cargo I sent by Captain Whright tooke damage by lying so long aboard upon your Coast before ye vesail could come up to London; I have two plants of betony groweth finely & ye Lysimake & orange mint but no ulmaria comes up tho sowed so often in severall situations but ye white briony I doubt will never grow to bear seed with mee   it allways dies root & branch & when it begins to flower tho I have tryed it in ye shade sun hedges north east & south exposures clay gravel & sandy soil & under talle plants   I have been with ye doctor to see that curious plant bearing a pod shaped like an Acron but full of insects but it proved nothing but our common golden rod[2] I suppose it was an excresence which some flying insect had darted & laid her egs therein which was hatched when ye doctor made his superficial observation who had rather believe allmost any thing then be at ye pains of accurate examinations   I have just been to wait upon Governour Morris[3] to deliver thy letter of recommendation (being hindered last year by a grievous wound) who treated me very civily

BP 1:20:5.
1. Undated, but written April 29, 1740 (see Collinson to Bartram, July 22, 1740).
2. Insect gall, very common on goldenrod, forming a hard knob which many a small boy has used to knock the heads of his companions.
3. Lewis Morris, governor of New Jersey.

From COLLINSON

Lond   June 10 1740

Dear frd

On the other sides are a miscellany of matters as they come into my Noddle.

I find in the Cargo of Martagons had from thee & others that there is apparently Two sorts and Two sorts of your Lillies with single Flowers. I have one open'd this Day that may be Called literally the Fiery Lillie   it is the Deepest Flame Colour I ever saw   it is really a fine Flower & I think of thy sending   The other Lillies will not flower this Month   the flower Leaves are Narrower   more Divided & Deeply Spotted

Thee sent Mee what we call the Atamasco Lillie from its shape   it has a blush of purple before the Flower opens   is white within, it is properly a Lillie-Narciss   the Leaves of the last & flower of the first   If in thy Rambles thee happens on this Flower pray send a root or two —

& please to remember a Lump of Sweet Gum, Sour Gum, Allspice Gum, if it bears any. Does the Red or White Cedar produce any   This last thrives finely the Leaves have a fine spicy smell.

I have bought of David Barclay the Goods thee Ordered as will appear p Inclosed Bill   pcells which I have Carried to thy Account   the Ballance I think to Send in half pence by first Convenient Conveyance

I shall Conclude with my best wishes for thy prosperity and am thy real Friend —

P. Collinson

In thine of July 24th pr Capt Williams Thee acquainted Mee that Thee intended to send Mee some specimens of Salt Marsh Musseles pr Capt Wright   I rec'd 2 shells   the one much broke & the other Injured   I would Desire thee when opportunity offers to send Mee one or Two good specimens, both Valves & Fellows[1] and Joyn'd by their natural Ligament if to be had, send the Largest   Thee undoubtedly for gott Specimens of your Fresh Water Mussels, send both valves & the Largest

What Intelligence has thee learnt relating to your Deer   have you Two Sorts of Fallow Deer or not   knows thee any Thing Certain and of thy own knowledge of the O'possum with a Double Belly and how the young are generated wether In the bag or in the matrix[2] and if the Last then how come they to the teats for there they are found in an Embryonic State   Pray what was ye explanation of our new Birth [illegible].

June 27 — none yett Hatched

Pray see what Further Mosses thee Canst Collect for Docr Dillenius   He defers completing his work till he sees what comes from thee, Clayton & Doc Mitchell

The Calceolus in the Last Cargo proves at last a fine Red One   a very Curious flower Indeed   Mr Catesby has painted It —

Amongst the Last things there is a very pretty Lychnis with pale Blew Flowers & sweet smell but a many of the Lumps of Mould don't yett appear   I wish the beasts of Ratts han't piss'd & kill'd them   The little box by Seymour[3] han't fared much better for they made a nest In that   There is only one thing appears of the herbaceous kind

BP 2:52; D. 135–36.
1. The two half-shells of a bivalve mollusc.
2. Womb.
3. A ship captain.

From COLLINSON[1]

Lond July 22d 1740

Dear frd

I had the pleasure of thine of April 29th 1740   Thy Experiment of the usefulness of the Farina is very Curious & Entertaining, where plants of a Class are growing near together they will mix & produce a mingled species   An instance we have in our Gardens raised by the late Thomas Fairchild who had a plant from seed that was Compounded of the Carnation & Sweet William   it has the Leaves of the First and its flowers double like the Carnation – the size of a Pink but in clusters like the Sweet William it is named a Mule per analogy to the mule produced from the Horse & Ass.

Writing on these matters brings to mind the Papaw – an Indian fruit, – which in our stoves is produced in great plenty   On this Tree is very remarkably distinct, male, female, and hermaphrodite blossoms which are very Extraordinary to see but whether the last is an assistant in generation or is a sport in nature is not yet agreed.

Thy Journey to the mountains must be very delightful and afford a double Gratification to please both thyself and friends. It is something perticular in your Yew's taking root as it trails on the ground. I never observed ours to do so   Pray Nail up Close the next growing Cargo leaving a few Inches of space between the Earth & the Top of the Case full of Holes for Air   I fancy this will in some Measure secure us from Ratts for they have Sadly Damaged the Cargoes for the Two Last years But if thee can think of a better pray Do

Of all the American people I ever talked with about your Mulberries (which we have in our gardens) that one of ours for Largeness & Flavour, is worth a many of yours but how it happens that Docr Kearsly thinks the Contrary I can't say. Different Mind Different —

I am glad to Heare that what came to Mee p name of Girandilla which is the true pellitory of Spain thrive so well   pray fail not to send Mee Some Seed   all I had was killed p the Last Severe Winter

Doc Witt's Hollow leafed Lavendar is no doubt the Side Saddle flower but what relation it has to Lavendar I must leave to Him   the plant with Tricolor leaves I am well assured is your fine Clinopodium   our Late severe winter has carried all Mine off so pray send me some more seed and of the Lychnis with Crosswort leaves.

The Doc did not carefully Distinguish or observe the fruite he mentions which I take to be no more than an Excrescence raised by Insects, like Galls & oke apples which have a pulpy Substance in them of a beautiful complexion sufficient to Sett a Breeding woman a longing and yett are raised only as a proper nidus & Vehicle to contain and nourish the Infant insect — till it is fitt to take wing and provide for it self   it is certainly so by the small white worm which he mentions which grows brown which is then in crysalis as the fruite grows riper

Wee have had no luck as yett with the fine Crysalis thee Sent last   none are yett Come Out   the Large Ones are alive so we have hopes but the Rings I am afraid are all killed by our Inclement Spring Season or were Suffocated coming over for the Varnish that Covers them appears Shineing & not broke which makes me think the Eggs are all addled in the Cells.

The Box by Stevenson after long Search & Long Lying I Rec'd att Last if thee hadst done the same thing thee commends Mee for, that is have writt my Name in Large Characters on the Top & Sides I had had it sooner and undoubtedly in better Order — pray for the future observe this   to writt my Name plain & where I Live — on the Tope & Side — the Sugar Birch Budded but went off   Do all I could only Two plants make their appearance   a pretty Maiden Hair and another plant with fine Tender Leaves but no Foxglove Root or Seed

I am Glad the Cutlery Ware & Whips are Come Safe to Hand   I well Remember the Receipt & Bill pcell   For the First I Inclosed in a Letter which has undoubtedly Miscarried — but p Capt Hargrave I sent another Bill pcells — with Directions for next year Collection & p Capt Wright   I Desired a Lump of the Sower Gum not the Wood and of the Sweet Gum or Liquid Ambar Tree & if the Benjamin or all Spice produced any Lump of that —

Now I will give the some account of the last Cargo of the 4 Roots of Chamaerhododendron   only one survives which is the Large one — the White Cedar trampled to Death   a great Loss   of the 4 Roots of the White pine all trampled or Eat p ye Ratts   of the two Roots of White Spirea one grows

I am in doubt about the Red Root   dont know what it is unless the Pecune an Indian name   I dont find a Specimen   if possible always send a Specimen of the plants sent   1 Root of Dwarf Willow grows   its a pretty plant   the Stump of Sugar Birch grows stoutly   Its Leaves Look very much Like our Horn Beane and I believe will prove the same Tree that I had some years agon from Docr Witt but under what Name I cant find   I cant tell what to Say to the blew Mountain Hasell   the Mitella grows and within this few Days there is a Leafe putt forth much Like the pretty Violet (I wish it may be)   the Flesh Colour Lychnis does not appear but in its Roome One with a pale Blew Flower phaps this may be that from Susquehannah   a new one and very Sweet Scented which I Esteeme much and I want when thee Increases It, that with a White flower with a Red Spott in the Center, & that Lychnoid with a Small white Flower   the Lady's Slipper flower'd strongly & proved that with a Red Flower which was a great Rarity   I had it painted   the yellow orchis Show Its Leaves but is so crowded with asters or Starwort wch I dare not pull away for fear it should be New — those asters Sure are in great plenty for no less than three Sodds Have them — I wish your Valerian may not prove our Greek Valerian with blew Flowers — the plant grows strong but does not flower   neither the Gensang or Tennants Snake Root yett appears   I am afraid them and others have suffer'd by the Ratts who had tore up the Sodds, tho more is alive than I Expected but great Care has been taken of them   I think I told thee I had the Genseng from Seed   I shall want [illegible] or Root of Orange Colour'd   if thee happens on any more Roots of the attamasco Lillie

The List of Seeds I have sent to Docr Delenius at Oxford hopeing the Variety of plants cultivated in the Physic Garden may furnish some of them   what I can I will but more of them grows Remote — it will be Difficult to do it

What thou obbserved in Phil. Miller is Just   att proper Time will give Him a Hint of It.

The Boxes of Mosses came safe p Capt Bell and was very acceptable to Docr Delenius for thee has outdone all his other Correspondents   Lady Petre is much obliged for thy present of Musk   pray send my Wife One   Pray are the Baggs Distinct Vessells to Receive the musk (as in the Civet Catt) or are the Testicles Lodged in them   but from whence does the Smell arise   from the Testicles themselves or from the Baggs that contain them or Secretions that are made from them   the Seeds of Ketmie that grows in the West Indies has the Like Smell and the Leaves of a Geranium has the Like Smell   the Muscovy Drake has the Like Smell   it is worth observing that this smell is produced from such a Variety of different Subjects   ambergrese has much of It

The Roots to the specimens p Capt Bell Seeme in very good Order   they are Curious pretty things   I am obliged to thee for them & shall take much care of them   So farr I think I have taken Due Notice of thine of aprill 29th   I now come to take Notice of thy Remarks on Docr Witts Curiosity

As you have such a Variety of Persimmons if wee had the first Ripe Sorts Wee might Expect to tast them in pfection with us   I have a very large Tree but it never bears wch makes me think it is of the Late sort   the Cardinal Flower, May Gilliflowers and King's Beard are agreeable to thy Sentiments   His Daisie or Double Mountain Ranunculus is a pretty Little plant   I have 3 Roots wch flower every year but I did not know that he call'd it his Daisie — Single one thee sent Mee but I cannot Increase It — I am glad to find that I had His upland Cranberry or Jersey Tea   I am glad of the Dens Canis — but did not know before it was Josselyn's yellow bastard Daffodill — I hope I shall see it in flower   pray did any of the Roots that I sent thee in a Bagg survive for it is a ticklish Root and great care have been taken of them

BP 2:53:1–4; D. 136–37.
1. The end of this letter is missing.

To CRESSY

July ye 24 1740

Respected friend

I received thy kind letter of May ye 26 with ye specimens seeds & other curiosities all which is very acceptable for I love anything that is curious in any branch of nature but indeed I did expect a letter from thee by Cp Bower which if I had received or if my friend Graham tould me that thee had mentioned me to him by letter Captain Bower should not have come to thee empty handed for I have mostly something by me to present A curious friend with when I have an appertunity to send it; but I haveing received no answer from thee for what I had sent I might reasonably conclude that what

I had sent did not ingage thy esteem so not worth answering unless in common civility to let me know thee had received them   By this opertunity I send thee 90 specimens of our native plants numbered so that I may know what kinds I have sent that I may not send thee ye same again unless thee sends for any of them   allso perhaps I may send thee many of ye seeds belonging to them which shall be numbered with ye same number of its respective specimen which I now send thee; I have sent thee A few seeds first gathered in my garden but most of our countrey seeds is not ripe yet nor ye great single oficinal popy but I hope to send it next opertunity with several other Curiosities   I am obliged to thee for thy generouse desire to send me some limes & if thay or any other present had come from thy hands I should have received it kindly but I am no admirer of acids   I had rather have A pound of sugar then A bushel of limes for my own use I have sent thee A little peice of Cotton stone but next opertunity I hope to send thee more for I design to take a journey to ye mountains where I hope to find some   of all ye seeds thee sent me none comes up but ye thistle popy & indian shot or Canacoral which we have had in curious gardens many years   ye jerusalem thorn & poinciana or flower of France [?] & scarletbery & musk melon & cashew I have had which growed 6 inches high & perished with ye first frost   by this thee may observe it is in vain for us to expect that any of your plants should produce either flower or seed with us that is above four months after planting before it arrives to this perfection

BP 1:20:1.

To COLLINSON[1]

In my Journey to Minisinks[2] on the Eastern Branch of Delaware att the foot of the paiqualian Mountains I saw a Grove of three Leaved pine and of Long Coned or Ld Weymouth pine that has Five Leaves in Each theca   this pine I saw some 150 feet high and between 5 & 6 Feet Diameter with a Quantity of Newfound Land Spruce-firr

The great three Leaved pine whose Cones open & sheds thair Seed in October grows in moist Swamps Butt the other 3 Leaved pine whose cones keep shut for one – Two – or 3 years, grows on Dry Sandy barren Hills, as also the bastard 3 Leafed pine, grows in the Same Sort of Ground —

I set out fifth day morning & at night reached to ye great swamps   then set out early in ye morning toward ye lakie hills which is A great ridge of mountains runing thorow ye countrey from whence I had A fine prospect of ye great blew or Paiqualian mountains over A great vail between 20 & 30 mile broad   ye western branch of delaware runs along it slainting a cross it so as to run thorow ye blew mountains near 40 mile distant from ye north eastward branch   I rode up ye west bank within about 8 mile of ye blew mountains   then rode 12 mile being choise land all ye way where George

Whitfield has 5000 acres of choise land where he is carrying on fine improvements of it   then I left this rich vail & made directly toward ye pasage over ye blew mountain   this was dismall traveling along A Indian path over hills swamps creeks barrens & grevous stoney all ye way for above 20 mille   no mankind to be seen all ye way no ground fit to settle on & glad I was when I got near ye foot of ye mountain where I saw A fine grove of pines of ye 3 leaved sort & five leaved & one of a spruice or fir which I climbed up to gather ye cones which was about as big as ye new found land sort but they had shed thair seed long before; ye pine cones was open & dry   I suppose that thay might be ripe when ye long coned pine was ripe in August   then I ascended ye Paiqualian mountains by winding passages between ye rocks so steep I could hardly lead my mare up   this pasage is A bout A mile of where ye river runs thorow but there is no pasing near ye river side   when at ye top I had a fine prospect over A hilly sort of A vale to A ridge still higher about 30 miles distant   then descending down ye other side I came to exceeding fine rich low lands on each side of ye river which is in some places A quarter or near half A mile broad   ye hills come so close to ye river that there is scarcely A road to go on   these low lands is finely watered with large streams of excelent water which comes tumbling down ye mountains in glistering Cascades from [springs] on ye tops of ye paiqualian & other high mountains by [illegible] some of these lakes is A mile or two long & replenished [illegible] which are when ye lakes overflows in great rains driven down & lodged in holows made by ye fall of water on ye sides of ye mountains where ye neighbors comes & gathers what thay will   it is setled on both sides of ye river above 40 mile above ye blew or Paiqualian mountains   I crosed ye river 3 times where it was 150 yards broad above ye mountains swiming my mare over that I might have an opertunity of searching both sides   on ye jersey side 10 mile beyond ye mountain ye hils is mostly good land & not very steep but on pensilvania 10 mile beyond ye blew mountains ye hills are very steep & barren with bare perpendicular scaly rocks very high espetially where that very high ridge comes to ye river; I climbed up one of these ridges where I found strange representations of snails & scalop shels with other curiosities which I desighn to send to thee & if one was to spend a day or two thay might find A prodigious vairiety for many miles for I believe this great ridge is full of them & ye high rocks is yearly tumbling down being composed of scaly mater which is penetrated by rains descending which in winter freezeth bursteth & tumbles down roling to ye bottom about ye bignes of ones fist & mostly of A flatish oval form; as I returned here I crosed ye Paiqualian mountains on Jersey side near the top of which I saw A heape of stone thrown together containing several wagon load   its said an indian king was laid there; I wanted badly to pull ye heap to peices to search what antiquities I could find laid with this royal body but I was afraid of disturbing ye Indians hard by   I crosed A stream of water 2 yards wide [flow]ing out of A pond on ye mountain   it is full 3 mille going up & down this mountain & many places for A long way nothing but hard stone   next day toward evening I went into A cave ye mouth of which began towards ye top of A lime stone hill & descended down untill I came to A pond of clear water then I set homeward as fast as I could conveniently having in all this journey observed abundance of sugar maple but not one key to be seen   I have since been in Jersey to ye sea on purpose to gather red & white cedar seeds & mirtle berries but to little purpose for ye red cedar bore hardly any good berries   I observed above A hundred trees & many very large but not a hand full of good berries but some bliths   ye white cedar I have seen thousands of but very few seeds this year   I gathered most that I could find in climbing high trees for A little handful of cones   ye mirtle near ye sea had A few berries tho not one in 20 bore this year but in travailing thorow Jersey A large plain 4 mile square it seem'd to be ye highest land between ye sea and delaware river   A poor barren plain   no trees to be seen from one side to ye other but on one side there was severall great white cedar swamps   I went to many of them but could not find A handfull of cones there growed in this plain A bundance of dwarf oaks about brest high full of acrons but ye chiefe bushes that growed in this plain were A strang kind of dwarf pine which growed 4 or 5 foot high   3 leaves growed in A sheath & bore abundance of Large cones   sometimes it would spread upon ye ground 3 or 4 foot square & half a foot high & as even at top as if it had been sheared   others would spread as broad from one root & growed some A foot   others two foot high & even at top producing many cones   others would spread as broad as A table A foot high & from ye midle shoot up on a regular stem two foot high bearing full of cones   I gathered as many as I thought my mare would carry home to send to you hoping it may bear but ye most surprising kind of pine I ever heard of was brought to Philadelphia   ye bush that produced it was 8 foot high & near ye top it branched into 4 equal branches as thick as ones thumb tapering to 14 inches long ye extremiti of which each 4 branches produced 24 cones set all round like A ball   each cone was full as big [as] your larch cones   ye midle cones was something larger & from ye center of these 4 branches sprang up another stem 14 inches long producing A ball at top of 24 cones as other branches   I measured them with A rule & found them 14 inches long & 14 inches distant at top   see ye figur[3]   ye sight of this raised my curiositie excedingly to find ye place where this was found for I believe it is very diferent in species from what I know   ye leaves was all droped of   ye man that found it lives I do not know where but If it be possible I intend to search him out   ye tre hath past thorow hands so its hard to find him that found it first

I have sent specimens of most virginia plants that growed in my garden raised from seed which I gathered in ye back of virginia   greatest part of which I sent you that fall but supposing some might mis coming up with you or if thay did you may by these specimens compare thair largeness of growth with yours being I have mentioned thair magnitude as thay have growed in my garden thee rote to me thee had sent from Carolina cones of A three leaved pine whose leaves were 6 inches long but ye leaves of ye pine which I send thee I measured some of them 7 inches long   how much more elegant must my pine be & then growing in A climate colder in winter then yours   it is likely to succeed ye better with you   as to going to new england next year I had rather stay a year longer & go next year up hudson's river as far as albany   I hear ye balm of gilead fir groweth near that river & arbor vita   I believe in new england thay are A pack of ungratefull clownish presbyterians

Linnean Society of London, Ms. 323, Collinson's Common Place Book, p. 314; BP 1:42:1, 1:1:16.
1. This letter is dated September 7, 1740, in Collinson's Common Place Book.
2. An island in the Delaware River in northwestern New Jersey.
3. Here Bartram drew a picture.

To CRESSY

September ye 10 1740

Respected friend Doctor Cressy

I am not willing our friend Bower should appear before thee empty handed when he returns my service to the [illegible] therefore I have sent thee above 40 specimens & 20 sorts of seeds which I Colected for thee but most of our autumnal seeds is not yet ripe   Allso I have sent thee A piece of fine stone cotton which lyeth in vains in ye solid rock; & to give thee A idea of ye prodigious variety of plants which grows upon our continent I have sent thee severall species of 3 classes of plants [illegible] eupatorium virga aurea & ye Capilaries or fern tribe & if thee desires it I may send thee next year several species of our asters hypericums & Corona solis which are large tribes   I observed in thy curious specimens A fine one of ye oficinal Cena   pray did it grow in your Island   if so I desire thee to send me some ripe seed by ye first opertunity or any other rare annual plants that soon comes to perfection   ye indian shot thee sent me is now begining to flower   its about 4 foot high A fine scarlet flower   ye ricinus galiosus last year growed 4 foot high & flowered long yet produced no perfect seed so I lost it with ye first frost   I sent by Captain Wall A Colection of specimens of plants & seeds with A letter which I hope thee hath received   thy specimen of the Casia fistula I have fixed on ye wall of my study as A prety curiosity   pray friend Cressy write often to me   let me know wherein I can oblige thee   we dont know how long either of us may live to Communicate   pray draw freely   I am not soon exhausted if I have health & prosperity; in travailling many thousand miles many thousand plants hath come under my observation   A brisk & lively friendship with mutual afection is very agreeable to thy Sincear friend   in hast

JB

BP 1:20:1.

To COLLINSON[1]

I Cant well forbear Recomending to thy notice our two leaved or Jersey pine for its exceeding toughness; this year I have made 4 prety long Journeys in Jersey & three times in ye desert whereby I have made perticular observations of great numbers of several sorts of pines & most of them very brittle wood except ye dwarf, & Long-Coned; & this two leaved which is ye toughest of them all so that one may twist bend or tie it in knots so that I know not any wood so pliable which is very extraordinary for A tree that will grow in any wast grounds   heath   commons   on cold north sides of barrain mountains. it allso branches out abundance of horizontal branches from ye bottom to ye top until it be Twenty-foot high as afords fine quantities of stuf for hoops or baskets   indeed it doth not grow alltogether so handsom as ye other sorts but its toughness makes sufitient amends for that defect   it grows near as larg as any of ye other kinds except ye long Coned Lord Weymouth pine which I have seen prodigious large 5 or 6 foot diameter & 150 foot high & ye great 3 leaved pine whose cones opens & sheds thair seed in october   groweth in moist swamp but ye other 3 leaved whose cones keeps shut for 2 or 3 year & ye bastard 3 leaved grows on dry sandy ground or poor hills — The Sugar birch is worthy of your Care to Cultivate it for its straight & lofty growth   sweet Juice & medicinall bark   it naturaly grows on cold north sides of hills where there is Springs or rivulets near or in moist ground at ye bottom of hills tho it often times groweth in ye clifts or rocks & no ground can be too stoney for them; I have walked for an hour together upon nothing but great stones & no soil to be seen: yet these trees & white pine growed finely there & being on ye north side of A mountain where ye rocks produced much moss which rotting with ye moisture (which hard rocks on North situations seldome fails producing) & being driven by great rains between ye cliffs of ye rocks afforded nourishment for these rare trees to subsist upon   Altho I have mentioned so often ye naturall places of growth of many trees yet I have admired to see trees & some plants which I never observed to grow naturaly any where but in moist swampy mossy [land] & many times in ponds & runs of water; these I have brought out of Jersey Virginia & several places in pensilvania planted in my garden & thay grow much better then in thair place of natural growth & yet some that groweth naturaly both in moist & dry ground when planted in A garden Languisheth away while others brought from such like soil improve finely by transplanting — I have put in ye box two yellow wasp nests being ye first that I have known for many years to escape ye Racoon one of these was built in a thorn bush so near ye house that ye thief durst not assault it; the other was built at ye end of A Chesnut tree limb over ye water — these venemous insects is very dexterous to form such a nest out of weather beaten wood & doubtless some of thair Glutinous moisture to sement it together

I have Colected for thee & Lord Petre about 60 sorts of mosses   his I have put in his box of Cones; thine is of the same sorts with his   pray if thee canst Conveniently let Doctor Dillenious see them   it may be there may be some new sorts: I endeavoured as much as I could to send such ripe moss of every kind as produced heads in order for your better satisfaction but some of ye different sorts I never could find any heads to them — I have sent a few specimens to doctor Lawson being he desired them in his paper which thee sent me   I could allso furnish him with many kinds of Reptile & animals or thair parts   allso many kinds of earth, stones, slates, &c but many of those things he mentions will not onely take upp a great deal of time to colect & put them in A condition to send as thay should be with proper remarks: but thay will take up much room in A ship: then who must pay ye freight   there is many of my friends that is curious is endeavouring to raise about fifty pound yearly to defray my loss of time & charges that I may spend most of my time in searching all ye english northern colonies in america for curiousities & to make my remarks upon them   if this should succeed I should have an opertunity to furnish europ with many curiosities.

Linnean Society of London, Ms. 323, Collinson's Common Place Book, pp. 177–78; partial copy in BP 1:16.
1. Undated, but written September 25, 1740 (see Collinson to Bartram, May 16, 1741).

From DILLENIUS

Oxford Oct. 15 1740

Good Mr Bartram

Herewith I send you some seeds of officinal plants & a plate of the Mosses; the sort marked * groweth on Trees, hath larger Diskes than any other known sort & was formerly observed in Maryland by Vernon. I dont doubt you will find it in your Country & shall be obliged if you will send me some specimens of this as well as other sorts.

Your last Parcell of Mosses letter from April 20 is safe come to Hands, by ye Care of P. Collinson   I return you thanks for them & remain your obligd friend & humble Servant

JJ Dillenius

BP 3:99; D. 309–10.

From COLLINSON

Londn. Octo 20 1740

Dear frd

Inclosed is the Mate's Receipt for a box of Bulbs directed for thee — Make Much of them for they are such a Collection as is Rarely to be met with all att once For all the Sorts of Bulbous Roots being taken up this year, there is some of Every sort. there is above 20 sorts of Crocus   as many of Narcissus   all our sorts of Martagons & Lillies, with Gladiolus   Ornithogalums   Moleys & Irises — with many other I don't now Remember wch

Time will show Thee — It is likely some sorts thee may Have but I believe there is More that you have not so pray take great Care of them, give them a good soil & keep them Clear from weeds which are a great prejudice to these flowers in the Spring —

I have several very Curious Flowers out of the Mixt Virginia seeds in pticular a New Jacea with hoary rough Leaves — a very pretty Dwarf Gentian with a large Blew Flower, the Extremity of the Flower-leaves all Notched or Jagged   the whole plant is not above 3 or 4 Inches High — I am afraid it is an Annual but there is a great Variety besides   a very pretty Gratiola & a Dracocephalon   it has a Labiated Flower like Snap Dragon and is very near akin to It   Lord Petre has had the greatest Luck haveing the Largest Quantity of seed   he has 2 or 3 sorts of fine Chrysanthemums or sun flowers   Asters   I have a fine New Sort — Your thickets must make a beautifull show in the Autumn wth these plants for I see they must be in great plenty for almost every sod has an Aster growing with the Curious plant that thee sent   a great Many of the plants grow of the Last Cargo but few show their Flower Except the Ladies Slipper with Red flower which was a fine thing, and the pale blew or Milk & Water colored Lychnis — and Asters   I dont remember any other Sort has flowered besides, I wish these may be the Lychnis with white flower & Red Eye, the Sugar birch grows and one Chamrhododendron — but the Sugar Birch in the small Case was Dead, but there was a pretty Fern and another plant with Leaves Something like Collumbine Leaves Survived and a pretty many seedling plants come up out of the Earth   I am in Hopes some may prove the Foxgloves   the other Box of Bulbs came Safe and in very good order   I hope I shall now see Josselyn's Daffodil or your Dens Canis with a yellow flower in pfection —

I am much obliged to thee for the account of Dr. Witt's Rarities — thee has unravelled the whole Mystery   pray tell Mee is the plant thee Calls a Valerian with blew Flowers which came in the last Cargo a Native of your Country for it has been Long in our gardens   Wee Call it Greek Valerian

Every Day I Expect thy Last Specimens from Holland — they have been long Delayed by many Accidents but I can't help my self — for Docr Gronovius is so kind to fix them Neatly on fine white paper that they look as beautifull as so many pictures and names them into the Bargain, Neither my Skill nor Time would permit Mee to do this — so I am glad to Comply with his own Time but this will prevent Mee giving Names to the last 2 Quires till next year — I can tell thee in the next Edition of Virginia plants[1] Thee will see Bartramia —

I shall be glad to Heare all thy Remittances are Come Safe to hand – I sent the General Account by Capt   but for fear of Miscarriage I again Repeat It on the other Side as I also have repeated several things in this Letter as I have before which I hope thou will take In good part as this is likely to be the Last opportunity this year. I wish thee Success in all thy affairs with the valuable Blessing of Health to thee & thy Family

I am thy true & sincere frd

P. Collinson

Gronovius note (Cortusae sive Verbascl Fl. Virg. pp 74, 75. This being a new genus may be called BARTRAMIA) Lond: Sept 12th:1739.

To Balln as p Capt Neat	3: 6: 9	
Mar 2 To Cash in Half pence remitted Him in the Library Company's Trunk p Capt Hargrave	10: 0: 0	
To the Insurance of ye above Money	0: 7: 0	
April 30 to Cash in halfpence per Capt Wright Enclosed the Mates Recept for the Box within his Letter	5: 0: 0	
May 23 To Cash in half pence in a box to J. Logan from Docr Fothergill	6: 0: 0	
June 7 Two Goods as Under pr Capt Clay		
117 Ells brown Ozinbriggs @ 8	3: 18: –	
Bundle 1 Demy ⅞ Garlix 12	1: 3: –	
J. B. 1 Demy printed Long bluesh purple	1: 5: 6	
N'S 3 Ells Hassen	2: 0	
pd freight	0: 5: 0	
	6: 13: 6	
Aug 11 in Thos Penn's Box in half pence	5: 0: 0	
Sent to John Samuells[2] care	5:	
12 To Cash in Silver in a Letter pr Ditto	0: 2: 9	
	31: 10: 0	

Lord Petre subscription	10 : 10	
Duke of Richmond	5 : 5	
Phil Miller	5 : 5	
Duke of Norfolk	10 : 10	
	31 : 10	

BP 2:54; D. 137–38.
1. *Flora Virginica,* by John Clayton and J. F. Gronovius.
2. Unidentified.

From COLLINSON

Londn Decemr 20:1740

Fr John

It is to be hoped that thy patience will be rewarded with some knowledge as the other part of the sheet will Informe thee   There are many Names not to be met with in Old Botanists, the Discoveries of such Numbers of plants in your World has oblyged has oblyged [sic] our Moderns, being new Genuses to give them New names   if thee hast any Complaint Docr Gronovius is answerable.

I am my Good Friend Much Thine in haste

P. Collinson

Wee are much In fear, lest the Rascally Spaniards should fall foul on our vegitable Cargos[1] I hope thee has Recd My Account Current and all Last Years Money to Satisfaction.

As thee has the Flora Virginica thee will find most if not all the plants Mentioned there   I have sent thee a Correct preface In our worthy Frd J:Logans pcell —

BP 2:55; D. 138–39.
1. The War of Jenkins' Ear (1739–41), a commercial war between Spain and England.

To BENJAMIN FRANKLIN[1]

Many Persons being at a Loss to know the Plant which is the true INDIAN PHYSICK, I thought it not amiss to give the Publick a distinct and plain Account of it.

The Root hath the Appearance of the true Ipecacuana, Branching from the Centre every Way near the Top of the Ground, or about two or three Inches deep, from which riseth one Stalk, finely chaneled with redish Lines; from the Sides of which grow alternately, about the Distance of two Inches; from near the Bottom to the Top, three distinct Leaves, two Inches long, and near an Inch broad, finely toothed round the Edges, and pointed at the Ends, but joined near the Stalk; out of the Bosom of which ariseth branches of every Side the Stalk, which are in large Plants again divided into several Branches, and three Leaves joined together accompany the Beginning of every Branch, both which diminish the nearer they are to the Top; where there is commonly, set upon Foot-stalks half an Inch long, three white flowers, consisting of five Leaves to each Flower: The Plant groweth from two Foot to four Foot high, in hilly Ground; on these Northern Provinces the whole Plant is bitter in Taste. This is the true INDIAN PHYSICK mentioned in that valuable little Book entituled, *Every Man his own Doctor,* written by a learned Gentleman in Virginia,[2] whom I had a Letter of Recommendation unto from London: I enquired of him, particularly, concerning the *Ipecacuana* mentioned in his Book, and he shewed me a large Quantity of it, which was gathered for his own Practice: He told me, that less than *Sixty Grains* was not a full Dose for a Man. This I mention because many in Pensilvania and Maryland use a Species of the Spurges, which yieldeth Milk, when broken, and is violent Medicine, instead of this which the Gentleman designed.

John Bartram

Benjamin Franklin, *Poor Richard's Almanack* (Philadelphia, 1741); *The Papers of Benjamin Franklin,* 20 vols. (New Haven, 1959), 3:298–99.

1. Undated in *Papers of Benjamin Franklin*; we have used the publication year of the *Almanack* in the absence of any other.
2. Dr. John Tennent.

From COLLINSON

Lond feby 25 1740/41

Dr frd

I now come to answer thine of 7 Sept 1740 and give thee some account of thy Cargoes — the three Long boxes of Seeds came all Safe and in very good Order & gave Content   the Two Boxes of plants in Earth, were of a Right Size and came in Excellent Order, every thing appearing as fresh & Lively as if that Minute taken out of the Woods — I wish Wee had been so Lucky to have thought of this Method before, thy pains & so many fine plants had not been lost. One Box I gave to Lord Petre & the other to M. Catesby, & Reserved only for my self the Ladies Slipper & Ipecacuana   the others I had before & the Little Box of Insects was in fine order   there is 3 or 4 Flies very fine   all Indeed are Curious & worth Seeing & possessing   The Box of Specimens with seeds & Nests[1] came very well   the first I have writt too & the Mechanism of the Last will afford much Contemplation   One I shall give Lord Petre & the other keep myself. the Indian Curiosity & piece of pott I shall speak more pticularly too at more Leisure for now is our greatest hurry   In Return for so many Rare things I Desire thy acceptance of four Vols of Natural History which I don't Doubt will Inlarge thy Ideas in many things and give thee great Entertainment   thee'l find the Account of the Sea Muscle will Explain what thee has formerly Observed & writt to Mee About, which I had Intended to have answerd but that I Intended to send thee these Books which are much Esteemed Here —

I can't Enough Commend thy Diligence in procureing Such a Noble Collection of Herbaceous Seeds, Lord Petre, P. Miller & Dr Delenius have principally shared in them   then I pick & Choose what plants I like   a few favourites I sow myself — but as theirs are Botanic Gardens, all Sorts are greatly Acceptable to them. I love all fine, showey specious plants —

I am Extremely Obliged to thee for the Crysaliss   It is wonderfull as thee observes, to see the Surprising Instinct and contrivance of the Creature to preserve It Self from being Lost & Trodden under foot, by the strong Webb, that both secures the Stalk of the Leafe to the Twigg   I wish Wee may have better Luck then Last year for wee hatch'd but one pfect one & that was New & very beautifull and the Adition of one new thing is a great Acquisition   there was Something very Remarkable in the comeing fourth of the Flies, One that was imperfect came out above a Month after the first that was pfect for these Creatures generally Observe one Season but that may be owing to the untoward Summer   Last Year wee had such Suney Dry weather but Little that was warm and Want of that Share of heat that you have may be the reson of Its so Long comeing to Maturity & Its

Imperfection — the Shell thee sent is very Curious, I shall remember thee for It — the petrifactions are as Extraordinary — shall att proper Time Further Consider them   but pray what Distance is the Mountain from the Sea   The Cavern thee was so Hardy to Ramble through Every Creek & Corner is a strange Phenomenon in Nature and what can be the original Cause & Intention or Real use of these Cavities in the Earth is best known to the Great Architect of them, Wee know of Little Else than to Raise our Admiration, they have indeed some times Served for a Retreat & place of Hideing but they are not Habitable tho some Creature thought fitt to use one of its Isles for its Magazine   this puts Mee in mind to Ask thee a Question if thee Ever Mett with a Harmless Land animal about the size of the Large Grey Fox Squirrel Call'd a Monack   it has a Long Brown Furr & seems to have Much of the Squirrel & Ratt in its composition   it has Lived several years running about house Like a Catt   Eats Green Roots & Fruits, was Sent Mee from Maryland where it is called One of the Seven Sleepers for it Buries itself In the Cealar in Sepr or October as the Season happens warmer or Colder & comes out again in March or Aprill, I never Met with any one mention this Creature but Lawson in his History of Carolina.[2]

Butt now I come to Take notice of the Main Article and tell thee that I have procured Twenty pound Tenn shillings in halfpence which I have putt up In a strong Cask, thy name is writt on the head at Length & undr and I have ordered D Barclay to putt up 2 pieces cloth in I. Pemberton, Junr Goods for thee — I had sent the brass kettle thee Desired but as freight is High it would come to too much unless thee had given Mee pticular Orders what to fill it up withall for thy telling mee Brass Ware is nothing without sending a pticular of the sorts & prices to Each   I could not Omitt Sending thee the Above mentioned £10.10s by Capt Wright who is a most Obliging Man and he knows thee & phaps may give the Carriage tho I shall not Receive the Money this Twelve month   nay I have now Some Standing Two years — for it is very hard getting Money of great people, tho I give them my Labour & pains into the bargain   They are glad of the Cargo, but are apt to forget all the Rest   they give good Words but that will not always do — but for thy Sake and if it will but Contribute to keep thee in thy Circumstances, I gladly will do all & much More if it will but be of Service to thee and to Encourage thy Ingenuity —

Wee have not had time to consider thy Cargoes for next year Butt thee must Look sharp out after the Balm of Gilead Firr   a quantity of this for all pties will be Acceptable & abundance of Long Coned white or Ld Weymouths pine wth 5 Leaves in Each sheath   Red Cedar, white do — Candle Berrys   Sugar maple & more of the Largest Coned pine that thee sent this year but these are hints, So Look out Early about the Balm of Gilead Firr & any other Firr

It is very Entertaining to survey the great Variety of Mosses that there is with you as well as with us   I have Sent Mine Down to the Docr, who admires att thy Diligence   He observes paper is scanty so has Desired mee to send thee half a Quire of writing paper which comes in a pcell per Capt

Wright with some paper for Specimens — the Books, Tournefort are a present from Lord Petre — wch I hope will make thee Easie   I sent all thou desired to Docr Lawson   doubt not but thee will hear from Him & Catesby — the Last has a Mind to Figure the Laurel or Chamaerhododendron and by the fine Specimens thee hast sent is pretty able to Do It, but Wee are att a Loss for the Exact figure & shape of the Flowers   thee says it is of a pale Red or Blush Colour but in thy last Letter thee says they are studded with green Spotts   now here wee are att a Loss again so if thee can help us pray do, thee tells Mee that the has a Mind to Draw or paint[3]   pray do   One single Flower is Sufficient, and some marks where the spots are   Wee can Easily add the Rest — Leaves & seed-vessels Wee have and also growing plants

Col Custis & I. Randolph Kindly remember thee.

the draft of the Cavern & Mapp of thy Journal, make each very Conceivable & Intelligent but pray what does Whitfield pretend to do with the 5000 acres of Land

I am surprised att what thou tells Mee that from Capt Wrights arrival to 9ber 7 the date of thy Letter thee had no Letters   then they must have Miscarried or been Delayed, this untoward Warr putts all things in Confusion and out of their usual Chanells   Wee have had a Tolerable Winter 2 smart frosts each of a Weeks Continuance but most of January and since fine open Weather but our Spring backward but the Corn Looks well on the Ground   abundance of wheat sown Last year, which if the Harvest be good will make great plenty   wheat is now 75:s p bushel but is Expected Lower   I am Dear John thy sincere Friend

P. Collinson

Inclosed is a seed Vessel of a plant, that may Deserve some Observations — it proves to be a species of Chamaerhododendron   It was sent mee with more seed & a specimen from Russia   It abounds in the woods that are found in the neighbourhood of the Lake of Baikal in Lat. 55° which lies in Eastern Tartary but now in the possession of Russia   another species of this fine plant is Found in the Country near Black Sea of the Euxine Sea in Turkey, and that found with you being nearly in the same Latitude it shows the unlimited power & goodness of the Creator that such fine plants so nearly related should be dispersed in places so remote from each other, to gratify & please mankind   It flowers beginning of May, the inside of the flower white, the outside of a faint Red or blush Colour   The green leaves are exactly like yours and the flowers come in Clusters like yours —

M. Catesby has sent thee his first part as a present. it is Tied up by it Self & Directed for thee as Is Docr Delenius paper, Specimen paper & Bookes in another Bundle is thy 2 ps Garlicks I think will not Come till next Ship which will be soone   I shall give thee notice

Inclosed is a letter to Docr Colden surveyor general of New york   He may be of great service to thee to inform thee where is the likeliest place to find the Firs. He is a very Ingenious man & has writt a very entertaining &

informing history of the Six Indian Nations which he has been so kind to send Mee — pray go soone and Look out sharp for the Balm of Gilead Firs, & Black, Red & White Spruce as Mr. Dudley Calls them   I hope thee will meet with more of the White Pine for our people are insatiable after them

The Cask of Half pence is Ship'd p Lawrence Williams and as I have Contrived to have it done without any Charge — it will be better to beare an Insurance wch will be 17:6 and as Capt Wright sails without Convoye I thought these precarious Times it would be most to thy Interest to do It there is 20:10:0 — Tied up in Two shilling papers   these things and others are writt twice over but thee must Excuse   I haveing att this juncture so many things to Do.

BP 2:57; the postscript from BP 4:17; D. 139–42.
1. The yellow wasp's nests mentioned in Bartram to Collinson, September 25, 1740.
2. John Lawson (d. 1711), author of *A New Voyage to Carolina; Containing the Exact Discription and Natural History of that Country* (London, 1709). Lawson was killed by the Tuscarora Indians.
3. This interest in drawing may have been encouraged by Mrs. William Byrd, of whom Bartram wrote: "Col. birds Lady persuaded me mytly to draw plants   she saw me draw ye iron flourishes on ye top of thair garden gates which pleased her so well that she said she was sure I could draw plants [if] I could but try" (BP 1:42, an undated fragment).

From CATESBY

February 25, 1740–1

Mr. Bartram: –

I have received from you a box of plants, containing a tree of the Sugar Birch, with others I could not tell, because I have no letter, or account of them. I conclude you had not received my letter, at your sending away the box of plants, otherwise I might have expected the favour of an answer.

The plants seem to be in good condition, and I heartily thank you for them; and in return, desire you'll accept the first part of my book; and for fear of Spanish depredations, I send, as above, a duplicate of my first letter.[1]

* * *

In the box you sent, I find there are two plants of Chamaerhododendron, which seem not to agree with our climate; therefore, please to send no more, till better encouragement.

Your beautiful Rock Cistus, which for many years I have received from Carolina, but could never make it blossom, last July we were favoured with a sight of its elegant flowers; the first, I dare say, that ever flowered in Europe. It was from a plant sent Mr. Collinson; – the Climate from which it came being nearer ours, than from whence those came that I was unsuccessful in. This plant is again set to blossom, though it increases not at all.

Wishing you all happiness, I conclude, sir,

Your obliged friend and servant,
M. Catesby

P.S. I must inform you that the part of my book I send you is in a more contracted manner, and smaller paper, than that you have seen of Mr. Penn's, but in other respects the same.

D. 320.
1. The asterisks on the following line were used by Darlington to indicate his omission of part of a letter.

To CATESBY[1]

friend Mark Catesby

I received thy kind letter of the 29th of november but thee not having inserted when or where it was written I am at A Loss to know where to direct my answer otherwise then to thee & to ye care of our well beloved & trusty friend Peter Collinson who merits ye esteem & ye friendship of most of ye Curious   Ye reading of thy acceptable letter incited in me ye diferent Passions of Joy in receiving a letter of friendship & request from one so much esteemed: & sorow in considering what time we have lost when we might have obliged each other   its A pity thee had not wrote to me years ago   I should by this time have furnished thee with many different species of plants & perhaps some animals; but ye time past cant be recalled therefore pray write often to me & inform mee in every perticular what thee wishes of me & wherein I can oblige thee for when I am a traveling sometimes on ye mountains or in ye valies and ye most desolate craggy dismal places I can find where no mortal ever trode I chiefly search out: not that I naturally delight in such solitudes but intirely to observe ye wonderfull production in nature of transformations & transmutations & by observing ye rocks & mountains in their [illegible] we may in some measure guess how thay was once wound up [illegible] & inclemency of weather I am travailing on ye low lands upon ye banke of rivers washed & reflex of ye tide on ye salt inlets & bays & sandy beeches where ye [ocean] storms ye sandy banks; breaking therein one place & filling up another   all these different observations there seems to be of universal [illegible] mentioned tho matter seems never at rest, but allways in a state of contraction or expantion; in these different objects & situations I have an opinion as makeing different observations suitable to different persons tasts — any person informs me with what perticulars he desires to be informed I generaly take ye most notice of that; & neglects others perticulars (I try to be as agreeable to some others tasts) for want of knowing which would be acceptable; & its possible both observations might have illucidated each as for instance before Doctor Delenius gave me a hint of it, I took no perticular notice of mosses but looked upon them as A cow looks at a pair of new barn doors; yet now he's pleased to say I have made A good progress in that branch of botany which realy is A very curious part of vegitation; I am exceedingly pleased with thy proposals & shall do what I can Conveniently to Comply with them   I have A great value for thy books; & esteem them as an excelant performance & an ornament of the finest Lybrary in the world   I have [illegible]

BP 1:42:2; D. 321.
1. This letter is incomplete and undated, but probably written in March 1740/41 (see Collinson to Bartram, June 6, 1741).

To CRESSY

March ye 29 1741

Respected friend Cressy
I have received thy present of two shugar loaves by ye hands of our trusty friend Captain Bowers   thay was very acceptable & I am obliged to thee for sending them   I wish thay had been accompanied with A letter from thee   I cant yet be certain whether thee received those 90 specimens & some seeds which I sent last summer by Capt wall   Pray lett me know what success thee hath with ye seeds that I sent the   by that I shall be informed what kinds to send that will be most like to prosper in your climate   for if thee or any of thy friends desired varieties of seeds or specimens of diferent natures I can furnish you with large Colections of Curiosities: Espetialy if a desighn succeeds which many gentlemen of generous tastes in several of our northern governments hath industriously endeavored to assist me in by raising anualy A sufficient sum by subscription to enable me to spend most of my time for several years in searching & observing natural production of ye mountains plains lakes rivers springs & grotoes in our four northern governments of york jersey pensilvania & maryland that I may oblige ye world with perticular account maps or pourtratur of the scituations of animals minerals & vegitables of ye before mentioned provinces but I cant yet know whether thay will raise A competent sum by reason of this grevous hard winter   the great losses of cattle generaly sustained & ye discouragement our merchants are under by difficulty of trade & loss of vesails in this war

BP 1:21:2.

From COLLINSON

Londn May 16:1741[1]

Dear John
   Having a Little Leisure it gives me great pleasure to Review thy Entertaining Letters, possibly the following Hints may have been made before but that I rely on thy candour to Excuse for I keep no Copys —
   Sepr 25:1740 & Sepr 7 Ditto are the first that comes to hand   I take them in order.

In thy Journey to Mennesink thou saw the 3 leaved & Long Coned pine & a swamp of Spruce or Firr like the Newfoundland sort   Query if this is not a proper place to Collect Cones being the sorts Wee Want —

pray send ½ doz: yellow Wasps to place with their Nests

I observe thou Mentions 3 sorts of 3 Leaved pines and they are thus Distinguished: first, the Great three Leafed pine — Second the Three Leafed pine whose Cones keep shutt for 1-2 or 3 years, Third the Bastard three Leafed pine — as our knowledge of these Noble Trees are very slender, Lord petre as well as my self Desires when opportunity offers, that thou will gather Fair Specimens of Each sort with their Pine Cones on them — Each Distinguished by Its Name   Send when the Cases come — they may be Laid on the Topp — Thou may Also send 2 specimens of the Long Coned or 5 leafed pine with the Cones hanging on

It is now a Rainy Day & being att Peckham[2] I & my wife was agreeably Entertained by reviewing thy Journey & thy Map to Mennesink   pray how farr from the sea is that Mountain where thou found the figu'd Stones

When the Larix was Discovered was there no old Trees that yielded Turpentine — for the finest & best sort is made by the Venetians from this Tree, whence it has the name of Venice Turpentine

pray have Wee had that new Mapple with Red Stalks & Leaves Rough, the large Red Flowering Raspberry thou found is a fine showy plant   has been long in our Gardens, but I never saw it bear any Fruit with us   the Conestogo Gooseberry also annually Flowers, but the Fruite does not Set —

I am much pleased with thy account of Docr Witt   It is confirmed to me in many Instances in his Letters   I believe He is very Credulous & Deals much in the marvellous   Its plain he was mistaken in the Golden Rod for no doubt the pod He mentions that plant Bore as thou well observes was but an Excresence — the Like I have often observed Here in several plants   His Daisy, or double Mountain Ranunculus is a pretty thing   It is a Vast Quantity of plants we Raised from the Willow-leafed Acorns — it is a fine Variety & makes a pretty Tree — I hope Wee shall have the Sugar Birch to Grow with us   it may make a fine Tree — I reced the Specimens of Sweet & Sour Gum   they are plants peculiar to themselves and Each a Distinct Genus — consult the Flora Virginica   Canst thee assign any Reasonable Conjecture why your House Wasps don't sting in october   Your Greek Valerian thrives well with Mee   I Like It because it comes before ours & grows Lower —

thy Account of the musk Ratt is very Just & Natural   Few can give any Reasonable account for their antipathys   Some Wee suck in with our nurses milk, that is when Wee are under their Documents they often Instil into our minds Dislikes, for things they Dislike & this we rarely gett over but retain as long as Wee Live, what parents are frightened att by their Example Children conceive the Same, phaps this may be thy Case in relation to the Oposum a prejudice arising from some of these Causes — or Else really I can see no Reason for It, for I have had the opportunity of seeing & handling & playing with a Female that had 3 young nearly as Large as her self and by frequent use was as docile as Catts and in Colour not much unlike this Contemptible Creature in thy Eyes has been remarkably Distinguished from other animals in the wonderfull provision contrived for the preservation of Its young (as if a Creature of Great Consequence) and another wonder attends It, is, how the young Comes so very small to the Teat This none has yett been able to Ascertain but by Conjecture and has puzzled all our Anatomists to find the Aparatus requisite to Carry on this Delicate operation — Docr: Mitchell[3] att Urbana in Virginia has Imploy'd some of his Leisure time in Examining the Internal structure of this wonderfull Creature & I doubt not but in time, will clear up the Doubtful points — Generating is Different from most animals there is reason to believe the other perticularities that attends this Creature have some foundation in Nature

BP 2:67; D. 154–56.
1. Darlington dated this letter May 16, 1742. The year on the original copy is no longer legible. It seems unlikely, however, that Collinson was answering Bartram's letters of September 7 and 25, 1740, in 1742.
2. Collinson's home at Peckham in Surrey.
3. Dr. John Mitchell. Europeans were not familiar with marsupials.

To PETER BAYARD[1]

I am now home having performed my Journey to ye falls of ye Mohawk river & back again in about two weeks after I parted with thee: I caled at Mr. Wilemans & Mr. Grasbecks at both which places I dined thay are civil people please to remember my respects to them I called upon francis Salsbury who was very kind & directed me to ye Katskill hills where ye balm of gilead fir groeth I engaged A man who Lived at ye foot of ye mountain to gather me A bushell of ye cones for ten shillings & leave them at Salsburys who promised me to send them to Derick skillers at brunswick where I am to send some curious seeds for mr depoister & John Shuyler[2] at Albany who showed much Civility to me; when I came [home] I had ye pleasure of receiving many entertaining letters from my Correspondents in europ & Sir hans sloan which was Constituted president of ye royal Society after Sir Isaac Newtons descease hath in perticular desired my asistance. But now friend Peter to come to our imediate afair; I have inquired weekly all endeavours for opertunity to send thee some roots & at last met with A gentleman at Philadelphia who is to live in York he promised to take them to Elizabeth town point & send them to thee or word where thay are left for thee thay Consist of A fine variety of double & breeding tulups of ye baget primors with curious hyacinths & Narcissus these are loos in ye box ye large round bulbs are hyacinths ye other kinds are lapt in perticular papers with thair names writ upon each respective paper; I think now I have fuly performed what I promised; thay are such a Curious colection as I never received nor can ever expect from any stranger

BP 1:21:2.
1. Probably written in June 1741, because Bartram's trip to New York began on May 20, 1741.
2. None of the aforementioned men has been identified.

From COLLINSON

Lond June 6, 1741

Dr Fr

I was glad to see thine of Decem 4 March 22d and am Sorry for the fate of the 2 boxes which are all spoilt   I shall answer thine fully by next ship Wee all hope thee has taken or will take a progress to Hudsons River to find the Balm of Gilead Firr   pray call on Docr Colden att albany who may Informe thee where these trees grow   Pray in thy Travels did thee ever Meet with the Monack or Seven Sleeper the Moose, the Martin, or the Cole blac Fox   I saw today att Sir Hans Sloanes a great Curiosity   a porcupine brought from Hudsons Bay   it was 2 foot 9 Inches from Head to Tail and a foot High with a young one   it was wonderfull to observe how this animal which is found in very Hott Countries was so Contrived to Endure & Subsist in the Coldest for it is provided with a very thick furr Coat Covered with Hairs and in this Its Quills are secreted so that unless the Hair is Turned up they are not Discovered but no doubt the Creature can Erect them for Defence   it is a wonderfull animal of a Dark Brown but its Little one was of a Shineing Sleek Black and had no Quills but there was Some appearance of their Coming   the porcupines from the South are Covered all over with Quills without any other Mixture of Hair or Down and their Quills 4 times as long   Mr. Catesby is wonderful pleased with his letter
   I am thine

P. Collinson

BP 2:50; D. 142-42.

From DILLENIUS

Oxford, June 22, 1741

Dear Friend Mr. Bartram: —

I received your letter of December 16, 1740, per post; and that of March 24, was sent to me by Samuel Whyting;[1] so that I had it, together with the Mosses, without any trouble. After two days looking over and comparing them with my own, and those I had formerly from you, I found but five or six new sorts. There might be some more, but as they were in an imperfect state, I could make nothing of them. However, I thank you for them, but desire, for the future, to send me nothing but what hath heads.

You complain, you never received any paper on my account. When I was in London, last Whitsunday, I paid to our friend, Mr. Collinson, amongst other things I had of him, for half a ream of writing paper, which he had bought for you, November 10, 1740, and I hope you have received that since. But, finding that you are wanting, and sparing paper in wrapping up Mosses, I have sent this day se'en night, by our carrier to Mr. Collinson, a large bundle of waste *Hortus Elthamensis* paper, upwards of ½ c, to be forwarded to you; which I hope you will receive in its time. When you have an opportunity, I shall be glad to have one of your Muskrat Skins.

The inclosed Moss, you said grew in a moist shady swamp. I should be glad to see it with his heads, – which I guess it bears in summer — as all swamp Mosses commonly do. I remain your obliged friend and servant

J. J. Dillenius

BP 1:26; D. 310.
1. Probably Captain Whiting.

From COLLINSON

Lond July 21 1741

Dear Frd J. Bartram

I have as thee Desired Shipt pr Capt Redman the Ball of thy Acct being 17:16:6 the Stockings & pt of the Cutlery comes in a Box Directed for thee and one pcell of Cutlery Comes in a Box to Sarah Read, Relict of Charles Read of Philadelphia, who will Deliver it thee with a Box & 2 or 3 paper pcells of Seeds In the Box I returne thee a Broken Fly that thou may know what the Large Crysalises wrap up in Leaves that thee Last sent produces It is a fine Moth when pfect as ours are

the other Two that Spun up against Board are both come forth and prove 2 Small but pretty Speckled or Mark's Black & White Moths Wee call them [Kittens] because Wee have a Larger Moth mottled or Tabbyed in the Same Manner that wee call the [Puss]

In Jno Amblers[1] Trunk is a Brown paper with Tulips & Double Colchicums &c I have been Obliged to Divide thy things to make thy Box the Less that there may be Less Freight to pay wch runs high

In thy Box on which I have Directed thy name att Length are Some Roots of Cyclamens 4 sorts peonys & Sundry other Roots that require to be sent in Mould these I have putt in a Small Box to prevent their hurting the other goods I have paid ready Money for every thing and have given a Strict Charge to putt the Lowest prices wch I hope thee will find so

The Last 2 Boxes by Dent who came in June most of the plants seemed alive & had sprouted and the Earth was Moist wch is wonderfull it should keep so, so long it being the beginning of July before I gott them into the ground – I am

In great Doubt about them — I took great care to water & Shade and as they came with Lumps of Earth phaps they may Do beyond Expectations   I most regret the Serpentaria or Snake Root which had Sprouted much out   what twas Mr. Catesby shall share In — The Calceolus thrives finely that thee sent Mee this year but did not flower wch I believe is owing to a Corona Solis that unluckily grows out of the Midst of It, which robs it of its nourishment, which I did not know when I planted it and now I can't remove it without Danger to both, Sure your Woods & Thickets are all Flowers   the Mitella has flowered strongly   it is a pretty odd thing — Consult Miller on it   the Lychnis with the flesh colour'd Flowers made a fine show and is Different from 2 fine Sorts I had before but Still I want that with a purple Flower & white Eye — the Willow & fine White Spiraea grows Finely but I want the Genseng & Tennants Snake Root or polygala (see Miller)   In answer to thine of December 4 1740 & March 22d ult. the Specimens of Sweet & Sour Gum I received and prove to satisfaction but I want the Gum of Each sort & the Gum of Arbor Benzoin or your Allspice Tree and pray send me a Wasp or two of that sort that Builds their Nests with Clay for that I had happened to be broke   Your Valerian is pretty & different from ours

Wee see the particular Effects of Resentment and antipathy in thy Contempt of the Opossum   I have both seen them & handled them and put my hand in her pouch and thought her a pretty creature without any offensive smell or anything disagreeable

Last Winter 2 of the best Roots of the marsh Martagon Died — What should be the Meaning   dont think for the Cold & Frost was nothing near So long or so Severe as that before — it is Extraordinary to hear of your Long Frost in lat 40° — I have a fine Delphinium or Larkheel from thy Seed & the Lychnis whose leaves are Sett Like the Cross worts finely in flower   I have filled the little Box with mould that came with Currant vines from the island of Zante in the Archipelago   In it I have sown seeds of Cyclamens and Tournefort's fine Armenium Poppy — In the Box is 4 Sorts of peonys – ½ Doz Cyclamen Roots — Double Sarsifrage   Boulbous Crowfoot, yellow & white Molys &c   Scatter the Mould thinly on a Bed in a Half Shady place and Expect a fine Stock of Cyclamens   their Seeds are originally Boulbs — so will not keep a Day or 2 out of Earth and being Just now Ripe hope will succeed — In one corner thee'l find a rough Burr Like Seed of a Water plant call'd Sagitaria   a pretty flower — Sow all the Seeds but the African Baurn Immediately   that Sowed Early in the Spring & some Later   it will have a great chance to ripen its Seed annually   it is a Delightful Smelling plant

the Bills of peices Belonging to Each sort of Goods are in Each pcell   I thought that best Least this Letter should Miscarry

My friend Charles Read acquainted me thou Intended to Sett out for Albany May 22d   a delightful month to Travel in when Nature is in all her beauty but I conclude that was purely for Discoveries against the Fall   I hope this will find thee safe Returned and everything answering to thy Wishes   the Last seeds came up very well   the pine seeds & Okes came up as thick as grass

Docr Delenius gives his service & has sent 3 or 4 reams of the Largest size paper being sheets of his Hortus Elthamensis wch will make noble Books for Specimens but as freight is dear & Captains strangers I shall Defer sending them till I have an opportunity by our worthy Generous Frd Capt Wright, to whom pray my Hearty Respects

Docr Lawson is likely to go physician to the next supply of Land forces that are Soon Intended for Jamaica to Recruit Admiral Vernon   whatever is sent for him must be directed to Mee.

pray has thee Ever seen the Monack or Seven Sleeper   the Moose Martin & Black Fox   Something of this I have hinted in my Former Letters   Should be glad att thy Leisure, of Some observations on them.

as there is great Risques now run In Navigation I thought it best for thy Interest to Insure Especialy as it comes to a Small Matter & I had the opportunity to Do without any Expence

Wee have had since the 7th of May the most Delightful summer I ever knew   Before that memorable Day there seemed a prospect of Dearth & Famine to all grass feeding Animals — for we had had no rain for months past that there was no more appearance of grass or herbage than in winter — but then it pleased God in his great Compassion to the work of his hands wch was perishing in numbers to open the Windows of heaven & Give us plenty of rain wch soon fill'd up the Gaping Crannies of the Thirsty Ground and an abundant plenty of grass Ensued & such a crop of Corn of all kinds was scarcely ever known in England and the Finest Harvest to get it in

Now Dear John with a Cheerful Heart I can bid thee Farewell and am thy sincere frd

P. Collinson

I have also added Some Seed of Viola Lunaria or White Satten flower by some called Honesty but for what reason I cannot Guess — the Seed Vessell when Ripe or near it splitts open   Leaves the Middle partition of it with a Delightfull shining white Satten like appearance   it makes a very pretty Lasting Winter ornament for Windows and to Sett on Hearths where there is no fire kept   a pyramid may be Composed 2 or 3 foot high which will Last for many years   my Grandmother I dare Saye had them much Longer by a Little rectifying or Redressing with Some New Materials Annually

Inclosed is my Kinsman James Collinsons (who is Chief Owner of Capt Redmans Ship) note to him to deliver thy Box without any Expence – I hope He will make no words about It   if He does Insist on anything It can be but for his own Share wch I presume is not more then a third or quarter part, for my Cousin by the note gives up all his right or Demand   this is doing all I can

Vale
P C

BP 2:59; D. 143–44.
1. Unidentified.

To SIR HANS SLOANE

Skulkill   July ye 22d 1741

Desired friend
My faithfull & beloved Friend Peter Collinson in his last letter to me which I received acquainted me that thee desired I would send thee some petrified Representations of sea shels; accordingly to his instruction I have sent thee A few; which I gathered toward ye northward ye latter end of last may: which was before I had ye least hint that thee tooke any notice of any thing that I sent or wanted any from me —

I hope these few things may meet with thy acceptance so as to introduce a further Correspondence which if thay do; Pray be so kind to favour me with A Letter Containing instructions what kind of Perticular Curiosities will be most agreeable. However I design to send thee Another Colection by Captain Whright when I hope to give thee A further demonstration that I am thy vigilant & industrious friend

John Bartram[1]

British Library, Sloane Ms., 4057, f. 56.
1. For comparative purposes, Bartram's first draft (the copy he kept) follows.

July ye 22d 1741

Respected friend Sir Hanse sloan
My faithfull & beloved friend Peter Collinson in his last letter to me that I received acquainted me that thee desired I would send thee some petrified representations of sea shels   accordingly I have sent the A few which I gathered toward ye northward ye latter end of last may which was before I received ye before mentioned letter   I hope these may find acceptance so as to introduce A further Correspondence   however I desighn to send thee another Colection by Captain Whright who talks of sailing ye latter end of August when I hope to give the A further demonstration that I am thy vigilant & industrious friend

D. 302; BP 1:22:4.

To COLLINSON

July ye 22 1741

To Peter Collinson
I received about ye midle of may thy letters of october ye 20th 1740 december ye 20th   February ye 25th   april the 7th 1741 with all ye cash goods & presents mentioned therein   I am obliged to my good friend Lord Peter for ye second parts of Tourneforts herball   it is an agreeable present for I delight to read his books   I am promised ye loan of one part of his Journal to ye levant   I am allso obliged to thee for ye four books of nature delineated   thay are fine performances   ye account of ye sea muscles is very Curious but seem very diferent from ours in thair nature   yours removes from place to place to seek thair food as other fishes tho thair method of

motion & feeding be remarkable but ours seem to pertake both of ye animal & vegitable nature in location feeding & growth as first thay are fixt two thirds of thair length fast to ye ground that one must pull as hard to eradicate them as plants secondly thay draw nourishment from ye solid soil by ye strong fibers which proceeds from ye bely of ye muscle as a plant doth by ye roots 3dly thay have ye animal muscular power of opening & shutting thair shells to take in ye salt water & what may swim in it when ye tide covers ye mash for thair feeding as an animal I suppose ye petrifactions I sent last year was

George Whitefield (1714–1770). *Harper's New Monthly Magazine* 103 (1901):120.

about a hundred miles direct from ye sea ye creature which I suppose the calls ye Monack wee cal with us A ground hog it is much biger with us near as thick as A fox but much shorter in legs body & tail A clumsy slow creature as to what Whitfield intends to do with his 5000 acres of land he proposed to bring as many as would make A township of his friends from England I suppose hee designs them to be such favorites as was elected before thay was born or begot or before ye foundations of ye worlds was laid & then when thay get up into heaven thay are to witness against us at ye great day of Judgment when our bodies must rise again after thay have been wonderfuly disolved & transformed in elemental & vegitable & often animal species & some of thair bretherin talks of being Judges; (I suppose then thay will send us Reprobates   hundreds & thousands if not millions to hell) nay one of them tould his auditorys he would Sit at ye right hand of ye father to Judge them (but surely first he must heav ye sun out of his seat) — enough of this   wish it were better   ye great stone house that was begun but I know not when it will be finished   is to teach young negroes a year I know not what: then return them to thair masters   if thay was elected so long ago what need he to trouble his head about them   If thay was damned what signifieth his tutoring   however this we may be sure he will teach them to think themselves as good or better then thair masters & too good for servants   the 2 sorts of nuts one larger then filberds   Governor Morris daughter shewed me those sort which was brought from beyond Oswego & I believe I saw A many of ye wild trees upon ye catskill mountains but ye sagamores head & ye fruite like your [illegible] I know nothing of ye variegated thorn flowers I sent thee about 2 years ago with ye specimens of our sweet & sour gum for you to observe what Class thay belong to but thee never informed me whether thee received them or not   I sent the variegated flowers & leaves on ye twigs with ye insects & nests that you might observe ye cause of thair extraordinary variegation   I have seen several trees this spring dilicately striped red white & green   this spring toward ye northward but it is caused in all by minute insects difusing A perticular juice in ye green leaves which soon flowed with ye vigative juice all over ye flower or in part acording to ye quantity of ye stinging juice of ye insect   whether there is any perticular qualities in these thorns from ye rest of thair species to attract these insects to them I leave at present   I never observed any of these flowers vairegated without ye adjoyning leaves was likewise & had insects or thair nest upon them   but now dear peter I Must give some account of my Journey to Albany   I set out about ye 20th of May   Caled at trentown in Jersey & waited upon Governor Morris who shewed me Abundance of kindness   Shewed me his Library which is ye very finest I ever saw except Col byrds & but little short of it neither   he shewed me an excelent performance of Sir Hans Sloane his history of Jamaica   he allso gave me A very good generall letter of recomendation desiring all Magistrates & Gentlemen to be friendly aiding & assisting me   his son who is Chief Justice gave me a letter to A gentleman that was of service to me so that now having ye sanction of these of ye first rank I travailed towards ye highlands as thay call them & which I take to be ye same ridge with ye Calie hills up delaware   there is several ponds amongst ye mountains   I crosed these about half way between delaware & hudsons river [near] ponds some 4 or 5 miles long 60 miles from ye sea   here I first observed sea shells in a sort of loam or rotten stone   then I descended down into ye prety rich vail intersperced with abundance of high hills on which are plenty of shells intersperced in large peices of stone   thence toward hudsons river round ye end of ye Shongo mountains which ye inhabytants says is ye end of our blew mountains   thence I travailed to ye Katskill mountains being ye highest I ever saw   Governor Morris tould me he took ye alltitude of them very carefuly & judged them to be A mile perpendicular   indeed it is A laborious walk to get up to ye top   it is accounted by ye mountaineers to be A good days Journey to travail up to ye top & down again   I left ye top of ye mountain about sun set & made what hast I could carefuly down by runing & sliping & tumbling & yet it was so dark before I reached ye bottom that I could hardly see ye brambles or rocks before I run against them   I am apt to believe thay are a half A mile perpendicular   there is numerous kinds of soil upon these mountains   where I ascended it was at first gradual then very steep for near a quarter part of ye way by a run which was headed under A perpendicular wall of rocks near 20 foot high   then a prety steep rise to ye foot of another 30 foot perpendicular & so until I came to ye top which was very thick of brush that I could hardly scramble thorow it   here growed many of ye red spruce & hemlock   at last I found ye balm of gilead fir   a lovely straight regular tree A foot diameter & 60 foot high & very smooth bark like ye white pine except where ye blisters are   we have had a grevous severe winter which kept our river frozen until ye 10th of March that men & horses passed over ye ice & no vesails could come in or go out   I put on board Captain dent two boxes of plants for thee & M Catesby one   the Captain said he would sail in A few days but ye frost stoped him & I would fain have got ye boxes again for there was several plants in them that I valued but he would not altho I tould him that ye plants would be spoiled & do you no service that all would be dead before thay arived at England   I am very sory such curious plants must be intirely lost you expected of ye fruits of my labour but there is no help for it at present it is not worth paying freight for them unless it be to see what pains I have taken to oblige you   onely ask for a little cedar box directed for thee at Carys[1]   in it there is A box of fosils sent by edmond wooley to dr Lawson a letter for M Catesby & one to dr dillenius with A large colection of mosses & some curiosities for thee

BP 1:21:1.
1. Probably Robert Cary and Company, London tobacco merchants.

To COLLINSON[1]

My good Friend,

I have observed something of an Extraordinary Nature in Our Salt-Marsh Muscle. By its fibrous Roots, which strike deep into the Soil, it seems to be of a Vegetative Nature; for, it is highly probable the Animal Draws some Part of its nourishment through them: They are fixed by these two thirds of their Length in the Sand with their Broad Ends uppermost which open att Every return of the Tide to be replenished by the Salt-Water — when it is retreated, they are Found Lodged in the Grass, Sedge, Creeks, and Banks, singly and together in plenty

I herewith send you a Specimen which will give you a better Idea of this wonderful Creature.

There you may plainly observe the Ligaments draw their Origin from the principal Parts of the animal and unite near the Extremity of the Shell which they pass through on that Side of the Muscle that opens to let in the Water, then they Divide again into many Capilary Roots or Fibres which penetrate and Extend themselves into the Mudd or Soil of the Marsh wch by long Observation, seem to me for Two uses   First, as I have above observed to Convey Part of their Nourishment wch seems probably by their being Dispersed through the Body of the Muscle   this is better seen when alive; but now they are Dry, one of the Specimens plainly show It

The other Use of these Fibrous Roots for so I must Call them, by their striking Deep into the Mudd or Sand is to secure the Creature from being Carried away by the rapidity of the Tides So that in this Circumstance, they are somewhat analogous to plants whose Roots both nourish them & secure them from the Injuries of Wind & Flood.

If these short Hints prove any Entertainmt It will be a pleasure to your
obliged frd
John Bartram

On the other side I will give you some of my observation on our Oysters & Fresh water Muscles.

Our Oysters are of an oblong Figure, they grow att the Sides and Bottoms of Creeks, Rivers, and Bayes, near the Sea but Mostly In such a Situation where they are near or quite dry at low Water   They have the Power of Opening and Shutting, like the Muscle to take In and Retain the Salt-Water, which is their principal nourishment tho they stick in the Mudd they are not so secured as the Salt Marsh Muscle before Mention'd; and tho' these Oysters grow in great Clusters or Heaps, commonly called Oyster Banks, yett every one that is alive hath Free Communication with the Air and Water & Liberty to open & shutt. If the Oysters Way of growing may be compared to that of a Plant I think there is great Similitude between It and the Opuntia or Indian Rigg, a Leaf produces & supports a Leafe, and so on —Thus the young Oyster grows on the Sides of the old one, which by degrees is so deep Imerged in the Mudd that it dieth, but yett it serves to support the young one upright untill it comes to Maturity to produce others; and then that by Degrees subsides so that by this Method Banks of dead & Living Oysters are Extended of an Inconceivable Length & Breadth — thro all our Coasts —

Our Common Fresh Water Muscles Differs from our Salt Marsh Muscle In that they are not Fixt to any place or thing but have a Method of Trailing along on the sandy Bottoms of Creeks and Rivers   they have the Power not only of opening & shutting their shells, at pleasure but have moreover the power of Creeping (a) along as it were Like a Snail by Turning upon the Upper Edge of the shell that opens and so work themselves along the soft yeilding Sand in Little Furrows about half an Inch Deep. I have traced them for several yards by these Little Channels When the Tide is down & left the Sands Bare

If these few Observations prove acceptable It will be a Pleasure to

Your friend,
John Bartram

Royal Society of London Archives, Letters and Papers, Decades 1–4, p. 309; Royal Society, *Philosophical Transactions* 43 (1744):157–59.

1. This letter was transcribed from Collinson's copy of Bartram's letter and differs a great deal from the printed version in capitalization and punctuation. The letter is undated but may have been part of the letter to which Collinson referred when, on February 3, 1741/2, he wrote: "In anser to thine of July 22d I am Delighted with thy Account of your Muscle." It was read before the society on November 8, 1744.

To COLLINSON[1]

but why did thee send me 2 pieces of doulas instead of garlicks which I sent for   I want a piece of good Garlick for my own use to travail with   Beside thay are charged so dear that I cant sell them for near double of what thay are charged to mee   I received thy letter of recommendation to Doctor Colden which I tooke with me when I went to albany; but he was not at home but was gone toward new England so I mist of an opertunity by which I expected to have gained A deal of intelligence   he lives in part of ye high lands   I was within 4 mile of his house but I kept ye letter carefuly in hopes I may meet with him another time but he is often abroad   I have just put on board of Captain smiter ye several Curiosities in ye same box directed at large for thee which thee sent me with such A fine Colection of bulbous roots last fall but thay did not arive here untill about ye midle of may & yet thay seemed prety fresh   I planted them carefuly but there is no more but one yet come up neither do I expect or desire any untill next spring except there is some autumnal flowers amongst them which I may expect to see A month or two hence   ye curious variety of seeds thee sent is hardly any come up   we have had such A dismall dry summer as I think we have not had this 30 year   ye soil hath not been thoroughly moistened since ye melting of ye snow but toward ye northward thay have had abundance of rain which I had a tast of to my sorow for in riding over A creek amongst ye mountains it proved deeper than I expected which obliged me & my mare to swim which spoiled many of my specimens & obliterated my notes in my pocket book   doth any of ye seeds of ye rose laurel   red and white cedar   sassafras   witch hazel   allspice   white pine   sheep turds & sugar maple which I sent come up that I may know better what to send thee   pray let mee know ye specimen 405 which I sent the last year   thee said it flowered with thee was A male & female flower   I have two from ye same parcel of seed I sent thee but thay are males & produceth no seed   I am obliged to thee for ye names of specimens for ye 2 last years   if thee hath Gronovius names for ye specimens I sent two years before I wish the would send them with thair numbers   it is very kind of thee to endeavor to Ingratiate mee into Sir Hans Sloans favour   it shows thy good will to me & as such I take it   there is many of thy friends in pensilvania maryland & jersey is industrious in promoting A yearly subscription for me that I may dispose of thy favours & spend my time chiefly in ye search after natural productions both animal mineral fosal & vegitable & to make a perticular map of all ye ridges of mountains   springs & branches of rivers within our English continent   if this should go forward I shall be able to furnish you with A prodigious variety for I should be for peeping at everything that is uncommon in order to satisfy ye curious

BP 1:22:1.
1. The first part of this letter is missing. It is undated, but probably written in the late summer of 1741, since Bartram says he hopes to see autumnal flowers within a month or two.

From CRESSY

Antigua August 20, 1741

Worthy Friend,

You have just Cause to Accuse me of Silence after your repeated favrs. first by Capt. Wall in a former Voyage and yr. last by Capt. Bowers; but I assure you it was not Occasioned by willfull neglect or disrespect, but by waiting for Opportunities of sending you some fresh Specimens from hence, wch. I am still prevented from by our long 8 months drought, wch. has not left us till abt. fourteen days ago, wch. not only proved distructive to a Botanist, but to the whole Island in Generall; so that yr. flower has Sold from 30 to 40 Shillings per Hund. & Corn at 10 Shillings the Bushell & still remains So.

I have tryed all manner of ways to raise the Poppy, the Rhubarb &c, but can get none of them to appear, pray advise me if possible how to proceed; I much want the Sunflower and true Turnsole[1] seed if you have them, and a little true leave Lettice, wch. seldom comes hither genuine nor indeed are the others Publickly vended here as good as might be hoped for. Here are Sevll. Gentlemen much in want for Garden Seeds and if it is worth your while to Send a quantity of each upon yr. recommendation I believe I could sell them for you at a good Price. You make Mention of a Generous design amongst yr. northern friends of settling an Annuity upon You, in Order to encourage your Botanicall Labours, wch. I heartily wish may be effected to yr. satisfaction, if my Mite will be Acceptable I shall with Pleasure add it. Pray my Love to Mr. Grayham to whom I wo'd have sent some Lymes if we had any, but we are obliged to the French Islands for what we use ourselves: However we hope in time to be able to oblige our friends again.

As soon as possibly I can oblige you wth. any plants worth notice I shall not fail any Opportunity, in the Interim pray believe Me to be

Sr, Your Obliged Humble Servt.
S. Cressy

If you have any fresh gather'd Buckthorn Berries pray oblige me wth a few, I think I sent you word that our last high wind had destroy'd two wch I had got above two foot high –

BP 3:92.
1. Plants that turn with the sun's movement.

From COLLINSON

Londn Sepr 1:1741

Fr John

I hope thou has all mine p Capt Redman   by him I sent the Ballance of thy account in Goods thou Order'd with thy Account Currt — part of the Cutlery & Seed &c I putt in Mrs. Sarah Reeds Box Some Tulip Roots &c in John Amblers Trunk of Goods & the Remainder in a Box Directed to thee att Length Marked JB — In which is another pcell of Cutlery & Hosiery with a Box of Roots in Earth —

Dear John I have little to add to former Accounts   I fully Expected thy Last Quire of Specimens from Holland In Time to send thee their names,[1] but they are not yett arrived — but phaps they may before this Ship Sails which I think will be the last from this port this year — I shall now wait with some Impatience to heare from thee & how thou fared in thy Expedition to Hudsons River — what Discoveries thou has made to Tempt thy subscribers to Continue their Subscriptions

the Trees & shrubbs raised from thy first seeds is grown to great maturity   Last year Ld petre planted out about Tenn thousand Americans wch being att the Same Time mixed wth about Twenty Thousand Europeans, & some Asians make a very beautifull appearance great Art & skill being shown in consulting Every one's pticular growth & the well blending the Variety of Greens   Dark green being a great Foil to Lighter ones & Blewish green to yellow ones & those Trees that have their Bark & back of their Leaves of white or Silver make a Beautifull Contrast with the others the whole is planted in thickets & Clumps and with these Mixtures are perfectly picturesque and have a Delightfull Effect — this will give thee a faint Idea of the Method Lord Petre plants In which has not been so happly Executed by any and Indeed they want the Materials whilst his lordship has them in plenty   His nursery being fully stocked with Flowering shrubs of all Sorts that can be procured, with these He borders the out skirts of all his plantations and He continues Annually Raising from Seed and Laying, budding, grafting that 20 Thousand Trees are hardly to be missed out of his Nurseries — when I walk amongst them, One cannot well help thinking He is in North American thickets — there are such Quantities — but to be att his Table one would think South America was really There to see a Servant come in Every Day with Tenn or a Dozen pine apples as much as He can Carry   I am lately come from thence Quite Cloyed with them — thee will not think I talk figuratively when I tell thee that his pine apple stove is 60 foot Long 20 foot Wide & height proportionable and if I further Tell thee that his guavas, papaws, Ginger & Limes are in such plenty, that yearly He makes abundance of Wett sweetmeats of his Own Growth that Serves his table & makes presents to his Friends   finer I never saw or Tasted from Barbadoes nor better Cured — but these Trees grow in Beds of Earth in Houses, Some 20 some 30 feet high — It is really wonderfull to see how Nature is helped & imitated by art — but besides, his Collection of the West & East India plants is beyond thy imagination   Here I must End because It is endless to Mention the great Variety of Contrivances in his gardens to produce all Fruites & plants in the greatest pfection.[2]

So Dear John Farewell

P. Collinson

I have Collected a pcell of Most Nectarine stones being a Fruite most wanted with you   Phaps they may thrive best on their own Stocks — the plum stones are most green Gage wch is the best plum that grows   I apprehend they will all come up the First year tho I am told some will not till the second

BP 2:60; D. 144–46.
1. These were being identified by Dr. J. F. Gronovius.
2. See Winifred Notman Prince, "John Bartram and Thorndon Park," *Garden Journal* 7 (1957): 141–43, 152, and 8 (1957): 189–91.

From COLLINSON[1]

London, Sept. 16th, 1741

Friend John: –

There came up amongst the new sort of Poplar seed, sent in last cargo, a pretty many plants that were formerly in our gardens, called the Jesuit's Bark Tree. It's a pithy plant, like Elder; but the leaves are longer, and of a deep green. Dost thou know anything of it?

Pray send some Ginseng seed; but roots will be better. I had great expectation I had this rare plant, but don't find it proves so. The young leaves of the *Prenanthus,* or Doctor Witt's Snakeroot, I took for it.

These are stones of the Katherine Peach; which is the best late peach we have.

I have sent thee some Horse Chestnuts, which are ripe earlier than usual; hope they will come fit for planting.

Thine,
P. Collinson

I am glad I can send you Doctor Gronovius's List of your plants, collected anno 1740.

Some Observations on Specimens, 1741

No 1—Sweet Fern   this seems to Mee a shrub but wether Ever Green or no cant tell   Should be Glad of a Root or Two

2—Its New & worth Haveing   seems a Spiraea for Lord Petre

3—This Balm of Gilead seems Different from Ours   I should be Glad to see the Cones

5—Some of the Cherry Stones would Determine if the Sort I had from the Northward

6—Is New   Seeds of this would be acceptable for Lord Petre

7—this Red Root blows or flowers finely Every year with Mee

8—pray send Mee 2 or 3 plants of this if to be Had Easily for the Seed is to small

11—I have had Long to Grow in the Garden   Thrives Well   a geum or Sanicle

13—is a pretty plant   pray send a Root

15—pray Send Mee 1 or 2 Growing plants of the *Gensing* (for I mightly Want   Every one Expects I have It)

24—is another Geum or Sanicle

28—is a pretty thing & maybe a Mitella

33—seems near akin to the Above

39—seems a dwarf Aconite   pretty plant

42–43—Honesuckles   Different from any I Ever Saw   plant or Seed

50—I take to be a Gentian

61—is a Charming flower   I am Glad of the Root so Hope I shall see It in perfection

62—Sea plum is a Curiosity Especially the Large One as big as a Nectarine

ye Holly I am pleased to see   have often heard of It

Remember seed of Collinsonia; for I want it much, for several correspondents.

The downy specimen, 69 of Lord Petre, that thou gathered near Cape May, is a plant that we have long had in our gardens, by the name of *Senecio arborescens,* or Groundsel Tree; but ours never seen in this beautiful downy state, for which reason we think it the male. If thee happens where this shrub grows, again, pray make some observation about it, – and if there is male and female plants. These in haste; I wish thou may guess at my meaning.

Send specimens of Black Gum, in flower. Hast thou observed the mechanism of the seed-vessel, when it chips or sprouts? It thrusts off a valve, to let the gemma come forth, which is so hard at first, as not to be opened without breaking. The power of vegitation is great.

I shall soon send thy specimens to Holland, to Doctor Gronovius, from whom thou may expect a good account; but only one must stay some time for it.

Pray Remember some seed of Collinsonia & Variegated Clinopodium.

BP 2:63; D. 146–47.
1. This letter was taken from Darlington except for the plant list (BP 2:63), which he omitted.

To COLLINSON

October ye 18th 1741

I have put aboard of Captain Whright two long boxes Containing beries & seeds in sand   Box No 1 PC is for ye Duke of norfolk in ye large pertition & duke of richmond in ye lesser   ye first layer is black gum berries   ye second is sugar maple seeds   ye third is myrtle   ye small cones is ye spruice fir   most of ye rest is put in separate bags with thair names writ upon them   in this box is a little box for dr Lawson sent by Edmond Wooley which should have gone by Capt Dent   Box No II is for Lord Peter & Philip Miller   ye same sorts as ye other in ye large pertition is some tulup tree Cones for Catesby in ye small pertition is A small paper bag of beach plum & chery stones   Several shels & A cluster of sea muscles for thee to observe how thay stick in ye soil   I have allso sent two boxes of roots in earth   one for ye No 1 PC NI mediola   II has specimen 56   III witch hazel   IIII sasafras   V sheep turds   VI snake root & fine gentian   se[e] specimen 61   VII red root & two curious plants brought from ye desert of cape may   VIII sea Limonium from ye cape & in ye midle skunk weed   Box No II PC & C on ye side for Catesby is sever[al] roots planted in ye bottom for him & on ye top of earth I have planted sods of several Curious plants with ye white lychnis with a red eye & several others   I have put on board a box of insects for thee & A box of specimens for Lord Petre   I am afraid thay will give a deal of trouble to separate them   I could not tell how to send them better in two boxes because my Cargo Consists of small seeds or berries that takes little room & some clay wasps nest for sir hans sloan   I have put A piece of wood in one end of the box with the nests built upon two sides of it that thee may observe ye dexterity of ye insect for ye propagation of its species   thay allways build them under some board   stone or shelter from rain   thay begin at first with ye end of ye cell so continue working until it is long enough to contain ye pup; & until it is strong enough to bite its way out   then thay lay an egg in ye bottom of ye cell   then crams it full of live spiders but so crippled & over powered that thay cant stir   then plasters ye cell close up & begins to build another such A cel by ye side of ye other or at ye end of it; soon after this cell is plastered up ye egg is hatched & a small embrio appears which feeds upon & devours all ye spiders there deposited & by october it hath spun A fine thin case wherein it lyeth all winter in its nymph state when at ye approach of warm weather it is strong enough to bite its way out   it breaks thorow its confinement & flyeth abroad

I have made three long Journeys since harvest   one to ye mountains of east Jersey to seek after & gather ye white pine Cones & firs   ye other to great Eg harbour to gather plum stones but this sumer being so grievous dry there was very few perfect ones to be found   allso another Journey to Cape may to gather mirtle berries & red & white Cedar but these was all scarce this year   I gathered most of what I could find   we cut down near 20 white Cedar trees & climbed many more to gather what I have   I could find very few white pine cones or rose laurel alltho I have observed hundreds of these trees this year   I heard in my Journey to Cape may of A great Curiosity of A strange sort of A defensative weapon which was out of A fishes nose which I ingaged A man to send to Philadelphia for me   there hath allso been A monster of the deer kind killed by a hunter about A month ago in ye swamp where I gathered white cedar seeds   it hath been seen this 4 year at several times by both indians & english & much admired but allways escaped til now: I was tould its neck was as big as A lusty mans midle & one of its horns had 12 snags & by ye best discription I could hear it was a Moose dear which thee wrote to mee about two year ago   I engaged ye man who related this to me to try if he could purchase ye horns and send them to mee   he tould me that thair governour had A pair of A large moose dears horns which was killed towards albany   I wish I had heard of it sooner   I should have enquired perticularly of ye Governor about them
I have been twice with him this sumer   he seems to delight to inform me of any thing that he knows that is Curious but next opertunity that I have with him I design that to be one of ye subjects of our discource   our hunters informs me that there is two kind of dear in our Countrey beside the elk   one kind is shorter both body legs & horns   ye other is larger longer legs & flater horns & keeps more in low grounds & [illegible] I was pleased with thy kind letter by via Boston, Pray what doth thee call A moose   what color & how big is the martin, is the fox like ours except ye Color   two days ago I rode several miles with A man in jersey that said he had A porcupine for A show for two months & then it dyed   he said it came into A garden & stayed several days & fed upon green pease   ye owner or his dogs durst not catch him but this man tould ye owner of ye garden he would give him ten shillings for him himself   so he tooke A tub & held it before him & whirled it over ye Creature & he soon became very tame & got 3 pence A person for ye sight of it   it was 2 foot long   ye quils 3 inches on its back 2 on ye sides wholy naked of hair   when it was pleased it would stroke it self against one like A Cat but when disturbed would set up its quils. if irritated discharge A number at once which would soon be succeeded by young ones in thair room   if A dog was so hardy as to advance to it after receiving several shots he ye porcupine would cram his nose between his legs & erect his darts all round so that no dog could bite him: how or from whence this creature came no body there could know some said he dropt down out of ye Clouds   others with more probability

supposed he swam A shore from some vesail either upon ye Coast or coming up ye river   I Can hear nothing yet of ye cones of ye balm of gilead altho I have wrote to several about albany   sent them presents in order to encourag them to send me some down   I have allso been at bruinswick & ofered one there Considerable who trades to albany to take care of any thing that comes to his hands for me   he promised me hee would   I have received two letters from A Gentleman near york who says he hath wrote to Col Salisbury to take care & send them down to bruinswick if thay be gathered & I think ye man who lived near them might aford to gather them for ten shilling or els I am sure thay will be very dear to me before I get them to my house but I believe if I have them I must gather them my self   If you think fit to order me, If I & my family hath our health I dont much Care if I go to new england next year to se what sort of A Clownish sanctified people thay are there   several of them hath come to my house   I showed them what Civility I was master of & desired[1]

BP 1:23:3.
1. The end of this letter is missing.

To COLLINSON[1]

Pensilvania Muscles

No 1—the Fibrous Veins Dispersed in the Body of the Muscle,
    2—the Strings or fibres that fasten it in the Mudd.
    3—the Ligament that Joyns the Shells together –
    4—part of the muscle that appears out of the mud

These are the Size of the Marsh Muscles   I call them so because I found them sticking Two thirds in the Mudd – with their broad side uppermost which they open when the sea overflows the marsh att high water which yeilds them their principal Nourishment – and then close up their Shells to Retain It, untill the Tide returns   they are Dispersed all over the Marsh amongst the Grass   Some perch distant from the Creeks – that brings in the Tide and are found on the Marsh which when I was there was firm enough to run a Horse on it — There is to my apprehension a Tuft of Fibrous Matter or Vessels that is Dispersed through the body of the Muscle and seems to Mee to be the Vessels that conveys parts of its Nourishment and is extended through that side of the muscles between the Two shells that opens to lett in the Water — When these strings or fibres are projected without the shell they are Divided into many branches which are fixt in the mud – by which the muscle seems to draw nourishment from the mud Like as plants by their Roots, when they are plucked up the fibres brings the mudd or soil with them – they will also adhere very strongly by those Fibres to old Loggs & Stones.

Linnean Society of London Archives, Ms. 323, Collinson's Common Place Book.
1. This description of salt marsh mussels may have accompanied Bartram's letter to Collinson of October 18, 1741, in which he said that he was sending "Several shels & A cluster of sea muscles for thee to observe how thay stick in ye soil." The numbered list at the beginning of this description refers to the numbered parts of a sketch he drew in the margin of the original. See also his letter of July 22, 1741.

To CRESSY[1]

To J. S. Cressy
Dear Friend I At last had ye pleasure of receiving thy letter of August ye 20 1741 after haveing long expected one & at last concluded patiently to submit [illegible] ye misfortune of haveing [illegible] ofended & lost a friend who I endeavoured by all Convenient means to ye utmost of my power to oblige   I am surprised to hear of ye loss of ye buck thorn trees surely that must be A terible wind to eradicate A bush two foot high   I did not hear of it before having not received any letter from thee Since that letter dated May ye 26th 1740   I very much admire what can be ye reason that so few of ye seed that I send thee grows   I am sure thay was ripe & carefuly packed up which is as far as I can assist being unacquainted with ye nature of your climate & soil it difering so much from europe & ours   wee have had A grievous dry sumer so that our ground was scarcely wet plow deep from march until about ye midle of august   at present my circumstances will not alow me time to raise any quantity of kitchen garden seeds   I am so often abroad upon long Journeys in making discoveries of animals & vegitables & fosils & insects to oblige my corespondents in England holand france & sweden so that my time is mostly spent this way in ye sommer season except in ye harvest time   I am obliged to thee for thy generous ofer for incouraging me in my general observations of all that is Curious in our northern governments tho I question whether I shall have subscribers suficient to make it worth while to leave of[f] farming & pursue this wholy   misfortune & martial Charge discourages our People from [illegible] desighns but what is for present necessity   about A week past I saw our friend Graham in Philadelphia   he lives in Chester & keeps A publick house or tavern where I hope he may improve his estate   I tould him thee desired me to remember thy love to him & that thee would have sent him some limes but that ye dry season hindered &c   this did not give him satisfaction   he though[t] thee might have sent him A better answer
I have sent some Buckthorn beries seeds of ye great oficinal white popy & Phapontick seed mixed in mould hoping this may preserve them until thay come to thy hands   ye may pick ye Buckthorn berries out & sow them by themselves   ye other seeds sow together with ye mould there sent in   I would have sent thee some Siberian rubarb seed but this dry summer

hindered it from seeding kindly   we have not true turnsole in our Country that I know of   I brought A Curious sun flower seed with me when I came from Virginia that growed in my garden A few months 16 foot high & bore many flowers near A foot diameter but A storm blowed it down before ye seed was ripe & I have lost it but I hope to send thee some & better seed another opertunity

BP 1:22:3.
1. Undated, but probably written in October 1741, when Bartram commonly shipped seeds of the types mentioned here.

To CATESBY[1]

october 1741

Respected friend Mark Catesby

I have according to thy desire planted in A box of earth these following roots[2]   these I hope may meet with thy acceptance   pray dear friend let me know yearly with what I can oblige thee & I shall use Convenient endeavours of Complyance   I hope the hath received my letter by Captn Smiley

BP 1:23.
1. In his letter of March 1741/42, Catesby thanks Bartram for his letter of the 15th of October.
2. There was no list in the letter, so it must have been sent separately.

To BAYARD[1]

Respected Friend Peter Bayard

I received thy kind & acceptable letter of Sepr wherein thee informs mee that thee hath wrote to francis Salisbury upon my account which was very kind but I can hear nothing from him nor of ye balm of Gilead cones   I am afraid thay will disapoint mee   I should have answered thy kind letter directly but could not meet with an opertunity to send it   I have been extreamly hurried in gathering seeds & herbs to send to several parts of europ as england holand sweden & ye royal garden at paris to oblige my Corespondents in these [illegible] thee seems to be unacquainted with ye bulbs of ye flaming lily as bradly[2] calls them   Parkinson calls it ye red fiery lily   Miller ye bulbous fiery lilly   it flowers 3 or 4 weeks before ye other english kinds for which it is esteemed by our florists   it produceth these bulbs between ye bosom of ye leaves & ye stalke which if planted whilst fresh will grow to fine plants in two years   as to ye evergreens for pyramids that which is called in europe ye silver fir in new england hemlock & our people spruice is esteemed one of ye most beautifull evergreens for showey pyramids & yew & holy is also much esteemed   I saw ye yew growing near ye head of ye easternmost branch of delaware & for hedges in A garden I like our red cedar or Juniper for tall natural pyramids   ye white or Lord weymouth pine & balm of gilead fir   ye larix & spruce fir & arbor vita which makes ye spruice [illegible] hath thair beauties but ye larix sheds its leaves in ye fall tho A resiniferous tree   these all except ye holy groweth amongst our mountains   I expect within A year or two to have A fine Colection of bulbous roots   I had this year near a thousand came in from london   my lavendar this year did not seed   I shifted it last spring & we have had A grievous dry summer but I send thee some sweet marjorum & musk seeds two fine sweet plants   sow ye seeds next spring   if thee hears of any thing that is fact in ye animal mineral or vegitable kingdom that is strange uncommon or curious if thee please to inform mee of it It shall be kindly accepted & gratefully acknowledged by thy sincear friend in hast

J B

BP 1:22:4.
1. Undated, but obviously written in the fall of 1741.
2. Richard Bradley (d. 1732), author of a treatise on gardening in which he dealt with plant hybridization.

To SLOANE[1]

Bees

  I This great wasp or bee   its feeding is upon flowers   its building is in boards or logs which it perforates after a wonderfull maner in which it layeth an egg which hatching it appeareth A nymph which biteth its way through a pertition of clay, then casteth its scin & flyeth away   thear is many such cels in one of these long perforations   see ye specimen

  II This is our Common bumble bee. it builds often in our medows sometimes in our fences or in houses amongst wool or flax making a cluster of about half A dozen cels of brittle wax to breed thair young in, which thay forsake at ye approach of cold weather

  III these bees feeds upon flowers & often times suck ye juice of several sorts of fresh dung   thay perforate 8 or 10 inches into Clay wals & at ye far end makes A Cavity large enough to contain a cluster of half A score of these clay cels   in every one of these cels thay lay an egg then fills it full of ye farina of male squashes or gourds as I judged by observing it in A microscope; then closeth it up with clay; this egg hatching produceth A worm which feedeth on ye farina: then resteth in its Nymph state   then breaketh thorow its Confinement & cometh forth A bee after its kind   Specimen III

IIII these   thair way of feeding & building are much like ye last onely ye nymph is inclosed in a rough Case within ye Cel of clay   see ye Specimen IIII

V these bees perforates deep in clay or stone walls that is laid in clay for lime cement is too hard for them; then thay form these separate Cels of ye rinds of plants into which thay lay an egg & doubtless puts some thing into each cel for ye worms nourishment, then closeth it up – then buildeth another such A Cel close to ye end of ye other & so on Successively for 5 or 6 in length, for these do not lay them in clusters as ye other two sorts, these three sorts my boys dug out of my own wall last July

VI this small sort of bumble bee is very scarce   it creeps into ye flowers of squashes gourds & convolvulus Coating it self with ye farina & doubtless sucks honey   I believe it builds in ye ground.

VII this little bee feeds chiefly upon ye Eupatoriums & small umbeliferous flowers   its building is chiefly in ould tres & logs.

VIII this generaly feeds as ye last but its building is in ye ground 5 or 6 inches deep in holes which I believe ye worms makes   thay makes little cels of clay in which thay lay an egg   then stops ye cel up   most of these breeds sometimes in holes perforated in rotten wood   sometimes in holes in stalks of large weeds

IX this in its feeding is much like ye last; but it perforates small holes horizontaly on ye side of a dich or where ye earth is dug away perpendicular in which I suppose thay lay thair eggs.

X this or one very like it I have seen go out & come in into small holes in corn fields where I suppose thay laid thair egs. I have dug after them but ye holes being so exceeding small I lost them before I came to ye far end. ye earth falling in tho great care taken   these ten different kinds I call bees by reason that thair hinder legs is hairy & thay gather ye farina of flowers in lumps about them as our common bees doth

XII[2] our anual locust   it is larger & makes a different noise from them which cometh in prodigious numbers once in 15, 16 or 17 years.

XII skin of one of them which he casteth ye morning that he cometh out of ye ground & will fly about ye same day.

XIII two locusts with a dart at his tail prety much like those that Comes in such great numbers some years in one part of ye country & other years in Another   I have known them in 3 or 4 diferant parts of ye Country since thay was in our parts near Philadelphia   XIII two scins of ye locusts with darts

WASPS

XIIII this wasp feeds chiefly upon umbeliferous flowers   this wasp is one of ye sorts builds with clay fastened to walls or boards

XV these feeds upon umbeliferous flowers & eupatoriums   I suppose thay build in ye ground but am not certain

XVI these sort is sometimes seen upon flowers but often running upon ye ground amongst ye grass. I think I have seen them catching spiders. I suppose thay breed in ye ground.

XVII these delights to suck umbeliferous flowers & calaminth & Clinopodiums

XVIII this is one of ye kinds of our yelow wasps   thay feed on most sorts of eatable fruits & many kinds of flowers & insects.

XIX this frequents umbeliferous flowers, builds with clay or in worm eaten wood.

XX this wasp frequents all sorts of tufted flowers & feeds also upon insects   it is this that builds them long clay nests in rows upon boards or logs.

XXI this is our common yelow wasp that builds sometimes in ye ground or sometimes hangs thair nest on A bough of A tree like our hornet   thay feed on all sorts of eatable fruits.

XXII this frequents ye flowers of ye origanums & Clynopodiums thay are scarce

XXIII these are rare   sometimes thay come into our orchards & sucks ye juice of aples & peaches   thair manner of breeding I have not observed –

XXIIII this is our hornet   builds large nests shaped like a heart: first in ye spring thay build a little nest about 3 inches diameter shaped as in ye margen with one comb of 8 or 10 cels in it for ye breeding of so many young which when thay are able to fly thay all forsake this little habitation & pitcheth upon a suitable branch of a tree or under ye roof of an out house for to build A City but at ye approach of Cold forsake it   also thay feed upon most sorts of fruits & many kinds of insects & many times enters very quietly into our houses to catch flies which we are no ways displeased with

XXV this is our common house wasp   builds under ye roofs of houses & in ye latter end of september or begining of october leaves thair nests & creeps about our windows in ye heat of ye day & at night hides themselves in ye chinks of ye wall

XXVI this wasp frequents umbeliferous flowers & keeps in swarms upon our corn till harvest time   thay breed in ye ground as I suppose

XXVII this monstrous kind of wasp was Catched on ye flowers in my garden   I dont remember to have observed it before.

Flies

XXVIII   this insect frequents paths and roads lighting down before [illegible] yet keeps at such a distance as its difficult to Catch them. there is some that is very green on thair backs which some thinks is Cantharids

XXIX   this is a species of our tumble turds who delights chiefly in human ordure.

XXX   this is our small tumble turd   delights chiefly in horse dung

XXXI   this tumbel turd had in ye latter end of october dug a hole in ye ground near A foot deep where I suppose it might have laid all winter if I had not removed him.

XXXII   this is our little tumble turd   it digs holes in ye ground to repose therein in ye daytime & in ye night labours

XXXIII   this tho it seems strange is certainly ye louse of A great hen hawk that I shot that was 2 foot 10 inches between ye end of one wing & ye end of ye other when extended & two foot between ye end of ye bill & that of ye tail; tho' this hath ye appearance of a fly it certainly was on ye body of our hawk. thay are full of them amongst ye feathers & sticking to thair skin & are exceeding nimble hiding amongst ye feathers –

these observations I have made last summer according to ye best of my judgment by ye few opertunities that I had being so thronged with business for ye support of my family or traveling in search after plants & such observations as these require A deal of time to come to A certainty; thair feeding & breeding is so various that it may take several years accurate observation before A full discovery can be made

British Library, Sloane Ms. 4019, ff. 132, 133.
1. Written on the outside: "John Bartrams remarks on ye insects sent in a box to Sir Hans Sloane in 1742, box no 9."
2. Bartram omitted number XI.

From SLOANE

January 16, 1741–2

Sir: —

I am very much obliged to you for several Natural Curiosities, Shells and Petrifactions, which my very good friend, Mr. Peter Collinson, hath delivered to me with great care; and for which I reckon myself very much obliged to you; especially on account of the remarks that you had sent along with them, in your letter to me.

The triangular arrow-head of white chrystal, or spar; the like of which, in green jasper, I have had from Tierre del Fuego, on the south side of the Straits of Magellan, used by the inhabitants of that country. The Indian instrument you sent, was the head of a hatchet, made of a sort of jasper. This, fitted to a handle, was made use of by the Indians of Jamaica, and several parts of the West Indies, for making their canoes, before they were taught the use of iron and steel. I have one of them fitted up for use by them. It's believed they could not make canoes, and large periaguas,[1] with these hatchets, before they had first with fire made the part of the log, to be hollowed, into coal, to be friable, and brought out by the hatchets.

I have, with the approbation of Mr. Collinson, sent you my Natural History of Jamaica together with the catalogue of the plants I found there, referred to in that History; whereby, you may find what has been said by any authors I have seen, that write of them. I should be glad to have some seeds, or samples of your plants, for my collections of dried herbs, fruits, &c.

I should be extremely pleased to know wherein I can be useful to you, and retaliate the obligations you have laid upon

Your most humble servant,
Hans Sloane

D. 302–3.
1. Obsolete spelling of *piragua,* being either a canoe fashioned from a hollow tree or a flat-bottomed boat with two masts.

From ALEXANDER STOPFORD CATCOTT

Bristol Febry 2 174$\frac{1}{2}$

Sir,

I gratefully acknowledge yr favour; and in order to make it as usefull as possible to yr native Country (as I presume England is) I have communicated & sent the seeds to Dr. Dillenius, professor of Botany in the University of Oxford   from him (who is my friend & correspondent) we may hope to have in due time, a just account of what the species may prove; & no doubt the plants when rais'd will be no small addition and ornament to the fine Collection already in the physic Garden. I would have sent some of the seed to Mr. Miller at the physic Garden at Chelsea (he being also my acquaintance) but suppose, as he has everything wch any member of the royal Society can furnish him with you have opportunity of sending any curiosities directly to him at first hand. John, I am no great botanist, but have had good experience in cultivating green house and garden plants & have a tolerable Collection of both; and shall be very ready to communicate to you or yr friends any you will be pleas'd to signify by name. But my favorite plants are the lily and Narcissus kind; I have 20 sorts in the open ground & several sorts from Jamaica, Barbadoes and the midle of Virginia in the green house; if yr travels furnish you with many of this tribe I should be equally obliged to you to share in yr pleasures, there is one fine sort of Martagon which we call the Canada martagon or lilly but it grows in the

English Colonies: I have a very small plant but Mr. Collinson of London I know has had that & several others from yr. part. I had likewise once some flag flowers from Carolina but the hard winter killed them; these likewise would be very acceptable. of these I have sent Mr. Chanceller[1] 10 or 12 different sorts. I heartily wish you success in yr botanic searches; not only as they may prove an agreeable amusement to yourself, but a benefit & pleasure to many others and am Sr

yr oblig'd humble servant
Alexr. Catcott

BP 1:98.
1. Dr. William Chancellor.

From COLLINSON

Londn: Feb 3d: 1741/2

Dr frd John

All thy Cargoes came safe and well by Capt Wright so shall Defer saying more till I come to answer thy other Letters in pticular —

I have thine before Mee of March 22d which if I remember right I have fully answer'd p Captain Breame In mine of Sept 16th —

I must also Inform you that the Box of seeds p Capt Brown and thy Letter are Come Safe   Wee have been very Fortunate to Escape the Spaniards in all our Cargoes on Both Sides —

In anser to thine of July 22d

I am Delighted with thy Account of your Muscle and with the Specimen thee has sent wch confirms all that thee has said On this Head & being on this subject I will send thee a rough sketch of a muscle that I discovered by Accident in one of our markets[1]   It is wonderfull to think that anything new is to be Discovered on our Coasts — but so it is, Wee have not been able to find this Discribed in any Book or Author of Natural History — In its nature it seems to Agree near with our and your Solen — by some called Razor-Shell, by others Finger Shell and what thou reckons a Sort of Clams — wch I delivered to Sr Hans per thy order

I observe that thou takes no notice of any Natural History relateing to the Monac or Groundhog   as the Creature will be as Tame as a Catt (for I gave one to Sr Hans Sloan who was much Delighted with it and became a Domestic Animall   ran up and down Like Dog or Catt for years)   It would be pretty to keep one and observe the provisions he Makes for his Winters abod for 6 or 7 Months Sleeping or Liveing all that time without food

I find thee has seen some of the Fruite or nutts I mentioned Butt I don't find the Butter Nut which is plenty in New England as a Gentn tells Mee has yett come under thy Notice with the Medlar & Sagamores head

I have much to do to read thy Letter for some Mischievous Insect has

Eaten thy Letter in large holes in four places   to prevent this wrap them up in dry tobacco Leaves —

I shall Indeavour to Look about the Sweet and Sour Gum — is this Last call'd Black Gum or are they different plants — I hope thee has Docr Gronoviuss names to thy Cargo, 1741   What Notice He takes of these plants I can't well Remember but will Look at my Leisure —

That some Variegations may be occasioned by Insects is Certain but then these are only Annual & Cease wth the year — But thos Variegations that are permanent In our Hollies & Phillyreas proceeds from a Distemper in the Juices (Like the jaundice in Men & Women)   take a Budd from a Variegated Jessamine & Insert it into a plain Jessamine, not only the Budd will continue the variegation but will also Infect & impregnate the Circulateing Juices, that the branches & Leaves above & below the Budd will appear Variegated   This is a plain Demonstration of the Circulation of the Sap and is a Vegetable Inoculation wch is very analogous to that practised on the Human Species which I hear is very successfully operated with you but Obtains Little with us — for Wee are fearful of Bringing on a Distemper wch oft proves Mortal on persons that never might have had it in a Natural Way. I have two Children but dare not Venter on the Experiment for fear of Consequences

I am now about Intering upon thy Journey to Albany, but must first stop to tell thee that the History that thou so much admired at our Good Fr Govr Morris thou may soon have the pleasure to Call thy own — for With what Thou sent and I have added Sr Hans was so pleased that He said what shall I send Mr. Bartram — I proposed His History — He paused, I said how Aceptable such a Thing would be — In short without entering into a Detail or a Little Contrivance — He has sent it thee as a present and will Come by Wright   The Mole I sent Him He was much pleased with It because it was New & Different from ours, but the Insects made Sad Havoc with It   a better specimen will please better — the Mole & blew Stone I sent Him & others   if thee hath a Specimen of petrifaction gathered on a Hill betwixt the high Lands & Shongo Mounts that I sent Sr Hans, I should like such another   the Wasps nests of both sorts was new, and pleased Much — He Desires & so do I specimens of the Wasps that are the Builders pticularly Distinguished.

I am Extremely Obliged to Gover Morris & his son for their kind assistance   pray did thee find no sort of Shells on the Verges of these Lakes on the Mountains

I am not a Little Concerned that thou Missed seeing Docr Colden — He is a very Ingenious Intelligent Man and also For thy Disaster in passing the River   pray be very Carefull for the Future and Look before thou Leaps

Of the Seeds thou Sent   the Rose Laurell are Come up and are very thriving, Red Cedar by thousands   White Cedar a few — Sheeps Turds none — must send a young Tree — 2 3 or 4 — White Pine some   Sassafras a few   Sugar Maple a few   All spice a few   witch Hasel one —what they belong too I can't say   Make these Queries to Docr Delenius, has thee

Consulted Miller — the Last being new He may know nothing of Rose Laurell   white Cedar   white pine & Sassafras thou Cannot send to much for Wee can never have Enough of them

I was out in the Country when specimen 105 flowerd but by makeing no seed fancy it is Male   I Heartily Wish a subscription may go on for thy Encouragement for thy Subscribers may soon be furnished and then will withdraw their Subscriptions, some talk of Doing It but more p Cap Wright —

So much I think for thine of July 22d — But before Wee part I must thank thee for thy Dessertation on Whitfield   it has afforded Some Entertainment   He has for Some time made no Noise Here which I presume is on the Account of a Rich Wife he has Lately gott — which may spoil his Spiritual Exercises for the Creature must be minded and gratified Else his bedfellow may Quote the Apostle paul on Him and from the Scripture can bring Cue that Husband should give a wife her due

It's now late and it is with much Difficulty I have Stole this Time to assure thee that I am thy sincere friend,

P. Collinson

BP 2:56; D. 147–50; American Philosophical Society Library, Wildman transcript.
1. The following, taken from Wildman, is probably the sketch to which Collinson referred: "Said to be caught in the Mouth of the River 9ber 10th 1741   going along the Borough Markett Southwark I saw these Shell Fish Lying in Baskett to sell They seem'd New to Mee   I putt them in Salt Water and to my surprise they putt forth at one end of the shell a long proboscis wch they draw In & putt out att pleasure and appears to have two perforations, att its Extreamity   When it is at its full extent (having Imbibed or suck'd In a Quantity of Water) it cannot contract or retire into its shell without first Discharging a Quantity of Water wch it does by Ejecting or Squirting it with some force to the Distance of Two Feet & more   it seems in some part to pertake of the nature & structure of the Solen att that End where the proboscis comes forth wch is Wide enough for it without opening the shells and by it undoubtedly it collects its nourishment   on Boiling was found to be very sweet food" (BP 2:62). This undated fragment probably accompanied the preceding letter.

From CATESBY[1]

Dear Friend
I am much obliged to you for two kind Letters, one of them dated the 20 of July 1741, the other the 15 of October following, the first contained a very accurate Account and dissection of the Chamaerhododendron which gives me so good an idea of its form and colours that are an assistance of the Specimens you Sent when occasion requires [I will] be enabled to give a tolerable figure of it which will be so much the more necessary as there being little probability of ever seeing it in blossom here: Those plants you have already Sent us, plainly show the avertion they have to our Soyl & climate, by their Slow progress & Stunted appearance. In answer to your conjecture of their growing here as well as with you in the like moist land I say that plants which in America grow in moist land are generally killed

when planted in Such [land] here. It is by experience found that a dry warm Soyl is most agreeable to American plants even Aquatics. This I conceive is not from our too great cold in Winter more than with you but from a difficulty of heat in our summers. Wherefore a situation by being warmer may compensate for that difference of heat in a wet situation.

It can hardly be imagined in the Agreement of American plants with our Climate. Though some growing here as well as if they were Native of England; others will not with all the Assistance of Art. The [illegible] is apparently a Cousin German[2] to the Chamaerhoes: and can no more than that be prevailed on to grow with us [illegible] after many years I have one plant that has produced some [illegible] of its beauty these two years past and yet the plant diminishes yearly. I am now to make my gratefull acknowledgements [of your] other Letter of October 1741 accompanying a Case of Plants [which] seemed to be alive and in good order but those Sent by Capt' Dent as you for told miscarryd. Yet I am nothing the [less] obliged to you, such accidents must be expected. When I [illegible] they are plants of ornament I most desire I must leave it to [you] what to send next tho' a few plants of Sassafras and Laurel [will be] acceptable as coming from a colder country than Carolina they will agree better with our Climate

Sassafras Plants taken out of the woods are so bare of roots [they] seldom arrive alive in England. Whereas if they are transplanted [to] a Garden and there remain a year their fibers will increase [and] endure a voyage much better. If the plants you send are somewhat larger it would be better and if it could be they [have] several stems arising from the root are better enabled to [survive the] voyage.

[one or more lines are illegible at the top of a page] that regard her commoner token to claim, and as she Scornes to be familiar with us we must be content with her nigardly floral favours, So that instead of many plants for increase we desire only one large bearing plant with the mould about the roots which may attract annually some Devotees who can no other way admire its beauties   This is also the Opinion of our Friend Pr. Collinson who desired me to mention it to you.

Mr. Clayton mentions a plant in the remote parts of Virg: called Leather Wood. It is a Thymelaea or Spurge Laurel   perhaps the Same of your Leather Wood? Among the Shell Animals of New England one is called the Signoe   its eyes are placed under a covert of thick shell but so ordered that the part above the Eyes is transparent that the creature can see its way tho' otherwise it is blinded these are somewhat like the Eyes of a Mole which are covered with a thin Skin to fit it for working under ground

In New England is also The Monkfish having a hood like a Fryer's cowl

In Baker's Cave in New England are Scarlet Mussels yielding a juice of a purple colour that gives so deep a dye that no water can wash it out.

I am told of an Animal in Pensilvania called a Monax and by some a Ground hog it lives and burrows under ground and Sleeps much   it is about the Size of a Rabbet   I shall be glad of what you know concerning it.

Have you Observed any other of the Deer kind, besides the Moose, Elk and common Deer? Do you think that the black Fox common in North America is a different Species or only varying in colour from the common gray fox?

There is a Bird in Virginia and Carolina and I suppose in Pensilvania that at Night calls Whipper Will & sometimes Whip Will's widdow by which names they are called (as the Bird clinketh, the fool thinketh). I have omitted to describe it & therefore should be glad of it. I believe it is a kind of Cukoo.

Your House Swallow is different from ours & singular in its tail & Nest which is artfully made with Small Sticks and cemented together with a kind of glue   the Bird with the nest would be acceptable

With what I now send of my Book you have all the American Small Birds that I have figured except 7 or 8 by which you may guess what other Birds your Country affords. But such observations may be too troublesome without a Strong inclination   New Animals of any kind are Always Acceptable   Birds are best preserved (if not too large) by drying them gradually in an Oven and when Sent cover them in Tobacco dust   There is no other way in preserving Fish and Reptiles than in Spirits or Rum which method will also do for Birds

I present you now the second and third part of my Book in retaliation of your kindness

Think not my good friend that I expect you to comply [with] all I mention, or anything more than what Suits your convenience, for tho' my method is to make a memorandum of what will be acceptable, it is with no other intent —Some things may offer or come in your Way when others   [do not]

Plants { A large plant of
Sasafras
Laurel
Wood Honeysuckle white }

Different kinds of Turtles
Fish etc

I am Mr Bartram With all Sincerity

Your Obliged Friend and Servant
M Catesby

BP 1:96; D. 321–23.
1. The date of this letter is obliterated, but it was written in March 1741/42 (see Collinson to Bartram, March 3, 1742). The right-hand margin is badly eroded, hence the many brackets.
2. A first cousin.

From COLLINSON

Lond March 3 1741/2

Dear frd John

By Our good friend Capt Wright I have sent Sr Hans kind psent of his Natural History of Jamaica in 2 Vols: these I have put in a Box I had made on purpose for them & Directed It on Two places for thee & with it I sent on board In a Canvass wrapper a Large Bundle of paper, a psent from Docr Delenius wch I think will furnish thee with paper for Specimens and for Seeds for thy Lifetime   it is fine Duch paper and very fitt for such purposes because it will bear ink   it is the printing of His Hortus Elthamensis   a very Curious Work when the Cuts are with It —

I thank thee for the pelitory of Spain seed   the Name Girondella was by mistake applyed to it. I had only one Root survived the hard Winter of 1739–40 — the Root is Esteem'd Excellent for the Tooth ache   if from a Cold Humour a little Slice Laid to the Tooth will draw out the Cold Rheum — Amongst the Many Curious Herbaceous seeds there is the Collinsonia Omitted which I am solicited for, both att Home & a broad and can't oblyge my Frds with — for tho Mine grows strong & flowers finely yett our summers are not Sufficient to bring its seed to perfection —

For this Reason thee must Send all sorts of Herbaceous seeds over again, as they happen ripe in thy Way — for unless such plants as Increase from the Root most others go off in a year or Two — Especially those beautiful small yellow flowering Sunflowers, Obeliscothecas, or Crysanthemums (all names nearly Synonymous) which are Biennials & flower & then die & by sliping or Laying or any other Art I have not been able to perannuat them, whereas the Low Dwarfe sort with a size Larger flower continues many years in the Ground and makes a fine show all summer, with Its yellow flowers with purplish bottoms, this Mr. Catesby brought first from Virginia   I think thou found it there also —

I am much obliged to thee for the noble root of Skunk Root   I divided it into 3 parts so that I hope I shall be now so furnished as not to want again all the other things was in fine order so that I now begin to Long to see them peep there being so many fine things amongst them   the Chamaerhododendrons move very slow   they seem to like Lord Petres Soil Better — they seem to Die Dayly with Mee & I have tried them in different Methods —

I was much delighted with the birds' nests in pticular with the Hanging Nests wch are most Wonderfully Fabricated & seem to be of Two Sorts — as M Catesby Intends to send thee his History of American Birds, Both he as well as myself Desire to know the Birds they belongs too them for He does not remember to have seen them and also that Bird thou Calls a Marsh Wren   these thou may send over to his Name & folio for I have the same by Mee and so when any Eggs comes pray tie a Label with the Bird's name according to his Catalogue   I Desire the Little Mans acceptance of the Picture Books that sent them Mee — the Swallows Nest is Exactly the same as Ours & Built in the Same Manner & with the same materials — but what I greatly want is the Swallow or Martins Nest that Builds in Chimneys these nests are of a Different Curious Make being a sort of Basket work very pretty and Different from any Nest I Ever saw, Mr Catesby had one sent him from Virginia & the Eggs are Different in shape from others — this is so nicely Constructed that it requires a very steady hand to take it without breaking —

The Two Humming Birds nests are neatly Built but it would be an Addition to their Curiosity to Cutt off the Twig that they are Built on with the Nest on It — pray from what do they gather that wolley or Downey composition that is inside of their Nests for it is much finer & softer then sheeps Wool — Lady Petre Wants a Nest & Eggs & an old dead Humming Bird   Cock & Hen

I observe In the Shells of your Museles there is Rudiments of perle —that is perle Like protuberances   Is there none ever found In them — I have some taken out of yr oysters but those from your Musele are of a Better Complection for they Generally ptake of the Complection of the Shell — I think I observed Three Different sorts of Museles found with you [illegible] pray from which Species of Firr or Pine was those Bladders Gatherd — our Balm Gilead Firr sweats out Tears of Balsame from the Budds in the Summer months

I thank thee for the Sweet Gum or Liquid Amber as we Call It & for the White Cedar Gum   I never Saw any before   It is odd to Call a plant souer Gum or Bla Gum and it not produce any — But when thou observes any Trees gum that Wee have not pray think of Mee, and to send Mee Two or Three Roots of Growing Gensang and Polygalla or Seneka Snake Root if they happen to be seen in thy Rout   I want them in my Garden & Serpentaria of the Shops

I have taken Care to putt the Clay Wasps Nests in Boxes to see their produce   they are Exceeding curious Especially the last Flatt ones wch are prettily Marked with Ribs &c pray are these a New Discovery —

Thy account of the Tumble Bug (Beetle) is very Curious and Entertaining But M Catesby says they have another sort that they Call so in Virginia pray send 2 or 3 More Specimens for I presume they are not scarce   one or Two for Sr Hans with thy Account will wonderfully please Him

the Mapple No 8 to the Leafe in the Small Quire of paper seems to be our English — I know I formerly sent thee some Seeds — all the Mapples thee Described Deserve a place in our plantations —

I thank thee for thy Curious present of thy Mapp & thy Draught of the Fall of the River Oswego   I was really both Delighted & Surprised to See it so Naturally Done and at thy Ingenuity in the performance — upon my Word Friend John I can't help Admiring thy Abilities in so many Instances   I shall be Sparing to say what more I think   A man of thy prudence will place this to a right account   to Encourage thee to proceed Gently in these Curious things wch belong to a Man of Leisure & not to a Man of business   the Main Chance must be minded — many an Ingeneous Man has Lost himself for want of this Regard — by Devoting too much of his Time to these Matters   a Hint thee will take in Friendship   thy obliging Grateful Disposition may Carry the to farr   I am glad & Delight much in all these things   none more   but then I would not purchase them at the Expense of my Friends precious Time to the Detriment of his Interest & Business — (now, Dear John, take me right)   I showed them Sr Hans   He was much pleased — Ld Petre Deservedly much admires them and indeed does Every one that sees them, when they are told who was the performer

All this is writt by rote or per Memory for I dare not, nay, I cannot Look into thy Letters for I have no time to Add More but to tell thee In the Trunk of the Liby Comp thee'll find a Suit of cloths for thy self this may serve to protect thy outward Man being a Druget Coat, Bla Colld Waistcoat & shagg[1] breeches and now that thou may See that I am not thoughtles of thy better part I send thee R. Barclay's Apology to replenish thy Inward man so farewell Success attend thee in all thy Expeditions, The first Leisure will Consider all thy Letters, thay are all Carefully laid up the chrysalises are all in fine order I am in hopes of some new Beauties I can now add no more but that I am thine

P. Collinson

as these are very precarious uncertain Times I have insured to the value of Tenn pounds that all may not be lost —

Inclosed is the mates receipt for Sr Hans Sloans Books & Docr Delenius paper — there is a Map & another pcell or Two beside for thee & Catesbys books & Docr Delenius will Send thee his history of Mosses

BP 2:58; D. 150–53.
1. Wool or silk cloth with a velvet finish.

From CATCOTT

Bristol March 13 1741/42

Sir,

This brings you my acknowledgments of yr favour by Capt. Davies; I have communicated of all ye seeds to my acquaintance Dr. Dillenious who (as I find by his Historia Muscorum just published) is not unknown to you. I presume Mr. Miller (who is also my acquaintance) is furnished via London. If in your travels you find any of the lily tribe I'd be glad to have ye good fortune & will be ready to make you amends in any way you will point out. Dr. Dillenius in one to me mentions a plant in Plukenet Tab. 79, Fig. 6 a cyclamen as a native of yr Colony which he sh'd be glad of. There is a martagon that blows a large yellow flower spotted with black call'd the Canada Martagon wch I think you have in plenty, I have a plant or two but very small. I am no great Botanist; but from the care of a garden have some knowledge of plants; but those I desire of any friend are such as to make something of an appearance in a collection. If I can any way serve you here you have a right to command me who am Sir

yr oblig'd humble servant
Alex. Catcott

I wrote you some time since via London

BP 1:100.

To BAYARD[1]

Many of my friends both in Jersey & pensilvania hath proposed A method to engage me devote my life chiefly to ye observation of natural productions & curious inqueries of ye formations & qualities of ye vegitable animal mineral & fosils with perticular descriptions of every curiosity that comes under my observation with A exact map draught or picture in ye four provincial governments of new york Jersey pensilvania & maryland with ye purpose to travail until I have observed ye course & productions of ye rivers creeks mountains & plains in each government & as in ye travails hitherto I have laboured under ye great inconveniency of being always in a hurry & care for my family which hindered me from making such accurate remarks as I otherways should have done if I had more leasure   In order to promote this designe several gentlemen hath subscribed to an annual sum & set their hands to A paper containing ye proposal[2] & A copy of which I send thee another to west[3]

> A COPY of the Subscription Paper, for the Encouragement of Mr. John Bartram promised in our last.
>
> Botany, or the Science of Herbs and Plants, has always been accounted in every Country, as well by the Illiterate as by the Learned, an useful Study and Labour to Mankind, as it has furnished them with Cures for many Diseases, and their Gardens, Groves and Fields with rare and pleasant Fruits, Flowers, Aromaticks, Shades and Hedges.
>
> And as the Wilderness, Mountains and Swamps in America, abound with Variety of Simples and Trees, whose Virtues and proper Uses are yet unknown to Physicians and curious Persons both here and in Europe; it should be esteem'd fortunate, and a general Benefit, if a Man could be found sufficiently skilful and hardy, who would undertake, as far as in his Power, a compleat Discovery of such Herbs, Roots, Shrubs and Trees, as are of the Native Growth of America, and not described in Herbals or other Books.
>
> And as John Bartram has had a Propensity to Botanicks from his Infancy, and to the Productions of Nature in general, and is an accurate Observator, well known in Pennsylvania, where he was born and resides, to be a Person fitted for this Employment: acquainted with Vegetables and Fossils, and Books treating of them; of great Industry and Temperance, and of unquestionable Veracity; and has by many Ships sent over to some of the Members of the Royal Society in London, at their Request, Plants, Seeds and Specimens, as were new and unknown to them (and received by them as Curiosities) in order to be farther discovered and made useful by the Learned and Ingenious there, who have yearly return'd him Names for them, and Accounts of some of their Virtues; we the Subscribers, to induce and enable him wholly to spend his Time and exert himself in these Employments, have proposed an annual Contribution for his Encouragement; with which he being made

acquainted, and it agreeing with his benevolent Temper, he has promised some of us, that if it appears by what shall be subscribed, that he can maintain himself and Family, and defray the Expences he must sometimes unavoidably be at in long Journies for Guides and Assistance, he will without delay dispose his Affairs at Home, and undertake what is desired of him; and that his Searches after Vegetables and Fossils, shall be throughout the Governments of New-York, the Jerseys, Pennsylvania and Maryland; and that whatsoever he meets with worthy of Notice, in the Places and Things before mentioned, and in the Form, Situation and Produce of Mountains, Lakes, Springs, Grottoes, Rivers, &c. he will describe and yearly communicate to the Subscribers in the best Manner he can.

We the Subscribers, do therefore severally promise, for Us, our Heirs, Executors and Administrators, to pay him yearly the Sums annex'd to our Names for three Years next ensuing, he for so long time industriously employing himself in the Premises.

N.B. *Subscriptions are taken in at the Post-Office in Philadelphia. Near £20 a Year is already subscribed.*

BP 1:20:4.
1. Addressee uncertain; letter undated, but ascertained to have been written around March 1742 because of the date of publication of the proposal.
2. The proposal was published in the *Pennsylvania Gazette,* March 17, 1741/42.
3. Unidentified.

From COLLINSON[1]

Lond March 20 174$\frac{1}{2}$

Frd John

I have Rece'd thy Orders as under for Seeds to be sent next Fall   a Duplicate of this will Come by Capt Wright but for Fear of Accidents and that thou may have thy Commission in Time I send this p Capt Gill via New York that thou may Have it in time Enough to Look for Seeds Required & pray Collect some Roots of Genseng & Seneca Root & other Snake Root if it happens to be Mett with in thy Rambles

I am Truly thine

P Collinson

all the Goods thou Desired will Come in the Library Companys Trunk of Books p Capt Wright & other Letter &c[2]

A Catalogue of Seeds for Year 1742

For the Duke Norfolk   To Send Two or Three Cases of pine Cones if kept to full size & well packed att Ten Guineas each but mind no Jersey or Dwarf pine for of these Wee have Enough

The Long Coned pine or Lord Weymouths pine with five Leaves   the Seed to be taken out of the Cones & Sent by it Self in Sand for hitherto att Rate the Seed is Sent it costs a Guinea or Two an ounce   all parties Desire Some of this pine Seed as much as can be afforded   also they Desire Winged Leafe Toxicodendron or Poison Oke   Treble spined Accacia or Honey Locust Chinquapins   I query wether these are found in any plenty with you   if they are be sure to send them   Send a Ten Guinea Case of these Seeds for Lord Petre and a Ten Guinea Case of the Same Sorts of Seeds for the Duke of Richmond & Phil Millar only add Some pine Cones to theirs but mind no Jersey or Dwarf pine   they all complain that their Last Cases & Cargoes were Less than Usuall   Seeds Balm Gilead Firr   all other sorts of Spruce Firrs   Small Coned or Hemlock Firr   Beech Lime Tree   all sorts of Hickories   Dog wood   Long Walnutts   all sorts of Maples & any New pine   Flowering Shrub or Forest Tree   Sassafras   Allspice   all Sorts of Herbaceous Seeds   for myself Growing Roots of Genseng   Seneca Root   Serpentaria or other Snake Root

BP 2:65; American Philosophical Society Library, Wildman transcript.
1. Addressed to "Joseph Breintnall Mercht in Philadelphia Pensilvania for J. Bartram p. Capt Gill via N. York."
2. From this point, the letter has been taken from Wildman.

From COLLINSON

Lond: Aprill 24, 1742

Fr John

   Mr Catesby Desires that thou wilt Look after a Night Bird call'd WipperWill — if this can be shot & sent in its Feathers being first Bowel'd, — & Dry'd in a slack Oven, & then Tie'd up in Tobacco Leaves or pack'd up in Tobacco Dust   pray observe if it is cock or Hen   this may be seen in takeing out its Gutts, if it has Testicles or No —

   What I have further to Desire is to Look after the Horns of that Monstrous Deer or Elk that thee Mentions to be Shot by an Indian in a Swamp.

   Possibly if thee makes Broad Hints to our worthy Friend Gover. Morris, He may send His pair – for they are Rare things Here & I want to Examine them with the Fossil Horns that are Dugg up in Ireland, for they do not Belong to our European Elk – and unless they do with yours the Species of Creature seems to be Lost — Wee should be glad to know something Certain of Its size or to See its Hoof —

   I have writt in perticular in J. Breitnall's Letter & Sent sundry things in their Trunk — & a Box of Sr Hans Books & a Bundle paper from Do. Delenius all wch I hope will Come Safe to hand —

   I also writt in perticular thy orders for Seeds this Year per Cap Wright & per the way of New York
   I am in Haste much thine

P Collinson

To Joseph Breintnall Mercht in Philadelphia
for John Bartram

Haverford College Library, Charles Roberts Autograph Letters Collection.

From COLLINSON

April 25 1742

Dr frd
    I have the pleasure of thine Inclosed in Frd Bland's Letter of March the 7th   I think I have answered all the articles per my sundry Letters however I will again take notice of them — the Clay Wasps Nests I admire much Especially those on the piece of Wood But ye Damp of the Ship made the Clay Moist so that they was Drop'd off   however it shows the Nature of the Insect they being pack'd with such Judgment came Safe to my hands, I admire much their fabrication and have putt them in proper boxes covered with gauze that I may see Their produce for by their make they seeme to be of Two sorts — Thou may Depend great Care is taken of Every thing thou Sends — wee are Dayly in Expectation & in hopes to see the Sundry Crysalis's produce if there is but Male & Female   we are Resolved to Lett them Unite & see their Eggs & Doubt not the Bringing them up So it may be always necessary to hint the Trees they are found on for the article is to procure proper food & now Wee have most of yr Common Trees in plenty that may be in pt removed
    There were some fine Insects in the Box & very Beautifull but the Major pt was sadly Eaten or Lacerated by some mischievous Insect   it is a thousand pitys it can't be prevented   If there was tobacco Dust or Leaves spread over the bottom & the Insects pinned on that it might be a Means to prevent it for the future — the first Leisure I shall show those relating to the Animals to our friend Catesby —
    The Monac I know well — proved a pretty Domestic Animal   Lived with Sr Hans Sloane many years and ran about House like a Catt — is one of the Sleepers for he made a Nest in the Cellar & went Into It in 9:ber & came out in March or Aprill   Wee were in hopes thee might have known something more pticular of It — being so remarkable in its Nature
    I am glad to know what you Call the Two Specimens I sent thee   the water birch & the Arrow Wood was sent Mee by Doc Witt but under what name I cant now Remember   the Last is a pretty flowering Tree & the first that was in England   Wee have this & another Species of it in plenty but if there is any other sorts Wee shall be glad of them —
    the Box of Berries & Map p Capt Bound came safe & Well — I much admire thy Performance   It really conveys a good Idea of that wonderfull Natural Cascade —
    to day I breakfasted with Sr Hans   He always Inquires after thee   I hope his Books p Wright will Come safe to hand and all other things   the

whips and other Goods I have putt in the Library Companys Trunk to save Charges & Mr Catesby's Books with many others —

Docr Lawson gives his Humble Service to thee & our Frd Wooley   I wish I could have a specimen of that Large piece of polished Iron ore sent Him Last pcell   He Intends a psent to Mr. Wooley but does not know what to Send   Docr Lawson tells Mee that he had recommended a very Curious Knowing Man in Ores to E Wooley   pray show Him to

M. Catesby Desires a Dry'd bird of a Night Bird who has a Note that sounds like whipperwill which he Chants all night Long

pray Look after the Elk Horns   Phaps a broad hint may procure a Gift of those from Governor Morris

My first Leisure I shall read over all thy Letters again & then will take further notice of them   I have sent thy order for next years Collection by this ship & p way of New York per Captain Gill

So hope there will be no occasion to say more but that I am thy sincere friend,

P Collinson

I shall be Delighted too heare that thy Subscription goes on   my Love to Frd Bland & thanks for his Care of thy Letter

BP 2:66; D. 153–54.

From DILLENIUS

Oxford May 13th 1742

Good Friend Mr. Bartram,

I received Yours of Novemb. 14th 1741. together with the Mosses and good Completely fair Specimens, except the Lycopodium, which seems to me as if it hath been [put] up damp. Tho' they were few in Number, yet I observe two new sorts, viz. one [from] an ould Tree that you gathered on the Laurel, upon the Mountains towards Susquehana of which if you have any left, I desire you will send me some more — the other is the above mentioned Lycopodium, which you found in Koves in a wet place at the foot of a Mountain near Susquehana, which I think, differs from that, which groweth in Jersey. I suppose you mean Lycopodium Tab. LXII. of my History of Mosses, from which it differs, in having slenderer Spikes & Stalks. The Specimen I had is whitish, withered & was mouldy therefore desire you should send me better ones & don't wrap them up like those, spread it so as it grows naturally. Describe it in what manner it grows & what colour the Leafes & Spikes be of, when fresh, whether the Spikes rises upright, lean, or whether they ly on the Ground. I should be glad to know [more] of the 8th sort, viz. whether the Spikes lean, or grow upright.

Per trusty Friend P. Collinson I have desired to send you this book in perusing of which you will frequently find mention made of your name of finds of yours & any as You found new ones, especially in the last Table, which I hope it will encourage you to look after those things, when you happen to wild Places, where they grow plentifull. You may send me from time to time, what comes to your Hands & what you think is new, which you may find easily out by the said History & comparing the figures of the plants, you find. If new Sorts comes in, I may perhaps [add] another Plate or two. But above all, let me have a share when you send any: There is a Clinopodium (Field or Wild Basil) in Virg. Maryl. & Pensylv. with a row of purple Leafes round the fine Yellow hooded Flowers, with red spots, which I should be glad [to have] Seeds of. I am not sure, what is meant by the Spinning Yucca? I want to know, whether it be that Sort, whose Leafs [illegible] – its 2th of Millers Dictionary & the Clinopodium is the 5th of the same. If you send to Mr. Collinson at London, or to Mr. Catcott at Bristol (whom I hear corresponds with you) will come safe to me. I am your obliged friend & Servant

J J Dillenius

You have sent once seeds of a Yucca from Virginia, pray was it the Spinning leav'd Yucca? I raised for 2-years plants of it, but are all gone off, should be glad to have some fresh seeds.[1]

American Philosophical Society Library, Miscellaneous Manuscripts Collection.
1. Collinson added the following note: "I think you have only that yucca that has threds coming from [illegible] for wch Reason Wee Call it the Spining yucca — Butt I have a [illegible] Leafed one that grows abt. 4 foot high from Canada and another with Leaves that grows 6 or 8 foot high from Carolina that has [illegible] and I have another with Narrower Leaves but where that is from I dont know — these 4 sorts I have and all I have."

To CATCOTT

May ye 26th 1742

Respected Friend Alexander Catcot
I have now before me thy two kind letters of February ye 2d & March ye 13th   I am well pleased those seeds I collected for thee was acceptable I find by thy letter thee supposeth I was born in England but I asure thee I was born in Pensilvania & never been out of sight of land since & I believe hath taken more pains after ye study of botany & ye operation of nature than any other that was born in english america notwithstanding my low fortune in ye world which laid me under ye necessity of very hard labour for ye support of my family having now a wife & seven smal children whose subsistance depends on ye produce that is raised on my farm which is scituate on A navigable river near Philadelphia but I have had ever since I was 12 years of age A great inclination to botany & natural history but could not make much improvement therein for want of bookes or other instruction until I entered into Correspondence with my good friend Peter

Collinson who ingaged first Lord peter then Philip Miller & ye duke of richmond & Norfolk to subscribe 30 guineas in order to enable me to travail into maryland virginia new Jersey & york Government to search for forest seeds roots & plants to adorn thair gardens & other apartments where thay thought proper to dispose of them   thay have allso sent me varieties of root & seeds for my garden & several books for my instruction   to my friends Doctor Dilenius & Mr. Catesby I send my observations on such things as will be proper Materials to assist them in composing thair fine history for which thay promised me one of thair books   Sir Hans Sloan desired I would send him some Curiosities which I did last fall for which I hear he hath sent me his two books of ye history of Jamaica which I expect every day   we have great variety of Martagons   I have sent my friend Collinson many which flowred finely in his garden   thee may expect a curious Colection of them & other fine flowers from me by ye first opertunity   Marchant Willing[1] expresses A mighty respect for thee & saith he will do any thing in assisting me to oblige thee   what plant plucnet[2] names A Cyclamen that is A native of our Colony I cant imagine   indeed we have several plants whose leaves somewhat resemble it but thay belong to other tribes & I saw A plant near ye mountains of virginia whose leaves had ye apearance of A Cyclamen in ye shape & marks of its leaves but realy was A species of ye asarum   if I knew how Plucnet discribed his Cyclamen I could Judge better but I could never yet have ye happiness to read any of ye valuable author's books, tho much desired   I believe there is not one of them in our parts   our americans hath very little tast for these amusements   I cant find one that will bear ye fatigues to accompany me in my peregrinations therefore Consequently thee may suppose I am often exposed to solitary & difficult travailing beyond our inhabitants & often under dangerous circumstances in passing over rivers climbing mountains and presipices amongst ye rattle snakes and often obliged to follow ye track or path of wild beasts for my guide through these desolate and gloomy thickets [remainder of letter torn off].

BP 1:28:4; D. 324–25.
1. Probably Charles Willing, Philadelphia merchant, born in England.
2. Leonard Plukenet.

To CATESBY[1]

thee mentions [illegible] I have heard of some being white as well as some haires   ye black fox I know nothing of   we have ye red fox much larger then [illegible] & seems more of ye nature of ye wolf & kills lambs   having long legs never climbs trees but when after A long chase takes into ye ground for safety   I have seen scores of black squirrels beyond ye mountains & one milk white with black eyes: our whipperwill our people takes to be ye same that thee Calls ye goat succer   one may see hundred of them flying about towards evening in ye fall or latter end of summer   if thay be not ye same thing thay are much alike[2]   I have often found thair nests which is A little Concave on ye bare ground in which thay lay large speckled eggs   I should be much obliged to thee if thee would be so kind to send me a little of your best Colors which tho Clumsily done might give you some idea of thair natural perfections   I shall endeaver to send thee whatever I can conveniently procure of those things thee mentioned   I believe we have many kinds of birds in our northern Colonies which thee hath not drawn in thy natural history but I hear nothing of thy two books which thee wrote mee the had sent   if I had them now this spring I could see what kinds thee had figured   we have a great white & gray owl   A raven   A large kite   gray & white heron   comorant   wood kock   mountain pheasant   crow   several kinds of ducks with many smaller birds   several kinds of snakes   many kinds of fishes & turtles   I am not sure that we have above four distinct kind to many variety of colors   I have formerly seen a fine red lyzard 5 or 6 inches long spotted with I think black spots   lives in & near cold springs of water   hath thee seen A muskrat none of these I dont remember to have seen in thy books

BP 1:29:3.
1. Incomplete and undated, but probably written in the late spring of 1742 (see Catesby to Bartram, March 1741/42).
2. The birds that Bartram saw flying at dusk were probably the common nighthawk, *Chordeiles minor*.

To COLLINSON[1]

[May 29, 1742]

[illegible] which groweth 3 or 4 foot Diameter & of A curious pyramidel shape whose plyant branches is bended by gentle zephyrs or [illegible] side of ye leave is everted & displayed being wafted to & fro which strikes ye eye agreably   this Charming natural disport which I have beheld on our northern rivers banks when Phoebus reflects his golden ray upon this pretty silver Colored object   ye other smaller key is our red Flowering maple being flowers   this tree groweth 5 foot diameter   most of the seeds of these is perfect whereas ye sugar maple not one in fifty often times that will vegetate   I am glad to hear of so many of ye forest seeds growing and as sorry to hear ye sheep turds miscarries   it is a charming bush when in full bloom 3 foot high & excellent for hedges   ye 30th of may 1742 yesterday I received thy kind letter of March ye 20th via New York which was very acceptable   I wish it had come sooner   I could have sent a fine parcel of early maple seeds which was ripe ye beginning of May or April   it was prudently done to send it via York for if it had come by Capt wright I should not have had it next month which would be two late

John Bartram

BP 1:28:5.
1. This letter is incomplete and without salutation or date, but the latter is evident from the content.

From COLLINSON

London: June 16: 1742

Dr John

not any of the Wasps belonging to the Clay Nests are yett Come out, nor any of the Crysalis — which wee much wonder at — Yett Wee are not yett without Hopes

And Hitherto as Bad Luck attends the growing plants   Several Curious things in the Clods of Earth dont appear — Especially those Iris Like flowers from Cape May wch Wee both so much admire which may be owing to our Long Cold Dry Spring — one Gentian with small narrow Leaves appears & I think 2 of the Witch Hazel   1 Snake Root   the Skunk weed thrives Well   one Lychnis but I have a Lychnis from docr Witt Different from any yett that I have seen   it seems to be the king of that Tribe   its Stalk is near as thick as my little finger (which is but small for a Man)   it is now about 2 foot high and yett no flowers appear   the Stalk is most finely Spotted wch is very Distinguishing from all the Rest that I have seen — one or two of the Sassafras sprout but I can't Depend on them for they will often go after that —

the Ground Hogg I presume may be the Monac of Lawson   does it ptake nothing of our Badger wch Gesner[1] Mentions, phaps our Learned Friend J Logan can show thee its Description

pray Remember some growing Roots of Genseng & Tennants Snake Root — what thou Calls a Black scinc,[2] Wee should be glad to know   Send a skin or draw his picture — whether it belongs to Rabbitt, or Squirrel Fox or what — I am delighted to Hear that thou has a prospect of a Subscription I wish it may operate   it will be a fine opportunity for us Both   I hope all things came safe p our good Frd Capt [illegible] Doc Delenius has sent the [illegible] of His History of Mosses   It comes in a Trunk of Books to James Read[3] and in a Little box some fresh Poppy seed

[The following is written on the outside of the letter.]
When any More Marsh Martagons happens in thy Road think on Mee & Send a Root or Two & Seed of Collinsonia

I am concerned thee Sent all the Lychnis with a Red Eye   it seems to Delicate a plant to bear Conveyance   all my Art could not Secure it   Mr Catesby would be glad to know the Birds Belonging to that Curious Nest thee Sent Mee, if in his Book   this I hinted before —

the Dayse Seed sow as Soone as thou Receives It by scattering it on Light Ground — I am sure there is Some I sent before — Take care of Weeds Choaking them   the may Expect Variety for they are from 5 or 6 Different Sorts

I have received none since thine of March 20th that I answer'd

[The last several lines are badly faded and impossible to read.]

BP 2:67; D. 156–57.
1. Conrad von Gesner's *Historia Animalium* (Zurich, 1551–58).
2. Possibly *skink,* a lizard.
3. Unidentified.

To COLLINSON[1]

I now have before me thy kind letter of February ye 3d [1741/42] & am glad to hear my cargo & letters is safe arived by Captains Whright & brown   I am well pleased my account of ye sea muscle is delightful to thee   I can at present give very little account of our ground hog   our people takes very little notice of them & thay are seen [illegible] our back inhabitants catcheth them & regales upon thair carcas as also ye wild cats & panthers which our mountaineers accounts as delicious [illegible] I have not seen one this year   ye butternut which you take to be what we call a white or long walnut grows in plenty up our rivers beyond our mountains where it is called ye butternut   I am pleased with thy caution about inoculating ye small pox   I now have 7 children alive & but two of them had it   I have wished often that thay had them but it seems a presumption if we believe in an over power that regards our actions to afflict ourselves we ought rather to implore his devine aid; to preserve himself is often ye cause of his own confusions   an example we have in ye words of Moses Come let us build us a City a tower whose top may reach up to heaven [illegible] be scattered abroad upon ye earth   there was two boys inoculated in our neiborhood with ye small pox & both died   one of them was his parents onely child ye other was forced by his parents against his will to be sacrificed   I am pleased to hear that ye mole was new   I hope soon to give you a Natural history of them   I have since I sent you that one found two ould ones & a nest of young ones before I received thy answer else I should have sent them   I have yet to learn thair ways of working which transports me with rage & admiration thay being ye most troublesome creature we are troubled with on any marsh banks & least taken notice of by reason of ye trouble to catch them indeed seeing them   we have allso a large marsh mouse near a half foot long in ye body   thay swim ye water as dry as a duck   I am heartily obliged to thee for thy trouble in procuring a present from Sir Hans Sloan   I long to see these books or any other natural history   it is very instructive (if embellished with accurate observations and matter of fact)   it enlargeth our idea exceedingly but we are poorly furnished with such books   few people are minding such amusements pray give my respects to Sir Hans for his kindness   I shall endeavor to oblige him again   Several of our Library Company talks of making me a present of a shair of thair Library which will be very acceptable to me but I dont think it will answer to give six pounds to purchase a shair & ten shillings yearly (they having few books of botany or natural history)   as to my spending so much for books I perticularly want from london. I did not observe any shels on ye verge of those lakes I saw whose banks was very steep but I was informed some of them had some   in ye specimen thee mentions 105 I have two roots what hath had abundance of male flowers I have another plant that hath not flowered nor I believe will not this year we have a chance for this   it may prove to be a female plant. Thee writes as if my subscribers would withdraw thair subscriptions   if it were to be so I would not accept of such a small one as I believe our people would make I have many small children to be provided for with food & raiment so that I can hardly leave home & ye chief motive of my accepting them was that I might have a better opertunity of furnishing you more abundantly in the Curiosities   I have a box of cedar berries that was sent to me from Carolina   thay are in ye bottom of ye box over which is ye keys of our great silver jaged leaved maple writ large on it

BP 1:29:4.
1. Undated, but written in the summer of 1742 (see Bartram to Collinson, December 18, 1742).

From COLLINSON

Londn: July 3: 1742

Oh Frd John

I can't Express the Concern of Mind that I am under on so many Accounts   I have lost my Frd – my Brother   the man I Loved & was dearer to Mee than all men – is no More, I could fill this Sheet, and many more, But oh my anxiety of mind is so great that I can hardly write & yett I must Tell thee that on Friday July 2d our dear friend Ld Petre was Carried off by the small-pox in the thirtieth year of His age   Hard hard Cruel Hard to be taken from his Frds His Family – His Country – in the prime of Life when He had so many thousand Things Locked up in Breast for the Benefit of them all, are now Lost in Embrio

I can go no further but to assure thee that I am thy Frd

P Collinson

All our Schemes are broke

Send no Seeds for him nor the Duke of Norfolk for now   He that gave motion is Motionless — all is att an End

As I know that this will be a great Disappointment to thee   If thee hast a mind to Send the Seeds as was orderd for Ld: P & Duke of Norfolk on thy own Account & Risque I will do what I Can to Dispose of them — the Duke of Norfolk shall have the preference but there is no obliging him to take them, as I had not the Order from Him but from Ld Petre[1]

Send those for the Duke of Richmond & P. Miller

Ld. Petre was a fine, Tall – comely personage Handsome — had the Presence of a Prince yett was so Happily mixt that Love and awe was begot at the same Time, the Affability & Sweetness of his Temper were beyond Expression without the least mixture of pride or haughtiness   Wth an Engaging Smile He always met his Frds — But oh the Indowments of his Mind are not to be Discribed   Few or None could excel Him In the Knowledge of the Liberal Arts & Sciences   He was a Great Mechanic as well as a Great Mathematician, Ready at Figures and Calculations — Elegant in his Tastes   In his Religious Way an Example of great piety, and in his Morals of Great Temperance & Sobriety   no Loose Word or Double Entendre did I Ever hear (this is something of the Man)   For his Virtues & his Excellencies and His Endowments I Loved Him & He Mee, more Like a Brother than a friend.

BP 2:68; D. 157–58.
1. Lord Petre had made plans for the reforestation of Worksop Manor, the estate of his cousin, the duke of Norfolk.

To COLLINSON

July ye 6th 1742

A few hours past I received thy letters of March ye 3d   ye 20th & April ye 25th 1742   yesterday ye ship arrived which our dear friend Captain Wright sailed in from London but alas! hath left her captain asleep in Neptunes Bosom & now such mortal sickness is on board that she is ordered to ride Quarantine below the town   no goods can be got of   I heartily thank Sir Hans Sloan for his kind remembrance of me   I long to see his history & perticularly M. Catesbys books to see what birds he hath figured before I set out next week for A journey along our sea coast where I believe there is many birds which he omited to draw which I shall be very perticular to observe thair dimensions, shape & colors, if I can compel them by the charms of sulphur & nitre & lead, to let me dispose of them as I think most suitable   I shall endeavour to procure lady Petre a humming birds nest & eggs as soon as possible   I have not heard of any being found this year   thay commonly build thair nest upright upon A limb of A tree, & a little shake with ye fall of ye tree separates them   ye fine downy composition is gathered from ye stalks of our Fern   ye bladders of balm which I sent the I gathered on ye Balm of Gilead tree on ye Katskill Mountain   A delicate fragrant liquor as clear as water   I desighn next month to go my self & gather some seed for you which I hope will be as much pleasure to you as fatigue & charge to me to get them   there is no more trust in our americans then curiosity   Colo Salisbury who lives near them sent me last winter A very loving letter afirming he did what he Could to procure them leaving orders when he went to York to gether them but at his return there is none gathered   He sent A man on purpose to ye mountains to gather them but he said ye birds had picked all ye seed out being very fond of them   I am glad my map & draught was acceptable altho Clumsily done having neither proper instruments nor Convenient time being most of them in part of A first day or by candle light haveing no whole original but nature nor time to take A copy being hurried in gathering of [&] packing of seeds   I am greatly obliged to thee for thy necessary present of A suite of clothes which just came in ye right time & Barclay's apology[1] I shall take care of for thy sake, it answers thy advice much better than if thee had sent me one of natural history or botany which I should have spent ten time ye hours in reading of while I might have laboured for ye maintenance of my family   indeed I have little respect to apologies & disputes about ye ceremonial parts of religion which often introduce animosities confusion & disorders in ye mind & sometimes body too but dear Peter let us live in love & innocency & worship ye one allmighty power with serenity of heart in resignation to his will doing to others as we would have them do to us if we was in thair circumstances   living in innocency we may die in hope   then if you dont go to heaven I believe we shant go to hell[2]

BP 1:40:1; D. 158–59.
1. Robert Barclay (1648–1690), Scottish Quaker and author of *An Apology for the True Christian Divinity*, which became one of the Friends' textbooks for many years.
2. Darlington ended the letter with "living in innocency we may die in hope," omitting any reference to heaven or hell!

From CATCOTT

July the 21st 1742

Yours of May 26 came to hand & since I am now informed of a vessell being to sail for Philadelphia on monday, the 22nd consequently have but bare time to write a short answer to yrs.

I have read yr. account of yrselfe & circumstances with pleasure; I fancy that way of life is some thing after the patriarchal manner; amidst plenty, and with simplicity of manners; & much happier, I believe; than that of those whose business lies amidst the hurry of a large City, or that exposes them to the dangers of the ocean; double much preferable to the pursuit of false pleasures, or the pageantry of greatness wch take all the whole time & thought of so many in our European world; the occupance on yr plantation; while it engageing Care, gives you also an opportunity of contemplating the goodness and greatness of the Creator.

Yr. account of the difficulties and dangers you incounter in yr search after plants, brings to my mind Tournefort's account of his climbing Mount Ararat where as he (pleasantly) says, he had like to have dyed a martyr to Botany. But in the midst of yr hardship is not the discovery of some beautifull vegetable. [Following line illegible.] have gone thru the fatigues of an Indian expedition; for the pleasure of taking the game but my constitution hath long been broken with weakness & the robust exercises of the field have given way to the amusements of my garden. My taste, I own, is rather is [sic] intrinsically valuable for its beauty, that wch, is so only because uncommon. And I do not scruple sometimes to transplant a field flower into my border if its beauty be sufficient to recommend it; plants as bear large colour'd flowers, & do not take up too much room in my garden are my fancy; principally lilys, narcissus, &c, that is, the bulbous tribe in generall; I wait with impatience for the Collection you promise me; that all discoveries are not only innocent & agreeable but may tend to the benefit of mankind by the discovery of usefull plants but undoubtedly engage every one to whom you communicate yr. rarities, to admire & acknowledge the beneficence & bounty of that Being who made the Earth for man's use, and covered it with such a pro[fuse] variety of beautifull productions.

Of the Seeds with which you favoured me, not more than six [?] have come up but I keep the rest carefully [illegible] next spring may effect. I have not plukenet [illegible] till I consult Professor Dillenius. As you correspond I fear my collection can offer you nothing but wt. his may supply something of interest, in due time to send you a Catalogue of the furniture [of my garden]. I desire you to let me have a Catalogue of wt. botanical authors in your possession; perhaps I may be able to add to the number. I am sir

Yr sincere friend
A Catcott

BP 1:101.

To COLLINSON

July ye 24th 1742

I am just returned from amboy & Shrewsbury having waited on Governor Morris & discoursed with him about those great horns which I was informed he kept as A curiosity   he tould me he had sent them to England several years ago   ye beast was killed near albany & was supposed to be above fifteen hundred pounds weight & was excelent good eating   ye horns differed much in shape from those figured in ye transactions of ye Society for ye moose deer   I desighn as soon as I have gathered ye Cones of rose laurel & white pine & sassafras berries to go to ye kats kill to gather ye balm seed & as soon as returned to gather what seed is ripe nearer home, then directly to ye five nations of indians up ye branches of Susquehanna having ingaged our Chief Interpreter[1] to go with me ye beginning of September from whence when I have returned home I hope to give you A good account of my Journey   yesterday & to-day I have been at Philadelphia looking after ye goods & presents thee & our friends sent me   I have found all that thee mentions in thy letter which I received ye goods answer as well as can be expected here – being such abundance of all sorts in our stores that thay stick on our hands   thy presents of clothes are fine & very acceptable as also ye curious presents from M. Catesby & Sir Hans   pray give my hearty thanks to them   I hope by next opertunity to write Largely to them which I hope will be accompanied with some curiosities   I should have sent you some now but ye ship sails sooner than I expected & I as aforesaid just returned home   By reason that there is no vesail that I know of to sail this fall from here directly to bristol but yet notwithstanding to alleviate thy disappointment I have sent about 50 different sorts of seeds of our finest wild flowers gathered in their best state of ripeness & well dried & sent with Doctor Dillenius parcel & directed for thee & if our winter should prove moderate any vesail should go from hence to bristol before spring I shall endeavour to send A box of roots

This comes, with sincere respect & good will, from thy friend,

J. B.

BP 1:40:2; D.159–60.
1. Conrad Weiser, interpreter for the province.

To COLLINSON

Sept 5th 1742

dear peter
I am lately returned from ye Cats kill Mountains – having gathered A fine parcel of ye Balm Cones Just at ye time of thair full ripeness with many other curious seeds and other fine Curiosities   this hath been A happy journey & I met with our friend doctor Colden who received & entertained me with all ye demonstrations of civility & respect that was Convenient   he is one of ye most facetious agreeable gentlemen I ever met with & his Capacity thee may Judge of by ye last account he gave thee of ye economy of ye 5 Nations & some other subjects which he may soon acquaint thee with   I hope to give thee A fuller account of him this fall when I delineate ye particularities of my Journey   I received thy kind letter of June ye 16th & ye seeds & book of Doctor Dillenius Last night   I take it to be ye Completest of that kind that ever was wrote for we don't read that Solomon wrote of any plants of humbler growth than the hysop so I conclude he knew as little of mosses as he did of ye plants that grew beyond Lebanon or in america   I am just setting out towards Susquehanna to gather seeds but I question whether I shall go to ye 5 Nations   Our interpreter was obliged

Cadwallader Colden (1688–1776). Portrait by Matthew Pratt. From Howard A. Kelly, *Some American Medical Botanists* (Troy, N.Y.: The Southworth Company, 1914).

to go with A gentleman from Maryland to treat with them while I was on my Journey from Hudsons river which baffled our conclusions

BP 1:28:5; D. 160–61.

To DILLENIUS

ye 14th of ye 9th month 1742

Respected Friend Doctor Dillenius
I received thy kind letter accompanied with thy kind present of thy book of mosses which is very acceptable; as allso A great parcel of paper for specimens and seeds   this summer I have not gathered any mosses because I thought thee wanted no more after thy book was published & this fall I have been long sick since I received thy letter   when I was upon ye Cats kill mountains last August I found A comical species of licopodium which I gathered but lost it upon ye mount in coming down but if I should ever go

there Again I intend to search ye mounts on purpose, having engaged a hearty young felow to go with me & concluded to stay on them A good share of A week day & night but since I have heard of ye death of my good friend Lord Petre I know not whether I shall be employed again & so my journeys may terminate but if I receive orders to travel again I shall endeavour to serve thee   I have Collected A large parcel of seeds for thee & sent in a box directed to P. Collinson   there is ye seed of ye variegated clinopodium & Virginia yuca   this & ye spining yuca is all ye yuca I know   I found A plant at ye falls of James river which I planted in my garden & ye second year shot up A stalk 4 foot high producing A long spike of flowers exceeding sweet smelling like spice but it had ye exact characteristics of an aloe   it hath not flowered this two years

BP 1:26:2; D. 310–11.

To CADWALLADER COLDEN

Philadelphia
ye 25th of Sept. 1742

Respected Friend Doctor Colden

A few days past I received A very Melancholy letter by ye way of New York which gave me an account of ye death of my great & good friend Lord Petre being in ye 30th year of his age & left but one son behind him & he but 9 months ould So that his fine improvements which is ye admiration of ye curious is very like to be laid waste before his son be in A Capacity to look after it: this Noble Lord was one of ye greatest promoters & encouragers of botany & gardening & embellishing of rural seats with exotick varieties of forrest trees & shrubs that perhaps ever lived in Europ & who was my Chief supporter & encourager in my botanical inquiries   This thee may suppose was but disconsolatory news to me who was but begining to recruite from A fit of sickness which Seised me upon ye banks of Susquehana so that I was constrained to return home while I had A little strength left to support me: but now to wave this unpleasant discourse I will enter into our affairs of mutual friendship ye thought of which & ye agreeable Conversation I had ye happy enjoyment of then in thy presence hath since afforded me many pleasant Amusements in Solitude. But now to give thee A little taste of ye regards I have for thy perticular Satisfaction or interest: I will proceed

Mr. Brown[1] after we left thy house concluded to put me in ye shortest way to Sopus went with me along A path leading to ye right hand of Wilemans[2] & when we came to A new Settlement where A Cart road Crossed this path Along which road Brown turned on ye left hand to go to Wilemans who directed me to continue this path about two miles farther & when this path divided in A plain to take ye right hand path ye other leading near browns farm   accordingly I folowed ye right hand path A Considerable way when being upon A plain I observed A large quantity of Seneca snake root growing on both sides ye path near A great dead oake on ye left hand marked as in ye Margent & A little foreward on ye right hand A clump of aspin trees near ye foot of ye hill still riding along I soon Came to A swampy place which I rode over then directly under A ash tree partly bent broke over ye path thence over a little plain ye snake roots still continuing this path soon lead me to ye Duch setlements & thence to ye Palts By these directions I hope thee may easily find these roots which I take October to be ye properest month to gather them in for medicine dear friend my hand is so weake I can hardly hold my pen pray accept these few lines thay being sent in Love from him who sincerely desires thee & thin[e] health & Prosperity

John Bartram

P.S. I am obliged to thee for thy care in sending those two boxes thay are come safe to William Allens I hope to send one of them back full of walnuts thine as before

JB

For Doctor Cadwalader Colden
Surveyor General living near ye High Lands

The Letters and Papers of Cadwallader Colden 1730–1742, 2:272–74 (hereafter, LPCC).
1. Unidentified.
2. Unidentified.

To COLDEN

october ye 23d 1742

Respected Friend Doctor Colden

I received thy kind letter of September ye 25 which was all very agreable Amusement to me as well as A demonstration of thy generous & Communicative disposition with so much Sincerity as if thee designed rather to inform thy friend by rational Conclusions from acurate & mature observation of facts then to impose upon him with incredible & wonderful relations from ye reports of those whose observations penetrated no deeper then ye superficies of nature.

Thy remarks upon ye Britanica as being A good antiscorbutick yet not to be depended upon in A genuin Cancer appears very reasonable but I am pleased with thy account of ye Phitolaca I wish it may be Confirmed by A successfull practice on A ulcerated Cancer pray make further enquiry of ye certainty of it. It hath A great volatil purgence while fresh but upon drying it looseth its emetick & cathartick virtue in A great degree I know not of any plant from my own observation that hath been used with greater success in ulcerated breasts then what Gronovius in flora virginica calls Saururus yet Notwithstanding I dont believe that it would cure an inveterate ulcerated Cancer & now to enlarge further upon specificks let me tel thee

I have known ye root of Colinsonia have A surprising efect in ye Cure of womens after pains & if thee please to accept of A report of an extrordinary Cure performed on ye bite of A rattle snake thee shall have it Cheap as I had it but ye accounts of ye many cures by so many plants of very different natures I perceive hath shocked thy ascent to so many specificks as well as mine. As I was A travailing with our chief interpreter which is one of thy brother turtles & reconed A cincear honest man   he tould me he was once with some indians when one of thair squaws was bit by A (rattle snake) to whom the indians applyed many remedies to none effect she still growing worse untill she was unsensible & ye indians said she would die   then he desired leave of them to try if he could cure her which was readily Granted   then he gathered some of ye leaves of Colinsonia (he showed me ye plant) & boiled them in water & gave her ye direction to drink & presently after she made sighns for more & that she felt ye poison to go from her heart   however as he tould me she soon got well   But to return to ye Britanica   I a few days ago perused A folio volume of botany which gave A perticular account of two species of Britanica   first ye Europian exhibiting A act with A perticular discription thereof quoated Abraham Munting[1] who enlarged much upon ye virtues of it: & after gave A curious discription of ye American or virginian Britanica which for thy Curiosity I send A coppy of it to thee that thee may if thee please Compare the Britanica with it

The American or Virginian Britanica hath A root consisting of A head thick & gouty but not of A round tuberous body like ye former from which head grows downward into ye earth several arms or branches which are thick brownish without & yelowish within   from this root riseth one upright stalk of several feet high which hath allso joynts upon it like knees from whence come forth very long & large leaves strong & hard not much unlike to monks rubarb but that these are much longer   ye stalk which is very like that of other docks riseth up sometimes to A considerable hight about ye midle of which it sends forth A great number of branches not much unlike ye europian which have some few leaves like ye other upon them but less   ye flowers grow in vast numbers upon all these branches single & each upon A short foot stalk even from thair begining up to thair very tops set on spaces at certain distances in A seeming uniform manner   after ye flowers are past away ye seed comes which is contained in A chafy husk like ye first & differs not much from it neither in shape color nor magnitude thus far my author   I have in my Journey to Susquehana received surprising discourses about ye retreat of ye bears in winter into dark Caverns in ye mountains   I am tould thay purge themselves until thair guts is wholy clean from any excrements after which thair fundament is naturaly stoped up & that thay then repose in these caverns in A sort of Lethargick state during ye winter season & are as fat at spring as in ye fall; but as to thair manner of breeding I can learn very little of our hunters   thay affirm never to have killed A bear with young ones in her: Now whether she bears as soon as thay are impregnated   retires into dark recesses until thay have brought forth thair young & reared them big enough to run about with them in search after prey & that ye bears that appears in ye winter are called runners are ye Males or such which are not impregnated Pray if thee can set me right it would oblige me to inform me in this knotty point which makes me uneasy with these doubtfull ruminations

Dear friend I am to set out tomorrow morning towards egg harbour & cape may being A little recruited from A grievous fit of sickness I did not know of going so soon untill this evening since which I have scrabled over these few lines in hast my kind respects to thy dear spouse & children This comes in sincear love from thy obliged friend

John Bartram

P.S. I hope thee hath received my letter with directions where to find ye Seneca root I have received ye two boxes & contents in good order from my friend Mr. Allen one box I intend to send full of our black wallnuts to York for thee by first opertunity after thay are dry enough to send

For Doctor Cadwalader Colden
at Coldenham near ye Highlands

BP 1:26:6; LPCC 2:274–77.
1. Abraham Munting, professor of botany at the University of Groningen, the Netherlands, and author of *Catalogus Plantarum Horti Groningensis* (1672).

To SLOANE

November ye 14, 1742

Respected Friend

I have received thy kind letter & curious books of thy History of Jamaica which is very acceptable to mee as are all such fine instructions for I delight exceedingly in reading books of natural History or botany this noble present engageth not onely my gratefull acknowledgement but allso my endeavours to oblige thee with any curiosity my small Capacity & Circumstance will Conveniently afford & in Complyance with thy modest request I have 1st sent thee A quire of paper filled with dry specimens of plants numbered so that if thee wants any more of any sort here please to mention it to each number 2dly I have sent thee A box of insects with thy name at large on ye box numbered & A sheet of paper with my remarks to each number 3dly I have sent thee a Colection of Curious stones figured with sea shells & some other Curiosities which if they should many of them prove new & acceptable I shall be well pleased; But when I read in thy second volume of thy extrordinary Colection of Curiosities: I thought it would be dificult to send thee any thing of that nature that would be new. I have procured an indian pipe made of soft stone intire: it was dug by chance out of an ould indian grave ye figure & dimensions see below[1] this I esteem as A great Curiosity & if I knowed that thee had none of this kind I should endeavour to give thee an opertunity of seeing it & calling it thy own.

this comes in love from thy obliged friend

John Bartram

ye hole of ye stem of ye pipe to put a reed into to smoak them

British Library, Sloane Ms. 4057, f. 157; D. 304; BP 1:26:3.
1. Bartram drew a picture of the pipe at the bottom of the letter.

To COLLINSON

November ye 17 1742

Dear Peter
I have put on board ye Constantine these folowing Boxes P C No 1 for Phillip Miller & ye Duke of richmond   in ye bottom is rose lawrel cones next is dogwood berries   next is sassafras berries   ye other seeds is put up in paper bags with ye name on each bag & some buternuts & two parcels of fosils   one in blew paper for M Catesby ye other in brown for Sir Hans & several Curious species for thee packed about here & there to fill up vacancies so look Atop sharp for them   Box P C No II is for the duke of Norfolk   ye one end is ye 3 leaved pine Cones which dont shed thair seeds ye first year & two specimens of perforated [illegible] one for thee ye other for Sir Hans   at ye bottom of ye other end ye Cones of ye 2 & 3 leaved pine   next is ye seeds of ye balm of gilead A fine parcel gathered at ye right time just when thay began to dry & shed & carefuly looked after   Box No III P C is for thee & boxes No IIII P C & V is for Catesby & No VI in thy name above Contains seeds & specimens for thee Sir Hans Catesby & Dillenius   thair names is writ upon each   pray be so kind as to send or help each party to thair respective parcels   I had gathered a fine parcel of rose lawrel cones sasafras & dogwood because or thare being prety many of them this year But upon hearing of ye death of our dear friend Lord Petre & I being taken sick upon Susquehana I thought it was better to let them have his share of these before mentioned which is more [illegible] so I think ye others which I omited [illegible] be excused for not sending them this year & ye duke of Norfolks order did not come to my hands until all ye pines had shed thair seeds but that sort which doth shed ye first year   these I went to eg harbour to gather to make up his want of other sorts   he has a double share of [illegible] seeds which is more to be valued then many bushels of ye other sorts of pine seeds both for thair value in service & for Catesby several bird nests & 2 or three bird scins stuft   there is also chimney swalow nests one for Catesby & ye other for thee   I thought ye glutinous matter which thay glued ye sticks together with was ye gum of our chery tree but yesterday when drying it with a coal fire held to it I found it was no gum but of animal production by ye stinking smell it emitted like burnt

animal substance   I believe it is a kind of saliva [illegible] perticular for that use but I think thay are ye foolishest of all birds in ye place thay chuse to build thair nests in which is in chimnies & when thair young is grown heavy allmost big enough to fly thair weight with ye first rain that comes relaxes ye glue & down cometh ye nest & ye young one two ye latter of which commonly makes a fine regale for our cats which hath soon notice of thair downfall by ye squaling noise thay make   I believe it is not one brood in 5 that escapes[1]   this day upon examining A hornets nest I observed ye lineing of each cell was of A different mater from ye outside which I was sure was made of wood & cemented with ye glutinous mater of ye insect   this would flame as clear as brown paper & ye ashes fall away without any ofensive smell but upon seperating ye lining from ye outside I admired what substance that could be of   I tryed it with A coal & found it to pertake on an animal substance by its curling up ratifying & burning ye glutinous substance before it was converted into a light coal as other animal parts doth & concluded that it might be of ye nature of silk by its apearance in A glass   I tryed a peice of our silk with a fire coal & observed ye same Phenomena   If I had observed this before I sent remark on Sir Hans Sloans insects I should have inscribed it there but we are never at ye end of this thing until death   therefore I believe ye hornet makes it or spins it out of themselves as ye silk worm makes A suitable substance being so fine

BP 1:24:2.
1. The remainder of this letter was written on BP 1:24:5.

To COLLINSON

November 18th 1742

Dear friend
I have put on board ye Constantine VI boxes which I hope will come to thy hands   I am very sory my last cargo of plants miscaried   I took as much care as posible in diging them up with sods & packing them & puting them on board with my own hands   I have sent thee A great number of insects in a botle of rum in box VI hoping this way thee may have them intire there is one of ye flies A yelow one with two long hairs for its tail   ye bird that belongs to ye [illegible] nest the mentioned friend Catesby wanted   I employed one to shoot me one which I scined & stufed & put in ye little box with ye Chimney martins nest   I have been informed of A cave up susquehana by one that was in it & saw a fine natural pillar fluted of A stone petrified from ye droping of water   he said it was 7 foot high & A foot diameter & if it was in london it would be of extrordinary value for A noble man to adorn one of his apartments with   but notwithstanding my grievous sickness as I was travailing home I observed on A great flat rock of limestone close by ye river side   ye ground level with ye rock on ye back side of A hard rock had A large hole made in it by ye indians about 18 inches

deep & 3 foot diameter shaped like A bowl in which I suppose thay pounded thair corn & about 18 or 20 year past Governour Keith & A company with him went to see it to please thair fancy thay made A large quantity of punch & since then it is caled Governours punch bowl now this is grown up near half a foot of ye top & instead of A holow smooth botom it is now flat & uneven with holows & ridges that deserve further observation like as limestone groweth now that it should grow ye bottom upwards it seems strange & confirmeth ye opinion of ye growth of limestone

friend breintnal wantes to be informed how high your elm tree groweth there is a hikery tree near Philadelphia which is measured 150 foot high & captain tould him [this is] nothing in height to thair elms that ye rooks build upon [illegible] whether dillenius intends to have cuts of plants to his Hortus elthamensis

[The remainder of the letter is illegible.]

BP 1:24:2.

To CATESBY

November ye 18th 1742

Dear Friend Mark Catesby
I have received thy letter & fine present of thy two books which was very acceptable & Layeth me under an obligation of Complyance to thy modest request I have sent A box No 5 with A fine lawrel planted in it & A root of what we call sweet fern allso another Containing red & white honey-suckle sasafras sheep turds & A rose laurel I have allso sent two paper parcels of fosils & minerals in Complyance to thy printed paper as for ye birds & turtles I have been sadly disapointed in procuring them I employed several to shoot me a whipper-will & our chimney swallows but thay did not get me any I have sent thee A nest of our chimney swallow & 20 [illegible] which I scined & stuft; ye marsh ren I have not seen one this year nor thair nests I hope next year I may be more fortunate I think to look out soon my self

BP 1:24:8.

To COLLINSON

December ye 18th 1742

Dear Peter
wee are daily expecting Captain Stephens from London & many is almost out of hopes & afraid the Spanyards hath catched him I hope my cargo went in ye Constantine will come safe to thy hands I sent 3 boxes of shrubs but could not conveniently dig up or find several plants which I thought to have sent by reason of ye great snow that fell on ye first day of

november & ye frost & several other snows that folowed within 2 weeks after & I had A grievous time to gather ye pine cones near Egg Harbor for ye Duke of norfolk I climbed ye trees in ye rain in A desert & loped of ye bows then must stand up to ye knees in snow to pluck of ye cones but now & for three weeks past we have had fine weather & yesterday ye frogs made A noise ye birds sung & ye bees flew about like as in spring & I doubt it will be worse in next march if not in Aprill we in pennsilvania, have had A fine plentiful harvest this year I have been with our ingenious friend Colden who treated me very Civily as I have related in two letters to thee he advised me to travel into ye mohawks Countrey & to Oswego & ye lakes & he would recommend me to ye inhabitants there He believes there is great variety of plants & other curiosities there but I suppose ye death of our dear friend Lord Petre will discourage such distant travails & our Americans hath not zeal enough to encourage any discoveries of this kind at thair expence Captain Davis by whom I sent ye box of red cedar berries & maple keys last summer Complains that thee took no care of it but let it stay on board untill he was loaded again Such delays will discourage ye captains for takeing things of that kind unless I pay here

BP 1:24:2; D. 161–62.

To COLDEN

January ye 16th 1742/43

Dear Friend Dr Colden

If I had not some Aquaintance with thy person & disposition I should be apt to think thee Could hardly believe ye pleasure I received in reading thy agreeable letter of december ye 22d which I received yesterday. It put me in mind of what our friend Collinson wrote to mee last fall desireing me to Call & see thee for I should find thee a man after my own heart, — I had before sent three letters to thee without receiving any answer which almost discouraged me from writing to thee, yet resolved to write once more. I am now prety well recovered from my sickness since which I have been twice at egg harbour once I gave thee an account of I think in my letter sent with ye wallnuts which I am glad to hear is under thy Sons Care but I had rather thay had been sent directly up to thee as soon as thay arived at York. I had taken Care to keep them in A moderate moist vigetative Condition until ye day that ye sloop Sailed with them but if thay dry or mould in ye box I doubt ye vigitive life will be distroyed before thay are planted; — which I would have performed after this manner. After A spot of ground is diged or plowed then how or plow A furrow two inches deeps & two foot between one furrow & another then drop ye nuts therein about six inches Asunder & cover them even with ye earth; next summer if thay grow well thay will be six eight or ten inches high & fit to transplant ye spring following (where thee would have them to remain) for thay shoot down A long tap root & are difficult to remove so as to live if thay grow several years before their removal; if thee plants them for standards for timber or bearing nuts then sixty foot will be near enough but if for hedges thay should be planted about three foot asunder & when thay are grown as thick as ones arm thay may be plashed[1] in ye begining of March or Just before ye sap interposeth between ye bark & wood, Pray hath your river been frosen so hard this winter so as to hinder boats from passing Along from your parts to York   our rivers hath been open all along & we have had warm weather for ye season, & I have now in my Garden ye Meserion, Black helebore, grounsel, hen bit, Esula & Veronica in flower & many others is budding; But wee had A very sharp time of frost & snow ye beginning of November   ye first day of which it fell with us A foot deep but A bout half way betwixt us & ye Sea it was near two feet deep, from which place it gradually diminished to ye shore where there was little or none; I write of my own knowledge for Above A week after it fell I stood near ye head of Egg harbour river up to ye knees gathering pine Cones of A perticular sort to send to Europ; & it rained fast from morning till night in which I was exposed all day at which time at my house it snowed, but from ye midle of november we have as Aforesd fine weather but rain once or twice A week.

I am obliged to thee for Recommending me to Captain Rutherford   I should Gladly embrace such an opertunity if I have health and Can leave my family so long especialy if I have orders from London next spring to Continue my Perigrinations   Our friend Peter informs me that he is looking out for A new Subscriber in Lord Petres room, it would be A great pleasure to me to accompany A gentleman of such learning & qualification & I suppose of A very Curious tast too that in his Circumstance would have undertaken A Journey to Oswego or resolve to venture down Susquehana as far as Conestogo amongst ye Indians   pray what perticular Motives induceth ye Captain to undertake such desolate difficulties   is it for Animal mineral vigetable or Geographical discoveries thus to hasard his life & health, what attendance doth he intend to take with him   what will he do for an interpreter amongst ye Indians or provisions between ye Christian settlements of your Government & ours, — these things ought to be considered where to meet & what course to take in order for our Journey & Communicate our resolutions to each other before wee fully conclude when to set out that we may not disapoint one another. I am obliged to thee for thy information of ye New Edition of Lineus Characters Plantarum   I design to send for it by ye first opertunity, — I have now under my Care A fine stone as Clear as Cristal but of A delicate purple   in dimention two inches long one & a half broad & one thick drawn to A point with six iregular angles ye basis seems to have been joyned to A whiteish spary flint   A boy found it in A cart rout about 20 miles from my house   this may give A hint that our province is not destitute of gems for our gould smiths takes it to be a fine Amethist   it indures ye fire; No doubt but your mountainous part of ye Country abound with vairietys, if thay could be found might aford pleasure if not Profit, ye 18th [sic] yesterday we had afternoon A storm of snow   it cleared up last night with A N.W. which Continueth exceeding Cold as commonly I have known it, — Now A little to manifest my regard I have for thy family, how doth thy dear spouse fare as to health, Part of ye bounty she was pleased to bestow upon me I enjoyed on ye top of ye Catts kill mountain & part I brought home for my wife to taste how dilicately you fared in ye north Countrey; How doth thy Son that liveth with the & thy other son & his wife that is settled by ye rivers bank   how doth thy Pretty daughters at home   I shall be glad to hear of your wellfare: Pray write as often to me as conveniency will permit: A brisk lively & free Corispondence is very agreable to thy sincear friend

John Bartram

BP 1:26; LPCC 3:3–6; D. 326–28.
1. Entwined.

To COLDEN

April ye 25th 1743

Dear friend

I received thine of December ye 22d which I answered directly & sent by ye post according to direction; but have not received yet any answer from thee wheather thee received it; which I have A Considerable time expected; But ye Opinion I have entertained of thy good nature leads me to find several excuses for this Omision (I do not [say] neglect) as ye difficult pasage from York to thy hands. For it may be thee waited to know more of ye Captains mind Concerning his tour down Susquehana in order to send me his answer; which may be A considerable time in obtaining; or mine might miscary; [illegible] I trust so much to thy generous disposition that thee will vouchsafe me an answer to my letters; tho thay contribute no way to thy instruction; but are rather impertinent yet this insufficiency is for want of Capacity & not inclynation to oblige thee. I have this day received several letters from London which informs me of ye great Satisfaction I gave my Correspondents in what I sent last fall so that I expect to travail A great way this summer & perhaps into your parts toward ye Mohocks Countrey; therefore pray let me know how ye Captain is disposed for travailing this Spring; as soon as conveniency will permit; that I may know how to provide to accompany him; if our affairs & time will suite each other — at present I am waiting for Perticular orders by ye next ship from London which I expect soon will arive haveing not received any answer to my two last letters; I have no more to write to thee at present but to asure thee that I am thy loving & Sincear Friend

John Bartram

For Dr Cadwalader Colden
at Coldenham
These with speed

LPCC 3:21–22.

To COLLINSON

May ye 27th 1743

Dear friend Peter

This day Captain Rutherford accompanied with several gentlemen of distinction from Philadelphia bestowed upon me ye honour of a visit   ye captain very generously offered to take care of any letter I should send to thee which opertunity I will make use of notwithstanding A vesail is to sail from Philadelphia in about two weeks   I have received all ye goods sent for last fall in good order & excellent good   ye thickset I have A suite made of which pleaseth me exceedingly   I am heartily thankfull to thee for it   it's A fine present   ye silk is very good   by thy good officiousness our Library Company hath made me A present with an unanimous consent of A share during life   dear friend by these demonstrations of thy pticular regard for my interest & satisfaction thee engages to thy self my grateful service & remembrance for such favours, but to proceed with thy letter of february ye 15th   I am sorry thee overlooked several roots of ginseng which I put in thy box & observed when I put them in just before ye vesail sailed A lively bud to each root   We have expected Captain Buden in so long that now his employer gives him over for lost by whom I expected to have had more perticular orders   ye Arbor Vitae which I gathered on Hudson's river I take to be ye same kind I gathered on James River I think upon Captain Isham Randolphs land or very near it   He went with & showed it to me supposing it to be A Juniper   within a few yards grew ye Leather bark or Mezercon both which I believe he would send thee ye seed of if thee write to him for it   he is A man of great humanity whom my heart opens to receive   when I think of him which is very often.

   in thine of december ye 20 these folowing observations
   that which ye doctor calls his Shad blows he thinks is our sheep turds his sweet scented gouldenrod is ye same which I sent thee but it will not grow with thee   ye bark of magnolia & leaves of ye sweet goldenrod I desighn to send you by Elias Bland   all ye three Jaceas that ye doctor [mentions] I have sent thee & another I found in Maryland   ye yelow snake root is A species of ye goldenrod & is what doctor Kersly[1] recommended to some in London several years past   ye rose I forgot to examine of him about last time he was at my house but I desine to go to his house in A day or two   I am A visit behind with him   I believe he was imposed upon   his summer Ivy is ye minespermum   there is male & female plants   his hoppany is A very good root   see Parkinsons page 1062   his other Clematis that bears triangular pods I sent the several years ago   the called it dioscorea male & female   his kings beard is our fine yelow orchis   as he informs me his melongela I have had many years for curiosity but is now lost & ye doctors hath shaired ye same fate   I saw one in Philadelphia many years ago that had A small sort that growed upon a vine 6 or 7 foot high supported by bushes so like cherries that he imposed upon ye people by tying them to his chery tree branches in ye latter part of

sumer thay taking it to be A rare tree that produces such late fruite   I think his upland cranberrie leaves hath A very diferent tast far from Cinamon   ye bulbs by redman² many of them grows   ye peony hath not flowered   ye Colchicums is all single   ye tulips is prety good but we have abundance finer   ye ulmaria seed is none of it come up nor ye eye bright   I despair of ever having them to grow in my garden   My wife is well pleased with ye silk the chose for her   she is much obliged to thee for thy Care   I am very thankful to my good friend Sir Hans Sloan for his fine present of 5 guineas being he hath so generously bestowed it upon me I desire thee would send me A silver Can or Cup as Big and good as thee can get for that sum which I or mine may keep to entertain our friends withal, in remembrance of my noble benefactor³

BP 1:27:3; D. 162–63.
1. Dr John Kearsley, a Philadelphia physician, naturalist and architect, was extremely popular with medical students.
2. A ship captain.
3. The cup was inscribed "The Gift of S. Hans Sloane Bart / to his Frd John Bartram Anno 1742." It is now in the Rare Book Room of the University of Pennsylvania Library.

To COLLINSON

June ye 11th 1743

friend Peter
I have lately been to visit our friend Doctor wit where I spent 4 or 5 hours very agreeable sometimes in his garden where I viewed every kind of plant I believe that grew therein which aforded me A Convenient opertunity of asking him whether he ever observed any kind of wild roses in this countrie that was double   he said he could not remember that ever he did   so being satisfied with this amusement we went into his study which was furnished with books containing diferent kinds of learning as Phylosophy natural Magic, Divinity, nay even Mystick divinity all of which was the subjects of our discourse within doors which allternately gave way to botany every time we walked in the garden   I could have wished thee the injoyment of so much diversion as to have heard our discourse provided thee had been well swathed from hips to armpits but it happened A little of our spiritual discourse was interupted by A material object within doors for the Doctor had lately purchased of A great traveller in spain & italy A sample of what was imposed upon him for Snake Stones[1] which took me up A little time beside laughing at him to convince the Doctor that they were nothing but calcined ould horse bones   indeed to give the Doctor his due he is very pleasant facetious & pliant & will exchange as many freedoms as most men of his years with those he respects   his understanding & judgment thee are not unaquainted with having had so long & frequent intercourse with him by letters   when we was upon ye topic of astrology magic & mystic divinity I am apt to be a little troublesome, by inquiring into ye foundation

& reasonableness of these notions which thee knows will not bear to be searched & examined into though I handle these fancies with more tenderness with him then I should with many others that are so superstitiously inclined because I respect ye man   he hath A considerable share of good in him   I observed perticularly ye Doctors famous Lychnis which thee hath dignified so highly, is I think unworthy of that Character   our swamps & low grounds is full of them   I had so contemptible an opinion of it as not to think it worth sending nor afford it room in my garden but I suppose by thy account your climate agreeth so well that it is much improved as ye other which I brought from virginia is as much debased which grows with me About 5 foot high, bearing large spikes of different coloured flowers for 3 or 4 months in ye year exceeding beautiful   I have another wild one finely specled & striped with red upon A white ground & a red eye in ye middle, ye only one I ever saw   now I will conclude this botanical discourse haveing answered thy queries in A letter via bristol   I believe my subscription our proprietor[2] inquired after is wholey dropt some people lay ye blame upon James Logan & not without cause   our worthy friend dr Colden wrote to me that he had received A new edition of Lineus Charateres Plantarum lately reprinted   he advised me to desire Gronovius to send it to me   I should be very glad to see it   ye first I saw was at ye doctor's & chiefly by it he hath attained to ye greatest knowledge in botany of any I have discoursed with

BP 1:27:3; D. 163–64.
1. A stone thought to be a cure for snakebite.
2. Thomas Penn.

To COLLINSON

June ye 21st 1743

dear peter

I have Just now received thy kind letter of march ye 12th wherein thee hath sent orders for A 35 guinea cargo   I hope this will aford opertunity of observing more of ye production of ye Kats kill mountains & transmit an account of my remarks as A small gratification of thy regard for my interest for I must go there if I get ye seeds of ye Balm of gilead & now to answer thy letter of March ye 12th which pleaseth me wonderfuly   I shall endeavour to oblige ye Yorkshire Gentleman   it was very kind to dispose of ye ceder berries   I wish the had reserved one half of ye profit to thy self   I am sure thee deserves it   it is two late to gather any of ye silver leaved maple seed this year   I design to try if I can send one this fall but it is very discouraging to have ye roots thrown out of ye earth by ye boxes being tumbled about If ever I can come to pay you A visit I would bring abundance of trees & shrubs with me which is very difficult if not impossible for you ever to have growing without one that understands them comes with them & takes perticular care of them in their pasage but I don't know how to leave my family   I have many small children & none yet grown up to take care of business & servants in this Country strive to do as little work & spend as much time as they can in carelessnes   that peice of thickset thee sent pleases me beyond any cloathing I ever had before   I have A full suite made of it tho what thee hath favored us with hath been extraordinarily good pray let me know by first opertunity how ye laurel flowered   suppose I should send A chamaerhododendron set with flowering buds after ye same manner   I am sorry thee mist of ye sweet fern & ginseng root   I am sure I sent it in good order   the chinquapins dont grow any plenty near us   I am sorry ye leaky bottle of insects did any damage   I thought to have sent them ye best that way   I am obliged to thee for recommending me to our proprietor   if he would please to be so honourable as alow me A annual salary worth while to furnish his walks with all ye natural production of trees shrubs & plants which grow in our four governments I would undertake to do it   it pleaseth me that what I sent to Sir Hans & M Catesby proved aceptable   I think that Hanging-bird's nest belongs to ye baltimore bird   the Aralia spinosa I brought from virginia   it grows well with me we have had 2 exceeding mild winters insomuch that ye xanthoxilum which I brought from ye capes of Chesapeake was not injured by ye frost (we have one sort growing all ye way from potomock to Hudsons river about 6 foot High but not so hot to ye tast but warm enough to be troublesome when chawed)   I sent it to thee last year ye specimen 46 which the called Acatia & that thee had large trees growing of it but thee was mistaken & that it never yet arived in Europ   my pomegranat is 4 foot high   figs loaded with fruite which was set last fall ye gors now full of seed   geranium maculatum survived & flowered last winter but doubtless these will be humbled under next winters severity   those brown striped muscle shells thee so much admired was brought from ye bottom of ye Sculkill by ye muskrats   thay feed chiefly upon them in ye winter when other food is scarce such as fish & ye water lily   I believe our river bottom is full of these muscels and at 8 or 9 fathom deep for there Lyeth thousand of these shells on shore & ye neck pooled clear out by ye rats   I have forgot what shell that was I sent that matched your fosils   ye indians bury at darby some pots which [rest of page illegible] boil victuals in ye holow round ye neck of it   I suppose thay tied a cord or twisted withe round it to hang it over ye fire or to carry it in ye hand like a bucket to fetch water   the fosill shells are found at ye distance of A hundred or 150 miles from ye sea most of ye way by places from Hudson's river to Susquahana   ye Katskill Mountains is in York government   I am apt to imagine our chimney swallows might build in holow trees before ye Europeans built chimneys. my rose is now producing its second crop out of ye centre of ye old flowers which many do & those that doth not is such as ye stem of ye ould rose withers away   for this rose bush produceth no seed   ye beginning of last winter we had warm foggy weather for several days in which time our persimon trees produced A considerable quantity of gum in ye form of A transparent Jelly   I gathered

Some of it & layed on A shelf in my study but what acidence came to it I dont know but I could never see it more   ye rains which came soon after disolved & washed it of ye trees so that I could gather no more altho we had much such like weather several times in ye winter   when it dryeth it looke very black   I have put into A box several Curiosities & delivered it into ye care of Elias Bland who promised to take good Care of it   in it is put A marsh mole for Sir Hans sloan & one of our great black birds which comes near to Catesbys purple Jackdaw but ye colors are much finer   pray let him see it   if I mistake not I saw A flock of birds in ye eastern shore of virginia that was more like his figure than this   I sent in ye box some of our rose laurel barck but ye sweet goldenrod is not fit to gather yet   I hope to send it in ye fall   I received a letter Lately from Dr. Colden (for we send letters to each by ye post free & A perticular favour) who informed mee he had received A letter by ye ship from thee that thee expressed more upon ye account of my being at his house then he deserved   I delivered an amethist & cristal stone into ye hands of Elias Bland for one of my aquaintance to be set in A ring of Gold ye charge of which I desire thee would answer to Elias if he calls for it & place to my account   In ye township of Darby several have joined together & signed articles of agreement pretty much like ye Library Company at Philadelphia   thay advised with me how thay [the books] should be procured   I tould them I thought thee could send them better than any that I knowed   if thee would favour such A design but thee had abundance of business other ways & that if thee condescended to oblige them so much it must be more for ye love and inclination thee bore to ye promotion of learning & thy generous disposition to assist those that was thereto inclined then ye benefit of what might be thought a reasonable sattisfaction for thy trouble in buying & shipping them   however thay being very desirous of having ye books assumed ye freedom of addressing the by letter with A catalogue of ye books thay want with A bill of exchange which I put in ye box directed to thee   if thee please to comply with their request pray pack them up with ye goods I sent for

John Bartram

BP 1:15:1; D. 164-65.

To COLDEN

June ye 26th 1743

Esteemed friend Colden
I have lately received thy kind letter of May ye 13th since which Captain Rutherford hath been at my house accompanied with several Gentlemen of ye Chiefest distinction in Philadelphia   he appears to be A fine accomplished Gentleman — I am much surprised that thy neibour should tell thee that he left A letter at my house in March which Could not be else I should have heard or of him which I have not[1]   I have lately received

orders from London to travail to gather ye seed of ye Balm of gilead cones & other species of evergreens; ye duke of Norfolk hath subscribed 20 guineas ye duke of richmond & an other Gentleman fifteen more besides our Proprietor hath sent me orders to procure Some Curiosities for him I am now providing for A Journey up Susquehana with our interpreter in order to introduce A peaceable understanding between ye Virginians & ye five nations we suppose ye meeting will be in ye Onondagues Countrey not far from your fort Oswego we are to set out in a week or two; & If thee would pleas to be so kind as to write to ye Captain of your fort or ye minister in ye Mohocks Countrey in my favour it might do me A kindness in A strange land if I should return home that way & thorow Albany which I cant yet know I do not yet know whether we shall ride up Susquehana any farther then ye great Branch (which runs westward toward Alegany) where one of thair chiefs lives whom we are to take with us to the treaty & according to his advice we are to proceed either on horseback or by water as far as navigable: thence by land to ye Onondagues river this Journey I hope if we have good success may aford us A fine opertunity of many Curious observations[2] however thee may be assured of ye real friendship of thy Sincear friend John Bartram I sent a letter in may by one of my acquaintances who promised to leave it at thy house or deliver it to thee

BP 1:27:2; LPCC 3:23–24; D. 328–29.
1. We have reproduced the letter sent to Colden. Bartram's copy, and hence Darlington, both begin at this point.
2. Bartram's copy ends here.

From COLDEN[1]

Sr
I was in Connecticut in the Execution of a Comissen. on an affair of Consequence to that colony when I receiv'd yours of the 2th of June & stay'd there till towards the end of August by which I was deprived of the pleasure of writing as you desired of me So far as I can learn you return'd without being in the Mohawks Country if you had I believe Mr. Barclay the Minister[2] there would have shown all the Civility in his Power on what I formerly wrote to him when you designed for that part of the Country I hope you have returned with ample Satisfaction to your own Curiosity by a Discovery of many New things in Natural History & that you will likewise take the Pleasure of Communication of your Discoveries to the Inquisitive part of the world.

These Avocations by Publick Business have entirely taken my thoughts from any subject in your way I have been taken off from viewing the agreable Phenomina of the beautiful varieties in Nature to the Disagreable phenomina of mens perverse Actions but as this can give you no pleasure no more of it However that this summer may not be entirely lost to our Correspondence I shall acquaint you with something which I thought worth taking note of. As we past through the Country we were with much Civility entertain'd a few hours at their Governor's house (Mr. Laws) & had the pleasure to see himself & his Children cloathed in a good handsom Silk of their own making & he told me that this year there would be above a hundred yards made in that little Town (Milford) They make silk Handkerchiefs & stockens as well as Stuffs He takes a great deal of pains in being inform'd himself in the Mystery of the Silk Manufacture & in instructing his Neighbours If I be not mistaken this little Town has done more without any publick incouragment than all the Colony of Georgia with the Incouragement of I dont know how many thousand pounds of the Publick Money & by this we may see how in any shape publick Spirit is more useful than money[3]

I believe you may have often heard a complaint of the Expensiveness of Lawsuits that Justice must in a manner be bought at a Dear rate They have no reason for complaint of this sort in Connecticut for I believe no where are lawyers fees & other Court charges lower than there but such is the misfortune of all human affairs that the avoiding of one evil generally occasions twice as many. As in no place a law suit can be carried on so cheap so in no other place do they abound in them so much, they assured me that in the County Court of the place where we were, above 600 Actions were then depending. This occasions a litigeous humour among the People a perpetual caballing & attendance on their Courts An Avocation of their Minds from their Business & the Interest of their Families & a great Defect in their Industry. Besides tho' every man allmost in that Colony thinks himself a Lawyer yet perhaps hardly one man in it thoroughly Understands the Principle of the Law. We may learn from this that nothing more prevents the advancement of any Art or Science than that of making it cheap & mean. We might observe the same as to their Religious Notions no where more talk of Religion or a greater pretence to skill in Theology to Sanctity among Individuals & no where are the Principles of Religeon less understood.

In digging a well about a mile from my house at about 9 foot depth we came to Water In some places between the points of a Slaty rock the water came out as Black as ink & upon examining the joint we found in it a black fluid of the consistencie of a Syrup & in the same joint we found several small irregularly shaped clear white flinty stones or Spar It had nothing remarkable either as to smell or taste. Please to let me know if you have at any time met with such & your thoughts of what this black Fluid may be. The Oar or Veins of Minerals are observ'd to grow & to have Sperm embryo (if I be not mistaken) in a Fluid State. If they grow like other Vegetives they must in time come to a State of Maturity & after that decay & at last dye come to Corruption So that this may likewise be the Mineral in a Corrupted State. Perhaps you can give me some light into this for I have no knowledge of the nature of Minerals.

As my son carried this I can have no doubt of its coming safe to your hands & gives me the pleasure of hoping that I cannot fail of having a full sheet at least from you after so long an Intermission in our Correspondence   I am very affectionately

LPCC 3:25–28.
1. Undated, but written in September 1743 (see Bartram to Colden, September 17, 1743).
2. The Reverend Henry Barclay, minister to the Indians and an authority on their languages.
3. For a discussion of attempts at silk culture in the colonies, see Brooke Hindle, *The Pursuit of Science in Revolutionary America, 1735–1789* (Chapel Hill, 1956), p. 200.

To COLDEN

September ye 17th 1743

Esteemed Friend
I am now returned from my tedious Journey   we[1] went up Susquehana to Shomokin about 160 mile from my house being an indian town of about a dozen cabins there   ye river forks one branch runs west by north ye other north N. east; wee traveled about 60 miles up ye west branch which cometh from near Aligany then crosed North east about 100 miles to ye N.N.E. branch up which we traveled crosed a large branch whose source was near ye Cayugas Country & hence to another branch up which we traveled towards ye Onondagues where we stayed near two weeks   onely four days going from thence to Oswego fort & back again most of ye way by water down & up ye Onondagues river   ye Captain was exceeding kind to us; so was ye traiders; I could not have expected such Civil treatment nor do I desire ever to meet with better wherever I may be engaged to travail; in gratitude to ye hospitality of Oswego I speak it   ye indians received us very kindly & entertained us with ye best they could aford & why should we expect more; I thought to have travailed home by ye way of Albany, but ye indians tould us we could not posibly take our horses to ye Mohocks river for deep miery swamps so we returned near ye same way back again that we came; I observed in ye forks of Susquehana a large species of Magnolia three foot diameter very strait & above 100 foot high growing on ye mountains & abundance of Gin Seng & curious fosils all over ye Country: at ye head of ye Onondague lake is a sandy plain of sand wherein one digs a hole 18 inches deep   it springs full of salt water a gallan of which yealds about a pound of salt by boiling[2]

ye 31 of October

this day I had ye agreeable enjoyment of thy sons Company & ye Pleasure of receiving a letter from thee by his hands   I took his visit & thy letter very kindly; & tho exceedingly pinched for time to answer ye desires of my Uropian Corespondents in sending them such curiosities as they wrote for yet Notwithstanding this hurry: ye great value I have for thy friendship engages me to steal so much time to write to thee having such a good opertunity to send it by thy son. I am pleased with thy remarks on ye Law & Religion in Connecticut: its very true ye expence of ye Law makes many people bear many afronts & strive to live more peasable than they are naturally inclined to rather then venture a certain expence for an uncertain satisfaction — and often where there is ye greatest talk & pretence religion & ye mind is taken up with a zeal in ye Performance of ye Ceremonial part and ye substantial part which is Love Resignation & humility to ye Eternal Power is often Neglected

I am glad to hear of ye improvement of ye Silk manufactory & ye Governours good inclination to promote it by an industrious example which is more powerful than any Precept to engage ye attention of ye commonality

it was by ye example & encouragement of industry that ye Mighty Monarchs of China first began & after caried on that ferment of Emulation in husbandry & manufactory whereby thay became so populous & rich & thair Princes So Powerfull

Severall in our Province made an attempt to raise Silk about 16 or 18 year ago but ye trouble in raising ye worms & winding ye silk Soon discouraged them & ye persons that was ye most eager to promote it hath since found a greater profit in raising Hemp & Tobaco so that now we have no inclination [to] try any farther experiments of ye Silk worms notwithstanding our plantations is full of Mulberry trees

But if our Neibouring colonys should Succeed its very Likely Some would make another tryall

We have in our Province lately had a flury of raising vineyards of ye Europian vines & some expected to be mad rich imediately by ye juice of ye grape: ye vines flourished & ye fruits grew finely till allmost its due magnitude: but alas ye graps dropt of unrip which deprived ye Proprietors of their beloved liquor   Indeed one gentleman at great expence raised so many grapes to perfection as made a few gallands of thin wine which he valued highly & for good reason too for I suppose it Cost him no less then ten pounds a galland — yet for all these discouragements I tasted such fine grapes up ye west branch of Susquehana toward Alegany as makes me uneasy when I consider ye difficulty of obtaining that delicate fruite with us; which grew in such plenty there; some lying in large Clusters upon ye beds of sand while others was pendulous scituated on ye adjacent Plum trees Loaded with scarlet fruit near ye rivers bank; which was above 20 foot perpendicular high above ye surface of ye water; — other vines grew upon ye sloaping bank where ye flowing river in vernal floods washed their superficiall roots but when I was there I saw them loaded with large delicious fruite as sweet & large as ye Burgundy Graps which indicates thair propensity to grow either in moist dry or Sandy ground — dear friend as to thy last query I have not time materials nor room at present to answer it according to thy desire   its a reasonable conjecture that if minerals hath a growth that thay have a time of maturity & consequently May have a time of decay but Mineralogy is out of my province   I am not capable to judge how long thay grow before thay arive to a mature state how long thay abide in this state & how long thay are decaying before thay are reduced to fluidity: but whether that black Juice be not a vegitable Juice disguised with a terestial matter descended between ye veins or Crevises of ye rocks & there detained as in a receptacle which you pierced and let out. I have often found a black matter in clefts of rocks which was ye sediment of corrupted moss & several other things: oak leaves & most barks meeting with a vitriolick Juice may descend very deep & appear in a black liquor   My good friend pray excuse my blunder in misplacing my pages as well as words & assure thy self of ye Sincear friendship of this friend

John Bartram

LPCC 6:339–42.
1. Bartram accompanied Conrad Weiser and Lewis Evans.
2. For a full account of the trip, see Bartram's *Observations,* published in London in 1751. Whitfield J. Bell, Jr., has combined Bartram's account with an extract from Evans's journal and Weiser's report in *A Journey from Pennsylvania to Onondaga in 1743* (Barre, Mass., 1973).

To COLLINSON[1]

Dear Peter

I am now returned from my long journey from ye country of ye Five Nations of Indians & ye Fort of Oswego on ye Ontario Lake having had A very prosperous journey   I also found several curious plants shrubs & trees perticularly A great mountain Magnolia 3 foot in diameter & above a hundred foot high very straight & very fine wood — specimens of which I hope to send by next ship with a perticular account of my journey & ye Indians' maner of living & order of thair councils having been at thair chief town & ye meeting of ye deputies & ye treaty of peace between ye virginians & them   I visited ye Salt springs & boiled ye water thereof into salt   I observed ye fossil shels all over ye country even on ye top of ye mountain that seperates ye waters of susquehanna & St. Lawrence in ye vail of Onondago & on ye banks of ye Lake Frontenak   I desighned when I went from home to have returned by ye way of albany then to travail from hudsons river & climb ye Katskill mountains to gather ye balm of gilead cones & Fir cones & on my way to delaware but found it impracticable to ride between Onondago & ye Mohoks river & I mist of them this year for there is none to be found where we traveled which was too far westward for them & ye paper Birch for I find more difference in ye kinds of plants in ye same distance of latitude than longitude & if I am imployed next year to gather seeds especialy of ye fir kinds I desighn to travail to ye kats kill mountains & thence back of new england northeastward whereof I believe I could find many curious evergreens that is not yet known for I cant learn that any botanist was ever there yet   I received thine of May ye eleventh writ in Sir Hans Sloanes letter by which I perceive that freedom & openess is exercised in our correspondency which I love   Doctor Gronovius hath sent me his Index Lapidae & Lineus second edition of his Caracters Plantarum with A very loving letter desiring my correspondence to furnish him with some natural Curiosities of our country. I hope by next ship to send him some   in the meantime if thee hath an opertunity pray return my thanks to him for that fine present   I am providing to set out to-morrow to travel up Delaware to gather some Jin Seng roots to send to thee by next ship so in great haste farewell

J. B.

BP 1:24:1; D. 169–70.
1. Undated, but written about September 1743 (see Bartram to Colden, September 17, 1743).

To SLOANE

September ye 23d 1743

respected Sir Hans Sloane
I received thy kind letter of April ye 4th 1743   I am glad what I sent last fall was acceptable   I have filled ye 2 quires of specimens of plants in thair perfect bloom & am Colecting A fine variety of mosses to send with them which I desighn to send with our dear Peters specimens   I have been A long journey this summer   unexpected till A few days before I set out but having such an opertunity as very likely never to have such another I embraced it so could not gather insects as I desighned   I am much obliged to thee for thy kindness in desiring me to send thee A catalogue of my botanical books   indeed it is soon done   I have so few of them on natural history which I love dearly to read

   The first authors I read were Salmon,[1] Culpeper[2] & Turner[3]   these James Logan gave me[4]   Doctor Dillenius sent me Miller's Dictionary, and his own book of Mosses   Lord Petre sent me Miller's Second Part, and the second book of Turner's complete Herbal; and thee kindly obliged me with thy History of Jamaica. Our friend Peter sent me them fine books of Nature Delineated. Catesby sent me his book of Birds, and some books of Physic and Surgery, which was my chief study in my youthful years   I have heard of Petivers fine collections of plants & animals which thee published   nay I am well aquainted with his Nephew, Captain Glentworth, who lived with his uncle Petiver   He tells me he used to change spread & dry his uncles specimens & carried many curiosities between thee & his uncle

BP 1:24:5; D. 304–5.
1. William Salmon, author of *Botanilogia, the English Herbal or History of Plants* (1710).
2. Nicholas Culpeper (1616–1654), English physician and apothecary, proponent of the "Doctrine of Signatures," and author of *English Physician Enlarged*.

3. William Turner (c. 1510–1568), doctor of physic at Oxford, published the first English herbal and was called the "father of English botany."
4. The next five lines are illegible in Bartram's copy, so were taken from Darlington.

To SLOANE

November ye 16th [1743]

Friend Sr Hans Sloan
I have received thy kind present of A silver Cup & am well pleased that thy name is engraved upon it at large so that when my friends drink out of it they may see who was my benefactor   I received thy kind letter of [illegible] & have endeavoured to answer thy desires   I have sent thee two quires of specimens gathered in thair full bloom — as many as I could but several that I found amongst ye indians could not be found with thair proper Caracteristics so pray except them as I found them rather than none of that species   I have colected several kinds of seeds belonging to ye specimens — numbered with ye same numbers that ye specimens is to which thay belong   I have also wrapped up in separate papers several of our north american mosses & packed them up with ye seeds & if thee wants more another year of mosses seeds or specimens pray let me know perticulary by A letter & I hope to endeavour to procure them for thee

I have put in ye box of specimens one of our yelow wasps nests that was built in my ditch bank   we have another sort like these that builds A hanging nest on ye twigs of bushes or trees like our hornets   I have wraped up in paper some of our humble Bee breeding cells or Combs & have procured A large hornet nest to send   dear Sir if these few Curiosities is acceptable to thee it will not onely encourage me to strive to oblige thee more but will exceedingly pleas thy Sincere & obliged friend

BP 1:24:6; D. 305–6.

To CATCOTT

November ye 24 1743

Respected Friend Catcot
I received thy kind Present of 3 books   Grew[1] & bradley[2] I had read before but now by thy favour I have them my own   before I borowed them   as for Lobel[3] I had his long ago   there is little in him but collections from others but I am obliged to thee for thy good will in sending them but I had rather thee had sent Tourneforts 3d book of his Compleat Herball or Botanical Institutions in English which I very much want having never seen it nor know not where to borrow it   I have now sent thee by friend Willing A Box of curious flowering plants in earth   one root of Yucca I slipped of one of my ould roots in ye spring & planted it for thee which I now send

it flowers 4 foot high with near A hundred flowers upon one stalk   thee will also receive A fine Collection of seeds of our best flowering wild plants with my remarks upon each perticular

BP 1:26:1; D. 325–26.
1. Nehemiah Grew (1640–1712), the English "father of plant anatomy," published *The Anatomy of Plants;* he studied at the University of Leiden.
2. On Richard Bradley, see Bartram to Bayard, fall of 1741.
3. Matthias de Lobel (1538–1616), Flemish botanist.

To DILLENIUS

November ye 29th 1743

Respected Friend Doc Dillenius
I have sent thee 2 or 3 sorts of mosses that I gathered in ye country of ye Five Nations which I think is A little different from any that thee has figured also I have sent thee A Large Collection of seeds of our Country plants gathered in thair proper season & carefully dryed which I hope many of them will grow with thee   in looking over thy Curious book of mosses I Cant find any figure of ye ould mans beard Moss[1] which I saw grow in virginia on ye trees   It groweth 6 or 7 foot long & is fine food for horses & deer   pray my good friend write to me & lett me know wherein I can do the any further service; which will oblige thy sincere friend

J.B.

BP 1:26:5; D. 311–12.
1. Although commonly known today as Spanish moss, this plant (*Tillandsia usneoides*) is not a true moss but a flowering plant of the pineapple family.

To COLLINSON

November ye 30th 1743

Dear friend Peter
this day I have received & have before me thy kind letter of September ye [illegible] I have sent thee several times seed of my great Lychnis both flesh colored & pale but never sent thee roots expecting thee had it long ago   I have planted A good root in ye box for thee   my speckled lychnis is yet very small but I desighn next year thee may expect one   my milk white I sent thee all I had   I hope my specimens this year will confirm my judgment of ye digetated Mallows   is not this ye onely one of that tribe that is male & female distinct   doctor Gronovius hath sent me ye second Edition of Lineus Caracters plantarum   if thee wants ye shels of our turtles intir dryed I hope to send thee as many as thee wants next summer   if I had known that would have done I Could have sent enough before now   I could preserve ye head feet & tail well enough   I desighn next year to send thair eggs nests or birds of our swalos we have beside ye chimney swalow

John F. Gronovius (1690–1762). Courtesy of the Linnean Society of London.

one with a white belly that breeds in holes in ye perpendicular banks by river sides & keeps flying over or near ye water for to catch flyes or small insects   we have allso A martin that breeds in boxes of under ye eaves of houses & some will hang A gourd with A hole in ye top of A pole in which thay will breed

BP 1:26:5.

To JOHN FREDERICK GRONOVIUS

November ye 30 1743

Respected friend Dr Gronovius
I received thy kind letter & Lineus Characters with thy index Lapidae by ye hands of my friend Phineas Bond   I have got them neatly bound up together in one book since which I have received ye second part of ye flora virginica[1] [illegible] all which I am very much obliged to thee for & shall

endeavour to send thee Specimens of what I suppose may be acceptable. I have put in ye box A glass bottle with one of our red-bellied snakes[2] [illegible] thus if thee please to make any remarks of any of ye perticular [specimens give ye] numbers and I shall understand which thee means for I keep a duplicate number of that I send to thee in Lineus Species Plantarum which thee sent me ye Order Genus species goes no further then Class   ye twelft icosandria monoginia ends with [illegible] desire thee would send it me by first Opertunity   My Booke binder hath left an [illegible] 2 or 3 leaves in ye book. I have sent thee in a little square box of several directed [illegible] Curiosities of Shells, stones & earth which I hope may be acceptable. I sent them to our dear friend Collinson & desired him to send them to thee. — I have this summer made a tour up our great river Susquehana & to ye Nation of Indians thence to ye great lake Ontario & I desighn in spare time to write A Journal up there & back again giving an Account of ye Soil timber mountains which came under my observation in that tedious journey with a map thereof

BP 1:24:7; D. 349.
1. The first part of *Flora Virginica's* first edition had been published in 1739, the second part in 1743. It was compiled from a catalogue of plants sent to Gronovius by John Clayton. Linnaeus helped with this first edition.
2. The preceding lines are taken from BP 1:24:7 (D. 349), which is incomplete. Those that follow are from BP 1:26, which seems to be a part of the same letter; unfortunately the first three lines are illegible.

From COLLINSON

Londn January 16 1743/44

My Dr frd John
I was mightily pleased to see the specimens of both sorts Arbor Vitae — That of Poor Ishams (*is much the finest*) — but the Good Man is gone to his long Home & I doubt not but is Happy — I have at this juncture writt to his wife to Send Some of her people to Gather & send Mee some Seed — Wee all Esteem it here to be an American plant and brought by the French from Canada for by all the Herbals that I have Examin'd they all make it a Native of America   I never knew it grew in Germany till thou Inform'd Mee of It —

the Specimens of Crabs was sufficient to see the Species   I had not the Sort before, but I have seen them discribed   if they had been perfect they would have been a Greater Curiosity but their make is so delicate it is scarcely to be Expected whole   if such a thing should happen doubt not of thy Care to send it Mee   there is a very Great Variety of this Species Every part of the world bounded by the sea furnishes new kinds —

The Eggs Thou has sent are very pretty & Curious to see such Variety — but what affords M. Catesby & Mee Great Matter of Speculation is to see so many sorts of Turtle which if Wee may Judge by the Eggs are Specifically

Different but this is like to bring some trouble on Thee for Wee Naturalists are Impatient & never easy untill Wee are Satisfied so what wee have to Request of thee is that when any of these kinds happen in thy Excursions thou will Send us a Shell or Two of these kinds viz

 The flatter back Red Bellied Water Turtle smaller long Eggs
 The Common Land Turtle the next Larger & long Eggs
 The Round back stinking Turtle the smallest with pretty long shining Eggs
 The Great Black Turtle – with Round Eggs
 The Great Red Bellied Turtle with largest sized Eggs of all

Mr. Catesby admires so many of these sorts Escaped Him but it is next to impossible that He could as a Sojourner make such Discoveries as a Curious Man that is a Native it really is True what my frd Sam Chew said (who recommended Thee to Mee) that nothing can well Escape thee —

The small Nest has this Singularity that it seems all Tied, Twisted & Wove together with Flaxen or Hempen Threads nay some white Thread Like Substance has assisted With the others to Tie the branch & Nest together as these seem to be all the Refuse of the Thread Spinners which may be thrown out & picked up by the Birds — for their use pray How may Wee conjecture these pretty artists was supply'd with Materials before the Europeans came and then how must Wee account for another observation that Birds never alter the original order of their Materials for Nests but the same Instinct In the Choice of them prevails through the whole Species I should further be glad to know the Name of the cunning Fabricator for I take It I had a peice or Two of his operations before which Wee much Admired The Loggs thou sent Mee perforated by the Species of Bees produced six Bees In May & June, very Lively & brisk but the Clay Wasp Nests that thou sent Mee from Time to Time None ever produced any more than One Wasp — the Reason I cannot account for I am now by thine & Col Custis obligeing Disposition well Furnished with Chimney Swallows Nests, which are deservedly to be admired, but now I want some Eggs to furnish my Nests and some Huming Birds Eggs for I have many Nests of this pretty Creature — But they are so cuning in their Contrivance that it is meerly by Chance when they are found but if old or young ones can be Caught pray send them.

The Substance thou sends Mee to guess is, I Conceive belonging to a Fungus Feb'y 5 This Day have gott all thy Cargo of 7 Boxes 6 very Safe & Secure, but No 2 being but very badly Nail'd, that it was all Broken Quite to peices — I have the great plants but the Earth shaken from their Roots which is very unlucky and I am afraid the pretty Digitalis & Gentian and Hopames are Dropt through & Lost — those Accidents Wee must Compound, for as the Root was in very Good Order —

Butt Wee have not yett found the Boxes of Specimens & Seeds &c — I have sent down again aboard for It — hope by Capt Hargraves ship to give thee some Account of It —

I have by Elias Blands Assistance as He tells Mee Sent thee by Roseanne 100 lbs. good Madder[1] which I hope will Come safe   the Garlick & Check[2] thee may Expect by Hargrave and the other things as I find Conviency — I have Defray thy Debt to Elias Bland   I cannot yett gett the Microscopes for the Maker Lives in the Country — I hope Lewis Evans has got the Book of Birds and with it the Rule with parralel Lines by Capt Bower because I hear nothing from Him or thee Concerning It —

I am In haste very much Thine

P. Collinson

BP 2:71; D. 166–67.
1. A dye prepared from the root of the madder plant (*Rubia tinctorum*).
2. Fabric printed or woven in a checked pattern.

From JOHN FOTHERGILL

London 22 XII mo 1743/4

Esteemed Friend John Bartram: –

I think myself highly obliged, in the first place to my Friend Dr. Bond for his favourable description of me, and in the next to thy self for thy acceptable present which came safe and yet more for thy generous offers of assisting me in procuring such natural production as your country affords I must own it was what I had long wanted, and must have intruded myself into the number of thy correspondents, had not my friend P Collinson frequently communicated whatever he could spare me. I always admired thy industry and exactness, as well as the surprising progress thou has made in the knowledge of plants, A branch of my profession, which I have just applied myself to, so as to be able to know the principal officinale of our own country, and to collect the best accounts I could meet with of their genuine effects — I retain this acquaintance with them by now & then taking a walk to Peckham or Chelsea[1] but cannot prevail upon myself to launch far into a study which would rob me of more time, to cultivate with success than my present situation will admit of. The fossil productions have always suited my inclination most but I have made but little progress; I don't so much collect with a view to have a great number of odd things together, as to have so many productions of different kinds, natures, compositions, figures &c as when laid together may assist me in forming some general Idea of the production of several of these kinds of substances, more consistent with the nature of things than I have yet met with from others. This is the entertainment of leisure hours, and is a structure which can only be erected from a multitude of materials, which time may supply me with, and the kindness of my friends: — The Amianthus or Cotton Stone, was very acceptable. E. Bland has sent me a very little bit, which was the only specimen I had till thine came to hand. The fossil shells are likewise very acceptable. Whatever of this kind comes to hand will always be welcome. Elias likewise sent me a little bit or two of Bolar[2] earth: I should be glad to know whether you have it in plenty: and to have a pound weight or two sent for experiment. He sent me likewise a small, square black Pyrite have you these in plenty? If you have, please to send a few of them. Crystals, spars, ores, sulphureous matters, liquid or solid bitumen if you have any Marcasites very singular earths, stones & fossil shells will be agreeable.

John Fothergill (1712–1780). Oil portrait by Gilbert Stuart. From Hingston Fox, *Dr. John Fothergill and His Friends* (London: Macmillan and Company, 1919).

But there is another affair of more consequence than these, in which I should be glad of thy assistance. Tis possible I say now and then have occasion to prescribe for persons in your country: I should be glad to be inform'd of what helps I might expect, which are peculiar to your country. In the first class of which I must mention mineral waters: Have you any of considerable note? & near the inhabited parts. Hot or Cold? Chalybeate, sulphureous, or not manifestly either, but salt & purgative? Tincture of Galls, oak bark or green tea leaves made in water will discover the first. If sulphureous, the smell will discover it and its changing silver black; if salt the taste will manifest it. After I am informed of these circumstances I can easily give the directions how to acquire a still more accurate knowledge of their nature & effects.

The next thing I should be glad to be inform'd abt. is, what simples[3] of considerable efficacy, peculiar to your clime, at least indigenous are in use among your practitioners: or even celebrated among the vulgar: I should be glad of some specimens of such, whether roots, leaves, fruits or what else; not barely as specimens to know the plants by, but an handfull or two of each carefully dryed, for experiments with the names they are commonly known by —

I am told that the Sassafras tree when in bloom, casts a most delightful fragance around it. Pray has ever any trial been made to procure a distilled water from the flowers? I fancy they would afford a gratefull and effeicacious one, unless the odoriferous particles are extremely fugitive indeed. I think if the experiment has not been made it would be worth while, to have some gather'd at the proper season and distilled. Some with water alone, some with the addition of a third part of Rum, molasses spirit or some other spirit if you have any clean & cheaper. I should be glad to have a few dry'd flowers sent over & some put into a quart bottle when fresh gathered & some molasses spirit or Rum pour'd upon them and then close cork'd.[4]

Thus thou sees my good Friend, that thy generous offer is like to be followed with not a little trouble & some expense, but whatever of this kind happens, shall be thankfully repaid, and thy trouble acknowledged in the best manner I can.

I am thy obliged friend,

John Fothergill, Jr.

P.S. Whatever figur'd stones as spar, Crystals, Talcs Pyrites &c comes in thy way with any other Remarkable fossils that occur will be very acceptable. It just now occurs to my thoughts & which I shall endeavour to think on again: that a collection of the several natural productions of your colony would be a fine addition to your Public Library. No one is fitter for the undertaking than J. Bartram and some means ought to be considered to make it worth his while. This hint may at least be so far useful as to induce thee to keep a part by thee of everything curious, lest thou should be called upon for that purpose.

Farewell,
J. F.

BP 4:15; D. 333–37.
1. Chelsea Physic Garden, founded by the Apothecaries Company in 1673.
2. Clayey earth.
3. Plants used for medicinal purposes.
4. Sassafras oil, extracted from the roots of *Sassafras albidum,* is used today as an aromatic, stimulant, diaphoretic, and flavoring agent.

From ELIAS BLAND

London 19th: 1st mo 1743/44

John Bartram
Esteemed Friend

Herewith hast Copy of mine pr Capt. Hargrave   Am sorry was detain'd in the Downs pr a Storm in which has Lost his Masts   am told [he] is almost refited & will sail in a few Days. Have presented to P. Collinson pr thy Request the Accot. of Sundrys sent thee which he will write thee abt. pr this Conveyance I believe. Any Service in my Power shall with Pleasure be Render'd thee at all times.

I am

Copy

Thy Reale Friend
E. B.

BP 1:90.

From DILLENIUS

Oxford Feb. 27. 1743/4

Dear Friend Mr. Bartram
I received yours of the 29th of Novem. 1743. together with 2 or 3 sorts of Mosses & the Seeds, you were so kind to send me, by the Care of Our Friend Mr. Collinson. As to the Mosses, they are not new, nor different from any I had before. But the Collection of Seeds is curious & good, I mean thy Seeds are plump & gathered when they were in Perfection, therefore hope to have better Success with them, than I have had before. I am infinitely obliged to you for them, & if I can serve You in any thing, pray let me know, that I may have an opportunity to shew that I am Your thankfull friend & humble Servant

J J Dillenius

Historical Society of Pennsylvania Library.

From COLLINSON

Lond 10 March 1743/4

Friend John
I wrote thee by Capt Breame and Expected our Frd Elias as He was so kind to ship the Madder that He would send thee a Bill of It but it was omitted so I send It here Inclosed   By Hargrave I just writt a Line to

233

acquaint thee I had sent the Scotch Check & Garlix but he happened to Loose his Masts by a Violent Storm in the Downs so Believe this may gett to thy Hands Before He arrives — In my Letter by Hargraves I Inclosed the Mates Receipt for the pcell on board — for I had not Time to attend the Capt for a Bill of Loading so no Freight is paid —

In the Library Companys Trunk there is 3 or four pcells for Thee, an Ingenious Gardener who shares in they Vegitable Collections of Seeds had a Mind to send thee some of His as a Token or His Respect

The prices of Microscopes are advanced to a Guinea So have only Sent Thee one for thy self & desire thy acceptance of It with a Book — thee will find it in a Long Box & the Little Glass Tube in ano'r and some Holly & pyrocanthos Berries   these are all the Ever greens I could procure this year & shall serch out against Next for some other Sorts

I have sent 3 of 4 sorts of Thread for Garlix   what is not fitt for your Use may be saleable

As for pins there is such great Variety of prices and not mentioning whether they was for Sale or your own use I did not know what to send — however I have putt up a Few which I Desire thy Good Wife to accept for her own use

The Fustians thou Desired I can gett none but Some Course old Shop-keepers for they are as much out of Ware Here as if they never had been, so fickle Wee are and yett I can remember the Time that there was scarcely one without a Fustian[1] coat —

I have paid the Several articles mention'd on Elias Blands account Current Here Enclosed — and placed them to Thy account — by Capt Bream I sent the Names of Last years Specimens &c

At present Can give Thee no assurance of any New Contributors, only the Duke of Richmond & P. Miller Continues who Love new Things, but wether so small a subscription will countervail thy Going among the saints in New England, I must submit to thy Consideration   I am looking for New Subscribers   am persuaded that many would be Glad of the opportunity if they knew where to apply but if the worst comes to the worst – if Thou sends over 3 or 4 five Guinea Cases prettyly sorted with something of every Thing but in perticular pine, Firr & Cedar, and Walnut Hickory, I fancy I shall find means to Dispose of Them amongst our seeds Men but Thou must be very pticular and send Mee an exact list of every Individual sort of seed in each of Them & the Number of the Large seeds & the Quantity of smaller sorts[2] — If Two of Them Contain variety of Okes, being pticular in the sorts & Numbers Acorns in Each, with pines, Firrs &c — I Really think I shall be able to Dispose of Them when They are Here – But Then Thou must pay the Freight &c for it will be Difficult to make the gardeners pay that, they would Expect Them Selves Freed of Charges – if the Cases are Larger they will not be so Easily Disposed off   be of great Heart   I doubt not but to succeed – But pray [Sett them] or see them Disposed in the ship where no Wett can come, for I am afraid that the Duke of Norfolks have sufferd Grately by the Salt Water   I open'd & Dryed them and did all I could but Yett I fear the

Vegitation is Destroyed & in the D. Richmond & P.M. one End was much Soak'd with wet for the Time to come, putt Every Sort in a bag by its self & put a White paper with the Name written on it in the Mouth of the Bag or write on a Smooth Chip and putt in the Mouth of the bag, for many of the Last was so rotten I could find no Name

[The next four lines are illegible.]

I am in great Hopes of seeing the Gensang Flower to [have] it painted Two Roots sprouted finely in the box [& shows] a pretty Countenance   I did not in the Least Disturb it and Turn'd it out whole but I was greatly Concern'd in the Dry Roots being what is so much Desir'd in growing & Soak'd them in Water they plump'd but yett was gone to Farr   The Ferns &c indeed Every thing in the Great box came very Well & I promise myself, much pleasure in seeing them come forward   the other box broke all to peices but I [illegible] the whole Case I could of the plants – the sugar maple is a fine plant, the rhododendron suffer'd but yett I hope it will [live] too I have try'd it in the house & expect they bloom Delightfully att Ld Petres — the Common Laurel for Catesby came off the best which I was Glad off because he [illegible] to Mee in Last years bud for all my Care could not make it Do   I attribute it to our very uncommon dry summer — and two good plants of Red & White Shrub grows — I have nothing Farther to Ask – another Root of Skunk Weed[3] —

I sent all the things to Sr Hans Sloane and writt Him a Letter to remind Him that a Ship was going if He had anything to send thee   Docr Delenius has writt Thee a Letter   is greatly delighted with the Last seeds   they are so good, sayes that thou art the only Man that Ever did Things to the purpose

The Curiosities for Docr Gronovius are gone for Holland with the Specimens, I have writt both to him & Linnaeus not to forget the pains & Travel of Indefatigable John Bartram but stick a Feather in his Cap who is as Deserving the Rest   Docr Colden our Worthy Ingenious Friend is Quite a proficient   I was surprised with his proficiency in the Linnean System.

I am in haste farewll

P. Collinson

Oh dear John I Long to see Thy Journal and sentiments and observations of thy Expedition to the Five Nations   It was a Lucky opportunity — I was glad to see Cones of the Fine Magnolia   The wood must be beautifull, I had Specimens before I saw thine from Docr Mitchell of Urbana in Virginia 2 or 3 years agone where there is a stately Tree on the plantation of Nicholas Smith[4] in Essex County on the Head of Piscataway, Rappahannock River, in his Pasture it is well known by all & visited by all Travellers —

I now come to take a little Notice of Thine of the 2d Decemr: I was pleased to See the Digitated Leafed plant prove a Mallow   I know it will be acceptable to Docr Gronovius   Thee need not trouble thyself to send Nests of the Swallows & martens but the eggs, the Chimeny one beats them all for Curiosity but Thou & Colo Custis have well supply'd Mee   I only want some whole Eggs

To be sure a Shell of Each sort of your Turtles, dry'd will be acceptable, and if anything Remarkable in their head & feet — they may be Easily Cured in a Slack oven after the Bread is out

pray how does Docr Witt Do   I have not heard from him this year

Inclosed is thy account with Elias Blands account of what he has done for thee

Now Dear John Farewell.

P. Collinson

BP 2:70; D. 170–72; American Philosophical Society Library, Wildman transcript.
1. A cotton and linen fabric used for bedding as well as for clothing.
2. From this point much of this letter was omitted by both Darlington and Wildman.
3. The rest of the letter is from Darlington.
4. Unidentified.

From SLOANE[1]

Chelsea March 14th
1743/44

Sr

I have received the Plants and Several Things mentioned in your Letter of December 2d which are all extreamly welcome to me, as will be the Hornets nest you mention or any additional things of the like Nature that you meet with. I have sent you all Mr. Petivers works which are very Scarce and may be useful to you and have added the Natural History of Ireland, Etmuller[2] Abridged in English, Herman's[3] Paradisus Batavus, & Selius's account of the Timber Worms that eats the Ships, which I perceive you may have not and which may be Diverting & Instructive to you who Love such Things. I wish you all Health & Happiness and remain

Your Obliged Humble Sert
Hans Sloan

Historical Society of Pennsylvania Library, Autograph Collection of Physicians and Chemists IV.
1. Signed by Sloane but written by an amanuensis.
2. Michael Ettmuller (1644–1683), German physician, professor of botany and surgery at Leipzig, and author of *Opera Omnia*.
3. Paul Herman, also author of *Horti Academici Lugduno-Batavia Catalogus* (Leiden, 1687).

To COLDEN[1]

March ye 27th 1744

Esteemed Frnd.

I have Long expected A Letter from thy hands & haveing received none since that sent by thy son which I answered by him   dear friend this neglect or misfortune gives me some uneasiness

I should be very glad to hear oftener from thee by letter. I have here sent thee one of our proposals for forming A Philosophical Society. we have already had three meetings & several Learned & Curious persons from our neibouring Colonies hath allready Joyned membership with us & we hope thee will pleas to do us ye honor to be involved in our number — I hope this undertaking may be of publick benefit to our american Colonies if we act with diligent application in this afair

I have little more to say at present haveing received no letters fr London this winter but a very learned & curious Clergy man from Bristol[2] sent me A long Catalogue of his garden furniture which did realy pleas me   My respects to thy dear spouse & children & asure thy selfe of the friendship & service of thy Sincere

friend John Bartram

Beinecke Rare Book and Manuscript Library, Yale University.
1. This letter was published in Carl Van Doren's "The Beginnings of the American Philosophical Society," *Proceedings of the American Philosophical Society* 87 (1943):284.
2. The Reverend Alexander Stopford Catcott.

From BLAND

London 28th 3 mo 174[1]

My Friend

The Preceeding is Copy of my Accts Inclos'd in a Letter from our Frd. P. Collinson. Also Sorry to Advise thee Capt. Reeve is taken by the French. Is a Disappointment & Loss to many Myself in[cluded] Particular being a Young Man in Trade. Write me what Approbation the Articles per Capt. Hargrave receiv'd.

I am Respectfully

Thy Friend
Elias Bland

BP 1:90.
1. The date of this letter is undoubtedly 1743/44. See Sloane to Bartram, January 19, 1743/44, in which he mentions his account; and also Darlington, p. 172, in which Bartram wrote to Collinson on July 24, 1744, that he had just heard that Reeves had been taken by the French.

To COLDEN

ye 29th of April 1744

Dear friend

I have now before me thy two letters of march ye 28th & april ye 23d ye latter of which I Just now received about 6 A clock this evening; as to thy inquiries about ye great plain of land up Susquehana I know nothing of it nor ever heard of it from our people or ye Indians except thee means ye

Common low land which is most of ye way up ye river & its many great branches: whose winding channels passeth thorow large rich plains covered with grass & weeds; in some places half a mile broad on each side; some places A mountain Joins close to ye banks on one side & A large fertil plain oposite to it & mostly where A great branch comes in there is a neck of rich low land most of which is or hath been Indian towns

the 2d part of ye Flora Virginica begins with page 129 & ends with 206 after ye same method of ye first part with ye virtues ascribed to some of them according to ye practice of ye common people

I shall be exceeding well pleased with some of thy botanical observations this season: I have received several letters from several of my correspondents in europ with their several observations on various subjects which affords me an opertunity I hope of enjoying ye secret pleasure of modestly informing them of some of their mistakes; & with ye like freedom tho not pleasure I would inform the that according to my Capacity   I am full as much hurried in business as our friend Benjamin for I can hardly get any time to write but by Candle light after A very hard days labour about my plantation for ye subsistence of my family. Our Philosophick Society increaseth finely. I think we had 7 members initiated last meeting of which thee was one by unanimous consent   as for those three thee mentioned they are persons of little curiosity & I belive was never acquainted with our proposals or not till very lately; indeed James Logan was acquainted with it as A Complement but I tould Benjamin that I believed he would not incourage it; & we should have been as well pleased with his name at ye top of our List, as his person in our meetings. however we resolved that his not favouring ye desighn should not hinder our attempt & if he would not go along with us we would Jog along without him

the next fifth night we are to have another meeting where Doctor spence[1] will accompany us. he exhibits Phylosophical lectures now at Philadelphia & approves of our desighn: offers to take our proposals with him to ye west indies with A favourable acount of our proceedings.

My sincear respects to thy Dear Spouse & children, I remain with great obligation thy Loving friend

John Bartram

Historical Society of Pennsylvania Library, Autograph Collection of Simon Gratz, Case 7, Box 21.
1. Dr. Archibald Spencer or Spence.

To JOHN MITCHELL

June ye 3d 1744

doctor Mitchel
I have now before me thy kind letter of may ye 5th which pleaseth me well. I should have been exceedingly pleased to have been aquainted with thee when

I traveled in your country in ye year 1738 when I lodged in frederichsburgh from whence I traveled near 60 miles down Rapahanock   thence over dragon bridge[1] to John Clatons where I was disapointed of seeing him he being gone towards ye mountains   thence to Williamsburgh   so up James river to goochland where I saw a prety little tree of ye arbor vita on ye west bank of ye river   it was about 6 inches diameter   thence travailling to your blew mountains headed rapahanock   fell upon ye branches of shenandoah A great branch of potomack   kept ye great vail between ye North & South mountains till crossing Susquehana took ye nearest way I could home   since which time I have traveled many times over East & West Jersey & up ye north river to ye great falls of ye mohocks river, & twice climbed up ye great Kats kill mountains (which is near 3 times as high as any other I ever climbed) where is A fine prospect over a great part of New England   these mountains produceth ye greatest vairiety of plants and trees of any perticular spot of ground I know of   ye Balm of gilead fir grows here A hundred foot high very straight   so doth 2 or 3 kinds of ye Newfound land spruce Firs with several kinds of curious pines & A fine species of ye paper birch whose bark yealding leaves above 3 foot square of fine paper for eather writing drawing or printing & several other species of birch, cherry trees 5 foot high, not of ye bird clustered kind   quicken tree 15 foot high   A fine species of Viburnum with broad leaves shaped like A heart   planes several species of ye Aralias & Araliastrums, christophorianas   Ladys Bowers   herb paris with many other very odd kinds of plants & shrubs & upon ye same ridge with your South Blew Mountain by Hudsons rivers bank grows large trees of ye arbor vita & in ye swamps fine Larch trees   this Last sheds its leaves in autumn, tho' A fine resinous tree   Last July I went with our interpreter to Onondaga to make peace between your people & ye 6 Nations on ye account of ye scirmish with your back inhabitants   from whence I went down ye river to ye great Lake Frontinack[2]   in this Journey I observed many curious trees shrubs & plants, perticularly A fine magnolia above 60 foot high & 3 diameter   ye cones 3 or 4 inches long   ye leaves A foot long & 6 inches broad a little hairy   ye winter bud covered with down or short hairs to defend it from ye severity of ye cold in that rigorous climate   I sent A specimen of it to our friend Peter last fall. he write me, thee sent him specimens of ye same species 3 years ago of a large tree growing near piscataway rapahanock but I believe [illegible]

BP 1:27:1; D. 363–64.
1. This bridge crossed Dragon Swamp between Urbanna and Clayton's home near Gloucester.
2. Lake Ontario.

To FOTHERGILL

July ye 24th 1744

Respected Friend Dr. Fothergil
I have now before me thy kind letter of ye 22d of 12th month, 1743–4. I am glad those things I sent thee prove acceptable   perhaps I may send some

few curiosities next fall but as times is so precarious & my subscriptions this year is small I shall hardly travail above one hundred mile from home on each quarter & consequently cant find many: ye Sassafras flowers was all fallen before I received thy letter   there is A very penetrating oil extracted from ye berries by frying them in a pan like as you do coffee   we have abundance of medicinal roots herbs & barks, used with success amongst ye common people which is extolled for wonderful specificks in many infirmities upon ye first discovery made by ye indians on most of them but when our people take them not considering age constitution season nor ye perticular progress or crisis of ye distemper but expect an imediate Cure upon ye first or second dose thay are sometimes disappointed — then it is directly discarded and thrown out of use (especialy if ye patient grows worse after taking it) & another famous specifick gains aplause for awhile then is subject to ye others fate & another taken into favour   we have several springs in our province on which many people have bestowed A large encomium but many of them being impregnated with iron & not agreeing with all constitutions so as to perfect A cure thay are of late neglected   one of them I believe might be of great use to mankind under proper regulations   it is A large spring allmost big enough to turn A mill   very cold clear when it springs up but when it runs away there is A great quantity of rediss or orange Colored crudled mater is mixed with ye current   we have other springs pertaking of vitriol & amongst ye mountains some of alum & some places black stinking sulphurous springs

BP 1:28:1; D. 337–38.

To COLLINSON

July ye 24th 1744

Dear Peter
I sent last spring by captn Reeves my Journal to ye 5 nations & ye Lake Ontario Containing a perticular account of ye soil productions mountains & lakes which I observed on our journey thither   allso ye daily proceedings of ye Indian chiefs in thair assembly while we was there but I have lately heard that Reeves is taken by ye french   I conclude that which I took so much pains about will never come to thy hands nor ye letter I sent in ye same ship which I have not time to write over again to send by this vessail in thy letter of January 16, 1743/44 I am glad ye specimens of Crabs were new to thee   I never could yet see any more perfect then those I sent thee if I find any I shall endeavour to send them   I endeavoured to send ye turtle shells by this ship but unfortunately have lost several that I had prepaired   ye birds nest the mentions with flax or hempen threads is mostly piled of our apocinums   we call it A yelow bird though it hath a little greenish cast   that substance which I sent thee to guess at was a kind of scum on ye water of A mill pond which had been drawn of & ye scum

settling on ye bottom & being bleached by ye rain dew & sun appears in that form   I am sorry ye box No 11 miscaried   I thought I nailed it well but ye sailors often handles such things very roughly   ye mader Garlick & check came well & was good   so was all that came by Reeves   Lewis Evans hath ye book & rulers but I have not yet had ye book nor ye money for ye last   hee is A quear fellow   thine of march ye tenth   I am heartily obliged to thy friend ye gardener for his kind endeavours yet am sorry he sent me such large quantity of seeds that might have fetched him something considerable in London which to me signified very little for we have great plenty of such things in allmost every kitchen garden   I sowed A little of most sorts but what I gave to our proprietors gardener but I see nothing come up [but] what we have very common: I am surprised ye price of ye Microscope is raised Contrary to what is published in print   I am very much obliged to thee for it ye book pins & ferrets[1]   these last is very usefull for my family of small children being 8 alive   I wish ye evergreens may come up   ye thread is good   its very well thee paid ye several articles to Elias bland upon my account   ye names of ye specimens were very welcom   I hope my great magnolia may be different from any thee hath yet seen. you are sometimes mistaken in specimens. our friend Doctor Wit is as well as usual   I have received thy accounts in good order & exact but am troubled that Sir Hans hath not sent me A few lines   I doubt what I sent him hath not given such satisfaction as I desired   I desighn to provide A box of seeds for Philip miller & am obliged to thee for thy very kind offer of selling other seeds that I should send if I pay ye freight here which is reasonable but as times is so precarious if thay should be taken I shall lose my labour & freight   if you pay ye freight when you receive them you are sure of something   I am surprised that my last cargo was damnified by wet   I thought I had chosen ye best place for them that is between decks I beged hard for it & was glad to obtain that favour hoping thay would have done well   I hope to send thee ye roots mentioned for thy self   it is very kind in thee to recommend me to Linneus and Gronovius   Dr Colden hath sent me A pretty draught of ye bell animal which thee drawed for him

BP 1:40:3; D. 172.
1. A type of narrow tape.

From GRONOVIUS

Leyden, 25th July 1744

Dear Sir: –

In the month of Jany I was surprised to see such a variety of natural things, which you are pleased to send to me. I assure you I shall always endeavour to deserve your favour, and not keep your observations for my own, but make them public to the learned world. And, to be short, I shall give you an account how I propose to go on. First, I propose to dispose all what you send me in their orders, vid., regnum lapideum, vegetabile and animal; and secondly, in their classes, genera, and species. This being done, I endeavour to explain every particular of which I give you the following scheme about the petrifactions.

Transundum nunc est ad tales lapides, qui simulacrum animalis, vel ejus tectum et domicilium representant, quales Petrificate appellare consueverunt authores, quaeque in veritatem diluvianae inundationes adducere no dubitarunt. Haec vario sita loco observavit vir egregius; alia quippe in superficie terrae, alia in profundo. Quae enim in Australi Pensilvaniae plaga, immensos Canadae lacus respiciens, occurrebant, in superficie terrae jacebant; imo in itinere, quo aliquot centum millaria absolvit, ea ubique sparsa reperit

And in this way I propose to go on with every particular subject you send me. In things now which are estra sphaeram meam I address my self to such gentlemans, which I know that have any notion of them. You never can believe how our Virtuosos are pleased to see the cells of the Wasp nests filled with Spiders, of which they never have heard before. Professor Muschenbroek and Lulofs cannot enough admire that mechanics. They hope with me to give you a good account of it only we wish you could send to us at an occasion one of the Humble Bees him self and also one long black Wasp num. 25 & 26. We have discovered that all the chrysalides of them, and those that are still in their silk folliculus are still in life. So that you see by this way everything will be welcome.

Pray can you tell me how goes the loadstone rok out of which you split the cotton stone, num. 67. doth she go from East to West, or from South to North, or else way. You send to me a shell with a sort of a Lapster in it. The shell is the Cochlea perlata Bonan. rar class 3, num. 167. The animal in it is the Heremite Krab of Catesby nat. Hist. vol. 2, tab. 33. fig. 2: the Soldger of Rochefort,[1] p. 122 The Cocinas of B but the paper where in it was involved, was inscribed with the name Antigua.[2] I wish to know if this is the Indian name. It will be very convenient always to have the Indian name. As much as possible you must endeavour of the conchae bivalves to get both valves. You never can believe what a great rarity there is amongst the muscles num. 1, and particular amongst the small ones, of which I find severall different varietys.

I believe upon strik enquiry that in your sea and rivers are to be found all the species of conchae and cochleas which are to be found every where, for I see that under num. 2 amongst the salt water shells you send a valva cava pectinis aurit, but the other ones are the most curious, to my knowledge only to be found at Curacao in the west indies, and at Amboina in East India: they are one of the valvae of the Ostrea perlata capite foraminoso Petiv. mus. n. 823 and concha subrotunda una valva perforata eujus multiplices sunt varietates Gualt. Ind. test. tab 97 ——

Your consideration upon the fragments of variety of pots num. 4 is really some things new   I don't find any mention about the earthen pots of the old Indians before they were acquainted with the Europeans in our Voyageurs except Sloane introd. p. 47 et 70. who tabula 2 gives the figure of an Urne found in Jamaica so that your pot is a great antiquity, worth to be set in a public Museum.

I admire so many things discovered by you in pensilvania, which are the same in Germany. it brings me in mind a problem of the Botanist, that plantae alpinae ubique eaedem, plantas ejusdem climatis fere eaedem, and at present by your observations we may conclude terram ejusdemque contenta sub eodem saepe eadem; for num. 7, the marble of your countrey is the stalactites calcis solidae, Supell. p. 15, No. 12 ——

In my next I shall give you an account of the rest. You shall very much oblige the learned world with your communications, particularly with your Journal to the 5 Nations. I am particularly desired by some learned Gentlemen to ask you about the Loadstone, of which they wish to know what the longest and the thikkest piece was you remember to have seen and if you could spare to have a little pieces of the same you send me, which is the most curious they ever have seen, to make experiments with it.

As soon I have an ocassion to send to Mr. Collinson something, I shall send to you the sheets you want to compleat your characters, beside another copy of the characters for a pocket book, and another copy of my index supellectilis   pray my service to Dr. phineas Bond.

we hath here this winter one of the Dutch ministers from pensilvania studying in physik. I have seen him once at my house, but seeing that he was a man of no knowledge of all, I would not los my time with him.

Now dear sir, I finish these, with many thanksgivings for so many curious things, which I hope in short to make public to the whole world, and do as Plinius says ingenum est profiteri per quem profeceris.

Wishing you all health and prosperity, I remain your most obedient servant.

J F Gronovius

BP 4:38; D. 349–52.
1. Charles de Rochefort, author of *Histoire Naturelle et Morale des Isles Antilles de l'Amerique*.
2. This had probably been sent by Dr. Cressy.

From COLLINSON

Augt: 5: 1744

Fr John

The Supposed Martigon is in full Flower — but to my Surprise the Petals do not reflect & Turn back as the Martigons but rather Hang down Like Crown Imperials — its of a Dun Yellow most finely Spotted with purple within Side So that by its way of Growing its greatest beauty is Hidd — Butt on the whole it is a Curious flower and being New is very Entertaining   the Lychnis makes a fine Show

I have Lately had a Letter from Doc Gronovius   he Desires his Humble Service and many Thanks for so many Curious Things wch was Very acceptable —

pray send some perennial Lupin seed — has the fine Spirea found in the Jersey[s] began to flourish in thy Garden   Does the Seedling Rose continue Hose in Hose[1] and does the Obeliscotheca continue its Sporting? Narrow & Broad Leaves   Clinopodium is Wanting

BP 2:72.
1. A double flower.

To JOHN CLAYTON

September ye first 1744

Dear friend John Claton
A few days ago I received thy obligeing letter of August ye 13 which I have read with great satisfaction & am very thankful for thy information about ye Stewartia & Smiths magnolia which agrees with ye description I have had of it from P Collinson   ye stager weed seed I gathered in October behind your blew mountains when some plants that had been cropt or broken & produced new shoots was in flower   it flowers early with me & at ye same time that ye true Napeta doth & is very like it   in this vail I found A curious perannual senecio growing high ye leaves very sweet & A strange species of ye mallow of alcea tribe growing perannual & male & female growing 7 foot high distinct of several plants & ye leaves near 18 inches diameter & A diminutive species of the zanthoxilum with other odd plants   ye two alaternus I cant remember perticularly where I found them in A dark thicket on cold clay moist ground not near any house [illegible] Dillenius & he called it Sene. I climbed on ye Katts Kill mountains first to discover ye Balm of Gilead fir in May   next to gather ye seeds thereof in august – I hired A guide to go up with me who was no man of curiosity so consequently was soon weary of staying there so that I had no opertunity of making full discovery of nearly all ye great vairity of curious plants thereon produced but if ever I go upon them again I desighn to be guide my self & stay on them as long as I please but as far as I went I found A surprising vairiety of trees as several sorts of ye new found land spruice firs pines birches various species   Quicken tree 12 foot high   chery trees besides ye cluster kinds   A curious species of Viburnum with A rough leaf shaped like A heart & queer kinds of maples some male & female distinct & some dwarf yew of plants several species of Cristophoriana   Aralia & araliastrums   Ladys bowers very beautiful   herb paris with many other odd kinds. as for animals I saw but few uncommon ones onely A fine kind of Lizard of an ash color with 4 Golden spots on each side & about 5 inches long   thay lay on top of ye water of a great Lake near ye top of ye mountain & when I drew near to observe them thay would dive down to ye bottom &

creep under ye stones but ye neibouring inhabitants tells strange stories of a little creature about ye bigness of A midling dog exactly ye shape of a Lion & another creature thay call A tiger that I dont give Abundance of credit to & as ye indians hath been setled for ages round them so ye game is much destroyed   but as thay appear next to ye north river in which ye tide flows to ye northward of them A hamock or spring tops very dificult of access by reason of Lakes Swamps thickets & prodigious ledges of rocks & craggy caverns in some of thair native inhabitants escapes ye vigilance of ye cunning hunter   indeed ye west & northwest sides (where is ye sources of ye great river Susquehana & ye head springs of your bay & our river Delaware) rises gradualy   ye common animals that resides in these northern parts as ye porcupin fisher an amphibious creature about ye bigness of A rackoon & A little creature about ye bigness of A squiril of A yelowish color & excelent furr & such multitudes of pidgeons that ye ground is covered A foot thick with thair dung   some say much more   ye Larix sheds its leaves in autumn   pray doth that tree the mentions on ye south branch of James river thee may easily know ye paper birch   do but Lanch ye bark perpendicularly on one side & thee may easily pil 8 or 10 foulds of paper as thin as parchment al round ye tree   I have put in this letter A specimen of ye birch paper & ye bark of a twig of another species of ye birch which may be ye same with what thee observed near ye fals of Potomack & one quil of A porcupine which [was] killed by ye indians up susquehana where I gathered A handfull of quils & brought home to oblige ye Curious   now dear friend I think I have answered thy letter in ever perticular & if I have not enlarge so much as thee expected pray let me know & I shall endeavour to mend it   in ye meantime thee may be asured I am thy real friend

BP 1:28:2.

From CATCOTT

Bristoll, Sept. 17. 1744.

Sir,

The product of seeds is as follows.

Sweet yellow flower from virginia annual with yellow flowers; grows very like a tamarind: perhaps an acacia (another plant growing not much unlike it, with pennated leaves, but larger; with some prickles, yellow blossom that cups, & black petals) white convolvulus [illegible] (Lychnis with crosswart leaf) an Hypericum / 2 Goldenrods / Virginia thistle / Clinopodium, wth. varieg: flowers / 2 plants that have not blomd; one with a trefoil leaf; the other's leaf shap'd like a heart / Cardinalis, I had both before

In looking over Miller & Catesby I looked over ye names of the following plants; any of wch. I should be glad to have. Silquastrum polygala, or Senegaw rattlesnake / great late red martigon / Helleborine or Calicolus majore / Anonis / Iris or flag flowers / yellow Jasmine / wild roses / broad leavd Guracum wth. blue flors. / Althea or Florida / 3 leavd solanum, wth a flor. of 6 leaves / of a carnation color., & a tuberous root / Anemone-flower shrub, wth. a spicy bark / Cistus with a honysuckle flor. / Coco-plum / Dahoon holly / Yellow ornithogalum / Gentiana / Rose Ketmia / spik'd Solanum, with borage leaf, blue-purplish flors. / Corallodendron, with leaves shap'd like a spear   I will not yet despair of some of the lily tribe; and with thanks for past favours, am Sr,

Yr. obliged humble Servant
Alexr. Catcott

BP 1:99.

From COLDEN[1]

Sr

I was so much longer at New York than I expected that I have been much longer deprived of the pleasure of continueing my Correspondence with you than I thought would happen for my private affairs since my return home have necessarily employ'd my thoughts. In the first place I must thank you for the Civilities I receiv'd while I was at Philadelphia   I am very sensible of them   And next I must excuse my not procuring the seed of the Arbor Vitae as you desired   the cones were all open before I return'd & the seed fallen But I shall have the greatest pleasure if I can be a means of persuading you to make your knowledge more publick & of consequence more Usefull & I persuade my self it will not be difficult for me to persuade you to it for the greatest pleasure a good man can have is in being usefull to the community & in what I am about to propose   I likewise hope that you'l find a private advantage in it. It is to communicate your knowledge of our American plants to the publick   This I believe may be done with most advantage to your self by publishing it by Subscription in monthly papers of about one shilling Value & to take Gronovius's Flora Virginica for the Foundation of your work & method. It will be necessary for you to have at least six months paper ready before you begin to publish that the work may be continued with sufficient care & without Interruption. I make no doubt you'l find severall forward to incourage & assist you where it may be necessary especially in such parts where you may be under difficulties by your not having had in your youth the advantages of Learning. I will very cheerfully contribute whatever shall be in my power & give you my thoughts as to the Method of presenting your design after I shall know that you are resolved to undertake it

LPCC 3:94–95.
1. This letter was written October 24, 1744, according to Bartram's reply on November 2, 1744.

To GRONOVIUS

November ye 1sr 1744[1]

Esteemed Friend
I have little at present to write haveing received no answer to my letter I sent last year; but as this fair oppertunity offers by my friend Samuel Shoomaker[2] who is a young man of a wealthy family Sivil behaviour of good Credit & well respected in ye Cyty of Philadelphia where he was born who is designhed to visit your parts: I desired him to bear a few lines from my self to thy hands accompanied with a few perfect seeds of our Sugar tree which produceth A sap little inferior to ye Canes & in great plenty   it is besides a beautiful regular-shaped tree   I hope these with my friends presence may find thy acceptance; I long to hear from thee by A letter

Friends Historical Library, Swarthmore College.
1. Under the date, Gronovius wrote: "Repondi per Shoomaker April 1745."
2. Unidentified.

To COLDEN

November ye 2d 1744

Dear Respected Friend
this day our Good natured friend Benjamin Franklin brought thy Letter of October ye 24th which I have read & read with pleasure & am well Satisfied that my endeavours to Gratifie thy former Civilities & present merit had ye much desired efect   I am sorry thee mist of procuring ye seeds of ye Arbor Vita   I long to have that growing in my Garden but such disapointments often hapens.

   I am obliged to thee for thy kind advice & offers to assist me in publishing A discription of our American plants which I have thought of Many times but am not yet very hasty in entering upon a Performance that requires mature consideration   I have had several years past A specimen of A performance of this kind from ye medical Society at Boston with an account that Doctor Douglass[1] had described (according to that specimen which was done well according to Turnforts method) eleven hundred plants growing round & adjacent to Boston — allso ye Ingenious Doctor Mitchel hath discribed curiously many of ye plants in virginia & hath promised me A book as soon as possible   he hath sent it to london to be printed   when I am furnished with these materials than I shall be better enable[d] to proceed warily in so difficult an affair But I cant Well pass by Giving thee some account of my friend Mitchel who is A Member of our Society   he did me ye honour of Calling at my house & staid all night. & next morning to demonstrate ye kindness & esteem I had for his Company went with him to town & he being an intire stranger I introduced him into ye company of our friend Benjamin to whose Care I left him for ye present. He staid in town near three weeks so that I had ye favour of his Company many times at my house in ye fields & in ye woods which I was well pleased with   he is an excelent Phisition & Botanist & hath dipped in ye Mathematicks which inclined A Gentleman in Town well known to us to say to me that our doctors was but novices to him, but another person more volatil & more extravagantly expressed his value for him tould me thay had not ye Millioneth part of his knowledge — But notwithstanding ye satisfaction I received in ye Doctors Company I could not help mentioning my friend Colden to him & set thy abilities & Character in such A clear light before him which together with some specimens of thy performance so inflamed ye doctors mind (that tho his Constitution is miserably racked) he said that if he was sure he could See thee at York he would venture so far for ye sake of A little of thy Company.

Sir Hans Sloane hath ordered me A fine parcel of books   some is come in & more I expect every day   I wish thee would please to put 10 or 12 good seeds of ye bush squash in ye next letter thee sends me   I think to send by this opertunity some seed of ye Siberian Rubarb   pray hath thee seen ye snough box or Bitter gourd   if not, I can send thee some seed this in hast from thine

John Bartram

LPCC 3:78–79.
1. William Douglass.

To COLDEN

ye 10th of ye 11th month 1744/5

Esteemed Friend
I have lately received thy kind letter of I dont know when it being without date   I am obliged to thee for ye bush squash seed & am glad to hear of thy correspondence with Gronovius & Linneus. I expect dayly to receive letters from Gronovius by A ship or two from London but it is so long Since thay left that port that I am under uneasy apprehention for them: I am obliged to thee for thy information of ye virtues of ye Uva ursi   I am afraid thay have not made sufficient experiments of it yet — I have seen ye berries as large as cherries & when verry rip near ye color of claret tho thay continue green till late in ye fall. I have eat of them on our mountains; our indian interpreter tould me that he had lived of them several days & reconed them wholsome   some of our people saith thay are poisonous & others that ye berries is very good to moderate A burning fevour; I cannot find that ye Collinsonia groweth in Maryland or virginia on ye south of ye mountains or else Clayton or Mitchel would have found it; when ye latter was at my house last fall he tooke seed & specimens from mee. he had never seen it before that Journey to Philadelphia; indeed Miller in his second part of his

Gardeners dictionary saith it came from Maryland which is ye place of its natural growth; but this is a shamefull error for I sent ye seed of it first to Peter Collinson with ye first seeds I sent to him; & when it growed & seeded with him it was observed to be a new Genus & in honour to its first propagator in Europ thay called it Collinsonia; & if I had not sent it out of Pensilvania I suppose Miller would not have known that there had been such A plant upon ye earth

Sir Hans sloan hath sent me this fall all Petivers works Hermans Parradisus Batavus. Sellii Historia Naturalis teredinis. Etmulerius on all diseases & ye natural history of Ireland which is prety amusement for this winter.

ye 25th of January

I have sent thee some of ye stones of ye best Plumbs in England as our friend Peter informs me thay are ye Orleans and Green Gage & apricots one nutmeg peach stone. I have Just received them. pray plant them as soon as possible if thay was soaked in bran & water A week it may accelerate thair Vigetation I am apt to believe thay would prosper finely in your countrey — have you any of ye little bitter gourd like Colocynthus I have some if thee want I can send thee some seed doth any of ye Saururus grow near thy house it is a wonderful specifick for ye cure of sore breasts

I have some thought of comeing into your parts & to ye katts kill mountains next august & should be glad of thy company there If it would suite with thy interest or satisfaction but Alas we dont know what disapointments we may meet with before that time. However in ye mean time if I can do thee any service pray let me know wherein which will much oblige thy Sincear friend

John Bartram

LPCC 3:189–90.

To COLLINSON

December 1744

Dear Peter

I have received thy kind letters of April ye 4th 16th 19th & 24th with all ye books mentioned in those letters very safe & in good order & ye Sesamum seed which I intend to try to propagate & give thee an account of my success I am afraid our sumers will be full short I am obliged to thee for thy kind endeavors to secure subscriptions for me but thy orders came too late to comply with any of them this year except that for ye duke of Richmond but I came under some infirmities this year & espetialy been discouraged by ye french thinking my labour would be lost as running all ye risque & its a chance if any vesails arives in London I desighn next year to try how I can bear traveling   if instances is no wers with us but I find most of my employers wants ye firs pine & ye balm of Gilead fir   ye spruice fir bear onely on ye very top of ye branches on high trees   ye first of which it is next to impossible to gather quantities as is wanted for it is not one in A thousand that bears & those that produces very few on A tree which is commonly 100 foot or 150 foot high & on ye extremities of ye uper branches & tops & mostly those trees that leans over a river that it is very tedious to cut down A tree 2 foot diameter for half A dozen seeds 100 or 200 miles from home   I believe I have traveled amongst them 300 miles square & gone thro ye thickest & larges groves of them & yet never as much as two hat fulls of clean seed upon ye trees   ye balm of gilead I believe grows nowhere to ye westward of new england but on ye Catts kill mountains at ye head of Delaware & hudsons river A long dangerous tedious Journey   both these shed thair seed directly as soon as ripe   our friend Doctor Colden hath been this fall at my house whom I received with much Satisfaction Allso Doctor Mitchel who stayed at Philadelphia near 3 weeks & made me several visits   he is A man of good parts but his constitution is miserably broken   I correspond very freely with him & Claton but how shall I do with Robert Fenwick[1]   its very rare that any vesail sails from Philadelphia to Liverpool or white haven or if thay do who will take care of them there how shall I direct them   I am glad those roots I sent last fall grows well I love to hear of ye prosperity of what I sent to thee   I have sent by this vesail by Capt Falkner 4 boxes directed to thee   N I for our friend Catesby   N II one of laurel   two roots of fern & A prety creeping spring Lychnioides   N III red & white honeysuckle   sasafras   tupelo   scunk root   roots of hopenies   A root of my great Lychnioides & A root of our great Silver Leavd maple   N IIII hornet nests   one for Sir Hans sloan & several parcels laped up in paper directed some for him & some for Doctor Fothergil   ye others are for thee or to whom thee pleas to bestow [them] there is a bag of good Sugar tree seed & several other kind with thair names writ upon them   I have put half a score little [illegible] which I take to be ye snough box gourd thee wanted some time past & I have put 2 or 3 handfull of ye seeds of A climbing species of euonymus Mitchel said thee wanted very much   its berries make A fine appearance in ye fall   it twists about ye trees or poles like hops   ye narrow leaved oblisco red spirea lupins & candle mirtle grows a long way off in Jersey & ye leatherwood back of our mountains so I cant send them by this opertunity   I have sent four quarters of Hickery in a bundle   one of them is of ye nut whiter then ye other   thay are ye best I could get of thair bigness but if thy friend finds that it will answer he had better have quarters of A tree [illegible] diameter which will split strait & free from knots if it be A kind [illegible]

BP 1:29:1; D. 173.
1. Unidentified except in Bartram to Collinson, December 10, 1745: "I am not so much surprized at fenwicks knaveing being [thee] tells me he is a lawyer."

To COLLINSON[1]

Dear Friend Peter Collinson
I have received thy kind letters of May ye 4th 16th 19th & 14th July ye 21 August ye 1st 20th 27th & 28th 1744 all which is very acceptable   I allso received ye paquet of seeds by ye care of Elias & ye plumb stones by Saml Chew   as all these letters came to my hands so late that I could not send ye articles mentioned that fall   I desighn if I am Able to try next summer what I can do   I have this winter been A great way in Jersey to fetch ye red flowered spirea & A fine birch with leaves somewhat like poplar & planted in my garden to send to you next fall & I desighned to go up to our mountains last week to fetch ye thymilea or leatherbark but I have had a sore blow on my back by A horse which drove one or more of my ribs out of joint & bruised mee inwardly grevously so that I was not able to turn myself in bed nor sufer any person to help me so that I was forced to lie upon my back which was a great affliction to mee who cant rest long without action and who cannot endure confinement but I am now much better & can sit up [illegible] I planted it once in my garden & it lived part of ye sumer then died   I am well pleased that so many of ye plants I sent thee grows   I love to hear of thair prosperity but thee sends me no account of them specimens which I gathered in my Journey to ye 5 Nations which I took for very curious   I desighn when I travel near to ye Larix in eastern york to bring home A billet of it for thee   there are trees near A [illegible]

BP 1:29:2.
1. The content of this letter indicates that it was written in the late winter or early spring of 1745.

To COLDEN

April ye 7th 1745

Esteemed Friend
two days past I received thy kind letter of March ye 19th. I wish ye plum apricot & peach stones may grow. thay are fine sorts & I believe would bear well in your Countrey, which is not so infested with destructive insects as ours is; I am obliged to thee for thy good will in endeavouring to send me A few great Spanish Chesnuts; I have had many of them from Europe at several times but not one of them ever came up; I have allso planted several times of ye large thin shelled french wallnuts without success. I now send one of ye little bitter Gourd and good seed in it. I am afraid it will be full late before thee gets it to plant, so as to come to maturity this year. I desighn to send thee some seed of Saururus   [plant] it in A moist place or marsh — if I travail to ye Catts kills next August I shall send thee information when & which way I intend to take my rout — we make at present but a poor

progress in our Phylosophick Society: ye tumultuous reports of wars Invasions & reprisals exercises most of our thoughts & discourses & many is under apprehensions of being more sensibly touched with these Calamities   altho we cant yet generaly agree to put our selves in any posture of defence notwithstanding many is very uneasy in our exposed Circumstance —

I am pleased with our friend Peters fine remarks on ye benefit that our Society might be of if it was carried on with A Zealous Emulation, who should make ye greatest discovery in ye secrets of nature. But most of our Members in Philadelphia embraces other amusements that bears A greater sway in thair minds — dear friend I sometimes observe that ye major part of our inhabitants may be ranked in three Classes   ye first Class are those whose thought & study is intirely upon geting & laying up large estates & any other attainment that dont turn immediately upon that hinge thay think it not worth thair notice. the second Class are those that are for spending in Luxury all thay can come at & are often ye children of avaritious Parents, [illegible] ye third class are those that necessity obliges to hard labour & Cares for A moderat & happy maintainance of thair family & these are many times ye most curious tho deprived mostly of time & material to pursue thair natural inclinations   I am much obliged to thee for thy little booke upon tar water. I had for A long time A great opinion of terebinthe preparations & am of opinion that tar water may be of good use to mankind yet am apt to think ye Bishop[1] carried it farther then it will generaly bear. I have known it used 30 year ago for ye small pox yet two persons that drank it freely A month or two before thay was seised both dyed; since then I have not known it much used. Our Governor lately drank prety freely of it for A pain of his stomack without any advantage, since which he hath sent to me three times for a root called in ye flora virginiana page 38 Starroot, by which he hath received great benefit. I have lately read ye Bishops [illegible] & I like his Philosophick enquiries better then any of that I have ever met with when he treats of vegetation, air eather, fire & light. in these subjects I think he hath made many Curious Reflections but towards ye latter part of his Book he hath dipped into such Confounded abstruse enquiries that I can hardly understand what he means & perhaps he doth not know himself or what he thinks — I have had this spring ye misfortune of A grievous kik of A horse on my back under my Shoulder blade that dislocated one or more of my ribs & was obliged to be helped into my house. as soon as I came in I was put to bed, being very fainty & A little stupified   I presently tooke ten drops of ye oil of turpentine in A little sugar. it was surprising that in three minutes time how spirits was raised & my eyes enlightened & had A good stomack to my victurals. I kept takeing 12 drops at A time every few hours for 2 or 3 days & by that time was able to walk about my room though was very much bruised inwardly   ye 4th day I walked about my plantation & ye 7th to Phyladelphia

Now dear friend I shall Conclude in love to thee. Respects to thy dear Spous & Children & remain thy Sincear friend

John Bartram

pray let me hear from thee as soon as conveniency will permit for I believe we must be ye most active members in our Society   adieu

Courtesy of the Trustees of the Boston Public Library.
1. George Berkeley, bishop of Cloyne (1685–1753), author of *A Treatise on Tar Water*.

From GRONOVIUS[1]

Yesterday I was favoured with a letter of Mr. Collinson, in which he communicates to me the loss of the Ship the Queen of Hungary, for wich I am very sorry. I hope your voyage was not there in.

Now dear Sir, as you are now setting up a Philosophical Society at Philadelphia I think you have the best occasion to propagate the Naturall History of Fishes, of which the Europeans are very wel described by Artedy.[2] But of the American ones we know nothing. Mr. Catesby hath indeed painted the American fishes very wel. But I wish to know of all them fishes, how many bones there are in the membrana branchiostega, which is sufficient to determine the genus together with the numerus pinnarum. as for an example in this species of cottus You see Letter A. is the membrana branchiostega, containing sex ossecula marked 1.2.3.4.5.6. Pinnae in universam Octo, nempe duae ventrales B. una utrinque. Dua pectorales C. una utrinque Pinnae dorsi duo, quarum pinna D. aculeata, secunda E. aculeis flexilibus praedita. pinus Ani una F. et cauda, quae semper ad numerum pinnarum refertat. Constans ossiculis octo ultra medium radiatis, prates extrema minora. Per consequens any fish which hath six bones in the membrana branchiostega, and 8 pinnae, must be referred to the Genus of Cottus. How easy it is to prepare the fishes this way, you may see in the philosoph. Transactions Numb. 463. I send to You for this purpose the specimen of Cottus, in hope You may find one amongst Your Countreymen, that will go on this way with Your fishes.

Pray You will so good at an' occasion to acquaint Dr. Colden of what I wrote before and that Mr. Collinson wrote to me in a letter dated the 24 of March, that he send to me by Mr: Hawkins a packet from D. Colden, which as soon I have received I shall give as speedely an answer, as possible.

[Large section missing] and that this Crab with a penostium is fixed to the shell.

Late in August I made a Society[3] with Mr. Reddy an Irish Gentleman and Monsour, the Gentleman traveler of Dr. Radlif,[4] to observe what the sea-coast would afford us in six days time, taking our lodging at Catwyk 2 hours from hence, when we hath the luck to meet a vast nummer of these Heremeet Crabs upon the Shoare, the most part living in a Shell, but however several naked. We carried a large number of them to our lodging, and put them upon a table, instantly we discovered that Swammerdam was mistaken for we found first

1: that this Eremite crab liveth in two different specie & genera shells, videlicet in the Cochlea infecens fascus maclatis maxime ad imes orbes distincta Litt. Cockl. mar. ang. st. 30, and in the Buccino crassum infiticous stratum et undatum List. 20, bit. 2. By these two different Lodgings it appeared that Swammerdem is mistaken, when he says, that this Crab liveth only in one sort of shel which is created only for his use: and it appears more that he is mistaken by the shell, You send to me, which is the Cochlea perlata Bonnari sect. Class. 3 n. 167 and a very different shell from that which Catesby painted Vol. 2. tab. 33 fig. 2, which is the Trochus maximus laevis ex negro maculatus, List. hist. com. tab. 90 num. 30   So that the Heremit Crab is found in two different species of shell as well in America, as in Europa.

2. that Swammerdam is mistaken that the Eremit krab is joyned with a penostium appeared very gratis dictum: for these creatures had no longer been upon the table, that we could hardly light our pipes, when they run out their shell, walked from one part of the table to another, creeping some of them in anothers Shell.

These two experiments we repeated in a second voyage, and succeeded the same way.

Therefore dear Sir, You shall obliged the whole world, if you will be so kind to observe when you meet any of these creatures, in what species of shells You find them, and if (when they are still in a perfect life) they dont come by themself out the shell, and thirdly if the pes cheliferus dextrus is constantly shorter and smaller than the sinister.[5] I found that in that, which you send to me, is the pes dexter, cheliferus minor, which I there fore call Cancellus abdomine nude, peditus Dex, destro-chelinfero minore. Contrary is with these at our Sea Coasts, which I there fore call Cancellus abdomines nudo, pedibus sex, dextro chelifero majore.

I propose to write a dissertation upon these animals, and to shew that Swammerdam was mistaken: I believe he never hath seen them a life, for they were send to him in a pot, so that they were al dead. I observed that ours did not life longer than 6 or 7 hourse.

In our Second voyage Mr. Reddy and I let these creatures boil like shrimps: we can assure you that we hath an exceeding good supper with them, eating them with vinegar and peper with a piece of bread and boter and two bottels good claret. All the people of the village run out, for they suppose falsely that thay are poison, but all our fishers at the Sea Coast thay are so phantable that they still believe it, notwithstanding they have seen us next day in a good health. I wish You could get the Bay clam and Sea clam (of which I give You the names in my account pag. 14) with the two Valves.

Now dear Sir a finish these, wishing You all health and prosperity, I remain, Dear Sir

Your most obedient Servant
John. fred. Gronovius

American Philosophical Society Library, Miscellaneous Manuscripts Collection.
1. April 14, 1745 (see Bartram to Gronovius, December 6, 1745).
2. Peter Artedi (1705–1735), author of *Ichthylogia,* published posthumously by Linnaeus.
3. This letter was forwarded to Bartram by Peter Collinson. Here Collinson has added: "went in Company."
4. Hawkins, Reddy, and Radlif have not been identified.
5. Collinson added: "I have acquaint the Docr. that I had Specimens of Hermit Crabs in near a Dozen Sorts of Shells."

To COLLINSON[1]

The plain Clay-Nest is fabricated by a small black wasp, of the same Species of that in *TAB*. III, *Fig.* 1, but less, that has a Speck or Stripe of Yellow in its Tail; and the Cells are made four or five together, joining Side by Side to each other. But the Clay-Nests that are so elegantly wrought are Built by a purplish Black Wasp, such as is figured *Tab.* III, *Fig.* 2: After one Cell is formed, they stop it up, and join another to its End, and then add another to that; which makes these wrought Clay Fabrics longer than the plain ones.

Their Method of Working is much alike, and it is very diverting to see them at it: Their Art and Contrivance is wonderful; and, as if it was given to chear them at their Labours, they make a very particular musical Noise, the Sound of which may be heard at ten Yards Distance.

Their Manner of working is, to moisten Clay, and temper it up into a little Lump, of the Size of Swan shot. This they carry to Build with; they begin first at the upper End of the Cell, and work downwards, until it is long enough to contain the Nymph or *Chrysalis:* After they have spread out the little Lump in a proper Manner to form their little Fabric, they set up their musical Notes, and return to temper and work up more Clay for the next Course. Thus they continue alternately singing and working, until a Cell is finished; which is made delicately smooth withinside; then, at the further end of each Cell, they lay an Egg; after this, by surprising Instinct, they go and catch spiders, and cram the Cell full of them; But it is further wonderful to observe, that they only in some manner disable the Spiders, but not kill them; which is to answer two Purposes; first that they should not crawl away before the Cell is finished; and next, that they may be preserved alive and fresh until the Egg hatches, which is soon.

The Spiders, by wonderful Instinct, are provided for the Embryos to feed on: Having stor'd up sufficient for its Support, she very securely closes up the Cell, and then proceeds to build the next in the same Manner.

The Maggot, or *Embryo,* having eat up all its Provision, before *October* prepares for its Change, and spins itself up in a fine soft silken Case, in which it lies all the Winter in the Chrysalis-State, until the Spring, when it eats its way out of its Clay-Dwelling.

"An Account of some very curious Wasps' Nests made of Clay in Pennsylvania, by Mr. John Bartram: Communicated by Mr. Peter Collinson, F.R.S," *Philosophical Transactions of the Royal Society* 43 (1745):363–65 (read at a meeting of the society, April 25, 1745); Letters and Papers of the Royal Society 1:386.

1. This account is based in part on that given by Bartram in his letter of October 18, 1741. Further information sent later by Bartram has not survived except in this paper, presented by Collinson to the Royal Society. In his presentation Collinson added: "Mr. *John Bartram,* a diligent Observer of natural Productions, sent me, from Pensilvania, two Sorts of curious wasps Nests made with Clay, which are commonly built against the Timber under the Roofs of Houses and Pales, to shelter them from the Weather. They feed as the Bees, on Flowers; but whether they sting like them I do not yet know."

From FOTHERGILL[1]

As the printed essay herewith sent will serve as a model to proceed upon, I shall not have occasion to say much here, having marked all those paragraphs which ought to be particularly observed in inquirys of this nature.

As the Tincture or rather the infusion of Galls must be made fresh from time to time, I have sent some powder of Galls which if kept dry will be good a long time.

Thirty grains of this powder may be put to an ounce of clear spring water, (Distilled water would do better) after they have stood 24 hours the water may be gently cleared off and sufferd to pass thro a clean peice of brownish paper and this kept for use.

This infusion always discovers if there be any Iron dissolved in mineral water. The deeper purple or black any water becomes upon putting in a few drops of it and the greater quantity of Iron, may in general be judged to be in it. Tho some mineral waters which contain Iron will not actually discover it at first by this change of colour, so that it is necessary that the tincture & water should stand in an open Vessel abt. 24 hours. If it does not change in this time, one may be almost certain there is no such thing as Iron dissolved in it. Such waters as these will generally bear carriage in closed vessels without much loss.

Syrup of violets, added in a small quantity to any mineral water becomes green, or red, or keeps its colour, only a little diluted. the first happens when any thing of an alcaline nature is contained in the water, the 2d. if an acid and it keeps its own colour, if neither.

Oil of Tartar likewise shews if there is any alcaline earth or of the nature of Limestone contained in any water by immediately turning it thickish white, and making it deposite in a little time, more or less of a white sediment.

If the water contains any thing of sulphur, it will soon tarnish Silver, either put into or held over its steam, it will likewise let fall a blackish coloured sediment or gray with a solution of Silver in Aqua Fortis.

After these experiments are try'd and their success noted down, it will be necessary to evaporate a quantity of it in order to obtain the sediment and to know what quantity of sediment a known quantity of the water affords. The greater quantity the better.

In evaporating the water great care is necessary, both that the Vessel yields nothing to it, that no dust gets in, nor that the heat does not any way destroy the salts contained in it. Glass is by much the best, but then it has serious inconveniences. Ile endeavor to procure a vessel of Block Tin,[2] which will communicate nothing to the water. The best way will be to fill any old Iron or earthern pot with common water, then set it on the fire placing the block tin vessel which holds the water to be evaporated, in the other upon straw &c so as to prevent the boiling water in the Iron pot from getting into the evaporating water. by this means a heat will be made by the boiling water in the Iron pot sufficient to evaporate the mineral water contained in the Block tin vessel without hazzard of injuring the sediment. Both vessels may be filled up as the water escapes till a sufficient quantity of the mineral water is exhaled. About 4 Gallons or 32 pounds will be necessary, the more the better and I should rather choose that the water is weighed than measured.

When the water is nearly gone both vessells may be taken off the fire; the remaining heat of the pot and the water it contains will be sufficient to dry it: it must then be carefully brushed off, or lightly scraped from the sides of the Tin, then weighed, put into a bottle and close corked or ty'd over.

This I should be glad to have sent over with the observations and experiments made upon each respective water and about 6 or 8 quarts of the same kind of water put into clean new bottles, well corked ty'd down and covered with pitch or resin. I shall from time to time draw up from these accounts a short view of the nature, quality and uses of the water which thou inquires after in order to their being published either here or with you, for general information and advantage.

The reason why I am so intent upon this part of the Natural History of your Country, I have partly expressed above and another is that from some successful inquiries into this perplexing affair I think I am able to give a tolerable account of them in a plain demonstrative usefull manner, more so perhaps as I have been more employed in thinking about this subject than some others.

Jno Fothergill

PS. I have marked with + all the places and paragraphs in the printed essay to which I should be glad that thou would attend in thy inquirys. Thou sees they are all of such a nature as can only be observed on the spot. As to the production of the sediment, I can easily examine that here as it will loose nothing by Carriage. And I believe it will be best to observe the directions No 6 p 19, in evaporation of the water.

I think to send either by this or the next Ship a proper vessel, which if it will not answer for these purposes may not be quite useless.

J. F.

BP 4:16.
1. Undated, but written in the summer of 1745 (see Bartram to Colden, July 15, 1745).
2. Commercial tin in blocks, unrefined.

To COLDEN

July ye 15th 1745

dear friend

I have received thy kind letter of June ye 30th   I am sorry ye Plumb apricot or Nectarin stones is not come up which I sent thee. no more is any of mine yet I have some hopes thay may come up next year. I intend to send ye seeds of ye Saururus & starroot when it is ripe in ye fall   ye roots of ye first is commonly called Brest root from its excellent vertues in curing sore brests being made into A poultise   I allso knowed A man that had been long affected with A grievous pain of his neck & brest with great weakness & could not find any relife from medicines until a Palatine man gave him ye leaves of this herb in powder which he called Oister Lacie or in our terms Aristo Lochis I suppose from ye Likeness of its leaves to that plant. this gave him immediate relief & as he tould me cured him in a few times takeing it. the star root is chiefly used by several for ye pain of ye stomack   thay boil ye root in water & drink ye decoction after ye method of our Indians from whome thay learned ye use of it, I should be mightily pleased with thy good Company (which I value very much) and Captain Rutherfords at ye Katskill mountains; if I durst venture on such A Journey this season I would rejoyce in ye favour of your Company but at present I am poorly & support my acking head on my hand & elbow leaning on ye table while I scribble over this paper   I hardly know how, my neibouring town ships is sorely distressed with Fluxes & fevers   in ye City many children dieth & in ye Countrey many lusty young men so that I think it not convenient to leave my family of little helpless children so far from home in so sickly A time I doubt our society will be so long A brooding that some of ye chickings will be starved if thay dont seek out themselves in ye fields for food

relating to ye vertue which I ascribed to oil of turpentine I think thee takes my expression after A different sence to what I intended it. indeed I wrote that letter in A hurry & had not time to take A coppy of it or scarcely look it over after I had wrote it. but as I remember I intended onely to let thee know how much it refreshed mee & helped my inward bruise & I thought might hinder ye blood from coagulating but I hope thee did not find any place in my letter wherein I ascribed ye reduction of ye dislocated rib to ye oil as thee seems to question my ribs being dislocated   I shall freely tell thee my reasons for believing thay was   eleven O'Clock Ant. merid   ye horse gave mee A kick with all his force by ye spine on my short ribs   I stood ye stroke but could not fetch my breath until I laid down on ye ground & roled about. & then I both felt & heard ye end of one or more of my ribs slip in & out of ye socket of my back bone as I drawed A full breath   then I got up & walked about A 100 yards to my house & was helped of with my cloathes & put to bed in great pain & very faintly   I presently took 8 drops of ye oil which as I believe refreshed mee exceedingly   then my wife looked at my back & where ye blow was given was turned black & sweled

& my pain was very sharp in my left side from ye Sternum to ye spine & on ye least motion my Diaphragma would be so contracted that I could hardly draw breath   my wife could hear my rib snap into its place again tho she was several yards of — she soon got some rum & salt & bathed my back which soon tooke away ye blackness & swelling & eased pain   she bathed it often with ye rum & salt for 2 days & nights & I took ye oil every 6 hours   this method I tooke in order to hinder ye blood from stagnating presently after ye first application of ye salt ye pain & blackness was removed but upon ye least motion my brest & under my short ribs would be pained & contracted so that I could hardly get breth   I suppose ye blow drove ye lowermost ribs forward & strained ye midrib for there ye pain & cramp seemed ye worst which engaged me to ly as still as A log which ye rib kept in place so well that we never heard it snap in after ye first day — ye reduction of my rib I ascribe to taking A full breath & keeping it in its right place to stillness & lying quiet   After I had passed 48 hours after this manner & perceiving no sighn of any blood stagnating in my brest (for I was very free from A fever) I ordered A strengthening plaster to my back & a discutient one to my brest which I kept on 3 weeks   now dear friend I have Candidly laid before thee ye symptoms & method of Cure & leave thee to Judge whether there was not a dislocation & whether I did not consider these symptoms reasonably & endeavour to apply proper means for thair Cure

some persons advised me to flebotony[1] but I trusted to the oil to answer that article – I have not room to take perticular observations of thy curious letter must defer it to another time — the seed which thee sent me for ye bush squash groweth finely but all runs about strongly yet I believe thee sent ye right sort for most of them growed upright at first but our heat drawed them out such A length that thay leaned to ye ground & now runs in long vines like others but very large   ye leaves near 18 inches diameter: if paper did not confine me I should wear out thy patience but I hope thy generosity will excuse thy friend

John Bartram

LPCC 3:129–32.
1. Phlebotomy, the letting of blood.

To COLDEN

october ye 4th 1745

Dear & esteemed friend
I received thy kind letter of september ye 13th since which I have received many letters from London Holland & Petersburgh some containing Matters of friendship other orders for seeds & curiosities   other curious remarks & usefull instructions of which those of Doctor Gronovius is very curious

I wish thee could see them; I would send thee a Coppy of them; if I could write it over exact; but as it is so mixed with Latin I cant read many of his words. altho I can understand his English prety well: if I could meet with safe conveyance I should be ready to send thee ye Original which I value much — Doctor Fothergill hath sent me A booke of ye enquiries of Lincom Spane[1] with large & curious directions & A box of spirits, oils syrops & Solutions for ye tryal of all medicinal springs that comes under my observation in my travels & to know what mineral thay are most empregnated with   he is pleased to say that he believes, from an observation that I sent him, upon his request, above A year ago, that I am ye most capable to manage such an undertaking of any: he uses many arguments to engage me to enter into it & to make diligent inquiry therein, But ye main spring of motion stil hath not its proper temper   but he saith he is not without hopes that he can engage some to assist him to remedy that defect, for thee may easily believe that it will take upp A great deal of time to make all those tryals that is requisit to come to A compleat judgment of ye different qualities of many mineral waters.

I received many letters that came with Captain Bream But I saw none directed to thee nor thy name mentioned in any of them. If I had I should [have] given thee an account of it by ye first Post; I find thy name mentioned in Gronovius letter after this manner — in April Last year I hath send for Dr Colden an answer to his characters, & besides send ye fundamenta Botanica: florum Virginica, & Index lapidum: and in November of ye year 1743 I hath send ye same things, but to my great sorrow I suspect that by ye uncarefulness of A friend of mine ye last mentioned is lost   However ye first I hope is come to his hand being by ye favour of Mr. Van Ingen principal Cornchanler in this town recommended to Mr. Hope at Rotterdam. Two or three pages following I find this Paragraph   Pray you will [be] so good at an ocation to acquaint Dr. Colden of what I wrote before & that Mr. Collinson wrote to me in A letter dated ye 24th of March that he send to me by Mr. Hawkins A packet from Dr. Colden which as soon as I have received I shall [forward] as speedy an answer as possible   I am obliged to thee for ye account of doctor Knights[2] extraordinary discovery of ye magnetick power of steel & improvment upon ye loadstone in return of which kindness I here send A coppy of a Paragraph or two out of A letter from Dr. Gmelin[3]   Petersburg october ye 13th 1744   I cant tel for what reason ye Government does not Publish ye expedition from Kamshatka to discover ye Eastern Coast of America. Notwithstanding all my endeavours I cant learn ye Perticulars of this voyage   neither can learn in what latitude where it was they landed on ye american shore but I know for certain is that our ships discovered America two weeks after thay Left Kamshatka toward ye east & landed on A Coast unknown to other Europians   they searched this Continent for A few days   after that thay returned to Kamshatka   ye expedition is kept secret by ye order of ye senate, — Have we not some reason to think from this account that this Surprising & Politick people who hath conquered & fortified ye chief passages from Petersburg to ye eastern sea hath an intention to engross to them selves ye trade of ye northwest part of america & perhaps ye spanish coast of ye south Sea   But suppose thay have discovered ye supposed straights of Anian   will not our Britans Be too late — suppose thay should find A passage from Button Bay thro to that Straight — I find by my correspondents in Europe that thay have been informed of our Phylosophycal Society & have great expectation of fine accounts therefrom tho I durst not so much as mention it to my correspondents for fear it should turn out but poorly; but I find the mentioned to Collinson, hee to Catesby, & hee to Gronovius, which was to him from Claton   these accounts I showed to franklin & he layeth ye blame on us; & Dr. Bond Saith Ben. Franklin is in fault; however wee three talks of carrying it on with more diligence then ever which we may very easily do if we could but exchange ye time that is spent in ye Club, Chess & Coffee House for ye Curious amusements of natural observations — I inclose seeds of ye saururus & star grass; I want some good seed of ye arbor vita   I long to have it in my garden & ye paper birch which grows on ye kattskill mountains whose seed is shed 6 weeks ago.

Dear friend with Salutes of kind love to thee & family I rest thy Real friend

John Bartram

LPCC 3:158–60.
1. Unidentified.
2. Gowin Knight (1713–1772), later first librarian of the British Museum. His research on magnetism improved the mariners' compass and won him the Copley Medal of the Royal Society.
3. Johann Georg Gmelin (1709–1765), German naturalist who was with Bering in Siberia.

From SLOANE

Chelsea Oct. 16:1745

Sr

I have received your Letter of the 8th of December 1744, which was sent me from France, by those who took the ship, but without the Hornet's Nest &c you sent with it. I am obliged to you for your good intentions as much as if it had come safe. I hope this will not discourage you from your observing the Works of Allmighty God in the Creations and continuing them and that amongst the rest of your Friends you will make me a sharer of your Discoveries, which will be a great additional favour to

Your most Sincerely
Obliged Humble Servt.
Hans Sloane

Historical Society of Pennsylvania Library.

From COLDEN

Coldengham, November 7th, 1745

Dear Mr. Bartram: –

I am much obliged to you for the information in yours of the 4th of October, which did not come to my hands till the 3d of this month. Mr. Collinson wrote to me that he had forwarded my packet to Doctor Gronovius; and mentioned the curious instructions Doctor Gronovius had sent you, and wished I could see them. Perhaps Lewis Evans may take the trouble to copy them for me.

The experiments Doctor Fothergill would set you upon, and has enabled you to make, may certainly be very useful, if carefully executed.

We have very few Mineral Springs in this Province. All that I have heard of, is a stream on the south side of Anthony's Nose, a mountain in the Highlands, between my house and New York. It runs down a precipice into Hudson's River. Sloop men, who use the river, say that they have always found it purgative; and lately I heard that a sloop, being in want of water, took in some from that stream. They had many passengers, men and women. The water proved purgative to all of them. [illegible] As there is no anchorage on that side of the river, near that stream, I never had any opportunity to observe it; and I doubted of the truth of the accounts I had casually received of it. But now, if I have any opportunity, I shall take some more notice of it.

There is a good deal of ore found in that hill – a mixture of iron and copper; and they being mixed, has made the ore of no use. I am not sufficiently acquainted with the methods of trying mineral waters. I have never thought on that subject; but I find that *Sal Ammoniac* will give a blue tincture to anything impregnated with copper, and galls give a black to the tincture from iron. If my memory do not fail me, I shall try this with galls, and *Sal Ammoniac*.

My son tells me, that upon a survey in the Mohawk's River, they met with a spring which let fall considerable quantities of sulphur; and that the Indians who were with him filled their kegs with water of this spring, to carry home for the use of some that were sick. It is not a hot spring. I have never heard of any hot springs in this country. Colonel Morris,[1] I remember, several years since told me of a very good chalybeate spring, in Monmouth County, in East Jersey; and this is all the information I can give you, on this subject. I forgot to mention the spring in Onondaga country, which, perhaps, you saw when you were there, which throws up a kind of Naphtha, or Petroleum, or Barbadoes Tar.

Mr. Collinson wrote to me, that he had directed my brother's letter to your care, and from thence I concluded that it was put up among your papers. I have received a letter from my brother since the date of that, which makes the loss of it of no consequence. I thank you for the piece of news, of the Russian Expedition to America, which is well worth the notice of Great Britain; as likewise for the seeds of *Saururus,* and Stargrass.

I inclose a few seeds of the *Arbor vitae*. When at my son's, in the end of September, I found the seed ripe, and gathered a little; but being obliged to return home speedily, I resolved to send my son John to gather more, who was then with me. Something made me delay it for five or six days; and when he came, the seed were everywhere fallen. I little suspected its being so soon gone, otherwise I should have taken care to have got you enough to send to your correspondents.

As to your Philosophical Society, I can say nothing but that, as it is certain that some have been too lazy, so others may have been too officious; which makes the more prudent afraid of them

Doctor Mitchell writes to me, that he has sent you some account of the Virginia Pines. I should be glad to see anything that comes from that curious and learned gentleman.

I heartily wish you and yours all health and prosperity; and am your affectionate friend and servant,

Cadwallader Colden

Since I wrote this, I received by way of London, Doctor Gronovius' packet, with Linnaeus's *Fundamenta Botanica, Critica Botanica*, and Gronovii. *Flor. Virg.*, 1st and 2d parts, and his *Index suppellect.* I have likewise sent away my letter for him and Mr. Collinson; therefore, when you write to Doctor Gronovius, tell him that I received, the 8th of November, those books, and his letters dated the 6th of August, and 3d of October, 1743, after I had wrote to him.

College of Physicians of Philadelphia, Historical Collections of the Library.
1. Unidentified.

To GRONOVIUS

November ye 16th 1745
Dear friend
I have received thy observations on ye curiosities I sent thee with 2 kind letters for which I am obliged to thee   my friend Peter acquaints me that thee hath sent mee A parcel but I have not yet received it: I have sent thy letter & book to our dear friend Colden by ye post, free. I have not had time to peruse thy curious observations to satisfaction having ever since I received them been much hurried in collecting seeds & curiosities for my correspondents in England; & many for thee which I have not time now to make proper remarks upon in order to send   ye vesail is Just A sailing which I thought would have stayed A week or two but I have sent thee A Muskrat skin with its feet tail & part of its head that thee may observe its Characters; but one of its under & some of its Jaw teeth is broke by accident   I hope to send A better specimen by next ship which is to sail in A month if not hindered by ye frost   [ye teeth was] so small I could not

263

preserve them so as to give you an idea of thair scituation   it was catched yesterday & carefully scinned & dryed it as well as time would afford; as times is now so difficult I thought it was better to send one little imperfect then none at all: shall endeavour to mend it with an ould one next opertunity. In ye mean time please to assure thy self that I shall use all possible means these discoureiging times to demonstrate that I am thy reall friend

John Bartram

P.S. I desire thee will be so kind when thee sends me any more observations thee will write in English   I can make but A poor hand of latin & we have very few or none that can assist Mee   thine as before

American Philosophical Society Library, Miscellaneous Manuscripts Collection.

To COLDEN[1]

Dear esteemed Friend
two days ago I received thy agreeable letter of November ye 7th with ye seed of ye Arbor Vita which seemed to be very good   it was A fine parcel & very acceptable   I sowed it carefully yesterday   I am obliged to thee for endeavouring to procure more for my correspondents but I dont know yet whether thay want any of it; thay have not wrote to mee for it; but I believe if my affairs falls out prety well next year, I must go to ye Katts kill Mountains. I desighn to lett thee know before I set out. thy accounts of ye mineral springs in your countrey is very acceptable. I am allways glad to meet with any materials to enlarg my knowledge withall. pray which side of Hudsons river is ye purgative spring. I never heard before that there was a bituminous spring at Onandaga but in ye Senecas Country, but am well informed there is one at Alegany; doth thee believe it is realy brimstone that ye spring up ye mohawks river lets fall. if so it must be of great virtue

in ye same ridge with your highlands in Pensilvania & virginia is great quantities of iron oar & often mixt with copper Sometimes Vitriol & Sometimes Sulpher. that mixed with copper or Sulpher Some people thinks will make very good pots   it runs easy, Some Says thay will be too brittle I have been lately at a Copper mine mixed with iron   ye earth or stones there about yealded fine Coperas & ye water preceeding therefrom would turn Iron into copper as ye owner affirmed to me who Shewed me his knife handle that seemed to be good Copper, which he said had been Iron. ye water is so corrosive as to Corode ye Iron that is put into it which being put into fusion by fire is transmuted into copper   ye mineral stones exposed to ye air falls to powder like slaked lime

I received A letter & A booke from Dr. Gronovius directed to thee & A letter from thy brother which I forwarded ye same day I received them: which I hope is before now come safe to thy hand. there was in Jersey A well dug about 14 foot deep in A stiff marly Clay which supply ye house with water for 40 years but these two dry falls it failed. this fall ye owner had ye well taken up & dug 14 foot deeper (through A black stinking sulphurous earth; interspersed with lumps of hard shining sulphur) but found no water, then he bored 12 foot deeper still found no water   then left off: its pitty but he had dug or bored 10 feet deeper to try what difference he might have found:

I have sent thee some of Gronovius observations on some things that I sent him: if thee thinks it is worth while keeping ye original, I wish thee would be so kind as to coppy it over in English which I can better understand & send it me by ye first opportunity — & I will try if Lewis Evans who is under obligations to thee will coppy over Dr. Mitchells history or treaties of ye pines in virginia which he left with me; but since hath sent for them   if Lewis will coppy it I or hee shall send it to thee: I have not yet received ye parcel from Gronovius   I suppose it is coming in ye next ship which I hope will not be long if ye french dont intercept

If I can do thee any further service thee art fully entitled to it & needs onely to let me know wherein I can serve thee which will exceedingly pleas thy Sincear friend who wisheth thee & thine prosperity & content

John Bartram

LPCC 3:178–80.
1. Undated, but written in December 1745, according to the Colden Papers.

To GRONOVIUS[1]

December ye 6th, 1745

Esteemed Friend Doctor Gronovius: –

I have received thy kind letters of July ye 25th, 1744, and April ye 14th, 1745, with thy observations on ye Shells that I sent thee, and ye skin of ye Fish, with its fins curiously displayed on paper; all which was very acceptable. But as I did not receive a line from thee since I sent those curiosities to thee, around two years ago, until late this fall, so I could not procure any Fish, nor Insects for thee. But since I received thy letters, I have rode about ye country to gather what I could for thee, and particularly to the Loadstone quarry, and bought a few Loadstones, two of which I send to thee for those two gentlemen who were so desirous of them; with whom I should be glad to correspond by letters: for I am ready to learn of any learned person that will be so kind as to instruct me in any branch of Natural History, which is my beloved amusement.

Ye Loadstone lieth in a vein of a particular kind of stone that runs near east and west for sixty or seventy miles or more, appearing even with, or a little higher than its surface, at three, five, eight, or ten miles distance, and from ten to twenty yards broad, generally mixed with some veins of cotton.

Ye earth of each side is very black, and produceth a very odd, pretty kind of *Lychnis,* with leaves as narrow and short as our Red Cedar, of humble growth, perennial, and so early as to flower, sometimes, while the snow is on ye ground; also, a very pretty *Alsine.* Hardly anything else grows here. Our people call them Barrens; but if this black light mould be spread upon other kinds of soil, it will produce corn and grass, finely. See more in ye papers in which I have wrapped some of both ye common rock and loadstone.

I have sent thee many curiosities in a box directed to thee: which I hope our worthy friend, Peter Collinson, will send to thee according to my direction, – if the French and Spaniards don't hinder him from ye opportunity of obliging us. Indeed, it is very discouraging to think that all my labour and charges, may very likely fall into such hands as will take no farther care of them, than to heave them overboard into ye sea, as I suppose they did all that I sent last year, by the Queen of Hungaria. If I could know that they fell into ye hands of men of learning and curiosity, I should be more easy about them. Though they are what is commonly called our enemies, yet, if they make proper use of what I have laboured for, let them enjoy it with ye blessing of God.

I have sent a variety of ye clay-cells, which ye stinging Wasps built last summer; but ye wasps were gone, or dead, before thy instructions came to my hands. I believe we have a great variety of these kinds. I design, next summer (if my affairs go on pretty well), to make a fine collection of insects and fishes for thee.

I sent by ye last ship, to Mr. Collinson, a Muskrat's skin, with its feet, tail, and part of its head, for thee to make particular observations thereof.[2] it is a young male but ye parts of generation at this time of ye year is scarcely discernable. I have here sent the a female more perfect & next spring perhaps I may send a perfect male when ye parts of generation is more enlarged.

I have sent thy observations on ye Shells, I sent thee, to our friend Dr. Colden; and thy letter to him, with ye book for ye Doctor at New York, – who died a few days before I received them.

Dr. Colden and I often send letters to one another. He is a worthy gentleman, of pleasant and agreeable conversation, and great humanity. He staid at my house one night, last year; and next day, I went with him to James Logan's, and from thence to Philadelphia.

Doctor Mitchell lodged several nights at my house. Last year, he came up to town for ye advantage of better health. He is an ingenious man: but his constitution is miserably broken, and if he don't remove soon from Virginia, he can't continue long in ye land of ye living.

Our friend, Dr. Phineas Bond, gives his service to thee. He hath a great respect for thee.

I have lately been upon ye branches of ye Susquehanna, to ye mountains, to fetch some roots of my great *Magnolia;* and measured a common dry leaf fourteen inches long, and seven broad, — the trees very large and straight. I have not yet received those books thee was so kind as to send, for which

I return my sincere love. I hope they are coming in ye next ship from London.

* * *

I shall be much obliged to thee, if thee would please to write all thy further observations — which thee pleases to communicate to me — in English which I can understand much better than Latin, which is troublesome to me to understand your sentiments. But now, dear sir, pray make use of every opportunity, that falls into thy hands, to write to me. A brisk and cheerful correspondence is very agreeable to thy sincere friend,

John Bartram

I have [sent] a copy of my Journal to Onondaga, twice, — which hath been taken; since which, I have not wrote it over again. Perhaps I may send it, next summer, again.

BP 1:31; D. 352–54; American Philosophical Society Library, Wildman transcript.
1. The original letter (BP 1:31) is now so badly faded that it is here copied from Darlington with the exception of substituting ye for the. There are minor differences between his version and that of Wildman.
2. Darlington omitted the two following sentences.

To FOTHERGILL

december ye 7th 1745

Dear friend Dr. Fothergil
I received thy letter & A box of vials & book of Lyncom spane which I am obliged to thee for   I sent to thee by Captain Lisle A box of sassafras flowers & other odd things which I hope Peter Collinson will give thee if thay come safe to his hands   Dr. Witt tells mee he got A good quantity of ye expressed oil of ye berries drawn at ye common oil mill & that it makes ye best minium plaster of all   he saith oxidation is nothing to it nor any plasters of ye shops is to be compaired with it for its wonderful penetrating vertue & discusion   I have not yet made much observation on our mineral waters for want of time to examine them being hurried in ye fall to procure forest seeds for my correspondents & indeed if I should make diligent & proper observations on all our mineral waters it would take up most of my time or I am sure more then I can spare beside serving my benefactors in Europe & my plantation at home & still worse, because most of ye trials must be made at great distances from home & which is still worse I like very well to serve my country but as I have nine children alive most of which are not able to help themselves it is my duty to provide for them   I have lately heard of many mineral waters on ye mohawk river that lets fall A quantity of sulphur on ye highlands by ye north river   the indians fetch ye water away in kegs for ye sick to drink   several men and women passengers that were going up ye river, drank at this spring to quench thair thirst which purged them stoutly & put them in a nasty trim on board ye ship   One

chalybeate spring in east jersey & Dr. Shaw A brewer in Burlington affirmed to me that A Spa water broke into his well which he brewed beer with, which affected ye beer so much that it purged those who drank it so much that thay thought he put A trick upon them so he was forced to throw away 50 pounds worth of beer & make use of other water to brew with   another doctor tould me of A spring near him that if any that had the ague should drink of it, thay would vomit, and cure them   And one that I was lately at, had a vitriolic taste, like cobbers water & indeed[1]

BP 1:30:5; D. 338–39.
1. Incomplete.

To SLOANE

December ye 8th 1745

Friend Hans Sloane: –

By our last ship to London I sent thee A hornets nest & A bag of our mosses with some other odd things   I wish thay may come safe to thy hands but if thay should miscarry I have sent another this time which I shall order Peter to let thee have if the other failed   if not to keep it himself he wrote to me last spring to send A quire or two of specimens but it came to my hands this fall & too late to send any this year   I desire thee would please to send to me what thee would in particular have me to send thee & I will use all reasonable endeavours to oblige thee with any curiosity that is in my power to procure   however in the mean time thee hath fully engaged by thy many favours & kindnesses – the respect with the hearty love & good will of thy sincere friend

John Bartram

BP 1:30:4; D. 306.

To COLLINSON

ye 10th of December 1745

Friend Peter

I have put on board Captain Mesnard one long cedar box containing A Hornet's nest & A variety of seeds for thee & A box of curiosities and Musk rat scin for Gronovius which I hope thee will take care to send him as soon & safe as possible   I have not nailed ye lid fast too because I would have thee to view them all for thy own satisfaction   his letter I have not sealed that thee may read it & send it to him   if thee observes any thing in his colection that the want let me know & I shall endeavour to send ye same sort to thee   there is an open letter in ye box to him which if thee thinks [illegible] I have sent by ye two last ships to London five boxes in each ship   three in each of forest seeds for those gentlemen thee sent me orders from & A box with roots in earth for thee in one ship   in the other A long cedar Box with A variety of seeds for thy self & some curiosities for Sir Hans & for thee   I have sent allso 2 quarters of hickory & A square box of plants in earth viz one root of my great mountain Magnolia   several roots of papaw   one fine root of our Laurel full of flower buds   one sod of sweet Persian Iris   one sod of ye fine creeping spring Lychnis & A sod of what you call Dracocethalum   pray give Catesby one root of papaw   I sent several in our last ship   I have received ye nails calico russian linen & ye clothes for my boys   all which are very good & well chosen & gives great satisfaction   ye only thing that gives me any uneasiness is that thee hath sent more than what is my due.

Now though oracles be ceased & thee hath not ye spirit of divination yet according to our friend Doctor Witt we friends that love one another sincerely may by an extraordinary spirit of sympathy not only know each others desires but may have a spiritual conversation at great distances one from another   now if this be truly so   if I love thee sincerely & thy love and friendship be so to me   thee must have a spiritual feeling and sense of what particular sorts of things will give satisfaction & doth not thy actions make it manifest? for what I send to thee for thee hath chosen of just such sorts & colours as I wanted   nay as my wife & I are one so she is initiated into this spiritual union for thee has sent her A piece of calico so directly to her mind that she saith that if she had been there herself she could not have pleased her fancy better   I am bravely recovered of ye blow on my back & that which I take to be A [illegible] is much better   ye first that I was Much uneasy with was about [illegible] but I heartily rejoice that my cargo sent last fall is safe arived I hope in good order   I am sure I took great pains to gather all in its full perfection & put them in fine order or board   pray let me know   ye fine magnol comes forward   thay cost me ready cash besides my Journey to ye mountains to fetch them & instructions to ye indians how & where to find them   it is ye statlies tree of all that tribe to be 3 foot diameter above an 100 foot high & as straight as an arrow   ye seed that I send thee was choice good & all I could get   my root is putting forth A fine green bud   ye laurel pine cones fabia & ulmary is very acceptable   I have a great desire for A large Colection of ever greens   ye allpin pine & evergreen thorn thee sent last year or year before last is not yet come up   indeed I believe not one evergreen thee sent me is alive   our extream heat or cold killed them but if I can get them again I hope to manage better   I have now better conveniency in opening those fine cones of Cluster Pine I observed how close the scales adhere which is contrary to all our Pines & Firs (except one species of ye three-leaved Pine); which, before thay are well dried, spring open & shed all ye seed out which makes them ye difficultest to gather   one may in ye beginning of ye week see ye cones green, & before ye latter end all ye seed that is good will be shed out, especially ye five-leaved, which you are so fond of: & which it is not possible for me to gather any great quantities thereof; as I wrote to thee last year I design to get what I can yearly, but as I cant be in three or four hundred distant places in three or four days time, I cant procure great quantities & if I depend upon others assistance I am sure of being deceived.

As our friend Miller seems to question my account of our Pines I now tell thee I generally take care to speak truth — even to those that I think will bestow no more pains of examination than to tell me it is not so — to whom silence suits better than arguments — as ignorance doth to thair capacity but as I have a great opinion of Miller's learning & judgment I am engaged in duty & friendship to inform him ye best I can at present.

All our Pine cones are two summers & one winter from thair first appearance to thair perfecting & casting thair seed but this one species — which open not till ye second or third year after thay seem perfectly ripe   I have been much surprised at observing these trees have upon one branch all ye cones of three, four or five years' growth at once   when shaken no seeds shed out as these trees grow mostly on sandy desert   I thought it might be due to [illegible] which inclines me to take it for a different species from ye other 3 leaved pine whose scales of ye cones do not onely open to let ye seed out but are reflexed yet stick fast on ye tree for many years after ye seed is shed which is different from ye 5 leaved pine which is A little while after sheding its seeds drops ye cones which our spruice or silver fir doth not until A year & a half after sheding its seed but ye balm of gilead fir lets drop both scales & seeds together & leaves ye centeral Cylinder of ye Cone sticking to ye tree before it is quite dry like our tulup tree [illegible] receive them [illegible]

as for ye plumbs apricots & Nectarines thay do but poorly with us as I tould thee many times   we have A mischievous Beetle that bites or darts ye young ones then lays an egg which hatcheth & becomes A grub that eats ye fruits to live   then ye fruite drops of before it is ripe   I cant se that grafting on a peach stock or by planting by water courses or ye north side of buildings signifieth anything   I have tryed all these ways   ye only way that I can find is to plant where ye ground is daly trod & kept bare of grass or weeds   in such places I have had fine plumbs   thair imperfection is owing to our heat of summer seeing thair berries shewed so plump & fair   we have many fruits that doth come to perfection yet hath seed & kernell too   our plumbs & apricots tho thay will not ripen fitt to eat yet thay have stones & kernell in them too & such as will grow fast enough when planted   ye gooseberries bears fast enough but ye fruit is so furry thay are not worth eating   yet thay are full of seeds but I design to try both dung moisture & shade for them   but all thay signifieth nothing to plumbs or nectarines   ye onely place I can find is in ye hard gravely parched ground which is commonly trod & ye tree shaken   I planted a plumb tree some years ago in ye moist ground near A spring which hath blossomed & set abundance of fruite but thay was bit & all dropped of last spring   I dug & cleaned all ye grass from about it but it signifieth nothing   but I had 3 trees one at ye south end of my house   another on ye north & another on ye west where thay was daly trod about which bore perfect ripe plumbs as thick as thay could crowd together   I have last spring planted A nectarine tree on ye north end close to my kitchen dore & I desighn to plant A apricot tree or two on A cold dark northern declivity by my stone quary where it is never heated with ye sun   I shall be glad to know what Dillenius & Lineus makes of ye burrage flower   I am glad ye shrub periclimenum grows with thee I like it for its long flowering   my great magnolia shot out near half A foot   I then thought I was sure of it when of A sudden it dyed root & branch to my sorow for I cant tell when I can get any more unless I can hire an indian to bring me some but thay wont stir without one gives them as much A day as thay can get in A month   if we wont give them six shillings A day thay will tell us we may go our selves & these trees grows in thair countrey   I know nothing of any oblescotheca with red flowers so that If I sent it I must have gathered it [in] my Journeys   I am not so much surprized at fenwicks knaveing being [thee] tells me he is a lawyer [illegible] to be a pest & perplex to mankind & I took with some degree of happiness not to be cheated with [illegible] however I am obliged to thee to endeavour so much for me   I have lost ye great blue berried Cristophoriana   I had it many years but it bore neither flowers nor fruite   it delighted in dark rich light & is A constant companion to ye ginseng   if I come across it again I shall endeavor to send thee A root   I am glad gordon[1] has raised one plant of ye great magnolia   take care of it for my sake   I dont know how you can get any more   but what proceeds from it   I thought you had Chinquapins enough by this time because thee wrote to me formerly that you could have them from Maryland where thay grow in plenty & I dont know where any quantity grows nearer to us then ye borders thereof from whence I desighn to try to procure what quantity I can to send thee   our locusts is not come out this year so could not make any remarks about them   there is abundance in ye ground which we find in diging

BP 1:30, 1:31; D. 173–75.
1. James Gordon, a gardener.

To COLDEN

January ye 25th 1745/6
Dear Friend Colden
I have received thy kind letter of december ye 31st with thy translation of Gronovius observations on ye fosils & shells that I sent him   I am much obliged to thee for doing it: now I can understand ye doctors meaning; before I was doubtfull; ye lattin pusels mee: I now send thee another of his letters in which is a Paragraph of lattin which I should be glad to have A little unfoulded; I hope ye letter may gratifie thy curiosity: – I have in my last letter to him mentioned what thee desired me to do
    as thee was so kind as to inform me of ye fine discovery of increasing ye vertue of ye load stone & of impregnating steel with an extraordinary magnetick virtue. I have now by me A bar of steel three inches & half A

quarter long & ¾ of A quarter diameter being octangular finely polished & very hard, so strongly impregnated that ye north end or pole will hold up A midle sized key or three large ten peny nails by thair points in A perpendicular position, & two nails after ye same manner at ye south pole; or if it be held horizontally like ye beam of A ballance it will hold at one end four large knitting needles perpendicular by thair points & at ye other ye key at once so that it will hold up ye same weight at each end and at once as it will hold at one end at twice   ye midle of ye bar hath no attraction but from thence ye attraction increaseth toward each end so that it will take up A nail within an inch of either end & A large needle within an inch & half these tryals I made upon this paper & thee may depend upon it for fact

    I delivered Dr. Mitchels treatice of ye pines of virginia to Lewis Evans to coppy over for thee which he hath done & I suppose will send them to thee by the first oppertunity; I have sent ye originall back again according to ye doctors desire   I have found on A branch of Susquehana A piece of excelent brimstone oar different from ye Marchasite or pyrites which by Sublimation[1] will yeald A small Quantity of brimstone; but this which I send thee here will yeald A great quantity of fine Brimstone onely with burning in crucibles as thay do in England or Sweden & ye ashes of which thay make vitriol; & by ye addition of urin by another process thay make allum but our blew mountains in some parts abounds with natural alum so that we need not mind ye factitious;[2] thy remark is curious that ye pots in new england hath A mixture of copper   we have an oar near Susquehana that hath A mixture of iron, copper & sulphur which is supposed will make good pots: indeed I believe ye sulphur will make it flux easyly but whether it will not render ye mettel more brittle [illegible] within Burlington was lately found four foot deep under A great stone some peices of human Bones & A large Cake of indian bread. Supposed to be by its form & consistency, being very much like ye shape ye indians makes them in these days; I have A bit of it now by me which I have examined by ye Microscope   it appears to be composed of materials reduced to very fine particles by grinding between two smooth stones   I believe ye kernels of hicory nuts entered into ye composition. if Indian corn was another it certainly underwent A laborious trittition[3]   I held A live Coal to it which imediately reduced to A Coal & ashes   it emitted A thick smoak & smelled like A burnt crust but A little earthish   how long it is since this was buried no person can give any certain account: but it is most certain that it is A great while since; ye ouldest indians there about saith there was formerly A great Indian king buried there – ye stone was very iregular as to breadth & thickness being in its natural shape but from whence transported or how cant be known there being none like it to be found in that part of ye country – in all appearance this Cake might Continued intire many hundreds of years longer   it seemed to have suferd very little change onely ye out side was A little discolored; ye sand in which it was buried was incrusted about it ye thickness of brown paper but as ye sand hereabout was not impregnated with any mineral Juices it did not penetrate into ye Cake to allter its nature or texture, – Now dear friend thee may se that I am so much in ye humour for Scribling that rather then send thee blank paper chuse to send it filled with rubish taken out of an ould Indian grave

I wish thee & thine health & prosperity & remain with much respect thy Sincear friend

John Bartram

Historical Society of Pennsylvania Library, Simon Gratz Autograph Collection, Case 7, Box 21.
1. Refining or purifying.
2. Artificially produced.
3. Grinding into powder.

To COLLINSON

april ye 12th 1746

Dear Peter
I have now but little to write haveing received no letter from thee since last fall. I sent A cargo of forest seeds for my correspondents & garden seeds for thee with many curiosities as presents for several of our friends in 3 ships but can hear nothing whether thay be arrived at London or not   we hear there be great troubles in england[1] & dread ye consequences   our friend Joseph Breintnall departed this life ye midle of last month so that now what letters thee sends for me let them be directed to me or to ye care of I. Pemberton, Jun. for every merchant of note in town knows me   I am mightily pleased with thy letter from Petersburgh giving an account of ye Russians discovery of america   pray doth thee hear any more of it   I love to hear of any new discovery of any kind

BP 1:30; D. 175.
1. The War of the Austrian Succession (1740–48) had involved England in a war with France, who was backing a return of England and Scotland to the house of Stuart.

From CATESBY

Ap: 15: 1746.

Dear Friend:
I own my Self your Debtor, not from design or inclination, but I have really been discouraged by my ill fortune of loosing not only what I sent to America but also the two last years cargoes you intended me which loss the deprivation of time doubles. Yet never the less your kind intentions equally oblige me as if attended with Success and require a retaliation which I shall endeavour the first opportunity, to acquit my Self of. In the mean time accept of this Book of Birds. As Mr. Collinson gives me the pleasure of reading your entertaining Letters, I find you have sent me a plant of your Anona, some seeds of your tall Magnolia, &c. for which I heartily thank you.

In a letter to you in April 1744 I have mentioned in general what will be acceptable: which I mention because I don't remember any of your succeeding Letters take any notice of your receiving it. In it was an acc't of the Sesamum, &c.

I am Sincerely

Your Obliged Friend &c
M. Catesby

BP 1:97; D. 323–24.

To COLLINSON

April ye 16th 1746

this day I received thy kind letters of October ye 12th 1745 & January ye 24th, 1745–46, and Sir Hans Sloane's of October ye 16th with all ye seeds mentioned in those letters except ye strawberry and sloe – ye last of which we have had in the country these fifty years   I plant them about my hedges where it grows to a large size. ye blossoms are prodigious full but never one ripe fruit   they are bit with ye insect as all our stone fruit is, but ye Peaches & some kinds of Cherries overgrow them   I have some hope of ye horse chestnuts tho most of them were blue moulded yet some seemed to be pretty sound but alas! ye four fine large roots of Madder had no more appearance of life then if thay had been drying in ye house A year. ye 3 pine cones was right sound & I have sown them & ye most of ye seed   this after which we have had several hours of fine showers after being A cold backward spring as most we have had   my great bay is now in full bloom both guilded & plain   my prety plant is just in flower that thee saith Dillenius calls A Borage which I think hath no affinity with it or likeness to it save only barely in the shape of A single flower & I believe is as much A new genus as any plant that ever was sent out of america & not ye only one that adorns that spacious vale of 6 hundred miles in length, S.W. by west in which I have gathered ye finest of my autumnal flowers & where by report of ye inhabitants it is like as if Flora sported here in solitary retirement as Sylva doth on ye kats kill mountains where there is ye greatest variety of uncommon trees & shrubs that I ever saw in such A compass of ground   I am glad ye white berried Cristophoriana grows with thee but thee should have that with great blew berries which is much ye finest plant   there is abundance of it growing by Rapahanock in virginia so made no question but our friend Mitchel or Claton had sent to thee long ago   it grows nowhere less than fifty miles of me

BP 1:30:3; D. 175–76.

To COLLINSON

april ye 23 1746

Dear Peter
I have packed up in A box directed to thee 4 of our turtles dried after thair bowels were taken out & well washed, having preserved thair shell head feet

& tail intire by which you may observe ye difference of them almost as well as if thay had been alive   I cannot get any other kinds   its too soon in ye year   These females had ye yolks of eggs in them almost at thair full bigness but no whites no shell to them   it is near A month to thair time of laying   I design this summer to collect all our kinds of turtles with ye eggs belonging to them with insects & fishes & send some or other by every ship that sails from here to London so that if some is taken others may escape   We had extraordinary luck last year   I doubt there will but few sail from here this year   I have expected by every ship since Hargrave came in last summer those books Gronovius sent me   pray what is become of them   All ye ships that sailed from London last year for Philadelphia arrived safe yet I have no account of them

How doth our friend Catesby do   he wont speak A word to me now a days   he hath had several opportunities within these two years of writing to me & I have sent some curiosities to him every year

The account of Reaumur[1] about bees & wasps was very entertaining   I love natural history dearly but how come ye female wasps impregnated in spring if all ye males die in ye fall or doth thay impregnate ye female before thay die & ye principle of [illegible] lie dormant all winter with ye female

BP 1:30:3; D. 176–77.
1. René Antoine Ferchault de Reamur (1683–1757), French naturalist and physicist.

From COLLINSON

London Aprill 26 [1746]

Now Frd John I come to consider further of some of thy observations by thine of the 10 Dec   I am glad to find that thee art so well Recover'd & that all the Goods are Come safe to hand & please, wch is more than I expected and ought not to Excuse thee from being more perticular & Exact in thy orders Next Time —

Tho' thou canst not see, yett have told Thee what Inoculating on a peach stock May Do — if I am not out in my Conjecture, as it is a free stock & sends up its sap plentifully it may assist the Nectarine & Apricot, att a season when Supplies are wanting   as thou has tried the north Side of Buildings & sides of Water Courses &c to no purpose with plums: pray give the other fruits as fair a Chance

To prevent the Depredations of the Beetle I confess is not so easy as some other Bad Effects yett as we know the Duration of this Insect is but short if while he is so Noxious some Contrivance Could be found out to disturb or Destroy Him you then Might hope to taste a Nectarine one of the most Delicious fruits in the Universe & much Exceeds a peach in a Rich Vinous flavour'd Juice and an Apricot is also one of the fine fruits, Last Year our Standards was overloaded, which are allowed to Excell the wall fruit —

Suppose as soon as this Beetle is Discovered if the Trees was to be

Smoaked with Burning Straw under them or at some Distance so as to Fumigate their Branches att a Time the Beetles are most liable to attack the Fruit — or if the Trees were to be squirted on by a hand Engine with water in which Tobacco Leaves was Soak'd, Either of these Two Methods I should think if they did not totally prevent, yett at least would Secure so much of these fine fruits as would be worth the Labour of people of Circumstances who are Curious to Taste these Delicious Fruits in perfection —

I take it the Reason the plumb succeeds so well is the Frequent Shaking the Trees by being planted in a Frequented place   the Beetles are tumbled off or else are Disturbed & Frightened from Settling on the Trees — and the Ground being Trod so much may be a great Help by keeping the Moisture wch is so Conducive to bring the fruit to Maturity –

This brings to my Mind a Contrivance I was told a few Days agone — an English Man went and Setled att Naples, about yr Latitude & writt over to P. Miller that apricots throve very Well but all the fruit Dropp'd off, which He was surprised att for He Expected the finest fruits in that fine Climate, but he was Mistaken; for the Natural Fruits of that Country are Figgs, Pomegranates, Olives Grapes Oranges & Lemons

my Friend Miller writt Him Word to Lay a great Deal of Mulch Rotten Dung & straw mixt or a Great Quantity of Fern Leaves or any Compost that would keep the Ground Moist & prevent the suns Action, which is very penetrating In that Country as well as with you — This had the Desired Effect & the Gentleman writes Him word that since He has practised It, He has never failed of Fruit in plenty in the Greatest pfection —

Now frd John Improve this Hint & if your apricots are too Forward, plant them under all Disadvantages possible, that is in the most Exposed places, & In all the Coldest shadiest aspects that can be found, phaps when Mountains come to be settled the north sides may succeed with this fruit & others and may not be so much frequented by the Beetles. I apprehend, if your Goose berries were littered it would prevent their dropping Off & if this litter was now and then watered both under the Apricot, &c., it would be of service.[1]

Frd John I have writt more fully by Captain Mesnard[2] — but this will hint to thee thy Good fortune of all thy Cargos coming safe which is great Luck these very perilous Times —

Notwithstanding all my Endeavours I can only raise thee one new Subscriber for 4 five Guinea Cargo who Desires a little of Everything & Duke of Richmond & P. Miller is Continued   Send them any sort of Pine but Jersey pine   some acorns a few of a sort   Sassafras   Sweet Gum Sweet flowering Bay or small Magnolia or Laurel & any New Tree or Shrub & some of all sorts of Wild flowers:

I thank thee for the fine Cones of Small Magnolia & the Great sort, they are so fresh I hope to raise some   is there no more Chinquapin to be Had, why Does thou not Raise a plantation in thy own Garden of Chinquapin Trees to serve thy Correspondents   From the first Wee wanted them & if they had been then Sown by this Time Thou would have had plenty to serve us for it is a tree that is not to be had here for Money

The Larix and Evergreen seeds that our Friend John Miller[3] has Collected for thee I have Divided & sent half by this Conveyance & half by Mesnard. Now farewell.

P. Collinson

The Larix must be kept until next Spring but sow all the Rest Immediately for then thou may Expect them next year to Come up — our new Correspondent Desires in perticular to have Cones of ye Small Magnolia sweet Swamp flowering Bay [illegible] & for Gordon Seeds of your pretty ivy or Bay   he has Raised several, I hope, Sent me Last with the other plants will Stand it but I despair of the creeping Lychnis but by Seed

vale in hast

BP 2:72; D. 177–79.
1. There is a copy of this letter to this point in another hand, on which Collinson has written: "Frd John this is a copy of mine p Capt Lisle   Inclosed is a pcell of seeds in Brown Paper pcell Directed for thee and Left with Jon Head to be packed up with his goods." (BP 2:78). (Jon Head has not been identified.)
2. Captain Stephen Mesnard.
3. Unidentified.

From COLDEN

Coldengham, May 9th, 1746

Dear Mr. Bartram: —
You must excuse my not answering your kind letter of the 25th of January sooner. It was above two months in coming to my hand; and since that time, I have had my head so much set on a certain affair, that I could not think of anything else.

I return inclosed to you Doctor Gronovius's letter to you, and am obliged to you for the perusal of it. That part of learning of which it treats, I am so little acquainted with, that if I were to translate what he writes, it is probable I may make nothing but a series of blunders; but for your satisfaction, I shall turn the first sentence the best I can, as it is to show the manner in which he intends to publish what you send him, viz.

"We must now pass to such stones as have a resemblance of some animal, or of its shell or covering, and which authors commonly call petrifactions, and which they make no doubt in producing them as proofs of the ancient deluge. This excellent man observed these, variously situated on the ground; some on the surface of the earth, others sunk deep; for what he found in the southern parts of Pennsylvania, towards the great Lakes of Canada, lay on the surface of the ground; and in a journey which he made of some hundreds of miles, he found them scattered everywhere."

Your account of the Indian grave, is so far from requiring any excuse for writing it, that I am much pleased with your account, as it discovers how long bread and corn may be preserved, when kept in dry sand from the air; and shows that the Indians did not get their Indian corn from the Europeans.

You may expect to see more from me, when I can obtain anything that I can think will be entertaining to you; and which may better serve to show how much I value your correspondence, than anything I can write at present.

I am, very affectionately,

Your humble servant,
Cadwallader Colden

D. 331–32.

From GRONOVIUS[1]

Leyden, 2 June 1746

Dear Sir: –

The 19 of May I hath the favour to get your letters, dated the 16 Novemb. and 6 December, 1745, with a good number of exceeding fine curiosities, which I partly, for a short time and several occupations, have examined, and of which I send to you my observations, having the occasion that my friend, Mr. Dundas,[2] is going to London. I wish you would examine if the Muskrat hath not four *Mammae* — two at the breast and two at the belly.

Professor Muschenbroek is much obliged to you for the account you have given of the loadstone, and the situation of the rocke — of which he at an occasion shall make use, and remember you as is decent.

I am sorry your voyage[3] is fallen into the hands of the French; but I hope this present warre may soon be turned into peace; and by that occasion we may see another copy.

I am sorry you hath not received the books I hath send to you: wherefore I send to you another copy of the *Characters* of Linnaeus; and an edition of the *Systema Naturae* in octavo, which is very convenient for the pocket: besides, two copies of the New Chimney,[4] translated into Dutch, of which you will be so kind to send one at an occasion to Dr. Colden, who hath been so kind to communicate that book, in English, to me. That invention hath found a great applause in this part of the world which is the reason that I could not hinder to let it be translated into Dutch, and no doubt soon into French. In the plate, you shall see a little alteration, what is occasioned by very skilfull people.

I send also a copy of my *Index Lapidae*; but at present my collection is three times larger, so that I think for a new edition.

All things you send to me came very well over, except the two fishes, which were spoiled. I take, therefore, the liberty to communicate you two prescriptions; of which one is a varnish that preserves the fishes, and any other thing, in a great perfection, viz.:

R Gumm. Copal, ℨiij
Mastiches,
Sandarach. a ℨij
Spirit. vini rectificatiss lbi jss
   M. lege artis

The other is a powder, by which any creature, as quadreupeds and birds, are preserved and become very hard. I have several times made the experiment with a fowl, larger than a duck, putting him, with his excrementae and all, into a box, which is well closed, and putting this dose of a powder all over it: when the creature became in a few weeks very hard.

Pulv. aloes ℨiij
Myrrhae ℨij
Sulphur
Alumin. a ℨj. – M.f. Pulvis

I don't doubt it will do very well with the fishes, without taking the intestines out of them, except they may not be too thick; then the intestina must be carefull (by a gentle hole, made in the side of the belly) taken out.[5]

* * *

N. 2 The sea [illegible] mussele, with a concha and the Eremite-krab that seems to be the same with ours viz. [illegible] but as they are a great deal more in latitude, they may perhaps be a quite other species. Wherefore I beg a large one. In my previous letter I have acquaint you how they are always joyned together by a filamentum, and always stick on to a stone or piece of wood or any other thing like shapes to the [illegible]

This is the same cochlas in which our Eremite crab commonly is found, and the same of which Swammerdam made mention, but he Errs prodigiously. He says the shell was created by God almighty for it [illegible] that is false, because thy concha has his proper [illegible] as did with us a [illegible]: this boild like shrimp and eaten with vinegar and peper, with bread and butter [illegible] supper which I frequently have hath when I go to live for [illegible] at the seacoast.

Thus he says that the Eremite crab is with ventriculas and fibres so joyned to the concha that by no means the crab can be taken out.

Two years ago I lived now and then for some days at the sea coast two hours from this town, in company of Dr. Reddy [illegible] Ireland [illegible] the son of the Dr. of Bentlicks. We filled several times our pocket with these creatures putting them upon a table we took up pipe tobacco, and before this was finished we had the pleasure to see the creatures coming out their shells, creeping over the tabel, and fyting one against another, and severall times creeping in one another's shell. We were the first in this country that eat them; after they were boild like shrimp, and realy they gived us a good supper. However the people at the sea coast thinks still that they are poysons.

Swammerdam also says that the Eremite crab is only to be found in this shell, and in no other; but we have found that it is a mistake, because we found them in a great number in the Bucc [illegible] undatum of Lister,[6] Such animals and crabs anointed with the varnish preserves very well.

I have a method to detecte in 12 hours what creatures are living in several places in different waters. I only take a long stick which is very rugged and nothing at al smooth, set it Fastly in the mud, after 12 hours take it softly out, then you may see adhering severall living creatures to it.

I am very much obliged to you for the *Bay Mussel* which has two valves and the account of his situation, but I suspect that in my precedent letter I have call it the Pectunculus maximus massasnostras agneus of Petiver, what is a great mistake, for it is the Pectunculus margae dease [illegible] When you open the shells you see the inward margins of exceeding fine [illegible]

The Common *Bay Mussel* is an [illegible] Virginia Lister

The part of another shell [illegible]

The two young ones [illegible] to the Bay Oyster are [illegible] but of what [illegible] send [illegible] shall give you the name.

Thus far, Dear Sir, I can give you an account of some Curiosities: of the rest you shall see in my next letter.[7]

I hope you received my Letter dated in April 1745 by Mr. Shoemaker to whom I pray my service; likewise to Dr. Colden Dr. Phineas Bond and James Logan. I hope that he will remember me concerning the desperate affairs of our Synodus, which are in the hands of Mr. Peters,[8] according to the last account of it.

I am sorry to hear that Dr. Mitchell is so ill. I hope he may recover soon.

yesterday night I got a letter from Mr. Collinson dated the 16 of May in which he acquaint me that Dr. Mitchell was taken by the Tiger privateer from St. Malo, Captain Pallier, who took from him all his learned observations: for which I am sorry.

As you do not mention a word of the Caracter of a new genus of plants I suspect that you know nothing of it. You must know that with the assistance of Linnaeus and other friends we discovered several new genera, quite different from all those which are known, and so there is made one Bartramia and another called Coldenia. I can't say positively in what book they with severall other new Characters are printed, but I am sure that they will be found in Fauna Suecica or the Acta Suecica; which books were in April send from Stockholm by sea, so that they are expected here every day; when I shall send to you that book, if there are sent duplicates of it. However, that you should know what plant it is, I send to you the characters:[9]

Pray, when you write to that learned gentleman send to him a copy of this Character, and acquaint him, that I with great pleasure, perceived by your letter that my packet is come to his hands, but that I am extremely sorry that his things for me were taken by the privateers.

Pray acquaint me in Your next, how it go's with your Learned newly erected society, and what improvements they have made.

This is all, Dear Sir, what I could perform since the 19 of May, being now obliged by the departure of my dear friend Doctor Dundas to finish these, wishing You and all friends Health and prosperity, wherewith I remain

Your most obedient servant
Johannes Fredericus Gronovius

BP 4:39; D. 354–57.
1. The Bartram Papers, 4:39, present a number of problems. There are four copies of original pages of what appears to have been a single letter from Gronovius to Bartram, a part of which was included in Darlington (pp. 354–57). There is no original of the first part of the letter as given by Darlington. Of the four pages in the Bartram Papers, a part was purposely omitted by Darlington, but we are including as much of it as we have been able to read. Almost a page of identifications of Bartram's specimens containing much Latin, which we have been unable to read with any certainty, has been omitted here, as have two lengthy Latin characters of the two new genera, *Bartramia* and *Coldenia,* included by Darlington. For Bartram's transcription of the Latin characters, see the following letter.
2. James Dundass of Dundee (a Petiver correspondent?).
3. Gronovius refers to Bartram's account of his expedition to Onondaga.
4. A description of the Franklin stove.
5. The material from this point to superscript 7 was not included by Darlington.
6. Dr. Martin Lister (1638–1712), English naturalist and a Fellow of the Royal Society.
7. All of the material following was included by Darlington.
8. Unidentified.
9. The Latin characters of *Bartramia* and *Coldenia,* which appear in the original at this point, may be found in Darlington on pages 356–57.

To COLDEN

October ye 6th 1746

Dear esteemed friend

I received thy kind letter of may ye 9th & am much obliged to thee for translating part of Gronovius letter   It is not for want of respect to thee that I did not answer sooner, but for want of entertaining subjects to work upon: I may still add another reason as great or greater: ye generall distress of our provinces   yours with ye invation of ye barbarous Indians[1] and ours with four different kinds of mortal distempers viz ye small pox which now begins to be very malignant   ye bloody flux   grievous lingring feavours commonly Called ye dumb ague & ye sore throat   all these is generaly thorow ye countrey   very few families escapes some or other of them & abundans dies both men women & children   as it is ye dryest Summer that ever was known since ye English setled here so it is ye sickliest so that we are daly prest by naturall affection or ye ingagements of humanity to condole our near relations & friends afflictions instead of amuseing or diverting our selves with curious speculations — A few days past arivd Captain Mesnard from London who brought me severall pacquets of letters from several of my Corespondents as our friend Collinson, Sir Hans sloan, M. Catesby & a Parcel of books & letters from our worthy friend Gronovius in one of which he mentions Docter Colden with great respect & desired me to transcribe part of it & send it to him which runs thus. "you must know that with ye assistance of Linneus & other friends we discovered several new genera quite different from these which are known & so there is made one Bartramia & another Coldenia. I cant Say positively in what book thay with several new characters are printed, but I am sure that they will be found in Fauna suevica or Acta Suevica which books were in april sent from Stockholm by sea so that thay are expected here every day: when I shall send to you that booke, if there are sent duplicates of it. However that you should know what plant it is I send to you ye Characters; Bartramia & its char then Coldenia. Teucrii facie Bisnagarica   tetracoccos rostra pitis scaten foliis profunde venosis pluk. alm p. 363, tab. 64. fig. 6.

CAL. perianthum tetraphyllum. foliolis Canceolatis erectis.

COR. monopetala infundibuli formis longitudine calycis. Limbo patale obtuso aequali quadrifido

STAM Filamenta quatuor. tubo corolla inserta Anthera subrotundo Pist germina Quatuor ovata Styli totidem capillaries   Longitudine stamen stigmata simplicia persistantia

PERIC nullum Fructus ovatus scabe compressus rostris quatuor

SEM quatuor acuminata hinc convega inde angulata

Facies Neurada sed diversissima planta

"Pray when you write to that Learned Gentleman send to him A Copy of this Character & acquaint him that I with great pleasure perceived by your letter that my paket is come to his hands but that I am extreamly sorry that his things for me were taken by ye privateers"; this my dear friend I have transcribed out of his letter to me, for thy sattisfaction but as I don't understand Lattin any thing like well I may have mist several letters for want of understanding ye sence of many that was blotted but I hope thy mature Judgment may assist that defect   Now I have one favour to request of thee which is to send me A few growing trees of ye arbor vita after this manner make A little box about A foot square   lay about two inches thick of earth at ye bottom   then dig up some young trees about 10 inches high of ye arbor vita if thay have A sod in which ye fibrous roots are fixed it would be better to plant these on ye mould as close as possible   then fill ye box half full of mould & press it hard about ye roots   then put more earth in ye box about ye stems pressing it pretty close then fill ye box with mould to ye top letting ye tops of ye branches be just above ye mould   then nail ye lid fast on   this way I believe will preserve them alive A month or two in this cool season when ye vigetive Juices is at rest & ye box being full it may be tumbled about like other goods without much damage to it   it will be better to write upon ye lid KEEP THIS SIDE UPPERMOST: if thee would be so kind as to direct it to Dr. John Bard in new york for me & send it thither for me I believe he will send it to Philadelphia ye first opertunity that seed thee sent me did not come up tho it seemed very good indeed   ye dry Summer might be A great hindrance   If I can do thee any service in our way pray use ye freedom to accept it which will be cheerfully performed to ye best of ye understanding of thy well wisher

John Bartram

LPCC 3:270–72.
1. The French were encouraging the Indians to attack the English settlers.

To COLLINSON

december ye 14th 1746

Dear Peter
I have put on board this vesail 2 boxes of forest seeds   one pine box of Ld weimouths pine for duke of richmond & philip Miller   ye other with an oak lid one half is several sorts for our new correspondent   ye other half is for thy selfe to dispose of as thee thinks proper among thy friends   ye seeds is right good & I trod ye cones down in ye boxes close as I could that thay might lie in as little compas as posible & as A good part of ye seed was shed out of ye Cones on ye chamber floor I proportioned ye loose seed as well as I could to its due quantity of cones: this year hath been ye greatest quantity of seeds of Ld weimouths pine that ever I knowed & imployed hands to gather as many as I could   I have allso put on board one cedar box directed to thee at large No 111 in which is some curiosities for Sir Hans   seeds for dr Dillenius & Gordon with thair names writ on them & seeds & other curiosities for thy selfe

BP 1:31:3.

To GRONOVIUS

ye 15th of 12th month 1746

dear friend Dr gronovius
I received thy kind letters of June ye second & September ye 9th 1746 allso ye second edition of Lineus characters & thy Index all which impressions thee sent me before but ye Systema Naturae which is now received I never had before   I have not traveled much abroad this year by reason of ye wars & troubles both in europ & on our back inhabitants   ye french indians hath been very troublesome which hath made travailing very dangerous beyond our inhabitants where I used to find many curiosities & indeed these troublesome times is a great hindrance to any curious enqueries   while we may daily expect invasions we have little heart or relish for speculations in natural history

BP 1:31:1; D. 358.

From COLDEN

Coldenham, January 27th, 1746-7.

Dear Mr. Bartram: —

It is so long that I have lost the pleasure of my wonted correspondence with you, that I am afraid of my having fallen under your censure; and which would give me more concern, than the censure of some great men in the world. But if you knew the true reason of my discontinuing to write, as usual, you would be so far from blaming me, that you would pity me.

I was unexpectedly engaged in the public business, and when I entered upon it, I expected it would only have been for one single piece of service; but one drew on another, and I was kept more months from my family, than I expected to have been weeks from them.

But at last I have got to my country retirement, and to thos amusements in which I place my delight; but not to enjoy them so fully as formerly, by reason of interruptions which unexpectedly break in upon me.

The distempers which you mention to have been epidemical with you, seem, by what you wrote to me, of the same nature with the malignant fever that was at Albany while I was there, and carried off many. It was of the remittant kind, accompanied with profuse sweating and prostration of appetite. Madeira wine proved the most effectual specific; which most people were surprised at, when I advised it; but I had so old an authority as Hippocrates for the use of wine in some kind of fevers. This was attended with so much success, that the use of it became common.

It gives me much pleasure to think that your name and mine may continue together, in remembrance of our friendship. I do not know the plant, of which you send me the description from Gronovius. It is none of them I described to him; and therefore I suppose you have sent it to him, and that he has honoured it with your name.

It was not possible for me to comply with your desire, of sending you a plant of the *Arbor vitae,* for it was the 14th of December before I returned home from New York.

All my botanical pleasures have been stopped this summer, while I was at Albany. We durst not go without the fortifications without a guard, for fear of having our scalps taken; and while I was at New York, I was perpetually in company, or upon business, so that I shall be a very dull correspondent. However, I designed to have sent you something of our transactions, by Mr. Franklin, at his return from Boston; but he stayed so long, that I left New York before he returned; and I was at last exceedingly hurried in leaving that place. If I had stayed one day longer, the river had become impassable.

Now, dear Mr. Bartram, take pity on me, and let me have some share of that pleasure which you receive from your correspondents. I have not a line from any, but a short one from Mr. Collinson, of the 3d of August. I expected to have heard from Gronovius, by a ship expected from Amsterdam, and by which I wrote to him; but I do not hear that she is arrived. I sowed some of the seed of the *Arbor vitae,* but it failed as yours did. Perhaps they may germinate next year.

Can you give me no hopes of seeing you, in your rambles next summer, in search of new knowledge of things? Pray, make my compliments to the good woman, your spouse, and be assured,

That I am your affectionate, Humble servant,

Cadwallader Colden

D. 332–33.

From COLLINSON

London March 2 1747

Frd John

I am very apprehensive that in the [illegible] all the Cargo thou sent is taken which I must confess is very disheartening & what Scheme to prevent it I do not know, but that for the future to insure them   half a Loaf is better than no Bread   Thou but resolve to get all ready to ship in one or two ships which is most suitable for thy Convenience   as the order is large, I think it may be worth thy while, but that I shall submit to thy consideration they are all five Guinea Boxes   let every one be packed by it self with the Persons Name upon it, then I shall have nothing to do but to get them from on board & throu the Customs House & send every one to its Owner

Pray send no more of anything curious but keep all untill a Peace which I hope cannot be a great Way off for all Sides have spent their Money & when the Sinews of War are broke then all Parties must agree.[1]

Dear John farewell
P Collinson

a very pleasant temperate Winter untill 15 Feb — & then two weeks cold & snow   My aconites began to flower Dec 17 untill now   nails Callico & Cloth will come by the first ship

For Duke of Richmond
     Duke of Argile
     Lord Deskford
     Lord Lincoln
     Sir Hugh Smithson
     Charles Hamilton
     Mr Williamson
     Phillip Miller
     Mr. Hall

Arthur Dobbs   2 Boxes to be sent by any Flax Ships bound to Dublin Directed in the Care of Mr. Hans Bailey Mercht in Dublin or what is better all Boxes by a Ship to Bell Fast near to Castle Dobbs the seat of Arthur Dobbs [if] the Consign'd them to Mr. John Gordon at Bell Fast the Money will be paid me Here. I shall write more pticulars p first pensilvania ship which will sail in abt a month & then I shall write to our Worthy Friend B. Franklin to whom pray my Respects

BP 2:73.
1. What Collinson predicted came about a year and a half later, when the Treaty of Aix-la-Chapelle was signed in October 1748.

To COLDEN

March ye 6th 1746–47

Dear & esteemed Friend Colden

I have severall times read thy agreable letter of January ye 27th with A deal of pleasure & notwithstanding I love to hear often from thee; ye was so far from harbouring any censure that I was very much Concerned for thee & thy dear spouse & children on ye account of ye apprehention of ye near approach of ye Canadians; & ye damage thay did in ye neighbourhood of Albany which as often as I heard of I was uneasy perticularly for thee & thine.

thy relation of ye good effect of Madera wine in ye fever at Albany puts me in mind of ye imediate reliefe I found by it when I was seised with A fever & painful loosness with suddain prostration of strength; by Susquehana at a house of plenty of either food or Phisick & other necessaries ye good woman would give me A dram of what she called A Cordial which I suppose might be good of its kind but very disagreeable to me after which she urged me to take some Madera wine I tould her to put two spoonful in A pint of cold water & thro A hot burning crust into it; I sipped most of it leasurly with A spoon but before I had quite finished it I found A cessation of that turbulent motion in my bowels & such an universal quiet that I could hardly hold my eyes open I desired to go to bed where I sweat freely & slept quiet for several hours & then arose & walked about ye plantation, at night rested well next day being prety hearty I eat two freely at dinner on roast & boiled flesh; then set out & rode 10 mile to another house, but my feavour & painfull looseness returned upon me grievously; before night & next morning was stil worse when I set out for directly home ye fever thirst & painfull looseness still Continuing; this day I travailed near 40 miles & called at ye taverns to get some madera wine but they said they had none; at my lodgings I asked for some thay brought me some black berry wine but it seemed very disagreeable & instead of uniting friendly with my spirits as ye Madera wine had done it raised A Perturbation. this was ye first time I knowed ye material difference betwixt our home made wines & ye Madera. Next day I reached home & soon got some Madera which seemed to refresh me.

I have received but one letter from Gronovius since I sent ye account of those plants that is to bear our names & that contained ye names of several kinds of fosils which I sent him

Peter Collinson sent in my packet A pamphlet treating of ye northern lights; & A paper of ye changing of ye poles of ye loadstone; & ye steel magnets which I left to ye care of our friend franklin to send to thee directly   I should esteem it as an extraordinary pleasure to be with the on ye Cats kill mountains but these troublesome times is A great interuption to such agreeable amusements: If I should determine to go to them I shall surely send thee my intentions   I suppose thee hath allready heard of ye Electrical experiments which thay can so efectualy apply to A man as well as to many other objects as to fill him so full of fire that if another man doth but put his finger to ye electrified person ye fire will fly out & strike that part which approacheth nearest I take this to be ye most Surpriseing Phoenomena that we have met with & is wholy incomprehensible to thy friend

John Bartram

LPCC 3:362–63.

From MITCHELL

London, June 2, 1747

Sir: –

I have a long while waited an opportunity of writing something to you that might be acceptable, and am glad of this opportunity of doing it. I am desired to get a parcel of seeds for the Duke of Argyle,[1] and know of none whom I would sooner depend upon then you to do it. He would have a large quantity but fears the season may be too far advanced before you receive this, to collect them and so desires you would send as many as you can afford for five pounds. If they please I doubt not but he will desire more — as well as my Lord Bute[2] who gave me this commission. they desire chiefly flowering trees and shrubs. Some of the new Magnolia if you can get it and particularly some of the white Cedar which I told them you would be sure to send. Mr. Collinson tells me he has sent for seven such parcels this year already so I doubt not but you may have some that are curious collected. He has many of the common things already and wants chiefly the Papaw Tree or Anona the two new Chamaerhododendrons, Sugar tree Orange Apocynum, Scarlet Spirea, Euonymous scandens, the large Ketmia with flowers like Cotton, Leonurus or Oswego Tea, the new Pines which I think you said you had seen, he has all the common sorts, &c.

I am glad to hear that your industry this way is like to be of some service to you. I hope it may be in my way to promote it, which you may depend upon. this is the only way I ever knew it of any service to anybody, for Botany is at a very low ebb in England, since the death of Lord Petre   Dr. Dillenius is likewise dead. I should be glad to hear from you & what new plants you find. I have wrote a long letter to Mr. Franklin which I hope he will receive & desired a specimen of the water that turns Iron to Copper & the earth, salts, &c. about it, which I would analyze & should be glad of an

Account of its effects with you & the way of operating with it there, to see if it would do the same here. I likewise desired some specimens (& a quantity of them) of the blew stones in your Yellow Springs, which pray tell him of, if mine to him should miscarry. I fancy it may be more in your way than his to procure them, by which you would highly oblige me. Remember me particularly to him & your good spouse & Dr. Bond. I have nothing worth while to say to them else should not fail to do it.

You may direct the Box of seeds, &c., to the care of Mr. Collinson with the others, from

Yr. hble Servt.
John Mitchell

BP 4:85; D. 364–66.
1. Archibald Campbell, Third Duke of Argyll.
2. John Stuart, Third Earl of Bute and nephew of Argyll.

From MITCHELL

June 2 1747

Sir

I have this day sent you a letter by Capt. Teffin, which, least it should miscarry, I have sent this abstract.

The Duke of Argyle desires some of your American seeds which I hope you will take Care to collect for him. he wants Chiefly the new Magnolia & particularly the white cedar & any other evergreen or flowering trees & shrubs, the Papaw two new chamaerhododendrons Sugar trees dwarf mapples orange apocynum scarlet Spirea, Euonymous scandens, large Ketmia, Leonurus or Oswego Tea, or any new Pines &c. would be acceptable. he has most of the common sorts — Send what you can afford for five pounds to the care of Mr. Collinson with the others he has wrote for (which are seven five pound boxes) & the money shall be paid to him or your order.

I likewise wrote some time ago to Mr. Franklin for some of the water that turns Iron to Copper with the Earths, Salts &c. & the manner of managing it there to see if it would do the same here, which no body hardly will believe, & to see if we could not make a good analysis of it, if mine to him should miscarry, pray remember him of it & my respects to him & both your families from

Yr. assured friend
John Mitchell

BP 4:86.

To COLLINSON

July ye 20 1747

Dear Peter

I have received Six of thy letters & two of Gronovius & some seeds which I sowed directly & tho A very warm wet season not one of them is come up: two of thy letters from ye way of boston & one by ye way of York I received by ye hands of our friend Benjamin franklin & several of ye others   he was so kind as to tell me to acquaint thee that any letters thee pleas to send to me if thee hath an opertunity by either Boston or york if the incloseth it in A letter directed to him he will deliver it to me post free which is very kind indeed & I hope to prevail with him to inclose one in his when he sends to thee by ye way of York by which means I hope we may hear often from one another. this is like to be A plentiful year for forrest seeds   I hope to gather A fine parcel; but how I shall have an opertunity of sending them I know not   thee adviseth me to send them by two vesails which would do very well if two vesails should sail from here to London   at present we know of none but Mesnard & he is too soon to send by. I am obliged to thee for taking so much pains with [illegible] let me know how much is due to me that I may know how much to draw or send for; The Cylindrical Columns[1] are certainly in new england Benjamin Franklin saw them at 3 miles distance but being very cold, did not care to turn out of his way. Our proprietor is allmost as crafty as covetous he wont sell land because ye people being necessitated for land to live upon raiseth its price prodigiously so that in a few years he may get 5 times as much as he could now or may set it at an extortionate ground rent: I design to go to ye sea-coast this fall, to fetch from thence curiosities of what kind soever I can find. I have wrote to my friend to gather what he can for me. I have wholy lost ye pyrethrum   it is a fine flower

BP 1:17:6; D. 179–80.
1. Unidentified.

To COLDEN

August ye 16th 1747

Esteemed Friend

I have received thy kind letter of July ye 27 by ye hands of our worthy friend B. F.   I have nothing new to acquaint thee with   I have received two letters from Gronovius concerning several Curiosities which I sent to him   he mentions A Curious book which he hath sent me which he calls ye Fauna medica wrote by Lineus but I have not received it yet — ye worm seed that Doctor Bard tould thee of is what is called chenopodium Botris or oak of Jerusalem   it grows very naturaly to ye southward; if thee hath it not I can easily put A few seeds in A letter whereby thee may soon raise enough   I want some seeds of ye arbor Vita & ye paper birch which grow on ye katts kill mountains   ye seeds of both is ripe near ye same time — I have delayed longer writing to thee in hopes of A ship coming from London whereby I might perhaps have picked out some curious observations from some of my letters that might have rendered this letter more agreeable: however I hope thee will believe that I am thy Sincear

Friend John Bartram

LPCC 3:419–20.

To COLLINSON[1]

I have another cargo to send by another vesail   she will not be ready to sail this six weeks or as likely not before spring [illegible] should be frose hard this winter   this fall hath been exceeding [sickly]   scarcely a family hath escaped either in town or countrey   what be ye reason no mortal knows Last year was very dry & most sickly that ever was known before. Some people suppose that was its cause   this year hath been very seasonable weather yet as bad health or worse. I have put in Williamsons[2] box a parcel for thee thy name writ at large & some fresh seed of our [illegible] & other seeds I have reserved to send by ye next ship   ye Locusts hath not appeared in any ground near us this many years   what should be ye reason I cant tell   I have put in ye bottom of each box tulup cones next sweet gum then spruice at ye top with a variety of black scarlet champain & mountain chestnut & swamp spanish & willow oak   ye other seeds in bags   let me know how much is due me   I dont know which is better to send for it in goods or draw upon thee or let it lie   we are in expectation of a visit from ye french next year & what injury thay may do us is uncertain   pray give my kind respects to our worthy friend mitchel I am providing some seeds for ye duke of Argile to him

BP 1:38.
1. Undated, but written in November 1747 (see Bartram to Collinson, January 30, 1747/48).
2. John Williamson.

From MITCHELL[1]

& observations about it   among other things I remember you told me of some virtues of the Collinsonia. have you observed any more effects of it since. Do you know, what the Indians dye their red & black colours with. their black is entirely unknown. their Red is made of a sort of Rubia with a fibrous root that grows in swamps. We have it in Virginia, where it was used by our Indians, but I suspect your northern one may be different. If you can send me a speciman of yours you will oblige me very much, & I shall return with an Account of it & of ours — It is said, in Philosophical Transactions, that sort of wild Pennyroyal or Dittany in Virginia will kill a Snake of any kind when held to its nose. This is supposed to be the sweet scented Dittany, which I have known tryed without effect. But by the Description of that Plant in Philosoph. Trans. I find that what is there said to have the effect, is the Trichostema flor. Virginica or the small fetid weed wt blue flower & is like Hypericum, which grows plentifully in your fields. Now our Society would be glad to have this matter tryed fairly again. I know of none more fit to do it than you, which if you have time to try, & transmit an account of, I will take care it shall be communicated to them, & inserted in their Transactions. I know it will kill worms in the body, & why not other reptiles? does it kill worms in water &c. If you find any thing in it pray send some of it dryed, that I may convince our Philosophers of the truth of it, for they are otherwise great Infidels in what they do not see.

I have many other such things to trust to you, but fear of giving you too much trouble. I have wrote to Mr. Franklin particularly to give me some Account of Shoote's[2] mineral water that turns Iron to copper which I trusted to his care as I know you have business enough beside your office   both he and I must be obliged for your promises for it. When I think of the many other Productions in the spring I cannot but think it as a sort of reflection on us among other things, that we should let it lye in obscurity, & not so much as acquaint those with it who should thank us so heartily for our pains, but might like to give us some better information of its nature & uses, if they were appraised of this thing. for this reason I have desired some of the water, & of every production about it which I shall put to the most exact tryalls that I or my acquaintance are able to make.

I know very well how much the tryall of those things must hinder your own Business, which must necessarily keep you from following them as you would. for this reason I think you ought to look out to see if there is not a small place that you could get to enable you to bestow more time on them. I think all such things should be bestowed on those who would make a good use of the leisure time they afford instead of feeding an excess & Luxury, Now if any such things should cast up at any time, to which you think you might be promoted by the Interest of your friends, I think you should acquaint them of it, & I hope you will rekon me one of them. I am pretty well acquainted wt. several in power, & can easily propose such a thing to them & even urge it, which you may well assure yourself shall not be wanting on my part. You know such things as to such success are ruled much by chance & an [illegible] so that we cannot depend upon them as they come but I do not see why you should not have that chance as well as others. Whatever may happen you may assure yourself of the good Intentions of

Your very humble servant
John Mitchell

BP 4:85.
1. The first page is missing and no date is given, but this letter was probably written in early 1748 (see Mitchell to Bartram, August 1, 1750).
2. Unidentified.

To COLLINSON

January ye 30th, 1747/8

Dear Peter
I have put on board ye ship Beulah 3 boxes of forest seeds: No. 1 for ye Duke of argile No. 2 for Squire Hamilton & No. 3 is for thyself. I sent in a vesail that sailed last november 4 boxes: No. 1 for smithson No. 2 for Williamson

No. 3 for Lord Deskford No. 4 for Lord Hopetoun. I have sent none for ye Dukes of Richmond and Bedford this year for I had nothing new to send them but what I had sent them several times before. I sent them A fine parcel of ye white Pine last spring by Seymour   I have not been at ye Cedar Swamps myself   I sent several to gather ye Cedar seeds but they found but few so I could send but A little seed to each correspondent that wanted & it was not safe going beyond our mountains for fear of ye French Indians. I have not received one letter from thee this long time   ye last was dated June ye 6th   we are surprised that we have no news from London this many months. We expect A visit from ye French early in ye spring & numbers of our people is daily exercising & learning ye Martial discipline in order to oppose them if thay should attempt to land & are makeing preparations for forts & bateries to stop any vesails that come in A hostile manner. ye clergy exercises thair talents with all thair force of eloquence to persuade thair hearers to defend thair country, liberties & families by ye sword & ye blessing of god but our society like fools or something worse opposeth them by pamphlets persuasion & threats of reading them out of our meetings for breach of our discipline in takeing up ye carnal weapon which unreasonable proceeding I suppose hath made one hundred hypocretes to one convert for thay cant bind ye freedom of thought

BP 1:17:4; D. 180.

To LOGAN

April ye 14 1748

Respected Friend,

I received thy letter & specimen with much pleasure; being glad of the oppertunity to gratify thy Curiosity. Ye plant is called Hen bit or ground Ivy leaved Chickweed or Alsine hederulae folio major

if my kind friend Logan would please to make so free as to write often to me concerning any subject that I am capable to give any information of I shall not only think it A pleasure to satisfy thy curious enqueries but an Honnor done to thy Sincere friend.

John Bartram

Historical Society of Pennsylvania, Maria Dickinson Collection.

To COLLINSON[1]

We have had the most dreadful mortality this last winter, through the Province (Pennsylvania), both town and country, that ever was known since the Christians settled it, and it still continues.

It is now very grievous in Jersey. It chiefly takes men in full strength, though women and children, in abundance, have died of it. Many families have been broken up, and in some the whole is turning to corruption. Some continue sick, twelve, some twenty-four hours; many three or four days, and some two weeks, before the fatal tragedy is completed.

These last two summers[2] have been the most sickly that ever we knew, but not quite so mortal as this spring. Last two summers, the Yellow-fever, and what we call Dumb-Ague[3] and Dutch Distemper (because the Dutch first brought it in many years ago, since which it rages in one part or another of the country, yearly, and baffles all physicians, prevailed). These two last seemed to be joined, and each prevails most according to the particular constitution. Either of them is able to finish the fatal stroke, or render the body so infirm as not to recover its former constitution for several months and maybe never.

Last summer (1747) the measles afflicted abundance of children, and a looseness following carried many off, in town (Philadelphia). Others a cough wasted away.

This winter a kind of pleurisy is followed with certain death. But the Yellow-Fever, the Dumb-Ague, and the Pleurisy joined, are the chief actors in this tragical scene.

"Notices of the Epidemics of Pennsylvania and New-Jersey, in the Years 1746, 1747, 1748, and 1749," *Philadelphia Medical and Physical Journal*, 1, pt. 1, (1804):3–5.
1. The editor of the *Journal*, Benjamin Smith Barton, introduced Bartram's letter to Collinson, written May 5, 1748, with this preface: "The following facts relative to the prevalence of certain very severe Epidemics in our country, many years since, are extracted from the manuscript letter of Mr. John Bartram (the Father), which have been kindly put into the hands of the Editor, by the family of that distinguished American botanist. Although these facts are by no means so particular as could be wished, yet, in the paucity of authentic materials for a history of the epidemics of our country, they cannot prove unacceptable to physicians."
2. The summers of 1746 and 1747.
3. An intermittent fever, without definite chills.

To CAROLUS LINNAEUS[1]

Respected & much esteemed friend
I received thy kind letter by the hands of our Curious friend Mr Kalm[2] whome I have had ye pleasure to converse with; & whom I value not onely for thy sake but for his own ingenuity

I have at thy request & his sent thee severall Curious seeds which I hope may meet with thy acceptance

I have formerly sent thee packets of seeds by ye swedish ministers of our provence. But whether thay came to thy hands I cant be certain, as I never had A line from thee before

these few lines I commit to ye Care of our friend hopeing it may reach thy hands. pray when opertunity offers send me A line or two which will oblige thy friend

John Bartram

Linnean Society of London Archives, Linnean Correspondence I, vol. 1, f. 355.
1. Undated, but written in the fall of 1748 (since Bartram refers to Kalm's visit of September 1748) and "Addressed to the Right Honourable Charles Linne Barronet at Upsala Sweden pr fav'r of The Revd John Wieksell."
2. Peter Kalm.

To FRANKLIN[1]

By a diligent observation in our province, and several adjacent, I apprehend, that timber will soon be very much destroyed, occasioned in part by the necessity that our farmers have to clear the greatest part of their land for tillage and pasture, and partly for fuel and fencing. The greatest quantity of our

Carolus Linnaeus (1707–1788). Portrait by T. Cardon (1835).
Courtesy of the Linnean Society of London.

timber for fencing is oak, which is long in growing to maturity, and at best is of short duration; therefore I believe it would be to our advantage to endeavour to raise some other kind of timber, that will grow faster, or come sooner to maturity, and continue longer before it decays.

The red cedar (a species of juniper) I take to be the most profitable tree for fencing, and several other uses, that we can raise in our country, considering how easily it may be raised from seed; its readiness to grow in most kinds of soil; its quick growth; the profits it will afford while it is arriving at maturity; and the long duration of the wood when grown to a proper size for the materials we want for our several occasions in husbandry or building. The way I propose at first to raise a nursery of them, is to dig a piece of ground, suppose two square rod, clear away the weeds and grass-roots, as you would prepare a bed for parsnips or onions; then sow half a gallon of good berries evenly upon it, and rake them well in; this may be done in the latter end of *October,* as soon as the berries are ripe; they genrally come up the Spring after the sowing. Take care to pull up the grass or weeds the first or second year. If the ground be poor, very little attendance will serve, and the cedars will grow well enough. The Seeds may be easily gathered in great quantities on the beaches by the sea-shore; but when you have got a few bearing trees, the birds will carry the berries all over your plantation, which will come up and grow finely, so that you may dig up as many as you please to plant, or leave as many as you think proper to grow where they came up, which will soon come to maturity, if the soil is suitable; But the most danger is their being broke or molested with horn cattle, nothing else is more hurtful to them. I know no other tree that will grow so well on such different soils as this will; for upon our sandy beaches, which are nothing but beds of sand, they grow as thick as possible, from whence many thousand posts for fencing, are brought into *Pennsylvania* and *York* governments; and I have seen, in a great miry swamp, upon a branch of Susquehana, great trees growing near 18 inches diameter, 70 foot high, and very straight. And the inhabitants near the mountains, up *Hudson's* river, make great use of them for making large hovels or barracks to put their corn in before it is threshed. They will grow well in high gravelly or clay soil, in rich or poor, or even upon a rock, if there be but half a foot of sand or earth upon it. It is much to be valued for its quick growth from seed, the little sap, and its much durable heart, which it acquireth sooner than any tree that we can raise on common land. Indeed the mulberry and locust are of quick growth in very rich land but not upon poor. A cedar tree, from the berry, will in eight years be fit for hoops, in ten for bean-poles, in twelve for hop-poles, in sixteen or eighteen for ladders, and in twenty will be big enough to make three posts, besides a good stake at top; with this care, that they are not removed, bruised or broken, which very much retards their growth, makes them deformed, and spoils their straight pyramidal growth; which form this tree naturally inclines to grow in more than most trees, and in which we must enjoy the greatest profit from it. And we may in this assist nature by art, in carefully trimming them every three or four years, cutting the branches close and smooth off to the bole; so that these wounds be closed, which will make the tree smooth on the surface and the grain strait, which will be of great service, if we make boards or rails of them, which will be much the better for being clear of knots; But if we let this tree grow without trimming, as it naturally shoots out branches on all sides in all the degrees of its growth, the lower ones die, but do not rot off near the bole, as in other trees; so that the sap can't close over them, but grows round which makes the grain crooked, and instead of being straight and even, it appears as if drove full of spikes, as we may observe by the posts (especially the second cut) that are brought from the sea-coast, where they grow naturally, tho' not so large or tall as those beyond our northern mountains. It is now generally used for posts, which, as I am informed, will last fifty years, or longer; so that one sett of these posts about a plantation, would last a mature age, which would be of great advantage to farmers, and at the first cost, with white cedar or chesnut rails, would be no dearer than a quick-set hedge and ditch, which must be often repaired; this wood would be of extraordinary service in building for sills for barns, stables and outhouses and for door and window cases, and boards for floors, I suppose one of the best of woods, as not being subject to swell with moisture, or shrink with dryness; whether or not it would be very good to make large cisterns for the malsters to steep their barley in, and for the brewers for coolers? I have seen sloops abuilding at *Albany* of this wood; indeed the bottom, as I remember, was made of oak; for as the river there is shallow and the vessels often strike upon sand or gravel, which oak, as being a stronger wood, is better able to bear such a shock than cedar, which is more tender, yet notwithstanding the *Bermudians* build fine durable vessels thereof; and I have seen cedar-trees growing in *Pennsylvania* large enough to make wider planks than any I have seen in a *Bermuda* built vessel. I believe it would make curious lasting boats, which would swim light, row well, and want but little repairs for many years. I don't doubt but my countrymen will think, if not say, What signifies telling us of such great advantages which we can't obtain? We don't know how to get either hoop or bean-poles of cedar, much less trees for house or ship-building; But I am of opinion, that with care, ingenuity and industry, we may make the very raising of them to a proper magnitude (exclusive of the value of them when cut down) to be easy, ornamental and profitable.

And first, I think it is easy to raise great numbers of them after this manner; Dig them out of the nursery when three or four years old, or about the plantation, as I mentioned before; and if you have an old worn-out field, which many of our country farmers already have, or I am apt to think they soon will have, a field of ten acres, which contains 1600 square perches, will hold as many trees; for a square perch[2] is sufficient room for each tree to stand in, while they are of middle growth; these trees thus planted in rows, when grown eight or ten feet high, which they will in five years after planting, will put forth their fragrant male blossoms; and the females will begin to produce their aromatick berries, which to behold in upright and regular rows, will be very ornamental. And now some or other of them will yearly want trimming, as I mentioned before, to make a smooth strait-grained bole; the branches thus cut, will make withes, poles, stakes, and furnish brush for dry hedges, and fuel for the fire, And if they stand too close you may cut every other one down for the several occasions mentioned before. When they have been thus order'd for twenty years, I believe one tree will make seven posts, and a rail or pole at top; and in forty or fifty years will make good boards for floors or planks for naval uses. I have a tree in an old field, which hath stood about eighteen years, that would now make seven good posts.

Note, A field thus planted, will yield good pasture while the trees are growing; for either grass or corn will grow very well near the cedars (but oaks and hickories are very destructive to both, as the walnut is to most fruit-trees) and when cut down will be fresh land for tillage. But the horn-cattle must be kept out until the trees are as thick as one's wrist, else they will break them to pieces with their horns; but horses and sheep may go in when you please.

There is another method I would propose, which I believe may be altogether as profitable: that is, To plant them close to all the fences belonging to our plantations; whereby we may not only preserve all our fields for tillage, but while they grow, they may support our fences from blowing down. They must be planted close to the fence, if planted young, and trimmed near the top every year, until they are out of the reach of the cattle, else they will break them with their horns. They may be planted, one to every pannel, or three to two rod. Then supposing a field of ten acres will take 160 rod of fence to inclose it, you may plant it round with 240 trees, at one to a pannel of fence: Supposing a farmer hath 150 acres within fence, divided into fields of 10 acres; but very likely he may have some fields above ten, and some under, and allowing for several partition fences: I will suppose he may plant by all the fences about his plantation 2400 trees; so that if he plants every year 100 trees, he may after 25 years cut down every year 100 successively; which, allowing every tree to yield eight posts, every post to fetch one shilling, which they will now readily do (and hereafter maybe more) which amounts to forty pounds; a fine yearly profit, considering we lose so little ground from tillage, and the trouble and expence of raising them is but little, and the profits so great, that I believe we can't generally fall into a method that will afford the farmer more profit with less expence, and more sure to hit. If we should fall into this method, it will be necessary, that two or three years before we cut a parcel down, we plant a young one between every one that we intend so that we may always have the same number of growing trees. One inconviency attending of planting them too close to the fence is, that the wind forcibly blowing the young tree to and fro, is apt to rub the bark off next the fence; but when they are grown pretty large, they stand too stiff to be moved by any common blast of wind, and will support the fence.

Vale et favore.

"An Essay for the improvement of estates, by raising a durable timber for fencing, and other uses," *Poor Richard Improved,* ed. Benjamin Franklin [Richard Saunders] (Philadelphia, 1749).
1. We have placed this letter at the end of 1748 by reason of its appearance in *Poor Richard* in 1749. Franklin's preface: "Kind Reader, By way of preface (for custom says there must be a preface to every almanack) I present thee with an essay wrote by a celebrated

naturalist of our country, which, if duly attended to, may be of more service to the publick, than 375 prefaces of my own writing."
2. 30¼ square yards.

From BLAND

London 10th 1 mo 1748/9

My Friend
John Bartram,

Inclos'd Receipt for a Bundle Shipt in the Delaware from our Frd. P Collinson, which hope will receive in Good Order. When thou meets with Some Clear Stones of a Brown Colour Would take very kind thy Sending me 3 or 4 pieces as Large as Cans't Get.

I am

Thy Ap^d Friend
Elias Bland

BP 1:89.

From ARTHUR DOBBS

London May the 5th 1749

Sr.

I wrote to you some time ago which I hope Mr. Collinson sent safe to you Desiring four Boxes such as you sent to me last year and which further variety of flower seeds shrubs or Trees you can light upon, – The Acorns sent last year I hear was most of them Rotten and the seeds very dry, so that I hope you will take the best care you can of sending them safe packed up and separate from each other next year, by as good ship as you can to Belfast to the care of Mr. John Gordon, and, in want of one there, to Dublin to the care of Messieurs Caleton & Jevers, if you can get any good seeds of the Magnolia and of the Tupelo and of the Mahogany or Red-wood of Carolina if it grows so far North as where you go, I desire you would send them in Earth in a Box or Basket 2 or 3 feet long, for we find they dont grow here if kept long out of the ground, if you light upon any Roots or Seeds of the Ginseng & of the Rattle-Snake Root and send them in Earth I would try to raise them here, if you have any seeds of *Curious Dying Woods,* Indigo &c or any Evergreen Honey Suckles or Cypress Canes, which I dont find were in the parcel sent, or a plant of the *Prickly Pear* – I hope you will have a good season for the seeds and wish you Success in all your affairs – I am Sr

Yr Most Humble Servant
Arthur Dobbs

Chicago Historical Society.

From COLLINSON[1]

May 6 [1749]

Frd John
Pray remember a Little Pcell of Small Magnolia & white Cedar & Red & Spruce Cones if to be had – for our Friend Hamilton – who had bad Luck by the Seeds comeing so Late to Him in the Last Sommer
   I am

P. Collinson

& Send Mee Specimens of all yr oakes & half a doz or ½ a Score Acorns of Each Sort for mySelf, put them in a Bagg or Sir Hugh Smithsons Box of acorns

Boxes of Seeds Next year

1 Box of Seeds all Sorts	for Sr Hugh
1 Ditto only acorns	Smithson
1 Box of Seeds	for Mr. Hall
1 Ditto	for Lord Marchmont
1 Do	for Lord Deskford
1 Do	for T. Penn
1 Do	for Duke Malbrough
1 Do	for Mr. Gynonder
8 boxes for England	
1 Ditto	for Mr. Nugent
9	
4 for Ireland	
13 in all	

Send the Acorns for Sr. H. Smythson by first ship after they are Ripe

Chicago Historical Society.
1. Enclosing Dobbs's letter of May 5, 1749.

To COLLINSON[1]

About the beginning of May I observed many deformed water Insects by Naturalists called an Hexapode — creep up out of the water and fix themselves on the Shrubs & rushes, in this Situation they continued but a few hours before their back splits open & from the deformed Case creep out a Beautifull Fly with Shineing Transparent Wings. At its first appearance there is only what one may call the Rudiments of Wings, but is a most Entertaining Sight to Observe how they shoot out & Expand themselves, Thus in Less than an Hour they have attained their compleat Dimentions, during all this operation the Creature Is Immovable & So continues untill their Wings are Dry & then It Swiftly Flys away, roving about the Sides of Roads & Rivers Seeking their Food, being Insects of Prey are Very Voracious & Like the Hawks amongst Birds are very Swift of flight, & nimbly Seize their prey which is mostly Flyes & small green grasshoppers   They delight in sunshine but in cloudy Weather they rarely are to be seen but seek protection under the Leaves & boughs of Trees

Towards the End of May the female is ready to deposite her Eggs, she then Seeks the Warm Quiet side of Ponds & Water Courses continuing in a hovering posture, dodging up & down in the Water   in this action the Male Seises her & with the End of his Tail catcheth fast hold by the back of her Head & Flieth away with Her   it is uncertain how long they continue in this position before the Female bends the End of her body so as to penetrate the part between the Belly & Breast of the Male — in this Singular & Surprising Manner she is Impregnated   then she repairs again to those still shallow Waters whose botoms are cover'd with Moss Sticks & Weeds which may be a Security to the Little Grubs — Here she in a Hovering position deposits her Eggs in the Water which Immediately Sink and find a proper Nidus in the aquatic Moss &c   the Eggs are Soon Hatch, the young reptiles creep amongst the Stones & Weeds &c & So continue water Animals the Greater part of the year[2]

Royal Society of London Archives, Letters and Papers II, 31, Rd. 1, February 1749/50; *Philosophical Transactions of the Royal Society* 46 (1750):324–25.
1. Published in *"Some Observations on the Dragon-Fly or Libella of Pensilvania, collected from Mr. John Bartram's Letters, communicated by Peter Collinson, F.R.S."*
2. Here Collinson added: "untill the Season comes round for their appearance in that Beautiful Fly before you which is different from our European but their process I think well agrees with ours, as It is curiously described & Delineated by that Excellent Naturalist Mr. Reaumore — they have a great Variety of this Tribe of Insects in America; as well as Wee have in Europe."

To COLLINSON[1]

May Flies

Their bodies being replenished with an Oily Matter they easily quit their Husks & rise up to the Surface of the Water, and disperse themselves A Mile or More back in the Woods, Whilst others stay near the Water.

May the 4:1749   I perceived Many had attained Wings and was very thick Spread on the Bushes & grass by the River Sides — the Second Day after their leaving their aquatic Abode they Cast another Skin, after which their Tails are Longer & their Wings Dryer & more Transparent.

The 5th & 6th was Rainey, the 7th Windy, so very few Came out — the 8th was Cool so few was seen but the 9th & 10th being warm many Swarmed late in ye Evening & the 11th:12th:13th they Swarmed abundantly —

What I call Swarming was the gathering thick as Bees, near the Rivers to lay their Eggs in the Water

In their Flight they mount to the Topps of Trees 20 or 30 feet High, their Motion is surprising — Hovering up and down riseing & falling 7 or 8 feet at a Time — this I take to be the Time & Manner of their Impregnation after which they flie to the Brooks cast out their Eggs & perish Immediately, their Eggs sink directly to the Bottoms & Lodge amongst the Mudd & Gravel & may be food for some Minute Water Animals. from their Eggs proceeds a deformed Grub wch subsists under Water & (is food for Eeles) untill next season – that it attains its Fly state & then is food for Fish & Fowl —

The reason of their being so long in Coming fourth this year was the Cold Chilly Weather   Other years in a Warm Season In Few days they would have performed all their Functions and disappeared

Wee have Two other Smaller kinds that very much resemble the Former but they come later by 2 or 3 Weeks, what is most remarkable the Males are Black & live several days after the Females ——

Royal Society of London Archives, Letters and Papers II, Decade 2, 112, Rd. 5, April 1750; *Philosophical Transactions of the Royal Society* 43 (1750): 400–402; Linnean Society of London Archives, Collinson's Common Place Book, pp. 69–70.

1. This letter, probably written in the summer of 1749 according to its contents, was published in the Royal Society's *Philosophical Transactions*. Accompanying Bartram's observations, Collinson sent the society the following note: "Some time agon I laid before the Royal Society My Observations on the wonderfull Appearance of the Libella or May-Flies of England. This Account being perused by my Ingenious Friend Jno. Bartram excited Him to make the following remarks on their Appearance in Pensilvania. By the Specimens before you — The May Flies of America have no very remarkable difference from ours Excepting a few Days in the Fly state, live all the year a Water Insect in the form of those on ye center of the glass —"

From DOBBS

Castle Dobbs near Carrick fergus
June 27th 1749

Sr

I wrote two Letters to you which were Communicated to you by our Ingenious good Friend Mr. Collinson to whom I paid ten guineas for the two Boxes you sent to me and Desired that you would send me four Boxes of all Nuts, Berrys & Roots next Season which I hope have got safe to your Hands, in which I mention such things as I then could think of which were not in the list of Seeds sent to me last year. Since my coming home finding there is a ship bound from Belfast for Philadelphia, which will be the convenient vessell to Bring back the Seeds &c from you I embrace this opportunity of writing more fully to you by the Captain and herein Inclose to you a List Extracted from Catesby and Miller of all shrubs, Trees, flowers &c as are to be found in the northern Continent as far as they knew them: Some of them as you can find in your neighborhood and Climate which were not in the Collection sent to Me I should be glad to have, a few of each Sort you can meet with to myself in a separate package because the 4 Boxes I wrote for of your general Collection are to be Divided among 5 or 6 of my acquaintance & friends of which I have only one eighth part.

I Hope you will be carefull in packing them & keeping the several Sorts Distinct and distinguishing the names of each Sort for since my coming home I find they were so Mixed and blended with each other that they could not be divided so as to know one kind from another And Many of the acorns were dry and failed so that very few of them have come up, Nor do we Desire so many kind of acorns, but only such as are the best Timber as the White, the Champaign, the Spanish & Chestnut Oaks and a few only of the others for variety: But the several kinds of Pines, particularly Ld. Weymouth or smooth pine. Fine cedars & Cypress we should all Desire as well as the Magnolia, Tulip Tree and other Curious flowering shrubs & Flowers in the List Inclosed and such others as you can meet with which are new & Curious. I shall also at the Bottom of this Letter send you some of the names of those you sent which have either been wrong taken by my Gardner or there are none such that I can find either in Catesby or Miller's Dictionary, so that I would have you explain them if you can if they are not mentioned in these Books. A great many of the kinds you sent me are come up, but many have not some of which I know ly in the ground until next spring, as the Cedar Black Walnut Cluster black Cherry and I believe some of the hard shelled Hiccory, Sassafras and phaps several others, so that I dont Despair of seeing them next year.

A Friend and neighbour of mine Mr. Dallway,[1] has had some very Curious young trees sent to him from Mr. James Alexander, gardener to Mr. Penn one of yr Lords proprietors, most of which are growing, particularly the Tulip Tree, Lord Weymouths pine, Sassafras, ginseng, Locust Trees, may apples an Ipecacuana, and several other, as probably you maynt have Nurseries of these kinds of your own as you are so much taken up in Collecting Curious varietys in the Distant mountains and in places at a distance in the season; I should be obliged to you if you could procure me some of the several kinds out of Mr. Alexanders Nurseries which I have mentioned at the end of the general Catalogue Inclosed, in which of them as he has in his nursery, Carefully made up, as that he has sent to Wm. Dallway and Charge me with the Cost, which I shall pay either to him on your order either in London, here or where you shall direct; I would desire only a few of each, where the seeds maynt be depended upon by being too long out of ground; and if you can procure any seeds from the Carolina Magnolias, mahogany, and other Trees growing there or in Bahama, which are not growing in your Climate, put them up in a Box of Earth or Sand and send them over as directed in my former Letter, and as far as you can let me know the soyle natural to the several sorts, of such new sorts you find not Included in millers Dictionary, that I may know how to treat them, what will require a Walled, bank Bed, or Stove and what I may venture in the open ground –

I should be glad to know how our Colonies Increase, and what numbers are gone this year from Germany &c now we have a Peace, whether our back settlements Increase and how far they are Extended, whether any number have got beyond Lord Fairfaxs Tract to the Branches of the Ohio or Allegany – beyond the springs of Potomac & the Apalachian Mountains in that Delightfull Country and Climate which I long to have Settled, to secure the [protection] of the Lakes from an Incroaching Neighbour, by Civility and well treating the Natives and giving them a beneficial Trade with us to secure their friendship.

As I believe so long a Letter and List will Heartily Tyre you, I shall add no more, but depend upon your Care in the package and Instructions with them, and that you would recommend to the Captain, where they may be kept safest on board, and hope they will have a speedy and safe voyage here, to have them put on early into the ground – I wish you success in your Searches after the Varieties of Creation and in all your Concerns and hope to live to visit the American Northern Colonies and see those Curiosities in perfection.

I am Sir

Yr Most obed. Humble
Servant Arthur Dobbs

I have found the several names of what you sent except Your Beech cherry the Correopsis   Sweet yellow

BP 3:100.
1. Unidentified.

To COLLINSON[1]

CICADAS

Towards the End of Aprill, the Hoggs give notice by their routing in the Ground, that the Insects draw near the Surface, (for they feed much on them, the Ground under the Hedges, Bushes & Trees is like a Honeycomb, with such Multitudes that creep out of Chrysales) in this State they are a Grub or Hexipode filled with a thick whiteish Matter, phaps their Eggs, Sperm, or what may serve to nourish them, when they come to be Flys; for I never could observe them to eat any thing in that State, & yett as they are furnished with a long proboscis I am apt to think, with it, they collect the Dew from the Leaves of Trees & flowers &c

May the 10th:1749   Early in the Morning was observed they had Quitted their Earthly aboads, at first they are all over White, except their Eyes, which are Red, in a few Hours the Air Changes them, into a Dark Brown, like the Specimen. they continued coming out Innumerable, to the 15th; the Grass, bushes & Trees &c are covered with them   When they are a Day or Two old, the Males begin to Sing, which is performed by a Tremoulous Motion of Two bladers, by the air under their Wings, and now there is a Continued Din (So great as to Interrupt Conversation) all over our Woods, & Orchards, flying too & fro Seeking the Females —

Soone after impregnation the Female begins to Dart Twiggs & Lay her Eggs: as it is difficult to give an Idea of this operation I have procured some specimens to lay before you to which I refer; To Enable Her to perform this work at the Extremity of her body she is furnished with a Dart or Peircer by wonderfull Instinct they generally Choose the second years Shoots, and then without distinction fix on all Sorts of Trees, in the Orchard or the Forests. It is surprising with what dexterity & quickness they work through the Toughest Bark, into the Close Wood, their Dart having An Orifice near the point, at the same time that they Penetrate the Wood, they lay an Egg from Twelve to Eighteen Close together, fixing them under the Bark, fast to the Wood, in order for their Nourishment, with the Sap, and thus they proceed on darting the Twiggs until their stock of Eggs is exhausted, In this work they Continued untill the 8th of June & then there was scarcely one to be seen, the greatest part of them become the prey of most four-footed animals, except Cows, Horse, & Sheep — Squirrels become wonderfull fatt with them, & all domestick Foule & most wild ones are extremely fond of them — those that survive these depradations, being spent with their several functions, pine away & die[2]

Royal Society of London Archives, Letters and Papers.
1. In his presentation to the Royal Society on May 17, 1750, of the following Bartram account, Collinson noted that parts of other letters had formerly been read concerning the periodical appearance in the northern colonies of insects known there as locusts. He believed that these had given the members an impression of "an insect of the Grasshopper kind." He had now received from Bartram specimens of two species of this insect and believed them to be cicadas, "an insect frequently found in Italy and other Southern Countries of Europe." The year 1749 had been remarkable for the appearance of these insects in great numbers.
2. Collinson at this point informed the society that Bartram had observed the hatching of cicada eggs on July 16, 1749. Many years later, on February 23, 1764, Collinson read another paper, "On the Cicada of North America."

From PETER KALM

Quebec, the 6th day of August, 1749

Because I have an opportunity of writing to you, sir, I would have the honour to tell you, that I have now come here to Quebec. I do now send my servant-man from me to Philadelphia, to gather there seeds of all trees and herbs he can find, or which I have found there before.

I am obliged to stay here myself to the middle of September, to have several seeds, which not can be ripe before; and when I have gathered them, I think to return from hence, and will have the honour to see you in the beginning or middle of October.

I have found great many trees and plants, which I not have seen before; but you have in Pensylvania, too, great many trees and herbs, that do not grow here; Poplar, Sweet and Sour Gum, Laurel, Chesnut, Mulberry trees,

Black Walnut, Sassafras, Magnolia, and great many others you can't find here. The Oaks of all sorts have taken leave, only some small shrubs of Black Oak do grow here by this town.

I have made great many observations in all parts of the Natural History. If you do see Mr. Evans, pray remember my most humble duty to him, and tell him that I hope to satisfy his curosity in true maps of Canada; but the map of Canada he was so kind and write for me, has once (it was not far from it) thrown me in the other world. The reason was, that he has not put down a great river between Fort Ann and Crown Point, that runs in Wood creek. My guides did not very well know the way, and we did go down this river, where such Indians live that do kill all the English they see; but to our happiness we did by good time find that we were wrong, and returned.

Fifteen years ago, when the French King did send several of his learned men to Swedland to measure there a degree of latitude by the North Pol, our King in Swedland did let them have all thing the[y] wanted gratis, or for nothing. In recompense thereof, the French King have given orders to his gouverneurs herein Canada, that I too shall have everything as victuals, lodgings, men to carry me to which place I will, &c., for nothing. It is not permitted to me to pay any thing, but the French King he pays that all.

You can, sir, inform my man in several things where he can find some rare plants, pray do it. Show him all places, where you have seen some small Mulberry Trees, or Grapes, but especielement Mulberry Trees, — these I cannot have too many. I am persuaded it will be a pleasure for you to assist me. When I do returne from hence, then I can inform and satisfy your curiosity in great many thing in all parts of Natural History. — My respects, sir, to madam, your wife. My man he can in great many things, too, satisfy your curiosity.

I am, sir, your most humble servant,

Peter Kalm

D. 367–69.

From WILLIAM SHIRLEY[1]

St James Street, May 5

Sir

Tho' I have not the Pleasure of being personally known to you, yet having heard much from the Secretary of the Royal Society,[2] and other Gentlemen here of your great Curiosity & Knowledge in all kinds of American Seeds & the Culture of 'em, and that you have made a general Collection of 'em in your Garden, I take the Liberty to beg the favour of your Assistance in a Collection of the Seeds of such American Trees or Shrubs as you esteem curious & can endure the Climate of England, for one of the Royal Family, who has laid his Commands upon me to produce him one for a Plantation of his own   in Return for the favour I ask, I shall be glad to receive your

Commands either here or upon my Return to my Government at Boston & serve you in any way within my Power

Whatever the Expence of the Seeds may be, I will pay to such Person as you shall appoint to receive it and would beg the favour of You to send'em some time this year by the first Opportunity after they are sav'd in two Parcels by two different Vessels directed for me & consigned to John Thomlinson Esq. Merchant in London, sending him a letter of Advice on the same ship, & another William Bolland, Esq.[3] advising him of the ship they are sent in. Mr. Bolland's letter to be left at Mr. Dodsley's Bookseller in Pall Mall: every kind of the seeds to be mark'd with their names on whatever they are put into and if no Opportunities should present soon to send them directly from Philadelphia for London, be pleased to send them to Boston by some Vessell directed to Eliakin Hutchinson Esq: in Dock Square with a line to him informing him of it, to be sent from thence to London.

If a Bundle or two of the most curious Trees or Shrubs could be sent in the Plant, besides what is sent of 'em in seeds, so as to be likely to grow upon their being put into the Ground here, I shall be glad.

I hope you will be so good as to excuse the Liberty I take in asking this favour of you & am, Sir,

Your Obedient, Humble Servant,
Wl Shirley

I should be glad of a sufficient Quantity of every Kind of seeds you send for four or five persons

BP 4:102.
1. This letter was written by or for Shirley, governor of Massachusetts, and is marked "Duplicate." The year is not legible, but Collinson's question concerning charges for plants sent to Shirley in his letter of February 22, 1750, suggests that Shirley's letter was written in 1749.
2. Dr. Cromwell Mortimer (d. 1752) was secretary of the society from 1730 to 1751.
3. Unidentified

From COLLINSON

Lond February 22 1750

Frd John
I have paid thy bill of £60 & sent The Two Quarto Bibles val. 14 s. each — £1:8s:0d.

Remember when thou Draws next year to Do it in £25 bills & let each Bill be a Month after the Other, as for Instance one at 30 Days one at 60 Days & at 90 Days after sight — for these great people are dilatory in paying and when thy Bills come I have a pretence to press hard for thy Money which I Choose not to mix with my other Cash as thine is a peticular & Seperate Account I keep it by it self

I am now deeply Engaged in Business so must excuse Entering into pticulars. The Bibles &c in a brown paper fully directed to thee are pack'd with Neats Goods by his partner or agent Neve[1] & come by Budden

The present order of seeds as now —

1 Box Richd Hall Esqr, —
1 Box for Christopher Gray Gardener
1 Box for North a Gardener
1 Box for Mr [illegible]
1 Box for William Pole Esqr to be Sent in a Ship to Dublin consigned to Alderman Daniel Cooke

pray forget not to putt Catalogues in Every Box for the future for it gives a great deal of Trouble if [omitted]

I Expect Dayly more orders for Boxes & I have thought [illegible]

To Cure Colegunthas

To Peel off the outer rind & then Gently press out the Juice & Dry it in Shade — [illegible] at most one makes great Distinction – yett as yours by all accounts is much smarter then ours I much doubt if any I have Mention'd would Survive yours — for I know Our Common Furze which is vulgarly Called French Furze which grows here on our most Exposed places & flowers all the Winter — yett with you is certainly killed with your Severe weather which plainly intimates to Mee — you are much Colder than Wee are   Its likely Furze may grow in the sandy soil in the Jerseys near the sea — but with us it is an observation the Furze is always found in good soil sometimes very rich — The plant Thou mentions of our Ingenious friend Kalm finding I know full well it is called the Faba Egyptica — It grows in Carolina, but I did not think it grew so farr to the Northward   the Seed Vessell is very Curious — I always thought the Colocasia was a Species of Arum   it is so Esteemed by the Moderns – pray if thou visits the place Send Mee a good Specimen of the Leaves &c. — what Blossom it has I cannot guess — if thee hast any young Chinquapins pray putt in 2 or 3 plants next Cargo — but I had almost forgot a Material article that is to Send Mee Some Terepins, for I have Two Gardens Walled In, that I can Secure them from runing away   they will come in the box of plants or by themselves as thee thinks best, the proprietors gardener Sent Two Sorts, the Yellow & Black I know not but there was a Black Flatt Shell Sort with most beautifull painted shell round the Edges, that is very nimble to the other — pray Lett thy Ladds look Sharp for Some for Mee but I rather that they put me up in a Box by it self some of odest, about the same Number of Each Species of Pines & 2 Doz of Each Species of Firr — for I have none to Serve my Self or oblige a Friend & Sorts of Hickerys &c and of that large Species of Magnolia that thou Observed with its Cones in October in the Desert   I wish thou had Send a Specimen of It – for I cannot Account for its Seeding at that Season unless owing to barren Soil & Sharp Winds that in the Spring keep Vegetation back   I was in hopes of some Cones for my own Sowing, the Enchanting Spot thou describes Makes Mee Wish to be there at that Time to see the Common Laurel & Rose Laurel together — is the Grass Leafed plant what thou Calls the Blazing Starr   I have given the seed to Gordon   if he does not raise It despair of seeing It   Has the Blazing Starr a Boulbous or Herbaceous Root   Wee want Much to Know — Next year pull up a plant in flower Root & all & Send it by way of Specimen — thou well Observes their untameable disposition wch will not Submitt to Culture for Mine makes no progress   I mean the Grassy Leafed plant sent Last year — So much for thine of Octo:14:   in answer to thine of October 28 — the Chinquapins all faild, I wait this year for the Sarsfras — I am att a great loss what Value to putt on the plants in Earth both to Shirley & E:Northumberland — I wish thou'd mention some thing for the future, I may under do but not over do — for there is more trouble in procureing those Cargos then can easily be conceived —

Our Ever Greens as the Several Species of Alatemas, Philarea, Laurustinas, Bayes, Laurels are by our Gardeners all Raised from Layers, an art they are very expert & Trees are soone raised for sale this Way — is one reason they rarely save any Seed and another Is, that as all these Trees are Exotics from Warm Climates, in ours their Seed is rarely Maturated but in some Long Warm Summers — for these reasons it is difficult to gett the Seeds of these Ever Greens — but I will look out this Summer   Some winters are very Mild unless once in about 20 yrs

An Account of the Butcher Bird

My Friend who Lived many Years in Russia — a very Ingenious Man of great Probity told Mee this remarkable Account — of their Gray or Ash coloured Butcher Bird which are caught in plenty in the Country about Petersburgh & made Tame to Show its extraordinary Way to provide for himself —

My Friend had one of these given to Him – the first thing He did was to fix a Sharp pointed Small Stick in the Wall of his Roome for the Bird to Perch on — as well as to Show Its singular Instict in desecting its prey when it was hungrey a Linnet or any Small bird was lett Fly, on Seeing this, he would Instantly dart from his perch & Seize the little bird in a perticular Manner by the Throat & Soone Choak Him — after he was dead, the Next wonderfull thing to be observed was his Carrying the dead bird and with great dexterity Spiting It on his Sharp pointed perch (abroad a Sharp long Thorn may Serve for the same purpose) which it Effected with its Bill & Claws, by degrees drawing it on his perch, where it hangs ready for Disection & thus, it will dispatch one Bird after another which affords much diversion to the Spectators – He may derive his Name of the Butcher Bird from these Actions which are performed to supply a want of Strength to pull the Bird to peices, as Hawks do — but being thus fast hung up; He Setts on his perch, picks them to peices as he wants Food. —

BP 2:61; D. 181–82.
1. Neats and Timothy Neve (1729–1798) were Philadelphia merchants.

From FOTHERGILL

London 3 mo 1750

Esteemed Friend,

I am more obliged to thy generosity than I can easily express for still remembering me, often with such strong appearances against me, might easily, in a less equitable mind, have wholly extinguished regard. Want of health, at some times, unavoidable engagements at others have defeated both inclination & duty. The only time I can set apart for writing is late in the evenings, and this is not always certain.

Sometimes the thought of the day have made me incapable of doing it, and this is the reason why Physicians are worse correspondents than others. We cannot, like Tradesmen, reserve proper times for proper business, but must go when and where called. In respect to J. Martin;[1] I took over the translation of his letter to Voltaire and don't find the quotations mentioned in it. I have not the book now at hand and cannot be too certain as I could wish. In the latter part of his life he was very remiss and inattentive, and I don't at all wonder if he suffered egregious mistakes to escape him. He had been under the necessity of subsisting on his books to a great measure for some years and had sold several at different times for between 3 & 400 £ at most.

I am still of the same opinion in regard to the origin of lumber that I formerly mentioned: I am obliged to thee for pointing out a passage that would not otherwise have fallen within the compass of my readings, but I hope to explain the affair in such a manner as to obviate every difficulty. It is agreed on all hands that the faults contained in the Essay on the generation of plants are curious and well conducted and to the theory built upon them; people doubt whether it will hold good; In some of the Latin Academical dispersions, printed lately at Upsal, I see the experiments are oftener than once quoted, which makes me think it is well received by the Botanists of that Country who are at present the most industrious of any in Europe.

I have sent by Jonah Thompson, a Friend in the Ministry of good repute amongst us, and I think well worthy of regard, Knight's discourses; a number of the Phil. Transats which contains the only copy I have of an Ac't of Siberia[2] and a little tract upon a medical subject which I laboured hard at, the winter before last.[3] The Disease of which it treats has committed great ravages in some places when a different method of management was pursued. It is not wholly extinct but seldom proves of Fatal consequence.

I hope this spring to get more leisure to answer some of thy unanswered favours, more particularly then at present I can do. I only beg leave to assure thee, as I am perfectly sensible of thy regard for me, and the honour I receive from such correspondence as well as advantage, so it gives me great uneasyness when the leisure I have devoted to make the best returns in my power is snatched unexpected[4]

My best [wishes] for the preservation of thy health and [thy] continuance amongst thy Friends and assure that I am

thine with gratitude & sincerity,
J. Fothergill

P.S. Please express my very kind respects to thy Son William. It is very painful to me that I cannot write to him by the present opportunity but hope to do so soon. J.F.

Historical Society of Pennsylvania Library, Maria Dickinson Collection.
1. Josiah Martin (1683–1747), Quaker classical scholar, widely known for "A Letter from one of the People Called Quakers . . ." to Voltaire.
2. Fothergill wrote "Account of Observations and Experiments" made in Siberia and submitted it to the Royal Society in 1748. It was published in their *Philosophical Transactions* 14 (1748):248.
3. Probably "An Account of the Sore Throat attended with Ulcers," published in 1748. This essay was Fothergill's best known of more than fifty memoirs. There were at least two English editions and one in French.
4. Badly torn.

From GRONOVIUS

Leyden, 2 July, 1750

Dear Friend: —

It is more than four years that I have not heard from you, of which the last war was the cause. I let you know by these that I am printing a new edition of my *Index Supellectilis lapideae;* wherein you shall find the names of all the minerals and fossils you ever had sent to me, with an encomium and thanks of all the benefits you have bestowed upon me. As soon as this book is printed, I shall send a copy of it for you to Mr. Collinson, who is now my only correspondent in London, being our good friend Mr. Catesby dead. You perceive how I expect to hear from you.

The bearer of these is Mr. Adolf Bensel, son to the Archbishop Eric Benzel, of Upsala, whom I recommend to you.

Wherewith, I remain

Your most obedient, humble servant,
John. Fred. Gronovius

D. 358.

From R. POOLE[1]

New Jersey July 3d 1750

Dear Sir —

I am this Evening safely ariv'd here in good Health; Yesterday I was with Governor Belcher[2] who appears to be very much of a Gentleman and a hearty Sincere Christian; I this Day saw Doctor Cadwallader[3] in this Place called Trent Town, who appears to me to be an ingenious Curious Gentleman and has a little imployed himself in the Botanic Way; but I have yet met with none nor do I indeed expect to meet with, any equal in Diligence and Knowledge herein to you my kind and much esteem'd Friend, who, I can't but highly esteem as the Wonder herein of the American Continent, and unto whom I heartily wish a Reward equal to your deserts in Labour and readiness to be useful to the Public, and communication of useful Knowledge. Since my leaving you, I have thought upon your Journal to the Indian Nations and hereby request it as a very acceptable Favour to be favour'd by you with a Copy of that Journal, which I hope will meet with much better success in coming to me then it did in its voyage to Holland; if it be your Pleasure to favour me with it please to send it by a trusty hand that may safely deliver it to me directed according to the Directions left with you which however lest you should have mislaid it is, For Saml. Govers near White Chaple, London. I heartily wish you all Health and Happiness and also your Spouse and the rest of your Family   I am much Obliged to you for the Pleasure receiv'd by your great readiness to oblige while at your House, and should be glad to have it in my Power to gratifie you in any thing agreeable to you.

I remain, Dear Sir, your affectionate humble Servt

R. Poole

BP 4:96.
1. Unidentified.
2. Jonathan Belcher (1681–1757), governor of New Jersey.
3. Dr. Thomas Cadwallader (1708–1779), a founder of the Pennsylvania Hospital.

From MITCHELL

London, Augt. 1, 1750

Sir: –

I have received several letters from you since my last, for which I return you thanks. The reason why I have been so long in writing to you is, that I have been in Scotland & over most of that country with the Duke of Argyll, since my last to you, and since my return here, have been so engaged in writing some other things, which has disagreed so with the state of my health, that it gives me pain even to set down to take a pen in my hand, & very often I am unable to do it, on account of a vertiginous disorder which it has occasioned & brings on so that you must excuse me from writing fully & particularly to you, till I can do it with more safety.

The Plants & Seeds which you sent for the Duke of Argyll, came safe to hand, & I have long ago paid Mr. Collinson for them. I lately likewise got two or three seeds of the new Magnolia from him which I carried to the Duke, but there is none of them come up, and it is to be feared that we cannot expect any from about 8 or 9 seeds which I had, as they are so apt to miscarry at the best

As the Duke of Argyll has all the Plants that are common & seed of his own from most of them, he does not desire any more, unless it be any thing that is new. I have lately got a commission from some other gentlemen for some seeds for you, while I told them was rather too late in the year, but they desired that you would do the best you could, they are

1 box of 5 Guineas for the Prince of Wales by Lord Boote.[1]
1 Do. for Lord Strafford
1 Do. for the Earl of Galloway

I have been obliged to give over my botanical pursuits for some time, so that I have not any thing to say to you on that head at present. But I have often mentioned you to several great men whom I have had an opportunity of seeing here, who are very glad to hear of Industry & laudable endeavours, but are backward in rewarding them, at least with any thing that is real & substantial, which is the most of what I can say on that head, altho if it lies in my power to recommend you to any thing, or to be of any service to you in any shape, you may freely command & depend upon

Your very hble servt.,
John Mitchell

Historical Society of Pennsylvania Library; D. 366.
1. Lord Bute.

From COLLINSON

London January 20: 1751

I am very much Obliged to my good Friend J. Bartram for so fine a Collection of growing plants — if they had all come to my Hand I should have troubled Thee no further but to my great Loss some prying knowing people Looked into the Cases and out of that No. 2: took the 3 Roots of Chamaerhododendrons, Red Honeysuckle   Laurel   Root of Silver Leafed Arum & the Spirea alni folio   these was the Most Valuable part & what I most Wanted, it is very vexatious   wether taken out on board or Coming up from the Ship I can't Say — but this is Certain they was gone — I wish Ld: Northumberland had not the Same bad luck for as I peeped In I could see but very Little — but as I have had no complaints I hope it was otherwise   how the Rose Laurels came I cannot Saye but I may Hear — I am Sensible of the great trouble & Difficulty to procure these plants as they grow So remote So cannot Desire thee to Renew them again — but if thy Friendship for Mee should prompt thee to Do It – then add some More Rose Laurel but yett unless thy Health permits and other agreeable Circumstances Concur — pray don't, think about them — I fancy some of the sailors having relatives gardeners seeing these plants so carefully boxed up took them for rarities so were tempted to steal them to give to their friends.

All the Boxes came Safe & Seem all in Good Order — I think they are well Sorted as I hope will please Everyone but the last ship was within a Week or Two of the first — I think it was running too great a Risque to Ship so Largly on the last, for fear of Accidents but the reason I apprehend was, the Seeds was not perfectly dry to go by first — but as they came Safe all is Well — they came in fine Time of year as our Winter happens to be Hitherto as warm & mild as Last — This day, I gathered the finest Nosegay January 16 to carry to town being plenty of Violets, Crocus   Snow drops   Polyanthos   Single Anemone   Double & Single Stocks and Wall flowers very Sweet Black Hellebore acconite, Lauras Tinus which flowers all winter — Double Hepaticas. I had formerly a Single Sort from thee but lost It.

I conceive the 3 Leafed pines growing in a Different forme is Entirely owing to the soil they grow in & Exposure to the sea Winds   I have Several Shrub Groundsel from thy Seed — but I should Like a plant or Seed of the Shrub Wormwood — which I presume growing near the Sea is of a Blewish Green as Most of our Sea plants are phaps from the Saline particles in the air & soil

Did the berries of the evergreen Rhamnus that was found in the great plains in the Desert — growing 5 or 6 Inches high amongst the Dwarf pines — Come up in thy Garden   none did with Mee   It was a very rare & Curious plant — I want Berries of your Native Holley & Seed of Erryngium Yucca folio and if any Obelescothecas of Virginia are left in thy Garden & Send Mee Some Seed — and of White Lychnis with Fringed Flower & Cross wort Leaves —

Thy Journal Is in the press — hope to send it by Next Ship.
I am thy Sincere frd.

P. Collinson

BP 2:84:2; D. 182.

To GRONOVIUS[1]

January ye 24th 1750/1

Dear Friend
I haveing now A fine opertunity of sending A letter directly to thee, by ye hands of my friend Slauter[2] who promised to deliver it with his own hands, so I readily embraced ye opertunity   I wrote to thee by ye way of London, Last november, & acknowledged ye recept of this kind letter of august   I have sent my Journal to ye five nations to our friend Peter Collinson who hath received it   if thee desireth to see it I doubt not but he will readily send it to thee: I tooke A Journey last fall beyond our blew mountains & passed thorow A gape which I believe had been A large water course, when ye waters covered all ye lower parts of ye countrey, & began to run off from ye mountains, this gape is about one half ye hight of ye mountain & near A

The Delaware Water Gap. *Harper's New Monthly Magazine* 32 (1863):456.

mile through; all ye way stone: as soon as we arive, near ye foot of ye mountain, we travel on nothing but loose stones, as close together as they could be paved about ten rod wide is 16 foot ½ wide & all ye way to ye top on both sides; of all dimentions from 10 tone weight to as big as my head. when we have passed ye gape & begins to descend down ye north side, we have soil all ye way mixed with ye stones, which shewed that ye waters gradually fell away & formed from this place two streams, on ye north side which emptied one into ye east, ye other into ye west branch through which ye waters run & drained ye countrey on ye north side, so that in time this gape was left dry, being so paved with stones, that ye waters could not wear it any deeper as it did in ye other channels. pray accept these short hints in love as thay are given which will oblige thy Sincear friend

John Bartram

Hunt Institute for Botanical Documentation, Carnegie-Mellon University.
1. Added to this letter was the following note from Peter Collinson to Gronovius:

> My Dear Friend, I can learn very little certain of the Cortex Peruvianus – for Wee have nothing certain printed about It – this is certain that the Quina Quina which was the first febrifuge of the Jesuits is quite a different plant from the Cortex now in Use – by the Specimens I have seen It is a Species of Lilac – and may be named Lilac Peruvianus flore Coccineo
>
> Docr. Mortimer our Secretary, has collected materials for a History of this curious plant and made a Variety of Drawings, of the Leafe flowers & seed vessell &c but is in hopes of more accurate accounts & then He will communicate them to the R. Society – Condemine [Charles Marie de la Condamine (1701–1774), French commander of a French and Spanish expedition to Peru in 1735–44] is the last that has mentioned it in print – that Wee know off – I have made all the Inquirys I can but to Very Little purpose – Its place of Growth, & it's Effects wee know but there is a many other perticulars required to give a general History of It – pray give my Respects to Docr. Brayne [unidentified] & his Grandson   I sent you Bartrams Journal per Mr. Slawter which I hope is come safe to hand   I am with sincere Respects
>
> Truly yrs
P Collinson

> pray if an oppertunity offers Buy the plants as under for Mee & send by any Friend:–
>   4 Roots of Geele Franse Roos Narcissus
>   4 Roots of Narcis campanelle flo: Luteo Reflexo
>   4 D— of — Comp —— flo albo reflexo
>   1 D— of Moly purpureo Major
>   2 Narciss Nana Minor —— 2 Shavers Huck
>   1 Narciss Nana Minima —— 10 Steven Huck
>   2 Ranunculas fol plantagines
>   12 Duc Vanloe Tulips
>
> this I had formerly from Van Hassen but in removing my Garden lost them – all the Charges I will repay with thanks

2. Unidentified.

From JAMES GORDON[1]

London, Mile-End, March 3, 1750–1.

Mr. Bartram: –

I return you my thanks for many curious seeds, which my good friend, Mr. Peter Collinson, has given me through your means. If there is any seeds here, which you think worth your having, please let me know, and I'll endeavour to procure you some of them; and I am,

Sir, your obliged servant,
James Gordon

D. 369–70.
1. Collinson wrote on the back of this letter: "Our friend Gordon is a very modest man, and can't speak himself; but a few Magnolia cones, or the two or three sorts growing with you, will be acceptable to him."

To COLLINSON[1]

Our pheasant was I believe wholy unknown to Catesby, it being more northern than Carolina, they have been Common (in Pensilvania) but now most of them are destroyed in the lower settlements, tho the back Indian Inhabitants bring them to market. when Living, they Erect their tails like turkey-cocks. and raise a ring of Feathers round their necks and walk very stately, making a noise a little like a turkey, when the hunter must fire. they thump in a very remarkable manner by clapping their wings against their sides, as is supposed standing on a fallen Tree. They begin their stroke at about 2 seconds of time distant from each other, and repeat them quicker and quicker, untill they sound like Thunder at a distance, which lasts about a minute, then ceases for 6 or 8 Minits, and begins again, They may be heard near half a Mile, by which the hunters find them. They exercise their thumping in a morning and Evening in the Spring and fall of the year. Their food is berrys and Seeds; their flesh is white and Good. I believe they breed but once a year in the Spring, and hatch 12 or 14 at a sitting and these keep together till the following Spring. They cannot be made Tame. many have to their disappoyntment attempted it by raising them under henns, but as soon as hatched they Escaped into the woods, where they either provided for themselves or perished.

Royal Society of London Archives, Letters and Papers, 2:469; *Philosophical Transactions of the Royal Society* 48 (1754):499–503; also quoted in George Edwards, *A Natural History of Uncommon Birds and Some Other Rare and Undescribed Animals,* 4 vols. (London, 1743–51), 188–93, and Thomas Pennant, *Arctic Zoology,* 1:302–3, with quite a bit more detail.
1. Apparently written early in 1751 (see Collinson to Bartram, March 5 and late summer, 1751). Pennant extracted part of Bartram's letter to Collinson and made a drawing of two grouse sent to Collinson from Bartram (Collinson's note on a copy of the sketch in the earl of Derby's library, Knowsley Hall).

From COLLINSON

March 5, 1750/1

My Good frd John —
pray what is the reason I have No Acorns from that particular Species of Oke that Docr Mitchell found in thy Meadow and I observe in thy Specimens 2 other Narrow Leafed okes — as I have now ground Enough I wish for a Dozen good Acorns of Each — a few Sugar Mapple Keys — unless *thou could send Mee a young plant* — the pticular sort of Hazel Nutt grows that was sent Mee 2 years agon but in removing my Garden[1] I lost the Early Sweet Iris & the Curious Species of Arum — pray repair these Losses besides a Sweet Spiraea alni folio named Clethra per Linnaeus which I much admire but that must come in a plant or Two & a plant or Two of Ivy or yr Laurel — my Soil is Some of it Light Sandy & moist — phaps they'l thrive in It and a few Small Magnolias or Swamp Roots flowering Laurel — I saw a few Days agon Some Charming Snugg[2] Bushey pretty Trees of this kind & Some Snugg Bushy Trees about a foot high all of your laurel or Ivy Sent by your proprietor Thos Penn's Gardener   I never saw such pretty plants nor Come finer   all full of Blossom Budds & their Leaves as green as if Just taken out of the Woods —with Divers other fine things & Some New plants I have not seen before thay was sent to one Scott a Gardener   prethee try what thee canst do Next year to repair my Losses which are great & make the old proverb good   those that have Little shall have Less   who would think it — but so it was, the Case No. II: was Robbed Either on Board or on the River and the Red Honeysuckle   all the Chaemododendrons the Silver Leafd Arum & the Sweet Spirea alni folio called Clethra by Linnaeus, was all taken Out

To Remedy this for the future Nail the Top Boards & Side Boards So Close that none shall Peep into It – for thou knowest in the Winter Months a Little Air or what comes through the Crevices of the Boards is sufficient to keep the plants alive — I am more concerned on thy Account, then my own because of the trouble and pains there was to procure them   the plants in the Other Box Came Safe & Well   I was amazed at the Length of the Convolvulus Roots   phaps they [are] the Mechochan mentioned by Some authors to be a Convolvulus –

on the other Side are things drawn up at Different Times in a Huddle,[3] pick out what thee canst — pray from what Quarter art thee Supplied with White & Red Spruce Cones — there is the black Spruce & the Balm of Gilead   I see not these Two sorts amongst them. I thank thee for the Mint Seeds – there seems great Variety and for So fine a Collection of Lillies & Martigons & for the Hunesuckle Seeds in the autumn   in return I putt up Some for thee but was Left behind by Reves not sailing

MEMORANDUMS

Besides I Desire Either plants or Seeds of Early Sweet Christophoriana – that I am now supplyed with thy last kindness   Digitalis & Solomons Seale of

which I see in the Specimens what I have not   Hast thee found the Evergreen Smilax Obeliscothecas all Sorts – Mountain Goats Rue   Leather Wood or Thymela   what Sorts of Clematis grows with you   Lychnids with fringed wt flowers & Cross wort Leaves   Eryngium with Yucca Leaves — seed pfoliated apocinon — best Species of Eupatoriums — Seed *your Hepatica I formerly had but lost* had no flower or seed   What are these I had formerly
    a plant growing in Rich Island up Skulkill   flowers in spring
    a plant whose Leaves are Indented with white   Myrtle Island in Skulkill
I had formerly a Perrenial Tall blew Larkspurr from the back of Virginia —with Acconite Leaves and a Species or Two of Acconite with blew flowers if they are left in your Garden send Mee Seed   Seed of Serratula & Early & Late Jacea   Seed of Jacea called by you Throat Wort for its Vertue in disorders of the Throat & Quinsies   *Roots of a Sort of Hyacinth with white flowers if Bulbous*   if the Roots of Orchis's was taken up in flower and planted in thy Garden & marked with a tobacco pipe or Stick they would be Easily found & come well in Mould with other things   *a yellow orchis* would be a rarity Here   ours are Either purple or white Ruellia –growed on a Branch of Potomack in the great Vail   if thee hast any of your Country Gentians growing in thy Garden please send Mee Some Seed   a Species of Alaternus found by thee on James River   a Viburnum with yellow Budds in Winter & Spring   What of the Above is Sent take no Notice of   I much question if your Heath Fowl & Pheasant is figured by Catesby or if they are known Here — it is possible to skin them & stuff their skins with Tobacco & Wool or Cotton or Tow or Flax — oh why had I not a few acorns of the broad leafed Willow Okes found in the Jerseys & the great broad leafed Oke by pond   all the Dwarfe Okes must be pretty in a garden —besides to Mortifie Mee the More I had none of the broad leafed Magnolia found in the Jerseys — I have no share in the boxes   all go as directed   pray to Remember to Send 2 Species of Terapins for my garden & Early Ripe Indian Corn & Send Mee Squash Seed for my own Eating
    Orders follow for seven customers

    1 Box for Duke [illegible]
    2 Boxes for Rich [illegible]
    1 Do for Christopher Gray Gardener
    1 Do for Norris a Gardener
    1 Do for Mr   the name forgott
    1 Do for William Cole Esqr to be sent in a Ship to Dublin consigned to
        Alderman Samuel Cooke
    1 Do for Robt Fraser at Brumton

BP 2:83; D. 183.
1. Collinson had moved his garden from Peckham to Mill Hill, outside of London.
2. Compact.
3. In haste.

From COLLINSON

London March 22d 1751

I hope my kind Frd John Bartram has mine by Budden   I am So engaged always at this time o'year, that I always write in a Hurry and write phaps the Same thing over & over again for my Memory is Burdened with a Thousand things —

Thy Bill of £60 is paid — remember when thou Draws next year draw in 20 or 25£ Bills a Month or Six weeks Distance Each — for then I have Time & a last pretence Summons those that have not paid — to pay their arears our Gentry &c are but Slow & I have So many things to think on that I forget — untill thy Bills come —

I have only had an order for Six boxes   pray putt Catalogues in them & Large Marks and Strong Baggs — but one for Duke of Marlbrough

I observe 4 Species of Hickery   Send Mee ½ score of Each for my own sowing —

I am much obliged to thee for the Cargo in the Little Box   it was well stuffed — all came in fine order.

The 2 Bibles I sent I think by Budden val 14s: Each

I believe I told thee of the great Loss of the Duke of Richmond, my Intimate & Familiar Friend next to Lord Petre   none so ardently Encouraged Gardening & plants & Every Laudable Design — both in Publick & private Life.

pray remember the Terrapins — one the Shell is Black beautifully marked with under the Brim & Edges of the Shell — & early ripe Indian Corn & Squash Seed

Thine,
P. Collinson

Bp 2:85; D. 183.

From MITCHELL

London, Mar: 30th 1751

Dear Sir,

I received yours in which you complain, that you had neither received any letter from me, nor any account of the seeds you sent me, which I am surprised at, I having wrote you a letter particularly for three boxes of seeds the last year of which I have received only two. Mr. Collinson indeed made some mistake about the payment of the seeds sent the year before this last for the Duke of Argyll, and demanded payment for them again, after I had his Receipt for it, by which I suppose he might forget to write you about the Receipt of that Money which he stands indebted to you for by his own Receipt to me, to wit £5..14.. charges included. I have likewise paid him lately twenty guineas for two Boxes received this year by the Duke of Argyll, & the Prince of Wales, and wanted another that I wrote for but could not get it.

This is to advise you of another Box of Seeds that is wanted by the Earl of Hyndford, for which he desired me to give you particular Instructions that they might be sent to him by the first opportunity, & of the best of your forrest Trees. He wants a box of Ten Guineas price, like the one you sent this year. You must excuse me if I do not write to you so often & fully as I would incline to do   I have had so much business of that kind upon my hands since I came to England, that I have contracted a disorder by it which makes me unable to puruse it any longer, or even to sit down to write a letter especially that requires any thought, without being sensibly the worse for it. I hope however to be able some time or other to make amends for my omissions of this kind.

We have had two great losses lately in Planting & Botany in England which will hardly be repaired I am afraid, and are rather greater than the loss they sustained by the death of Lord Petre. The Duke of Richmond & the Prince of Wales, are suspected both to have lost their lives by it, by being out in their gardens to see the work forwarded in very bad weather. The Prince of Wales, whose death you will hear of by these ships, manifestly lost his life by this means, he contracted a cold by standing in the wet to see some trees planted (thro' a sort of obstinacy agst. any precaution of that kind which it seems the whole family are blamed for) which brought on a Pleurisy, that he dyed of lately. If anything occurs worthy of your notice I shall consider of it at more leisure by next opportunity. I am Sir

Your most humble servt.
John Mitchell

BP 4:87; D. 367

To ELIOT[1]

In Pensilvania & ye Adjacent Colonies I have observed these severall different Soils on ye surface; ye variety of stratas under & ye kinds of stone & rock on what way are supported;

first near ye sea in West Jersey is chiefly Course Sand & gravel & very poor ground. onely where it is covered with Oister Shells which enricheth ye fields on which thay was spread by ye Indians;

2dly near ye Sea in Pensilvania: where ye sand is Course it is poor. but where it is finer & mixed with loam A bed of oister shells from 15 to 20 foot under ye surface it is generaly very rich.

3dly Near ye sea in Maryland coars Sand. on A stratum of Shells 10 or 12 foot under ye surface: ye land is poor but if covered with shells by ye Indians, or fine sand mixed with loam then ye soil is rich;

4thly near ye Sea in Virginia fine sand on A stratum of Shells   10 or 12 foot deep the land is rich:

5thly Virginia near ye bay on ye east side. fine black sand of very good land especialy in ye necks On ye west side near ye bay. on ye necks fine sand mixed with loam on A Strata of Shells 10 or 15 foot under ye surface is generaly rich. but where A stif clay prevails or ye sand is coarse there ye land is poor;

6thly in Maryland on ye east Side of ye bay fine sand & rich in ye Necks. between ye mouths of ye rivers on A stratum of shells: but toward ye heads of ye rivers poor white sand & many swamps; on ye western shore & in ye necks is A fine sand & Loam very rich & black generaly is fine Loamy soil on A bed of shells, from ye bay to ye hills: which consists of Loamy Soil & loose stones intermixed:

7thly Pensilvania for near 100 mile up ye river Delaware ye soil is sand & loam mixed. upon A strata of Shells; at uncertain depth from 10 to 20 foot under ye surfacte & generaly very good land level to ye head of ye bay of Chesapeak

8thly Jersey near ye River where it is fine sand mixed with Loam is choice land but where it is coarse Sand upon A bed of marl or clay at 16 or 20 foot deep gneraly poor   sometimes under this stratum there is A deep strata of A black sulphurous matter sometimes vitriolick with abundance of yelow markasites mixed with it: this I have observed if it be near ye surface & 2 or 3 foot of loam upon it is choice Soil but too much destroys vegitation as all salts do in great quantity. There is A stratum of A red rock runs from 2 to 5 foot under ye surface & from 1 to 2 miles wide extending its length from near New York & runs A west by north course through East Jersey & Pensilvania toward ye Lake Erie   this is generaly good Soil, espetialy where there is several feet of Loam upon ye rock. which is very full of fissures: but where it is covered with A deep stif Clay its but indeferent.

10th[2] I have observed that deep stif clay upon an Isinglass rock is generaly very bad corn ground. this rock mostly Lyeth in vast masses of miles extent & very deep without any perpendicular fissures & ye lamina is placed horizontaly.

11thly Above ye head of ye tide in Jersey. Pensilvania. Maryland & virginia & for 20 mile Back A loamy soil generaly prevails on A strata of gray or black stones of all dimentions from as big as A nut to 20 ton with some vails of lime stone land intermixed: which is generaly good corn land. ye hills producing Oak   Hicory & chesnut: ye vails wallnut & Hasel. but when we are over that ridg of high hills about 50 mile above york (up Hudsons river) which thay call ye high Lands which ridges strecheth west by South all ye way back of South Carolina & is ye South bound of A fine rich lime stone vail bounded on ye North with our great blew mountains. beyond which is very broken mountainous land all ye way to ye 6 nations; who is setled on A choice large tract of land most of it limestone land on ye branches of susquehana Mohooks Onondagoes & Ohio rivers; So far I have given A short account of ye nature of ye diferent parts of our Province & those adjacent to it from my own observations. Now I will take ye freedom to Communicate some of my conjectures concerning ye Natural fertility of ye different Soils as thay occured in my botanising travels:

there is several natural causes (as I apprehend) of ye fertility as well as sterility of all ye different Soils. One cause is very obvious in rich low lands. by ye banks of rivers that are fresh. which are Already enriched by ye floods that brings down mud & trash deposited there where ye stream doth not run very strong or in eddy or back water or where there grows bushes weeds of brambles &c to retain ye leaves or trash that is brought down: I have observed that in Pensilvania East Jersey & York government their rich low lands before thay was cleared: produced abundance of hasels, weeds & vines which entangled ye trash which ye floods brought there; & in time rotting kept it very rich: but when cleared & plowed thay had A contrary effect upon it instead of bringing A rich supply & leaving it thay often bore away some of ye best of ye soil which as A fine black sandy Loam: & if ye stream hath A fall & Consequently runs swift it often leaves A coars sand which impoverisheth it; & moreover as ye higher ground & hills is trod & pastured ye water in great rains washeth ye earth much more in gullies, bringing down more course sand or clay then formerly. as I have observed when I was in ye back parts of ye Countrey above 20 year past when ye woods was not pastured & full of high weeds & ye ground light   then ye rain sunk much more into ye earth & did not wash & tear ye surface (as now)   ye runs & brooks in floods would be black with mud but now ye rains runs most of it off on ye surface is colected into ye hollows which it wears to ye sand & clay, which it bears away with ye swift current down to brooks & rivers, whose banks it overflows & where ye current runs swift it leaves ye sand behind but where ye stream is checked some of ye rich sedimen remains & enricheth it greatly   An example of which is very Conspicuous near Albany where Hudsons River brings down anualy A very rich sediment which meeting with ye tide or swelling water which checks ye current is deposited on ye low lands on each side which so fertiliseth them as never to be worn out no more than Egypt's   so is it with our tide marshes by thair diurnal Overflow   all this is plain to any common observer how ye low ground is enriched by an addition of rich composts on its Surfaces:

but how shall we account for ye exceeding fertility of ye high & hilly ground – I have been many times upon A branch of Susquehana I suppose 50 mile above ye tide where ye surface of ye soil was elevated 150 foot above ye bed of ye river which soil was so exceeding rich for many miles square that it was like A rotten dung hill, produceing Locust two foot diameter, Sumachs big enough to make 8 rails apiece, Large plumb trees, grape vines 6 inches diamater: very large Judas tree & papaws, walnut & mulbery vastly large; & weeds eight foot high such kinds as our richest marshes produces & ye soil black & rich 4 foot deep: but now it is much of it cleared & ye rest trod & pastured so that it hath now quite another appearance. I knowed one field that bore strong hemp for 12 years Succesivly after which it was sowed with wheat which for many years growed so rank that it could not stand but lay down before it ripened producing A very light grain yet indian corn & rye would prosper exceedingly.

now what must be ye cause of this wonderfull richness of Soil Some supposed it to be caused by turkey or Pidgeons dung; but that could not be ye natural cause; if thay had laid thair dung 10 foot deep on clay or course sand it would in A few years have assimilated it into its own nature it must be fed as I Conjecture from fertilising Saline streams which ye perticular modification of ye Soil which was Qualified to attract either from below or retain as thay transpired & perhaps allso ye contents of ye atmosphere may contribute to help considerably. We see ye works of providence are wisely Adapted so as mutualy to assist each other & now to illucidate this my notion I will give thee A perticular account of ye rock & ye strata of earth lying upon it in this exceding rich piece of land

ye rock is A very deep bed of limestone which is covered with A fine Sandy loam of a brown Color with some shineing particles intermixed about 11 or 12 foot deep.

Beinecke Rare Book and Manuscript Library, Yale University, Jared Eliot Collection.
1. Probably written in spring 1751 (see Bartram to Eliot, February 12, 1753).
2. "9thly" was apparently omitted.

From COLLINSON

London April 24 1751

To My Esteemed Friend John Bartram

Lest my Letters by other Vessels Should Miscarry, I here Renew my orders for Seeds, with aditions but Desire these may be putt in Cloth bags Especially the Small sorts & Large Labels or Ticketts — for there is great complaints of the paper Bags rotting Tickets not found & running one Into another as I know the account will bear It, Thou ought to do all thou cans't to Encourage so Beneficial an article to all parties — & be sure forgett not to putt a Catalogue wraped in brown paper to prevent the Moisture Effecting It in Each Box for I was ticked for Lists and for Names of Seeds — but besides Inclose Mee several Lists that I may know what is in Each Box — and it Serves to Show Strangers wt sort they may Expect another Time

as for My own garden pray my good frd Revers my Losses — as these Large orders will engage, to make some distant Excursions it may be the Less trouble to procure what I want of Growing plants, Chamerhododen-drons, Magnolia, Shrub Honesuckles Your flowering [illegible] timely notice to Collect in what is owing — for our Great people are very Dilatory — & wont bear Duning — I sent thy account by Last Ship — the Bill being — 9:22; which [illegible] for it suits thee, Lett all be for the Exact Sum that Wee may not break into another years Account —

Powel[1] paid Mee — 8 Guineas I conclude he has given an order this year — & sent a bundle of Baggs which with the Bibles &c I sent per Neal & Neaves ship — Williamson paid Mee — 7:17:6

Our spring is Late — I watch Dayly to see the success of the last growing

Cargo — only the blew berried Christophoriana appears — & some of the plants in the great Sodd begin to Budd as the Huckle berries, Some Warm Weather will I hope make them sprout — the Laurel or Ivy is Dead   I have raised Several Grounsel Trees   I saw what plants the Earl had in Moss & they Look likely to grow — but yett I think in Case of a long Voyage its Safer to cover their Roots with earth & a Good Deal of Moss over it will keep the Earth Moist & the plants Fresh — remember the Beach Cherries & some plants or Seeds of Shrub Wormwood & Send Mee in a Little box a few Select Seed for myself as Pine Cones, Magnolia &c & flower Seeds, Clinopodiums, & Oberlecothecas, Red flowered Eupatorium, pfoliate Eupatorium, the white Gentian   I have 3 or 4 Roots so think no more about It — pray remember a plant or Cones of that Rose Laurel with broad Large Leaves, thou found in October last — Send a Specimen of It — I cant think it a New Species   its Cold Baren Situation might retard its growth & prevent its Maturity Sooner   It is very Extraordinary what thou writes of the Larch it grows very fast Here on all Soils

pray remember the Faba Egyptica that our Friend Kalm found in West Jersey — specimens of Leafe flower & fruite — He & His Wife arrived Safe Here — Wee have had many Conferences — He Desires his Service commends Thee in Most things, but much blames thee for not Enriching thy Journal with a Many Curious Articles which He has collected from thy Mouth — & which had He come time Enough He would have added

the Persian Iris thou sent Mee Twice is the Same Wee have had Long in our Gardens & it is a Charming flower — but what I wanted & was in hopes it was Early Sweet Dwarf Iris of Virginia which I had formerly & Lost

this concludes answers to thy 4 Letters Last year June 1st: July 14: Oct 14: ye 18th which was all Received Last Year — the Sarsifras & Chinquapins did not come up   the First will Lay untill the second year so I may hope to See it Soone

In mentioning Boxes to Governor Shirley Mitchell & Powell & Williamson but not a Word on what Value to Either so that I am obliged to take what they pay Mee   Govr Shirley has not yett paid any thing & I know not what to ask of Him   He is now at Paris setling the Limits of Nova Scotia

Write to Williamson for what Ever Green seeds Thou wants or to Gordon   the last has sent thee Turnip & Cabbage seeds Desired

The death of our Late Excellent Prince of Wales has cast a great damp over all the Nation   Gardening & planting has lost its best Friend & Encourager for the Prince had Delighted in that Rational amusement a long while but Lately He had a Laudable & princely ambition to Excel all others —

But the good thing will not Die with Him for there is Such a Spirit & Love of It amongst the Nobility & Gentry and the pleasure & profit that attends It will render It a lasting Delight —

I admire in thine & Kalm's Travels, that you gott no Intelligence of the Great Moose Deer — so celebrated by the first Settlers — this Great Formidable animal cannot be Extinct — I wish only to See a pair of Its horns to compare with the Great fossil Horns found in Ireland, which is certainly Extinct in that Kingdom — now my Dear John It's time to Conclude with my Sincere Wishes for thine and familys preservation

thy real friend
P. Collinson

BP 2:86; D. 183–84.
1. Nathaniel Powell, a nurseryman.

From COLLINSON[1]

a List of Seeds to be sent this Autumn —

- a Box by Order of Mr. Hamilton Directed for William Pole Esq to be consigned to *Alderman Daniel Cooke in Dublin*
- a *small Box of a Guinea price only Great & Small Magnolias for Mr. Hamilton*
- a Small Box of Seeds of 5 Guineas for Ld: Northumberland of Mountain & Small Magnolias, wht Cedars, Tupelo, Honesuckles, Roses, Hollys & any Uncommon Tree & Shrub & Seed & of all Wild Flowers that Make a good Show   this box is not Expected size of ye other but a small Box with Curious things
- A Box of Growing plants in Mould for Ld: Northumberland – of Great & Small Magnolias, Mountain Chamaerhododendron & Smaller Species as the Ivy &c Shrub Honesuckles, Ginseng or any other rare plant that is not Easyly to be *raised by seed*

Much less mould will do within boxes, barely to Cover the Roots & a Many planted togetherer [sic] in the same box & then Cover'd — thick & Deep with Moss will make them Lighter & answer all purposes and Nail them up on Top to prevent purloining or Seeing them — for really I am in doubt if the Earls box was not pillfer'd this year — there seem'd so Little In It —since the Earl is willing to give five Guineas for the box of Growing plants as I sent before Those yr proprietors Gardener sent, much Exceeded [yours] chiefly living plants

Orders for Seeds Continued –

a Box for Mr. Hall
a Box for Christopher Gray Gardener   } Something
a Box for Robert Frazier Gardener   } of
a Box for Mr. Bercley   } Every
a Box for Duke of Malbrough   } thing
2 Boxes for Mr. Jackson   }

— and 4 Boxes Tenn Guineas Each for the Friends of Mr. Williamson Gardener at Kensington   his order went by Last ship —

Take one General hint, that all Sorts of Pines – Especially 5 & 3 Leafed pines both Species of Magnolias, White & Red Cedar Honey Locusts sweet Gum & all Species of Firrs, will be Acceptable (Common Tulip Tree) to Every Subscriber   Sugar Maples   Myrtle berries   add what Else thou please aralia spinosa, acorns, &c   *New Subscribers Desire Every thing*

Acorns should be packed in the bottome of the Boxes to prevent their Drying   I do not encourage the sending for growing plants because a good Deal of trouble attends them.

BP 3:5.
1. Undated but probably enclosed with his letter of April 24, 1751. See reference to the duke of Marlborough in Collinson to Bartram, March 22, 1751, and to the proprietor's gardener in Collinson to Bartram, March 5, 1751.

Moses Bartram (1732–1809). (Philadelphia) *North American,* December 20, 1908.

Young Billy Bartram (1739–1823). (Philadelphia) *North American,* December 20, 1908.

From COLLINSON[1]

I was delighted to See the Son[2] of my Old Friend John Bartram   the Honesty & good disposition of the youth pleases Mee as well as his Industrious disposition — the ship being sold, the poor Lad Is adrift & no passage to be had back without paying for It   He thinks it a hard Case & I think so too, for at this time there are very few ships going until about Xmas, which is too long to stay, & then will only have the Chance to go to

Mary Land or Virginia or West Indies, which He had been very Industrious to find out   He would willingly give his Labour for his passage, but neither to yr port or to New York will they take him on those Terms — and His Hireing himself to the West Indies I can no ways Agree to It tho he is very Desirous of It. But I shall persuade Him off of It for it will be exposing his virtue to too severe trials, for he must associate with our London common Sailors who are a most profligate Crew and if possible will never be Easy until they make Him like Themselves & then our Wages are very Low   the best sailor has but 25s a Month — the only Method I can advise is to get Him in a Setled Imploy in Some of your own Ships either tradeing here or to the West Indies that He may return & pass the Winter (if from London) under thy Inspection — as He was very bear of Clothes & those he had in a ragged Condition I have according to thy order fitted him up in the most frugal manner I could   I must say for Him that He was even contented in his Raggs & thought I did too much & yett in his poor Equipment, I could not see how I could do less & have gone as near as I could which I hope will meet with thy Aprobation.

I must Acknowledge my good Friend has taken great pains to Oblige Mee with so many Entertaining Letters — Thy Observations on the Faba Egyptica are well worth Our Notice   Docr Gronovius will be delighted with it   I have had Specimens from South Carolina but never imagined it grew so far to the Northward; the Specimens are fine   I will send one to Holland the first opportunity   Next year if it is not too remote gett More Leaves, Fruit & the flower *in its full size* which will make the whole Compleat & I have some Curious Botanical Friends to Oblige with Specimens   It must certainly be Some other Sharp Strong pointed production, that could annoye the scally Sides of the Crocodile, indeed its Belly is Easier penetrated   The Tribulus equaticus is much harder & sharper   It is possible this rare plant may have been Eradicated from Egypt &c by the great Increase of people animals & Traffick — But in China it subsists with a Variety of Rare Species as I have seen & showed Moses from a Chinese Herbal containing near a Thousand Vegetables — all most Curiously drawn & painted in their Natural Colours — there is Delineated 3 Species, with Large White, Yellow, & purple flowers   These have their Seed vessels represented upright   that yours should hang down is very singular — all aquatic Leaves have the property Thou Mentions I presume from their downey Surfaces tho not pceptible to our Eyes without a Glass & as all webfooted Fowls shoot off the water from the oily downiness that is on the Surface   Thy Expedition up the Creek shows with what energy Thou pursues Nature   the Hidden deeps cannot secure her treasure   She rewards thy labours with her Spoils

There is great reason to Believe from the Beds of Petryfied Shells that are found all over the Level Country below the Mountains & confined by the Ocean — that Its Waves once wash'd the feet of those Hills, but on some great revolution retreated & Left those Memorials behind It — Indeed Wee refer all such Phenomena to the Effects of the Deluge — but it is Believed &

also known that there has been great alterations on the Face of Nature from Earthquakes, &c, — That Belemnites are found with Sea Shells I think is a confirmation that they are Marine productions wch many Doubt, but think them stones, after their own kind — which, for many reasons, I can by no Means agree too — It may Seem wonderfull to Thee that New Shells are found, not known before, but who can tell what lies concealed in the fathomless depths of the Ocean   the belemnites may lie concealed there their weight may prevent their being washed on the Shores.

We have a Clift in England near Limington that Abounds with such Variety of Shells, I have at least 20 Different Species Large & Small all unknown on our Coasts being from the East & West Indies, what a renversement must this have been   the productions of the South East & West thrown so far to the North.

I observe Well In thine of the 26th June thy Account of the Original Building of the Swallows   I think it very feasible but it is pretty singular none should continue their original Institution. [several lines illegible]

What thee calls Water Swallows — Wee call Sand Martins — from their building in sandy precipices — near Rivers & in inland places remote from Them   They are with us of a Different Colour from our Chimney Martins or House Swallows

as to thy Desire of an Assistant, it would to be sure be of Great Service to Relieve & Assist thee — but Such as thou'd like is not to be had — for none care to Leave their Native Land, but those that from their bad principles & Morals cannot Live In It

As to the Yellow Orchis I am not So deprived of that, or any Variety Else, that is not Easie to be secur'd   I only mention'd It that making coming Collecting seeds It happened in thy Way Well & Good

By thine of July 19th: both thy son & myself was glad to find Some degree of Health restor'd to thy Family — as Catesby only Resided in Virginia & Carolina It was Impossible He could describe only the animals of those provinces & not all them neither

I shall be pleased to see both your Pheasant & Heath Cock — as it may not be possible to procure both Cock & Hen of each Species, pray be carefull to Examine their internal parts that Wee may be sure for In Birds as the Cock & Hen varies so much for want of certainly knowing which, has made confusion and Multiplied Species — their Thumping is a very Extraordinary action & Moses confirms thy account   possibly it is a piece of Gallantry the Cock uses to recommend himself to the Hen   I admire I never heard of It Before   when the skin is stuffed gentle Drying in an oven after the bread is out, will preserve them packed in dry Tobacco leaves, or dust   Vale

P. Collinson

BP 2:79; D. 184–87.
1. The content of this letter suggests that it was written in late summer 1751.
2. Twenty-one-year-old Moses Bartram.

From GRONOVIUS[1]

Leyden June 26, 1751

Mr. Bartram
Dear Friend

It was in Decemb. laste year, that I hath the favour to get a letter from Mr. Collinson, whereby he acquaint me, that he was sending to me your Journal. The frost and snow hindered that ships upon the Mase-river could not reach up to Rotterdam, but were obliged for the Ice to stay two months betwixt the Sea and Rotterdam, which was very tedious for me. But at last I got that Journal, written by your own hands, reading it over and over very judiciously, and I don't give it any farther encomium, but refer my self to the preface of your printed Journal at London, which I got yesterday from Mr. Collinson, by the care of Mr. Slatter from pensilvania, by whom also I got the favour of your letter dated the 30 of Novemb. 1750. The last war hath spoiled our correspondence for some years, which I hope will now revive. I was forced to make a new edition of my Index,[2] in which I made mention of you in a decent way. That time I hath a prospect to get again some of the goods [curiosities] you sent to me, and Mr. Collinson, by a ship (if I remember well The Queen of Hungary) which was taken by the French or Spanyards, being some of the things sold at Diepe in France: being all come in the hands of Mr. Jussieu at Paris: but all what I could get bak, were only some seeds. Else I hath [had] a mind to print after my Index a treatise with the Title of Bartramia, that is your Journal in Latin, with notes to it containing the places where you hath found so many curious pieces [articles] which realy are an ornament to my Supellea, particular your great River shells. I got also your letter of the 24 January 1750/51, with the fine drawing of the gape at the blew mountains, which indeed is very curious. It is now the 26th of June, when Dr. Thomson acquaint me of his going to London. So I take this opportunity to send to you a copy of my Index, and also a copy of the Bibliotheca Botanica of Linneus, lately printed at Amsterdam, much enlarged and in better order, than the first edition. It is pity we had not, before this Bibliotheca was printed, your Journal, else you would have hath a place in it at the 163 page, under this title

PENSILVANIA
Bartram Johannes
Observations in itinere ex pensilvania in canadam
Lond. 1751. oct. pag. 79 tab I. fig. 2

You have realy obliged the world with such curious observations, as you have [made in] most every page. What hath been a great work about 50 years ago to find out the place where the Ninzi [Genseng] is growing, which you have discovered so easily. It was to be wished that all Travelers hath been so curious about the nature of the ground, as you have showed.

Linnaeus has printed his Philosophia Botanica, which I expect with the first ship from Sweden. He wrote to me that they have sent a Learned Botanist to China, and another to the Holy Land, to discover plants. So that in few years the garden at Upsal will be the finest of all [if they had more sun and a milder climate]

I sent at this occasion to you few specimens of dryed fishes, to be kept as plants in an Herbarium; the great misfortune is, that the colour perish; else it shows a good way to find out their characters 1. by nummer of the bones in the Membrane branchiostega, which you see in flying Trigla marked with blak; 2. by the nummer and position of the Fins, and the bones in them. 3. by the Course of the linez lateralis running in each fish from the bak part of the head to the tail. *Hebenstreit* a professor at Leipsich hath invented this methode, but he never would communicate the way to prepare them so; till at last I found it out a few years ago, and communicate it to our good friend Mr. Collinson, by whose care it is printed in the philos. Transact. num. 463. I send also to you a bit of what Tournefort calls *Fucus manum referems,* and which is exceding wel represented. Docr. Boerhave taketh it for a fucus. this body is frequent at our sea coast, having at first a great reference to the Spongia, being full of water, but this once being pressed out, it never soaks water again, but then it appears that it is a congeries of pipes, wherein breeds the polypi, but four times larger than the sweet water polypi of Mr. Trembly,[3] and so plentifull that I believe in this little bit were more than a million of these creatures, which being cut in four or five pieces, do live, grow and become the same posture [shape] as the First was.

Now I give you the witch names of the shells you was pleased to send to me.

1. Large fresh water muscle breeding in the creeks in the hilly part of the countrey. Concha testa oblonga, media antice contracta. Linn. faun. 1331,

34. Antiqua. this creature is the [Crab] Heremite Cancer macrourus cauda molli testa cochles inclusa; chela dextra minore. We have such a creature to at our sea coast, but differs that the chela dextra is much larger.

35. Under this nummer you sent to me 3 sorts of shells
    a. cochlea oblonga fluviatilis. petiv. gazoph. t. 18 v. 8
    b. cochlea trium orbrum. List. conch. t. 140 n. 16
    c. cochlea testa subglobosa glabra, carnei coloris, sulco transversale. Linn. faun. 1336

39. Sea clam, chama fusca lata planor. List. conch. t. 423 f. 259

40. Bay clam. pectunculus margine dense crenato, velut ex viola purpurascens ib. t. 271 f. 117

41. Oyster. Ostrea virginiana List. conch. t. 200 n.35

2. Sea blak small muscle. concha testa laevi subviolacea Linn. faun. 1333.

6. Shining Sea snails.
    a. Buccinum brevirostrum clavicula breviore, labio interno insigniter repando, ore atro purpureo splendente.
    b. — brevirostrum striatum & cancellatum, labro interno repando et splendente, mucrone costato, atro purpureum.

There is a good prospect for the affairs of *Mr. Slauter,* being very happy for him, that I hath the occasion to gain the favour of the Deputys of the Synode for him.

Now Dear Sir wishing You and Your family all health and prosperity I remain

Your most obliged Servant
Joh. Fred. Gronovius

[as all the Goods etc. was ship'd on Board I don't know wether I can send the roots etc. by this ship]

William Allan Neilson Library, Rare Book Room, Smith College; *Torreya* 16:116-20.
1. We are indebted to Alison M. Scott, assistant curator of rare books at the Neilson Library, for painstakingly copying this now-fragile letter for us. Her transcription differs in some details from that printed in *Torreya,* and has been followed here. There are several interlineal insertions by someone other than Gronovius, and also a postcript, these appear to have been made by Collinson, and are here rendered in brackets.
2. *Index Suppelactilis Lapidae quam collegit* (Leiden, 1750).
3. Abraham Trembley (1710–1784), Swiss zoologist.

From DOBBS

Castle Dobbs June 29th 1751

Sir

I received your Letter and Catalogue of the Seeds you Sent over by Captn Blair, which was delivered to me tho the Captain and Ship was lost with the Box in which the Seeds were which I am very sorry for as it greatly disapointed me and was a great Loss to you, and as this year I shall be abroad I shant want any Seeds this year: a great many seeds I had the year before never Came up nor one of those which should have been two years in the Ground Came up this year, nor do I find any one white Cedar has Come up here in any of the Boxes you have sent over which has greatly disapointed all who were Concerned. I Communicated your account of the American trees which I had last Spring as well as the account I had the year before, relative to the White Cedar, to the Dublin Society[1] and have here Inclosed to you Mr. Prions answer, our Secretary, whereby they accept of your kind offer of Corresponding with you and getting some of your Seeds, So that if you direct a Box with Seeds &c to Mr. Prion in Dublin for the use of the Society it will be agreeable to them and he will pay your ordr. for them; I shall only want a parcell of white Cedar Berries, and American Cypress Cones if such you have with you, for which I shall pay you what you Charge for them. My Friend Collinson sent me over yr Book of your Journal to Oswego which with the Letter of the Niagara Falls[2] was very agreeable and as I had Mr. Evans Chart which he was so kind as to send me it Cleared up that Journey very agreeably. I wish you better success in the Next parcels you send to Ireland, and am glad to hear that those you sent to England all arrived safe, and that the demand Increases there, which I hope will make some Amends for your Loss here, which was the more provoking as it happened within 5 or 6 Leagues of the port she was bound for, and Im afraid was occasioned by her Calling at Isle of Man to get some goods and Spirits to run into Ireland and fear some were drunk or they could not have made such a false Course in a run of 14 or 15 Leagues from thence to Belfast. I wish you all Happyness and am Sr

Yr Most Humble Servat
Arthur Dobbs

I delayed writing till a Ship from hence Sail for Philadelphia

BP 3:101.
1. The Dublin Society was founded in 1731 by Dobbs and several of his friends to promote agriculture. He presented Bartram's account of American trees to the Society on February 28, 1751.
2. Probably Peter Kalm's article on Niagara Falls, published in the *Pennsylvania Gazette*, September 20, 1750.

From COLLINSON[1]

My Dr frd
I have now thine of the 18: June before Mee & Moses by my Side So I cannot fail of many Intelligences   He has Surveyed my Garden and finds many things wanting   as the Weather has proved very fine I believe He will think his Trip hither no ways disagreeable —

Our Good Frd B:Franklin has Some papers on Husbandry from a Curious Friend[2] of Mine from wch Its Likely thou may borrow some Usefull Hints, Butt great allowances must be made for the Difference of our Soil & Climate with yours — I have Also Desired Him to Lett Mr Elliot of Connecticut See them for they may tend to the Improvement of that Colony. —

As thy Sons Inclination is bent to the Sea and He is very Desirous to Quallifie himself for that Business It would be much to his Advantage to be Setled in some Regular certain Imploye   then his Industry & diligence will be taken Notice of & will be a Means for His Advancement — whereas if He is from Time to Time Changing his Masters & his Ships he will be lost among ye Vulgar at first, It might be well Enough to go abroad and see the World but when his Curiosity has been Sufficiently gratified, a Settled Employe is to be preferred —

He will Informe How He Imployed his time Here   He was not Idle —

Thy Bills will [be] met with Due Honour   I here returne thy account which I hope will prove right — I have not mixed the other years account with It because Mind what I writt to draw for the Ballance 9:12:0 in a Bill by it Self — and then I shall place it to thy Last years account   thy Son Carried both Williamsons & Gordons shoots of the Sweet Service Berries   I apprehend if the Larix Seed was Shaded with Green Boughs stuck thick on the South Side of the Bed it would screen them from the Scorching Sun and prevent their going off

I have often with thankfulness observed how Good providence has Checked the Devouring Caterpiller by a Course of Natural Causes & preserved a Ballance of his Creatures in the Creation, — Each Species has its Natural Check which arrises from Accidents wee Cannot for See or prevent —

If it raises thy wonder to See how the Caterpiller Lies in the Egg what will It do if thou was to see the Oke Existing in the Acorn

I am glad the Snakes did not Come   there is a Sort of Natural aversion in Human Nature against this Creature.

But any of the Species of Turtles & Terapins would be Innocent & pretty in My Garden and are Easily sent in the Fall in a Box of Leaves &c when they have done Eating —

poor Moses is Suddenly Concern'd about paying his passage & yett there is no remedy — It may be of Service to Him in future Life to take Care & make a Sure Bargain & not trust to any Mans promises, but have it under their Hand writeing

now friend John Farewell & remember that I am

thy Friend P Collinson

Moses can give an account of my place & Garden   I should be glad of some Roots of your Common Snake Root   Is it not possible to send Mee a lump of your Cranberry roots tied up in Wett Moss

BP 3:7; D. 187.
1. The date has faded but appears to be either September 20 or 22, 1751.
2. Probably Richard Jackson, barrister and agriculturist.

To COLLINSON[1]

I am much pleased with my kind friend P. C's reasons for ranking *Belemnites* among marine productions. – I doubt not but there is a great variety of animals in the deep seas, both swimming and creeping; and many species of shell-fish on shoals very remote from the shores, never yet exposed to our sight or knowledge, which may agree with many fossil bodies found very far in land, which carry the strongest marks of their having once existed in another element.

I am apt to think that there are interspersed throughout the ocean sub-marine ridges, or mountains as we may call them, the tops of many of which rising above the water, form islands of various sizes and elevations.

If the captains of the king's ships, (for trading ships have not the time in sailing to the East and West Indies) would take the pains to sound every day with long lines, I doubt not but they would find many ridges, shoals, and banks, where they now suppose unfathomable depths; which banks and ridges have very probably their proper inhabitants and productions, and where various kinds of known fish resort to prey or feed upon them, for their respective nourishment.

And it appears to me not unlikely, that the deep sub-marine valleys between these great ridges, may extend many hundred miles or leagues, and be in part the cause of the great currents, which our seamen complain of in most of their voyages.[2]

All my observations confirm me in another opinion, that the sea once washed near the foot of the hills of this country, seeing there are strata of sea shells all over most of the low grounds, which are covered with clay, marle, sand, or gravel, of unequall depths, by being gradually raised, either by the rivers bringing down great quantities of soil from the mountains, or the sea, continually driving up large banks of sand; for in stormy weather the sea washes up sand-hills to the height of 20 or 30 feet above the highest water-mark, which being kept from falling back, by the grass and bushes, are now become terra firma. Thus the sea has most evidently retreated lower than formerly, and left our low lands in the condition we find them at present.

By observing the beds and banks of our rivers it plainly appears, that they are not really worn deeper than they were originally, but that they have contained much more water, as will be manifest by viewing the wide passages through the mountains, where the violent currents have for ages past washed and worn away all the soil to the bare roots, and must have began when the waters gradually diminished after the great deluge, and possible, have been decreasing by slow degrees ever since.

As for the vast body of sea shells, some petrified, some not, which are found beyond our blue mountains, included in rocks, I take them to be of an earlier date than the Noachin deluge itself. These I rather suppose to have been deposited where we now find them, after the spirit of God had moved on the face of the waters, and light was separate from darkness; before beasts lived on dry land, or fowls flew in the air. Moses does not particularly mention shell-fish, or when the sea produced them, but I take this to be the likeliest time. For when the terrestial particles of matter began to subside and coalesce, might not those shells be mixed and tumbled together in various directions in the confused manner they are found? where marle or clay prevailed, the shells entered into the formation of lime stone, marble, or flint; but where sand superabounded, there these shells entered into the composition of gritty rock which hath, by degrees, cemented into the hard compact state that we now find them in unless where the currents of water have worn them away, or where they have been exposed to the air, rain, or frost, which have dissolved their original cement.

At that great separation of the fluid from the more solid parts of matter, the terrestial womb of nature was wonderfully qualified to be impregnated with the universal principle of life, which hath since been maintained by particular matrices, foecundated by their respective seeds; which order, 'tis like, may continue until another great change.

I cannot agree with Dr. Woodward, that the rocks and mountains were so dissolved at the deluge as he represents; nor with Burnet,[3] that there were no rocks before the flood. – Moses expressly says, that *all the hills were covered.*

In most of the northern countries may be found fossil bodies, both animal and vegetable, which are well known entirely to agree with others found in warmer climates. The great variety of fossil shells near Limington in Hampshire is a farther confirmation, as they were altogether like those found in the West and East Indies. This to me seems a demonstration, that our earth's axis was in a different position to the sun before the flood; and if *our country,* as well as *yours,* hath received much alteration by earthquakes, might it not be some very violent shock that altered its poles? – These hints and conjectures I submit to more mature consideration.

JOHN BARTRAM

"A Letter from Mr. John Bartram of Pensylvania, to P. Collinson, Esq., F.R.S., in which there is a remarkable Conformity of Sentiments with the Author of some Physico-mechanical Conjectures on the Propagation of the shocks of Earthquakes (see p. 221) tho' it is impossible they could borrow one from another," Gentleman's Magazine 26 (October 1756):474–75.

1. Written November 14, 1751, according to the *Gentleman's Magazine.*
2. The first detailed sea-floor maps were recently drawn. In June 1977 the National Science Foundation announced the discovery in the South Atlantic of "two submarine Canyons more than twice as deep as the Grand Canyon."
3. John Woodward (1665–1728), F.R.S., English botanist and geologist, and Bishop Thomas Burnet (1635–1715), English geologist, were noted diluvialists.

From COLLINSON

1:December 1751

Had Specimens accompanied thy Curious account of your Okes, it had been worth printing — but it is all a Dead Letter without a View of the Real Subjects — & that is the Case of the fine Specimen of Pine at the head Delaware   no Cone so is useless   prethee Dear John for the future never send an Account of any plant without a Specimen   I should be glad to see Specimens of those anonimous plants thou observed in the beautifull plain of Egg Harbour   I have Specimens of Sower Gum & Sweet Gum   thine of Feby & March I will consider my first Leisure

I have by Several Ships sent an order for Seven Boxes of Seeds — and a Guinea worth of White Mulberry seed for the King of prussia for his goeing on a Silk Manufacture

I fancy some of the sailors having relations gardeners — seeing those plants so carefully Boxed up thot them for Rarities so was tempted to steal them to give to their friends

Thy Son Moses has so diligently attended his Business on Ship board, on its New Riging &c that He cannot find Time to See Mee in the Country & I rarely see Him but in an Evening — His Industry is to be commended — and in the End must turn to his advantage —

I Directed thee to Draw for fifty pounds in Two 25£ Bills — at one Month & Two Months & thou may Draw for 25£ More at 3 Months or in such a Manner as it may come in Course of payment a Month after that for the 2 months & they shall be all Honour'd —

I have Expressly Desired over & over again that thou would Draw for the Ballance of the year 1750 being 9£:12:0 as p account sent & yett no notice is taken off Itt which I take very much amiss — for I Love to Ballance accounts & keep them Even — I cannot yett gett all the Money Due on the year 1751 which Vexes Mee much So I cannot order thee to Draw for the Ballance —

But Draw for the above 9£:12:0 in this Manner — att a Month after sight pay to — or order Nine pound twelve shillings being the Ballance of my Account for the year 1750

I am thy Sincear frd

P Collinson

BP 2:84.

To ELIOT

february the 4th 1752

Respected friend

I received thine by the hands of William franklin which I read with pleasure: in answer to thy desireing to know my opinion of Mr. Maxwels & Tulls[1] repeated plowing. its very likely thay found benefit by it (believe thay are honest men & earnest in promoteing the good of thair Countrey) in thair northern Climate sorounded with Marine moist vapours. the Atraction of the sun very moderate so as not to exhale the volatile fertiliseing particles: But with us & to the southward our suns heat atracts the terestial exhalations forceably & the more the surface is comminated[2] & exposed to the scorching rays the greater is the exhalation   Spread rotten or other dung on the plain or plowed field in May & let it be exposed to the sunshine until August in a dry summer & it will have little more fertility in it then stuble: but if it be turned under furrow so as to hide it from the sun how doth it disolve & inrich the ground: thee may say it doth that by fermenting with the earth which I alow: for without we can raise a proper fermentation to the roots of the vigetable we want to nourish. all our tillage will help but little more then Just to prepare the soil to receive the seed that is sown – I take tillage to be helpful in these respects following – first to open pulverise & destroy the grass & weeds making the ground fit to receive the seed & that the tender roots may spread in the earth to receive proper nourishment for the growth of its respective plant. 2ly to destroy the weeds or grass that thay dont check or draw nourishment from the plants we would raise & rather turn the weeds under that thay may rot & ferment   3ly we should bring a sufitient proportion of fermenting matter to the extremities of these delicate imperceptable fibres to divide the particles of water & earth in several hundreds smaller particles then all our art can do by plowing or hoeing any more then to loosen the ground after the vigetables is sowed or planted when the earth is setled too sad[3] for the tender fibres to penetrate it, or aford suffitient nourishment to them as we may observe indian Corn cabbages peas & beans; what poor increas thay yeald without the plow or hoe – yet Notwithstanding if we continue to plant & till one spot of ground annually for many years (tho the crops may mend for one or two years according to the stock of fermenting matter with which it was replinished when we began to plant it) the fertiliseing materialls will be exhausted tho we artifitialy pulverise the earth as much as we please without we plow deeper & raise the impregnated & before unmoved earth to the surface which will allso by frequent pulveriseing be rendred as steril as the other unless it be of such A quality & so scituated as to attract or retain the subteranian fertiliseing efluviums or the contents of the atmosphere, some of which certainly promotes vigetation: or we apply natural Composts to help it

if we pulverise stif clay ground over much before wee sow it, So much the more stif hard & compact it settles like a brick after much rain or frost   in this case Tulls hoeing may help greatly to loosen the baked earth that the fibers may spread to draw nourishment besides covering some of the roots that may be washed bare or spued out by the frost as frequently hapens in our clay ground   An ingenious man in Jersey tould me several years past that he had when his ground was fresh plowed three times for his wheat & had good crops but after it was wore many years his crops failed so much that he had thought of leaveing his farm when he tryed how once plowing would answer which suceeded so well that then he had good crops & was much incouraged to pursue this method which was to plow up his grasse field after harvest then sow his wheat & harrow it well in all one way because cross harrowing would draw the sward back again; in this method he found these advantages: first he had the spring pasture till after harvest: 2d he had time before harvest to dress his Indian corn well: his ground is a prety loamy Soil inclineing to sand & no stones to drive the plow out so that he could turn all the sward clean under. I suppose the grass rotting did mellow the ground so that the roots of the corn in the spring drawed nourishment when the stalks & ear most wanted to be fed

in east Jersey & part of york Government & some parts of Pensilvania thay harrow thair wheat in after two plowings. When I was in virginia rideing by James river amongst the second crop of tobaco as high as my head which thay are forbid to top or make use of, I asked the inhabitants whether it would not be better to have hoed it up when thay cut the first crop that thay might not draw the vertue out of the ground. thay answered the sun would draw more if the light pulverised earth was exposed to its rays.

all the low land of west Jersey our three lower Countys Maryland & virginia to the hills I suppose was formerly covered with the Sea which hath left A strata of sea Shels of various strange kinds & magnitudes some wonder full large. the strata is from 12 to 18 inches thick & in some places thay are petrified in other places cemented into A mass with a kind of feruginous matter & in other places loose in beds   thay are covered from 10 to 40 feet with different soils as fine or Course sand gravel clay marl & sometimes Sulfurious or vitriolick earth & bog oar   no mountain rocks to be found but sometimes A sandy rock with gravel cemented with A feruginous matter.

this soil appears to have been brought from the mountains by the many great rivers that is discharged into the sea in these several Provinces & deposited thair contents on its shallow Shoals many of which of vast extent is still to be seen on all the coast of North & South Carolina both of which seems to have had the same original   I mean the lower parts: I suppose the waves of the sea drove toward shore by furious storms heaving up the sand & mixing with the soil brought down (after the waters of the flood was considerably diminished) contributed to raise the soil above the sea which no doubt is since setled lower: allso the high winds often blows the dry sand up to A great hight which the grass weeds or bushes entangles & forms great sand banks as is very commonly observed on the low sea coast

this account may seem very odd to some people who is unaquainted with the rough raged dress our great mountains (towards the sources of our great rivers) apears in but I think these Suggestions may be indulged to one that hath so often (with deep humility & adoration to the allmighty power) viewed those exalted towers. those dreadfull Precipices. the rocks washed bare. many undermined by furious torrents & tumbled down into the water cources. others hanging over or standing tottering on the others shoulders. deep valeys wore to the solid rock the mighty ridges wore through that vast bodies of water might pass with thair muddy or sandy contents which here appears to have been in such large quantities that one may wonder as much where it could be deposited as when we are on the low lands where so much soil could be fetched from as to raise so large A tract so high above the surface of the sea shore.

Now dear friend I have been so free to thee as to communicate my thoughts upon thy queries   I hope thee will be so free with me as to lett me have thy opinion thereof which will oblige thy friend   in hast

John Bartram

Beinecke Rare Book and Manuscript Library, Yale University, Jared Eliot Collection.
1. Robert Maxwell (1695–1750), author of *A Treatise Concerning the Manner of Fallowing the Ground;* Jethro Tull (1674–1741), author of *Horse Hoeing Husbandry.*
2. Pulverized.
3. Compacted.

To GRONOVIUS

March ye 14th 1752
Dear Friend
I received thy kind letter June 16th 1751 & thy Index with ye *Bibliotheca Botanica* of Linnaeus with ye curious specimens of fishes, all which I am

very thankful to thee for. I designed to have answered this last fall by A ship bound from Philadelphia to Rotterdam, but she went sooner than I expected, while I was up at our great mountains, beyond which I was thrice this fall & twice at or near ye sea

I shall have been for above a month & still am weak by reason of A cough & fever that I can hardly hold my pen. I have sent thee, within A little box directed to thee at large, several strange sea shells, belemnites & besides several different stones which I gathered on ye ridges of our mountains which I hope may meet with thy acceptance. I am heartily sorry I had not more acquaintance with Mr. Slater before he went to Holland. I should have endeavored to have sent thee many curiosities by him, who seems to be A good sort of A man.

There [are] in Jersey our low country [of] Maryland, Virginia North & South Carolina great strata of strange sea shells of prodigious size & various forms at uncertain depths from twenty to forty foot under ye surface & ye strata in depths from one to two foot thick, which demonstrates that ye sea once flowed there & that those strange shells lay either on its bottom or shore, & that it flowed quite to ye hills which was then its bounds. Now ye query is when this time was & how it came to be covered with such an even bed of sand loam or clay as to overspread them for near 1000 miles in length & in many places above 100 in breadth – so much for our low lands.

But when we ascend to our mountainous country, then we view nature in her ragged torn & tattered crags, in beholding ye exalted rocky towers, those dreadful precipices of rocks washed bare, many undermined by furious torrents & tumbled down into ye water courses; others hanging over or standing tottering on ye other's shoulders, [In] deep valleys more of ye solid rock ye mighty ridges move through that vast bodies of water might pass through with their sandy or muddy contents; vast lakes drained dry at ye bottom of which is now excellent rich soil & many that is so filled up by ye wash of ye adjacent mountains as to become marshes of large extent, many great lakes very much diminished in depth & extent by wearing ye falls below deeper so as to drain ye water so much off ye adjacent shores is now become rich low land

Your opinion of these great mutations would much oblige your friend,

John Bartram

New York Public Library, Miscellaneous Papers, Rare Books and Manuscripts Division, Astor, Lenox, and Tilden Foundations.

To GRONOVIUS

November ye 30 1752

Dear Friend
I received thy kind letter of March ye 24th by Mr Schlater, which pleased me well: Pray how doth ye water mill prove doth it anser expectation after

what manner doth it work   I should be glad to know something of the nature of it   I am in expectation of enjoying great satisfaction by thy next letter & Kalm's Catalogue of plants which thee mentions thee desighns to send me: I sent thee Last spring A box of fosils & curious stones with A letter: but hath not yet received any answer

I have not traveled much this year it being A very bad seed year: I hope next may be better & I desighn to travail most of ye season if providence affords me health & opertunity when I hope to pick up some curosities for thee of ye fosil kind   I have had several accounts from curious observers of many fish which have been catched near ye midle of ye Sea in which there have been found shell fish & sand reptils & several such like submarine fish whose abode is on sandy shoals which inclines me to quere whether there may not be vast chains of mountains of many hundreds of miles extent in ye sea as well as at land & whether ye tops of these may not be large sand banks which may produce food for many kinds of fish (that never swims near ye shore) which resorts to these banks for thair daly food   whose summits may be nearer ye surface then most people may expect & where thay may suppose it to be unfathomable: as there is islands allready known many of which is dispersed in most parts of ye sea at unequal distances where ships takes thair Course in Sailing to ye east & west indies; & its very likely many more is yet undiscovered by reason ye vast tract of sea where ships hath not yet sailed as may be observed by consulting ye sea Journals; these iselands being ye tops of vast mountains apearing above ye surface so I think its very likely that hundreds of them may be placed as different in altitude as magnitude or distance so consequently many of them may be in ye reach of common sounding, not yet known by reason that ye navigators never sounds but when thay expect thay are near some coast but if our cruising vesails (for merchant ships cant loose so much time unless in A calm) was to sound every day far from shoar perhaps thay might find fine banks where many kinds of fish frequent for food & might be improved for good fisheries for ye benefit of mankind

quere whether those vast chains of mountains if there be such may not be in part ye cause of ye currents in ye sea, which our navigators complain so much of. & is it not probable that there may be various kinds of fish in ye great vails between these ridges which never appeared nor can live near ye surface of ye water   thy answer to these queries will be very acceptable to thy Sincear friend & well-wisher

John Bartram

P S our worthy friend Benjamin Franklin desires the to send him A dutch translation of his new invented stove or fire place; & one book of his Electrical experiments if it be translated into dutch[1]   he wants to make A present of them to A friend in York   he is willing to settisfie thee for them cost what thay may & thine as before

J B

Gray Herbarium Library Archives, Harvard University; D. 359–60.
1. Franklin's *Experiments and Observations on Electricity* had been published by Edward Cave in 1751 and was translated into French, Italian, and German. For his work in electricity Franklin was awarded the prestigious Copley Medal by the Royal Society of London.

From COLLINSON

Jany 11th 1753

I have only Just time now to [thank] My Good frd J Bartram for his three kind letters — the seven boxes are Come Safe & all the others — But Docr Mitchell is displeased that he has no Letter Neither the Seeds, which he says he gave thee orders for to the Value of £35

pray thank Moses for his Letter & pray look out this year for Land Terrapins for my Son is very Desirous of them — our water ones I believe will do very Well for they have been very brisk all Summer

Docr Kearsly is very much mistaken to take the Mechoacan for the True Scammony for I have seen it growing Several Times raised from True Seed Sent from Aleppo — I will not deny but it may be a Species as they are both Convolvuluses

pray send Mee a good Specimen of evergreen privet in blossome & fruit if to be Easily had   I dont hear it is raised

Is the Charming Autumn blew Gentian an Annual or biennial or pennial —

I shall Acquaint Docr Mitchell with thy reasons for not sending his order

I hope thou has mine of Sep 27 p the Triton with thy Goods to the Value of [illegible] old Ballances.

This Day the young Man deliver'd thy Letter for Gordon which I immediately sent him

I want to know if the Laurell & the Horse chestnutts that Moses carried grow and suit your Climate

The Difference is very remarkable between our Country & yours — for I have heard Thunder but once this year & that at a Distance whilst you have had it so Terrible all over yr Continent as our Frd Clayton writes Mee from Virginia & Wee have scarcely had Sufficient to make our Ingenious Frd Franklins Experiment — our Summer was Wet but our Harvest Good & our Autumn Long & fine   I gather'd Such a Nosegay on Xmas day would have delighted thee to have see It. Some of your Golden Rod   Asters, Varigated & Narrow leafed Clinopodium   Obelescathecas Joyn'd with Anemone – Double & Single Stock July flowers in abundance   Polyanthus variety & charming Violets that pfumed the whole, so that In England vegitation may be said never to Cease for the Spring flowers tread so on the heels of the Autumn flowers that the Ring is Carried on without Intermission & then such a Quantity of Species of Lacrustinas & Arbutus added to the Rest — made a great bundle of flowers for the Season

I am, in hast thine

P Collinson

I had formerly Seed of the Larkspur from thee   have lost It   pray send some more

BP 2:87; D. 188–89.

To ELIOT

February ye 12th 1753

Respected friend Eliot
I have been long waiting for an answer to my letter which I sent last spring but lately our good friend Benjamin tould me our letters had miscaried so now I venture to trouble thee with a few more of my rambling observations   pray how did ye rape prosper with thee   mine growed 3 or 4 foot high but produced neither seed nor flower   I sent thee several Curious seeds which I dont know whether thee received or not: I have in my travails abroad but much more near home observed with concern our approaching distress on ye account of our want of timber for fencing & indeed many of our necessary uses   A great Part of ye country that was first settled hath not neare timber enough on each tract for one set of new fence nor one half of ye old good enough to keep A cow in ye field or A horse out   ditching helps us very little & A quick hedge less by reason of ye horned Cattle & sheep   ye latter kill ye quickest with croping ye tender shoots & ye first not onely with browsing but when it is grown thay twist and brak ye bushes & tears down ye bank with thair horns tho never so well turfed with grass
I have made great deep ditches & consequently high banks   if I made them steep ye frost & rain would moulder & wash ye bank down   if I made them wide & slanting ye cattle would climb up & tread them down   if ye ditch narrow thay step over   about 16 year past I planted A hedge of red Cedars one foot long on a small bank About 2 foot asunder   thay growed so well that in 3 or 4 years I had A fine hedge 4 foot high 2 foot thick, & so close that A bird could not fly thro it   then I thought I had been furnished with the onely material that was requisite for A strong lasting beautiful fence that had all ye good properties that ye others wanted as, first, it would grow well on all our different soils; 2dly, none of our cattle would crop them; 3dly[1]

BP 1:34:1; D. 372–73.
1. Incomplete.

From COLLINSON[1]

Your Proprietors Gardiner[2] has Collected 2 Quires of Specimens, I had the pleasure of looking over them
   No 94   He names Goats Rue   these are all fine plants
   107   He gives no Name   and I cant remember them
   115   He names Coluta   in all thy Specimens

For thy better Information I procured Small Samples of Each in paper with his Name & number   if thou Canst not recollect them Carry the Samples to Him and He will no doubt Informe thee, that 107 without Name has a Lovely Spike of Flowers   I could only gett one or two Just to give thee an Idea of It   No 115 that He names Coluta is very pretty but wether a Shrub or Herbaceous I cannot tell — No 94 His Goats Rue, I thought at first had been a Lupin but I think otherwise — the Large Specimen has a Charming Spike of Red flowers   all these three plants must be fine Ornaments in a Flower Garden — I cannot say the Argeratum is a shrub It is what is called Bastard Jesuit Bark   It grows Woody Sometimes, but goes off in the Winter   I will send a specimen next year   I shall be glad if the Digitalis grows for I believe they never was in England before & you have several species — I have sent seed of ours   did it ever Come up   I take it to be the finest Wild Flower Wee have

I want much to know if the Laurel & Horse Chestnutts grow that Moses Carried — for the Laurel is a great favourite is easily Increased from Cuttings planted in Warm shady place (but not Drip'd on by Trees) in October —

Wee want Berries of your Native Holly — Broad Leafed Clinopodium Lychnis with white Fringed Flowers & Tupelo Seed   If it is suitable replenish these plants [that] did not come up last year — Viz silver leafed Arum   Odd Harts Tongue, Seneca Snake root   Maiden Hair & Orchis I presume bfore this thou has Received Dr Butners remarks on thy Appendix to the Medica Britanica[3]   I thank thee for It & will take Care & Send the other to Linnaeus —

I can't Imagine at the Long Silence of Docr Gronovius   whether it is his Imploye on the Governmt — or whether his tast for Natural History Abates I cant Saye but this our Friend Clayton tells Mee that He write Him a Letter Complaining of the Expence that attended the Conveyance of His Specimens to Holland and as good as forbid his sending More So that It seems to Mee the last Vice that attacks Human Nature has laid hold on Him & that is Covetousness   I wish it may not be So, but it is more then probable, postage becomes chargeable & so he is Silent   He is Two Letters in my Debt and used to be the most punctual Correspondent

Many are asking Mee why the name Hemlock is given to the Smallest Coned Firr which Wee call yew Leafed Firr —

Thee sayeth that the Water Turtle feeds on the Seed of the Nenufaris — this is a name I never heard of before   pray what is It —

the Gentian flower'd finely   pray is there any other species that is perennial   I should be glad to have them —

Inclosed is a specimen of a Delphinium that if I remember right thou gather'd in thy Expedition beyond the Blew Mountains in Virginia   its a fine plant perennial but I lost it in the removeing my Garden   I wish thou may be able to recruit Mee with it again —

It gives Mee Great Concern to hear Williamson & his friends complain He is a very Honest Man. I am persuaded there is a Cause to it but is that thou art Like to Loose thy best Chapman[4] who always pays well   I inclose his Letter which is a short Hint — but hope he will write to thee more fully — it is always better to send none, then to send not to the purpose, Especially to those that are to make their money again   Some Satisfaction is necessary to restore thee to their favour — but they are not the firm that I have had complaints from so pray be very Carefull for the future Else Wee looses all our Credit —

I am so engaged I cannot answer Moses letter but pray give my thanks for his pott of persimons & beaker [of] Cyder but only Bottle No 2 was Deliver'd being boild & Ginger'd is not agreable to our palates   I have heard so many bragg & talk of the Goodness of american Cyder that I Wished for a Bottle of true Genuine Cyder without Mixture but the pson He intrusted it with took Care to Drink the best bottle & give Mee the other nay I wonder they gave Mee any

Boxes Wanting next year
   one Box for Gardener Greening
   one Do for Wood
   one Do for Julian Beckford
   one Do for Mears
   one Do for Lord Marchmont
   One Box for Lord Fitzmaurice in Ireland consigned to Mr. Mitchell Barker at Dublin   Give Mr: Barker a Letter of Advice & Invoice Inclosed

BP 3:6; D. 190–92.
1. Written February 13, 1753, according to Darlington, who omitted large portions of the letter.
2. James Alexander.
3. This was the third edition of Thomas Short's work (Philadelphia: B. Franklin and Hall, 1751), with a preface by Bartram as well as notes on British plants and an appendix giving medicinal plants from the northern part of America. Dr. David-Sigismund-August Buettner (1724–1768) succeeded Albrecht von Haller (1708–1777) in the botany chair at the University of Gottingen.
4. Customer.

From JOHN SWINHOE[1]

                                            Brumpton Park near London
                                                     March 7th. 1753

Mr John Bartram
   I rec'd yours of ye 3d of last December, and was sorry to be disappointed of the Seeds I writt to you about, for if you had but sent me part or a few of the sorts it would have been some satisfaction — but losing an entire season in all of them gave me concern. I have again enclosed a list which is partly yours & ye rest I had from other hands, and must desire you to send me all you can of them; otherwise to lett me know by ye speediest opportunity

what I may expect. As to the large quantity of Lord Weymouths pine & some other sorts I mentioned I find I was mistaken in supposing you had them in such plenty but I could never have thought you had them so scarce as not to be able to collect 3rd of seed in three of ye Colonys for at that rate we save in England Ten Times as much of that commodity Yearly as you do and I was inclined to think you have one hundred trees in a bearing Condition to one here, but you must know best, and all I can expect is that you will let me have a fair proportion of everything you can get in this list, or of any other sorts not therein mentioned that are Curious. I have left out the Walnuts, Hiccories & most of the Oaks & Chestnuts, because I have had already a great many of these from different hands & abound in most of them, but if you should happen to meet with any thing uncommon of these Tribes may send a few such. And lett me have a Ten Guinea Box filled with all the variety you can procure except Walnut Hiccories &c as before mentioned, and Consign them to your friend Mr. Peter Collinson directed for me, with a letter of advice & Catalogues from you of their being sent, and I'll pay Mr. Collinson for the same before he delivers them, or any other pson as you may direct, pray dont disappoint me, and lett me hear from you as soon as you can which will much oblige

Sir
Yr Most Humble Servt
Jno Swinhoe

P.S. I have sent you a Duplicate of this by another Vessell; but you are only to have regard for the first that comes to hand; for it is only meant as one Commission but repeated for fear one of them happening to miscarry

BP 4:108.
1. A nurseryman.

To LINNAEUS

March ye 20th 1753

I received about two months past thy letter dated August ye 10th 1750 I was exceedingly pleased to receive so kind a letter from one that so deservedly bears a superior Character for Botanical Learning, but was very much concerned that I could not have had it sooner then above two year after it was wrote; & much ye same misfortune happened to those pamflets thee sent to Dr. Colden & Mr. Claton which our worthy friend Benjamin Franklin shewed me last week haveing just then received them, which he intended to send according to direction by next Post: I traveled in 1751 most part of ye Autumn & found several new species of plants & shrubs which I should have sent to thee if I had known they would have been acceptable: Wee have four or five species of Jacobea that you have not in Europe. one species grows in marshes, another in flat low ground another on cold shady banks of great rivers another on loose slaty soil on ye great mountains: & most of these species is used by ye back inhabitants for ye cure of ye same diseases that ye antients did tho they know nothing of ye name of ye plant. I hope thee hath received ye Medica Britanica   I design to send thee some specimens next fall   pray let me know what sorts of seeds thee wants   I am glad those that I sent thee grows   If I can any ways oblige thee with specimens seeds or plants or any information My poor Capacity can contribute, none can do it more Cherefully then thy sincear friend

John Bartram

P.S. We are all surprised that we have not one letter from Peter Kalm whome we are ready to tax with ingratitude   thine as before —

JB

Linnean Society of London Archives, Linnean Correspondence I, 356/57; BP 1:31:1; D. 371.

To COLLINSON[1]

Our friend Doctor Butner hath mistaken several plants which I mentioned in ye Medica Britanica as first ye [illegible] Canadensis which some call wild liqerises is what is caled in ye flora virginica Aralia folis pinatis amplis lobis cordiformibus floribus parvis albis racematim &c page 34

10 alichrysum folis dilute flavescentibus longis angustis tomentosis capitulis luteus &c page 95 flora vig.

15 orchis a fine species with one or two large striped leaves which I cant make to grow in my garden nor live in ye box of plants I send to you   it is not discribed by any that I know   it is scarce   grows on good soil

20 Eupatorium perfoliatum Aquaticum folis rugosis longis longissimis &c flor. vir. page 94

BP 1:32:2.
1. Undated, but written in the spring of 1753 (see Collinson to Bartram, February 13, 1753).

To COLLINSON[1]

I have employed my time this spring near Ponds & Rivulets to observe the various notes & tones of our Froggs which I apprehend is modulated by A Hesitant or Quivering Organ that directs their Breath or the air against a Blader under their Chin which produces a sound in General like a Team of Horse Bells but with a greater variety of Notes higher and Lower, which are greatly diversified as proceeding from a number of different species. Each have its peculiar note which may be heard in consort a quarter of a mile distance.

It is very difficult & requires much Time and great attention to Distinguish the note of each species for on A near approach they dart under the Water – they are of all tones from the Bull Frogg as big as ones foot to the small species the size of one joint of one little Finger & of various colors according to the species.

Those that make the continual ringing that one Frogg continueth his sound not above 2 or 3 minutes before he resteth for the space of 5 or 6 & then begineth again & while he resteth others supply his place during the time of the most general Cry which is Commonly from six o'clock to midnight sooner or longer according to the Coolness of the morning or most of the day in warm weather   thay commonly begin in February   some one or other is heard in the Middle of the Day: if the Weather is warm & ends in Aprille sooner or later according to the [illegible] this is their Time of generation & laying thair spawn   some in long trains like small guts others in lumps of jelly as big as A childs head — we have many other kinds that makes very different noises   some in the Water, on the Land and on Trees, Day & Night at different Times most part of the summer.

The Bull Frogg makes a noise something like that animal may be heard a Mile off. He sounds his Blader day and Night at different Periods – is recon'd by our nice City Palates a Dainty Morcell. whether would not some of these Noisy curiosities be prety amusements in thy ponds as thay are some of the most innocent of natives living upon flies insects & reptiles

BP 1:33 (most parts of which are illegible); American Philosophical Society Library, Carlotta Herring-Brown's copy made from Collinson's abstract of Bartram's letter in his copy of Catesby's *Carolina*, in the earl of Derby's library, Knowsley Hall.
1. Dated May 27, 1753, by Carlotta Herring-Brown.

To COLLINSON[1]

Dear Aflicted friend
As I have been once near in some respect in the same gloomy disconsolate Circumstances with thine[2] I believe I am in some measure qualified to sympathize with one of my dearest friends in his close & tender afliction it seems hard to have one's dearest consort A loving spouse an afectionate wife an object that we love above all terrestrial enjoyment taken from our arms   how grievous is it for one that is thus agreable to be torn from our hearts! her dear sweet bosom is cold   her tender heart the center of mutual love is motionless   her dear arms are no more extended to embrace her beloved, the partner of his cares & sharer of his pleasures must no more sit down with her husband at his table   Oh! my dear friend: let us resign all to God almighty   his will be done! he knows what is best for our ultimate good   we dont know what blessings he may yet bestow upon us   I lost an innocent loveing wife which I lived with above 4 years   I thought my loss could never have been made up   It was[3]

BP 1:33:2; D. 194.

1. Undated but written July 8, 1753 (see Collinson to Bartram, August 21, 1753). Mary Collinson died in March.
2. Bartram's first wife, Mary Maris, died in 1727.
3. Incomplete.

From COLLINSON

Londn July 19:1753

 If My Friend John Bartram knew better My Affairs, my Situation in Life, My publick Business my Many Engagements & Incumbrances — Instead of Being in a pett that I answer not the Letter He sends by one Ship — by the Next that sails He would wonder I do so well as I do — tho' He thinks it so Ill, — and Had he but Faith and patience I Wipe the Score off at last —tho not in his punctillio — & therefore he should never Suspect His Friend untill he has better foundation for so Doing — to Serve Him I often Neglect my Own Affairs — but as his Surmises all are Well meant — Yett they arise from his Want of Experience & not knowing Mee & the Share I have in the Busy World, So Well as I could wish then he would not think Mee so bad a Correspondent – and I dare Venter, now I have given Him these Friendly Hints, He will not think Mee So Again — Butt continue His Friendly & Informing as well as his entertaining Correspondence & not break off the Thred of his Designs because I have not in a Sett Time Acknowledg'd them in the Manner he Expects — making no allowance for Letters Miscarrying — I thought He had known Mee Better to think any thing He sends Mee Either lost or Neglected — for which reason I shall tell Him notwithstanding his Supposition that his seeds & his plants laid so Neglected

 I All Nature Lock[ed] up with with [sic] Cold Winds Frost or Snow that Neither Seeds can be sown or Plants planted, so full as Well in their Several packages which will be Seen by the annex'd account I shall begin with his Numbers & have the pleasure to tell Him that the Seed of Sarsifras has shot out strong and finely but such is the deception of this Tree that nobody can tell how it will stand it untill a Summer or two is over — I have seen many Sarsifras Trees in England but never saw any Spawn about their Roots . . . .

 II the Sea Wormwood could never find

 III the Saracena Grows wonderfully in an Artifical bog but most unfortunately a Black Snail Eat of the flower bud before it was discover'd, but the Leaves are great Rarities for their wonderfull Structures & much admired

 IV the Evergreen privet came as fresh & fine as if Just taken out of the woods with the original Mould to its Roots & yett with all my Skill so weak is its Nature it Dwindled away, possibly it may spring from Root now our Rains are come In for wee have above a Month & not any Rain fell so that all new planted things suffer'd Greatly & but half a Crop of Hay & but the Wheat promises a Vast Crop — the pretty grass leafed plant is Stubborn but has made Some progress — So I have hopes — The other Evergreens grow prettyly —

V the Perrenual Digitalis made Little progress but the Late Rains brings them forward —

VI the Boggy Evergreen Hellibore with Little leaves thrives well & gives Mee hopes of its flowers

VII the Cranberry thrives wonderfull & is in blossome — Every way agreeing with ours but much Larger —

VIII the Gnaphaleum I had in plenty   a pretty plant but I Esteem thy kindness not the Less of many Things   a Stone is [illegible] for your plants rarly Seed with us —

The Highland Turtles came in fine order — Creep about very Briskly — My Gardener saw the Great one have a large black naked Snail in its Mouth and the Water ones are very brisk — seem very well reconcil'd to their Habitations

I thank thee for the Early Indian Corn & Squash Seed — they both thrive Well —

This Letter I answered the First of february

Agnus Castus is a tender plant   will not Endure your Climate & never Seeds in England   I will remember Seed of our Great Mapple   it is a fine Tree & Seed of Sherrils, but as Dwarf Elder grows very remote I Dispair of that   it is rare, Except in some particular places —

X   Sod of Maiden Hair grows [IX omitted by Collinson]

XI the broad Leafd Linaria continues Green but has not made the least Effort — the Nole me Tangere that came in the sod of the Great Marsh Fern Last year is come up Spontaneously from the Seed then Scater'd — which I dispard of Ever Seeing

the season was So Wett but now I think Wee are secure of It for Ever, it is a fine Showey Stately plant — and in the Same Sod came a Fragard or black-berry very Different from ours; Thou quite Mistooke Mee — I am very fond of sods, for many things come up unexpected (pray trye & send Mee a Sod of Snake Root) but your proprietors gardener send all his plants without Sodd packing [line illegible] He Sent a very Curious Geranium with tuberous roots of which I had part & it flower'd finely — is Quite a New Species — the Great Chamaerhododendron & the Laurel or Ivy have shot very finely this year —

Now to Business

Thy years' account for year 1751	116: : 6
Ditto for year 1752	133: 7:
	249: 7: 6
Credit	214: 5: 9
Ball	35: 1: 9

Thy Last bill to Nordica Yamak [?] is paid for £25   Now draw for the Exact Ballance in Two Bills   one at 1 Mo. & 2 Mo   by that Time I hope to have the Money in my hands — It was but a few Weeks agon that I received the Last on the year 1751 — Some Noble people are very Delitory & must be often reminded before they pay —

I could never Learn if the Dublin Society had the plants Thou Sent them

I have not yett gott the Insurance but I have sent the Same Goods to pay the old Ballance

pray give my thanks to Moses for his Two Letters   In the box with the other things I have sent Two fine Cedar Lebanon Cones, Just come from thence   they all come in a Box for the Academy

I have thy Several kind Letters of March 13 May 17 & another without Date which was very acceptable to Mee & I shall answer first Leisure —

There is a Little token in a Box for Billey[1] whose pretty performances please Mee Much —

Thy account of the Froggs is very humerous but would it not be more so to Import a Cargo of them and had I a park or place Inclosed I would wish It, but it is stroling people and boyes would Destroye them   A Bull frog would Surprise the whole village but then it would be certainly killed.

Dear John, farewell
P. Collinson

BP 2:89; D. 192–93.
1. John Bartram's son William.

From COLLINSON

Augt. 10:1753

This will acquaint my Dear frd J:Bartram that I have ship'd the Ballance of his acct for the year 1750 being £ 9:12 In a Box marked xx^{y}xx for the Academy — I have receed the Insurance, but the Insurors made some ^{xx} Deduction so I receed 2s Less which I have Caried to thy new Account

The Ballance of the year 1751
                      1752
           Is — 35: 1: 9
paid & in goods   214: 5: 7   Seeds 249: 7: 6
                  249: 7: 6

Be sure Mind & Draw for the Exact Sum of 35: 1: 9 — in one or Two Bills — wch will keep our account from runing over into Another —

I must defer taking notice of thy Several kind Letters   I have had great troubles in my Family   the Loss of the best of Wives — now Marrying my Daughter & many others

Accot of Goods in the Box July 5

5 Yd Cloth	1:6 marked	2:17:6
6 y shall	1:6	9:9
Buttons Silk Twist		7:2
20 yd fine Damask	2:3	2:14:–
25 yd Irish Holland	2:10	2:10:–
for Lawn		–:14:–
		£9:12:5

sent in Box xxxx^y
xx

There is a Little Token to my pretty artist Billey   His Drawings has been much admir'd & better then could be expected for his first Tryalls   I have not yett my Friend Edwards observations

Send 8 Boxes of Seeds – In Warr the Hazard was Double when sending in Two Ships & was Responsible but now its Peace the Risque is much Less — and when they come in one Ship one Trouble to Mee for all, was these Seeds a regular Commodity I could Imploy an agent — but now I must petition the Commissioners my Self, to gett them from on board   then I must have them Examined & the Officers Report — then an Order for Delivery   all this Takes up the best part of 3 Days at a Time of year if I had 4 pr hands I could Employ them and Sometimes if they Do Stay on board all week or Two after they arrive I can't help It — I can do no More then I can Do — So that all comeing in one Ship Saves Mee much trouble which is nothing to the Time I am obliged to spend about them & yett my friend John is in a pett because I Desire in one ship & that they Lay so Long on board — without considering my affairs & how much I am obliged to neglect my own to Serve Him & his Family which I would do for no Man Liveing under any Consideration.

My Last by Mitchell I hope is come to Hand —

Our Friend Gordon Desires the favour of Some Seed of the Orang Col'd Apocinon –

In January 1751–52 sent Beach Cherries   He Desires Some More & a Specimen of the Tree, for he thinks he has raised one but if he saw a Specimen then he could be sure — & if he had Sodds of Ever Green Rhamnus & Privet, He thinks he could Manage those untameable plants & Indeed He has a Superior Skill to any one I ever knew, It would give thee great Entertainment to See his Performances   publick & private affairs so Occupy my Mind Dayly — but when the Long [hours] of Evening Come, then I shall take thy Letters into Due Consideration —

So Dear John for the present

Farewell
P Collinson

Wee have had a very Long fine but Dry Summer that I have had Enough to Do to Save the Cargo this year & yett I hope I shall — all but the Evergreen privet — which no Art could tempt to Staye for I cover'd it with Glasses & only gave it the Dews & Rains — & shaded It — but all to no purpose —Thy Bill of £25 is paid

BP 2:91; D. 577-78.

From NATHANIEL POWELL

London Aug; 14 1753

Mr. John Bartram
Sir:

    I desire you will send me a box of seeds   pray let me have as great a variety of new sorts as possible   consider that I have them to sell again let me have larger quantities then you send to Gentlemen for thare own youse   if you want any of ower English seeds for your self or friends, pleas to let me know what sorts you like   I will make you a present of them I have paid your friend Mr. Peter Collinson for the last box   pray take care to pack them well   the papers are comonly brock and the seeds mixt thay should be put in Cloth bags. your care in packing and sending all fresh and good will Oblige Sir

your Most Humble
Servt   Nath Powell

BP 4:97.

From CHRISTOPHER GRAY[1]

Fullham
Augt. the 16 *1753*

Mr Battarm —
    I Desire you will Send me as Maney as you Can of those Sorts of Seeds for Me and put My Name upon the box — a goode Maney of the other Sorts as you Sent before — I do not like thorn   put Whole you Can of those Mention from

Sir Your very humble Servt
Christopher Gray

[I told Him I was in doubt if this order would come Soon enough   if it does it will make Nine Boxes —][2]

      1 Virginia Tulip [Common Tulip poplar]
      Ld way Mouth pine
      3 Leaves pine
      Jersey pine
      Ditto pines 3 leaves
      [he might have said pine of all spcies –]

2 Leaves Mountain pine
Mountain Red-Spurs
   Black Spurs –
   Whit Cedors
   Red Cedors –
   Arbor Julia
   virg Dog Wood
   Benjamins
   Tupelae 2 Sorts –
   Swamp Magnolia Minor
the ~~Larg Magnolia~~
the New Sort Magnolia [Desseduius –]
~~Swamp pine~~ [or Caroline]
arbor vitia
Balm Gilard [Firr]
Anona [papaw or]
Honey Succus – [Honeysuckles]
Sassfaryos – [Sarsifrass]
Scarlet Oakes – [Scarlet Oke acorns]

BP 2:91.
1. Christopher Gray (c. 1694–1764), a nurseryman and friend of Catesby. His garden was on the road between Parson's Green and Fulham.
2. All notes in brackets were added by Collinson.

To COLLINSON

                                                          august ye 20th 1753

Dear Peter
I am now very intent upon examining ye true distinguishing characters of our forest trees finding it A very difficult task as I can have no help from neither ancient or modern authors   thay haveing taken no perticular observation worth notice   I expect by our worthy friend Benjamin specimens of ye evergreens of new england which I intend to compair with ours & those of york Government so that I may give A perticular account of ye evergreens natural to our northern parts which I hope to send thee this fall or next spring with A fuller account of our oaks and Hickories & for thy Present amusement I here send thee as A specimen of my method of preceeding A near perfect description of ye characters of our Hop Hornbeam from A pointed single bud comes forth A spring shoot set alternately on each oposite horizontal side with single oval but sharp pointed leaves finely indented round   from ye midle rib or nerve of ye leaf proceed straight lateral ones which terminate at ye point of ye main indentation between which is 2 or 3 smaller ones near ye point of ye leaf but 3 or 4 toward ye base each of which is terminated by A small nerve branching directly from its perimeter   each springs shoot is terminated by ye summer either by A

single bud at ye base of its respective leafe or A pedicle with Catkins on it by ye bottom of ye bud oposite   partly by ye hop which is A number of pointed vesicles ranged regularly round an axis or continuation of ye shoot & foulding one over ye base of three like ye scales of fish containing one oval smooth sharp pointed seed. there is A number of very sharp hairs adhering to ye base of ye vesicle which sticks on ye fingers of ye gatherer being very troublesome   ye Catkins that is formed in ye fall opens next spring & sheds its farina impregnating ye young hop that is formed on ye springs shoot that grows from ye bud that was formed in ye fall before at ye bosom of ye uper leaf   ye tree grows 30 foot high & 8 or 10 diameter   ye bark brownish in ould trees with shallow perpendicular furrows   in young, smooth & spoted   it grows commonly by ye banks of rivers near ye tide   is A fine branched regular shaped tree   ye wood is tough & pretty strong but ye scarcity of it renders ye use thereof to be but little observed   I am prepairing for A Journey to dr Coldens & ye mountains   I desighn to set out with my little botanist[1] ye first of September which is 10 days sooner than usual hoping to gather ye Balm of Gilead & Larix seed which was genraly fallen before I got there   neither do I desighn to be in such A hurry as I have been.

A List of Specimens sent to Peter Collinson

I	A prety shrub by ye lake on katskill mountain	XI	great broad leaved Euonimus
II	quick bean mountain	XII	aralia spinosa mountain
III	opulus mulberry leaf	XIII	ash leaved maple
IIII	mountain striped maple	XIIII	black ash
V	mountain red maple dwarf	XV	wild chery mountain
		XVI	our beech chery
VI	dwarf cluster chery	XVII	sweet fern
VII	tree chery	XVIII	tough viburnum
VIII	silver colored alder	XIX	pawpaw
IX	horn beam	XX	white ash
X	paper birch		

BP 1:33:1; D. 193–94.
1. Bartram's son William.

From COLLINSON[1]

Augt:21:1753

Dear frd

I have just received thine of July 8th   wether this will catch the Ship in the Downs I cant say but I have another order for a box of seeds — so this will make 10 Boxes — and if thou hast a mind to add 2 More if there [is] such a plenty then Do — Send a Dozen boxes — I believe I shant want

Chaps   I shall be heartyly glad to hear of thy safe return from thy Expedition to the Mountains —

So farewell
P. Collinson

BP 2:91:5.
1. On the envelope: "Addressed to Capt Peter Reeve on Board the Lydia to Philadelphia, Downs, Kent   If sailed then Burn It   For B. Franklin Esq."

To LINNAEUS[1]

November ye 11th 1753

Much Esteemed & worthy friend
Whereas I wrote to thee last spring & have yet received no answer therefore I have not much to write at present But haveing an opertunity I send thee A small specimen of a plant which I discovered fourteen years ago but supposeing it would not grow in A garden & not knowing what it was or what flower it bore I tooke but little notice of it but haveing now found out ye way to raise any plant or shrub (but ye great magnolia) I transplanted it last fall & ye succeeding spring produced this specimen but by an untimely frost it was niped so that it could not open to ye top; it is an evergreen veratrum   it grows in wet boggy shady cold ground   ye root is white & fibrous from which proceeds 16 more or less of longish leaves broadest toward thair extremity yet sharp pointed. the leaves of last years growth lyeth flat on ye ground in rays round this summers leaves which stand more erect yet bending toward ye ground & sorrounding a centeral bud which is set in ye fall & if for flowering is like A pointed Cone whose base is near an inch diameter which next spring shoots up A single stalk eighteen inches high with short pointed leaves but round it without order gradually diminishing in magnitude unto ye spike of flowers which is two or three inches long. ye petals is A flesh color ye apicies blewish & standing out longer then ye Petals which makeing A prety appearance.

Pray how doth our friend Peter Kalm go on with ye discription of ye plants of our Country   He promised to send me one as soon as printed & that he would do me Justice in mentioning what Plants or specimens I shewed him. But I can never get A letter from him since he left my house I should be very well Pleased to see what he hath wrote on our Plants. I have sent Mr. Collinson A perticular discription of our Evergreens which he desires to Publish   thay are so discribed from ye green specimen before me that you may easily know each Perticular species by their distinguishing Characters & when that is Printed none will be more ready to oblig thee with one then thy friend in hast

John Bartram

Linnean Society of London Archives, Linnean Correspondence I:358–59.
1. It is interesting to compare this letter with the copy Bartram retained, which follows.

To LINNAEUS

[November 11, 1753]

dr Linneus
Respected friend
as I wrote to thee last spring & have yet received no answer I have not much to say Pray how doth our friend Kalm go on with his history of our countrey Plants He promised mee to send me one as soon as printed & that he would do me Justice in mentioning what plants or specimens I shewed him. But I never can get A letter from him since he left my house I should be very well Pleased to see what he hath wrote of our plants. I here send thee A specimen of a curious evergreen veratrum it grows in wett swampy shady cold ground the root is white & fibrous from which proceeds 16 more or less of longish narrow leaves pointed at ye extremity ye leaves of ye second year lyeth on ye ground spread in rays round ye summer leaves which stand more erect yet bending towards ye ground & sorounding A center bud this is set in ye fall & if for flowering is like a painted cone whose base is near an inch diameter which next spring shoots up A single stalk eight inches high with short pointed leaves set without order round it gradually diminishing in magnitude unto ye spike of flowers two or 3 inches long ye petals of a flesh color ye apices blewish & standing out longer then ye petals which makes A prety appearance see ye imperfect specimen as it flowered ye spring after transplanting

BP 1:36:1; D. 371–72.

To GRONOVIUS

December ye 6th 1753

Sir:
I haveing not received a letter from thee for a long time discouraged me from writeing any more to thee. But haveing this good oportunity by my good friend Mr. Slator who promised me to deliver it to thee. Hee is a person well respected by good & honest people. He appears to be a pious innocent Christian I wish he may meet with incouragement amongst you.

I have sent thee almost two years ago a Box of curious stones & fosils with a letter & last year I wrote to thee again, but have received no answer; since which I have had complaints from thy ould correspondents of thy neglect in writing to them, which inclined me to excuse thy forgetfulness of me supposing it may be caused by multiplicity of business. Thee gave me an expectation of sending me Peter Calm's Catalogue of Our American Plants but I have heard no more about it. I have sent to our friend Peter Collinson a perticular description of all our species of oaks & evergreens: by which you may easily know how many we have & how to distinguish one from another. I have some thoughts of going through with all our forrest trees &

shrubs which will amount to near one hundred & fifty different species; in the describing of which I have the green specimens before me, taken from trees of midling growth neither too young or ould, too luxuriant or declineing. I first give the general character of each genus; then the description of each species with its perticular distinguishing character by which it may be certainly known from other species, in what soil or situation soever it is found growing in.

I remain thy Sincear Loving friend

John Bartram

American Philosophical Society Library, West Collection.

To COLLINSON[1]

after 2 weeks sickness being prety well recovered but still a lurking fever hanged on me known by A very bad tast in my mouth & urin high colored & A weekness & dullness in stiring but hopeing this would wear off by travelling in change of air   we set out ye first of September & traveled 40 mile   ye next day we traveled near 50 & ye next day crossed ye south chains being 3 ridges of our blew mountains on Jersey side where we stayed about noon to rest ourselves & observe ye vigetables that growed thereon which was mountain chestnut   oak   sassafras   mountain or champain red oak & some spanish oak   chestnut   ash   black & white maple   wild cherrie   persimon   3 leaved pine. Shrubs sweet fern & in swampy places prinos & very good fox grapes which I ate very plentifully & seemed to relish better then any thing I had tasted in my Journey for my feever returned no more upon me & my tast was much depraved yet ye quantity I eat did not make me sick but I cared no more for them in that Journey   we descended down toward ye river & low lands of ye minisinks in which way my son spyed A large rattle snake quoiled up in ye compas of ones hat   we dismounted & cut A stick to try to anger him drawing him out at length but he ofered to run away from us   I stopped him & put him back & he drawed in his quoil again ratled & flattened his body by which his colors brightened much & I wished my son had brought his box of paints with him (which A Switzer Gentleman made him A present of with A quire of fine drawing paper) to have drawn him in his greatest beauty for he was A yellow one such as Catesby drawed but I believe he drawed him dead   but we could not make him offer to bite so we mercyfully let him go without harm   now many laughs at ye story of changing color which is realy matter of fact as I shall demonstrate by reason as well as common observation   I was reaping this summer & found A great black viper   we took notice that it was blacker then common   we tryed to vex it to make it swell & hiss several times that we might observe its change of color   it spread its head & neck near three fingers broad & swelled its body & we observed its color to come & go as it drawed ye air in & hissed it out for as it filled its body it stretched its scin which drawed its scales farther asunder & shewed ye white membrane that is in its natural state covered with which ye scales are foulding over part of another whereby ye snake appears speckled & when any of our common striped snakes hath swallowed A frog or any thing that swells ye body it appears finely spotted in that place for ye same reason my brother in law was very much surprised at thair approach to A great blacksnake that had newly swallowed A large [illegible] that distended his belly & skin so much that ye black scales was so drawn apart that ye white membrane appeared but that it was so much distended that ye red flesh or blood appeared through it which made ye snake look very strange by its enormous bulk & diferent colors of black whit & red: we traveled that day to A tavern by sunset whose house stood on A peple [pebble] stone hill about 20 or 30 foot higher then ye level of ye low lands   this hill had ye blew mountains about 2 or 3 mile distant   on my right hand & on my left ye low lands of ye minisinks river & A ridge of high hills near half as high as ye blew mountains with very raged rocky tops: we ordered our horses to pasture & walked to ye river about A quarter of A mile over ye low grounds being near A level from ye foot of ye hill to ye river which I suppose may be here 300 yards over from one bank to ye other which is about 10 or 12 foot perpendicular above ye bed of ye river which now was so low that wee walked three quarters of ye way over on round oval & oblong peples of all shapes but angular & dimentions from one inch to A foot diameter of various colors & compositions as ye adjacent hills was stored with as we found by A strict examination   ye bed of ye river runs in A serpentine manner as all ye fresh rivers I have observed do from one hill to ye other so that ye low grounds is in some places on one side & some places on ye other   ye hills on ye west side is as aforsd very high but of pretty easy ascent 2/3 of ye way to ye top being all shivered scales ye spoil of ye rocks above which is continualy shivering & mouldering away & tumbling down for 30 or 40 mile in length   ye low grounds is composed of A fine black loamy sand & very rich where ye low land is wide but where ye hills closeth nearer together ye low grounds is of A yellower courser sand & ye banks higher & much poorer allmost barren sand where narrowest   I have observed where ye inhabitants have dug wells that thay come to A bed of round Smooth peples exactly like those in ye bed of ye river even near ye foot of ye hills in this strata thay find water   now I have given A perticular discription of this various Phenomina   next I will shew my wandering conjectures of what was ye Subordinate cause of this appearance. in ye first place I will suppose that ye waters flowed down this vale in very great quantity to what it is now   that it flowed thorow ye gap of ye mountain to be discribed in our return   this gap I suppose is near A level with this peply hill & ye Menisinks allowing A proper fall for such A distance   ye pebles & gravel of this hill is all wore smooth & without acute angles as those in ye bed of ye river & consequently was wore smooth by ye current of ye water & sand as ye other; that after ye water broke thorow ye mountain where it now runs in A great perpendicular chasm from top to bottom of ye mountain where ye water is very deep (which shows that A varst body of water once passed thro it) where this pebly hill riseth A little higher or Joynes to another higher ye stones all of all forms as well as dimentions with very acute angles which shews ye water there had no great current or never reached them after it was gathered in ye vail   now let us pass over ye river to examine ye other high hill which seems to consist of A vast body of once prety solid & near perpendicular rock composed in ye general formation of A slime & aqueous productions & doubtless cloathed with fosil as very like all rocks then was   this rock of 30 or 40 miles in Length I suppose then was washed & scoured & laid bare by ye rapid current of A large body of water that then filled ye whole vail from one hill to ye other when it broked thro ye mountain whereby in process of time ye north east & east winter rains beat against ye naked rock disolved ye natural cement & penetrated it after which ye frost burst it to pieces & it fell down in shivers which anual operation hath continued to this day diminishing ye rock & enlarging its base so that in ages to come it may come to A declination of 45 degrees from ye top of ye rock or hill to ye low grounds below   next to account for ye low rich soil below   I suppose that when this great body of water broke thro ye mountain that it ye bed of ye river reached most of ye breadth between ye hills on each side & occupied most of what is now ye rich low ground or else how came ye round smooth stones all under ye rich low ground and level with these in ye bed of ye river   but when ye water gradualy abated in A long process of time & returned to A much narrower space to run in it must form banks on ye verge of ye water course & these would make eddies & stagnate places which would fill up with trash slime mud & fine sand till it was raised above ye surface of ye common flowing on which would soon grow great quantities of herbage & bushes which would still entangle ye trash & slime that was anualy brought down in floods which gradualy would still rais it above ye common floods as we behold it now   I am more perticular in this discription as it will answer for ye formation of most low lands I have yet observed   early in ye morning we set out & our road leading us round A hill back of ye inhabitants by good land I spied A plant of wild lovage which I was well pleased with but could not find any seed   this prety species of lovage grows 3 foot high bearing an umbel of seeds about ye bigness of fenel seed   it hath A very strong tast & smell of lovage   I saw this species in my first travels near 50 miles from home but could never find it since that year tho diligently looked for it   we continued our traveling till eleven A clock near ye river & then turned on our right hand along A road that crossed ye blew mountain agin being ye road ye people takes to goshen: I tooke this road to show my son ye broken mountainous desolate part of ye countrey where we took ye first perticular notice of ye allder with A silver color on ye under side of ye leaf which is plentifull in this part of ye countrey on ye branches of ye North river   I saw it plentifuly in my first Journey but took no perticular notice of it but its largness   it grows 15 or 20 foot high & 4 inches diameter whereas ours grows about 2   as we came down ye mountain on A sunny rich bank I found many roots of this wild lovage & brought its seed to so in my garden after dispairing 15 years of ever seeing it again   at last we came to A little cottage one hour by sun & ordered our horses to pasture   our host said there was ye strangest plants growed on his land that growed any where in ye countrey   we went directly but thay all proved to be but common plants to me tho indeed there was such as did not grow amongst ye inhabitants at night we lodged 7 or 8 of us (thay being two families) in ye hut hardly big enough for A hen roost   I & billy on ye ground   after A piece of A musty supper slept but little in this lousey hut which wee left as soon as we could well see our path in ye morning haveing paid him half A crown which he charged & reached Dr Coldens by noon   got our dinner & set out to gather seeds & did not get back till 2 hours within night   then looked over some of ye Dr daughters botanical curious observations[2]   next morning as soon as I could see we hunted plants till breakfast   then ye doctors son went with me to dr Jones[3] where we observed ye pines on a high hill near ye doctors   after dinner we went to ye river to gather arbor vita seeds   then returned to dr Coldens by 2 hours within night   in ye morning gathered seeds till breakfast   these two days I could have refreshed my self finely if ye doctor had been at home or durst have eaten freely of what was set before me for thay all was very kind but A burning feavor hanging on me I durst not eat any strong victuals & yet what I eat was too strong for my feavor was worse after   I set out as soon as we had breakfast for ye Katts kill & nothing remarkable happened till I came there   I hired A Guide for 4 shillings A day   we got our breakfast & set out & had 3 mile to walk carying our provisions on our backs to ye foot of ye mountain most of ye way was rising ground   I found it heavy climbing up with A strong feavor & heavy boots & A great thirst   most of ye springs was dryed up but when near half way up we found water where we rested a few minits   then set all our strength to climb making us of every bush in our way to pull ourselves up   our guide more kind then any I had before   he carried my baggs here   I found ye odd between sick & well   I was more foiled to get up now then I used to be when I carried my baggage with me   we got up to ye top about noon & sat down by ye lake when my son & guide dined while I loathed food but my eager desire to see ye great falls three long miles of animated me to travail stoutly: going round ye lower end of ye lake we found abundance of ye prety opulas with yellow buds growing between ye rocks under ye spruice balm of gilead & hemlock firrs where ye sun hardly ever shines   here was A large ledge of rocks that projected over 5 foot above ye surface that above A 100 men might have lodged dry in A shower of rain we left our baggage here while we went to ye falls   leaving this lake we followed ye water cours which was dry tho A rod wide   in half A mile we came to ye second lake scarce A mile long & half broad   good traveling under ye shade of lofty firs being prety open under [illegible] below this lower lake we found water runing in ye water cours which now began to descend fast about A mile farther another larger creek came into this which agmented ye stream which now became more rapid with falling one or two feet perpendicular every few yards which in A great rain must certainly make A great noise   at last we came to ye great gulph that swallowed all down   we Judged it to be about 100 foot perpendicular alltho it had three falls perpendicular ye ofset being about 4 or 5 foot each   ye water cours scarcely two rod wide when it pours over ye rocks   A hill on each side coming close to ye banks   we throwed down stones to ye bottom   could count 20 while going down   haveing observed all we thought worth taking notice of we returned   I wanted my Guide to go & search ye North branch which we did for near A mile but seeing nothing new we left & climbing up A hill steered toward our lodging at ye lower end of ye uper lake   ye ground was prety level dry & shady being under large firs & beech being very pleasant walking   our guide going first billy next & I the last for two reasons   one because I could not well keep up with them   ye other for stairing round about to observe ye trees & plants   billy saw A great black rattle snake quoiled up   thought at first sight it had been A great mushroom was going to kick it but found his error before he came too near it & called out A rattle snake   I cut A stick & laped my handkerchiefe about one end of it presenting it to ye snakes mouth but he would not stir   I then took my hat & held it near his mouth   he slided his head over his quoil & seemed to smell at my hat   then drawed his head back again   I then pushed him out of his quoil & he crept away   our guide stroke [him] over ye neck with A stick & said he never let any escape   he then began to rattle which he continued as long as he lived   we soon came to ye north side of ye lower lake   then crossing ye water cours between them came to our lodging kindled A fire & I being very weary tumbled down on ye moss that was spread on ye ground for our bed while my guide & son gathered wood to keep A good fire all night & A fine pleasant lodging we had   A great rock between us & ye lake which served for A back to kindle ye fire against which reflected heat to ye under side of ye rock that projected over us   A bright moonshine night & nothing wanting render all agreeable but ye absence of my feavour which rather increased in ye morning   we compassed round ye uper lake gathering seeds where we could find them which was but few   I never saw seeds so scarce here before   I climbed several high mountain firs or spruice & trimed them   my guide would not for any consideration climb one   he would cut any down but all would not make A hat full of cones   we fell several trees of ye paper birch but could not get A spoonfull of seed & we could see but one cone of ye two leaved pine & very few of ye 3 leaved   very few of ye balm bore & very few berries to be found   we brought several of ye prety opulas down with us & got home about sunset & being much tired & loathing any food I went to bed without my supper but could not rest for A looseness seized me so that I was forced to call one of ye house up to let me out of ye house   next morning early I set out homeward   my looseness continuing made me very weak but my feaver abated   this day it rained very fast yet we traveled 50 mile. nothing remarkable happened untill we crossed ye Viskill & rode along ye foot of ye high hills which rocks is anualy mouldering & tumbling down to ye low land below where we often dismounted & walked up ye scaly declivity to look for ye curiosities   one morning rideing by A point of easier ascent then common tied our horses at ye foot of ye hill & ascended prety steep till we came prety near ye top where ye rocks was perpendicular but very loose & shivering   we tooke ye advantage of ye cliffs & with much ado reached ye top where we found abundance of impresions of sea shell fish in ye rocks which was so loose & shattered that we could pull them all to pieces with our hands & allmost as easy as A stone wall without mortar thay haveing lost thair original cement   we brought down as many odd figured stones as ye distance of ye way & ye rest of our load would allow us to carry home   it was a fine diversion   after we had descended safe by ye clefts of ye rock to run or slip or role down ye scaleing declivity often sinking to ye ancles in ye mouldering scaley spoils of ye perpendicular rock   soon after we reached ye plain it began to rain first moderately then exceeding fast so that we was force to call at A house & turn our horses out & dry ourselves by ye fire but my son was presently seized with A bad fit of ye fever which did not go off till ye evening so we stayed all night & next morning rode many miles ye river as ye day before on our left hand & high shivering rocks on our right   I wanted much to climb again but ye bushes being very wet & billy now as well as myself being weak & afraid he would be worse made us post home as fast as possible while he had strength & Just before night crosed ye gap of ye blew mountain which by ye present appearances seems very likely to have been one of ye outlets of ye waters that flowed down ye vail above which its very probable was A great lake before it broke down its present pasage   we set out early & in two days reached home

Observations on ye Katts kill mountains

my staying on these mountains for ye best part of two days enabled me to have A better Idea of them then I had before   thay are A body of ye biggest land on this side of St. Lawrence river between Lake Ontario & Lake Champlain   thay are ye united cluster of ye southwestern mountains united from ye blew to ye alegany mountains & butts against ye North river for ye length of 30 mile or more containing ye sources of ye branches or heads of ye adjacent rivers whose waters rusheth down ye declivities & perpendicular rocks in glistering Cascades in as various forms & dimentions as numbers which being many of them united together hath worn & divided ye mountain into deep narrow valeys into many spireing ridges on all sides of which as well as ye valleys is for ye most part prety well stored with wood by reason of ye long continued perpendicular banks of rocks which supporteth ye fertil soil with gentle declivity of 45 degrees to ye foot of another bank   this is ye outward prospect at A distance from ye foot of it now let us ascend & examine ye top which is not so frightful & shocking as ye outward view seemeth to threaten us with: ye ascent indeed is tiresome enough to one that is used to walk on level ground & dangerous enough to

A Careless heavy lubber who may have frequent opertunity of breaking his neck but to A nimble carefull person ye way is pleasant & safe   one half of ye way is shady of A reasonable ascent & plenty of good water except in dry weather in most places   I ascended it in four diferent places & had good water every time   ye other half way is more steep, & more ledges of rocks which are deeper & longer   many 20 or 30 foot perpendicular & 100 or more yards long which we must go round unless we can find some cliffs to climb up & then steep bushy ground to another bank & so on up to ye top some places all covered with sweet Gale asplenofolia or bushes of oak or pine & some places high trees   most of ye top is much pleasanter then one would imagine that had not travail on it   ye soil in general is of A brownish color & but few stones on ye surface which is composed of rotten wood rocks moss & fallen leaves except on ye high points & water courses which is full of stones of all dimentions & som places all solid rock at bottom which indicated to me that ye main body of these mountains is rock & that ye soil is very shallow above it & which ye more confirms it is ye sudden running & draining of ye rains & dryness of large water courses   ye rain water soon pasing thro ye rotten rooty soil to ye rock which by its declivity guides it to ye declining water courses or where at ye surface ye rocks is concave it holds ye water like A basen as is plain in ye lakes whose borders is solid hard gray rock like very cours limestone   ye general appearance of this elevated Mass is diversified in its gentle riseing hills & descending vails where ye rain water is colected forming streams first gentle & as it has aproach nearer ye verge of ye hill or mountain thair rapidity increaseth with thair dense acumulation of several streams rushing together in some places where ye ground was flat at ye foot of A hill there will be an oosey mossy shallow swamp full of paper birch balm of gilead & hemlock firs   ye hilly ground produceth pines   ye champion[4] of easy ascent produceth hemlock spruce mountain fir champain red oak beech & white pine (all very lofty & pleasant open travelling under in thair shade)   this is ye general appearance of ye tops as far as I traveled on them   I would gladly have traveled farther but for 2 reasons   first ye gathering what I could of seeds secondly I was weak with A feavor which seemed to increase so that I wanted to return home   this is ye general appearance where I was but as ye several great chains that ends here or begins which you will & runs to ye S W to ye back parts of Carolina these chains I have crossed several hundred miles to ye southwestward & found each chain consisted of different soils ye alegany mountains is all ye way good land as far as I can find which thay continue till thay joyn this great body where as I am informed thay are very rich land to ye southwest of albany so that ye several parts of these mountains is very like as diferent soils as ye diferent chains that compose them

    ye tree & shrub of ye mountain
        white pine
        three leaved pine

    two long leaved pine
    great mountain firr or spruice
    Balm of Gilead fir
    hemlock fir or silver short leaved
    Beech
    Champain red oak
    paper birch
    maple
    wild cherry
    ash
    aspin
    sweet service
    sugar birch
shrubs
    striped mountain maple
    allders
    quick bean
    opulas with A heart shaped leaf & yellow buds
    Marsh broad leaved viburnum
    Laurel or Ivy
    Caprifolium
    prinos
    aralia spinosa
    red mountain maple
    common shrub honeysuckle
    willow
    white spruice
    hammelis
    purple spirea

BP 1:35:1–9; D. 194–95.
1. Undated, but undoubtedly written in the fall of 1753, judging by his references to a September trip.
2. Jane Colden, an able botanist.
3. Unidentified.
4. Flat, open country.

To COLLINSON[1]

"A List of Seeds of Forest Trees and flowering Shrubs gather'd in Pensilvania, the Jerseys and New York, by John and William Bartram, and sent over the last year to their Correspondent, being the largest Collection that has ever before been imported into this Kingdom."

1. Benjamin or all-spice tree	3. Red cedar
2. Magnolia	4. Wh. cedar or cypress

5. Broad leaved euonymus
6. Cephalanthus, or button wood
7. Judas tree
8. Sugar maple
9.10 Myrtle
11. Dogwood
12. Holly
13. Evergreen rhamnus
14. Jersey tea plant
15. Nissa or tupelo tree
16. Downey sumach
17. Hemlock silver spruce firr
18. Sarsafrass
19. Three leafed or frankincense pine
20. Tulip tree
21. Two leafed tough pine
22. North American black larix
23. Swamp services
24. Viburnum with black fruit
25. Poplar leafed birch
26. Female cornus
27. Beach sumach
28. Arrow wood
29. Ever green privet or ink berries
30. Accacia or locust tree
31. Horn beam
32. Hop hoon [sic] beam
33. Two leafed pine
34. White ash
35. Balm of gilead fir
36. Lesser chamaerhododendron or mountain laurel
37. Greater ditto
38. Dwarf pine
39. Beach nutts
40. Toxicodendron
41. Hamamelis witch hazel
42. Mountain spruce fir
43. White wallnuts
44. Celtis or nettle tree
45. Arbor vitae
46. Aralia spinosa angelica
47. Scrubby White oak
48. Tough twigg'd viburnum
49. Azalea or honeysuckle
50. Mountain red oak
51. Great shagbark hickery or butter nut
52. Scarlet oak
53. Willow leafed oak
54. Broad willow leafed oak.
55. Great female cornus
56. White oak
57. Dwarf red oak
58. Prinos or red winter berry
59. Clethra sweet spirea
60. Mountain red oak
61. Three leaved mountain pine
62. Anona or pawpaw apple
63. Black mulberry
64. Great cranberries
65. Beach cherry
66. Spanish swamp oak
67. Bastard ditto
68. Climbing euonymus
69. Swamp chesnut oak
70. Mountain ditto.
71. Swamp broadleafed ditto
72. Sweet gum tree
73. Honey locust tree
74. Sumach
75. Black wallnuts
76. Ever green euonymus
77. Dwarf cluster berry
78. Early harsh service
79. Sweetservice
80. Andromeda
81. Lime tree
82. Alder tree
83. Staphalodendron
84. Dissiduous cypress
85. Platanus plane tree
86. Ash leafed maple
87. Red and white pinxter broom
88. Persimond fruit
89. Upland roses
90. Mountain laurel with thyme leaves
91. Broad leafed Andromeda
92. Narrow leafed thorn

93. Great cluster cherry.
94. Dwarf round leaved cherry
95. Menispermum
96. Swamp spruce firr
97. Five leafed Canada pine
98. Dwarf chesnut oak
99. Tall chesnut oak
100. Toxicodendron

Gentleman's Magazine 24 (February 1754):65.
1. Bartram enclosed lists of the seeds in his boxes sent to England. Collinson considered this one so impressive that he sent it to the *Gentleman's Magazine*.

To THOMAS D'ALIBARD[1]

To Monsieur Dalibard at Paris
Our very worthy friend Benjamin Franklin esq. whom I have ye pleasure (as well as honour) to be intimately acquainted with showed me A letter wherein thee mentioned A book thee desighned to send me[2] which will be very acceptable for I love Botany & Natural History exceedingly   I shall be well pleased to correspond with one so curious & shall make use of all opertunities to oblige & as an introduction I have sent A little parcel of seeds & specimens which I gathered but as you are posest of so large A part of North america I suppose it will be difficult to send you any plant that you have not alltho I believe wee have several which you want but the difficulty is to know which they are   if I had A Catalogue either of what you have or what you want I will endeavour to supply you which I suppose must be carried on by the good offices of Benjamin Franklin here or my first Correspondent in London the Generous Mr. Peter Collinson who is ready to oblige all men.

BP 1:36:2; D. 370.
1. Letter undated, but probably written in 1754, judging by its content.
2. D'Alibard wrote to Franklin on January 14, 1754, that he was sending Bartram his *Flora Parisiensis Prodromus* (Paris, 1749); see Franklin, *Papers of Benjamin Franklin,* 5:192.

From GRONOVIUS

Leyden, 10 Jany 1754

Dear Friend
I received your Letters dated January and November 1751 March and November 1752; besides one of your son Moses and lately by my good friend Mr. Collinson, yours of 6 of Novemb. 1753.

My own and public affairs and an indifferent health have hindered me to show my thankfulness to all my friends and benefactors, being in great fear to become totaly paralytic but since I turn my self to a way of living, as our old patriarchs did, I am quite recovered, for I drink no wine, coffee or thé but only small beer, and milk mixed with water. My dinner consisted in gruttos and greens boiled in water without butter [illegible] some roasted and boiled meat: avoiding all the delicate aromata which the East and West

Indies send to us. What a change it must make in my body, that was from his youth customed at dinner and supper, to a bottle and a half wine, besides the rest when I get a friend   However I can tell to you, that I left it all at once, in three days the swelling of my feets and cruel pains went off and I my self became not at all week, but contrary I get a great strength and sleep exceeding wel. So that I at present am entirely at the service of my friends and now my worthy Friend, the Rev. Mr. Schlatter, returning to you, I take the opportunity to send these to you.

I am obliged to you for the description of the gape near the blew Mountains, all filled with stones. Betwixt Utrecht and the Loo a country place builded by King William the III, is the country all covered with sandhills for about eighteen Dutch miles but heer and there some low places for a quarter of an hour, which are all fild with stones, les and great some larger than my head and most part Flint stones. I believe realy all the country under the sand there is covered with such stones. I have seen in Flanders when the King of France made a new rode about Brussels, that they removed some immense sandhills, and found at last the ground all filled with loose stones all roundish, and here and there some petrifactions of a yellowish colour, but not separated: but shells of a different kind and cochles joyned to one another by the same calcarea materis of which the stones consist, so as Rymphius represents in tab. 58, E.

I am infinitely obliged to you for the petrified shells with the belemnites and other stones. I was surprised to see these shells, for as much as I know they are originally from the coast of Sicily and that way, under the name of Bucardia, of which several other species are to be found upon the Alpes in Switzerland, and upon the Mounts of [illegible] in Italy, but this particular species was never met calcinated or petrifyed. It is pity it was broken. Question is, how now, and when, these creatures are brought from Sicily to your country. It must be agreed, that there must have been a passage by water betwixt these two places but what time it was so, no body can say. That all the petrifications should be attribute to the general deluge, is what I never shall agree; but I think that with good reason we may derive them from the time of the creation of the world, so that they should not be taken for diluviana but antediluviana

It is also probable that after the creation there have been as well storms, as in our time, when the sea overflowed severall countrys. To those overflowings I attribute the strata, and per consequence, so many strata there are, so many overflowings there have been. We see that confirmed in this country, for when we dig three feet, we find a stratum all of shells, the same as we have at our seacoaste, under it a stratum of clay, and then again a stratum of shells. It is also confirmed, that before the same sandhills were thrown up by a great storm, this country was not habitable in winter time by the overflowing of the sea, and that the few inhabitants of it were obliged to remove to Batavodurum which is 36 miles from hence.

So farther I suppose the sea had overflown the land, and left there a stratum of shells, this was easily overspread by the flying sand, upon which the waters coming or by the rain or by any other way, and standing there make a sedimentum, out of which there becomes by time a marshy ground, being the matrix of the Sphagnum and likely sort of plants, and from which in time by the accession of other particulars are produced the different sorts of clay and humus, and so by succesion we get a fertile ground.

It is a great hardship to me I must tell you that the watermill of Mr. Genete[1] is well finished, but the experiment is not yet taken with it. Every one talks very indifferently of it, and the most part have no opinion of it. . . .

That there are vast chains of mountains in the sea where they are called islands and banks is not to be contradicted, and I believe several petrified subjects are the prove of it . . .

Yes, I believe that Majorca and Minorca are only the tops of mountains standing in a large province under sea, where many fishes find their food. We know by Mr. Cleghorn's observations,[2] that there is no places where more variety of fishes is, than at Minorca, and I have by reports of some of our sea officers the confirmation of it.

And now lastely to your Letter dated the 6 of Decemb. 1753 which I get by our good friend Mr. Slatter, I hope you shall hear from him, that he hath been here with good success, at least I have contributed what is in my power! He hath a great patrone [in] Mr. Thomson the minister at Amsterdam, to whom I communicated Mr. Peters[3] Letters, having Mr. Thomson promised me to give answers to them in my name. When you see Mr. Peters tell him that.

I send you a copy of the new invented stove, but of a dutch translation of his experiments upon the electricite I don't know anything.[4] But in a few days I go to Amsterdam, if I find it there, I shall send it immediately to Mr. Collinson by a friend that goes in a few weeks to London. Pray my service to Mr. Franklin, I wish I could do to you and him any services. I wish you good success with your book about Trees. Wherewith wishing to you all health and prosperity

I remain dear Friend

Your most obedient servant,
Joh. Fred. Gronovius

BP 4:42; D. 360–63.
1. Unidentified.
2. Dr. George Cleghorn (1716–?), an anatomist and writer who spent thirteen years in Minorca.
3. Unidentified.
4. See Bartram to Gronovius, November 30, 1752.

From COLLINSON

February 13, 1753/54

From my country cottage, called Ridgeway House — under that Title it is to be found in our old maps so I conclude it Little less than 200 years standing but yett is a tolerable Dwelling

Dear John

Being Retreated here from the Hurries of the Town while Snow covers the Ground in this Alpine Situation (the Country near the Town being Clear of It), I retired to my Study with a Good Fire and found great Serenity and pleasure of Mind in conversing with my distant friends   thy sundry pacquets lay before mee, as often as I peruse them I still find Entertainment & much Matter for Speculation & Reflection

The first that I laid my hands on was the Well wrote desertation on your Okes & Hickerys   I am pswaded I have taken Notice of this paper before but allow Me to do it again as my pacquet by Neats ship never came to hand, possibly it might be therein for amidst my many Affairs of Business it is impossible to Charge my Memory with Such Matters

The Discriptions are so exact and Natural that I am always delighted with reading them but my Good Friend I must Impart to thee my doubts — I am afraid the Species are so multiplied that it will be a difficult task to distinguish them Here

the Difference between the Low Land White Oke & the Mountain White Oke is purely owing to their Situation & that cannot be determined but by Experiments, take the acorns of Each & plant in thy Garden   a few years observation will putt that Matter out of Doubt, & the Like may be in the Swamp & Mountain Chesnutt a Difference owing to Soil & situation not Sufficient to constitute Two distinct Species & so of the Spanish & Swamp Spanish Oke   I know this Tribe of Trees Sport so in their Leaves that it is easy for thee to collect Specimens that shall have a great appearance of a distinct Species but the question is will this hold through the Forest. In England Wee have but Two Species of Oake & yett in the Course of my observation I could extend them to Variety of Species from the different figure of their Leaves & shape & size of their acorns.

As an Account of your Forest Trees is a very Desireable piece of knowledge Here, with their properties & uses Since the Humour of Cultivating Them is so much Indulged — but when the Lowland & Mountain Oak grows up here together & no very remarkable difference then our Ingenious Friend John Bartram will be araigned with want of Judgement to distinguish things aright   to prevent such an Impeachment of his Skill, I much Wish he would revise his Account Again — & Confirm his Opinion with fair Specimens & Acorns, *Impartially Collected* — for I have a great Desire to have them Ingraved & published   our Frd Catesby has Indeed exhibited Variety but then his work is so expensive few can Afford to buy It[1]

There can be I hope no Exception to Hickeries but good Specimens & Nutts with their Husks on will be very Necessare to be Ingraved for Hickery Nutt are more Sent over than other Seed but How to distinguish them wee know not — unless wee have thy Assistance, that care ought to be taken in gathering Specimans neither from a too [illegible] Tree or a Stunted One, — pray remember Mee if the Oak observed in thy Island bears Acorns to send Some — I wish to see Specimens of Red, White & black Mulberrie

— as this Fruit is very pulpy it may be gather'd a Little before it is full ripe & putt in a Phyal that I shall send in Liquor half rum & half spring Water which will preserve them for Wee know Little of them Here & so....

I now come next to examine thine of June 7th, perhaps over again — thy Account of the Roses please Mee   I have the marsh Rose Raised some years agon from thy Seed & flowers annually with this advantage   after other Roses except the Monthly damask which keeps flowering untill near Xmas, nay for several years I have gather'd Budds on that Day when the Season has been Mild — pray send Mee Seed of the upland Roses — and now I am on this article remember to make a Layer of that Seedling Rose which thou Sent Mee the Specimen of   it continues its pticular Manner of flowering — Wee have one Here that Sometimes bear flowers like it but is Different   the Evergreen privet I shall be glad to See   pray at least send Mee good Specimens in flower if thou goes at that Season   it is a new & Valuable plant   I wonder Wee have not heard of it but so Lately, I long to see it in my Garden; the Evergreen Rhamnus is another Favourite of Mine as is all Evergreens, thine June 7th

Thy Account of the Water & Land Terapins is very Entertaining in thine of June 21 but pray at thy Leisure be particular in the amorous Scene of the last & pray collect Some land ones & then I shall have the pleasure of Seeing them in my Garden   the Water ones but only Those with the painted shells Wee see often   I before told how my Son caught one a fishing with a Earth Worm, pray what is become of the Land ones in thy Cellar — this letter I think I answered by the Tryton 27 7br

thy Expedition to the Mountains must be an agreeable Jaunt to one of thy Tast & Mine   in these Expeditions forget not to Collect any Insects or Observations on them that I have not had before for some frequent the Hills   others the Dales — I don't remember thou ever sent Mee any of your Land Snails of which there must be different Species in Different places it delights Mee to see the boundless Variety that fills every Corner of the Earth & the Sea

by thy Description I have one plant of the Red Spruce   a Specimen of thine with the Cones or Else there is no Determining   Dip'd in thin Gum Water & Dry'd I apprehend will preserve the Leaves on

What Thou names the Sea beach Cherry by its leaves Seems rather a plum if we are right in the plant   pray send a Specimen of the beach Cherry, which will sett us right

I commend thy method of Sowing parsley &c with the Firr Seed — In the northern province of Germany where it is Sandy & Barren & will produce Little but Firrs & pines to prevent the Seedling being Burnt up they sow Oats with their Seed to Screen it in the Summer & its Dry Straw protects it in the Winter — for they do not reap the Oats, and one Reason may be in such a Barren Soil they are not worth It.

I am pswaded if Cuttings Skillfully taken from your Wild Vines, there is no doubt of their Growing   alway take off a Cutting at a Joynt with a Knott or Knub of the Old Wood to It — in length 3 Joynts & then bury the whole in the Ground only covering the upper bud with an Inch of Mould over it that it may Easily strike through   Lett the place be Shady & the ground well Digged   as I know your Vines are long Joynted they may be laid a Slant   this work Should be done in the Autumn, but Here Wee think it better to make Cuttings in the Winter & tie them in bundles & Stick them half Deep in Shallow Water & So Lett them lay until the Mid of March or Aprill & not one will Miss that has a Knot of 2 or 3 years Wood at its End if Curious knowing people was to search your Country there is no doubt they would find Grapes of Various Excellencys & worth Cultivating & Carry Some old White or Red Cloth & tie to them, that they might be the Easier found at a proper Season to make Layers or Cuttings — for from Seed there is no dependance   not one in a hundred will come up to the Original — the Grape as Green as Grass may be a great Curiosity Here for those that ripen them in Stoves without much assistance   our Climate will not ripen fruits that require so much a Warmer Sun   so much for Sepr.

In thine of Octo first Convolvulus or Mechoachan is Recon'd a Southern plant but as it is also a native of yr Continent — for many years agon I had a great root sent Mee from South Carolina — it may be proper for your Constitutions if tryed with Judgement & prepared by a Skillful Hand —

Docr Colden has lately confirmed to Mee the success of the Phytolacca in Cancers — as it is to be apply'd outwardly the Danger is the Less —

I find the Mistake lies Here   I writt to Dublin thinking it was a box of Seeds but as it was plants and Intended as a psent to the Society that affair is all Sett to rights[2]

I am glad of the Information about the Horns of the Moose Deer   I intend to Visit the Hudson Bay Companys Hall & See theirs & then thou shall hear my oppinion — I much Suspect Our Frd Swain[3] is too precipitate & recons to fast — I would wish to know In what part of Hudson bay He intends to push his discovery, that is Easily pointed out on the Maps to the Voyages of Middleton, Smith, Ellis & Dobbs Maps.[4] If wee may depend on their Accounts there is very little left undescribed for him to make the Experiment on   if He can Settle a Trade with the remote Indians it may be more for his private Interest & that of his owners —

the White Cedar Expedition must be pleasant — but it would Spoil Trade to tell how Easie the White Cedar is propagated from Cuttings   not one will Miss. I have 2 Dozen of the finest Straight upright plants from Cutting thou ever saw but this Gordon & I keep a great Secret —

In thine of Novem'r:14 thou advises of 7 Boxes of Seeds which are all come Safe & Well   Docr Mitchell is much concerned for want of his   I told him the Reason & Desired him to send later this year

The Uniforme & Admirable Order in the Creation speakes the unlimited power & Wisdome of the Great [God] to preserve the Chain of Beings, the Fish in the Sea the Fowls in the Air the Beasts in the Forests are all Directed in their Migrations in Search of food as the Insects, Fruits &c are produced in their Seasons and as thou well Observes have their several gradation of Maturity — the like I have frequently taken notice of Here and in the very remote Northern Countries where These Supplies Cease many animals are disposed to Sleep through that Terrible Season as the Black Bears & Dear are affirmed to Do in Green Land &c

In thine of Novem:28:1752 adviseing of a Box of plants & Seeds, I wish these had been sent with the others for It takes up as much Time & Trouble & Expence to gett these from abroad through the Custome House as the other seven boxes   if it is possible Send all that I am concerned in together — next year — those for Mitchell or Powell or Williamson as thou Chooses   I have not yett gott them from on board   Thy bill of 10:15 & 30 will be paid   I have some Heavy people that I cannot gett the Money for Some of the Cargos last year & but a few Days agon some that was Due for the year 1751 — but Time & patience brings things to bear —

the Agnes Castus is tender   never bears seed with us   Dwarf Elder grows very remote I can't tell where   the Great Mapple is rarely loved by anyone   it is a stately Fine [Tree] but not admired by Every one   remind Mee of It against next fall — Now No more Complain of thy Sincere frd

P. Collinson

BP 2:88; D. 189–92.
1. Collinson was mistaken about the number of species of oak in Bartram's collecting region, and Bartram's descriptions were never published. Gray's *Manual of Botany,* which covers the same area, recognizes twenty-seven species of oak.
2. See Dobbs to Bartram, June 25, 1751.
3. Captain Charles Swaine led one of two expeditions sent from Philadelphia in 1753/54 by the North West Company in search of a northwest passage to the Pacific. Eskimo utensils that he brought back were given to the Library Company of Philadelphia.
4. In 1746 Parliament had offered a prize of £20,000 to any ship commander who discovered a northwest passage to the Pacific. Captain Christopher Middleton of the Hudson's Bay Company made a dozen voyages to this area. Later, as commander in the British Navy, he sailed again to try to find a northwest passage. Arthur Dobbs, surveyor-general of Ireland, accused the Hudson's Bay Company of lethargy in their efforts to discover a passage, and Middleton was suspected of cooperating with Dobbs in his criticisms. Henry Ellis (1724–1806), governor of Nova Scotia, had little hope of discovering such a passage, although he made an expedition to Hudson's Bay.

To COLLINSON

March ye 10th 1754

we have had a very wet winter generaly rain twice A week ever since last October   many times A fine clear serene evening till after midnight yet rain in ye morning   in general very warm weather with South or S W winds but we had 2 or 3 very sharp spels for 20 or 30 hours with keen winds at No west which killed abundance of wheat & distroyed my figs. ye mercury fell 20 degrees in ye barrometer in five hours time   ye 4th & 5th of march was warmer then I have known some days in June but we had rain hail & snow with very could north east wind ever since & when it will clear up I know not but ye N W wind begins to blow hard so we may hope for A clear cold day tomorrow   so very uncertain is our weather that this day two weeks was like may   ye wind at S W but toward night n w about dark north soon after it began to rain & hail   next day cold n e wind & snow & rain great part of ye week   in rainy seasons espetialy in winter ye S West wind is sure to bring rain but seldom continueth long unless it taks about suddenly (as it often doth to ye N E then we often have much rain)   from whence should these frequent S. W. rains come seeing there is such A large body of land between us & ye S W sea & no great lakes nor rivers   some years ye S & S W winds is very dry for many months in summer   ye reason of our extream heat & cold is owing chiefly to ye winds as we are so near ye Southern latitude that if ye wind blows above 24 hours so we are sure of very warm weather in ye midst of winter   I once set out from home to visit a relation 20 miles off one seventh day about noon ye snow being half A foot deep   ye wind soon turned So [South] & continued all night   next morning ye snow was most of it gone   ye creeks & runs was raised prodigiously   great cakes of ice half A foot thick was drove on ye banks or low grounds   next night ye wind turned N W & froze so intensly next day that ye road was all in ice so as to bear my horse. but what can be ye reason that our N & N W winds is so extream cold to what it is in europ & asia in ye same latitude   many reasons hath been given by diferent persons but none to my satisfaction but I have thought of offering one to your consideration that I take to be more probable   all our continent from new england to carolina is all open as we may say to ye most northern cold   perpetuell mountains of snow & ice that is there is no high ridges of mountains high enough to intercept ye north & n west winds in thair pasage from ye north of hudsons & Baffins bay to us but that those frozen north winds hath allways A full stroak at us unless over powered by our south winds   for ye highest of all our northern mountains is but like mole hills in comparison to ye lofty ridges that runs thorow europ & Asia which I suppose intercept ye cold north winds of ye continent of europ & Asia which hath allso another advantage which is that ye sea is all Along on ye north of both europ & asia whereas ye forever cold winds from ye north of greenland comes directly over ye cold regions to us   indeed our n e winds is chilling & piercing but never very freesing   I have been informed that at hudsons bay ye wind in winter is generaly due north or N W   if so it is probable our cold west winds is A compound of thair N W there & overpowering thairs & our south meeting after this manner   our west winds is sometimes exceedingly cold for several days   then if it will incline A little southward it is soon warmer

BP 1:35:3.

To COLLINSON

Dear Peter   July 1754

I have had very good luck with many of ye young trees that I planted last fall   my magnolia is shot from A young root near two foot high with leaves near half A foot broad   my uva ursa or thy evergreen ramnus this spring bore flowers pitcher shaped from ye Catskil mountain   this grows finely ye heart shaped viburnums   one odd shrub toxicodendron   one strange honey suckel   two longe narrow leaved pines   one mountain spirea   I have now Just come up A fine young Ceder of lebanon but alass A hot scorching day in ye midst of harvest killed it tho shaded & two cypress scotch firs & larixes from this years seed but ye acrons was all nought   I have now two european larix has shot out this spring near A foot   seeds wanted Cornelian cherry   great chestnut   norway maple   stone pine   norway spruice   I have examined Hill[1] now prety well & am very well pleased that I have got him alltho it be very far from being exact true or fully inteligible   on ye contrary he hath not gone half way thro with it   there is many great omisions & errors I suppose for want of opertunity to examine ye subjects himself & doubtless there is also neglects by being concerned with other business which diverted him from takeing so much notice of ye minute perticulars as he might otherways have done yet notwithstanding these deficiencies there is many curious observations & certain truths contained in it   I am much pleased with dr Parson's Analogy[2]   I look upon it to be an introduction to a very extensive field of observations   I should be glad to correspond with him & if he lives near thee or comes to thy house I wish thee would show him my description of our forrest trees but dont hinder thy own affairs about them   I have just now received thy letter of May ye 2d 1754   I am glad of your remarks on my deficiencies which I hope you will favourably excuse & consider that my descriptions were done & specimens placed, in the greatest hurry most of them by candle light or first days being hurried in travailing & gathering, drying & sorting seeds or labour about my farm

BP 1:33:3; D. 195–96.
1. John Hill's *The British Herbal* and *A History of Plants*.
2. Dr. James Parsons wrote *Philosophical Observations on the Analogy Between the Propagation of Animals and Vegetables* (London, 1752).

To COLLINSON

Dear peter   November 3 1754

I received thy kind letter of July ye 30th   good grammar & good spelling may please those that are more taken with A fine superficial flourish then real truth but my chief aim was to inform my readers of ye true real distinguishing characters of each genus & where & how each species differed from one another of ye same genus & if you find that my discriptions is not agreeable with ye specimens, pray let me know where the disagreement is & send my discriptions back again that I may correct them or if they prove defitient that I may add farther observations for I have no coppies & you have ye original   So by all means send my discriptions back again by ye first oppertunity for I have forgot what I wrote

the microscope I like very well   it is prety adapted to ye observation of plants   its pity the should not be able to answer my two letters of april & may   I fancy I was as much straitened for time to write them as thee art to answer them

ye great water turtle of new england I take to be our great mud turtle which is much hunted for to feast our gentry withall & is reconed to be as delicious A morsel as those brought from ye sumer Islands with this advantage that thay have ye same sauce & many of our Common people is fond of them who adds nothing to disguise ye tast but plain stewing & a good apetite   thay are very large   of A dark muddy color   large rough tail, feet with claws   ye ould ones mossy on ye back & often several Large hors leeches sucking the superfluous blood   A large head, sharp nose & mouth wide enough to cram ones fist in   very sharp gums or lips which you will with which thay will catch hold of A stick offered to them or if you had rather your finger which thay will hold so fast as you may lift ye turtle by it as high as your head if you have strength or courage enough to lift them up so high by it   but as for their barking I believe thy relator barked instead of ye turtle   thay creep all over in ye mud where thay lie perdu & when A duck or fish swims near them thay dart out thair head as quick as light & snap him up.   thair eggs are round as A bullet & choice eating.

as for ye Opossums I cant endure to touch them or hardly look at them without sickness at stomach & I question whether any beast of prey is so fond of them as to kill them for food & as they make but little resistance, but by thair loathsome scent, few creatures will kill them for sport except dogs but if wolves or panthers should chase them thay can creep into less holes in A hollow tree or between rocks then thair pursuers can or if suddenly surprised there is A tree or bush mostly at hand where thay can be secure for thay can run to the extremity of a horizontal branch & lap thair tail round A slender twig which thay will hang pendulous out of ye reach of larger animals

I have sent thee & gordon several evergreen privits & evergreen ramnas with one or two of our hairy mountain hasels wel wraped up in your dear mossy conveyance   pray let me know what success   by many experiments we gain knowledge   if moss will do as well as earth it is much lighter   I laid some moss in ye bottom   then I laid ye roots close & strewed some fine mould   then I throwed some water on ye mould to settle it round ye small fibers   then I placed ye moss as close to roots as I could & about ye lower part of ye stems then sprinkled more water on ye moss then put more moss toward ye top december ye 16th 1754

I have sent by Captain ridall 10 boxes all consigned to the   one for the & gordon   one Box of plants for thomas Kirkham[1] one for swinhoe & ye other seven for thy friends as thee ordered me & now I have shiped on ye Mirtilla Buden two ten guiney boxes & two five guiney boxes for John Williamson & two boxes of five guiney for Powel & one for Ann Conoley[2] to Dublin on board Captain [illegible] & for thy self one box of plants in moss & A box of A great variety of seeds & A quire of specimens of our oaks with thair acorns on in perfection acording to thy desire beside my son William hath drawn most of our real species of oaks and all our real species of birches with an exact description of thair perticular characters not according to grammar rules, or science but nature. the hath our oaks & my distinguishing characters of them   pray compair them with Catesbys draughts & see how wildly unnaturaly he has placed ye acrons   he makes no distinction of summer & winter acrons nor how that thay or ye leaves grows on ye twig or how ye nerves projects   yet how is his work applauded   indeed his birds snakes & fishes may be excelent as far as I know for I am not so acquainted with them as with plants of which he seems to know little of thair natural growth but hath done all at random except outlines of ye leaves

BP 1:37:1; D. 196–97.
1. A London nurseryman at the Woolneck and Crown.
2. Of Castleton.

To COLLINSON[1]

Draught & discription of ye drounded lands & great vale

all ye draughts & discriptions after thee hath Just looked them over pray send them to our friend Dr. Gronovius by ye first safe opertunity for his perusal   there is A letter to him in ye box which I desire thee to inclose in thine to him   thee often year after year desired me to send thee specimens of our evergreens for that you knowed but little of that tribe (little to your Credit)   in compliance I collected with much pains at great distances most if not all ye evergreen trees & shrubs natural to our three or 4 governments in thair perfectest state & sent them carefully above A year past & yet never since received one line mentioning whether thee received them or not & all the reason I have to hope thee hath received them is that thee writes no more to ask about them onely those two or three I sent after from terra Labrodore   I have put A split piece of black ash into the Box   I have discribed after my fashion several other kinds of forrest trees but no time enough to send them when — I received A small letter with an imperfect balance of accounts. I think what I sent to Dr Mitchel for his friends is not in it   pray take notice of it again in more perticularity   I searched diligently for A bull frog or two to send thee hopeing if thay came safe to thy hand that thay would have barked louder then ye New england turtle but thay was retreated into thair winter quarters I and billy ascended ye Katskill mountain in A new place several miles from where wee used formerly & found ye ground allmost covered with lillium convalium & mountain cherry trees 30 or 40 feet high one diameter & very straight allso ye striped maple 20 foot high & one diameter & thousands of ye paper birch but not one good seed & but one two leaved pine but barren we lodged on top of ye highest point by ye side of A rock A horrible ground drawed [illegible] way to get to it to see two lakes

BP 1:47.
1. Probably written December 16, 1754, enclosing the following letter (Bartram to Gronovius, December 16, 1754).

To GRONOVIUS[1]

december ye 16th 1754

Dear & well beloved friend
Docr Gronovius
I have received thy kind letter of January ye 10th 1754 which was indeed very acceptable & more so being I thought thee had forgotten me. I am very glad the approves of my notions about several of my observations.

    I have A little Son about fifteen years of age that has traveled with me now three years & readyly knows most of ye plants that grows in our four governments. he hath drawn most of our oaks & birches with a draught of ye drownded lands & several of ye adjacent mountains & rivers as they appeared to him in his Journey by them: this is his first essay in drawing plants & A map he hath drawn several birds before when he could find a little time from school where he Learns Lattin. I now send these draughts to our friend Peter Collinson whom I shall desire to send thee as soon as A Convenient opertunity offers to thee with our description of ye Birches, their general & perticular Characters & Wherein one species really differs one from another in any soil or situation: these I send to thee to have thy opinion of ye method I have fallen into. & if thee can inform me of A better; I shall readily embrace it — & whether it would not be better to have it published in Lattin. I design next spring to set my son to draw some of our flowering trees & shrubs in thair flourishing state. Our friend Slater tells me that thy son[2] is like to be A great Curioso if he will write to me & let me know what will be acceptable I can furnish him with several Curiosities.

    I have some thoughts of traveling to Carolina next spring, however pray write to me as soon as possible which will oblige much thy friend

John Bartram

Linnean Society of London Archives, Ward Ms. 17, 1874; Ms. 325.
1. Collinson added a note (dated June 5, 1755) on the back of this letter. He wrote that he

had forwarded Bartram's papers, drawings of oaks, and his "system." He added that Bartram's "son's Drawings are very fine"; also "very fine Specimens of all the Oaks & Acorns and another Quire of all the evergreens of North America."
2. Laurenz Théodor Gronovius (1730?–1778) published the second edition of the *Flora Virginica* in 1762.

To COLLINSON

March 6 1755

Dear Peter

I have received thy kind letters of october ye 2d 8th 14th & 24th 1754 am well pleased with ye description of ye agreeable situation of thy countrey seat & more so that thy heart flows with gratitude to our heavenly father & great benefactor   it gives me much sattisfaction that billys drawings is so well received & that thee hath so much regard for my son moses & his wellfare but what is thy reason that billy must learn surveying   I should be glad to try ye Ceder of lebanon once more   we have not one of ye stone pine growing in our countrey   one growed in our Proprietors vineyard about 5 foot high & then perished tho planted on A fine south bank   I never could have one good seed yet   thay was all mouldy or shriveled   I admire that Clatons tree perished in such A warm climate   I question whether it was ye cold that killed it   our Proprietors tree had survived several colder winters then that wherein it perished but ye sudden extreams of our winters spoils ye exoticks   I wholy purposed last fall to go to ye virginia & Carolina mountains but now being certainly informed of ye great danger of travelling near those delightfull scituations I must forbear at present but am sadly afraid your ministrey will be fooled by ye french who no doubt will pretend thay will not act in A hostil manner in order that you may forbid us to drive them back that thay may in ye mean time not onely incroach upon us but allso fortifie themselves stronger there in thair incroachments   Joseph Lees[1] went with 2 more last year up to our blew mountains in east & west Jersey to gather seeds & hath allso been this year to gather more   he now minds nothing but his garden & travelling & boast much how my ould faithfull Correspondent helps him out in A hard life

thine of october ye 2d   certainly you have fine temporate seasons to what we have   we had ye hottest fall I ever knowed   ye fore part of January ye ice drove in ye river several days   ye latter part was very warm so that ye cattle stood in ye shade from ye heat of ye sunshine but since february come in we have had very unconstant weather   some days so hot as to sweat & next day ye wind North cold & snowy & succeeded next day by very sharp wind at North then west   next day south & very warm   I am glad thee approves of my notion about our winds in which I am convinced by observation this winter but there is A great error in ye magazin   I wrote thee that our So west winds is A compound of ye N W & our South & gave thee a figure of it   thy observation is very good about ye snow   to be sure it protects vegitables exceedingly against ye extream frosts & we suffer most winters for want of it to our sorrow   our black wallnuts rarely grows beyond ye 41 or 42 degree Northward but ye white or butter nut grows much further north   I thought ye 3 thorned acatia had been A native of virginia but I believe ye sweet smelling locust is   thay wont grow naturaly & but rarely by planting much above A degree northward then our parts   pleas to read lineus dalibard or hill who well & naturaly explain what thay call Petiole drupe & gemma   I am much obliged to thee for thy kindness to my son moses   the helebor which thee mentions was sent from new york with A redish purple flower I take to be our mountain narrow leaved kind ye seed of which I have sent to thee allmost every year but its being light & chaffy it may not come up   it grows 4 or 5 foot high with A sparse spike of flowers A foot long & 6 inches broad at ye base   I am obliged to thee for thy kind advice about our french correspondents   hitherto thay have been grateful but I shall proceed with Caution   I have read owens[2] observations on stones which is very ingenious but I think ye reasons he assighns for ye warmness & vertues of ye bath waters is very weak   hot springs A strange phenomina far from volcanos

this should have gone by Hargrave

BP 1:36:7; D. 197–98.
1. Perhaps a relative of Thomas Lees, Philadelphia plant collector.
2. Unidentified.

To PHILIP MILLER

April ye 20th 1755

worthy Friend Philip Miller
I have received thy kind letter of February ye 19th 1755 which gave me much Satisfaction & some uneasiness that so many years have elapsed wherein wee might have reciprocaly have communicated our observations to each other & alltho thee had incomparably ye advantage over me yet notwithstanding I love to peep into ye abstruse operations of nature perhaps I might by thy familiar instruction have made some remarks that might have been satisfactory but for the time to come I hope we may double our diligence if ye war with France[1] do not obstruct our endeavours   ye Catalogue of shrubs and trees is very acceptable or any other books of natural history   I have thy first & second book of ye Gardeners Dictionary   one sent me by Ld Petre   ye other by Dr Dilenius   I design to take perticular Care to send those seeds thee mentioned which I can procure & if thee please to send by ye first opertunity it may come to me soon enough to send next fall   any other curiosity thee pleas to mention for time is so far spent past our Meridian that ye afair calls for diligence   I design to colect specimens of our pines just when thay are in flower & ye young cone just impregnated, which is to ripen not this ensuing fall but ye next

when it immediately dischargeth its seed before it is well dry whereas other trees keep thair cones shut for several years containing perfect ripe seeds & then discharge thair seed   pray does all your europian pines set thair cones on ye same springs shoot & perfect them ye succeeding year or certain several ye second years wood as by thair cones in europe thay are no distinguishing characters in your draught the scotch pine doth? Although the species of pines & fir may, many of them, be distinguished by thair cones in Europe thay are no certain distinguishing character in America except Ld weimouths pine & firs   ye balm of gilead fir & ye hemlock spruice fir as for example ye great 3 leaved pine two & 3 leaved ye dwarf 3 leaved & ye long two leaved pine of ye Katskil mountains   these all varieth so prodigeously in thair cones in each species espetialy ye great & dwarf 3 leaved that rarely two trees bears cones alike some near as big as my fist others no biger then A pullets egg & so various shapes as dimentions some exceedingly prickley others much smoother   in short we must call in all ye assistance of leaves bark & form of growth to perfectly distinguish each real species in thair different ages soils & scituations   thy observation on ye leaves of ye pine is very good   I have seen ye 3 leaved pine some with 4 leaves in A sheath but not one in A hundred thousand that is so   I have seen in ye 2 & 3 leaved pine one branch with 2 3 & 4 leaves in A sheath & Ld weimoths pine with but 4 but these diferences happens rarely   thay generaly hold ye same number to each species with us   I am obliged to thee for thy good advise to contract my descriptions   I own ye leaves acorns & especially ye cups are very material in ascertaining ye diferent species of our oaks   yet ye discription of ye bark & form of growth is usefull helps in our mature oaks   I can often discover our diferent species of oaks one from Another by thair form of growth half or A whole mile distance & I am sure he must be very sharp sighted that can know them at half that distance by thair leaves acorns & cups all together

I take thy ofer very kindly to assist me in understanding lineus sistem which I am A little acquainted with in some degree haveing several books of his setting forth which Dr gronovius my good friend hath sent me & Mons. dalibard sent me his Catalogue of plants growing near Paris & hill hath nearly translated Lineus Characters but I find abundance of many plants that do not answer to any of his Genera & is really A new genus   I have an account that he hath published lately   two books containing all our north american plants which Kalm observed when he was with us   I shewed him many that he said was A new genus & that Lineus must make many alterations when he was by him more truly informed of thair true Characters as I should soon see when thay were printed   I long to see these books to see if thay have done me justice as Kalm promised me   Dr Gronovius promised to send them to me as soon as thay came to his hand   I shall be much obliged to thee for thy figures of plants as soon as finished   I love to see nature displayed in all its branches   I shall be glad to assist thee with any new plant or shrub either dead or Alive   in substance or A perticular discription as thee pleaseth to inform me after what manner it will answer thy intention the best & I shall I hope endeavor to comply with thy desire I have observed in all ye firs I have examined that ye vestiges of ye winter buds or base of ye spring shoot remains very plain for several years but in your draught of ye Cornish fir I cant see any thing of it tho it is so visible in ye balm of gilead & small coned fir tree   in a specimen I had from china it was very plain   whether may not this be taken for a certain character of ye Genus of ye fir   if your draught of ye balm of gilead fir be exact it is very diferant from ours on ye Katkil mountains whose leaves is more patent[2] & ye cones much thicker at ye base & grows erect   Pray doth all your european pines set thair [cones] on ye same springs shoot & perfect them ye succeeding year or certain general ye second years wood as by your draught ye scotch pine doth   alltho ye species of pines & fir may many of them be distinguished by thair cones in europe thay are no distinguishing characters in america except Ld weimouth pine & for firs ye balm of gilead fir & ye hemlock spruice fir

BP 1:35:4; D. 376–78.
1. The French and Indian War of 1754–63, a part of the Seven Years War in Europe.
2. Spreading.

To COLLINSON

April 27th 1755

I have received thy kind letters of January ye 5th February ye 1st 12th & 19th   I am well pleased with ye relation of thy fine curious flowers in thy garden   thy agreable discription of thy greenhouse & its furniture but oh my dear dear friend thy sweet disposition thy Humility adoration & resignation to universal power supream   our eternal father ye one true & living god   I was ready to wish myself with thee to assist in such an acceptable sacrifice to have held ye Censor or blowed ye coal to kindle ye incence or else to have had thy company in my little library or Chapel as I call it or rather in ye grand & spacious temple amongst ye lofty chains of mountains ye craggy precipices of elevated rock embellished with various shrubs pliant evergreens out of thair uneven surfaces & ye gloomy shaded vails with ye variety of ye ferny tribe or various shrubs & plants of quiet recess   ye purling streams & glittering cascades ye level plains ye concealed humid bosoms discharging numerous pearly drops perpetualy trickling down   or ye shore of ye mighty ocean ye great metropolis of ye finy tribe where we view ye rolling waves dashing against ye shore & breaking into steam rising up in vapour which is colected in humid fleeces in ye vast expance   all ye objects all these variety of scituations demonstrates ye power & wisdom of an allmighty power ye contemplation of which with humble adoration we sincerely resign our will to his   I design to set billy to draw all our turtles with remarks as he has time which is only on seventh days in ye afternoon & first day mornings for he is constantly kept to scool to learn Latin & french   we intend to take notice of ye frogs & lizards as thay come our way or we know where to find them   I have often sent thee ye seed of our great aster   next expect A root   We sent A letter to moses by A young man in mesnard that promised to deliver it to him   I am much obliged to thee & Gordon for your kindness to him as he expressed it in A letter I suppose from Lisbon but we cant so much as guess where he is now   we expect him in every day   I am well pleased that thee let Philip Miller see my specimens of oaks & evergreens   its pitty but he had wrote to me many years Ago   time is now far spent with us both   I hope Dr fothergill wont condemn me without giveing me liberty to plead my own cause   I have abundance of undigested thought to communicate if I could explain my sentiments so as you could understand my meaning   Dr mitchel sent A letter to Franklin I believe by Hargrave in which he desired me to send him several boxes of seeds   I wish he would write to me more perticular before it is too late   thee write to me to draw 50 pounds but if there should be A war with france I had rather have it in thy hands if it could be secured to my children if thee or I should die as we are all mortal   Our Philadelphia people seems at ease & dissolved in luxury I think two 20 gun ships could take ye town in two hours time   I hope to send thy 10 or 15 boxes   ye rock goat I dont think liks [licks] ye soft sandy stone to excite their apetite for wild Creatures in ye forrest hath no temptation to eat more then nature requires for thair proper nourishment & thay allways when well hath apetite sufficient   its man that by over chargeing his stomach spoils his digestion & still wants sauce to sharpen his apetite to devour more then nature requires   I dont think thay have need to clean thair tongues with rock sand   ye goats food is commonly rough as bushes & leaves   if thay eat grass or herbs thay mostly grow so close to ye rocks & sand thay must lick up sand enough to scour thair tongues & help digestion if sand will do it but I rather suppose that there is some nitrous or saline particles in ye soft sandy rock that ingages those creatures to lick ye rock   I take it to be so with ours   most of our liking places is A black stinking sort of mud   stinks like ye washing of A gun barrel & may be smelt A distance off   there is some places that is called white licks that is like clay that is sweeter yet may be impregnated with some saline matter that may induce them to lick there; thee acuseth me for not paying due regard to thy letters relating to ye packing up roots in moss when I punctualy pack them up according to thy directions except ye fine heart shaped leave Viburnums which I took more perticular care of because I did not know how to get another so good   I put a little wet mould about it & tied A cloath close round it & then packed it in ye moss which is ye very exact method the hath directed me to this spring & then I desired thee to let me know ye success & that if moss will do   it must be much better as it is much lighter   thee art very much mistaken in the striped Maple being a seminal variety or an accidental one either   it is a very perticular distinct species both in its manner & place of growth   it hath ye most constant appearance of any species I know & place of growth being perticular to ye northern ridges of our blew mountains from ye no river to Susquehana   I never observed one naturaly to grow on ye three southern ridges or between them & ye sea   Kalm looked for them on ye Kats kill

I hope to send the seeds of ye bartsia & christophoriana with white seeds   I shall remember ye heleborine   I think powel need not make such A bluster being his orders was dated ye 15th of august & I think came in novr & had I not been better provided then common he would not have had any but he had two good ones   as to thy queries concerning ye variety of ferns in slate & ye natilus in clay ye one being natural to ye east & others to ye west doth not perticularly belong to my hypothesis which chiefly related to ye appearance of ye fossil in rocks or shells [illegible] our great chains of mountains & that thay was deposited & fixed there at ye mosaical creation when ye waters was seperated from ye land & ye mountains appeared that ye great deluge did not alter ye scituation of ye great midle ridges of ye continents without it was to cut Chanels between & thorow them in many places by furious Currents   however to come to thy query I cant have time now to answer otherwise then by quering too   we may suppose ye flood made prodigious allteration in ye plains & ye lesser hills that ye waters covered ye vast quantities of ye lower lands washed & broke ye lesser hills with which thay covered ye vast bodies of level ground   what & where was ye atlantis that Plato mentions which ye Priests tould him as A very antient tradition   indeed altho I have A very indiferent opinion of what ye priests have tould us in all ages & nations of ye world relating to thair imported & imaginary notions of thair superstitious worship & atributes of thair gods yet I think it is very probable that thay was ye most likely to have ye most antient true tradition of natural efects handed from generation to generation from time immemorial   how do [we] know but that was part of america & Joyned to or near ireland & that to England that to France & is it not probable that Spain joined to Africa at ye straights of gibralter   that asia & Europe Joyned at ye propontis   that ye mediteranian was high enough to cover great part of ye islands contained therein & might not ye deserts of libia & Arabia be ye sandy bottoms of ye sea 100 or 200 fathom deep might not waters of ye flood or not long after cut its way thorow ye straights of gibralter & ye black sea through ye propontise   might not britain be separated from france & ireland & ye atlantis which be low loose & sandy be washed away or sunk   there is found in several northern countreys plants & shells which appears to be ye production of prety warm climates I cant at present see how this can be accounted for better then by these two ways that I shall mention   either that thay growed in or near where we find them or that thay was brought from ye southeastward or southwest from ye places of thair original growth by very strong winds & currents; if thair original growth was where we now find them or near it & by winds & mighty currents of water such A vast body of soils covered them we may reasonably suppose ye countrey there was once A warmer climate & consequently ye earth run paralel with its equinox   this will perhaps make some start   but pray consider we read in ye booke of Joshua that ye sun & earth stood still A whole day & I think it would require no greater power to incline ye earth 25 degrees then to stop its or ye suns motion   now dear Peter I have sent A confused heap of broken links   I doubt it will puzzle the all to make A tough chain of such brittle materials   might not ye deluge cause great allterations in ye nature of ye soil

my good friend thee judges me two hard in thine of february ye 19th if I did say ye letter was small & ye balance was imperfect was it not true there was but half A sheet & in ye balance the wrote received of Powel 5-5 & he wrote to me by ye same ship that he had paid thee seven pounds & seven shillings but as I thought that he might pay the two pounds after ye other 5-5 & it might be out of thy mind so I tould thee that I thought Dr Mitchels account was not in it & desired thee to take notice of it again more perticularly   I was in no pet about it   I am A plain countrey fellow & is for useing freedom & sincerity without being in A pet   I do what I can to oblige thee in every respect

I am sadly puzled about finding out ye cause of ye hot springs far from volcanos & cant hit upon any satisfactory way of account for it   most other Phoenomina I Can fix upon something that seems to pleas my fancy with ye appearance of A probability that it may be so rather then otherwise but all my attempts to account for this is so far from affording any sattisfaction that if I had not heard credible persons affirme it I should be ready to conclud there could be no such A thing in nature   it is like shooting arrows against A rock   thay all fly back again at my face   pray what is ye opinion your learned men concerning this as I take it obstruse Phenomina   I desire some of you would be so kind as to help me out with this dead lift — I am glad of ye specimens of acron cups   My son William is just turned of sixteen   it is now time to propose some way for him to get his liveing by. I dont want him to be what is commonly called A gentleman   I want to put him to some business by which he may with care & industry get A temperate resonable liveing   I am afraid Botany & drawing will not afford him one & hard labour does not agree with him   I have desighned several years to put him to A doctor to learn Phisick & surgery but that will take him from his drawing which he takes perticular delight in   pray my dear Peter let me have thy opinion about it   I am glad My friend fothergil hath ye perusal of my notion of ye antediluvian impressions of marine shels & our mountainous rocks or any other of my rambling observations   I hope if I can stand ye test with his trial I shall come out like gold well purified I had rather undergo now a rough purging than to have my dross left behind   Dear friend if thee propose to me any questions of Philosophy pray let me have as many as thee pleas in ye fall   it will be a fine winter divertion & questions in botany in spring that I may have ye summer to make proper observations of vegitables in   if there should be a war with france how shall I send my discriptions & billys drawing without falling into ignorant hands that will not take any notice of them or may be thrown out Suppose I should direct them to Mr delebard Bufan[1] Jessieu[2] or dr gronovius as if ye french should take them & seeing them directed to such noted men thay might take care to send them to them   last war thay tooke care & sent my letters & part of ye curiosities to gronovius as directed   ye rest jussieu kept himself   pray direct me how to act for ye best for I suppose little can be sent in merchant ships without A convoy but what will fall into ye enemies hands & I had rather that ye discriptions & drawings should fall into learned then ignorant hands

pray send me A pair of globes about 3 guineas price which will be about A foot diameter as Benjamin informed me & instead of ye gentlemans Magazines send those by Benjamin Martin[3]   in ye Magazine Dr Alston[4] account of ye spinage mercury & hemp seems very curious & to appearance might be true yet I cant yet believe that ye female parts is very much influenced by ye male & as providence acts wisely in all his operations in case of accident its not unlikely but some provision might be made in ye female anual plants that is distinct male & female   that if ye female should by chance or accident are sown or set at too great distance to attract ye farina from A male plant there may be produced some latent anthers to em-pregnate ye female part tho wholy invisible & inactive & would have remained so unless roused up & called to assist ye greatest necessity (& is very frequent in ye latent buds of trees & plants where ye top of ye shoot is destroyed) as these poor fixed vegitables hath no locomotion to approach one another as animals: as many Genus of plants is distinct male & female I have observed many of them that are females trees hath ye male anthers but doth not discharge any farina unless at A great distance from A male tree   but plants or trees that hath ye male & female parts on ye same tree but at remote distances are generaly intirely male or female[5]

D. 198–200; BP 1:35:5.
1. Georges Louis Leclerk, Comte de Buffon.
2. Bernard de Jussieu (1698–1777), demonstrator at the Jardin des Plantes.
3. Benjamin Martin (1704–1782) published *Martin's Magazine* from 1755 to 1764, "a new and comprehensive Philosophy, Natural History, Philology, Mathematical Institutions and biography."
4. Dr. Charles Alston.
5. Darlington treated this as a single letter, as we have done. There is some reason to believe that part of it might have been a separate letter of June 10, 1755. The *Gentleman's Magazine* for September 25, 1755, under the heading: "Some Remarks made on Dr. Alston's Dissertation on the Sexes of Plants . . . by two celebrated botanists of North America, both dated June 10, 1755," quotes from letters evidently written by John Clayton and John Bartram. The letter published in the magazine contains essentially the same comments made by Bartram in this letter, with some further elaboration; that letter follows.

To COLLINSON[1]

In the Magazine I read Dr. Alston's observations on the mercury, spinage and hemp, the female produceing good seed at great distance from the male, which seems curious, and may be true to appearance; yet I can't believe but that the female must be influenced by the male, tho' at a very great distance, as providence acts uniformly in all its operations; But yet it is not impossible, in case of accidents, but that some provision may be made in the female to act in both capacities, especially in what we call annual plants, that are male and female in distinct, separate plants; that if the female grow at too great a distance from the male to attract his farina, there may be produc'd some latent farina to impregnate the female part, altho' before invisible and inactive, and would have remain'd so unless called and roused up to assist in the greatest end of nature.

Many genuses of plants are male and female in distinct trees; of which I have observed many of the fem. trees to have the same anthera, but not to discharge the farina, unless at a great distance from the male tree; but this is not always the case; for the roots of *English* briony that I raised bore abundance of fine red berries, but all imperfect being nothing but skin, and watery juice.

I found a fine stalk of *Indian* corn, at a great distance; I cut off the male tessel as soon as it appeared, and there was produced a large ear, but no good grains upon it.

If we plant cucumbers, squashes or melons near the bitter gourd, the fruits of the first will be as bitter as gall. — These experiments show how necessary the male farina is to the fructification of all seeds, and how liable plants are to be bastardized by bad neighbours of their own kindred.

This will give a hint how careful a curious gardener ought to be. The way to preserve a good species of any plant is to keep it separate from others of the same kind, that is not of so good a quality.

Gentleman's Magazine 25 (September 1755):408.
1. Undated, but possibly June 10, 1755; see note 5 of previous letter (Bartram to Collinson, April 27, 1755).

To COLLINSON[1]

both town & countrey is now in ye utmost astonishment & moved as ye leaves on ye trees with A wind & ye sea with A storm at ye relation of such A tragical sceen tho it is confirmed by several letters daly for near a week yet it is so incredible that it seems more like A dream then real fact: but I doubt ye dreadfull consequences will soon convince us that it is too true: General Bradock is overthrown   600 of his men slain & wounded   most of his officers killed & ye artilery taken by 300 Indians   Oh stupid obstinate Briton: that would not be moved By his soldiers falling round him in garments stained with blood   not ye agonies & groans of his valient Captains at his feet roling in gore nor ye earnest entreaty of those more superficially wounded who begged leave to take 200 or 300 men & rouse ye hidden enemy up from behind ye trees & bushes from whence thay took such sure aim that thair Balls seldom failed of opening canals for ye efusion of sanguin streams while our mens offenceless bead onely saluted its mother earth or graised ye bark of senseless trees: general would not break his ranks or turn out of his ould beaten path   his foot [soldiers] he kept in A lump his captains on horseback all exposed to ye fire of ye secreated enemy who could not desire A better opertunity to embrace ye limbs of those who if thay had liberty could have bound them hand & foot   oh how are ye french now strengthened by our spoil & enriched by our treasure   thay have arms to fight us with & cloathes to keep them warm all brought to thair dore & A great road ready cut at ye great toll of ye provinces   this is now common report

BP 1:34:2; American Philosophical Society Library, Wildman transcript.
1. Dated July 10, 1755, by Wildman.

To COLLINSON

September ye 28th 1755

Dear Peter
I have received thy kind letters of March 25, April 23d June ye 17th & July ye 3d sent on by Captain Budden, also one by N. E. & one by N York   I have been at Killingsworth with our friend Eliot who is A good sort of A man & endeavours for ye general good of mankind   his time is fully employed in visiting ye sick looking after his farm supplication & thanksgiving in his family praying & preaching in ye Pulpit & very agreeable in his conversation with his friends   In my return home I traveled more back in ye countrey & crossed ye north river below ye highlands & went with my billy to observe ye falls of second river which are very remarkable for such A body of water to precipitate about 60 foot perpendicular into A narrow gulf between two rocks about 10 foot distance. I have A cruell spel of ye dry gripes since I came home but am so far recovered   I am well pleased that Billy gives you such satisfaction in his drawing. I wish he could get A handsom livelyhood by it   Botany & drawing are his darling delight   am afraid he cant settle to any business also   indeed Surveying may afford an opertunity to exercise his botany but we have five times more surveyors allready then can get half employ   If he could get A surveyor generals office for life it might do   the specimen of your oak comes near our White oak yet differs prety much in its acron cups: seems to be of the summer kind is there no winter ones but what grows in No america   ye other oak specimen comes near our scrubby oak but ye leaves is longer & slenderer I suppose thine was gathered from A young tree   so I suppose was ye paper birch   ye twig is very slender   I am glad ye Boggy evergreen Andromeda hath flowered   hath thee observed ye prety texture of its Shagreen[1] leaves   ye heleborin from york I sent thee in my first specimens   it grows common in wet gravely ground   I doubt Dr Colden cant find that stone

composed of sand and cockle-shells   I found it on ye South side of ye drownded lands near ye mountain on much higher ground then it is where ye doctor lives where most of ye stones is composed of A coarse sandy limestone & scallop shels of A large size & perticular form peculiar to this vail & antideluvium layer for I find in our present bays or sea ye scalops lyeth much deeper then ye cockle which lyeth in ye sandy shores   if I should travail to ye doctors again I desighn to search ye south side & try to find that stone; but there is now great allteration since I was there & very like ye woods in which I found it may now be corn fields & it will be like searching A needle in a bundle of hay   We have had ye most grievous dry season for 2 months or 10 weeks that I believe was ever known in this countrey at this time of year since ye English setled here   about ye begining of June we had so severe A frost & froze many plants that was grown A foot long so that thay imediately turned black & broke off & yet before & since ye Mercury rose to 80 or 90 degrees where it is now generaly   ye ground is now so hot as not to be suffered to tread upon with bare feet & ye stones cant be held long in ye hand thay are so hot   our meadows where we used to mow two good crops which growed from ye begining of may to ye begining of august old stile is now burnt up brown so that it will rub to powder under foot   ye plants are perishing & ye leaves of ye trees turned brown & withered & ye branches dryed   all winter & till April we had scarcely 3 days without rain which with ye evening frosts spewed ye corn out of ye ground so that many plowed ye ground up & sowed it with spring grain which is now scorched with extream heat & drought   I have out 3 cedars of lebanon & two of ye manured pine & many fine pines & firs which I daly water & nourse & as I can now gard against ye heat & drought with [illegible]

BP 1:35:6; D. 200–201.
1. Covered with small granules.

To ALEXANDER GARDEN

October ye 12th 1755
Respected Friend dr. Garden
I received thy kind letter of May ye 18th 1755 which was very acceptable as will allso be any of your countrey seeds of plants or shrubs some of which is hardy enough to endure our severe winters   Of ye Catalpa I have enough from Dr. Witt   very few of those seeds thee sent me came up   onely ye Indica & Thea which I find to be a Sida   2 or 3 plants of A smooth oblong thick shineing leaf growing opposite   pray what is your Palmato royal how high doth it grow before it bears fruite which is very prety tasted   I am apt to think I have 3 come up   ye leaves is shineing something like parsley & growing opposite   I hope thee art falen into good business   being so much confined in town I shall be glad if it dont endanger thy health   as to

ye sudden changes of heat & cold in your climate as well as ours I suppose are caused by our open exposition to both as we are scituated so near ye open sea & southern heats so we are allso exposed to ye greatest extremity of ye northern blasts a little tempered by ye intermediate heat in adequate degrees to ye power & progress of ye southern currents of air for I cant find that there is in all No America any chains of mountins so high as to intercept ye currents of ye air of ye frigid zones from ye highest latitudes all ye way over land as there is in Europe & Asia which hath allso ye great advantage of haveing ye sea north of them except about Nova Zembla.[1]

as for rain I suppose it to be collected from ye Sea ye rivers & lakes, vegetables & mountains: ye sea afords materials abundantly for ye formation of rain as it is continualy in agitation espetialy near ye shore   ye waves dashing & breaking against into steam & rising in vapor   ye rivers affords large quantities of vapor both from their even Surface thair agitated waves & at thair falls as may be observed in A frosty morning in A thick fog plants & trees sends up great quantities of vapor from which perhaps most of dews are formed: & lastly ye mountains not onely colects and condenses ye vapours by thair coldness & hight but allso directs ye course of ye rains in some scituations as is evident on ye coast of Coromandel in Asia, Mount Atlas in Africa ye Ripheous in siberia & ye Cordeliars in america with many others to tedious to name   all which is doubtless very instrumental in furnishing ye in land parts of ye globe with ye necessary liquid element but I take ye more imediate general cause of rain to be A proper disposition & araingment of ye form & density of ye vapours & clouds was to act organicaly to form A vacuum & consequently to be in A state of strong atraction in one part & A plenum of discharge in ye other part in A regular succession for many miles so as to water ye countrey which I suppose is in part caused by ye proper disposition & scituation of colder regions of air with respect to its various distance from ye different parts of ye earth at different seasons of ye year according to ye disposition of ye surface of ye globe to reflect ye solar heat   mountains reflect little   ye plains much in hot weather   ye sea but little   wheather is not this ye reason that in ye great heats there is but little rain in Egypt & peru & several flat countries except near ye sea coast which reflect ye heat & warming ye atmosphere to a great hight to what ye sea & mountains do, so that ye vapours pass thro without being condensed into drops   doth not most of our rains in hot weather come in thunder gusts from ye mountains & our winter rains from ye sea   sometimes thay come from ye west but I take these to have come from ye sea & turned upon us by ye n.w. wind which mostly blows very hard soon after — wheather is not most of ye powerful motions of fluids in ye universe caried on by ye organised vacuum & plenum attraction & repultion such as for instance ye heart when one ventricle is contracted ye blood is expeled   A vacuum is made & ye venal blood rushes in   ye fire ingean by casting cold water condenses ye steam in ye tube & forms A vacuum & ye Piston comes violently down & ye siphon as ye liquid runs out of ye longer leg forms A vacuum & ye water rushes in at ye other & ye syringe operates by drawing up ye piston & forming A vacuum & ye vegetables by transpiration of ye vapour by thair leaves & twigs causeth ye roots to attract moisture to supply that expence but there is another method by which nature acts very powerfully in ye conveyance of fluides which alltho it is by organised vacuum yet not by direct tubes but by ye proper araingment of numerous vesicles as in sponges & in many parts of animals & vegetables seems espetialy ye fructification, buds & leaves to be A mass of organised vesicles   ye bud is such A surprising organised part of proper araingement as to transmute any common juices of ye same Genus in its one species & metals & minerals is purified & maturated in ye ore & stone much after ye same manner by slow degrees   how forceably doth humidity enter & suck dry wood or ropes ye first so as to split rocks & last to draw up ponderous masses

BP 1:47:2; D. 390–92.
1. Possibly Novaya Zemlya.

To COLLINSON[1]

none knows how to catch them [moles] but laying bare & watching when thay rais ye surface again but few hath time or Patience to watch them & many times thay work A foot deep to hide themselves   thay chiefly work in ye night   all my cedars of lebanon is dead do what I could   ye root perished while ye leaves & stalk looked fresh & green   ye manured pine growed finely untill I travailed to new england but when I came home thay was all perished   I am sory ye time [thyme] leaved Chamerhododendron Languishes   mine grows finely which now I send thee set full of blooming buds   I wish ye Bartsia may flower with you   I sent ye seed as soon as ripe that you might sow it in ye summer it being A bienial as many of our curious flowers is as ye great fringed autumnly gentian ye fine yellow poligala centery Elicrysom   spring fall aster &c   but pray oblige thyself by letting me know whether thee hath that ruellia   ye seed I have often sent without any account of in ye spring success which beareth A fine large blewish flower spotted or streaked with white on ye inside & in ye summer & fall bears ye hermaphrodite flowers which produce good seed as several of other genus of plants doth ye like tho little notice hath been taken of them by botanists

I am glad my Epilobium flowered with thee & ye clethra   thay are fine flowers   I am heartily sorry that I should cause any uneasiness in my good friend   I have wrote formerly to thee that I had received both thy letters by Captain Wall & allso by Captain Garrison by new york   ye last of which gave me full satisfaction   I acknowledge every Letter received & answer it by ye next ship   indeed I am sensible of ye great care thee takes for my benefit & I am as ready to do any thing that I know will gratify thee   in answer to thine Sept ye 20th I have received ye globes in very good order &

delivered ye packet for Mr Smith[2] to Benjamin whose prints came in good order & billy has got them all except ye last letter   so for thine of september ye 20   now to ye 1st letter   ye doctor hath often tould me of ye baked apple & pear which he eat plentilly of at new found land but I never imagined it to be ye fruit of ye yellow root which I think grows not so far north   I am sure it grows to ye sowest [southwest] of us & bears its fruite in perfection four times as big as what ye doctor discribes his baked apple there is two species of ye herb paris discribed by Catesby which likewise produceth A single fruit out of ye center of three leaves but these groweth 2 foot high & ye fruit is large   one of these grows plentifully at ye katts kill & in one I saw it between ye mountains in New England & at ye surprising fall of ye second river   but what ye dr thinks is near if not ye same   with ye baked apple or pear is A more humble plant I showed him which I brought from ye top of ye Catts kill mountains about 3 or 4 inches high with leaves like A cornus placed crossways & horizontal out of ye center of which grows A prety red berry of a pleasant tast   ye root is fibrous & runs horizontaly under ye surface & shoots up at allmost every half foot distance so that there is near an acre allmost covered with it   this is ye onely place I remember ever to have seen it but I shall not at present determine which of these or whether any of them be ye right but as these mountains produce most sorts of plants that grow at new found land or Acadia (or perhaps most northern countreys) in one part or another of them (for thay have never yet been searched far in)   it seems more probable this humble northern plant may be it   I sent thee fair specimens of all these kinds above A dozen years past   I sent Philip Miller A root this fall & if I had knowed that thee wanted it I would have sent thee 3 or 4 tho thay grow nine or ten mile off   most of what ye dr writes for we stil want tho many of them we have had but most is gone off   ye dr as fully believes ye ould womans voyage to bermudas & back again in A night as that thee lives in London   so far in answer to letters received last

BP 1:36:3.
1. Undated, but written late fall 1755 or early 1756, judging by the content. The beginning of this letter is missing.
2. Unidentified.

From COLLINSON[1]

I have the pleasure to Tell my Dear Frd that His Boxes plants came in fine order by Buddens ship   it is really the best way of sending plants only to keep as much of the native mould about the Roots by Tieing them on a Corse Linnen Cloth, or else tieing the mould or Sods to the Roots with Course flax or Hemp thread, being wrap'd over & over would keep all Tite

My son & I were both surprised at the sight of the Great Mud Turtle   it is really a formidable animal   He bit very fierce at a Stick, he had near bit my finger   thy former description is very good excepting His sharp hook at the point of Its Bill, & his shell being very jagged or Notch'd near his tail   it made an uncouth noise, I can't say barking but what a full grown one might do I can't say   it is really a Curiosity & Wee are oblig'd to thee for sending it for Wee had no Notion of such an Animal — for writers in General content themselves by Saying theres Terrapins or Land & Water turtles &c   I wish Billy could gett one this Size and Draw it, in its Natural Dress — but pray Lett the Shell be well Wash'd that the Sutures of the shell may be well expressed, What Eye it has Wee can't say for they Seem'd closed up as if Asleep. All the Species of Turtles Drawn as they come in yr way with some Account of them would prove a New piece of Natural History well worth knowing

the pretty Frogg came safe & well & very Brisk but more of these Inocent Creatures should not be amiss: the other Water Turtle is a pretty species came very Well but pray send no more Mud Turtle   one is Enough   All sorts of Helebores, Ladies Slippers, & lillies & Martagons are all my Favourites — the Evergreen privets & Rhamnus had no Sods to their roots so I doubt if they do well — now dont say they was as I Desired them — for that I never did, for my Self (but for Ld. Northumberland)[2] I looked hard for the Mediola   my Species that thou formerly sent Mee will flower this year — I conclude that pretty plant with Variegated evergreen Leaves is what Thou Calls the sweet rooted Sanicle, it came in very fine order, it was always a favourite of Mine   the Elder had shot 4 or 5 Inches so I find it a forward shrub with you as With Us — I had once the [illegible] with very large flowers — I wish thell send more to Mee as also that the Lilly of the Valley may be that fine sort   it may be Curious, — the Viburnums all look well but I am afraid the Heart shaped one is not amongst them   the Snake Root & Gale aspenifolia   I took every Thing out of the Boxes Myself and planted every one with My own Hands for I never trust the Servants with such Curiositys procur'd with Care & Trouble & I Carefully Search every Lump of Moss, least a small root should escape   They came in a fine Season for the Weather was Mild as aprill   the Robin Red Breasts serenaded Mee as I was planting them *January 20:1755*   Wee have had a Surpriseing Mild Jan no frost but Abundance of Rain & Wind

I have too many Spring Flowers in the garden to Mention their Names, the Species of Oke of which I Inclose a Specimen is now in As fulle Leafe as at Mid Summer   Your tough twig'd Viburnum is quite an Evergreen while I don't see even a plant of the Heart Shap'd Leafe Viburnum   Besides thy Seeds, Alexander had 52 Boxes & these is Consigned to one Stephenson[3] I don't know   Several More Boxes for yr proprietor & other people I don't know, after this Rate England must be turned up side down & America transplanted Heither — prithee with what Sorts does Alexander fill so many Boxes — it must require a Number of hands to make Sufficient Collection for such a Cargo & then again I am as much Surprised how He finds Customers for them   I saw the Ship's Manifesto or List of her Cargo & there is in her 80 odd Boxes of Seeds — a prodigious Quantity Indeed —

Both thy Bills are come to hand and Will be paid   I am pleased to Hear thy Daughter is Like to be disposed of to thy Mind — poor Moses has been tumbling and tossing about the World — Inclosed is his letter from Gibralter   Indeed by what Wee can learn the whole Globe had been shaken terribly in Some Places as I find It has Reached your Continent also which thou takes no Notice off so I presume could not be very remarkable — The Terrible Lott of Lisbon being totally ruin'd & other places too long Even to Touch upon[4] — thou'll See in the Magazines or your public Newspapers I observe there is no Acorns in this years Collection of Seeds which makes a great gap in the Catalogue and will be a considerable Disappointment to most of thy purchasers as your Okes most of them Differ much from Ours & no Balm of Gilead Fir

Billy's Drawing & painting of the Tupelo is fine & is Deservedly admired by Every one   There is a Delightfull natural freedom through the whole, & no minute pticular omitted   the Insects on the Leaves &c   it's a pity he had not kept it, to add the Flowers & to have Disected a Flower showing the Stile & Stamina &c each part distinct by it self after Linnaeus Method which seems to be the prevailing Tast   our Friend Coldens Daughter Has in a Scientificall Manner Sent over Several sheets of plants very Curiously Anatomised after his Method   I believe she is the first Lady that has Attempted any thing of this Nature   they are to be sent to Doc Gronovius & He poor Man I believe is in a bad State of Health for I cannot gett a Line from Him (who used to be very punctual) if He has received Billys fine Drawings of Oaks & thy System — Tho I have writt Several Letters I shall this Day send Another

I shall be Carefull to Look into J. Swinhoe's Box of plants for the fine Water Turtle — thou did well to consign it to Mee because one trouble I never had but one thing — thou has omitted what the Value of his Box of plants is to be

I am really concerned there are no Acorns   I am afraid Wee shall be out done by that Alexander   I must not print thy List this year for that Reason   By the Common Laurel — does thou Mean the small Magnolia — if thou does thou should say so, for the name Magnolia will sell a box of Seeds — if this is wanting Wee shall be undone —

By all means make Billy a Printer   it is a pretty Ingenious Imploy — never lett him reproach thee & say Father if thou had putt Mee to some Business by which I might gett my Bread I should have by my Industry Lived in Life as well as other people   Lett the fault be his, not thine, if he Does nott   So for this time Dear John Farewell

P. Collinson

BP 2:82; D. 201–2.
1. Darlington dated this letter January 20, 1756. The date is no longer legible on the original, but the reference in the letter to planting on January 20, 1755, is very clear. Bartram's reply (May 30, 1756), however, makes evident that this letter was written in 1756 and that Collinson wrote "1755" by mistake.
2. Hugh Percy.
3. Unidentified.

4. A devastating earthquake had occurred at Lisbon on November 1, 1755. It was felt in New Jersey on November 18; that same day Colden's house was badly shaken. Apparently it was not felt in Pennsylvania.

From COLLINSON

Londn Feby 1756

My Dear frd John's Next letter is May 17th which I answered July 8th p Cap Richey — I therein hinted that the Flowering Ash which consists of Clusters or bunches of small reddish Flowers is not a Native & Never bears Seed its more Likely the Norway Mapple may produce Seeds the only great Tree that I know is in Chelsea Physick Garden So P:Miller may Supply thee

The next is that of June 16

It is true, I have been in the Hott bath & Just over the spring it is really as hot as one can bear it but what is that to Some Hott springs in other pts of the world — that the natives boil their Eggs & Dress their victuals with the Hott water it would be exceding my Time & the Extent of this paper to relate the Various opinions about this wonderfull operation so my dear John content thy self this is one of the many things that's concealed from us.

I before hinted my opinion with relation to Billey He is now come to years of understanding & therefore it is time for Him to consider how he Must Live in the world — & give up his Darling amusements in some Degree, that he may Attain a Knowledge in some art, or Business by which He may with Care & Industry, Support himself in Life. — and as printing is an Ingenious Art, Drawing and Engraving may with advantage be applyed to It. I would fain Have thee Embrace our kind Friend B. Franklins obligeing offer — but unless Billey will determine to Settle Close & apply Himself it will never answer the good purpose Intended

In case of a war I approve thy plan of Directing all to Mr Buffon at the Royal Garden Paris and then, underneath direct for Mee then I should have it, one Time or other but our affairs are So Surprisingly Situated, that none knows yet wether it will be War or Peace — Wee continue taking the French ships but they take none of ours So reconcile this peice of French Policy if thou can & foretell its consequences

I have wrote to Phil. Miller for [illegible] from Ships [illegible] Raised Indigo of S carolina I never Knew [it to] seed here tho' it flowers finely Narcis Polyanthos will not Endure your Frosts, tho' they have flowr'd all this Winter which hitherto is the Mildest I have known no frosts or snow but Blustering Rainey Weather

the 19th Jany Hepaticas, [illegible] Crocus, Polyanthos, Anemonies, Hyacinths, [illegible] Helebore, Cyclamens, Acconites & many others in fine flower thou would wonder to see it, Daffodills 4:5 Inches High

The Epilobium never set Seed, so pray send some I thought thine &

our Friend Claytons observations so material on Docr Alstons System that I putt them in the Gentn: Magazine

I believe I before told thee there was a Female Palm Date Tree in the Berlin Garden which annually made Efforts to produce fruit but for want of ye Male Farina none was Mature — but hearing of a Male palm grew at Leipsic, they at Berlin Sent for some of the bunches of Male Blossoms & wrap them up carefully & then shook them over the Female Blossoms The Consequence was Ripe fruit was produced, this Marriage between the Two Trees in consumation arrived to such Effort that I am told young Trees have been raised from the stones. Thee must understand these Date Palms grow in Large Cages & are kept in warm Stoves in winter — but I have Two that Stands well in my Green House without that art.

The Box with Seeds for Swinhoe, Gray &c was received & Sent as Directed

In thine of July 24th

the Medeola that Wee have named so, is not the old Sort in the flora Virginica viz Medeola foliys Lanceolatis fructu Barseto, or Lillium pusyllum floribiis (of Banister)[1] neither that pretty Veratrum thou Mentions which flowers Annually & bears a fine spike of Sweet white flowers with very remarkable shineing Nectarions as it Decays it turns redish — but this that flowers with Mee thou will Soone know by the Leaves which grows round the plant close to the Ground & keeps green all the Winter, from its Center arises the flower Close Headed of a bright red on a stalk 4 or 6 Inches — it now has much sweld its' Center Bud   My Dear John what shall I say to the Great Vale, but admire thy Account of It — & think how happy will those in future times be whose Lott it is to Cultivate so rich & fertile a Tract   My Medeola which thou formerly Sent Mee — I cannot find Described in the Flora Virginica — of which is Inclosed the Leaves

Thy Observations on the removeing your Holley is Just — I wonder from Seed so often sent — that Wee have not Raised yr Holley —

Docr Garden is the Man for the all Spice Tree   it Thrives & flowers wonderfully for Mee — the Docr writt Mee a Long Letter but I was obliged to Cutt it Short

Thy observation on the birches & other Trees is peculiarly thy own, pray how does it agree with the Sentiments of our Great Botanist Phil Miller pray run not the risque of harming thy Little finger for a Paper Birch — but pray mind seed of the great Meadia Acconite & perennial Centory

Phil Miller promised to send more Cones of Cedar of Lebanon — These and all Sorts of pines will come up freely — but are very liable to go off abt June or July — some looking green on Top, while the root is perish'd & gone   We have a never failing Way to prevent It, for is sooner than July Wee pceive, but one to go off, or to be certain (*if none goes off*) Wee prepare a fresh Bed of proper Soil & then Draw the young plants out of the seed bed, & plant them in the new bed, watering them as soon as planted, then Turn Some Hoops or Twigs over the bed & Cover with a Matt or Coarse Cloth to shade them from the Sun in the Daytime but open at Nights to receive the Dews & Rains — Treat'em in this Manner for a Week   by that time they will Loose their Tap & make Colateral Roots & then Expose them to the sun by Degrees — Thou will find they will thrive finely & make a fresh Shoot before this   Wee rarely Loose one plant in a Hundred, by this means being planted a foot asunder & their makeing Side Roots, they may be transplanted safely in 2 or 3 years Time — whereas if the Tap root remains so Long in the Seed bed, — they can be rarely removed with Safety & it is the same in pines

no one Doubts but that the Marble of Tadmor was hewn out of the Neighboring Mountains, but thy Notion of its formation by a Mixture of Slime or mud with what thee calls Nitrous or Marine salts Enters not into my Comprehension, So thou hath it all to thy Self

but I am thy frd,
P. Collinson

BP 2:92; D. 203–4.
1. The Reverend John Banister (1650–1692) collected Virginia plants from 1678 to 1692. His plant catalogue was published in John Ray's *Historia Plantarum,* 3 vols. (London: Royal Society, 1686–1704).

From MILLER

Chelsea, Feb. 2, 1756

Dear Mr. Bartram: –

I have been favoured with your three kind letters and the two boxes of plants which you was so good as to send me for which I return you my thanks. to the first of your letters I returned an answer in September last but for fear it may miscarry I beg leave to repeat the substance of that here. I am sorry so many years have passed without our having had an intercourse by letters as I am sensible how many observations I have lost which must have fallen in your way to have made. As I seek after truth so I shall always be glad to receive any information from my friends, even if they should contradict what I may have published, yet I shall never think it derogatory to my character to own my mistakes, and rectify them for in large works consisting [illegible] Dictionary it's not possible to avoid mistakes, and opportunity enlarging and correcting the character of the Ice Plant to grow as to [illegible] will assist in more additions as also the [illegible] in your letters which shall not be passed over and whatever communication you shall be so good as send me either of your desires for plants shall be [illegible]

I have not seen what Dr. Linnaeus has published from Kalm's observations which he had mentioned in his Species of Plants, where he has added many new names to them, and inserted some which may probably be new.

Kalm has published two volumes of his observations, in the Swedish language; but as I do not understand it, so I have not been curious enough to send for the book, nor do I hear any good character of it from [others?]

I sent you four numbers of my Figures of Plants, some time since, by our friend Mr. Collinson: and should have now sent you the others which are published, had I not waited for some which will be better coloured; for the persons employed to have the care of this work, have not done me justice, so I have been obliged to take it out of their hands

I have also sent you a few plants of some of our best sorts of Roses, which I wish may prove such as you have not already; for, as I am unacquainted with what has been sent you from England, so I am at a loss to guess what I should send; but this, I hope, you will soon set me right about. So I shall add no more, at present, but to assure you I am your sincere friend and servant,

Philip Miller

BP 4:79; D. 378–79.

From COLLINSON

Feby 18 1756

My First Letter to my Worthy Frd was of January 20th which was a Sort of general Letter writt in hast to send by first oppertunity — Now I come to consider thine in Course — & I shall begin with thy Favour of March 6th

In none of thine since is any Notice taken of what success was had with the Stone Pine or Pinaster   I intend to send more this year least that should Fail as I have said before our severest Cold does not Hurt them

I commend putt'g off thy Expedition to the Western Provinces   Joseph Lees is a prateing Fellow — He may Thank an accident & not Mee, for the sale of his Seeds. We think our Weather very inconstant but yrs is much more so. — the Carelessness & Inexactness of Martins [*Martin's Magazine*] is a material reason to have nothing to do with them — If I don't forget I will Enclose some of the Heleborus with a red tinted flower   I doubt but it is the same Billy has painted with the Spotted Turtle.

I am of this Mind, the Heat of Bath Water is out of the Heat of our Long Season

I am well pleas'd to Hear that Billey will undertake the Turtles and of the Lizards & other Lesser animals. I hope the paper for Drawing that I sent wound up in Mitchells Map[1] is Deliver'd to Him.

Thy Soliloquy is very Pathetic, no part of God's Works but raise Rapturous Ideas in a Well Disposed Mind.

I have many great asters   pray send Mee a small Specimen of that thou Extols —

I dont know what to conclude about the 5 Boxes that thou mentions Docr Mitchel had writt to thee about in B:F Letters – in thy Letter to Mee of Aprill 29th Last — wether they are sent or not — for not the least Notice is taken any Further about them — or any of thy Letters since.

The Lillie of the Valley of the Katskill Mont. is a very tempting plant — but by no means run another Risque

Hast Thee observed at what time a year ye Deer Like to repair to the Licking places — may it not be a Means to Excite Venery — no doubt but it conduces to some spectacular Ends In Nature or Else there would not be such an Instinct in this Tribe of Creatures, as well in Europe as with you

It is said how true I don't know that your vast Flocks of Pigeons once a year, return from ye Inland parts to Regale themselves on the Sea Shore this I know that our Pigeons are great Lovers of Salts — for our Columbarians make Salt Cakes to Engage them to stay at Home

Since the Striped Bark Mapple will afford us none of its Seeds I wish Thou would gently bend down thy 10 foot Tree & Layer it on the Ground to Strike Root since it is Like to bear no seed — I have served my fine Large Silver Leafed Mapple So with great Success I have a fine sort of Mapple thou formerly Sent Mee — I can't find by Billey's Drawings which it is I shall He[re] Enclose a Leafe it comes nearest our Norway Mapple

pray remember Seeds of the Basti & Christophoriana beans

My Dear John Sayes truely His Hypothesis is Composed of Broken Links for I cannot unite Them but yett there is many Ingenious Conjectures but as Suppositions are Endless & Wee are still in the Dark relateing to the Many wonderful Phenomena In Nature — the Great Author of our Being has Sett Bounds to our reasoning Faculty that Wee may be sensible of our Imperfections — yett has permitted us Mental Excursions & those the best conceived & to us, most probable — may be nearest the Mark This answers thine Aprill 27 — I thank Billey for his Letter, am pleased to see that He Imp. In his writeing & spelling — I admire at what He Sayes about the Drawing paper which was both Great & Small fine Paper rowl'd within side the Map with other Drawings if I remember right — and as the Case of the Mapp was consigned to our Friend Ben Franklin I did not in the Least Doubt the Delivery of the paper &c which I think was Directed — but this I am Sure of that I wrote our Friend Franklin, the paper was for Billey I Intended it for the Drawing of the tortoises, there was a pretty Quantity

I am greatly obliged for the Last Box of Seeds thee sent in pticular the Galega which Wee never could Raise tho Wee have had Seed so often so pray send 2 or 3 roots More next year — but my Dear John how canst thou Imagine I could remember a Specimen sent so many years agon – but Billy's fine painting has give Mee a Complete Idea of its Beauty & that fine Red Helleborine which I have long wanted the Female Cornus is Exquisitely done it resembles ours & yett there is a Difference I am very sensible of the great pains Billey has taken about the Turtles — I can't reward him Equall to his Merrit I send him a Small Token & some fine Drawing paper all in the Lib:Com's Box to B:Franklin, with sundry pcells for thee — the Marsh Hawk is admirable I dont see that either Edwards[2] or Ehret[3] can much excell it — but I wish He would paint the Pond Turtle over again, it is the Most Indifferently performed, the Shell is made almost white whereas it is Black but then, Again I must do Him Justice nothing can be finer

Executed then the Horned Turtle   Such Ingenuity brings Truth to Light time won't permit what I could Say on this Strange Creature, what can be the use of its horn   To strike its prey — I have another request to Billey – that is to Draw the wrong side of the Spotted Turtle he has sent with fine Red Helleborine — So paint all the belly-side of all the Turtles for there is always something remarkable There   Thou art my Dear John Extreamly obliging in thy kind offer about the Evergreen Shrub   I should like it much — I send the seed of a Great Leaved Evergreen Sort   I wish thou may have so Warm a Season makes almost all thy plants sent this year to Bud — an Evergreen Andromeda sent 2 years agon is finely in flower tho I have one with a Broad Leafe that Flowers Latter — I hope this Last is the Red flowering Shrub Honeysckle   I have the white   it buds finely & the pretty Fine Leaved Chamaerodn is just in flower   all the plants came admirably

But as I hope Billey will go into the printing Business I Desire He will apply himself Diligently & not think on Mee or his Favourite amusement —

But yesterday I had a Letter from Docr Gronovius   He Admires much the Drawings of the Oakes but He can gett nobody to Engrave & print them so will Return them to Mee   Our Friend Ehret will do them he Tells Mee but I can't say when   those original Drawings of plants was our Ingenious Friend Catesbys

I am my Dear Friend thine in great Sincerity

P Collinson

Lord Kildares[4] Box Came Safe

BP 2:93; D. 204–5.
1. John Mitchell's *Map of the British and French Settlements in North America* (London, 1755).
2. George Edwards.
3. Georg Dionysius Ehret.
4. James Fitzgerald, Lord Kildare, of Ireland.

From MILLER

Chelsea, Feb. 18, 1756

Dear Mr. Bartram: —

I have just now been favoured with your kind letter, dated the ninth of December; and although I wrote a long letter to you a few days past, yet I take this opportunity to acknowledge the receipt of yours, especially as I made a mistake in my last, in the name of the ship by which I have sent you some seeds, with a basket of Roses and Cedar cones. This mistake was occasioned by my waterman, who carried the things to the ship; but the enclosed note will set that right.

I am glad you like my Figures. I hope to send you some much better done, having changed my engraver.

You mention that you want the Norway Maple. Had I known this sooner, you should have been supplied; for we have a large tree in our garden, which produces plenty of seeds, and young plants come up in all the borders near it. The cuttings will also grow, like willows. If another ship departs from hence, soon, I will send you plants of it.

As you desire to know my wants, that you may supply them, so I must desire you will acquaint me with what things you want from hence, that I may make you some returns; and although in my other letter I pretty fully told what would be acceptable yet have I here sent you a list of some things taken out of the *Flora Virginica,* which book I suppose you have, so will soon know what I mean by the names. Some of these you was so good as to send me, in the last box; but as they were in a bad condition, so I can't tell, yet, which of them are alive, as they had no titles to them.

I shall take every opportunity to write to you, and shall always be glad to hear from you, being your obliged friend and servant,

Philip Miller

BP 4:80; D. 379.

To COLLINSON

February ye 21 1756

Dear Peter

we are now in A grievous distressed condition   ye barbarous inhuman ungratefull natives weekly murdering our back inhabitants & those few Indians that profess some friendship to us are mostly watching for an opertunity to ruin us & we that is near ye city is under apprehentions too from ye neutral french which is sent amongst us full of resentment & revenge alltho thay yet appear tolerably civil when we feed them with ye best we can afford   thay are very fond of thair brethren ye Irish & dutch romans which is very numerous amongst us many of which openly declare thair wishes that ye french & indians would destroy us all & others of them privately rejoice at our calamities   0 deplorable condition that we suspect our friend of treachery while he is willing to assist us & cant discover our enemy till it is too late   by what we can understand by ye reports of our back inhabitants most of ye indians which are so cruel are such as was allmost dayly familiars at thair houses   eat drank cursed & swore together   were even intimate play mates & now without any provokation destroyeth all before them with fire ball & tomahawk   thay commonly now shoot with rifles with which thay will at A great distance from behind A tree fence ditch or rock or under ye covert of leaves take such sure aim as seldom miseth thair mark   if thay attack A house that is prety well maned thay creep behind some fence or hedge or tree & shoot red hot slugs or punk into ye roof & fire ye house over thair heads & if thay run out thay are sure to be shot at & most or all of them killed   if thay come to A house where ye most of ye family is women & children thay break into it   kills them all plunder ye house & burn it with ye dead in it or if any escape out thay pursueth & kills them   if ye cattle is in ye stable thay fire it & burn ye cattle   if thay are out thay are shot & ye barn burnt   If our captains pursue them if in ye level woods thay skip from tree to tree like monkies if in ye mountains like wild goats thay leap from rock to rock or hide themselves & attack us in flank & rear, when, but ye minute before, we pursued thair track & thought thay were all before us   thay are like ye angle of death   give us ye mortal stroak when we think our selves secure from danger   O: Pensilvania thou that was ye most florishing & peaceable province in North America is now scourged by ye most barbarous creatures in ye universe   all ages sex & stations hath no mercy extended to them ye young man with vigor & activity perhaps with hasty steps heart filled with raptures of love is going to visit his intended   is unexpectedly pierced by A silent ball shot by A distant secreted enemy   his active arms is unbraced   his vigorous sinews is relaxed   his body rouled in blood & exposed to ye fouls of ye air   our tender Infants hath thair brains dashed out   our wives big with child hath thair bellies ript open   Those killed within thair houses is mostly burned with them   ye beautifull & modest virgin obtains no more mercy then indeed a decripet   if thay fly into ye woods or hideth in ye hedges ye murderers then find them plunges thair hatchets either into thair breast or skull   when thay are exposed to ye inclemency of ye weather day & night thair once proud Cheeks & lips now stained with dust & blood & thair bosom filled with clotted gore until by chance thay are found by Companions who comits them to A private grave without winding sheet or Coffin & surrounding grieving relations.

We have had A fine moderate winter hitherto   ye first of February my crocus was out & ye aconite A week before   ye red flowered & silver leaved maple   ye hazel filbert & alder   much about ye same time ye double snow drop   claytonia & paronychis hath been out about two weeks   ye seeds of mustard arrock & lettice is come up but now I suppose thay will be nipped last night A snow fell 10 inches deep & now ye west wind blows very cold but perhaps it may not hold in that quarter too long   ye most prevailing winds this winter hath been S or SW   ye day be fine yesterday very early   it blowed A very strong NW wind   toward night it turned to ye North & frese   yesterday wind NE but very mild   did not frees much great part of January & February was so mild that working people striped to thair shirts

BP 1:44:8; D. 205–7.

To ELIOT

March ye 14th 1756

dear friend Eliot
I have, since I left thy home been very much hurried in traveling & sending my curiosities to Europe   after which I married my daughter to A worthy

young man whose house is in sight of mine & about half an hours walk. Since which our friend Benjamin Franklin hath been A great while in ye back parts of our countrey building forts   since his return home, is so much ingaged in publick Business that we had no convenient opertunity of sending A letter until now but I assure thee I have not forgot thee nor ye agreeable hours I spent with thee   I have often thought that your salt marsh mud may be so ordered as to be of extraordinary benefit to your countrey & you have enough of it   suppose you were to dig A large quantity of it & haul it to shore as you may easily do in ye winter when ye ground is froze   our ditchers chuses to do it in winter   thay are not so subject to catch cold and thay have strong tight boots   thay dig ditches 12 or 14 foot wide & four foot deep to drain our marshes & we commonly dig pits 8 foot deep to mend them or to haul ye mud on our fast land to inrich it which will last near 20 years   you should put A layer of mud half a foot or more thick   then such a quantity of common mould then A layer of mud super stratum until your bed is 4 foot thick   let it lie & ferment A year, then cut down to ye bottom & toss it all together unto another bed & let it remain half A year longer or more   then spread it on your ground   I have had an account from Sicille that thay manure thair wheat ground there with salt mixed after this manner with mould but it is observed that ye salt fetched from one place doth not agree with all sorts of soil on the island but thay adapt ye salts made in different parts to ye different soils   perhaps if required I may give thee A more particular account but our travellers into different parts of ye world are very deficient in relating ye true methods of agriculture which ye inhabitants practise in thair respective countries   thay think if thay relate thair observations of ye old ruins   ye extravagant diversions of ye people   thair government & superstition   then thay think thay have done much although it is little more than what many of ye former travellers have done before them

BP 1:44:1; D. 373–74.

To GARDEN[1]

March ye 14th 1756

Respected Friend Doctor Garden
I have just received thy very kind letter of February ye 13 1756 but alas very short   I am glad that ye bulbous roots flourish with thee   I send thee A fine variety of Tulip roots but thay all come too late though sent by ye first opertunity   I long to see thy Journal to & from Saluda[2]   pray what is your Palmetto Royal   Is ye fruit wholesom to eat   Is it A tree or shrub   How soon doth it bear from seed   I am glad thee art so well settled in business & I hope art possessed of A sweet dear agreeable consort   This winter I have married my daughter Mary to A very worthy rich young man who lives in sight & about half an hour's walk distant from my house   I am much

obliged to thee for thy kindness to my son William   He longs to be with thee but it is more for ye sake of Botany then Physic or Surgery neither of which he seems to have any delight in   I have several books of both but can't persuade him to read A page of either   Botany & drawing are his delight but I'm afraid won't get him his living   I have some thoughts of putting him to A merchant   I have wrote several times last fall to Peter Collinson about him & expect an answer by ye first ships who wrote to me last fall thee had sent him A very Cyvil letter which he had answered

I have often thought of proposing A scheme which I am apt to believe would be of general benefit to most of our colonies if put in practice & as a perticular curious friend I first acquaint thee with it   & perhaps I may mention it to my friend Peter Collinson   It is to bore ye ground to great depths in all ye different soils in ye several provinces with an instrument fit for ye purpose about four inches diamater; ye benefit which I shall propose from these trials is to search for marls or rich earths to manure ye surface of ye poor ground with it   2dly to search for all kinds of medicinal earth sulphers bitumens coal peat salts vitriols marcasites fosills as well as minerals   3dly to find ye various kinds of springs to know whether thay are potable or medicinal or mechanical   Now to bring this into practice suppose there was appointed in every province A curious judicious honest careful man as overseer that he should choose such men as understood boring in rocks & earth & furnish them with proper instruments   that he or any whom that he may depute under him shall take perticular care to write down in A book for that purpose ye time & place   when & where thay began to bore & ye perticular depth of every strata thay bore through examining curiously ye contents of ye bit every time ye augure is drawn out & ye depth from whence it was drawn   Minit it down so that thay may know ye exact depth whether it be marl chalk coal salt or any other mineral or ye springs of water & how deep thay are from ye surface so that every proprietor may know what riches is in his possession & may guess what expense he must bear to come at ye benefit of them   I am persuaded that most sandy desert soil hath under it A large bed of marl or saline earth which if brought on ye sandy surface would make ye surface fruitful & most countrys far from ye sea have vast beds of rock salt at uncertain depths which if thay was discovered would be of great advantage to ye inhabitant   Moreover how exceeding usefull & satisfactory will it be to curious Philosophical inquirers to know ye various terrestial composition that we daily walk over   By this method we may compose A curious subterranean map.[3]

There was A vessel sent lately from Philadelphia to ye Azores or western islands but could not find any of them & after sailing about A week in ye latitude & longitude thay used to find them she returned without finding them   Ye Captain as I am informed supposeth that thay are sunk   if it will be so it will coroborate my former opinion that thay was ye remaining mountainous ruins of ye antient Atlantis that ye egyptian priests tould Solon of that was sunk by earthquakes or washed away by them

I want much to come to Carolina to observe ye curiosities toward ye mountains but ye mischievous Indians is so treacherous that it is not safe trusting them even in thair greatest pretence of friendship thay have destroyed all our back inhabitants No travelling now to Dr Colden's nor ye back parts of Pennsylvania Maryland nor Virginia Pray how far do you commonly reckon it from Charleston to ye Cherokee Mountains I should be glad to search them if it could be done safely but must wait till these troublesome times is over You have growing with you A prety sort of A red flower ye tap root of which is A soverain cure for worms as I am informed Pray send it me I want it much Have you ye right Sene growing plentifully Thee promised me some seed I believe I can make most of your perenial plants live over our winters by covering them over with straw but some of your shrubs & trees will not I suppose thay are such that naturally grow to ye southward of you & though thay seem to grow A seed with you yet can't bear much cold.

D. 392–94; BP 1:44.
1. The first part of the original letter is essentially illegible, so it has been taken from Darlington.
2. Alexander Garden had accompanied Governor James Glen of South Carolina to Saluda Old Town in the Cherokee Indian territory. Garden hoped that his journal would be presented to the Royal Society.
3. Some of Bartram's speculations were investigated in the Mohole Project, the National Science Foundation's 1960s study of the earth's crust.

To COLLINSON

may ye 30th 1756

Dear Peter

I have received thy kind letters of January ye 20th & february ye 28th by Mesnard & since some seeds brought & two books of natural history all which is very acceptable I am well pleased with thy choice of ye magaseens I expected greater matters of philosophy & new discovery in natural history, in Martins then I found Billy is much obliged to thee for his drawing paper he hath drawn many rare birds in order to send to thee & dryed ye birds to send to his friend edwards to whome he is much obliged for those two curious bookes he spent his time this spring in shooting & drawing ye rare birds of quick pasage which stayed with us but a few days to rest & fill thair bellies on thair flight northward where they breed as he observed by ye hens haveing immature eggs in thair bellies which thair quick passage thro our countrey before rendered them unobserved we propose to send them by Captain Mesnard by whom we intend to write largely Last night I was with our friend Benjamin & desired his farther advice about Billy & reasoned with him about ye difficulty of falling into good business & that as he well observed he was ye only printer that did ever make A good livelyhood by it in this place though many had set up both before & since he did & that was by his extraordinary & superior abilities & close application & merchandizing was very precarious & extream difficult to make remittances to europe: he sate & paused A while   then said that there was A profitable business which he thought was now upon ye increase; that there was A very ingenious man in town who had more business than he could well manage himself & that was engraving & which he thought would suit billy well   thine of January ye 20th   I am glad ye box of plants & turtles came in good order   ye evergreen rhamnus & privet could not be sent in sods   ye first grows in course sand which in diging falls clean from ye roots & ye latter runs several feet under ye surface of ye earth   we had A small shock of an earthquake   it awakened me but many was not sensible of it   I did not send many acrons because several of my correspondents wrote to me that thay was common & did not want them   else thay was ye easiest article I could send & ye magnolia thay said seldom comes up so not worth sending   ye box of shrubs to Swinhoe I left it to him to allow me what he pleased for them   I have not yet this year had A line from him or williamson   by ye common Laurel I mean what you sometimes [call] ivy   ye stone pine & pinaster perished while I traveled to yr northward   I have nurst them up finely until then   ye Cedar of Lebanon came up well but ye roots rotted in ye ground while ye top was green   I have had no further order from dr Mitchel   Billy is much obliged to thee for ye drawing paper & landskips   ye specimen of maple is our true sugar maple   ye great long leaved birch is ye black sweet or sugar birch   ye other with A spotted stalk is ye poplar leaved birch   ye oak seems to be A kind of water oak

BP 1:44; D. 207–8.

From COLLINSON

Londn June 8 1756

I am obliged to my kind Friend for his Letter of the 21st of February   Wee here are greatly Effected at the Ravages and cruelties Exercised by your ungratefull perfidious Indians   Wee hope proper measures will be taken to prevent their Depredations for the future — Inclosed Thou will find a Bill of pcells & Loading for the Goods Thou Desired — As I am no judge of these things I ordered them from a pson of Repute   I paid Him ready Money & Said everything I could to Induce Him to use thee Well — So I hope they will be found to Content — if not — I will try others if any more is wanted — I am pleased to hear that thy Son Isaac has So good a prospect[1] —

Why may not a Murrain fall upon Dogs as well as amongst our Bulls & Cows — which has now been many years in Several parts of this Nation   at first the Distemper made great Havoc but it grows Less & Less — & we hope is now gone off —

Great & many are the Calamities of War & the Expences that attend It It is new to you   the yoke Setts very uneasie, but we have felt it in Every Sence — Wee all wish for peace   the ways of Providence are unsearchable; it may be nearer than we imagine   I am concerned that I hear nothing From Moses — Since the Letter from Him that I sent thee   How does my friend Billey go on — I shall be glad to Hear that he is with our Friend Franklin —

Our Frd Colden has writt me how He was obliged to Leave his habitation — I truly sympathize with Him under such severe Calamities   Oh the Delight of Peace, when every man can Sitt under his own Vine & Fig Tree & none make him afraid — He has sent Mee the Curious Stone Thou Mentions that is Impressed with a species of Bivalve shells that I don't remember to have seen   About a week agon I dined with your New Governor[2]   If I may Judge by his countenance He seems a Mild Moderate Man — He Assur'd Mee He went over Determined if possible to heal all Differences, I heartily wish he may be so happy.

Our Last Winter was very Mild — the Acconites was in Flower about the Middle of December, Many of your American Deciduous Trees never Lost their Leaves

I have your fine yellow Calceolus Maria in full Beauty & the Saracena —but I wait with Impatience to See the Appearance of the Calceolus maria sent with the last Plants   with the first Rains for Wee have had for about 3 Weeks Drying Easterly Winds & Hott Sun & no Rain — so that Vegitation Stood Still — Thou must needs Think my Dear frd what great pleasure I have every Time I go into the Country to go & See what new thing appears —

I wish if without much trouble thou could procure for Mee Half a Dozn plants of the small Magnolia or Sweet Flowering Bay or Swamp Laurel — I wish they could be plants of about 2 foot high with sods to them — I saw some most Delightful fine young plants of that size sent by J. Alexander & if a young papaw or Two of that size, I Should Like it Well & a Sod or Two of thy Dittany & Snake Root but if these things must be Sought for where skulking Indians molest never think more on them —

Send Mee Tenn 5 Guinea Boxes of Seeds & one 5 Guinea box of Scarlet Oake Acorns & some pine Cones

I have many of thy Letters lays behind wch I shall take notice of at my Leisure So for this Time, my Dear John, Farewell.

P. Collinson

The Governor will want Seeds &c to send Home   I have recommended Him to thee for them —

As thou art an admirer of Docr Hills performance I persuade myself his History of Plants will not be unacceptable to thee & to do Him Justice I think Hee has handled the Subject skillfully & Treated our Frd Linnaeus Decently — as Ingenious men should always do another when they differ in Judgment   There are only 18 numbers yett published   these are sent with

Doc Russels[3] History of Aleppo, for the Lib Company — they are all putt in the box of Druggs So I hope will Come Safe
   pray send Some Red Cardinal Seed to Gordon

BP 2:94; D. 208–9.
1. Isaac Bartram had served an apprenticeship to an apothecary. In 1756, he went into partnership with Thomas Say.
2. William Denny (d. 1765), governor of Pennsylvania from 1756 to 1759.
3. Alexander Russell.

To COLLINSON

                                                                          June ye 12 1756

dear peter
I wrote lately & answered thy letters & presents & sent it by Samuel Fothergill[1] by ye way of ireland & now since by Reeves I have received thine of february 10th & April 3d   thee mentions ye bath water being warm & severall springs in other parts of ye world being exceeding hot of which we have frequent accounts but to render ye Phenomon more surprising & ye works of eternal wisdom more wonderfull there is as I have read A very cold spring within A few yards of ye hot one   nay even in Iceland near ye base of Mount Hecla there is A very hot spring & A cold one near one another: what different Sources these rises from or what alteration thay undergo in thair passage to ye surface God Almighty knows   I cant imagine how or after what manner or with what James alexander fills so many boxes but this I know he frequents ye market & discourses with all ye people   he can get any intelligence of where any trees grow that he wants & offers them money for any quantity thay can gather of ye seeds if thay will bring them to town so that when I go to gather seeds where I used to find them ye people near where thay grow will not lett me have them but tell me thay will gather them all to send to London   phaps where he gets so much bog moss to pack up his trees with unless he fetcheth it from Jersey   I know not nor what variety he puts in his boxes   we always speak friendly together & visit one another but do not communicate ye affairs of our correspondents
   my dear worthy friend thee cant bang me out of ye notion that limestone & marble was originally mud impregnated by A marine salt which I take to be ye original of all our terrestrial soils   I think I have now ye barba Jovis growing from my friend Garden   if I had ye narcis Polyanthos I would try to protect it from frost   I should be glad of A variety of your kinds of Cyclomens anemonies & ranunculus   what A lovely temperate winter you have but Our No & N W winds the begining of June   ye first part of ye day so hot as to work without A Jacket   ye wind at S W but ye wind taking about at north so cold as to wear 2 or 3 coats on & next morning frose & killed ye beans & cucumbers   thy account is very good concerning ye date tree   Miller never gave me any perticular account how he liked my method of describing trees   I am now finely furnished with ye seeds of evergreen

trees from thee gordon & miller   thy account is excelent & advices very natural & good about ye transplanting of ye pines & cedar   we received all those humorous & other prints last fall thee mentions & gratefuly acknowledged them in general & this spring we have received ye fossils seeds prints & two books natural history & Edwards for all of which we are very thankfull   I love natural history dearly   I shall endeavour to send those articles which gordon desires   I wish he would send me next fall A few of your very best earliest pease which I am very fond of   I am very sorry thee had so much trouble with ye Box that had no list with it   I thought I had certainly put A list in every one   My billy hath sent in A band Box directed to thee & to ye care of neeve who promised to put it in his chest & be very carefull of it   several drawings of rare birds of passage for thee & some of ye Birds & A letter he sent to edwards & A letter & A drawing of ye flower of my evergreen veratrum for miller which pray send to Him

BP 1:45; D. 209–10.
1. Samuel Fothergill (1715–1772), brother of John Fothergill; gifted Quaker preacher who visited in North America from 1754 to 1756.

From COLLINSON

Londn July 20:1756

Dear John

I have been Just perusing Docr Douglass Summary — pray tell Mee what are those Pines He calls American Pitch Pine, with Leaves about 3 Inches long with a prominent Longitudinal Rib instead of a Sulcus   In New England there is another distinct Pitch Pine Called the yellow Pine   if these are peculiar to this Country, phaps our Frd Elliot or Some of his Frds may Inform us   He was mightily pleased with thy Visit —

This Day I received thy Letter of 30 May   It gives Mee pleasure to Hear my old Friend is well   I hope He will not Expose himself to Indian Cruelties & yett I want a Doz Boxes of Seeds   Thou should always remember those that give orders for no Oaks should have none but as these Boxes are for new Beginners those never had their Orders from Mee   They should never be without all the Variety thou Can — I am glad the Trifles came Safe & that Billey has a Business offer that may Suit his Genius — By all means don't Delay it for I think Engraving a Curious Art & if he succeeds In it, will not Want Encouragemt. Wee want one very much Here Skillfull in Engraving Birds plants &c — Edwards has in a manner left off   We have Engravers enough — I may Call them Scratchers but a fine Hand is much wanted — See Ellis Book of Corallines[1] at the *Lib:Com*. it was with great dificulty & a Long time, to Do it as well as it is, which is reckon'd well done in Comparison with Others —

I have sent Millers Letter   I have 2 plants of the Ever Green Privet that grows finely   the Rhamnus Gordon has raised so shall have it from Him be sure Send Seeds or Cones of Small Magnolia in all Boxes — have seen them come up thick as Grass & people are fond of the Names as well as the plant

pray good John look out for Mee & send Mee Some plants   a Dozen at least for removing my Garden   mine kept Dwindling — till now they are come almost to nothing   Send them with Sodds if thee can but Send Some — I saw at Scotts Garden, the finest Jersey Trees about 2 foot high sent by Alexander that flowered the first year

I wish thou would Send a Large Case of only these Small Magnolias or Swamp Sweet flowering Bay to Gordon — I will take care thou shall be paid to thy Satisfaction   well pack'd in Moss — but send mine by themselves —in the Gardens of some of my Friends they thrive & flower Delightfully this year the Great Chaemerhododendron flowered for the first Time   it is a Charming plant & the 4 Leaved Bignonia runs up against my Green House in full flower   a fine thing   I think this does not grow with you but in Virginia

I had a Martagon from Siberia flowered this year a very Singular Colour'd flower approaching the nearest to Black of any flower I know — I have 4 different Species of Hurtle Berries flower'd this year, that with broad Leaves & Long white Tubular flowers is now in prime   a fine plant Raised by Gordon from thy seed   I have lost Claytonia   I had it with a Redish flower   Send a Root and he has a many fine plants raised from thy Seed of the Great Chaemerhododendron so thou sees Some Body can Raise them

The Mediola thou Sent Mee Last Cargo flower'd prettyly   it is Singular & very Different from what thou sent before   in the Sod with it came up an Heleborine of so Singular Structure I cant Describe it — Ehret came to paint but came a Week to Late & was ready to beat himself by seeing what remained of the flower, these Singular Bogg or Swamp plants rarely flowers 2d Time — it is a many odd plants comes up out of the Sodds   now me thinks I hear thee say Oh my Dear Peters minds much alter'd   it was Ld Northumberlands mind *was mistaken* by Dear John for Mine   I always Loved Sodds for the sake of accidental plants Ferns &c comes in them

I hope thou has mine by Capt Rench June 5 In which I took some Notice of Thine of feby 21 & Aprill 25th   By Him I sent thee Druggs &c the value of

```
                26:0:0
pd. insurance    3:2:2
                29:2:2
```

My Dr Jno Dogs are quite out of my Way But if Moses comes thou may happen to have one but to send by Strangers is to no purpose

I have a great opinion of your New Governor   He assured Mee he went over with a Heart full of Good Will & that He would Spare no pains to reconcile all pties & hoped our Friends would decline a majority for the present in the next assembly, & Choose Moderate Churchmen & then He doubted not but to putt the province in such a Posture of Defence as to be able to repel your Enemies

and John Hunt and Christopher Wilson are sailed from Bristol as Deputies from the Society who come over in a Spirit of Brotherly Love with out fee or reward to restore it amongst you — Wee Rely on good Providence to operate with them in the Restoring Love & unity

I am thy Sincere frd

P Collinson

I am vastly Concerned at the Coppy here Inclosed of what Williamson writes because I know Him to be a Man of Honour & would not complain without a Cause — & used to have the highest opinion of thy Integrity — Some reparation must be made for I cannot bear my Frd John should be under such a reflection & besides will do Him Infinite prejudice & throw all the Seed Business into Alexanders Hands who sent over last year 52 Boxes for I saw the Ships Manifesto consigned to one Stephenson   So my Dear John wipe off this Slurr whatever thee Does — I am glad to find Moses after so many Perils Safe with thee   I shall be pleas'd to see Him Here remember Mee to Billy   Wee are obliged to Him for his Indefatigable application to furnish us with New & Rare things — but I advise to leave all his Darling Delights to Quallifie Himself to live in the World

BP 2:95; D. 210–11.
1. John Ellis.

To MILLER

November ye 3 1756

Respected friend Miller

ye last letter I received from thee was date February ye 25 1755 which I have answered & now haveing an opertunity to write but no answer from thee I will send thee some of my observations on forrest trees tho its likely others have done it allready but I have not yet seen any such observations on ye female parts which is distinct on diferent branches on ye same tree from ye male parts   ye first I took notice of was ye black spruice fir ye black larix & ye bald Cypress of Carolina all which hath for several years produced ye female cones to appearance as large & plump as ye most fruitfull with ye appearance of ye seed between each squama but no kernel in them   ye black spruice hath for two years produced ye male cones & good seed   ye black larix did produce male cones & good seed one year but hath since perished by an extream dry summer   I have some younger ones that this summer bore several female cones fruiteless by reason that there was no male parts   in ye spring my cypres tre hath many large balls but no good seed in them   it hath not yet produced any male Catkins   what it will do this fall I cant say   I have A young tree of ye paper birch 4 year ould from seed which this spring set 7 cones which this fall appears to be as large & plump as any I ever saw but ye seed is chaffy & destitute of kernals but this fall there is Abundance of male Catkins set so may hope for good seed next year   my scotch pine of 3 years ould produced last spring several little cones (a specimen of which I sent thee last summer) which fell off ye later end of summer I suppose for want of being empregnated in ye spring whether any male katkins will be produced next spring I cant say   most of our Viburnums rather improves by being transplanted in a garden but ye fine one with heart shaped leaves from ye top of ye Catskill mountains & ye dwarf one terminating ye summer shoot with a bud growing on ye dry vale at thair [foot]   these two Viburnums with all my art I can but just raise 2 summer oposite buds & in one ye succeeding spring leaves formed in ye fall & ye other A pointed bud set for A shoot next spring   my chamacerasus & ye 2 leaved pine with long slender leaves & ye mountain red spruice fir ye balm of gilead fir & 3 young striped maples brought from ye top of those mountains doth prety well   I have 3 or 4 inch shoots of most of them this summer & good buds set this fall but I have from those mountains an odd kind of A woody shrub growing about 5 or 6 foot high & regular   it seems by its common appearance & smell to be A species of ye toxicodendron tripliton but it sends forth A many katkins in ye fall which in ye spring produceth numbers of yellow flowers but no seed   I am much pleased with my silver leaved alder from ye mountains   ye midle nerve with its pedicale & most of ye laterals is of A fine scarlet color [illegible] which is A fine silver color [illegible] shot out four stems of which one is grown 2 foot long & has vigorous buds for next springs shoots   last year I found growing in an ould drained beavour pond near Connecticut river in new england A fine dwarf Crategus about 2 foot high exceeding full of large sweet very Jucy black fruite of an excelent tast   I put ye berries in A bag & squeezed out ye Juice (as red as claret) that I might carry ye seed home ye better to send to my correspondents   I brought A small root home which now hath shot forth 4 or 5 stems one about A foot high with thick finely crenated leaves   ye pedicile & midle nerve is A deep purple color [illegible] & this year being A few miles from ye blew mountains in east Jersey in A black Larix & spruice swamp I found A curious species of crategus growing 8 or 9 foot high bearing A prodigious quantity of A large black sweet juicy fruit A little roughish in tast   thay grew on ye tops of ye branches in such bunches that I could pull them off by double handfulls   I gathered as A proportionable share with ye other seeds to carry home   I & my little son John eat our belly full of them   thay was very wholesom & quenched our thirst finely it being an extream hot day & no water near but what induced me chiefly to search these swamps was A certain information that ye lesser or northern xanthoxilum growed plentifully about here where I hoped to find ye female kind that bore seed for alltho it grows between ye mountains of virginia pensilvania in ye great vale & york government about dr Coldens yet I never saw any bear seed but A few bushes between Coldens & Goshen but in these swamps in east Jersey it grows 9 or 10 foot high as thick as my arm & full of red berries or rather capsula for when ye capsula turns red ye seed is most of it cast out as I found to my disapointment that A hatfull of red capsula would not afford half A spoonfull of seed   but when ye capsula is Just turning from flesh color to red then gather them as thay spread prodigiously & sends forth stems from ye roots at remote distances from ye mother stock   I brought several of them home & planted which hath since shot out green leaves   we have two other species of crategus growing with us ye one grows 2 foot high & bears A few dark colored berries early ripe very dry choaking & harsh   ye other grows 7 or 8 foot high   ye berries red & very late ripe & as harsh as ye other   ye leaves is hoary under side ye flowers is very prety & thay was so oily & smelt so strong in gathering as caused A sickness at my stomack & head ach   there is in one of these great swamps ye dwarf birch growing 4 or 5 foot high   by chance where it is is too wet for ye fire to burn but it spreads over acres of ground about half A foot high   that is one summers growth for ye inhabitants anualy sets fire to ye dead grass & burns all clean to ye groun

BP 1:48:2.

To COLLINSON

November ye 7th 1756

Dear Peter

I having not received any letter from thee for A long time so haveing none to answer I have little to write but to let thee know I have provided A fine cargo to send & is now ready to pack against ye departure [illegible] presents to send them   we have expected Capt Mesnard in for some time & Capn Rankin   I am in A poor state of health & hath been so for A month   my son William is apprenticed to A merchant[1] & I have onely A couple of little boys to help me that I have been [illegible] foiled to death & had ye seeds been as scarce as thay was last year I could not have gathered half enough   I thought to have sent thee 2 Boxes of plants in earth but I could not persuade ye Captain to take them   he is so full loaded with lumber   pray if Moses is in London when thee received this letter lett him know that all his relations is prety well but my self   I have A slow fever every day yet makes A shift to keep up & allmost every day gathering seeds   I should be glad to see him or hear of his wellfare   we have now ye worst kind of small pox that ever was in our countrey   it baffles all ye skill of our doctors   ye indians is weekly making inroads in ye pleasant vail of tulpehocon & if not speedily stopped will doubtless clear all that pleasant vail of its inhabitants before spring & drives us all on heaps   indeed Dear Peter if our afairs is not conducted much better another summer then thay have been ye last we may reasonably expect that by ye succeeding winter all pensilvania & york government will be taken under ye french power & then all ye northern countries will naturely soon fall to ye french   O what doth our Proprietor think of his fine estate   what doth our King think of his flourishing colonies

BP 1:48:1.
1. Captain James Child, former master of the *Beulah*, who had opened a store on Water Street in 1750.

To COLLINSON

January ye 22 1757

dear peter
I have shiped on ye carolina Cpt duncan & consigned to thee 26 boxes   ye first ten marked on ye sides, is for our Governor   ye freight of which comes to three pound 8 at 16 per foot which thee must charge to his account with thy trouble   he will give thee perticular orders about them   P C # xi & s on ye side is for swinhoe if he sends for it soon   if not dispose of it   it is A very good box of ye choicest seed but not many acrons in it or nuts   ye other 12 boxes is according to thy own orders   ye general list answers to thair numbers   No 22 is A box of seeds for thy self   onely A packet for miller of seeds & some letters which pray send as directed   XXV a Box of plants for miller   XXVI is A box of plants for thy selfe in which is plant roots of red flowered Azalea   several roots of papaw   13 roots of magnolia   one root of shrub st Johns wort   2 sods of perenial yellow digitalis   of dittany one sod of pirola repens folis scabra   I should have put more in but ye ground was frose so hard I could not dig them up   I wrote to our friend Edwards something about our snow birds as thee may see for I did not seal ye letter that thee may read it. for 3 days we had extream cold weather with A north wind & ye snow birds plenty next morning ye wind turned south & ye larks singing merrily & not one snow bird to be seen this day nor ye next which was warm & rainy wind east in ye morning then south   then west at night   strong north west next morning ye snow birds flittering about in every bush & tree about ye house   by these observations I am apt to suppose these snow birds retire at ye approach of A warm day behind or on ye north west side of our north mountains or in ye cool & shady valeys & in summer still farther north to breed   Billy saith he saw many of them in new England when we was there in September   many birds in thair migrations are observed to go in flocks as ye geese brants pigeons & blackbirds   others flutters & hop about from tree to tree or upon ye ground & feeding backwards & forwards, interspersed so that thair progressive motion is not commonly observed   our blue or rather ash-coloured great herons & ye white ones do not observe A direct progresion but follow ye banks of rivers sometimes flying from one side to ye other sometimes A little backwards but generally northward until all places be supplied sufficiently where there is conveniency of food   for when some arrive at A perticular place & finds as many there before them as can readily find food some of them move forward & some stay behind   for all these wild

creatures of one species generaly seem of one community & rather then quarrel will move still A farther distance where there is more plenty of food like abraham and lot but most of our domestic animals are more like thair masters every one contends for his own dunghill & is for driving all off that come to encroach upon them it is very probable that many kinds of birds in thair migration flieth out of our sight so high & so is unobserved as for instance our hooping cranes in thair passage from florida to hudsons bay thay fly in flocks of about half A score so exceeding high as scarcely to be observed but by thair perticular noise of thair loud hooping we can but just see them tho so perticularly directed where to look for them all tho such A very large bird thair flight is near circular with A progresion in lines after this manner [here Bartram made a drawing of loops] one after ye other by which we have an opertunity of observing thair motion by seeing & hearing for several minits time (but there may be millions of smaller birds fly over our heads much lower then these & not one of them seen) next to these of our larger fowl flyeth lower ye brant then ye geese then pidgeons then black birds I mean in thair highest stages of flight in thair migrations I want ye rest of hills English herbal that I may have them bound up all together. I have received twenty-one numbers it seems odd that in his history of plants he kept to close to Lineus & now in this hee pulls him all to pieces & seemingly with good reason too Poor Lineus he is an industrious [illegible] but I always thought he crowded too many species into one genus

BP 1:45:2; D. 211–12.

To JANE COLDEN

January ye 24th 1757

Respected Friend Jane Colden
I received thine of october ye 26th 1756 & read it several times with agreeable sattisfaction indeed I am very carefull of it & it keeps company with ye choicest correspondents, ye european letters ye viney plant thee so well discribes I take to be ye dioscoria of hill & Gronovius tho I never searched ye characters of ye flower so curiously as I find thee hath done but pray search them books thee may presently find that article I should be extreamly glad to see thee at my house & to shew thee my garden My Billy is gone from me to learn to be A merchant in Philadelphia & I hope A choice good place too Captain Childs I shewed him thy letter & he was so well pleased with it that he presently made A pockit of very fine drawings for the far beyond Catesbys took them to town & tould me he would send them very soon I was then in A poor state of health but am now well recovered we very gratefully receive thy kind remembrance & my two dear friends thy father & mother I want once more to climb ye Catskils but I think it is not safe to venture these troublesome times

I have several kinds of ye Cockleat or snail trefoil & trigonels or fenugreck but being anual plants thay are gone off   ye species of persicary thee mentions is what turnfort brought from ye three churches at ye foot of mount Arearat   ye amorpha is A beautifull flower but whether wont your cold winters kill it   if ye Rhubarb from London be ye Siberian I have it I had ye perenial flax from rusia livonia   it growed 4 foot high & I dont know but 50 stalks from A root but ye flax was very rotten & course   ye flowers large & blew   it lived many years & died   neither what you will want this   I am quite at A loss what seeds to gather & what quantity of each to preserve.

John Bartram

BP 1:44:4; D. 400–401.

To ELIOT

January ye 24th 1757

Dear worthy Friend
I did not receive thy kind letter of march ye 14 until lately   our friend Benjamin had put it in his drawer & could not find it when looked for   I am sorry thee did not get my son's drawings   ye rector[1] of ye coledge got all of them   my son I believe wrote thy name on those he intended for thee   ye stick was hollow   I filled it with indigo seed. I am often recollecting thy agreable conversation with pleasure. I am apt to think that if your drained salt marsh was plowed several times & planted with indian corn & sowed with wheat after several years planting it would bring it in good order for grass or corn; ye crude saline nature of your marshes should be exposed to ye alternative of dews sun rain & frost. but then ye salt water must be kept wholy out — I tould thee that I had been informed that ye grinding & mill stones was split in some countreys with driveing woden pegs round A cilinder but not that your rocks would split after that manner but that I could split them & that I had been used to split rocks to make steps, dore-sills & large windo cases & stone pig troughs   I have split rocks 17 foot long & built five houses of hewn stone split out of ye rock with my own hands & very easy pleasant work it is but ye raising them up is very hard & must be done with iron bars & levers: my method is to draw A line upon ye rock that I want to split from one end to ye other in ye midle in which I bore holes according to ye depth or toughness thereof   if ye rock be 2 foot thich 6 inches deep one diameter & A foot or 18 inches distant will generaly do but if ye rock be 4, 5 or 6 foot deep ye holes should be A foot or 15 inches deep & ½ or ¾ diameter   ye depth of ye rock adds to ye difficulty but ye length & breadth nothing, onely more wedges is required. there must be twice as many wedges as holes & one half made rather longer than ye hole is deep & rounded at one end   Just fit to drop down to ye bottom of ye hole: ye others A little longer & bigger one way to open ye stone both blunted pointed ye upper one sharp & all ye holes must have

thair wedges drove together one after another gently that ye rock may be strained equaly alike from one end to ye other   you may hear by thair sound when thay all strain alike   then with ye sharp end of your Sledge or maul strike several smart stroaks in ye line between every one of ye wedges & at each end where you would have ye rock to split   then drive all ye wedges again & it mostly will open from end to end if ye rock be sound. then with iron bars or long levers rais them up & lay ye pieces flat   then bore & split them in what shape & dimentions you please: if ye rock is any thing free thay will split allmost as true as hewed timber & by this method you may split allmost any rock for you may add what power you please by boreing ye holes deeper & closer together; ye cheapest way is to buy 30 or 40 pound weight of bar iron some one inch square for shorter wedgs & some 1½ or 1¾ inches for ye longer wedges & ye bars for priseing up ye stones   take ye bars to ye smith & get him to cut ye wedges in proper lengths & beat one end round & taper ye other end to A wedge & beat ye bar for resting ye stones asunder   one end beveling both ways prety sharp. ye other end flat & straight one side, ye other side beveling to prise up ye stones   all this takes but little smith work as thay take no welding heat ye best iron for ye wedges is what ye forge men rakes off ye hearth which is near as hard as steel & prety tough   our men charges no more for it then ye common iron   ye iron bar or crow should be rounded so with 6 inches off each end   I suppose I need not give any directions about boreing as thee saith thee tryed twice: I believe all things considered this method is as cheap as blowing with powder which bursts ye stone all to pieces very iregularly takes much time in raming   many times misseth & allways dangerous but by this method you may split ye stone to what sise & shape you chuse   ye boreing takes ye most time   ye splitting is soon done

dear beloved friend I am thy sinceer

John Bartram

Beinecke Rare Book and Manuscript Library, Yale University, Jared Eliot Collection; BP 1:46:1; D. 274–75.
1. Dr. Thomas Clap (1703–1767).

From COLLINSON

10 February 1757

I wish my Good Friend J: Bartram would peruse a Little tract called New England's Rarities by John Josselyn[1] and see his account of *the White Mountain & sugar loaf Mountain* which are very Extraordinary   if it was peaceable Times who knows how thou might be Tempted to make them a Visit —

What was his bird Pilhannaw — a Monstrous great Bird   He must have a fine Palate & a good Digestion to say a Turke Buzzard was good meat — the porcupine shooting his quills is a vulger Error

pray see his account of the Moose Dear   they was plenty in his Time in that remote part where his Brother Lived unless he recons the deer holding up his head with a full grown pair of horns on   itt could not be 12 foot high — by the Method of measuring a Horse   the width of their Horns and their being palmate agrees nearly with the Irish Fossil Horns   phaps the same Animal by their being found always in Boggs & Marshes   it was thought that they was all killed by some Murrain or Pestillent Distemper — for the Horns was not shed but found with the skull adhering to them which is surpriseing Small compar'd to the Horns it Sustains the Vertebra & Muscels of the neck must be immensely Strong to Support them —

I don't know how to Distinguish between his Raccoon & His Jaccal — are they all one or is these with you the Two distinct animals, as in other Countries of the World —

I presume they must have mistooke a panther for a Lion Especially a She Lion — But Lions are never found in such Cold Climates, —

By his Cataloge of Fish He takes it for granted that you have all the Fishes, He could collect Names, from Pliny and other Naturalists of Later Date – there is no doubt but that you have great Variety unknown to Us

His notion of the origin of Ambergrise near akin to our Modern one & that is that it is a Natural Bitumen washed up from the Bottom of the Sea

The Tyrian Dye was collected from a vein found in a species of [whelk] and I know some other fish beside his Scarlet Muscle that has the red vein that will stain Linen Effectually, but being so Long gathering a Quantity to Dye a Cloak or Mantle made it of such value as only to array princes — but the Discovery of Cochineal reduced the price so that every Common pson can Wear scarlet

Does he not exaggerate in his article of Frogs a foot high   His rattle snake vappor shows him to be a vapporer

What is his Lillie of the Valey with yellow flowers   neither Oake of Jerusalem nor Cappadocia — will stand our Winters   Sure the Snow must protect their Roots in New England where the Cold is much more Severe than with us

Hollow Leafed Lavendar, & Side Saddle Flower, are Names Equally Observ'd & farr from giveing any Idea of the plants

Page 67 – the Two Leaves of what he calls Pirola I take to be thy Perennial Sanicle sent last year

but what the Singular plant fig 12 fol 68 I must submit to thy knowledge to find out

Fig 3 I take to be Skunk Root — Fig. A *Nole tangere*

His Tree low Thistle I once had & it flower'd well by being Biennial it went off & Did not ripen seed

What his No. 5 is I cant recollect alltho He gives 2 Figures

Figure 6 is Chelone with White flower but the Red is much more Beautifull —

Figure 7 is a pretty plant, but I never saw it   Neither do I know his Small Sun flower No 8 — nor on what plant his Cochineal is found, it may make a fine Colour for Billy are his Two Standing Dishes of New Engl'd now in use   the Morse is the Largest Species of Seal   the Sea Horse or Manaty is the Hippopotamus found in Warm Countries

He seems enamour'd with the young Indian Nymphs   What sayeth Thee to these originals in their native Dress?   Have they ever been able to Charm an English man as they do the French — who are not so Delicate

As thou loves Curiosities and Novelties I herewith send thee a book will let thee see the notions of a virtuoso, about one hundred years agone but to thee it may be most valuable   In the Article relateing to the Improvement of land

I am much concern'd for the Loss of the Lydia outward bound by whom I had sent thy Account Current & had writt thee Largely on many other Matters which I have not Leisure now to Do again, & indeed when Once my Budget is Empty the Memory is discharged so one cannot Easily Recollect again

I have paid thy 25£ Bill favour of Capt Child but as the whole Bill was not of thy writing no advice came off It   I Demur'd some time to pay it for I have before expressly told thee unless the whole Bill is of thy own hand writeing I intended not to pay it, it is so Easie to Counterfeit Two Words of a Man's Name & had it not been to Capt Child I had not paid It   So now mind for the future   if bills with only thy Name to them & no advice — come back protested thank thyself for I am not Warranted by Law to pay Them

I was so Extreamly pleased with thy Letter to Phil Miller that I had it Coppyed — My observations on it are Lost —

I have Lately had a Letter from Docr Linnaeus & He gives his Service & Desired Mee not to forgett to tell thee with what Respect Docr P. Kalm mentions Thee in his Books of Travels in ye Country & Canada — there is only 2 Books publish'd — Thine of February 2 Last year I answer'd by Capt Rench June 1   is there no saving seed of thy pretty Rock Lychniss nor of Earliest Dwarfe Spring Iris   this is a sort that grows plenty in Virginia but if with you cant Saye   Thy letter of 8th Novem mentions nothing of the arrival of Capt Wrench on the William with Cargo of Drugs

Our friend Neve Carefully Delivered Billeys Drawings which are very Elegant & much admired — I am glad he has found out that He may be in a way to rise in the world — probably there may be at Times Some Leisure Hours in which He may Divert Himself in his Favourite amusement So have Sent Him the best Book Wee have extant by which he may Improve Himself — Moses, no doubt will write, he is waiting for a proper oppertunity to Return — I have a notion 8 books of Hills was taken on the Lydia so write Mee Word what thou has, that I may not send duplicates for the Book is quite Finish'd —

I writt thee Two letters relateing to the Complaints of Swinhoe & Williamson — they greatly Resent thy usage of them in sending Such wreched Cargo's which has given Mee great Concern — as they are Men of probity & will not Complain without a real Cause — thy Letters of Last year are Feby 21: Aprill 15: June 15: May 30 & Novemr 8th all which I have regularly answered   hope some will Come to thy Hands — the Ball[ance]

Due to thee and not Last years Seeds Included is 69:19:11 — if I have Time will send the particulars —

It is now the 10th of February & no Seeds are yett arrived but Wee expect a ship Dayly from your parts & then I hope they'l come — if you know our Distress for Wheat   Wee should have your Merchants run all Risques the profit is So Great and Insurance with you on the prime Cost would be Inconsiderable   Wheat is now & has been for some Time from Eight Shillings to Eight shill: & 6d. a Bushel Sterling   this makes it very Hard for the poor & if it Should please God that the present Crop on the Ground should by accidents prove Bad — a famine must Ensue unless Relieved by you for there is very Little old Corn in Store & the Last Years was so bad from a Wett Harvest Neither that nor the price will allow to pay it up   Thou seest Wee are not without our Calamities no more than you   So Dear John Letts be resignd. Trust in providence & hope & Do all Wee can for the best

I am thy real frd

P. Collinson

BP 3:11; D. 212–14.
1. John Josselyn (c. 1608–1675), English naturalist who spent over eight years in New England; author of *New England's Rarities* (London, 1672) and *An Account of Two Voyages to New England* (London, 1674).

From MILLER

Chelsea, Feb. 15, 1757

I received your letter dated the third of November last. I have the disagreeable account that neither of my letters wrote last summer have come to your hands for which I am extremely sorry because there were some queries therein which I should have been glad to be informed about, especially at this time, when I am revising the Gardeners Dictionary. one was to know the characters of the *Gale asplendii folio* which you say is not of the same genus with the Candleberry bush. I find there are authors who have ranged it with the *Liquid ambar* but I doubt much of their being right so I shall be much obliged to you, if you can send me a perfect specimen that I may determine its proper genus.

In my former letters I acquainted you that the basket which you mentioned had been sent to German town and was returned to Philadelphia was directed . . . with it a bag of Cones of Cedar of Lebanon, on both which there was full directions for you and at the same time a letter of advice sent you which I apprehend you did not receive. in the basket there were two plants of the Norway Maple which you seemed to want.

The notice of departure of this ship from London is so short that I have no time to put some plants which I intended to send you nor do I find the Captain very willing to take these things on board, but if I find any oppertunity to do so they shall be forwarded to you. at present I have sent you the numbers of plates of plants which have been published since those which you have received and all the numbers of the Gardeners Dictionary which are printed, as the others come out they shall be forwarded to you and whatever you are so good as to furnish me with, shall have place in this performance if they come in time; but as seeds require time to raise plants to flower so if you have any dried specimens of remarkable plants which you will be so good as to send me, they shall be inserted and justice done to the discoverer.

You are so good as to mention in your last that you intended me a parcell but hearing nothing more of them I fear you have missed the oppertunity of sending or they are lost.

Your observations on the male and female flowers on the same, and also on different trees are fully confirmed by many repeated observations and Experiments as you will see in this Edition of the Dictionary however I shall not omit mentioning yours with the others. The Viburnums which you mention appear new to me. I know but few sorts from your country: one is the *Black Haw,* the other two are *Tinus* Flor. Virg. and the *opulus* of the same book. if you have any dried samples of these they will be most welcome to me as also of your new Crataegus or in short any of your late discovered plants

Pray to what size does the Balm of Gilead Fir grow in your country and what is the soil in which it lasts longest for there is but one place in England where the trees live more than ten or twelve years.

I am much in want of a few seeds of *Zanthoxylum* for I have but one in the Garden I have several [line and a half missing] gotten it finely painted, intending a plate for it: for I do not find any in our Books the yellow root and *veratrum* put out leaves but no flowers. I wish they may flower this summer, that I may have the oppertunity of inserting them. The *Clethra* flowered, but there was another low shrub, which put out three or four obtuse leaves, which I do not know where to place till it makes a farther appearance.

Which of the sorts is it you call the Paper birch? I have two sorts growing from *America,* one of which approaches near our Common sort; the other hath leaves are heart shaped.

The *Chamaecerasus* which you mention to have brought from the mountains seems to be the same which you will find figured in one of my plates. I received the seeds from *Paris* without name or any account of the Country from whence it came but have since been informed it came from *Canada.* it is certainly the cherry mentioned by *Gerard.*[1]

I shall be glad to know if any of the seeds which I sent you last year have grown and if they were agreable, because I can supply you with many other sorts if I know they are acceptable.

Pray let me hear from you soon which will greatly oblige

Your sincere friend & servant
Philip Miller

P.S. I shall send with this a dozen Cones of Cedar for fear the last miscarried.

BP 4:80; D. 380.

1. John Gerard (1545–1612), author of *The Herball, or General Historie of Plantes* (London, 1597).

From COLLINSON[1]

London March 3 1757

Dear John

I am very apprehensive that in the Event the Ships with the Cargo thou sent are taken which I must confess is very disheartening, & what Scheme to prevent it I cannot say but that for the future to insure them   half a Loaf is better then no Bread —

If thee can but resolve to get all ready to ship in one or two Ships which is most suitable for thy Convenience as the labor is large I think it may be worth thy while but that I shall submit to thy Consideration, they are all five guinea Boxes   let every one be packed by its self with the Persons Name upon it, then I shall have nothing to do but to get them from on board & thro' the Custom House & send every one to its Owner.

Pray send no more of any Thing curious but keep all untill a Peace which I hope cannot be a great way off for all Sides have spent their Money & when the Sinews of war are broke then all Parties must agree   Dear Jon. farewell

P Collinson

A very pleasant temperate winter untill Feby. & then a week of Cold & Snow — My Aconites began to flower Dec. 17. untill now

Nails. Callico & Cloth will come by the first Ship

12 boxes of 5 Guineas	For Duke of Richmond
63 Lb. – Sterling which I wish in thy pocket	Duke of Argyle
	Lord Deskford
	Lord Lincoln
It may be worth saving such a sum	Lord Leicester
	Sr. Hugh Smithson
	Charles Hamilton
	Mr. Williamson
	Philip Miller
	Mr. Hall
	Arthur Dobbs – 2 Boxes to be sent by any

Ships bound for Dublin Directed to the Care of Mr. Hans Bailey, Mercht. in Dublin or what is better I shall write more perticular per first Pensilvania Ship which will Sail in abt. a Month & then I shall write to our Worthy Friend B. Franklin to whom pray my Respects

BP 2:73.
1. The first half of this letter was written by a scribe.

From COLLINSON

Londn March 18 1757

Dear John

I was glad at my heart that the ship is come that Brings the Seeds Where she delivered her Letters I can not Saye but hope she will come Safe into our River — There is a fine Cargo of Seeds &c Indeed

I See a Box for Swinhoe — I hope thou hath wrote to Williamson — for really I believe his Complaints to be Well founded — for I believe Him to be a very Honest & Just Man   his own Letter I sent thee by one Ship & a Coppy by Another so it will be hard if Neither is fallen into thy hands because thou takes not the Least Notice about in thy Letter now come of the 22d January —

I am extreamly pleased with thy account of the Migration of Birds   I shall add Each to Its Bird in Catesby's History which will help much to their Natural History   By Frd Carmalt[1] comes, with other parcells a large brown paper bundle from P. Miller   I presume that may prove the Books thou wants, & there is more of Hill's Herbal   I know some were taken on the Lydia   those Comes to hand & I can be Informed of the Exact Number thou wants   I know not what to send   Such accidents will happen these perilous Times   I think there are 3 New York ships taken — which is a hard lott for those Concern'd

The Book of Husbandry thou Inquires after is as thy Frd well observes a Book Letters Book [sic] patch'd together from many authors, very probably a pson may pick something out of it worth knowing but wether that will answer the expence of the purchase must be taken as it Happens

But by Fd Carmalt there comes a book of Husbandry by Lile[2] in quarto a Dear book but I hope there is an Equivalent in It — thou may Easily see it & if thou Likes it & the Price thou may Have it sent thee

My Frd Edwards has a fifth book published — When complete & Delivered, I think he intends to send it to Billy   I have sent him a fine Drawing book which I hope will come safe for I know it will please Him. I have just scrawled this, as it will be long before any other goes.

So, dear John, farewell

P. Collinson

the Skunk Weed (arum Beta Folio) began to show its flowers seventh of February though wee have had a very severe winter yett the small Magnolias have kept all their Leaves & I think they shed them with you

the Elder thou sent Mee last year began to show its Green Budds at the Same Time   it makes a pretty Variety being very different from ours in its Leaves —

Our last Summer was very Wett which is the Occation of the Great Rise of Corn & no Seed Ripen'd — will remember to send more of Large St Johns Wort &c next Season

I shall be heartily Glad your Treaty with the Indians may produce a

Settled peace that Bloodshed may Cease —

Moses is yett Here — I wish'd He had gone Home in some of those ships but He will Try his Fortune in an adventure I dont understand — So now I hope thou will be pleased with my Blotting so much paper to Little purpose

Frd Carmalt went hence Feb'y 21st in the Eagle   Since I have wrote thee by the Royal American Capt Telly & sent Larg Case of Instruments for Academy & a Box Books for Lib: Com with some pinaster Cones for thee[3]

BP 2:96; D. 214–15.
1. Unidentified.
2. Unidentified.
3. In the margin at the end of this letter, Bartram wrote: "sent Peter Collinson by Buden One great Sod containing spiked andromeda   our alder   red flowered maple   one root of silver leaved arum   many heleborines   Itea   dwarf spring cretegus   seedling sassafras   various kinds of bulbous & tuberous Orchis with other plants in ye sods   snakeroot   ginseng   variegated leaved Orchis   se Joslins pirola page 67 & our striped pirola   a sod of sasaperila & snakeroot."

To MILLER

June ye 20th, 1757

Dear friend Phillip Miller

I have received thy kind letter of february ye 15th 1757 with six good cones of ye cedar of lebanon as allso A fine parcel of ye numbers of ye Gardeners dictionary & of the figures adapted to them for which favour I am much obliged to my worthy friend   I am very much concerned for ye loss of thy two letters sent last fall   I sent thee last fall many curious seeds & A box of plants letter & specimens which I shall rejoyce to hear thee hath received   I have now sent thee as thee desired some specimens of ye gale aplenia folium   it differs much from ye gale candlebery mirtle & from ye liquid amber & is I believe A new Genus with good flower specimens desected   yr basket thee mentions with ye norway maple had allso some roses in it. I tould my friend dr bond if he would take care of them he should have one half of them if no others could shew A better right to them: Ye roses all died but 2 or 3 of ye maples is alive as ye doctor tells me, & one or two is enough for me of A sort. the roses thee sent me in A basket directed & advised to me most of them grows prodigiously & is now full of flowers I think there is one sort Something differing from ours but I cant see ye austrian nor ye single nor double yellow rose which would be a rarity as I think we have them not   above half of ye sorts of ye seeds thee sent me last year grow finely   some laid in ye ground A year & then came up   there is A half dozen kinds that I had not before which is A fine acquisition   I have three kinds of xiphions that is ye early persian   ye large blew & A lesser with A yelowish spot on ye falling leaves but I have none of ye white red or yellow   I should be very glad of A variety of these as thay are easily sent & dont take much tending   two roots of a sort is enough   I dont want much of any one species but variety pleaseth me   I had formerly ye xeranthimum & ye Pyrethrum & phlomis which growed well for several years but for want of care went off ye last in A sharp winter   I dont greatly like tender plants what wont bear our severe winters but perhaps anual plants that would perfect thair seed with you without ye help of A hot bed in ye spring will do with us in ye open ground as our heat is 3 or 4 months extreamly hot   I want your white poplar   ye pyracantha berries I have often sowed but never came up   ye acrons & berries seldom do   Any kind of foreign trees & shrubs that is not native to America & will bear our frost will be acceptable   I have sent thee some specimens & seeds in A paper parcel directed for thee to ye care of P. Collinson   pray my good friend write often to me & let me know wherein I can perticularly oblige.

BP 1:44:2; D. 380–81.

To COLLINSON

July ye 29th 1757

Dear Peter
by ye favour & good disposition of our friend I take this opertunity of communicating my unsuccessful endeavors of raising ye Cedar of lebanon & pinasters   Last year by thy direction of transplanting ye pinaster 3 or 4 of them kept very green all ye winter & looked very fresh in ye spring with one cluster pine but in May thay all perished   thay had not sent forth any lateral roots from ye stem: ye little cluster pine is Just alive but I cant see any bud set for next years shoot; this spring several hundreds of pines firs & pinasters & cedars of lebanon came up in various scituations   most of them perished & disolved to slime in 2 or 3 days after thay came up   nay many with ye seed on ye leaves   few stood one week   some I let ye sun shine upon for 2 or 3 hours in ye morning   some none at all   some I transplanted & shaded them in ye day & let ye dew on at night   some neither sun dew or rain; yet with all this care few survived one week   at last I dug up 3 or 4 cedars of lebanon at first appearance planted them with ye earth about thair roots in A pot watered them & carried them to ye falls of A run & set them under ye cool shade of ye great rocks hopeing this cool scituation might agree better with them then our common air which was about this time extreamly damp sultry & sometimes very hot but in A few days I went to see what success   thay was all perished   there is one firr in A box that is yet alive   I have received ye 6 pinaster cones & ye prety little pamphlet of ye conjectures on ye cause of thunder which I receive kindly   I have planted some of ye seed & intend to plant ye rest at different seasons: ye Arbor vita of china & Cypress grows finely but how thay will bear next winter I cant say   I gave them A little protection last winter: but ye Siberian larix notwithstanding it is shaded from ye meridian heat makes but A poor shoot about one inch this 2 summers   many seeds of europ &

from Carolina showed last year is come up this spring   nay several kinds of ye seeds abode in ye ground all winter & came up this spring which will not endure our winter when in ye plant without protection as ye palmetto royal   I have received my son Moses 3 letters this spring but cant learn certainly which way he is gone   he is wanted here much   two of our marchants is building A vesail & would put him master directly & if he behaved well keep him in if ye french did not hinder or was cast away   thay inquired of Captain child about his conduct & thay tould me he gave him A very good character   thay was Shoemaker[1] & peninkton[2]   moses knows them well   my family is in good health   onely my wife & son John hath A fever lurking about them but thay keep mostly up   I have 4 or 5 humble plants[3] growing finely   thair motion seems astonishing & I think it is no more heresay to inquire whether thay as well as most vegitables hath not as much sence as our marsh muscles which is fixed as firm in ye ground & as hard to pull up & will bring as much earth with thair roots as ye sensative plant will   I have not had any account yet how my last cargo & presents was received nor no orders what more to provide to send this year   I wrote both to thee & Miller by Lyon & sent you A packet of seeds specimens &c

BP 1:44:10.
1. Benjamin Shoemaker (1704–1767), Philadelphia merchant; provincial counselor and mayor of Philadelphia (1746–1764).
2. Unidentified.
3. Several species of plants (e.g., *Mimosa pudica*) commonly called "sensitive plants" were also called "humble plants."

To FRANKLIN

July ye 29th 1757

Dear Benjamin
I now take ye freedom of thy usual Benevolence & favour of thy wife to inclose this letter in hers hopeing this way we may keep ye chain of friendship bright while thee art diverting thy self with ye generous conversation of our worthy friends in europ[1] & adding dayly new acquisitions to thy former extensive stock of knowledge by thair free communication of thair experimental improvements while thy poor yet honest friend Bartram is daly in mourning for ye Calamities of our provinces   vast sums spent & nothing done to ye advantage of ye king or countrey   how should I leap for Joy to see or hear that ye British Officers would prove by thair actions ye seal & duty to thair prince & nation thay so much pretend in words   I am not unsensible of ye burden thee art charged with & perhaps thee may meet with some that is not so sincear as our dear Peter whome Captain Lyon tould me in A gratefull zeal was he believed one of ye best men in London   pray my dear friend bestow A few lines upon thy ould friend such like as those sent from wood bridge. thay have A magical

Benjamin Franklin (1706–1790). Oil portrait by Joseph Wright. From Hingston Fox, *Dr. John Fothergill and His Friends* (London: Macmillan and Company, 1919).

power of dispelling melancholy fumes & chearing my spirits   thay are so like thy facetious discourse in thy southern chamber when we used to be together   we have had this summer Abundance of thunder which hath done much damage   several houses hath been much shattered. in one house 2 young women was killed one of which had A child in her lap two weeks ould which was found on ye floor & still liveth   all in ye room was so stupified that thay [can't] give any account how thay was hurt   One saith he saw A ball of fire break [into ye room &] spread about   Several was singed as with fire.

BP 1:44:3; D. 401–2.
1. Franklin had gone to England as agent of the Pennsylvania Assembly.

To COLLINSON

September ye 25 1757   by Captain Duncan

Dear Peter
I have received thy kind letter of June ye 16 1757   I am glad that my cargo came safe to your hands & was in some degree acceptable yet must reckon

myself in several cases unfortunate & in perticular in this that when I have endeavoured to give ye greatest satisfaction my labours hath been ye least valued   last year thee wrote to me to send thee A variety of seeds of forest trees shrubs & plants for to give to thy friends, for that thay expected thee was able to supply them with variety & accordingly to thy earnest request I did what I could to oblige both thee & friends & freely sent A variety which came safe to thy hands but when I read these lines in thy letter (What didst mean to send me so large A box of seeds   it made much trouble & time to part it)   this answer quite astonished me to think it A trouble to part A few seeds sent ready to hand to ones intimate friends   I reflected upon my self what pains I had taken to collect those seeds in several hundred miles travail drying packing boxing & shipping to put my friend in trouble   indeed my good friend if thee was not A widower I should be inclined to tell thee that old age advanced as fast upon thee as upon myself & perhaps these lines may give offence for as times go now we must not complain of either private or public disappointment no not to ones perticular friends   I am glad my evergreen veratrum flowers this year & that ye seed vesails may incline you to call it by some other name then mediola
I have been on ye mountains & plains of east Jersey & brought down several seeds of orchises to send to thy son by Captain Budden who is to sail by ye latter end of October by whome I hope to send A cargo of seeds but ye black larix hemlock spruice & sugar maple not one good seed to be found   black birch & pine cones very scarce   ye sweet crategus found in east Jersey last year I never observed before or since but this year I observed a very different sort about A foot high with black fruite as large as cherries & very juicy
I sent you our late red fruited crategus very often   we have A great variety of this tribe all bearing very prety blosoms   I take ye reason of some of our deciduous trees keeping on thair leaves till spring with you is because of your temperate autumnal heats which doth not attract ye moisture so much as our untemperat fall which is one part or night in A week frosty & ye greatest part very hot   our summer is very hot & sends forth ye shoot fast with its leaves which carrieth off much sap & bosom buds groweth fast & crampith ye pores of ye base of ye leaf so that ye Juices cant flow so fast into ye leafe (espetialy such as is of a loose texture) — as is exhaled by our autumnal heats so that ye leafe must dry & fall off espetialy ye penated leaves & those foreward bosom buds   some other that is quite dry in ye fall & on could ground will stick in till late in ye spring when ye bosom buds swells & drives them off but with you ye fall & winter is temperate & moist & where ye leaves is of A compact consistency & ye surface not so porous thay exhale but little moisture & ye bosom bud doth not swell much till spring to deprive ye leafe of nourishment or cast it of   you have certainly all ye advantages of our countrey   seeds germinate with you & we have A great disadvantage   ye great magnolia is A charming tree   ye leaves of mine is 8 inches broad & hath shot this year 3 foot but have seen it shoot 5 or 6 foot in one season   The St. Johns wort thee sent me is come up this spring & grows finely   so doth ye Cornus mas & I think ye russian

alaternus but ye Pyracanthus & Laurel never comes up with mee   my family is generally prety well at present but it is I believe ye most grievous time for general sickness in ye provinces that Have ever been since thair settlement   abundance dies of fluxes & fever & I believe towards winter many will be afflicted with troublesome coughs   my billy comes on finely with Captain Child who is very kind to him & keeps him very close to his business   he hath sent thee A letter & acknowledges thy kind present of ye drawing book   we want to know how poor Moses fares & where he is   we were glad to see his letter to thee & that he showed so much respect to his worthy friend

BP 1:44:11; D. 215–16.

To COLLINSON

October ye 16th 1757

Dear worthy friend

I have received thy two kind letters february ye 15th & June ye 3d 1757 with ye figures & dictionary all which pleaseth me well   I wrote to thee by Captain Lyon by whome I sent ye spruice which thee desired in thair perfect state of flowering   I allso wrote my worthy friend Benjamin Franklin   I have now sent thee a Box Marked P C N 11 on ye top & M on ye side containing a great variety of shrubs & plants as folows

my great red leaved viburnum	a sod at bottom containing
crategus from new england	dwarf red kalmia
mountain hary hazelnut	& broad andromeda
a root of rough evergreen viburnum	& other plants
	a sod containing Dwarf
broad leaved marsh viburnum	chamerododendron olive leaved
roots of our Sarsaparila	Kalmia autumn gentian
root of sasafras	& I think spiked andromeda
time leaved chamerododendron	a cutting of my great
itea: toxicodendron varnis	toxicodendron triphylon
gale espleni folia; Martagons	northern this shot from
striped leaved orchis	one shoot this summer near
virginia snake root yelow	30 branches many of which was
roots several Jersey tea	from 4 to 6 foot long
ginseng & some other	ye tops of most branches is
ye smell very heady	full of male katkins which is to
	open in ye spring

I sent thee by the Lyon specimens in full flower   this doth not seem to spread by sending forth suckers at various remote distances from ye Mother plant as I observed another species very like this — toward albany where it covered several rod of ground as thick as thay could well stand & about a foot high but these bore some seed   some of them but its many years agon since so that I cant remember wheather ye male had katkins on or not or thay was male & female distinct   I thought when I brought this from that province that thay was both one species but I now am doubtful   if it was safe on ye road going there I should be for fetching some home & planting   these mischievous Indians is in ye way   pray write often to me & let me know perticulars wherein I can oblige thee   our time can be but short —[1]

Library of the Academy of Natural Sciences of Philadelphia, John Bartram (1699–1777) Papers, 1757–1941. Collection 15, Manuscript/Archives Unit.
1. The few remaining lines of this letter are too badly faded to transcribe.

To COLLINSON

october ye 16th 1757   By Captain Budden
Dear friend Peter
I have sent by Captain Budden two Boxes of plants in earth   No 1 is for thy self   ye other for Philip Miller   in the number 1 is ye folowing shrubs   one great sod containing many heleborins & others mixed with ye roots of liveing shrubs of spiked andromeda   our alder   red flowering maple &c   these all delight in moist soil   one root of silver leaved Arum with its ripe seed pod in ye moss   be sure plant these in very wet soil else thay will not prosper   ye leaf & flower is very Curious   A fine root of Itea that may be divided; dwarf Crategus   a young seedling sasafras wraped up in Moss   various kinds of bulbous & tuberous orchis & other plants in ye sods   ginseng wraped in moss   snake root   striped leaved orchis & with variegated leaves   See Joslin's pirola page 67 & A great sod on ye top of our rare pyrola   a root of sarsaparila   I thought to have sent ye rest of my cargo by Budden but he sails too soon but another talks of sailing in three weeks by whome I hope to send ye Boxes of Seeds   there is the appearance of abundance of sugar maple   black birch   hemlock spruice   pine   toxicodendron   hammamelis & others which this year is imposible to find but winter acrons is exceedingly plenty & ye summer as sparse   ye St Johns wort thee sent me grows finely   it came up this summer   so doth ye Cornus & rushia alatemus   ye silver Larix grows very slow   ye italian Cypress & China arbor vita grows well but how they will fare next winter (which I expect will be hard enough) I cant say   it seems strange that thee never heard of [or] saw ever green shrub st Johns wort & I sent thee full specimens of it & Seeds many times & gave thee A very perticular description of it with our evergreens   it grows generaly 4 or 5 foot high in moist ground near as thick as my wrist & spreads its top 2 foot diameter producing hundreds of prety yelow flowers   never saw it naturaly in high or dry ground   I wrote largely by Captain Lyon by whome I sent thee &

miller some Curiosities & lately by captain duncan   I hear our dear Benjamin franklin is safe arived   pray give my very kind respects to him & let him know that all ye family is at present in good health   my dear Moses is in new york in good health after a prosperous voyage & seeing many of ye northern ports

Library of the Academy of Natural Sciences of Philadelphia, John Bartram Papers.

To COLLINSON

november ye 11th 1757   by Captain sneade

Dear Peter

I have not received any letter from thee since that of June ye 16th which seems A great while since   I have wrote to thee by Captain duncan & last by budden by whome I sent thee & Miller each A box of plants & now by Captain sneade I send thee 14 boxes of five guineas each   12 of which is according to thy order & ye other two is for our worthy friend Benjamin franklin according to his order   ye little box N 15 is for John Kell[1] thy kinsman on Captain [illegible] account. thay are all so near alike that I know not which is best   all packed in good order by my one self but in ye greatest hurry ye Captain sails so soon

I am doubtfull one box wants A list but cant so much as guess which it is   I thought I took ye greatest care to put lists in every one before I nailed them up: I nailed up this day 19 boxes & cant recon above 18 lists made use of   have put A box of seeds in ye Collectors Store in order to be sent to dublin for Kildare[2] by Captain reach who is to sail soon as ye Collector informs me   my son Moses hath had a prosperous & pleasant voyage to several of ye northern ports of europe   he is dayly ordering ye finishing of a vesail of which he is to be Captain to whome ye vesail & Cargo is consigned   I sent by Captain budden two boxes of plants in earth   one for thee & ye other for Miller   we expect three vesails from london every day   one of which its supposed will sail back this winter by whome I design to send thee a Collection of Seeds & perhaps a box of plants but it is very uncertain wheather any will sail this winter which was ye occation that I was in such A hurry to send all ye forest seeds by this vesail   I got a promise of ye Captain to take in mine before ye ship was cleaned but as she is loaded with logwood he sett mine in ye Cabin   James[3] spoke a few days after & hath got but two boxes aboard as ye Captn tould me that he would take no more but if these should be taken & another ship should sail for london this winter & get there safe James would have ye advantage of me My good friend Dr Bond hath lately got A book writ if I mistake not by ye king of prussias Physition who exceedingly Commends ye Solanum Lethale as a perfect cure of A Cancer without danger of ye patients life   pray if it be posible Send me Some of ye Seed of ye true Sort but perhaps it may be hard to get any it being generaly supposed to be so dangerous to keep near

A house for fear of ye unadvised takeing it but I find my doctor is on ye query wether such medicine is as capable of doing ye greatest mischief is not allso capable of doing ye greatest good when prudently applyed   but I think these edged tools should be handled carefuly   I will alow ye keener ye instrument ye quicker ye operation but then ye artist should have such absolute Command of it as to direct it to ye very spot & that it shall go no farther but our Constitutions is so different one from another & ye fluides of each person is often so variously vitiated that often when A medicine is directed to a peticular part it Joynes with fluides in their Course to other parts much to ye patients harm   Our affairs from year to year grows wors & worse   fort william henery is lost & some few of ye men that ought to have defended it   our back inhabitants is weekly murdered carried into Captivity or drove away: ye finest enemy fleet & artilery that ever Came into north america which was sufficient to have shaken all of Canada & destroyed ye whole french fleet merely sported themselves at halifax in erecting & takeing a sham battery until ye french fleet got safe into lewisburge   then thay sailed out of halifax to meet ye news of ye french [illegible] arival when thay presently peaceably returned back & is now come [into] winter quarters   but this mock seege set honest Ld Hay[4] into such A flame that I hope europe [will see] by its light what is done in america   I read our newspaper [illegible] several gentlemen in london laid wagers that Cape breton of Quebec [illegible] time in the hands of the english [illegible] surely you dont know that [illegible]

Library of the Academy of Natural Sciences of Philadelphia, John Bartram Papers.
1. Unidentified.
2. James Fitzgerald, Lord Kildare, of Ireland.
3. James Alexander.
4. Lord Charles Hay (d. 1760) had been sent with the English forces to Halifax under the command of General Hobson, Lord Loudon. Hay accused Loudon of making sham sieges and planting cabbages when he should have been fighting the French. Such remarks resulted in Hay being returned to England for court-martial.

To FRANKLIN[1]

Philadelphia, Nov. 12, 1757

Here is a visible Aurora Borealis; at 7 o'clock, it was about two hours high, to the northward pretty bright   Soon after Daylight disappeared, it was much more East where it was redder, with some faint streamers, whose Points reached near 45 degrees Elevation, which soon disappeared, and the Light descended by degrees under the Pole, and by 10 oClock was near extinct   I should be very glad to know whether (and how) it appeared this Night with you, which may assist in some Philosophical Enquiries. I have not observed any, this fall, before. Yesterday the weather was cold & clear, and the wind pretty strong at north; and I believe this the coldest evening we have had this Fall, though this week we had ice as thick as a Dollar.

Royal Society of London Archives, Letters and Papers IV, 97; Royal Society, *Philosophical Transactions* 52 (1762):474.
1. Read before the Royal Society on February 25, 1762.

To COLLINSON

december ye 15th 1757

Dear peter
I have sent thee two Boxes   one of seeds with other plants in earth   one sod of galega at ye bottome   one dwarf red kalmia   one root of silver leaved allder & sasafras   a little bag with A few roots of Clatonia all I could find with diligent searching & one sod of dwarf early Lychnis two Sorts in ye box of seeds there is a fine parcell of swamp magnolia seed for thee & gordon; & A paper parcell for Phillip Miller

I dont remember to have known one English man to have married an Indian nymph   it would [be] reconed a horrid crime with us but indeed if thay was well dressed & as cleanly as our women thay would make as handsom dutyfull industrious loveing & faithfull wives as many of our own women if we could whiten thair scin a little & persuade or compel them not to use strong drink but most of our Indian traders debaucheth them shamefully which is one cause of many that hath alienated thair respect from us   ye young girls & women are generaly very modest unless debauched by Europeans   then sometimes thay throw of all restraint   I have heard that ye ship is safe arived in which I sent my last cargo of seeds which I think is ye very best that I ever sent & if it do not give general satisfaction I utterly despair of ever doing it for as much as it was a very plentifull year as ever I observed & I was very diligent in gathering & carefull in drying & packing but as there was such plenty of pines & fir seeds last there is a great scarcity of them this but as I have no account what satisfaction thay gave neither what you will want this [year] I am quite at a loss what seeds to gather & what quantity of each to procure

Library of the Academy of Natural Sciences of Philadelphia, John Bartram Papers; BP 1:44:9.

To COLLINSON

January ye 3d 1758

Dear Peter
haveing now an opertunity & not knowing when I shall have another I now trouble thee with another letter tho I hardly know what to write haveing wrote 4 or 5 times last fall & this winter & haveing received no letters from thee of later date then august ye 25th

I sent all my Cargo of forest seeds by Captain snead there being at that time no other vesail put up for London   also I should not have sent all my

Cargo in him but if he should arive safe to London its well   I sent before by Captn Budden two boxes of plants   one for thee & ye other for Miller & by ye last ship I sent thee two boxes More with a paper bag of seeds for Miller   we have now exceeding warm weather like May after A short spel of snow & frost which hath killed ye tops of my Italian Cypress that was planted in A south exposition while ye one that was exposed to ye north is not hurt   our meridian sunshine is so hot that it opens ye pores & sets ye sap in motion & when ye night aproacheth ye frost is so intense that it congealeth & puts all in disorder & ye tender shrub perisheth   so that these kind of tenderish plants that will endure your winters frosts must be planted in our eastern exposition   I desighn to try how our figs will bear such treatment for in A warm situation thay are killed to ye root every winter; my tough twiged viburnum hath cast all its leaves but ye siberian larix is yet green   I have two diferent kinds of very stif woody shrubs brought from ye northward that growed erect ye first year very stiff but of their own accord   ye 2d & 3d year thay bow down & takest root but on ye Contrary our white Cedar & common spruice their slender shoots of ye year is wafted about with any blast of air & is bent to A square of near A semicircle but ye second year thay grow upright so strong as to support another long bended shoot   Can this be performed merely by mechanical power or originall motion   I wrote an answer to thy queries on Joslins new england varieties; his No 5 I take to be our great Cacalia A noble plant growed with me seven or 8 foot high & as thick as my arm & two redish stalks from one root. [I h]ave often observed that in plants [illegible]

Library of the Academy of Natural Sciences of Philadelphia, John Bartram Papers.

From FRANKLIN[1]

London, Jan. 11, 1758

I Thank you for your Acct. of the Aurora. A very considerable one appeared here the same Evening being Saturday, November 12. I did not see it, but have heard of it from several. If it was the same, that you saw, it must have been very high, or very extensive, as the two places are 1000 leagues asunder.

Royal Society of London Archives, Letters and Papers IV, 97; Royal Society, *Philosophical Transactions* 52 (1762):474.
1. Read before the Royal Society on February 25, 1762.

From MILLER

January the 12, 1758

Dear Mr: Bartram
  I received your letters the first dated October the 13 and the other November the 12 as also the box of plants   many of which I hope will succeed

but some of those in the bottom of the Box were rotten particularly the Snake root and yellow root. for these I return you my thanks. the Specimens you was so good as to send me by Captain Lyon would have been a Treasure, had they arrived safe but his ship was taken by the French so those are all lost. which is a great misfortune at this time when they would have been of great service to me in ascertaining the names of some plants which remain doubtful: for tho' many of the plants of your country do begin to thrive here in several gardens yet they are not come to the state of flowering or producing their fruit, for which reason fair specimens of them are of more value here than they would be, if they could be obtained here, and as my Hortus siccus is now replete with near ten thousand specimens, so I am very solicitous to make it as complete as I can.

I am afraid the cuting of the great Toxicodendron is perished, for it lay at the bottom of the box where there had been wet. I am very desirous to get all the species of this genus which I can and am making observations on their flowers and fruit, for Doctor Linnaeus has joined these to his Genus of *Rhus*, with which all the species of *Toxicodendron*, which I have yet examined will by no means agree; for these are either Male and female in distinct plants or have Male flowers in separate parts from the fruit on the same plant, which according to his own system must remove them to a great distance from the *Rhus*. the species I have at present in our Garden are these viz, *Toxicodendron triphyllum glabrum – triphyllum folio pinnato pubescente – rectum foliis minoribus, glabris,* and the *– foliis alatis fructu rhomboide, Hort. Eltham.* If you can add to these you will greatly oblige me.

When you are so good as to send me any roots for the future if you will be so good as to put each sort in some Moss separate, and put a label or number to this, I shall then know which comes safe and what are lost, in the same manner as I have sent the plants you desired.

As the notice was short of the departure of the ship so I had not time to put up so many things for you as I could wish, but the rest shall come by the very next oppertunity, with some seeds which I hope may prove acceptable to you and if our friend Mr. Collinson thinks this is a good oppertunity for me to send you the remaining numbers of my Figures of Plants they shall come now, but if he judges otherwise, they shall be sent by the first oppertunity.

I believe we have at present but two sorts of *Crataegus* from your Country. the old one with the *Arbutus* leaf, and another with mealy leaf: if you have any varieties of the Genus to spare they will be very welcome. The Martagon you was so good as to send me now I suspect to be the same you sent me two years ago which has flowered and perfected seed with me. I have given a figure of it in my plants and have mentioned you as the benefactor. There are several other Species of this genus which grow naturally in your Country that I should be glad to receive.

I cannot judge of the plant you described to arch to the ground, by the single leaf in your letter; but if you will be so good as to send me a fair specimen of it in flower I shall then probably inform you of its name. I have the plant which Doctor Linnaeus has named *Bartramia*, just beginning to flower in our stove so I propose to send you a specimen of it when it is perfectly dry. The flowers are so small as not to be discerned by my eyes, without a glass.

In your last letter you complained of not having received any letter from me for some time, how it happens I know not, for I have missed no oppertunity of writing to you. I sent you two letters in the Summer and another since Michaelmas I sent for you to Mr. Collinson who I suppose forwarded it with things to you. The *Mountain Magnolia* which you mention, we have not in our garden, so if you can spare me a plant of it you will much oblige me.

I shall miss no oppertunity of writing to you, and shall send you plants of any other sorts you desire from hence and therefore wish you will send me a list of them that I may have an oppertunity of showing you the pleasure I shall have in supplying you, for as you observe we may not long have it in our power to oblige. But you complain of age too soon   I am now entering on my sixty fourth year, and bless God, I am still hearty and well, tho' not so active as formerly, yet can go thro' fatigue, and so long as I have health am contented with doing what is in my power.

I sincerely wish you health and happiness; and remain your sincere friend
Philip Miller

BP 4:81; D. 381–82.

To MILLER

June ye 16 1758

worthy friend Miller
I have received two very kind letters from my dear friend this spring one dated august ye 26th 1757 & ye other January ye 12th 1758   I received last summer thy figures of plants to ye number XXIII & with them ye gardeners dictionary to number XXV & this spring I have received from Number XXVI April ye 3d 1757 to number 43 August ye 17 1757   Now how ye eight numbers miscarried I know not. I have received every article our worthy friend Peter mentioned in ye letters I received from him & I have always ever since I corresponded with him found him to be as faithful careful punctual & true a Correspondent as I believe ever lived so That notwithstanding ye extensive correspondence he carries on to most of ye trading ports   if thay had ever come to his hands he would have given me some account of them   I am much obliged to thee for thy kind endeavours in sending me such A fine collection of plants but alas thay was so long stifled in ye vesail in hot weather that most of them was so rotten as hardly to be separated from ye mould in which thay was sent   some that was planted near ye out side that could breath A little air lived of which ye hound wort was shot 2 foot thro ye box   those that are alive by thair appearance

I take to be (for ye bandage that bound ye labels was rotten) ye master wort bistort tormentalis & spignell & orpine   ye mould in which thay was sent I spread carefully on A bed & out of it come up abundance of gramcils several thisles vervains & several others that is so small yet that I cant know them which shows that ye plants whose seed will rarely come up when sent in paper will readily come up when sent in earth   I took so much care not to break ye roots or buds that I took ye box to pieces & spread ye earth carefully on A bed that ye labels might not be broke from ye roots thay was tied to   I have got A root of mader that was sent from hollands grows finely & I hope soon to have ye valerian   ye great gentian I want much   ye fig cutting had A little green in ye bark but in A few days after planting it turned black   I believe all cuttings should be stuck onely half way in ye earth but what can live (except bulbous roots) in close hot stowage   ye three spring months you have all ye advantage to have them come to you in winter while ye roots sleepeth   when thee sent ye roses I spread ye earth carefully & in it came up after harvest A plant I took to be mercury   it grew well & there was ye appearance of seed but before it ripened ye frost killed it   last summer very late another came up but before it flowered it was killed   this spring another came up & grows finely & another came up in ye new earth sent this year so that now I expect increas   strange it is but very true that many seeds of plants we take little care of as not being of general use will keep good in ye ground for seven years or more before thay all come up & perhaps ye ground tilled every year too but ye nutritious grains pulse & other esculents that is adapted for our general support generally comes up ye first year thay are sown — Oh the wisdom of Divine providence   ye more we search into it ye more wonderfull we discover its powerfull influence to be; I shall endeavour I hope next fall to send thee those roots thee mentions in thy letter   I hope thee hath received those seeds I sent thee last fall in A paper bag by Captain robinson which was taken & retaken I think twice but whether ye letters of advice came to hand I know not

BP 1:42:3; D. 382–83.

To COLLINSON

June ye 16th 1758

dear peter

I have now before me thy agreeable by Budden letters unanswered of october ye 6th 1757 November ye 10 december ye 8th & 25th february ye 4th & I have received all ye seeds & presents mentioned therein   ye seeds are many of them such as I wanted & most very good & grows well. I am much obliged to thee for them & for purches pilgrimage[1]   I borrowed it formerly & read it with pleasure   those antient books whether Sacred or prophain mostly contains truth mixed with (I was going to say error) which is to be discovered onely by an unprejudiced & experienced reader: we have but four kinds of swallows that I know   that is ye barn swallow I believe like yours builds his nest with mud in A barn & ye chimny swallow makes his basket nest & ye water swallow very numerous makes deep holes in perpendicular banks by rivers   4th ye great black martin very scarce builds in boxes or under eaves of houses none of which stay in winter   I received thy account [illegible] which was to my satisfaction both by Captain Bolitho & presents by him [illegible] lives in much more luxury then thay can afford but many poor people among ye sick inhabitants as well as those that lives near ye frontier have not ye opertunity of liveing to any great excess yet is as much afflicted with fevers as others. I rather take it to be caused from ye sudden allteration of our air & atmosfere as to heat & etc. you have A fine temperate climate to what we have & yet with care & industry ye people may live well   ye newtown Pipin is realy a fine apple & yet our pensilvanians hath not propagated them so generaly as thay might have done we have such a great variety of good aples which we like nearly as well. If I had received thy letter before grafting season was over I would have grafted some in ye small roots & transplanted them in order to be seen next fall but ye best way now will be to stick some grafts in A box of earth with ye plants & you may have them as fresh as if thay was new cut & if you graft them in ye spring in A young bearing tree thay may bear in two years   I frequently cut grafts in september carrieth them several hundred miles & graft them next spring & thay grow finely   I hope to send ye single, & perhaps ye double ranunculus   ye little dwarf plum I have been acquainted with this 40 year   it is very scarce   I have not observed it this many years tho looked much for it but last season it was sent me as A great variety   ye fruite full ripe   A little roughish tast but not so rough as clarret   I sent word to them to drive A stake by them & I would come & take them up in ye winter accordingly I went   ye stake was broke down & Cattle had cropt ye bush but thay shewed me ye place near where thay growed & several bushes which thay thought was right   Last I observed two stumps whose outward bark run horizontaly as ye cherry & plumb   I took them up & planted them & thay begin to grow finely   I have received ye Fossills of our friend Joseph Morris[2] who is a very pleasant agreeable man & offered his service to me & said he would take perticular care of any thing directed to him for me so will any of ye Benezets[3] which are great merchants in ye London trade. ye fossils are very curious & well chosen   I esteem them as A great ornament to my study or chapel which thee pleas   thay are sure demonstrations of ye great changes our earth hath suffered   it was prudently done to chuse such as had ye originall shell in part remaining upon them   ye echinus with ye flint growing to it is wonderful   See Bevan[4] page 11

Library of the Academy of Natural Sciences of Philadelphia, John Bartram Papers.
1. *Hakluytus Posthumous or Purchas His Pilgrims* (London, 1625), by Samuel Purchas (1575?–1626).
2. Unidentified.

3. Anthony Benezet (1713–1784), English Quaker philanthropist and writer who settled in Philadelphia.
4. Unidentified.

From MILLER

Chelsea, Aug. 28, 1758

Sir: –

I was yesterday favoured with your letter, dated June 16th 1758 by which I am informed that part of the numbers of my Figures of plants which I sent you miscarried, which gives me some concern, because they were duly sent as oppertunities offered. how the parcel in brown paper was sent, which you mention to have been in a Box directed to the Academy I know not; for I always sent them to Mr. Collinson, who tells me he put them in a box directed for you. the day that I was favoured with your letter I sent to Mr. Collinson all the remaining numbers of my figures of plants and allso those of the Gardeners Dictionary, which have been printed since the last I sent you, which are directed for you, and Mr. Collinson promised me to forward them immediately to you so I hope you will receive them safely. in your next pray inform me what numbers are wanting in each that I may replace these which are lost.

I am sorry to find the plants which I sent you arrived in so bad state; if there should be an oppertunity offer earlier in the winter, I shall send you a [illegible] and shall add to them the others mentioned in your letter, for if they fail to get to you before the warmth of the spring, there will be small hopes of their succeeding and I shall be more careful in fixing the labels to each, that they may be more certainly known.

The following roots which you was so good as to send me are entirely lost. if you can supply me with them in the Autumn you will greatly oblige me. *Ever-green Helliborine, Ladies Slipper* and *Orchis.* in my last I mentioned some other roots which would be very acceptable and you are so good as to write me that you will send them next Autumn.

In the clod of earth which you sent me, there came up one sort of *Crataegus,* which flowered last Spring, and has now ripe fruit upon it, which is small round and black, but it came too late to be inserted in the *Dictionary,* so may be brought into a supplement. there is no determining the difference between *Crataegus Mespilus* and *Sorbus,* either by the number of their styles or those of their seeds, the latter is very inconsistant in all the pomiferous fruites, *Apples* and *Pears,* have sometimes five or others, six or seven seeds in each; so that to make that a character of the Genus is very absurd. *Doctor Linnaeus,* has joyned so many genera together as occasions confusion. The Apple and Pear are undoubtedly of different genera they will not take upon each other either by buding or grafting; and it is well known from experience, that all trees and shrubs of the same genus will grow upon each other.

I shall be glad to receive Specimens and seeds of these, but hope what you are so good as to send me, may not meet with the same fate, as the specimens which you last sent me, which were carried to France. I shall be obliged if you will supply me with them and also for one of your large *Toxicodendron*. the Toxicodendron I believe are all *Male* and *Female* in different plants, the Sumacks have male and hermaphrodite flowers on the same panicles, in which [illegible] place their difference but I want to make farther examination of the various species of each Genus. pray have you the narrow leaved climbing Toxicodendron with pinnated leaves? I should be glad to have a specimen and some seeds of it. the root of *Veratrum* which you sent me is quite dead, I believe it will be a new genus for so far as I can judge from an imperfect specimen sent me by Mr. Collinson it cannot be a *Veratrum* nor can it be a *Medeola* as some have imagined. for *Veratrum* has male and female flowers in the same spike, which in the imperfect specimen which I have examined I could not find the flowers of your plant are monopetalous whereas those of the Medeola are either tetrapetalous or hexapetalous and I believe the flowers of yours have but one style.

I want much to see a specimen of a female plant of the *Gale Aspleni folio*. I have only yet seen the male with its catkins, for we have not any female plants here, so far as I can learn and I am in great doubt about the character of it. If you have any of the female plants, and will be so good as to send me a plant or two as also a dried specimen you will much oblige me. If you make a collection of dried specimens yourself, I will send you in return any you may want from hence.

The method in which I was under a necessity of publishing the Gardeners Dictionary has in some measure prevented my inserting several new plants which have come to my hands after the initial letters of their title was passed over. I shall be obliged to add an Appendix to it, in which I propose to take notice of as many plants as shall come to my knowledge, so that whatever you are so good as to send to me shall be gratefully therein mentioned. I am
your obedient humble servant,
Philip Miller

BP 4:82; D. 388–89.

To COLLINSON

November ye 13th 1758

Dear Peter

I have wrote about two weeks past & acknowledged thy letters received to ye 4 of may   I wrote allso to our friend miller from whome I have not received one letter since april but have received A fine parcel which thee mentioned of his figures & dictionary with ye Box of bulbous roots; yesterday I put on Board ye Dragon Captain Hamet ten boxes Consigned to thee   No. 1 is for George fernat[1]   it is A great long ten guinea Box   ye

No II is for Powel   this & No III is ye largest & best filled   ye two Boxes of acrons is marked on ye side near one end with A C   ye little Box N X is plants for thy self Containing two dwarf black oaks & three dwarf scarlet oaks from ye desert   one perfoliated honeysuckel grows as thick as my arm & will run up A tree 20 foot high   several branches well rooted of A northern shrub that bends down & takes root its Self [new?] genus   a branch or two well rooted of A northern shrub or tree   trifoliate toxicodendron   one years shoot was 5 foot   it smells very strong   a bunch of ye roots of itea a prety flowering shrub   a root of ye prety Crategus from new england   my bush produced hundreds of berries   I observed them to be turning black A month sooner then thay did in new england   after which I went to gather them to send to you but ye birds had not left one for us to tast tho thay was not quite ripe   A root of our perenial indigo   a root of our red twablade Calceolus from west Jersey   A root of our great white spotted kind from ye mountains of east Jersey   two roots of ye yellow root & ye blaseing star   this hath been A scarce & late seed year that I had much ado to gather enough to dry that I have sent by this ship in ye greatest hurry   I should [send] a dozen boxes by next ship which we dayly expect in from London Captain Duncan but we are afraid ye french frigate which hath done much mischief to us hath or will catch her   I hope to send thee & miller A Box of plants seeds & specimens   thee makes no mention of receiving a Box of seeds for thee & Miller, which I sent with ye last box of plants last winter   the thorny elder thee was tould of is ye aralia spinosa which ye owner of ye place thee mentions got of me Above A dozen years past   I brought it from John Clatons in virginia when I was there   if thee wants it I can easily send thee enough but I thought you had it in plenty long ago   I intend this winter to board in A little convenient spot to keep ye most curious plants I can get to out do our Dutch in flowers pleasure to myself under lock so that I s[hall] hope to raise ye most curious plants of each kind my friends will please to bestow upon me. I am delighted today brought me A fine root of ulinary with [illegible] I am promised A root of ye wild valerian from Madera [illegible] lived over last winter in ye open ground   the two fine roots of Cyclamen thee sent me two years past flowered this fall wonderfully   many young ones from thy seed grows finely & ye [illegible] thee sent with them flowered finely last spring have had long in our gardens   A prety Sweet which sends up in ye fall long green leaves which abides all winter & flowers in May or June   these two is all I have but you have many other sorts which I should be glad of   thay are easily sent & keep them but from ye fire, water, rats & french thay will do well enough   I have had ye double Xeranthemum A prety flower   I want all ye different species   ye geranium Moschatum I had 40 years ago in plenty but I cant now find it in any of our provinces   I have seen ye winter sweet marjoram & winter savory but it hath been lost long ago   this day I measured my young striped maple which I brought about 7 years since from beyond our blew mountains & had advanced one foot in height & this year it shot 3 foot 8 inches two foot whereof is delicately striped with white

& red 4 inches farther ye white gradualy diminisheth from whence ye remainder is A fine red to ye top. last years shoot is A silver stripe on A light green & ye other years' shoot is A silver on A dark green   James[2] admires it exceedingly   my ould tree continues its bright silver stripes down to ye root intermixed with dark green   light green brown & yelow is intermixed for ye bark is quite smooth in ould trees ye largest of which I saw by A pond in ye very body of ye katskil mountains & was 6 or 8 inches diameter & very regular with A spreading top   I should not be so perticular in its description to set thee A longing for it if thee had not given me strong hopes that thee hath one growing & I am sure I sent thee one or two some years past   I can have nothing of any great magnolia seed this year   I am told ye poor man is killed   he said last year that he ventured his life then which I know he must as ye indians is often A hunting where thay grow   I gave him 20 shillings for A little parcel he brought me & entertained him as well as I could to encourage him   he promised to gather me all he could get yet one seed of ye aconite parsatilla or Ladies bower came up last year & he [illegible] seed came right well & seemed very good   I desighn next box to send the ye dwarf chesnut oak   I can get it nearer then ye desert which is 70 miles distance from my house   it is A prety bush but ye acrons ye scarcest of all oaks for as thay are sweet ye fowls, hogs or grub falls upon them while thay are green. I have two plants of that plant I found on an Island by skillkit one of which I desighn to send thee in ye next box   I believe there hath not one grown there this dozen years since it was cleared & mowed   Indeed most of our curious native plants shrubs & trees is destroyed for 80, 90 or 100 mile back this year   I went up sculkil toward ye mountains to gather ye shugar maple seeds where grew A fine grove of them whose fallen tops lay thick upon ye ground there I could hardly ride along & was forced to return without seeing one seed. I took another course about 30 mile to gather some perticular forrest seeds that I used to gather there but ye trees was cut down & ye land cleared is [planted?] with green corn this year   I went into east Jersey to gather curious seeds [illegible].

I have often seen peach, aple, cherry & mulbery trees planted with out any branches & but 2 or three buds which have in A few years made fine flourishing trees   it is very common that even english cherry trees when planted in ye open ground & not sheltered by A fence & growed about 6 or 8 inches diameter that ye sun will so scorch ye bark of ye bole on ye south side as to rot & fall off   ye wood will decay & in few years will be by high winds broke down   my narcisus polianthos is now all green & one in full flower but if it should come A very hard spel I must cover them or thay will perrish but I desighn next summer to take them up & plant them About this time or later   I can hear nothing of ye crocus seeds thee mentioned in thy letter   I went many times to enquire for them at Colemans   I received Baker[3] on microsopes pamphlets & ye fine draught of Halesia which I have growing sent by dr Garden   I can get A root of madder of my neibour I believe who hath planted near an acre of it so neither thee nor Miller need send me any

Library of the Academy of Natural Sciences of Philadelphia, John Bartram Papers.
1. Unidentified.
2. James Alexander.
3. Henry Baker (1698–1774), son-in-law of Daniel Defoe and author of *The Microscope Made Easy* (London, 1769).

To HIS CHILDREN[1]

blessings Rejoice in a harmonious quiet with Gratfull thanksgiving and praises to ye living God, your Sitting Down to ye meals Should be with a composed thankfull heart: & your going to bed with humble prostration of mind & adoration to that Eternal being who Lives for Evermore — This is our Duty to God and may be Caled true piety or walking humbly. The other Command Regards our Duty to one another or Love to our neibour and may be Called Virtue & by some morality but if it be performed (as it Should be without sinester views) with a Design to please God & in his Love and fear I think it merits ye name of Pious morality of Doing Justly and Loving mercy; ye basis or Root of which is this noble and just Command to Do to others as you would have them Do to us if we were in their Circumstance from this root proceed many branches of Excelent actions ye nature of this difficult but main article of Practical Virtues I am doubtfull is so little thought of and understood & Less punctualy fulfiled espetially by those that is inclined to Self Conceat and Covetiousness which Spreads an Impenetrable mist or darkness Round them that they Cant See an others circumstances Clearly and their own but very Confusedly — but that method I found to Come nearest the truth was to Sit Down in a Cool Deliberate frame of mind and maturely weigh and Consider in present Circumstance with his motives as well as my own, then supposing my Self in his Circumstance and he in mine then I should be in a Condition to Judge how I would have him act with me and Consequently how I should act by him. Ye other Great Qualification mentioned to Render us exceptable to God is to Love mercy that is to Shew mercy to others (most is Very Willing to have Mercy Extended to them selves) this Excellent Virtue near akin to Charity which is by the apostle recommend as the main act of Piety — some may Enquire how and to whome we may Extend our Charity and mercy   I anser Shew mercy to the Distressed and Charity to necessitious in a restrain Sence but Love to all men. But the proper objects of mercy are those that have a dependency upon us and are Reduced to Distress by accidents & misfortunes which was not in their Power to avoid and that the[y] Come to Crave our Compassion as also that have highly offended us and Come to beg Pardon. the proper and immediate objects of Charity is those that is industrious and Just setting up in business & hath Little to begin with   poor aged honest persons and Poor Widows and those that by fire water or Sickness is Reduced to Poverty But the Drunkard indolent Extravigant & vitious are no objects of Private Charity   ye more we give such as these the more we incurriage them in their Vitious habits. the next virtuous qualifications are meekness humility and Innocency all which are fine Dispositions of the mind, the meek and humble man can simpathise with all men in their afflictions Ready to assist them in their Distresses in the Love of God his Compasion is Extended according to his abilities to all that Craves his assistance; the innocent man Cant bear to opress any, he takes no advantage of peoples necessities no extortioner but Rejoyseth to have an opertunity of helping the needy without much injury to himself or family.

he Receives his naibour with arms Extended with Love & his Enemy with bowels of mercy when he Cometh to Submit & beg Pardon; he when alone Enjoys a Calm Quietude and tranquility of mind praising and glorifying the Eternall majesty and power in Seraphick Love.

My Dear Children I recommend a stil quietude in an Evening   it refresheth the Soul & prepares the mind to receive Divine Instructions pray make tryall of it my Little Children   it will be more profitable than noisey vain Discourses & you that are married take what opertunity you Can Conveniently to sit hand in hand together in calm Stilness & Quiet praising the Living God & Returning him Grateful thanks for his blessings and praying that if it be agreeable to his will to Continue you Longer together that you may instruct your Children temperance and moderation. the apostle Saith Let your moderation be known seen in all things   this I recommend to you for your Daily Practice through the whole Course of your Lives not only in eating and Drinking but also in Cloathing and in Every action both of body and mind   in your Pasions and Desires practice the universal Golden mean   in Eating Let it be wholsome and plain   use not high Sauces to Excite the apitite to crave more then nature requires or the Stomach Can digest to Suitable nourishment   a good apitite is the best Sauce — Let your drink be week and mild which is more agreable to our nature then Strong Spiritous Liquors   Rise from the table with an Easy meal and thankfull heart and you may obtain three Great advantages thereby   that is Please god Enjoy a good State of health and afford to give your poor neibour a mess now and then whose poor innocent children may be crying for bread   Let your Cloathing be plain strong and neat   then the[y] will last longer so as before you may spare some help to the neady now as to ye temperance and moderation of the mind we ought to have a perticular regard to keep within its proper bounds, some is naturly very hasty & rash both with their tongues and hands   others is more Still Sullen and Revengfull, ye first I take to be much the better temper for when the[y] have given vent to their passions by their mouths it is soon over like a cask whose bung is open'd   the Liquor subsides in Good order but the Later keeps freting and fermenting within and we hardly know what ails them or how to help them before the Cask bursts and the Liquor is Spoiled — the best Remedy against these infortunate passions is to Live in the fear & Love of God which will keep us meek and humble and soon Quench the flame and also the Kindled Coals —

another intemperince of the mind is the Strong Desire to obtain injoyments quite out of their Reach such as honour perferment and Riches

These People often meet with Disappointments and their Expectation not being answered Causes much uneasiness and Disquiets the mind Rendering it very unfit to Receive Divine instruction.

Industry is a very Commendable practice without which we can neither well searve our King benefit our Country honestly maintain our families (man is to get his bread by the sweat of his brow)   moderate Labour and industry is necessary to our Subsistance and it is much more honorable & virtuous to Labour to maintain our Selves and families and Give to the nedy then to opress and Grieve others for our Support: I have often observd many Idle headed Enthusiasts abstain from their Daley Labour under ye pretence of Serving God but Soon Came to Poverty and Confusion unless they Look to their Labour again but I believe we may follow our Dayly Labour in moderation and have our minds sharp and Devoted so Closely to God as to be Scarcely Sensible of the Pain or wariness of Labour   frugality is so very necessary that many for wont of it Can hardly keep the Wheel turning Round   living very Poorly upon a reasonable means which is owing Chiefly to their not puting things to the best advantage or wast: (Remember the fragments were all to be gathered up and nothing Lost)   Beware of wasting Eny of the blessings of Providence you are favord with that may be of Eny Good Service to you or to your neibours or the beasts that is under your Care. if you have no present occasion of it your Selves it is better to give it to give it [sic] to your nabour than Let it be waisted. Live in Love with him   Lend a hand of assistance to them in their wants   bear with them if the[y] trespas upon you. Try to bring them to Reason by fair means before you use harsher methods — to Come to treat of the Government of a famely; this Requires the most prudent Care and Consideration as it generally Relates to the future benefit of your off Spring. My Son Love your wife as you should   be you fellows and Draw both one way Should be both of one mind: if misunderstandings should happen dont be angry both at one & Suppress your Rising Passion at all times & with Every body more Espetialy with your Dear Wife; ye very moment you preceive its motions in your breast be watchfull of it in the fear of god   by no means provoke one another but in Love and mildness, Let each other know Soon what it was that Gave the offence before you let in hard thoughts between you which to often is the Cause of Great uneasiness; But in Love and mildness strive to gratify Each other by Sweet Effectionate Condisention   it is a great Encouragement of a loving wife to ask her advices. Reason together on the advantage or Disadvantage of any important transaction you have a mind to be Concerned with   a prudent wife's advice is often beneficiall and many times Husbands that have rejected it have plunged themselves and family into grevious inconveniences   true Love should be mutuall: Woman suffers much in child bearing and nursing their children and looking after their families wch is apt to make them fretfull: but you should bear with them and treat them mildly: remember that a soft answer pasifieth anger
a Kind husband ought to Deal tenderly with them and not Cross their Desires in Reasonable Demands but Strive to please Each other which is the

way to make both your Lives Comfortable; if you should differ in your opinions about Common actions and Each of you should Contend for your own so Earnestly that you should perceive the Least Spark of Anger kindled let it Immediately Drop: condescention is better than Strife   if Providence please to bless your Endeavours so that you are like to get afforehand in ye world Dont Raise your Expences to the full of your incomes nor fall into Luxury and indolence but be thankfull to God for his mercy: humbly frugall and temperate and lay by the Rest for a time or need   perhaps Providence may see fit to try you with losses but if you are Still favored with prosperity help your children or the distressed or if old age or infirmity Should Call for Ease from incumbrance then make use of it in moderation; but many People when they have got into a good way of business or trade will Live to the full Extent of their income Expecting it will always hold or increase more so & they by higher Living gets more indolent are apt to frequent more or higher Company and Conceave they Can Live without such hard work or Care, then if their business or trade should fall or not be so profitable to them as before and perhaps owing in some measure to their own neglect these people then must be in A poor miserable Circumstance for they cant tell how to Lower their Expences or take to Close Industry as before: — beware of Jealousies or letting in any hard thoughts of Diskindness one towards another, Communicate your thoughts freely one to the other in mildness tenderness and Love at the begining of Eny uneasiness; many men hath through inadvertense been Rather to free with other women introduced Some times by Lawfull Concearns & perhaps with no Criminal Design yet for want of watchfulness his mind may waver; now if his wife Should mistrust Eny such thing by some unpleasing behaviour She Should in a mild tender frame let him know her uneasiness that his Case may be Explained and both Reconciled; a little Spark is sooner quenched then A flaming fire and a little Leak in a bark is Sooner stopt than a great break   We are apt to Suspect ye worst by appearances of some behaviors until ye Reason of it is Known but when a wife by a too nice scrutinous observation of her husbands Conduct Grows Sullen Reserved Disobliging out of humour is in a ready way of alienating her husbands Love for Ever, therefore take Care and not wilfully Give your wife Occation of mistrust   a dear Sweet Loving industrious carefull wife thinks She hath the only Right above all her Sex to her husbands Love, take great Care in showing the Least Slight, Disesteem or misunderstanding between Each other before your Children   it will very much [affect] their Regard to one or both of you: the Little Dears Cunning Creatures very soon observe the Conduct of their Parents — The greatest affair of family occuring is the training up your Children; which as it Concearns the happiness of our offspring we ought to be Carefull to begin Early to instruct them   they will soon take ye impression of virtue or vice on their tender minds very Deep and Lasting; I am apt to think the vitious and Exorbitant practice of the Present age is greatly owing to the neglect of ye Early inculcating of truth and virtue in their tender age [of] Childhood: we ought Strictly to observe ye golden mean and true temperate medium in all our conduct and instructions to them both as to Love and anger, indulgence and Restriction, heat & cold, meat and Drink, Cloathing and Physick: as also the perticular nature and Disposition of the Child must be Duly Observed. Soon after the Child is born it is swathed up not quite so tight as an egyptian mummy then fed high: often with Spiritous food and suks from its mother unwholesom milk occasioned by her feeding on too high and spiritous food   this Causes Gripes and Pains in the Child which deprives it of Rest and makes it fretfull which to Relieve the[y] give it anodines which I take to be a pernicious practice; and for a demonstration of the truth of this assertion Doe but observe our Indians and almost all the Northern and temperate nations of the world; how Straight the[y] goe how Regular their features and handsome shaped bodies vigorous and healthy yet how Loose and hardy are the[y] brought up without Swathing any thick Cloaths about them or Lacing   no spiritous foods nor anodines yet these in all ages hath Been the Common terror and Conquerors of the indulgent and affemenant. Keeping Children to warm giving them much Spicy Sweet food and forcing more into them than nature requires is the Way to make them catch Cold, weakness gripes and indigestion and nerves Disorders Commonly attend those who are tenderly brought up   it is by temperance that the[y] Can get over them: — Of the improvement of the mind the principal Part of man I have often observed a very imprudent method many Parents take when their Children is forward and Ready to Spoil themselves with Crying, to offer them play things or money to be quiet which hardens them by Degrees that the[y] Expect still Greater Rewards & if thair Parents Dont presently Comply the[y] throw what the[y] have Given them away and set aroaring Still Louder untill they obtain what they wanted which they Receive with a very Sower ill humour takeing it to be but as a Scanty Reward for being a little while Quiet which advantage thay improve untill often when they are Grown up allways teasing their parents to give them where withall to gratify their Lustfull Desires to their own distruction; and if their Parents will not assist them the[y] Do not Care how soon he is in his grave   another bad method parents and nurses use to hinder their Children from crying or Committing faults or to make them do as they bid them is, by frightening them by telling them that such & such bug bears will Catch them if the[y] Dont Doe as they Bid them   this Seldom answers to Eny good purpose but on the Contrary Exceedingly terefies ye Child and leaves a lasting Empression of terror upon him and if He be of a fearfull disposition he can hardly Ever get over it so as to go boldly about his lawfull and needfull occations espetially in a dark night without some uneasiness; besides parents by these foolish proceedings looseth much of their authority over their Children and often their Love to. But the best method I have tried according to my maxim is not to let a good Deed pass without praise nor a bad one without Rebuke; that is to inculcate a good Idea of Virtue and Love and a bad one of Vice and Shame: begin very Early with them   they Can understand before they Can talk   tel them how pretty it is to love father and mother   how good it is to do as thay bid them & how bad and

Shamefull it is to Cry to be Stubborn and not do as they are bid: & if you see it Do any Pretty actions as you see it then hug it and prais it but never show any pleasant Countinance to any froward action unless it be to give it the breast to quiet it and when it can begin to talk play and run about then talk often with it alone in a pleasant tender manner telling it how pretty it is to love father and mother and its Sisters and brothers (if it have Eny) and what a pretty Sweet Child it is to Do as they Bid it: and how ugly and Shamefull it is to be Cross Stubborn quarrelsom & ill humord: thus by Slow Degrees you may work out ye Sour, Stubborn, pevish Disposition so naturall to Children; and infuse the love of virtue & quiet condissention but then you must Show them ye Like Example between your Selves; and what one Says the other must not Contradict; for the Child will not know which to obey; if he wants you to give him any plaything make him ask for it in a quiet Pleasant modest manner which if he Do; then give it him and Carais him for his Pretty behaviour; at four or five years old and so on it may be well to inform him in a solid yet pleasant manner of the power majesty and mercy of God & ye Dependency we have upon him and how he favours the good & Virtuous and is Displeased with the wicked and vitious and those that Dont live in his fear; advise him to take perticular notice of what he Reads in his bible & often Discourse with him about the ill Effects of Lying Cheating and useing bad words or Sausy Expressions Shewing him that god nor good people will have Eny Regard for those that follows such bad practice; allso explain to them the benefit & advantage of a pious Life & how lovely & commendable it is to be modest and Speak the truth, to be loving to all the family   to do to others as the[y] would be Done unto   to strive to please Each other, and Espetially gratitude and thankfulness for benefit Received both from god and man which is the main Piller under God that supports that noble structure of Piety, love humility and Justice without which practices no man can be Exceptable to god let his pretence or faith be what it will — by this plain Simple method with the blessing of god you will gain by Slow Degrees the love of your Children and not onely Cherish the Seeds of virtue but Cultivate the Pious Plants in this virgin Soil and leave Little room for vitious ones to grow in — this method (I have found much better then all ye whiping thumping boxing and Scolding & I know not what that is Commonly used by Parents.) when taken in time secures their veneration authority & Effection to parents   the other inclines them to Carelessness when out of Sight & Coolness of love & Regard if not hatred: Espetially if thay have let them have their own will to long, and then Suddenly Restrain them; if you find that fair means alone will not Do let your Chastisements or Rebukes be adequat to the fault Committed & the Repetion of them after your advice & threatning to ye Contrary; Let it be Short and Sharp with a Stearn Countinance which Last hath more Effect on Some Children then Either words or blows   Take Care in your anger of wishing bad wishes to your Children or Eny Ill undecent Expression which is to Common Evan amongst great professors; I Knew a very Religious woman that with great indulgence raised many Children & most to men and womans Estate to their Ruin and hers too when they vexed her and that was very often; she frequently Said to them that she wished they was Dead or in their graves they all Died Long before herself tho they Lived to Spend all she had; If you have Several Children train them up in love to one another & while under age the younger should be Directed by the Elder if he have as good or better Judgment; and both by their Parents ye younger is very apt to think himself as good as his Elder brother and will have his own way but he should be taught otherwise or the[y] will be apt to Quarrell which if thay does you Should hear their Complaints together if ye younger be in fault reprimand him; but if ye elder ordered ye younger to do anything unreasonable, or gave the younger just occasion according to the nature of the affair that they was set about then by himself show him the unreasonableness of his proceeding & in a tender loving manner instruct him how to behave better for the future; — When your Children comes to about the age of twelve or fourteen & so on then have a Continual watch over them; their minds then begins to open their understanding to Expand & they begin to look abroad & too apt to incline to worldly vanities; get into Company & take notice of the Superfluities and undue liberties and Diversions of the times all which is vary apt to hurry their minds away from the Love of god: harbour no bad Currupt Company about your houses which will Endeavor to Seduce or intice them to Desire greater Liberties then you are willing to allow them now is the time to fix the Love of Piety and virtue in their Will and Desires; & an abhorrance of vice in them selves & others now is the time to lead them out to See the variety of necessary temporall affairs like the bees that Lead their young out to the fields groves and pastures to gather the Sweet nourishment not only from the Sweet and fragrant plants but also from ye Sower and bitter. now take them amongst your friends & Relations or other ways where your business may call you that they may observe other peoples method of managing their Lawfull affairs Some of which may perhaps better Suit to their inclination than what you may Practice it also emboldens them and makes them more familiar with Strangers and Different branches of business, and much improves their Carridg and behaviour both to their Superiors and inferiors to the aged as well as to the youth and is a great incouragement of them to Display their naturall talents as also to acquire more Excellent qualifications from the observation of many Peoples Ingenious actions now Parents Should be watchfull as well as free with their advice in a pleasant agreeable familiar way to Explain to them the Credit honour and advantage of virtue temperance, moderation, Justice, and being Punctual to their word; as also the henious Distructive pernicious Shamefull effects of vice and the Dangerous Consequences of Keeping of vicious Company, and the benefits and Credit of those that frequent the pious and virtuous, the Extraordinary value of the Esteem ofred good Character of wise Prudent men — tell him it is now time to qualify him Self for mens Company and take notice of their Discourse about the manedgment of their Common affairs call him to Come into the Room with your visitors to Speak directly & Chearfully to

them: then Sit Down on one Side of the Room with a Modest pleasant Countinance & harken Diligently what the[y] are Discoursing upon and if Eny questions be asked him let him give a modest answer to the best of his understanding & then be silent. this will please your friends so well that the[y] will Delight with talking more with him or you may introduce a little discourse to him: this will incouridg and improve him but it is a shame for youth to interrupt discourse of Either his parents or friends and much more so to argue or Contradict them; it is a great burthen to the Company and makes their Parents Even Dispisable as I have often observd in my travels
I believe the ages of 16 & 20 is the time to instruct him into natural Phylosophy & the wisdom of god manifested in the Creation   Explain unto them the numberless number of the fixed stars ye Planitary sistem and their vast Dementions roling in the vast expance of heaven all supported by the all mighty Creator of the universe   this will Raise their ideas of the adorable infinite majesty and the inability and insignifigences of themselves — if you perceive any inclination to bad habits or Idleness use all Endeavors to make him Sensible of the Evil tendency thereof: and the advantage of a frugall industrious Carefull life without which there is no living credebly; or happly in the World. all honest minded people that Liveth in the fear of God will industriously follow some necessary Employ either for Private interest or Public benefit. None is more Exposed to the vitious lustfull temptations of various Kinds then the Lasy and indolent who is very apt to get in to bad Company which often Draw insensably the unwary. many innocent good natured young men have been beguiled to their Ruin   wise men mostly take notice what Company People keep and accordingly is very apt to Judg of their virtue or vice   See that your Children behave in moderation to your Servants: the[y] should not find fault with them without very Just Cause   the[y] should not Quarrell with them on purposely nor give them Eny Contemptable Saucy or Domineering Expressions: neither on the other hand associate as Common Saying is Hail fellow well met but preserve a degree of Dignity above them; but with a familiar air of pleasantness   thus they will gain the Sarvants good will: which may be of more future advantage to them then the[y] may be aware of for the good Character of a young man or woman by a good sarvant is taken a Pretty Deal of notice of.
these My Dear Children are the observations meditations and Reflections I have made in the Cource of my travels abroad and I am now in the 59th year of my age and you know I have kept strictly to temperance and moderation both in body and mind before men; but now I hath need to Keep as strict a watch as Ever. I have three Patent Enemies to war against that usualy assault old age   that is drunkeness; Covetousness & Pevish and fretfull humour, how many wise understanding men that hath been of great Service in Publick affairs, others that have Lived prety Credebly in a private Capacity hath occupied their Elder years with the Excess of Strong Drink and instead of obtaining ye venerable honour of Gray hairs they have been dispised & had in Contempt: many Elder people is overcome with Covetousness and more is so pevish there is hardly Eny such thing as pleasing them and hate

to please anybody Else and I doubt think little of god or their own happiness: — but on the Contrary, how amiable it is to See one Covered with gray hairs, to set in a temporate moderate free Disposition a discoursing with his Children or friends   Sometimes in Pious meditation thanksgiving and Praises to the living god for his mercys   other times a loving meek and pleasant frame of mind, advising his Children or grand Children to follow his Example in industry, moderation Justice Reverence and Charity incouraidging them to live in the fear and love of god and one towards another; Sometimes in a chearfull Sometimes in a Thankfull factious manner Relate to them the various transactions of his life and the Favours of Providence the curious observation you have made upon the various affairs that have Come under your notice that have Eny tendency to inform the people to become wiser or better   it is a great favour to People that is past hard Labours to have their Eye Sight that they may Devert themselves with Reading writing or observing ye various innocent diversions of the field meadows and groves which imediate visable objects of the Creator of wonder and wisdom may Excite the mind to Pious meditations   but the greatest blessing of old age, with gods assistance to be favored with Reason and the brightliness of our intellectual faculty that we may guard against the pevish fretful disposition which so Commonly attends the aged — My Dear Friends and Children if I should Live to more advanced years and you should observe that I begin to give way to this weakness pray Doe in a loving tender manner advise me of it before it [is] too habituall   god almighty grant that I may keepe a diligent watch over this naturall passion and Live in great humility Love and Resignation to him that I may dayly Serve him in stillness and uprightness of heart praising and glorifying him in a harmonious Quiet — this Pious frame of mind will in great measure aleviate ye Pain and uneasiness that our Decayed nature will be subject too   this is living to day as if we Expected to die tomorrow. If we make up our accounts Every Evening we shall have the Shorter reconing hereafter   what great Satisfaction must we have that we have lived a virtuous pious innocent harmless life when he Reflects upon his former action: how his heavenly father hath from time to time delivered him from the Snares temptations and alurment of this life and preserved him in innocency and moderation. What Consolation it must be to Se his friends & neibours and those whom he hath assisted in their necesities Come Round about him with Respect for the Services the[y] have received from him   his Children and grandchildren he can with Joyfull tenderness Embrace in his withered arms and sincerely say "the Living god, my Eternal father who hath protected & Blessed me if it be his will bless all you my Dear Children." Such beautiful qualifications is the greatest ornament of the aged & a glorious Diadem Round the hoary head and altho he appears in a Shrivel'd skin and his Eyes are dim with age yet is he Serounded with Rays of Light   thair pious minds are waiting to hear the midnight Cry with thair Lamps trimed Ready to meet their god whom they have Loved hoping he will Receive them into the glorious mansions where the wicked must cease from troubling them and all tears be wiped from their Eyes where they may Praise and glorify ye Eternal Supream majesty of heaven their only beloved which was and is and is to come with Seraphick Love Eternally in ye Heavens.

Friends Historical Library, Swarthmore College.
1. This is a copy of BP 1:76 (now largely illegible), marked 1758, and obviously much edited.

To COLLINSON[1]

Introduced Plants Troublesome in Pennsylvania Pastures and Fields

A brief account of those plants that is most troublesom in our pastures & fields in Pensilvania most of which was brought from europe ye most mischievous of which is first ye stinking yellow linarya it is ye most hurtfall plant in our pastures that can grow in our Northern climate. neither the spade plow nor hoe can destroy (eradicate) it when it is spread in a pasture every little fiber that is left will increase prodigiously nay some people have roled great heaps of logs upon it & burnt them to ashes whereby ye earth was burnt half A foot deep yet it put up again as fresh as ever covering ye ground so close as not to let any grass to grow amongst it & ye cattle cant abide it but it doth not injure corn so much as grass because ye plow cuts of ye stalks & it doth not grow so high before harvest as to choak ye corn it is now spread over great part of ye inhabited parts of pensilvania it was at first introduced as a fine garden flower but never was a plant more heartily cursed by those that sufers by its incroachment

the common english hipericum is a very pernicious weed it spreads over whole fields & spoils their pasturage not only by choaking ye grass but infecting our horses & sheep with scabed noses & feet especially those that have white hair on thair face & legs this is certain fact as generally affirmed but this is not so bad as ye linaria ye hoe & plow will destroy it

wild camomile called Mathen is another mischievous weed it runs about & spreads much choaking not only ye grass but ye wheat more then ye other two but hath not yet spread so generally as thay but this may be killed by planting indian corn or sowing buckwheat on ye ground for several year successively I had it brought many times in dung but when I find it I burn it root & branch

Leucanthemum this is a very destructive weed in medow & pasture ground choaking ye grass & takeing full posession of ye ground so that ye fields wd looke as white as if covered with snow but ye hoe & plow will destroy this weed

ye great english single stalked mullein this grows generally in most of our ould fields & with its broad spreading leaves takes up some room in the pastures but its easily destroyed with ye plow or sithe having only single tap roots.

Saponary this is more difficult to eradicate as it runs deep & spreads much underground but it is not yet spread much in ye country   with care we may keep it under

great double dandelion is very troublesom in our medow ground & difficult to eradicate it but ye hoe & plow will destroy it

crow garlick   this is greatly loved by ye horses cows & sheep & very wholesom early pasture for thim yet our people generaly hates it because it makes ye milk butter cheese & indeed the flesh of thos cattle that feeds much upon it tast so strong that we can hardly eat of it but for horses & young cattle it doth very well but our millers cant abide it amongst corn it clogs up their mills so that it is impossible to make good flower

docks is very troublesom in our mowing ground & without care thay spread much by seed   thay stifle ye grass by thair Luxuriant broad leaves

scotch thistle   this is very troublesom weed along our sea coast   ye people say A scotch minister brought with him A bed stuffed with thistle down in which was contained some seed   ye inhabitants having plenty of feathers soon turned out the down & filled the bed with feathers   ye seed coming up filled that part of the country with thistles

these are most of ye english plants that hath escaped out of our gardens and taken possession of our fields & medows very much to our detriment

I now make A few observations on some of our native plants that is very troublesom in our fields & medows & is with difficulty eradicated

we have four kinds of ye Rubus beside our common black rasberry   ye great upright Bramble grows near an inch diameter and eight feet high in good ground tho commonly about two thirds of that magnitude   this grows in our old fields and hedges   bears berries plentifuly & spreads much under ground sending up abundance of shoots at uncertain distances   another kind is much like ye former but grows more weake & leaning but bears plentifully & spreads as ye other any piece of ye root left in ye ground tho a foot deep will soone send up a shoot   another kind we call ye running Bryer & is ye most troublesom kind   it roots very deep & if we grub them up half A foot deep thay will shoot from ye remaining root in ye ground several branches which will run on ye surface 2 3 or four yards in one summer & dip into ye ground where thay take firm root   from whence thay will run & take root as before whereby thay soon spread over much ground & neither ye plow nor mattock can easily destroy them   mowing will kill them in a few years if repeated 3 or 4 times A year   A large black berrie & as good as ye others & is ye first ripe near ye latter end of June   ye 4th sort grows about 3 or 4 foot high upright & one side of ye leaves of A fine silver   these grows in few places but where thay take root thay seem to spread & covers ye ground

ye next native that is troublesom in our ould fields is A late flowering peranual white aster with A spreading top   ye flower much like your single dasy   these will spread all over a field so thick as to destroy all ye grass & most herbs too except your hipericom which onely is A fit match for it both which no creature likes to eat   plowing destroys most of ye ould roots but increaseth ye young ones from seed for A year after a crop of wheat is cut A field will appear as white as snow when ye plants is in flower

ye lesser ambrosia is A very troublesom weed in plantations where it hath got A head   it is an anual & grows with corn & after harvest it shoots above ye stuble growing 3 or 4 foot high & so thick that one can hardly walk through   it tasts very bitter & if milch cows feeds upon it (for want of enough of grass) thair milk will tast very loathsom   it seldom grows to any head next year nor until ye field is plowed or sowed again

we have another weed called Cotton groundsel which grows with us 6 or 7 foot high & ye stalk at bottom near as thick as my wrist   in our new cleared land after ye first plowing in ye spring or in our marshes ye year after thay are drained It grows there all over so close that there is no pasing along without breaking it down to walk or ride through it but in ould fields or medows there is not one stalk to be seen now   if we put ye question how comes this to grow so prodigiously on ye new land plowed ground & perhaps not one root growing within several miles ye answer is very ready it is natural to new land & not to ould but our Phylosophers saith that every plant is produced from ye seed of ye same species   but how came ye small seeds of this plant there in such quantity as to fill A field or medow of 100 acres as full of plants as thay can stand   one day when ye sun shined bright a little after its meridian my billy was looking up at it when he discovered an innumerable quantity of downey motes floating in ye air between him & ye sun   He immediately called me out of my study to see what thay were thay rose higher & lower as thay was wafted to & from in ye air   some very high & progressive with a fine breeze   some lowered & fell into my garden where we observed every perticular detachment of down spread in 4 or 5 rays with A seed of ye grounsel in its center   how far these was carried by that breeze cant be known but I think thay must have come near five miles from a medow to reach my garden   as those are annual plants they do but little harm in ye countrey

ye Phytolaca is troublesom in our new cleared medows and new fields which comes up from ye seeds being carried all over ye settled parts of ye countrey by ye birds which is fond of them but these may be easily destroyed by grubbing them up   sometimes A very severe winter kills many of them as thay natives of southward provinces   when I first travailed beyond ye blew mountains I saw not one but now there is enough of them

our Elder is exceeding troublesom in our medows   ye roots run under ground & spread much & I do not know that mowing will ever kill it & grubing will kill little more than ye mattocks takes up for if there is but A little bit of ye root left in ye ground it will grow   I have had a root growing in my kitchen garden about thirty year   it was plowed once every year & generaly grubed & howed once or mostly twice every Summer yet last summer two stalks put [up] & if there is an inch of root left in ye ground if it be two foot deep it will put up again   in short I believe there is not a shrub in ye world harder to eradicate then our Elder   I wish I had some of your Elder seed to sow   I hear it grows much larger then ours   these here mentioned are most of ye troublesom weeds that frequent our medows & pastures & corn fields but in our kitchen gardens we have many that are troublesom enough of which ye chickweed which was brought from England   there is no getting rid of it   it flowers & seeds most part of ye year ye hen bit is allso another that flowers & seeds most of ye summer   sheppard purs is very plentyfull in good ground but many people makes a good boiled sallad of it so is our wild purslain very troublesom tho good when boiled

ye small running mallow is pestering enough & two or three kinds of ye veronica   ye malvinda is very bad & so is ye Moluga

one very tall species of Amaranth is very troublesom but some boils it to eat & A species of arack which we call lamb quarter is very tender when boiled   docks & sorrel is plague enough   boath in our pastures medows & gardens   ye last of which is very hard to root out   these are most of ye noxious weeds of our gardens that makes us have much work to destroy every year beside ye grass

BP 1:42:4; D. 382–89.
1. This was sent to Collinson early in 1759; he expressed his pleasure with it on July 20, 1759. Darlington published it as a letter to Philip Miller.

From COLLINSON

Londn. Jany 14 1759

Dear John

Thou art a very lucky Man   I have both thy Letters with bills of loading one ship the Albion is come up, with the seven Boxes & in a few Days I had advise of the arrival of the other — it is wonderfull they Escaped when so many Virginia ships are Taken – I am glad thou Sent so many Boxes of Seeds for I have a purchaser for every One – but I have not yett an Order for One Next year

I shall be glad to Hear as good new[s] of the Vegetable Cargoes sent by Gordon by the Myrtilla Capt Bolitho[1] —

I send thee Some Fresh Silver Firr & Larches from the Alps — Sure their Cold must be Equall I should think may Exceed any of yours —

The Pines Thou hast raised I take to be pinasters   an Elegant Quick growing Pine as any Wee have   our Last Autumn so much Rain the Siberia Cypress did not ripen seed.

pray my Good Frd. what plant dost thou Mean when thou tells Mee of thy double Wild Crocus now Improved to an Inch & Quarter Diameter. I sent the Autumn Narcis I think in the box of Books for the Library Company — be that as it will, this I am certain I sent It, & by some good Conveyance & sent no common jonquils —

The Belladone, Jacobean & Gurnsey Lillies I shall send this year as soone as fitt to remove

23d – Jany 26 – hitherto Wee have had no Winter — the Like I never remember for Early Spring Flowers — for three Week & More thats past I have had plenty of Acconites, Violets, primeroses Polyanthos anemones Narcis polyantris, Snow Drops Periwinkle Hepaticas   What is very remarkable the 4 or 5 slight frosts, have not carried off the autumn flowers, as the Yellow & White Double Chrysanthemums, Rudbecias or Dwarf Sunflower in high beauty of which I have abundance, All that tribe being my favorites — Our Peaches have not Absolutely Lost their Leaves — a peach stone come up out of Dry Earth but not lost a Leafe   Seems a perfect Evergreen   My Clethra has new Leaves & flowers on It & so has had all the Autumn   the Itea not lost a Leafe — my small Magnolia lost but few Leaves — for what Weather has happened my oranges might have staid out to this Time — but Wee shall pay Dear for this Summer in Winter — our Long South & South West Winds — I expect will be Succeed with a Long range sharp Cutting Easterly Wind, which will blight all our Early Budds which are now Surprisingly Swelld — So wee shall have no fruit — Last year was exceedingly Fruitfull So wee must [hope] for the Next —

I have sent pcell with the Seeds to the Care of Mr Neal

From thy old frd
P Collinson

Remember Mee to Billy Moses & Johnny

In the Quire of Specimens by Budden there are Some that Sett Mee a Longing as their Tribe always my Favourites —

No 1 – the odd Golden Rod from the Jerseys —

3 – this Rudbecias is my great favourite   be sure send seed annually the branching small white flowery anis is pretty   The New Aconite don't forget —

5, 6 & 7 are pretty things

10   The Two Floxes are favourites

11   is a singular Leafe   I have had the 2d flower of my [illegible] Larkspur as fine as Thine

13   Seed of the Stager Weed —

17   from Susquehannah a pretty plant

18   Great Wild Anemony I should Like much

20   and the milk white Flox is my favourite

19   Huckle berry is new to Mee

22   This fine blew or purple Eupatorium I have had Specimens from Time to Time from Virginia but never Could procure Either Seed or plants though I have long'd for it   I hope it will ripen Seed so Send Mee Some I am afraid it is biennial —

24   this Double Mountain Aster is fine   Send Seed or root

25   but this Charming Obeliscotheca or [illegible] is what above all I Desire   I am persuaded it is a biennial so every Year I must be reconciled for it will not ripen with us.

No 2 – 7 – 8 – 21 – 23 I have in my Garden

I had writt the Long Letter by New York Packet which I hear is taken I am much concerned there is no Mention of any Accacia or Locust Seed – if none come I shall almost fall to pieces

BP 2:102.
1. John Boletho.

To MILLER

February ye 18[1]

friend Miller

yesterday I received thy kind letter of August ye 28th postage 2 – 10   I was very well pleased with ye letter & its contents   I would not for three times what it cost me have mised it but should have wished that all ye inclosed letter had been filled   ye numbers that have miscarried are[2]   I have received thy Gardeners dictionary from No 1 to XVI but ye numbers between XVII & XXVI is wanting   No XLIII is twice sent   thy figures of plants I have received to num-XLI but ye numbers between XXIII & XXX is wanting   neither have I ye least hint how thay miscarried   the last letter I received from thee was dated January ye 10th 1758   I am very desirous of one little root of ixias & moreas from ye cape & indeed all bulbous roots most of which may be sent in A little box of sand in which perhaps some cuttings of your hardiest cape plants might be sent Alive but now our correspondence is atended with difficulties   your vesails waits so long for convoys that ye plants perisheth before we receive them as was that fine collection thee sent last winter which did not arive hear before hot weather   we have hitherto been unfortunate in receiving ye presents from each other   hope for better luck   in the mean time I must desire thee to let me know what I can oblige thee with in seeds roots or specimens. I have sent thee one root of our perenial Ludwigia as thee wrote thine to be an annual plant mine must be different   thee mentions but one kind of our scutelaria & that is ye tall broad leaved but our narrow leaved which is intensely bitter is ye most beautifull   have you got our dwarf yew   it is A shrub for low thick hedges   I have one in my garden whose branches is nearly 5 foot diameter regularly & about 4 foot high   plain on ye top tho never sheared   last fall I brought in our martagon roots from ye great meadows in east Jersey   if there be variety next summer I hope to send some of them   perhaps next spring I may take A [torn]

I am glad the crategus I brought from New england grows with thee   it was A fine sweet Jusey fruite A little roughis the 11th of September but when it bore fruite with me thay were devoured in A day or two by ye birds tho ye bushes was as full from ye top allmost to ye bottom in July before thay was quite turned black   this is ye onely species of this genus that I have observed that bears fruits upon all ye lateral numberous branches   another species I found in East Jersey three years past that bore its fruit large in horizontal great branches on ye ramified sumits of ye stem which growed 6 foot high   I sowed ye seed which never came up but last fall I went to fetch some roots & expected to have feasted on ye fruite as before but I could not find one single berry   I hope to send thee A root next season If mine grows   we have A great variety of this tribe perplexing unconstant   ye mespilus & all make A pretty neat appearance in flower   ye pears I have grafted in aples thorns & our crab stocks & growed well for a year or two   I have seen an aple tree bear both aples & pears at once   there is no general rules without some exceptions   so it is with Lineus sistem   he erred on one hand as Turnfort did on ye other   thee art right in my observation ye male & female toxicodendron so I allways took all our sumachs to be but this   I am sure we have many patches never bears seed & others every year all over ye countrey of I think every sort but I intend next summer to search more accurately   thy observation on ye veratrum & ye mediola is very Just   I desighn to send thee another next fall   it is A sweet flower   ye gale espleni folia rarely bears seed not one in hundreds or thousands but I sent both specimens with Lion[3] & desighns to send more by first opertunity   but I have A notion that ye male & female plant is distinct on ye same plant   it grows on very poor ground in ye Jerseys   I hope next summer to collect A fine little volume of specimens for thee   I am obliged to thee for ye very kind ofer of ye specimens which I am asured is very curious but at present my fancy runs all upon ye living plants   therefore thee would oblige me most in sending mee some of thy curious seeds cuttings or bulbous roots   fibrous roots is difficult to send when I have sent thee A new variety of specimens I will talk farther about that affair   this winter I have very diligently perused thy figures & gardeners dictionary believing them to be ye compleatest work of that kind extant but I find many of our countrey plants omitted by reason of not being fully acquainted with them which I hope in A few years to furnish thee with specimens or growing plants in order to compleat A useful apendix   as I wrote to thee [by] ye mirtila by whome I [illegible] formerly Dr Witt used to tell me he used commonly to dream of fine flowers   I delighted most to dream of flying from ye top of one mountain to another   now ye doctors sight fails him he cant entertain flora any longer   dont thee think he is fled to me for now every few nights I dream of seeing & gathering ye finest flowers & roots to plant in my garden

pray my dear friend oblige me with one or two of thy best sorts   I want but one of A sort but I love variety   pray dont let our dutch outdo me but I hope I have engaged A prety good humoured dutchman so that he will get what he can of his countreymen for me & he is well beloved with thou   he is an ingenious man but he likes to have his stove room hotter then I do & thinks his plants loves it two, but most of ye native plants of ye temporate zone loves to breath ye natural fresh air & in thair dormant season ye Juces will bear A Congelation like pismires[4] or ye worms in wood & thair organical vesails not be lacerated provided ye congelation comes on gradualy & ye fluidity is restored as gradualy for I believe more foreign plants is destroyed by our suns heat then by our cold in common winters   but most certain that our most intense frosts will congeal ye juices of some plants more then thay can bear in such A case thay should have some light covering which should in moderate weather be A little raised to let in fresh air but not sun shine before hard frost is past & then it should not in ye hottest time of ye day until ye buds begin to swell   but to bring these plants into A hot stove heat makes them so tender & sickly that thay hardly recovers in ye whole summer season but ye native plants of ye torrid zone is adapted not onely to A high degree of warm air to thair leaves but warm earth for ye roots to draw nourishment through

American Philosophical Society Library, John Bartram Collection.
1. The year of this letter, 1759, is clear from its content.
2. Bartram added a description of the missing numbers on the other side of the sheet.
3. Captain Lyon.
4. Ants.

From COLLINSON[1]

I have answer'd largely my Good Friend Johns Letters of 9br 1 & 13 by the Dragon acquainting Him that the seeds & plants came Safe   I only wish there had been 7 or 10 boxes more of Seeds — thy Two Letters came Mee On New Years Day & none Since is come to hand – next year send about fifteen boxes of seeds — perhaps Twenty   it is all a Chance & thou must risque It   I could now sell Tenn or 12 boxes if I had them — next year they may not be in that Humour — I heartyly Wish that Capt Duncan[2] was come for the Season advances and people are Impatient for them —

amongst the plants Wee could not find the yellow Blaseing Starr, & but one Root of Calciolus which are favourites, Look out for them & more Orchis, especially the yellow flowering — I cannot recollect that the box seeds & specimens was received by Mee last Spring — I think I could not forget such a Thing

There is Two Species of a Aralia Spinosa or Angelica Tree from Virginia — but you have another prickly plant the New York pelitory or prickly ash — and there is another Species in Virginia called the pelitory or Tooth Ache Tree a fine plant & what I want — send seed of the Aralia spinosa or Angelica Tree or Some young plants

Alexander['s][3] Purple Ulmaria must be a fine plant — I hope Care will be taken to Increase It

My Striped Bark Mapple has not all the Colours thou mentions   phaps it may as it grows older

I have in my other Letter told thee the uncertainty & risques of Laying out Money this Warr Time — I have some Thousands Laying by Mee & am fearfull to Lay it out — for if Warr Lasts every Stock will be much Lower —and I dont see any prospect of peace — for more perticulars see my other Letter

I am now much Engaged

Thine
P. Collinson

The Magazine comes in debt on Frank.

As the Ship has had so Quick a passage I hope the grafts will be alive — but Trees of thy grafting is more Certain

Send 2 Boxes Seed to Ireland as under

1 box for Lord Farnham to be consigned to Mr. Charles Hamilton Mercht in Dublin

1 box for Charles O'Hara to be Consigned to Mr. Robert Birch Grocer in Dublin — give both them & Mee Letters of Advice

As the Myrtilla is so happyly arrived in a Month & 2 Days – with the Seeds — Send but *10 or 12* Boxes next year

Thou Surprises Mee to hear the Talk of your Rivers being Frozen!! February Wee had the Warmest Finest Weather ever known & Gardens full spring flowers —

I am obliged to thee for thy trouble about the Governors Bill – I have heard He is a Man of great Indolence

I have heard nothing from Wm Borthwick[4] of Edinburgh nor from Elias Bland for the Hambro box

BP 3:25.
1. The date of this letter is uncertain. Collinson's reference to his "other Letter" (concerning the uncertainty of investments in wartime) seems to refer to his of February 25, 1759, and suggests that this letter may have been written in March of that year. He is replying to Bartram's letters of November 1 and 13, 1758.
2. Captain Robert Duncan.
3. James Alexander.
4. A merchant and seedsman.

From COLLINSON

March 10 1759

I now come to Thank my Good Friend Jno Bartram for his cargo of plants & Congratulate him on the success that has attended all his Cargo of Seeds during this Warr — all the plants Seemed in good order but why was I tantalized about the Dwarfe Oaks — I & my Son examined everything with great attention but could find nothing Wee could liken to them except 2 or 3 sticks with knobs at their End but neither the Least Root or fibre we could discern — Wee therefore conclude they was by Accident Left behind for we was persuaded our Ingenious knowing friend knew better than to Send such rootless Sticks for to produce growing plants —

Wee have great Hopes as fort Duquesne is in our hands & if Crown point is as happyly surrendered, all the Nations of Indians will see it their interest to join us & Establish peace in all our Borders — Then Thou will be able to sally forth again on New Discoveries & I think with Safety, thou may Venture to Fort Duquesne, as there will be continual traffick thither, both from your Country & from Virginia — as there is a fine Straight road now made, it will be very Easie of access, — Inquire in Time, what parties of

Trading people, or Troops, are going thither, and then Joyn thy Self with them, from the Fort Little Excursions may be made every Day & come & lie there at Night, that fine Country has been unsearch'd   So Rich a Soil will be productive of New & Rare Vegitables that Wee are strangers to — but as Thou art a better Judge how Safe & practicable such an Expedition may be, I submit to thee — But for Certain it must be a pleasant one & what may be Discovered would recompense the Length of such a Journey —

Wee have had hither To one of the Mildest Winters that can possibly happen in this Country — all January South Winds warm & mild only 2 frosty Days — & now this 25th feby the Itea, Sweet Bay Dogwood &c have as Green Leaves on them as in Summer — the Tough Twig'd Viburnum is quite an Evergreen   the Gardens full of flowers — but such Early Warm Seasons rarely prove a fruitfull year for apricots & almonds have been in Blossome & peaches are ready to Open — then come Sniping Sharp winds in March & Cutts all off — Wee have had more than a Month without Rain   Warm & Dry which is good for the Corn   Wee may be thankfull to providence for our great plenty —

Wee was Sadly Disappointed being in hopes of Seeing Some Grafts of the True New Town pippin but there was none   pray remember another year — for what comes from you are Delicious Fruit   if our Sun will ripen them to such perfection — our Frd Benjamin had a fine pcell of the apples came over this year in wch I shared —

I received Billey's Letter   I am pleased to see him Improved in his Writeing   I wish I could say as much in his spelling — which will be Easily attain'd with application   I send Him 2 books to assist Him —

I wish it could be any ways contrived for him to give us a Draught of your Great Mud Turtle   Our friend Edwards wants to see It — I thought I had Lost that Thou Sent Mee — but last year I saw it several Times on the Water — but there is no catching It — & then I would Wish to have a Larger painted — and also to have its Shell for in all my Collection it has been forgot to send Mee that shell which at least I should be glad off — if a Drawing cannot be had but its upper & under Side Should be Drawn   send 15 or 20 boxes next year but be sure Early   I am in sad distress for more Seeds   I wish the next ship may come Safe & bring Some   I want Tenn Boxes more — I don't Hear of any yett come from Alexander —

Wee are of various Opinions about Swallows   Some assert they take their winter abode under Water   others say they resort in great numbers into Caves or Caverns, & sleep all Winter but the prevailing opinion is, that when food grows Scarce they retire to other Countries to the Southward & return in our Spring   Many want to know if your Swallows are the same as ours   Wee agree on the Number of the 4 Species — So if it can be conveniently done Send a Cock and Hen of those that can be caught   I have writt in my former Letters but by thy answers I know some have miscarried these precarious Times.

I have lately been reading Hennepin's Travels[1] who first Discover'd the great River Mississippi   He often mentions they were sustained by killing goats   Now I don't remember ever reading of any in the country about the lakes nor with you   they must be aborigines, because met with in countries very remote & where no Europeans had been before

the present situation of our public affairs makes it very Difficult how to advise Laying out Money   our stocks Fall Every Day   I have some Thousands Lying by Mee & have done for some Time and I don't know how to Lay it Out — there is more a prospect of Looseing then Getting in times of peace the Hazard is much Less —

Besides I should not venter to Lay out any of thy Money — unless I had an Instrument in writeing under thy bond & the publick Seal & Legally Wittnessed — by which thou Impowers Mee to Lay out thy Money in the publick Funds, and that I should not be Subject or accountable for any Losses thereon for if such be the Case which often happens & thou should Die thy Executors may call Mee to account for so Doing

I am thy old friend,

P. Collinson

Send by the First ships for Ireland one five guinea Box Seeds Directed for Lord Farnham and consigned to Mr. Charles Hamilton Mercht in Dublin one Box 5 guineas of Seeds, for Charles O'Hara Esqr consigned to Mr. Robert Birch Grocer in Dublin

Give both the people bills of Loading and Letter of Advice, & *Mee also, or Else I shant know* they are sent — *pray mark another Skunk Root & Send Mee next year*   Magazine for last year comes in Lib Com Trunk

I am concerned for poor Moses's bad Luck   March 10th 1759 this day I had a letter of thine of Feby 8 with advice of the Seeds

As these are arrived send Mee but Tenn Boxes next year for if these had nott arrived, they must have staid untill then but as they are now Supplyed 10 or 12 may be Enough for I have not yett orders for any so they may be to much, so dont know how to go   fast or too slow   for the freight will fall on us if they are not sold so Dear John I must leave it to thee

BP 2:97; D. 216–18.
1. Father Louis Hennepin, French explorer and writer, accompanied La Salle on explorations along the Great Lakes and upper Mississippi. He published *Description de la Louisiana* (Paris, 1682) and *Nouveau Voyage* (Paris, 1696).

From COLLINSON

Londn April 6th 1759[1]

Dear John
I have writt Largely by Captain Hammet in the Dragon & another Ship in answer to all thine — they are dated March 10th —

I am much obliged for the Box of plants & Seeds wch last was more acceptable as I have several friends to Oblige — the Specimens for Miller no doubt He'l give some account of

The Truss Thou Desired is packed up in a Box   Inclosed is the Key, sent to the Care of our Friend Neve — in the James, Capt Simpson which I wish Safe to hand & that it may answer

In the Lib:Com Trunk by this Ship is the Magazine for Last year & another pcell with Books & some printes for thy Study

I am in haste thy old frd

P. Collinson

James Gordon gives his Respects and Desires Seed the great & olive Leave Chamerododendron, of Kalmias, Andromedas Ivy or Azalea Huckleberries & will send any thing thou Desires

there was I remember a Box plants come Late Last year — with Silver Leaved Alder which did Well but being So Late in the Season the others did not do notwithstanding all my Care

Truss	2:12:6
Insurance	5:3
	2:17:9

Miller & Gordon have both shared in the Little Box Seeds   this very Mild year our Crocuses began to flower the Middle of January

I want five Guinea Box of Pines, Firrs & Every other Evergreen that can be procured — so the Box is to contain no other seeds but Evergreens

one Does not know how to go to fast or too Slow   I have no orders for any more then the above Box

however Send Eight Boxes — besides   If it was not that Wee must pay freight if unsold I would run the Risque of More

I have had the pleasure of my Friend John's Letters of Dece. 17, Jany 18 — Feby 8th and Two Sheets of January 28 — which was very Informing & Entertaining — I have sent them to Miller for his perusal & shall take more notice of them when I have the Leisure

Friend John I have great Luck before I seal this to answer thine of Feby 28 this 9 aprill   I before wrote thee thy laying out thy Money whilst Warr Lasts is very precarious but in the First place if thou will send Mee power of attourney to Impower Mee so to Do — & next that I shall not be made liable to any Loss on the Purchase of Such Stocks in the Bank &c for if for Instance I should Buy Hundred Pound Stock, for a Hundred pound Sterling and in a while thou or thy Children in Case of thy Decease should order Mee to Sell thy Stock, and by that Time from some bleak accidents, it may fal to 90 £ as is the Case Now a Tenn pound Loss on a 100 — I must not be Liable for that —

as it happens in thy Way think of these as under

Orchis, Heleborines, Calceolus Marias, & any od plants   pray send a sod or Two More of thy pretty Pyrola with variegated leaves   It flowered finely last year but I see no young shoots which makes me think it will go off after flowering

Fail not to send 3 boxes of Seeds to Ireland
1 for Lord Farnham consigned to Charles Hamilton in Dublin
1 for Charles O'Hara Esq consigned to Robert North Grocer in Dublin
1 for Lord Kildare in Dublin

giveing Each a Letter of Advice & Mee also — pray look out against next Season for 2 or 3 flowering plants of your Ivy, Bay or Azalea   Inclosed is a Leafe for Wee have now so many Names of plants it is Difficlt to explain one Self, this Beautifull Evergreen Shrub thou has sent Mee several Times over   it will Flater one & shoot a few Leaves & even Flowers and will go off, as is the Case Now — It requires a peculiar soil — to hit it, for the future, what Earth is requir'd in the Box, pray Lett it be of the Identical kind in which it grew

Billy sent Mee a Delightful drawing of what is called with you the Yellow Root — pray Look out & Send Mee a plant or Two for it seems a New genus — J. Alexander sent over last year some Roots — but not knowing it by that name I neglected to buy them — phaps He can inform thee where it grows in plenty —

this last Box of plants came admirably well — though I search with utmost Care Could not find all the plants Mention'd in pticular the Dwarfe mountain Ranunculas, the single sort is pretty but the Double from Doc Witt is much more so — for the small things putt in moss & then Tie up in a Little [illegible]

We are all much Entertained with thy draught of thy House and Garden   the situation most delightful and that for our plants is well chosen I shall endeavour to furnish it   my pen & ink is so bad so [illegible] pray remember me to Moses   after all his [illegible] am glad he is well   pray give my kind love to my worthy old friend Doctor Witt   I am concerned for the loss of his outward sight   May his inward receive a flow of Divine illumination

prethee tell Mee at thy Leisure the Story of those Lying Hypocrites — I am glad thou hast got the Money of the Governor, He is an unworthy man to oblige Mee to Dun Him in his Government —

Oftentimes after people has bought stock at a 100 and it rises to 105 then thou will have the advantage so thou must take thy Chances but I must be secure in what I do or else thy Executors May call Mee & mine to account if it prove a loosing bargain

BP 2:98; D. 218.
1. The postscript that comprises most of this letter was written on April 9, as noted therein.

From COLLINSON

Some Notes on Specimens Sent P:Miller

the Pavia is common in our Gardens, grafted on the Horse Chesnutt, for it flowers freely but never ripens Seed — which would be Acceptable —

Bartram's drawing of his house and garden, sent to Peter Collinson (see Collinson to Bartram, April 6, 1759). Reproduced by permission of the Earl of Derby, Knowsley, England.

the Red bud Andromeda is pretty   I should like a plant or Two off but does not come up to the Evergreen with olive Leaves thee formerly sent Mee which began to flower beginning of March but bears no fruite so cannot Increase It —

the Different Species or Hydrophillon should be glad to see — I want much the Yellow Root   if a Stranger to thee ask Alexander —

of the Olive Tree Chamaerhododendron I have had a Tree Some years but makes no progress — should like one or Two More

thy New England Crategus or Service I much Like — send some of its Suckers if rooted —

our Early Tree Service and another Specimen Like it without Name — our Swamp Spring Service	Send Specimens with Fruit on them — Gordon is Doubtfull if Wee have these sorts send plants

our Tree Early Sweet Service   this Wee have & thrives finelyly [sic] — but thy Specimen wants the flowers —

Our Dwarfe Summer Crategus   send Specimens & berries   all the Sorts Wee have flower freely but rarely fruit — that pretty shrub was raised by the Late Lord Chancelors Lady in Compliment to Her is called Lady Hardwick's[1] Shrub   Wee query if the Dwarfe Plum is not what Wee formerly Had for the Beach Cherry — Sett us right but by the Size of the Fruit it must be Different   So pray Send us Stones of Dwarfe plum

I should be glad to have 2 or 3 plants of that pritty Shrub, that is Like a Huckle Berry & which bears a flesh Colour Fruit big as a Morella Cherry — is not a Species Oxyacocus or Ozacorus or Cranberry —

the Dessiduous Magnolia thrives So with Mee that it will Match thy Leafe for Size — I have all the 4 Species of Magnolia in great prosperity

Gordon Desires Some Seed of the Climbing Toxicodendron Triphilum. — He thinks it a New Sort

the Spring flowering State of this Shrub Toxicodendron Triphilon & its Winter State — this Wee have wanted many Years — if the Can Send a Tree & Seed — the Northern Shrub has Shoot finely   it Seems a New Genus

I shall send in the Box with the Truss[2] a Little Galipot to putt the Misleto berries In — they get too much Dryed comeing in paper   However Wee planted & sowed them on the bark of Several Trees

Thee Disappointed sending only 3 or 4 grafts of Newtown pippins Be Sure send Trees of Each Sort & more grafts for they Look Fresh & Well, would have been better Tied up in Moss — these Sent was Loose —

Send more Specimens *for my Self* off all your Services or Crategus or Mespila's   Wee are not truly acquainted with all the Species — and without Flower & fruit can determine nothing Certain

& Such is your Variety of Huckleberries Andromedas, Vitis Idea's — Wee are at a Very great Loss to [identify] them without seeing them in thear Flowering & Fruiting State —

BP 3:29.
1. Wife of Philip Yorke, First Earl of Hardwicke (1690–1764).
2. This mention of sending the truss indicates that these "Notes on Specimens Sent P:Miller" were enclosed in Collinson's letter of April 6, 1759.

From HENRY de PONTHIEU[1]

London April the 12th 1759

Mr. John Bartram
Sir

Being informed by my friends Mr. Collinson & Mr. Ellis[2] that I cannot apply for American Plants to a properer Person than yourself I take the liberty to trouble you with this, to desire you'd send me next autumn the following Plants

4 or a half dozen of the Evergreen Andromeda such as Mr. Collinson of which I send you inclosed part of a branch with the flowers on it.

4 or a half dozen Plants of the Pensilvania Privet such as the other sample You'll find here inclosed: You'll know again the leaf tho' the colours are faded   The leaves on the tree are of a bright green.

Half a dozen Plants of the Ivy leaved Azaleas such as Mr. Collinsons. I believe it is called with you the Mountain Ivy   It is a dwarfe Plant the leaves are small & of a bright green   If you could send me a branch of this tree & one of the American Privet in flower it might serve me better to determine their Genus which is not perfectly known at present as they dont flower here.

Half a dozen Plants of your Mountain Laurel known by the name of Camerododendron or Rhododendron.

Half a dozen Plants of the Sweet Flowering Bay or Smaller Magnolia   I should like too to have any sort of Evergreen You may have lately discovered   As to other trees I am not so curious in them tho' if it be agreeable to you I could recommend you several of my friends — I should like to have fresh seed of each of the above sorts   Mr. Lewis Pintard[3] of New York will pay you for whatever you send me   He or Mr. Collinson can inform you whom I am —

If you'll please to trouble yourself with the executing the above Commission I shall be glad in return to be of Service to you here — Sir,

Your humble Serv't.
Henry de Ponthieu

I beg the above may be the best plants you can get.

BP 3:95.
1. Henry and John de Ponthieu were neighbors of Collinson.
2. John Ellis.
3. Pintard (1708–1778) was a wealthy New York merchant.

From COLLINSON

Lond May 29th 1759

I have now only Leisure to thank my Good Friend John for his Entertaining Letters of the January 28 of Two Sheets of paper which I shall take more Notice off In process of Time & I have since Received thine of Feby 28 March 15 & April 6th —

Both thy Cargoes by Capt Hammet and Capt Bolitho came safe — of the Living plants Sent I can give but a poor account   many of them was Stumps without Fibers so I had no hopes of them but Live in Expectation they may shoot — there is a Calceolus Maria that raised our Expectations it is a strong plant with roughish Leaves but Wee cannot yett procure the flowers   the Grafts was such poor slender weak things I am afraid they will Come to Nothing besides there was so few of Them our Chance was the Less

I am glad your Gover[1] has paid his Bill — I Design to have no more to do with So unworthy a Person — What I have writt before I will repeat again if Thou will Impower Mee by a proper Writeing Sign'd & Attest'd under your Citty Seal — in which I may be Indemnified if any Loss should happen on thy Money Laid out on Bank Stock or Annuities I will readyly do It — I have not the least Suspicion of Thee my Dear Friend but I don't think It reasonable to be Called to account by thy Executors for what I did as an act of Kindness haveing only my Labour for my Pains

I writt the March 10th & 16th Capt Hammett for 8 Boxes of Seeds tho i have no Orders but from Two — that is One for the Duke of Richmond to be all Sorts of Ever Greens as Pines Firrs Cedars Holley Arbor Vita & any other Ever Green thou can procure   Lett this Box have a pticular Mark —

Another Box for Lord Clifford — of all Sorts of Forest Trees   pines firrs Oakes &c — very few Shrubs except Some that are rare & New

The other Six Boxes to Contain all Sorts as usual   remember Three Boxes for Dublin   1 for Lord Kildare at Dublin Consigned to Him   1 for Lord Farnham Consign'd to Charles Hamilton, Merch't Dublin   1 to Charles O'Hara Esq Consign'd to Robert Birch Grocer in Dublin   Send Every one Letters & Bills of Loading & also give Mee a Letter

If any Land or Water Terrepins happen in thy Way Save them and Send them but not the Great Mud Turtle — I only want his Shell & if Billy would paint his Curious figure it would be better   if any Orchis Calceolus Marias Martigons Lillies or any other Curious plant think of thy old frd

P Collinson

I wish Moses good Success in his Jamaica Voyage

In Jared Eliots Letter I pceive thou has a Method of Splitting Rocks with Water   pray tell Mee how that Is pformed & give mee thy answer to his 5 Queries about that operation   A fine pcell of Seeds with the List 50 Sorts of thy own Hand writing have been presented to Mee — by One that Sought to do Mee a favour   amongst them are Curious Sorts — that was not sent Mee in thy Box Seeds [illegible] plants growing   first Cargo [illegible]

The perfoliated honesuckel grows finely   Two Oaks Northern Shrub grows, what to make of it don't know   Itea grows & Crategus, these have been Long in my Garden   The Tall Calceolus [illegible]

Plants in 2nd Cargo

Perenial Indigo   Creeping Syringa   Some others may come yett   I sent thy Letter to Phillip Miller   pray send 3 or 4 flowering plants of this Leafe or what thou Calls Ivy or Lessor Chamerhododendron   Lett the Box have only the Earth it grows in & no other that I may plant it on that Earth & then See what Success I shall have for they don't Like our Soil   tell Mee in what Sort of Situation it grows   In High or Low Wett or Dry   for of all plants it is my Favourite   So pray try & gett Mee good strong plants with Sodds to them, carry some String in thy pockett & tie it round It to keep the Earth to the Roots & putt 2 or 3 plants of broad Leaved Andromeda with Large white flowers   I had a fine Large plant went off from our great Drowth — next I will plant in a Bogg & Time [Thyme] Leaved Andromeda a plant or Two   these all are favorites, pray what is the plant thou calls Red leaved Andromeda   Send a plant or Two that I may See and give Mee a Little account in what Soil & Situation Each plant grows — if any Papaw Tree happens in thy Way putt in 2 or 3 — I have not received thy Letter So if any where Obscure guess att the Meaning — I sent the Truss by the Care of Merchant Neve Ship the James, Capt Simpson & I think I putt in a pcell for thee in the Lib Com Trunk of books

BP 2:49; D. 218–19.
1. Governor William Denny of Pennsylvania.

From MILLER[1]

Chelsea May 30 1759

Mr: Bartram

I was favoured with your letter and received the Box you was so good as to send me in which I found your rooted plants and four small branches of plants cut off without any title, neither of which [illegible] it is hardly worth while to send cuttings of plants   I likewise received from Mr. Collinson a paper of seeds without any titles   these I have sown in two or three different places and at different times to see what may be produced from them. Few of the seeds you sent me last year came up and in most of the parcels there are come up a mixture of two or three sorts of plants only so that they are scarce worth the trouble of raising. I was in hope to have received a root or two of your Veratrum, having lost that which you sent me before and also a root or two of your different kinds of Martagons; for those which rise from seed here make so little progress that they will be many years before they flower. I shall also be much obliged to you for a plant or two of the Gale with spleenwort leaves and a dried specimen of the male and female plant for in the garden here I have only seen the male. A root or two of your Orchis's Ladies Slipper Evergreen Pyrola &c will be very acceptable to me; or any uncommon plants you may meet with which are not common already in your Gardens. The Tetragonotheca is also rare here; if you can find me either roots or seeds of thos you will greatly oblige me and in return I will send you the plants which you desire from hence, with some seeds which I hope may prove acceptable to you and by the first oppertunity will forward the remainder of the Gardeners Dictionary to you which is now finished with those numbers of the figures of plants you want but I am surprised how those numbers which you write were not received because I regularly sent them to you as I found oppertunities

The speciman which you sent of the Pavia is of the same sort with ours, but in your climate it produces more flowers than here. Fair specimens of your polygalas, Gerardias and such plants as we have not here will be a great plesure to

Your humble servant
Philip Miller

American Philosophical Society Library, Wildman transcript; BP 4:83.
1. Wildman's copy has been used for this letter because much of the original is illegible. On the back of this letter Bartram wrote a list of the plants sent to Collinson by Buden in 1759.

From COLLINSON

Lond July 20th:1759

I answerd my Dr Jnos Letter of the 28 Jany & feby 8th per Capt Simpson Aprill 9th & by the James Neaves ship sent thy Truss May 29 To which I refer'd — & now send thy Acct on the other side

of thy 2 Cargos of plants — I have only one Root of Great Cocalia but did not flower this year   Two Dwarfe okes are shot out from rootless stumps so dont expect they will hold

one Root of Calceolas that flatter'd my expectations & came   Perrenial Indigo — up very strong but did not flower   the non described shrub that grows downward — 1 Christophoriana, 1 Itea 1 Service   these last I had before   the perfolioated Honesuckle grows finely   I wish it may prove different from what Wee have

I am greatly pleased with thy Account of our English wild plants — So early as Josselyn He makes an article or List of our plants growing in New England in his Time, which came in grass seeds or by Strange accidents as the Willow & the Scotch Thistle which I think a fine plant. I had it once in my Garden   See what Climate & Soil does, the Yellow Linaria is no pest with us — I keep it in my Garden & it is very orderly, for the sake of its fine Spike of orange & yellow flowers —

The Hypericum keeps always on the border of our Fields — but the Leucanthemum or Ox-eye Daisie over runs some fields — but then it makes a fine show   for that reason I give it a proper place in my Garden as I love all flowers

I intended this a Long Letter but must cutt it short for the Capt goes to Morrow & I am just going out of Town

My Friend Daniel Mildred is Owner to Capt Friends ship — He has promised his Care of a Little Box of Roots the Great White & Yellow Asphodel fine flowers — with other Bulbous Roots & Some Sweet Scented great pale Blew Iris 3 or 4 Roots of Calcedonian Iris   these are smaller then the other & must have care taken of them in Frosts — they sprought up Soone & show their Long Narrow Leaves   Take Care & plant the Least Root for there is Some pretty odd things amongst them —

1757 Aug. 15 By Ball.		225:14
to Aprill 1758		
By 13 Boxes Seeds by Cap Duncan		68:51
1758 By 12 boxes Do. By Salley Cap Nead		63:01
1759 By 9 boxes The Dragon Cap Hamett		52:10
1759 By 1 box paid by Mennon & Mason		5: 5:
1759 by 6 boxes seeds by the Myrtella		31:10
	£	440: 4:
DR		
1758 To Cash pd J Bevan for his Son		10: 0:
Feby 3		
March 19 To Do. pd Cap Child		15: 0:
To Magazine 1758		6: 2:
To Cash pd for a Truss		2:12: 6
To Do pd Insurance		5: 3
To my Bill on Govr Denny		6: 2: 6
To Ball July 20:1759		415:17: 7
	£	446: 4: 5

I have before writt, send Mee a proper authority to Lay out thy Money, and Indemnification, if any Loss arises on It for so Doing – & I will Lay it out in the funds —

please to tell Joseph Morris there is a pacquet of Magazines &c for the Lib: Com — in Capt Friend Deliver'd in the Care of Daniel Mildred his owner as is thy Box &c   thy House & Garden Delights Mee Much —

don't trouble thy Self to send any more plants in Earth but what is Rare or Curious — I am afraid it will be to Late for Lillies, Martagons Coleolas &c.

Remember to Moses & Billey & Johney

BP 2:99; D. 219–20.

To COLLINSON[1]

13th day Saturday to 28th day Tuesday

Some good land   crossed Opecon   it rained prodigiously most of ye way   held up in ye afternoon   found several curiosities which I saw thereabout before   it is wonderfull how ye english hounds tongue is spread over this countrey in most of thair rich lands   here we saw ye effects of ye incrusting limestone waters which is of that nature that where it runs it incrusts round brush or leaves or stones or any thing in its course frequently stoping its course & overflowing ye adjacent low grounds amongst ye leaves brush or grass or weeds which it incrusteth & when ye winters frosts is sharp it penetrates this crust which falls in scales & enricheth ye ground exceedingly   I observed A bank 8 foot deep at A mill race all of this incrusted limestone matter converted into firm soil & many times of such A firm consistency as to make numerous dams quite cross large creeks so that ye floods frequently overflowed large quantities of low grounds & enriched them much with its Calcareous matter when disolved by ye frosts rains dews & sun   rode through winchester & tiffins town midling land most of ye way over & between limestone ridges   some places very stoney & rocky limestone reached 4 mile beyond ye town   rain most of ye day   ye roads very dirty & slipery by ye great rain   other wise prety good & prety well inhabited & people sivil

14: set out & rode over very stoney ground produceing great red Cedar pines   2 leaved   2 & 3 leaved   broad leaved willow oak   Ptelia & lodge by North shenadore this day was cloudy & bad roads

15: rode 4 mile   crossed ye river   found ye great indigo on its banks prety good road & land with pines   came to thomas loukins[2] about noon who was very kind   had a fine plantation & choice medow   here our horses was finely refreshed with A belly of good grass

16: set out   prety good land & rodes   sometimes rockey   some piney land   crossed south Shenadore   larger then A branch of brandywine at ye forks   saw ye great shrub St Johns wort & lodged at thomas stevensons near ye stone meeting house   Irish setlers   heard of ye mischief ye indians had done a few days before

17: came before noon to Augusta court house or stenton[3] where ye people discouraged me from going any farther along ye road toward looneys ferry   that ye Indians had murdered many white people about 30 mile distance in ye same vail so I turned to ye left toward ye South mountain intending to take ye Pedlers gap & travail on ye south side toward Roan oak but before ye midle of ye afternoon our horses was so tired that we could hardly get them along espetialy ye young horse that my son had   he had A very sore back   in his distress A woman overtook us & very kindly invited us to her house about A mile farther which we gladly accepted — our horses being so tired that when we came by A neibours barn my sons horse could go no farther until he had A sheafe of oats & rested A little   frosty morning

18: then we reached ye good womans house where we stayed all night &

next day where our horses rested & was much refreshed with grass & oats

19: We set out from our very kind friend John stills house he riding with us several miles to put us on ye right road to woods gap   he hath A choice tract of land wel watered & very good meadow good road & land to ye gap

lodged at John Ramsey by ye south branch of Shanondo as big as ye brandywine at ye forks   here I bought an elks horn which he promised to send to Philadelphia for me   in his field I found thair wild angelica ye running clematis A prety campanela & I think A small granadila.

20: set out thro ye gap where we gathered much seed of Angelica & ulmaria   we passed thro several ridges along A water coarse until ye southern ridge which was very high   much higher then ye highlands by ye north river or flying hills up skukill being ye same chain   we descended down ye South side near A run where I saw ye ginseng   thence a good road & land most of ye way   at ivy run we found A lovely aconite five or 6 foot high   redish soil   we lodged at Tirels   here ye negro was very merry playing on ye Banjo great part of ye night

21: Set out   crossed two large branches of James river ye eastern branch   had A fine bridge hanging over it 38 paces broad   here I found ye spotted leaved asarabaca   midling land some places poorish & stoney prety good road   soil red   road by orange court house   town like darby   lodged hard by

22: Set out   ye Soil red producing broad & narrow leaved willow oak & pine   crossed A large branch of Rapahana   rained most part of ye afternoon   lodge at Joseph normans   very rainy stormy night & rainy morning

23: Set out   poor soil   crossed A large branch of Rapahana as large as big brandywine   then poor flat stoney soil   broad leaved wiilow oak & barren black oak til noon   German Town   then midling to A new house where we lodged

24: Set out   poorish gravely ground   came in ye afternoon to william wests where we stayed to rest our horses all night   he is an ingenious man & hath A fine large farm & improvements well about it

25: Set out   rode over red poor soil most of ye way till ten mile of potomack where was limestone composed of peples & flatish stone & prety good land but rocky in places to ye river A quarter [mile] wide   thence rich to Molata toms where we lodged   A civil man   had A white wife & negroes cloathed   A good farm & things well about him

26: We set out   good road to frederick town   land good to Manachipie   lodge between ye pipe creeks

27: Came to crown & stayed all night where we had good pasture

28: Stayed to rest & refresh our horses

29: Set out & rode to york & came to ye widow wales where it rained dined there & got over ye river & lodged at James Whites   it rained exceedingly great part of ye night

BP 1:54.

1. This letter comprises part of Bartram's journal of his Virginia trip in October 1759 with his son Johnny.
2. It has not been possible to identify the various persons at whose houses the Bartrams spent the night on this trip.
3. Staunton.

From COLLINSON

Londn Octr:10:1759

I received my Dear John's Letter of the 16th:June   His Hodge podge digests very Well with Mee   I may give him as good as he Sends — thy Letter came to Late to mark the Hephions — but I like good Old Names best that Is the Bulbous Iris — I sent Some Variety of tuberous Iris &c

I am glad to Hear the Spanish Broom & Late peas are prosperous — I now Send More Laurel Berries — I wish Some may come up for it is one of the finest of Evergreens   I also Send to Some Ripe Berries of Portugal Laurel wch I think exceeds It & is Equally as Hardy — as Thou has ground Enough I Send More of our best Peach & Nectarine Stones, possibly Some being worth thy Culture may proceed from them —

Polyanthos is my Delight for they Anticipate the Spring for they have been Some first in flower & So will Continue through our Winter — their Variety is always Entertaining & Some thing New always comes from Seed — I shall be pleased if the white Campanella is come up   it is a stately fine plant but I have lost it by Some accident, tho it is perennial So Send Mee Seed again —

Ah, John, I thought thou had been too cunning to be Deceived by a Deborah — I have no Collection of tomatoes   I will try to gett Some from Gordon —

The Specimens came Safe & have been Deliver'd to P Miller — I wrote thee my Observations on them   I am much obliged to thee for Grafting the Newtown Pippins, what fruit comes from you is Excellent — I wish our sun may bring it to the Like perfection   Wee will give them a fair Tryal — in different situations —

I think thy Query Needless, (if the Punch-bowl in the Blew Rock was that fill'd by Governor Keith[1]) — Doth not thy own Memory Confirm It — It is really a very remarkable Instance of the Growth of Stone, in thy own Memory of 15 years — to be grown up within 3 Inches of its Surface —

It was very Curious to observe those Stone Basons & the Method of their formation — at my Leisure I may Consider more pticularly all thy remarks deserve my attention for these wonders in Nature would be Lost if it was not for thy happy Genius & turn of Mind for these Discoveries —

I hope the Boxes of Seeds will come in Time   if this is not too Late I can Dispose of 2 or 3 More — people come at all seasons   pray, sir, Let Mee have a box or Two of Seeds — Just as if I could write into the Country for them — never thinking they must come near 4000 Miles — So very thoughtless are the generality of Mankind so that I am at a great Loss what orders to give thee for I know not, who are to be my Customers for they most times come unexpected

Now, my Dear John Farewell

In hast
P Collinson

p Cap Marsden on 2 Brothers

Laurel Berries } Tied in Brown paper
Portugal Laurel Berries } in a Box to the Care
Peaches & Nectarines } of Elias Bland
Sow all as Soon as possible
the Small Berries that hang in Long Bunches Is the Portugal Laurell

Turn out all the Box at once on a Cloth phaps they may come out without breaking off — remember the yellow Root & Small Monolaca Ranunculus

In the Box I have Scatter'd variety of Seeds in the Sand — in perticular yellow Foxglove so take Care of It — & Spread or rather Sow it thinly over a Bed, haveing first Loosen'd Earth & Laid it very Smooth — Then Sift very thinly some mould over the Sand — & be carefull to Suffer no Weeds to grow on It

BP 2:100; D. 220–21.
1. William Keith (1680–1749).

From COLLINSON

Londn:Novemr:3:1759

I answered my Worthy Friends Letter of June 18 Augst:20 & Sent a Box of variety of Seeds on board By Capt Marsden on the 2 Brothers as Laurell & Portugal Laurel Berries well ripen'd & many other Seeds to the Care of Elias Bland & allso a Letter with Some Anemony Roots & Ferula from Island of Menorca   Since I have received thine of the 8th August — I am pleased to find thee in Such High Spirits, now I am convinced more than Ever that thou art a Deep rooted Botanist for a little Enthusiastic turn, probably the Effect of your Hott weather has sett thy Ideas a rambling — in the Wide Fields of Nature, she is not so Docile as thou Imagines and will be putt very Little out of her Course by all thy Inventions — however by the Tryals thou proposes to make thou will be convinced of the Weakness of thy Efforts to produce any Setled or remarkable Change in Her Laws

pray Lett Mee know the Success of thy Experiments — it is frequent with us after Long Summer Droughts Rains the begining of Augst & Warm Dry Weather Insuing Many Trees will blossom   to many to Enumerate but this is the Effect of a pticular Season & does not Happen every year — this year I Saw a Cherry Tree in Blossoms in Augst, but that Tree may never do so again — it is Accidental & not to be brought into practice by Art in the common Course of Nature   It is frequent in Curious Gardens whose Owners are Men of fortune to plant Fruit Trees & Vines in warm Stoves to bring them very Early into Blossome to have Early Fruite but this so exhaust the Trees, that new trees must be planted every year —

I hope the Obelescotheca & 3 Leaved Passion Flower – comeing so Early will ripen good seed for Wee want them Both — their great growth may be owing to a pticular Soil that Suites them   The great Aralia Spinosa I have Two Trees   the old[er] they Grow the more remarkable they are for their Thorney Bark   the Dwarfe Aralia grows flowers & bears plenty of Berries   I am psuaded from the Warm Aromatic flavour the Root may have Singular Virtues   the Large Xanthoxylum — fine plant but Tender   will not do abroad unless planted against a Wall — but the Dwarfe Northward Species lives & grows wonderfully — Thou frequently Talks of Sending Specimens to Mee & Lord Petre of this, That, & the other Species — as if it was but a year or Two agon — when Alas He has been Dead 14 or 15 years — all such Items are but wasting Paper & Ink — I am psuaded my Dear John there is great Difficulty in finding your Dwarfe Oakes proper to remove & that Thou did thy Best, — for the future plant all Such Stumps in thy own Garden for a year or Two in their own Native Country to make New Roots, then they may be removed with a prospect of growing — or Else Wee are only flater'd with fine Things as to very Little purpose — my Dear John I don't remember the Stone of the Bird Cherry & Dwarfe plum nor can I charge my Memory when the Specimens of yellow Root Came but as it was a rare plant if Thee hadst but Sent Some Roots — That I never could have forgot —

It must be a Surprising fine Sight to See the White Calceolus near 3 foot high — but your Warmth & Soil greatly promotes Vegetation — my plant flattered Mee with 2 strong Stems but no flower — phaps next year may bring It — what Seeds are Collected I presume are put up before this come to hand — I could now Sell more than first ordered —

I am my dear John

Thy sincere frd
P. Collinson

I don't understand the Nature of the fine variegated pyrola but after it flowered it went off — when another happens in thy Way I will try again —

Our Ingenious Friend Elliot has long desir'd to Try Turkey Wheat after many Essays & many Difficulties in procuring It — So is at Length come to my hand   I have Sent thee a Sample of It for a Tryal   It may come to Late for a Sowing this year — however Late as it may be Try 2 or 3 Rows in thy Garden   I have putt it in a paper pcell in a Box of Books for the Library Company that comes by this ship

prethee Frd John when thou goes to the Library ask for Josselyns Two Voyages, a little book of the size of his New England Rarities — & a Book well worth thy perusal   In Pag:61 He mentions an admirable Creature

— that the Indians call a Tree Buck   pray tell me what thou cans't of It which he says he often found —

the York Ships are gone so I cannot send Elliot his Turky Wheat untill next year

I have the pleasure to Inform my Dear frd I am Agreeably entertained with his kind letter of Sepr:28: — as the Ship Come safe so I hope the Box of plants are in Good Condition —

July 20th by Capt Friend[1] I sent thy pticular account — and the Totall all the Boxes out this year

16 Boxes – a Double To Fern[2]   I make 89 when I am paid for all the Boxes – thy acct –

Is 446:4:0 — paid — 34: 6:57
Totall Due to thee   411:17: 3
                    446: 4: 0

I received the Box by Budden — But Billy's Elegant Performance makes the shell alive   They are Dead Lumps without It —

More in my Next — the Carnation Seed is all my best   have Divided it & Sent Some by Each ship viz the Friendship & the Juliana

I am Concern'd for poor Moses — now He had Eat his Brown Bread but which will come next   I wish He would write a Little Journal in his own Way & stile from his first going to Sea to this present Time — *Short Hints will Do* — I question if it is to be paralled, Wee don't know what Human nature will Bear untill it is Tried   I have Sent a Large Letter   Seeds by Neets ship   I think [it is] called the Friendship

BP 2:101; D. 221–22.
1. James Friend.
2. A nursery gardener and seedsman.

From MILLER

Chelsea, Nov. 10, 1759

Dear Mr: Bartram

I was this day favoured with your letter dated 28th of September last, by which I am informed you have not received any letter from me since that bearing date of the 30th of May last. I wrote to you the 16th of July to acknowledge the receipt of the Specimens you was so good as to send me in Mr. Collinsons Box and to return you my thanks for them; and as you was so kind as to offer me plants of those sorts which you had in your Garden, so I must earnestly wish to have of them, as I believe there are some new Genera amongst them. The plant with a long spike of white flowers and grass leaves appears to me to be an Ornithogalum, but the flowers are so much compressed as to render the distinguishing characters very doubtful.

The Box of plants which I received from you last year I do assure were most of them cuttings, and if ever they had roots, they were cut off before they arrived here for there was no appearance of their having been in the ground, and except two herbaceous plants they all miscarried: they lay in the Box as if they were thrust into it without care and no labels on them to distinguish them.

In your letter you mention that you have sent me a book of plants, but as the Ship is not yet arrived in the River so I cannot give you any account of them but will do it as soon as I receive the Box.

You mention that none of my numbers have been sent you this year, the reason of which is I waited to have an account of the numbers which you have received of the Gardeners Dictionary and the Figures of plants, and in my two last letters I desired the favour of you to send me that account for as my Booksellers have changed hands the account of those numbers which were sent to you is either mislayed or lost & I must beg you to send it to me as soon as possible that I may make them compleat.

With this I send you a parcel of Bulbous rooted flowers from the Cape of Good Hope. If they succeed as well with you as they have done in the Chelsea Garden,[1] I am sure they will give you pleasure, but I imagine they will not live thro the winter without protection, which is the case here. They are a pretty tribe of plants   their flowers [seem] to be of a very singular structure   I have also in this parcel sent you some seed of the Scarlet Colutes which you desired in your last, this plant will flower and produce seeds with you, if you sow the seeds in the spring but they will not live thro' the winter in the open air in your Country —

The yellow-root has flowered and ripened seeds in our garden two years past, from some roots which were sent me from the Inland parts of your Country. it is a New Genus   I have figured and described it by the title of *Warneria*   the Gale Asplenii folio has produced male flowers in our Garden the last year, but as there was no appearance of female or hermaphrodite flowers, nor any rudiment of fruit, so I suppose it to be male and female in different plants. the two specimens you was so kind as to send me were one male and the other female so I shall be glad to be informed if they were taken from the same plant.

The Pavia which you sent me a specimen is the same with ours here   the flowers of which are some years more beautiful than others and sometimes it produces fruit here. I should be glad to have specimens of your new sorts of Toxicodendron   if they flower with you for those two which you sent me are not likely to flower here in some years. one of them is the Toxicodendron folio sinerato subscenti of Tournefort, the other with five and seven lobes to each leaf is new to me. it is that which you sent by the title of Great Toxicodendron, this makes but little progress with me as yet and seems to be a trailing plant which will not rise with a stem.

Your dwarf Cherry I believe is the same which I have figured. The stones came from Canada to Paris, and were sent me from thence. it produces great numbers of flowers along the branches, so makes a good appearance in the spring and the fruit is black about the size of our small black Cherries here, but of a disagreeable flavour. The plant propagates so fast by cuttings and layers that it is now common in our Gardens.

I am greatly deficient in your Martagons, having at present only one root of the common sort, that with two flowers upon a stalk which I have figured perished last year. Indeed I have many seedlings which came up last spring but it will be many years before they come to flower here. if you want any of our European sorts I can supply you and beg to have of all your kinds.

The Tricostema came up this year from the seeds which were sown the last, but it was so late in the Autumn before the plants flowered that I shall get no seeds from them, and I believe it is an annual plant   not one plant of the Gerardia has appeared tho' I sowed the seeds at different times and in different soils and situations, so I should be glad to have a fair specimen of each sort, as also of your Polygala's neither of which have succeeded with me, tho' I have left the ground unstired two years to see if the seeds will vegetate.

I propose to send you by the next oppertunity a parcel of plants and seeds of such sorts as will be very ornamental to your Gardens, but the notice of this Ships departure was so short as that I had not time to put them up and as soon as you favour me with an account of the numbers which you have of the Dictionary and figures of plants, the other shall be sent you.

I am

your friend and servant
Philip Miller

BP 4:84; D. 389–90.
1. Chelsea Physic Garden, founded in 1673 by the Apothecaries Company and still in existence.

From COLLINSON

garden full of Flowers
Lond feby 1760

By Capt Hamet I wrote my Dear John of his good Success for both Cargo of Seeds arrived safe in proper Time & without any Damage   in the same Vessel with them 11 boxes I was told was from Alexander   I can't think how they [illegible]

I apprehend my Letter miscarried that I wrote on receiving the two Large tortoise Shells: Thine and Billeys account of the Snaping Turtle with his fine Drawing, would make a Curious piece of Natural History, but our Authors of the Magazine are so careless, on these affairs, that I Don't know how to trust them & yett It is with regret I cannot find a better way to communicate them to the publick

I was amazed to See so great a Shell to the great *red Bellied Turtle* for they are the very *ones Sent Mee* & Billeys paintings is probably Lost   I have been in trouble for the Last of May [illegible]

This reminds Mee of the Elegant species of the Water Lillie that is in the Jerseys   Does it occupy such a depth of Water that the Roots can't be come att — Thou art ambitious of plants from Us, but here is the most Charming plant of Asia including China & *of Egypt* in thy Neighbourhood, & yett so Little is thy Curiosity, or Industry, that thou cannot avail thy Self of so great a Curiosity — Thou that hast Springs in thy Garden to make a Pond for its reception — or a River so Close by, if more proper for its Culture   prethee John never more Let Mee reproach thy want of Tast, & Curiosity in this article — I wish thou could employ some pson to gather the seeds when ripe, & putt in a Bottle of Water with a Little sand or earth in its Bottome — I conceive thus preserved they would come in a growing state to us   This I have mentioned often before but *Roots* well pack'd in a great Deal of wet moss in a Box would do better —

If I was in thy place, I should spare no pains or expense to be possessed of a Curiosity that none in the province could boast off besides thy self, which thou are ambitious off in other plants, in no comparison so Charming when in flower

Thou Mentions the Bay Terrapins   should be glad of a Shell   phaps Billey may be tempted to give a Sketch of it, I hope Billey has received the present of our Frd Edwards book that I sent in the Liby Com: Box of Books in which Mention is made of Many of thy Letters

Billey Sent Mee a Drawing of a Shell of the Salt & the Pond Turtle but neither shows any tail [illegible] Query, how does this *Pond Turtle* differ from the great *Red bellied Turtle* to which [illegible] Is this Last a *New species* with a Red Belly [illegible]

Dear John, farewell

P. Collinson

BP 3:13; D. 222–23.

From COLLINSON

Lond Feby 10:1760

I am now So much in a Hurry of Business that I can only acknowledge My Dear Johns Letter by Capt Budden with box plants — I sent them into the Country but Have not been able for Some Weeks to go down to see the Spring flowers which is Mortification enough for Mee —

Since Capt Friend[1] is fortunately arrived & all thy Cargo Landed & Seems in good Order which is owing to their being Stowed in a Dry place   Fern tells Mee Alexanders was much Damaged by Wett — and that Box of thine Suffered much by putting in that unripe Squash   it was all so putrid & Nasty there was no touching It which much Damaged the Seed, Birds & Specimens that Lay next to It   they was wett as much   It rent Mee to the Heart — never trust any thing of this Nature with Dry things —

the Birds is sent to Edwards that with the white Breast is Stain'd all yellow with the Squash & Letters are sent & Millers Specimens will be Sent as Soon as paper is Dry   thy 15:£ bill will be paid and as the Seeds are Come Safe thy Two orders on Mee from Bevan will be paid — so Dear John Farewell.

P Collinson

the box of seeds in sand with a pacquet of Seeds come in the Beulah Capt Gibbon

the 2 Little Baggs writt Gordon on & 2 papers of Shrub Seeds as I think butt all four without Name — Lay Near the gourd   Its moisture has rotted the very Cloth   the seeds all Mouldy must be renewed another year but pray putt some sort of name on Every thing   1 Peper Mint seed   the Martagon seeds & branch jacea all Damaged   Query if any will grow   by good Luck the Magnolia Escaped & Millers Bagg of Seeds & some others that Lay on the other side of the Box — pray send seed of the Smaller flowerd Rudbecia for that is my Favourite — as is the Large flower but that I have in plenty & flowers till Xmas

Denys Rolle[2]
at Hudscot
near Southmoulton

Make up a Box

Devon
For the Right Honourable Lord Viscount
Sudly — St. Stephens Green Dublin
and Wm. Gallagher at his House in Grays Alley
or at the Admiralty Office will pay you —

BP 3:14.
1. Charles Friend was master of the *James and Mary* in 1760.
2. Lord Denys Rolle, former M.P. from Barnstable.

To COLLINSON

february ye 20th 1760

Dear Peter
I have just received thy kind letter of october ye 10 1759 but ye vesail has not yet come to town   our river hath been shut above A month   Captain friend Just slipt out in time & put us in such A hurry that we hardly knowed what we did   I sent A box to John web[1] & forgot to have it inserted on ye Bill of loading But I sent him A letter of advice of it by him   we have had prety cold weather in general this winter & fall but little snow   I sent thee & gordon each A box of plants & A variety of seeds & to miller   I

answered thy letter & roots by Captain friend   I did not send by him all ye Boxes thee wrote for   thee said thay was not all bespoke & our merchants would have some   thay paid me 5 guineas A Box ready down & no risque run   I must next season gather more quantity I am exceedingly pleased with ye laurel berries espetialy ye Portugal   If but one of each will grow well I would not take ten guineas A piece for them (as poor as I am)   I believe there is not one growing in our 4 or 5 governments   I wish ye yellow digitalis & ferula may come up   I have one ferula yet alive from thy first seed   hope this may be different   I love variety   I have not yet received A line from Miller nor seed this winter or last fall   is he dead   I shall be very well pleased if ye anemony roots grows   our climate doth not agree with them by chance thay will appear in surprising glory for one or two springs then leave flowering & next year die   we have no hopes of ever seeing them flourish with us or ye best sorts of ranunculus   should be glad of some of your common sorts   perhaps thay may do better   I have sent in ye ship Rebeka Captain Linsay ye three boxes for Dublin according to thy order

BP 1:49:6.
1. John Webb, nurseryman at the Acorn, Bridge Street, London.

From COLLINSON

Mill Hill feby 25:1760

My Good Friend John Desir'd to know the Success of His Cargo by Budden   now I will tell Him – & Thank Him for His great Care in takeing up the Kalmias with Such large Sodds — which was all they had in their Favour for undoubtedly the Season was too Early for their removal for there was not a Green Leafe on Them – but when they come latter their Leaves are always as fresh as if taken Just then out of the Woods   However Wee took the utmost care to plant them to give them a Chance tho there was little appearance of Life in the Wood but phaps there may come up Some thing out of the Sods to reward our pains —

but to Thine & our Comfort the Branch of Dwarfe plum has all the Appearance of Life so doubt not but it will Do — & the Newton Pipins are all alive and promise well, time must Discover wether their Excellency is derived from your fine Climate —

with the outmost Care Wee Search for the Sundry Roots of Curious odd plants, — but the bagg was So rotten wee could neither make Head or Tail of It, — but I hope wee found the Roots   I was much Delighted to See what I take for the Yellow Root & my old acquaintance Docr Witts Mountain Ranunculus — it is a pretty thing   I hope the odd Anonis is amongst them, the Snake root which I wanted & the Orchis is I think Easily discovered all were planted in the Mould they came In, with a mixture of ours — to bring them to Like ours by Degrees pray Frd John Look out Sharp for Two Such fine Kalmias agt: next year & pray don't break the blossome Budds & give it Box Room & pack it up with a great Deal of green Moss for that keeps the Bark & Leaves Fresh & the Less Mould Does, for when they are very Heavy they Run great Risques from our Careless Porters.

Thy Fine Description of the Charming Calceolas with great White Spotted Flowers — O that Billy had been well Enough to have painted them with his inimitable Pencil — Such a Rare thing which I Scarcely can hope to See, I then might have always seen It — for I have Observed too Often that if these rare plants do not flower the first year — Seldome do afterwards & Yett your Yellow has taken such a likeing to Our Soil & Situation that I believe it cannot flower stronger with you than it does with Mee — So I may Cherish Some Hope to See the White one this year —

It is surpriseing thy Account of the Ivy or Lesser Kalmias growing in all Soils & yett so Churlish with that It will not Accept of our best Entertainment Except for 2 or 3 years — So much for thy kind Letter of 28th Sepr —

I now Come to the Perusal of thine of ye 18th Novem   commend thy resolution to Turn thy Horse about & Jogg Homewards — the doing It I know must be Mortifieing as Thou was Advanced so farr — but Wee have no Doubt you have Authentic Accounts that the Govern of So Carolina has Established a Secure Peace with ye Cherokees   this then restores a General Tranquility Through all your Borders — However don't venter Again untill thou art well Satisfied it can be done in Safety —

Oh John hadst thou known the Nature of the Ranunculas & Anemony Roots — thou wouldst have rejoyced to have seen them as Dry as a Stick — Docr Witts complaint was they always came Mouldy — but being Dry they would have kept untill your severe frosts was over but planting them So Soone, I wish they Survive them

I plant my Last but this Day, as Dry as Sticks could be, however lett Mee hear how they succeed —

The Tortoise Shells are wonderfull   Billys fine Draught admirable — these I have taken proper notice of in a former Letter

I must Endeavour to think of asking both B: Franklin & Bland about the Boxes of Seeds — the best way is to write to Each thy Self for I have a thousand things that Incumber my Noddle — that if these & many other things are forgot thou must Excuse It —

I am not Clear about what thou Calls & Wee Call New England Services — when thou Sends Mee a Compleat Sett of Specimens, both in flower & Fruit wee shall Settle that point & know what Each Means   I have one of your Services whose blossome budds are very much Swell'd ready to break   this Seems to be the Earliest Efforts of any of your Trees or Shrubs

Thy experiments on transplanting Trees from the Northward — may afford thee much Speculation but unless thou could transplant the Soil & Situation as well as the Tree — thy Kindness to It may be Ill bestowed —

Powel wrote for Seeds but his Letter Miscarried   if I had not Spar'd him a box Seeds would have been a great Disappointmt —

I much regretted the Loss of Williamson   He was the best Chapp thou had   He is returned again   take Care in the Paccage of his Boxes & that they are Sett in a Dry place in the Ship   I told thee before how Sadly Alexanders are Spoil'd —

I have a Friend at Prague in Bohemia that Desires about 4 ounces of your Common Accacia & Locust Seed — Lett it be taken out of the podds & Sent Mee   He would like More but I know there is trouble in Getting so Much, how you are Stock'd with this Delightfull Tree I don't know — however Send Mee Some that I may make good my Engagemt. —

on the 28 Feby I Paid Bevans by thy Order one hundred & Thirteen pounds

9ber 3d the Friendship Capt Cleland ⎱ sent Carnation Seed
10th p the Juliana Capt House   ⎰ by Each

Is it possible to procure Some Seeds of your fine great Nymphea or Faba Egyptica from the Jerseys & putt them Directly in a Bottle of Water & Cork it up — Certainly they must keep in their Natural Element & Come good

I have wrote by the Beulah & Sent to the Care of Merchant Neat a Box of Seeds in sand & a paper pcell of Seeds — & Seed enclosed in my Letter —So dont find fault & say thou are forgott   I have orders for Seeds as under

2 Boxes for one Balk to go to Germany
2 Boxes for our Friend Williamson
2 Boxes for Powel & Eddie ptners[1]
2 Boxes for Fern as usual I presume

Remember Mee to Moses & Billy —

BP 3:15.
1. The nurseryman Nathaniel Powell became a partner with Edie in 1760.

From POWELL

London April 21 1760

Mr. John Bartram
Sir
I write you last year for a Box of Seeds and plants but was disapointed I suppose my Letter miscaried or the Ship was taken. I have given Comisson to our good friend Mr. Collinson to send me Two Boxes of American seeds and Two Boxes of Plants   if his miscarys this will be your Comisson   let them be fresh and good as many new sorts as posable   you know I trade in seeds   you will let me have larger boxes and more in quantity then you comonly send to Gentlemen for thare own youse. as below have sent a Catalogue of what plants wold have you send with any other sorts you think

483

proper that are curious. let the seeds be all fresh and good   have named some sorts that I would have larger quantitys of   wold have some of all the sorts as you send to others   your care in sending every thing good carfully packt and [as soon] as posable will oblige

Sir

Your Old frind and Humble Servt
Nath: Powell

American Plants
Magnolias   many plants
Chamarodendren   Great and Small
Kelmias   all the sorts
Azalias   all the sorts
Sweet Gale with Farn Leaves
Andromeda   all the sorts
Papaw
Red flowring and Dwarfe Laurels
Stript Calcolus
Sarasina
Chiononthus
Ever green American Privet
Uva Ursi
Some others that are Curious
Send Large quantitys of the following Seeds
Magnolia
Red and White Cedar
Weymouth Pine
Bald Cypress
all the sorts of Pines
Two thornd Acatia
Sasafras
Benjamin Tree
Chionanthus
Maples   all the sorts
Myrtle
Red Cardinal
Great Chamorodendron
Chinqypins
all sorts of Wall nuts & Hecory with as many more new sorts as are to be got.

P.S. If you have my Comissons from Mr. Collinson you are only to send me two Boxes of Seeds and two Boxes of plants.

I want a Large quantity of Weymouth Pine   I believe the best way will be when the seed is Ripe to spred the Cones on a Cloth or Matt and lay them in the Sun   the seed will easley come out   you may send the seed without the Cones. I shall be pleas if you will send me a large bag of the seed as much as you can get.[1]

BP 4:98.

1. Bartram made the following notes on the above letter. He had traveled to North Carolina by ship in early March 1760 and had visited his half-brother William, of Ashwood, a Bladen County farmer and member of the General Assembly. At this time Bartram met Arthur Dobbs, who had become governor of North Carolina.

> Sent Brother 1760 several roots of Buckthorn two roots of angelica 4 roots of white rasberry one root of althea one of helibore a Sod of lily of ye valley a bunch of ye true safforn A root of cowslips A root of liquorish
> Sent Dobbs 4 kinds of iris A sod of Peony several roots of white rasberry a root of ye true savin A sod of violet A sod of cowslips A root of columbines roots of crown imperiall roots of ye great red lilly & ye flowering lilly A Sod of Lilly of ye valey two roots of angelica & seed sown in ye mould

From COLLINSON

London June 6:1760

I hope this will find my Good Frd. arrived Safe at his own Dwelling, from His Carolina Expedition — Thine from thence came safe to my Hands & I thank thy good wife for Hers — I have writt Largely by Budden — but for fear of Miscarriage I write this per Way of New York to Inform Thee what Seeds will be wanting next fall

& am thy old Frd.
P. Collinson

2 five guinea Boxes for Gordon who hath sett up a Seed Shop
2 five guinea for Powell & Eddie
2 Ditto for Williamson
2 Ditto for Fern
1 Do — for Webb
5 Do for Sundry people
1 Do for Bush
<u>2 Do</u> — for Bush but pray mind & be Exact for these are only to [be] fill'd
17 boxes   with pines, Firrs, Acorns, Beach, Chesnut and all Other Trees — but no Shrubs   putt a particular Mark on these two Boxes   Catalpa & Alders, Junipers, Cedars, Mapples, Birches, Services, Wallnutts, Hickeries, Planes, Padus Cherry, poplars, Tulip Tree, small Magnolia, Mountain Magnolia, &c.

June 10th

I am Charm'd, nay in Extasie to See the White Calceolus Marina Thou sent Mee in flower with Mountain Laurel, Red Acacia & Fringe Tree & all spice of Carolina, all in flower together —

Remember Mee ½ pound or a pound of Acacia or Locust Seed taken out off the pods.

Remember Mee to Billey Moses & Johnny

BP 3:16; D. 223.

To COLLINSON

June ye 24th 1760

Dear Peter

I have now my dear worthy Peters letter before me of february ye 10th   I am very sorry that ye seeds were damaged by ye rotten squash   it seemed when I put it in ye Box to be ripe enough & I thought to oblige my dear friend with ye best sort I ever eat but I believe misfortune will pursue me to ye grave let my intention & care be ever so good   ye seeds that I collected on ye south mountains on ye branches of James river was excelent good those that I sowed is come up as close as thay can grow except ye mountain Angelica which Claton[1] tells me will never come up but I hope yet to find him mistaken tho he is A worthy ingenious man   I took such care to gather ye seed in several degrees of ripeness   if none of mine cometh up I shall be allmost ready to believe it will not come up in A garden   I have received ye laurel beries & arbutus in good order   ye acrons was every one rotten   ye packet of seeds was good   I sowed them directly after receiving them which was A week in June   ye seed thee sent last fall was choice good & most of them come up   ye ranunculus & anemony roots grows finely & several bore fine flowers   ye flag iris grows well & two of ye bulbous is ready to flower   many aconites is come up & ye polianthus by hundreds balm of gilead & several prety anual linary hath been long in flower   sowed last february   I hope ye yelow digitalis & double blosom celendine & rubarb is come up but how glad should I be if ye doronicum gentian & laurels would come up which I sowed carefully last winter under shelter   all these are very acceptable   above 30 Carnations grows finely   several of ye bulbous roots & polianthus flowered pretty as my wife tould me while I was gone   dear friend I am A going to build A green-house   stone is got & hope as soon as harvest is over to begin to build it to put some pretty flowering winter shrubs & plants for winters diversion   not to be crowded with orange trees or those natural to ye torrid zone but such as will do being protected from frost   ye pretty little flowering rudbeccia is A charming flower but difficult to raise by seed   I have often sent it   it grows prodigiously big in A garden   in ye woods commonly it sends up but one stalk from A root & one or two flowers on it but one I have hath now about 100 stalks from one root   I planted A pretty oenothera out of A medow & it hath now shot up [illegible] stalks each being full of flowers & hope both these will continue to flower till frost   my Aconite that I brought from James river last fall if it be it grows finely & tho in its native place sends forth but one stalk from one root yet mine hath now five stalks & by its forward growth it may flower 2 month sooner then it did last fall yet I hope to continue it in flower till frost if I dont let it seed to send to you

BP 1:49:1; D. 223–24.
1. Bartram borrowed a horse from his brother and rode home from North Carolina, visiting John Clayton on the way.

From EDWARD GROSS[1]

Sr,

If you can Oblidge me with a Larger Quantity of those sorts of seeds here mentioned, in my 5 Guinea Case & Lesser Quantity of ye other sorts mentiond then you have Usually sent and as to ye pines shall be Glad if you wd. Let ye Seed be Took out of ye Cones & put up in bags — which will Oblidge

Yr Hble Servt.
E. Gross

Sorts of seeds that I wd. Chuse ye Largest Quantity of	
Red Ceedar	A small Quantity of those
White Ceedar	under mentiond will be suficient
Cypress's of all sorts	Virginia Dogwood
Pines, of all sorts	Cluster Cherry —
New England in perticular	Birches
spruce Firrs	Tupelo
Hemlock Do	Viburnams
Magnolia both sorts	maple Leav'd Tulip Tree
Red flowering maple	Judas Tree
Lotus	Sumachs
Chionanthas	Sweet Gum
Ceanothus	
Kalmia	
Chesnuts	
With any New sorts[2]	

BP 2:103.
1. London seedsman.
2. Collinson added:

> In short Friend John make the Whole Number of Two Guinea Boxes Twenty Boxes —
>
> P. Collinson
July 1:1760

as thou hast so great Luck to raise so good a pear from seed I sent thee — I have in the pcell Sent some more of our best pears in a Little Box of sand   in it is some Wood Sage   the names of the pears is the Marquis & St. Germain

Wee find it improves the Fruit to graft all our pears on Quince Stocks except one or Two which do better on their own

To COLLINSON

July ye 20th 1760

Dear Peter

I have wrote several letters to thee which I hope is come to hand altho I cant yet expect an answer to them   I have not received any letters from thee since that dated february ye 25th   I am realy very uneasy about those two boxes of plants I sent to thee & Gordon by Captain friend with my last Cargo which thee never mentioned ye receiving   alltho we have had four ships arived from london without bringing me any letter from thee; two year past thee sent me seed marked yellow foxglove & white campanella   this summer thay flowered   one turned out A common mallow   ye other A little blew ordinary campanela & thy white aconite is metamorphosed into ye common siberian delphinium & an evergreen which I was near half in hopes might be A portegall padus is nothing but our evergreen uonimos from my seed accidentally scattered   in short there is nothing come up of all this summers seed sent that I had not before but ye french honeysuckel   ye other seeds came up fast enough   thay had A wonderfull moist & warm season   I admire ye bays & arbutus doth not come up   thay seemed very fresh   ye pulsatilla I believe will never come up   I have now united double to upright larkspur & thay have produced not onely A monstrous but A gigantick monster of A flower upon ye top of ye central shoot   it is in form & magnitude like ye double nigela   above 30 petals compose ye lower part of ye flower & is blew & measures an inch & half diameter like ye double larkspur   ye midle part is composed of above 80 petals delicately striped purple & white spread horisontaly upon ye other   ye other or uper courss is composed of 40 petals standing more upright & darker purple

another plant stood Just by it which had such A like flower but hanged perpendicular & two common flowers growed out of ye oposite side of ye stalk   both these plants had many curious common flowers growing on several branches under them; another prety striped red & white plant grows near   it is got out of ye common road which I hope to lead to advantage that is to his honour & my pleasure   I have been several years nursing A purple stalked Martagon   last year it shot up A stalk near an inch diameter but by accident it was broke off before any flower buds appeared   this year it shot up three stalks   one produced 30 flower buds   another 22 & ye last 6 which are now several of them opened   I have now A martagon from ye great medows Just 7 foot long which I hope to improve so as to make A fine fellow of him: many years past I chanced to spie A martagon   steping A little out of my way my curiosity tempted me to try if I could not lead him farther to suite my purpose which was to make his leaves striped which succeeded but every year instead of forming flowers ye leaves & stalks all perished in ye begining of summer yet increased by ye roots: two winters past I took up A root & put him under another sort of discipline & last summer it growed stoutly held its stripes but produced no flowers   this summer it is grown wonderfully   ye leaves very long & curiosly striped & ye flowers is 3 inches & half long   but ye most stubborn plant that I have to deal with is our narrow leaved Casida   I cant get one to produce its fine large flowers in my garden   this summer I tooke up two roots of ye broad leaved in full bloom which naturaly droped off & is succeeded by good seed & now it is sending forth numerous seed pods which will produce good seed & ye narrow leaved which I planted last year & hath been all thru summer seeding without any [illegible] of ye large flowers   next year I desighn to take up root in ye spring to try if [it] will produce its large flowers which [illegible]

BP 1:49:4.

From CLAYTON

Gloucester July 23d, 1760

Dear Sir

Having so fine an opportunity by my neighbour, Capt Richard Bentley,[1] I have sent you inclosed some of the seeds you seemed desirous of having, when I had the pleasure of your agreeable company here. I hope you got safe and well home and that you found yr good wife and family all in perfect health   as we were just beginning an acquaintance, the parting with you so soon made me very melancholy for some time, and I have since frequently wished that I could have prevailed with you, by some means or other to have stayed with me much longer. I quite forgot to show you my specimens of dried plants, of wch I have a pretty large collection, also a few other natural curiosities. Several plants too in my garden wch I wanted much to have yr opinion of, were intirely forgot to be shown you but I hope if ever providence orders it so that you should have a call into this province again, you will make me ample amends for this last transient visit. If you have any of the seeds ready of the underwritten plants, the bearer will give'em a safe conveyance to, Dear friend, your most sincere friend and humble servant,

John Clayton

Monarda with red flowers
Meadia   true betony
Carolina Lupins with entire leaves & arranged 2 at a joint
Carolina Anonius   Phaseloides with fine yellow flowers
Loblolly Bay

BP 3:1; D. 406–7.
1. Unidentified.

From CLAYTON

August 30, 1760

Dear Sir: –

Captain Bentley not setting out for Philadelphia as soon as he intended, gives me the further opportunity of writing to you, and, as he tells me, he believes he shall stay there till the latter end of September, and promises me to take particular care of anything you shall please to send by him, I think it is happened very luckily for me, especially as the season will be tolerably good for removing rooted plants; and he proposes coming from your city in a vessel down Delaware, and then in his own vessel down Chesapeake Bay, quite within about three miles of my house. It will do much better than sending by the shallop to Colonel Hunter's[1] as was concluded upon, when I had the pleasure of your company here.

I presume there will be no occasion to put you in mind of the plant you were so kind to promise me; yet I can't forbear mentioning that the *Meadia, Arbor Vitae,* and Northern Spruce Fir, were to be among'em. I shall be always very ready to retaliate your favours, and am, dear sir, your sincere friend and most humble servant

John Clayton

D. 407–8.
1. Colonel William Hunter, of Hampton, Virginia, appointed co-deputy postmaster-general of the colonies with Franklin in 1753; public printer and editor of the *Virginia Gazette*.

From WILLIAM BARTRAM[1]

At the General Assembly now held at Wilmington

Dr Brother

I recd yours with great Satisfaction to hear of your Safe Arrival to your family; & to hear of your family Being in Health: I am Sorry I had not timely Notice to Send you: & my Cousens Answers: by the Same Vessel: that yours Came in: I hope my Cousen William[2] will come and see us next fall: I am glad to hear the horse Held out Very Well: as for Selling him: if you Dont want Him I am Satisfied: and keep the Money or Send Any things that you can Buy Cheap: And Send it by Cousen William: if he comes; or Any Safe hand; if I meet with no Bad Misfortunes I Expect my Polly or Bille: or Both will Com to your Parts next Spring: But I am Very Unfortunate in many things: I had my Sawmill Burnt: with Lumber & many other things of Value: in the time I was at the Assembly at Newbern in May last: to the Value of three Hundred Pounds Proch: Dr Brother I believe you may Rember I Desired you Inquire for one Jonathan Brown who I expect is in Notingham: he told me his frds. & Relations Liveth there   he Lived in our Parts Several years & went of from us with his wife & Children & was Met Near Pensilvania by John Cruse[3] who knew him Very well   if you Can find he is in them Parts; pray Inquire what Circumstances he is in or Likely to be in a Short time and Please to Let me know as Soon as Possible: But I Desire you not to Let him know that I Inquire after him: I have no News: But what I expect you have heard   we hear the Creek Indians have joind the Cherocees Against us: and have drove of hundreds of the westward Inhabitants: as we Expect Very Troublesome times: in that part of the Cuntry:

But Cousn Bille Need Not be Discouraged on that Account: I am Certain I Can Clear him from going out: Except Every Body Else goeth: I hope youl Excuse my Long Epistle   I conclude wishing you all health & Prosperity is the Hearty Desire of your Lovg Brothr:

William Bartram

P.S. Pray Remember me to Sister Cousins & all frds in hopes your all in health as we Injoy at Presnt thanks be to God.

BP 1:73.
1. Probably written in the summer of 1759, since he refers to "next fall."
2. John's son William; this letter is from John's half-brother.
3. Neither Brown nor Cruse has been identified.

From CLAYTON

September 1st, 1760

Dear Friend: –

I have sent you, inclosed, some seed of a new plant, which I presume is a stranger in your northern part of the world. Indeed, it grows here only in the southern parts of the colony. I have it in my garden, but have quite forgot whether I showed it to you, when I had the great favour of your company. If I did, I believe I told you that it was to be called *Amsonia,* after a doctor,[1] here; but I think the name inscribed upon the inclosed more proper, as it answers to the perticular form of its seed.

I intend to send you some seed of our thorny Sensitive Plant, by the first opportunity that offers, after it is ripe;

And remain, dear sir, your most sincere friend and most humble servant,

John Clayton

D. 408.
1. Dr. Amson of Williamsburg.

From COLLINSON

Londn:Sepr:15:1760

I am highly pleased with my Frd Johns expedition to Carolina — because I know how he would be delighted with the Striking Beauties of that fine

Climate, one of the principal No 18, the great Laurel Leaved Magnolia complimented Mee this morning with a Glorious Large white Flower — which I raised from Seed about 20 years agon — it is now about 16 feet high — This fine Tree is grown pretty Common & flowers in Several places, — but will never arrive to the Heighth they do in their Native Country — for they go much into flowering & that Checks the Growth —

The Atamasco Lille has flower'd often with Mee but thou sees how plants that are most common are neglected by those that see them every Day — they are like our wild Daffodils in our fields — no one regards them — but a pson of thy Curiosity who never saw them before would admire them but thou must not accuse Catesby for he has figured the Atamasco Lillie — so much for thine of 21 of March

Next I must Thank thee for thy Entertaining Letter of June 24 — I was glad to find thee Safe Return'd to thy pleasant Dwelling — by the Success thou hast had with the seeds from the South Mountains thou sees plainly how they are impaired by transportation — for very few comes up with us — it gives Mee pleasure to hear that some of the Seeds altho [dry] still come up   I am glad of Polyanthos succeeding it being a very desirable seed & send over — of the Success your Hot Dry Summer   thou will be Delighted with their Variety — they begin to grow with us & Continue for Six months   the Carnations are from New Sorts — pray Lett Mee hear how they growe — I wonder the Laurels don't Succeed — did thou See the Laurel at Claytons that he raised from my Seed

I am pleased thou will build a Green House   I will send thee seeds of Geraniums to furnish It — they have a charming Variety & make a pretty show in a Green House but contrive and Make a stove in it to give heat in Severe Weather

No marvel that the Scotch have sent thee some Heath as it grows at their door but Wee must send many miles for It   it is a favourite plant of Mine — I sent thee Boulbous Ivy I have but if thou will have Variety during the year Sow the Seed & thou will find thy self gratified — If Millers Cape Roots are planted on open ground — they must be taken up & sett in potts & then in thy Green House — or Else your Winters will kill them — Andrew Lamb[1] very obligeingly Deliver'd Mee the Specimens, as Soon as I have looked them over — I will send them to Miller — but I was Surprised att the Sight of the White Calceolus — pray thank Billey for so Elegantly painting It — my Flowers are not quite so Large & Whiter than yours —

pray Lett Mee [know] the success of the Turky Corn   Thou Sayes the Library Keeper said he saw Josselyns Voyages with the rest of the Books — then how happened It was not placed in the Library — it is sad Management if they loose books as soon as they Have Them —

Well, my Dear John never considers the Accounts that attends shiping & how precarious is the conveyance of Letters — and not bounce out with a positive Assertion — *Thee had not yett answer'd my remarks on Henepins Book concerning Goats*   Where as that was Long agon in Converse therefore I shall refer on thee, *that common Civility* would Induce thee to be

Less Censoring — in the Course of our Correspondence I have Observed that my Letters have miscarried or I concluded so because no answers has come to Them — but my Friend John never found Mee reproach Him for Neglect   great allowance is to be made on both sides for such accidents — & modest Queries is to be made on both sides — not accusations that doth not Sett well on Either side

I sent Some Siberian Pines & Firrs & pinasters as they grow strong send specimens of Each & then I may know Them —

thy Contemplative Soliloquy on the [illegible] mile walk is very Entertaining   full of Thy Imagination Ariseing from a Mind Overflowing with Gratitude & Admiration of the wonderfull productions of Almighty Power – but had the Season of the year been further Advanced the Charm of the Vegetable Race would have been Displayed with Greater Variety — this may tempt thee to make Another Visit — at a Time when no reigning Calamity can Interrupt thy Discoveries, when all Blooming Nature will open to thy view New Scenes of Wonders — the Two Sensitives are Astonishing — not be concerned — Govern. Dobbs has promised to Send Mee Seed of Each — if the Loblolly Bay was in Flower it must be a Delightful Sight — the Scarlet & white flowering Andromedas — are they different from yrs —

Wee want the long leaved Pine with Cones 9 Inches Long   I have one Tree of this Remarkable Pine in my Garden but I want more for my Self & Friends but I will write to the Governor for It —

in my Former Letters I gave the an Account of the Success of the Last Cargo of plants by which thou will pcieve I had those by Capt Friend & Budden

By no means forgett a good Quantity of your Common Locust Seed or Acacia, Charge what thou will for It — Send it in or out of Pods — it is to Send to Prague in Bohemia to be Sown to raise fodder for Cows & Horses During the Drought & Heat of the summer in that Country that burns up the Grass   they propose planting the Trees at small Distances & keeping them Low & Cutting them 4 or 6 Times in a Season as it is a great Grower

Horse Sugar seems to be the Ligustrum of Catesby   among the Specimens are many Charming plants   Could Garden send seeds of them — the fine Clematis with Blewish reflex'd Flowers grows Luxuriously in my Garden as Does the Spice Tree which keeps flowering all the Summer & perfumes all the Garden   cannot be more Vigorous in its own Climate Wee have Two Sorts of Padus   Yours & One called an Evergreen from So Carolina   I have known both   when yours is Vigorous keep their Leaves untill Spring — but now it being Grown Old It sheds all Leaves, thou sent the first Over to Lord Petre in 1736:37 or 38 which are now the Oldest In England — I had the Loblolly Bay sent by my Friend Lambol[2] of Charles Town but [does] not shoot away for want of Sun & Moisture but it is a Charming plant, as is the purple Berried Bay   the privet or Ligustrum of Catesby   I have the Red Sweet Bay — but thou hath brought many specious plants to Light — Gordon longs for them but cannot see how he can gett them unless Docr Garden can help Him — pray recommend Gordon to

Him — He will not prove ungratefull if the Docr will inform Him of his Wants in the Vegitable Way — Send his List to Him   I am a Little surprised thou should be unacquainted with the progressive annual growth of oranges & lemons   the great [illegible] is a real Indulgence to Mankind has prolong'd the Continuance of the Trees   both gratifie our [illegible] as well as our palates   as your proprietor has a Green House & Oranges & Lemmons in It   Little thought but thou was acquainted with

I am my Dear John thy sincere Friend

P Collinson

wrote by the Intcana Cap House that was taken

BP 3:17; D. 224–25.
1. Unidentified.
2. Thomas Lamboll.

From PETER TEMPLEMAN

Strand
London, September 16, 1760

Sir

As the surest Method of improving science is by a generous intercourse of the learned in different countries, and a free Communication of knowledge; the Society established at London for the Encouragement of Art, Manufactures & Commerce take this Liberty of addressing themselves to you to intreat the favour of an answer to the following Inquiry

Do any Herbs or *Species* of grass grow in your Country during the most inclement part of the year (which we consider to be the Months of December, January, February, March & April) so as to supply all sorts of Cattle at that time with a vegetating food?

Induced by reason & analogy we are inclined to think that the common Parent of all has not left the preservation of such animals solely to the care & Industry of man, to furnish them at that season of the year with dry fodder only but that proper herbs & Vegetables are afforded them to support themselves at least in some tolerable Condition.

We know that Nature has disseminated her Bounties variously through the habitable World so that some species of fruits and herbs arise spontaneously in one country and others in another but that most of them are capable of being transplanted and will thrive in the most Distant Regions.

It is the business of the Philosopher and Naturalist to explore these treasures of Nature and spread the knowledge and use of them for the benefit of mankind.

Such are the sentiments of the Society I have the honour to be secretary to, and they address themselves to you as animated with the same generous way of thinking.

All the Plants, Herbs & Grasses, which grow here in England both in Winter and Summer, are enumerated in Ray's[1] synopsis.

If there are any other Species, that flourish in the Winter Season with you, not cited by Ray, and proper for the food of Cattle in the above mentioned Months; the Society beg the favour of you to transmitt an Account of them with the nature of the Soil they grow in, and the Culture they require: and intreat you to procure a sufficient Quantity of the seeds of each kind to try the Experiment of their thriving here in England, and to send at the same time a Botanical Description of them.

Your kindness in answering these requests will lay an indispensable obligation on the Society to requite the favour, whenever they shall have it in their Power, and with greatest pleasure, they will embrace the opportunity.

I have the honour to subscribe myself in the name of the Society,

Your most obedient hble servant,
Peter Templeman,
Secretary

BP 4:110; D. 412–13.
1. John Ray.

To HUMPHRY MARSHALL[1]

September ye 17th 1760

Dear Cousen

thee would oblige me much If thee would be so kind as to gather me A parcel of fring tree seeds & if it happens in thy way some black ash & A fair specimen of that plant so like ye mediola that I hardly know ye difference[2] — I hope to come up in ye fall to thy house & if thee comes up to town soon I hope thee will not go by without calling upon me. My garden now makes A glorious appearance with ye virginia & Carolina flowers —

my kind love to thy wife & to uncle & aunt   we are all my family in good health, God Almighty be praised who alone is worthy of all Glory & honour to endless eternity

pray accept ye respects & friendship of thy sincer Cousen

in hast
John Bartram

D. 58.
1. Humphry Marshall (1722–1801), botanist and author of *Arbustum Americanum* (1785); son of Abraham Marshall and Mary Hunt, whose sister Elizah married William Bartram, John's father. Darlington reproduced the original letter, which is now in the Linnean Society of London, Autographs of Foreign Botanists, Mrs. Isabella James and Thomas Potts James Collection.
2. Someone has here added a note: "Probably Pogonia verticillata, Nutt."

From COLLINSON

Lond Octo:2d:1760

By Capt Boletho I answered my dear Johns Letter of June 16 — before that I wrote Two Letters of July 10 for seeds   for fear of Miscarriage Inclos'd it to my friend Colden[1] Postmaster of New York in his packett to forward to thee & yett thou art always Complaining for want of Letters makeing no allowance for miscariages   Thine of March the 21st I answered Sept 15th & yett the good man is never Easie, if all my Correspondents was of thy Restless turn of Mind — I would never sett Pen to paper   In Mine of 25 feby I wrote but for 8 boxes of seeds but 9 March I have doubled it since for I keep no Coppy

Now I come to thank my kind friend for his Letter of the 28 July — I am delighted with his operations on the Larkspurr   the produce is wonderfull   if these Charming flowers can be continued by seed they will be the greatest ornament to the Garden In their season of blowing

This purple stalked Martagon is the glory of that Tribe   in my soil & Climate I had it grow above 6 foot high & had 28 flowers on the Spike — by all means sow the seed Directly, for it Deserves all our Care but it never produces seed in our Climate — it was what was formerly sent Mee — the yellow spotted Martagon thou formerly sent Mee — Catesby figurd His from my plant — after some years it went off — I shall be glad to have It Again — pray send the seed — If by thy Cunning Thou could Marry these Two together offspring must be Curious — the striped Leaves will have a pretty Effect —

I have your purple & white Casseda that flowers annually & the flowers of an Inch Long — which Looks very well

It has been Long my Sentiments that plants and animals as they Advance northward they Decline in their size

For Instance the Crocodiles of Carolina which is the highest Latitude they are found In, — are diminutives to those found in Countries between the Tropicks — So this pancratium which I have had from my friend Lambol as it comes Lower down may grow Less — yett it is a Very Different Species from that which grows in the Bahama Islands which I have seen flower often   they have a fine smell

In the Library Companys Box May 28 Capt Budden I sent thee some Curious Roots: Bulb codeurs, Dub & long Fritilarys, Vantol Tulip first flower — Wood Anemones — the other Book which I find by thine of July 28 was not come to hand   I wish they may keep Clear of the French

I shall be glad of the Yellow Root, for it did not come up & for some Blew & Red Cardinal seed   on the other side is what success I have had with the Last Cargo — which I have mention'd before but as Letters May be Lost I mention again   In the Box there was a parcell of Edwards book to Billy & Magazine for year 1759 — pray send Mee some of your Mistletoe berry in a Little Box or Gally pott cover with Leaves on Top   I sent thee before in another pcell our Late yellow Crocus Narcissus *which is now in flower* pray what is become of the fine purple Ulmaria fr the Madeira   I am glad of the success of the Carnation seed — I Divided it in halves & sent by the Freadth & by the Juliena which last was taken — make much of it & save seed & Sow it — for I don't know when I can Send thee any More

Plants that Grows p Buddens Boxes

2 Sods of Calmias — the great one is come out Vigorous if it does but hold It
5 Grafted pippins — grows finely
the Dwarfe plum flowers finely — & yet went off which I much regretted
an odd Anonis & Jersey orchis — did not appear
a Ranunculus Appeared   it did not flower   I wish it may be Dr. Witts
2 Roots of Canada True   grew finely
not a yellow Root or Orchis came up & yett great care was taken
the sweet snake root sprouted one Leafe
I am afraid it was too soone in the year that many of these plants was taken up, Else they had not failed so   Sept is to Early a Month to take up plants of some kinds —
a pretty perrenial Sparge came up but a wicked snail eat it up —

By Capt Friend

The Skunk Weed flowerd Freely — is now this 6 Octr shot and much above ground
White Azalea grows as Does the Red
Red Budd andromeda Grows
the papaw plants all shot   if they do but Hold   the seeds I gave to Gordon
the Climbing Toxecodendron grows
the Striped pyrola my favourite went off   the Rough Leaved flowerd & grew finely but take in thy first, plant it in a Dry place but our sun carried it off, notwithstanding it was often water'd —
The Aralia spinosa grows finely
The pippin & grafts grows — so hope it forms Fruite
Broad Leaved Andromeda grows
Olive Leaved Kalmia grows
Thy Toxecodendron grows finely *a Choice plant*   where was it found growing
The Hydrophylon grows strongly   is new Species   Thus thou sees my dear John Wee have had pretty good success in our Vegitable Cargo of fine plants which gives much pleasure to thy Sincere frd
P Collinson

the Specimens for Miller I received safe & thy Letter by thy kind Neighr the Sweed — but I happen'd to be out of Town every Time he call'd so did not see Him — or Else I should have paid him due Respect — He is gone to Sweden — pray when may I hope to see thy Journal to Carolina —

The British Chronicle is Inclosed for the sake of Wm Penn's Letter How customs & manners in the Indians are altered since that Time thou canst best tell or be informed — So att thy leisure thy remarks wil be acceptable to thy friend PC

B. Franklin & son are Well   are gone a Tour into Wales   may expect them in the spring ships

BP 3:19; D. 225–26.
1. Alexander Colden, son of Cadwallader Colden.

From GARDEN

Octr 25th 1760

My Dr Friend

I have received two very kind letters from you since you left this place, neither of which it has yet been in my power to answer. Ever since I saw you I have lived in a greater hurry than when I had the pleasure of your agreeable company. Often since our parting have I reflected with concern that I had then so little time to enjoy you. I read with great satisfaction your acct of the rarities of North Carolina — I examined the tree in my garden which I formerly took to be a holly like Mr. Wragg's[1] but I find it quite different as is likewise that one in Governor Glen's garden which is of the same kind as mine. It is a new genus and a Beautiful enough Evergreen.

My Close Confinement deprives me of that happiness which I would have in searching our woods —

Your plants in my Garden[2] thrive surprisingly well & they are now ready for your Boxes — one or two are dead — As I met Lately with Lee[3] on Botany I bought two copies one of which I have sent you & beg you'll accept of it, from

Your Sincere Friend
Alexander Garden

Inclosed you have a letter from Mrs. Logan[4] which has been with me some time for want of an opportunity

BP 4:10; D. 394–95.
1. William Wragg.
2. Plants collected by Bartram to be forwarded to Philadelphia by Garden.
3. James Lee (1715–1795), nurseryman who owned a garden at Hammersmith in London (in partnership with Lewis Kennedy).
4. Martha Logan.

From AL MONEYPENNY[1]

New York 1st December 1760

Sir

In September last Mr. Peters a Surgeons Mate of the Hospital wrote to you from Montreal to provide for me, Parcels of seeds or bulbous roots of any Trees, Shrubs or Flowers peculiar to this Country, that have any Merit or Beauty in them or any near Species of such as grows in England, to the value of about ten pounds New York Money.

If you have got them or can procure them I shall be much obliged to you if you will send them to Major Moneypenny at General Amherst's House in New York with a note mentioning to whom the price is to be paid; which shall be done most thankfully.

I shall be glad to have them rather in the Natural Legument than cleaned & the name of each sort along with them; but to have them at any Rate,

I am Sir,

Your most obedient Servant
Al Moneypenny

BP 4:88.
1. Unidentified.

From DOBBS

Brunswick December 13 1760

Sr

I had ye Letter with the roots and seeds by Capt Mulford which are all safe and the roots planted out, but I have lost my gardener who died about a month ago, so shall be at a Loss how to find out the roots &c. you wrote for that goes by Mr. Nagel to new york and from thence to Philadelphia —

I have before sent you a list of those seeds as I shall want for my Kitchen Garden in which I desire you will send by the first vessil and I shall send your pine in return as I have lost the season in growing Myrtle Wax, in the Spring I shall endeavour to procure my annual flowers and plants as they open and know what they are, you may compute how much of each to send

I am so tardy sending off dispatches and the vessils that goes is ready to sail so I have only time to add that I am Sr

yr Humble Servant
Arthur Dobbs

BP 3:102.

From MARTHA LOGAN

Charleston, 20 December 1760

Sir: –

I have, last week, received both your favours, with the seeds therein mentioned, for which am much obliged; and wish you had been so kind to let me know what we have that would have been most acceptable to you; but, as you did not, have sent, inclosed, the little bag, which contains some variety, but few of a kind (as you requested). The middle division is flowering shrubs, trees, and vines, which we esteem, and wish they may be new to you.

I doubt not you have many things which I should be glad of as I am particularly fond of Double flowering & if you could send me a fue Seeds of white Stock gilly flowers & yellow Wall flowers which would produce the Double flowers or any of the Sweet or other Pease of the Like kinds they would be much Esteemed. or a fue fine Carnations as I have only the common kinds.

I was so unlucky this last summer to Loose all the Roots of Ranunculists anemony Tulips & fine Double Hyacinths by Laying them in a Closit to Dry after they were taken up for the mice Devoured them before I had a thought of it.

If these Seed with you & can Spair them I shall be vastly glad to make the any Return for a fue. Other roots or Seeds Wee have several Sorts Bulbous roots & I could Easily Convey them to the if they would be an adision to your Collection of plants. I should be Likewise glad of your kinds of hesperis they may differ from mine also a little Double Chine Aster seed.

I do again assure you of the truth of my assertion, relating to the striped Stock Gilly flowers. If the seed should produce you flowers of a plain red, I beg you'd not be discouraged, but make a second trial the next season; by which I am persuaded you will be convinced of the truth.

The seeds I sent you, by the name of Virginia Stock, was of the same little flower you so much admired in my garden, and hope they have succeeded with you; but have again sent a few more, for fear of any accidents; and am, with greatest sincerity, sir

Your assured friend and humble servant,
Martha Logan

BP 4:71; D. 414.

From WILLIAM BARTRAM[1]

Dr Brother

I came So far from home in a hurry in Chase after the Vessel that was Capt Mulford as I had my Box of plants now gon for Philadelphia; My Son lw: Anthony Gully[2] is to have the Command of her I am informd; he went from my house A few days agone to town: Not Expecting to go to Sea Before he Came home Again: the Vessil Being Ready Loaded for Sailing the Owners Insisted on his going immediately: I wanted to have seen him Very Much to have Sent two or three Plants and Sent Som Messages & Letters   Neither He nor I Expected Any thing of his Going when I saw him Last: I sent A Box of Plants & trees & Bagg of Seeds: by him to Wilmington of a Passage: they are Som of Such as you Desired me & my wife to Send: the Frost Killed Several [illegible] My Markes were Broke Down: that I did on the Roots; otherways should sent a Deal [if] Known in time of such a fine oppertunity; – informed my Son Lw Capt Gulley has the Box & Bagg of Seeds: with him which I Expect he'll bring you Safe if it is in his Power: I hope your all in health as my family as we Enjoy at Present thanks be to God: But we have been very Sickly & Mortal time with the Plurises   But I am in hopes it is a good Deal Abated tho [now]   I have no Strange news to Acquaint you with: Our Gov & Assembly Differ Very Much: We have had three [illegible] for Assemblymen in Less than one year & 5 or six Assemblies called in sd time & Little Business Don: I have had the Honr of Being Chosen Ever time: But a Deal Agst: I hope Cousin William will Com with Capt Gulley as this is a fine oppertunity; it will suit to bring Rum Molasses if anything Reasonable there   Som Powder & Lead & Som [illegible] not much at first Coming; Captain Gully can tell which   Pray give my respects to my Sister & Cousins & all friends

Not time to write to them   I have wrote Several times but afraid miscarried as I had no Answer; the Lord All Mighty [bless] all with health & Happyness is the Hearty Desire of your Brother

Wm Bartram

P.S. As I dont expect Polley nor Billey[3] to Com your way soon please to Sell ye horse you had from me as you wrote to me & Send the value in good Rum by Captn Gulley if anything reasonable. I would have sent you a Barrel or two of good Rice & Som good Indigow of my own make if I had known of Such oppertunity.

BP 1:75.
1. Written in the fall of 1760, judging by its content.
2. Husband of William's stepdaughter, Susanna Smith.
3. William's son.

To ARCHIBALD BARTRAM[1]

1761

friend Archibald Bartram
My friend George Bartram[2] shewed me two letters & two coats of arms that thee sent him wherein thee desired me to write an account of our family but as I was but young when my father & uncle died so ye best account I could have was from my grandmother who lived some years after   she tould me that my great grandfathers name was Richard Bartram   he lived in Derby

shire & his father before him: Richard had one son called John, who married my Grandmother in Derby   thay settled in ye town of ashburn in ye Peak where thay lived & had three sons & one daughter   from thence thay removed to Pennsilvania before there was one house in Philadelphia   my grandfather & his elder son John, died about 60 years past & my uncle Isaac a few years after   both bachelors   my father maried & had three sons & one daughter who died A young woman   we three sons are at present all liveing   I am ye eldest & have 6 sons & 3 daughters alive   my brother James is the next, hath had one son and two daughters, which are all dead.

The Bartram coat of arms.

His eldest daughter left five daughters. My youngest brother, William, liveth in North Carolina, hath one sone and two daughters.[3]

    this is ye best account I can give of our family   there was here some years past a Presbyterian minister come from Scotland — he said that two brothers of our name came with william ye Conqueror one of which setled in ye north of england of which I suppose my family came & ye other setled in scotland of which, I suppose, your family came which corresponds with thy relation,[4]

BP 1:53:1, 1:55:2; D. 416–18.

1. A very distant relative of Bartram. No month is given, nor indicated by the letter's content.
2. Husband of Bartram's daughter Anne, but no relation. A Scot, George was a Philadelphia merchant in partnership with his brother Alexander.
3. The letter to this point is from BP 1:53:1.
4. This paragraph is from BP 1:55:2.

From JOHN ST. CLAIR

Belleville Febry 11th 1761

Sir

I have received your obliging Letter of the 24th of last month with some seeds of the Mimosa for which I return you my most hearty thanks. I shall send to you the End of this Month for the things you mention in your Letter, please to let me know any day you are to be at Home and I shall be punctual in sending that Day.

I should be extremely glad of a visit from you. I can promise you a hearty welcome & to show you the best Garden in America which I have neither spared labour or expence to finish. You may easily believe that I have not been able to stock it wt great variety, but what trees I have are good and this Season will show if my flowers answer my Expectation.

I have prepared everything for the reception of the West India Trees & Plants: and have wrote to Charles Willing[1] at Barbadoes to send me the Avocado Pear, the Guava, & Chaddock, with any other curious Plants or trees. As a Ship is just going freighted by Mr. Plumsted, if you'll send Mr. Charles Willing a list in my Name he will send any thing you write for.

I shall send to Holland for some flowers this Summer, and I have an acquaintance who is Rear Admiral of North Holland by his means I can get of all the sorts of the Cape of Good Hope, so that I should be obliged to you for a list & the sooner I get it the better. I imagine the Dutch flowers will answer better than the Genoese, I am perfectly acquainted with both these climates having been five years in each place and the latter always degenerates tho planted in the same degree of latitude this I have experienced in Minorca, the first year they were good, but the second good for nothing excepting the Carnations. The King of Prussia kept up the Price of flowers at Genoa by having the Root of every good flower bought up, and a bargain made for it when the flower was in Blow; & even this was practiced by the first Genoese Nobility, so that one was not at liberty to present a Lady wt a Nose Gay. The Genoese flowers do last but one season in the Gardens of San-Soucis at Potsdam, and I believe not so long as that, at Present. I shall never attempt to give a reason for the changes that a Climate makes on the Animal World. For sow English Carrots in Spain the first crop is good, the 2d. white wit. out taste & the 3d. Purple of an Earthy taste. I know three farmers in Spain all become Bankrups by purchasing a farm of Hott sandy ground, at last a Mad-Man made the purchase of it, and planted Vineyards on it, it not only succeeded but produced the best wine which enriched him and his family; this was the more Singular as there was neither Stone nor Rock on the Ground

I wish you could help me to a Couple of Nectarine trees and as many Pomgrenates, I am plagued with the Shrubby kind of the latter & have sent to Boston for the former   I want to propagate the Red China Orange wt the Nectarine flavour, in this place wc[h] I have formerly succeeded in. My only doubt is that the Nectarine or peach Stock will not bear the green house in Winter. Should you have any Plants to preserve in a green-house or bark Stove you are welcome to send them to me and great care shall be taken of them untill you can send them to England. I would call on you when the Weather is good but at that time I am unwilling to leave my Garden & farm. I am with Sincerity Sr

Your most obedient and most humble Servant
John St Clair

BP 4:104.
1. Perhaps a son of Charles Willing (1710–1754), a prosperous Philadelphia merchant.

From THOMAS LAMBOLL

Chas. Town in So. Carolina, Febry 16th 1761
Worthy & Esteemed Friend

You will very likely think much of my Silence after receiving three Letters from you, vizt. of June 18th p. Mr. Rolles; of Septr. 2 & Novr. 2nd. 1760 (for all which and the Contents of them, I now thank you)   But the real Cause of the delay in acknoledging the Receipt of the same was partly sickness in my Family and partly being unprepared for sending somewhat more than a bare Letter.

When Mr. Rolles did me the honour to Call at my Home (which was the only time I saw him) it was towards the latter End of August & exceeding Sultry Weather; his Visit was Short yet he gave me some hopes of his dining with me before he went but meeting with a fine Vessel ready to depart he imbark'd in her, and soon after sail'd. He sent me & several others Billets to Dine with him in Publick just before his Departure; but the State of my Family at the Time debarr'd me of that Pleasure. I heard afterwards that he was supposed to be of Noble Descent. And I know nothing further concerning him.

The manner Mrs. Lamboll manages her Ranunculas & Anemonies every Year, is thus: She prepares Beds of good Rich Mould at least Two Months before she takes up the Flower Roots; that the Earth may be well settled by Rain. Wherever the Ground is low, she raised the Flower Beds, at least half a foot in heighth, and where high flattens them. In Summer time, the leaves of the Flower Roots being thoroughly dry, immediately after a Shower of Rain happens, she takes up the said Roots, divides & cleanses them (but not by washing) from Insects, then makes slight holes with the Fingers on the

Tops of the prepared Beds, places the Roots about four inches asunder and covers them over with Dirt, Scrap'd from the Paths, about half an Inch deep; strewing it over with the Fingers. And if the Rain fails she afterwards causes the Beds of Flower Roots to be Watered gently, such Water having first stood a Convenient time in the Sun. In Cold Weather she causes the Flower Beds to be Cover'd and Shelter'd; especially when they have begun to Sprout.

I have at length Got a Box of Earth, containing the under mentioned Roots, Plants and Herbs vizt. a small Root Winter Savory: a Root Winter Sweet Marjoram; a Root blew Flagg, two Roots white Iris; two Roots Grape Hyacinths, a few Roots Early white Spanish Hyacinths; a Root of white Feather'd Hyacinths; a Root of Starry Hyacinths; a few Plants of Water Oak; a few Ditto live-Oak; two Plants white Broom; two Ditto Oleander; Six Roots Narcissus, wch you call Pancratium, and a few Plants of Great Garden Cresses; for as to Seed we were prevented from Saving any last summer. the Box is put on Board the Brig[anti]ne Hannah, George Noarth Commander: directed for you, Freight paid, and I hope in due Time you'l receive it safe.

In this Letter is also inclosed for Alexander white Broom, & Narcissus (Qu. Pancratium) Seeds   I have not seen or heard any thing concerning the two Ministers you mentioned to have written by   Perhaps they altered their intentions of coming this Way.

My good Friend I must now Close my Letter. Capt. Noarth is being near sailing, but be assured that I retain a gratefull sense of all your Favours, and desire very much to Continue & Cultivate our mutual Correspondence, tho' I am not so luckily situated as some other your Acquaintance here for collecting the Shrubs &c which Our Climate yields; Nevertheless I shall Gladly embrace all opportunitys of doing you all the good Offices that I can: I will endeavor to shew that I am, with due Respect Sir

your most Obligd
Friend and Servt.
Thos. Lamboll

P.S. Does the Peony Flower grow with you? we have none of it here.

BP 4:60.

From MARTHA LOGAN

February 20, 1761

Sir: –

I wrote you, some little time since, requesting your instructions in my flower garden, which I hope you will grant.

I make no doubt you have received the seeds I sent by Dr. Garden's conveyance, and wish they may succeed to the uttermost of your desires;

and if it is in my power to oblige you with anything in this province, only let me know, and you shall find no person more ready.

When you favour me again with a line Pray be so kinde to tell me whither the following Roots are to be Purchased with you as the Passage is so much Shorter I should Chuse it Rather then Sending to England for them Such as Tulips. Ranunculists. Anemonyes Narsissus, Hyacinths & Horsenecks, the Last Named & a little Seed or Slips of the Tree you Call the Snowball is what I am particularly Desirous of & they are not to be had from England for I have sent for them In several of my Lists but Never gott one. I find they Doe very well with us for Doctor Garden has a good many roots Now bluming.

If the afore mentioned are to be purchased (& you'd give me Leave) shall trouble you with a short List by the time ye Seeds are ripe, & Roots out of the Ground.

In the Meantime I remain with true Regard sr your assured friend and humble Servt.

Martha Logan

BP 4:73; D. 414–15.

From CLAYTON

February the 23d, 1761

Dear friend

I recivd. yr agreeable letters of the 16th of November last about a month ago, and am very much obliged to you for the seed therein inclosed. it was a long time in coming & had passed through various hands insomuch that the folds were quite worn out & some person or other had taken out the paper with the striped Stock July flower seed, the Loss of wch I regret very much, as it is so great a curiosity. I was a little doubtful of my Pyrethrum seed; but, as you guess, it was really the very best I had. if hereafter, I should happen to save any better, you may depend upon participating with me in that, as well as in the others you mention in the letter, for at present I have not one grain of the seed of Stoechas nor of the Tetragonotheca nor Staphisagria.

I am very glad to hear that you are perfectly well recovered of your troublesome cough & fever. I assure you I was under a good deal of concern for your going away with such a disorder upon you.

There was one paper of seed you were so kind to send me, inscribed Dracocephalum, which by the appearance & smell of the dry calyces, I take to be the same plant wch I have had several years in my garden. it is called three-leaved American Moldavica with a strong scent of Balm of Gilead. I have a species of Aconite in my garden wch grows about five feet high. I found it at our little S. West mountains. The flowers are blue & grow in the same manner as those on your large tall species, according to your description. in its natural place of growth it blossoms in October but in my garden it is about three weeks forwarder. You say you never found any real species of the true Aconite except that tall one near our South mountains. now I should be glad to know what you take our Stagger weed to be? The places you mention for our meeting at again, are, my dear friend, such as I fear I shall never be able to travel to. Capt. Bentley, at his return told me he was at your house but could not see you, because, as some of yr. family informed him, you were gone a long journey in search of plants, &c., and could not be expected home while he stayed. when Mr. Franklin was at Wmburg. he desired me, if I had occasion to write to you or Doctor Garden, by the way of Philadelphia, to send the letters under a cover directed for him, in order to save paying postage; but now, as he is not in America, I don't know very well how to act, if I should have no other way of writing to you then by the post. I have sent you, here inclosed, three papers of seeds, such as I judged would be most acceptable. they are all natives of Virginia —

this comes by a young gentleman, a friend and neighbour of mine, whose name is Richard Blacknall, who I am confident may be relied upon for his utmost care of a box of rooted plants if you'll please to be so kind as to send it by him to, dear friend,

your most sincere and affectionate friend,
John Clayton

Pray don't forget to put a root or two of Madder in the box.

BP 3:2; D. 408–9.

From GARDEN

Feb 23d 1761

Dr Sir

I received your kind letter with your present of apples & plants for both which please to accept of my thanks. The apples were extremely good & have kept much beyond any that ever I had before. You made me very happy in the Newfoundland spruce, Hemlock Fir & Kalmia, I wanted these very much & you gave me fine thriving plants; The others viz the Lavendar, Sabina & Rhamnus with the Fraxinellas are all growing beautifully so that I expect to have great pleasure in them all Summer

I hope you may have like pleasure in those that I now send you I need not tell you to plant them out immediately & in a shady moist place — The Box is rather too full, but the reason is, my not choosing to remove the earth from the roots of the plants as they grew, so that earth taken up with them soon filled up the Box. Your four Umbrellas are all alive & very thriving as is the great magnolia The Atamasco Lillies are all alive the Four-Leaved Bignonia & the fine blue Purple flower — I could not find the Worm grass root so that I'm afraid it is dead, but I shall soon replace it to you with some others. The Asarum & Solanum triphyllum are both in good health & blooming

I sincerely wish they may arrive safe — I have watered them again, to Day & the Capt says that he'll sail to morrow. May God grant him a speedy & prosperous voyage & thus give you a further opportunity of viewing & admiring the beauties of some more of his amazing & Wonderful works —How eminently happy are these hours which the humble & philosophic mind spends in investigating & Contemplating the inconceivable beauties & mechanism of the works of nature the true manifestation of that supremely wise & powerful Agent who daily upholds & blesses us — May that Fatherly Being continue to enlighten your mind till that hour come, when the parting of this Veil will lay before your Eyes a new & more glorious field of Contemplation & still more unutterable sights of Bliss —

Be assured that I offer in great sincerity my kind Respects to all your family & am Dr Friend

Your's
Alexander Garden

N.B. I should be much obliged to you for some Hyacinths, some Narcissus with the largest Nectariums — we call these Horsenecks. I have one or two Persian irises that blossom beautifully. If you could spare some more I should be glad of them or any other bulbous root —

I have put on board a letter from Mrs. Logan with some seeds in it.

Yours
A. G.

BP 4:11; D. 395–96.

From ST. CLAIR

Belleville Febry 27 1761

Sir

On my Arrival home from New York and Phila. I found your Letter of the 19th Inst. for which I return you my hearty thanks. I have sent my Gardener Mr Marshall for the Trees and any other things you are pleased to send me, and I shall take it kind if you'll please to let me know the Value of them & I shall order Mr. Leenan to pay unto your Son at Phila.

I shall send to Holland this year for a parcel of Flower Roots: Hyacinths & Auriculass are what they run the most upon at Harlem, which far exceeds any thing of the kind at Lyden.

The Harlem florists vye wh. one another who should produce the greatest Varietys of the above flowers and when any appears that have not been seen before all curious People flock to see it.

For my part I shall never give my self so much trouble but shall content my self with some of the best Sorts of each kind as likewise of the Tulip. I shall now begin to make my Compost for flowers, but I am at a loss to know the Soil that will suit best in this Climate, but I think one third Cow dung, one third saw dust and one third black mould. half virgin Earth of Rotten leaves will do. I am afraid of rotten Tan. If you are of opinion that any thing is better say so & I shall prepare it. I am of opinion that the plants & Shrubs of the Cape of Good Hope will not be very dear the only way to deal with the Dutch is to give them 50 or 100 Guilders & desire them to give you Roots and Shrubs for it. The price of flowers is regulated every Year by the florists as each has a Catalogue of what the other has, and is the same as the Exchge. at Philadelphia.

Let me know if you have read Justice on Gardening.[1] It seems to be well wrote, if you desire to see it I shall send it you.

What is the reason that Gooseberrys grow scabby, is there no remedy for it? Would planting them in marl do? or would it do for plumbs. I am obliged to you for the Stock of Gilliflower Seed. tell me if they will stand the Winter out of doors. I should be glad of a visit from you whenever it is convenient, I can give you a good Bed in my Library Room above my Green house where a Gardiner ought to be lodged, and a very hearty wellcome. I am Sir

Your most humble Servt.
John St Clair

BP 4:105.
1. Unidentified.

From WILLIAM POWELL

Brunswick 10 March 1761

Sir

By this Opportunity Capt. Lambson in a Schooner from hence for Philadelphia, I send you a Box containing some pine Trees, purple berry Bays the holly Saracina, the bulbous root out of the Marsh which by the Acct. I recd. of it on my Return seems to be the Lilio Mariposas – polyanthus of Catesby, and some peach Stones, chiefly the Kennedy, part of which last if you send with my Compliments to Dr. Percival[1] of German Town you'l oblige me. In the paper in the box the Govr. sends you Paradisa Berries, broad & narrow leaved Myrtle berries, & some dates lately recd. from his son at Gibralter and which he sends you for planting.

This is the first Vessel from us to you since Novr. and the Assembly then sitting I cod. send nothing. I asked your broth. for the Atamasco Lily & some Chesnuts of the Scarlet flower, but he had neither, I must now tell you that I am not a little Jealous with you in writing to the Govr. for those things wch. I had promised you and again to assure you that you will find me ready to oblige you

Last Jany. I sent Mr. Collinson some finest Saracenas, & the bulbous root, taking it as above; and then undoubtedly a Curiosity. His Excy. desires his Complimts. to you. I am

Your most hble Sert.
Wm. Powell

BP 4:99.
1. Unidentified.

From CLAYTON

March 30, 1761

Dear friend

Capt Bentley has talked of sending a vessel to your City for above these six weeks past, upon which I gave him a letter for you dated the 23d of last month, but I fear the Spring will be so far advanced before he sets off, that it will not be safe moving the rooted plants mentioned in that Letter. This now comes by one Mr Caleb Hundley who lives near the side of Chesapeake Bay about twenty miles from me, he had promised me to take particular care of anything you'l be so kind to send me, and if he's come, in a vessel quite up to Philadelphia, and arriving there before you see Capt Bentley, I should be much obliged to you for a box of plants, and a little of the Striped Gilly flower Seeds, (as the first you sent me was lost) by him upon his return, and am most sincerely

Your affectionate friend
and very humble servant
John Clayton

Historical Society of Pennsylvania Library, Autograph Collection of Simon Gratz.

From ST. CLAIR

Belleville April 13th 1761

My Dear Sir

I received your obliging Letter with a Couple of fresh Dates, I have planted them in a pot & plunged them in the back bed, they are not so good as the fruit of Turkey which I have in great plenty, but many reasons make me think the Palm tree (of wc the date is the fruit) cannot bear in this Climate.

I am under a necessity of beging you'll come out to me on Saturday the 18th and I shall return wt you either Sunday or Monday, the benefit arising to me from that visit is that you are the best Judge of the plants I can raise from the Conveniencys I have; and I in return shall give you any trees I have for ornamenting your Green house.

I shall be obliged to you if you will bring a plant of the Stinking weed you so much value   I shall use it to garnish Dishes for delicate Palates.

I shall please my self all this week with the Hopes of seeing you and am wt a most Sincere regard My dear Sir

Your most obedient and most humble Servant John St Clair

BP 4:106.

From LAMBOLL

So. Carolina, Chas: Town, April 30th: 1761

Worthy Friend.

By Capt. Noarth I received your Favour of the 30th Ultimate, with the Seeds there-in-closed; which are now Sowed; but don't know how they will come up. Most of those that I received heretofore never sprouted, therefor suppose they were overheated in bringing hither.

The Season of the Year puts it out of my Power to remit you any Seeds etc., even if you had let me know what to send, so that I can only trouble you now with this bare Letter of acknowledgment, saying that as Mrs. Lamboll desires to have specified the Names of some Flowers & Herbs, that she is fond of procuring. They are under mentioned, but if your Garden don't produce them, I hope my good Friend won't put himself to the Trouble of seeking for the same elsewhere; Alexander, Angelica, Anniseed, Camomile (that will flower), Clary (common sort), Colchicum, Cow-Slip, Crown-Imperial, Elicampe, Martagon, MarshMallow, Polyanthos, Self-Heal, Snow Drops (the double kind), Solomon-Seal, Sultan, Tulips, Bloud-wort.[1]

But I think I have already been too troublesome, and shall only superadd our kind Respects to your Self and Family, and remain

Your obliged Friend to serve Thos: Lamboll

BP 4:61.
1. Bartram noted on the back of this letter: "sent lambol 1761 novem Several roots of peoney, Solomon seal, polianthos, rasbery, angelica, One root of current, clary, cowslips, selfheal, enula, compane, arbor vita, marsh mallow, dasies."

From WILLIAM BARTRAM

May 6th 1761
Brunswick   Cape Fear

Dear Father

I am just arived at this Place after a most severe attack from that most dangerous Disorder of Sea sickness, we had a tedious Passage of about Seven days from the Capes, we rode out two dangerous Gales of Wind   the first was last Thursday night a little to the east of Cape Hatteras & was miraculously delivered from them dangerous Shouls & the last two days Past near the Fryin Pan & likewise escaped that shole & next day several dismal appearances of a Wreck appeared   A Bowsprit of a Fine Bermuda Sloop cast away just before & some casks of Rice Part of her cargo.

This Morning I waited on his Excellency Gover. Dobbs with Cap Gulley & Mr. Powell But am Prevented from accepting of ther Generous Invitations of spending some hours with them. Our Capt. going imediately to weigh Anchor for Wilmington which I hope to see this Night & tomorrow My Unkle   Tire & time prevents saying any more

Thy son
Wm Bartram

I should be glad to Hear from Dear Mother Sisters & Brothers

BP 1:68.

From COLLINSON

Londn May 7th:1761

I wrote to my good frd Decemr 6:via New York but I think the pacquet was taken   pray what is become of the moderica purple ulmaria or Valerian of which thou was to send Mee seed — & of thy fine Double upright Larkspurr &c

I have no Letters from thee Since those with Seeds which came to my Hands in Last January —

The Last Winter has been the Mildest I Ever knew — so dry Warm & Delightfull So Early was my Garden cover'd wth flowers from Autumn Wee skip'd over Winter and Catch'd Spring unexpectedly — In our Field Wee had & I saw it a Wood Larks nest with Two Eggs — 21st february Old Stile   4 March new Stile — my Small Magnolias Clethra, Itea, Myrica Did not Loose their Leaves & Some others — I very much want the Yellow Root — all have it but Mee a sad Case indeed

It is a long while since I heard from my Good friend John Bartram   I hope no illness has prevented him giving Mee that pleasure   not for want of materials for those are always ready to a speculative Genius Like his

for my part I have been So engaged I had little room for speculations

as I have left off transacting the Library Companys Business I miss the opportunity of sending thy last year's Magazine; however I hope to do it by our friend Franklin who is very well & his son. I have the pleasure to see them often.

The seeds came admirably well & gave satisfaction   I heard quite otherwise of Alexanders

My son sayes, "Father, what is the Matter   friend John has quite forgot you who take so much pains to Dispose of his seeds &c   what no plants this year   sure He might have sent them having two opportunities by the

Two ships in which He sent seeds" Indeed friend John I leave thee to settle this account with my son who is an Enthusiast after Orchis, Lady's Slippers, Hellebores, Lilies & all new things

the Yellow Slipper is now in glorious flower five shoots from a Root & 2 flowers on a stalk & the white one just now peeping out of ground not half an inch High   What singular difference in plants of the same tribe

Send Double Boxes for Pike & Powell & Williamson & 6 single ones for I have only orders for One   Powell & Edie desires but half the Quantity of Walnutts & Hickerys but all Desire new things   they say they are Tired of old ones   Gordon and Myself want to hear how his 2 Vegitable cargos came to hand

Alexander has sent the Yellow Root & the largest finest Mountain Laurells or Rhododendrons & Calmias to our Neighbr Ponthieu & Many other rare plants came in Excellent order (this gives me mortification)   it is very unlucky these fine plants should never happen in my Friend Johns Way & I have seen before this as fine come from Alexander — these plants Two foot high & Some More — & there is Twelve of Each sort —

I have not a good Azalea or the Shrubby White & Red Honesuckle — which are my favourites but — Little plants of Five or 6 Inches that don't flower — prethee Dear John don't be out done by this Fellow, — but Look Mee out against next year — Some Fine Azaleas & Calmia — Tie up the Roots with Sodds, or Moss & Pack them up well in Moss in a Long Box I think Alexanders came so — & they Look as fresh & fine as if Just taken from their native place   a Root or Two of Genseng will be acceptable to

Thy Old Frd P Collinson

the Box of plants open'd for the King   they are in order & a fine Collection as is Mine, but there is some formality to Deliver the Kings which [goes] to Kew Garden[1] where all Vegitables are treated [with] utmost Care & all that Art can do to bring them [illegible] in our Climate

BP 3:79; D. 226.
1. As a result of the interest of Frederick, Prince of Wales, and his wife, the Royal Botanic Gardens were established at Kew.

From SAMUEL GREEN

Wilmington May 18th 1761

Mr. Bartram

Sir. I read yours dated Novr. 18th Last past which was very agreeable to me. I intended to write to you many a time since I had the pleasure of seeing you but one thing or another allways put it off. I wish I could be so happy as to make you a friendly Visit (agreeable to you) but alass that will never be I am apt to think for I have been here 21 years and never was further than fisher people were pleased to send for me   But to make up for that deficiency as well as I can I should be glad to keep up a correspondence with you. Whatever you may have to send your brother or any other person here I hope youl please to send it in my Care and that shall not be wanting till delivered agreeable to your orders. I asked your brother a while ago if he had sent you any flowering shrubs   he told me he had   I then concluded it was not necessary to send you any nor do I know what to send but I think the best method I can fall upon will be that whenever I see some very uncommon thing to send that and I think I have done that pretty well in sending you the Moss in yr Pil box for I imagin you have no sand for it to grow upon for it grows upon nothing else than being not ye least sign of soil under it   nothing but a white bed of sand. I took it up about Christmas last in full bloom the flowers being a beautiful red and I think the smallest in ye world some of which are upon the stem none but shriveled up pritty much. The flower I send I took in November   it grows in Sou west Savannah Land but when in bloom is a very pretty flower but I have not any name for it. The Pod and beans I send are from a very pretty flowering shrub but I suppose you have it already. This is but a poor collection and not worth your acceptance, how ever of some service to me as a proofe that I have not forgot you. I make use of a Root of a Red Colour (have no name) and finds it of much service in some cases   if it would be agreeable would send some either green or dry   I saw about Novemr an Evergreen with red berries growing in a pond in a Savannah, water 15 Inches or more deep, it was a different sort from any I had ever seen before and some of my friends say the same. If this would be agreeable please to let me know whether to send ye root or berry or leafe. This is all at present from thy best wisher and humle servt

Samll Green

BP 4:30.

From WILLIAM BARTRAM

May 18th 1761

Dear Brother

I am in hopes these few Lines will meet with you all in good Health: as we Enjoy at Present: Thanks be to the Allmighty: I Rec'd your Last with More Satisfaction than Ever I Did Any Before: by Reason that I had the Pleasure of Receiveing: it from the hands of my Dr: Cousen[1] Wm: Bartram: who is Very Well: And I hope will be Blessed with health and Prosperity in our Cuntry: I have No News: Nor Nothing Strange to hardly worth Acquainting you with: only our Genrl: Assembly Met Last March at Wilmington And we have Agreed to grant an Aid of twenty Thousand Pounds Prock: to Raise 550 Men Exclusive of Officers: to go where Genrl: Amherst shall think Proper to order them: But I am afraid they:l be So Long a Raising that they:l do Nothing but Spend the Cuntry's Money: But good hands to Set it a

Circulating. We have had within these few Days the Largest fresh in our River: that Ever was Known Ever Since the Cuntry was Setled: which has Don Many Thousands of Pounds Damage: I Expect I shall Loos Neer two Hundred Pounds worth my Selfe. I Did Not Know of Captn: Gulleys going of in Such A hurry Last time; or Should Sent more Roots & Seeds: & wrote more Perticularly: But I: & Cousen: Bill have Sent the Sensitive Plant & White Nettle Bryer: which I hope will Com Safe Alive to your hand: by Captn: Gully, I Shall take Perticular Cear to Send Several More Next winter if I have an Oppertunity: I Recd: the Magazeen by Robeson[2] & Shall be Very glad of More: Pray give Harty Respects to Sister: & Cousens: from your Loving Brother &:c.

William Bartram

I hope youl: Excuse my Not writeing at this time to my Cousens, having But a Short time — A Boat goin Down Sooner than I Expected: I Believe I Can Be of Service to them in the Sale of Drugs in this Province:[3] I Shall give farther Notice I hope in A Short time

from W:B

BP 1:69.
1. His nephew, John's son William.
2. Probably his son-in-law Thomas Robeson, husband of his daughter Mary.
3. Isaac and Moses had gone into partnership as apothecaries. To expand their business they were seeking wholesale drug outlets in nearby provinces.

From WILLIAM BARTRAM

Wilmington   Cape Fear   May 20th 1761

Hond Father

I am just puting off from Willming: with Part of my Goods bound to Ashwood where I intend to dispose of them as well as I can to make the best Returns, I am unfortunate in ariving to a bad Market, a wrong Season of the Year, and the excessive rains has allmost destroyed the Country. They continued Incessantly for 7 or 8 days and kept me in Idleness & Unkles Boat on which I put a dependence for the carying of my Goods up he had just lent to a Gentleman & after waiting about a Week at his House was put to the necessity of hiring a Boat at the Rate of Ten Shillings p Day which will cost me allmost as much to get my Goods up as their Freight here — Unkle has been a Greate Sufferer by this Inundation, has destroyed all His Wheat, which was a Pretty Parcell as ever I saw. The banks of the River being overflowed spread over the Low Lands to a greate distance   many People are drove from their Dwellings & forced to seek shelter in the Woods & Sandhills — should be glad to hear from thee & Mother   Please to give my love to Brothers and sisters & all those that'll except it. I have my Health will thank Heaven   hope I may Injoy it in this Country God Willing — I have sent you p Capt Golly the most extraordinary Beauty in the Vegitable

Kingdom that Comicle Sensitive Plant which grows in the Savannas & the Nettle with the white Flower — Thay are Good roots —

Dear Father here no Preaching   But Unkle seems a Gods man and we enjoy some Pleasant & Inosent conversation — Men are allowed the Liberty to Worship God her[e] according to the dictates of right Reason

BP 1:70.

To COLLINSON

May ye 22nd 1761

Dear Peter
I received thy kind letter of february ye 2d 1760   I never received any account of ye tortoise shells   ye great red bellied one I take to be very diferent from those small ones I sent which is ye lesser red bellied or that which Billy drawed tail & head in ye shel & ye terrapin is very different from all ye others: if I can get a shel of these I desighn to send one   it is often 1 or 2 years after I send such curiosities before I get an answer & many times never that   ye perticulars is forgot & Billy is now gone to Carolina but whether he is arived or when he will come back I know not   was it ye loss of ye yellow or white water Lillies that troubled thee   it is ye root of ye yellow one that ye snaping tortise feeds on   I can help thee to either of them   thee very unjustly reproacheth me for want of curiosity in ye article of ye colocasia   I have made three tryals of it at diferent times   twice it miscarried & ye last it grows so slow as scarcely to be seen: it will be very difficult to send ye roots   thay are allmost as brittle as glass & runs two or three foot deep in ye mud   I hope to send ye seeds next fall & perhaps A root: Doctor witt & Alexander went on purpose & fetched seeds & roots but both miscaried: spring water kills them & ye marsh weeds choaks them: Billy received ye fine present of Edwards & promised me to send A letter of thanks or else I should have done it   I received ye pear seeds & sowed them directly but I expect never to see ye fruite   if A graft had been sent alive perhaps I might but I believe no body ever had worse luck with vegitables from London then I for of ye cargo which I have wrote for 20 years past these are all that lives: 3 roots of poplar as I take them   4 cuttings of willows which I take to be ye real white which I had long from New England   one root of Oleander   cyclamen which I had from Carolina   one root of mandrake   spignel & one something like ulmaria these are all which grows which ye Captain charged me (no list or letter of advice) 3 Pound freight   how thay all came to perish I cant say unless ye sailors watered them with salt water   of ye seeds thee sent ye globe thisle come up by ye hundreds as ye tessel but it proves to be ye common wild tessel common about Philadelphia   ye wild anemony roots never came up   one fritilary flowered A dul green Flower   ye asphodels narsisus

autumnal yellow crocus & four flag iris   common little ornithogala grows prodigiously   we have had them in plenty long & I must dig them up & make A burnt sacrifice of them to bad fortune after one or two years carefull nursing in hopes of something rare   this puts me in mind of Doctor witts common saying that you send us all ye worst & will not let us have ye rare ones   indeed I am quite out of heart for sending for any perticulars which rarely come & afraid to sow or plant what is sent least it should prove common: but yet by chance one or two comes in A year very curious   ye Chalcedonian Iris made A glorious appearance & ye poleanthus such A surprising variety that I could no more tell which was ye most beautifull then I could before have imagined there had been such varieties   I have planted out this spring over 200   I had two prety early tulups blowed well   what was sent me for ye red & yellow digitalis & ye carnations is near blowing but my heart akes when I look at them lest thay should be common: ye seed of ye cape aster   oriental red mallow   narrow leaved asters   nicotiana & Iron colored digitalis comes up well but from ye Carolinas I have had as extraordinary good luck as ye other is bad   I have received 5 large boxes well stuft with curious plants & shrubs all which came as good as if taken up ye day before besides A variety of seeds but A curious dark smooth leaved holly pleaseth me much   now I find it differs greatly from ye dahoon holly   I dug up one last spring in April & planted it in A garden   it was just sent this spring & now it hath scores of blosoms   there is still two sorts of smooth leaved hollys or A new genus but very beautifull in two gardens   one came from towards ye mountains   fine bearing trees which I hope to have by ye favour of an elderly widow Lady[1] which spares no pains or cost to oblige me   her garden is her delight & she hath a fine [one]   I was with her about 5 minits in much company yet we contracted much mutual Correspondence that one silk bag hath past & repast full of seeds several times last fall   I desired her last march to send me some seeds of ye hors sugar or yellow leaf   she directly sent me A box with 2 fine growing plants mixt with several other sorts that she thought would pleas & paid freight with promises to send any vegitable in her power to procure & thay thrive finely   several roots of ye long leaved Saracena dug out of thair savanas grows finely in my uper dry gravely garden   so doth thair sweet scented asarbaca which I dug up out of ye side of A pond   Dr. Garden is so hurried as he knows plants well & where thay grow   I am sory to hear that ye ship is taken that I sent four boxes in   one large box of plants for Powel one for Henry de ponthieu one for thy self & another containing specimens & seeds for thee & Gordon   I sent him A fine parcel of holley berries ye geting of which had like to broke my bones I fell on ye top of ye tree where ye top that I had hold of & ye branch I stood on broke & I fel to ye ground   my little son Benjamin was not able to help me up   my pain was grevous after very sick   then in A wet sweat in A dark thicket   no house near & A very could sharp wind & above 20 mile to ride home   the may Judge what A poor circumstance I was in & yet my arm is so weak that sometimes I can hardly pull on my cloaths   yet I have A great mind to go next fall to Pitsburgh in hope to find some curious plants there

BP 1:53:2; D. 227.
1. Martha Logan.

To WILLIAM BARTRAM[1]

dear son
I received thy kind letters of April ye 27th May ye 6th & 20th May [illegible] hear of thy safe arival tho sorry of thy disapointment by ye great rains   I am obliged for thy care in sending ye plants tho thay miscaried being washed overboard which if thay had not thay could not have survived ye improper time for sending them: ye onely time of sending roots is between september & April or May, well packed in earth & watered then nailed up & placed in ye Cabin or uper course of ye hold with lid upermost as A box of marchandise: so most came from both no & So carolina & most all grows as in thair native countrey   pray gather what seeds thee can   those sent me few comes up: ye Convolvulus in plenty   one of ye long leaved lupin & two of ye yellow spiked flower with leaves like our indigo   4 more is come up from last years sowing which is enough if thay live: ye horse sugar I received from Mrs. Logan since thee went   ye grape vine which brother sent grows finely as all ye rest   it looks just like our little odius grape which perhaps it is   A degenerate northern kind   pray take good notice of its magnitude & tast that I may know what honor to bestow upon it. Brother commends it much   he sent me A fine parcel of shrubs in excelent order & good roots but omited several that I much wanted perticularly   A lovely flowering shrub which I shewed thee A specimen Just before thee went   A new genus grows on ye bank at Ashwood & many other places   ye leaves is roundish & not serated   not ye halesia   ye lobloly Bay or alcea floridiana & ye dwarf palm that grows up A little creek at ashwood & that pretty flowering shrub growing in brothers medow above his ould house in great plenty & I think ye water tupelo is not sent nor a pretty flowering shrub growing near ye sides of branches about 5 foot high   ye seeds growing in whorles these is most that I want which I saw near Brothers of ye tree & shrub kind & ye little deciduous bay grows in moist places but nearer to Brunswick & fort Jonson there grows many of ye evergreen oak with leaves allmost like ye prickely holly but narrower & not so sharp which I should be glad of; ye seed of ye sensative Brier & Nettle will do better then thair roots which is long & difficult to grow   I am now all in A flame to go to Pittsburg if Providence permits   I desighn to set out ye latter part of August or ye begining of September as opertunity offers   I want much to see ye productions of that Countrey   if I get home well by ye last of october I shall be very thankfull to our heavenly father,   My dear Child I have no new advice to give thee but to remind thee of my former general instructions;

fear God & walk humble before him; practice all virtues & eschew all vice take care of being beguiled by vain recreations   thay are like ye hornets hath A sting in thair tail   but keep close to industry temperance & frugality; thee hath left A good character behind in town   pray dont forget it   now is ye time to gain it there & establish it in both provinces by makeing good remittances to thy Creditors here; be Complaisant & obligeing to all so far as consistent with thy credit & no honest man will desire more: thy master & mistris gives thee an extrordinary good word & laments thair loss as one of thair family: I have thy wellfare much at heart. take thy uncles advice   he is both Capable & I doubt not willing to advise thee for ye Best as to thy general Conduct but in ye perticular Branch of Marchandise thee ought to know best but I think it might be well if thee would at convenient times pay A Complaisant visit to ye Governour & most of ye chief persons letting them know that thee art come to thair Countrey in ye way of trade & that thee would if thee could make A suitable remittance   settle such a Correspondence at Philadelphia or London as thee might be enabled to furnish them with any goods thay wanted & as thee was A stranger & A young beginer & in A pleasant Cheerful obligeing manner desire thair good will & concurrance therein: advise with thy uncle about it   he knows ye disposition & ye Abilitys of ye people as well as most   while our vesail lay at Anchor A little below Brunswick I went on shore where ther was A narrow strip of low land between high water mark & ye bank. I walked on ye shore downward until ye bank came to the shore whereabout I saw A patch or number of shrubs four foot high & ye thickness of my finger very close together as if Joyned at ye roots   thay had no leaves nor vestiges of fruite but thay seemed to be new to me   if thee goes to Bruinswick & has time I wish thee would take A walk about half A mile & examine them what Genus thay are   just about high water mark perhaps thay are a fine flowering shrub   Dear Son ye Captain is here waiting   I must close up with much love

thy affectionate father
John Bartram

BP 1:39:1.
1. Undated, but written in early summer of 1761, probably June, judging by the content.

From MARTHA LOGAN

June 6 1761
Sr
   I have the Pleasure of yours by Capt North & am much Obliged for the Roots therein Promised   they will be quite Acceptable   If you have any Sweet or other Peas of the Double kinds shoulde be Very glade of a fue
   I am Sorry the Holly Did not Prove what you Wanted but shall make Inquirey after the trees in Mrs Wraggs, & by Mr Rapers[1] garden & send you

Some of theire Berryes as soon Ripe. as Likewise all the other things you Mention in theire Season for Removing   I doe not know if the Scarlet flowered Vine I have be what you heard   what I call Cannary [Vine] Saide to be Lylass. perhaps you may know it by this   how Ever shall send boath with the others & hope they will be an adision to yr Collections —

I have been a little unlucky in the Seeds though hast be so kinde to send. Several never Come up. Amongst which Weire the Sweet Sultains Purple Molly & Sibera Rocket. If the are well stocked with seeds shall be glad to try them once more. Pray lett me know how yr Stock gilly flowers turned out and thou wilt much Oblige Sr Your Assured friend & Humble Servant

Martha Logan

BP 4:74.
1. Unidentified.

From COLLINSON

Londn June 12:1761

I have no Letters from my Dear frd John since Decemr 6 & Novemr 8th, — that came with the seeds

I don't think I am forgotten, as my frd John is often apt to Imagine; (if no Letter comes), — I always make Allowance for accidents – of Ships being taken or Castaway — as I am psuaded is now the Case — Gordon longs to know in what state his plants arrived — as the New York pacquet is more safe & Convenient I write by that, as Alexr Colden the post Master is my pticular friend — the few seeds of the fine great Acconite root come up Remember more Seeds of It — & the Delphinium; Sibirea Larkspur, — several Rudbekias, & a fine long Close spiked blew flower — an odd sort a new Genus — all from Virginia Mountains — pray what is the Double Wild Crocus — I thought you had none of this Species in your Country — if thou canst not send a Root send a Specimen of it that I may see this marvelous fine thing — in thine of Decemr 6 thou mentions of sending a box of plants by next ship — but none is come to hand   I take it the pine seed I sent was the pinaster — a fine species —

The Ivy, Laurel or Broad Leaved Kalmia is now in Flower — certainly is one of the finest Ever Green shrubs that is in the World — the stamina are Elegantly disposed in the angles of the Flowers — & what a pretty blush its Bullated[1] Flower Budds — But in a few Days will the Glorious Mountain Laurel or great Chamaerhododendron appear with its Charming Clusters of flowers   prethee Friend John look out sharp for some more of these Two fine plants — for one can Never have too Many — but they are so delicate in their Natures — of the Many I have had how few can be tempted can be reconciled to Our Soil & Climate   if one out of 3 or 4 Succeeds it is Well — & the Shrub Honesuckles or Azaleas are almost as Ticklish in their

Natures — in some places they do Well in others not at all — So pray Look out for More & if one Box will not hold them Send Two — I have a sprig in flower of the Kalmia in water & it stares mee in the face all the while I am writing — saying, or Seems to say, as you are so fond of Mee tell my Frd J Bartram who sent Mee to send some More to keep me Company for they will be sure to be well nursed & Well treated and don't forgett the Yellow Root & Genseng if it happens in thy way

Thy Correspondents — Fern, Bartram [sic] Powell & Co & Williamson — Desires Double Boxes — I have orders only for One Single Box however send five more I may hope to Dispose [illegible]

The seeds came in fine order last year & gave Satisfaction — Alexanders was in bad condition & as Indifferently sorted as I am told but when He sends plants for size & Vigor they Excell all I ever Saw   I cannot Bear that my Indefatigable Frd Bartram should be outdone by Him   prethee find out his haunts where He gott such good & perfect things

There has been much talk of a peace & Wee have a Frenchman Here that is said to Come about It & yett it seems a great way off   What Millions of Men are slaughtered to gratifie the Wicked, Cruel Ambition of princes   O dear John I am much affected to see & hear the annual sacrifice of our brave Country Men   But the necessity of our affairs was such from French Perfidy & treachery that it was not to be avoided   May the God of Peace send Peace again on the Earth is the earnest prayer of thy frd

P Collinson

when they are proper to remove I intend to send Gernsey, Jacobea & Belladonna Lillies & Autumn Narcissus

BP 3:20; D. 227–28.
1. Puckered.

From GARDEN

June 17th, 1761

My worthy Friend

I received your obliging letter informing me of the safe arrival of the plants. I rejoice with you on your Encreasing collection of these Curious productions of the alwise hand of our omnipotent Creator, May your Soul be daily more filled with an humble admiration of his works & your lips exercised in his praise. How glorious are those hours of Contemplation & enjoyment that the ravished soul passes thro when viewing the wonderfull manifestation of his Power, Wisdom & Goodness. When this scene of things passes away & the Great & first Author of all leads us to fields of a more rich & fertile Clime, there shall we proceed with fresh vigour & enlarged faculties to view him nearer, worship & adore more strongly & live more willingly within the Peal of universal Love. How great is our God — How wonderfull are his works sought out of all them that take pleasure therein — Your letters particularly give me pleasure, they always contain something new & Entertaining on some new discovered work of God — I admire your variety of pancratiums & rejoice in your happiness — The Loblolly Bay, Dwarf Pomegranete & yellow wood have perished & all but those I Sent you — I could not get Beureria when I sent the Box & my own had died in the winter, but I'll try to get two or three plants this year — Pray remember to let me have some of your fine Bulbs especially Hyacinths, & the Daffodil with the large long pinched nectatium & whatever Else you please. Let me know your sons Duration & Address & I'll send him some Pink root.

This will be delivered to you by a Lady[1] whom I have the honour to be acquainted with, & who has a very pretty taste for flowers & the Culture of Curious plants. She intends to pay you a visit while she stays at Philadelphia & I take the liberty to beg your Civilities to her, not doubting but it will give you joy to see a Lady coming so far to view & Admire your Curiosities. My wife offers along with me our best respects to your wife & all the rest of your good family.

Believe me to be

Yours
Alexander Garden

BP 4:12; D. 396–97.
1. Unidentified.

From MARTHA LOGAN[1]

Sr

I received yours dated 1 March with the seeds Enclosed & am much Obliged for them. I hope for better sucess with these than those before having never a seed of the Sweet Sultaine or the Humble plant that Come up. the roots & Seeds you Mention will be Very Exceptable & if the Crocusts are blue I shall Like them Still better as I have 2 roots of yellow allready —

You may Sertinly Depend on my Sending the Holly berries & Seeds of the Savana Locust you saw in Mr. Rapers Garden as soon as they are ripe, & I will doe my Endeaviour to gett a root of the Starry Hyacinth of Mrs. Wragg but doe not know of any other person that has it in Charles town   The yellow Wood bears no seed & Grows Wilde when it is Propagated, 'tis only from its Slips. Wherefore have sent you some in a box of Earth (though tis Rather late to move it) but as tis not Difficult to grow hope they will Live. If not I can with Ease Send you some more Next Winter — In the same box you have 2 roots of another kinde of Starry Hyacinth & some fue other things of which you have a list at Last as allso a list of many things which I could with Ease furnish you with If I knew what would be Exceptable theirfore begg you will without Serimony tell me what to send thee, for am sure no person will moore readyly Comply with your Requests. I am with Respect Sr yr Well Wisher & Humble Servt

Martha Logan

A list of things which may be sent
   Trees & Flowring Shrubs –
   Oliander   Sweet Shrub   Cassena
   Double flowered Pumgranete
   Dwarfe Pumgraned. Nutmeg Mirtles.
   Scopesene (a shrub)
   Olive tree
   A Catalpa. one with white & other red flowers
   Canary Shrub (purple flowers)
   flowring bays & Layrels
   English Honey Suckles
   Chine Indigo
   Pasion flower
   the feathered leaf   One with Scarlet flowr
   Snaile flower
   Rose Cassia
   Turkey Balm
   alloways two Sorts one flors. Constantly the other very seldom
      (if ever)
   Ice plant.
   White Crocusts
   grape Hyacinth (blue)
   Chine & Turkey Pinks   Caldonian Iris.
   Guise [?] Narciss. Double White. Sweet scented Cypress narssis. Tuby
      roses

A list of whats Sent in the box

6 plants of yellow wood 2 Do Holly. Do the tree in Rapers garden, 1 Turff of striped grass (Much Esteemed hear) two sorts of smale purple flower you See in Mrs Bees garden, the which you liked   1 Plant of Italian Jesinmine 2 Starry Hyacinth but not of the Bulbous kind.

P.S. When you Send or Wright to me againe be pleased to Direct for me to the Caire of John Logan Marchant in Charles Town. for Dr. Garden has so much business he has not time to Think of me, Wherefore your Letters have Some times Layen a good While & I never Known of them

Captain North here is the person brings your box   will be a Safe hand when you faviour me with the roots & Seeds you mentioned.

BP 4:72.
1. The content of this letter suggests that it was written in the early summer of 1761.

To WILLIAM BARTRAM[1]

My Dear Billy
I was lately tould by a man that rides express that he saw in No Carolina not far from Cape Fear A strange plant About as big as a dasy & much like it in flower   I think he called it ye wonderful flower whose properties was such that if thay looked earnestly at it ye petals of ye flower would close up   he said ye moors near Bruinswick knowed it well: if it lieth in thy way to speak with Moris More:[2] ask him about it   if it be true it will be A fine curiosity & furnish matter for phylosofical contemplation   I want seed & roots of ye lobloly bay & ye pretty sensitives at A proper season   I sent by Captain Gulley A barrel of rum for my brother & A large parcel of bulbous roots for sister   pray gather every sort of seeds that dont grow in our countrey those that sister sent me dont come up onely ye convolvulus in plenty never mind keeping ye seeds seperate   cram them all into A bag & send them in ye fall   I am still resolved if providence permits me to travail to Pittsburg & down ye Ohio if safe   pray send me A young long leaved hoary lupin & some seed   I had two of them came up but our scorching sun killed them   seed & roots of ye lobloly bay & horse sugar as I wrote largely by Captain Gully   I have little to write onely all our loves to thee & Broth Sister & Cousens Adieu

P. S. I propose to set out ye begining of september & return ye last of october if our heavenly father please to favour me with A prosperous Journey   however his will be done: his will be done in all things

BP 1:61.
1. Undated, but written in late May or early June 1761. Bartram's son Billy reached North Carolina on May 6.
2. Maurice Moore, of New Hanover, North Carolina.

To TEMPLEMAN

July ye 6th 1761

Worthy Friend
I received thy kind letter of September ye 16th 1760 in ye name of ye Society for ye encouragement of Arts & commerce: we have in our northern Provinces no natural herbs or grass that will keep cows in any tolerable degree of heart all winter (supposeing no snow lay upon ye ground) except on ye salt beech by ye seashore where several kinds of Asters & golden rods: limonium & A broad leaved marsh grass   these being covered with A quantity of dead dry marsh grass which ye cattle eat All together by which thay make A shift to Just keep alive untill spring in A poor weak condition; ye inhabitants burn some of the dead grass very early that ye green grass may shoot up soon; ye other part of ye marsh thay reserve with ye ould & new grass for present feeding while ye other fresh grass & herbs is comeing

forward for A more full support   it is my opinion that Providence placed Cows originaly in A warm Climate where ye grass grew long & herbs flourished all ye year as we may Judge by ye form of thair mouths with no upper fore teeth (as other Cattle) & thair rough toung to lick or pull in to thair mouth such grass or herbs that are long grown & if we will bring them out of thair natural Climate & keep them there for our use we ought to feed them well during ye inclement seasons.

Indeed Buffeloes of ye same Genus doth travell from ye Southward in ye summer season in quest of food as far as our Latitude to ye rich intervail lands but then in ye fall & at ye approach of winter thay retire to ye southward again where ye green reeds is in plenty & ye grass long

Horses Sheep & Goats hath thair upper fore teeth & bites Close to ye ground & will live tolerable all ye winter if ye ground is bare from snow either in our fields or medows or in ye back woods where grows Asters & broad leaved grass which being covered with dead grass keeps green near ye roots all winter   thay allso brouse on young Sasafras shoots: Ceanothus & other shrubs – I observed on ye rich lands near Susquehana river after A very hard winter & much snow, ye horses had striped ye mulberie trees from near ye root to as high as thay could reach of thair bark for food but nearer to ye southward there grows on ye trees A long kind of Moss or viscum which is good food for Cattle or dear in ye winter with ye reeds & tops of ye yellow wood, A new Genus.

there grows in west Jersey A lovely plant with grassy leaves which spreads in tufts A foot diameter & is allway as green in winter as summer it shoots up A stalk four foot high & terminates with A spike of fine white flowers which nearly bears ye Characters of an Asphodel   ye spike of flowers is extended by gradual succesion to 6 or 8 inches in length   ye cattle will eat ye leaves in winter   I take it to be a new Genus & one of ye most dificult to transplant so as to flourish that I know   I went (after 20 years trial to no purpose) in ye heat of summer to fetch one out of Jersey it now succeds & lookes as well as in its native place   I have sent seeds & roots of it every year to England but I believe not one grows   ye roots is extoled for ye quinsey

I design to set out towards Pittsburgh ye first of September next   I would fain go down ye Ohio & up to Lake Erie but must have a good Escort for fear of the skulking Jealous Indians. thay watch all our motions even our eyes if we look at A Compass thay think we are searching thair Land to Posses it   if at A tree or rock thay think it is for A Corner Mark & ye creeks or hills for boundaries of different tracts of land

I hope to find if thay dont hinder mee many Curious trees shrubs & plants besides many fossils to add to my Collection from So. & north Carolina to Nova scotia   very few is wanting of ye vegitable productions of ye intermediate space & from ye sea coast to Lake Ontario   this success I say heated by ye Botanick fire set me in such A flame as is not to be quenched untill death or I explore most of ye South western vegitive treasures in No. America or perish in ye attempt   but if Providence favours

Worthy Friend 60.   July yͤ 6 1761

I received thy kind leter of September yͤ 16 1760 in yͤ name of yͤ
Society for yͤ encouragement of Arts & comerce. we have in our northern Provinces no natural herbs or grass that will keep cows in any
tolerable degree of heart all winter (supposeing no snow lay upon yͤ
ground) except on yͤ salt beech by yͤ sea shore where grows several
kinds of elsters & golden rods: Limonium & a broad leaved marsh grass
these being covered with a quantity of dead dry marsh grass which yͤ
cattle eat all together by which thay make a shift to just keep alive untill spring in a poor weak condition: yͤ inhabitants burn some of the dead
grass very early that green grass may shoot up soon, yͤ other part of
yͤ marsh thay reserve with yͤ auld & new grass for present feeding
while yͤ other fresh grass & herbs is comeing foreward for a more full
support   it is my oppinion that Providence placed Cows originaly
onely in a warm Climate where yͤ grass grew long & herbs flowrished
all yͤ year as we may Judge by yͤ form of thair mouths with no upper
fore teeth as other Cattle & thair rough toung to lick or pull in to thair
mouths such grass or herbs that are long grown & if we will bring them
out of thair natural Climate & keep them there for our use we ought
to feed them well during yͤ inclement seasons
indeed Buffaloes of yͤ same Genus doth travel from yͤ Southward in yͤ
summer season in quest of food as far as our Latitude to yͤ rich intervail
lands but then in yͤ fall & at yͤ approach of winter thay retire to yͤ southward again where yͤ green reeds is in plenty & yͤ grass long
Horses sheep & goats hath thair upper fore teeth & bites close to yͤ ground
& will live tolerable all yͤ winter if yͤ ground is bare from snow either in
our fields or medows or in yͤ back woods where grows elsters & broad leaved
grass which being covered with dead grass keeps green near yͤ roots
all winter thay also brouse on young Sasafras shoots. Ceanothus & other
shrubs:——   I observed on yͤ rich lands near Susquehana river after a very hard winter & much snow. yͤ horses had striped yͤ mulberie
trees from near yͤ root to as high as thay could reach of thair bark
for food but nearer to yͤ southward there grows on yͤ trees a long
kind of moss or viscum which is good food for Cattle or dear in yͤ winter
with yͤ reeds & tops of yͤ yellow wood a new Genus:
there grows in west Jersey a lovely plant with grassy leaves which
spreads in tufts a foot diameter & is alway as green in winter as
summer it shoots up a stalk four foot high & terminates with a spike
of fine white flowers which nearly bears yͤ Characters of an asphodel yͤ
spike of flowers is extended by gradual succesion to 6 or 8 inches in
length yͤ cattle will eat yͤ leaves in winter I take it to be a new Genus
& one of yͤ most dificult to transplant so as to flowrish that I know
I went after 20 years trial to no purpose in yͤ heat of summer to fetch
one out of Jersey it now succeeds & lookes as well as in its native
                                                                    place

I have sent seeds & roots of it every year to England but I believe not one grows if roots is extoled for y: gumsey I desighn to set out towards Pittsburgh y: first of September next I would fain go down y: Ohio & up to Lake Erie but m[ust] have a good escort for fear of the skulking jealous Indians. th[ey] watch all our motions even our eyes if we look at a compass thay think we are searching thair Land to Posses it if at a tree or rock thay think it is for a Corner mark & y: cheeks or hills for boundaries of diferent tracts of land I hope to find if thay dont hinder mee many Curious trees shrubs & plants besides many fossils to add to my Collection from So. & north Carolina to Nova Scotia very few is wanting of y: vegitable productions of y: intermediate space & from y: sea coast to Lake Ontario this success I say heated by y: Botanick fire set me in such a flame as is not to be quenched until death or I explore most of y: South western vegitive treasures in No: America or perish in y: attempt but if Providence favours me with success & a safe return I hope to give a good account of soil & scituation & also its visible productions as far as I travail in y: mean time I remain your Sincear friend

John Bartram

Bartram's letter to Peter Templeman, July 6, 1761. The number 60 at the top appears to have been added later. Courtesy of the Royal Society of Arts, London.

me with success & A safe return I hope to give A good account of ye soil & scituation & allso its visible productions as far as I travail   in ye mean time I remain your Sincear friend

John Bartram

Library of the Royal Society for the Encouragement of Arts, Manufactures and Commerce.

From JOHN de PONTHIEU

London July 16th 1761

dear Sir

We are Sorry to hear by your favour of the 20th May that your intended present was taken by the French. We are however not the less obliged to you & kindly thank you. we heartily wish we knew what plants of this Country's would be Agreeable to you   we shou'd send them immediately as likewise those from Italy, Spain, Portugal & a very great Variety we have from the Alps some of which we believe would please you very much, as nobody in England has them but ourselves. We keep a General correspondence all over the World & can assure you that nothing will give us greater pleasure than to accomodate you. We believe your best way will be to send us an account of all the European plants you have & then we shall see what you want & send them by first Oppertunity.

We shall be Glad of the same plants you sent us last year but beg you'd send'em with good roots & if possible to ball about their roots with a Good deal of Moss to keep'em Fresh   We want a fine plant of ye larger Magnolia & seeds of all kinds   We should be glad you would try some seeds in a box & send us the box   put in all kinds promiscuously — they stand this way a better chance of coming up

If you cou'd meet with any new Evergreens in your Travels we should esteem it a Great Acquisition or any Odd Plant that is new   we want some of the Calceolas maria of ye two Sorts & some of the [illegible] and flowering dwarff Accacia [illegible] ye tough twigged Viburnum white Hypericum would be very acceptable to make sure of some very good plants if you was to remove'em when this letter comes to hand in pots & leave them there till ship'd, desiring the Captain to water them now and then.

I dare say many Curious things may be met with in Canada —

In what ever I can be of service pray Command   you'll please to write by return of post, that we may send you what you want before winter   My Brother Henry is in the Country which makes me write — believe him as well as myself dear Sir,

Your most Sincere S'rv't
John de Ponthieu

BP 3:96.

To COLLINSON

July ye 19th 1761

Dear Peter

I answered thy letter of february ye 2d by Buden & have now little to write therefore now I must send a miselanious letter   I now send my Journal to carolina & some specimens which my friend Dr Chancelor hath promised to deliver safe to thy hands   Ye specimens is most of them from ye seed I gathered from ye So mountains of virginia most of which come up last year, ye rest this spring. thay grow prodigiously. So doth my No & south carolina plants even ye laururus & long leaved Saracena & ye clematis dug up this year in a carolina swampe is now full of flowers like martagons   each petal measures Above two inches long grows on ye dryest bank in my garden   this extraordinary success with our American plants hath set me all in A flame to go to Pittsburg & down ye ohio as far as I can get A safe escort   I desighn to set out ye begining of september   I have now A glorious appearance of Carnations from thy seed — ye brightest colors that ever eyes beheld   now, what with thine dr. Witts & others I can chalenge any garden in America for variety   Poor ould man: he was lately in my garden but could not distinguish A leaf from A flower   My great blew — hath increased prodigiously & I think thy white one is come up   thy white campanula grows finely but I have one by accident from [A] blew one is as white as snow   thine is cream color   I desighn to try if ye seed will produce white or blew flowers   I have had several double larkspurs but cant get any seed from them   ye seed thee sent me four years past for white betony produced red Flowers like what I had before   I raised from seed from Switzerland A very double sweet william of such A high blush as is dasling to look at   I planted him at A great distance from any other that he may not be corrupted, My son William is safely arrived at Cape Fear & met with A kind reception from Governour Dobbs & his uncle   I have but one root Alive that gordon sent in ye box & that is ye oleander   I think the same with what I had from Carolina ye cuttings of ye willow grows & 4 roots that came in ye basket   I think there is 3 plants of ye yellow foxgloves come up   it is quite surprising how ye Carolina plants grows tho we have very hot dry weather   ye hollys smooth leaved is shot to 10 inches long & ye savana locust sent in may is now shot 2 foot   every one of ye bays magnolias & hollys that was sent me that I planted in both Carolinas grows finely

BP 1:53; D. 228–29.

From COLLINSON

Londn:Augt:1:1761

My dear John

Is always in the same strain, of grumbling & Complaining   makes no allowance for Accidents although I have often admonish'd so to do — I writt him a long Letter soone after I received the Tortoise Shells with my observations on them but right or wrong He upbraids Mee with not doing it in Two years   This frequent censorious Temper is not becomeing our Friendship — the very same positive assertion goes on (No List or Letter with the plants from Gordon) — whereas I inclosed Gordon's List & advice of the plants — but if Letters miscarry as both these certainly did is it friendly to Censure us so severely with neglect   pray Lett Mee never more find occasion to remonstrate on this Head for it is disagreeable to Mee & much more to Read what thou writes after Gordon has taken so much Pains & sent Two such valuable Cargoes to find no Thankfulness no acknowledgments for who can help long Passages & accidents at sea   I saw the plants Growing in the Box & Basket in the finest order Imaginable [illegible]

Well Gordon is so good natured He forgives all thy complaints & will try another Cargo this fall

As times are so Perilous pray don't send thy Journal untill a Peace which Wee are in hopes of for though I long to see It It would grieve Mee to the heart to Hear of its being taken as I do for the Cargo of plants and then again I consolate my self to think how many have Escaped this War   Indeed my good friend thou hast much reason to be thankful since all thy Cargoes of seeds have come safe   the loss of thy Box of plants for my near neighbour Ponthieu was the more Bearable as they had so fine a Cargo of Alexander. The great Chamaerhododendron & Kalmia Laurel were the largest and finest I ever saw & so Fresh   I can't imagine where he getts them, with besides a Variety of your other plants such as the Evergreen Andromeda of which I have fine plants which thou sent, but was not in any other Garden, untill these arrived, & the yellow Root I saw in fruit but there is great complaints of Alexander seeds. — Thine Bears the Bell but his does well enough for the Scots

Thou sees my Dear John how Necessary it is to persevere & mind no complaints, for If I had thou hadst never had the Meadow Sweet Amoria & Polyanthos which I have been sending at Times off & on for 30 years past, how often has Docr Witt upbraided Mee (for He was an everlasting grumbler) that the seeds was musty & bad   sometimes came to soon & then too late so that I believe little or none was Raised & yett thou finds I hit the lucky Time at Last, Make much of It for I dare say none in your province can show the like [illegible] really friend John complain on — I am now so used to that I shall not mind it for the future [illegible]

But as thou canst write diverting and curious observations, in this manner I expect to be Entertained for the future which will always give pleasure to thy old friend P Collinson

I am greatly concerned to Hear of thy Dangerous fall, reflect on thy many narrow Escapes & be thankfull it was no Worse but Lett Mee advise thee to be very carefull for the future –

I plainly see thou knowest how to fascinate the Longing Widow by so close a Correspondence — When the Women enter into these amusements I ever found them the best assistants, now I shall not wonder if thy Garden abounds with all the Rarities of Carolina

Govr Dobbs & his Secretary sent Mee a Box with Swamp Pines — 2 or 3 of the Great Sarracenia which grows admirably & has shot Leaves of a surpriseing Length   I planted your sort, in the same Bogg that the difference in the species may be an agreeable sight & I had besides them Roots of a Narcissus or pancreatium that was found growing in a Bogg — that flower'd finely   it is a singular shoot with White flower & as thou well observes in the Lowest Lat these Charming Bulbs are found In —

I have often taken notice to thee how very few of the Bulbous Tribe are found through all the Colony Countrys but who knows what stores of wonderfull productions may be Discovered about the Lakes — if thou are able to make an expedition to Pittsburgh thy Penetrateing Eye will bring Hidden things to Light & come Home fraught with Vegetable Treasures

The Great Mountain Laurel or Rhodon. has been most Beautifully in Flower as is now my Great Magnolia — the small Magnolia flowerd freely the Umbrella & Mountain have not yett flower'd with Mee altho the Last is a Large Delightfull Tree of a Conic Figure wch strikes every one with admiration   the Clematis with reflected Petalls near Twelve feet high makes a pretty show in flower — as has been the 4 leaved Ever green Bignonia which thrives, makes lovely show & in fall decor Bore a Podd & Ripe seeds

In thine of May 4 — Thou Sayes in a hurry [illegible] no such Letters came to hand   Wee think [illegible] again finely this year

Now Dear John so much for thine of May 24 & 22d — haveing had none since Novemr & Decemr 10 grievous owing to the Charges of Warr — a Day or two agon I was fishing in one of my ponds — I caught a Perch — the hook was swallowed so Deep I cutt the Perch in halves to gett it out but instead of doing It I threw in my Line with the half perch on the hook — to try what would take it & Let it Lay in all night   So when I came to pull it out, up comes the Great Mud Turtle — that I had not seen for a year & a half — much grown   by this experiment I know how to catch the devourer – My fish has much decreased & now I know the poacher — I believe I must transport him

My son in law has built him a Large fine House & has Every thing to plant — prithee send a box of your more rare Trees — for I have none to spare of Rhododendrons, Kalmias, Azaleas, Small Magnolia & Sassafras   I can help Him with all others — of the Mountain Magnolia I have fine plants from layers

I presume Billy will return laden with curiosities

BP 3:21; D. 229–31.

From WILLIAM BARTRAM

Augt 5th, 1761

Dear Brother

I hope you're all in good health, as we Injoy at present thanks be to the Allmighty: I have Nothing strange to Acquaint you with: I send my son Bill[1]

by Captn Gulley: I Expect he will Incline to stay with you a while to go to School: Dr: Brother I make Bold to Trouble you for one favour more: which shall allways be Acknowledged: that is that you: & your sons: Isaac & Moses will take Into your Cear My Son Bille hopeing & not Doubting but you'l: Instruct & Advise him for the Best: to his Advantage and Credit: Cousin Bille Adviseth me to Put my son Bill to School in Philadelphia for Several Reasons Afsd: But I shall Leave that to your Judgment: if he stayeth in Philadelphia: I have wrote my Cousins Isaac & Moses to Let him Live with them: if out of Town: beg you'l let him live with you: this Notion has happened so Suddenly: that I am unprovided to Send But Little with him: But What ever Charge & Trouble you're at on his Acct: shall be As Soon as Possible Paid: with Many Thanks for your Cear & Trouble.

From your brother: &c
William Bartram

P.S. Pray Excuse hast
on Board ye Vessel
I wrote Some time Agone to Acquaint you I reced. the Gentlmn:Magazean: I and Cousen Bille should be glad of an other by Captn: Gulley: my hasty Respects to my Sister & Cousens & Brother James: I hope you'l: Excuse My Not Writing to them all haveing such short time: Pray write by all oppertunityes as I hope Cousin Isaac & Moses will do   I Intend to Send you Several Roots & Seeds Next fall or winter; if have oppertunity

BP 1:70; D. 415.
1. William's son was to study medicine in Philadelphia.

From GREEN

Wilmington Augst 7 1761
Sir
Your kind Favour recd by Captn Gully of Jan 22d in which I had a Satisfactory account of what I sent as also the Asia Rhubarb Seed. I have not had time to see after that flowering Shrub you mention   it being a little sickly, had 17 sick under my care but not so many now   will Assume to send it with ye other evergreen I mentioned when a proper time offers. A Gentleman of my acquaintance told me ye other day he saw the shrub and was full of Red berrys and thinks they are on all ye year round   I am sure they were on about Christmas. I have contrived a method that will be a pleasure to me   that is to number every thing I send and keep one and send one by which contrivance I can learn its name if you please to continue ye correspondence which I think will not be my fault if God spares life. I had the pleasure of your Brother and Sons company at my house about 10 days ago   both very well and spent the evening agreeably. The flowers I now

send I gathered since Capt Gully came   they all grow in Savanaha and Savannah land excepting the flowering shrub which seems to be very common. I thought I had found the Andromeda till I compared them as I have had No. 4 described to me. I now begin with No. 5   I gathered it out of a Ditch putting ye flowers about 4 Inches above ye surface of ye water about 10 or 12 Inches deep   I cannot think they recd any nutrament from ye earth   however I could not observe it and taking a side View I had a pleasing sight of a bed of flowers of a Crimson Colour. No. six is a bunch of Extremely white flowers   I thought many years ago they were a Species of the Lilly of the Valley but on Smelling I found my self deceived   I tasted the flower and it burned my tongue black when I touched it. No. 7 is the same specie only of a orange colour.   No. 8 is a kind of flag, growing in a wett place. No 9 grows on high Dry good Pine land. I imagine it to be a wild hore hound if there be such a herb   No. 10 a flowering shrub.   No. 11 a favorite of mine   I much want to know what it is   the flowers are of a white with a yellowish cast   seems to be very tender. They grow pretty high from two to three feet. We had ye other day about 40 or 50 in full bloom in Garden and when they went away one of my Negroes went to their camps and brought me some roots one of which I send to you   No. 12 whether for food or Physick I cannot say nor shall I Venture till I have name from you   This is all I have to send at this collection which I hope will give you no offence

from friend
Samll Green

BP 4:31.

To COLLINSON

August ye 14th 1761

Dear Peter
I have just now received two letters that came by ye packet   I shall first answer May ye 7th   ye purple ulmaria & mader grows prodigiously   I hope to send roots next fall of ye double upright larkspur now seeded   I wrote largely this spring by Captain Robinson who I hear is taken   allso by ye way of liverpool & since by Budden by whom I sent my Botanical Journal to Carolina & some specimens of ye mountain virginia plants raised from seed sowed in '59   I cannot understand how ye yellow root miscarrieth with thee   I have sent every year this several years & now in this letter I send good seed of this years growth   sow it directly   we had A very cold winter last but I have known it much worse   I am very glad ye seed came well & gave satisfaction   I strained my hip so with lifting ye Large boxes that I did not get over it til spring   I sent by ye last ship in ye winter which was taken in which I sent several Boxes to thee & Gordon &

one to Ponthieu as presents filled with Calmias all sorts azaleas & evergreen privit & one to Powel   allso A box of seed to thee & Gordon in which was A fine parcel of holley berries by ye getting of which I had like to have broke my bones & now my arm is so weak that I can hardly pull off my cloathes so that climbing trees is over with me in this world & in ye next I rather chuse to fly like an angel to search for vegitables in realms unknown to mortals   my yellow slipper improves well but ye white declines   sent double Boxes for Pine & Powel & Williamson (who is this Pine)   Powel & Edie desires but half ye quantity of walnut   who is this Edie   but all desire new things: they are tired of old ones   do they think I can make new ones   I have sent them seeds of allmost every tree & shrub from Nova scotia to Carolina   very few is wanting & from ye sea across ye continent to ye lakes   its very like ignorant people may give strange names to tickle your ears withall but as I have traveled through most of these provinces & have specimens by ye best hands   I know well what grows there   indeed I have not yet been at ye Ohio but have many specimens from there but in about two weeks I hope to set out to search my self if ye barbarous indians dont hinder me & if I die A martar to Botany Gods will be done   his will be done in all things   thay domineer threaten & stealls most of ye best horses thay can   none could have worse luck then I with your roots sent last fall & this spring   not one wild animone came up   one green fritilary flowered ye most ordinary I ever saw   yr asphodels & Narsisus I had before: in Gordons box one oleander lives & ye cuttings of willow   in ye great basket I think 4 roots grows   ye rest roots & ye tops & moss thay was lapped in as dry as if baked in an oven   ye Captain charges thee [illegible] freight & sailors thay must certainly have very well drenched with salt water   thay could not have perished so   I wish thee would give me A perticular account how Alexander packs up his roots   I believe he digs his up with soil & I think he useth more hay then moss which he must get from Jersey   As for thy first letter; thy letter of June ye 12th ye double wild crocus was A mistake   I suppose I meant ye ranunculus   thee writes thy correspondents Fern Bartram Powel & Co & Williamson desires double Boxes   who doth thee mean by Bartram   is it Gordon; what signifieth sending Williamson any to be reconed not worth two pense   he is a strange creature   I am glad Mr Powel[1] sent thee those curious plants when I was there he tould me thee had obliged him & he wanted to make the some returns but did not know what would be acceptable   I tould him what to send   he wrote to me this spring that he had sent them   he is A clever man: he was at my house last year   my second crop of flowers of ye kidney bean tre makes A fine show   ye spikes of flowers 4 inches & half long   I have three kinds of Quamoclit   from Carolina   ye heart shaped leaf is in A fine blush that with angular leaves is Just ready to flower & ye fine oliander leafe grows well

BP 1:55:2; D. 231–32.
1. William Powell.

To WILLIAM BARTRAM

September ye first 1761

Dear Son

I should have been glad of A letter & to have had an account of thy Success in merchandise which I have very much at heart; I was glad to hear that thee kept but little Company but that of ye best, & that thee was going to wait on ye Governour & hope thee will meet with Mr Powel his secretary A fine man   I should be glad to hear how thee was received there or any where Dear Billy keep to vertue, piety, moderation & frugality   be obligeing to all but dont Joyn with ye vitious; beware of the deludeing snares of excess. keep in ye narrow paths of strick temperance in all things which leads to ye Bowers of Tranquility.

Cousen Billy tels me thee & Brother intends to go to Georgia this fall: if so pray do so much to oblige thy father as to gather all ye seeds thee can find in that Journey or indeed any where else   you certainly have A great variety that I want much; A bag 6 inches square will hould abundance of all sorts mixed: never mind putting them seperate: when thay come up I shall know them thay are light carriage: if thee could save specimens of ye rare sorts I should like them well: ye flowering shrubs I am allways pleased with & evergreens above All; pray dont forget ye hors sugar, loblolly bay seed & roots; & of ye fine flowering shrubs as that pretty shrub growing in brothers swamp above his ould house & A pretty little deciduous bay & A shrub 3 foot high with whorled flowers both grows near brothers ould house by ye run; & ye shrub at ashwood bank with flowers like Syringa with roundish leaves A specimen of which I send   ye water tupelo   young ones grows near Singletaries there is A shrub grows near ye overseers house at ye bottom of ye hill   some call it Casena & some of your dwarf oaks I should be glad off as I suppose Captain Gully who seems to be A carefull honest man will come back to Philadelphia about ye latter end of october which will be A good time to take up roots & to send them: thee knows how I send & pack up ye shrubs & roots to London. Just so do mine & order them to be set upermost in ye hold those sent by him in ye spring came finely & grows well & that will be A fine time & opertunity to send all ye seed thee can gather   I hope ye sensitive bryer will be one   Dear billy I hearty wish thee well in all thy undertakeings & remain thy loveing father

John Bartram

Dear bill   I joyn with thy father in the good counsel hee give thee wishing thee health and prosperity in all thy undertaking desiring to hear from thee at all opertunitys and if I have anny in thy fathers absence I shall write to thee

from thy loving mother
Ann Bartram

this grows plentyfully at Ashwood below ye house

New-York Historical Society, Bartram Folder.

To WILLIAM BARTRAM

October ye 5th 1761

My dear son Billy
I am safe returned in very good health from Pittsburgh God Allmighty be praised: haveing been down ye Ohio below Bever Creek & up ye monogahela to above redstone Creek then to fort Cumberland thence to ye warm springs in virginia near great Cape Capon & Potomack then to ye great Cave near ye south mountain: haveing crawled over many deep wrinkles on ye face of our antient mother earth haveing not observed one tree or shrub but what I have growing on my own land except a vine very Aromatick which is very curious   I found allso some very pretty plants: but your countrey abounds with variety such as I much want   your hors sugar & lobloly bay I cant have too much or more ye long leaved pine seeds & roots of most of your flowering shrubs except ye halesia amorpha & kidney bean tree & Johnsonia & Petelia   allmost every thing else shrubs & plants I want   I lost ye pretty long leaved lupin   I wish thee could send me seed & A midling root or two: there grows near ye Governours house (& doubtles in other places near ye river) A pretty dwarf mirtle with little leaves Just by ye swamp on ye sandy bank above his house   I want it much   I wrote to Mr Powel for it but perhaps he may forget it   pray send A deal of ye seed of that pretty shrub 8 foot high that bears its seeds & flowers in whorls near ye tops of its branches   grows in or by every run or swamp & its companion ye little diciduus bay   if it is possible pray send what seed thee can this fall   all native seeds should be sown before spring: has thee been to observe that cluster of shrubs below Bruinswick about half A mile between ye steep bank & ye water which often washeth it   I should be glad to have A root of it if it be new & some roots of your dwarf spring sweet iris — I brought A kind of it from pittsburgh but hope it may [illegible] Captain Gully by whom I intend to send [illegible] of young plumb trees to Brother William: I am pleased with his son   he is allways wellcom to my house where he behaveth sober inocently & discreet   I hope he will Make A fine young man & be A credit to ye name of Bartram which I hope thee will never forfeit   pray give my kind love to my Brother sister & Cousens   I remain thy affectionate father

John Bartram

we are all in good health at present & hath been this fall   God be praised

BP 1:51:1.

To ELIOT[1]

Dear Worthy friend
I am lately returned from Pittsburgh & down ye Ohio by water A great way below Logs town & bever Creek & up ye Monongahela above redstone

creek then to fort Cumberland then to Col. Cresops,[2] thence to ye warm springs & allum rocks, then to ye great cave by ye south mountain thence home after travailing by land near 800 mile & ten days on ye water & lodged in ye woods on ye banks of ye Ohio & monongahela six nights; twice crossed ye great Alegany mountain & Laurel hill at about 30 mile distance, one crossing from ye other: saw many of ye banks of Coal, slate, limestone, whetstone, marl & Cole of which this countrey is well replenished & some very curious plants but strange it is but yet Almost true that in all this Journey I did not observe one tree or shrub growing but what I had growing of ye same kind & specie on my own land beside what I [illegible] both from ye more northern & southern Climates which is as different as Curious: I have not received any letter from thee never since that which our friend Richard smith[3] brought which I answered soon after but whether thee received it I dont know: I have sent thee now some good seed of ye true Mars[h]mallow, sweet Basil & broad leaved sweet lavendar which I hope will be acceptable with my respects to thy self & thy son in law ye Doctor

I remain thy true friend

John Bartram

Beinecke Rare Book and Manuscript Library, Yale University, Jared Eliot Collection.
1. Undated, but written in early October, when Bartram returned from Pittsburgh.
2. Thomas Cresap, justice of the peace and militia captain.
3. Unidentified.

From WILLIAM BARTRAM

Octr: 31st: 1761

Dr: Brother

I hope you've Returned: in good health from your Long Journey: [to] Pittsburg: I should be glad to hear from you: What Incouragement I could have to go and Settle there: or there About: I thought to have Sent Som Choice good Pork Beef & Rice: for my Bille But the weather Being warm for Meat & our New Rice Not yet Clean: Must take an other Oppertunity: I hope Bille is at School: & Likely to Do well: I hope his Uncle: or who he Liveth with will Keep him Well Imployed: in Service: when he's from School: And I Shall Endeavour to Make you Any Satisfaction in my Power for your Cear and Charge: as I Am One Appointed by our Gen'l Assembly to go with Som other Gentlm: high up our [illegible] on Business of Consequence & obligd: to go this Day; otherways Should wrote More: But am in hopes to go Down Before the Vessel goeth: if I Should Not Com Down in time Enough to write more to my Cousens & Billy I hope you Excuse me: & hope theyl: write to me. Pray Excuse hast: my harty Respects to you all

from your Brother: &:C:
William Bartram

P.S. Cousen Bill is in A Brave State of health

I hope my Sister Cousens & all is in good health   it is not out of Disrespect I Dont write to all: But in hope theyl: write to me; Pray Put my Bille in Mind of his Duty: his Mother wants much to hear from him.

BP 1:71.

To COLLINSON

November ye 8th 1761

Dear Peter
A box of specimens & seeds   in ye little box No IX I have packed up these plants 4 roots of mountain Calmia   A sod of evergreen andromeda of saracenia of low Calceolus, of A lovely evergreen grassy plant   perhaps an asphodel   evergreen privit   A great root of warneria   in A bag an odd orchis   in A bag sod of my Aconite   martagons   purple eupatorium & A root of striped pirola & A long box No VIII I have laid in several large roots of laurel of Ivy full of flower buds   magnolias   evergreen privit   green Andromedas   kalmias   Sasafras   white & red flowering Azalias   A great sod of purple ulmeria & madera   wild valerian   I wish I could get some good seed of your best Auriculas to try how thay would prosper with me   our duch florists have some of them but thay dont increas   thay have lately got A fine variety of Polianthes & have had two summers of fine flowers of ye Chalcedonian Iris & this year A large list of ye best flowering plants & bulbous roots is sent for to ye Harlem gardens & no reasonable cost is to be spared to purchase them   I went About two weeks past to se our brother dr Witt   he had A glorious sight of ye beladony lilys in flower   ye stalk near 18 inches high & many flowers on A stalk   he gave me one root two year ago but it hath not flowered yet but I never yet saw ye guernsey lilly in flower tho several hath had ye roots growing   it is very difficult to manage with us   I have just received two fine Cargoes of fresh plants from South Carolina from two diferent Correspondents but dr Garden hath sent me nothing this fall but thanks in A letter to my son for A large parcel of bulbous roots I sent him   he is so hurried in his practice that he can hardly go out of town but I am packing up A chest of Aples for him which I hope will make him speak by next spring   but I can't yet get one plant from billy   he sent me some in ye summer but thay were washed over board by A storm & I am dayly expecting another cargo but we have such continual Contrary winds that its much if thay come safe   my correspondents near London writes to me as freely for ye Carolina plants as if thay thought I could get them as easy as thay do ye plants in ye European gardens   that is to walk at their leisure along ye alleys & dig what thay please out of ye beds, without ye danger of life or limb. when I was in Newbern I searched ye adjacent woods with a doctor where I found plenty of ye Sorrel tree or great Andromeda   I shewed him ye plant I wanted

sent   He promised me roundly to do it without fail yet he never sent it tho not above half A mile to ye shiping   there is A man that lives up that river that frequent my house yearly who promised me to send me A root in A box & to ingage him to perform his promise I tould him I would fill ye same Box back again with ye roots that he wanted much   so much trouble I have to get one root that will cost me 40 shillings; & one in London wants A dozen of them & perhaps would think 40 pence to much to give for them   ye shrubs now in flower in my garden are ye rose: Honeysuckle   tough viburnum   dwarf service & ye lovely shineing evergreen mountain Hypericum   plants are ye red valerian Anual stock   ye pretty blew aster from ye Cape thee sent me   very double Marygold   scabios to [two] sorts.   daisy   tall canaria   blew Cyclamen & from Carolina A pretty stock. A fine purple flowering creeping plant   red geranium   pretty aster ye rays white & dark redish; from virginia my lovely Aconite & dracocephalon   Rudbeckia   sun flower & A tall perenial Groundsel & mountain Delphinium; ye Polyanthos very rarely flower nor ye polianthos Narcisus

BP 1:55:5; D. 232.

From GREEN

                                                    Wilmington Nov 3d 1761
Sir
   Yours recd which affords me a deal of pleasure. I am quite pleased to know the names of those trifles I send you As I never studied Botany so I cannot write in the Botanic way but I should be glad to keep up a Correspondence with you   I am greatly pleased to see you admire the few I send for I am at a Loss how to send the agreeable. I will (if God pleases) send what you want this winter — I send a Stem with seed but I believe imature of an Evergreen which I call No 14; it grows in our River swamps & I have seen it hundreds of times but never saw it put out Seed before   I knowing you was intending for Ohio made me leave off my Searches but will when I hear of your Return brighten up again   When I am in want of anything your way from your kind Repeated offers I will ask a favour. I know from your kind invitation and description of your Garden to have a desire to see you and it but being bound down with a great family I cannot say when that will be But if it should happen that you should come this way and not call on me I believe you will be very apt to be brought back again when on your march for I am not very much hated   therefore for a few words I can make a collection and bring you back to your assured friend
                                                              Samll Green

BP 4:32.

From ST. CLAIR

Belville, Novr. 4th 1761

My Dear Sir

I congratulate you on your safe arrival from Pittsburg, but at the same time I am vexed they should have let you go thither alone; this I must atribute to Capt. Currys[1] not being at Bedford when you passed that way; and I am afraid you met with nothing worth your while during your Migration. That you found everything in good order at home I am thoroughly persuaded of from Mrs. Bartrams great care; in this you have the advantage of me that have no wife.

My Greenhouse & stove are in a very flourishing state, I want you much to see them & to consult you about many things, and before Winter is over I will come to pass a Couple of Days with you. The geraniums thrive wonderfully. I lost the Scarlet Horse Chestnut and the Quamclid was killed t'other morning wt the frost by having the window it stood in left open it was just going to blow: So that I shall want some of the seed of it.

I must depend on you for some of the Seeds of the Paper Birch, Horse Chestnut, Root of Spanish Broom Hemlock Pine or any thing curious you have: I give you many thanks for the valuable Hickory Nuts I should have thanked you sooner for them; but I waited to see if I was to go on the Expedition that is fitting out, now I find that I am not to go; but from my numerous acquaintances that are going to that Climate, I may expect every thing in May that grows in our Islands so that if you want anything (be what it will) from these parts let me know it: I have sent a venture of strong Beer and the choice pieces of Beef to my good friend Govr. Worge at Senegal he is to make me the Return in African trees shrubs plants & seeds he is an Excellent Gardiner, and I am sure will do me Justice as far as lie in his Power.

If you will send any Body to this place to bring a cow for Mrs. Bartram she will oblige me in accepting of her. She is of the famous Rhode Island breed and will calve at Christmas; they are of a very large Size, if her Calf is not a Bull I shall rear one of mine for you that you may preserve that valuable breed which cost me a deal of trouble to get.

I am with great esteem dear sir,

your most obedient and
most obliged humble Servt
John St Clair

P.S. anything you send to me let it be directed to Mr [illegible] at his store in Water Street near the draw Bridge

BP 4:107; D. 418.
1. Unidentified.

From DOBBS

Brunswick Novembr 9th 1761

Sr

I take the oppertunity of a ship going off to Philadelphia to acknowledge yr. last favour with the seeds and I have Included a memo. of some seeds I shall want for my garden and in it a Pistole[1] to lay out in what manner you please to send such a quantity of each as it will bring. I cant at present send you any thing from hence, Mr. Powel being at New Bern as I have no Gardener   the great hurricane we had here the 22d of Septr which has broke in and carryd away our Eastern Bank at the [illegible] and has given us a new Channel, has demolished my Garden so that I shall have it all to do over again next spring   It rose near 6 feet higher than ever known, it carried away all our wharfs and drove all our vessils on shore. I have sent a letter from Mr. Powel to Mr. Wakely[2] to advertise my Lands in the back Country for sale to be put into your news paper   if he should not be in Philadelphia, I desire that you would take it from the Captain and open the Letter and print the advertisement.

We have made peace with the Cherokees and expect daily to have heard that it was ratified — I am

yr Humble Servant
Arthur Dobbs

This goes by the Newbery Capt Shanfield —

BP 3:103.
1. Old quarter-doubloon gold piece of Spain.
2. Unidentified.

From HENRY BOUQUET[1]

Fort Pitt   15th December 1761

Dear Sir

I was favoured with your Letter of the 9th Instant, & sent the Inclosed to Mr. Kenny.[2]

It gave me great Pleasure to hear of your Safe Return to your family, & that you have not lost intirely your Trouble in discovering some Noveltys about Fort Cumberland.

I expect soon the Serjeant from Fort Burd & shall inquire after the Hesperia Seed you mention & forward it to you.

I wish you good success in your Expedition to South Carolina, the best country for a curious Botanist, & hope to see you next fall in your own Garden.

Believe me with a true Regard Dear Sir

Your most obed. hble serv.
H. Bouquet

Mr. Kenny sends you Some Seeds by this Express

Henry Bouquet (1719–1765). *Harper's New Monthly Magazine* 23 (1861):586.

New York Public Library, Emmet Collection, Rare Books and Manuscripts Division, Astor, Lenox, and Tilden Foundations.
1. Colonel Henry Bouquet, later general.
2. James Kenny, a Quaker friend of Bartram who lived at Kennett Square. He was with the army at Fort Pitt.

To WILLIAM BARTRAM

December ye 27th, 1761

Dear Brother
    we have now very sharp weather   our navigation is quite stoped   I sent thee A Box of plumb suckers & young seedlings of my english kinds & wrote to thee: Billy: Dr. Green, & ye Governor & delivered ye letters into Captain Sharpless hands But whether he is got out, I cant say   he set out from Philadelphia A little before ye cold set in & was to take some loading in at Cohansey. Cousen Billy is now at my house, where I love to see him But he keeps very close to school   he tells me you have A root you call

taniers which I have often heard ye carolina people talk of   I wish thee would put one or two in A box of plants for me   we have had as healthy A fall as ever I knowed but now I am afraid of mortal sickness: two of my neibours is to be buried to day, by 2 or 3 days sickness. I and most of my son Billys relations is concerned that he never writes how his trade affairs succeeds   we are afraid he doth not make out so well as he expected   I should be glad he could gain Credit as Isaac & moses has   they began with A little & have unexpectedly dropt into fine business: fulfilled ye aged Proverb, first creep & then go. I have a great mind to drink next fall out of ye springs at ye head of Cape fear river & Pedee if God allmighty please to aford me an opertunity   Cousen Billy desires to be remembered to thee & sister so I conclude with much love to thee & Sister & remain your afectionate Brother

John Bartram

BP 1:50:1; D. 420–21.

To WILLIAM BARTRAM

December ye 27th 1761

My dear Son
Cousen Billy tells me that your loblolly Bay or Alcea bears A very sweet blossom   I wish thee would look well out for some of its seed   perhaps it is not all shed nor ye water tupelo   I want seed of every thing we have not & thee is a good Judge of that: ye Alcea & ye horse sugar I want much thay are very dificult to transplant   I had them from Charlstown but thay are gone off   perhaps your northern one may do better; it is strange that ye red sweet bay some of which grows naturaly in virginia should not bear our frost & yet ye great Magnolia that grows naturaly on ye south of Pede seems to bear our frost tolerably. what havoc our present frost will make with ye rest, I cant yet say but however I want to try all to be enabled to Judge which of your plants will bear our rigorous frost & what will not   thee disapointed my expectation much in not sending to me any seeds by Capt Sharpless & know your seeds was some or other ripening from ye day thee set foot on Carolina shore to Sharpless departure & such as was within A mile or two of thy common walks: or most of them within sight & yet I have not received one single seed from my son who glories so much in ye knowledge of plants & whom I have been at so much charge to instruct therein   ye fall be ye best time to sow ye native seeds   spring may do but many miss comeing up that year   I dont want thee to hinder thy own affairs to oblige me but thee might easly gather A few seeds when thee need not hinder half an hours time to gather them or turn 20 yards out of thy way to pluck them.
   I remain thy loveing father,

John Bartram

BP 1:50:1; D. 421.

From WILLIAM BARTRAM[1]

Newbern at the Genrl: assembly

Loving Brother

I take this oppertunity to write Hopeing these will meet with you all in good health: I am Now much Better in health than I have Bene for Som time Past: thankes be to the allmighty: as for my family I Cannot Informe you at Present haveing Bene from home About three weeks at ye Assembly: they were But Poorly when I Came from home   we have had a Very Sickly fall in our Parts: But Not very Mortal thanks be to god: I have Nothing Strange or New to Acquaint you with: only Bad News if it is so; that the 5 or Six Nations of Indians that has Pretended friendship: has Now Joyned the french: But we hope it is Not So: I wrote from Cape feare to you by a Vessel in October last: And Desired you to Encourage Som good tradesmen to Com to A new town: our neighbours are Encourageing thats Neer me: A good Smith & hatter & tanner Shoemaker Carpender & Tayler: I have a good Sett of Smith tools and More or Less of Proper tools for the other trades: which the[y] may have for their work   from your Loving Brother

William Bartram

Pray Rembr: me to all frd: your favr: as Above will very much oblig W:B — Pray Excuse hast and Manr: of writeing time by this opertunity being Very Short —

BP 1:71.
1. The content of this undated letter suggests that it was written in late 1761 or early 1762.

From GREEN

Wilmington Feby 2d 1762

Sir

Yours recd dated Septr 1st which I answered Novr 3d following since which I have not heard from you. I have had the pleasure of your Sons company at my house severall times   from him I heard you was going to ye Ohio, I should be glad to know what success.

I am now writing upon my bed where I have been confined 8 weeks, was almost Dead with a Violent bloody flux and whether I shall not die yet of a Consumption occasioned thereby I cant say but I am in a very doubtful state. This is the reason why I cannot send the evergreen Andromeda, or lily No 13 at this time but if it pleases ye Allmighty that I get better I do then intend to fulfill my promise. The Indian returned from ye [illegible] and called on me but I was too sick to get any information about that root but we do see them sometimes and if I possibly can will Learn what it is good for. If you should want one whole not more I can spare you one. your Brother tells me it puts out a vine and he is sure thee knows it. This spring I suppose will determine. How I long to see your garden you little know but I never expect it. I wish you could send me a few parsnips carrot savoy and cabbage seed, for my own garden. Your son sent a box and a little bag of seeds which I have taken care to send on board Captn Wills Brg. I hope they will arrive safe and am in hopes you will do me the favour to let me hear from you ere long.

Am your well wisher and humbl Serv.

Samll Green

PS Your brother's wife has had a very dangerous spell of a Pleurasy but is got on ye recovering hand.

BP 4:33.

From THOMAS GREER[1]

Wilmington feby: 2: 1762

Esteemed Friend

I take this oppertunity to inform thee that I got well home, and found my family all well through mercy, after an absence of two years and eight months. I have Delivered to Doctor Green to be forwarded to thee, three pieces of Petrified pine, I take it to be pine as the outer part of it was soft and mouldered & Smeled Strong of turpentine —

In my coming down ye river I called to see thy Brother and Son who were well and ye family, Except thy Brother's wife who is Just recovering from a Strange Spell of Sickness — he would have wrote to thee but was not Certain of an oppertunity wch he desired me to mention to thee in case I wrote, he and thy Son present their best regards to thee thy wife and family, and please to accept the same from thy asured friend with due respects.

Tho Greer

P.S. I have planted ye things thee favored me with & dont doubt they will grow as I put them in good soil.

BP 4:35.
1. Unidentified.

From COLLINSON

Londn: 3: Feby 1743/4[1]

I wrote my Dear John by the King of Prussia under Cover to our friend Franklin – Now I shall give Thee some Acct of the Cargo   the old Proverb is that there is no fence against a Flail so there is no Securing them from the Teeth of Ratts for att the Corner of Each box, they had Made a proper Hole for Access & in Each box was a Warm Nest of Straw & the Leaves & Stalks of the Shrubs   It grieved Mee to see how they had stripped the Great Rhododendron & Lesser Calmias but the Rhododendron they had gnawed of the branches – it was a fine thrifty plant when Putt Into the Box but at takeing out made a sad figure   however the Root is Good   Wee hope the head will shoot again – The Deciduous shrubs were in Good Order   all the sods of Curious Roots & the Martagons was not hurt   Warneria on Yellow Root is so remarkable that if it had been in the Last Cargo I could not help seeing it — it is impossible to Account for its Absence   Loblolly was Eat by the Ratts but I hope will Shoot from the Root, it is one of the Charming Evergreens   does it stand your winters —

Your Skunk Root is now in full flower —

I hope the Calceolus, Gentians &c will grow well   great pains hath been taken in the planting —

the Vitis Idea with so Large a fruit is new to Mee   I wish some Tallies had been tied to the Trees of New Sorts – then a more particular Care would have been taken of them & Wee should have the pleasure of knowing them —

Pray tell Mee how many Species of Solomons Seal hath thee observed in all thy Travells —

The 2 Sweet [illegible] bays of Carolina I was pleased to see because they will repair my Loss —

I find I have 3 Distinct Speices of Epigaes   this Last sent differs from the others — the Striped Pyrola is a pretty plant & my Favourite   I fancy it is very scarce or Else there had been another sod – Gentians are allso my Favourites   I hope I shall see it Flower —

Thy fine Collection of Specimens is under Docr Solanders[2] Examination — your Autumn flowers I pretty well know, but pray tell Mee what are your Spring flowers, besides the Pocune or Sanguinaria the little white Ranunculus & Meadia & Orchis   pray what are the Other Species with which your Woods, Thicketts Swamps, Fields, & Meadows are adorned in the Spring months of March, Aprill & May — I wish for my Satisfaction thy good son John would put a Quire of Specimens of all your Flowers, for only those 3 months — I mean only Herbaceous or bulbous flowers — no Trees or shrubs — for though I have been so many years conversant with your Vegitables, yett think my Self intirely Ignorant, (except the above mentioned) of Flora's Beauties in your Spring Months

Our Fields so abound with flowers in those Months, that they are a flowery Carpet   the primroses, Daisies & Pilewort, are now begining — will be succeeded by the 2 or 3 Species of Crowfoots, called Butter Flowers, Dandelion makes a great Show, then the fields are rich with Cowslips Lady Smocks, Caltha palustris or Marsh Marygolds   then they are covered with blew Hyacinths, Daffodils, Saxifrage, Stitchwoort & Blew & white Violets and a great Variety of Orchis   our Woods cover'd with Anemones & Periwinkle & Woodroff with its white Flowers

now I want to know what you abound with instead of our Flowers, for I presume you have not one of them that are Natural to your Country but have a progressive Set of Flowers, for every Spring month that differs from Ours & is peculiar to your Soil and Climate   I cant add more but that I am

thy sincere friend
P Collinson

BP 2:69; D. 167–68.
1. Collinson misdated this letter. He undoubtedly meant to write 1762.
2. Daniel Carl Solander.

From BOUQUET

Fort Pitt 3d February 1762

Dear Sir

The Gentleman who will have the Pleasure to deliver you this is Lieut. Brehm an engineer sent by General Amherst to our most remote Posts to the westward. He has been round Lake Erie, and thro' Lake Huron, in Lake Michigan — I thought it might be agreeable to you to know what Nature produces in those Wildernesses and tho' the Gentleman had observations of another kind to make, he may perhaps Satisfy in some respects your Curiosity as you will certainly do his by the large Collection you have in your garden.

I should be much obliged to you to send me at your Leisure a Catalogue of Trees & Plants peculiar to this Country which are not natural to the soil of Europe; as I propose to send a Collection to a friend, when we have more peaceable Times.

I expected to have had the Pleasure to see you this spring but I find I am to be confined here Sometime longer.

I am with great truth Dear Sir

Your obdt. hble. sert.
H. Bouquet

BP 1:93; D. 427.

From MARTHA LOGAN

February 13 1762

Sr

I Received your faviour by Capt North with the Box & things therein mentioned for which am much Obliged, I have now sent you the underwritten in your Own Box & hope you will have them alive — the tree in Mr. Glens garden is the same with that of Rapers of which I have sent you a plant & some Seeds   the Latter Comes in a small Bagg — If the Season is Proper I should be very glad of a tree ye Kalmia & Tulap of Diffring kinds from Our for we have none Other but the Purplish red flowrd Tulaps & red & white Kellmia which blooms in Bunches. but I finde from Mrs. Hopton you have 4 or 5 Sorts. the rare shrub & a root or two of Piconeis (or seeds) I should be Very thankfull for. Mr. Ratlive Brought of these latter for him self by Land & they Seem quite Alive & springing. I have filled the Earth in the box with Seeds as I finde you take Caire of it & wish you Better Success with them. the Snaile flower will not Bear Our Winters without gourding it by Shelters Maide Over theire roots, so that yours will require to be moved in the fall into a green house for they will not flower till the Second year —

If we have any thing Else you Desire pray lett me know & will doe my Endeavour to gett them, In the meantime Conclude me your assured friend & well Wisher

Martha Logan

P.S. My Respects attend yr Spouse & family
   Memorandum   Plants in the Box
   1 plant from Mr. Rapers tree with a tally on it —
   2 Dwarf Pumgranets   1 Olive   1 Sweet Shrub   6 yellow wood
   4 Loblolly bays   3 Slips Bounceing bessies   3 Mrs. Bees flower
   2 Nutts of Ollives in the Earth in box
When you have any Cyclans to spaire Shall be Very glade of root Each Sort of them   Mrs. Hopton Just Enformed me you was desirous of a root of our Wilde Lilly which is Called the golden. allso the Wragged Lilly wheirfore have put 3 or 4 roots in the Box with 3 roots the foxtaile Hyacinths which she sends thee   allso 1 hyacinth Perue & 4 plants Pride Chine. the Hyacinths are planted in the Box[1]

BP 4:76.
1. Bartram wrote on the back of this letter:

> two roots of Ivy or calmia
> dwarf double rose
> flowering rasbery
> dwarf plum, A prety shrub
> crategus from new england flowering
> one tree box sod of white lychnis
> several root of striped Peonea

From GARDEN[1]

My very worthy Friend

I have this moment finished a letter for your Sons,[2] for whom I have much esteem on your Acct. and likewise for their own merit; It will give me much pleasure to serve them in any thing that I can from this place & I hope our acquaintance will be for our mutual advantage —

By Capt Noarth I received your most obliging & very agreeable letter. I rejoice at your safe return & sincerely desire to bless the name of God for his care & protection of you   Your observations are many valuable, curious & diverting   I have read them over & over with much satisfaction & would willingly enter upon a discussion of each particular if my Continual hurry of business permitted me to have a leisure hour, but alas my Dr Friend ever since I had the pleasure of seeing you here I have lived in that same hurried life in which you saw me. — I have never been three miles from town since that time so that now Botany is quite neglected by me, but I rejoice to hear of the keeness & Ardor with which you daily advance in the Science & cultivate your mind & that Study — The unbounded treasures of the Wisdom of the Great Father in the works of nature is a field of research & Contemplation worthy the rational mind & is the noblest subject on which you can meditate — Happy — thrice Happy are you whose comfortable easy & retired situation gives you this noble opportunity of exercising those faculties with which God has blessed you.

Advance & be doing — The time may come when I will follow with more care & quickness than my present situation will permit. —

I have sent you a small quantity of Rice which I hope you will please to accept of as some small acknowledgt of the many favours which I have received at your hand

Believe me your friend
Alexr. Garden

BP 2:4:1.
1. Written February 15, 1762 (see Bartram to Garden, March 25, 1762).
2. Isaac and Moses.

From LAMBOLL

Charles Town, Febry 17th 1762

My dear Friend,

As Capt: Noarth is about to return to Philadelphia I sit down to acknowledge the Receipt of your obligeing Letters of the 6th & 21st: Novr:last, received by him, the 22d: Decr, following, together with the Box of Plants and Roots, which came in good order: some of the Flowers therein blown; all were immediately set out, and are alive, except the two Cowslips, which are dead. I am much beholden to you, for so great and such a Variety as you have sent me. Mrs. Lamboll has made up a Box with Earth (which is now to be put on board Captain Noarth's Vessel) for you, of such Trees and Flowers as she can procure: vizt: a few Trees of Live Oaks, Water Oaks, Red [Oaks?] and Bay: one red and white striped Rose and one Virginia Rose (all our yellow Roses are dead) one Rose Acacia, one Italian Jessamin, some Roots of Button Snake Root   some of healing & some of the true semper Viva or Aloes, one Bella donna Lilly, some Roots of ragged Lilly or Pancratium & a few Nutmeggs. Most of the Trees have been some time set in this Box, & lately had a fine Rain. There is also a little Chip Box of Seeds, French honey Suckle, Great Valerian, Lunaria or Moon wort, Honesty or Sattin flower, Scarlet Lychnis, Dwarf Lychnis, double Columbine   double Rose   Lark Spur, dwarf Stock Flower

Striped Stock July Flower, Queen Stock July Flower, double blue China Aster, double red Aster, double white China Aster, Purple Stock July Flower, Bladder Ketmia, Purple Hawk Weed, Brumpton Stock, White Sweet Pease, Cresses, Rocket, Persicaria, Canterbury Bells, Purple Stramonium, Sweet Sultan, Auricula, Opopino (being a Beautiful flowering Tree), and Cucumber for Pickleing   Both the one and the other Box are directed to you, and to induce the Master to take more Care, the Freight is paid at putting on board.

And we both wish they may get safe, and meet your Self and Family, in good Health, which we shall be glad to hear of, and that we may oblige you with any thing that can be got here   My Wife and family join in Respects to you and yours; and I remain

Your real Friend, to serve
Thos. Lamboll

BP 4:57.

From SARAH HOPTON

Charles Town 18 February 1762

Mr. Bartram
Sir

By favour of Mrs. Logan I have sent you 3 fox Tailed hiacinths 1 large white hiacinth of Peru & 4 roots of pride of India dwarf. should have sent you the rest of the things contained in your list, but as Mrs. Logan tels me she has supplyd you with them, thought It would be needless for us both to send the same things, by the return of Capt Noarth it will be a fine Time to take up the evergreens, if we have any here that you have not got, pleas to let me know & will send some   Please to pay my best respects to Mrs Bartram & thanks for all favours & accept the same from

Sir
your humble Servant
Sarah Hopton

The golden Lilly is not out of the ground

BP 4:52.

To GARDEN

March ye 25th 1762

to Doctor Garden
I received thy very kind letter of February ye 15   am glad my remarks on ye Ohio gave thee such satisfaction but thee makes no mention whether thee received ye present of Aples or that thay kept sound   I picked them &

packed them with my own hands ye day before I put them on board but as thee mentions nothing about them I fear thay miscarried   I received[1] thy kind present of rice in good order   it was very good & I gave my daughter Mary & son James share of it & we all return thee grateful respects

I have Just received two very loving letters from new england   one from Doctor Gale   ye other from doctor Eliot a very worthy presbyterian minister one that spends his time in pious exercise & in promoting ye general good of mankind   he found out ye method about three months past to make out of sea sand excellent iron   one hundred weight of sand will yeald 40 of good iron   I think little coal will do it   it was advertised in ye York paper A month past & many curious people thought it so very improbable that thay gave little or no credit to it   he sent me A specimen of both ye sand and iron   I showed it not onely to our smiths but to ye owners of ye furnaces & forges & thay alowed it to be very fine & some thought it would make choice steel.   & now dear friend not to keep thee too long upon ye rack & as mutual friends should Allways ease & not torment explain and not perplex one another   ye sand out of which he makes his iron is not ye white crystalin sand but A Black bright fine mixed sand in great beds that will adhear to ye magnet as ye fileings of iron but ye grand quere is from whence it came & how it got there.   my dear worthy friend I am much affected every time that I often read thy pious reflections on ye wonderfull works of ye omnipotent & omniscient creator   ye more we search & accurately examine his works in nature ye more wisdom we discover whether we observe either ye mineral vegitable or animal kingdom but as I am chiefly employed with ye vegitable I shall enlarge more upon it. what charming colors appears in ye various tribes in ye regular succession of ye vernal & autumnal flowers   these so nobly bold   those so delicately languid   what A glow is inkindled in some   what A gloss shines in others   with what A masterly skill is every one of ye varying tints disposed: here thay seem to be thrown on with an easy dash of security & freedom there thay are adjusted by ye nicest touches   ye verdure of ye empalement of ye shadings of ye petals impart new liveliness to ye whole   whether thay are blended or arranged   some are intersected with elegant stripes or studed with radiant spots   others affect to be genteely powdered or neatly fringed   others are plain in thair aspect & pleaseth with their naked simplicity. some are arrayed in purple   some charms with ye virgins white. others are dashed with crimson while others are robed in scarlet   some glitter like silver lace: others shines as if embroydered with gold. some rise with curious cups or pendulent bels; some are disposed in spreading umbels   others crowd in spiked clusters   some are dispersed on spreading branches of lofty trees, on dangling Katkins   others sit contented on ye humble shrub   some seated on high on ye twineing vine & wafted to & fro   others garnish ye prostrate creeping plant   all these have their perticular excelencies   some for ye beauty of thair flowers   others thair sweet scent   many ye elegance of thair foliage or ye goodness of thair fruite   some ye nourishment that thair roots aford us   others please ye fancy with thair regular growth   some is admired for thair odd appearance & many that offends ye taste, smell & sight too is of vertue in Phisik —

but when we nearly examine ye various motions of plants & flowers, in thair evening contraction & morning expantion thay seem to be operated upon by something superior to only heat & cold or shade & sunshine such as ye surprising tribes of ye sensitive plants & ye petals of many flowers shutting close up in rainy weather or in ye evening until ye female part is fully impregnated & if we wont allow them real feeling or what we call sense, it must be some action next degree inferior to it for which we want A proper epithet or ye immediate finger of god to whome be all Glory & praise   John Ennis one that rides express hath tould me several times that when he rode between Lockwoods folly & pedee He & William Moore[2] saw A plant much like A dasy that if A person looked at ye flower when open it would imediately shut up. this surely must be A very modest flower & A great curiosity   I dont in dwelling so long in ye vegitable kingdom, as though I thought ye wisdom & power of God was onely Manifested therein: ye Contemplation of ye mineral & especially ye animal will equaly incline ye pious heart to overflow with daly adorations & praises to ye grand giver & supporter of universal life but what amaising distant glories is disclosed in A mid night scene: Vast are ye bodies which role in ye imence expance   orbs beyond orbs without number   suns beyond suns   sistems beyond sistems with thair proper inhabitants of ye great Jehovahs Empire   how can we look at these without amaisement, or contemplate ye divine Majesty that rules them without ye most humble adoration   Esteeming our selves with all our wisdom but as one of ye smallest atoms of dust prasing ye living God, the great I am.

BP 1:55:6, 1:60:5; D. 397–99.
1. To this point the letter is taken from BP 1:55:6; the remainder is from BP 1:60:5.
2. Unidentified.

From COLLINSON

Londn Aprill 1:1762

I had my Dear Johns Letter of Nobr 12th which is always Acceptable — but what Have I to do with Ponthieu that I must be Charged Double postage 20s. for his Bill of Loading, why had I the trouble of It — & then what is very Singular, thou mentions no price for Either his Box of plants or for that to Powel & Eddys but if thou art so generous to give both, all that is at once setled —

I really believe my Honest John is a *great Wagg* & has sent 7 hard stony seeds, something shaped like an Acorn to puzzle Us for there is no Name to them   I have a vast Collection of seeds but none like them — I do laugh at Gordon for he guesses them to be a species of Hickery   Phaps I may be

Laughed at, in my Turn, for I think they may be *what I wish*, seeds of the Bonduc Tree which thou Picked up in thy Rambles on the Ohio — for thou must know there is Trees of this rare species that grows in the French Settlements in Canada & Called by the French[1]   but whether it grows near Quebeck Montreal or Near the Lakes I cannot learn   Wee have three in our English Gardens that thrive finely & if the Warr had not broke out Mine would have been the fourth – a few Days agon I had a Letter from Paris informing Mee they keep 2 Trees for Mee when it shall please God to send a Peace — This Elegant Tree has Large Leaves divided into many Portions very much resembling the Angelica Tree — It bears its Fruit in podds like the West India Bonduc or Nicker Tree — but what Blossom I could never Learn — this is the only fine Tree in which the French Rival us — but now Wee have got possession Wee shall rival them

I am pleased with the monthly progress of thy flower Garden — Wee are never without but Since Wee have Sett thy plants, our weather has been Cool, Wett, & Cloudy   theres very Little progress in Vegetation which prolongs the Flowers for those blown in January & February are not yett gone off altho' others are added to them

the most of the Month of January was Mild & Warm yett Wee had frequent Snow & Frost in February & March for which reason a Month Later then Last year for on the 10 or 12 March our Elms had almost Leavd but now not a bud Swells this 27 March — & yett my Garden has something Creeping on   What is very Extraordinary My pink Root has been near this month in flower & makes a pretty odd show & is much admired —

I am always carefull of your Earth, for I have raised many odd plants out of It, that thou never would think to send seeds of

There is a great Difference when Grumbling & Complaining against what happens loss, & could not be foreseen — and a liable observation that the Delay of the box of Bulbs will prevent their flowering as they was not arrived the 21 10ber   Thou seeth the Delays & Difficulty that attends sending any growing plants from Hence yett great preservation was used that could be, the Evergreens taken up as Early as Wee could & ship'd by first ship — but the Sea is against you but always for Us — for how quick the plants come from you — In the Course of more then 20 years correspondence with Docr Witt [two illegible lines]   Delays happened to them in Times killed with sea Water & then kill'd for Want — Lost or thrown over board &c

Thy Hypothetical Systems on the Phenomena in nature shows a fertile conception & a Fruitfull Genius — but as I have neither Leisure nor Inclination to oppose thy Sentiments I subscribe to them & if I had, it would be fruitless, for when Wee had both said our say out it would be all conjecture at Last — What I desire to see is thy Diary which consists of facts, that cannot fail to give sensible pleasure by Instilling some knowledge into the Mind, & Inlarging my Ideas of the Inconceivable power & Wisdom of the Great Creator

The Dearest of Friends must part, with Regret to lose so Valuable a Member of Society — I see our Friend Franklin preparing to Depart — by Him I send the Magazine & Two Books which will give Entertainment to thy

Speculative Genius — Thou must take this Letter as an Instance of great Friendship, for I am so Hurried in business that I write a bitt & a scrap now and then to show thee how much thou has the Esteem of thy real frd

P Collinson

My love to thy wife

When thou writes by the packet always inclose it to my friend Alexander Colden Esq Post master at New York, & then it costs Mee Nothing   I have heard nothing a long time from Moses, Billey, or Johnny — *I don't want them to write Mee Letters* but for thee to Tell Mee how they go on & how they Do.

BP 3:22; D. 233–34.
1. Collinson left a blank for the French name. He was referring to the Kentucky Coffee-Tree (*Gymnocladus dioica*).

From HUMPHREY SIBTHORP

Oxford, April 30, 1762

Sir: –

As a correspondence, and communication of seeds and specimens, might be serviceable to both of us, I've the more particularly been desirous of cultivating such, and for that purpose have forwarded letters, by friend Collinson and others, to you heretofore, in hopes of an answer

* * *

As no part of Europe has a larger collection than the Sherardian[1] and Du Bois's, many from Catesby, Houston,[2] Gronovius, Clayton, and others, are a further addition, with Morison and Bobart's[3] Collections. And the North American plants thrive well in our soil, being swampy, or low. Many from different parts, gardeners and others, send seed. Many boxes come through your friend Collinson's hands, which are often, by our custom officers and others, too much jumbled together, and, in regard to their quantity, oft best suitable to nurserymen, than those more curious. Could you favour our garden with a small box of a few of each sort you may have gathered, fresh and good, and any seeds of perennial plants, the more ornamental the more preferable, any pains you take shall be most gratefully acknowledged and requited. Nothing is more agreeable than the variety of Firs, Evergreens, or forest trees to us. Some of the Spruce and Balm of Gilead we have. The Weymouth Pine seed has miscarried, as well as the *Magnolias*. But nothing, indeed, can come amiss; and as I understand from your neighbour, Mr. Franklin, who has done us the honour, today, of taking a degree, and now ranks Doctor of Civil Law, with us, you are about entering on a large excursion, I heartily wish you a safe return, and that you may meet with many curious plants. And as he encourages me to write again, and promises more particularly to forward this, I flatter myself I may have the satisfaction of adopting your name in our public garden.

* * *

I shall add no further, at present, than my best wishes for your health, and a prosperous journey and hopes of hearing from you by letter, directed, as below, to your faithful friend,

And very humble servant,
Humphrey Sibthorp

D. 428–29.
1. William Sherard had established a botany professorship at Oxford, the first holder of which was Dillenius.
2. Dr. William Houston (1695–1733), plant collector employed by Sherard, Lord Petre, and others to gather plants in the West Indies and other places.
3. Jacob Bobart (1641–1719), author of volume 2 of *Plantarum Historiae* . . . (Oxford, 1699); volume 1 was published by Robert Morison in 1680.

To BOUQUET

May ye 3d 1762

Dear worthy friend
I received thy kind letter of february ye 3d 1762 but not by ye Gentleman whom thee mentioned that was to deliver it to me. he hath not been at my house nor I have not seen him. I went to town next day after I received ye letter to invite him to my house but he was gone to York   I have here sent A list of our North American trees & shrubs as they occured to my memory most of which I have growing on my land but to send A list of plants of All ye species which I collected from new England to Carolina & from ye sea coast to Lake Ontario would take up more time then I have to spare at present besides I have many plants that is so young that thair proper Characters is not so visible as to ascertain thair Genus & many that is A quite new Genus but when I have ye pleasure of thy promised visit we will talk farther about it. in ye mean time thee may be assured that I am thy Sincear friend

John Bartram

N 1 Lord weimoths pine.
  2 Swamp pine
  3 two & 3 leaved pine
  4 two leaved pine
  5 long leaved Carolina pine
  6 long leaved Pinaster from ye mountains
  7 Hemlock spruice
  8 Liriodendron
  9 white Ash
 10 black Ash
 11 red flowering Maple
 12 Silver leaved Maple
 13 striped bark Maple
 14 Ash leaved Maple
 15 Sugar Maple
 16 dwarf mountain Maple
 17 Mountain Magnolia deciduous
 18 great evergreen Magnolia of Carolina
 19 deciduous Magnolia or umbrella tree Caroli
 20 swamp Magnolia

21 Chinkapin
23 chesnut [22 omitted by Bartram]
24 poplar leaved Birch
25 paper birch
26 black sweet birch
27 red birch
28 dwarf birch
29 Sasafras
30 Benjamin
31 tree Cornus
32 white berried Cornus
33 purple berried Cornus
34 spotted barked Cornus
35 great round leaved Viburnum
36 red berried Viburnum
37 swamp long leaved Viburnum
38 tough twiged Viburnum
39 spiney Viburnum
40 crenateed leaved Viburnum
41 tall mountain Viburnum
42 small twiged mountain Viburnum
43 broad leaved Andromeda
44 Spiked andromeda
45 red flowered evergreen Andromeda
46 white flowered evergreen Andromeda
47 Sorrel tree or the tallest Andromeda
48 tall red berried Crategus
49 dwarf red berried Crategus
50 tall black berried Crategus
51 dwarf black berried Crategus
52 red Ceder
53 white Ceder
54 Black mountain Quick bean
55 Linden
56 black newfound spruice
57 red spruice or fir
58 Mountain chesnut Oak
59 dwarf chesnut Oak
60 great scarlet Oak
61 dwarf scarlet Oak
62 great barren Black Oak
63 dwarf barren Black Oak
64 white Oak
65 swamp white Oak
66 highland spanish oak
67 swamp spanish Oak
68 bastard Champain Oak
69 great Champain oak
70 broad leaved willow oak
71 narrow leaved willow oak
72 scrubby white oak
73 great black oak
74 olive leaved oak evergreen
75 evergreen oak with prickle leaves
76 dwarf evergreen oak
77 swamp oak
78 dwarf narrow leaved oak
79 narrow leaved evergreen oak
80 great downey Sumach
81 common smooth Sumach
82 beech Sumach
83 great Shell bark Hicory
84 lesser Shell bark Hicory
85 common rough Leaved Hicory
86 small sweet twiged Hicory
87 balsamick Hicory
88 white Hicory or Pignut
89 tupelo
90 water tupelo
91 Sily quastrum
92 great Mountain Kalmia
93 olive leaved Kalmia
94 thime leaved Kalmia
95 our laurel or lesser Kalmia
96 Candle berry Myrtle
97 dwarf candle berrie mirtle
98 great prinos
99 evergreen prinos
100 Elder
101 Arbor vita
102 clethra
103 Itea
104 papaw
105 chionanthus
106 ceanothus

107 hop horn bean
108 common horn beam
109 red buded andromeda
110 white spirea
111 purple spirea
112 spirea epuli folia
113 Petelia
114 Halesia
115 silver leaved Alder
116 common Alder
117 large coned Alder
118 Aralia spinosa
119 Cephalanthus
120 beech cherrie
121 mountain cherrie
122 dwarf cherrie
123 Hamamelis
124 sweet gum or Liquid Amber
125 boggy evergreen Andromeda
126 minispermum
127 Johnsonia
128 great mountain Elm
129 river Elm
130 lesser tree Cornus with blue berries
131 Marsh rose
132 upland rose
133 black Rasberie
134 flowering Rasberie with red fruite
135 our common hazel
136 dwarf mountain Hazel
137 dwarf yew
138 Balm of Gilead Fir
139 red ever green Honeysuckel
140 redish deciduous Honeysuckel
141 yelowish deciduous Honey suckel
142 great Horse chesnut or Hipcastanum
143 scarlet Hors chesnut or Pavia
144 stewartia
145 the great willow
146 runing marsh willow
147 dwarf willow
148 great Robinia
149 dwarf Robinia
150 Hydrangia
151 Gleditsia
152 great early sweet service
153 dwarf sweet service
154 swamp sweet service
155 parsly legged thorn
156 dwarf thorn
157 long leaved thorn
158 ye great thorn with sweet fruit
159 great leaved heart shaped poplar
160 aspin tree
161 black wallnut
162 white wallnut
163 black mulberrie
164 white mulberie
165 red mulberie
166 bald Cypress
167 narrow leaved candle myrtle
168 chymilea
169 silver leaved bryer

British Library, Add. Ms. 21648, f. 129.

To COLLINSON

May ye 10th 1762

Dear Peter
I have received thy kind letter of december ye 31, 1761
    I am glad my Journal to Carolina is acceptable   I wish my remarks on ye Ohio may be so too   I have roughly wrote my Journal to Pittsburg but

I should write it over again before I send it but when I can get time to do it I cant say nor how to send it safe   it is larger then that to Carolina:

as thee hath made little mention of insects these many years I thought thee had lost thy taste for them long ago & ye nets being broke I bent my mind to ye search of minerals & espetially vegitables   as for ye animals & insects it is very few that I touch of choice & most with uneasiness. neither can I behould any of them that have not done me A manifest injury in thair agonizing mortal pains without pity   I allso am of opinion that ye creatures commonly called brutes possess higher qualifications & more exalted ideas then our traditional mistery mongers is willing to allow them

ye back parts of ye countrey where I chiefly travail do not abound with such A great variety of insects as nearer ye sea coast that seems to be in most nations ye first & main scituation or resort for most animals   indeed many wild creatures is drove back by mankind first setling near ye coast   others resort to ye mountains & some to feed at perticular season & in some large continents where great rivers may run north & south   some animals that is natural to hot or cold climates may live alltogether at ye heads of very long rivers & is never seen near its mouth on ye coast. but my sons John & Benjamin is not so squeamish   thay can handle & kill them without any emotion

we had this winter two sharp spels one in december & ye other in february & march but I have known colder weather: January was prety mild   ye rivers was open & ye frost generaly out of ye ground but ye last spell disrobed all my carolina evergreens & shrubs except what was [not] out of green house & killed most to ye ground & some root & branch   ye purple berried bay dahoon holly & magnolia is putting out fresh leaves from ye branches   ye deciduous shrubs is little hurt not so much as ye basteria which my worthy Lambol sent last fall is now just flowering & ye red bay is killed to ye root   so is ye evergreen oaks   ye spotted asarabaca stood it but ye solanius triphilium with spoted leaves & most of ye pancratiums is gone   ye atamasco lives   I have had thre fine boxes well filled sent this spring but ye rats got into one box & gnawed every leaf & twig but I hope all ye roots is living[1]   Lamboll sent A stout beladone lilly which hath now leaves A foot long & many stout pancratiums but all that Powel sent is dead   I think there is in Carolina two sorts of sweet bay & three or more sorts of Candle berry mirtle & A wonderfull variety of oaks   Oh Carolina Carolina A ravishing place for A curious Botanist   your warm winters is really surprising as ours is for extream cold considering what latitude each is in   it would be dificult to make A catalog of all ye plants trees & shrubs in my garden as I try to procure A great variety of species of each genus & I have many plants growing that is many year before thay flower to ascertain ye Genus & many new ones as ye three Gigantick plants   first ye vine with A great heart shaped leaf near Pittsburgh ye seed of which was sent to me this spring not yet come up & 2d ye great plant I found down ye Ohio 7 foot high ye stalk growing throw ye base of oposite leaves   3d ye great leaved tall plant I found behind ye mountains of Virginia which grows very strong

but will not flower this year to which may be added ye mountain Angelica which is now A foot high with but one leaf & I suppose will not flower for several years   I received thy box of bulbs in good order & out of gordons basket I have one shrub as grows fine as if it had not been removed   I was in hopes it was an arbutus   now I fear it is A pomegranate of which we have plenty   it is talied No 7 which in ye list is two clumps of Aria of which many came up last year & more this   I have spread ye earth on A border hopeing some accidental seed may come up   it will not do to send living shrubs   ye pasage is so long & waiting for A convoy   seeds is ye onely thing to send most of which if thay be good will come up   scores of Gordons wild teasel seeds came up last year which I destroyed & numerous others are come up this spring which I must eradicate   my seeds from Pittsburg comes up as close as thay can stand & many from North & South Carolina sown this spring & many which I brought from there & sowed about two year past   my upright violet from red stone creek is in full bloom & ye dwarf flag iris grows wonderfuly   I think it difers much from that at ye mountains of virginia & both from that in carolina   if so it will be A fine variety   that which I brought from virginia lived about A year with me then perished but as I intend if Providence affords me an opertunity to make another attempt to new river & then to cross ye south mountains to ye branches of Pedee & then return crossing ye head branches of Cape fear roan oke & James rivers near ye south mountains   my siberian cytisis planted in ye coldest shadyist in my garden is shooting out fresh   ye top sprigs is perished   ye chalcedonian iris & fritalary spreads wonderfuly
I have at last after above 20 years tryal brought ye fine grassy plant to flourish better then I ever saw it in Jersey   it is now sending out 3 large spikes of flowers   I take it to be A asphodel & ye most glorious of that tribe   ye iron colored & yelow foxgloves grows lustyly   there is 5 of thy portugal come up

now I hope to be stocked with padus as I have received A lovely parcel this spring from mistris Logan my fascinated widow   I saw ye lovely tree growing in governour Glens garden   she allso sent me A young tre from there but ye ratts allmost demolished it   I have allso facinated two mens wives alltho one I never saw   that is mistris Lambol who hath sent me two noble cargoes   one last fall ye other this spring   ye other sent me I think A great curiosity   she calls it A golden lilly   I thought when I planted it to be ye attamasco but ye bulb seems diferent   I am apt to think I have not yet got ye true lobloly bay or alcea tho several say thay have sent it but I believe thay are species of sweet bay   tho I have walked & rode by thousands of them yet I could not find one good root   ye sorrel tree & 3 or 4 more that I am very fond of I cant yet procure tho I believe my correspondents strive which can oblige me most

BP 1:60:1, 1:57; D. 234–35.
1. This letter is taken from BP 1:60:1 to this point; the remainder is from BP 1:57.

From COLLINSON

Londn May:22:1762

Whilst my Dear John is in Melancholy Mood for the loss of Pitt — I keep myself to equal poise, putt the successes *in One* scale & His Two Rash French expeditions on their Coasts, *in the Other,* In which He wantonly sacrificed so many brave English men to answer no purpose but his vain Glory — Had they been sent *then* to Martinico, some Millions had been the Difference to England. If Wee consider the Number of our ships Taken, & their rich Cargoes, the Men useless, & the Vast produce of that Island kept From us – So all things putt together (for this is a short sketch) I dont find any Cause to Lament his abdication   Wee go on full as well without Him So prithee my Dear John revive & don't sink & be lost in dolefull dumps, under so terrible an Event which portends no Harm that I can See, for Wee Have a Brave King & Good Men at the Helm — never fear, Wee shall keep Canada, & have a Good Peace & Pitt is as well pleased with his Mercenary pension of £3000 per annum & a Title in reversion & has cleverly slip'd his neck out of the Coller, when it most became Him to keep In — to serve his Country, but he preferred serving himself before it —

From one Melancholy Story Wee come to Another — thy Account of the loss of so many fine plants which Effects Mee more then the Loss of Pitt — It is a fair probation how far the principles of Vegitation may be maintain'd when removed from a Warmer Latitude to a Colder — Art will assist Nature — There is many fine plants that grow on this side the Tropicks, if we will bestow a South Wall on them, will thrive & flower well in our Northern Climate — The Red Sweet Bay & Great Magnolias & Long Leaved Pine have not suffered in the Least — What Thou calls their Oleander, I presume was had from Us — I some years agon sent a fine Tree of the Oleander to Docr Witt which throve finely by being protected in Winter — by thy Myrtle Changing its Colour in thy Green House its Evident that the Walls are not of a Sufficient thickness to keep out the Frosts – or Thick Close Shutters are wanting in the Front to Cover the Glass, phaps a stove may be necessary in very severe Weather — Thy Last Cargo — the Azalea and shrub Honesuckles is finely in flower & the Calmias will Do & all the fine plants the fine Red Calceolas flatter'd us, came up very Strong but alas the flower was aborted, & the White one does not yett appear — the Fall Arum or Indian Turnip I but this day, perceived his point above ground — whilst others of your plants are quite gone off as the Fumitory with a White Breeches like flower — but I have been much Delighted with the small Mountain Double flowerd white ranunculus sent last year —

I am [glad] at Last the Box Bulbs are come to thy hand at Last   in better Condition they could not be expected as they had been so long —

The Ponthieus will pay for the box Seeds but they make Light & Trivial what has been sent besides — for whose Letters & Bills of Loading I paid so much postage they don't offer to pay even part though wholely on their own account —

I cannot advise for I am fearfull thy grand Expedition to the Lakes will be too Much to undertake without suitable Companions for Accidents may happen in so Long a Journey — but if it was thy Resolution my advice will come to Late — So, my Dear John Farewell

P Collinson

Lord Kildare's 3 boxes came safe   Docr Solander wrote by a Swedish parson on the last specimens   I formerly corresponded with Docr Witt your neighbour & his son in Law Docr More — this answers thine of Jany 17 & Feb 5 —

I don't know what to say about Bushes[1] 2 Boxes of Seeds for he has never been near to Mee in this Spring & I have writ to him for he Lives in the Country — He may be dead for ought I know, so pray send no Boxes of seeds or Woods for him — I hope Gordon will Raise the fine aromatick Vine for the fall seeds were good

It may be 20 years agon since I gave the White Broom to our Frd Lamboll which was sent me from Portugal

Docr Gronovius has sent Thee a present of a new Edition of his Flora Virginica[2] which I have gott bound & given our friend Franklin to convey to thy hands with two other tracts

I make the Ballance of thy Accts Exclusive of the Seeds sent February 1762 of which I have received but for one Box paid by Bush £460:19:9 — it is well thy money was not laid out in stocks which have fell Thirty % — untill a peace is made publick [several lines illegible]   only one Root of Warneria comes up   Thy fine Aconite is come up and will shoot his flower

BP 3:23; D. 235–36.
1. John Bush (Busch) Hackney, Middlesex nurseryman.
2. This second edition was completed by Gronovius's son, Laurenz Théodor (1730?–1778).

From WILLIAM BARTRAM

June 11th 1762

Dear Brother

the Parting with your Son Bille this Day felt: harder to Me than the Parting with My own son: his Behaviour to me: & my family has Bene so Agreeable as well: as to others: which gave A Concern to Many. But one Comfort to me is: I am in great hopes he will Return & Live with us Again: as Soon as he Can Settle his affares there: which I hope & Doubt Not But will be to his Advantage: I have Nothing Strange to Acquaint you with: I have wrote Several times & Not Bene Answered: I hope my Son Bille Behaves himselfe well: I am afraid he is Troublesom Among you: I do not Doubt your good Advice & other Services for his Advantage: I wish he May

Behave in Such a Dutifull Manner: So as to Deserve your favour, – I hope youre all in good Health: as we Injoy at Present: thanks be to our Mercifull God – as Cousen: Bille is in a hurry for going I Conclude: wishing your all health & Prosperity is the Harty Desire of your Brother:

Willm: Bartram

P:S Pray Dr: Brother write by all oppertunities to Acquaint me of all your welfare: And my Billes Behaviour & Progress – from W:B

I hope hel: Like his Cousens Imployment & they to Instruct him: Untill hees Capable of Business: I hope to hear Certain when your Son Bille: Returns Again

BP 1:77.

From COLLINSON

Lond: June 11th 1762

Notwithstanding I have wrote so lately by Docr Shippen May 22: in answer to those of 17 January feby 5 yett I can't lett the Packet Sail without a few Lines   I forgot in my Last to tell thee my Discidious Mountain Magnolia I have raised from Seed about 20 years agon flowers for the First Time with Mee & I presume is the first of that species that ever flowerd in England & the Largest & Tallest, the Flowers come Early Soone after the Leaves are formed – The Great Laurel Magnolia & umbrella both fine trees in my Garden showed their flower Budds the first of June — my Red flowering Acacia is now in full flower & makes a glorious show as well as the White but above all is the Great Mountain Laurel or Rhododendron in all its Glory — this 10th June, what a Ravishing Sight will the Mountains appear when alive with this rich embroiderie   How Glorious are thy Works o Lord, they inspire Mee with Admiration & Praise — in the Sod with thy Saracena is come up a Seeming species of Orchis, a very singular flower. It would be worth while importing from wild boggy swampy places where so many odd & Rare plants grow for the sake of the uncommon plants they produce   the Tradescantia now shows its flower   it is new & I am Impatient to see the new production

My Dear John If thou knowest the pleasure thou so often Gives to thy old Friend by peruseing thy Journals   the Time taken in digesting them cannot be said to be thrown away, as they Afford an Endless fund of Entertainment & Reflection from the various Incidents & Objects that Diversifie Every Page —

By thy Discription Pittsburgh must be a Delightful Situation both for Health, Conveniance & Trade — No Doubt but our people will avail Themselves of these Advantages when the Country grows populus, & Wood Scarce & Dear, Coal may be of Infinite Service to Supply that Difficiency

What shall Wee Saye to the Strata abounding with fossil Sea Shells Petrefactions   very probably as thou conceives the sea flowed higher, or once overflowed all   all our Conjectures may be beside the mark as Wee know not the true Causes of these phenomena.

The Want of Fish in the Ohio may be as thou observes from its great distance from the sea but this cannot be the absolute Cause for it is well known that Inland lakes in many parts of the World abound with Fish —

The New Species of Turtle I should like to see, but there is another four footed amphibious Creature that is pecular to the R Ohio, that may deserve thy further inquiry — I printed an Accot of It, & the figure the best I could procure in the Gent Mag abt 2 or 3 years Ago   A skin of this rare Creature would be a Great Curiosity as well as an addition to Natural History & some more particular Observations on the Great Buffalo, Their Bones or skeletons are now standing in a Licking place not far from the Ohio of which I have Two of their Teeth   One Greenwood[1] an Indian Trader & my friend Geo:Croghan   both saw them & gave Mee relation of them but they omitted to Take Notice what Hoofs they had, & what Horns, these two Material Articles known, would help to determine their Genus or Species – prethee inquire after them, for they are wonderful beyond description if what is related of them may be depended on — I heartily wish Thou had been properly Informed of them & the place they was found In — then we should have had some Certainty —

Thus, Dear John I scrawl on but now I must conclude.

thy real Frd
P. Collinson

I heard nothing from Bush, & thought him Dead but now he has been with Mee & has paid Mee for one Box – & now He Desires another – what is that spiked Indigo thou mentions   send a Specimen of It – I want much Seeds or Root of [Classiane?]   My Attamasco lillies are now in bloom

The last pacquet from New York, was taken So I am afraid I have lost one of thy letters, always write by the pacquet under Cover to my Friend Alexander Colden, Esq Post Master of New York & then I have thy Letter with out Charge

Sassafras has blown abundantly – The Fringe Tree is now in flower & Ever Green fern Leaved Bignonia in plenty makes a final show — yellow Root grows but Weakly — Look out for another — my ginseng I raised from Seed is gone off — Striped Bark Maple has been in Blossom —

BP 3:24; D. 236–38.
1. J. Greenwood made a map of his Ohio travels.

From BOUQUET

Fort Pitt, 15th July, 1762

Dear Sir: –

I received your letters of May the 3d, and June the 11th, which have given me great pleasure. I am much obliged to you for the curious list of North

American Trees and Shrubs you sent me. I hope to understand it better, when I see the originals in your garden.

This war will not last for ever; and I hope we shall have some leisure, hereafter, to study the productions of nature, and bestow some time in cultivating plants, instead of destroying men.

I am glad of the success you have had, in the few plants you got, hereabout; and wish New River and Pedee may reward you for your trouble, if you undertake that journey, which, I fear, must be attended with great trouble and fatigue.

I got, a few days ago, a very great curiosity, from about six hundred miles down the Ohio; – an elephant's tooth, weighing six pounds and three quarters, and a large piece of one of the tusks; which puts it beyond doubt, that those animals have formerly existed on this continent.

I sent your letter to Mr. Kenny.

I am, with great regard and friendship, dear sir, your most humble servant,

Henry Bouquet

D. 427–28.

To COLLINSON[1]

Dear Peter
we have had ever since last fall great extreams of unseasonable weather last fall was very wet   december very cold & every few days snow: January mild   great floods & high tides   february extream cold & dry to ye midle of march   then to ye midle of april extream wet & could   thence to ye midle of may very dry & cool   thence to June extream hot & dry   then ye heat abated but ye dry weather continued; this unseasonable & inclement weather hath done much hurt to Corn & fruite & several plants hath suffered much espetialy ye ever greens from Carolina all of which except ye long leaved pine was disrobed & ye stocks killed to ye ground except ye Holly & great Magnolia: but ye deciduous trees was not at all hurt   I have A fine species of buglos now in full bloom & hath been near A month & will yet continue   hundreds of flowers blew & purple is out at once   I esteem it as one of my Capital plants but I cant tel when I got it or who to thank for it but it is A glorious plant   I have yet four fine portugals alive & as many from Carolina of thair evergreen Padus which I take to be what miller calls mahogany   ye spigelia is in full bloom & thair clematis hath been A month & will continue till frost   I am realy astonished at ye prodigious variety I have of thair trees shrubs & plants & yet I want many that I saw there as ye sorrel trees   a species of box thorn   two species of evergreen andromeda with red & white flowers & I am not certain whether I have yet ye lobloly bay or alcea Altho several hath sent me shrubs by that name which I esteem next to ye great magnolia & several charming flowering shrubs & several

very odd plants new genus & several sensitives one of which I have from ye congerees I set no price upon Edies & ponthieus Boxes but left it to them to give me what thay pleas being willing to try thair honesty & generosity for once that I may know how it will answer to send them more if thay want: but I had rather not send them any growing plants I can sell them here for twice what thay will care to give & have my mony directly without any risk or ensurance I received thy kind letters of April ye 10th & 11 1762 ye hard nuts I sent was given me at Pittsburgh by Colonel Bouquet he called them hicory nuts he had them from ye countrey of ye Ilinois thair kernel was very sweet I am afraid thay wont sprout as being A year ould many of my Carolina & Pittsburgh seeds is come up except ye hard seed which I expect next year I long to be on ye Cherokee mountains but I doubt those indians is mischievously bent which discourages me much in my intended Journey thee did well to Caution me not to enclose any letters in thine to de ponthieu I did not know but you had been intimate friends & he might have as good or better kindness

BP 1:57.
1. Undated, but probably written in late summer of 1762 (see Collinson to Bartram, April 1 and December 10, 1762).

From COLLINSON

London July 25:1762

I cannot lett our dear Franklin pass over without a Line to my Dear John — In my last of July 9th by pacquet I acknowledged the receipt of thine 10th of May

I know thy Many avocations therefore will patiently wait thy own Time for thy Journal to Pittsburg —

There is no end of the Wonders In Nature the More I see the more I covet to see not to gratifie a trifling curiosity but to raise my Mind in Sublime Contemplation on the unlimited power & Wisdom of the Great Creator of all things — I am glad to Hear my Two pretty Friends John & Benjamin are not so squeamish as their Father How is my Frds William & Moses, I expect some Discoveries from William who has curiosity & Ingenuity — I much wish He could give a sketch of the Sensitive Leafe if He is with his uncle it may then be no Difficult thing to procure — I wish I could hear it was Once in thy own Garden & that I had good Specimens I then could forme some Idea of this Wagish plant, — as Wagishly Described.

Birds & Insects have their certain periods at the Time thou was on the Ohio most of the first was absent & the Last in their Chrysalis state It requires a year's adjournment to have a tolerable knowledge of the Animals of a Country

The Severity of Last Winter will teach the Experience, as Thou was not aware of its Effects, some protection, as Wee use, may prevent its fatal Consequences — South Country plants or the seed [from] the Tropicks grow well against South Walls   these Wee can cover with Matts & Lay Litter all about the Roots to keep out the Frosts — Those that stand in the open Ground Wee first take care to plant where they may be screen'd by Trees, Hedges or they [are killed] from the fierce and Freeseing Winds then Wee will litter that & cover the ground [several illegible lines]

The Basteria my good Friend Lambol sent Mee many years agon   it is a fine Bush & flowers plentyfully every year   its fragrance is smelt at a great Distance   is very Hardy — as its Wood is very Aromatic, certainly has Eminent Vertues   is it no ways applyed as a Medicine

My Great Magnolia is full of flowers this year, in which Wee have had the least rain & Longest Warm sultry Weather I ever remember — I have had much to do with all our watering to keep many of your plants alive   Wee have pomegranates against South Walls   the fruit as Large as an Egg — no doubt will ripen Well this year   all Fruits are very forward & in great pfection   Figg & Apricotts Excellent   our Wheat never finer [illegible] thou mentioned into Flowering but this Hott Dry year is very bad for seeds, very few are Come up of the Pittsburgh Seeds. I wish they may [bear] Strong fruit   they come in Autumn   the Winter may kill them

the Grassy Plant sent last stands at a stay   Send Mee More & give Mee a hint how to Manage this intractable Vegitable & I much Want that very Earlyest root Iris   I have Two New Asters come up out of the sods   the one pfoliated, wch I never saw before   Sure your Country is Inexhaustible in Asters   Virga Aureas   Coronoa Solis, I forgett if I ever Mention'd two Monstrous Teeth I had sent Mee by the Govr of Virginia   one tooth Weighs 3¾ pds 15 Inches round   the other 1¾ pound — 13½ inches round one other has Docr Fothergill & T. Pen another   One Greenwood, well known to B. Franklin an Indian Trader knocked some of the Teeth out of their Jaws, & Geo:Croghan has been att the Licking Place near the Ohio where the skelletons of six Monstrous animals was standing as they will inform thee   Croghan is well known to B:Franklin   to Him I wrote a Long Letter which I have Desir'd B:Franklin to show thee before He sends it to Crogan of which thou Take a Coppy if thou thinks worthwhile   I Briefly mention these Wonders of Wonders that in thy next Excursion to the Heads of the Rivers if thou art within an Hundred Miles of them they Deserve a Vissit to see what no body knows is to be seen in the World besides — The Indian Tradition that the Monstrous Buffaloes so called by the Indians was all struck dead with Lightning at this licking place but is it likely to think all the Race was Here Collected & was Extinguished at one Stroke —

P Collinson

BP 3:35; D. 238–40.

To COLLINSON

Dear Peter   august ye 15th 1762 by ye packet

I wrote by Budden last By whom I sent my Journal to Pittsburg haveing A fine opertunity by my friend Taylor[1] who promised to deliver them to thee with his own hands   there is two large roots one from Carolina ye other from Pitts.   doubtless of as great vertues as most medicinal roots   our extreme hot dry weather still continueth alltho we have once in 2 or 3 weeks A shower that wets ye ground 2 or 3 inches deep but yet ye ground is 3 foot deep as dry as dust   yet some plants that grows naturaly in or near water bears ye dry weather as well as any I have   I have one lobloly bay that came over in hot dry weather that grows ye best of any of ye Carolina evergreens sent this year notwithstanding I planted it in ye highest border of my upper garden not knowing it was ye Alcea so that now I am in hopes it will do well with me if ye hard frosts dont kill & disrobe it as ye other evergreens   I am obliged to Solander for ye names of ye specimens of my last colection   ye names of most are very just, & show ye great learning and ingenuity of ye doctor but as dried specimens is not to be depended upon like ye growing plant so he hath mistaken several   I shall begin with remarking A very odd new genus 54.   ye doctor calls it Asclepias linifolia   I found one with broad leaves near ye coast of no carolina   ye leaves is milky & I thought it had been an Asclepias at first but observing ye leaves growing alternately: ye flowers & seeds being so very different from that or any other known genus I concluded it was new   it is surprising how it casts its long rough mishapen seeds like bits of rotten wood out of ye top of its long upright pods   I take it ye lower part of ye pod contracts as it dries & by slow degrees, squeezeth ye seed out of ye top of ye pod which openeth by its contraction below: 41 A new species of anthemis this I take to be A true Silphium: 45 tragia volubiles   this is a severe stinging upright netle little difering from ye europian but ye roots strikes very deep in ye ground perpendicularly: 16 perhaps A viburnum is ye Basteria: 18 crategus [Lydslas?] Haw which thee said was ye parsley thorn from ye divisions of ye leaves but this leaf is [illegible] & directly oposite to ye other both in its natural growth leaves thorns & fruite   32 chirenia engularis   this I took to be ye lesser centory with white flowers bienial   I received ye history of florida Edwards 7th volume magazines & Gordons catalogue of seeds with thy letter of June ye 30 & that in franklins letter & July ye 8th   ye saith letters from germany complains heavyly of but 8 sorts of seeds being in A Box but none complains of haveing ye others above A double shair of such curious seeds as thay never came before which with ye 3 with 8 or 10 sorts made up ye whole complement of 3 double Boxes

BP 1:58:1; D. 240.
1. Unidentified.

From JAMES WRIGHT[1]

Respected friend　　　　　　　　　　　　　　　　　　August 22nd 1762

pursuant to thy request, I have made as particular an enquiry relating to those bones thou mentions, as I possibly could from two Sincible Shawanese Indians, assisted by an Interpreter, And the Substance of what they Say is as follows – the place where they lye is about 3 miles from the Ohio, salt & moist, as well as I could Judge by their description of it seems to contain 30 or 40 Acres, in the Midst of a large Savannah, 4 days Journey Below the lower Shawanese town, on the East Side of the River, that there appear to be the remains of 5 entire Scelatons, with their heads all pointing towards each other, and near together, supposed to have fallen at the same time; when they were desired to describe their several parts, they began with their heads, of which two were larger than the rest. One of these, they said a man could but Just grasp in Both his Arms, with a long nose, and the mouth on the under side, they next mentioned the shoulder blade, which when set on end, reached to their shoulders, and they were both tall men, what they call'd the cup (or socket) of this bone, was Equal in size to a large bowl, the thigh bone when broke asunder, would admit of a little boy's Creeping into it – they were asked if they had seen those long bones they call'd horns, they Answered they had, And by the distance from where they stood to the door, Showd them to be 10 or 12 feet long, and added that by the Bones, they Judged the creature when alive must have been the Size of a Small house; pointing from the Window to a Stable in Sight; I asked them if the place where they lay was Surrounded with mountains, so as to admit a probability of its Ever having been a lake, they answered, the place was Salt and wettish, and by having been much trod & Licked, was something lower then the adjacent land, which however, was so level, to a prodigious extent, that the licks as they calld it, could never have been coverd with water; and that there were many roads thro this extent of land, larger & more beaten by Buffalos and other creatures, that had made them to go to it, than any Roads they saw in this Part of the Country.

on being Questioned if they had seen such bones in Any other place, they said they had seen many such, Scattered here & there in that large tract of land mentioned before, some upon the surface, and some partly buried but all much more decayed by time, then those they had been describing, and not any entire Sceleton; I asked if they had ever heard from their old men, when these 5 were first observed or if they, or their fathers, had ever seen any such large creatures living, as these bones were supposed to have been a part of, they answerd they had never heard them spoken of, other then as in the condition they are at present, nor ever heard of any such creature having been seen by the oldest man, or his father – that they had indeed a tradition, such mighty creatures once frequented those Savannahs, that there were then men of a size proportionable to them, who used to kill them and tye them in Their noppusses and throw them upon their Backs As an Indian now does a deer, that they had seen marks in rocks, which tradition said, were made by these

Mastodon. *Popular Science Monthly* 1 (1872):209.

great & strong men, when they sate down with their Burthens, such as a Man makes by sitting down on the Snow, that when there were no more of these strong men left alive, God kild these mighty creatures, that they should not hurt the present race of Indians, and added, God had killd these last 5 they had been questioned about, which the Interpreter said was to be understood, they supposed them to have been Kild by lightning – these the Shawanese said were their traditions, and as to what they knew, they had told it – the man who Interpreted, was well Acquainted with their language, and as I have known him from a boy, I am confident he would do it faithfully. I shall be pleased if what smal Information I have gain'd will be agreable to thee, and shal be glad to oblige thee at any time to the Utmost of my Power

I am thy assured friend

James Wright

British Library, Add. Ms. 21648, ff. 333–34; George Gaylord Simpson, "The Beginnings of Vertebrate Paleontology in North America," *Proceedings of the American Philosophical Society* 86 (September 1942):130–88 (edited).
1. A Quaker friend of Bartram, living in Delaware County.

To COLLINSON[1]

I am now provideing to go to ye new river & if we can hould out & ye indians dont stop us we desighn to cross ye mountains & come to ye Moravian settlements on ye yadkin & if I can drink water out of ye springs of ye wateree it will pleas me much where I hope to find A fine variety of plants but I dont expect to find so many different from ours in A hundred mile rideing there as I should in one near ye sea coast   but ye last I have & hope soon to have but those near ye mountains I must fetch myself if I get them   My son Billy is to set out with me in about two weeks   we desighn to travail together to ye Yadkin about 200 miles from his uncles   he hath traveled much in that countrey yet never saw ye umbrela tree there   I lately received a letter from John Bush   he wants young ones & seed of that lovely tree but I think he must give more pounds then he is willing to give shillings before he gets it   I have two growing but then I planted them in ye doctors garden & he sent them ye year folowing   thay grow very slow but its strange that all dont perish while our aple trees is withering with thair fruite on them for want of moisture   I would have all these Chaps that wants quantities of these curious shrubs to go to Carolina themselves to fetch them & then thay will know how to get A proper value of them   I had A sensitive plant seed sent me from ye congaree   one came up before harvest but ye hot weather killed it tho I watered it every night & since harvest I have two more come up but I [don't] dare let A drop of water touch ye plant but I make A hole in ye ground A little distance from ye fibers of its root & fills ye hole full of water in ye evening & thay grow yet well   it differs much from ye sensitive bryer which onely closeth its leaves at ye touch & from ye humble plant both which is very prickley but this is quite smooth slender stalked & both closeth its leaves & gently prostrates: my little tipitiwitchet sensitive stimulates laughter in all ye beholders   there was lately a french gentleman from Montreal which was so agitated that he could hardly stand & said it was enough to make one burst with laughing   it seems to grow as well as in carolina   how it will bear ye winter I cant say   ye long leaved Saracena grows well: ye four portugal padus grows finely   so doth those from Carolina & ye stone pine from Madera   thay seem to stand our hotest sun & dryest weather to which I add that it soon produceth flowers haveing observed ye seed pods on trees no higher then my head which considering ye luxuriant growth of [illegible] ye geraniums is come up thee sent

BP 1:56:3.
1. Undated but written August 29, 1762 (see Collinson to Bartram, December 10, 1762).

From COLLINSON

London, October 5, 1762

My dear John

What good Luck attends thy Journals For thy last was carefully deliver'd by Mr. Taylor in a very obliging manner — There is an everlasting fund of Entertainment & Information wch will be subjects of consideration at more

Leisure — but I remark how few or none of your wild animals came under thy notice except snakes — I expected often to hear the Panther had sprung out of a Thickett or a bear wakened from his Den or a beaverdam broke up to observe its structure and artful contrivance &c.

Your weather has remarkable vicissitudes   Ours has been more certain for all our summer has been a constant Hott dry season, all burnt up longer than ever I knew. Plants languishing and perishing for want of rains & many totally killed but my greatest loss has been from a villain who came & robbed Mee of twenty-two different species of my most rare & beautifull plants   took all my fine tall Marsh Martagons that thee sent me last year which was different in colour from any I have had before   all my fine yellow Lady's Slippers that I have had so long & flowered so finely every year. These I regret most for they are not to be had again, but by thy Assistance & though I Doubt not of thy inclination, yett, as I apprehend they are found accidentally so it may not be in thy power to assist Mee.

the Anchusa is undoubtedly of my Sending for it is my favourite but Endures not long in my Garden   I think it is bienial   I have been in the Country & Collected fresh Seed   have just sown It

I am glad to hear of the Portugal Laurels   they are fine Evergreens & Beautifull in flower   the Bastard Mahogany must be another Tree   I have what is called the Evergreen Padus, of South Carolina but I doubt if it will hold when it grows older & in our climate   I have observed many young vigorous plants will keep their leaves for 2 or 3 years & then become deciduous.

Undoubtedly Carolina is the Country for Wonderfull Vegetative productions   Wee have numbers of them & yett Wee want many More — the Loblolly Bay sent Mee by our good Friend Lambol thrives finely but has not flower'd & the Sorrell Tree thrives — July 25 the first Blossom of my great Magnolia open & has continued Flowering untill this 3d October is the last Blossom   a Singular Circumstance belonging to this Tribe   their long flowering which is an Excellency to be admired

I am impatient to see a specimen of the leaves and flower of thy Tipitiwitchet   pray good John never lett a Letter pass without a Specimen as it advances, is it possible for Billie to paint It   I am much concerned that his affairs are Incumbered — pray take care of this singular plant & protect the root carefully agst your sever Weather — I should like the Six or 7 Temperate Months of Carolina but should be exhausted & Die with the Heat — for I am & have been this Summer over done for I Lay with my Chamber Door & Window Open under a sheet & Silk Quilt & yett could not rest & in our hardest Winter lay with no Blanket only a Wollen Quilt & Sheet — Now think how I would bear even your Sultry Season much less the Scalding Sun & fiery Air of the Summer months in Carolina

Our Neighbor Ponthieu takes no notice of the Case of plants but Sayes he will pay for the Box Seeds, Wee are on Good Terms as Neighbors   often Visit, but yett I see the Nature of People

I wish thou could gett more of the hard nutts of Col Bouquet   if they are

Hickories, they are very different from what thou has sent or what I have ever seen — I flatered myself they were the Bonduc a most Elegant Leaved Tree found by the French some Where in Canada — is in all the rare gardens of France, & in some Gardens in England, if the war had not broke out I should have had it sent Mee from thence & now I shall have it with a Peace which I hope is not far off

Is the Striped Rose a Native of Carolina, the Double Hawkweed with a pale red flower I have often sent Thee, the Long Leaved Saracena Grows finely but Does not flower   yours has often flowered   these plants are well worth Our Care for their Singularity

How Early your harvest is to ours which Shows your Fertile soil & warm Climate & although so much advanced to the North, yett there is many Concurring Circumstances that gives the plentiful Crops & a Successfull Harvest.

The Roots I have Deliver'd Solander   He thanks thee for them & will be pleased to Hear from thee —

My Dear John I have been Walking in *thy Garden* & cannot pceive where there is so much shade   none of the pines Love It, but the Scotch, will Endure Moisture but as all the Pines in Europe & Assia Grow principally on Mountains, where from the Strata of the Air, from Snow & Rain — the earth must be Saturated with Moisture So I think it could not Hurt them growing in an open Situation as thee has often seen in your pine Swamps —

I hope thou will not undertake so long a Journey without Moral Assurance of Safety — Gout-wort or what is called Podagraria is a notorious running Weed in a garden, for which reason Wee rarely save seed of It   it is only a native of Europe   you do not abound in umbelliferous plants which are plentyfull & in Variety with us, our fields & Banks are overrun with Them, — but your Tribe of Asters exceed Them — almost every Sod brings over a New one, In the last Cargo is Two fine new Species of Aster I never saw before   one Great Sod with the Saracena & the other with an Azalea   the purple Ulmaria keeps alive but the Dry Weather prevented it flowering   the Madiera Palenanos flower'd   is a curious plant & Different from ours — the Acconite & purple Eupatorium have shot finely & the first will certainly flower if our Weather proves Mild, but the Last I am doubtfull of — the Warneria grew but went of with the Drowth   but I hope that It is alive, the pyrola very Week   it is very extraordinary that Considering So Hott a Summer that all the other plants Survive It & I hope will hold It

Accidentally an Invoice of Alexanders fell into my hands   I hear Inclose it for thy Amusement — He makes but a poor figure when Compared with thine & there is great Complaint of his package — pray what is his brown & yellow Pine, Spice Wood, Evergreen Prinos

I have paid thy Draught to Benezet bill of 60£   pray Draw more if it is to thy Advantage —

By Docr Shippen I sent thy Account[1] who I shall be glad to hear is arrived, & now at thy request I send it again which I Doubt not but will prove right and the old Proverb says, right reckonings makes long Friends Lett those that Inquire my age know that I am thy Senior Some Months.

The Inclosed Specimen of Toxicodendron thou sent Mee last year   it is a new Species to us — pray where was it found — for it seems Tender being the Only plant killed down last Winter but is sprouted finely Since

Dear John thou must guess at my Meaning in many places   I write a piece now & then haveing variety of affairs on my hands but I am thy sincere friend,

P. Collinson

BP 3:36; D. 241–42.
1. Collinson showed receipts for £ 590.7 for the years 1760 and 1761.

To SIBTHORP[1]

To doctor Sibthorp profesor at Oxford
Worthy Friend
I have received thy kind letter of April ye 30 1762 which is ye second letter I ever received from thee ye first of which was left in town by ye person that should have delivered it long after it was dated   I thought to have Answered it but no opertunity ofering soon I drove it off from time to time till I was ashamed of it & now beg pardon & now if peaceable times come I intend to double my diligence for I am better stocked with materials than formerly haveing now searched our north America from New england to near georgia & from ye seacoast to Lake ontario & many branches of ye Ohio so that now there is very few plants in all that space of ground but what I have observed   nay have most of them growing in my own garden   I am Just returned home from A very successful Journey over ye congaree near Georgia & then up across ye country to ye Moravian settlements, up to ye head of ye Yadkin & over ye south & Alegany mountains to ye new river A great branch of ye Ohio on which I traveled four days & toward holstons river   in this journey I found many rare plants & shrubs & gathered much seed part of which I send to thee   it is very good & ripe & when I was upon ye wateree I dug up many curious roots of sorts which I could not gather seed from   these I planted in A Box to be sent one hundred and twenty mile to Charls town to be sent to Philadelphia which I have not yet received.

I was several years ago at charls town & Cape fear & setled such correspondence there that I have most of thair evergreens & plants growing in my garden & hopes to have all that our climate will bear

BP 1:56:5; D. 429–30.
1. Undated, but written in late October or early November of 1762; Bartram returned from his southern trip near the end of November.

To MOSES and WILLIAM BARTRAM

November ye 9th 1762

Dear Children,
I am now returned home in good health in which I allso found my family God Allmighty alone be praised   I had ye most prosperous Journey that ever I was favoured with   every thing succeeded beyond my expectation & my Gardien Angel seemed to direct my steps to discover ye greatest curiosities: ye presence of God was with me: & my heart overflowed with praises & humble adoration to him both day & night in my wakefull hours   I met with mendenhall[1] a few miles after we parted 60 miles from his house so I set off directly to ye Wateree to Samuel Wylys where I was recommended but he was not at home nor was expected for many days   he was gone A surveying; but it soon rained after I come & he soon came home & received me very friendly & next day lent me his horse to ride over ye congaree about 70 miles to Georgia   in this ride I found A wonderfull variety of rare plants & shrubs perticularly A glorious evergreen about 4 or 5 foot high & much branched in very small twigs growing upright   ye leaves is much like ye new found land spruice, rather smaller & grows around ye twigs close like it   ye seed is very small in little capsules as big as mustard   staid at wylys 2 whole days to rest my horse, then set forward to ye Moravian town which is 250 mile from Charlestown   Wylys is 120 ye ferry over ye Congaree is 140 to Charlestown   from the Moravian town it is 30 long mile to ye settlements in ye bottom & very bad road. ye bottom is near 20 mile broad & pretty good land   when I cam to ye last house I enquired ye way to ye mountain about 10 mile off   thay said there was 4 hunters Just going over to ye mine[2] & to Houlstons river   this I tooke as A great providential favour indeed so I set out & I suppose we headed to ye east branch of ye Yadkin, in ye mountain & lodged on A little branch of ye new river at ye distance of 7 miles or as some said 15 from ye head of Dan so that I believe haw river doth not reach ye south mountain but heads in ye high hills on ye south side of ye bottom which is near 10 mile across   these South or Alegany mountains is realy very high on carolina side & steep full as high if not higher then our blew mountains & still grow much higher against Georgia   there is much middling good land & fine savannas & plentiful streams on these mountains but it's so could & wet & ye snow frequently two foot deep in winter (some say in october & November but I believe not commonly then) that it must be uncomfortable liveing   it is commonly said that it allways snows or rains here   it rained ye first day but then it cleared up: we set out after Killing A dear & breakfasting on it   then rode A good pace till toward night   one of ye hunters killed 2 dear part of which we ate & left ye rest   next morning we set out & cleared ye mountain about noon   thence had 4 or 5 miles to ye mine   ye afternoon was spent about ye mine & ye banks of new river about 100 yards over   next morning ye overseer rode with me   crossed ye river in A boat & away to fort Cheswell toward Holstons river   then to ye Ferry 30 miles where it

was 300 yards broad, it was quite dark before we got to ye house   the next day we traveled till dark & went supperless to bed on ye ground by ye east branch of new river   set out early & by noon my guide parted with me & I set forward alone being obliged to my guide & very thankful to providence being now on ye branches of stanton & amongst ye inhabitants.

pray give my love to Brother sister & cousens. I was pleased with Billys temperance & patience in his Journey & shall soon be daly expecting A packet of seeds & A box of plants from you which with hearing of your wellfare will make glad ye heart of your loveing father

John Bartram

Moses pray take good notice of some of ye most convenient land about Brothers   I had rather Ben should settle in ye lower part of it if it was not for ye floods   I dont like ye uper parts

BP 1:52:1; D. 422–23.
1. Probably a relative of Bartram's wife.
2. Chiswell's mine near today's Wytheville, Virginia.

From LAMBOLL[1]

I am indebted to you for both y [our letters] the one of May 24th, the other of August past with Roots & Seeds, wch Doctor Garden carefully sent me

answering each of yours till now: the former because I could [get] nothing to remit; and the latter, on account of your intended Journey and Absence from home; but, from what you intimated have reason to expect this may meet you return'd: home, and I hope safe, and to your great Satisfaction, after having overcome the Fatigue of so long a Journey, and had the Pleasure of discovering new Curiosities; such as all your Friends now impatiently desire to hear and know of —

All the Roots and Seeds above mentioned have been sometime Planted and Sowd: and tho' we had here a long Drought at and after the Time I recd: them, have good Reason to think there's Life in them all: several of the Roots shot up Flowers presently after they were put into the Ground: the Weather being then Warm; I wish they may not be weakened & spent thereby. — This is intended by Capt: Noarth (who made his last Voyage hither, in Three days) in whose Vessel, I send in a little Box of Earth, directed for you, what Shrubs could be got ready, vizt: Sweet Shrub; two Sorts Pink-Root (of wch the narrow leaf is the right Sort for Worms) and three Sorts of Snake Root, with a very small Laurel-Tree: and in a small Chip-box, about four inches long & 3 wide, wth: this Letter tyd: thereto, the following seeds, vizt: Persicaria, Blood-wort, white-Iris, great Garden Cresses, Dwarf-Poppy, Winter Savory, Virginia-Stock, Ranunculas, Holly-Berries (from Mrs: Wragg) and what is calld: here Cocks-Comb, but guess may be your

Xeranthemum or double Ptcarmica, by the description; but if mistaken, your Candor will excuse it; it bears a large Purple head, wch: kept dry in Pots, hold the Natural Colour all Winter. If the Stalks of the Pink-Root should dy away in the Box of Earth, you Can trace their Roots by the hairy Fibres. My worthy Friend, I must conclude now: lest I should be too late for Capt: Noarth, who I hear is about to Sail; but with my wife's and my own best Respects, to you and yours, am dear Sir —

Your real Friend, to serv:
Thos: Lamboll

BP 4:67.
1. Undated, but probably written in late fall of 1762, judging by the content.

To ELIOT

december ye first 1762
Dear worthy friend
I received thy kind letter of march ye 25th 1762 by ye hands of Captain Smith with A specimen of iron sand & part of A bar which is Judged by our smiths to be very fine Iron. I should be very glad to know ye scituation of those iron sand banks thee mentions: are thay near ye mouth of large rivers from whence was thay brought: what was thair original & how was thay deposited there. I am very curious in searching into natural operations: but it is with great humility & resignation to ye great disposer of universal nature: hopeing it is no way disagreable to his divine will to search & Contemplate ye works of his Creation in which ye deeper we search ye more we discover ye unfathomable depth of Consumate wisdom not onely in Combineing: giveing motion: but preserving all material nature   this meditation dayly Nay hourly inclineth us to A Seraphic Love & Adoration of his Omnipotencey & Mercy: – I am apt to think that when our American Colonies comes to be cleared & Cultivated more generaly that ye state of our Atmosphere which is now very fluctuating may be more setled & more adapted to ye fruites of Asia & Europe   in the mean time I believe ye best of our own grapes would answer best for profit as thay make A stronge wine if ye birds would but let them ripen

Since I received thy Agreeable letter I have been in Maryland Virginia North & So Carolina & within a days Journey of Georgia between ye Congaree & Savana rivers   then Crossed ye Countrey to ye south or Cherokee mountains   then over ye Alegany mountain to New river 100 yards broad which I crossed   then toward Holstons   then crossed new river Again 300 yards broad   then the Alegany mountain traveling along new Virginia between ye North & So mountains to Potomack river: this great vale of rich limestone land of 300 mile long is A fine part of Virginia watered by ye many large branches of three great rivers Potomock, Staunton A great branch of Roan oak: & two large branchs of James river all of which heads in ye several ridges of ye North mountain: ye largest branch of James river is caled Jacksons river: on which is 5 wonders or great curiosities first A natural bridge or arch 200 foot high 30 broad & 68 long that unites two mountains   2 A vast cave in a mountain seven mile long   3d A stream on A mountain where water plunges down 200 foot perpendicular   4 a great spring flowing out of ye mountain runing & stoping periodicaly: 5th A great warm spring 30 foot diameter & those people that sitts in it A little time will be all in A sweat & another about seven mile farther is so hot as to harden eggs as is affirmed by those that have been there: when I set out this Journey I took A steel magnet with me to try ye sand & Iron oar; after I had crossed Rapahana river & past ye limestone ground I travailed mosly on A red tenatious soil generaly about 200 mile from ye sea Coast sometimes 150; ye sands here in ye road that was washed by floods out of ye red soil contained so much iron that it would adhere to ye magnet Just like that which thee sent me   ye road was full of it for about 400 mile until I came near ye 34th degree of Latitude where ye soil became very sandy; ye iron sand in many places had larger particles of Iron oar as big as Radish seed that adheared freely to ye Magnet; in my Journey from carolina & since I have thought much on ye cultivateing of our native grape; as ye generality of people is so eager after strong liquors & spirits ye markets is not to be overdone with wine & brandy: & some of our grapes is excellent for both if we could raise A sufficient quantity of vines either by layers, cuttings or grafting of ye best sorts: I intend to make several tryals of these methods this spring: I have A good opinion of the great sumer or bull grape of Carolina as I know it will live well by transplanting & I hope by layers or cuttings ye Joynts is very close together & will bear our more rigorous season   I have had it near two years   last summer it shot out near twenty branches & expect it will bear fruite either this approaching season or next

if I should go down ye Ohio & Misisipia this summer I hope to find some curious grapes & many other useful materials —

ye worthy Colonel Boquet hath orders from ye general to go to take possession & settle ye affairs in our new acquisitions to ye southward   he asked me to go with him   said I should never have such an opertunity he talks of takeing several hundreds with him so that I hope (if Providence please to favour my undertaking) to make greater discoveries then ever; as I shall have ye Leasure & not be so hurried as when I went alone for thay will take thair time & I suppose make A summers voyage of it

ye Colonel tould me that as soon as he had express orders he will let me know but tould me to prepare to set out ye latter end of april   I hear a number of carpenters is going to Pittsburgh to build Boats for ye voyage.

January ye 30

as this was ye longest Journey that I ever travailed at one stretch so was it ye most favourable; it seemed as if Providence ordered allmost every Circumstance both as to ye safety of my person & satisfaction of my mind:

I found A wonderfull variety of curious plants; & above all my dear friend: ye Presence of our God I had reason to hope was with me & my heart flowed in praises & thanksgiving to him both day & night in Humble Adoration & resignation to his will: our friend William Logan hath been proposeing to me to go with him to ye lower Shawnee town down ye Ohio to demand ye Prisoners & bring them up. how it will be I cant yet say   I have not spoke to him since I heard of peace being agreed to: so when its proclaimed its very likely some of our chiefs may be ordered to take possesion of ye banks of ye Mesisipia or to invite the Indians to A treaty & if so perhaps I may join thair company expetialy if William goes; we want much to see thos surpriseing bones near ye Ohio so much talked of & I should be glad to see & drink water out of ye famous river Mesisipia as I have out of many of its branches: I have sent me from ye Ohio A very odd kind of A turtle without A hard shell   it hath a back bone & 12 ribs   A broad fin is placed all round its body & is web footed & very small head & short tail   there was sent with it as strange A creature amphibious   A head like A catt fish   four short feet with flat nails on its toes like A man   its tail flat like A muskrat with A fin round it & A membranous fin one each side Joyning ye fore & hind feet   thay scratch holes in ye banks where thay lay thair eggs   many of them is allso in ye new river   thair called by ye inhabitants an Aligator   there is lately found in west Jersey A curious species of amber near ye surface in detatched masses near A pound weight not far from ye river delaware   it is inflamable.   near transparant   of A very tough consistency allmost as horn   of a yelowish color   it makes fine cane cane [sic] heads. what quantity there is of it is not known   neither hath it been much searched for yet. I have seen several bits of it but cant learn ye direct place where it was found   I heard it was plowed up in an ould field. I desighn to inquire farther about it; I am obliged to thy Son in law Doctor Gale for his very kind letter   ye specimen he sent me is called in Parkinson Christophoriana or herb Christopher   it differs A little from ye Europian & not much. our common tall black snake root or as some call it rich weed is near A kin to it in form & virtue   see Parkinsons figuer but thine is A true Christophoriana A churlish but good medicine Judiciously used: I never saw it grow south of philadelphia but its now quite destroyed in our parts   I should be very glad of A few ripe berries next fall for if kept til spring I doubt thay will not vegitate: my kind respects to Doctor Gale which I pray accept thy self which will oblige thy friend

in hast
John Bartram

Beinecke Rare Book and Manuscript Library, Yale University, Jared Eliot Collection.

To COLLINSON

december ye 3d 1762   by friend
Dear Peter
in answer to thine of may ye 22d brought me by doctor Shippin; I should be glad of an honourable peace but if Louisiana be not delivered to us we on

ye continent can hardly call it A peace for ye french will directly [by] encouraging & supplying ye indians set them against us & allso incroaching them selves which will soon cause first quarreling & next A war. I cant find in our countrey Latitude that south walls is much protection against our could for if we cover so close as to keep out ye frost thay are sufocated. I observed at ye distance of 120 miles from Charls town all ye fig trees is yearly killed down to ye ground   that is exposed to ye s or west but those in ye same garden that faced ye north & were shaded from ye sun did well   ye hot sun in ye day & sharp frosts in ye night, kills them   I have two flues in ye back wall of my green house   ye red & white calceolus & ye grassy plant white orchis & autumnal gentian & A pretty ornithogalon perticular to ye desert of Jersey is ye most difficult plants I know to prosper in a garden   I have one grassy plant grows finely but I have planted abundance of them & all failed   I brought it in ye midle of summer & planted it in ye dryest part of my garden tho thay grow naturaly onely in moist places   none of thy last bulbous roots flowered yet & many is perished but ye beladona & gurnsey lillys put out finely   I am glad ye sweet vine is like to prosper with gordon   he had many curious plants which I am sure he could not have had of any other neither for love nor money nor both: I think gratitude might ingage him to send me A root of each of his best bulbous roots which may be easily sent & would live tho thay was half a year in comeing   I have not one single curiosity from him but what is common & very few of them too that he sent me for ye persian Cyclamen two years past grows stoutly at my house & hath put out several flower buds so is not ye true persian   I am glad thee sent ye account of what money thee hath in thy hands of mine which I make no doubt is very Just   I am obliged to thee for ye Books & prints thee sent me   ye print of ye bastard pheasent, and Cinemon I had not before   that fine piece of Stillingfleets[1] I had two years ago   the miscellanies no way suited my tast except ye calendar of flora   my head runs all upon ye works of God in nature   it is through that telescope I see god in his glory. ye strawberry seed I sowed directly   ye apricot stones I gave away   thay do no good with us nor nectarines & peaches very little   if my Ben or John had nets perhaps thay would catch some insects   southern perenial roots whose top dies down to ye ground may be easily protected from frost but trees cant   indeed ye roots may very well, so as to shoot out anualy from ye ould root for ye curiosity of seeing it grow in ye summer but then most of them will not flower on one summer shoot   ye Johnsonia both flowers & fruites   ye dwarf iris one root perished & ye other is very poor occationed by ye dry weather   I believe many of our seeds I sent thee never comes up or else two new Asters could not have come in sods for there is hardly one plant between New england & Carolina & between ye sea & lakes of Canada but what I sent thee   there is some of your seeds that rarely comes up here as ye eye bright pulsatilla Aconite & gentian but yet ye most certain way to obtain your plants is by seed & if you would but sow your good seed in A box of moist earth in ye fall & send it directly I believe few would miss   as for those monstrous skeletons on ye

Ohio I have wrote to thee largely just before I set out for Carolina & since my return but by thy letter thee seems to think ye skeletons stand in ye posture ye beasts stood in when Alive which is impossible   ye ligaments would rot & ye bones fall out of Joints & tumble confusedly on ye ground but its A great pity & shame to ye learned curiosos that hath great estates that thay dont send some person that will take pains to measure every bone exactly before thay are broken & carried away which thay will soon be by ignorant careless people for gain. I take ye account of ye thick target to be ye scin of A bull Buphelo   his description of that Journey is very wild

My thanks to Gronovius for his new edition of the Flora Virginica. Its pity ye plants beyond ye South Mountain & ye draft of that fine country had not been in it

BP 1:56:4; D. 242.
1. Benjamin Stillingfleet (1702–1777), naturalist and author of *Miscellaneous Tracts Relating to Natural History, Husbandry and Physick* (1759).

From COLLINSON

Mill Hill   December 10th 1762

I am here all alone & yett I have the Company of my Friends with Mee, This will be no paradox when I tell thee on the Table lays their speaking Letters in that silent Language which conveys their most intimate Thoughts to my Mind — In course thine My Dear John comes First — I thank thee for thine of the 15 Augst — I have in my former Letters acknowledged the receipt of thy Journal wch is a lasting fund of Entertainment to Mee and my son these long Evenings   I am pleas'd to Hear thou has gott the loblolly Bay   I had it formerly   I know it is a Charming Tree — There is one now at Gordons & who has been some years Increasing It   My Umbrella flower'd this year & the flower Budds are strong for next — Whilst the French Man was ready to burst with Laughing I am ready to Burst with Desire for Root, Seed, or Specimen of the Wagish Tipitiwitchet Sensitive I wish Billie when he was with thee had taken but the least sketch of it to save my Longing — but if I have not a Specimen in thy next Letter — never write Mee more for it is Cruel to tantalize Mee with relations & not to send Mee a Little Specimen, in thine of the 15 of Augst nor in thine of the 29th — it shows thou hast no sympathy or Compassion for a Virtuoso — I wish it was in my power to Mortifie thee as much —

Don't use the Pomegranate inhospitably   a stranger that has come so farr to pay his respects to thee, don't turn him adrift in the wide world, but plant it against the South side of thy House, nail it close to the Wall, in this manner It thrives wonderfully with us, & flowers Beautifully & Bears fruit this Hott year   I have 24 on One Tree & some well ripen'd — Docr Fothergill says of all Trees this is the most Salutiferous to mankind —

I am glad the Portugal Laurel Thrives, thou will be Delighted with Them when it comes to flower   I heartily wish Billie may have every Way Success at Carolina   could he Pick up some Insects there in that hott Country that you have not —

Thy Letter — my dear John of the 29 Augst I am much obliged to thee, for takeing so much Pains to inform Mee, in so many Interesting Articles It is fortunate for thee & Mee through this Means to have so Curious Man as Col Bouquet   I hope He will continue There, now Peace is Secured under thy Instructions to Observe & Collect [five illegible lines]

I have often Seen they are a pretty domestic native animals such as your Wolf, differs from our European I am not able to Saye   Wild Catts must be a Curiosity as they is of the Tiger Species — send a Short description — but I want to know more of what you Call the Panther — now all Panthers are spotted, but yours is not, therefore It will be called *a Linx* — I have been regaling my Mind Every Evening I am Here, in reading over & makeing Abstracts from thy Entertaining Letters, beginning with the first & so on — I have collected all thou sayist of your Panther but no mention is made of his Colour, his Size, Length, or Height, shape of his head & Ears — Length of his Tail &c —

By my Beloved Friend Benn Franklin I wrote a Long letter relateing to the Skeletons of the Animals who are standing in the Licking place down the Ohio — I Desired Him to show it Thee for There In, is all I have been able to collect relateing to the Existence of thos Surprising Animals — that thou might collect what thou thought deserving Notice before The Letter was Delivered — I have Three of the Monstrous Teeth — but Thou well Observed Teeth [illegible] to Determine what these Animals are, or what Class they belong not, [illegible] is their Hoofs & Horns, if they had any — the Good Colonel thought them Elephants Teeth but they have no relation to them for I saw Elephants' Teeth & they are in the British Museum and can be certain on that point — but what they really are is [impossible] to Determine unless there was the strictest Examination by a Man well Qualified & then its more then [likely] they may be found to be an unknown Creature — unless it may be the Rhinoceras whose teeth I have not Seen —

thy Queries sett by J Wright to the Indians [eight illegible lines]

It is very probable that Colo Bouquet may have under Him Junior officers, espetialy in the Artillery, that can design & draw animals, I know that all the officers of that department have drawing Masters to learn them to take all manner of Designs — Now as I before observed there will be Leisure & nothing to fear in a profound peace with the Indians, now the French are striped of all that Fruitfull Country [illegible] the Re Maping — the Colo being a Gentleman of Curiosity & to bring one of the Wonders of the World to Light, may be excited to go & take a Survey of these Amazing Subjects [illegible]

I was much comforted with thy Good Wives Postscript that thou wast got to the Congaree in Health Sep 14   I trust that a good Providence will be with thee, in so Laudable an undertaking as to explore & discover the wonders of his creative power, and bring thee home in safety, to the joy of thy Wife and Family & in particular of thy affectionate friend

P Collinson

Now my Dear John look on the Map & see by this glorious Peace what an immense Country is added to our long, narrow slip of colonies from the banks of the Mississippi to Terra Labrador & Newfoundland &c See what a Complete Empire Wee have now got within ourselves what a grand Figure it will now make in the map of North America

I find by thy Letter of 1734 that thou sent Mee three kinds of Solomon's Seal Somehow or Other those have been Intirely Lost for I have them not pray to recruit Mee with these next year for they are plants I like

Roots came Safe & was soon deliverd to Docr Solander Extraordinary year that ripen'd our Peas to highest perfection & that they have yeilded perfect Ripe seed — they are the most Excellent Sow them Directly, Thee or thy Children I hope will test the Fruit of them

BP 3:38; D. 243–44.

To COLLINSON

January ye 6th 1763

Dear Peter
I received thy kind letter of October ye 5th 1762 I am glad thee received my rough Journal by mr. Talor, he was always ready to do me all ye kindness he could I did not see any wild animals in All that Journey, except 2 or 3 dear onely one tame bear at ye fort nor so much as A wolf or fox to be seen or heard alltho I lay six nights in ye woods on ye banks of ye Ohio & mononhahela & was two nights very late on ye Alegany mountains. I am much Astonished in reading ye historys of Europe & Asia, those ould settled clear countreys that thay should Abound so much with wild beasts of preay & others for food as travelers gives relation of as allso much wild water foul & plenty of fish: all which we had in great plenty 60 years Ago but now very few is to be seen all our small creeks used to abound with trouts but I have not seen one catched this 3 or 4 year tho traveled more then ever I did not see one fish catched in all my last Journey but at ye Wateree so many great rivers as I crossed nor one wild goos & very few ducks & but 3 or 4 small flocks of turkeys: its very provokeing to have so many of thy curious roots stole that rogue was too greedy to take all however: My dear friend I shall endeavour to furnish thee again though thay are now very scarce with us as most of ye land is cleared where thay used to grow quite to ye mountains. what our people will do for fencing & firewood 50 years hence I cant imagine

my fine anchusa long flowered & seeded then perished but many young ones is come up from ye scattered seed   two of my portugal laurels I took into ye greenhouse & two I left out under shelter but that from charls town I venture out but ye seedlings I have sheltered   ye Magnolia is A fine tree for long flowering   ye ponthieus promised to send me A wonderfull sight of curiosities but none comes yet   neither have I sent them any thing last fall not so much as A letter   I sent by Captain friend all my fall cargo   A Box of plants for thee & gordon   A fine parcel of Carolina specimens & seeds by my friend Fisher[1] by whom I wrote   largely I sent ye leaves & flower of my pretty Tipitiwitchet   I every day expect Col Boquet at my house where I intend to mention the hickory nuts from Ilinois   by ye Indians' discription I am apt to think ye Bonduc grows down ye Ohio, toward ye Shawnee town. I believe ye striped rose is not A native of Carolina. Its pretty double & smells like ye garden roses

 ye long leaved Saracena is A charming plant   grows near two feet high but I found one of that kind on ye wateree that growed six inches high was delicately striped with red & green   I dug up several roots & planted them in A box, with many other curious plants that I could not find in seed to be sent down to Charlstown for Philadelphia but I cant hear any thing of them   I doubt thay are lost or spoiled: thy observation is very good Concerning ye moisture of ye mountains by vapours & snow   I generaly find that mountain plants doth best with me in moist soil   I observed that ye high hills between Wateree & congeree was moist alltho ye flat ground was very dry   as thee observes we have very few umbelliferous plants   I did not see one new in all ye last Journey   perhaps next fall I may send thee specimens of all ye kinds we have. I am glad ye sent me James list   his swamp pine is ye 3 leaved pine which grows chiefly in swamps in Jersey but it grows on ye hilly ground from New England to Carolina   his yellow pine is ye 2 & 3 leaved pine   spice wood is ye Benjamin   Evergreen Prinos is what I call Evergreen Privet or Ink berries in Jersey   I am well pleased with thy account of ballance   ye specimens of toxicodendron that I sent thee I brought from near ye foot of ye catkill mountain   it is A male so cant get any seed of it   there is another smaller kind of this genus over potomock as well as toward Albany that is male & female distinck but that grows about 4 foot high in running patches: I admire your moderate winters should kill it & it grows naturaly in our coldest exposition & no frost hurts it   its realy A curious species   I sowed ye pulsatila seed & pears directly   it seems as fresh as if gathered yesterday   I intended to have sent thee Another Box of plants this winter   ye ship was put up but hath since changed her voiage   I question whether any vesail will sail before it is too late in ye spring   I doubt friend will be in danger of being taken this time

 I cant find thy amphibious creature that thee published in ye Magazine: my Billy has stole two from me to carry to his uncle at Cape Fear   perhaps it was in one of them   those in ye Ohio are very odd creature   amber of A very curious sort is found in west Jersey lately in detached masses near ye surface of ye ground & not far from ye river delaware   it is inflamable nearly transparent & allmost as tough as horn & will turn very smooth for

Cane heads of a yelowish color waved or checkerd with a lighter color   I think it was plowed up in A field, but I cant yet learn, certainly where it was found but I intend to make more enquiry about it.

BP 1:59:5; D. 244–46.
1. Probably Thomas Fisher (d. 1793), Philadelphia merchant.

To COLLINSON[1]

Apt to believe there is something to it   my landlord which is A knowing good sort of man affirmed to me that there was a great spring near ye head of James river that ebed & flowed as ye sea   that it turned A mill Just by where it came out of ye rocks. that he had been there to see it   that it ran six hours & stoped as long   that he saw it when no water came out & stayed till ye water come forth in A body & turn ye mill   that thay watched it coming day or night to grind while ye stream ran   now if this be realy true as he relates it it may pass for as great A wonder as any in your Peake of darbyshire (I have heard several times of this spring   there is another on ye branches of potomack in ye north mountains)   he allso tould me of A warm spring which had excelent virtues as he & many others had experienced that ran either into green bryer or James river   thay are here near together   this if true is valuable   my next neibour did live on new river before ye indians broke out   he is an understanding man   he gave me A list of all ye houses along ye road & ye distance of miles from house to house to Holstons river which I found surpriseing exact as far as I went he says there growed on his land A great tree 2 foot over & very high with A smooth bark that was exceeding soft wood which bore chesnuts but not fit to eat   this must be according to his discription ye Hipochastanum or Pavia. But I thought ye Pavia had not been A tree but A shrub   I have had A nut brought from green bryer several years Ago that was certainly one of them   if this should be A variety of either it will be A curiosity   he says there is abundance of different sorts that he never saw any where els & that if he be in life he will go & see his place again in 4 years   ye river is 180 yards wide against his land deep & rapid   Lewises[2] map is very exact there   I admired where so much water could be collected in that vail from ye south mountain but on looking on his map I found it headed most of ye Carolina rivers runing farther south then ye heads of holstons river   my neibour said there was monstrous Catt fish in that river but he saw none Above foot long but very few other sorts   I suppose ye falls at ye Mountain hinders them from comeing up. he says that holstons river is well furnished with fish   I suppose thay are not interupted with falls as by ye map it seems A fine level Countrey in its Course   my neibour tels me that there is on new river bank an excelent mine of silver mixed with lead which glitters so bright as to reflect it into ye river. I saw A man in my Journey that had buttons made of ye mettal which looked well   now to return to my own observation   on my return which was over ye South mountain along A wagon road we followed A run through two of ye ridges but ye third ridge was very high & so steep that ye wagoners when on ye top cuts down A great saplin & fastens ye smaller end to ye tail of ye wagon to hinder it from runing too fast down which thee may suppose scrats ye mountains back & sides finely   many hundreds of loads of wood is piled on ye sides of ye road toward ye bottom on each side of ye ridge & great fires is made to consume it out of ye way   I have crost this South mountain in many places allmost every 10 or 20 mile in york government East Jersey pensilvania & several places in virginia & Maryland but I think it is much higher in this part of ye countrey   from york river to Paiqualian there is very little difference in ye plants all ye way along this mountain   thence southward every 100 miles produceth one or more different plants: when I had crossed ye mountain I came both to different Soil & inhabitants both being some very rich but ye greatest part poor: ye low lands on ye rivers very rich & most of it in rich peoples hands: ye other land is some midling some poor   so is ye people on ye north side ye people most of them came from Jersey or Pensilvania & sows wheat & oats flax & hemp on ye high grounds & hath fine medows on ye low   ye south side on ye high grounds we se Indian corn & on ye best low lands tobaco but many lately sows wheat & some oats: & hath good orchards both peaches & Aples which thay distil & calls ye liquor brandy: when we come within 12 miles of Potomock ye land was much better & full of limestone   ye low lands very rich from whence to Susquehanna was generaly very good land   we traveled generaly near paralel with ye south mountain about ye distance of 15 mile; on ye high grounds between James river & Potomock grows abundance of flag Iris   ye leaves 10 inches long & half broad   I could not find one stalk nor seed so cant guess what flower it produceth   I brought A root home   it doth not spread in large compact bunches as our flag kinds do   I never observed between Conecticut river & Susquehana one Iris growing naturaly on dry land   hope it may be curious   I did not observe in all this Journey one lily or martagon calceolus or orchis tho looked for them diligently but this day have been observing perticularly A very odd yearling heifer haveing six feet: four of them was near like ye natural as to scituation, magnitude & form but ye back bone seemeth to have two spines from 3 inches behind ye scapulas in ye neck so as to lay most part of one hand & finger between ye scin covering each separate & from ye top of each chine near ye top of each scapula proceeds A ligament to which is Joyned ye round ball of ye os which naturaly fits ye socket of ye scapula: this bone is shorter then ye natural one & pretty closely surrounded with scin & hair   ye bone is articulated with ye radius (so as to bend something like A Joint) & that with ye carpus & A single hoof which is growed rather longer then common as it doth not touche ye ground to wear it shorter   one of these legs is 12 & ye other 14 inches long from ye round ball of humery to ye end of ye hoofe   ye bones is closely covered with scin & shortish brown hair ye color of ye beast   if we hould ye legs paralel together: ye two single hoofs seems to make A compleat natural one in shape & magnitude   as each leg hangs onely by a ligament & ye natural scin to ye uper part of ye chine & scapula so thay swing about & when ye heifer leaps or runs thay are sometimes thrown both on one side but generaly thay hang on each side without detriment to ye beast   thay seem to grow in proportion to ye other parts but with little flesh chiefly scin & bone

BP 1:66.
1. Undated, but written January 13, 1763 (see Collinson to Bartram, June 15, 1763); the first part is missing.
2. Lewis Evans.

From COLLINSON

Londn: February 23s 1763

I am greatly rejoiced to read in thine of the 31st of October of thy safe return from thy delightful Journey from the Terrestrial Paradise for such it must be that could raise such Ecstasies of Joy at viewing those Charming Scenes enriched with such Elegant productions — I long to see a sketch of thy Journal.

The Pyramid of Eden must be a glorious sight in full flower   Linnaeus makes it a Swertia — is the next Genus to the Gentians and differs from them by having beautifull nectariums consisting of Little tufts of small hairs in the hollow of Each Petal   Docr Garden calls it the Glory of the Blue Mountains   I hope we shall have seed of it that Gordon may raise it.

Wee now begin to grow Impatient for to hear of the Ship that brings the Seeds for us   notice is taken in thine of the 31st Octor. which is the Last I have received

I delivered thy letter into Doctor Shippen's hands   I admire he should delay giving it to thee   It is very unpolite to keep a Letter Two or Three months by him, it is not Gentleman Like to treat thee in this Manner   My Letter was dated May the 12th   December 10th wrote a long letter by Pacquet.

I inclose Docr Witts Letter which may be some Entertainment as thou knows the Man.

I am thy sincere frd

P Collinson

I thank thy wife for her kind Intelligence of our Frd Franklins arrival. I hope Thou hast gott the Book &c that I sent by Him — give my Love to Him & that of our Family   Wee are all well   I shall be Glad to hear of his Sons Safe Arrival

Thy Obligeing Letter of Augt:29 relateing to the Great Skelletons I Answered fully

If the small Alagator caught at Pittsburgh has a remarkable flatt proboscis — then it is the animal I published in the Magazine.

a complete skin of that animal would be a Great & a New Curiosity to all Naturalists   Look back to the Magazine, & thou will find what I say about it, I fancy 3 yrs agon.

BP 3:40; D. 246–47.

From COLLINSON

Lond March 11:1763

Being much engaged, I mist the last Paquet but by the Sally Cap Patrick of Philad — I thanked my Dear John for the Acceptable Letter that gave Mee advice of his safe Return from the Garden of Eden —

Since then I have suffered Much Concern for the Carolina Capt Friend, being Taken by the Spaniards & Carried into Belboa — but as she was taken 11 or 12 days after the Treaty was signed — she has been Claimed & I hear this Day she will be Delivered — I presume all our seed boxes are on board — but as is Customary all Letters were thrown over board — so shall be at a great Loss to find things — So pray write by very first & send to our friend Al Colden Postmaster at New York to go by first Mail from thence which sails every Month.

I am in a hurry of business   thine

P. Collinson

BP 3:42; D. 247.

From CLAYTON

March 16, 1763

Dear worthy Friend

I have been in great expectation, a long tedious time of having the satisfaction of receiving a letter from you, but alas! my wishes and expectation have hitherto been quite disappointed, and if it was not for my correspondence with Mr. Collinson and now and then meeting persons from Philadelphia I should be totally in the dark as to your being still in the land of the living.

I have wrote to you several times, since I received your entertaining, agreeable letter and the last I sent, was (I think) by one Mr. Adcock, who, I am informed lives in your City and is in partnership with one Mr. John Peyton, an elderly man and I have great reason to believe that that letter, with several sorts of seed inclosed, got safe to your hands.

I hear by common fame that you have made some excursions in quest of vegetables, as far as the Lakes Michigan and Superior, and should be highly delighted with some few sketches, or an epitome of your travels and discoveries in the vegetable kingdom. I had much rather have it from you, than at second hand from our friend Collinson who is generally, upon such a topic, too concise. I should, in particular, be very glad to know if you saw anything of the Canada Bonduc, or Nickertree, and if you brought any of the seed home with you. I should esteem it a great favour to be admitted to participate with you in that, or any other curious seed, where your stock is sufficient.

This comes by a gentleman of Philadelphia, Mr. Willing[1] who, I understand, sets off from Colo Byrd's the beginning of next month & who, I dare say, will take particular care of any letter or parcel you shall please to send me, and forward it (in case he should not return soon to Virginia) by a safe, careful hand, to Colo Byrd, whom I have the honour to be well acquainted with, and without vanity, esteem him one of my friends.

I wish you and all your family, health and prosperity; and am, dear Sir,

Your sincere, affectionate friend, and humble servant,
John Clayton

BP 3:3; D. 410.
1. Thomas Willing, William Byrd's brother-in-law.

From COLLINSON

London, April 7th, 1763

I am exceedingly engaged in business for your world, yet, as I know, it must be very satisfactory to hear that thy boxes arrived, and delivered the 6th, though late, it's better than never, and that all Louisiana is yielded to us by an honourable peace. I hope my dear John will recover his spirits and be no longer in melancholy mood. He sees a good peace can be made without his worthy Pitt, who deserted the helm to become a pensioner, with £3000 per annum, and his wife made a lady. So he is now known by the name of Grand Pensioner, — a blast on his reputation that will last forever.

Now, my dear John, does not the ardour of curiosity burn in thy mind to explore the wonders of Louisiana?

I joyfully received thine of December 3d, by the hands of Friend Fisher, but I have not yet got the turtle, &c., and the seeds. I hope there is some of the Pyramids of Eden

* * *

Last warm summer ripened our pears. I never had such good seed before. They are of the most delicious sorts; so either thee or thine may hope for choice fruits. They come late, but soak them a night in water, that will plump them, and they'll soon vegetate.

Pray my love to B. Franklin. I received his kind letter, but cannot write more than that I am thine,

P. Collinson

D. 247–48.

To DANIEL SOLANDER

April ye 26th 1763

Dear doctor Solander
I received thy kind & agreeable letter of february ye 10th 1762 & A number of curious pamphlets which I wish had been in English, for Latin is too hard for me — I was so hurried last year in travailing that I had not time to answer thy letter to my desire, but desired our worthy friend Peter to return my respects & shew thee ye specimens I colected in ye Carolinas & new virginia which I sent last fall   I have a glorious sight of curious plants from ye carolina & Alegany mountain seeds coming up which in time may furnish my friend with variety of specimens & I have ingaged to go with Colonel Bouquet down ye Ohio to ye Misisipi when peace is proclaimed & he hath perticular orders where to go & what to do for which he is in daily expectation so that at present it is uncertain whether he will set out or return but I shall not like to be at new Orleans or Mobile in ye latter part of summer when fevers is dangerous   if I should perform this Journey & providence grant me A safe return in health I hope to make fine discoveries in this wilderness countrey   as ye Colonel will take time to do his business well, so I shall have time to make ful discovery of what comes in my way. we have had A Cold constant winter & late spring but I have known it much colder   we have had one days hail that congealed into such A mass of ice that it bore both man & horse to walk upon & people skated alonge ye road or open fields as on ye rivers   ye efect it had on vegitables I shall relate as I observed it   ye bay & double pomegranate that used to be killed every winter to ye ground tho covered with boards & leaves is Now green even those branches that was exposed to ye full cold   so was ye English broom   ye scotch stood it both winters   ye gorse that used to be killed close to ye ground is now ready to bloom but I covered it all over with earth in ye fall but A native holly that stood two winters in my garden unhurt is now dead as far as to where ye snow covered it yet one from So Carolina set in A cool shady corner is green which with ye long leaved pine is all thair trees that will hold thair leaves green all winter   all thair bays   evergreen oaks   padus   yelow leafe   yapon magnolia & dahoon holy not onely casts thair leaves but ye tops of ye branches perisheth allmost to ye root but[1] most of ye trees or shrubs that cast thair leaves anually there will bear our frosts tolerably well   the Bignonia foliis conjugatis ran up ye northeast corner of my house last summer 20 foot high, ye leaves & vines of which is now very green but one at ye south west end is bare of leaves though ye vine is green   ye Carolina mirtles several sorts all growing near ye coast, keeps thair leaves green all winter but I think shed them in ye spring, when young leaves put forth: thay cast them in ye winter with me altho I have one sort from Jersey that keeps them on till summer   the whitled tree & fartleberry keeps thair leaves on all winter near ye coast but in ye midle settlements thay cast thair leaves in winter so thay do with me   the Basteria, or sweet wood, was exposed to ye severity of last winter yet I find not one bud hurt

but ye bignonia, or yelow Jasmine being an evergreen is hurt tho under shelter   ye Melia that I left out is wholy killed   ye Alcea is killed root and branch

BP 1:59:1, 1:58:3; D. 430–31.
1. From this point the letter is taken from BP 1:58:3.

To COLLINSON

May ye first 1763

Few days past with great Joy I received thy agreeable letter of december 10th 1762 & three days after another dated february ye 23 1763   I was realy afraid my dear friend was dead but I next thought surely his son would have let me know before now: my lobloly bay tho growed prodigiously in ye summer is intirely killed last winter tho in A warm place   it is in vain for us to expect to have ye broad leaved evergreens of Carolina to flourish in ye winter unless in A green house   I have at last got ye evergreen Andromeda & A great allcea from Mis Logan with ye olive & many others   I have but one root of ye tipitiwitchet   it bears our winter   is strong this spring   I sent thee twice of its leaves last fall by fisher   I sent both flower & leafe with A noble colection of Carolina specimens   this day I dug up ye pomogranate & planted it close by ye wall to be killed down to ye ground every sharp winter as ye rest have done for 20 year: ye root that gordon sent me for ye Persian Cyclamin is now in full flower   milk white & very different from ye beautiful persian   its strange that he should take so much pains to send such A large Cargo of plants & shrubs so difficult to live & yet will not send me A few of his best bulbous roots for I have thousands of ye common sorts that may be sent alive to ye utmost parts of ye earth with onely nailing up in A dry box   two of ye portigall Padua flourishes in ye greenhouse but ye other tho under cover of leaves & boards is kiled root & branch but ye Carolina ye tops & leaves. I sent ye turtle I got at ye Ohio last fall by fisher that thay call an Alegator   I take to be as much A water lizard but I believe a new genus   very odd   mouth like A cat fish & tail like A musk rat with A fin round it   nails like A man with A membrane on each side reaching from ye fore to ye hind foot like A flying squiril   I take our wild Cat to be A links in every respect   like A cat but A short tail   Kalm tould me it is like thairs   our Panther is in most respects A cat except its magnitude   in york government thay call it A tiger   thay have all ye actions of A cat   thay spring up A tree & upon thair prey like a Cat   have A head whisker short ears & long tail & sparkling eyes in ye night like A Cat   ye young ones I have stroaked will purr & meaow like a Cat   thay are very scarce   I never had a fair sight of an ould one   thay soon spring out of sight   thay are ye color of a dear   3 foot high 5 long   thair tail 3 foot long   I am wholy of ye opinion that ye Ohio Bones is ye remains of A creature unknown there is no likelyhood of ye Rinoceros its as difficult to account for thair comeing there as ye Elephant & ye bones as much too large for one as ye other but if I should go there & have A proper opertunity to observe them I believe I should want A many bones to make up an intire skeleton notwithstanding ye rash superficial reports of those incurious persons that hath been there: if I be at home in ye fall intend to send thee ye roots mentioned or my son John may send them he knows how to suply my place thine of February I hope my pyramid may differ from Lineus swertia ye doctor brought me ye letter of May 12 last fall I have near finished my Journal to Carolina but I have no opertunity to send it if I should go with Col Bouquet down ye Ohio & return in health next fall perhaps I may send it but it will very much differ from ye voluminous Journals into Asia & ye tour of Europe first it opens to your view ye works of God in nature 2d it discribes ye virgin nature & products of A countrey never before discribed after that manner & not stuffed with antique ruins & thair different methods of government which have been near as well discribed as ye historical part related by numbers of different authors long before: we have many accounts from ye different parts of europ of ye severe cold of last winter nay even from rome & yet dear Peter mentions not a silable how it fared with his garden I have now five fritilaries in bloom two double ones is coming out which is A great curiosity thay increase prodigiously I should be glad of other varieties

BP 1:59:2; D. 248–49.

From COLLINSON

Londn May 10: 1763

I have pleasure upon Pleasure beyond Measure with Peruseing my Dear Johns Letters of October 31 with the Rare Plants in Eden — which I answered 23 of feby then I have to thank Thee for thine Decemr. 3d & January 6th my last to thee was Aprill 7th by Pacquet giveing an account of the Arrival of the Seeds after a Vissit to Spain But for want of thy Usuall Care & Exactness or perhaps left to some Careless person to pack up one of the Boxes had but Eight Sorts of Seeds for 104 according to thy Catalogue — hapyly & Luckkyly this fell into Gordons Hands — Had it fell in to any one Elce, I should have been ashamed & Confounded for my Honour lay at Stake for I assured every One there was in the Boxes Seeds according to the Catalogue — Gordon had 3 Boxes to go Abroad & is terribly afraid least any of them should be so packed up — when a Box fails so Egregiously of the Catalogue — the full price cannot be Expected So pray tell Mee how I must Setile that Point — and now I don't know what to Do or Say, for nobody has given Mee yett any Order for Seeds — as I have Left writeing by Ship I hope by next Pacquet I may be more Certain

But very possibly before this Comes to hand Thou may have taken so Tempting a Journey   I Long to be with thee — It gives Mee much Comfort to think Thou will travel so Comodiously & so Safely — & what is beyond all that thy Eyes will see those Wonders of Wonders those Monstrous Skeletons — I need Say nothing to thee   thy Curiosity & thy Instincts will Dictate to thee [illegible] will be in Every Respect, the things to be desired — if a Horn could be procured & Sent Over — I am afraid a hoof cannot be come at or Elce that would be a principal Article to Settle what Tribe they belong too — I hope the Noble Colo. has some body in his Train that can Draw & I know thy Exactness in Measuring – How rich will Natural Knowledge be by your Means — Good Providence has reserved thee for this Great Work

Here is Just published Two Authentic Historys of Florida in Neat Pocket Vols — I wish they may Come time Enough by Capt Friend for Thee to take with thee as there is much information in them

It is really very Wonderfull, that as thy rambles was amongst the Wasts, Wilds, & unfrequented Countrys that no more Wild Animals was seen from whence then Comes that vast quantity & Great Variety of Skins Of Animals that I have this year Seen in Our publick Sales   What does thou Think of 2 or 3 Thousand Raccoon Skins — where do they hide themselves that thou didst not see One

as thou formerly Obliged Mee with the Natural History of your Panther I will in my Turn Oblige thee (Setting in my Elbow Chair) with Its Dimensions, from a very fine perfect Skin Lately Given to Mee —

	foot		Inches	
From the tip of the Nose to the Anus	5	:	4	Long
His Tail with a Black Tip	2	:	6	Long
Length of its fore feet	1	:	–	
Length of its hind feet	1	:	3	
Over the Shoulder from Toe to Toe	4	:	–	
Over the Rump & back from Toe to Toe	3	:	8	
Breadth of ye Skin over the belly	2	:	3	

Difficulty in Measuring a Dry'd Skin So Allowance Must be made   thou has Seen this Animal, but by what I can Judge from its Skin it is too Long & Slender for its Height which att Most cannot exceed two feet   as it is Sharp snouted, like a Wolf or Fox, it Differs in that External Mark from all the Tribe of Panthers, Leopard, Ounces[1] & Tigers which have all Catts Faces & are all spotted except the Last which is Streaked – it Seems a Species by its Self but comes Nearest to the Lynx of Assia which is all one Colour Like yours — but has a Catish Face — the Lynx of Europe is partly plain & spotted Like your wild Catt which is a True Lynx in all Characters   I have had a fine skin given Mee so can give thee the pticulars   Ye panther is found in the Brazils & is there Called the Cougar — the French call it the Red Tiger

I forgot to Mention the Box of plants Came Safe & Well & are all Growing — I gave Gordon 2 Roots of the Myrica & kept One for I much wanted It — for what I formerly had by Degrees went off — I tryd this on a Different Soil   pray send More   I can only now Acknowledge thy peice of Natural History of the Countries thou has passed through and the Mapp anext is both Entertaining & Informing

Yesterday I saw at my Neighr Ponthieus the Warneria or Yellow Root in flower, it is Singular to have no Petals   mine don't appear this year So pray Look out for Mee against Next — the Seeds are Sown   I hope Wee shall Raise the pyramid of Eden — it must be a Strikeing beauty – I am very much Obliged for the Ohio Turtle, it is a Singular Shell   Thy Mountain Magnolia is a Glorious Tree   will this year be a Pyramid of Flowers — & my Umbrella is near flowering   those Two Come in the spring — the Laurel Leafed & small Magnolia are Summer & Autumn flowering with us — I have had Two fine Bonduc Trees sent Mee from Paris — very Likely on this expedition thou will find them & the rare sort of Hickery — My Short Leaved Saracena is going into flower   the Long Leaved is Strong so I may hope to see It — the Striped One must be a Rarity — that fine Toxicodendron shot Out & Flowered finely

Think my Dear John with what Amazement & Delight I with Docr Solander surveyd the Quire of Specimens — He thinks near Half are New Genuss   this will Enrich the Fountain of Knowledge — The Docr is very Busie examining them — I hope soon to send thee a List of them — but they Laye so Remote their Seeds cannot be Expected from them   but what surprises us Most is the Tipitiwitchet Sensative   it is quite a new Species & New Genus, it was impossible to Comprehend It from any Description made Mee very Impatient to See It   I wish Wee had Good Seed   I doubt not but Gordon will raise It but so many Seeds Loose their Vegitation Comeing over that few are raised (notwithstanding all His Skill) in Consideration of the Infinite Quantity of Seeds that Wee have received from thee in Thirty years Passt   thee would be Delighted to see his Mixture of Moulds   Heats of even Temperature, Shades & Shelters, by these Means He has attained a regular Method of Raiseing all the Species of Calmia, Azaleas, &c   a few Days agon I see them Coming up as thick as Grass & yett the Small Magnolia a more Likelier Seed to Come up Eludes His skill which He Concluded is from the Seed spending its Self before it Comes to his Hands   yett He keeps Trying on but I will try thy Patience no Longer than to Assure Thee I am

thy Sincere Friend
P Collinson

BP 3:41; D. 249–50.
1. Any of various moderate-size wildcats (as the ocelot or lynx).

To COLLINSON

May ye 30 1763

Dear Peter
My garden now makes A glorious appearance   I have A fine anonis with A large spike of blew flowers in full bloom which I gathered in Potemack 3 years ago   whether that from Pittsburgh will prove ye same I cant yet say I expect next year that will bloom & ye 3 curious sorts I gathered last fall in eden is daly comming up with numerous other kinds from that inchanting place: my great carolina saracena is in full bloom & my wife tooke one to town yesterday which was much admired   it is a glorious odd flower   A goldish color & striped   my dwarf ones from Wateree grows finely   so doth my Aple haw & tree of life from Eden   ye last from seed   ye shrubs all perished   my sons lately sent me A box of plants from cape fear but I cant yet get ye sorrel tree which with ye lycium is what I still want   ye last I can give Mrs. Logan direction where to find it   she will pass thro fire or water to get any curiosity for mee alltho our personal acquaintance was but A few minits & with much company   my europian & scarlet horse chesnut is in full bloom & five of ye new river ones grows finely & is very different from ye other   A stately tree: ye deponthus sent me ye finest & rarest collection of plants that I believe ever was sent to America   100 different sorts but most of them perished before thay cam to my hands except ye hedge hog hollys hepaticas 3 kinds of ruscus, orpine double saponaria & some bulbous roots   of ye roots thee sent me two years past I had one tulip flower A pale yellow & ye common double dafodil after long expectation of something curious   ye attamasco lilly is now in flower & ye spoted leaved asarum & bignonia with two leaves   it run near 30 foot up A stone piller last year

BP 1:59:4.

From COLLINSON

London June 8 1763

My Dear John
I am in high Delight   my two Mountain Magnolias are Pyramids of Flowers — almost the Extremity of Every Branch is a flower   My Short & Long Leafed Saracena Growing Close together are both in Flower & make a Charming Contrast   the One Red the other a Golden Hue   Well mightest thou say, how fine they looked to see a Number together
   I have yett only Orders for

   2 Boxes for Mr. Bush single boxes
   2 Boxes for Gordon   Double
   4 Boxes Send at Venter for to dispose off

1 Box for Fern   He Desires ½ doz Ears of Large Indian Corn
I hear Nothing from Powell or Edie

I received thy acceptable Letters of April 24th and May 1st — My good John makes no allowance for one or Two Packets that was taken   thinks Enemies, Wind & tide should obey His wishes — I never had thy Letter with the Leaves of Tipitiwichet yett I never Complain & think my Dear Friend Dead & Buried — Sad news comes Fast enough & therefore I always think the best
Thy Bill I was pleased [to] See   it is Acceptable & will be paid —
I rarely ever write by Ships So thou should not expect Letters by them I Chuse the Packet because of Its certainty & I rarely Miss One   this packet takes the Mail the 18th   Capt Friend in the Carolina will not sale before the End of this Month or beginning of Next   By Her comes A box of Books   Some for thee consign'd to our Frd Franklin   if I have time may write more Largely by Her — if not by next packet   Bushes Seed must be all Forest Trees   I cannot get Solander who has thy list to settle the Names of the last specimens for I want to send them to thee
Gordon has raised the fine periploca from the Ohio, it is growing in my Garden
Pray Look where *grows nearest* some Azaleas, Kalmias, & Rhododendrons for my son in law who has Lately bought a fine Estate & Built a noble House & made Extensive plantations & is quite Cracked after plants — Has plundered my Garden all he can & looks with such Longing Eye on what remains, that unless thou sends Mee a Box of those plants to keep all Quiet for my own son is so ardent to keep what I have that I shall have something to do to Manage my Two Sons   they are so fond of plants & take such care in planting in proper soil & situation it gives Mee Much Entertainment to see their Ingenuity and Emulation but my son Cater deserves Encouragement — for when He married my Daughter — about 10 years agon, He scarcely knew an Apple tree from an Oak but by seeing often my Garden & Conversing with Mee & His Bro — is now resolved if He Can to rival Us — in his new fresh soil plants thrive finely   I wish thou may pick out what I mean being much Engaged, can add no more but that I am thy sincere
Frd P. Collinson

BP 3:43; D. 250–51.

From WILLIAM BORTHWICK

Edinburgh 8th June 1763

Mr. John Bartram
Sir
I have Engaged the bearer hereof Robert King to Serve Captain McPherson of your place as Gardiner and in case I should want some Tree

Seeds he'll put you on the Best way of geting your money. He is very Sober Clever lad, if you can be of any Service to him I hope you'll do it

I am Sir

Your most Humble Servt
Will: Borthwick

BP 1:91.

From COLLINSON

June 15: 1763

I now come to Thank my Kind Friend John for His Two Boxes of growing plants & Letter of Decem 13th & 18th which came in fine order — the grafted apples finely rooted — & the Cions fresh — I gave some to Gordon — every thing is carefully planted —

What pleased Mee much when I opend the Box to see the Skunk Weed in full flower — and the rough Leafed Pyrola showed its tufts of pretty white Flowers — which I never saw before — the papayas are fine young plants I wish they may take — the roots did not Look very promising haveing a very Dry blackish Look — phaps that is the Nature of them — they was planted in a Deep rich Soil which I know they Love — the Red Bud Andromeda's look well   the Evergreen one Thou Sent Mee Some years agon is now going into flower — I think now my Dear John thou has amply Furnished Mee — I only Want some good flowering plants of the Ivy or Kalmia   I have only one plant that stands It — and I Love more then one string to my Bow — and a Sod or two of Striped Pyrola — this pretty plant stands & flowers & then goes off but Orchis's Lady Slippers, & Martagons Wee can Never have to Many — I heartyly wish thou had brought some roots of that pretty fern found in Virginia by the Specimens to P. Millar   it is the same sent Mee Some years agon by Docr Mitchel   it throve so wonderfully but by an accident I lost It — I wish to have it again or any other New Fern, for it is a very pretty Tribe of plants and a Root or Two of Vitis Idea with red flesh coloured Fruite and if happens on a Root or Two of Genseng

Our Friend Gordon would Gladly Gratifie our Friend Bartram with a Box of Growing plants — but unless there is a pson on Board that would Water & Tend em in so Long a Voyage as Ships are Sailing to you It is plants & Labour thrown away — & then if any came Alive to you it would be an improper time to transplant them — Butt yett if Wee live to the Fall Wee intend to try our Luck by some of our Last ships — but I shall remind Gordon of some Hyacinths &c to be sent sooner —

I lately received thy Entertaining Letter January 13th — I wish the Iris may prove a new Species for its a favourite Tribe & a great Variety   I shall be pleased to hear those Iris's I sent prosper in perticular the Calcedonean Iris —

I am obliged to thee for So well Describing the Strange Heifer — No doubt Nature Intended Twins but failed in her operation — The use I make of Monstrous Births — Is, when I reflect that so very Wonderfull a Work wrought in So Secret a Manner should so seldom miss of produceing a perfect Being, Demonstrates the Power & Wisdome of the Great Creator, in the original Plan of Generation that it continues the same through all her Creatures to this Day

as the Laurel Berries came in a good time certainly some will grow   they come up here free enough but I can tell thee our Friend Clayton has a fine Laurel that he raised from seed I sent him about five years agon

I doubt not but the Anemonies will flower if they survive your Cold — do as Wee do: take them up after flowering when the leaves turn yellow — Wash them in Water & then Lay them out to Dry in an airy place out of the Sun — untill they are Dry as the Roots I sent thee   then Lay in a Box in a Dry place & then plant early in the Spring after your severest Frosts are over   In our Climate & in my Garden they keep flowering all the Winter long — especially those with single flowers —

Capt Lowrey has Delivered Mee thy Journal which gives us much Entertainmt —

Thy Cape Fear Expedition must have been very Entertaining, Governor Dobbs is my perticular Friend   a very Worthy Good Man & of great abilities

Webb the Seeds man received the Box & has paid Mee —

a pticular Account of the flowering of Trees will be entertaining — but they are Earlier or Later as the Seasons happen — this year Wee are at least a fortnight or Three Weeks Later then some years, from a Cold Winter our River was near Frozen over — When this Happens it is call'd a severe Frost but that I dont remember above four Times in my Lifetime — and yett many of your shrubs did not Loose their Leaves as Candleberry Myrtle Itea Dogwood, & one Species of Oak, — Is it possible to gett a Sodd of the Charming Red flowering Heleborine that Billey has so finely painted

I have orders for Eleven Boxes of Seeds for Fern, Webb, Powell & Williamson & others, add five more for I hope to find Chaps for them Now my Dear John Farewell

P. Collinson

My great Cacalia makes a fine appearance

If thou happens near where the Water Lillie or faba Egyptica grows in the Jerseys gett some Seeds & putt in a pint bottle of Water corked up for Wee have Mind to try to Raise it.[1]

pray tell Mee what I must do about the plundered Box & that Box with only 8 Sorts of Seeds in It — for they expect Some Allowance as they both had not a Sortment of Seeds agreeable to the Catalogue that thou Inclosed to Mee

In my former Letters by last Pacquet I gave thee an account how the Ship Escaped from the Spaniards   one Box was open'd & plundered & another Box unopen'd had but Eight Sorts of Seeds, in It — How that Happened I don't know   it was well it fell into Gordons Hands but He was greatly Disappointed — for It had not a Sortment to Supply His Customers & had many of these Sorts Left on his Hands —

I would not for any Consideration that Box had fell into private Hands, who I told was above 100 Sorts of Seeds — & finding but Eight I should have Lost my Credit & been so confounded that I know not what Excuse I could Make   pray take Care for the Future & be Exact & putt in catalogues into Every Box for some was wanting   this makes Mee trouble to Coppy & the Tallies with the Numbers so small they could not be found, which made Mee have 2 or 3 Letters to answer about them   Mind always to send Mee a Catalogue because if by Accident one is not putt in the Box, I can Supply It as I did in the Last Boxes

BP 3:33, 3:44.
1. To this point the letter is taken from BP 3:33, the remainder from BP 3:44.

From HENRY de PONTHIEU

London June the 20th 1763

Mr John Bartram
Sir

I have received your favour of the 26 of April   I am sorry the large parcel of plants I sent you came to hand in such bad condition   It has not been for want of care here, for It was kept in a friends Garden by the waterside till the Ship was ready to sail   How she came to be so very long in her passage is what I cant account for. I hope another time I shall be more lucky, I shall observe yr directions & send you a parcel of curious seeds & plants but should be glad that you would first send me back the list of what was in ye basket passing a line over what you have already that I may send nothing but what will prove acceptable   I thank you for ye plants you intend me. The Mountain & Umbrella Magnolias I have not, Nor the Loblolly Bay. But I have good plants of the Dahoon Holly, Laurel leav'd Magnolia, Sweet Bay, & purple berried Bay so that you need not send them   I should be glad of another Sod of ye fine Grassy plant that I had, being killed likewise the Great & Lesser Sarracena Evergreen tough twigg'd Viburnum, ye Ladies Slipper or Calceolus Marina or any new Seed or plant   also the Chincapin & some evergreen Prinos

I am, Sir

Your very humble Serv't
Henry de Ponthieu

If you should want a recommendation to Montreal I could give you a very good one   Perhaps your curiosity may lead you there   I have many rare plants from the Alps of wch I shall send you seeds.

BP 3:97.

From COLLINSON

June 28:1763

My Dear John's Letters are out of My hands, Haveing Sent them to Gordon to Read —

This only serves Just to acquaint him that His Letter with the 100 £ Bill is come to hand & is Acceptable & will be paid

Edward Cross Seedsman in Fleet Street — Desires a Single Box of seeds & a Box of Plants — Inclosed is his Order[1]

Thine
P. Collinson

pray remember a Box Azaleas, Calmias, & Rhododendrons to keep Peace in my Family   some sods of odd plants for my self &c & a few Gale esplini folia grass leaved plants &c

Boxes Seeds for next year
  2 Boxes for Gordon
  2 for Bush   Most Forrest Trees
  1 Box for Fern, few heads of Indian Corn
  1 Box for Cross
  4 Boxes for private sale   put in Catalogs   I have yett no orders for one

I hear nothing from Powell or Eddie   I writt by last Pacquet   By this Vessell Capt Friend In a Box to B Franklin is Books for thee   My Rhododendrons make a Glorious Show 24 Blossoms   A sod or two of Variegated Leaved Pyrola   it is hard to keep   think how Wee can do It

2 Bush[2]	3 other
2 Gordon	1 major ord
1 Fern	1 Calega
1 Cross	3 Clark
4 Collinson	3 [illegible]
1 Borthwick	2 [illegible]
1 Web	1 Bush
2 eddie	

BP 3:45; American Philosophical Society Library, Wildman transcript.
1. Wildman noted in his copy: "this order was not preserved."
2. The following list was added to the page by Bartram.

From COLLINSON

                                                        Londn: June 30: 1763

I am glad my Dear John I can Send thee Our Friend Solanders Catalogue of the Last Curious Collection of Specimens — there Is wonderfull things Amongst them Especially the Sensitive & Empetrum &c   Others marked with a Cross, but these are not to be Expected   they Lay so remote — but as Its Specimens they Enrich our Knowledge & anticipate our Treasures and Give us a Good Idea of the Riches there is in Store to attract the Botanists of after Ages   O, Botany Delightfullest of all Sciences   there is no End of thy Gratifications — All Botanists will Joyn with Mee in thanking my Dear John for his unwearied Pains to Gratifie every Inquisitive Genius — I have sent Linnaeus a Specimen & one Leafe of Tipitiwitchet-Sensitive — Only to Him, would I spare Such a Jewel — pray Send More Specimens   I am afraid Wee can never Raise It — Linnaeus will be In raptures at the Sight of It — How happens it in thy Journal that thou did not give a Sketch or Mapp of the Rivers, Wateree & Congaree, names I never heard off   these Rivers do they Joyn before they come to the Sea

Yesterday I putt in a Short Letter Inclosed in our frd B:Franklins to Informe the of Some Books for thee in a Box by Capt Friend Directed to B:Franklin   My Two Mountain Magnolias have flowered finely   I Dare Say the first in England that have flowered, but are different in the Colour of the flower from that figured by Catesby in his Supplement

thine
P. Collinson

pray dear John a Good pcell of Locust or Accacia Seed out of the Podds to Value of a Guinea to Prague in Germany   it is to be sown and time to time Cutt down to Feed their Cattle Summer months, for all the Country is burnt Except by Rivers — they are in great Distress to find food for those months for the Cows &c in the upland Country

It is something Singular & I dare Saye the first attempt of the kind but the Mud Turtle had clamberd up a whole pair of Stairs out of my Hall into the next floor. Led by what Instinct I don't know, but there was no water upstairs   There is no End to Creative Power & Infinite Wisdom in the Creation & formation of such Variety of Creatures — the Ohio Turtle I view with Astonishment   I hope by the Means of the Good Colo one may be Caught more Mature where the parts are more perfectly Formed — a few Weeks agon Wee Caught the Great Mud Turtle thou formerly Sent Us — It is much grown & so fierce Wee was much Diverted with It — After some days Wee will putt him again in his Watery Habitation

BP 3:46; D. 251.

From SOLANDER

London, July the 1st, 1763

Sir: —

Mr. Haeggblad, that delivers this letter, is a Swedish clergyman, that proposes to stay among you for some time. He is a lover of Natural Philosophy, and goes now into a country so well known to you, that nobody's friendship can be to more advantage to him than yours. I therefore will make myself so free, and beg the favour that you will give him how he best may employ the hours he can spend in collecting plants, insects, and other curiosities.

How much I have been delighted in looking over the specimens you last sent to Mr. Collinson, I shall tell you in a letter that I intend to write next week. At the same time, our mutual friend, Mr. Collinson, likewise proposes to send you a letter.

Just now, at present, I am so hurried, that I have no more time than only to recommend the above-mentioned clergyman to your friendship, and to assure you that I always with great regard, remain,

Your most affectionate and sincere friend,
Daniel C. Solander

D.432.

From COLLINSON

Londn:Aug:4:1763

I had the pleasure of My Dear Johns Letter of May 30th which was sensibly abated by the severe Disorder Thou hast to Encounter with — I shall be glad to Hear thou hast got the Victory — at the same Time it raises in my Mind Thankfullness for a Long Series of Health, without any such Calamities or Indeed any other —

My garden like thine, makes a Glorious appearance with fine Long spiked Purple Anonis with the allspice of Carolina Abundantly in flower, spreading its perfumes abroad, the Delectable Red flowering Accacia, the roots of two species of [illegible] & Back Red [illegible] flower, my laurel leafed Magnolia with its noble Blossoms which will continue for two months or More — the great Rhododen has been Glorious beyond Expression   before I told thee of the Mountain Magnolia and the surpriseing flowers of the red & yellow Sarracenia   Thus my Dear John thou sees I am not much behind thee in a fine Show but when thy Eden plants flower I shall not be able to bear the report of them —

But what Delights me Is to hear that our Horse Chesnutt has flowered but I think it much excells the Virginia if the spikes of flowers are as Large with you as with us — To see a Long avenue of them at Hampton Court of Trees 50 feet High being perfect Pyramids of Flowers from top to bottome for all the spikes of flowers are at the Extremities — is one of the grandest & most Charming Sights in the World   Thou doth not Mention the Colour of the New River Horse Chesnutt flower — Wee have Two Species the one Red the other White Flowers — could not a Leafe & flower be sent in a specimen that I may see the New River Sort

My Dear John what art thou Talking of   Wait 2 years for the Double White Daffodil — Think Man & know how to Value so great a Rarity, for I waited almost all my Lifetime for to get this Rare flower, I Read of It & Seen It figur'd in Books, but despaired of ever Possessing It — Butt about seven years agon Happening in a Tour forty Miles from London my Botanic Genius carried Mee into a Garden where I expected to find Nothing — on a Sudden my Eyes was ravished with the Sight of this flower & my Heart leaped for Joy — that I should find it at last — and never saw it since in any Garden but my own and I tell thee for thy Comfort — If thou had not been John Bartram, thou hadst not Possessed such a Rarity — but as thou grudgest the Time & so Little Esteems It I shall be Carefull where I cast my pearls another Time

[The next paragraph is illegible].

Consider my Dear John what a pleasure I feel now I can give thee an Order for a Tenn guinea Box for young Lord Petre   Little did I think when I gave thee the first like Order for his Valuable Father, in the year 1735 or 1736 that I should Live to give the Like for his Son   It may be Truly said the Spirit of Elijah rests on Elisha for he began this year with a Box of thy seeds —

I am Delighted with thy Desertation on the Good Old Doctor — it is very much the Idea I had formed of him from the numerous Letters of a Long Correspondence which has given Mee much Entertainment   when He tells of the fascinating power of Some women over Men & of the effects a fatal Consequence of the Penetrating Look of an evil eye from Some Women — but as thou has summed up his Character, upon the whole I believe He Meant Well, Did what good he could, & Lived up to the Convictions of his own Mind — so I hope will Meet with a suitable Reward —

May we persevere in the Path of Verity & uprightness that our End may be happy is the sincere Desire of thy real Friend

P. Collinson

I wrote by last Packet which is made up Every second Saturday in the Month [illegible] Account of Bill I had Paid   thy Bill of £ 100 — when thou writes by the Pacquet always Inclose thy Letter to Alexander Colden P M at New York & then He putts it in his private Letters & franks it to Mee or Else Every Letter by the Packet costs a Shilling as Did thy List — this Hint the'll not forget —

Lord Petre Desires his 10 Guinea Box may Contain all Sorts of Forest Trees — in particular all kinds of Oaks Black & White that is all species & including Beech   a few Pines only the Three Leafed [illegible]

package of Two Boxes — for 110 sorts as by thy Catalogue there was but 10 or 12 Sorts in Each Box — to one I was an Eye Witness — the other went to Germany — who have writt a very angry Letter — and will have to be indimnified for the Dificiency which I think is but realistick this is a very odd affair & will ruin our business.

pray Tell Mee what adjustment. [Several lines partially illegible.]

Be sure Send Mee a Guineas's worth of Common Accacia seed Taken out of the Podds to go to Prague

Boxes for Next Year

2 Boxes for Gordon
2 Single Boxes for Bush   Most Forest Trees of all Sorts
1 Single Box for Bush of all Sorts
1 Box for Fern & a dozn Ears of Indian Corn
1 Box single Box for Cross seedman & box plants
1 Double Box for Lord Petres   most all sorts Forest Trees
<u>4</u> Single Boxes for my self to Dispose off
12

3 Boxes of all sorts of Seeds for Separate people to Lett Each contain Excellent Variety of Sorts & putt in List of them Consigned to Lord Kildare in Dublin —

What is the Probable Methode to Establish a Last Peace with the Indians Phaps in my former Letters I have been perticular for Bushes Boxes — they must be all Single Boxes for Him

BP 3:47; D. 251–53.

To COLLINSON

August ye 8th 1763

Dear Peter
I have this week received my dear peters letter of may by ye packet which at first sight made my heart allmost leap for Joy but when I read *but for want of care & exactness* or perhaps left to some careless *person to pack up one of ye Boxes had but 8 sorts* of seeds instead of 104 this knocked me down at once but considering this was not ye 1st or 2d or third time that I have been rashly censored & reproached when I have hazarded life & limb both my own & children using my utmost endeavour to oblige my correspondents I revived again   surely you must think I am A careless fool When I know from long experience that ye least neglect will heap coals of fire upon my head: but by ye method I take its impossible to make such A mistake   I make up ye Boxes ready before I begin to pack   then I set one half in my room where I pack them & mark those which is for perticular persons then I divide my seeds in two parts then measures or numbers each box its

share with its number which is entered in ye catalogue as thay are put in I assist in every box & trust no living creature but my two sons which is very carefull   I dayly searcheth every box while thay are packing & placeth every list & lid to every box & marks them myself   helps to load every one & sees thair shiped but I cant watch them all along after until thay come to your hands nor keep them from being rifeled neither on board ye ship nor after thay are landed: my leg is healed up fine but it was A rebellious ulcer ye Colonel was much concerned about it   so was ye doctor lest it should have hindered my Journey down ye Missipia which thay said would be A national loss but Alas we are all disappointed   ye doctor could not cure my leg but (God be praised) after some simple applications it got well: but ye good Colonel instead of going to ye Misisipia is in great peril of his life in leading A few regiments with amunition & provisions to relieve fort Pitt which is surrounded with Mercyless Savages which seems determined to cut us off or drive us into ye sea! I went to Carolina in ye right time   I cant tell when ye Indians can be trusted again   not before thay are soundly banged!   I am much afraid our ministry will send orders to make A pretended peace with them which will be exposing our boasted Conquered country to ruin so far from Louisiana being ours that we cant keep our ould narrow strip of land   I am glad you have those specimens I colected in carolina   ye seeds of most I sowed & many is come up of several sorts that I did not send specimens of by reason of thair largeness or decay but notwithstanding my care in colecting bringing hom & directly sowing of them many of ye rare sorts is not come up (but those that I was indiferent whether thay come up or not are in plenty) tho we had A very moist cool spring & summer but for A month past but little rain   perhaps next year some others may come up   there is not yet ye 20 part that I sowed   I was in hopes ye evergreen shrub of eden was come but it proved to be ye evergreen from ye mine on new river which I am not displeased at as now its imposible to obtain it but that in eden may be had at great expence   my monstrous broad leaved Sylphium from new virginia is in flower   ye stalk is 10 foot long & produced 60 on one & that from ye ohio is 8 foot   thay make a grand apearance producing near A 100 flowers on A stalk but that from Pedee 12 foot long is not come up tho I sowed much seed but I cant find one of ye Alegany mountain plant whose leaves resemble convalaria but is A new Genus   great quantity I gathered ye two last years & sowed them directly as plump & Jucy as on ye mountain: yet not one comes up   we wonder so many fails with you   I have two kinds of Rudbekia with leopards bane leafe & peach colored petals   one from virginia with narrow long petals ye other with broad but shorter petals ye disk of A lovely changeable purple & gold Color   this dont grow quite so high as ye other   I like it better   I brought another from new river which is lately come up which if differs from ye other two as much as thay from one another I shall be pleased   thy italian strawberry is now in blosom & ripe fruite & ye pineaple grows finely   these I am proud of as I think I am ye onely Proprietor of them in ye country   I have had for many years what is

The Indians talk with Colonel Bouquet. (Philadelphia) *North American*, December 20, 1908.

called ye hoby but thay are all rogues & bears no fruite if I had some good seed & it produced honest ones I would endeavour to keep them so ye iron colored digitalis is realy A comical flower but that in millers figures & ye canary one I want ye pear pipins I steeped & sowed directly I have two from thy seed sent two years past that is grown 18 inches high ye Racoons generaly hides in ye day & rangeth in ye night for food when ye hunters catcheth them   sometimes thay stir in ye day as happened A little before we ascended ye south mountain   ye hunters dogs barked at 2 or 3 which had climbed up a high tree A distance from ye road   ye hunters turned out of ye path to shoot them & I kept along ye path looking for plants   thay shot them for sport & left thair karkases   but I cant understand why thy Panther skin having a sharp nose like A wolf had not it been stretched out   all I have seen or heard of hath A head & mouth like A cat which it in every part resembles onely in magnitude   thee wrote for double Boxes for Gordon powel & fern but A double box being so heavy & cumbersome to every one that hath ye handling of them so I thought to send ye seeds that should have been packed in A large one in two single ones so I put ye seeds of ye greatest quantity & bulk in one box & bags & lesse quantities in ye other & ye catalogue answered ye numbers of both   so I did those for fern & others & never heard A silable of complaint & I am sure gordon had as large A share if not larger then any other of ye articles mentioned in ye list espetialy of ye rarer sorts & must I be answerable for his actions after he received his full complement & was no way acquainted with his desighn   I thought thay was for himself & then it was better for him to have ye same quantity of seeds in larger or in one parcel then in smaller & in two   if he had gave me any notice of his desighn I would have divided ye seeds & ye numbers in every box should have answered its respectif list   I have often reflected on ye great advantage ye wild beasts both ye cat & dog kinds have above us that have near one half of our time involved in darkness unless we are at ye expence of artifitial light   what is it that illuminated them in ye night even in ye darkness yet thay seems to see as well as in ye day   its what we call light falling upon ye object that makes it visible to us but what makes it visable to them   have they A perticular light in thair eyes that reflects upon ye object   if it be so from whence doth it proceed   is it ye production of ye animal or is it an emanation from some other being   we can see ye eyes of A cat in ye darkest situation when she is much disturbed so I observed A Polecat in ye night   I could se his eye very plain tho it was too dark to see his body & our hunters say that thay can see ye eye of A panther A great distance in A dark night & ye people of Surinam say thair tigers eye shines in ye night

BP 1:59:63.

From COLLINSON

London, August 23d, 1763

I Received my Dear Johns Letter of July 3d. Assure Him his Complaint is not founded on my Neglect for I have writt Long Letters by Every Pacquet & by the Caroline I sent Him Books &c —
I am Concerned for the fatal Effects of the Rising of the Indians but the

Instructions that are gone over I hope will bring them again into Friendship —

But my Dear John I am sorry to say Thou art of that unhappy Cast of Mind there is no pleasing —

Look into Pitt's Peace & see what a pitty full figure Wee should have Made when he adopted Montcalm's Boundary for our Colonies   as Pitt did it & accepted it and made it, the foundations of his peace — it was glorious

pray Look back & see what slaughter & Destruction the Indians Made (when Pitts, British Glory was Lost in Germany) on the Back settlements of Carolina but every Thing the Turn Coat did was Glorious with my Dear John — He Heard all their Crueltys but did not then open his Lips to Complain —whilst He was sacrificing thousands of the best British heroes to his projects on the Coast of France, to gratifie his Vanity but all was glorious

My Dear John take heart and don't be Carried away with reports   Revive thy drooping spirits & Look forward & hope for the best

I have thy Charming blue Campanella in flower — six foot high branches on Every side   pray where was the Identical spot it was found & the Red or Purple Ulmaria has flowered: a sweet pretty thing & quite new [illegible] pray how is the ulcer — that affects Mee with true sympathy   I hope it is better as no Mention is made of it   Glorious Pitt, so presides in my Dear Johns mind   he is insensible to Complaints, except on the *Sorry Peace* that hath given so great an Empire to Britain

I am cordially thine,

P. Collinson

I have a respect for Mr Pitt & he has his Merrits, but every Thing he did was not glorious — tho my friend john thinks So

Wee had a Long Dry Spring which is succeeded by a short Wett summer   Farm [should] harvest a great plenty if the weather favours to gett in

BP 3:48; D. 253.

From GORDON

London August 28 1763

No 1   2 Martagons pompong
    2   2 double Martagons
    3   2 white Martagons
    4   6 white persian Cyclamens
    5   6 late starry hyacinths
    6   6 Early do
    7   1 Corona Regalis
    8   2 Yellow alpine Gentians

The Corona Regalis & the persian Cyclamens are Green House plants

Sir —

I have sent by Captain Budden the Philadelphis packet the above in a Box, which I hope that you will receive safe. I am under obligation to you for several Seeds given to me by my good Friend Mr. Peter Collinson

I am with much Esteem

Your Obedient Serv't
James Gordon

BP 4:32.

To COLLINSON

September ye 30th 1763

Dear Peter

my garden now makes A glorious appearance of A number of odd flowers & plants   I have 4 kind of Sylphiums in flower   one from ye Ohio new virginia   1 Ould virginia & one from ye Congaree   ye last seldom grows above 2 or 3 foot high but whether that monstrous tall one from ye branches of Pedee is come up am not sure   there is many plants grows finely that I am allmost in hope may be them but ye leaves is too long for thair breadth perhaps next year thay may be broader   A full grown one is near two foot broad   it is remarkable that not one species of this fine genus should grow naturaly to ye northeast of Maryland but from thence so [south] west such great variety of species   I have now from last colection in full bloom two odd kinds of sun flowers   A lovely Coreopsis   broad leaved Comelina with 3 petals   A curious Clitoria & tetragonotheca & one odd genus going to flower & a curious yellow Aster which I dispaired of haveing ripe seed when I gathered it yet near A dozen of curious sorts of seeds that seemed full ripe is not yet come up   another remarkable instance is that I have now travailed near 30 year throw our Provinces & in some 20 times in ye same provinces & yet never as I remember once found one single species in all ye after times that I did not observe in my first Journey through ye same province but many times I found that plant ye first that I nor any person could find after which plants I suppose was distroyed by ye cattle   I never found one person that ever found one new plant after I had been there that I did not observe   ye first time I crosed ye Shenando I saw one or two plants or rather stalk & seed of ye Meadia on its bank   I jumped off got ye seed & brought it home   sent part to thee & part I sowed my self both which succeeded & if I had not gone to that spot perhaps it had been wholly lost to ye world   John clayton asked me where I found it   I discribed ye very spot to him but he nor any person from him could find it after   O what A noble discovery I could have made on ye banks of ye Ohio & misisipi if I had gone down & ye indians had been peaceable inclined as I knowed many plants that growed on its No East branches but we are at present all disapointed   my son William wanted to go as draughtsman

I read lately in our news paper of A noble & absolutely necessary scheme that was proposed in england if it was practicable that was to search all ye countrey of Canada & Louisiana for all natural productions convenient scituations for manufactories & different soils minerals & vegitables ye last of which I dare take upon my self as I know more of North American plants then any others but this would alarm ye Indians to the highest degree   all ye discoverers would be exposed to greatest Savage cruelty ye gun tomahawk torture or revengeful devouring Jaws   before this scheme can be executed ye Indians must be subdued or drove above 1000 mile back   No treaty will make discoverer safe; many years past in our most peaceable times far beyond our mountains as I was walking in A path with an indian guide hired for two dollars an Indian man met me & pulled off my hat in a great pashion & chewed it all round   I suppose to shew me that thay would eat me if I came in that countrey again   I steped up to him & twisted it out of his hands & ran after him [illegible] 100 yards before [illegible] I admire thee should not know the Congaree and Wateree, seeing thay are in all the late maps of South Carolina both being branches of the great Santee River.

BP 1:56:1; D. 254–55.

From THOMAS ORD

Woolwich October 10th 1763

Sir

Since my arrival in England from North America, a Friend of mine has desired I would write for some of the newest, and last found out, Plants and seeds, of flowering Shrubs, and any thing that is curious in your way: I therefore desire You will be pleased to send over by the first Conveyances, at different Times, Six five-Pound-Boxes, or, three Ten Pound Boxes, in as compleat a manner as you possibly Can, with an Account of the Nature of the Soil they grow upon, and any other Necessary remarks that you may think proper; causing them to be carefully pack'd up, and well secured from the Injurys of the Weather; amongst the rest I would have you send the Azalea with red flowers, the Azalea with white Flowers, the Magnolia with annual large Leaves commonly call'd the Umbrella Tree, the Magnolia with annual Leaves with a Blew Flower, Gale, or Candle Berry Mirtle with Fern Leaves, the Kalmia, or Dwarf Laurel with a Sinus Leaf, call'd in America the Ivy Tree, Kalmia with a narrower Leafe, Prinos with evergreen Leaves, Acacia dwarf with Scarlet Flowers, the Soft Shell'd Nut from Canada, or the Ilinoise Country, if You can get them, or any thing else from that large Field; I likewise desire You will be pleased to let us taste of your modern Fruit, by putting up some Cuttings of the Spitsenberg Aples, and New Town Pippin — And You will be pleased to direct all these Boxes for Edwin Lascelles Esqr to be left with Lascelles Clark and Dalins Merchts. in Philpot Lane London, and with every Box you will please to Send an Invoice of the Contents, and at the same time that You send the last Box, you may draw upon Messrs. Lascelles Clerke and Dalin for the Amount not exceeding thirty Pounds Sterling, which they have Orders to pay You, on Acct. of Edwin Lascelles Esqr. and on the receipt of this, I shall be glad to hear from You, I desire you will be pleased to make my best Compliments to Mr. and Mrs. Samuel Miflin,[1] and to Mr. Giles Miridith[2] and Family, I am Sir

Your most Obedient Humble Servant
Thomas Ord
Lieutt. Colonel of the Royal Regiment
of Artillery at Woolwich in Kent

Mr. Bartram Master Gardener[3]
at Philadelphia in the Province of
Pensilvania North America
One Box Value £ 5 5 Guineas sterl.
For B. Hammet in London
to Care of Mr. Philip Boneret

Mr. Hammet, begs Mr. Bartram will send the same sort of things among the rest that Coll. Ord has mentioned & begs Mr. Bartram will favor him with a letter telling him what soil suits best, what time they blow & with any other directtions — Slip of Newtown Pipping   One Box of flowering Shrubs that grow quick & Show — for a guinea   April the first, the Apricot in bloom[4]

PC	I	for Edy	1 W	John Webb
PC	II	for Edy	G	Galliger
PC	III	F for Fern	WB for William Borthwik	
PC	IIII	B for bush	A IIII for allen	
PC	V	B for bush	R for Ralf	
PC	VI	G for Gordon	B for Benez	
PC	VII	G for Gordon	W for ward	
PC	Viii	P for Peters		
PC	IX	P for Peters		
PC	X	C for Cross		
PC	XI	for self		
PC	XII	for self		

BP 4:93.
1. Members of a prominent Philadelphia family.
2. Unidentified.
3. The following order was enclosed in Ord's letter.
4. Bartram made the following notes on the envelope.

To COLLINSON

october ye 23d 1763

Dear Peter
last night I received thy kind letter of august ye 4th, 1763   ye ulcer in my right leg is finely healed up, but I have A much worse in my left occationed by A cut to or into my shin bone which is now much exasperated by travailing two Journeys   one to little Eg harbour   ye other to great with my John to shew him ye very spot where growed A pretty ornithogalum I saw growing 3 years past but now not one is to be found   I saw it ye first time I ever went to eg harbour   I planted it in my garden but it went off in a year or two I believe for want of moisture sufitient   I have been ye subject of many misfortunes all my lifetime but as many has had worse & many better then I so I praise our God in leading me about ye middle way   your hors chesnut is realy A noble flower   what ye new river kind is I cant say haveing never seen it   If I had known ye white double dafodil had been such A rarity with the I could have sent thee large quantities 30 years ago   our first settlers brought them with them & thay multiply so that thousands is thrown away thay rarely perfect thair flowers with us   thay send forth A stalk A foot long with ye appearance of A fine large flower but not one in A hundred opens but rots or disolves to A slime   but last spring one or two of mine did perfect its large sweet flower which I compaired with thine   ye tree of life or Eden is N 6 you say it is like Empetrum one of ye finest evergreens I ever saw of ye shrub kind   I thought it had come up but it proved to be another pretty evergreen humble shrub you call illecebrum   I am heartily glad that young Lord Petre is posesed of ye Botanical genius of his father   I wish he may in vertue too I have intended to have inquired after him & his mother in every last letter ye pear raised from her seed hath bore here A number of ye finest relished fruite that I think A better is not in ye world & intend next spring to graft several of them   perhaps it may make ye tree retain its fruite better til thay are full ripe which is its onely defect that above half its fruite drops before thay are anyway fit for use & not A quarter stays on till thay are full ripe which is about ye begining to ye midle of october   I am much pleased that my disertation on ye doctors Character gives my dear friend delight & that by my expresing some words several times thee tooke my meaning as I intended it as for instance in saying he had as much practice as most & doing as much good as most my meaning is that in general that fewer had more practice then he had   to those that had less or that had better success &c so when I speak of distance in time means messurement or quantity when I say near it I mean between ¾ & ye whole mentioned   I dont remember sending any letter by ye packet but thro Coldens hands except one through Mistris Franklins hands & she promised to frank it   however I take thy hint kindly as it should be allowed between good correspondents   as for ye complaints about ye boxes I have answered them several times   ye plundered box I cant Judge ye value of it but I make no doubt of thy doing me Justice   as for Gordons he had one of ye best if not ye very best in ye whole cargo as to goodness & quantity &

makeing no doubt thay was all for himself so I sent them after ye best maner I thought possible   he ought to have examined them himself before he sent them   I have often sent seed of ye evergreen mountain hypericum   its one of ye pretiest flowering evergreens of no America   that prety fern I gathered on a rock near Monogahala   I did not see one ever since about 30 years ago I saw some growing on a rock toward Susquehana but I have searched that place many times since but cant find one   I have answered thy letter by Captain friend   I am glad ye 100 bill is paid   I hope to get some seed of ye locust but very few bears & thay are very brittle & dangerous climbing

ye most probable & only method to establish A lasting peace with ye barbarous Indians is to bang them stoutly & make them sensible that we are men whom thay for many years despised as women   untill then, it is onely throwing away men blood & treasure to make peace with them   thay will not keep to any treaty of peace   thay all are with thair fathers, ye french, resolved to drive ye english out of north America & altho some nations pretend to be neutral or friends it is onely with A desighn to supply ye rest with amunition to murder us   perhaps now & onely now is ye critical time offered to Britain to secure not onely her ould possessions But her so much Boasted new acquisitions by sending us suffitient supplies to repel effectually those barbarous savages

BP 1:58:4; D. 255–56.

From JOHN HOPE

Edinburgh, 4th November, 1763.

Sir: —

The great reputation which you have justly acquired, by many faithful and accurate observations, and that most extraordinary thirst of knowledge which has distinguished you, makes me extremely desirous of your correspondence.

If you will be so kind as send me a few seeds of your new discovered plants, I shall on my part make a return of whatever is in my power, that I shall judge agreeable to you.

It will be agreeable to you to hear that Mr. Samuel Bard, son of your friend Mr. Bard, of New York, is making most wonderful progress in Botany, and has made beautiful collection of near four hundred Scots plants; by which he undoubtedly will gain the annual premium.

I am, sir, with very great regard,

Your most obedient servant,
John Hope,
Professor of Medicine and Botany,
in University of Edinburgh

D. 432–33.

To COLLINSON

November ye 11th, 1763 by friend

Dear worthy Peter

I have received my dear friends letter of august 23d, 1763   I think most of our people here looks upon all our boasted acquisitions in north america to be titular & that onely of short duration as ye French still claims all one side of ye misisipi & part of our side. thay will draw ye chief of ye fur trade near them & will allway be setting ye indians against us   suppose we do keep possession of ye Lakes but unless we bang ye indians stoutly & make them fear us, thay will never love us nor keep peace long with us   thay are now got so cunning thay will not sell thair land & stand so to thair bargain as to let ye people live quietly upon it but when thay want goods it is but rob ye traders steal horses plunder & insult ye back inhabitants & instead of calling them to account for thair mischief we sue to them for peace & give them great presents to kill no more white people for 3 or 4 years   by such proceedings thay have us in ye greatest contempt believing thay may do us all ye mischief thay please & we are ready at any time to buy A peace with them for A few years under great insults   I am glad thee art pleased with my favorites   ye branched Campanela & purple ulmaria I found them both in plenty between Potomock & James river between ye South & north mountain — quite so westward towards Holstons River but how A single root could be found in James Alexanders swamp by Skulkil I cant say unless some bird shed its seed there in its dung   my leg got well of that troublesom ulcer but ye other is as bad or worse by A cut into ye bone about two months past & cant say whether its yet on ye mending hand   I have shiped on Captain friend two boxes for thee   N 1 PC is A present from my son John for thy son in law containing several laurels   2 sweet bays   red azalea   A fine autumnal gentian   calceolus   St. Johns shrub   orchis palmed striped pyrola   vitis idea   its fruite as large as cherries   convolvulus   several little roots: in Box PC II great chamero   white azalea   red bud   andromeda   shrub hypericum   lobloly bay   martagons & yelow root in A woolen bag   grassy plant   laurels   solomons seal   blew berrid cristopher   A curious Cynoglosum   sod of arbutus   you may divide ye spoil between you   there may be some plants & articles in thy sons Box that may better suite thee & some in thine that may better suite him   we planted them as thay best fitted ye Boxes but I admire how thee mised ye yellow root & rose   ye yellow root was large   had grown several years in my garden ye onely one   I had dug it up & planted it directly in thy box & I sent no other plants last year so there could be no mistake   I sent by friend now one box to web & another to de ponthieu in return for ye finest colection but thay most or all ye curious ones miscaried but I am much pleased with gordons present of bulbous roots   thay came in fine order & are most if not all such as much wanted   that which he sent me for ye persian lilly A year or two past is A charming sweet flower milk white produced abundance of flowers last spring [illegible] shooting up of flower buds but I have I hope A wonderful curiosity from South Carolina [A] species of autumnal gentian but not bitter   Mis Logan sent it last spring & its now near flowering if cold weather dont stop it   its above a foot high two branches from one root   ye flower bud is one inch & half long tending toward A purple & seems plaited at ye top as if it would open wide but it is yet not near perfected   tho we have had a dozen severe frosts & frose hard yet plant & flower is as fresh as in June in ye most open exposure   if ye flower is as fine as I expect it I should despise 5 guineas for it poor as I am as it seems very easy to raise   I have another species of ye same genus I think from No Carolina but it grows eighteen inches high sending out side branches crowned with flowers on thair sumits which seem not to be so large as ye other but ye multiplicity of flowers perhaps will render it equally valuable as it seems as hardy   Oh my dear worthy friend ye variety of plants & flowers in our So western continent is beyond expresion   is not it dear Peter ye very palace garden of ould Madam flora   Oh if I could but spend 6 months on ye Ohio misisipia & florida in health I believe I could find more curiosities then ye English french & spaniards have done in 6 score years but ye indians instigated by ye french wil not let us look at so much as A plant or tree in this great british empire   I have ingaged Captain Buden to take my seeds

BP 1:58:3; D. 256.

From LAMBOLL

South Carolina, Chas:Town, Novr:11th:1763

Dear Friend Bartram

Since my last of the 8th instant per Captain Mayson, he told me he should not Sail before Saturday: so I have got one other Flour Barrel, filled for you with Potatoes, mostly what are called Brimstone: and another Box with some young Loblolly-Bays, one Senna Bush & the Shrub you desired in Earth. As to the barrel of China Oranges, in haste I mention'd, about Twenty Four dozen: but should have said Twenty Seven dozen. All are directed for you, as before observed: Freight paid: and I wish they get well to your hands, and prove Acceptable   Docr: Garden is in a very dangerous and Critical State, with an Abcess in his Lungs, and intends to leave this Province soon, for his health. I remain, with Compliments, Your real Friend to serve,

Thomas Lamboll

P.S. The Capts: Receipt is herein inclosed.

BP 4:61; D. 436; American Philosophical Society Library, Wildman transcript.

From COLLINSON

> Ridgeway House
> Dec:6:1763

I am here retir'd all alone, from the Bustle & hurry of the Town Meditateing on the Comforts I enjoy; and whilst the old Log is Burning the fire of friendship is blazeing — warms my Imagination with reflecting on the variety of Incidents that hath attended our long and agreeable Correspondence

[The next four paragraphs are illegible.]

My dear John, thou does not consider the law of right, and doing to others as we would be done unto.

We, every manner of way, trick, cheat, and abuse these Indians with impunity. They were notoriously jockeyed and cheated out of their land in your province, by a man's walking a tract of ground in one day, that was to be purchased of them.

Your Governor promised the Indians if they would not join the French, that when the war was over, our troops should withdraw from Pittsburg. They sent to claim his promise, but were shuffled off. They resented it, as that fortress was situated on their hunting country.

I could fill this letter with our arbitrary proceedings, all the colonies through; with our arbitrary, illegal taking their lands from them, making them drunk, and cheating them of their property. As their merciless, barbarous method of revenge and resentment are so well known, our people should be more careful how they provoke them.

Lett a person of Power come & take 5 or 10 Acres of my Friend Johns Land from Him & give him half price, or no price for It — How Easy & resigned He would be & tamely submitt to such useage: — but if an Indian resents it, in his way, Instead of Doing Him Justice & makeing Peace with Him, nothing but Fire & Fagot will do with my Friend John — He Does not search into the bottom of these Insurrections, They are smothered up because Wee are the Agressors, But see my two proposals in the Oct Gentn's Magazine for a peace with the Indians

My Dear John I am glad thou art so happily recovered from that Cruel Complaint & that our Good Colonel escaped those Terrible Fellows   I hope such prudent Measures will be Taken as will putt a stop to their Ravages & Establish a Lasting peace —

The Peace thou art so merry with in your Mock Mourning is only glorious by comparison   I mean by comparing It with that Peace that Pitt would have made (But Thanks to our enemies could not). Then you must have been Thankful to Him & the French that they would allow you to keep your old narrow strip of Land — but now your Bounds are so extensively enlarged — how ungrateful how unthankful you are forever grumbling, never pleased. I refer thee to the Preliminary of Pitts Peace & Butes — Facts speak Louder than Faction   Wee all know here what Pitts Peace would have been and what Butes is

So much for a touch of Politicks   Now we change the Scene to something that Pleases us both   I can tell thee Gordon has raised the fine stately broad-leafed Silphium, but thou mentions three fine species from New Virginia by the Ohio & from Pedee River but which of them ours is I don't know but thy specimens will set us right.   I often reflect with what a numerous train of yellow flowers your Continent abounds, Seeds of the two fine Red Petal Rudbeckias will be very acceptable   I have one many years in my Garden but then it never ripened seed —

What a glorious scene is opened in that rich Country About Pensacola if that despised Country is worthy thy Visitation — but Because Pitt did not gett It thou canst not venter there on any Pretense, All beyond the Carolinas is forbided Ground, They are none of thy Darling Pitts Acquisition but thy son John may go with a good Grace. I am glad to find the Spirit of Elijah rests upon him — Thou Cheers my heart & flatters my Hopes with thy kind & Freindly Donations but Wee are under all the disadvantages to show our Gratitude — a run of Cross accidents always attends our Cargo & I never could contrive any Ways to prevent it unless a Person skilled in those Matters could attend upon them & make it his delight to nurse them Dayly —

I lament with thee the Disappointment of so promising an Expedition on the Ohio — take Heart   other Doors may Open to gratifie thy Inquisitive Genius

I was Delighted to see the Tipitiwichet Sensitive   I instantly sent it to Gordon for his skill Exceeds all others in raising seeds   pray where is poor Will & Moses   as for John I find he is our right hand Man   How happy is it to have children of so agreeable a Cast   I speak it feelingly by my own son.

I hope what I have writt will be read with Candour   Our long friendship will allow us to rally one another & Crack a joke without offence as none was intennded by

Thy sincere friend,
P. Collinson[1]

Doctor Solander gives his service; he is obliged to thee for remembering him. Our Crops of Wheat was Good but our Harvest Bad yett it turns out better than was Expected   Such as it is very great has been the Demand from Abroad   Some weeks nine or Ten thousand Quarters hath been Shipped off   What great Providence it is as Well as Advantage (for all is paid in ready money) when Wee can Help our neighbours without prejudice to our Selves   Wheat is now 4:6 a Bushel   If this great Call had not happen'd its Likely it would have been at 3:6   this would have been hard for the Farmers to pay rents at so low a price

This wheat Trade brings great Sums into England almost may be said to be Clear Gains.

The first paragraph in my Proposals is shamefully printed, — by omissions is made unintelligible,   No remedy but patience; though it vexes me to the heart to have it read as my genuine copy; for it is impossible for me to tell the printer's carelessness   nothing of the redoubled Boxes that thee mentioned — pray what is it is in them, who has those Boxes — for that is no expense to them for their Difficiencys — so they will be Considered and as [illegible] brought all their Loss — by thy actions the paccage [illegible] at our Order — So it Lays at thy Door —

BP 3:49; D. 257–59; American Philosophical Society Library, Wildman transcript.
1. From this point the letter was taken from Wildman; the original is now mostly illegible.

From MARTHA LOGAN

1763[1]

Sr
    I have the Pleasure of yrs 9th of November & hartly Congratulate yr Safe return to yr family which I hope you found well. I am much Obligd for the Enclosed Seeds & Promised Roots, which will be quite Exceptable   I heare with Send you A Box, which Contains the Under written Plants & in the Earth Several Roots (without Tops) of wilde roses of Diffring kinds which Hope will be Such as you'ld like being the best I could gett. allso in same Case is a tin Can of Seeds a fue Young Stockgilly flowers which weire [ripe] at the Critical time in Septr, to Stripe them, & begg yould set [them] out at Some time in March in order to see if they will [bloom] with you for they Never faile with me.
    I am Very Sorry tis not in my Power to send you any Seeds of the Ice plant   it died Last Summer with Out Seeding, but will Endeaviour to Gett Some for you. the Seeds of Mrs. Bees flowers are moste all fallen before I Received yrs so have sent you a very fue of them, but will Remember it another year   I have Sent a large Sod of the Shrub you see beyond the quarter house & also 4 young Evergreen which I hope is the Paudus you mentioned in yr last. it is Called with us Oliander a Very Pritty flowring Shrub. Likewise 2 Slips of Olive as I Could not gett them with Roots, & we frequently have these grow with us. Shoulde they faile I make no Doubt the Nutts I Send will Supply you as they are of the Last Summers Growth & weire well Rippned, — the Spung tree is a Native of Jamaca & will not bear much Colde but is a Delightful Sweet flowring Shrub & well worth a place [in a gr]een house. in the Same Case is 2 Loblolly bays & a fue roots of Mrs. [illegible] & hope they will Succeed with you   My best wishes attend & am Very Sincearly your friend & Humble Servnt

Martha Logan

PS   Wee have had Several Vessels from yr Port since I Received the above mentioned Letter from you, but have not had a line or the roots which makes me feare the French or Spanyards has Disappointed me of them. There is two Other Trees in the Case which is not a Evergreen but I think it a Pritty Shrub & the Lillyes, I make no doubt, will doe with great Ease for they grow wilde with us.

BP 4:77.
1. Probably December, because of the reference to November 9 in the first line.

From COLLINSON

London January 1 1764

I am very Thankfull to the Great Author of my Being that I enter the New year In perfect Good Health & Spirits — I hearty wish the Like comfortable Situation may Attend my Dear Friend & his Family

It was a pleasure to Mee to receive thine of the 30th Sepr but that Joy was alayed by the sad accident which I hope will not prove of bad Consequence —

I don't wonder your Autumn Gardens are So delightfull as your country more abounds with Stately fine flowers than in the spring

and Wee through thine & other friends' Benevolence have many of these Beauties in great perfection wch makes our Gardens Gay to the Depth of Winter & if mild the Autumn Flowers join the Spring, as they Do now

Gordon has been fortunate enough to raise one of the fine tall Silphiums with scaly heads and Wee hope some others that have not yet flower'd —

the broad Leaved Comelyna I take to be what was formerly Called John Tradescants Spider Wort — Wee have 3 Species

Thy Quick Discernment of Plants is a knack peculiar to thy self & is attained by the Long exercise of thy Faculties in that amusement — and is like the Hare finders with us — Some can't discover them if close under their feet — others see them at a great Distance

Indeed my Dear John I must congratulate thee on that Happy Discovery of my Favourite Meadia   It is really remarkable none should be found Since   I hear nothing More of that proposal thou Mentions but if there was any real Intention of carrying it into execution no one properer than thy self for Natural History & Botany — that the Indians would be alarm'd at our Sounding or Measuring — I don't wonder they should be Jealous of the Invasion of their property — Every Man is tenatious of his native Rights — & if you Invade their Rights, you must take the Consequences —

Lett those be well banged, I may say well Hanged that by their unjust proceedings provoked the Indians to Hostilities — knowing beforehand their Cruel resentments.

I am greatly pleased the long expected Horse Chesnutt has gratified thee with its beautifull flowers, I think it Exceeds an Hyacinth but to see a pyramid fifty foot high & every extreem bud a Blossom is beyond thy Imagination — but is one of the finest sights in the World — but pray tell

Mee if your Curious people have not had these fine trees long before, in your province   is none at yr proprietor's

I perceive what Thou calls the Double Sweet Daffodil — Wee call the Sweet White Narcis that indeed may be common but yett how could I know It. remove & part the Roots, every other year & they will blow strong & fine — but Lett them grow in great Numbers together — the Roots are weaken'd & rarely bring their flowers to perfection —

It has been thy Patience to Wait, but my pleasure to Hear of the Delitious Pear raised from Lady Petres Seed — but she Dear Good woman is gone to Rest — what I am persuaded will prevent its Droping its Fruits — if some Quinces was planted in the Lower part of thy Garden near the Spring & Graft them with the pear — it Melliorites the Fruit, & by long experience all our pears are grafted on Quince stocks & succeed better than on pear stocks with us

It is very strange I should not know the Broad Leafed Evergreen Hypericum   I hope a Root will come in the Next plants   if none is sent pray send Mee a good Specimen in the Autumn of next year that I may see It

John, Thou needest not be Glad the £100 bill is paid for I am not runing away — any bill thou Draws will be allways paid — if there is any Gladness in the Case — It is I, that am to be glad to Do It, so far as thine of Octr 23

In thine of Sept 30th is mentioned so many fine new flowers   be so good always to Send Specimens as Soon as conveniently can be for that will anticipate the pleasure I am to expect

It is with concern I hear of the Insurrection at Pittsburgh   in such a hurry I don't wonder the Curious things sufferd — the loss of the alegator is most to be regretted if it is an Alegator — which I much doubt, as these animals have never been found in such Cold Latitudes, but few in Nor Carolina & none ever heard of in Virginia —

There is Something very strange in the loss of the Yellow Root, I suffer no body to unpack those Cargoes   every particle of Earth goes through my Fingers & Missing It, I search it over & over again   its possible to rott by the Way but unlikely in So Short a passage —

It is a great comfort to the Poor Mariners & to Capt Friend & Passengers after so Terrible a Passage to find themselves Safe on English Ground — I have not yett gott the Boxes but they are Noble Cargoes — & will amply gratifie us all & Relieve thee from the Great Pains & Trouble & makeing so fine a Collection — I wish the Boxes of Seeds was Safe Here   I must Defer answering thy kind letter of the 11th 9ber being much engaged Packing goods for your Country — I meane Virginia & Maryland, — and am thy sincere friend

P Collinson

Pray hast thou got trees in thy garden of that odd kind of Hazel nut that was found in the forks of Schuylkill, beyond the Blue Mountains, of which there was plenty? It seems a different species from the Cuckolds nutt — which I take to be your Common Sort, but the Schuylkill Nutt is very diferent but could only find 4 Nutts & 2 was sent to Mee

I brought Friend Fisher to Day the 10 Janry 2 species of your Oakes Myrica & Myrtle with fine Green Leaves as in Summer because he scarcely could believe what thou formerly told Him my Fringe Tree has green leaves on it & Sarsifras is burstin out

Our Winter is Most uncommon I ever remember Warm, Mild, continued Rains & Wind no Frosts — this 10 January — plenty of Aconites, Hepaticas polyanthos Violets — Snow Drops & Crocus Anemonies all Winter if this may be called Winter —

the Country in many parts & in Wales great Numbers Sheep Drown'd — Wee Scarcely See the Suns Glorious face once a week but our fields green like aprill with young Lambs playing in them

BP 3:39; D. 159–60.

From LAMBOLL

Chas:Town, So:Carolina, Febry:20th:1764

Dear Friend Bartram

I am now to acknowledge the Receipt of your acceptable Letter of the 12th Decr. Last, p. Capt Dingie, with the Box of Plants, and Roots, &c and barrel of Apples & Pears, for all which Favours my self and wife return you and Mrs. Bartram our hearty thanks. It was Eleven days after the Vessel's Arrival here, before we heard of them, and yet the Contents of the Box was in the finest Order that could be imagined, and the Fruit much Sounder and better than might be expected — Out of the same Vessel and at the same time (vizt. the 21st Ultimate) I received the Letter, Box of Plants, and Packets of Seeds, you sent for Friend Wyly, which shall be all forwarded to him by first Oppertunity that offers for the Waterees; and you may depend on my best Endeavours to procure and send you some young Umbrella Trees, as soon as possible. We have had a Sharp, hard Winter hitherto; neither is it yet over, and it may be doubted whether Noarth's Brigantine has, or this Schooner will [,] get up to Philadelphia, so soon as hoped for. My Wife joins in Respects to your Self and Spouse; and I remain —
Your oblig'd Friend
Thos. Lamboll

P.S. I have lost the fine wte Broom Tree you saw in my Garden and have none of its' Seed.   T.L.

BP 4:62.

From CLAYTON

February 25, 1764

Dear Friend

I received your agreeable letters of the 16th of June & 3d of Decbr last about ten days ago and am really concerned to hear that my last letter went to you by the Post, for I fully intended and directed it to go by the favour of Mr. Willing, brother to Colonel Byrd's lady, who was at that time setting off for Philadelphia but the person I intrusted it with, instead of sending it to Westover (Coll. Byrd's seat upon the James River) put it into the Post office at Williamsburgh. The reading the account of your travels & the many curious & uncommon vegetables which you discovered in your long journey, gave me a vast deal of pleasure, & at the same time excited in me a longing to partake of the seeds or roots of such of 'em as are not too great favourites with you to be parted with. by your short description of the Evergreen shrub, growing over Colo Chiswell's lead mine, I conjecture it may perhaps be a species of the Taxus (English yew); for we have some of those trees more shrubby than the European kinds, growing in the western parts of what you call Old Virginia. Your new osteospermums, Silphiums & Chrysanthemums must certainly be delightful plants and flowering shrubs; at the same time, too, to have the conversation of my worthy friend in his garden. I sow always my Stavesacre seed in the autumn for if it is kept till spring, not one seed in a hundred will come up & those that do, make poor stunted plants, & flower so late that the frost kills 'em before the seed is perfected. I have not, at this time, any of the seed nor of the red Chelone, but will take care to save some of both this year, in order to be sent you by the first opportunity, or by the Post under cover as this goes, to Mr. Franklin. I should be very glad of a little seed of the Carolina Tipitiwitchet or Sensitive Plant, with a few directions as to the time of planting, and the soil it most delights in, &c. I dare say, my friend Mr. Franklin would be kind enough to frank a small parcel of seeds from you to him, who is your sincere and affectionate Friend,

John Clayton[1]

BP 3:4; D. 411.
1. The postscript of this letter is illegible.

To COLLINSON

March ye 4th 1764

Dear Peter
We have had A prety temperate winter after A severe early cold fall but much broken with rain & snow two of which was A foot deep but did not stay on ye ground long for we had several warm spells between several prety

smart frosts which hath done much damage to young plants by drawing them out of ye ground even those that was run 4 or 5 inches deep   my true correspondent, Mis Logan hath lately sent me two bulbous roots of what shee calls A white Iris which she had from Georgia, which I hope will be fine curiosity with several other seeds & roots   I received thy kind letter of November ye 11th 1763   our friend Benjamin sent it with Gerard Eliots[1] son who came to visit me   he is A good sort of A sensible gentleman   am glad to hear of thy health & wellfare & now my other leg is got well & I have ye great pleasure in praiseing our God when I go to bed & ye many times I awake in bed free from pain with great humility & thankfulness as I did before in resignation to him   I wish ye tipitiwitchet may do well with thee   ye seed was good & fresh   I doubt mine is drawn so often out of ye ground this winter that it will perish but if I can get it again I will endeavour to keep ye winters sun wholy from it   my John is A worthy sober industrious son & delights in plants but I doubt Will[iam] he will be ruined in Carolina   every thing goes wrong with him there   pray give my respects to ye worthy Dr solander   I hope you have examined ye specimens I sent by Captain Budden by whome I sent my cargo   I sent 3 boxes to Lord Kildare March ye 16th   we have had about A week could weather & snow & this night is as cold as most in ye winter   this evening our friend Benjamin sent mee thy kind letter of december ye 6th 1763 wherein thee writes Gordon is satisfied with ye package of ye Boxes & so well he may with above A double share of ye chiefest curious seeds at my loss: I think our Indians received A full value for that cheating walk & pretended to be fully satisfied with what thay received above ye first agreement & as for Pittsburgh they let ye french settle & build there then why may not ye English after thay had drove ye French out, keep possession of it & as ye Indians have committed such barbarous destruction on our people, we have more reason to destroy them & possess thair land then you have to keep Canada & must all our Provinces suffer A prodigious yearly expence & have thousands of our inocent people be barbarously murdered because some of our traders made them drunk to get A scin cheap or an irishman setles on A bit of thair land which thay will never make use of & if we must not settle any more land on any of ye branches of ye Misisipi: pray say no more about our great British empire while we must not be A farthing ye better for it   I should be exceedingly pleased if I could afford it, to make A thorough search not only at pensacola but ye coast of florida alabama, Georgia & ye banks of ye Misisipi   I make no difference who got it, if I could but travail safely in it   if you cant send plants to live in my garden bulbous roots & those that are large & succulent will do & most good seeds may do if sent early in spring or fall

    I acknowledge ye recept of every letter my worthy peter sent me so he might well know I received his orders for seeds contained therein   My dear friend I am so far from taking offence at thy familiar way of writeing that it gives me much pleasure   I received this winter A fine parcel of seeds of ye fine empetrum from ye wateree & sowed it directly   some in my greenhouse some in an east exposition & ye rest in A south one   we had as plentiful harvest last as most in this country but ye indian corn & buckwheat was much hurt with ye early frosts   Aples & pears more then ever

BP 1:60:2; D. 261–62.
1. Jared Eliot.

From COLLINSON

Londn: March 7th: 1764

My dear John,
Disafected, Ignorant People are always supposing Improbabilities, & putting worst Constructions on the best Intended schemes — so do not deserve further Notice

In thine of Augst the 6th: there was a Query why some Animals saw Clear in the night others not   Inclosed is my Frd Docr Parsons answer & I have added something

Is it reasonable to think the Indians will Love us after such a Cruel unprovoked slaughter at Lancaster &c   I hope the Authors will be made Examples of Justice

I congratulate thee on so Elegant a psent as the Charming Autumn Gentian — the specimen is fine, I was in hopes to send the Names of the Last Specimens — but I cannot get them from Solander but I hope to do it by next Conveyance

My Dear John Providence orders all things for the best — have patience & see how things will Turn   I don't d'spair of thy treading Paradisical Ground & returning loaded with spoils — nothing concerns Mee but that unlucky stroke on thy Legg

I have had 3 flowers on the Skunk Root which have made a pretty show for a month past, the Sheeps turd Viburnum is ready to burst in flower this answers thine of 9br the 11th   Mine of Jany 1 I hope is come to hand by Pacquett

I am thine sincerely,

P. Collinson

The Little Pacquett of Seeds was very Acceptable as they contain delightfull flowers — Save More   I hope Wee shall Raise the Red Obelescothecas — I have Two Roots already but I want more — they will not ripen Seed with us —

I before requested Specimens of all your Spring flowers — In March, April & May — that Grow wild in all manner of places for I am very Ignorant of these productions

the Capt hath very obligeingly Delivered the Accacia Seed   now the Difficulty is How to Gett it to Prague

pray how goes Moses — William was a very Ingenius Lad, but I am afraid made some Mistakes, that I hear nothing of him

Johnny seems now to be our sheet anchor, I hope He will Inherit his Father's virtues & at Leisure and suiteable opportunities, Make Nature his studies

pray how many Species of Solomons Seals hath thou Discovered — the Box leafed Lycium must be very Curious if it doth survive & will come under thy Documents

I will remember the watch by Friend Fisher mention'd in thine of 10br 17 — He Lodges within a few Doors of Mee & yett He is so taken up He has not yett found Leisure to spend an Evening   I have often asked Him but he has 2 or 3 Times Drank Tea   He is a pretty sensible Lad, will make a fine man when all His Ideas are Ripened of Men & Things

BP 3:50; D. 262–63.

Red Lyon Square
4th Jany 1764

Dear Friend[1]

Having Changed my Cloaths the day I received yrs which I think was the 20th Xbr or thereabout I could not devise where I had put yr Lett. till this very morning, I found it in the pocket of the Coat I now have on. I wish yu. many happy years and will now gratifye yu as my opin'n will allow: perhaps Others may fancy Some intrinsic light inherent in the Eyes of Cats, Dogs and Beasts of Prey, having for an Example the luminous property of the Flies that in the varying parts of the world, Shine in the night. But I think no probable Argum't for it can be drawn from this phenomenon because the luminous particles which emanate from this insect are made up of native *Phosphorus* placed by the Creator in it, thro' every part, which is only coexistent with the life of the Animal, for I have learn'd from Davis's Translation of the History of the Carribby Islands,[2] that their light is extinguished with their lives.

Now as to the power of Seeing in the dark in those animals mention'd, I am more inclined to think, that they see more clearly than we do, in the night, from their manner of Life. They lurk in dark places all, or most part, of the day: their Eyes are not fatigued as ours are by the glaring light of every day: and therefore they are habituated to profit of much less light, than we are, in disserning Objects.

If we consider the Structure of the Eyes of animals we see how curiously they are contrived for refracting the reflected rays from objects and painting them upon the Retina, and, except some very trifling differences in the form of their pupils, or such like, the principal fabric is the same in every animal, for optical principles must be the same everywhere.

I have often Seem'd to myself quite blind, in entering a darkened room, to visit the sick, but ten minutes or a quarter of an hour made me capable of Seeing every Object in the room, and what was profound darkness to me upon entering, was a Competent light, when the pupils came to be gradually dilated; and upon returning to the light my Eyes suffer a painful Stimulus til the proper contraction is settled again.

We might therefore remark that an absolute darkness is scarse to be found above ground; and as what appears like profound Obscurity to me or any other animal immediately after Strong light we see, in a little time becomes familiarly light enough for most purposes. We must also remark that the Rays of light which represent the Object to the perception must come to the Eye from the Object & not vice versa, in the act of Vision. I would say more regarding the inhabitants in some Northern Latitudes, where the light is very dull for several weeks together, but much concerning them may be deduced from the principles just mentioned; I may be mistaken in my Sentiments but Dr Peter, Humanum est errare, and so I am

with truth yr Sincere friend and Ser't
J Parsons

In anser to thy Query of aug ye 6 — The Eyes of Men & Animals have the same structure. Mankind from continual beholding the Glaring Light the Pupil of the Eye is so contracted they cannot see in the Dark. Wild Animals that sleep most part of the Day have the pupil of the Eye greatly enlarged to Collect the scattered particles of Light & by that means see so Well in the Dark.[3]

BP 4:95.
1. This letter from Parsons to Collinson was enclosed in Collinson's letter of March 7, 1764, to Bartram.
2. John Davies' translation of Charles de Rochefort's *Histoire Naturelle et Morale des Isles Antilles de l'Amerique* (Rotterdam, 1665) was published in English as *The History of the Caribby Islands* (London, 1666).
3. This last paragraph is a message to Bartram added by Collinson.

From SOLANDER

Busbridge
April the 17th 1764

Flora virginica p. 20; & I think is in North America called Swamp-Dogwood[1]

No. 24 Senecio canadensis. Linn Spec. plant. 2. p. 1219. 24

No. 25. Amsonia alternifolia; a new plant first mentioned by Clayton in his Manuscript Flora.[2] It is now in our curious gardens & flowers freely.

No. 26. Sophora caerulea, a plant that has been in the european gardens a good while but confounded by the Botanists with a species of Crotalaria.

No. 27. Scutellaria variegata, a plant not described by Linnaeus but mentioned by Dr. Gronovius in his flora virginia p. 92 under the name of Scutellaria foliis ovatis utrinque acutis, obtuse serratis

No. 28. is a very extraordinary kind of Delphinium without the Spur like nectariums. I wish you would try to send the Seeds, because I think one might by that find out if it is a monstrous variety come up by accident. There are hardly any of such accidental productions that can be multiplied by

Seeds; some few excepted, where none of the parts of the blossoms is intirely destroyed; but only alter'd[3]

No. 29. Aesculus Hippocastanum Linn. Spec. plant. 2. p. 488. n. 1.

No. 30. Aesculus Pavia. Linn. Spec. plant. 2. p. 488. n. 2.

No. 31. Aesculus media, not taken notice of by Dr. Linnaeus

No. 32. Serratula spicata. Linn. Spec. pl. 2. p. 1147, n. 11. Send the bottom leaves of this, & of No. 3, should be very agreable & seed of Both

No. 33. Salvia linifolia, a quite new & curious plant, not described before by any Botanists.

No. 34. Cleome dodecandra. Linn. Spec. plant. 2. p. 939. n. 7.

No. 35. is without flower & fruit, so it cannot be described, but accordingly to your observation seems to be a Memspermum.

No. 36. Seems to be Aster linifolius. Linn. Spec. plant. 2. p. 1228, n. 16 but for want of the bottom leaves cannot be determined for certain.

I am with great esteem Dear Sir

Your most humble servant
Daniel C. Solander

P.S. as soon as I come to town, I will have the pleasure of waiting on you with an other Letter

I[4] have Lately received from Govr. Dobbs plenty of Seed of the Tree of Life of Eden which I hope Gordon will Raise. I shall now be looking Sharp for to See the Tipitiwitchet. I am very Well but have not Leisure to add More but that I am thine P. Collinson, the Leontice or purple berried Christophoriana is come up – the pretty Double Mountain ranunculus is full flower, Martigons Just peep Aprill 21:1764 I expect the rest every Day — with Impatience —

To Mr. John Bartram at the Skullkyll Near Philadelphia
Mr. Franklin
Encld. under Cover and fordd. by ye humble Servt Alex Colden

BP 4:103.
1. Unnumbered by Solander.
2. Clayton, despairing of the appearance the new edition of *Flora Virginica* by Gronovius, had prepared a manuscript himself and sent it to Collinson in 1758, but it was never published.
3. Collinson added here: "can it not be increased by offsets from the Root in Spring."
4. Beginning here, the rest of this letter is a note added by Collinson.

From BORTHWICK

Edinburgh 19th April 1764

Mr. John Bartram
Sir

I received the Box of Tree Seeds you Sent me in Ja[n] last in very good order, and the money was paid at London as soon as it was deliver'd and I make no doubt you've got the money Remitted you Long before now — you

may Send me a Box of Same — by any Ship that first offers either for London, Greenock or Leith   if for London direct to the care of Kinier J. Mason who paid thee Last and will likewise pay thee; for Greenock to the Care of Mr. James McNeill & if for Leith will Receive them myself   let most of the Seeds be of the pines and wall Nuts, Magnolias, Oaks   in short I leave this Choice to yourself   only if there is any New Curious things you'll send me a part   pray send some of the New England pines either in Cones or seed   I need not bid you send them fresh and good as I make no doubt you will, and be so kind as to make my Compts. to Mr. Cowan[1] and tell him I'm glad to hear he has enter'd into a matrimonial state of life and heartily wish him Success. I saw his Brother last day who is well   I am Sir
your most hble Servt
Will: Borthwick

P.S. Please deliver the Inclos'd

BP 1:90.
1. Unidentified.

To COLLINSON

May ye 1st 1764

Dear Peter

I have received my worthy friends letter of January ye 1st 1763   I suppose it should be 64 & two of february ye 3rd   one dated 1764 ye other 44 I suppose by mistake   with ye packet of seeds which is very acceptable but one paper called acconite I take to be a campanele   I wish it may be ye piramidalis which I never had yet growing tho often rote for it   ye broad leaved Carolina Comelina & our narrow leaved is A late fall flower & very diferent from ye spring tradescants spiderwort   I had allways since 10 years ould A great inclination to plants & knowed all that I once observed by sight tho not thair proper names haveing no person or books to instruct me. I am concerned ye Callmias was hurt by ye ratts   thay was set full of flower buds   ye Box was strong & well nailed upp   I have many Carolina seeds come up this spring in ye bed I sowed when I cam home   I have several fine plants growing of ye monstrous Sylphium from ye branches of Pedee & ye piramid of Eden which came up last year but dont expect them to flower this year & ye latter not of several years   I hope there is one come up of that odd plant from ye Alegany mountains with leaves like convalaria   if it be it I should esteem A Jewel   its certainly A new genus my New river hors chestnuts is shot finely & alltho thay grow up on ye north side of my garden wall where ye sun seldom shines upon them yet thay are extended near thair anual shoot before ye europian had opened thair buds with ye benefit of ye whole days sunshine   my dear friend is much mistaken to think what we call ye Cuckold nut to be ye common sort with us   one may travail A 1000 miles & not see one of them whereas formerly in that distance we might not travail half an hour without being surrounded with them   thay covered ye surface of most of ye best ground for which reason thair allready allmost eradicated among ye inhabitants except in fence rows & very rocky ground but ye others grows on ye steep[1] precipices of rocky mountains tho sometimes on declineing ground   I observed ye hazel plant in ye forks of skulkil 30 years ago & since in york government & virginia in several places   ye fire burns them down to ye ground every few years & ye ould roots sending up shoots which in A year or two bears nuts   some 3 or four foot high but where thay grow in rich low land thay commonly grow 6 or 8 foot high bearing nuts 4 or 6 in bunches   I thought you had this sort long ago in plenty   Doctor Shippen gave me some seed last summer which he brought from ye south of Europe   one fine sumach grew 18 inches [illegible] I sheltered them with boards & thay are now very fresh   ye first I transplanted to one side of my walks & this spring there is two mespillies come up from his seed. last summer there came up in my greenhouse from east India seed formerly sowed there   an odd kind of Sumach (as I take it to be)   it growed in A few months near 4 foot high & continued green & growing all winter & this spring I planted it out to take its chance   it shoots vigorously & allmost as red as crimson   how it will stand next winter I cant say but I intend to cover ye ground well about its root   we have had A moderate winter   A cool rainy spring: ye tops of ye carolina bays evergreen oaks & your bay is kiled   ye magnolia mirtle lobloly bay & Dahoon holly hath some green leaves   ye evergreen bignonia folio conjugatis is not much hurt but ye sweet one tho under A boarded shelter is killed to ye root   ye bark bursts from ye stalks but one I have in ye greenhouse is very fresh   Gordons Pomegranate tho planted in A suny bank is killed to ye root as ye figs & azedarach   ye Broome & Gorse is little hurt   I have not yet consulted ye Doctors letter about snakes   I never had an opertunity of examining ye afair my self & I cant believe reports like his   I intend to consider it better

BP 1:60:3, 1:55:7; D. 263.
1. To this point the letter was taken from BP 1:60:3; the remainder is from BP 1:55:7.

To COLLINSON

May ye 10th 1764

Dear Peter

I haveing wrote largely by Captain robinson & haveing not received any letter from thee since I have little to write at present   ye seeds I brought from Carolina & new virginia & sowed soon after I came home is now coming up finely & ye iris dwarf from Pittsburg is in full bloom & very pretty   I have now borrowed from A woman in Philadelphia part of A monstrous tooth weighing three pounds & three quarters   one half was braked of & stole   that part which I have is in length nine inches & A half long & good part was broke off ye root   ye hole for ye marrow was A triangle whose two sides was one inch & quarter & ye base one inch   ye part that went in ye Jaw was 6 inches long   ye outward indenting was one inch & ¾ ye iner one inch   where it entered ye gums it was 14 inches round   it was 4 inches thick   it seems as sound as if it was lately living no way petrified but near as heavy as brass: what A monstrous creature must this belong to that is utterly extinct as ye great palmed horns of ye Irish [elk] but those are found under ground where thay was preserved but these of ours is exposed to all ye inclemency of ye weather for ye young man as I am tould found this about 20 mile beyond ye Alegany mountain as his master was tradeing with ye indians   he said there was one whole skeleton   he measured one of ye ribs & said it was 16 foot long   he reconed by ye bones it was of ye bufalos kind but it be what it is it must be by its teeth surpriseing large for ye grinding teeth of all creatures bears A proportion to ye bulk of ye body which ye ears & tail do not   neither is[1]

BP 1:55:3.
1. The remainder of this letter is missing.

From COLLINSON

Londn: June ye 1st: 1764

I thank my Dear frd for his obligeing Letter of the 4th March — it gives Mee comfort to hear thy Leg is Healed   as wounds are fatal things to some constitutions, take great care for the future

Your season in March is something like ours for then the sharp Cutting Winds do our plants more Damage than all the Winter before

I ought not to envy my Friends Happiness but I should Like such a Mistress as Thou hath got who is always treating Thee with Dainties   a new yellow Lillie & white Iris will be fine things —

Before this comes to hand I hope Thou will have received Docr Solanders Names of the specimens, sent by last Pacquet

I have the pleasure to Tell thee all thy Plants thrive Except the 2 Carolina Bayes   the Gentian & Orchis, the Loblolly Bay Grows — This must be as agreeable for thee to hear that thy Great pains Is not thrown away — as for Mee to see new wonders arise — My Mountain Magnolia is finely in Flower & my umbrella show the flowering Budd

I want to go to Gordon's, to see if he has any luck with the Tipitiwitchet, and the Tree of Life of Eden.

I wish Wee had some Wealthy publick Spirited People who would encourage a search of those fine countries — our new Acquisitions   No One so well Accomplished for that work as thy self but Court politicks so engross the attention of the Great Men thay have no room to think of any thing Else   it is by no Means advisable to undertake it att thy own Expense   besides unless a settled peace with Indians who would venter I shall be Glad to hear thou hath success with the Empetrum —

I have from China a Tree of surprising growth that much resembles a Sumach which is the Admiration of all that see It   Phaps thine may be same — It Endoures all our Winters   Thou Sayes thine came from the East but mentions not what Country: We call ours the Varnish Tree

I am really concern'd at the present Situation of your province under the Arbitrary proceeding of the Presbyterians & the Ill concerted plan of opposition in the Goverr & his Party, I hope good Providence will Open a Way to settle these comotions

I have read the able spirited Resolutions of your Assembly & commend their Zeal for equity and Justice   hope it will have a good Effect

I am pleased with the account of thy Family & am glad John inherits the spirit of his father   He will find his advantage in It But I am concerned that Billy so Ingenious a Lad — is as it were Lost in Indolence & obscurity   I am pleased to hear poor Moses after so many Imminent Dangers is gott into a safe Harbour where I hope he will Do Well —

Spare not to Draw on Mee when thou can do it to advantage —

I am thy sincere friend,

P. Collinson

pray don't forget thy Journal when Opportunity offers

June 5   the Rich Flower Budds of Great Rhododendron Disclose themselves, my Umbrella shows Blossom

pray remember seeds of Obolistothecas & a specimen of thy fine Broad Leaved St Johns Wort   I have 2 species nay 3 species & yett I am doubtfull if I have the Broad Leaved —

I have Indeed a broad Leaved One that is perennial that Died down every year Close to the Ground & Comes up the next —

BP 3:51; D. 264–65.

From JOHN BUSH[1]

London 8th June 1764

Sir

the last years 3 Boxes of Seeds proved not to Expectation so that in one of them were but Eight Sorts of seeds in the whole Box   ye other not above half full   my friends in Germany are not willing to pay me the full price for them but I am in Hopes I shall get payd for two Boxes for which I shall be accountable For

as to this years boxes I have had no Complaints for which I shall make my payment good for them to Mr. Collinson

please to send me 3 Boxes next year 1765

that is 2 Boxes all of the Large forrest tree kind and no shruby small kinds mixt with them and one Box of the Common with all the kinds of seeds with so douing you will oblige your

Humble Servant
John Bush[2]

BP 3:52.
1. A London nurseryman at Hackney.
2. At the end of this letter Collinson added:

> I dont know what to Do with these Germans Some of the Boxes was open'd, & plundered, by the Spaniard one of Gordons I saw was served So, possibly these might be so too.
>
> P Collinson

From COLLINSON

London June 30th 1764

I was agreably Entertain'd with my Dear John's Letters of May 5th & 10th Those late Comelinas p Carolina & Jerseys I dont recollect to have seen in our Gardens so pray send us seed of them I thought there was only John Tradescants My Umbrella is now in Flower

I have often heard of the Sensitive Briar pray send Mee a Specimen of It & thy Broad Leaved St. Johns Wort I have a perrenial One thou formerly sent Mee that goes down to the Ground & Springs up again next year I am afraid Wee shall not raise one of the Many Vegitable Wonders (the Tippitiwichet) for Gordon with all his skill cannot bring it to light I want much to go to his Garden to See what Luck he has with the Empetrum &c the New River Horse Chestnutt I Know only by Leafe I shall be glad to see it for flowers

I have a Good Tree of the Cuckold Nutt but I dont remember to have Seen your Common Hazel Nutt Thou hath sett Mee right in that point Send some nutts over in thy Collections in the Boxes

I am pleased to hear of thy success from Docr Shipps[1] Seeds the Sumach I take to be what we Called the Elm Leaved it is rare in our Gardens, because it is too delicate for our winters but what is more Extraordinary is raising the China Sumach it seems to be the Same that has been raised Here for Tenn years I have Two fine Straight Tall Trees thirty foot high which from the Large long Leaves hath a strikeing appearance [three lines illegible] any where offer'd to Flower or Seed So Wee name a Sumach by guess the Evergreen Bignonia is finely in flower it is pretty remarkable that the plants of Carolina should be so effected with your weather my Great Magnolia that has now stood abroad 15 years is not so Touched it now shows its Flower Budds but I have the pleasure to tell thee thy Loblolly Bay Shoots finely & thy Solomons Seal is now in flower I never saw it before its like ours but of a more Delicate Habit 3 Roots of the purple berried Christophoriana has been in flower but what I most wished for the Gentian does not appear   the Periploca from the Ohio thrives finely   in another year may hope for to see It flower   pray write for some seed of the Sweet bignonia   I formerly had such plenty that I grew careless of them so they slighted Mee   If I gett it again I will Treat It as becomes so elegant a plant

Pray what is the fine Carolina Evergreen andromeda   In what doth it differ from your Ever Green one which thrives & flowers well with us Send a Specimen of the Carolina & of the Dwarf Carolina Myrtle   Gordon wants seed of it

I hope wee shall not forget the Mandrake & Briony but there is little chance of Campanella pyramidalis as it is a Biennial & rarely ripens Seed is Increased Here by Cutting a good root to piece but Gordon may try a Root or two

Thou Sayes Plants with Tap Roots, Bulbous & Tuberous Roots may be sent in Box of Earth of which you have a great Variety in your Gardens, but this is Saying with uncertainty for Wee may send what you have already as I have often done from Millers Dictionary   thou may select the kinds thou wants So pray list anything thou desires & if Wee have them thou may hope for them

Thy Bill of £80 will be paid, thou need not at any Time Hope for a payment to be made, of any bill of mine, which I am glad to pay   I never yett could be Possessed of any of your Dwarfe Iris tho I have many years sought from Clayton &c especially the Early Sweet Sort   I have 3 Species of the Taller Sorts by thy Favour which flower finely   the Pale vein'd Blew, Docr Witt & others said was a grand specific for the Pox &c

The Monstrous Tooth thou so well describes is no doubt a Companion to Three I have of the Like Kind, that was taken from the Recent Skeletons that was found by Greenwood, Cleghorn & others. I wish Billey was at Home to Draw It   it is much longer rooted then any of mine as Teeth vary in the Length & Number of Roots according to their use & Situation in the Jaw bone   Mine was taken from the Animals in a Licking place not farr from the Ohio, but this being found beyond the Alegany Mountains I presume is a different place from the Others but the Bones, like the others, are above ground Else the Rib, could not be measured   I wish some pson of Skill & accuracy was to fall in their Way that Wee might have a more particular & Exact account and mensurations of the parts, of these Wonderful Animals which raises our admiration & Speculation

Boxes of Seed wanting on the other Side

Adieu my Good Friend
P Collinson

Friend Fisher – Brings the Watch for thy Son price four Guineas which is carried to thy acct.

Boxes for Next Year
  1 Box for Powell
  1 Box for Wilcox

1 Box for Fern
1 Box for Cross
1 Box for Germany   see his Letter
3 Boxes for Bush   see his Letter
3 Boxes for Gordon   the Last gave him great Satisfaction   was a true Variety
4 Boxes for my Disposal

Gordon is putting up a Cargo of Plants & Roots for Frd Fisher has promised the Care for them

I had the great pleasure of Receiving Safe thy Journal p Capt Friend of that in my next

Mr Web called to pay for Box of Seeds & plants but as thou sett no price for the Plants could not pay Mee untill He knew the price of the whole charge   send it with ye next

This Strawberry Seed should have been sent Sooner but I have so many things to think on, that I may be Excused if I forget some   sow it in the Shade   it may come up with the Autumn Rains

I hear my Friend Dobbs at 73 had gott a Colts Tooth in his Head & has married a young lady of 22   It is now in vain to write to Him for seeds or plants of Tipitiwitchit now He has gott one of his Own to play with

but I have writt to his Secretary to beg his Assistance but it is so rare that a Ship comes from thence to London that I almost Despair   I want the Loblolly Bay much & Seed of the very Long Leaved Pine that thou saw in such plenty   if thou passes there on thy Journey pray remind them of It

Dear John adieu   the Blew Ulmeria thrive well but I dont see it make attempt to flower   does it flower with you   the Madeora flowers freely the purple or blew grows well & thy aconite thrives again   this year it will flower strongly

I should like some more of the Red Bud andromeda   it is a favorite with my Son & Mee

My Son is gone on a Journey of above an Hundred Miles to Collect our rare bee, Fly & Frogg Orchis so pray look for Him for He takes true pains to adapt Soils & Situation to them   these untractiable plants will scarcely do long without our utmost Care   pray give my Love to our Worthy Friend B: Franklin   I cannot write now but shall by Capt Friend to advise Him of the Box of Books for Him & thee & the Libr. Com

Free
Alexr Colden

for
John Bartam
on Skulkill
Near Philadelphia

BP 3:53, 3:58.
1. Shippen's.

From CLAYTON

June 30, 1764

Dear worthy friend

Having so good an opportunity I could not forbear laying hold of it to acknowledge myself highly obliged to you for your agreeable letter of the first of last month. The seeds of the Meadiae & specimen of one of its flowers inclosed. Since I wrote to you in February last, I find I have several of that plant come up in my Garden, the largest pushed out 4 or 5 leaves, but gave not the least sign of blossoming. I placed 'em in a cool, shady situation, yet, though we have had hitherto the coolest summer I ever knew in Virginia, their leaves are all mouldered away & gone. I think they appeared to be eaten by some imperceptible insects. It pleases me to hear of your fine collection of vegetables, although I am debarred from gratifying my eyes with the sight of 'em, or my heart with the company and conversation of the esteemed collector. The young gentleman[1] who brings this, is the only son of a very worthy clergyman, very lately deceased, who was minister of the parish where I live, now thrity years, during all which time there was a particular intimate friendship between us. He comes to seek after an estate in your Province, which was purchased, as I am informed, by his grandfather and consists of a tract of land lying near a place called the Walch Tract[2] and when his grandfather dyed, there were some slaves upon it. He has got a considerable estate in this County and is a very honest, well disposed, good-natured young man. The Stavesacre seed is not near ripe, but you may depend upon my saving a sufficient quantity of it for you and of any other plant in my garden that you'l let me know will be acceptable. If you have any of the seed of the Carolina Sensitive leaf to spare, or of any other curious plant or shrub, I shall be very much obliged to you for a small quantity by the return of Mr. John Fox, who will wait upon you and take great [care] of anything you will be so kind as to send to Dear Sir

Your most sincere and affectionate friend
John Clayton

I fancy he would take the trouble of bringing me a small box with some roots of that sensitive leaf planted in earth as he goes up our Bay to Delaware in a very good vessel

College of Physicians of Philadelphia, Historical Collections of the Library.
1. Son of the Reverend John Fox, minister of Ware Parish.
2. The Walch Tract comprised 40,000 acres between Derby Creek and the Schuylkill River, purchased from William Penn by the Welsh settlers. Young Fox inherited 3,000 acres known as Greenwich, in Gloucester County, Virginia.

From LAMBOLL

South Carolina, Chas:Town, July 25th:1764

Dear Friend Bartram:

I was fav'd: with yors. of the 24th of Febry:past, pr:Capt. Mason, last Voyage; and on the 1st of March dispatch'd Friend Wyly's box [of] Plants,

Parcel [of] Seed, and Letter to him; and doubt not but he recd: the same, notwithstanding he has sent me no Answer. I am inform'd of the likeliest Place for getting the Umbrella Tree: it is about 14 Miles off, and must be done in the Fall or beginning of Winter. Our Pomegranates are not quite Ripe; however as some People begin to gather theirs, Mrs. Lamboll chose to send Mrs. Bartram a Bisket Cagg full (say 53) of the best she could Pick, for her Acceptance; directed for you, now by Capt: Mason, who is just about to return, and may possibly be with you by the End of next Week. The Freight is not paid. Our best Respects to you & yours is all that offers at present from Your real Friend —

Thos: Lamboll

P.S. Last Week I had a good Oppertunity and wrote to our friend Collinson, and sent him some of Friend Wyly's Heath Seed. Every Plant of it that he sent me died & only a Single Seed Sprouted: but that flourished finely and I hope will do well. T:L: —

BP 4:63.

To COLLINSON

august ye 19th 1764

Dear Peter
I received thine of March ye 7th 1764, with Dr Parsons' letter both which is very acceptable & since I received Dr. Solander's names to ye specimens I sent last fall for which I paid half A crown postage from new york   pray send in ye merchant ships or under cover to our friend Benjamin & then I shall have them directly as I had thine of June ye first. I am glad ye shrubs I sent thee prospers but I cant hear A word how any of ye boxes of forrest [seeds] gave satisfaction   there was ye greates variety I ever sent. I sent by Captain Friend my Journal to Carolina & new river   pray let our worthy mutual friend Solander peruse it   he sent several letters under cover to me from Sweadland,[1] which this day I delivered to Dr. wrangel who is I believe ye most indefatigable & zealous minister that ever crossed ye seas of any sect whatsoever   this day as usual he preached in our township   then came to my house dined read ye letters I gave him walked in ye garden discoursed a few hours   then forced to part to visit ye sick in ye neibourhood & then tho A very rainy stormy day he must go to town   its surpriseing what pains he takes to reform ye people by tender preaching innocent persuasion & pious practice that he gains ye love of all societies. I think I have two sorts of ye dwarf hairy stalked robinia from carolina   one flowers onely in ye spring & grows low   ye other shoots vigorously has produced me 3 crops of flowers & sent forth one sucker 4 foot distant from its mother 3 foot high producing 10 bunches of flowers & 8 very large flowers — now in full bloom notwithstanding our dreadful dry season   ye Persian bermudiana is A charm-

ing flower now in bloom   I hope still I have one of ye tallest Silphyums come up but those I mentioned in my spring letters proves to be that from new river much like the ohio one but ye stalk & main pedicle of ye leafe is purple & hairy & ye angles not so acute   my lobloly bay hath 4 fine buds for blosoms but this stormy day broke of ye branch that produced them   I admire ye sweet bay perished with thee   it seems very easy to transplant but will not bear our cold   I had A pretty broad leafed mirtle from Gibralter   it lived 2 years & growed finely but last spring it perished root & branch & seemed dead & dry   I then pulled it up cut of ye whole root & planted ye branches in moist ground & now ye branches put out green leaves & in ye fall I desighn to plant one in ye full ground in my green house & an other in A pot   its strange how ye pretty empetrum is procured   since I brought it to Justice Wyly & tould him where I got it he has sent it several times to charls town but none grows   onely Lambol has raised one from seed   I suppose Governor Dobbs got his seed from ye Justices as they are both Irish & thay & all ye scots will hang together like bees   many of my pyramids of eden intirely perished a month ago but hopes ye roots is allive   its odd ye leaves of this noble plant should be of such short duration & yet ye robust stalk will keep its magnitude & form for several years after both root & stalk is quite dead   ye sweet shrub from ye wateree grows finely   after I parted with my friend Wyly my botanik genius led me off of ye road near A mile where I found that shrub without flowers or seed   when I came home I wrote to my friend describing ye spot so well that he sent it 120 mile by land to charlestown from whence I had it   I am mighty fond of flowering or sweet shrubs   I think nothing in vegitable nature adorns borders better under trees   dear Peter thee can hardly conceive how it wounds me to think of 2 more shrubs I found at A great distance from my house that I mist getting to grow   one had berries which I brought home but thay are not yet come up   ye other I brought 3 roots home but being runners thay dyed in ye summer   most will do without good fibres which is hard to get if mother root is too big to carry[2]

BP 1:55:4; D. 265.
1. Sweden.
2. The remainder of this letter is torn and faded.

From MARTHA LOGAN

Septr ye 14d 1764

Sr

I have received your faviour with the Bagg of roots for which am much Obligd & doe now send you a Small parsel of Seeds which are Cheafly Natives. Those with Out Names are what a friend of mine Sent me from the Country so that I cannot tell what they are. I am in hopes it will be in my Power to send you Some Verity which I am to have from the Same hand as Soon they ripen, the tops of the Plant you mentioned by the quarter house are now dryed of so that I Cannot find it till Spring when you Shall Certainly have it if I live till then. you weire so kinde to ask what would be Exceptable to me. the mainy Shrubs & plants you have bestowed on me have Suceeded so badly that I am quite dishartned from trying Verity & shall Confine my desires to what I know will doe theirfore if you have any Single Hyacinths of Verry Deep blues or reeds nothing would be moore Exceptable & as I am frequently Disappointed in my Seeds from England Shoulde be verry glad to be Suppl[ied] from yr Part with about half pound good Orang Carrotts & 4 Ounces Parsnips, 2 Cabage 2 Reed beats 2 good Savoy Cabage for which would be willing to Pay the Cosst & return the favour if in my Power. this I Coulde gett done by any Capt of Vessel but it would not be in theire Power to know whither they weire good ones of theire kindes, so that I might be disappointed & Perhaps have as good at home. Else should not give you any trouble on this head which hope you will Excuse this Liberty

Sr Your well wisher & Humble Servt
Martha Logan

PS my good wishes & Complyments attend your family I shall be glad of the Plants you offer

Historical Society of Pennsylvania Library, Gratz Collection of Notable Americans, Case 7, Box 20.

From LAMBOLL

South Carolina   Chas:Town, Sepr:15th:1764

Dear Friend Bartram:

Your renew'd Favour of the 14th:ultimate with a box containing Mrs. Bartrams kind & acceptable Present of Angelica & some dried Apples came safe to hand the 5th inst: On receipt whereof I open'd the Box & sent Mrs. Garden her Parcel: What we had is excellent good, & well deserves mine, Mrs. Lambolls and our Family's Thanks which we hope you will both accept of. I flatterd my Self (and therefore delayd writing until this day) I should have got the Umbrella Trees, to send by this opptunity but the Person I depended on, does not yet appear, and I would not miss Writing. Mrs. Lamboll, however, by way of Return has, in the mean time, filled your Barrel with Pomegranates, China Oranges and Sour Oranges, directed for you, on one of the heads and I have got it put on board Capt: Mason's Brigantine, as you'l see by his Mate's Receipt here Inclosed. Mr. Dennis Rolle, Member of Parliament for Barnstable, who arrivd here some Weeks ago, from London, has honoured me with a Visit or two; he proposes settling a little Colony of his own, in Florida. I conclude with my Wife's and own Compliments, to your self and Spouse; —

Your sincere Friend, to serve
Thomas Lamboll

BP 4:64; D. 436–37.

From LAMBOLL

South Carolina, Chas: Town, Sept: 15: 1764

Dear Friend Bartram:

Soon after I had sent my letter of this date, on board Capt: Mason's Vessel (who is to Sail To Morrow Morning) came the long look'd for Umbrella Trees, and I hope time enough to get Packd: and put on board; there are Six of them, in a long Cagg, set in Earth, wetted with Rain-Water and the Cagg directed for you. they were drawn but yesterday out of the Ground where they grew, in the Woods not yet 24 hours since: so you'l probably have them in a Fortnight from their drawing. I can only add that to comply with anything which may oblige you, is a real Pleasure, to

Your sincere and Cordial friend
Thos: Lamboll

BP 4:64.

To COLLINSON

September 23d 1764

Dear Peter

I received thy kind letter of June ye 30th with ye Strawberry seed   the Commelyns I wrote to thee about many years past   presently after I found it   I have sent thee specimens of both in Buden with ye sensitive bryer perhaps I may send thee A root of each   we sent two roots of my broad leaved shrub Hypericum   ye tipitywitchet is very difficult to raise or keep mine that I thought intirely killed last winter is revived but is so small & weak as hardly to [be] sensible of being tickled   I hope I have ye cistus lacinifera come up from Dr shipins seed & A prety geranium from thy seed but none of ye aconite come up   I have sent by yong[1] A specimen of ye Carolina andromeda – ye briony mandrak & canary Capela came in fine order   buds as fresh as if just taken up & all ye bulbous roots; but ye [illegible] is not sent   I desighn to send ye pittsburg iris   I sent thee A specimen   ye great teeth is quite astonishing   I wish I could have an opertunity of measuring them   I sent by yong a viol of chinkapins Just gathered & put in   corked it tight   let me know ye success   I hope thay come to hand as fresh as when I put them in   thay will no bear drying so it is with ye white & chesnut oak   pray let Gordon & webb have a share   my neighbour yongs sudden preferment has astonished great part of our inhabitants   thay are daily talking to me about him   that he has got more honour by A few miles traveling to pick up A few common plants than I have by near 30 years travail with great danger & peril   it is shocking ye plants you have had many of them known 100 years & most 20 or 30 should be esteemed at court as new discoveries   several of my friends put me upon sending my new discovered specimens to ye king to try my success accordngly I have put A little Box of such specimens as I am sure he never found & I believe never came to England before I sent them ye Box I sent to thy care with A letter to ye king under cover to thee which pray deliver to his majesty or if thee hath not freedom to do it pray deliver it to Dr. Pringle[2] whom Benjamin Franklin promises to acquaint with ye whole afair I nailed thick paper upon ye Box with thy name at large which thee may easily take off as thee thinks fit pray be careful ye Box is not tumbled about there is flowers in it that may be shaken loose If I should be appointed by authority [or] private subscription to travail thro florida or ye illinois I am too ould to go alone & I think my son william will be A fit person to accompany me as he by this time I believe can draw well. there is a subscription set on foot at Edinburgh for to enable A person to send them plants & seeds for thair new public garden thay wrote to Benjamin to see if I would undertake it which I did but how it goes on I cant yet say but I cant expect to be able many years to perform such A Journey. I should spend A whole year there to make full discoverys hitherto I have travailed at my own expence except at Onondaga so was obliged to make hast home

BP 1:53:5; D. 266.
1. William Young, Jr.
2. John Pringle.

To LOUISA ULRIKA DROTTING

September ye 23, 1764

May it please ye Queen

The high Character which the Queen at Present bears in ye learned world for her many great Abilities & amiable acomplishments but perticularly for her surprising Progress in all kinds of natural Knowledge, encourages A Pensilvania Botanist with ye Greatest Humility to approach her Throne & lay ye Produce of his industrious Labours & Searches at her Royal feet.

the Collection of Plants which is herewith transmitted to the Queen is ye fruite of near thirty years Travel thro New England New York East & West Jersey Pensilvania Maryland Virginia North & South Carolina, from ye Sea Coast to the great Lake Ontario & for many hundred miles to ye north of ye great Alegany mountains back of all ye above mentioned Provinces, & on both sides of all ye great rivers that waters them; in these Journeys I became acquainted with most if not all the plants shrubs & trees of that vast tract of land in all thair different degrees of growth: many curious Plants may however without doubt be still found in Georgia East & West Florida Misisipia, the Country of ye illinois the lake Mitchigan & in ye Rest of our Kings new acquisitions.

I flatter my self that the Queen will honour my Collection with A place

in her Royal Cabinet and happy indeed shall I deem my self to find my labours rewarded by ye Aprobation of so learned & illustrious A Princess
I am may it Please ye Queen

> with all due Reverance & Respect
> the Queens most Obedient Servant
> John Bartram

University of Uppsala Library, Uppsala, Sweden.

To HOPE

October the 4th, 1764

Worthy Friend:—

I have received your proposals by the hands of our dear friend Benjamin; and since, by a letter from the worthy, humane Dr. Bard, of New York, in which he inserts a paragraph of a letter from his son (whose person and activity I am not a stranger to), wherein he writes to the same effect as thee wrot to Benjamin Franklin, signifying that you had laid a new botanic garden, to be stored with exotics; that you were forming a laudable and very necessary plan of storing your bare country with variety of forest trees; that many gentlemen of rank and fortune had countenanced this scheme with an annual subscription, to enable a botanist to make your desired collections; and that my answer was desired, whether I would undertake to supply your demands, which I consent to do, if your generosity is equal to them; for the charges of collecting rare vegetables are in proportion to the distance from home, and hazards and dangers in collecting them. I have, in thirty years' travels, acquired a perfect knowledge of most, if not all of the vegetables between New England and Georgia, and from the sea-coast to Lake Ontario and Erie.

Now what I have not yet discovered, is our new acquisitions in the mountains of Georgia, in East and West Florida, up the Mississippi and the country of the Illinois, Lakes Michigan and Huron, the upper lake. I suppose no great variety there.

All the plants north of 33 degrees will grow in the open ground at Edinburgh, and those in Georgia and East and West Florida with a protection from hard frost.

I have now sent, as a present, for thy curious amusement, one hundred specimens, some rare, with my remarks upon them, and to your new garden a parcel of curious seeds, near one hundred and fifty different species; and our friend, Mr. Franklin, engaged me to send you a box of forest trees and shrubs, in which I am going to pack above one hundred different kinds, and send them in the next ship for London, which will sail in three weeks.

In the box of seeds I have put a capsula of the true *Colocasia [Nelumbium luteum,* Willd.][1] with some nuts, just gathered. Plant them in wet mire; they will not live anywhere else. The stalk and leaves grow five feet high, and often that depth in water.

D. 433–34.
1. Darlington added identification in brackets.

To COLLINSON

October ye 15th 1764

Dear Peter
I received thy kind letter of July ye 30th 1764 with ye seeds which was very acceptable since which Cap faulkner is arived by whome I have received no letters   I sent by Captain Budden by my neibour young my spring specimens & A vial of chinquapins to try how thay will do that way: Various are ye opinions of his success   some think he will make such an awkward appearance at Court that he will soon come back again. others that ye Queen will take care of ye german Gentleman   I think that if he is put under dr Hills care that he will make A Botanist as he is very industrious & hath A good share of ingenuity   I hope thee will find some way to forward ye box I sent to thee for ye king   not that I depend on having any such preferment as Young but chiefly as A curiosity to see what differences will be made betwixt such rare plants as never grew in Europe or asia & such as have been growing in ye English gardens between 20 & 100 [years] past; for such I believe were most that young sent but I & several others should be greatly pleased with A list of what he sent if it could readily be obtained: My good ould friend I am well assured that thee is well acquainted with many of ye nobility, some of whom no doubt is men of curiosity   could not thay be prevailed upon to enable me to travail A year or two through our kings new acquisitions to make A thoro natural & vegitable search either by publick authority or private subscription & I must insist on 2 articles: 1 is that I have one to accompany me   2 to have an allowance sufficient to make full discovery & not be hurried for time to make remarks & carriage to transport what I discover but I cant expect to be able to perform such A task many years hence   I must yield to ye infirmities of age or death

BP 1:53:6; D. 266–67.

To COLLINSON

November ye 22d 1764   By friend

Dear Peter
I wrote lately by our dear worthy friend Benjamin Franklin who was sent of here with ye greatest demonstration of respect — in accompanying him to ye ship — far beyond any that ever sailed from America   I being no party man but wishing for ye general good of ye province stayed at home being

extremely hurried in packing   praying for ye desired success & that he may at his return home be received with as much or more applause & triumph over his enemies

I have since [sent] the & Gordon each A Box of plants & shrubs & now I send twenty-two Boxes Consigned to thee. thay are all marked on ye side for each person   thay are desighned for PC III X & BF on ye side for Benjamin Franklin. I have allso sent a little Box, with thy name at large containing above 100 different kinds of seeds for thee & gordon   there is A parcel of chinquapins & willow oak acorns that was mised in ye last packed 16 Boxes By ye extreme hurry we was in for above two weeks day & night First day not excepted   Ye Captain positively affirmed he would sail by such A day & leave them if thay was not brought before & now he stays for sailors   if I had known he would have stayed so long I might have sent every article in order

BP 1:53:2; D. 267–68.

From CLAYTON

Feb. 6, 1765

Dear worthy Friend

I received the favour of your letter by Mr. Fox with some curious seeds inclosed, for wch I am much obliged to you and return my hearty thanks. I now send you the seed of the red flowered Chelone and the Staphisagria which I saved this last year out of my garden and hope they will prove acceptable. We have had hitherto a very severe winter. The frost set in about the latter end of December and has continued with very few & short intermissions and now and then very intense & accompanied with abundance of snow to this day; and even now, there is no prospect of its breaking up. I was taken with an intermitting fever, about the latter end of October, wch reduced me so low, that I have been confined to my house almost ever since. all my hopes are, that I shall recover my usual good health in the spring. my Garden is entirely ruined with the cold piercing winds and frosts. All the flowers which were in the leaf, tender, as Narcissus, Polyanthus, Ixia, Leucojum, &c., are destroyed. I fear much that it has been severe with you. I sincerely wish you health and happiness; & remain, dear friend

your affectionate friend, and most humble servant,
John Clayton

BP 3:5; D. 412.

From FRANKLIN

London, Feb. 14. 1765

Dear Friend,

I received your Kind Letter of December 19. Our Friend Peter is not dead, as you apprehended; but, Thanks to Heaven, as well as ever I knew him, hearty, brisk, and active as a Youth. I show'd him your Letter, and he told me he had wrote to you, and that you must have been long before this time put out of your Pain on his Account. I have order'd the Box of Seeds to Edinburgh, and shall take care to satisfy our Friend for the same. He has wrote you all the News of the Reception your Present to the King met with. I hear from other Hands that it was much lik'd. I pray for a Continuance of your Health, that you may be able to perform the great Journey, if it should be concluded on. In the pleasing Expectation of a happy Meeting with you after your Return, hearing your curious and judicious Observations, and enjoying your agreable and instructive Conversation, I remain, Dear Friend

Yours affectionately
B. Franklin

Papers of Benjamin Franklin, 12:61–62.

From HOPE

Edinburgh, March 7, 1765

Sir: —

I was favoured with your letter of the 4th of October, and soon thereafter had the pleasure of receiving the small box of seeds and specimens of rare plants, which you was so good as to send me, and for which I heartily thank you, and shall be very glad of an opportunity of testifying my sense of your kindness.

The Society which was established here about a twelvemonth ago for importing foreign seeds, has it chiefly in view to import the seeds of useful trees, and in the second place ornamental shrubs.

As the members of this Society reside in very different and distant parts of Scotland, it is impracticable to attempt the importation of young trees or shrubs, and on this and other accounts have entirely laid aside all thought of importing them, confining themselves entirely to the importation of seeds.

* * *

As there is annually a ship or ships loaded with lintseed, which come from Pennsylvania to Leith, or some other part of Scotland, you will have an easy opportunity of sending such seeds as are ready at the departure of these ships.

* * *

If it is not inconvenient, we would be glad to have specimens of the wood of every tree of which you send us seeds; and you have an easy way of executing this, by making the tops, bottoms, sides, and divisions of the boxes of different wood, numbering each with reference to the catalogue: the whole constituted in the same rough way packing boxes are usually made, beginning with all the woods of one genus, as the Pines, and then the Oaks, &c.

* * *

Although, from the tenor of this letter, trees and shrubs only are the general objects of the Society, yet some of us are desirous of having a few of new and curious plants, particularly those used in medicine or in dyeing. I should be particularly fond of having the seeds of the *Lobelia syphilitica*.

* * *

Wishing you much health and success, I am your most obedient servant,

John Hope

D. 434–35.

From COLLINSON

Londn:Aprill 9th:1765

I have the pleasure to Inform my Good Friend that my Repeated Solicitations have not been in Vain for this Day I received certain Intelligence from our Gracious King that He had appointed thee His Botanist with a salary of Fifty pounds a Year & in pursuance thereof I received thy first half years payment of thy Salary, Being Twenty five pounds to Lady Day last — which I have carried to thy Account.

Now Dear John – thy Wishes are in some Degree Accomplished to Range over Georgia & the Floridas   as this is a great Work, & must be accomplished by Degrees it must be Left to thy own Judgment how to proceed

I hope by this Packet or by Next to procure Letters of Recommendation to the Governors of East & West Florida; because Either from them or by the aid of our Friend Lamboll seeds & specimens may be sent directly to Mee for the King

It is a great Work but thou must contract It & not Hurry but take time to make observations on the soil, the Country, or to gather Specimens of plants, fossils, Ores, &c., where they can conveniently be done, & not too remote for Conveyance, Either to Charles Town, St. Augustine, or Pensacola

Thou will do well to provide Large Paper, for the Reception of Specimens & to gett a Leather Cover to the size of the paper to secure the Specimens from Wett & Leather bags for to secure the seeds from the rain

As for Living plants it will be Impossible unless they grow not far from the sea port

Now as thou knows my love for Natural History I Desire thou will provide thy self with Little flat Boxes fitt for the pocket & with Pins, that if thou sees any species of Insects to have some Contrivance to Catch them, such as all sorts of Beetles, Bees, Wasps, Locusts (that is Grasshoppers) for the Cicadas that you call Locusts, I have Enough   Butter Flies & Moths are too Difficult to Manage — pray Look out for all sorts of Land Snails & River Shells one, 2 or 3 of a sort is Enough, & any other production that I may see the Wonderful Creatures of this New World – a Many of these may be stuck thick together in a little Box

Being Like to be So long & so Remote from Home I don't know what will be done about Collecting Seeds for the Boxes   the last came all in good Order but thy Correspondents wants New Things, I have still no Orders

Whether it will not be better to go by sea to Carolina takeing thy son or a servant with thee & there hire horses for the Expedition, then takeing so long a Journey by Land over & over again without meeting with anything new   this must be submitted to thy better Judgment and Experience to Determine — for thy health and preservation thou has

the best wishes of thy sincere Friend
P Collinson

About a Month agon I advis'd my Friend John of the Kings Intention by a Pennsylvania ship & a New York ship

At the same time that thou art collecting seeds for the King where thou finds plenty thou may think on Mee & thy other Correspondents —

Lord Kildare Desires Two Boxes of seeds may be sent to Him at Dublin A Duplicate is sent by Capt Friend or Carton   Letters of recommendation are not Yett Come & they are uncertain when they will   so do not delay for them —

BP 3:54; D. 268–69.

To BERNARD de JUSSIEU[1]

Philadelphia 25th April 1765

Worthy Friend Jussieu
I had entertained many years ago the thoughts of opening a Correspondence with thee, in the year 1755. I was going to Send thee a few Specimens of our American Plants, & Shrubs, when War broke out & put a stop to my design. Since that time my great Age, the difficulty of having in London proper Correspondents; & distance of both Countrys has discouraged me still more. when a Gentm. lately arrived from London determined to undertake it by his Easing me the means of Conveyance. my design in doing this proceeds entirely from the Veneration I Entertain for thy learning & from a particular Esteem I have had always for thee. Since thou hath so happily began thy Race in the Botanick Carrieer, I have at various Times visited all the Provinces of our American Continent & to Convince thee of the Sincerity I profess will not fail Sending thee by a Vessell that is to sail in a few days — Some Samples of our Springs Plants, Intending next fall to forward thee as Compleat a Collection of whatever we have rare & Curious I possibly can; as what I send yearly to Denmark Germany Sweden Scotland &c thrive well I am in hopes it will equally well grow in the beautiful

Garden of thy king, who has so Justly reposed the Care of so valuable a repository in so Capable hands as thine. the number of our Shrubs is amasing that of our Plants infinite. now that peace is returned to Europe I hope nothing will prevent me from having the pleasure of hearing soon from thee, for I must own that among the valuable Correspondents I have already in Europe I should think myself happy to count Monsieur De Jussieu.

May Health enable thee to attend without interruption to thy Studies, & may thou attain to an age Sufficient to give thee the time to Instruct thy Country & diffuse through it So usefull a knowledge as that of Botany, & by thy labours to Enlighten mankind

These are the Sincere wishes of thy admirer & Friend —

John Bartram

P. S. my Friend St. John who profess as great & as high an Esteem for thee as myself promises me to forward thee this & to Let thee know how thou art to direct to me in London

Laboratoire de Phanerogamie, Museum National d'Histoire Naturelle, Paris.
1. Written in another hand but signed by Bartram. Addressed "A Monsieur de Jussieu premier, Botaniste de Sa Majesté Paris."

From COLLINSON

Londn: May 1765

I wrote my Dear John by the Pacquet of Aprill 12th & by Way of New york informing of Him that He was appointed the Kings Botanist at £50 p annum & that I have received the first payment of £25 which is Carried to account

John thou knows nothing what it is to Solicit at Court any favour, nay though it is for their own Interest they are so taken up with public affairs Little things Slip through their Fingers — For all I can do, I cannot gett these Letters of recommendation to any of the Governors —

All I can at present Do is our good friend Ellis[1] who is appointed to an office in the Floridas has writt to the Governors in thy Favour I send one Here Inclosed & will send the others by next ship by Capt Carton & this by Capt Friend — So thou must Make the best of It & do what seems most agreeable to thy own Inclination — Thou may think the appointment not Enough — I did not Expect any thing — So thou may use It, or Refuse It, as thou likes Best or Search as far as the Salary will go to support It — in this Case I cannot advise thee as thou Grows in years thou will do well to consider if thy present Constitution & Habit of body can undergo the fatigue of such an Expedition.

I have not had good luck I could wish with the Last Cargo.

Carolina Sweet Bay ⎫
Thyme leaved Calmia ⎪
Carola. Sweet bignonia ⎬ gone off
Deciduous Carolina Bay ⎪
Spotted autumn Gentian ⎪
sensitive Bryer gone off ⎭
Pittsburg Iris flowered finely, a Sweet thing
Mountain Hypericum grows
Cluster Solomon Seal grows
3 Yellow Roots grows
2 Martagons both grows
pretty fern grows
fine plant
Hazel tree grows
striped Pyrola grows fine
and the sod of Orchis &c promises very Well

As the Colocasia seed falls into the water, and finds nourishment and protection untill it shoots forth in the Spring so if the seeds had been put immediately in a bottle of Water there would have been a probability of their growing. I put them as soon as they came to Hand in Water & mud but none makes an offer to shoot. Pray tell me, what colour is the flower?

I have not seen Young for some time   I conclude he is prosecuting his Botanic studies.

I sent the fine seed-vessel of Faba Egyptiaca to the Queen but heard nothing More of It.

What are the Methodes observed by the Indians to procure fire before the Europeans came amongst them

Remember Seed of sensitive bryar   Was not the Dwarfe Sumach in thy Journal owing to the barren Soil   Specimen & Seed of the yellow Leafe or Horse Sugar why so Called, must be a pretty shrub

From thy Journal

Query what sort of flowers bears the Northern Aloe or Agave   must be a rare plant   did the seed grow   bring More & Specimens of the Flower if Billy goes the Expedition, He may take slight sketches of such odd things & finish afterwards   A single flower coloured is sufficient to carry the Idea.

Remember Fartle Berries not yet in our Gardens   Good Ripe Seed of Pyramid of Eden & other new fine Shrubs   did the seed come up of the Curious plant found on the Wateree   what is become of the Apple Haw why was no Specimen of the pretty narrow Leaved Shrub on the Sand Hills near Congaree

What information has been received from Geof Lewis relateing to the Periodical Springs & other Phenomenon & in what particular part of the

Country they are found   What is become of the Bull Grape   what is its colour, and is it short jointed

Octr: 6 gathered seed of a Tall plant Species of Ranunculas   is it come up   Is there a Specimen of that Singular plant Observed on the Top of Colo. Chisels Mine & Does the barberry found near the Cols differe from the English one

the Clematis found in Seed   is it come up   doth it prove New Species

What is become of fine Astragalus from Col Lewis   Doth the Roots of perennial Spurge grow

These Hints are to refresh thy Memory   answer at thy Leisure

I am thine sincerely,

P. Collinson

I lament the loss of my oldest Correspondent Docr Witt   What was his age   our good frd B Franklin grows fat & Jolly   There is hope of accomodation. The Receipt of my Dear Johns Letters gave Mee great pleasure to find thee in such good Health & Spirits   I was just Closing up when thy acceptable Letter came of December & 12 March   Many of my Queries in this are answer'd in that   the Agave is mentioned in thy Journal but I never heard it was in thy Garden or Else I should have solicited for so rare a plant before Now   what colour is its flower

2 Boxes for Lord Kildare at Dublin
3 Boxes for Gordon
1 Box for Wilson
1 Box for Cross Seedsman
1 Box for Fern
1 Box for Bush

none for my own disposal for I have no orders for any

BP 3:55; D. 269–70.
1. John Ellis had been appointed agent for the new province of West Florida in 1764.

From LAMBOLL

So. Carolina   Chas:Town   1 May 1765

Dear Friend Bartram

I should be glad to hear of your Health and whether the two barrels and two boxes I sent for you by Capt. Mason, last Voyage, and my Letter therewith, came to hand. Yesterday I received a Letter from our mutual good Friend, Wyley Esqr. of Wateree with some Seed of the Heath-shrub and he desires that part of it may be sent to you: and it [came] just in time for this Oppertunity   I have herein inclosed some [for] you; which I hope you'l receive Safe. The Indians have begun to Murder our frontier Inhabitants to a considerable Nu[mber]

I remain

Your real Friend, to Serve —
Thos. Lamboll

P:S: I suppose you have heard of Doctr. Garden's Recovery

BP 4:59.

To WILLIAM BARTRAM

May ye 19th 1765

Dear Son:

I haveing now A fine opportunity by my friend Smith send these few lines to let thee know we are all well at present & hath been all winter God all-mighty be praised   Lord Gordon[1] was twice at my house last week general Bouquet ye Governour & many of ye chief gentlemen came with him & yesterday I waited upon them at ye Generals   his lordship is going to Quebeck takeing all ye sea ports in his way   he earnestly invited me to go with him in this journey & he would bring me back again all at his own expense   at ye same time & place ye General has several times before offered to take me with him to Pensacola — to find me A man to wait upon me & an escort through ye dangerous passes & it should not cost me A farthing   these are very generous offers   I should rather choose ye last & now cant Comply with it

I waite to hear further from Europe. we have expected two vesails & ye packet to York, for several weeks   my last letter was dated ye 10th of February mentioning that Lord Bute & ye Earl of northumberland declared that it was nessesary that ye floridas should be searched & that I was ye Properest person to do it   how this affair will turn out I cant yet say but I have just wrote to Peter that I must have A Companion   My eye sight is so well returned, that I wrote this by candlelight & without spectacles   Pray remember my love to Brother Sister & cousins which allso receive thyself from thy affectionate father,

John Bartram

BP 1:63; D. 423–24.
1. Lord Adam Gordon (1726–1801?), colonel of the Sixty-sixth Regiment of Foot.

From CLAYTON

May 22d 1765

Dear Worthy friend —

I have just reced notice from my friend Mr. Fox that he returns to Pennsylvania tomorrow, so I thought I could not by any means let so good an opportunity Slip by without writing to my worth[y] friend. I sent you by the Post under cover directed to Mr. Franklyn, in February or March last, some Seed of the red Chelone and Starsacre both fresh & good, which I hope you have received long ago. The Meadia begins to thrive and flourish very well with me. I had two plants flowered in April last, one had fifteen or sixteen blossoms upon a stalk near twenty inches high, the other was lower and had not more than eight or nine flowers, from those two plants I expected to be plentifully supplied with seed. I reced a letter from our friend Mr. Collinson about two months ago & he tells me you are to be imployed by his majesty in making discoveries in the vegetable way in East and West Florida and if this takes effect I heartily wish you health and safety in yr long Journey and success in this undertaking and am Dr friend

Your most sincere friend
Jon. Clayton

Historical Society of Pennsylvania Library, Dreer Scientists, II.

From LAMBOLL

Charles Town, in South Carolina June 1st 1765

Dear Friend Bartram:

I received your agreeable and consolating Letter[1] of the 12th by Capt. Eastwicke and am greatly oblig'd to my worthy friend for his condolences. When Streams are cut off it should lead us to the Fountain of all Mercies; in Providences and Government 'tis our duty to acquiesce while we are in th[is Life]

The Eastwickes Brigantine returns crowded with Passengers   I doubt if (our friend) Johnson will be one of them: the inauspiciousness of the Weather, and Moisture has much retarded his Electrical Exhibitions and Experiments   not withstanding [he] hath not wanted for Company at every Performance, and if he can but get [illegible] Monies and overcome his present Cold and Hoarseness I believe he'll have [no] Regret his visiting this Town; his Conduct here has been unexceptionable and [he has] general Esteem and Friendship. In about Eight days another Vessel is to proceed to Philadelphia and perhaps he may imbark in her —

My dear Friend, I now take the Liberty of informing you that five days ago a letter from our mutual Friend Mr. Peter Collinson, of London, dated [illegible] wherein, among other pleasing things, he has these words: "Our Friend John was appointed the Kings botanist, with a Salery, in order to search out the [illegible] and other Natural Production of E. & W. Florida; so very probably you may [see him] towards the Autumn."

Wherefore I embrace the first Opportunity of sincerely [congratulating] you on this just Reward of your Merit; and shall at present conclude. Wishing you a Continuance of health, and enjoyment of the Royal Favour and Bounty. [illegible] joins with me in Compliments and best Respects, to your self and Spouse, and

Your oblig'd and [sic]
Thos Lamboll

P:S: not a seed of the Chelone has come up.

BP 4:58.
1. Concerning Lamboll's son, Thomas Lamboll, Jr., who had died February 5, 1765.

From MARTHA LOGAN

June 2d 1765

Sr
    As your friend Mr. Johnson was so kind to take the trouble of a letter Coulde not Omitt wrighting (though am not indebte having writt two since I recived yrs by him. I shall Send you a few Shrubs &c, in the fall & Should be glad to know if you have the Fring tree. If not I will Send one as I think them a Very Pritty thing. I am sorry Mr. Johnson happened to Come hear at this Season of the Year for he has bein much disappointed in not being able to Performe so many Operations as he designed from the Dampness & thickness of the Weither & wish he has made it Answer his trouble & Expence   had it bein winter his Profit would bein Double, for he gave Greatest-Satisfaction to the Spectators. If we have any thing you Particularly desire I should Send, pray lett me know & will doe my Endeaviour to Gett it & am with Sincearst good wishes Sr

your friend & Humble Servt.
Martha Logan

P.S. I took the Liberty Sending a list in Each of my former letters so shall not mention them now & hope you have recived the Seeds then Sent

Historical Society of Pennsylvania Library, Dreer Scientists, I.

To WILLIAM BARTRAM

June ye 7th 1765

Dear Son William: –
Soon after Cousen Smith set off for Cape Fear, I received a perticular account that our King had appointed me his chief Botanist & I am ordered to go directly to florida & I have taken passage in A vesail bound to Augustine & thence to Pensacola with my good friend General Bouquet for whose sake I go sooner than I intended: perhaps the vesail may touch at

Charlestown. its some question whether I shall not stay about Augustine or Georgia this summer & perhaps winter in ye peninsula or East florida but I cant yet tell which till I speak with Governour Grant[1] & ye superintendent of Indian Afairs[2] whome I must consult   I am daily waiting for further orders & recommendations from Court but our friend Peter ordered me to take my son or A servant with me & as thee wrote to me last winter & seemed so very desirous to go there: now thee hath A fair opertunity so pray let me know as soon as possible   our vesail is to sail in about two or three weeks   therefore I advise thee to sell of all thy goods at A public vendu & give thy account into ye hands of an attorney there properly proved who will recover thy debts better & with A quicker dispatch then thee can thyself & write directly to thy Creditors to let them know how ye affairs stand   I believe thy best way to meet with me will be about St. Augustine   I wish thee could send A letter to me there as soon as posible   I intend to hover about there or Georgia till near winter   direct thy letters to ye Care of ye Governours at both places for me which will be ye likeliest places for me to meet with them or thee   I suppose that vesails passes frequently between Charles town & Georgia or Augustine   please to send them directly to Augustine or Georgia but pray let me know soon whether thee will come or not that I may provide myself with another Companion. perhaps next spring I may go to west florida but cant say where yet but in ye main time assure thy selfe that I remain thy loveing father

John Bartram

thy Brother George[3] or his brother who wants thee to come home & Joyn in partnership with them, desired me to write to thee

BP 1:64; D. 424–25.
1. General James Grant.
2. Colonel John Stuart, superintendent of Indian Affairs, Southern Department, based at Charleston, South Carolina.
3. Billy's brother-in-law.

From ISAAC BARTRAM

Philada. August 15th 1765

Dear Father

Through Divine Mercy We are all in a Good State of health, (except my young sun which is Unwell). I pray that these few Lines through Favour of that Divine Power, in which thee Trusts, may find thee in a Good State of health, and that thee may be Inabled from Day to day to Prosicute thy Botanic Resarches with Ease and safty thro' the many Difficultys thee may meet with – – –

We Recived thy Letter from Charles town Giving an Account of thy Quick but hard Passage, but was glad to find thee was kindly Recived by thy old Friends Dr. Garden & Mr. Lambol, for which kindness we think our selves in Duty bound to serve when in our Power. – – –

I was Glad to see thy Accurat Observation of the heat and Temperature of the Air at Charlestown, since by it I find, it was far short of what it was hear; about the same time, the 31st of July at 2 o'Clock in the afternoon I Observed by a Thermometer of Dr. Evans[1] which was situated Justly to Assertain the proper Degrees of heat, being hung up in a Cool Entry at such a distance from the street dore as not to be affected by the Reflection of the sun from the Pavement, and found the mercury at 93 Degrees hot, he told me it had been at 94   What I saw my self I have Wrought. I have nothing further to Mention any way material. I should be Glad to hear from thee by all Oppertunity, any Short account of any new Discoverys and Observations Will afford me much Pleasure. I could say a Great Deal more were I certain it would Reach thee. I will Just mention I recived A Letter from Brother Bill wherein he Expresses A Great desire in Going with thee, as he says to be a help and Comfort to thee in what Ever afflictions or trouble thee should meet with in thy Long and tedious Jurney. Please to Give my Kind Love to him, and Let him know I should be Glad to have a specimen from him, in the Curious way, all at Present from thy most Dutifull sun,

Isaac Bartram

P.S. My wife Desires her Love to be Rememd.

New-York Historical Society, Bartram Folder.
1. Probably Dr. Cadwalader Evans, a Philadelphia Quaker.

To ANN BARTRAM

Savannah   September ye 4th 1765

My dear Spouse
this day we arrived at Savanna town in georgia by 10 oclock   this was reconed A very hot day here with thunder & showers   thermometer 86 thay have had here as well as at Charles town ye hottest summer & dryest; & wettest August that hath been for many years   many great bridges is broken down & we were forced to swim our horses over but God all mighty be praised we are got safe into Georgia & strange it is that in all this dreadful season for thunder & prodigious rain we have not had occation to put A great coat on in both ye Carolinas nor rested one day on ye account of rain but we cant expect to be favoured so long; however Gods will be done: we are now hearty & has A good stomack   the people say that if we can weather this month we need not fear: we have been pestered these two mornings & evenings with very large muskitos but thair bite is not near so venemous as ye small sort at Charles town: the land in general is pretty good most of ye way from Charles town to this town & ye people very civil to us   we have Just been with one of ye Governours Counsel Mr Habersham,[1]

to whom our worthy friend doctor Wrangel recommended me: to wait on ye Governour who received us with exceeding civility offering to do me all ye kindness that lay in his power   nay that [if] any unforseen accident should happen if I wanted anything that he could help me to, he would immediately do it: we desighn to set out to-morrow toward Augusta, 150 miles up ye river where I have many great recommendations from ye chiefs in Charles town but whether I shall set out from there through part of ye Creek nation to Augustine or come back again to this town I cant say untill I consult some very knowing Gentlemen at or near Augusta

we are obliged to be at or near Augustine by ye first of october or thereabouts so that we have but about A month to travel 500 miles in

My dear love: my love is to all our children & friends as if perticularly named which I have not time nor room at present to do & its by ye Governours favour as well as information that I met with this opertunity to deliver it to his care in A letter to Mr Lambol

our Son Billy I hope if we have our health will be of great service to me he desires to be remembered to his mother, brothers, sisters & friends

September ye 5th. — Thermo 80°   just ready to set out toward augusta when we have breakfasted   perhaps the next letter may be dated from Augustine; but if we come back to this town we shall be for writeing here.

however dear love in ye mean time I remain thy affectionate husband,

John Bartram in grat hast

this town is pretily situate on dry sandy ground & generaly good water great ships ly close too & safe harbour

BP 1:65; D. 425–27.
1. James Habersham (1712–1775), secretary and acting governor of the colony of Georgia.

From COLLINSON

Londn: 19th: Sept: 1765

It was highly Acceptable to Mee to hear of my Dear Johns safe Arrival in Carolina & to find his Botanic Genius began to Exert It self in New Discoveries — I wish Thou may Temper thy Zeal with Prudence but I do not think it an Instance of It when thou & Mrs. Lambol — rambled in the Intense Heat of a Mid Day sun — phaps it was to Procure thee a seasoning —

A Horse is a Necessary article for a Kings Botanist   but doth thou know who thou art to Thank for that title   Between our selves an old Friend who knew thou Deserved It but under what Character the King is pleased to rank thee, I do not know   only this I know He allows thee £50 per annum Forty pounds Sink Deep if it was sterling — but I presume that may be about Tenn pounds sterling   I should think Horses cheaper where they breed

Wild & are had for Catching   however when thou hast done with Him, the Horse will be worth some thing —

Keep an Exact account of all thy Expenses   I know thy oeconomy & moderation but want for nothing that Nature requires, if it is to be had.

I wish thou may Gett thy son William to go with thee who is a very Ingenious young Man & I believe has a general knowledge in Natural Things & will be very Assistant in procuring Them

Wee have Such revolutions at Court and so unsettled I have not Deliver'd thy Specimens — until more settled Times to take Due care & Notice of them

Thy Brothers makeing so free with the King[1] is ridiculous and giveing Mee a great Deal of Trouble at the Custom House & himself to the Expense of 6: 6: which I have Charged to thy account or Else I must dispose of the ores to pay it   You don't know the Difficulty, trouble & attendance to gett things to the King   Tho' I undertook it for thee I shall not for any Body Else

Wee have had a Long Hott dry Summer   Fahrenheits thermometer in my Parlour was often at 95 & in the open air in the shade at 84 & 85   I have had little comfort this summer for I cannot endure hott weather

the Sod of Orchis is now in flower   thee expected a new species for thou will know what is called the Ladies Tresses, being a spiral spike of very small white flowers, [illegible] with buds, at the same time in flower but no Heleborines   the Martigons flowerd finely & the Pittsburg Iris which is now as large again as thy Specimen and Increases finely — is a great acquisition, one of the Martigons proved the yellow which I wanted, besides grows Mountain Hypericum, Solomons Seal, pretty Fern, Desiduous bay, Striped Pyrola, Hazel, Warneria or yellow Root & ripe berry

Docr Solander is a strange Idle Man   I cannot gett thy spring specimens from Him, is the Reason thou hears nothing from Mee about Them —

It is wonderfull to see the fertility of your Country in Phlox & Viburnums   there is many things in the Kings Specimens that set Mee a Longing which I Hinted to thy son John of this Date —

Thine of May 29th & June 16th I answered Directed to General Bouquet in Florida   pray remember Mee respectfully to him   the like to my most worthy Friend Mr. Lambol not forgetting my Ingenious friend Docr Garden —

Now my Dear John Farewell   Thou hast the best wishes of thy old Friend

P. Collinson

BP 3:57; D. 270–72.
1. Bartram's brother William had shipped a heavy box of mineral specimens to the king.

From COLLINSON

Londn Novemr 13:1765

I Received my Dear Johns Letter — of the 28th Augst on the 13th Novemr I Delayed not a minute to return this answer —

I am concerned for thy Disorder — but more to think a Wise Man should have so Little prudence to ramble about with Mrs. Lambol in your Mid Day sun with such a Distemper on Him. *What cannot be Cured must be Endured* — for I see no remedy. Wee are now again on a Change of the Ministry — whilst the members of the Helm are thus fluctuating, no application can be made, for those by whom thou was appointed have been out some Time — & the set that is come in their Room is Expected to be Changed every Day — So pray make no more Remonstrances on that Head for I am tired with a repetition of them in Every Letter —

Thou knows the Length of the Chain of 50 Links, go as far as that goes — when thats at an End Cease to go any farther —

I have received Two ½ yrs sallary £50 & shall receive £25 More in March & so on — & if Wee live to Michaelmas there will be 25 more   this will on the whole be £100   Keep within this compass & be not a loser, nay if the King Lives and thou gives him Credit, thou may be no loser   phaps a gainer, if you both live long Enough

I allow all thou sayes   the premium is not Equal to the Risque but in these precarious unsetled Times there is no Hope for an alteration

I beg of thee don't expose thy Health but return Home & wait untill thy allowance amounts to a sum in Hand & then begin again.

I am glad Billey is with thee to take Care of thee   pray give my kind Respects to him.

I Doubt not of our good Friend Mr Lambolls Care of the Box — My kind Respects to Him

I am my Dear John thy sincere Fri —

P. *Collinson*

Our friend Mr. Ellis writt a Letter recommending thee to Gov Grant wch I hope he hath Received — He also wrote to the Govr of Pensacola to the same purpose.

BP 3:58; D. 272–73.

From COLLINSON

Londn:Decemr:28:1765

Dear John —

I don't know what to add to Mine of November 13th, by Last ship Minerva — but to inform thee of my Welfare and my Hope for thine — we hear with concern with what riotous Mobs the publick Tranquility is Disturbed, I hope when our Parliament Meets some happy Medium will be found to alay such unjustifiable proceedings & prevent them for the future[1]

I condole with Thee on the Great Loss of that worthy Man General Bouquet[2] I am sensible How It afflicts thee to be bereaved of so Generous & kind a Friend Especially in a Country where His Notice & regard gave such a reputation to thy undertaking, However I hope Good Providence Will raise thee up some other Friend to assist thee

I have had a Letter from thy son Informing Mee he was preparing the seeds but was fearful they would fall short to supply all my orders which will be a great disappointment to some —

I lately saw a quire of specimens sent by Docr Garden to Docr Russell amongst them are some Curious new species   When thine comes to hand which I conclude may Hourly Expect — what high spirits will attend our Friends Solander & Ellis on the survey of such Rare & New productions —

I hope by that Time this Comes to hand the fine Temperate season will be near Concluding   be sure make a retreat in time before the Great Heats comes on & sit down under thy own Vine & enjoy thy Family, contemplating on the Wonders Thou has seen & when the evenings grow long give thy old Friend a Tast of these Dainties who thou knowest will relish them as they Deserve & Treasure them up with the Rest of thy Curious & Ingenious Observations

As there is few pleasures in this Life but what are subject to alloys & Disappoints – this I have lately experienced to my no small Mortification, haveing been again robbed of my Most Curious plants   What I most regret was thy kind present of Loblolly Bays which throve finely, thy sod of Orchis in full flower & a too long a list to Mention Here — but amongst others, I regret the loss of the Long Leafed Sarracenia   as it is a plant of the south Countries where thou art or may Meet with it in thy Passage Home — pray Contrive to gett 3 or 4 plants & send Mee   thou knowest packed up all over in Moss & tied up with moss round Each plant is the way to send them securely —

my Last was by the Minerva — Novr 13 which I hope is come to hand I therein hinted our change of Ministry so no hopes of aditional salary — I therein Advised to retire with what Discoveries & Collections thou has Made & Wait untill thou art reimbursed all thy Charges & untill thou has gott stock in hand & then if in health & strength — may Make another expedition for I dont see there is any Reason, neither is it required that a Man should Wear himself out to serve others on so Slender an Encouragement — but I was willing to gett that, with pretty Good Hopes of Doubling It, if that Ministry had Continued

I am impatient to hear from thee for I am fearfull of the Climate & that thy ardency will push thee beyond thy strength & I shall be glad to hear thou art gott safe Home & yett I believe it must be Delightfull passing an Autumn a Winter & spring in so fine a Climate   thy last is of the 28th of August which I received 12th of November —

I wrote May 20 & June 30th with Mr. Ellis Letters Recommending [thee]   I wrote Aug. 8 under Cover to Genl. Bouquet in Georgia & wrote Sept:19 under Cover to our friend Lambol

Letters received this year 1765 from Bartram	May 11 May 29 June 19	sent under cover to Genl Bouquet by Lambol	June 29 July 12 Augst 28

Capt Oreys was so obliging as to Deliver the quire of specimens but times are so unsettled I keep them by Mee untill there is a probability of more Leisure to Examine Them — in the mean time Doctor Solander will settle them after the Linnaean System — [next paragraph illegible]

pray remember Mee sincerely & Heartily to Dear Friend Mr. Lambol — I feel for Him & sympathize with Him for the great loss that he has sustained in his son.

I hear with concern the great Commotions in the Provinces but I hope our new Ministry will set all to rights. My Dear John farewell — take care of thyself.

P. Collinson

My love to Billey [several lines illegible]

BP 3:59; D. 273–75.
1. Collinson refers to the riotous reception in the colonies to the infamous Stamp Act of 1765.
2. General Bouquet arrived in Florida on August 23 and died of a fever ten days later.

From GARDEN

S. Carolina, February 12th, 1766

My dear old Friend: –

How do you do? It is so long since I had a line from you, and then it was so short, containing no botanical news, that I scarcely could believe it came from you.

Think that I am here, confined to the sandy streets of Charleston, where the ox, where the ass, and where men as stupid as either, fill up the vacant space, while you range the green fields of Florida, where the bountiful hand of Nature has spread every beautiful and fair plant and flower, that can give food to animals, or pleasure to the spectator.

Pray, out of the abundance of what you see, send me some curiosities, particularly seeds for my garden. But let these be confined wholly to what is new and curious. Some young plants, in a box, would be very acceptable.

My best wishes always attend you and I am, dear sir,

Yours, &c.,
Alex. Garden

D. 399–400.

From GARDEN[1]

My dear Friend: –

It appears to me to be an age since I have had the pleasure of hearing from you. Pray, write me, and tell me what you are doing; for I know you can't be idle. Tell me what you are discovering, for I know your imagination and genius can't be still. How many wonders of creation do you daily see? Why won't you let me know a few?

Some time since, I had the inclosed from your wife, which I now send to you.

Your friend, Mr. Lamboll, informed me of this conveyance, and I am just to send him this letter. Remember me to your son: and I am, dear sir,

Yours, &c.,
Alex. Garden

I have your letter to your son, which I shall send by first opportunity; but at present all communication is stopped.

D. 400.
1. Undated; we have used Darlington's chronological placement. The original of this letter, like the preceding one, is missing from the Bartram Papers.

From COLLINSON

Londn:March 26th:1766

I Received My Dear John's Letter of Sepr 28th — Highly Delighted with the Rich Cargo that the Letter promised (but sad story to Tell) When I came to see Capt Arbuckle — He said no Such Box directed for Mee was putt on Board Him — but He promised to search everywhere & next Time I saw Him could find Nothing & was sure that there was no such Box putt on board Him — Think my Dear Frd — what Disappointment & Vexation I was under at this Great Loss —the only way to have prevented it Lay at thy Door — & that by haveing a Receipt of the captain for the Box & Inclosing it In thy Letter to Mee   Then I should have demanded the Box with authority, & made Him pay Damages if it was Lost — but now I had only thy Letter to show & that He Did not regard & said thou might Intend to putt the Box on board, but never did it.

The Boxes of seeds came all safe & Well & thy son had packed them very carefull   I was pleased to find He was so capable to supply Thy place & the Box of Seeds forwarded to be putt on board Capt Arbuckles ship [illegible]

One trouble seldome comes alone for it gives Mee much Concern to hear of your Troublesome Dangerous Journey from Georgia to St. Augustine   It was a great pitty you atempted It at so unseasonable a Time

Thou Vexes thyself & Mee with perpetual Complaints, thinking it is in my power to redress Them — but Really it lays too much at thy own Door — in being so Hasty for the expedition   Thou should have staid & got 2 or 3 hundred pounds before hand & then sett out, but as I told thee before if thou Lives, & the King lives, thou will be no Loser — so pray do not tire Mee any more with repetition of Complaints but return Home as soon as thou Can & sit down & gather strength & receive thy Income —

It is very fortunate to have so good an opportunity to go to the Congress at Picolatta

Your work for the Duke of Cumberland[1] is fruitless, for the British Hero is no more.

The odd scene that an old Spanish town must make to an English Man must afford him Entertainment to see the Different modes of the Two nations in their buildings, &c., & I apprehend the rural prospects must be fine & afford a Variety of rare plants &c   In this Happy Climate Turn where one Will new Beauties rise, — little did I think some months agon, Natures Virgin Charms were reserved to be Rifled by an Enterprising Bartram — but pray take Care that we are not deprived of these precious spoils — the loss of the Last hangs Heavily on the Mind of thy old Friend

P. Collinson

Picolata. *Harper's New Monthly Magazine* 41 (1870):659.

pray remember Mee to Billy   I am much concern'd for the Disasters that befell him.

March 27th — My Dear John I have good News to tell thee   the box that thou Intended by Captain Arbuckle is safe arrived in Capt Ball at Dover — advised of it by a very Civil Letter from Mr. Graham Inclosing the Capt's Receipt for it —

BP 3:62; D. 276–77.
1. William Augustus, Duke of Cumberland (1721–1765), British general and George III's brother.

To WILLIAM BARTRAM[1]

April ye 5th 1766

I have procured 4 good yams two white & two red A present from ye colonel & sent. A west india gentleman said thay cut of one half of ye yam & planted ye upper part of it in A prety large hill of loose earth prety deep & when ye vine shot up A foot high thay set it A pole deep in ye hill 8 or 9 foot high for ye vine to run up   he says ye whole root dont do so well as ye upper part cut of ye lower part thay eate   how this will do I cant say   to make ye pumkins & cowcumbers large thay cut of ye top when thay run several yards which makes them branch & bear prodigiously. thay say ye potatoes is ye best that is raised from ye cuttings of ye vines   if so here surely in florida this method will produce well. I believe if the setts fire to ye 20 acre marsh will be ye place to plant rice in this year if it be two wett hoe it up in narrow ridges & plant ye rice on ye ridge for all agree if ye water covers ye young blade it will kill it: most here thinks that where ye grass grows so rank as about thy house amongst tall pines such ground will bear good corn when ye pines is fallen & ye tops burnt but above all take care ye negroes dont fall ye trees upon one another   thee hath sufficient warning   its supposed here that half A bushel of rice will plant an acre of rich new land but ould land takes twice as much   I have packed up A rice barrel marked B containing 3 bushels of seed rice one cov. pot one iron pot one heavy pensylvania ax A broad ax. adze. shovel much better than any spade. saw. rag whetsone bass line & hook. leading chisell: & mistris Lambol hath sent 3 stone cups A bed Cloath for thee to fill with feathers of ducks & turkey. A kettle A bushel & half or two of pease. taniers A pot of sugar ground nuts & several garden seeds beans &c. I have sent 20 yards of crocus & hesing for bags to fill with moss which ye people here say makes good beds   I have ordered by ye procurement of Col. Laurance two barrels of corn one of rice A barrel of poark & ye Colonel sent thee A cask of salt gratis. provisions here is strangely risen within A week or two. rice is double what it was indian corn twenty shillings per bushel & both it & peas wholy prohibited sending out but by ye Col. favour he spared us some   Captain hardy did bring thy watch to be mended & took it away to Philadelphia   promised to leave it with thy mother: Narney[2] saith it will not go long well. that it is not worth much. all thy friends here laments thy resolute choice to live at St johns & leave off drawing or writing   thay say ye negros will run away or murder thee   thay all seem to have A miserable opinion of negroes & recons ye new ye best as not yet haveing learnt ye mischievous practices of ye negroes born in ye countrey & town which the people generaly represents as if thay was all either murderers runaways or robers or theeves: espetialy ye Plantation negroes   I have at last by ye dayly assistance & choice of Doctor garden Major Moultrey[3] Mr. Sanders[4] & Col: Lawrans[5] all which tooke A great deal of pains to examine them   ye Colonel is owned by all to be ye best Judge in town as to thair appearance & ye doctor examined thair health   thay chose these out of several hundred of both publick & private sail: ould Mr Lambol hath been very sick & could do nothing but give his advice which runs all upon haveing nothing to do with them & declares thay are ye greatest curse that ever came to america yet owns that there is no raiseing rice without them   this is Menegots[6] & Narneys story   Colonel Lawrance bought ye two new negroes for me & ye doctor examined them as to thair health   thay have chose each other for man & wife & she is with child & the other woman I chose for A wife for Jacob   she is allso supposed to be with child so that if thay do well thee may boldly claim A pattent from ye Governour

I have shiped on board ye East florida Captain Bachop 6 likely negroes called Jack A lusty man A new negro 5 foot 8 inches high & 1/4: Siby his wife new 5 foot one inch 3/4: Jacob 5 foot high & Sam 4 foot 7 inches 1/2   allso flora A lusty woman not so black as many A cromantee which her master & mistris solemnly declares to be incorupted with ye vices of ye town being never sufered to go out at night or any negroes to come to her but ye family   she has A general good character & Bachus her son is A prety boy 3 or 4 years ould   I have allso sent A pair of good millstones & A grind stone: & A pair of smoothing irons delivered to ye care of slaves   half A dozen Sickles or hooks   A choice good Jack plain   A bar of lead for to make slugs which many guns will shoot truer then A round bullet   we cutt it about A quarter longer then its thickness which should slip down ye barrel prety easy: our friend Lambol tels me ye way to catch mullets is to take ye cano[e] in ye night with A stick of lightwood 3 or 4 foot long well lighted which one must hould in his hand as far as he can reach toward ye grass or reed about 2 or 3 foot water where ye mullets sleep   ye other strikes on ye side of ye cano to waken them   thay seeing ye light Jump from it into ye cano which must be heded whereby multitudes is catched   if the thinks thee can safely let ye negroes blood let me know & I will send thee A lancet
                                                                                                              John Bartram

Doctor garden & others say that when ye negroes pounds rice thay will be all in A sweat   then thay run out or to ye dore with thair brest open   then they catch cold & often fall into A pleurisy which he rates with ye flux two of ye most dangerous diseases & adviseth thee to take great care of them & thair cloathes which thay are now well furnished with   for thay will not take any care of themselves

To
Mr William Bartram in
St Augustine in
East florida

BP 1:62.
1. John Bartram and his son William had left Charleston, South Carolina (Charles Town) on August 31, 1765, bound for Florida. Bartram had returned there alone on March 22,

1766. No letters from them after that of John to Ann, September 4, 1765, have been found. Their travels and discoveries during that time are recounted in John Bartram's "Diary of a Journey Through the Carolinas, Georgia, and Florida from July 1, 1765, to April 10, 1766," annotated by Francis Harper, in *Transactions of the American Philosophical Society,* n.s., 32 (December 1942), pt. 1. A brief outline of their travels may be helpful to readers of these letters. They went first to Savannah, made a side trip to Augusta, returned to Savannah, then continued to St. Augustine by way of Fort Barrington. They reached St. Augustine October 11 and remained there until late December. In mid-November they accompanied Governor James Grant to a conference with the Creek Indians at Picolata. On December 19 they began an exploration by boat of the St. Johns River to its source. A guide for the trip had been furnished by the governor. After eight weeks they returned to St. Augustine, where Bartram spent the next month recuperating and completing his journal. He delivered the journal and a map of the river to Governor Grant in mid-March and took passage for Charleston. Billy had decided, against the advice of his father and others, to remain in Florida and become a planter. He located a tract of land, which was to be patented when he had imported a number of slaves. His father very reluctantly agreed to purchase both slaves and supplies for him at Charleston.

2. Unidentified.
3. Probably John Moultrie (d. 1773), Scottish physician and planter.
4. Unidentified.
5. Henry Laurens.
6. Gabriel Manigault (1704–1781), wealthy South Carolina merchant.

From JOHN LANE[1]

London 7 April 1766

Mr. John Bartram
Sir

Your Esteemed favour of the 7 of November is now before me & in answer thereto I am to inform you that I have received in good order the Case of seeds you packt for me, they are now in the Ground & hope they will turn out well. I am greatly oblig'd to you for the plants, there is but one Dead, the rest are in a flourishing state. If I should have any occasion for any more I shall take the freedom of Sending to you in the Interim I remain with great Respect Sir

Your most hum'le Servt
John Lane

BP 4:69.
1. Unidentified. This order was filled by John, Jr., in his father's absence.

To WILLIAM BARTRAM

April the 9th 1766

Dear billy
I have now A most greevous cough that teaseth me night & day yet I have sent thee six likely young negroes amongst which is two young breeding

wenches thee desired   one A new guiney negro & ye other A cormantie which is here reconed ye best of slaves & shee Can wash & Iron cloaths & as thay say she was never corrupted with vices of ye town shee perhaps may be trusted with ye care of ye rest in thy absence   shee hath a prety boy between 3 or 4 year ould   shee perhaps may make A wife for Jacob   but how thee will get ye provisions on shore on thy land   two large barrels of corn one of rice one of ruf rice for planting. peas taniers &c wth pot kettle & tools packed up in A large barrell   A barrel of pork mill stone & grind stone; there is one mr kinlaw[1] Comes with 16 negroes & provisions to settle at Duns creek above rolls town[2] which will be A fine opertunity of bringing thy provisions up with his but what place will be fit to land them without getting wet & preserving ye barrels which will be of great use to thee; suppose thee should take ye negroes by land up & search A place in ye cove below thy house & if it not be deep enough to come with ye boat close to shore thee may drive strong forked sticks into ye mud on which lay cross pieces close & next to ye water on which 3 ft. high poles may be laid 3 or 4 in. width to shore on which as far as ye swamp reacheth should be laid poles to role ye barrels on or else ye moistur will squees to ye corn & spoil it. I am apt to believe it will be best for thee to plant as many pease as possible for ye negroes   thay say here that thay are ye most profitable of any thing thee can plant & will grow well in new poor ground & thee hath plenty of seed I suppose two rails high on forked sticks will make suffitent fence of A log or two at bottom with A rail & stakes at top on high ground will do   there hath been so much rain here & thair rice ground in many places is 4 foot deep in water which thay think will not be dry enough to plant in season but thay say if thee plants any time in may or begining of June it will do at St Johns   I have sent thee A good adze for makeing troughs for washing & other uses which thee will much want for makeing lye to wash with, trays & bowls as well for other uses   I have not sent thee ye Bills of sail for the negroes. I am advised to ye contrary until I have setled ye affair at home in altering my will & as thee hath ye full use of them as much as if thee had them never so firm as to their labours   it can be no detriment to thee; to forbear makeing them thy own property until I can settle my affairs at home, for I intend no other than thay & thair issue to be made firm to thee   I should have sent thee some potatoes to plant but I am afraid that thay will be all rotten before thay reach thy place, which I doubt will not be before may. I have sent thee another parcel of garden seeds ye gift of Mistris Lambol [sewed?] round ye half A dozen sickles with ye bar of lead & A Jack plain sent by ye care of mr. Learons. I have paid Captain Bechops by Col Laurens for ye negros diet of 15 days begining ye 5th of April   he tooke them on board I believe ye night before when thay had been kept at my charge 6 pence sterling A piece per day — for one barrel of rice   15 pound for two barrels of corn   14-4-6 for one barrel of pork — 11-10 for 15 days keeping ye negros 11 lbs — 5s on board   this is Col. Laurans account

April 10   this morning I was with Mr Kinlaw   he thinks he can prevail with ye Governour to let Captain Bachop take both of our provisions together up St Johns   if so thee had better put thy chest on board of him which will be a fine opertunity of haveing it home if thee can be so lucky as to be in town when he lands   if so thee must keep A good looke out when ye vesail ankors against thy point for Mr Kinlaw will not like to wait there long

tomorrow I am to embark for Philadelphia expecting to be very sick all ye while at sea as I was in comeing here. pray write to me at Philadelphia by ye first opertunity & let me know how thy affairs stands & how thee likes thy scituation & what is most wanted: ye negros in charlstown is excessive dear so is ye plantation negroes which is dayly running away   ye people was forced to hire ye Catawba indians to hunt them & if thay can take them alive to do it for double price of those thay killed which made several to come home again but yet many lurketh about in ye swamps amongst ye inhabitants   I have been tould to-day another method to catch mullet is to go with A Cano in ye darkest night & one at each end of ye cano to hold A torch of light wood while A third stroak smartly on ye heeled side & ye fish would soon in great numbers Jump into ye Cano   thay went chiefly among ye thin grass in shallowish water or ye mouths of little creeks, where ye fish resorts to sleep which are wakened by ye stroaks of the cano which must often change place to surprise other dormant fish   here is A vesail Just arived from Augustine but no letter from my son   Mistris Lambol hath taken such pains to get things for thee & when thee hath time in hot weather & cant work out dore thee may draw some prety bird butterfly or plant for Mrs. Polly which will pleas them prodigiously   every body that sees thy drawings admires them exceedingly   I would have thee to plant A great many wild limes   many thinks thay will be one of ye greatest improvements in all east florida & ye market for oil or tallow can never be over stated   you need never trouble your selves about ye oil or wine while you can raise such quantities of oil without half ye pains ye others require   besides ye kernell after ye oil is extracted out would be ye richest feeding for h[ogs] & thay may be easily raised in fence rows & perhaps would make good [illegible] & will come soon to bear & perhaps thay would make us good Chokolet   I have sent thee for thy further incouragement two guineas which thee will take care of & lay it out in that most needful & shall still remain thy loveing father

John Bartram

New-York Historical Society, Bartram Folder.
1. Francis Kinloch, planter in South Carolina and Georgia.
2. The colony Lord Denys Rolle founded on St. Johns River; also known as Charlotia.

From COLLINSON

Mill Hill   May 28th: 1766

I received my Dear Johns from Carolina and Accepd thy Bill for £150:5:8 — I think thou hast done prudently to settle thy Son William for He is an

Ingenious young Man & I hope his Ingenuity will prompt Him to Industry, to Improve the Talent that in thy Paternal Goodness thou hast bestowed on him   I wish I could tell how to write to him without — any expense to Him, to give him my Friendly Advice as I have a great respect for Him — but one Thing is not to be omitted & that is to get him a Virtuous Industrious Wife such as knows how to share the Toils as well as the Comforts of a Marriage State   He will not settle rightly to Business untill this is done for then Home will be always agreeable to Him, if this is not done he'll fall into the snares of a Loose unlawfull way of Life from whence no good can come but much evil & Inconvenience.

I have read thy Journal over & over with much Entertainment but observe by the specimens that Nature seems to have Exhausted her stores in the Carolina's in the variety of Magnolias, Loblolly Bays, All spice, Stuartia, Red Acacias, Halesias &c   I think Georgia affords no new plants Equal to any of these — there is indeed some pretty things but they are not striking flowering Trees like the above.

My Dear John I wonder thou should trouble thy self about the Queen as she has Young, & Everything will be shown Him   it cannot be expected he will favour any Ones Interest but his own, He is now so new modelled & grown so fine & fashionable with his Hair Curled & tied in a Black bag, that my people that have seen Him often, did not know Him, I happened not to be at Home so could not Inquire what scheme he is upon —

I shall be Glad to hear that thou art safely returned Home & in such good Health & spirits as will permit thee to sit down calmly to reflect with Thankfullness on the pleasures & Danger past —

I have sent the 3 quires of specimens to the King with the seeds   It was a great disadvantage to the specimens that they had sufferd by the Wet, however, Docr Solander could discover many new undescribed articles amongst them as well as those from Georgia & Florida.

Thy short account of St. Augustine was very acceptable to thee as Well as to Mee to see the buildings of the Spaniards & other of their contrivances   pray tell Mee what sort of Improvements they had made in the Country for the support of themselves & their cattle, what sort of fabric was their church, no doubt all the ornaments they carried away — & further tell Mee if there are any True genuine Spaniards tempted by their possessions to remain there   I think its situation is pleasant   if no Spaniards are left it must be a great advantage to the English new settlers to enter on their premises & possess their Improvements, which I suspect from their native sloth & laziness, are Inconsiderable for a Spaniard is content with a very Little provided he can but indulge himself with sitting in the sun and doing next to nothing.

In all thy expedition didst thee fall in with any Indians, What nation & how did they behave   Is there a disposition in them to continue in peace & friendship   there is much talk of civilizing them, A good sensible man named Hammerer[1] a foreigner who was long in London could not be easy without going to reside among the Cherokees, in order to try to bring them to a sense of Moral duties

I have heard that the Opuntia or Indian Fig grows in such abundance at Augustine that the fruit was a great food of the Inhabitants   Is it a Different species from those at New York   I conclude the Palmetto arrives to a greater size than those Our poor Friend Dickinson[2] & his family that was cast away on the Coast was obliged to subsist on the Palmetto & Cassena Berries & though such is the force of Necessity   If thee hath not this History I will send it thee

June 3d: this Day I accepted thy bill for 14:3:13 drawn from St. Augustine — I shall be glad to hear thou art safe Home   the Pittsburgh dwarfe Iris made a [illegible] show this year & all the Solomons seals grow [illegible] — but the Rogues came the Second Time & stole my Two Loblolly bays Magnolia Minor & great Rhododendrons & many others — the Great Sylphinon

Billys Elegant drawings are admired by all that see them   When He comes to be setled I must get Him to Look out for Insects of any kind for in His warm southern situation these Creatures increase in size & beauty with many new species that you have not — When thou writes to Him pray give my Respects & thanks for his Curious presents

I dont forget my honest Friend Moses who sent Mee a very Sensible respectful Letter & remember Mee to our young Botanist thy son Johnny

People begin to be tired with the same seeds over & over again   could no plan be formed for Billy to send seeds from Georgia to make a Little new Variety in your Cargoes

I have no orders for seeds but from Fern — probably the other seedsmen write to thee & send their Orders — I have only on my my [sic] private Sale on order for Two Boxes & Two Single Boxes for Gordon —

So now Dear John Farewell

P. Collinson

Mr Ehret our famous flower painter was with Mee & I showed Him Billys paintings, He admired as Wee do all, his fine Red Centaury a most Elegant plant, if Wee can but gett it in our Gardens — His Butterflies, Locust are Nature itself his yellow Fly is admirable   I am pleased to see that He had got so pretty a Way of drying Fish — by it wee may have a Hortus siccus or rather Oceanous siccous of Fish   when I see Solander He will tell Mee the species & if it is new will inform thee — I have had only three Letters   Sepr 28 Augustine Octo 15 & Charles Town March 27   I hope None have miscarried — the Two Inclosed specimens I received From young   if they are Different from what thou has Sent I should like to have them for I love all the tribe of Andromeda & [illegible] or Hurtle berries of which I have several that thrive & Flowers well but never Fruits in our Climate   What a Glorious Variety of New plants   I hope to have Docr Solanders remarks on them

It is Impossible I suppose, to get plants of the Inclosed Leaves of N 13 a Charming Species of Kalmia – pray Desire Johnny to Look out for a plant or Two of the Broad Leaved Ever Green Andromeda – of the Narrow I have

Enough Leaves – and Red Bud Andromeda   both the sorts I want much I had them formerly, but now I know their Culture

BP 3:64; D. 278–81.
1. Unidentified.
2. Jonathan Dickinson, a Jamaica Quaker, was wrecked off Jupiter Island on the way to Philadelphia with his family; he wrote about the experience in *Ship-wreck in the Gulf of Florida* (London, 1699).

To COLLINSON

June ye   1766[1] Skulkil at my own house

Dear Peter

I am now returned to my family all whome I found in good health   God almighty be Praised for his favours. I am at present tolerable well but can hardly get over ye dreadful sea sickness & ye Southward fever   I have left my son Billy in florida. nothing will do with him now but he will be A planter upon St Johns river about 24 mile from Augustine & 6 from ye fort of Picolata   this frolick of his hath & our maintenance drove me to great straits so that I was forced to draw upon thee at st Augustine & twice at charls town all of which I sent thee letters of advice either with or in ye bills of exchange which I hope thee will answer for thy ould & yet true friend but I should be well pleased if thee will let me know perticularly how our account stands now   I have not had it of several years; my sons tels me that thee objected against my bills of 40 pound not being indorsed   ye meaning of which we cant understand   I think thay was sent as usual   this makes me very uneasy lest some or all those bills of exchange I drawed upon thee in florida & charles town should not answer thy critical examination alltho thay was drawn by men of very good Characters & learning & I am sure Intend nothing but strict Justice & very willing if thay be not drawn right to thy mind to have them mended   I have packed up in A little box directed to thee at large ye seeds I brought from florida which I should have sent sooner but had not A good opertunity but yet thay are good   dont dispair of thair coming up if not this year yet may come in 3 year as many of ye southern Plants do   those that I brought from New river & ye wateree 3 years past & sowed directly when I cam home is come up this spring & some others every spring since I sowed them   many of my florida plants & those of georgia is come up but I dont expect thay will all come up in less then one or two springs more: ye undermost seeds I send for ye king & those above ye pertition paper is for thy self except A little lining bag directed to John Web who hath sent A fine Collection of curious garden seeds by Captain friend whom we dayly expect at Philadelphia   pray send ye little bag to him or let him know of it   if ye vesail sails tomorrow I will not have time to write to him   I am grated ye cargo my son John sent last fall is come safe & in good order as thy letter by Captain shirley mentions   John is in high spirits about it   I have brought home with me A fine Collection of strange florida plants which perhaps I may send sometime this summer some for ye king & some for thy self but I want to know how those I sent from charles town & georgia is accepted or those I sent last spring to ye king from home   I hope what specimens I sent for thy self will give thee great pleasure as many of them is intirely new ye collecting of which hath cost thy friend many score pounds pains & sickness which held me constantly near or quite two months in florida   ye fever & Jaundice & A looseness thro No & So Carolina & georgia yet some how or other I lost not an hours time of travailing thro those provinces & when at Augustine with ye fever & Jaundice I traveled both by water & land all round ye town for many miles & to Picolata to ye congress altho so weak as hard set to get up to small bed chamber & during ye meeting of ye governor & indians in ye Pavilion I was forced to sit or ly down upon ye ground, close by its side that I might observe what passed

BP 1:49:2; D. 281.
1. Probably June 30 (see Collinson to Bartram, August 21, 1766).

To WILLIAM BARTRAM

July ye 3d 1766

Dear Son William
I received thy letter of June ye 6th   I wish it had come A little sooner before Mr. Rundle sent A cargo to Augustine by which I wrote to thee. he was at my house with his wife A little while past & promised to let me know when he had orders from Mr. Cummins to send another Cargo to Augustine   that what I pleased to send to thee he would take care to send it carefully; thee write that thee received my letter but I sent two — one enclosed to Parson forbs[1] & in one of ye two I sent thee two guineas which the doth not mention nor ye grindstone & millstones nor ye tools & other things I sent which I suppose thy usual ingratitude would not suffer the to mention: thay cost me dear & so much that I am still in debt for them: money being so very scarce that I cant get it when it is owing many years & ye expensive wall & bank of near half A mile is not near compleated which must be done before winter or most of it will be washed away by ye tide   I am very sorry thee was so hindred by ye bad weather as to loose A crop but I hope thee may plant some corn if not rice if it be but two or 3 acres it will help some & the hath been & is very indolent if the hath not planted much garde[n] truck —squash pomkins peas beans melons & taniers which I sent from town if thine at davises[2] should not come Mrs. Lambol sent the all ye garden seed she had which may be sowed any time of ye year with you as thay grow as well or better then in summer   I expected thee had bought A couple of cows with ye money I left in Mr. Cummins hands for that purpose: if A mare & colt could be bought reasonably thee should have them   thay will be of use & profit if thay will increase. thay tould me at augustine that Fish[3] has

allways some to sell cheape; when Daniel rundle sends next from Philadelphia to Augustine I hope to send provision & cloath & an order to Mr. Cummins if not some money but thee should let me know what thee has had of him allready for I will not answer any extravagant draught   I am not against finding thee real nessesaries this year but thee must expect to suffer ye first year as all do in new settlements   in ye mean time I remain thy loving father

John Bartram

I have a grievous painfull ulcer in each leg that I cant rest night or day mother brothers & sisters love to thee wishing thee health & prosperity

New-York Historical Society, Bartram Folder.
1. Rundle, Cummins, and Forbes have not been identified.
2. Probably Robert Davis, whose son acted as a guide for the Bartrams on their exploration of the St. Johns River.
3. Unidentified.

From HENRY LAURENS

Charleston, S.C., 9th August 1766

Sir:-

I have had the pleasure of hearing, from some of our acquaintance here, that you were safely arrived in Philadelphia, but that good news has been somewhat abated by Captain Eastwick's account, that you were very sick, when he left that city. I hope soon to know, from your own hand, that you are recovered, and as well re-established as we poor brittle clay-shells can expect to be, at three-score and ten.

Since you left Carolina, I have prosecuted my long-intended voyage and journey through the southern parts of this country, and Georgia, to East Florida; and was near five weeks in the last mentioned province; in which time I thrice visited the River St. John, often landed upon each shore, exploring the swamps and hummocks, pine barens, and sand barrens, between the great lake and the ocean; and you may be sure I did not carelessly pass by your son's habitation. I called upon him twice; and as a confirmation of it, you will find inclosed in this, a letter from him, wrote after my second visit.

Your knowledge of that country, together with the addition of Mr. William Bartram's remarks upon his further experience, renders it unnecessary, as it would be unedifying, for me to trouble you with my few general observations; but I hope you will not think me quite impertinent, if I detain you to say a word or two touching the particular situation and circumstances of that poor young man; and the less so, when you know that it is done partly at his request.

His situation on the river is the least agreeable of all the places that I have seen, — on a low sheet of sandy pine barren, verging on the swamp, which before his door is very narrow, in a bight or cove of the river, so shoal, and covered with umbrellas, that the common current is lost and the water almost stagnated, exceedingly foul, and absolutely stank when stirred up by our oars, on both days of my landing there, though, at the same times, the river was said to be rather high, and the stream running down strong, beyond the cove. This, I should think, must make the place always unhealthy, as well as troublesome to come at, by water carriage, especially in dry seasons.

The swamp and adjoining marsh which I walked into, will, without doubt, produce good rice, when properly cleared and cultivated: but both

Henry Laurens (1723–1792). *Harper's New Monthly Magazine* 56 (1882–83):41.

seem to be narrow, and will require more strength to put them in tolerable order, than Mr. Bartram is at present possessed of, to make any progress above daily bread, and that of a coarse kind, too.

There is some Cypress, which, if he had a little more strength, he might soon convert into shingles and ready money.

The Pine land (I am sorry to differ in opinion with you) is very ordinary; indeed, I saw none good in the whole country; but that piece of his may justly be ranked in an inferior class, even there.

At my first visit, your son showed me the growth of some peas, beans, corn and yams, planted only four days before, in the sand on the swamp-edge, which then looked very flourishing; but when I called three weeks after, although there had been much rain in the mean time, the progress was barely perceptible; a remark that we both concurred in.

I found that he had, according to my advice, continued to clear the swamp, and in that time cut down part of an acre of trees; but that sort of work goes on very heavily, for want of strong hands. He assured me that he had but two, among the six negroes that you gave him, that could handle an axe tolerably; and one of those two had been exceedingly insolent. I encouraged and pressed him to put a little rice in the ground, even at that late day (5th or 6th July); and he promised to do so the day following.

The house, or rather hovel, that he lives in, is extremely confined, and not proof against the weather. He had not proper assistance to make a better, and from its situation it is very hot, the only disagreeably hot place that I found in East Florida: but it should be remarked, that the weather had been uncommonly temperate. His provision of grain, flesh, and spirits, is scanty, even to penury, the latter article very much so. His own health very imperfect. He had the fever, when I was first with him, and looked very poorly the second visit. I am determined, by the next conveyance, to send him a little rum, wine, sugar, tea, cheese, biscuit, and other articles, and charge the small amount to your account; though I would most freely give him the whole, but for fear that you should take it amiss.

Possibly, sir, your son, though a worthy, ingenious man, may not have resolution, or not that sort of resolution, that is necessary to encounter the difficulties incident to, and unavoidable in his present state of life. You and I, probably, could surmount all those hardships without much chagrin. I verily believe that I could. But, at the same time, I protest that I should think it less grievous to disinherit my own son, and turn him into the wide world, if he was of a tender and delicate frame of body and intellects, as yours seems to be, than to restrict him, in my favour, just in the state that your son is reduced to. This is no doubt more than ever you apprehended; and admitting that my account is in part erroneous (which I do not admit, meaning to speak nothing but truth), yet the general outlines of the foregoing description must affect and grieve you. But it is by no means my design, or intention, to compass any particular end by colouring too strongly. In fact, according to my ideas, no colouring can do justice to the forlorn state of poor Billy Bartram. A gentle, mild young man, no human inhabitant within nine miles of him, the nearest by water, no boat to come at them, and those only common soldiers seated upon a beggarly spot of land, scant of the bare necessaries, and totally void of all the comforts of life, except an inimitable degree of patience, for which he deserves a thousand times better fate; an unpleasant, unhealthy situation; six negroes, rather plagues than aids to him, of whom one is so insolent as to threaten his life, one a useless expense, one a helpless child in arms;

* * *

distant thirty long miles from the metropolis, no money to pay the expense of a journey there upon the most important occasions, over a road always bad, and in wet weather wholly impassable, to which might be enumerated a great many smaller, and perhaps some imaginary evils, the natural offspring of so many substantial ones; these, I say, are discouragements enough to break the spirit of any modest young man; and more than any man should be exposed to, without his own free acceptance, unless his crimes had been so great as to merit a state of exile.

I had been informed, indeed, before my visit to Mr. W. B., that he had felt the pressure of his solitary and hopeless condition so heavily, as almost to drive him to despondency. He expressed an inclination to decamp from the place that I have endeavoured to describe; but was supported, by advice of a friend, to wait until he should see me, who was then daily expected in East Florida. He did not open his mind so fully to myself; but rather modestly appealed to me, upon his circumstances and situation, accompanying his complaints with the most dutiful and affectionate mention of his father, to whom he requested I would take some notice of them in my next letter: in answer to which, I gave him my sentiments very candidly, encouraging him at the same time to persevere until he should hear from you. I have presumed to say so much, in consequence of my promise to him upon that request, as well as from a natural and irresistible inclination to relieve every virtuous man in distress; and as the foregoing representation can have no evil effects, however it may be imperfect, or appear to be officious, I trust that I shall not suffer under your candid interpretation.

After this account of your son's circumstances, I might add a list of several necessary articles beside exchange of good negroes, in place of almost useless ones, that are wanting and will be wanted to mend them a little; but no doubt he has given some needul hints on that head, and if his modesty has restrained his pen, you will, if you pay any regard to what I have been so bold as to write upon so slight an acquaintance as ours, cheerfully and quickly give orders to supply him with such things as shall be necessary to make his banishment less galling, and present him with some prospect of reaping the fruit of his labours.

Here I shall drop the subject; and, after presenting Mrs. Laurens's and my own hearty good wishes, put an end to this long letter, subscribing myself, sir

Your most obedient servant,
Henry Laurens

D. 438–42.

From COLLINSON

Londn August 21: 1766 —

I Received my Dear Johns Letter of June 30th and really am at a loss to say any thing unless thou was more perticular as to the Specimens where they was Collected — I have received only Two Quire of specimens one that had been Wett & another I think collected on St Johns River — but I have sent both Quires to Phil: Miller so can not be Exact — if Thou hath sent More then they have not come to Hand — besides I have no Letter & Advice about them & By what ship sent & thou knows our Friend Lambol He is a punctual Man, all this I have hinted in a former Letter

The Florida Seeds & fossils came safe & were delivered to the King who is pleased with them.

I am much concerned for thy ulcer Docr Fothergill is gone out of town for months Else would have sent thee his advice but you have I should think skilful people at Philadelphia though a Good Old Womans nostrum has carried the prize from them all — pray consult some Indians, they have done Wonders in Obstinate Cases by their simples — I believe our Friend Wm Logans Correspondent is Gordon no one packs better although thou had bad Luck write to Him again & see if better Success will attend it I am pleas'd to hear my Friend Warners Jessamin[1] Thrives so Well it is Easily Inarched by Layering or Cuttings — the Double I have had Many Many Years [several lines illegible] Climate by such flowers in December it is the True Accacia Egyptica My friend John makes no allowance for letters miscarrying when seeds dont come that he writ for Repeat them every Letter Remember the widow in the Gospel succeeded at last by her Importunity

The Stuartia flowered for the first Time in the Princess of Wales' Garden at Kew which is the Paradise of our world where all plants are found that money or Interest can procure when I am there I am transported with the novelty & Variety & dont know which to admire first or most — I am Ruined with Two Great Roberies, so I cannot stand in any Competition once I bore the Bell, but now I very humbly condescend to be on an Equall footing with my neighbours — Wee have got an Act passed this session to transport the Rogues — but Wee must first catch them & thats not Easily done, as they come by night —

My new beauty beside Red Obelescotheca or Rudbekia flowers — the petals are much broader & shorter silver Colour'd then that Wee had before pray send more seed for they will not Ripen with us

I have Inclosed some seed of a Perannual [illegible] but a very uncommon Sort, for it Dies Back Every year but rises to Six foot high & makes a fine show of garden Flowers

Now my Dear John farewell

P Collinson

I wrote thee the 10th instant & sent thy Account Current by the Packet for more safety Wee have had a tedious uncommon Wett Summer which threatened Distress & famine but more than Two weeks passed Good Providence has sent us fine seasonable Warm Dry Weather for our Harvest and our Crops are reported to be plentifull I dare say thou wonders at my Ignorance in this Matter but thy wonder will Cease when I tell thee I go

Every week Twelve Miles & don't see a Corn field   I may go 2 or 3 Miles further & not see It for our Country is an Ever Green Country   all grass for sheep but no Daireys   our Fields feeds Cattle for the slaughter, and after its pasturage for sheep who suckle Lambs all the Winter — at Xmas I see the Lambs playing on the open Fields all around Mee & hear their Tender bleating which is Pastoral & Rural

BP 3:65; D. 282–83.
1. This was the gardenia, brought from the Cape of Good Hope by a ship captain and presented to his friend Richard Warner of London.

To COLLINSON

august ye 26th 1766

Dear Peter

I wrote to thee last week by ye Brig Elizabeth Captain Colley ye day after which I received thy kind letter: ye last date of which was June ye 6th   am glad to hear of thy acceptance of my bill for £150 5s. 8d. & that from augustine & shall be pleased with ye acceptance of another from augustine & charlstown & to know how our accounts stands but I am afraid all will be thrown away upon him he is so whimsical & so unhappy as not to take any of his friends advice   mr. De Bram[1] wanted him to go with him to draw draughts for him in his survey of florida but Billy would not tho by that Journey he would have had ye finest opertunity of seeing ye countrey & its productions   I have forgot what part of my Journal I sent thee from augustine except ye thermometrical observations. I alow that those flowering trees thee mentions, in Carolina is very fine most of which grow in georgia & florida but then there grows in both these last places many more curious evergreen trees & shrubs which if not so beautifull in flowers comes fully up with those & perhaps surpassed them in beauty of fruit & sweet scent as may be observed by my specimens gathered on ye banks of St Johns river   I am obliged to thee for sending ye specimens to ye King & also for thy advice about ye Queen   I sent last spring ye seeds I collected in east florida   Augustine now is in A very ruinous Condition to what it was when ye Spaniards lived there   ye soldiers has pulled down above half ye town for ye sake of ye timber to burn   most of ye best houses stands yet several of which is much altered by ye english who drives ye chimney thro ye tops of ye house roofs & ye sun begins to shine thro glass where before its light was admitted between ye bannisters & where ye well cultivated gardens was is now grown over with weeds & is ye common pasture for Cattle   many of ye orange trees & figs near or quite A foot in diameter cut down or grubbed up for firewood for ye english dont make much use of ye sour oranges as ye spaniards   Nor ye Citrons or sweet lemons but now ye sweet lemons limes & guavas is chiefly taken care of but ye two latter is most of them killed (espetialy ye branches) last winter   so was ye bananas   as for ye figs & pomegranates ye english is not very fond   I saw two of ye Opuntias as thick as my midle & 6 foot high much branched thay seemed to be near ye same kind with ours but I am apt to think ye fruit ye spaniards eat so much off was ye species of huica with terrible sharp spines at ye ends of thair leaves which some call adams needles   others palmeto Royal & some bananas from thair fruite which is sweet with A little bitterness & is ye chief fencing about augustine both against man & beast & is frequently planted on thair sandy ditch banks but as for ye spanish improvements I suppose formerly thay had made some both considerable & extensive: there being ye vestiges of large roads to several distant parts of St. Johns river & many miles beyond it but since ye creek indians by ye help of ye English turned thair arms against ye spaniards thay have been couped up within thair own fortifications & could not till any ground out of ye reach of thair cannon Balls   neither could thay keep any kattle out of sight or cut A stick without A guard   ye Indians in both these provinces above profess A strict friendship & perhaps will keep to it if ye english dont give them just occation to break out: there is but very few spaniards at augustine   I think not one of any account   there are four churches belonged to ye town   two in it & ye others very near   one was ye dutch church with A steeple & stone cupola   thair built of hewn stone   the more perticular description of them se in my Journal. I am glad ye pittsburgh iris pleaseth thee   I like it so doth ye sweet Carolina sort   Perhaps I may send thee A slip of it next fall

BP 1:49:3; D. 283–85.
1. William Gerard De Brahm.

To COLLINSON

december ye 5th 1766
Dear friend Peter
I have packed up & shiped & consighned these following Boxes to thy care   N 1.2 PC at top & at ye end for Powel   PC N 3 at top & on side for bush: PC N 11 on ye top is plants in earth for ye king: PC N 13.14 for Gordon: PC N 15:16 Boxes of seeds for thy self   PC N 17 plants in earth A present to thee   if it is disagreeable to thee to have so many boxes consighned to thee of other peoples pray let me know & I shall forbear: My son last year sent to Doctor Hope at Edinburgh 3 boxes & consighned them to Ld Kildare with two of his & he was so obligeing as to take ye utmost care of them: to send them to Kinloch in London but unfortunately thay was landed in chester & taken to ye custom house. but whether Hope has got them I cant say   he wrote to me to send him more this year but I have sent him but one for I have bad luck in sending seeds to Edinburgh & several in york & Philadelphia & Maryland want Boxes of seeds who pays well for them & I run no risk   I have packed up A great variety of curious seeds for thee & gordon & A little parcel of very curious fresh florida seeds for our

friend Ellis in remembrance of his kind recommendation to ye governour of florida   thay was sent to me by ms Lambol with whome I left A share which she sowed imediately & some of them produced good seed of which I send thee A share as allso A few to our Gracious king which pray send to him with ye box No XI of plants: I am surprised that young is come back so soon   he cuts ye greatest figure in town   struts along ye streets whisling with his sword & gold lace &c   he hath been 3 times to visit me pretends a grat respect for me   he is Just going to winter in ye Carolinas sayeth there is 300 pound sterling annualy settled upon him But Captain chancelor tels odd stories of him   that he was put in prison from whence he was taken by two officers & put on board ship but his friends utterly denieth it   its pity but ye truth was known & ye lying partly snubed   my aple haw & ye dwarf berbery grows finely but neither hath yet sent forth suckers by which thay may be increased in feby my son John sent by order one 5 guinea Box to Col william Ganzel in craven street westminster & one Box to lord John murrey consighned to Henry drummond great George street westminster   one to andrew fletcher esquire to ye care of henry foot   strand London[1]   these thre was ordered to pay ye fifteen Guineas to thee   pray let me know if thay have   thy little Box of plants contains ye greatest part most of ye sorts I put in ye kings Box besides I put A sod of mrs bees flower (as it is called in Carolina & is ye greatest spring beauty of all thair natives & with me A fall & winter ornament) & A desiduous bay wraped in leather: A root of long leaved Saracena (which languisheth with me) ye striped leaved leaved [sic] with A sweet flower from ye wateree which prospereth well   its wraped in A bag   in another veratrum & martagons   one sod of Carolina Phlox flowers winter & spring summer A very early Phlox; ye latest fall aster & sea golden rod: pray have you ye [illegible] scented goldenrod & spigelia   I quite forgot till it was too late to [illegible] Agave in thy box   no flower hath such A spicy scent as ye [illegible]

BP 1:66; D. 285.
1. Ganzel has not been identified; Andrew Fletcher was the duke of Argyll's secretary.

From JOHN HILL

London, Dec. 6, 1766

Sir: —

There is wanted here, on a very particular occasion, four pounds of the root of *Lobelia syphilitica,* or the Blue Cardinal, dry'd, to be used in medicine. My Lord Bute has given me permission to desire you to gather and send it over.

The same occasion wants, also, two ounces of the root of *Actaea racemosa;* and eight ounces of *Collinsonia* root. If you will take the trouble of adding these, it will also be very acceptable.

I believe the name of Doctor Hill is known to you, although we never corresponded. I always have, and always shall espouse your interest.

I am your faithful, humble servant,

John Hill

Please direct the roots to me, at my house in Arlington Street, St. James's.

D. 442.

To COLLINSON

december ye 18th 1766

Dear Peter

I have just received thy kind letter of september ye 16th 1766 & thy letter of false accusation of ye 18th with Dr fothergills to thee with ye Boxes of pills   I am much obliged to thee & him for your care   I am glad I shipt A box of curious plants for him about A week past as A small recompence for his trouble   but God allmighty be praised I am now as hearty & sound as I have been this 20 years   I have sores this & last year occationed by cuts or bruises on my shins by accident that began with A small blow with A little stick   it began with A little black spot no biger then A pea but increased to be as big as A shilling with excesive pain night & day   it would not digest with any application   every one seemed to inflame & enrage it   ye doctor gave me mercurials pills & diet drinks   it still grew worse   at last ye doctor said I must enter into A course of Physick   otherwise he could do no more   I asked him if I might stir about & drink water   he said I must do neither   I tould him then I would take my own way & in about A months time my leg was well & next fall I cut ye other shin with an adze   this would never digest but corroded ye flesh till it was near as large as ye other with grievous pain but after 2 or 3 months it got well without any doctor or internal medicine or one days rest from labour   & this spring my shin was hurt with A stone   it spread & became A corosive ulcer with proud flesh which would not yeild to precipitate or any digestives but remained dry & inflamed with continual extream pain   I applyed to another doctor that pretended to do wonders with antimonial preparation which I took till all was gone that was to have perfected ye cure but still my shin went worse & no cesation of pain but when I stired about & laboured hard: if I stood still sate or lay down ye pain was untolerable except A little before day   however at last a fine very mild applications it got well   A month or more after In steping out of A boat I bruised my shin worse then ever & it was extream painfull night & day except when I stirred brisk about my labour & much superfluous flesh arose which I kept down with burnt alum & by very simple applications it got very sound: I must inform my dear friend that I have been subject ever from my infancy or birth to grievous sour acrimonious acid humours which is called wind & heart burnings for which I took chalk which generaly stoped it imediately   diareus but no disentereas grevous racking cough espetialy in my younger years but no asthmas or pleuritick pains but its remarkable that while my ulcers was in thair raging state prety free from ye heart burn but since thay was well I have had it worse then ever night & day that I was forced to get out of my bed to take chalk but about two weeks past I eat A large piece of pickled cowcumber it was very sour with vinegar & hot with Capsicum which I used formerly to eat sparingly for fear of giveing ye heart burn but then I thought I could not be much worse then I was so I indulged myself presently after which I felt A glowing warmth in my stomach & never had ye heartburn since this day I met Captain falconer in ye street he spoke very civily to me & tould me he had been with thee & seemed to be wonderfully pleased with thy agreeable company & entertainment he tould me he intended to sail for London early next spring this I hope will be A fine opertunity of sending thee my true & general Journal & ye plants I found up St Johns river he is so taken with thy behavior to him that I believe he will take ye utmost care of them to deliver them safe to thy hand as I hope Captain Goley will those for ye King which I gathered between Georgia & about Augustine

BP 1:66:3.

From COLLINSON[1]

Some Observations & Remarks on thy Journal   A Reply at Leisure

— As Wee are Certain the first New England Setlers transported Bees from England but these of Florida I am apt to think are not Native & peculiar to that part of the Country for Wee hear of none in Maryland Virginia or Carolina   was any notice taken if they Differ in Size or Colour from ye European — the River Scenes must be Inchanting Enriched with the Charming prospect of the Orange Groves but no mention in all the Voyage is made of Limons   I think the Spaniards would not Neglect them but Stork[2] speaks of them —

It is a pitty the Wood Rat made His Escape   that a More pticular Description of It could not be taken for by its Great Nest & young hanging to its tail it seems to be an undescribed Species —

I have my Friend Johns Letter of 9br 3d   am pleased to hear he has got the better of his Ulcer   the Recipe is simple   is the plantain Leaves & Rosin Laid on the Sore or on the Oyled Rag that covers the Sore & how often Changed

My Sight continues very Good with Spectacles   the foregoing [illegible] & Inquiries I Drew up in perusing thy Journal which I could not Borrow before the 4th of January for few will Buy so Dear a Book but as my Friend John did not think Mee Worthy of the Original I found no Obligation to Purchase a Coppy

If thou hadst Intended to Lett Stork puff off his Book with thy Journal[3] to publish the Same as Kings Botanist to the World which by the way is a Title thou assumes without the Kings Leave or License which is makeing very free with Majesty   it is possible for this undue Liberty thy annuity may be withdrawn but I hope Not because thou Well Deserves It and as thy Eyes are bad & the Coppy of the Journal to send to Mee might have been Ill convenient to thee yett if thou hadst had an inclination to oblige a Friend that has Served thee & Family for so many years I should expect to have heard thee saye   I know my Friend Peter would like to Peruse the Journal but my Eyes are bad & I Cant undertake it   Come Moses Do thou Do It to oblige an Old Friend   I know Moses would have readily undertaken It but if this was to great a Favour the Least thou couldest have done was to Engage Stork to Send & Complement Mee with a Book but not the least Notice is taken of Mee   Doth not this show a Gratefull Friendly Mind Such kind usage I never Expected from John Bartram

I am really Concern'd Billey does not settle but as I told thee before that will not be unless He was Married to Some notable Farmers Daughter who has been brought up remote from Towns for then Bills plantation will not Seem Irksome to Her & when He has gott a Help Mate that will Mutually Share the pleasures & Toils of Life his Life will be Comfortable but to Expect he will Settle without an Agreeable Companion to Mee seems very Unlikely

Docr Stork is very Superficial in many things & some Improbabilities but I have not Time to point them out

I read one Davis was killed by the Cherokee Indians   I hope it was not that Davis that went with thee —

I shall be glad of some of thy Observations on the Indians at the Congress of Picolata   I saw no Nutts of the Guilandia which I should have been glad to see if in the seed Vessells   pray what is that Tallow Tree thou Mentions is it from China or America   the Tythymal of Billys Drawing is Elegant   I see in thine of Aug:17 the fine Colocasia does not grow in Florida

Vale
P Collinson

BP 3:80.
1. Undated, but probably written February 3, 1767 (see Collinson to Bartram, July 31, 1767).
2. A physician sent to Florida by the British government to write a promotional description in order to encourage settlers.
3. Bartram's report to Governor Grant had been sent to the Board of Trade. It had been added, without Bartram's knowledge, to William Stork's second edition of his *Account of East Florida* with the title *An Account of East Florida with a Journal kept by John Bartram of Philadelphia, Botanist to His Majesty for the Floridas.* . . .

From COLLINSON

Londn:Feby 10th:1767

On the 4th Feby I received my Friend Johns Letters of the Decemr 6th & 10th which came very seasonable to relieve all our Fears, for the seeds the

People were impatient and indeed I was very uneasie for thy welfare under such Terrible Disorders — it gives Mee Comfort to find Thou are perfectly Restored — as I know the value of Health and partake of it in a Degree beyond most Men, therefore I feel the more for my Friends who are deprived of that Blessing of Blessings

I am glad thou has sent some plants & seeds to our Gracious King, as thy annuity is Regularly paid   I dare say any of thy Journals would be very acceptable to Him; could they be Copied Fair, – Send Him Every year one for he must not be Cloyed by too much at once   Begin with the First, after Thou received the Salary — This would keep thee in His Memory —

I presume Docr Hope Professor of Botany hath wrote to thee of the Boxes being Detained at Chester & had them not untill this Winter — by which He thinks the seeds are spoilt and Hopes as it was not owing to any fault or Neglect of His, thou will consider & take Half the Value   Bad luck could never attend Sending Seeds to Edinburgh   if they was shiped with the other Boxes to London they can be Sent Every week by sea to Edinburgh   the Charges & Carriage from Dublin to Chester, from thence by Wagon to London & then Home I Dare Say Comes to half the Value of the Seeds   If Lord Kildare had Sent them by Sea to Glasgow or London it would have Saved a Great Expence & prevented their being Stoped by the Officers at Chester which ruined all

Neither Col Ganzel Ld Murray Esq Fletcher have Called on Mee to pay for the Boxes — and Indeed all thine Sent Mee last year remain unpaid except Bush & another — they require writeing & Sending After   Gordon[1] will pay for his this Week   as He is a young beginner & a very Honest fellow I don't press Him

I am glad the Colocasia is putt in Water. Now there is Hope of Success in my Ponds. I Long for a good painting of the Flower but am much concerned for William's unsteady Conduct   nothing but Marrying will settle Him With a prudent Discreet Woman, he may return to Florida and amend his Conduct

I writt the a Long Rambling Letter by one of the First Ships & putt it into the Bag about a Week agon

Wee have had for Two Weeks the Severest Winter for some years, but now & for a week past as warm & mild as Aprill   the Skunk Root is in fine flower — Some Crocus, Heleborines & Aconite in Abundance Snow drops & Violets & polyanthos &c   pray Send Mee Specimens of Mrs Bees flower Agave Apple Haw in flower Dwarf Barberry

I had rather all the plants had been left than the Agave which I have longed to see all my life Long   writ to Claton & others but never could gett It   did not think it grew so far to the northward as with you   pray send a good specimen of it in full flower   pray what is the seed-vessel?

I Don't see any Red Bud Andromeda in the List which I writt to Johnny to Send in particular with others

pray in particular Send Mee specimens of all the species of Andromeda you Have or Whortleberries of all species in flower if it can be   if not as they Can be Gott for my Son & I much Admire all this Class for they Thrive well with us — and against next year another Root or two of Thyme Calmia — it is a Sweet little shrub, that thee sent last year   thrives & flowers finely

I doubt whether Wee have the True Sweet Scented Golden Rod & Spigelia   none of the Seed or plants are yett gott from on board

It is late so my Dear John adieu —

P Collinson

I believe there is too Much Truth in what the Capt sayes about Young — He may Live to repent His folly & Extravagance   Such an opportunity Lost is never to be regained unless He has better fortune than He deserves as a friend I advised Him often to Oeconomy & Industry & not sacrifice every thing to his pleasures for I foresaw by his way of going on how it must end for I knew his salary could by no Means support his Expensive Way of Liveing.

Thou Mentions sending Box plants to Docr Fothergill but not the vesell or Captains name so may [be presumed] to be Lost

BP 3:66; D. 286–87.
1. James Gordon, Jr., started his own garden in 1767.

From COLLINSON

Mill Hill Aprill 10 1767

I wrote my old Friend Largely of February 10th: so have not a great Deal to Add – but least that should Miscarry this will Informe thee, all the Boxes came safe & in good order   That for Docr Hope I forwarded to Edinburgh & I am obliged to thee for the Box of plants which promise Well — the Viburnum was the Least acceptable as I believe I have them already —

Think my Dear John by length of Time your Country productions are Most if not all Naturalized in our gardens, but some few Delicate things will be always acceptable as Thyme Leaved Calmia, I have a sweet plant thy son John sent Mee Last year which thrives finely & flower'd as beautifull & is now sett thick with flower Buds   Calceolus Maria Orchises Helebore, Gentians, Lillies, Martigons & many other pretty odd Perrenial flowers, as they Happen to be Mett with, must make our Cargoes for the future — as for new plants &c Wee must Expect them from Georgia & Florida & the mountainous parts of Carolina

The Plants & seeds for the King was Carefuly delivered & no Doubt was acceptable   the Honour of giveing is sufficient — but there is no notice taken of the Freight & other charges so I believe must be Carried to thy Account but then, Consider thy salary is regularly paid —

No body has called to pay for the 3 Boxes sent by thy son to Col Ganzel, Ld Murray &c — Each that sent Him the order should take Care of paying

& without the person was well known to Him, it was very Imprudent to send them, but people are very Delinquent in payment — for I can not yett gett the Money for Several of the Boxes sent Last year tho' I have wrote to remind them

& the unlucky Business of Docr Hopes 2 Boxes, I believe after a good deal of Expence He gott them last Month but in what Condition I Don't know   he proposed if I remember right paying Half — Our Friend Ellis thanks thee for his present of seeds

Johnny sent Mee what thou calls a Deciduous Bay which thrives well — but pray tell Mee how it comes by that Name — the Sarracena promises well   I was glad to see it come for the Rogues stole our fine old plants

It was well Judged, putting the Colacasia seed in a Bottle of Water — but they had sucked it all up, — & was fat & plump & Two or Three of them was Soked open & that one might see the Germ putting fourth   I took all Imaginable Care by putting them on ground in mud in a Pott that is always covered with Water in my Green House window which is shut down at Night but has the full sun on Days — so I have hopes & am Dayly looking for their appearance — if the Bottle had been putt in the Box of plants, being well secured from Breaking all had been Well in all probability — but it being packed in the seeds & what was most unlucky was the most Curious that was rotted & spoilt   the paper turned Black, from the Moist Effluvia that proceded from the Dampness of the Bottle, for it was well stoped, but Bottles packed with seeds hath been always fatal to them   I remember Once or Twice before thou sent Mee some thing in a Bottle of Rum, & that had the same Effect, so never trust any thing again in a Box of seeds but what is of a Dry Nature — Docr Fothergill tells Mee He has ordered some Roots of Coloccasia to be Dragged up for Him & sent over in a Cask of Water — do I hope by one way or Another, Wee shall see this beautifull plant, but I have had no Description of the Flower from any one that has seen It   I want much a perticular Description but much more a drawing from Billys Inimitable Pencil — but if He is with you, I am afraid He is under such Dejection from his Late disappointments that He has not spirits to undertake such a Business — I have often thought what a pity it is, that his Ingenuity could not be of service to Him, I have for years past been looking out for Him but no opening has offered, the Difficulties to Introduce an Entire stranger are insurmountable, for whilst He is attempting to make himself known, He may be starving, which has been the Case of some Ingenious People in his way (that I have known) that have been Foreigners; if my advice may have any Weight with Him, it is to get Him a Good Notable Wife, a Farmers Daughter & return to his Estate & sett his shoulders Heartily to work to Improve It, a moderate Industry goes a great Way, (to in so fine a Climate) to supply the Belly, as little is wanting for the Back.

The Spigelia I have in great prosperity, but I lament the loss of the Agave — for more than 30 years passed I have wished for it — if all the plants had been left & that sent I should not have regretted so much   I see the Heart must not be set on any thing, I dare say it never was in England — a Drawing of it in flower would be quite New   I suppose it is so succulent there is no curing a specimen —

I am concerned for your Eden [illegible] Specimens without thy Notes are little Value [several lines illegible]

I am in great Hope that the fine climbing plant fr Pittsburgh [rest of paragraph illegible]

Puccoon & Claytonia in flower Aprill 5th —

Dont it make thee smile   I sett out to say Little & now I scrawl on for I know thou loves long stories   Its past Tenn o Clock so good night —

P Collinson

pray send specimen of Bee's flower   Lord Kildare Desires a Box next year   I have not yett an order for a Box

BP 3:67; D. 287–88.

From COLLINSON

Mill Hill July 31st 1767

My Dear John hath at Last gratified my Longing wishes with the sight & perusal of his Laborious Entertaining Journal full of fine Discoveries, usefull reflections & pertinent observations

I can take a squib from John Bartram without the Least resentment, Friends may be allowed to rally one another when it is not done in Anger or sharp resentment which I never intended, however my words may be taken

If I can be thought to quick, my Dear John, thou wast too slow & so we will Let the Matter go

the Kings specimens came safe & are Delivered and thats all I ever know about them, I am much obliged for those Directed to Mee   there are many new Curious plants amongst them   if I have time I will give thee Docr Solanders observations on them who is a very acute Botanist little Inferior to Linnaeus & not only in Botany but in all branches of Natural History Think how happy I am at this present writing, to have the Two Doctors, Franklin & Solander My Guests, for a few Days, to enjoy the Delights of Mill Hill.

The first oppertunity I shall write to proffessor Hope that thou art willing to accept of one half of their Value   it is a hard case on both Sides

the Agave I have long known but never Imagined it was to be found so farr North East as with you, was the reason I never mentioned It & what I wonder thou hast never sent Mee a specimen of so singular & so rare a plant, in all thy Collections — the Spigelia is a pretty plant & a Curious flower   I have 3 roots by the generosity of our Common Friend Lamboll it is Just now going to flower — I had it many years agon but in Dividing the

Root lost It, as I once did the Evergreen Veratrum & Skunk Weed — so I shall never try the Experiment again as I have the two last in good Condition, my Rhododendron or Mountain Laurel makes a grand show with 45 bunches of Flowers to be seen at one View   our Moles when they come into the Garden never Do us any Damage but disturbing the Earth which looks unsightly, but I never had any Sort of Roots eat by them. I conclude that they eat only on worms & Roots of Grass for they can find nothing Else in our fields which are most infested by them but yours Seems of a More Mischievous Nature   pray catch one   Skin Him & Stuff it with Okum or old Tarr'd ropes untwisted that I may See if Different from ours.

I apprehend the Portugal Laurel will Endure your winter for Wee have no Instance of its being Effected Even in Scotland   it takes freely of Layers or Cuttings in September —

I Dare say the Guilandina will be the Bonduc that I & others have in our gardens, I conclude some Indian Traders brought the Nutts to Quebec from thence to France & so the French believe it Grows in Canada, but they never could tell where — I always believed it a southern Tree yett it Endures all our Winters — How could my Dear John forget to send Mee some Nutts one at Least   It would help to Guess what it is. My tree shoots strongly, I think its Pinnated leaves are some thing akin to the Angelica Tree

The Wild Limes is a singular Plant, Docr Solander Wishes for its fructifications   at that season the flowers could not be expected, but probably the Fruit lay under the Trees & yett none sent, it is a great Disappointment because the like oppertunity may not offer Again, Some of these Nutts should have been carefully sent to the King for the Kew Garden where are all Conveniences for raising & protection –

It is well known the New England people brought over Bees & they may have spread to the Blue Mountains but they never could have reach'd to the Wilds of Florida — and it is well known the Spaniards have no Curiosity & but little Industry — I take the Florida Bees to be Aborigines   I am surprized at the Size of the Small Magnolia &c &c &c   I was a long Time in hopes of the Faba Egyptica but now I Doubt   The Nutts have been kept constantly in Water & are yett very fresh but they do not Germinate   I was in Hopes the Colour was like the Chinese, a fine Red shade – if Billy Comes I wish a drawing could be Made as there is no Drying the Flower so as to give a good idea of it, being so rare a plant. Suppose a drawing [of] the Faba was made & sent to the King — of the leaf, flower & seed-vessel, in a picturesque figure as growing in the water; but it must be on a contracted scale, for no sized paper will take in the leaves, &c.

I have Billy's seven charming Drawings before Mee — have been just now pasting them on paper to Secure them   as I have writt to Billey peculiarly on them I sent his Letter open to Save Mee the trouble of writeing on them in this Letter   Hope Either Thee or Him will give Mee Some Acc't of them — pray Seal Billey's Letter before it is Delivered to Him or Else He may not take it well to send it open —

As thou keeps a Correspondence with our Good Friend Lambol pray write to Him to Send Some Fartle Berries for I think they grow on His Island for I admire all that Tribe.

Our paper mentions a Bear killed at Boston weighing between Eleven or Twelve Hundred Score, doth thee think it True

These Plants of Last Cargo grow well — the Great Horse Chestnut from Kanawa River & most of the Viburnums that I had before & some other besides Roots of Ever Green Veratrum wch I wanted   2 Roots of Martagons, Late Aster, & Sea Golden Rod   an Andromeda what sort it is don't know — I am glad of It   Both the Saracenas grows finely, & the Disciduous Northern Zanthoxilon — had many years agon & the Disciduous Bay Bidens is now in flower, a very pretty novelty & Excells all that Tribe, but I doubt if the Seed ripens so send more —

But Last, the pretty Dwarfe Early Iris wch is my favourite — So pray Send the Two Sorts thou Mentions — but remember I don't want ye Pittsburgh Iris for that has Increased Wonderfully: — its a Sweet Flower —

But I have lost Carolina Bees Flower — if thee cannot spare a Root Send a Specimen that I may see what it is Lost   Carolina Lychnis   they are a fine Class of Flowers, make a fine Show in a Garden

the Aromatic vine grows amain with Mee, But is like to flower this year for the first Time in ye Kew Garden

I have Read thy Journal Once Over & am beginning again to make my Remarks as I go along & shall communicate as opportunity offers

So my Dear John wishing thee health which I am much concern'd to Hear is so precarious   Cupping used to Relieve much my Bror: for Diziness in his Head. Doctor Fothergill is gone out of Town for 2 Months   However I shall write to him for advice — am in the Interim thy
Sincere Friend in perfect health
P. Collinson

I don't remember thy finding the Red Acacia, It has been so loaded with flowers I am obliged to prop up the branches   it is the glory of our gardens & flowers twice a year   I think it is one of the finest trees of America. Could not our Friend Lambol send some plants of the Fartle Berry in Some of your Tradeing Vessels   I Long for It   give my Love & respects to Him

I am pleased to hear the Polyanthos Succeeds So Well   I carefully save the Seed & Sow it every year from whence I have a Delightful Variety that amply rewards our Expectation   Consult Miller on this article   Thou refers to Specimens of Pines but there is only one Specimen, the Spruce pine but the Cone was not Mature so could not Determine anything from It but it seems akin to the Jersey pine   If I can gett the Magazine for last year & Tulip & Hyacinth Roots Time Enough I shall send them to the care of Capt Falconer —

My being so much out of Town things are unavoidably Delayed & Indeed forgot & yett I believe I am not the only pson liable to omissions

I have sent thy case to Docr Fothergill who resides in Cheshire for Two Months to gett rid of too Much practice   if it comes time Enough will send it by this ship, I wish it may for thou art in a bad way

Boxes Desired next Fall
— One Double Box for Fern
        for Gordon

BP 3:69; D. 291–93.

From FOTHERGILL

1/8 1767

Respected Friend
J. Bartram

I am informed by our mutual friend P. Collinson, that since thy return from Florida, thou has been much indisposed. I have that part of thy letter before me wch describes thy case, and I should be glad to assist in removing it.

To do this I think it will be necessary to lose a few ounces of blood from the arm, and to repeat small bleedings once in two or three weeks, or months, as occasion may require.

Avoid being costive at any rate, and if this should be thy natural habit, take every day a little before dinner about half a table spoonfull of the Tincture of Husa Peisa in a spoonfull or two of small beer or wine and water. Take so much as to promise an early motion to stool the next morning. This is the proper quantity, and it may be continued for any length of time.

Keep thy feet and legs very warm: and if the disorder still continues, small blisters applied successively above & below the knees may be of considerable use. Most probably a part of the same sharpness wch gave thee so much trouble in thy legs before, now creates this disorder in thy head, & the stomach by consent of parts.

I gladly embrace this opportunity of acknowledging the kind present thee was pleased to send me. The plants came safe, prosper well, and are the greatest curiosity in my garden.

I am with much respect

Thy obliged Friend
John Fothergill[1]

College of Physicians of Philadelphia, Historical Collections of the Library, University of Pennsylvania Manuscript Collections, 1:71.
1. Collinson added at the end of this letter: "Dear John   This letter came soon enough to save the Conveyance & a Box of Bulbs came by same   Thine in Hall   P. Collinson." The closing ("Thine in Hall") was an old British expression meaning "From the manor house of a landed proprietor."

From COLLINSON

Mill Hill Sepr:19:1767 —

I cannot let this ship sail without Enquiring after my Dear John & familys Welfare & acquainting Him with Mine   I am thank God, in perfect Health   no complaints of any sort attending Mee, I wish my Old Friend could say the Like — I hope thou hath mine with Docr Fothergills Advice, by, I think, Capt Falconer with a box of Tulips & Hyacinths a present from James Gordon Junior an Ingenious young Man who deserves thy Encouragement for he has a garden of his own.

This Day thy Country Man Docr Kuhn[1] & Docr Solander dined with Mee Here — He will tell the of the prosperity of my garden & how all thy kind presents flourish being now arrived to some magnitude & perfection. Unless something new & rare don't trouble thyself in my behalf   I much want the Early Sweet Iris, some peculiar Lycheders, Ladys Slipper   Red Bud Andromeda   but I wish for the Faba Egyptica — as I study thy List it grows in our Dear Friend Lambol's Island — I should think berries or plants might be sent uninjured in your Carolina Vessells — or if He would please to Send Mee some roots directly in Some of the ships to London by wraping up the roots with some Moss & a Little Earth & then fill the Box well with Moss —if sent by very first Ships is no doubt but their Coming safe.

The Colocasia was carefully kept under Water yett none buds forth, I now have little hopes of seeing It — but by the means of Docr Fothergill who has some Friends that He hath Instructed how to Collect the Roots & then send in large Casks of Water — for he has large ponds of Water to plant them In — I was in hopes of the flower had been Redish like the China, I was glad of thy account of It   in my Former Letter I gave thee an Account of the Success of this years Vegitable Cargo, the Kanawa Horse Chesnutt thrives   pray what is the Flower — I could not find the dwarfe Early Andromeda from Carolina — which would have pleased Mee much   it must be in the Kings Cargo but was not in Mine   My son as well as my self admire all the Tribes of Andromeda & Apocinums   neither could Wee find Red Andromeda — pray send Mee some Saracenas, there is Some I have Seen Sent over – very red veined Leaves which looks very pretty – the long Leaved kind that thrives well as doth the Red Veratrums —

Thou canst scarcly think my Dear John what I have been for some Time employed about — then I will tell thee   after perusing thy Entertaining Journal Two or Three Times I found so many Curious Articles blended together in the Length of 79 pages that it was impossible to find them out after a tedious Search — if there had been a large Margin left on the sheets — then notes of the principal Matters would have lead to the principal subjects on that Page — but as there was no room left for this — I then determined to compose Three Indexes — in the first I selected all thy Botanic discoveries, in the first Column the page of thy Journal, next the particular Place, then Enumerating of the plants there found, this is contained in Two sheets of paper which I can presently run over & see the produce of Each place in Each province

The second contained all thy remarks & observations Abridged on the Petrified Rocks & Bluffs   this comprehends a sheet & from this view it is wonderfull to think what was the Original State of all the Lower Country throughout all our Colonies — once undoubtedly Covered by the sea, but what great Revolution in Nature brought about this Extensive retreat of the Ocean who can pretend to say — the Third Index contains all the remarkable things not comprehended under the other two Indexes — all have the pages anexed; so that for a further explanation I can immediately have recourse to the article it self

Now any Curious Friend can be entertain'd that hath not leisure to peruse 79 pages — & yett what I have done can only serve for my private amusement

it is too short an abstract for publication & the Original wants more pains & Leisure than I am master off — to dress it fit for the Public which gives Mee no little concern that so many useful Discoveries should lie concealed

What fills us with admiration is the wonderfull fossil presents of Elephants Teeth &c, sent over to Lord Shelburn & our Frd Benj Franklin by George Croghan — that Elephants was never known in America & yett the Great Fossill Teeth of Elephants found under a high Bank on the sides of the Great Lick near the River Ohio would force one to believe by their vast remains that they once Existed there — Some of these Great Tusks or Teeth were intire near seven foot long and of the thickness of common Elephants teeth of that Size & Length But what Increases the wonder & Surprise, Is that with these long Teeth (which are fine Ivory), is found great numbers of Grinding Teeth, but the marvel is they are not the Grinding Teeth of Elephants, as wee have recent Elephant grinders to compare them with — So that this phenomenon must be resolved into this Conclusion

That these Remains, that Geo:Crogan says, are at least of Thirty Animals — are some Vast Creatures with the long Teeth or Tusks of Elephants but with Great Grinders belonging to some animal not yett known, this affords room for Endless reflection & Admiration, these Grinding forked teeth, I am persuaded thou hath seen for I remember the mention of a portion of One thou has seen but I have 3 Intire, and I daresay a Dozen have come Over & Two of them in the Original Jaw which is of Monstrous size.

I think Inclosed in thine, I wrote to Billey & Moses by Capt Falconer – I have wrote to Edinburgh to Docr Hope about the abatement on the boxes but have had no Answer — neither have I received any thing for those Boxes sent by Johnny in thy absence —

We have had a Continual Driping summer but yett some Intervals to get in the Harvest which is plentifull that I hope will soon reduce the high price of Bread.

Now dear John farewell,

P Collinson

BP 3:70; D. 293–94.
1. Adam Kuhn.

To BENJAMIN RUSH

december ye 5th 1767

Respected Friend

I saw ye letter thee wrote to my son Isack & am much pleased with your discovery of ye nerves in plants & thair sensation which I hope by A more diligent search will lead you into ye knowledge of more certain truths then all ye pretended Revelations of our Mistrey mongers & thair inspirations; its certain many Animals hath A large degree of Cunning & is endowed with

Benjamin Rush (1746–1813). Portrait by Edward Savage.
Courtesy of the William Bradley Collection, Historical Collections of the Library, College of Physicians of Philadelphia.

most of our faculties & pashions & several perticular intelect beyond many of our species: but I have been many years upon the enquiry after ye operation of plants & wrote to curious persons upon ye subject, that if thay had not absolute sence yet thay has such faculties as came so near to it that we wanted A proper Epithet or explanation   I have been allso much delighted in ye curious observation of minerals, thair wonderfull Combination & thair long & exquisit intestine Purifications, duration & decay, in which contemplations I have queried whether there is not a portion of ye universal intelect difused in all life & self motion Adequate to its perticular Organisation. But plants hath ye appearance of A wonderfull sensation perticularly in ye Mimosas & ye Tipiwitchit of Carolina – nay even most of ye plants with Penated leaves close up in ye evening & many flowers opens & shuts at diferent hours both night & day, some opening but once then perish in 2 – 4 – 12 or 24 hours — we have a silene that flowers after dark & shuts up before morning — but most of these gratifies us with A long succession   some on ye same stalk as ye Sisrinchiums & Ephemera   some on winding vines as ye Convolvulus & Ipomea   Many on branched stalks, some single roots puts forth A single stalk & flowers as ye upright spotted lillys of Carolina & Pensilvania. But ye most Remarkable is ye blew Ixia of florida which my son William (who resided there near A year & half) hath fully described in this letter for your Amusement. — I have often admired ye explosive force of many Capsulas in dischargeing thair contents to A proper distance. the Balsamin by Contraction. the hammamelis by dilation. yet by A private spring in ye base ejects ye seed to many yards distance. ye Amsonia hath Cyllindrical pods 4 or 5 inches long yet will eject seed out at the opening of ye top of ye pod; Our mountain Chesnut Oak & white oak Acrons when fallen on ye ground A few days will alltho thay rest on one side or upon thair base shoot out of thair point A radical sprout which will make A short curve & shoot directly into the earth 3, 4 or 5 inches   ye same fall thay ripen alltho thay are summer acrons & ripens ye same summer thay are set. But ye Black red & spanish oaks is winter acrons & ripens ye succeding year after thay are set & impregnated of which I made ye first discovery to Mr. Peter Collinson about 20 year past: – ye strawberry & Cinqufoil sends forth runners to uncertain distance from ye main root before ye organical parts is formed to take fresh root for increase; our running Bryer send forth Cylindrical branches like vines running on Bushes, fences or plain ground for several yards but when at A natural distance from ye mother root thay form ye organical part, dips down & take firm root in A few weeks from which several Branches spring next season

Quere   what instinct or nature or what you please to call it directs our shrubs that spreads much under ye surface of ye ground when thay first come up from seed   thay establish themselves by tap roots & thair lateral branches which terminates in ye smallest Fibers that Can be imagined by which thay draw nourishment for ye whole shrub or tree, but as soon as this is performed ye root sends forth long Cylindrical roots with perpendicular organisations to A proper distance from ye mother root under ye surface then shoots up & forms another scion of younger shrubs

I remain with much respect in great hast

John Bartram

Purple Flower'd Ixia of St. Johns Rivr. Et. Florida[1]

Every Species or variety of this Tribe of Plants exhibet very eminent beauties, but this with applause claims the preeminence, its elegant form of growth with the brilliant colouring of its Flowers strikes on the imagination delight; and one can't look on it but with admiration. — The flowers open in the Morning soon after the day breaketh, whose Petals appear as a transparent Film framed with singular beauty consisting of a number of longitudinal fibres, which take their rise from the bottom departing from each other gradually to near the middle there they divide thus again to the end, and are so very minute presenting altogether an appearance of the finest webby Membrane, of so tender and delicate an excellence, they are bruised and ruffled, by the gentlest breathe of wind, and no sooner then the slightest glance of the Sun beams pass over them then they disapear, tho Acres of Ground were partly cover'd in such manner as to cast a glowing purple around soon after the sun is above the horison it would be almost impossible to find a flower; and one would be apt to conjecture all the beauty seen this moment to be mere dilution —

The colour of this most delightfull of flowers is a lively blue reflecting a slite dash of purple. The delicate texture of these Flowers is admirable beyond anything that Vigitation presents besides. Having cropt's a many plants with a view of preserving a specimen of such beauty but was as often baffled in the attempt for as often as they were placed in the Book the leaves quickly absorbed the purple juice from the Petals, leaving the transparent film colourless. This purple tint is of such strength and penitration; I have a Gena. Plantm. by me at present wherein a specimen has been laid, the juice of which has struck thro and coloured five leaves & remains a fast and most perfect purple colour —

But tho' these flowers are of so short a durance that seeming difect is amply compensated by a most liberal succession for the next morning the curious Botanist is delighted by a seeming return of those fugitives or he would rather imagine himself beholding a new creation & in the midst of thousands. —

The Root is a small and nearly round Bulb with a brown scaley covering from whence rises first one or 2 leaves 6 inches in length and very narow very like a blade of common Grass soon after the stalk for Flowers which is very small and round, rising 8 or 9 inches high   a single Flower breaks out from a Spath formed of a single lanciolated leaf   the foot stalk of the Flower is more than an inch long, bending downwards   The flower is composed of six equal oblong petals narrower toward their bases. The Stamina are three very short bending a little inwards & on their sharp points are placed the Anthera which are long and crooked. The Germen is partly oval swelling near the top & three cornered, seated beneath the receptacle of the Flower. the Stile is in the midst rising from the apex of the Germen very small but inlarging upwards when it divides into three stigma which are thick. Pericm: is sub-oval shaped composed of three valves contain three cell each having several seeds.

The maner which Nature hath assigned the Plant in producing the wonderfull succession of Flowers which presents the sight every morning a new, continuing for the space of three weeks is very singular and perticular to it.

The root is a nearly round Bulb & from the center of which rises the Flowering stalk producing commonly only one tho sometimes two flowers there being one a Spath & if two the stalk [illegible] shoots forward & terminated by the second flower proceeding [illegible] more than One flower from a Spatha & the Stalk never divided — whether this succession of flowers, may not be caus'd by the Older Roots flowering first & so the next in Succession according as their situation of growth may be more or less favourable for Nature to bring them forward to proper season

The preceeding descriptions and observations are the result of repeated oppertunities of Tryal, and there was nothing in this rare plant exclusive of its beauty, that would recommend it to perticular notice. I hope its merit on that head will gain the attention of the curious and in some degree plead the excuse of one who in every object finds the greatest pleasure in following nature in search of knowledge that may tend to publick advantage or speculation

William Bartram

Historical Society of Pennsylvania Library, Library Company of Philadelphia Deposit.
1. The remainder of the letter was written by William.

From COLLINSON

Mill Hill, 25th December, 1767

I had the pleasure of my Dear Johns Letter of the 14th Sepr which is full of many Entertaining articles   It is with you as it is with us — it was Long while before some of your plants could be reconciled to our Culture — but since we have found that planting them in our Bog Earth & makeing artificial Bogs I don't remember any plant of yours now but what takes a liking to our Country   it may be the same with you when you have found a proper soil & management   I dont see why Ranunculas, Auriculas & Anemonies should [not] thrive with you as with us if there was the same pains taken — the Two first are the peculiar Delight of perticular People — who Cultivate no other flowers — So these have their whole Attention and Nursing which so Northerly Climate as ours requires, for those articles look into Millers Dictionary & thou will find some Idea of It & so for Tulips & Carnations   Virtuosi in these flowers so regard all others as Trifleing these are properly our Florists   for my Part, I believe I can Like them Love them & Content my Self with them with the Common Hardy Sorts of these four species of Charming flowers that will Grow with little Trouble wch these fine Florists Dispise —

But it is amazeing to what a perfection these articles have arrived at when One sees a bed of Rich Tulips or Ranunculas   a stand of Some 100 pots of Auriculas & as many of Carnations & the prices they Value them at & yett so great is the Itch that a poor Raged Shoemaker a Weaver or a Baker will give half a Guinea or a whole one for a New flower   such is the infatuation

I am pleased to hear that Thou was Gratified with with [sic] seeing

Warners Jessamin in flower who could think that fine plant had travelled so soon to your world this Engaging Vegitable exercises the skill of all our Naturalists & yett I dont know any one has hit its Culture, for a year or Two it seems prosperous & then flags & Declines My Dear John don't be astonished at any Thing Wee remember & forget, forget & remember, Some years agon I wanted the Agave being disappointed I thought no more of It but looking over the Flora Virginica, it revived again, & so we go on, untill we forget our Selves, & are soon forgot.

We have no luck with the Colocasia so give it over Billys fine Drawing will supply that Defect About the Latitude 40° is generally allowed to be the finest Climate for Habitation, Rome, Constantinople & Madrid & others under it, is Celebrated by Travellers for their Temperature & Choice Vegitable productions. to find so remarkable a Difference with you is very Incomprehensible with Mee the severities of your Last Winter exceeds any I have known here, about 12 Degrees to the northward I never knew a Privet killed by our Cold, pray was it our privet or some native plant of yours like it — is it possible the Cold would kill our Friend Lambols vine to the ground in So Carolina of how penetrating a Nature must your cold be for I never knew an Instance here of a Vine killed by It — These surprising Extreams will never Tempt Mee to change Climates, for every Fruit seems degenerating that Comes from Europe, but Cherries — is it not possible these Defects can not be prevented by art For as you Increase, Luxury will Increase — Riches will increase then rewards will Encourage Ingenious Artists to find ways & Means to produce our Fruits in perfection this is now something the Case in England, Cucumbers at Xmas, Green Peas & Beans in feby, March & Aprill ripe Grapes in plenty in May, I have my self seen more than once some hundred Bunches of the finest ripe grapes in May, Cherries ripe in March, or Aprill, at a guinea or two a pound This golden Gain stimulates every artist to be first at Market

It Grieves Mee Much to Hear of Poor Billys adversity but I hope his Virtuous Mind will support him under it amongst thy Numerous Acquaintance it will be very hard if He cannot be got into some Business above the Servile drudgery of a Day Labourer – but that, should operate in his favour as an Instance of his Industry & Humility which I hope will be rewarded at last with something more Suitable to his abilities

Thy account of Augustine was very pleasing but the walling is so complicated I can not form a tolerable Idea of the Place — pray at thy Leisure with Billys assistance Just draw Mee the outlines on paper marking each place with its Name & the rivers that surround it on the one side & the other this I hope will not give much trouble as it is only composed of Lines, if the situation of the Forts, Churches, governors House & other publick buildings are added & numbered with figures will make it more compleat

I wish Much to have some Berries of the Fartle Berry to sow – Plants would be better but they are Difficult to Gett, but at least I should be Glad to see it in flower & in Berry, in Good specimens   as it grows in our Friend Lambols Island   pray write in Time to his Lady for the Women Deny the Nothing   thou hath such an Art of wrigling into their Good Graces to Drag specimens in Flower & then in Fruit & then to Send Some Ripe Berries for this pretty shrub is not in our Gardens   neither in all thy specimens, do I recollect ever to have seen It — pray mention if, it is an Ever Green, or not, that Wee may see what Class it Belongs too —

Wee have had a Smart, I may say Severe frost for 3 weeks before 21 Decemr & Ended the 11th January   Since Open Warm Weather   what is very Remarkable the Swamp Magnolias kept on their Green Leaves & so Continue Feby 1st 1768 which would make one think it is an Ever Green, altho' I know it is not with you   I have heard nothing from Lord Murrey, Ganzel & fletcher   they should be wrote to by Every Ship & if a Letter to Each sent Mee Directed to Each, I will have it lawfull Delivered   phaps they have forgot to whom to pay their Money for the seeds —

In all thy specimens, I cannot find a specimen of the Deciduous Bay — Doth it bear a Berry, the Leaves are much to Small to Compare it to Bay: it is more like our Narrow Leaved Philereas, the Last Thrives finely

BP 3:71; D. 295–96.

From BENJAMIN GALE

Killingworth, 3d Jany 1768

Dear Sr

I have not had the pleasure of a Line from You for a Long time, & had I not Accidently seen in one of the publick papers you was set out to visit Pensicola or West Florida, I should have been inclined to think you either had lost all remembrance of me, or that you had taken Your Leave of this world & called to have Acted Your part in some happier State of Existence, But by the Favour of a visit from my good friend, Capt Smith I am informed you are still alive & well & that you, not long before was enquiring for an oppty to write me —

I should be Infinitely delighted to spend one evening with you (I mean a Winter Evening), to hear the Journal of your Travails into that southern part of America & the just remarks you must have made in your Tour. I want to know whether in any of your Travails either in the Alegehany Mountains or Elsewhere, you have ever found any evident traces of the Deluge or monuments of Antiquity — if there ever was an Universal Deluge, I cannot but think it must have left some evident traces of it yet to be seen in every part of the Globe   Have they any Animals, Serpents, or beasts of prey, in those southern Colonies, not common to us — have you ever had such a description of the Cortex Peruvianus as that you would know the tree from whence it is taken — I have heard much of the stones[1] made use of to extract the poyson of vipers, are those stones Natural or Factitious.

I wrote you some time since wr [whether] ever you received it or not, am not able to say, to request of you Ever you have met with the Cicuta of Dr. Stork, or the Meadow Saffron   a Description of the Latter I now Inclose you, if but one half of the vertues he ascribed to it are in the plant I should think it a Happy discovery to find it in america — if found in America pray send me the seeds of Both — I want to know the Botanical name of the American Blood Root   its vertues are great & many, particularly I look upon it a specific in the Nervous Head ack or sick head ack as it is Commonly Calld — Inclosed I send you a News letter in which is Inserted the Natural History of Black Grass at ye request of our good Friend Mr. Collinson — have you ever met with any grass similar to it, in any of the Interior parts of this Continent — the conjecture I make as to its origin appears to me somewhat probable   perhaps your knowledge in that matter may determine the Affair —

When your Leisure will admit & any opportunity presents I should be pleasd to receive a line from You   my best regards to your son & believe me Dear Sr that I am your most obedient & most humble Servt

Benjn Gale

My spouse requests her regards may be presented to her Father's Friend.

BP 4:13; D. 443–44.
1. Snakestone (ammonite), popularly thought to be helpful when applied to a snakebite.

To COLLINSON

Jan ye 24 1768

I have lately received thy kind letter of September 19th which gives me much pleasure in these cold winter days & long nights   I hope ye Colocasia nuts will succeed   mine that I sowed ye same fall & parcel with thine [never] came up but I hope to see ye leaves above water next summer   those that flowered — by my pond came up ye second spring after sowing   I doubt Dr. Fothergill — with roots will not succeed   I desighn next spring to transplant a layer [illegible] andromeda to take root for thee against next fall   I thought thee had [illegible] surprising bones near ye Ohio   seems to be a Northern species of elephant of enormous size & very different from ye Asia & Africa ones   how much these [illegible] which is found by ye banks of Northern rivers of ye Icey sea caled [illegible] & perhaps all these differs one from another as much as [illegible] unless these frigid scituations had formerly been [illegible]

BP 1:54.

From COLLINSON

Feby: 12: 1768

I have Little to ad to my Last by Capt Sparks but that I have had opend the Kings & my Box but attempting to Call over the plants to the List to our great Disappointmt not one tally but was rotted intirely off & by the Shaking of the Boxes in Carriage was Drop'd to the bottom   this is a Grevious Loss, for Wee know not the blind Cane the agave & Mrs Bees Flower which I long to see   I Desird the Last year to Save Mee a good Specimen that at least I might have the Idea of It   But all the plants Look well but more Moss is requisite for it shrinks away

I have at Last gott thine & Moses Small Box   have not time to open them in Town so have sent them in the Country

I am in hast thine

P Collinson[1]

BP 3:72.
1. On the back of this letter is a note: "May 27 1768 Received of Jno Bartram Six pound for Halling one thousand Rails at twenty shillings a hundred — [signed] Benjamin Cheesman."

From COLLINSON

Mill Hill 17th February 1768

My Dear John

I have received thy Ingenious son Billys Wonderfull performances but what surpases all is the Colocasia   now I am amply gratified & wish for no More

I am sensible there has been much paper, paint, &c Expended on my account   I request that thou will pay to thy son William the Value of a guinea sterling, in your currency   I intended to have put it in a Letter but I recollected I had formerly lost the Letter for the sake of the Money & that to Post for the low officers that have the handling & sorting the Letters can Easily feel & cannot resist pocketing a weighty Letter   for that reason I ask the favour & I will make myself Debtor in the acct   What pleasure it must give thee to have such Ingenious sons — William & Moses in his Way has obliged Mee with his Curious observations & Johnny in his Way for plants & insects — are all very gratefull to Mee their Fathers old Friend — I shall take Care of his box to Mr. Lewin, my Friend Moses Box I had not Time to open in Town Comes in Trunk into the Country where I hope soone to have the Pleasure to Dissect It   My Love to them all

I saw the Box of plants open'd for the King   they are in good Order & a fine Collection as is Mine, but there is some formality to Deliver the Kings Box which will go to Kew garden where all vegetables are treated with the utmost Care & all that art can do to bring them to perfection in our Climate   the

Kings Specimens will be [illegible] I thank thee for mine   at my first Leisure shall take notice of them   I was pleased to See a Specimen of Mrs Bees flower & not the Root yellowish & fibrous   I gave young Gordon a Saracenia   if his Tulips & Hyacinth prove Well He will Desire a Box of plants next year   its Late so Adieu

P Collinson

the Dry Summers have killed all our Dircas, If I had it again I would plant it on a Bog, I want seed of spotted flower Monarda

When I go to Mark Orchises — I fill my pock[1] with the Broken part of tobacco pipes with the Boles to them   these I thrust into the Ground close to the stem of the plant   I intend to come again to take up   if Two is putt one on Each side the Rim then one is more Certain if the Leafe is quite Decayed — & be sure the pipes inclosed, that they may not be taken notice of by some unlucky people who may pull them up or trample & break them   Orchises of all plants must be marked for if taken in flower will come to Nothing, pray send Orange Col'd apocinon seed

P Collinson had forgot these few seeds – – Amongst the Last Specimens I see the Pyrola   send us a Root or 2 for it is such od plants that Wee want & Low pretty Bog plants — & your Hepatica, & roots, Single or Double of the Dwarfe White Mountain Ranuncula   Doc Witt sent Mee the Double wch continued some years but removing made us Loos It

I pray thy Son John, If He could not contrive to Mark those in flower Some of your Orchis's of which you have Variety, yellow ones which should be Glad to See — For they are my sons favourites   Once thee was so Lucky   If thou remembers I think 3 years agon Thou Sent Mee a Large sod to produce Heleborinites Ladies Slipper — but Instead of them shot out a Cluster of Orchises with sweet White spiral flowers but in the Heighth of Beauty came the Rogues stole them, Guess what could be more Vexatious & Mortifying — I wish thou could remember the spot & then I wish it may be Near   those fine grass Leaved Star of Bethlehems — I also wish it that they are not to farr to gett strong Roots & the Starr of the Earth — all your Common Trees & Shrubs Wee have Except phaps some odd Little Low ones which have not been taken notice off — if any More plants are sent the King Lett them be new odd plants as above from Woods & Bogs   all sort of Solomons Seals — your Common Solomons Seal thou sent Mee 2 or 3 years ago, flower'd finely but is Different from it — yet looke pitt[ed?] & went off — pray in thy next send another — I will try it in another Situation   the skunk is in fine flower — the King wants it, and all Sorts Arums Aquatic & Land Ones from Woods & Thickets — the Root of the Agave if I guess it right promises Well — send the King Saracenas — for they we can never raise from seed & they grow & flower well with us; I thank thee for that sent Mee for they are my favourites —

You have a sweet Heleborine with red flowers   Any Sorts of Gentians will be acceptable & pray a short account of the soil & place of growth — for such fine plants require our most Care

I wish Johnny will be so kind to Make a List of the plants Contain'd in this Rambling Letter which Just as it comes to my noodle I write down as Hints whatever not remote but when they are remote & Difficulties & much trouble attends them they are not expected by thy sincere friend

P Collinson

be sure add Sweet Early Low Spring Iris   the Pitsburgh Increases wonderfully[2]

BP 3:79; postscript, BP 3:74.
1. The word "pock" came from "poke," a sack or bag.
2. This letter was addressed to James Gordon, Jr., with the following note: "pray Inclose & send to Pensilvania Coffee House for John Bartram."

From COLLINSON

Feby 29 1768

On the Kings Specimens

N: 2   Wee are much Obliged to Billey for giveing us so perfect an Idea of this Glorious Hibiscus as it grows in Carolina   pray gett Seeds for Kings Garden   it will make a Charming show in their Stoves for I Dare Say it will not flower out of Doors in our Climate

3 — Pirola — I should Like 2 or 3 Roots in next Cargo with good Sods for there often comes up od plants out of them as did formerly the fine White sweet Orchis & a very Stately Cyperus Grass   they stole the first

8   the Crimson & Blew Florida Sages are Lovely Plants   I hope the Blew will come up & produce seed next year

13   thy fine Monks Hood Increases Greatly with us   flowers a month Earlier & Continues in December for our Sharper Frosts rarely begin untill abt Christmas, for on the 20th Decemr was in fine Flower in my Garden Several very fine yellow Tall Obeliscothecas and many Roots of the Dwarfe Sort, I luckily gather'd some flowers for my Parlor before the Frost & they Kept full 2 Months in Water — besides there was some fine Asters & Golden Rods Red & yellow Lupins Double Chrysanthemums in abundance   these keep long in Water   plenty of Primroses & Polyanthos Some Violets & Single Anemonies & Wall flowers & Stocks in abundance — of all these I gather'd plentifully for I saw the Frost was coming and Dureing its 3 weeks Continuance I was Delighted with these Beauties on My Table within Doors, whilst snow covered the Garden without & then out of my Parlour I go into my Greenhouse 42 foot long which makes a pretty walk to smell the sweets of so many odoriferous plants, Winter without but Summer within, many plants Flowering — My Dear John thou Loves my Long Stories but I should be ashamed to write such insignificent stuff to anybody Else   commit it to the flames —

N: 18 I presume there is no Chance of getting this fine Shrub —

21 — this fine Carolina Ketmia I never saw flower any w[h]ere but in the

Chelsea Garden, it barely makes it[s] appearance with Mee & Soone went off but if Wee had Seen I Dare say would flower in the Kew Garden which is a Warm soil & a very Warm Situation

23   Largest Vitis Idea   have had some years of thy sending flowers freely but never offers to Fruit   wee want your fructificateing sun —

27 — Is there any hopes of the pretty Low Andromeda of Carolina — the flowers are much Closer but yett some thing Like the Evergreen in shape

29 — Seems a Species of Lonicera or Fly Honesuckle   I have from France & from Tartary — & I should Like one from Pensilvania

34 — Can't Wee have Seed of that Delicate Painted Leaved Spurge Dwarfe Flox I must not expect unless from Seed

In my Specimens

N 31 — is a most Singular Grass   the flowers growing all on one side — Could I not have a Root of It for it is not to be expected from seed

30   I am mightly pleased with Mrs Bees flower   I hope the plant will grow   the fine Red Leaved Barbary I should Like   our Barbary is not near so fine

There is a very fine Plant in flower with very Broad Pointed Leaves, what Docr Solander will call It I know not for he has not yett seen the Specimens, it is only in my Quire of specimens & not in the Kings — but no Name or Description which I regret

There is 2 flowers of the Saracena in my specimens but no Leaves as farr as Wee can Judge (for there is no remarks on them)   It Seems a Lesser Species & the flower much Redder — Wee should be glad of a Root, for it is one of our Favourites   Some of the Leaves of the Common Sort are much redder Vein'd than others, this is an aditional Beauty, if such happens in Johnnys Way, pray Mark a plant or Two for us

I am much obliged to those that took the Pains to Dry the Flower of the Colocasia   that with the [sic] Billys Exquisite Drawing gives Us a Compleat Idea of that Wonderful plant —

Is that Beautiful Ixia with Blew Flowers become an additional ornament to thy Garden   Bulbous rooted Flowers that abound so much in Europe & Asia are very few in some Latitudes in North America   pray tell Mee how many thou canst recon up   the atamasco Lillie Seems the Chief & an ornathogolon   can Wee list the Clatonia & what others   the Swamp Narciss of Carolina

My next Leisure will be to bestow some regard to Billeys very Curious Disertations on the Productions of Florida

& Moses his entertaining Letter must not be forgot for there are many judicious Observations   His Box had happyly reach'd our Hands by the Obligeing Captains great Care   Every thing wee found in perfect Good Order   the Chrysalis found in his Garden moved briskly about so no Doubt Wee shall see this rare production   Tell Johnny His Box of Flies has been Carefully Delivered as Directed   am obliged to him for a sight of them   He is so kind to offer to collect Some for Mee but I Desire no Moths, or Butterflies — but Libellas or Dragon Flies, all sorts, of Beetles, Wasps, Bees, Hornets, Locusts or Grass Hopper &c as they happen in his Way always when he goes from Home take a little box in his Pocket, with a Pin cushion with pins

It is right & Respectfull to send every Year a Quire of Specimens for the King as thy Annuity is Duly paid but remember the King is no Botanist, so a Quire of Specimens showing flowering plants with flowers on them carefully Dryed & Neatly Laid on the paper of those flowers growing in thy Garden &c will please him better than Botanic Niceties, without show   but then remember to name them every year

BP 3:75.

From COLLINSON

Mill Hill May 17:1768

I had the pleasure of my Dear Johns Two Letters on Decemr: 20th & Jany 24   these I received Aprill 15th

My Colocasia nuts don't appear — I despair of them — They are in a Pot in a pond, always cover'd with Water — if any Fresh nuts offer again put them instantly in a Bottle of Water & so send them over tho Billys lively drawing gives a Clear idea of it yett to be sure, the real thing is to be preferred to the most perfect Work of Art

pray send a Twig or a Leafe of the Castena Andromeda for Mee to See for I apprehend a Layer will not be sufficient root to be removed in one Summer   I want the Fartle Berries from our Friend Lambols Island & I wish for a good Specimen in Leafe &c

I had some Doubts so Carefully Examined the Ohio Elephants Long Teeth with a Great Number (at a Ware House) from Asia & from Africa & found them agree to Every Circumstance & they agree with what is called the Mammots Teeth, from Siberia of which I have many fine Specimens, sent Mee from thence

It is all a wonder how they came to America & yett a greater is that no Elephants Grinding Teeth are found with them but very Large forked or pronged Teeth that have no relation to Elephants   I have One weighs near four pound, with as fine an enamel on It as if a Recent tooth just taken out of the head of the Animal, this puzzles beyond Measure, from whence no other conclusion can be Drawn but that they may belong to a New Species of Elephant that has Long Teeth, with these pronged or Forked Grinders —

or Else they Belong to some Vast Animal that has these Forked Grinders, Different from any other Animal yett known — but how they came mixt with the Elephants is incomprehensible

As to the Fossil Horns Dig'd up in Ireland, that Long contested Point, is now setled — for Last year my Friend the Duke of Richmond[1] had a Large Pair of Your Country Moose Deer Horns sent Him from Quebec, at the first Sight they have not any Affinity with the Irish Fossil Horns but come very near to the European Elk —

So Here is two Animals, the Creature to which the Irish Horns belong & the Creature to which the Great forked of pronged Teeth Belong — wether they Exist, God Almighty knows, — for no Man knows, wether Antedeluveans, or if in Being since the Flood, but it is contrary to the common Course of Providence to suffer any of his Creatures to be Annihilated

By comparing thy Horns from Terre Labrodore to the Rein Deer — It belongs to an Animal of the deer kind called by the French Caribou — & not to the Moose but is a real species of Rein Deer — which wee Here know nothing off, but for the Lame report of French Indian Travels, but since Wee have had Quebec their skins come over every year & is said to Differ very Little if anything from the European or Lapland Rein Deer

the Duke of Richmond has a young Moose & a young Caribou both alive came over last year   the foot of the Last is remarkably Thick with Large Spreading Hoofs to facilitate His Roaming on the snow   these are both Females but Wee want a better Discription, & a Pair of full grown Horns of the Caribou — the French for Colour & Size compare it to an elk which shows they are more asses by their Comparison

I have not Seen our European or African Bufalos but I have seen them From China & they Differ Much from Yours, which I have seen both Bull & Cow but you have Two Species of Buffalo, a Northern species which Inhabits the Country in the Latitude of Hudsons Bay which from its Smell, is called the Musk Buffalo, & a Lesser Size then those to the Southward

It is wonderfull the snakes should forget their mutual animosity for the means of keeping one another warm —

Thy suggestions on the Decrease of your animals is very Likely to be the Cause that so few are now found —

I have the pleasure to tell thee that the Agave prospers wonderfully   I shall have Solander here to Morrow   will show it to Him as a great Rarity being, I believe the first that has been seen Here — but I am not so great a favourite with the Ladies as my Frd John for Mrs Bee, notwithstanding all my Care & Indulgence remains quite Inactive — yett I live in hopes   the Sweet Golden Cedar not a Firr   the Andromeda and Vitis Idea [several lines illegible]

[illegible] & the Kanawa Horse Chesnut grows — pray remember Roots of the Early Sweet Iris but the Pittsburgh Increases greatly — is very pretty, Red Azaleas are in full flower a delightful shrub — the white Sweet scented will not flower In a Month   I now have Two fine Bushes of It which I admire & the broad Leavd Calmias or your Laurel will make a fine show in a few Weeks — this Last Winter has been the severest since 1740 — Has killed down to the Root & Some Totally of the arbutus, San [illegible] & Bays, in most Gardens Except ours but by Virtue of their being Bred up in a Colder Region, and for that Reason Hardier — for Wee have in those

Evergreens scarsly a Leafe amiss which is the Domination of all — but for this arrangement, in those Gardens where there was such distruction was the Least affected so I think thou may venter to plant it out – but if thou art fearfull plant it out against the South side of thy House, where it can be Easely protected with Laying litter abt its Roots & may be Easily cover'd with a Good Matt or Blankets in the sharper Weather — tho' I think by the Winters protection, it will Endure all Weathers

If the Pensilvania first setlers Naturalized Bees in their province then I have no Doubt of their extending themselves in so fine a Climate, but thought it too farr to come from New England — as the Indians have no Name for a Bee that is a plain proof they was foreigners

I am very Glad to hear thou art Sound [in] Wind & Limb: Wash thy Eyes with the best Brandy or mixed with a Little Spring Water is excellent to strengthen the sight, don't be afraid [illegible] going to Bed & Resting — I thank God my sight is so good, I can see an Object 20 or 30 Miles as Soon as any of my Children do & those which is the Brim of the Horizon in View, from over [illegible] as Mill Hills, but the Great Beauty of the Vales below Enriched with a Rural Scene, with riseing Hills between &c

Docr Hope has paid Mee 7:10 being half for the 3 Boxes that was Detained att Chester   most of the seeds was spoilt — & have paid for 2 Boxes this year   thy annuity is regularly paid

I am my Dear friend thine whilst I am

P Collinson

pray my Respects to Billy   His fine Drawing is Much admired by Docr Solander

pray my Respects to Moses & tell Him none of the Chrysalis have yett produced flies, but Wee still are not so Hott as you are at this Time year The Chrysalis in Earth, is alive & fresh   expect it out Every Day

The Marsh Mole Difers from ours in the length of its tail & it is a lighter Colour – Wee have but one species, expect your species Differ one from another

pray my Respects to thy Son John   I must not forget Him who take pains to gett me rare plants &c

BP 3:76; D. 298–300.
1. Charles Lennox, Third Duke of Richmond and Lennox (1735–1806), English statesman.

To COLLINSON

May the 20th 1768

Dear Peter
my rare kind of Pinaster hath now formed several beautiful Cones as red as scarlet & near half an inch long, near ye extremity of this springs shoot one

on each side opposite which makes A fine but very uncommon appearance. I never saw or heard of this exceeding beautiful Pinaster growing naturaly any where but on one part of ye Katts kill mountains from whence I brought two of them one of which is now near 20 foot high & A very handsom shape

my Burrea or sweet wood of Carolina grows & spreads finely & every branch is delicately gilded

I have drawn upon thee for 100 pound sterling for my son in law George Bartram which I hope thee will answer & place it to my account

pray at thy leasure draw out our accounts and send it by ye first opertunity, I want to know how those affaires stand between us which will oblige thy real friend

John Bartram

British Library, Add. Ms. 28727.

From COLLINSON

Mill Hill July 6:1768

This Day I was delighted with the sight of my Dear Johns Letter of ye 15th May — the Two prospects of St Augustine gives Mee & my Son great Satisfaction for now thy accurate Descriptions are perfectly Intelligible It is conveniently situate for trade & a safe Harbour if the Barr could admit vessels of greater Burthen the Island must have a pretty Effect from the Town

I am much obliged for Billys assistance in drawing the Plan — the Duchess of Portland dined here this Day She is a great virtuoso, in shells & all marine productions I took the opportunity to show her Billys drawings She admired them as they deserve — she Desires to bestow twenty guineas on his performances *for a trial* She would wish to have the Faba Egyptica drawn of the size of that he sent and drawings of all Land, River, & your Sea Shells *from the very least to the greatest* don't crowd to many Together in a half Sheet of paper for then they do not show them selves to advantage & a short description of the Colour & size of Each & where found — *and be sure to give no Shade to the Drawing* of the Shells *which only Confounds their Shape* — I have further Views for Billy if I can bring them to bare —

Thou hast told Mee a very pleasing story of your Mocking Bird which I have often seen & heard sing & some of my Lady Friends have kept them 7, 8 & 10 years but require to be Delicately & nicely fed Every Day, with fresh provisions yett his song, they thought, amply rewarded them for Their pains & Care about them — the Augustine scarlet Sage & Betony are finely in flower — all fine things, as plants advance to the southward they put on Gayer Colours & Birds gayer plumage

But now I will tell thee Some Thing Marvelous of the Great Mud Turtle

Thou formerly sent   Wee put him into a Great pond behind our House & there Wee thought Him safe & secure — Last Autumn Wee Emptyed a pond in our Field at a Great Distance & in a Bottome   the other was high on the Hill fenced in with a Pale & other Difficulties — as the Man was throwing out the Mud, he Sayes he felt as something Alive   What should it be but the Mud Turtle had notwithstanding found his way heither & Chose it for his Winter Quarters — Wee had him out & made him bite & Hiss & then putt him in Again — Wee was never more pleased then to see his Slow & Solomn March untill He came to Deep Mud where Wee saw Him with all the Calmness Imaginable go in with his Head fore most untill all the Mud cover'd Him that not a bit was to be seen — then Wee Left Him safe & secure for the Winter – but how long He kept his resolution of staying there Wee don't know — for a few Days after Draining the Upper pond with a strong Nett to the surprise of all He was drawn out, as a wonderfull Phenomenon – wee Teased Him & made Him Hiss & bite & putt him in again — there is something Surprising in the Instinct & Sagacity of this Creature — He must Certainly Smell water — or Else it is a thousand to one He could sett his way to the pond — in his first Essay & his Second Attempt was as extraordinary   Every one would think that saw the Situation & Distance of the Two ponds, — now it draws near to Eleven att night so is time to conclude from thy Real Friend

P Collinson

It is something Extraordinary to hear how Warners Jessamine Thrives It Increases both by Cuttings & Layers   it is the most ticklish plant that can be raised   Here No one (*no not Gordon*) has hit the Culture when exported Abroad, whilst it is kept under Frames in a Bark Heat it grows & flowers to Admiration but when exposed to the Air Looses its Vigor & is stunted & barely Lives

It is a sad thing to be so plagued with moles   they will come into our Gardens & Disturb our Beds but never known to Eat any Roots —

I am much obliged for thy Care of the Fartle berries   pray when thou writes my Respect to Friend Lambol & his wife — thy Sorrel Trees are Like the Agave by Accounts, Cross purposes & forget them   Wee have got them both at Last — the Sorrel Tree is an Andromeda —

the Grassy Starr of Bethlehem I saw a few Days agon in flower in Kew Garden — There & with us most of your flowers & plants thrive wonderfull in our black Bog Earth, the azaleas & Calmias make a fine show —

I have seen often Oranges Bear fruit in 2 years from the kernel — Draw the Stock with string the first year – but Insert with a Branch with Blossoms on it

I can't think thy Siberia Sage the same species. Mine has a Great Tuberous Root & has not increased for 20 years

Golden rod went off & Bees flower gone   don't forget root of sweet Early Dwarfe iris — The Tallies made larger, & tied with Thread of silk, will not Rot —

the Advice of thy 100 £ Bill came regular so no trouble, but thou should, Also, have mentioned it in thy Letter for fear of accidents

Wee could not help smiling when I read my Dear Johns Escape for not writeing a Bill of 4 or 5 Lines when to oblige Mee he could write a Letter of More then Two Sides of Paper   is not this fancy full, or are the most always in the same Humour to do the Same Thing

Wee have a very Melancholy Time   Rain more or Less at least Every Day   if it continues I don't know what will become of Us, a very great Crop on the Ground, but Wett & rainy weather runs it up all to Stock & Little poor, Thin Grain or none in the Ear – this was the Case the 2 preceeding years, a Third, which this is like to have, was never known to Come so together — I hope good Providence will fill up your Granaries — that you may relieve us — a very bad time [illegible] but there is a good Stock of old Hay — [illegible] neither the King or Queen would see Young or Take any of his plants, for his part [illegible] but Young has brought over I think from Carolina is many plants of [illegible] & the other rare plants which He Sett in Eight [illegible] red Potts, (Think on This) for which he asked Six hundred pounds — Money Enough — besides to make them Sell the Better He has painted or Drawn them in their Natural Colours (the most I hear he has been Bid is 40 pounds) but Mr. Ellis sayes this was wretchedly printed & He brought a Many seeds, your proprietor Thomas his great friend presented them to the Duchess of Portland & she [illegible] & *which I could not give six shillings for*

3 Boxes of Seeds for Bush —

2 Boxes for Gordon — *I have no Orders for any more*

[illegible] he can draw all your shells for that Money but only Don't Lett Bill draw any shells but what he can find are on your Continent [illegible] where there is variety of them &c and all from fresh live shells or [illegible]

BP 3:77; D. 300.

From FOTHERGILL

London. 29.10.1768

Respected Friend,

The loss which we have both sustained by the death of our late very valuable Friend Peter Collinson[1] is the principal occasion of my writing to thee at this time. I must in the first place however acknowledge my self indebted to thee for a box of very curious plants which I received some time ago, and which are most of them prosperous, and all of them would have been so had my gardener taken the care of them he ought for they came in a very prosperous condition. The Pittsburgh Iris I lost, and indeed I ought not to think of increasing my collection for my leisure to attend to it seems to lessen every day — for on one account or another so many people seem to have claims to my assistance that I have less leisure than ever. However

I keep a garden still and have an able young natural gardener to take care of it, and though I see it not once a week now, yet when I do see it, it is always with so much satisfaction that I cannot relinquish it but live in hopes of enjoying it one time or another.

I could have wished to offer thee my services in lieu of our deceased Friend but foresee that I cannot be half so punctual or useful a correspondent. But if in anything I can assist, for his sake as well as thy own, let me know and I will do everything I can.

I called upon my Friend one morning this summer, when he showed me some exquisite drawings of thy son's. He proposed that I should engage thy son to make drawings of all your land tortoises. I wish he would be kind enough to undertake this for me, and at the same time to make some short notes, with respect to their natural history, way of life, places of abode, generation and whatever occurs to him. Twenty guineas was mentioned but I will not restrict him to this sum. Let him take his own time. Send me a drawing or two as time and opportunities offer. If he has been able to divide them into classes or fit proper names, he will be kind enough to make them, and I'll either pay what he requires, as he may have occasion for it here, or remit it together as he chooses.

I shall be glad likewise to make thee any acknowledgement thou pleases, for any curious plants that may occur to thee. I think it would be a great advantage if thou was to sow a considerable part of most of the seeds thou collects. I mean the new discovered plants, in a little garden at home, and to send over young plants of two years old in boxes, several sorts of plants in one box. Many seeds wholly miscarry with us. The young plants would always find a good market. Seeds might be sent likewise, but young plants I think would be better. I should be glad of a colection of your American Martagons. It has happened that I have seen but a few. Would it not be practicable to send over a root or two of the Colocasia in autumn in a tub of mud or in wet Moss? The seeds mostly germinate but the plant perishes, at least all that I have made trial of. I shall be glad to hear from thee when convenient. Direct to me in Harpur Street, near Red Lion Square, London. Anything sent to me to the care of Daniel Mildred, Merchant, will come safe. Let me know what kind of return and how I shall repay thee for thy trouble, and I shall gladly repay. I propose if time permits to give some little account of our deceased Friend[2] in some of our public printes; if I do I shall send one for thyself.

Accept my kind acknowlegement for thy kind present, and believe me to be

Thy very respectful Friend
John Fothergill

Historical Society of Pennsylvania Library, Gratz Collection of European Physicians, Case 12, Box 20.
1. Collinson became ill with a kidney ailment at young Lord Petre's home and returned to London, where he died a week later, in mid-August 1768.
2. *Some Account of the Late Peter Collinson* (London, 1770).

To FRANKLIN

November ye 5th 1768

Dear ould friend

I have often intended to have wrote to thee this several years but has often been tould thee was soon to return to thy family and friends so I omitted it, but lately hearing that thee was likely to stay longer I now not onely write a letter of friendship but allso request a favour which ye death of our worthy dear friend Peter Collinson hath obliged me to crave. He wrote to me last summer that ye King desired me to send him some roots of arums but now I hear Peter is dead and I have not received a line from his son or any of my other Correspondents since; so that now at present I have not any so intimate or capable as my dear Benjamin to take care of ye Box I directed to ye King at large on ye lid it will oblige me much if thee will please to send or convey it to ye King or to his order as thee thinks most suitable; I expect dayly to hear from his son or some of my Correspondents how my affairs stand and whether any is to succeed in his room to receive ye Kings bounty to me or whether I must send anualy more plants to ye King and to whome I must direct them. Captain Falconor promiseth to take great care of ye Kings Box.

Alltho I have been long deprived of thy agreeable conversation yet for several years I have had thy pretty exact picture hanging by my bed which gives a dayly fresh remembrance of intimate friendship to thy sincear friend
John Bartram

American Philosophical Society Library, Benjamin Franklin Papers, vol. 2, f. 147.

From FRANKLIN

London, January 9, 1769

My Dear old Friend:

I received your kind letter of November 5, and the box directed to the King is since come to hand. I have written a line to our late dear friend's son (who must be best acquainted with the usual manner of transacting your affairs here,) to know whether he will take charge of the delivery of it; if not, to request he would inform me how, or to whom, it is to be sent for the King. I expect his answer in a day or two, and I shall when I see him, inquire how your pension is hereafter to be applied for and received; though I suppose he has written to you before this time.

I hope your health continues – as mine does, hitherto; but I wish you would now decline your long and dangerous peregrinations, in search of your plants, and remain safe and quiet at home, employing your leisure hours in a work that is much wanted, and which no one besides is so capable of performing – I mean the writing a Natural History of our country. I imagine it would prove profitable to you, and I am sure it would do you honour.

My respects and best wishes attend Mrs. Bartram, and your family. With sincere esteem, I am, as ever,

Your affectionate friend,
B. Franklin

P.S. January 28. The box is delivered, according to Mr. Michael Collinson's directions, at Lord Bute's. Mr. Collinson takes it amiss that you did not write to him.

I have sent over some seed of Naked Oats, and some of Swiss Barley, six rows to an ear. If you would choose to try some of it, call on Mrs. Franklin.

D. 402–3.

To FRANKLIN

April ye 10th 1769

My much Respected ould and Constant Friend

I received with great pleasure my dear friends letter of January ye 9th 1769 and am much obliged to him for his kindness in takeing care of ye Box for ye King. I should have wrote to Michael Collinson Last fall but I did not know then his name alltho I asked several that had frequented his fathers house but towards this spring I received a very kindly expressed letter from him dated September ye 22 wherein he gave me A perticular account of his father's death and ye friendship that had subsisted between us but mentioned nothing of our Correspondent affairs how thay stand. I allso by ye same Vesail received A kind letter from Dr. Fothergill who ofered to do me what kindness he could consistant with his great hurry of Business. But stil I am at A loss to know whether I must send any more plants or seeds to his Majesty and whether he is pleased to continue his bounty to me or not. I wrote to Mr. Collinson and the Doctor by ye first opertunity after I received thairs and desired Mr. Collinson to let me know how our accounts stands (which I expect is Considerable) and whether he inclines to Correspond with me as his father did for upwards of thirty years. I am at present in good health but hath been afflicted all winter with sore ancles   one is healed and the other is mending occationed by a small bruise which turned to painfull ulcers so that my travails as to any distant provinces is at an end. I sent my Journal thro the Carolinas Georgia and florida wherein I wrote my observations daly of the perticular soils rivers and natural vegetable production with which our friend Peter expressed Much satisfaction but there was no artificial curiosities in those provinces as temples, theaters, piramids palaces bridges catacoms oblisks picturs and different methods of government and customs to be discribed; which fills up the greatest part of all our modern travailers Journals alltho thay have been ten times near as well or better related many years before.

We have had the appearance of the Borealis twice last winter   one the most vivid ye last of february and lately two severe thunder storms with allmost continual flashes of lightning for near two hours   ye streams of which ran in a horizontal direction generaly.

My dear beloved friend thy kind letter moved me much   it was not for want of respect that I did not write to thee before but supposeing that thy publick afairs for the Provincial good took up so much of thy time as an hour was not to be spared to read or write a letter to thy ould friend

John Bartram

PS   I am much obliged to thee for ye barley and naked oats and I expect tomorow to receive some naked barley brought from Carolina

American Philosophical Society Library, Benjamin Franklin Papers, vol. 2, f. 169.

From FOTHERGILL

Lond 5th mo. 1st 1769

Esteemed Friend

I received thy acceptable letter of 26/1 on the 17th last Mo: and in a short time after, I also received the box of plants in pretty good condition. Most of them will live and divers of them are new to me. One of the Ginseng plants is coming up very vigorously. I am much obliged to thee for this valuable present and shall be glad to make returns for it as well as I can. If a copy of Purver's translation of the Bible will be acceptable please to call upon Thomas Fisher in Philadelphia and desire him to deliver one bound, and place it to my account. The author of this great undertaking like thyself is self taught and instructed. Almost without any assistance but from books he has acquired the knowledge of many languages and the best judges allow that this translation is the most faithfull one of the original Scripture that ever was made in the English tongue. Let me know if there is anything here in which I can make thee proper satisfaction and I will do it cheerfully. I don't want my friends should make brick without straw. There will be a considerable demand for American seeds to various parts of Germany, and were there any in town I know they might be disposed of. I have a nephew, by marriage, who lives in our deceased Friend P. Collinson's house and carries on the business of a mercer. If Michael Collinson does not choose to engage in the business of disposing of the seeds, I know I can readily prevail upon him to undertake it. He has no skill in these matters but he would take care to render a faithful account of the sales, and make due remittances. I am afraid of intrusting these things to the care of the seedsmen: J. Gordon, Junr., is I believe one of the best, yet one cannot be sure they will always continue to be faithful and honest. — If Michael Collinson will be kind enough to undertake the affair no person is more proper, I will see him as soon as I can and endeavour to prevail upon him. Should he decline it, and no other person seem more suitable send thy boxes to James Freeman Mercer in Gracious Street, and any instructions thou thinks proper to me and I will take care they shall be duly executed. —

I am pleased that thy son William is engaged in describing the Tortoises of your country. America seems to abound with this species of Animal, more than any other country. As the inhabitants increase, these as well as the native plants will be thinned, and it is therefore of some consequence to begin their history as soon as possible. — I would not limit him, either in respect to time or expense. He may send me his drawings and accounts of their history as he finishes them, and I will pay his demands to his order.[1]

It gives me satisfaction to find that our opinions are alike in respect to propagation of plants by seeds on your side. I think there is a shorter method and less expensive of making a natural soil for all your wild plants than is generally known. In the Autumn collect a large quantity of the new fallen leaves of all sorts of trees. Dig a large hole in any vacant spot and fill it with layers of leaves and layers of earth dug out of the hole. Do this every fall of the leaves and a good compost will be formed in which all sorts of seeds and plants will flourish that are natives to the country. If the earth dug out of the hole is not sandy this had better be thrown away and the hole filled with leaves and sand. It will be proper that this should lye to rot two years before it is used, but by making such a preparation annually enough will be at hand for every pur.[2] I judge that most of the flat country from Canada to Florida has been the last of all redeemed from the Ocean. The soil of these flat countrys consists of decayed vegetable and sea sand. In some parts the sand prevails and with it barrenness; in other places corrupted vegetables and with them fertility. The soil is good or bad or indifferent as it partakes of the riches of corrupted vegetables or the poverty of mere sea sand. This I only hint as my opinion, and on this opinion I found my theory of this species of Fertility. Put me to rights if I am wrong. My gardener has directions every fall to collect a quantity of leaves and treat them in this manner. We reserve this for the use of our wild American Seeds and succeed with them. Be kind enough to get us some plants of those curious oakes & chestnuts. Take them up with large balls of earth; tye moss about them plant them in similar earth at home till they begin to prosper. The branches of the old plants may be laid down, and a numerous progeny may be seen [to] bee raised to oblige and benefit our Country.

If all the more curious plants & shrubs were to be taken up while very young, and planted in boxes, & kept in them, often water'd during sunmmer, for one year they would succeed with us much better and deserve a better price than by any other management.

I shall expect the Colocasia when convenient to send it and shall do my best to preserve it. I doubt not but my Friend B Franklin has executed his commission. However, I hope to see him shortly and shall endeavour to inform my self of what is done and acquaint thee with it. The present gardener at Kew is from general account a very ingenious, sensible, honest man. It will be much in his power to determine the Royal personnages: and I think it would not be improper to write to him. If any plants are sent His name is Aiton and if a line or two are sent I will take care to convey it safely.

As I wish to make thee adequate satisfaction for the trouble thou has taken and may take on my account I should be glad to know in what way I can most satisfactorily make thee compensation. Through the favour of Providence and much careful labour, I want for nothing and therefore would desire that all due satisfaction may be given to those who are kind enough to do anything for me.

This perhaps will be delivered by Doctor Rush, a young man who has employed his time with great diligence and success, in prosecuting his studies here; who has led a blameless life, so far as I know; and it seems but just that those who have endeavoured to deserve a good character should have it when it may be of use to them.

My engagements in the duties of my station, may perhaps render me a very irregular correspondent; But my inclination to show regard to every person who was the friend of my deceased Friend, P. Collinson, will always lead me to be as diligent as I can. I am thy obliged, respectful friend,

J. Fothergill.

Direct for me in Harpur Street near Red Lion Square London

BP 4:21; D. 339–41.
1. Darlington omitted the remainder of this letter.
2. Abbreviation of "purpose."

From C. M. WRANGEL

Stockholm in Sweden July ye 2d 1769.
Dear Sir & beloved Friend
Whenever I think of America (which I do every day of my life), I think at the same time of you & your House & as ingratitude is what I detest I cannot but bear you the warmest gratitude, for all the civilities you were pleased to show me, while I had the pleasure to cultivat a Friendship with you at a nearer distance. I always looked upon myself as one of your Family, being happy enough to be counted so by you and yours. It grieved me when I was in America that your great merit had not in my native land recieved the marks of Esteem in the public as it deserved & therefor it gives me great satisfaction, when I now assure you that you are well known hear from the Throne to every one that regards Learning & the Society of Science in Stockholm, which has from its first institution been known for the greatest delicacy in choosing members of distinction & note, has manifested their great regard for you, by choosing you a member unanimously, at the proposal of Professor Bergius.[1] I had the pleasure to be present in the

Society that same day, when you were proposed & to deliver to the Society the drafts of your son & some other things in your name, which were received with much satisfaction. Doctor Linaeus is so used to receive presents from all quarters, that he hardly thinks of it, & therefore I took the liberty to give what was intended for him, to the Society as I expected, that they would show more gratitude & I hope to have your approbation in it. Your son's[2] corespondence with Professor Bergius will no doubt be of great use to him & do him much honour. I have not been like Professor Kalm in taking the honour to my self of what belongs to others. I have given my Dear Friend Mr. John Bartram, Junr. his due & I hope he will not repent of what he had done for Professor Bergius, who is a Man hear & abroad of great repute & at the same time very attentive to any thing that is done for him. He expects that his Correspondent will send him some seeds. You will no doubt be glad to hear that I have been recieved in my Native Land in the best manner I could wish for. His Majesty the King has shown me the greatest marks of clemency & I am now officiating at his Court as first Chaplain with great satisfaction & have a prospect of being extremely well settled at Home & the poor state of my Health in which I have been for some time hinders me from thinking of ever returning to America. Indeed, I should not be able to go through the hardships any more which a Faction of ungratefull hearers laid me under. Notwithstanding all this my heart is allways in America & when I think of my Friends there it makes me wish to be amongst them. I wish you & yours all the prosperity which this troublesom life will admit of & beg to be kindly remembered to your Dear Spouse & all the Family & am with greatest sincerity Dear sir & beloved Friend

Your most humble & affectionate servant,
C. M. Wrangel

BP 4:114; D. 444–46.
1. Dr. Peter Bergius (1730–1790), botanist and professor of natural history at the University of Stockholm.
2. John Bartram, Jr.

From FRANKLIN

London July 9, 1769

Dear Friend,

It is with great Pleasure I understand by your Favour of April 10, that you continue to enjoy so good a Share of Health. I hope it will long continue, And altho' it may not now be suitable for you [to make] such wide Excursions as heretofore, you may yet be very useful to your Country and to Mankind, if you [sit] down quietly at home, digest the Knowledge you [have] acquired, compile and publish the many Observations you have made, and point out the Advantages that may be drawn from the whole, in publick Undertakings or particular private Practice. It is true many People are fond of Accounts of old Buildings, Monuments, &c. but there is a

Number who would be much better pleas'd with such Accounts as you could afford them; And for one I confess that if I could find in any Italian Travels a Receipt for making Parmesan Cheese, it would give me more Satisfaction than a Transcript of any Inscription from any old Stone whatever.

I suppose Mr. Michael Collinson, or Dr. Fothergill have written to you what may be necessary for your Informaton relating to your Affairs here. I imagine there is no doubt but the King's Bounty to you will be continued; and that it will be proper for you to continue sending now and then a few such curious Seeds as you can procure to keep up your Claim. And now I mention Seeds, I wish you would send me a few of such as are least common, to the Value of a Guinea, which Mr. Foxcroft will pay you for me. They are for a particular Friend who is very curious. If in any thing I can serve you here, command freely Your affectionate Friend

B Franklin

P.S. Pray let me know whether you have had sent you any of the Seeds of the Rhubarb describ'd in the enclo'd Prints. It is said to be of the true kind. If you have it not, I can procure some Seeds for you.

D. 403–4.

From THOMAS JONES[1]

New York July 27th:1769

To Mr. Bartram Sen'r.,
2nd St. Phila.
favor of Mr. Abbotte

Sir

You will be so good to Collect a large Compleat Box of Garden Seeds with the most Valuable Plants in the Curious Way being for a Person of Distinction in England who has it in his Power to Recommend you Strongly to a more extensive Custom; The Last Collection I had from you turned out well & flourished & I assure you has gained you universal Applause & Credit — You will not forget to Minute down in a paper the Nature of Soil the Seeds require & the proper Season for Sowing or planting them: The Box will be sent here directed to Capt. Th. Jones of the Royal Artillery & the Cash shall be paid in any channel you desire   I could wish you at the same time put up in another Small Box a little Quantity of the most Curious Seeds you think will happily grow in England that will cost abt. a Guinea or so — Your Reply to this will Oblige him who is with wishing you prosperity
    Sir

Yours &c.
Thomas Jones

If you have any friends that have Collected any Ground Squirrel Skins during the Winter or who could get me some I will pay them what is reasonable for their trouble. The Squirrels must be caught in Traps & not shot as that will tear the Skin & render them unsuitable —

Farewell.

If skins of this kind can be procured for Capt. Jones he will be much obliged to Mr. Bartram but would be glad to know the price he is to give for them

BP 4:55.
1. Unidentified.

To FOTHERGILL

August ye 12th 1769

My dear worthy friend
I received thy kind friendly letter of ye 5th month 1769 & was surprised to find so much kindness expressed in it to one who so little deserved it. I have not received any answer from Michel Collinson or Benjamin franklin or any others to those letters I sent to them with ye Captain that brought thine but with Michel there is prety large accounts to settle between us which I desired his father A little time before his discease to send me an account how thay stood which he had not done of two or thre year before. I am glad ye Box of plants was acceptable & came prety well under ye greatest disadvantage being packed in frosen clods, lay shiped at ye warf — frose frose [sic] up A month after thay might have sailed & at last wind bound at our Capes. I never was so disapointed as last fall   all our vesails that sailed in ye fall for London went to soon   one I expected to sail after changed her voyage   one was to sail to Bristol but she proved Leaky & could not get out till spring; I am much obliged for thy valuable present of Purvurs translation   I called at Fishers for them   ye bound ones was all disposed of thay offered to get bound & charge thee with it but I would [not] Concent being satisfied that ye unbound present was more then I deserved   I like it much   he hath molified many harsh Calvinestical expressions in thair ould translation

I am much obliged to thee for thy kind offer of service   I dont know yet whether ye King continues his bounty nor who receives it   My Colocasia now makes A glorious Appearance: I intend to try if I cant assist ye King & my friend Fothergill in being Proprietors of it. — it rarely grows by seed I must try to send ye roots in A Cask of mud but it must have A pond of water   it will grow from two foot to 12 deep in water where thay will soon spread with thair rushy creeping roots 2 or 3 rod square & ye leaves wholy cover ye water

it is very kind in the to ingage thy Nephew to take Care of ye seeds I send   I must inlarge my nurcery garden   I like thy proposal of sowing or transplanting our native plants into it but I cant resolve upon any thing till I hear from Collinson Franklin Gordon or Webb: doth thee want A natural history of all our turtles   water as well as land; we have A great variety of ye first & but two real kinds of ye last

thy proposal of makeing natural mould by an artifitial means may answer very well in many cases but then we should be perticular in ye choice of earth & leaves to suite perticular vegitables if we want a rich melow soil we must chuse that amongst hard dark gray iron stones limeston & marble & ye leaves must be wallnut Mulbery Sumach Papaw hasel & locust; if we want A lean stif mould we must chuse white clay & gravel with chesnut & white oak leaves; if A hungry light mould chuse sand mixed with isinglas with chesnut beech & Hicory leaves: but all our kind of Oak leaves is long in disolving — I take one of ye Causes of natural fertility to be Saline efluviums out of ye earth & perhaps ye atmospher may contribute something to it as well as several other Causes for ye wisdom of Providence is manifested in his incomprehensible works in nature for ye general support of ye universe by such A wise structur that many causes mutualy contribute to one effect each of which under ye direction of Allmighty Power promotes ye general balance of ye Universe   ye sterility of different soils hath numerous causes beside wet & dry, cold & heat, as A deep compact bed of clay near ye surface or A flat rock of great extent of isinglas or as in Carolina Georgia & Florida A vast strata of whiteish clay near ye surface of A vast body of concreted sea shels   some by A Calcarious matter   some by A ferriginous & in some places sand & hard Compacted so with A feriginous matter as to be impenitrable by water unless by A long continued pressure which is the cause of the great extensive Savanas in Carolina Georgia & Florida where in moist seasons water continualy lyeth on ye surface untill ye sun in a long dry season exhales ye greatest part & the other descinds by slow degrees through ye compact strata below & furnisheth ye great fountains that breaks out allmost level with ye sea in Florida & banks of rivers in Carolina   It is very clearly demonstrable that our low lands to Florida from ye North river hath been raised since ye sea retired from between our mountains A little on our side York   its near twenty miles from ye hills to ye sea. Against Philadelphia its 50   Against Maryland 60. against virginia 100. No. Carolina 150   south carolina 200 some places more or less   Georgia much like Florida 3 & 400. from ye hills to ye point   all this extent of countrey hath been raised by ye wash of ye Sea & high winds blowing the sands A great Hight on shore above 40 foot high as I have observed in one stage & from thence still higher as ye back ground is leveled to receive it. allso ye great rivers brings down much soil in great floods   it is clearly evident that all our great chains of mountains was once so covered with sea or salt water for A long time before the earth was habitable to beasts: as Many of them & most of the vails between them is covered with seashels embodied in vast masses of rocks most of which is lime stone; these great vails doubtless was great bays of ye sea long after ye high hills was dry; indeed upon A very close examination our back mountainous countrey seems much resembling our sea coasts except in ye elevation ye position rocks, ye materials of which thay are composed as sand stone, pebles, gravel & sea shells ye same as on our Coast except in magnitude nay even ye very sea & salt marsh mud in its exact position but now is converted into sulphurious vitriolick & aluminous rocks but I take that Cordelior mountains & high piked vulcanos to be raised to thair vast hight by fire: but I dont deny ye Noachian flood but I believe by ye account we have of it being mixed with so much fresh water those shells was neither bredd in it, nor was it natural for such prodigious numbers to be then formed in such masses of rocks all over ye back Countrey

I am very much obliged to thee for thy kind offer of service to me its strange that Michel Collinson hath not wrote to me but one letter & that mentioned Not A word how ye affairs stands between us which is considerable as his father had not setled with me for years

I like thy advice much to write to ye Kings gardener at Kew in my next to thee I intend to inclose one to him

in ye meantime I remain thy gratefull & much obliged friend

John Bartram

Natural History Museum, London.

From WILLIAM CULLEN[1]

not say for what reasons my chief dependance is upon you. You will find by the Queries subjoined that it is chiefly information Mr. Pennant wants & as he has already made large collections he does not desire Specimens except the Subjects are very new & little known. I have now left so little room for Mr. Pennant that I must conclude with assuring you that I am with great regard Do. Do.

Your most obedient humble servant
William Cullen

Edinr. 16th Septr. 1769

To favor me with any rare Birds, small quadrupeds, fish reptiles or insects as yet undescribed would oblige me greatly. The Bats are unknown to me & would be very acceptable: The sorex cristatus, & aquaticus, all of them preserved in spirits. I am given to understand that a Mr. Bartram makes it his business to collect Things of this nature. I should be glad of his aid; & would gratify him in all That is reasonable: it will do me a service would you be so good as to speak to him on the subject; & inform me whether he is a person of observation. I am also recommended to Mr. Allen of Philadelphia, whose searches you will perhaps have the goodness to assist.

I hope you will soon favor me with an answer; & that you would please to send any curiosities you oblige me with properly packed up either to me at Mr. [illegible]

BP 3:93.
1. The first part of this letter is missing.

From JOHN LEWIN

London Oct 23 1769

Mr. John Bartram
Dr Sr

I received in due Course by the hand of Mr. Collinson your Box of Insects[1] I think myself obliged to you for them. I had not so long before writing to you, but on account of the Death of this Worthy Friend; as I could not till very lately find anybody to whom I cou'd pay a little money on your account, when I accidently heard of Dr. Fothergill having a correspondence to whom I immediately paid Six Guineas as you will see by his Receipt annexed for the same.[2] I propose 2 Guineas for the Insects, & 4 more I send for some plants & seeds as Dr. Fothergill tells me you are Curious in your Collecting them. I have a pretty large Shrubery, tho' but thinly stocked that I shall be obliged to you for a good Collection. I would not have more than 5 or Six plants of a sort, nor woud I have any of the Tree kind nothing but Dwarf trees or Shrubs & Perenial plants, such as you cant send in plants shall be glad to have them in seeds — I have a good many of the very common American plants &c already.

I shall esteem it a favour you woud send them next Spring if possible & let there be a great variety as you can of what is Curious & If you charge me more than the ten Guineas, I will pay it immediately, in to any persons hands you will be pleased to mention —

The Insects you sent me were a many of them very Curious, but a Good deal damaged in coming. I woud not trouble you any more for insects as I confine my Collection entirely to Insects of this Country — If there is any Service I can render you pray freely command me whom is Dr Sir

Your obliged Friend & hble Servant
John Lewin

Please to direct to me
Merchant in London

BP 4:70.
1. John Bartram, Jr., sent the insects.
2. Attached is Fothergill's receipt: "Received of John Lewin Ten pounds Six shillings on Account of John Bartram of Philadelphia John Fothergill."

To LINNAEUS[1]

To the Right Honorable Charles Linne Barronet
at Upsala in Sweden per favr.
The Revd. John Weiskell[2]

My Honorable & worthy friend
    I am much obliged to your illustrious Philosophical Society at Stockholm for nominating me A member of it & to shew my gratitude to them I now transmit my private conjectures upon two different Phanomena that have been ye subjects of much dispute with ye Learned: and allso A few observations which I made in my Botanical travails which I now lay before ye great Virtuoso & head of ye Respectable Body; not that I think that I have explained those Phanomenas as fact but as queries to move ye learned & Juditious to dig deeper for treasure or as ye saying is I started ye hare for ye hunters to catch. the ingenious Dr. Kally[3] hath taken such pains in Calculating ye dimentions of ye surface of ye Mediteranian Sea from whence he concludes that ye evaporation into ye atmosphere is greater then all ye great rivers beside ye numerous rivolets furnisheth ye sea with water. then if there be such A great evaporation of water in this little spot of surface what must there be in ye surface of ye Main Ocean, which is above 30 times as large & perhaps hath not above 20 or 25 times as much water flows into it as doth into ye Mediteranian   then what must supply ye vast evaporation of ye Main Ocean which is in some places 10000 miles broad & 16000 mile long from North to So. in some places & ye main body of it warm or ye warmest climates subject to violent storms to break its surface int[o] ye minutest parts fittest for evaporation which it must increase more then ye more stiller water in ye Mediteranian unless we suppose ye evaporation to be greater near ye shore then in ye midst between them
    But what shall we say of ye red sea being 1000 mile long & hath but one little river ye Mocha belonging to it with A few little rivulets & ye sand border of Arabia on one side of it as ye sand of Africk doth on ye so. side of ye Mediteranean: what then supplies its evaporation   doth ye Ocean pour in as much water at ye straight of Babelmondel as supplies it; so much concerning evapouration.
    But there is another pretty generaly received opinion in ye sea affair that I cant yet acquiesce with that is that ye moon is ye material Cause of ye ebing & flowing of ye sea which we call ye tide   if ye moon hath any influence on our main Ocean it must be by atraction or repultion; Can ye swift rotation of ye earth Admit instantly so much of ye lunar power as to move such A body of ye main ocean regularly as for instance it is reconed to be 3000 miles from our coast to that of England where suppose ye moon was perpendicular to thair horizon at noon or 12 A'clock then it will be same to us at five   Can you think ye moon moved all ye surface of that sea 3000 miles in five hours time regularly or doth it skip over some parts & take

fresh hold again   for ye motion of ye tide in ye sea I suppose to be not above 3 or 4 miles an hour: & is it not likely that when ye moon is in ye Southern Sighns our Northern Sea should be more effected with it then thay are. how can such A little remote body as ye moon in such A little time move ye far greater part of ye surface of our much greater Globe: I should rather think that our earth & waters hath much greater influence upon ye moon then it hath upon us: Perhaps our tides may be in A little degree under ye Lunar influence as allso ye earth & its productions but its A sure maxim all smaller beings is subservient or subordinate to ye greater   we read ye earth & sea produced plentifuly (we dont know how long) before ye moon was placed in our sight   was there no tides then

But many noted Philosophers hath been wrecked upon that rock   that is thay often ascribed one material cause to produce one particular effect upon ye All-wise Eternal Soverain Cause is often pleased to appropriate several material causes to mutualy assist each other in produceing one effect; we observe in plants how absolutely necessary water earth & warmth is to raise ye plant from seed   yt ye air & sun is necessary to make it produce flowers & good seed

but why may we not suppose ye glorious luminary (subordinate to Almighty power) may have a share in ye motion of ye tides   are we not sure he hath great influence on our globe & is ye Natural cause of its living productions; but to Come nearer home is not ye earth that surrounds ye Ocean (except its surface) capable to hould a prety good shair by its rotation to move its own water under divine apointment

the farthest I have travailed northward was to Lake Ontario about 43 degrees No. latitude between which & Latitude 42 I observed these folowing trees & shrubs   Sasafras, Liriodendron very small growing little further northward; white, red, spanish & chesnut Oak; black beried tupelo, grapes, alder   ash, dirka, Elder, Cephalanthus, prinos, viburnums, lotus, two leaved pine, three leaved pine, plum tree, Gale Espleni folio, Hamamelis, red flowered Maple, Hickories several sorts, birch, beech, willow, hornbeam, azalea, spirea, these continueth all ye way to floridas; silver leaved maple   sugar maple   hasel, toxicodendron   dwarf plum   striped bark maple   Larix, Balm of Gilead fir, black & red spruice of newfoundland, silver leaved spruice, white pine, arbor vita, yew, dwarf birch, paper birch, red birch, red currants, gooseberries, dwarf Zoxilam, long walnut, yew dwarf Kalmia, cornus, red rod viburnum with heart shaped leaves, Hidrangea, holly rhus lentis folio, mountain magnolia, mountain chestnut Oak, pinast with narrow long leaves, Rhododendron, Azalea Benzoin;

42   here begins several of ye southward trees as Liquid amber, candle berried mirtle, Robinia, cluster cherry, large & dwarf spirea   opuli folio, viburnum with red & large black fruite, silver leaved alder, chestnut & dwarf oak, & large chestnut, poplar leaved birch, swamp magnolia, white cedar, crategus, Vitis idea; many kinds poplar, small viburnum   black Butternut, Diervilla

41   here ends several of our northern plants & Trees as ye white striped

maple Larix, red & black spruice of new foundland   sweet gale   white pine   white long walnut & ye black   begins ink berries, evergreen prinos, poplar leaved birch, poison sumach or toxicodendron anona   diospiros Clethra   ash leaved maple   willow leaved oak   swamp spanish & swamp white oak   various kinds of andromedas   fring tree itea   chinkapins thime leaved Kalmia   olive leaved Kalmia   Siliquastrum   great hors chestnut with yelowish flowers   Uva uray senecio arborescens   here ends to ye southward dwarf yew   Rhododendron   red currants   gooseberries   silver leaved alder   Larix   firs & spruice   hidrangia   striped bark maple   balm of Gilead fir   pinaster   viburnum with heart shaped leaves, dwarf birch & dwarf cluster cherry & wild cherry

39   these following continueth most of them all way to florida anona, bald cypress,

38   narrow leaved shrub hypericum, beech plums   here ends ye white long walnut, broad leaved shrub Hypericum, Ptelia, Gleditsia & here ye mountain magnolia ends

37   sorrel tree, yapon, evergreen oak, periclimenum; here ends ye arbor vita, Carolina

36   canes, dwarf berberry, Burrea or sweet wood & ye shrub yelow root

35   here ye silver leaved maple ends unless on ye north side of A mountain by chance   umbrella tree, kidney bean tree; stewartia, loblolly bay, sweet red bay, purple berried bay, halesia, several sorts of evergreen oaks, Philadelphus, horse sugar or yelow leafe pavia, small palmeto, dionea or flytrap   this grows near ye sea coast near which it extends about 60 miles & near 50 miles up ye countrey   I have been several times round where it grows   it prospers there in A moistish ground in an open suny savanah chiefly on ye So. side of Cape fear river but there is no general plant   here & there a patch at 5 10 or 15 miles distance & will bear ye cold that freeseth water an inch thick in one nights time & will bear ye heat of 88 degrees farenheits thermometer

34   long leaved pine, great magnolia, dwarf bay with ye scent of Sasafras

33   small narrow leaved bay, great palmeto, Adams needle or palmeto royal so called & A thorny little tree with box leaves falsly called wild olive

32   great red water tupelo with red acid fruite, short poded Gleditsia & catalpa with short pods no longer then acrons & A dwarf running oak with smooth shineing leaves about A foot high & A curious kind of andromeda three foot high

31   ye bonduck & ye several curious evergreen shrubs   A fine variety

30   is a little patch of ye star Annis shrub   grows ten foot high, a sweet evergreen

I have here given A prety near account where I observed ye natural growth generaly of ye several genus of trees & shrubs of North America where I have travailed from North to South & where I first observed ye southern trees to grow naturaly toward ye north ye sea coast but as our great mountains generaly run N E & S W our Northern trees will grow on ye top of Northern expositions of them 2 or 3 degrees farther South then on ye plains & many times some odd seeds will be brought down ye rivers by floods from ye mountains yerely & be deposited on thair overflowed banks where thay may vegitate where thay make A feble growth & those seeds that is carried by ye birds from ye South, altho thay grow & flower northward yet ye cold nips them before ye seed is perfected

I could have extended this relation to herbs but as thay are numerous would take up much time & perhaps be little curious to those that have more able Correspondents

as our Country of North America is quite exposed from 30 degrees north quite to ye Pole without any mountains but what generaly may be walked to ye top in two hours but generaly in one or A half an hour so that wee as wel as china hath no[ne] high enough to screen us from ye severe cold of ye polar regions of snow & ice   so it is with part of China which is in A similar scituation as to ye sea & Land & mountains with us. I take it to be as cold in 40 degrees with us in North America & China as in 50 in Europe. that is when ye No. west wind blows but if A so. wind blows 48 hours it will be warm any time in winter   when ye warm wind towards ye tropicks reacheth us but generaly when it happen so ye air is so rarified   then presently ye condensed Northern air rusheth upon us & is extreme cold. I have seen it frees ye ground in one nights time one inch thick on A No. bank about 29 degrees no. latitude

I have in all my travails taken great pleasure in searching & contemplating ye usefulness of mountains   there we may observe how nature was wound & now how it is unwinding since ye sea retired from them   it is much satisfaction to me to observe its gradual decrease since ye grand seperation when ye wheel of nature was set in regular motion to accomodate the present animal race. I cant but indulge a Conjecture that all limestone & marble is of marine origine as well as alum & vitriol when thay be deposited in A proper matrix for thair seed & organical power to operate; I have searched diligently our coast & from thence up our many rivers beyond ye head of them   I find ye rocks composed of sea shells all along ye coast from Maryland & Carolina & cemented with A calcarious matter & will burn to lime but at florida thay abounding so much with sand ye shels in mighty masses is cemented with A soft cristalin spar & made up of ye same species found now upon our Coasts & ye same kinds of shels compose ye vast rocks of limestone in all ye back parts of our countrey quite to & on ye branches of Misisipia & St Lawrence rivers with this diference that most of our valey limestone between ye great mountains is of A very strong tough consistance being composed of A more maturated calcarious metter & those on our Coasts hath a greater mixture of sand & are more recent

I suppose ye true Calcarious Cement to be originaly sea shels & by ye sepage of ye sea into ye very minutest particles (as I have seen prodigious masses of it 100 mile up ye countrey under vast strata of Oister shels) this being impregnated with proper salts & Oils mutualy Combineing to make A firm Contexture   I have travailed many 100 miles several times along A limestone valey which terminated at a large ridg of gravely ground of very smooth round & oval shaped stones as big as hens eggs more or less & for several miles. first A few stones was interspersed in ye solid limestone rock but gradualy increased in number & ye Calcarious matter still cemented them in A solid mass until ye gravel became so plentifull that ye Calcarious cement could not hold ye gravel together but fel to pieces where ye mould was washed off ye rock & it exposed it to frost & rain   here ye inhabitants split them to burn them for lime & it being weak ye lime burnt before ye peples run to glass as thay would in A hot kiln   thay ridled ye stones out & used ye lime

When I was in florida A way up St Johns river I observed how well he had plaistered his house and asking where he got his lime he said he would show me   I got A hoe & went with him to ye river bank about three foot in ye water which was near as solid as chalk   I struck ye hoe into it which was A solid mass of fine groun Oister shels that I have seen great quantities of finer A vast way up ye country in strata with ye shels; for want of ye grand workman ye sea & its materia was converted into limestone

I have no more room at present to enlarge then to assure you that I remain your real & sincere friend

John Bartram

Linnean Society of London Archives, Linnean Correspondence I, 360–61.
1. Undated, but written in the fall of 1769.
2. Unidentified.
3. Unidentified.

To FOTHERGILL

November ye 26 1769

Dear worthy friend
I answered thy very kind letter of ye 5th month 1769 & now I have sent thee A small box of plants   thy name at large on ye lid   allso in it A couple of small snakes which my son William found Just before I began to pack: ye biger one was swallowing ye lesser as thee may see in his draught   he pulled it out of ye snakes mouth with some difficulty for fear of hurting either, after which thay both crawled about in a bucket without any hostility for many hours till I put them in ye box with ye plants supposeing that will be ye best way of conveyance allive to thy hands for thy more curious inspection   then if thay were dead thay are both so little & young that we cant tell to what species thay belong. take care how you unpack ye Box; not for fear of being bit by them, but least thay should be entangled in ye Moss & miss finding them

I have allso sent A Barrel in which I packed many roots of ye Colocasia which my son dug out of my fish pond   thair roots is exceeding tender part of them. I intend for ye King & part for thy self   there is enough for both for if one root for each grows it will soon increas prodigiously   I had but one nut came up which in two year, spread several yards square so as to cover ye water   thay will grow from 12 foot deep to one but perhaps it may be best to plant them two or three foot deep but be sure to plant them where ye water allways covers them & where no other vegitable grows for she is so Coy A Lady as not to bear A touch from any other species of plants without fainting

I allso put into ye Barrel two of our Bull frogs for ye King   I think thay are male and female   thay came into my Milk house well or spring to winter   there is numbers of them in my fish pond amongst ye Colocasia on whose broad leaves which spreads on ye surface of ye water   thay love to sit to air themselves under other broad leaves that riseth two foot above like A canopy but here thay seldom roar   its on ye borders of ye pond amongst ye grass or where thay can rest thair fore feet with thair heads out of water. thay may be heard near or quite half A mile roaring like A bull & when half a dosen is roaring at A minits distance of time between each at A perticular noise made by one all is hushed in A minute until perhaps half A quarter of an hour. then thay roar again until ye common signal for cessation is given. we suppose it is onely ye males that roars which is very diverting to some an Irish girl tould me that soon after she came into ye country she was sent to A neibours house back in ye woods where she lost her way in a swamp in ye night when ye Bull frogs set A roaring she thought she was surrounded with bears or beasts of prey   she then down on her knees in prayer to God to deliver her from those revenous beasts   I asked her if she did not thank him heartyly for his deliverance   thay are very innocent feeding on insects or slimy moss   if we find them traveling from one pond to Another strike them with A small switch   thay will hump up their back & cry like A child   our Gentry Catcheth numbers of them, Cuts of thair hind quarter of which thay make fricasees & esteems them A more delitious morsell then any chicken   if thay should increas in ye pond in St James park thay would surprise & divert all ye adjacent inhabitants of London but I think at present it would be better to turn them into ye pond at kew garden as being more private until thay have increased thair number   if you have none allready perhaps ye best way will be to convey by Barrel to ye Kings Garden at Kew to ye edge of ye pond   then take out ye head of ye Cask & pour out together water, mud, roots & bull frogs   then seperate what roots thee thinks suffitient for thy self putting them in A bucket with water ready to be conveyed to thy pond, then plant ye others directly in ye Kings pond in which turn ye frogs att liberty where doubtless thay will increas if ye pond is shoal on any side that ye sun may hatch ye spawn

I am exceedingly obliged to thee for thy kind information concerning thy Nephews assistance in ye room of our dear deceased Peter   if he will please to accept my offer I will give my correspondents orders to pay what thay ow me to him & very willingly allow him reasonable commisions.

Michael Collinson hath sent me A very loveing letter in which he offers to assist me or mine with his intimate acquaintance & interest with ye Earls of Bute & Northumberland her grace ye Dutches &c &c But declines ye trouble of ye seed business   he writes that ye privy purse had ofered to pay ye Kings annual Bounty for me but he desired him to take it back again until thay received orders from me to whome I chose to have it paid

ye Colocasia is A noble plant   its leaves grows above two foot diameter & is very diverting to observe ye water sprinkled upon them to run & dance upon them exactly like ye globules of quick silver. so is ye unfoulding & expantion of them when thay Just arise above ye surface of ye water. ye flowers is 10 or 12 inches diameter of A cream color   ye pod 6 inches diameter   ye kernel of ye nuts as sweet as chesnuts or more so:

I have according to thy kind advice inclosed A letter to ye Kings gardener at Kew   I sent it open that thee might see what I wrote to him. pray seal, subscribe & send it to him. thy list of ye plants in thy Box is inclosed in it — I have sent some of my son Williams drawings roled upon A stick & delivered to ye Captains care   part for thy self with thy name writ on ye back of each. the others for ye Dutches according thy & our dear friend Peter Collinsons order which pray deliver to her or to Michell Collinson for her

my dear friend I think I am heartier now then ever I was in all my life which I attribute in A great measure to very temperate liveing & much exercise of body being born with A bad Constitution, all my younger years being subject to grip   grievous coughs   heartburne, acrimonious Loosness, disiness & Rheumatism, yet never had ye disenterea Pleurisy or gravel. ye two first very fatal in our provinces yearly. I dont remember ever to have had A neibour to sit up with me or so reduced with sickness but allways able to get out of bed put on my clothes & walk about ye room. I am now turned of seventy & this near four years or since I left Carolina I have not drank A glass of wine or A gill of rum or two mugs of strong bear   my chief afliction is ye failing of my sight & no glasses helps me   I cant know A person five foot distance   neither can I know my humble garden plants without stooping to view them near & if I looke at ye moon before ye first quarter there appears to be five. Notwithstanding I can write & read ye Magazeen By candlelight but not so well as daylight, & which is remarkeable I have had many bruises & ribs broken in searching after plants tumbling over perpendicular rocks & from ye tops & branches of high trees yet I feel no pains on ye changes of weather in or near ye bruised members no more then if thay had never been hurt which is different from all elderly people with whome I have conversed who generaly complain of pains from hurts received in thair younger years, before or at ye changes of weather or wind which has not other effect upon me but when it is very could I love to be near ye fire, or when ye sun shines very hot I love ye shade or rain A dry house   I am unfeanedly thy obliged friend

John Bartram

Natural History Museum, London.

To FOTHERGILL

November the 28th 1769

Dear Beloved Friend

I have now little to write haveing wrote largely by Captain Falconer by whome I sent for thee A box of plants & shrubs in which I put two small harmless snakes   I sent allso A Barrel in which I planted many Colocasia roots for ye King & thy self & allso put two of our large Bull frogs perhaps male & female, which if thay come safe & you have none of them before will be A great inocent Curiosity for ye King: thay are very harmless   if thee wants any of them or any of our tortises I will endeavor to send them. we have a great variety of ye water kinds that is harmless beside ye mischievous snaping one that lives mostly on fish & fowls when thay can catch them by surprise & thay are very dexterous at it. thay creep all over in ye mud except thair nose & when A fish swims over them thay snap him into thair mouths   allso when young ducks or goslings swims over or near them thay catch hould of thair feet   draws them under water & devours them & mankind catcheth all thay can of them not onely to destroy them but thay esteem ye stewed soup to be A delitious morsel, as most of ye others are.

I shall be well pleased if thy Nephew will undertake to receive my salary & ye Cash for ye seed Boxes I shall send: for which I am very willing to alow him full Comisions. if thee will please to let me know by first opertunity. I intend to give him orders to receive & give proper discharges

I remain thy true friend

John Bartram

Natural History Museum, London.

To FRANKLIN

November ye 29th 1769

Dear worthy Friend

Yesterday I had ye pleasure of takeing Mrs. Franklin by ye hand in her own house as allso thy daughter and grandson A fine boy. Likewise thy sister from Boston all whome I expect at my house according to promise. I have now before me thy dear affectionate letter of July ye 9th 1769. My health and familys still continueth: (God allmighty be praised and adored)   I sent my Journal of No. and So. Carolina Georgia and florida to Peter Collinson who aproved of it. I dont doubt but Michael Collinson if thee desireth it would readyly lend it to thee and if thee should think it worth printing it I have nothing against it with proper correction which I know thee is very capable to do

I have received doctor Fothergills and Michael Collinsons letters   ye latter declines haveing any thing to do in ye seeds affair. The doctor recommends his nephew as A very honest person to supply our dear Peters place with relation to disposeing of ye seeds and receiving and remiting ye money. I have thoughts of giveing him orders for ye same purpose if he pleas to accept it. This is one of ye worst seed year I ever knowed   ye excesive dry summer [and] terible storm hath demolished most: I have collected what I could but cant assure them all to vegitate   such as thay are I offer freely to my dear friend.

I have not any of that rhubarb growing of which thee kindly sent me A draught, if thee please to send me A few seeds it would much oblige thy sincear friend

John Bartram

I have [sent] A couple of Bull frogs in A Barrel with Colocasia roots to Doctor Fothergill for ye King. I wish thay may come safe and be ye first.

American Philosophical Society Library, Benjamin Franklin Papers, vol. 2, f. 202.

From FRANKLIN

London, 11 January, 1770

My ever dear Friend,

I received your kind letter of November 29th, with the parcel of seeds, for which I am greatly obliged to you. I cannot make you adequate returns in kind; but I send you however some of the true rhubarb seeds, which you desire. I had it from Mr. English[1] who lately received a medal of the Society of Arts for propagating it. I send also some green dry peas, highly esteemed here as the best for making pea soup; and also some Chinese *caravances*,[2] with Father Navarett's[3] account of the universal use of a cheese made of them in China, which so excited my curiosity, that I caused inquiry to be made of Mr. Flint, who lived many years there, in what manner the cheese was made, and I send you his answer.[4] I have since learned, that some runnings of salt (I suppose runnet) is put into water, when the meal is in it, to turn it to curds. I think we have *caravances* with us, but I know not whether they are the same with them, which actually came from China. They are said to be of great increase.

I shall inquire of Mr. Collinson for your *Journal*. I see that of East Florida is printed with Stork's *Account*. My love to good Mrs. Bartram and your children. With esteem I am ever, my dear friend, yours affectionately,

B. Franklin.

Capringe
Jan 3d 1770

Dear Sir
1st Process
  The method the Chinese convert Callivances into Towfu. They first steep the Grain in warm water ten or twelve Hours to soften a little, that it may

grind easily. It is a stone Mill with a hole in the top to receive a small Gram of warm water which passes between the two Stones the time of grinding to carry off the flower from between & keeps draining into a Tub which has a Sieve or Cloth at the top to stop the gross parts from mixing with the flower.

2d Process

Then they stir up the flower & put the Water over the Fire just for it to simmer, keeping stirring till it thickens & then taken out & put into a frame that has a Cloth which will hold the Substance, & press the Water from it, & when the Water is gone off the Frame with the Contents with a Weight on it must be put over the Steam of boiling Water for half an hour to harden or something longer. The pressing & boiling over the Steam brings it into the Form you see it carried about at Canton. This is the process as I always understood.

Now I shall give you my Opinion in what Manner I should proceed in the first Process   I would send my Callevances to the mill to be ground, then I would put the Flower into water & stir it well very thin. Then strain the gross parts from the Flour & then you proceed to the 2d. For I look upon the reason they steep the Grain & grind it with Water is that it is so hard they could not grind it with their little Stones. I hope you understand it, & wish the Complts of the Season   I remain Dr Sr

Your most obedt Servant
J Flint

The Works of Benjamin Franklin, ed. Jared Sparks, 10 vols. (Boston, 1856), 7:464; D. 404–5; Flint letter, BP 4:14.
1. Unidentified.
2. Chick peas.
3. Domingo Fernandez Navarette (1698–1786), Jesuit missionary to China; author of *A Collection of Voyages and Travels,* 6 vols. (English translation, 1744–46).
4. Flint's letter to Franklin follows this letter.

From FOTHERGILL

London 13 1 mo 1770

Dear Friend

I have now before me thy two kind letters of the 26 & 28th Nov. last. I have received later the box of Plants, the cask of Colocasia and the Bull frogs alive. I likewise received a Roll of Drawings directed to me all safe and very acceptable —

The plants came in good condition. The roots of the Colocasia seemed but in a doubtfull situation, however they are planted, part at Kew and part in a little piece of water at Upton, my little residence, exactly agreeable to thy instructions: We first filled a basket with light loamy earth. we then put in the roots and just covered them with the earth. we then let the basket gently down to the water, where they will always continue covered with about two feet and a half of water.

A place is not yet fixed upon for the Bull frogs to be put in   in the mean time however they are kept in a shallow vessel of water the bottom covered with moss where they may either put their heads above or under water as they like. We have severe frost but when this goes off they will be set at large somewhere and in safety   We have none of the kind in England   the King is acquainted with their arrival; also the Colocasia and from whom they come.

My Nephew will endeavour to serve thee to the best of his power; and on the same terms that our worthy Frd Peter Collinson did. as he is a stranger to many of the things sent him please to mention at what prices they should be disposed of. I will assist him to the utmost of my power, for thy sake, and for my deceased Friend. I have received Six lbs. which I shall pay into his hands soon. I could wish to know likewise how much [is owed] to Date to thyself for the curious plants [illegible] Mention is made in thy letter of some drawings designed for the Duchess of Portland. I received only one roll, and those directed to me consisting of drawings of the Colocasia, a New species of Momordica, shells &c 6 in number. If any of them are designed for the Duchess be pleased to inform me. If they are for me which I hope be kind enough to give me some intimation of their value, which I will pay to my kinsman. I must still desire that thy son will favour me with drawings of the rest of your American Tortoises with such remarks on them as occur to him. As the inhabitants increase the species of this and some other animals as well as some vegitables will perhaps be extinguished or exist only in some still more distant parts.

It would therefore be of great advantage to natural History to have everything of a fugitive nature consigned to paper with as much accuracy as possible, and inquiring into the value of these drawings, I do not so much want to know at how low a price he can send them as what is his own opinion will be a proper compensation for his labour and his time. and whatever he attempts of the kind let it be well finished and I hope he will not find me niggardly. He will continue to give me all the land and river shells he meets with. and to send me specimens of the real ones as he can —

I should be glad of a few seeds of the Momordica he has drawn if convenient — You have I doubt not a great variety of Ferns and all that tribe of Plants in America. I have a few very curious by the favour of Michael Collinson from his father's Garden. When any of them fall in thy way please to send them, I have good conveniences for their preservation. I think we have been too negligent in inquiring after your Herbaceous plants. We have many of your trees; many of your shrubs, some of [illegible]

I wish it was in my power to assist [restoring thee] to thy sight; but in part it is effect of years which effects I must likewise feel if I live to thy age. Are no glasses of use? Pray was thee short sighted when young? If this was the case [glasses] would rather injure than help thy sight. If thou can point out any way for me to enquire after better glasses I will do it with satisfaction.

I hope to send thee in the spring some little account of our late kind Frd P. Collinson's life, and service in respect to Botany. For several years past I have left London about ten weeks in the summer and got about 160 miles from it, in order to [renew] my strength against winter for the duties of [my] station. It was in one of these intervals that our Friend was carried off by the suppresion of urine. Had I been present I know not that any thing more could have been done to have saved him. When I was informed of his decease, partly to indulge my sorrow, partly to pay tribute to his memory, I employed myself in drawing a short account of his character. A few copies will I believe be printed this spring for the satisfaction of his Friends and I will take care that a few be sent to thee.

I have not leisure to become a perfect botanist but I love the vegetable creation. I love its variety and cultivate it as an amusement. every new [plant] is an addition to my pleasure. I have most of the common products of America and they [prosper] with me more than any where else. I have a Garden in a low sheltered situation where [all] prospers. My Kalmias make shoots of 5 or 6 [inches] in a summer. The large magnolia has [shot inches] and the smaller near 2 feet; others thrive in proportion. This is owing [to the] soil   Let me know as soon as may

BP 4:19; D. 342–43.

From MICHAEL COLLINSON

London March 1st 1770
Manchester Buildings

Dear Sir

Your Favour of the 1st Nov is before Me inclosing the Account between your self & my dearest Father which I find to agree with the Account Current as per ledger and which I have at last been lucky enough to discover. I must beg you will let Billy continue the Account up to the time of my poor Father's disease — I mean as far as he is able mentioning the number of Boxes, if sent and if you are furnished with the names of the persons for whom they were designed, I shall be glad to have them. I was my dear Sir so entirely a stranger to my dear father's Money affairs that I positively assure you I was uncertain on wch side the Ballance lay between you   judge then of my Amazement when I discovered by you & confirmed by the Account which has but just appeared, what an astonishing ballance was against Me and in Consequence of the Idea I entertained of something very inconsiderable subsisting betwixt you I ventured upon that Supposition long since to settle everything, and should have been highly obliged to have had earlier information how things stood, soon after the News of my dear Father's demise reached Philadelphia, as very disagreeably the Book which alone could afford matter of Information was unaccountably mislaid at the time of my Father's removal from Grace Church Street, and only very lately come to light, I am projecting a little Tour thro'

France, part of Spain and Italy but this will not be attended with the least postponement to finally ballancing the above Acct as I shall take care your drafts on Me shall be properly honoured so that you may draw how and when you please for it   When you draw do it for near the whole if you please at once   It will be the most agreeable to Me to finish at once if we can   If I go it will be in a Month's time and my absence will be abt. 6 or 7 months.

You have Sir of Course, I conclude heard from Dr. Fothergill that I have let my premises at Mill Hill for two years with a reserve in the lease that not a Single Plant or the soil that contains them is upon any terms to be moved, for even yet there are still some very few fine Plants remaining of the rich Collection which your Bounty furnished us with   the miserable remains of three most cruel robberies wch have torn the Garden all to Pieces & left me only the wretched Apprehension of finding fresh devastation on every little Absence from home, This with some other unimagined and disagreeable Circumstances operating, rendered a Residence at Mill Hill both uncomfortable & inconvenient at present —

As no notice has been taken to Me of the draft of the Colocasia I conclude the Doctor will convey the same to the Duchess of Portland, agreeably to your orders. Sr Wm. Bretton[1] is acquainted with your pleasure respecting the King's Bounty.

I should think some very singular kinds of fresh water shells might be met with on the shores of your vast interior Lakes and some of the Land tribe as well as river   I think must be a Curiosity here even in the best Cabinets   I should be very glad to see a specimen or two of them —

I shall always find myself happy in hearing of the Prosperity and health of a Gentn for whom my most valued Parent felt the Sincerest Regard & Friendship to his latest hour & I am sure it will be ever with the truest Respect that I shall be dear sir,

Your faithful & most obliged servant,
Michael Collinson

BP 3:81; D. 446–47.
1. Possibly a member of the king's Household.

From FOTHERGILL

Harpur Street
19th 3 1770

Esteemed Friend
Having an opportunity of sending thee the inclosed performance of my Friend John Ellis[1] is by a young man who comes over as an Apothecary to your Hospital, I could not well avoid just sending thee two or three lines tho' much straitened for time

In a letter I wrote to thee some time since I informed thee that my Nephew James Freeman had undertaken to transact thy money affairs here, and to assist thee as far as he is capable. That I had paid into his hands Ten guineas on my own account and six more that I had received from John Lewin of which I believe he will inform thee himself.

The Frogs are alive and well but not delivered. The K. has been acquainted that they are here and from whom they come, but the present state of the publick affairs leaves him not a moments time to think of any thing else. I will endeavour to provide a place for them in my own garden. I have no express request to make for any plants in particular, but if any thing new occurs, either plants or seeds, I should be very glad to be a sharer.

Thy son will be kind enough to continue his drawings of any non descripta he may meet with either plant or animals and I shall endeavour to make him proper satisfaction. I hope soon to send thee a short account of the life of our late worthy Frd P Collinson at least an essay towards his character   a few copies will be printed to give amongst his Friends and no one is more entitled to this epithet than thy self.

I am with much esteem

Thy assured Frd.
John Fothergill

BP 4:22; D. 343.
1. Possibly "An Account of the Male and Female Cochineal Insects that breed on the *Cactus Opuntia* . . . In a Letter from John Ellis, Esq. to Peter Wych, Esq." *Philosophical Transactions of the Royal Society* 52 (1762):661–66.

To FOTHERGILL

June ye 10th 1770

Dear worthy Kind friend,
I have now before me thy kind letter of ye 13th of ye 1 month 1770 & ye 19th of ye 3d month   am glad thee received ye Colocasia & frogs   shall be glad to hear of thair success — it is kind yea very kind my dear friend to ingage thy self so much for my interest as to recommend thy nephew to take care of my affairs in ye room of our disceased friend & allso to assist him therein. am very willing to allow him full Commisions for his trouble   I had several ways to oblige dear Peter but at Present I know of none to gratifie thy Nephew in ye same way. I take his offer very kindly & have given orders to all my Corespondents to pay what is owing to me to him & that his recept shall be thair suffitient discharge from me: ye six guineas from John Lewin is for my son John who sent him insects formerly: I can assure thee my dear friend that I recon my self in thy debt for books & much other kindness; as for my son Williams drawings he modestly declines setting A price upon them but leaves it to thy generosity & ye Dutches of Portland for whome he desighned ye draught of ye Colocasia & shels   ye rest for thy self.

as for several ferns of which we have variety I intend to send them next fall if a convenient opertunity offers. as to my sight I never was near sighted. about 45 years ould I began to use spectacles which helped my sight by which I could discover objects as clear as usual when without them I could not see to read A good print but about 60 thay failed, but then I could see prety well without them but I must have ye object within 4 or 6 inches near my eyes. for at 2 or 3 foot distance objects seem magnified but surrounded with A mist & multiplied. ye moon appears as five before ye first quarter & ye planets or ye blaze of A Candle 4 or 5 times as big as formerly yet I can read & write by Candle light when ye Candle & letters is very near & when I weed my garden my knees & elbow must Kiss the ground   it seems rather to go worse every year; but I am resigned to ye disposal of Allmighty Power   his will be done. I am obliged to thee for our friend Ellis's Performance   its A prety Pamphlet. he makes some mention of destructive insects but it would fill A prety large volume to give A full & acurate description of all our American insects   it would be attended with long & laborious search & observation as many of them makes thair most destructive havock in ye night & secreets themselves in ye day. some feeds on ye roots of several plants   some on stalks others on leaves   some on flowers   others on fruites & many on grains & seeds but I think thair greatest mischief & detriment to us is in ye way of generation in preparing a proper nidus in which thay lay thair Eggs & ye prodigious ravage ye embryo makes in ye vegitable while it is growing to such perfection as to disengage itself so as to rove at large in ye open Air.

    I have not received any letter from ye kings gardener at Kew in answer to ye letter I wrote to him desireing to be informed what plants would be most acceptable   would any or All our turtles sent Alive be acceptable to thee I could send most of them in a Box with Moss or leaves

    I have tryed all spectacles that came in my way or that I could come at but cant find one that helps my sight   I here there is one pair in town lately come over. thay are exceeding clear & one sees an object at A great distance clearly   I called at ye gentlemans house who brought them over to see them but he was not at home   he holds them at an excessive price as I am informed

    I remain with A grateful respect for exceeding favours received thy sincear friend

John Bartram

P.S. I have received A kind letter from Michel Collinson dated March ye first acquainting me that he intended to take ye tour to france & Italy & be out 6 or 7 months: in his first letter he wrote that Sir William Bretton came to him to pay ye anual Bounty from ye King   that he desired him to take it back & keep it till I gave further orders   I wrote to Michal that I had not fixed upon any person yet but that I should give perticular orders this year & Michall wrote in his last letter that he had acquainted Sr William with it so that now James hath undertaken to succeed our dear Peter I should be obliged to you to let him know how ye case stands

thine as before

Natural History Museum, London.

To FOTHERGILL

September ye 30th 1770

Dear worthy friend

I have before me thy kind letter of ye 19th of ye 3d month 1770 since which I have received none from thee   neither Have I received any from thy nephew Freeman which makes me very uneasy & so many opertunities offered since I suppose he received my letter so that I am utterly in ye dark relateing to my affairs in England   whether ye King continueth his bounty or how ye Frogs or Colocasias prospers. nor any answer from ye gardener at Kew: as to ye drawings my son William sent last fall. I think three of them he desighned for ye Duches of Portland viz. ye Colocasia & I think ye snails   I put A note upon them: Poor Billy hath had ye greatest misfortunes in trade that could be & gone thro ye most grievous disapointments & is now absconded I know not whither. he would not take his friends advice yet kept very temperate — thee mentions paying ten guineas on thy own account to James Freeman but dont mention whether it was for my sons drawing or not: I received A letter from Michel Collinson last spring who signified his great desire to settle accounts with me but he was so ignorant of his fathers accounts with me that I doubt it will be very dificult to do it Justly. & I trusted so much to my other Correspondents honesty, that I Cant affirm who has paid & who hath not.

Michel wrote to me that he desighned to take A tour to france & Italy this summer so that I did not write to him by the vesail that I sent thine in but I desighn to send one to him now

I am at present in as good health as I ever was God Allmighty be praised in great humility, but my sight still grows worse but my great respect & desire to gratifie thy exceeding kindness stil increases & assure thy self that I remain thy loveing & sincear Friend

John Bartram

Natural History Museum, London.

To FOTHERGILL

October ye 11th 1770

My dear friend

it is long since I received A letter from my fried [sic] Fothergill & none yet from his nephew & if I dont receive one from one or both this fall I shall be very uneasy on that head. I have had A very healthy summer & is now so, God Allmighty be Praised. But my sight fails me much & no glasses helps me   yesterday I tryed Joshua Fishers Cristall spectacles but thay helped me none at all. I have according thy desire sent in A Box all ye ferns we could procure which are in number eight or nine   allso these folowing shrubs

  No I[1]
   II mountain Kalmia
   III thime leaved do
   IV Saracena common
   V spotted leaved do Carolina
   VI Calcolus red flowered
   VII fringed gentian
  VIII Mediola
   IX & ten new shrubs the names not known
   X huica
   XII Agave

  in ye bottle is Colocasia nuts I have put ye Colocasia nuts in two bottles before & ye swelling of ye nuts broke them both I hope this bottle will hould them in ye box of plants there is many of them pray give part of them to John Ellis who sent me ye same impression that thee was so kind to send me before but his good will is accepted & so I remain your true friend
                      John Bartram

Natural History Museum, London.
1. Bartram omitted numbers I and XI.

To FRANKLIN

                      November ye 24th 1770
My dear worthy friend
I have thy Kind letter of August ye 26th before me which Comforted me as coming from my dear intimate ould friend ye pamphlet & espetially ye picture of my dear Peter was very acceptable & now I am furnished with four of our worthies Linneus, Franklin, Edwards & Collinson (but I want Dr. Fothergill) to adorn my new stove & lodging room which I have made very Convenient for thair reception alltho I am no picture Enthusiast, yet I love to looke at ye representation of men of inocency integrity ingenuity & Humanity. I can hear nothing this year whether ye King continueth his bounty to me or not: William Young Blusters stoutly & publishes it in ye news & perticular advertisements all over ye countrey that he is Botanist to thair Majesties ye King & Queen of Great Britain I have sent according to thy desire A small Box of seeds with a list of them in ye Box which I have Consighned to James Freeman who hath two Boxes to dispose of for me he lives in ye same house where our dear Peter formerly lived this comes with great love & respect from thy Sincear friend
                       John Bartram

pray my dear friend squeeze out a few lines as often as Convenience will alow to comfort thy ould friend in his new stove room

American Philosophical Society Library, Benjamin Franklin Papers, vol. 3, f. 34.

From MICHAEL COLLINSON

Manchester Builds. Jany 9th 1771

My dear Sir

It was with great pleasure soon after my return home from the Continent that I received your agreeable favour of the 1st of Ocr last and believe the account of Boxes sent in 1767 & 8 to be right, though I have not been able to ascertain it to a Box, which is of little importance as I have a most implicit Confidence in your honour and shall instantly direct the payment of the ballance of the Account whenever you please to order it to be paid to Mr. Freeman or otherwise which I shall not be sorry for as it is a kind of weight upon Mee especially as it is so very considerable and unexpected to Mee However, I have a principle of honour in my heart which if I know it can never be capable of a shuffling or dishonest Action. You may therefore my dear Sir be entirely Satisfied and make your demands whenever it suits you best

In the course of my late Tour the Objects that most struck me were the following: the Forrest of Fontainebleau abt 35 miles South of Paris, in wch there is a most romantic Range of Rocks not lying in strata but roughly piled one upon Another and Coverd with Silver Bark Birch and our common Juniper growing 10 and 15 Feet high — the Wonders of Pont du Gard a Roman Work being an astonishing Aqueduct thrown across a deep valley and joining two rocky Mountains, this is situated near Nimes and Montpelier   here among the Rocks grew Myrtle; what we have by the name of the Lycian Cedar Arbutus; a fine species of prickly Broom, and wild Figs — the beautiful Mountain Esterelles which lies between Toulon and Nice, bore green Pinasters, also what we call Aleppo Pine, broad leaved Myrtle narrow and true Philarea, Cork Oak   Laurus Tinus   Arbutus and a most glorious heath rising 10 and 12 feet high and dispensing from the White Bloom the most delicate fragrance possible, nothing could exceed the Views through these Evergreen Bowers of the Mediterranean Sea on one hand and the Alps rearing up their Cloud Capp'd Snowy Summits on the other   a little farther on the South side of this fine hill are growing condiginously Pomegranate the Donax and our common Ever Green Aloe   I was my dear Sir delighted beyond measure at perceiving the line wch Nature had drawn in the different Latitudes, where one species and Tribe of plants ceased, and another commenced — I shall epitimize only the remaining Objects such as the Grandeur of Genoa — the astonishing Collections of the Florentine Gallery, the Magnificence of Old Rome, the delightful Scenes surrounding the Bolsenan, Arvennes and Albanian Lakes – Vesuvius smoking away and proudly overlooking the City of Naples   the Isle of Capria and the whole Neopolitan Harbour — to these succeeds, the [illegible] of the Appenines with their Evergreen Oak and Chesnut and Italian Cork Woods rising in the Clouds — The Superstition of Venice floating in the Sea — the Elegant comliness and Curiosities of Bologna, Florence and Turin particularly the latter wch is eligible place to Live in. There saw the city laid out at right Angles and nobly built parks are well planted as are the [illegible] of the most striking Region of the Alps [illegible] the Great among wch are seen the great Chamonix & Resserection mountains stand far above the Rest, with their heads and great part of their Declivities deeply immersed in everlasting winter — The lakes Garda of Geneva and Maggiore are noble little Caspians here but yet how diminutive they appear in Comparison with your Huron, Superior &c &c. upon a very lofty Tyrolese mountain wch with great labour I ascended   I found two Species of Rhododendron one in full bloom and tinging the highest crags with the richest glow of Colouring   many other rare plants grow here & upon Mount Cenis the Specimens of which and Acct. of, would have given infinite Pleasure to my most dear Parent had Providence spared his life a little longer   I make no doubt but you have seen the little pamphlet of some anecdotes of his life for the principle part of wch I think myself highly obligated to my valued friend Dr. Fothergill   If you have not, I have any number of copies at your service; and am, dearest sir, with true affection and esteem, your obliged and very faithful friend and servant,

Michael Collinson

BP 3:83; D. 447–49.

From HOPE

Edinburgh, 23d March 1771

Sir: —
You will recollect that some years ago, you sent to a society at Edinburgh, a parcel of seeds, of crop 1765, amounting in all to £15, which seeds, by being sent to Ireland, instead of the port of London, according to directions, occasioned not only very great trouble and expense, but likewise the loss of the seeds; as, upon their being re-shipped and landed at Chester, they were there seized by the Custom-house officers, and, after a deal of work to obtain their release, sent by land to London; from whence they were again reshipped for Edinburgh; but so late, that they only came in time to be sown in the year 1767, and the greater part of them good for nothing, to the great disappointment of the members of the Society.

When I talked of this subject to my much esteemed friend, Mr. Peter Collinson, and informed him how discouraging this would be to the Society for importing foreign seeds, which had been lately established, and the funds of which at that time narrow, the excellent old man insisted that the Society and you should bear an equal loss, on this unlucky occasion. Accordingly, one half of the charge, viz., £7:10, was paid by the Society to Mr. Collinson on your behoof. And the managers of the Society, in order to make some amends to you for your loss, had intended to enlarge their commissions, annually; but you, discouraged, as it would seem by that loss, somehow declined answering their commissions to the full, which necessarily behooved to stop all further correspondence.

The funds of the Society being now fully sufficient to answer all demands, cannot be so properly applied as to make up to you the loss you sustained, on the above parcel of seeds. I shall therefore pay to any person you please to name, the above sum of £7:10.

The managers of this Society are very sensible of your great botanical merits, and would incline that the payment presently be made to you, should in some degree convey with it the sense they have of your merit; and therefore, would include, instead of the £7:10 in specie, to send you a gold medal,[1] or piece of silver plate, of at least equal value, with a suitable inscription thereupon.

Be pleased, therefore, to inform me which will be most agreeable.

I heartily wish every good thing to you and to your family, and am, with much regard, sir,

Your most obedient, humble servant,
John Hope.

D. 435–36.
1. The gold medal weighed 487 grams. One side was inscribed "To John Bartram from a Society of Gentlemen at Edinburgh 1772." The reverse side had a laurel wreath surrounding the word "Merenti."

To WILLIAM BARTRAM

April ye 25th 1771

Dear son Billy

I received thy letter of september about three months after ye date & never heard ye least account of thee after thee left us so unaturaly. but it was satisfaction to hear where thee was but it concerned us to hear of Cousen Williams death in ye prime of life[1]   I have sent thy Chest to town to be put on board of Captain Dyer. we have prevailed on thy Creditors to take one hundred pounds ready Cash & give A full discharge forever & George Bartram hath paid it on my account   he allso paid that troublesome man who threatened thee on his own account I think ye day before thee went away. all thy papers is to be sent according to thy desire. we are all well as when the left us but my sight is much worse but my Brother James is very poorly & very likely to go off soon   has not had one well day since thee went away

I expect thy brothers will write more fully   its with difficulty I can see to write att all. we have had ye most constant winds & high tides I ever Knew   hath tore our banks from end to end so that they wont be got in good order again this year. thy Brother John hath passed one meeting & intends to pass ye other in A few days.[2] thy mother Joyns with me in love to thee sister & Cousens & remain & remain [sic] thy loveing Parents

John Bartram

ye key of thy Chest is taken to town & is to be inclosed in A letter by Isaac or Moses

To
Mr. William Bartram at Ashwood
up Cape Fear River
By Captain Dyer

American Philosophical Society Library, Bartram-Collinson Papers.
1. Bartram's half-brother Colonel William Bartram had died on October 24, a few weeks after Billy had arrived in North Carolina. Not long afterward the colonel's son Dr. William Bartram had also died.
2. Johnny married his Uncle James's grand-daughter Eliza Howell on May 9. According to custom, the banns had to be read twice before the wedding.

To FRANKLIN

April ye 29th 1771

Dear worthy ould Friend
I have very little to write beside A repetition of real friendship haveing received never A line from thee since I sent thee A box of seeds & A letter last fall, wherein I desired to be acquainted whether ye King Continued his bounty still to me or droped it   I Cant yet hear ye least tittle concerning it except that William Young stiles him self thair Majesties Botanist. I should be glad to hear how ye affair stands. but it astonisheth me very much that I cant have A line from any of my Correspondents this spring (alltho 3 or 4 ships is arived here from London) & all thair last letters contained expressions of real friendship: my Daughter Elizabeth hath saved several thousands of eggs of silkworms which she expects will hatch in A few days   she intends to give them A fair tryal this spring

my eye sight fails me very much & I am going to thro all my business into my son Johns hands except part of my Garden but still thee may be assured of ye love friendship & best wishes of thy Sincear friend

John Bartram

American Philosophical Society Library, Benjamin Franklin Papers, vol. 3, f. 54.

To FOTHERGILL

May ye 9th 1771

Dear Worthy Friend

I have long expected to have received A letter from my dear friend Doctor Fothergill in answer to two letters sent last summer & fall with A Box of plants: it seems strange to Me that A few minits time could not be spared to sattisfie thy friend whether thee received them & whether thee intended to break off all Correspondence with me or to continue it & thy Nephew is near as far behind for I have not had A line from him this spring nor no account what is become of ye Cargo which I sent last fall consighned to him or whether he is dead or alive. & such A number of ships is arived here from London which inclines me to conjecture he has taken some afront which if he hath I am intirely inocent & ignorant which way & he should candidly & friendly advertised me thereof, & if I did not give him satisfaction he should have let me know by ye first opertunity that he declined houlding any further Correspondency with me. I can yet have no account whether his Majesty continueth his bounty to me since our worthy friend Collinsons death or not William Young stiles himself Botanist to thair Majesties the King & Queen of Great Britain. Pray dear friend do favour me with A letter by ye first convenient opertunity which will much oblige thy real friend

John Bartram

Natural History Museum, London.

From MICHAEL COLLINSON

Manchester Buildgs: June 28th 1771 —

Dear Sir

Both your favours of the 29th Apl and 3d of May are come to hand for the last of wch my best Acknowledgments are due I have accepted the bill for £200 and shall punctually discharge it when due — I have also inclosed the Acct between us according to the best lights I can obtain, for the furnishing of which I am obliged to have recourse to the Acct you sent me in Oct. last of the Boxes sent in 1767 & 1768 for my Fathers Memorandums were so perplexed that without yours and Gordon's assistance could have made nothing out — as I have a full Confidence in your honour I can implicitly rely on what you say is right: and will to the best of my Ability faithfully on my side discharge the Demand upon me which being so very considerable had I confess been a stroke upon Me, especially being unacquainted with my dear Father's Concerns and neither for so considerable a time hearing anything from yourself or being able to discover the Account itself, wch was somehow mislaid at the time of my Fathers breaking up in Grace Church Street I really judged the Ballance, if anything, to be but very trifling the truth is, latterly my dear Parent found those things a Trouble to him wch was none a few years since as he evinced on many Occasions and which has occasioned Me much Confusion and Trouble — his situation too in point of Circumstance were likewise mortifying — his Business at last totally declined and you will Sir I am sure from the goodness and humanity of your own heart and your long and unremitted Friendship for him be shocked when I tell you that he solicited a small pension for an Age near 75 — great part of which was employed in pursuits advantageous to his Country — and was refused —

I am very certain that the King's Bounty is regularly and will always Continue to be paid   my Father received the half year to Lady Day 1768 which was the last payment due in his Life time and in the Sepr following the Depty Privy Purse applied to me to know whether I would receive the 6 months due, wch I declined and I have since introduced Mr. Freeman to Mr. Matthias[1] and I heard Mr. Matthias assure Mr. Freeman that it should be regularly paid, and that with as Little trouble to Mr. Freeman as possible —

I think myself equally honoured and obliged by your favourable Sentiments on my little remarks whilst abroad   I kept a daily Journal of what struck me most during the whole Expedition for the advantages of my future Memory and hours — Your most sensible and pertinent Remarks on Your important Quarter of the globe, I shall beg leave to Consider some future Opportunity for neither my head nor Paper will permit me to say more, but that I am with high esteem & affection dear sir

Very faithfully yrs
Michael Collinson

BP 3:84; D. 449–50.
1. Unidentified.

To WRANGEL

July ye 6th 1771

Dear worthy & beloved friend
I have long waited for an opertunity of acknowledging ye recept of thy kind letter wherein thee mentions ye great honor your Academia of Sciences hath confered upon me for which favour I return you my most gratefull obligations & thanks   But I much lament that such a respectable favour had not been confered upon me in a time of life when I could have made a more suitable return for now my eyes is so dim that I cant know my children six foot distance from me (yet God Allmighty be praised in great Humility sincerely:) I can yet read tolerable & hold ye book very near my eyes. I greatly rejoyced to here of the kind reception thee met with in Sweden & ye Royall favour ye King was pleased to bestow upon thy merit: But alass ye Church thee had so much at heart in our town is much neglected   ye congregation is much squandered. Oh, they want Doctor Wrangle to come

& gather them together Again   they never will be favoured again with such another Pastor!

I did not know of Mr. Coons[1] going to Sweedland this summer until late last night & I here is to sail tomorow & its now harvest time   I would have sent to ye Society some of ye rarest seeds I could have procured if he had stayed to ye fall when thay was ripe & it is very rare that we can have an opertunity of sending at a proper season.

thee mentions in a Postscript a list of some plants of which thee & thy friend should be glad to have specimens which list I never had, we should be well pleased if we could have a good opertunity of sending seeds specimens, &c. safely every autumn to ye Honorable Society at Stockholm but at present wee are intirely ignorant what method to take to send them safe to your hands.

I take it very kindly & I think it manifested true & sincere friendship in thee to deliver all those curiosities which I sent to ye Society in my name & if I had known of thair gratitude I should have endeavoured to have sent more by ye same opertunity.

ye great Doctor lineus sent me a kind letter by ye same opertunity which I gratefuly acknowledge   he desires to know what soil & situation ye diferent species of our American plants generaly grows in: if he will pleas to send me A list of ye perticular species I will indeavour to inform him: I suppose when Mr. Coone returns it will be a good opertunity to send any letters or instructions you pleas to send to us.

I have now in full Bloom a number of ye flowers of ye Cape J'esamin or Gardenia measuring four inches & three quarters diameter very double white as snow & very sweet.

I have seeds of ye meadea just ripe   some of which I have put into thy letter desiring thee to deliver them in my name to whome thee believes to be most deserving; yet time is so short warning or else I had a mind to send some indian Curiosities but I dont know who to trust with them:

My hearty respects to Doctor Lineus Profesor Bergeus & ye rest of your chief members of your worthy Academie of Science at Stockholm.

My wife & John & his wife joyns with me in gratefull respect to thee & remain thy sincear loveing friend

John Bartram

My much respected & beloved friend & one of our family it seems reasonable to let thee know how ye remaining part of thy familys affairs is circumstanced here

it is something remarkable that I had a few months past two sons Courting & two daughters Courted at ye same time. John is safely married to my Brothers grandaughter much to our likeing & lives with us   Benjamin is to all appearance likely to have John Knowles daughter with a large fortune. Elizabeth is likely in a few weeks to have a man liveing near Lancaster of good Character[2] & Mary is a widow & was courted by a man of tolerable Character but with indiferent Connections & I suppose will not succeed.

My son William is gone to North Carolina to Collect in his debts which is a difficult task in that poor Countrey:

Library of the Royal Swedish Academy of Sciences, Stockholm.
1. Possibly Dr. Adam Kuhn.
2. Elizabeth, Billy's twin, married William Wright of Lancaster County on August 2, 1771; Benjamin married Elizabeth Hunt February 4, 1773.

From JAMES FREEMAN

London, 7th mo. 13th 1771

Est Frd John Bartram

By Return of Capn Sparkes, I now reply to thine 29th 4 mo since which date thou will have received mine dated 16th 4 mo Copy p Captain Osborn Williams which I doubt not will fully satisfy thee that I have been neither unmindfull of thy Interest nor the Trust reposed in me, Since which I have received as per stat of Act annexed from the King's Dispenser of the Privy Purse which will no doubt be continued to thee in future, and be paid Punctually to me as it becomes due on thy Act   I have also received as p Annual Acct. for the seeds sent last Excepting the Executor of Luwin & Executor [of] Webb who will settle in a little time, — & therefore I have not included what is due from them in the same Act. Bush is ingaged as Gardener to the Empress of Russia for 6 years & is desirous that thou would send him to England if no immediate traffick from your Parts to Petersburg: Box Seeds & of Plants & also to his Successor whose name is Luthers at Hackney 2 Box of Seeds — Bush did not pay me for the last Box of plants alledging that thou Always presented them to him in Consideration of Plants from England sent by him to thee without Charge, And I could wish in Future thou would be kind enough to hint terms in thy letter when thou gives any of them the Plants that they may not take offence, at my asking for the Money. Fearne would also have a Number of seeds as last sent him — Doctor Franklin has not (but will) when he comes into the City pay the Charges for the Box that thou sent him as a present   I have asked all the other Seedsmen if any Order for the next year but have received no other than what I have above mentioned, Nevertheless if thou sends a few more than Ordered & they come as early in season as last years did I think I can dispose of them   Uncle Doctor is well but much Hurryed, am affraid he has not time to write to thee by this Ship

I am thy real & assured Frd

James Freeman

This is Copy of the Letters sent By Captain Sparks

BP 4:3; D. 461.

From FRANKLIN

London, 17 July, 1771

My good and dear old Friend,

I received your kind letter of April 29th, wherein you complain of your friends here not writing to you. I had written a letter to you on the 20th of the same month, which I hope is long since come to hand; but I confess I ought to have written sooner, to acknowledge the receipt of the box of seeds, whereby I was much obliged. As to your pension, there is not, I believe, the least reason for you to apprehend its being stopped. I know not who receives it for you here, or I should quicken them in writing to you. But there is no instance in this King's reign of taking away a pension once granted, unless for some great offence. Young is in no esteem here as far as I can learn.

I wish your daughter success with her silkworms. I am persuaded nothing is wanting to our country for the produce of silk, but skill; which will be obtained by persevering till we are instructed by experience.

You take notice of the failing of your eyesight. Perhaps you have not spectacles that suit you, and it is not easy there to provide one's self. People too, when they go to a shop for glasses, seldom give themselves time to choose with care; and, if their eyes are not rightly suited, they are injured. Therefore I send you a complete set, from number one to thirteen, that you may try them at your ease; and, having pitched on such as suit you best at present, reserve those of higher numbers for future use, as your eyes grow still older; and with the lower numbers, which are for younger people, you may oblige some other friends. My love to good Mrs. Bartram and your children. I am, as ever, your faithful friend and servant,

B. Franklin

P.S. On inquiry, I find your pension continues, and will be regularly paid, as it becomes due, to the person you empower to receive it for you.

Sparks, *Works of Benjamin Franklin,* 7:534–35.

To WILLIAM BARTRAM

July ye 21st 1771

Dear Billy,

I received thy kind letter of April last by Captain Dyer in which thee signifies that thee had not received my letter which much surprised me how it missed comming to thy hands I cant say   in it I gave thee an account that I had paid one hundred pounds to thy Creditors to compound for ye whole & that they had given A full discharge for all thee owed them; we are all in good health but my brother James is near death to all appearance.[1]

hath been near A year & half in A poor state of health: John is married to Eliza & I hope will do well   My eyes is so dim that I cant know my own children A foot distance & I write with trouble & must hould my face within 2 or 3 inches of ye paper. I received A letter from Cousin Sarah[2] wherein she demanded ye rest of Gullies wives[3] cloaths which I know nothing off. My wife returned every article to her husband that she thought was worth sending & never charged A farthing neither for doctor nursing coffin nor buriall charges. ye Coffin I paid fifty shillings for after I came   we shall be glad to hear of thy welfare   thy mother brothers & sisters Joyns with [me] in love to thee & I remain thy affectionate father

John Bartram

College of Physicians of Philadelphia, Historical Collections of the Library, Z10–18, 1:59.
1. James died shortly after this letter was written, around August 1, 1771, and his will was proved August 5.
2. Colonel William's daughter, Sarah.
3. Captain Anthony Gulley's wife had died at the Bartram home. She is thought to have been Colonel William's stepdaughter, Sussanna.

From MICHAEL COLLINSON

Manchester Buildgs Augt. 16th 1771

Dear Sir

I wrote you a few Weeks since inclosing the Acct as well as I could make it out and also Mentioning that I should duly discharge your draft upon me for £200 Sterlg wch I have since done and shall be very glad to settle as soon as may be the remainder of an Acct. concerning which I have such uncertain Documents to direct me and in wch I have so much to trust to your honour. Mr. Gordon has just paid me £5.5 for a Box of Seeds which was sent in 1768, the Remainder of the Acct. being the last Boxe. Mr. Freeman has received the £5.5 from me him self and for which I must be debited and may be added to the Acct. sent & drawn for accordingly —

I am highly delighted and obliged by your partial Comment on my little Remarks of Italy &c   My notes wch I am recopying in order to serve for an occasional Retrospect, and to assist my memory hereafter of past scenes are indeed so multitudinous that I am on the revisal surprised at my past Labours which were indeed daily nay frequently hourly repeated, as on such Occasions the Memory is too fallible to be depended much on and I wished in particular to preserve the general idea of the Country through which we passed and the spontaneous productions of it.

Our Route my dear sir comprehended a tract of about seven thousand miles in which there was much to admire and observe [illegible]

The Orange & Limon & Pomegranate Gardens the last of which is also indigenous every where first made their appearance about Toulon and Nice and afterwards in greater plenty between Rome and Naples on the very beach of the Mediterranean Sea, particularly near Mola de Caeta and

Terracins, perfuming the air after sunset with their excessive Fragrance, on the quays at Marseilles we met with a very singular and most excellent species of China orange, brought from the Isles of Hieres just by the pulp of which is of the deepest Crimson possible and which we met with nowhere else   but for magnificence of size surely the Limons of Naples exceed everything wch the common people devour at a vast rate sour as they are and with as high a *goût* as ours here do the China orange. This operating with the salubrity of the sea and Mountain air I think is a great means of preservation to this filthy generation and secures them from the effects of their own excessive Nastiness. I am well assured that the Alps and even Apennines in point of elevation much exceed any of the mountains of North America though at the same time, they fall greatly short of the tremendous region of the Andes or Cordilleras and the Lakes of Italy though far surpassing any here, in this island are yet but as the drop of the bucket in comparison with your amazing inland oceans Erie Huron &c., &c. The largest in Italy are Lake Garda and Lake Maggiore the banks of which abound with the common eating Spanish Chestnut and a few Italian and English Oak. That of Garda is about 35 miles long and 10 and 15 broad, and abounds with Tench and Perch   Maggiore near Milan is near 50 miles in length, and about seven, four & three broad.

I am, my dear sir, very respectfully, and very affectionately yours,
Michael Collinson

BP 3:85; D. 450–51.

To MICHAEL COLLINSON

december ye 17th 1771
Dear worthy friend
I have now thy kind letter of august ye 16th which gives me great satisfaction to receive such an affectionate letter from ye son of my dear & ouldest Correspondent: it was kind in thee to receive the 5 lbs. of gordon & place it to my account, but as bills is now very low I shall not draw this winter, being very easy that is in such A good honest hand: I have Just been reading Condamins travels[1] thro Italy & France & smolets travails[2] near ye same rout but neither of them nor thy self makes any mention of ye famous Canal dug in Lewis ye 14th reighn: called ye royal Canal of Languedock which if it be now much used is worth A perticular observation   perhaps its fallen to decay: we have had this fall ye most surprising numbers of bears, rabits & partridges that hath been known these 60 years   partridges hath been sould in our market at three half pence apiece & rabits at two pence A piece: which used to be ninepence & partridges 3 or 4 pence A piece: it is surpriseing where all ye bears could come from   thay seemed to come

from ye west or N. West   thay must have come A great way as now thay are become very scarce in all ye indian countries where we have any trade. thay are so much hunted by all ye indian nations both for thair scins & flesh for food & if thay come from beyond ye head of St. Lawrance, Misisipia or its great branch ye Misoury, we may reasonably suppose many of them would be killed by ye many nations of Indians thay must pass thro before thay come to our parts but what should incline them to come toward ye ocean once in 50 or 60 years. some say its for want of acrons or grapes thair chief food but its strange thay should be so scarce for so many hundreds or thousands of miles   thay was no more plentifull with us this year then usual but what should incline such prodigious number of partridges to make to ye tidal shores   thay feed chiefly on berries & herbatious seeds & hath been exceeding scarce for many years in all ye inhabited parts of ye countrey. as for the Rabits thair plenty seem to be partly caused by ye very mild winters we have had of late but our inhabitants expects now A very hard winter: thee mentions our great lakes which is wonderfull. I think for great rivers, bays, lakes & high mountains America can boast superiority to any part of ye globe. where is such A river as St Lawrance with its five lakes in extent: or Amasones, Aronoco   La Plata or misisipia for its length depth & narrownes   for bays where is such A one as Chesepeak & hudsons with such A number of large rivers entering it on each side & where is so many great Lakes all communicateing one with another as ye canada lakes & where is such mountains as ye Cordeliors[3] but as for north america there is no mountains comparable to what is in europe Asia or africa & deserves to be dignified with no greater Apelation then common hills as we experience to our sorrow haveing no mountain to screen us from ye dreadfull Cold of ye Polar Circle   I take ye misisipia to be ye most odd & useless river in ye world for navigation on account of its wonderfull depth, narrowness, crookedness & yet its very swift heavy Current too strong to sail up it too deep to set up it with poles & too many bushy points to draw up ye vessails with horses & two narrow to tak about to sail up it so that if it ever be inhabited on each side as ye goodness of ye soil will admit of thay must build vesails up ye river & load them with ye countrey produce send them down ye river & sell both vesail & cargo – I have not room to give A rational Account of ye many different Phoenomena of this river from most other but please to be assured of ye great respect of thy sincere friend

John Bartram

British Library, Add. Ms. 28727.
1. Charles Marie de la Condamine (1701–1774), "Journal du Voyage Fait par Ordre du Roi a l'Equateur," *Histoire de l'Academie Royal des Sciences* 51 (Paris, 1751).
2. Tobias George Smollett (1721–1771), *Travels Through France and Italy* (London, 1766).
3. The Cordilleros include all North American mountains from Alaska to Panama. All South American mountains from Panama to Cape Horn are known as the Cordilleros dos Andes. Bartram seems to refer to the latter.

From MICHAEL COLLINSON

Manchester Buildings March the 6th 1772

My dear Sir

Your two most acceptable Favours of the 12th Octr. and 17th of Decmr, came safe to hand and I wish you to believe that no Person whatever can receive greater Satisfaction then I feel from the very pleasing picture you have drawn in the former of the domestic felicity of your family which I hope will be as permanent as I am sure the cordiality of my wishes are truly sincere for its long, very long continuance. Condamine is a very instructing little Book but I have never met with any work that is fully satisfactory respecting the Country of France and Italy &c. The traveller has generally exerted his abilities in deciphering some obsolete vestige of antiquity or in describing the works of Art whilst the natural history of each Kingdom is quite neglected — he is wafted from City to City and all the intermediate space which I think a Naturalist would wish to know something about is, for what he says of It a mere vacuum, or little better.

Were not my dear Sir nearer to the grand Canal of Languedoc to my great regret than Montpellier and which is but a short distance from it   I very particularly wished to see it as well for its own Importance as for the reason of botanizing in the hills of Narborne through which place we should of course have passed and which are famous for most valuable productions in the Vegitable world and remarkably so for the Orchis Tribe — my Favourites — if we are to believe Parkinson's Herbal, many very Curious fossil shells are likewise picked up in the chalky Hills of Narbonne. there is however a most magnificent work lately finished at Montpellier and of miles in extent being a noble Aqueduct constructed of an elegant white stone and designed to convey water from the Mountains to a grand reservoir for the Service of the City, and I think I never tasted any water so deliciously pure and sweet — It is built on the principle of the famous Roman One, at Nimes, not many miles distant, with this difference only, — the former One consists of only two Tiers, or Rows of Arches, whereas the Roman One has three — my Companions trembled for the imagined Fervour of an Italian sun, and therefore were impatient to push away before the Heats commenced, so that Montpellier was our furthest point west in the whole Journey.

Your account of the Migration of the Bears, Rabbits and Partridges is really wonderful but I believe in a manner local as Cadr. Colden, Esq., of New York from whom I have just received a letter takes no notice of any such Circumstance in those parts of the Country   considering the destruction that is perpetually going on, I should not be surprised if the whole race of Bears should become extinct, and still more so with regard to the Beaver there being an annual sale here only of between 40 and 50,000 of their skins and I make no doubt with Camden[1] but that we formerly had the Beaver among the unfrequented mountains and Lakes in Wales, which, in the course of time have been utterly destroyed   You will please to draw for the

Ballance whenever it suits you, and the sooner, the more agreeable to, my Dear sir

Your most affectionate Frd. & servt,
Michl Collinson

BP 3:86; D. 451–53.
1. William Camden (1551–1623), English historian and antiquarian.

To WILLIAM BARTRAM

July 15, 1772

Dear Billy,

I wrote last week but I am afraid it miscarried so I now write a few lines lest ye other mist   we are surprised at thy wild notion of going to Augustine   indeed I don't intend to have any more of my estate spent there or to ye southward upon any pretense whatever   I think it much better for the to come home and dwell amongst thy relatives & friends who I doubt not will endeavour to put thee in A way of profitable business if thee will take their advice & be industrious and carefull   My eye sight is gone very dim & I have thrown of all plantation business to John & we live with him. Betty is married to Conestoga. Mother & John & benny remember their love to thee & remain thy loving father

John Bartram

Historical Society of Pennsylvania Library, Society Collection of Photostats.

From FRANKLIN

London, Aug. 22, 1772

My dear old Friend,

I received your kind Letter of May 10. I am glad the Rhubarb Seed got safe to hand. I make no doubt of its Thriving well in our Country, where the Climate is the same with that of the Chinese Wall, just without which it grows in plenty and of the best Quality. I shall be glad to know how you find the Turnips. — I ask'd Solander about the Lucern Seed you wrote for. He could give me no Account of it, nor can I learn any thing of it from others. You may rely on my Friendship in recommending your Seeds. I send all that enquire of me about American Seeds to Mr. Freeman. He should advertise them when they come. I hear nothing lately of Young, and think him not of much Consequence. With Love to Mrs. Bartram & your Children, I am ever, my dear Friend,

Yours most affectionately
B F

City of Salford Arts and Leisure Department, Salford, England.

From FOTHERGILL[1]

Esteemed Friend

Constant and various engagements have long prevented me from writing to thee. For some years past I have retired from London to a considerable distance for about two months in order to recover strength sufficient to undergo the dutys of my profession. Here I used to have a little time to correspond with my distant Friends; but last year I was wholly prevented.

I desired my nephew James Freeman to acquaint thee with this and to desire thy indulgence hoping to be able at some time or other to acknowledge thy kind remembrance. I hope he acquits himself to thy Satisfaction. He is a sober diligent young man and wishes to oblige me and my Friends.

The frogs came safe and lively. I transcribed thy account of them and had it delivered to the King with an intimation that they were in my hands and should be sent whenever he would please to order. No order ever came to me — In a little place where I keep a few Gold fish I put the frogs and fenced it in in such a manner as I thought they would be forth coming whensoever they were called for   A small Communication between the place I had allotted for them and a large Canal underground and of which I was ignorant afforded one of them the means of getting more liberty   The other is still a prisoner   it is still alive and my gardener who sees him frequently tells me he has increased in size   I imagine they are quite forgot and will never be called for. And having once made the offer through a channel of some Consequence I shall make no further overture.

As I have no chance of recovering the animal that has escaped, I think to let the one that is confined to escape likewise into the same water; perhaps they may find one another.

In a letter to my Nephew thou intimates the probability W: Young may have endeavored to raise some prejudice against thee. He has not, he durst not attempt it as he knows my esteem for thee. He never spoke one word to thy disadvantage. My silence has been solely owing to my incessant occupation — I have endeavourd to assist this poor man and have aided him considerably. But he will not succeed, nor can he be supported —

A few weeks ago I received a letter and some drawings from thy Son William in Carolina   For his sake as well as thine, I should be glad to assist him. He draws neatly, has a strong relish for natural History and it is pity that such a genius should sink under distress. Is he sober & diligent? This may be an uncommon question to ask a Father of his Son & yet I know thy integrity will not suffer thee to mislead me. I would not have it understood that I mean to support him. I would lend however some little assistance if he is worthy — He proposes to go to Florida   It is a country abounding with great variety of plants and many of them unknown. To search for these will be of use to Science in general but I am a little selfish   I wish to introduce into this country the more hardy American plants, such as will bear our winters without much shelter   However I shall endeavour to assist his inclination for a tour of Florida, and if he succeeds shall perhaps wish him to see the back parts of Canada — Many curious flowering plants will doubtless be found about the lakes that will grow any where —

We have totally lost in this Country the Tetragonetheca   Will it be possible to get some seeds or a few roots of it? I believe nobody in America knows it or where it is to be found but thy self —

My garden is pretty large, well sheltered & a good Soil   The North American plants flourish with me exceedingly — I have most of the common plants usually sent over, but we have room for everything; I am fond of the Ferns. I have several from America but not all. I do not want to have a specimen of everything that grows in my garden but plants that are remarkable for their figure, their fragrance or their use are exceedingly acceptable. I must own that with this inclination to increase my Collection of plants, I have very little time to spend amongst them. I see them now and then transiently. But I look forward to and it is not impossible but I may live long enough to think it proper to decline all business. Then an amusement of this kind will have its use. To lessen the tediousness of old age and call me out to a little exercise, when subsiding vigor prompts to too much indulgence. I hope thou will perceive from this that my regard for thy deserts is undiminished, and that for thy own sake as well as my deceased Frd P. Collinson I am thy assured Friend

John Fothergill

BP 4:18; D. 343–45.
1. Undated, but written in September or October 1772, judging by the content.

From FRANKLIN

London Oct. 17. 1772

My dear old Friend,

I received sometime since the enclosed Letter from Dr. Hope, and lately the Gold Medal it mentions was delivered to me for you. By the first Ship directly to Philadelphia I shall send it in the Care of some safe Hand, thinking it not so well to hazard it with this letter round through New York. Dr. Hope's Letter to you is not yet come to my hands —

I hope the Rhubarb you have sown and distributed will be taken care of. — There seems to me no doubt of its doing as well with us as in Scotland. Remember that for Use the Root does not come to its Perfection of Power & Virtue in less than Seven Years. The Physicians here who have try'd the Scotch, approve it much, and say it is fully equal to the best imported.

I send you enclos'd a small Box of Upland Rice, brought from Cochin China. It grows there on dry Grounds, and not in Water like the common Sort. Also a few Seeds of the Chinese Tallow Tree. They have been carefully preserv'd in bringing hither, by Mr. Ellis's Method.[1] I had them from him, &

he tells me they are in good Condition fit to vegetate. I hope they may grow under your skilful Care. My Love to Mrs. Bartram and all yours from
Your affectionate Friend
B Franklin

Haverford College Library, Charles Roberts Autograph Letters Collection.
1. John Ellis imbedded seeds in balls of wax to prevent deterioration in shipment.

To MICHAEL COLLINSON

November ye 11th 1772

Dear Friend
I have long waited for a kind loveing letter as usual from my worthy friend Michael Collinson: haveing received no answer from thee all this long summer & fall & not one word of comfort to thy loveing friend: ye notion of basilisks, Dragons & unicorns is disbelieved by many never to have existed on our globe but I shall not deny thair being in considering how many remains of many creatures is frequently found in our days which have existed tho not living within ye reach of history as ye monstrous bones on ye banks of ye Ohio, ye horns dug up in Ireland, ye Mamuts teeth on ye banks of ye Oby.lena & Jenesea on ye Icey sea & our Bufeloes beavours & rattle snakes is so like all to be distroyed that if thay are so continualy destroyed for A Centry to come as thay have been for ye last 50 year there will be but few left & ye story of A rattle snake & its fascinating power will be in A few hundred years as little credited as ye cokstrice[1] killing at A distance by its eyes.

ye reason of ye great decreas of ye rattle snakes is thair slow motion in runing away & thair gathering together from distant parts in ye fall to lodge together in ye winter where thay are found & multitudes of them killed when all enmity seems to cease with others & those snakes that at other times is food for each other now lieth twined & entangled together so here ye Lyon & lamb lies down together; ye beavour is continualy hunted for its skin & thay hord together in thair houses & so great numbers is destroyed & ye great bulk of ye Bufelo exposeth him to ye sight of his enemy as doth ye Elk & doubtless that was ye chief cause of ye utter extirpation of ye beasts that bore those monstrous horns before mentioned

My dear friend thee writes that it is agreeable to thee to wholy settle our accounts but I hope not our Correspondence by letters so that if thee please to pay ye ballance to James freeman & his recept shall be thy sufficient discharge from thy obliged friend

John Bartram

British Library, Add. Ms. 28727.
1. Cockatrice, legendary serpent with a "deadly glance."

To FRANKLIN

November ye 11th, 1772

My dear ould worthy Friend:

I have before me thy kind letter of august 22, 1772   I sowed ye rhubarb in two places, ye one in ye sun, ye other in a shady cool place   That which was in ye cool place growed ye leaves was as big as ye palm of my hand but not palmated   Perhaps it may be next year

Ye Turnip seed came up well, growed large & tasted well & is by some admired & expect it may be A fine improvement

I hear no more of ye medal from Edenboro nor from Dr. Hope

We have had several bright Aurora Borealis last summer & in ye heat of harvest which is very uncommon at that season & we have had two slight shakes of an earthquake, very little thunder or rain but much hail in several parts distant from Philadelphia.

A late cold dry spring temperate summer & now A warm very dry fall Very few troubled with agues   Some bad nervous fevers but not very mortal but ye favorablest Measels I ever knew & as yet the slowest in spreading Perhaps when cold weather approacheth it may be more severe & spread more

I remain dear friend with much love & respect thy sincearly well wisher as

John Bartram

PS I can hardly see to write or read

Papers of Benjamin Franklin, vol. 19, ed. William B. Willcox.

From FOTHERGILL

London 1772[1]

My Esteemed Friend

I received thy kind letter, and am pleased that my employing thy son affords both him and thy self some satisfaction. He may perhaps in the space of two or three years, if his life is spared get into a good livelihood by sending boxes of plants and seeds to Europe from those less frequented parts of America. The money advanced on his account viz., £17, I will pay James Freeman for thy use. a correspondent of mine at Charlestown[2] has direction to accomodate him, as his occasions may require. — I have lately wrote to Wm. pointing out what I would principally wish him to attend to: and I hope he will meet with suitable assistance in journeying thro those provinces, which at present are almost an unknown country. — It was late this year before he set out. I cannot expect much from him; but the observations he will be able to make in this journey will enable him to do much another [year] if his life and health be spared. — If thy son John meets with any new plants or flowering shrubs in his search after seeds, and will be kind enough to send me a few, I shall endeavour to make him satisfaction. — The K. was acquainted that thou had sent over the Bull frogs, and that they were in my possession, till he was pleased to give orders concerning them wch he never did. I put them in a little pond of water and fenced it round in such a manner as they could not get out. But there was a small communication under ground between this and a larger piece of water which I did not know of, and thro' which one of them made its escape. My gardener sees them sometimes, and I have directed him to let the other escape its confinement. —

By the kindness of my Friends and some expence, I have got together a pretty large collection of valuable plants. The North americans prosper with me full as well as they do anywhere else. I have likewise got a fine young Tea tree from China. It is planted in ground under a west wall but is [illegible] a glass cover in the winter. It has [illegible] this summer near two feet long. Its [illegible] five inches and a half long by two [illegible] broad. There are plants likewise of [the same kind] in divers gardens, but none [illegible] that I know of as mine. I do not yet [dare] hurt the plant by making layers as [illegible] but when it is grown stronger, I shall endeavour [to propagate] it. It would suit the hilly part of [South] Carolina well. —

I have a good collection of Ferns; many of wch are Americans but not all, by many. This is a despised plant but its foliage to me is pleasing. If any cast up in thy sons excursions, he will dig up the Turf with them, and send along with the seeds of the Tetragonotheca, if he can spare any.

Earnestly desiring for thee all kind of Comfort and satisfaction, I remain
Thy assured friend
John Fothergill

BP 4:25; D. 347.
1. This letter was written after Fothergill wrote to Lionel Chalmers on October 23, 1772.
2. Lionel Chalmers.

From MICHAEL COLLINSON

Manchr. Buildgs Jan 8 1773
Dear Sir

Your kind favor of the 11th of November last is now before [me] the Contents of which, however equally surprize and Concern Me in finding that neither of the two Letters I troubled you with the 6th March and 14th June, have come to hand, which I am indeed astonished at as I delivered them both Myself at the post office, which Conveyance I never found fail before in any Letter either Sir to you or my Frd Cadr. Colden of New York and till your present favour I have not my dear friend heard a single tittle from you since the 17th December, 1771, to wch I had long since replied —

This present Scrawl shall be conveyed from the Pensilv. Coffee house which may possibly be the surest mode of Conveyance.

with regard to my Letters in point of Consequence they are less than Nothing — on the Contrary yours sir, are invaluable — Your sentiments are Original ingenious and to the last Degree pertinent on the subjects on wch they treat. They were held in a manner sacred by my dearest father, nor is their Consequence sunk in the hands of his Son, by whom they are Considered as an inestimable treasure of American Natural History: –

Tho' I never take any copies of my own insignificant Epistles to my Frds yet I always memorandum the date of my Letters to them or the day they are consigned to the Office, wch makes Me positive to the above wch have somehow strangely miscarried   I have paid into Mr. Freeman's Hands £22:2:3 being the Ballance of the Acct including £10:10:0 for 2 Boxes for Gordon wch is the only Money I have ever received from any One on the Acct. I mentioned 1 Box before but in the Whole I rec'd from Gordon as Above but not knowing of the second Box at first — Your ingenious Idea respecting the former Existence of certain kinds of Animals now Extinct I confess carries great Weight with it and yet my dear Sir I cannot implicitly give my Assent to It in the whole. With regard to the Unicorn I am rather divided in my Judgment even in respect to their present Existence, in the interior Region of Africa of which at this Period we are extremely ignorant — I have an old Histy of Abyssinia that speaks positively to the Fact: and there are other Authorities on Record, if they deserve Credit, that support the same Opinion — I much fear the Extirpation of that dreadful Animal the Rattle Snake will be never accomplished notwithstanding the perpetual war against the Race — the Continent of America is so vast, the Retreats so many — and so secluded from human Approach, that if it ever should take place it must, I think be many Centuries first: for please to remember those Reptiles are found as far south as the Line Itself — an Immense Tract, and how much farther We know not —pray is the Rattle Snake found as far North as the Labrador Coast? And if not where is the Line of Termination drawn? As to the poor Bufalo and Beaver I believe their days are Numbered; and sorry I am for the Belief especially with respect to the latter which from its extreme inoffensiveness, and ingenuity deserves a better Fate. I shall follow this Letter very shortly by Another, wishing to Communicate something relative to a Species of Snake I observed in Italy &c. &c. I have therefore only to add that if Wishes could have any Effect, I would never cease wishing new numberless and happy years to You and your worthy Family, till I had not room enough left in my Paper, to crowd in the useless name of

Dearest sir,
Your truly affecte. friend,
Michael Collinson

BP 3:82; D. 453–54.

From FRANKLIN

London, 10 February 1773

My dear good old Friend,

I am glad to learn that the turnip seed and the rhubarb grow with you, and that the turnip is approved. It may be depended on, that the rhubarb is the genuine sort. But, to have the root in perfection, it ought not to be taken out of the ground in less than seven years. Herewith I send you a few seeds of what is called the cabbage turnip. They say that it will stand the frost of the severest winter, and so make a fine early feed for cattle in the spring, when their other fodder may be scarce. I send also some seed of the Scotch cabbage; and some peas that are much applauded here, but I forget for what purpose, and shall inquire and let you know in my next.

I think there has been no good opportunity of sending your medal since I received it, until now. It goes in a box to my son Bache, with the seeds. I wish you joy of it. Notwithstanding the failure of your eyes, you write as distinctly as ever. With great esteem and respect, I am, my dear friend, yours most affectionately.

B. Franklin

Works of Benjamin Franklin, 8:32–33; D. 405–6.

From FREEMAN

Lond 2 mo. 16th 1773

Esteemed Frd
Jno Bartram

I recd thine, & shall duly honour thy draught & that of thy sons, the seeds he sent this year am affraid will not all answer there being much Complaint   not so well put up as last year, however I hope to do my best Uncle Doctor is bravely considering his hurry. by this time thou will have recd a Letter from him wch he told me he wrote some time back wherein he mentions thy son who was at Carolina   I tho't it wod not be right to omit writing by thy countryman Dr. Parke[1] who has been our Intimate during his stay in London and by his good Conduct gained the Esteem of many Friends here   I am thy real Frd

Ja Freeman

Thy salary is continued   After the next Payt: I shall transmit the Account.

BP 4:5; D. 461.
1. Dr. Thomas Parke, one of several colonial students befriended by Fothergill.

From MICHAEL COLLINSON

Manchester Buildgs. Feby 25th 1773

My dear Sir

I troubled you with a Letter dated the 8th ulto and I hope with better success than my two preceeding Letters met with —

Our winter to this date has been uncommonly Mild there having been nothing equal to It since 1750 one continued series of mild S.W. winds having blown for four months past with an Intermission only of about a fortnights moderate Frost so that whilst vegetation has been surprisingly pushed forward the rich and the Great have been put to it, to fill their Ice houses — I am however afraid there is a Scouring yet in store for Us, but I hope not so intolerable a One as we experienced last May when the severity of the N.E. Winds not only blasted all the Bloom in our Orchards but our Grass to such a Degree as to double the price of hay — Your American Apples have been an admirable Substitute this season some of our Merchants having imported great Quantities of Them they are notwithstanding too expensive for common Eating being sold for two pence, three pence, and even four pence an apple.[1] But their flavour is much superior to anything we can pretend to, and I even think superior to the apples of Italy. In Italy, I observed four species of the serpent kind; viz., our common Snake, Viper, Slow-worm, and a very singular species of snake, which I do not believe has been described by any one; the first three only being common to England. The first of this last kind, I met with at Rome, where a couple of Italians were showing tricks with it, having rendered it extremely familiar and tame. This was above six feet long.

I soon after met with another, near the celebrated cataract of Terni, which the guides despatched, in spite of my wishes to the contrary. I found, on examining the mouth, in which there were no fangs, and from its whole appearance, that it was but a simple snake. The colour—head, belly, and all, was of a plain shining ash colour, as glossy and free from Scales as the slow-worm but not partaking of its brittle quality — Besides the common Toad, that is the same as Ours they have One of an enormous Size and frightfully deformed these the peasants destroy whenever they meet them and then suspend them by the leg to the next tree: in which situation I have contemplated many. They are all over of a dusky brown, with scarce any spots discernible; a broad, rough, furrowed head, and a mouth wide enough to ingulf a moderate-sized Toad. Upon the whole, it is the ugliest creature I ever beheld.

Beside our English Frog, they have also, in astonishing abundance, the Tree Frog, whose appearance is far from disagreeable. The males only are green and the females gray

* * *

These gentry ascend trees by millions, and serenade till the autumn, living upon dews and insects. I have many times laboured to shake them from the saplings; but they stick so close, I was never able to accomplish it but once; and could only bring one home, which I presented to Dr. Fothergill.

You could not, my dear friend, oblige me so much, as to send me a few specimens of your different kinds of Oyster, and River and Land Shells, of any sorts that may happen easily to come in your way, without hurrying yourself, or taking too much trouble. They might be packed in a box, and consigned with the Seeds to Gordon or Mr. Freeman, marked M C the Freight of which and other Expenses, would be instantly paid by dear Sir

Your truly Affectionate servant,
Michael Collinson

BP 3:87; D. 454–56.
1. From this point much of this letter is illegible, so the remainder has been taken from Darlington.

From LIONEL CHALMERS

Charlestown, 1st April 1773

Dear Sir: —

I last night received your favour of the 13th ultimo, by your son William, who is to dine with me this day, together with Dr. Morgan,[1] of your city, and some other Friends. According to our mutual good friend Dr. Fothergill's desire, I shall immediately advance him ten guineas, to set him a going; & I doubt not but by his Diligence & skill in Botany as well as Zoology he will pass his time agreeably to himself as well as to the Docr who, besides the £50 sterling per annum, will pay him for his drawings. In the mean time be assured that whatever may be in my power shall not be wanting to assist him in his progress.

I am much obliged to you for the promise you make me of sending Bulbous Roots, when the season comes for taking them up. [illegible paragraph]

Our friend Fothergill has often sent me varieties of flower-seeds, and plants: but the former never grew, and the latter were perished before they came to hand. My Carnations were all destroyed by a severe frost and snow we had about the 20th of February last, when they were shooting out strongly; so that a few seeds, or slips of them, will be welcome to, dear sir,

Your friend and servant,
Lionel Chalmers

BP 1:102; D. 464.
1. John Morgan (1735–1789), prominent Philadelphia physician.

From CHALMERS

Charlestown 7th April 1773

Dear Sir

The Letter I wrote you Some Days ago, will probably come to Your Hands together with this. In my first I told you, I should advance Your Son William Ten Guineas, by way of outset, which I did. But as that Sum with all his Frugality, would not go far, I desired at the end of six months or Sooner, that he would draw on me for £25 ster. more, which I would Pay, as well as the remaining £25 at the Years End; for it could not be expected that he could travel & maintain himself for 12 months on the first Ten Guineas Dr

Fothergill desired might be paid him — so far as this I have ventured on the Dr's Generosity, to shorten the Time of William's being supplied with Money.

As your Son inclined much to pursue his Researches into the Indian Country; & as our Superintendent in these Affairs will set off towards the End of this Month to hold a Congress above Augusta with the Creeks & Cherokees, about some Lands that are to be ceded to us, I spoke to Mr Stuart to take him in his Retinue, & recommend him to the Protection of the Several Indian Tribes — Mr Stuart not only agreed with me, that he would assist him with his whole Interest in this way, but also that he should travel with him without Expense — Mr Stuart himself being an Excellent Painter & Draughtsman, and in many Respects a Virtuoso —

As it is now but early in April, & Mr Stuart, probably will not set off, till about the Beginning of May, William this Morning told me, he intended to go to Augusta in a trading Boat, in order to prosecute his Plan; & then to stay for Mr Stuart, as by that time he might do something to please Dr Fothergill —This I Highly Approve as I hope you will; for the Season for Flowers will soon be over, & besides it will save the Expence of stabling his Horse &c, should he buy one, & wait for Mr. Stuart's departure from home — All this I hope will meet with your Approbation; & as he dines with me this Day, I shall speak further to him & he himself will undoubtedly inform you more of these things —

He certainly has a good Notion of Painting; & might take an excellent Representation of Things, were he more exact in his colourings after Nature; which from a sample he gave of the Starry Anise Flower; I had occasion to caution him to be — a painted Finch which flew on board of the Vessel in his Passage hither, he painted beautifully — On the whole, I doubt not, he will fully answer Dr. Fothergill's Expectation, & make it answer well for himself, considering he is to be paid separately for all his Drawings —

I am Dear Sir

Your obedt. humble Servt
Lionel Chalmers

So far of our Proceedure hitherto, I thought it proper to inform you & shall from Time to Time acquaint you how we go on, which I hope will wholey be to William's advantage & the Dr's Satisfaction; for your son has all the Requisite & Application to Researches of this sort, that his Father had before him — And indeed it surprises me, that you should not have encouraged this Genius of his as a Naturalist sooner; for, tho' you endeavour'd to cure it by putting him to a Mercht &c, yet Nature prevailed so far as to disqualify him from Pursuits of this sort — On the whole, John Bartram has a Son, who I hope will perpetuate both his Father's & his own Name, for the Advancement of Natural Philosophy, as well as of Science in General

LC

Historical Society of Pennsylvania Library, Gratz Collection of Notable Americans, Case 7, Box 27.

From MICHAEL COLLINSON

Manchester Buildgs. July 21st 1773

My dear Sir

I am to thank you for your very obliging and instructive Letter of the 10th May last, and sit down to reply to it as well as I am able; but in the first place beg you will never think of troubling Yourself to make any future Apology in regard to writing &c nothing can be more clear and comprehensive notwithstanding the increased imperfection of sight complained of and which I shall be most heartily rejoiced to hear proves only a temporary complaint and I cannot help adding that if the sincere & ardent wishes of an Individual can avail there are many, very many happy years yet to be added to a Life not more justly prized by its dearer and nearer Connexions than it Has I am sure proved an honour to Humanity and the Public at large the Consideration you have been pleased to show to the communications of reciprocal friendship for a series of years past was mutual between my dearest Father and yourself. He also preserved the Letters of his old and beloved Friend he considered them as they justly were an invaluable mine of original American knowledge and I trust at least that the Treasure will not sink in its Value in the hands of his son —

The general remarks you make respecting the Extirpation of the native inhabitants of your vast Forrests are striking and curious and carry Conviction along with them and indeed I cannot help thinking but that in the period you mention notwithstanding the amazing Recesses your prodigious Continent affords many of the present Species will become extinct and perhaps the Indians themselves but of the humbler Tribe I feel most for the poor ingenious Beaver and read with Indignation and concern the many many thousands of their Furs imported from America annually, advertised for sale in the Papers — I honour and admire the Tenderness of your Sentiments even with regard to that frequently fatal Reptile the Rattle Snake; and the more so, as it is correspondent with my own Feelings; for it is some years since except in one or two instances only that I have even deprived the minutist Individual of life, I consider it as a heavenly spark derived from the great author and Fountain of Life, which is to be held sacred and which I have no right to injure or destroy. — The new species of Viper you mention must have been a prodigious Curiosity. what a dreadful Creature! Pity he could not have been preserved or at least his head, — to have comtemplated the structure of his enormous Fangs [remainder of paragraph illegible]

Though we have every year very considerable importation of the Italian viper yet our apothecaries also employ their Viper-Catchers here tho as our Sun is less fervent 'tis possible the virtue of Ours may not be equal to those from Abroad with respect to Size and Appearance they are the same, as I have had proof enough in my botanic Rambles, having seen several of the former both Male and Female not only in the Campania of Rome where they abound, but elsewhere; — one of our British Viper Catchers since dead I

knew well and having seen him turn out of a Bag into a Room 50 or 60 of them at once all alive and vigorous   he informed Me that as soon as he seiz'd a Viper for which he was accoutred with a cleft stick and an almost impenetrable pair of Gloves with a Steel Instrument he immediately wrenched out the Fangs in which Operation in spite of all, he was now and then bit and had many scars to show — but a little warm Olive Oil with wch he always went provided rub'd into the Wound presently blunted the Effects of the Venom — the proper distinction my dear Friend, between the Male & Female of this Species is — the *Adder* is the Male the *Viper* the Female and very different they are — The adder is thicker in proportion to its length than the Female and is of an unvaried Colour a dusky reddish-brown with scarcely any perceptable marks on his Back, on the contrary the Female or Viper has a very singular, irregular light Coloured List something resembling in its Configuration a chain of Death's Head that runs quite down the back to the extremity of the Tail and she is also on the upper parts of a brighter Colour all over and likewise more susceptable of Danger and livelier than the Male. on the Belly they are both Male and Female of a dun or darkish Ash Colour — Mr. Banks' and Dr. Solanders Circumnavigation of the globe[1] is just published by which it appears that in the Islands of the So Seas within the Tropics — Nature has been as sparing of the Animal Productions as of her vegetable — in the delightful Isle of Otaheite in I think 19 Degrees S Lt the natives possess'd no other quadrupeds than Hogs and Dogs the latter of wch they preferr'd to the former. Fish indeed was the grand Article — their principal Support which abounded, and excepting the Bread Fruit mentioned in Ansons Voyage,[2] and the cocoa-nut they had little else to boast of — the Adventurers However, left them abundance of European pulse, stones of Peaches, kernels of various kinds particularly Orange & Lemon, &c. &c., wch promised to enrich the Island as many of them sprouted with great luxuriance before their departure: I have now only just room to add, that it is with equal respect & Affection I remain Dear Sir
your very gratefull obliged Frd & Servant
Michl. Collinson

BP 3:88; D. 456–58.
1. Sir Joseph Banks (1743–1820) and Solander accompanied Captain James Cook on a voyage around the world in 1768–72.
2. Baron George Anson (1697–1762), British admiral who circumnavigated the globe.

From REVEREND JOHN WEIKSELL

Philadelphia August 31. 1773

For esteemed and much Honoured Sir

I rejoice of hearing you nominated a member of the illustrious Philosophical Society at Stockholm, and wish you might reap much Satisfaction from that Learned and Respectable Body. I wanted yesterday to wait on you personally in order to acquaint you that I, at last, have obtained a gracious

Repeal from His Majesty the present King of Sweden, to return to my Native Country; And that I am determined to obey the same Call, & leave this Country yet this fall, after 5. or 6. weeks, with any of the London Vessels. I offer my Service unto You generous Sir; in any commands you may have to that quarter, or London & what ever lays in my power to Conveigh, to your Friends on your behalf, shall be a pleasure to me. I humbly beg you would also bestow on me your devoted Servant such share of your natural curiosities as yourselves think proper would suite, and your own noble & generous heart could lavish away on me, I promise my Self the pleasure to wait on you the next time I come up to the City. The young Virtuoso, your Son, Sir John Bartram, wrote me, last fall, in your absence, also a generous promise, of some natural Collections suiting our Zone. I beg you would recommend me into his favour, & revive his generous promise. In this hope, & even without the fullfilling of it, I always Shall remain much Honoured Sir

Your most humble & affectionate Servt.
John Weiksell   late Rect: at [?]

In great haste

BP 4:112.

From FREEMAN

Lond:12 mo:1773

John Bartram Senr.
Esteemed Friend: —

I recd thine & thy sons Letter by Capt. All with the seeds wch thou mayst tell thy Son I believe are all disposed of; and by the 1st Conveyance after the Accounts are settled I shall transmit the general Account to him. I am oblig'd to thee for delivering the List of Goods to thy son from whom thou givest me Reason to have expected p the same Shipps on Order but I have received None   It has been a great Favour to be favor'd with such a share of Wealth & Facultys to thy time of Life & no doubt what thou must expect the Gradual Decay of Nature, but its Happiness thou mayst enjoy in having Children grown up & well disposed to render thee every filial Comfort for thy past Care & Attention during their Tender Years, wch I hope will be continued to thee to the latest Period. Uncle Desires his Respects & that I wo'd acquaint thee He wrote to Doctor Chalmers of Charles town to supply thy son with some Money and he will draw on Him, viz., Dr. Fothergill for the same which may now make thee quite easy in that Respect. It will, to be sure, be the second Month ere I can write again when I hope to write to thy son.

In the interim I remain thy friend,

Js. Freeman.

BP 4:6; D. 462.

From FREEMAN

London 2d mo 19th 1774 —

Esteemed Fr.
John Bartram, senr.

This being the usual season of the year to exchange Accounts as beneath is thine which I daresay thou will find right. I received no orders from thy son as hinted in thine — If I had been so favoured I should have made a point of serving him on as good Terms as any of thine. Doctor Fothergill is much as usual considering his hurrying life which must apologize for his not keeping up a constant Correspondence, with his Friends abroad, whom he nevertheless has greatest Esteem for. The Doctor has written to Dr. Chalmers to supply thy son William with some money on his Account   My Wishes for thy Continued Happyness attend thee & believe me thy Real Friend

J. Freeman

The account due John Bartram S'n'r.		Sent Act Curt. Jm. Freeman
1774 To Ballance due to JB 431.7.2		1773
2 mo. 19		
Dr. By Ballance as P Act delivered		£388.16.8
1773 9 mo. 29 By cash Pension		25
10 mo. 30 By cash P Doctor Fothergill		17.10.6
		£431.7.2

Errors excepted.
J. Freeman

BP 4:7.

From MICHAEL COLLINSON

Manchester Buildings
March 5th. 1774

My dear Friend

Your most acceptable Favor of the 8 of November last came safe to hand; and I am to thank you for all your ingenious and obliging Communications wch never fail to make me a wiser Man whilst at the same time they are the sources of much Entertainment. the few Things you gave Me the hopes of receiving this Autumn, I imagine You was disappointed in procuring tho' what I principally wish'd was only a few perfect Specimens of your Oysters, to which, if a Land or River shell, or so, had been added, I should have been more than contented, and have paid Freight, and any Expense in procuring that might have arisen —

With respect to Natural History tho' I am at present from various wayward Reasons prevented from enjoying my beloved Amusement in botanical Researches, yet I still flatter Myself (perhaps vainly) with passing the Autumn or at least Winter of my Days in some sequestered Situation far removed from the Tumult and Confusion of this Metropolis which are the utter aversion of my soul — In the mean while I indulge in the Contemplation of what my Cabinets afford — many very curious Materials of which I am highly indebted to your Bounty for —

We have had an exceeding Tempestuous Time for a fortnight past attended with violent Rains   otherwise the Winter has been mild upon the whole, the severe weather seldom lasting above two or three days, and then changing with a S.W. Wind — we have also had one of our Spring Cries already that of Primroses, — which the lower Class of People at this Season usually plunder the Woods of a few Miles from the City, for yet, my dear Sir, there are a few woods left tho' in my Remembrance many fine Ones have been grub'd up and turned into Pasture to supply the enormous increase of Horses, which luxury and riches have found necessary of their Use —

Things seem to be wearing a very serious face here in regard to the Colonies; — in respect to the Business at Boston, concerning the Tea that was certainly the act of a lawless Rabble, and in that light only I believe the Administration views it. — Indeed it is the general belief here that much of the present disposition of the Colonies has originated from the incendiary Arts of some interested People here, *not* American born, but who delight to inflame and hope to find their Account in fishing in troubled waters. — the times are certainly eventful and distempered, and I should be very glad that something consistent could be adopted, to heal this Breech agreeable to the Wishes of America and yet not derogatory to the Honour of the Mother Country. —

I remain with great Respect and Regard Dear Sir [your] affect Frd.

Michl Collinson

BP 3:90, D.458–59.

From FOTHERGILL

London, 8th., 7th month, 1774

Esteemed Friend:–

I received thy very acceptable letter of the 14th, 4th month last, and am pleased to find thy health so well preserved, — so well in the evening of life.

I had a letter the other day from Doctor Chalmers, who mentions that he had a letter lately from William, who was going towards East Florida, and well. I have received from him about one hundred dried specimens of plants, and some of them very curious; a very few drawings, but neither a seed nor a plant.

I am sensible of the difficulty he is at in travelling through those inhospitable countries; but I think he should have sent me some few things as he went along. I have paid the bills he drew upon me; but must be greatly out of pocket, if he does not take some opportunity of doing what I expressly directed, which was, to send me seeds or roots of such plants, as either by their beauty, fragrance, or other properties, might claim attention. However, I shall hope he will find means of fulfilling my orders, better than he has done hitherto.

If thy son John meets with anything new in his travels about the country, I should be glad if he would send me at least a part of his discoveries; and I hope I may be able to content him for his trouble. I am obliged to him for the seeds of the Orange-coloured *Hibiscus*. I have a good many plants of the *Illicium*. I have planted these in the natural ground, and shall give them a little shelter in the winter. It has a most grateful fragrance, and will be a pleasing greenhouse plant.

Please let him know that I received the Turtle in good health; and shall be much obliged to him if he will procure me a male and female Bull-frog. Mine are strayed away notwithstanding my best endeavours. If they are put up in a little box of wet moss, they will come safe; at least, I received a little American Frog, the *Rana ocellata,* in a box of plants, filled up with moss. They should be sent in autumn;

I shall be much pleased to see the *Tetragonotheca*. There is not, I believe, a plant of it now in England.

We have got the true Green Tea. I have a plant in the natural ground near five feet high. Mine has been sheltered in the winter, but old James Gordon left his exposed to all weathers, this last winter, and yet it thrives very well. We shall propagate it as fast as we can.

Do not imagine that all the people in this country are against America. We sympathize with you much. It may be our turn to suffer next. We hope however, that the impending storm may blow over, and that you may be enabled to act your part properly.

I am thy assured friend,

John Fothergill

D. 347–48.

From CHALMERS

Charlestown 12th July 1774

Friend John
I rec'd your favour of the 4th ulto, & now inform you that [the] last Letter I had from your son William, was dated at St. Johns river in Georgia   But where he is now I know not; having not heard from him for 3 months — Be where he will, an excellent Oeconomist he certainly must be; for he has not drawn on me for more than £12 since the first Money I advanced for him. So

that, by this Time, he must have near £40 due — As to bulbous Roots, I leave the Choice of them to Yourself, but should you have any of the best flowering Peonys; the larger sort of Canterbury Bells, or seeds of true Rhubarb, I shall be obliged to you for a few of each — I forgot Carnations in sorts, if you can spare some. I am so pestered with a swarm of Pidgeons about here that I can raise nothing for the Kitchen in my small garden, so that I am obliged to throw it into Flowers. Scarcely anything that is sightly will [not] come amiss

Yr Assured Friend & Servant
Lionel Chalmers

BP 1:104.

From FREEMAN

Lond:16 7 mo: 1774

Est'm'd.,
J. Bartram sen'r:

Thou are quite right in embracing every Oppertunity to invest thy Property to Advantage & the draughts drawn shall be duly honoured tho think it might have been an Advantage to thy Son or Sons in the Merchantile Way to have allow'd me to have sent a few dry Goods wch might have been charg'd already   No Price as thou could have settled with them and its now not too late for a Part of the whole of thy Act remaining in My Hands of wch as annex'd is the Copy. the last Money they genteely asked to see thy Letter thinking thee a great Age   However I hope to receive for thee many years yet. May every Comfort requisite at thy Period of Life attend thee is the best wish of thy Frd —

J. Freeman

J. Bartram Snr. Act with J. Freeman

1774
6 mo:10 To Dis. to

W Bertram accepted —	160	By Ballce p last act.	382.16
To. Do. Isaac Bertram	25	1773 9,29 Per yr ½ Pension	25.
To Postage —	1	10.30 Per Cash in full of	
To Ball due JBSenr	271:6:2	Mr. Collinson's act	17.10
	456:7:2	1774 3,25 per ½ yr Pension	25.
			£456:7:2

Errors Excepted 7 mo. 12th 1774
J. Freeman

BP 4:17.

From MICHAEL COLLINSON

Manchestr. Buildgs. Sepr. 22d 1774

My dear Friend

Your very kind Favor of the 7th June is before me and I am to thank you for its very obliging Contents — in regard to the critical Situation of America I Sincerely join with You in Sentiments — and I am sure I most sensibly feel of the distresses of the innocent Part of its Inhabitants but in certain Situations it is very difficult to separate the punishment of the guilty from the Innocent — as to the Conduct of the Bostonians it ought I think to excite the Indignation of Every honest Mind — in all their late Resolves and Meetings We hear of no Proposal whatever to pay the E. I. Company for the Goods they rob'd and plundered them of but Retribution they will be obliged to make, I firmly believe some Way or other as they have now to deal with an Administration firm and Persevering   if Lord Chatham's[1] Word is to be believ'd "America was conquered in Germany," if so We are not now to learn the Price of Blood and Treasure we have paid on its' Account and for it's Security and Advantage — but the Conduct of part of the Colonies, and their Wishes for an illicit contraband Trade to the prejudice of the Mother Country, and their own separate Emolument, is now pretty well understood here, and who are their principal Abettors, on both sides the Water — but enough my Dear Sir of this   it is a disagreeable Subject and we will if you please Drop it —

When the Lease of my Habitation here expires which will be in little more than a Year I shall if I live I hope once more breathe the salubrious Gale of the Country, at my Mansion at Mill Hill wch I am once more the Proprietor of —and tho' no more than ten Miles from the Metropolis, commands distant and home views of several Counties. — I well remember my old Friend Mr. Moses Bartram being there — and I hope he is well and alive, I have not heard a Word of him for many Years past. the principal Reasons of my leaving it at all, were the depredations Committed in my Garden, from whence all the fine Plants possible to remove were Carried off and wch almost all derived from your Bounty, to which may be added my Resolution of going into France & Italy &c — on the loss of a most revered and beloved Parent but even now the blue Mountain Magnolias are still flourishing with amazing Vigour, and are above (for there are two of them) thirty feet high, and flower prodigiously but the seed Vessel is the most beautiful part of the plant, being when ripe of a rich deep Crimson but I have this from report for I shall not have Courage to look into the Premises Myself till I go to reside for Good, having a good Tenant for a year who rents it ready furnished — the more I see and reflect the more I am satisfied in the justness of your remark and think I cannot too soon retire from "the extravagant confused Inventions of Men."

I remain dear Sir with great Respt most affecionately yours,

Michl Collinson

BP 3:89; D. 459–60.
1. William Pitt, First Earl of Chatham.

From FREEMAN

London 12 mo. 18 1774

J Bartram Senr.
Esteemed Friend

I received thine 29th 9th mo. last & was glad to find thee yet able to write And the Pleasure to look back to thy infancy & on good Grounds I hope to feel such comfortable Reflection on the several Parts of thy Life, now in advanc'd Age, & must be unspeakably great & I sincerely wish it may continue to thy Conclusion.

I am obliged to thee for the application to thy Son but he is mistaken in his Conjecture tho I now & then buy an odd Article of the Warehouses, as they also do of me, yet in a day our Goods at the first Hand as well as them. However I wo'd give thee no further Trouble on this Head in future

I sincerely sympathize wth the Children of an ungrateful Mother in their Present dilemna   their Resolves seem to be not hastily, but deliberately adopted & some of them I sho'd hope wo'd be steadily abode by (even if the Mother sho'd repent her severity towards Her Children & again restore to them their Natural Rights) those I mean are, the Abolition of the Slave Trade, and that of Horse Racing, Stage Plays &c., wch in the first Case wo'd be full Proof of their true Idea of Liberty and in the last, of their Affection to their Children in preserving their Morals from Corruption as far as in their power lyes for surely nothing can tend more to corrupt the youth than these dissipating Pleasures. On the other side is thy acct: wch: thee will find rightly stated by

thy obliged & sincere Frd
Js. Freeman

BP 4:8½; D. 462–63.

From WILLIAM BARTRAM

Charles Town March 27th 1775

Honord & Benevolent Father

I am happy by the blessing of the Almighty God by whose care I have been protected & led safe through a Pilgrimage these three & twenty months till my return to Charlestown two days since. I am now lodged most kindly in the Family of your deceased Friend Lambol; his daughter Mrs. Thomas excellent in goodness beyond her sex with expressions of the same affable & cordial friendship so particular in the character of her antient excellent Parent asked me to her house while I stay in this Province which believe will be but a few days. I wrote to my Father soon after my return to Savanah from Tugilo River which letter gave an account of my proceedings there in that journey which I traveled upwards of 300 Miles. I collected a large number of specimens & sent to Doctr Fothergill with some drawings in answer to which the Doctr was pleased to send me a list of the new & nondescript which I was glad to find were many, & hear he was pleased to express his satisfaction with the success of my labours & his willingness that I should continue my researches this Packet I received in Et. Florida. Soon after my return to Savanah in order to forward my collections to Doctr Fothergill, I intended to go back into the Cherokee & Creek Countries when the alarm from the Frontiers of hostilities commencing between the Indians & the whites put a stop to that scheme. I then turned my views toward Et. Florida & prepared for it. I put my baggage on board a Vessell bound for Savanah To Mr. Spauldings Store on St. Johns intending to go by land there & set off accordingly got safe to the Allatamaha where I was taken Ill of Fever of which I did not recover so as to be able to travel for near 2 months when I sett off again but was turned back again by expresses from Et Florida that the Indians were up in Arms against us in that Province having killed & captivated several white People & the Inhabitants were flying in to Augustine & all the Indian stores except one were robed & broken up so I stayed in the So Parts of Georgia waiting for a favorable turn & here I discovered & collected many valuable & new Vegitables. hearing that the Lower Creeks were dealing with the Governor of St. Augustine I resolved to make the second attempt. I left my home in Georgia & went down the Alatamaha to Frederica on the Island of St Simons; waited on Mr. Spaulding who was pleased to give me letters to his Agent in Et Florida & in a few days went on board his vessell bound to his store on St. Johns. 2nd day after we left Frederica we met another of his vessells. We came too, went on board. this vessell was returned from the Store having on board Numbers of Traders returning from the Indian Country being drove away by the Indians they brot very bad talks & had on board the vessell all the Goods of the Trading houses except a few which the Governor of Florida purchased of Mr. Spauldings Agent at the request of the Siminole Indians they being desirous to have the lower Store kept up these goods were landed on an island a few miles below the Store in the River St. Johns where my Chest & baggage was with them; the vessell returned back to Frederica & I prevailed on them to sett me on Amelia Island near the mouth of St Marys being determined to pursue my journey into Florida at all events & having some papers & books in my Chest which I stood in need of, so I walked the Beach until I came to a Plantation where I was friendly received by Lord Egmonts[1] Agent & stayed with him 3 or 4 days on his promising me a passage to St Johns in a boat he going to St Augustine went on board a boat rowed by 5 negroes & in about thirty hours arived at St Johns near the Cowfords & here I was again put to my shift being once again left alone however this Gentleman sent me to a Plantation in his Boat higher up the River where I purchased a small canoe & having furnished myself with a sail & Paddle set off on my Voyage up the River St Johns & got safe to the Island where I found my Chest went to the Store where I heard much more favourable accounts of the Indian affairs & on confering with Mr Spauldings Agent he encouraged me to stay a while until the Indians were quiet a short time after this some of the Traders thought fit to risque a Journey out to Alatchua in quest of horses which they had amongst the Indians & having an inclination to see the Simonole Indian Town of Cusceola on the great Alatchua Savanah I went with them. The Savanah is vast & beautiful beyond description. The Chief of the Town received us most friendly, assured us of his protection & gave the Traders liberty to hunt up their horses   I rode with them near 50 Miles round the green verge of this beautiful Savanah & went to the sink or Vortex where the waters are discharged   the Savanah is sorounded by hamocks of rich land planted with Orange Groves   Palm Trees   Morus   Magnolia grandiflora   Telia vera   Laurus Cerasus & a variety of other Trees & shrubs   after a week or ten days returned from Alatchua to the Store   continued my excursions about this country, took a trip in my Canoe up St. Johns about 100 Miles above the Store to the uppermost plantation   returned down to the Store & after some time an opertunity offered to an Indian Town on little St Juane River at the Bay of Apalache about 100 Miles W. from the Store across the Istmous   this was a pleasant Journey & afforded me a many Curiosities   The Face & constitution of the country is Indian wild now & pleasing.

The Indians at the Town received us with the complaisance & good breeding peculiar to them   treated us with the best they had & assured us of their protection whilst with them   returned to the Store & took another Voyage up St. Johns   returned with some fine roots & seeds which together with my former Collections made up 3 large boxes of roots & one of seeds which I caried safe with me to Sundbery in Georgia where I put them on board a Vessell to London for Doct Fothergill having collected a number of curious roots in Georgia

Dear Father it is the greatest pleasure that I hear by my worthy Doctr Chalmers that you are alive & well with my Dear Mother which I pray may continue   I beg leave to acquaint my benevolent Parents that I am resolved with the concurence of Doctr Chalmers to continue my travels another year. I intend to go through the Cherokee & Creek Countries to Pensacola where I shall send my necessary baggage & if it please God to spare my life & health I may go the Mississipe River. I have been often with the Doctr concerning it & he promises to assist me with proper recommendatory letters through the Nations. please to excuse this long tedious Letter

I am ever your faithful son

I have not had the favour of a line from my Father or Mother whom God ever preserve.

BP 1:78.
1. John James Percival, Earl of Egmont (1683–1748), Georgia trustee.

From FREEMAN

London, 7 mo: 15th 1775

Dear Frd —

I think myself obliged to thee for thy kind Intelligence tho at the same time exceeding sorry from Humanity as well as Interest that a Civil War has taken place & great effusion of Blood already been the Consequence   Penn is just come over, 'tis conjectured, with some kind of Offers from the Congress   if they are any ways concessory so that the grand point in Question the Right of Taxation — be settled in your favour, we hope the King whose benevolence has been exhibited in many Cases & who, I'm persuaded feels deeply for his Subjects who fell lately near Boston & thereby occasioned great distress to many worthy Familys wod if possible sheath the Sword to wch I have also heard his servants are not averse, but that some Concession — must first come from you. This is the Point of Honour they stick on — Yet I still think in every private society if the first man among them commits an Error wch renders him Obnoctious to his inferiors when he becomes convinc'd if but in part, of his Mistake, the Acknowledgmt & Concession to his Inferiors ennobles the more in their View. Why not so in a Monarch & his Ministers? That a speedy issue to our troubles may be the result of your deliberations & ours both sides being open to Conviction is the best wish of thy Affectionate

J. Freeman

I think, when I wrote last, £296.5s.10d. was the balance in thy favour; since which, having received £25 Lady Day last, the balance is increased to £321.5s.10d.

Dr. F. is well, and desires his love.

BP 4:9; D. 463.

From FRANKLIN

Paris,[1] May 27, 1777

My dear old Friend:—

The communication between Britain and North America being cut off, the French botanists cannot, in that channel, be supplied as formerly with American seeds, &c. If you, or one of your sons, incline to continue that business, you may, I believe, send the same number of boxes here, that you used to send to England; because England will then send here, for what it wants in that way. Inclosed, is a list of the sorts wished for here. If you consign them to me, I will take care of the sale, and returns, for you. There will be no difficulty in the importation, as the matter is countenanced by the ministry, from whom I received the list.

My love to Mrs. Bartram, and your children. I am ever, my dear friend,

Yours most affectionately,
B. Franklin

D. 406.

1. Franklin had represented the Second Continental Congress in Paris and was later to help negotiate the Treaty of Paris.

To HIS CHILDREN

[several lines missing] & by all means speak ye truth   let your ye [yea] be ye & ne [nay] be ne in all things   Ye first principles that we should inculcate in ye minds of our children is ye love & fear of ye eternal unbegoten supream liveing God & next punctualy to observe to do to others as we should desire they should do to us & to love one another & our neibour as our selves   this is ye foundation of ye true religion   we ought to love & fear God not only for fear of punishment or hope of reward but in awful reverance & humility worship him in sincear adoration & thanks giving & praise in true faith which is not received by ye force of education or ye vain traditions of man but is manifested to us in A great degree by pious contemplation of his power Majesty & Wisdom in ye incomprehensible swiftness magnitude & numbers & distance of ye Celestial orbs & thair regular actions & proper distances one from another which orders ye mediate government of A soveraign power power [sic] over all creation & hourly stir up our minds to adore in ye lowest prostrations yt omnipotent power   Now we come to come [sic] to ye formation of Animals ye wisdom & power of ye deity is perspicuously manifested in all thair tribes as is discovered by disection which discovers numberless numbers of vessels & tubes for ye Conveyance of fluids & organs separating ye diferent liquids absolutely necessary to ye health of ye animal & ye continuation of life & ye vegitable tribes is no less wonderfull in displaying eternal wisdom after such A maner that ye deeper we search into thair texter growth & motions in thair buds flowers & seed ye more we discover of thair surprising motions many of [which] by A very accurate search we can by close reason understand but some of thair fluides is conveyed after such A maner as seems more misterious than those of animals & seem beyond ye power of mere machinism & if thay has not perception & sence thay have A quality so near it that we want A proper term to explain it to one another & are under ye divine power which clothes them with such innocent beauty which may invite us to adore that infinite power which arrays them with such dasling beauty   I shall now conclude this section with ye words of paul to timothy   now to ye King of eternity incoruptible invisible onely wise God be honor & glory forevermore

Next is to do unto others as we would have them do to us in ye same Circumstance which is [ye] same as loveing thair neibour as thy self which is positively commanded as ye foundation of true Justice after Paul to ye galatians tels us what is ye deeds of ye flesh & declares that those that do them shall never inherit ye Kingdom of God   he then enumerates ye fruites of ye spirit which is temperance meekness love gentleness goodness & against such there is no law   temperance moderation meekness & inocency are excelent practical qualifications of ye mind & relative terms & very conducive to ye hapines of society as well as individuals   by Temperance I don't mean onely as to meat or drink but its A guard against all excessive actions both of body or mind or unreasonable use or disuse of any of ye natural blesings of god that is given for our benefit is A breach of temperance   so is ye unreassonable pashions of ye mind as love hatred anger &c according to ye circumstance of us & ye object we fix it upon Meekness inocency & humility seems near of one nature & highly pleasing to God yet are alowed to be angry with those that practice injustice vice & wickedness but let not ye sun go down upon thy wrath without reason.

Moderation or ye golden mean is an excelent practical human qualification a ballance against all extreams   A vertue that governs all pashons   A sweet calmness of mind fit to receive by contemplation divine influences: it will lead us from pride extra[va]gancy highmindedness ye common attendents of prosperity & such aleviate ye gloomy anxious aflictions of adversity

Piety takes in all that Paul calls ye fruit of ye spirit   ye truly pious man worships ye father in spirit & truth   fears god with thankful reverence he is ye center of his affections even in ye midst of his lawfull worldly affairs   he soon returns to ye center again so that he may be said to meditate upon ye love & mercy of God both day & night in great humility & adoration of ye Soveraighn being   ye pious man cant commit willfuly any known evil   he cant let either man woman or child suffer unjustly by him that he can help   he will be punctual to his word without evations he wont undermine any in bargain nor take any unreasonable advantage against them but will do them what good he can without injury to him self or family which we are advised to protect

Gratitude is A noble principle & highly acceptable both to God & man & ungratitude is so much condemnd in scripture that all ye calamities of ye Jews is ascribed to this sin of idolitry which is ye very highest degree of ungratitude   Gratitude hath been ye very foundation of all religious worship & sacrifice in all ye Europion & Asiatic nations   what was ye sacrifice of ye Jews and other nations long before but A gratefull acknowledgement of benefits received from ye deity thay sacrificed to   True gratitude to God is A sincear humble thankfullness of heart & mind to our supream God for his mercy & benefits confered upon us   it is strongly recommended by all holy writers of ye new testament & is ye chief tenet of Jesus & ye apostles

prudence & vertue ye last of which lies solely in ye right applycation of our powers   prudence is A disposition of mind to regard distant good equally with present pleasure estimating both according to thair real not apparent magnitude & will incline him allways to that which is best before that which will immediately please his sences or gratifie his desire or indolence but is ready to follow ye dictates of reason & constitutes ye esence of moral wisdom which would shew ye drunkard's folly in prefering momentary pleasure of pouring down hastily A quantity of strong liquor down his throat & ye permanent satisfaction of A temperate life & creditable liveing but will grieve A tender loveing wife be an ill example & shame to thair children   dispised by his friends & dispised by every body of account   ye liquors for ye sake of deceiving A few persons two or three times act so imprudently that what he affirms cant be believed in anything he says unless thay know it to be true other ways as is not fit to be trusted in any matter of consequence & generally despised espetialy by all honest people

ye adulterer how imprudently doth he act to leave ye sweet bosom of A tender loveing wife that loves him intirely & is true to his interest & perhaps several loveing pretty children   how unatural it is to grieve such A dear tender Creature & cast off A great degree of affection of his children & stray away to another & perhaps rob another man of his dearest property or if A single person he may be sure thay will not pretend any friendship to him any longer than expence feeds them with what he robs from his dear wife & children to his disgrace with honest people.[1]

& now, Dear Children, to Sum up all, there is no duties we owe to God more Recommended than to Love, to Fear, to Worship, to praise & to pray to him, and to thank him for his Blessings. We should love him as proceeding from him and his fatherly love for us. We should fear him with awful reverence & sincerity of Heart in Love as being ye only Sovereign of Eternity, past, present & to come. We should worship him as being ye Supreme Power & Governor of ye Whole Universe. We ought to pray to him as being Omnipotent and Omnipresent imploring his direction to shew us ye right way to worship & adore him acceptable. We ought to praise him as ye Eternal Majesty of ye heaven & earth; we ought to return what is owing to him in profound humility of heart and mind, at our Laying down and uprising, at our eating and drinking, in our Labours in the field and in our waking hours in the Bid for his mercy, in profound humility of heart & mind. That is the true religion of the first ages of the world, of the Patriarchs, of Moses, of the Prophets, of Jesus, of the Apostles and the primative Christians for Eleven Hundred Years and ye Religion of

Your Father
JOHN BARTRAM

There is no visible operation of Superior power More instantaneous & errisitable than Lightning in our air & so Near the Surface of our earth & its effects Many times Very fatale & Tremendous; when I was Young & desired to Live to Maturity I [was] almost In a Slavish fear of its dreadful Stroak   I used to sit in Solemn stillness prayer & Awful Reverence to the Living Eternal God; During the Clouds passing over the house & when wholy past Returned humble thanks to the Onely Supreme Commander of Universal Nature for my Safety & when grown up & had Children to provide for altho ye Slavish fear wore off   gradually I had still a desire to Live (if it pleased ye Allmighty) to see My Children Settled; and when a Storm approached I in awfully Reverence supplicated the true God in resignation to his Will To grant me Longer Life & when the Storm was over returned him Thanksgiving & praises as before.

But Now for Several Years I have Not desired Long life, but is intirely Resigned to the divine Will & Waiting for his Call: & as it is one of the Easiest deaths so to[o] it may be attended With a happy Consequence; how Many that goeth of[f] this Stage by sickness, Pains or old age by its severity of Defeciency rendered Insensible both Before & at their departure &

uncapable of prayer gloryfying or Praising God. But when a person of pious Virtuous & inocent Life When ye thunder is Near as well as Many other times is Wrapt up in A still awfull reverence & humble adoration & prayer desiring to glorify ye Superior Majesty of Heaven in ye highest; & if This Condition ye Grose incumbering Mortal Body is instantly separated by a Blasting Stream of Light may not our immortal part be Transplanted to Regens of Bliss where without the Material Infirmities We may praise and Glorify the Eternal Allmighty God; Whome We Loved & Worshiped with a Single & sincear heart while we lived in Health?

My Dear Child I should be glad if thee could in a good degree Overcome thy Slavish fear of thunder   it is a weakness but who is without a Weak Side; perhaps there is Not above one that is killed by Thunder to five thousand that dieth by Sickness or other accidents, Then Why Should thee be so very fearful of a danger that happens So seldom. If the[e] Lives a Virtuous inocent Life the[e] may with a humble sinsere heart bouldly trust in God; & in awful supplication Hope that he will hear thy prayer & Mercyfull Grant thy Request & allso accept thy gratefull thanks for thy deliverence in Solemn Composure of Mind in Reverence to ye Divine power; Moderate fear is a very useful passion & was Given for a Very Necessary purpose Even for Self preservation unto all Creatures.

But to Give Way too much to Neadless unreasonable & Slavish Fear of Danger which a fearfull Disposition is Subject to; and which all human prudence and power Can with Difficulty Intirely Overcome it, often times will cause Uneasy apprehension.

I speak this from Experience, being Naturaly one of the fearfull Mortals from my Infancy. But Altho this passion is affecting And troublesome to the mind Yet to a pious Person that fears God in Sincerity & truth it is of all the other passions (except Love) The Most Excellent as it generally Excites us to the four Greatest duties to God: that frail Men is Capable of performing: That is adoration, Prayer, Praises & Thanksgiving, for all ye blessings Bestowed upon us in Life as depending upon him. But most of the other passions rather diverts us from the Close Applications to ye before mentioned duties to our Heavenly father: The one God & Father of All, who is above all & through all And in all. Ephesians the 5th.[2]

BP 1:102; Friends Historical Library, Swarthmore College.
1. This letter was obtained from two sources. To this point it is taken from BP 1:102; the remainder is from a copy made by Billy, now in the Friends Historical Library of Swarthmore College. The first several lines of the original are missing. Billy's copy begins: "The Last written Instruction of John Bartram to his Children in order to incourage them to the practice of piety & Virtue. 1777. The first principals we should inculcate in the minds of our young children is the love fear & reverance of the eternal Supreme Living God & next to observe punctually to do to others as we would desire the[y] Should do to us, in the Same Circumstance & to Love one another & our Neighbor as ourselves."
2. Bartram remained active until almost his last hours and died following a very brief illness on September 22, 1777.

APPENDIX I

*Bartram's descriptions of
North American forest trees and shrubs*

IN OCTOBER OF 1744 Cadwallader Colden urged John Bartram to communicate his knowledge of American plants to the public. He replied that he had often thought of doing so but did not want to be too hasty. Nine years later he decided that he was ready to undertake at least the publication of descriptions of native trees and shrubs. In August 1753 he wrote to Peter Collinson that he had begun seriously to work on this project. He planned to start with the evergreen trees native to Pennsylvania and New York, and would follow with the oaks and hickories. His correspondence for the next several years contained references to this undertaking.

There are today among the Bartram Papers at the library of the Historical Society of Pennsylvania Bartram's descriptions of most American trees and some shrubs (BP 1:32:1 and BP 1:41:1–14). Why were these never published? Part of the answer lies in Collinson's hesitation. In February 1754 he wrote to Bartram, acknowledging that an account of North American trees was much needed. He stated that he had been enjoying Bartram's very exact descriptions, but feared that he had mistaken environmentally induced variations for true species distinctions among the oaks. He helpfully suggested that Bartram plant acorns of all the supposed species and raise trees, which he might then compare to see if the distinctions were environmental or genetic. He asked Bartram to check his specimens again, and to send both specimens and acorns, as he was eager to have them engraved and published. In July of that year he wrote Bartram a letter that has not survived, criticizing his grammar and spelling in the descriptions. Bartram replied, with uncharacteristic heat, that these details might be important to those readers more concerned with superficial things than with truth, but that his concern had been to give readers accurate descriptions by which they could distinguish one species from another. If Collinson did not believe that his descriptions agreed with the specimens he had sent, he should tell him in what way they differed, and to return the descriptions, because he had kept no copies.

In November 1754 he commented in a letter to Linnaeus that he had sent Collinson a description of American evergreens, which Collinson desired to publish. When he had done so Bartram would take pleasure in sending a copy to Linnaeus. Shortly after this he wrote to Gronovius that he had sent Collinson descriptions of all species of American oaks and evergreens, and was giving some thought to continuing with all forest trees and shrubs.

In December 1754 Bartram sent to Gronovius, via Collinson, descriptions of birches and drawings of oaks done by his son Billy. He wanted Gronovius's opinion of his method of description, and whether or not they should be published in Latin. In January 1755, Collinson wrote that he had not heard whether or not Gronovius had received the descriptions and Billy's fine drawings. In February he wrote that he had heard from Gronovius, who admired the drawings but could find no one to engrave them. He returned them to Collinson, who asked the artist Georg Ehret to engrave them. Ehret had agreed, but could not say when he would be able to do them.

Strangely, at this point all mention of the project disappears from the correspondence and does not recur. Perhaps the concern over the French and Indian War partly explains this. At some point Collinson must have returned the descriptions to Bartram. What became of Billy's drawings seems to be unknown. The beginning of Bartram's "Treatise" follows to illustrate his method. Perhaps someday all of his descriptions may yet be published.

A Treatise of ye Evergreens of Pensilvania York & Jersey

A treatise of ye evergreens of pensilvania york & Jersey of which ye great white or long coned pine is ye champien. Ye long coned pine is very beautiful grows very straight tall & thick of A regular pyramidal figure 5 or 6 feet diameter & 150 foot high mostly near ye rivers or if far of it is mostly in moist flats on high ground exceeding close together in clumps of several acres sometimes 20 30 or 40 sometimes A quarter of A mile distant from ye current promiscuosly with oak & hicory   ye bark is very smooth on young trees on ould A little rough

perticular distinguishing characters of this species —
Ye cones is 6 7 or 8 inches long hanging down by a pedicel with scales one inch long thinly set round ye axis which springs open as soon or before thay are well dry, which is about the last of July, between which ye seed loosens & drops out & by a fin adhearing to it is whirled about &

drops at various proper distances from ye tree according to ye strength of ye air by which it is carried   after which ye cones hang on till towards fall & then drops

ye leaves is 3 or 4 inches long triangular 5 in one sheath   one is shining green ye other two angles hath each A line of white full ye length   thay closely sorund ye twig, on which thay grow very close ye wood is white & softer then our other pines midling durable & is used for planks boards shingles & stoves masts & yards   it is a northern tree growing chiefly from 42 degrees of N Latitude to Hudsons bay & hath little variety

APPENDIX II

Bartram's notes in the Medicina Britannica

ON JUNE 27, 1751, the *Pennsylvania Gazette* carried the following notice to the public: "Speedily will be published and sold by B. Franklin and D. Hall at the Post Office in Market Street MEDICINA BRITANNICA, with a Preface by MR JOHN BARTRAM, Botanist of Philadelphia, and his Notes throughout the Work, shewing the Places where many of the described Plants are to be found in these Parts of America, their Differences in Name, Appearance and Virtue, from those of the same kind in Europe; and an Appendix containing a Description of a number of plants peculiar to America, their uses, Virtues, etc."

The *Medicina Brittanica* had been published in England by Thomas Short (1690?–1772), a Scot then living in Sussex. The publication advertised by Benjamin Franklin and David Hall appeared in early September. Following are Bartram's preface and his appendix from this work.

Bartram's preface

The first man that was famous for the practice of physick in the Grecian history was Aesculapius, the son of Apollo, who practiced an age before the Trojan War, and, as they say, was so skillful in his applications as to cure diseases and raise the dead, Whereby he gained so great a fame as to have a temple built to him, where those people who were afterwards cured of their infirmities, either by his former directions or their own discoveries, wrote their method of cure particularly and reposed it in that temple. From whence, after six hundred years, and about the time of the captivity of the Jews, the famous Hippocrates, who was born and lived near the temple, in the Island of Coos, searched the medicinal receipts and by those informations and his own ingenuity so enlarged his knowledge in practice of physick as to be, to this day, called the Divine Hippocrates. But the Christians say that he learned his wonderful knowledge from the writings of Solomon and his treatise of plants, which was procured from the captive Jews, or the Chaldeans, after they had burned the Temple. However, it is certain that most nations, tho' never so barbarous, have made use chiefly of vegetables for the cure of their diseases, and doubtless with good success. And certainly we have in our country a great variety of good medicinal plants which may be administered to the people with great advantage, if properly adapted to the season, age, and constitution of the patient, and to the nature, time, and progress of the disease; without which caution, it is not likely that the practice should succeed generally. But it is very common with our people, when a root or herb hath been given with good success several times in a particular disease, and the patient recovered soon after the taking of the medicine, to applaud that medicine exceedingly. Then many that are sick of the same disease, or any other that hath near the like symptoms, apply directly to this famed specific, expecting immediate relief; which often failing by reason of its improper application, as to time, constitution, or nature of the disease, many choice medicines grow out of repute again, are disregarded and little use made of them, especially if they are common and easy to come at; wheras, if their virtues were well known, and a skillful person had the administering of them, who knew how to properly correct and fit them to the constitution of the patients, and join suitable vehicles or companions with them, to lead them to the parts of the body where the distemper lies, then those very herbs or roots, I suppose, might continue or increase their reputation.

Bartram's appendix

Containing Descriptions, Virtues, and Uses, of Sundry Plants of these Northern Parts of America; and particularly of the newly discovered Indian Cure for the Venereal.

Aralia, called by some *Spikenard,* by others *Wild Liquorice;* this bears large clusters of Berries, ripe in September, which are pleasant and wholesome to eat: The Roots are of a balsamick Nature; the back Inhabitants use them to cure fresh Wounds; they bruise the Roots, then pour a little Spring Water to them, mixing them together, which brings the Mass to a mucilaginous Balsam, which they apply with good Success; the Roots chewed, and the Juice swallowed, help the Pains of the Loins.

Aralia Caula Nudo, commonly called Sarsaparilla, hath a long creeping Root, something like the Spanish, but is really a very different Plant, yet of great Virtue. The decoction daily drank as Diet-drink, is much commended for cleansing the Blood, and curing a Dropsy; and outwardly applied is extoll'd for curing the Shingles, and cleansing and healing of Ulcers.

Virga-aurea, or that Species of *Golden Rod,* that is so famous for the Bite of a *Rattle-Snake.* This elegant Species hath slender purple Stalks, rising a Foot high, with a Spike of fine yellow Flowers for near one third Part of the Length of the Plant; the Flowers grow out of the Bosom of the Leaves, three or four in little Tufts. This is extolled as a very effectual Cure for the Bite of a Rattle-Snake; the Herb boiled, and the Decoction drank, and the warm Herb applied to the Wound. It is used with good success to cure the Swelling of the Throat and Neck, and Pains of the Breast, it being a powerful Dissolver of viscid Humours.

Triosteospermum, called in our Northern Colonies *Dr. Tinker's Weed;* in Pennsylvania, *Gentian;* and to the Southward *Fever Root,* where it is used for the Fever and Ague: With us it was used with good Success for the Pleurisy, and in *New England,* for a Vomit: It is a powerful Worker, a little churlish, yet may be a noble Medicin in skilful Hands. Blazing-Star, as it is called by the back Inhabitants, by others Devil's-bit, both fanciful Names: the Leaves spread on the Ground, four or five from one Root, and are three or four inches long, and near one Broad; in *June* it shoots up a Stalk eighteen inches long; it grows plentifully in the back Parts of the Country, on dry rich Soil: the Root is white, and about as thick as a Pipeshank, and extremely bitter.

This precious Root is a great Resister of fermenting Poisons, and the grievous Pains of Bowels, taken in Powder, or the Root bruised and steeped in Rum, of which take a Spoonful at once, and as often as Need requires until the Pains remit.

Lobelia. This curious Plant riseth from a fibrous Root to three or four Feet high, with a Spike of blue Flowers surrounding the Stalk for near a Foot in Length: It grows in rich shady Ground; it is a scarce Plant in many Parts of the Country.

The learned *Peter Kalm* (who gained knowledge of it from Colonel *Johnson,* who learned it of the *Indians,* who, after great Rewards bestowed on several of them, revealed the Secret to him) saith, That the Roots of this Plant cureth the Pox much more perfectly and easily than any Mercurial Preparations, and is generally used by the *Canada Indians,* for the Cure of themselves, and the *French* that trade amongst them, tho' deeply infected with it. They take a Handful of the Roots, and boil them in a Quart of Water, and drink the Decoction, beginning with Half a Pint at first, if the Patient be weak, then increase the Dose every Day as he can bear its purging; but if he can't bear it every Day, let him omit a Day or two, then take to it again, as he finds Occasion, until he is cured: They wash the Ulcer with the Decoction; but if it be deep and rotten, they put some Powder of the inner Bark of the Sprucetree into it, which helps to dry it up; but if the Disease is inveterate, they drink the Decoction of *Ranunculus Folio Reniformis,* an old *Sachem* told Colonel *Johnson* of another Shrub, with a red Root, from which proceeds several slender Branches eighteen Inches or two Feet long, on which grow Spikes of white Flowers, which produce three-square black Seed-Pods; the Leaves some of our People drink as Tea, and some smoak it with Tobacco; the Roots of this, bruised and boiled, and the Decoction drank, the *Sachem* said he rather preferred to the *Lobelia;* but the *Lobelia* seems to be of the most general Use, and with extraordinary Success.

More particular Directions how to use the Lobelia-Root for the Venereal Disorder obtained from the Indians, by Col. J.

"After making a Decoction of it, the Patient is to drink about two Gills of it very early in the Morning, fasting, the same before Dinner, and Bed-time. Add or diminish as you find it agree with the Patient's Constitution. The third Day begin Bathing, and continue it twice a Day, until the Sores are well cleansed, and partly healed, then use the Lotion but once a Day till quite well; observing all the Time to use a slender Diet (vegetable Food, and small Drink) as in other Courses of Physick, a Salivation is excepted. These are the Directions I have had from the Person who gave me the Secret."

GLOSSARY OF NAMES

Aiton, William (1731–1793): director of the Royal Botanic Gardens at Kew; author of *Hortus Kewensis.*
Alexander, James (d. 1778): Thomas Penn's gardener.
Allen, William (1704–1780): Philadelphia merchant; served as mayor and as chief justice of Pennsylvania.
Alston, Dr. Charles (1683–1760): professor of botany at the University of Edinburgh.
Argyll, Duke of. *See* Campbell, Archibald.

Bard, Dr. John (1717–1799): apprentice of Dr. John Kearsley at Philadelphia; practiced there until 1746, when he moved to New York.
Bard, Dr. Samuel (1742–1781): son of Dr. John Bard; later, physician to George Washington.
Bartram, Ann Mendenhall: John's wife.
Bartram, George: Scottish merchant in Philadelphia, in partnership with his brother Alexander; married John Bartram's daughter Ann.
Bartram, Isaac (1725–1801): son of John Bartram and his first wife, Mary Maris. He and his brother Moses were partners in an apothecary shop, 1759–72.
Bartram, John, Jr. (1743–1812): John Bartram's sixth son; took over his father's business, and made the first catalogue of the Bartram garden.
Bartram, Moses (1732–1809): John Bartram's fourth son; after an early career as a merchant seaman became a partner with his half-brother, Isaac, in an apothecary shop in 1759.
Bartram, William (1673–1711): father of John Bartram; killed by Indians.
Bartram, William (1711–1770?): half-brother of John Bartram; a planter at Ashwood, Bladen County, North Carolina, and member of General Assembly.

Bartram, William (1739–1823): John Bartram's fifth son; naturalist, artist, and author.

Bartram, William: son of John Bartram's half-brother William; studied medicine in Philadelphia.

Bentinck, Margaret Cavendish, Duchess of Portland (1715–1785): owner of finest shell collection in England.

Bland, Elias: London merchant; came to North America c. 1746.

Bond, Dr. Thomas (1712–1784): studied medicine in Paris and practiced in Philadelphia with brother Phineas; joined Benjamin Franklin in founding the Pennsylvania Hospital, the first in North America.

Borthwick, William: merchant and seedsman of Edinburgh.

Bouquet, General Henry (1719–1765): a Swiss officer in the British Army; commanding officer at Fort Pitt.

Breintnall, Joseph (d. 1746): Quaker merchant in Philadelphia; secretary of the Library Company; original member of Franklin's Junto.

Buffon. *See* Leclerc, Georges Louis.

Bute, Earl of. See Stuart, John.

Byrd, William II (1674–1744): wealthy planter; born in Virginia, but educated in England and spent many years there; Fellow of the Royal Society.

Campbell, Archibald, Third Duke of Argyll (1682–1761): developed a thirty-acre garden at Whitton, near London, and was very much interested in reforestation of Scotland.

Catcott, Alexander Stopford (1692–1749): minister and poet in Bristol, England.

Catesby, Mark (1683–1750): English artist and naturalist who spent seven years in Virginia, visiting also Carolina and the Bahamas; author of *Natural History of Carolina, Florida, and the Bahama Islands* (1748).

Cator, John: son-in-law of Peter Collinson; resided in Beckenham, Kent.

Chalmers, Lionel (1715–1777): Scottish physician in Charleston, South Carolina; graduate of the University of Edinburgh.

Chancellor, Dr. William (d. 1763): assessor for Philadelphia County, 1729.

Chelsea Physic Garden: founded in 1673 by the Apothecaries Company, and still in existence.

Chew, Samuel (b. 1693): physician who practiced in Maryland before moving to Philadelphia in 1732; introduced John Bartram to Peter Collinson.

Clayton, John (1685–1773): clerk of court for Gloucester County, Virginia; planter and botanist; author (with J. F. Gronovius) of the *Flora Virginica*.

Colden, Alexander: son of Cadwallader Colden; postmaster of New York.

Colden, Cadwallader (1688–1776): physician and naturalist; governor of New York; author of *The History of the Five Indian Nations* and *The Principles of Action in Matter*.

Colden, Jane (1724–1766): daughter of Cadwallader Colden; botanist, prepared a "Flora of New York" with 340 illustrations, an unpublished manuscript now deposited in the Natural History Museum, London.

Collinson, Michael (1729–1795): London merchant; son of Peter Collinson.

Collinson, Peter (1694–1768): London woolen draper; avid gardener and correspondent of John Bartram (see introduction).

Cressy, J. Slingsby: physician in Antigua.

Croghan, George (d. 1782): native of Ireland; Indian trader and deputy superintendent of Indian affairs.

Cullen, Dr. William (1710–1790): professor of medicine at the University of Edinburgh.

Custis, John (1678–1749): wealthy Virginia planter; member of the Governor's Council.

D'Alibard, Thomas Francis (1703–1779): French botanist; author of *Flora Parisiensis*.

De Brahm, William Gerard (1717–1799): cartographer who surveyed Florida; author of *The Atlantic Pilot* and other publications.

De Jussieu, Bernard (1698–1777): French botanist; demonstrator at the Jardin des Plantes in Paris.

Denny, William (d. 1765): governor of Pennsylvania, 1756–59.

De Ponthieu, Henry: neighbor of Peter Collinson, along with his brother John de Ponthieu.

Dillenius, Johann Jacob (1687–1747): German botanist; professor of botany at Oxford University.

Dobbs, Arthur (1689–1765): surveyor-general of Ireland; later governor of North Carolina.

Douglass, William (1691?–1752): Scottish physician in Boston; enthusiastic naturalist.

Drotting, Louisa Ulrika (1720–1782): queen of Sweden; sister of Frederick II of Prussia and wife of King Adolph Frederick of Sweden.

Dubois, Charles (1656–1740): Georgia trustee; patron of Mark Catesby; officer of the East India Company; Fellow of the Royal Society.

Dudley, Paul (1675–1751): graduate of Harvard, studied law at the Inner Temple; attorney-general of Massachusetts and later chief justice; Fellow of the Royal Society.

Edwards, George (1693–1773): English naturalist, author of *A Natural History of Uncommon Birds* (4 vols.) and *Gleanings of Natural History* (3 vols.).

Ehret, Georg Dionysius (1710–1770): German artist; illustrated Linnaeus's *Hortus Cliffortianus*; later settled in England.

Eliot, Jared (1685–1763): Connecticut clergyman, physician, botanist, and agriculturist; alumnus of Yale University.

Ellis, John (1710–1776): London merchant and naturalist; author of *Essay Towards a Natural History of the Corallines* (1755); Fellow of the Royal Society.

Evans, Lewis (1700–1756): Philadelphia surveyor and cartographer; accompanied John Bartram and Conrad Weiser to Onondaga.

Fairchild, Thomas (d. 1729): Hoxton nurseryman to whom Mark Catesby sent seeds from America, and for whom he later worked; experimented with cross-pollination.

Fitzgerald, James, Lord Kildare: native of Ireland; one of John Bartram's best customers for thirteen years.

Fletcher, Andrew: secretary to the duke of Argyll, and friend of John Mitchell.

Fothergill, John (1712–1780): distinguished Quaker physician in London; Edinburgh graduate; had broad scientific interests, and corresponded with European and North American men with similar interests; Fellow of the Royal Society.

Franklin, Benjamin (1706–1790): publisher and scientist, interested in all aspects of natural science; Fellow of the Royal Society.

Franklin, William (c. 1730–1813): son of Benjamin Franklin; controller of general post office, 1754–56; accompanied his father to England in 1757 and studied law there; Loyalist and last royal governor of New Jersey.

Frederick, Prince of Wales: son of George II and father of George III.

Freeman, James: nephew of John Fothergill; merchant of London; lived in Peter Collinson's old home after the latter's death.

French and Indian War, 1755–63: one of the North American colonial wars, in which the French and Indians drove all English traders out of the valleys along the Ohio and Monongahela rivers and built Fort Duquesne. General Braddock was sent to displace them, but his forces were destroyed and Braddock killed in July 1755.

Gale, Benjamin (1715–1790): Connecticut physician; son-in-law of Jared Eliot.

Garden, Alexander (1730–1791): Scottish physician who practiced at Charleston, South Carolina; graduate of University of Edinburgh; enthusiastic naturalist; Fellow of the Royal Society.

Gordon, James (1708–1780): gardener at Mile End, London; trained by Lord Petre and others; credited with introduction of *Ginkgo biloba* into England.

Grant, James (1720–1806): general, appointed governor of East Florida in 1760; led expeditions against "the mountaineers of Carolina" and the Cherokees in 1761.

Green, Samuel (1707–1771): physician in Wilmington, North Carolina.

Gronovius, John Frederick (1690–1762): physician in Leiden, the Netherlands; naturalist, friend of Linnaeus; edited and published Clayton's *Flora Virginica*.

Hill, John (1716–1775): English physician; author of *The British Herbal* (London, 1756) and *A History of Plants* (London, 1750).

Hope, Dr. John (1725–1786): professor of botany at the University of Edinburgh.

Hopton, Sarah: wife of William Hopton, prominent merchant in Charleston, South Carolina, and planter at Starved Gut Hall.

Johnson, William (d. 1768): Irish Quaker who gave popular lectures on electricity, 1763–68.

Kalm, Peter (1715–1779): naturalist, student of Linnaeus; professor of agriculture at the University of Abo, Finland.

Kearsley, John (1684–1772): Philadelphia physician, naturalist, and architect.

Kenny, James: Quaker friend of John Bartram who lived at Kennett Square, near Philadelphia, but was stationed with the army at Fort Pitt.

Kildare, Lord. *See* Fitzgerald.

Kuhn, Adam (1741–1817): Philadelphia physician; former student of Linnaeus.

Lamboll, Thomas (1694–1774): planter in Charleston, South Carolina.

Laurens, Henry (1723–1792): distinguished citizen of Charleston, South Carolina; later president of the Continental Congress, and American commissioner at the Treaty of Paris.

Leclerc, Georges Louis, Comte de Buffon (1707–1788): French naturalist; keeper of the Jardin du Roi, 1739; author of *Histoire Naturelle* (44 vols.).

Lennox, Charles, Second Duke of Richmond (1701–1750): patron of John Bartram.

Lewin, John William: English entomologist and author.

Library Company of Philadelphia: organization that originated as Benjamin Franklin's Junto, a group of friends who met to share books and read papers. Members of the group first pooled their books, and later made annual contributions to buy books, which Collinson purchased for them.

Linnaeus, Carolus (1707–1778): Swedish botanist; author of *Systema Naturae* and other works; considered the founder of the binomial system of nomenclature that is universally used today in the scientific naming of plants and animals.

Logan, James (1674–1751): generally considered Philadelphia's foremost scholar; he came there as William Penn's secretary and remained there as his deputy, holding such offices as president of the Governor's Council and chief justice of Pennsylvania.

Logan, Martha (1704–1781): owner of nursery at Trott's Point, Charleston, South Carolina; author of *A Garden Calendar* (1751–60), the first published in America.

Logan, William (1718–1776): eldest son of James Logan; educated in England; friend of the Indians; member of the Provincial Council.

Miller, Philip (1691–1771): director of the Chelsea Physic Garden; author of the *Gardener's Dictionary*.

Mitchell, John (1690–1768): Fellow of the Royal Society; physician, botanist, and cartographer; graduate of the University of Edinburgh; practiced medicine in his native Virginia until poor health sent him back to England, where he assisted Lord Bute in development of Kew Gardens; prepared a highly regarded map of North America.

Morison, Robert (1620–1683): Scottish professor of botany at Oxford in 1669; author of *Hortus Regius Blesensis* and volume 1 of *Plantarum Historiae Universalis Oxoniensis* (Oxford, 1680).

Morris, Lewis (1671–1746): governor of New Jersey, 1738–46.

Morris, Robert Hunter (1700–1764): governor of Pennsylvania, 1754–56; son of Lewis Morris.

Mortimer, Dr. Cromwell (d. 1752): secretary of the Royal Society of London.

Musschenbrock, Peter Van (1692–1761): physician in Leiden; mathematician and physicist; co-discoverer of the Leiden Jar.

Norris, Isaac (1671–1735): Quaker merchant and prominent politician in Philadelphia; owned an estate where he raised many unusual plants.

Norris, Isaac, Jr. (1701–1766): Philadelphia merchant; important Quaker leader.

Northumberland, First Duke of. *See* Percy, Hugh (Smithson).

Parkinson, John (1567–1650): author of the herbal *Theatricum Botanicum* (London, 1640).

Parsons, James (1705–1770): English physician; one of the sponsors of Franklin for election to membership in the Royal Society.

Pemberton, Israel, Jr. (1715–1779): Philadelphia merchant known as "King of the Quakers"; interested in the Indians; member of the General Assembly.

Penn, Thomas (1702–1775): one of three sons of William Penn; inherited proprietary rights in Pennsylvania and was in charge of the colony's interests in England.

Penn, William (1644–1718): English Quaker and founder of the Pennsylvania colony; Fellow of the Royal Society.

Pennant, Thomas (1726–1798): author of *British Zoology* (1766) and *Arctic Zoology* (1784); Fellow of the Royal Society.

Percy, Hugh (Smithson), First Duke of Northumberland (1715–1786): former Sir Hugh Smithson; gave plants to the Royal Botanic Garden at Kew, many of which he ordered from Bartram; his illegitimate son Sir James Smithson gave money for the Smithsonian Institution.

Petiver, James (1663–1718): apothecary, collector, and famous correspondent; publisher of some of John Banister's plant descriptions.

Petre, Robert James, Eighth Baron (1713–1742): patron of John Bartram; owner of Thorndon Hall near Brentwood, Essex; elected Fellow of the Royal Society at the age of eighteen.

Pitt, William, Earl of Chatham (1708–1778): English statesman; prime minister, 1766–68.

Plukenet, Leonard (1642–1706): administrator of Hampton Court Gardens with the title of Regius professor; published four volumes describing his plant collections.

Portland, Duchess of. *See* Bentinck, Margaret Cavendish.

Powell, Nathaniel: nurseryman at The King's Head, Fetter Lane (Powell and Edie after 1760).

Powell, William: deputy secretary of state for North Carolina.

Prince of Wales. *See* Frederick.

Pringle, John (1707–1782): physician-general of the British armies in the Low Countries; author of a book on army diseases which had 13 editions; friend of Benjamin Franklin.

Purver, Anthony (1702–1777): translator who completed translation of the Bible "with critical notes" in 1754; John Fothergill paid him £1000 for the original and paid for printing it.

Randolph, Isham (1685–1742): Virginia planter and merchant; represented Goochland County in the General Assembly.

Ray, John (1627–1705): English botanist and naturalist; author of *Historia Plantarum* (3 vols., 1686–1704).

Richmond, Second Duke of. *See* Lennox, Charles.

Rolle, Lord Denys: former member of Parliament from Barnstable; founded a colony on St. Johns River in Florida.

Rush, Benjamin (1746–1813): Philadelphia physician and professor at the University of Pennsylvania Medical School; author of *Medical Inquiries and Observations* and other essays.

Russell, Alexander (1715–1768): physician and author; practiced in Turkey before settling in London; author of *Natural History of Aleppo*, 2 vols. (London, 1794).

Rutherford, Captain John, British army officer, son of Sir John Rutherford; retired to Albany, New York.

St. Clair, Sir John (d. 1767): quartermaster general in North America under Braddock; acquired an estate near Trenton, New Jersey.

Shelburne, William Petty Fitzmaurice (1737–1805): Second Earl of Shelburne; British statesman.

Sherard, William (1659–1728): overseer of the Duchess of Beaufort's garden; sponsor of Mark Catesby.

Shippen, William, Jr. (1736–1808): Philadelphia physician; returned to America from medical school in Edinburgh in 1762.

Short, Thomas (1690?–1772): Scottish physician who settled in Sheffield, England; author of *Medicina Britannica*.

Sibthorp, Humphrey (1713?–1797): successor to Dillenius as professor of botany at Oxford and in charge of the Oxford Physic Garden.
Sloane, Sir Hans (1660–1753): Irish-born physician and naturalist who spent most of his life in England; president of the Royal College of Physicians (1719–35) and of the Royal Society (1727–40); author of *Voyage to the Islands* (London, 1704, 1725). His collections became the foundation of the British Museum.
Smithson, Sir Hugh. See Percy, Hugh (Smithson).
Solander, Daniel Carl (1736–1782): Swedish botanist and student of Linnaeus; came to England in 1759 and became under-librarian of the British Museum and secretary of Sir Joseph Banks; traveled with Banks and Captain James Cook around the world.
Spaulding, James: storekeeper at St. Simons and elsewhere in Georgia.
Spencer (or Spence), Archibald: physician trained at Edinburgh and London; gave a course in Experimental Philosophy in Boston, Philadelphia and Charleston in 1743.
Stuart, John, Third Earl of Bute (1713–1792): statesman and botanist; author of *Botanical Tables;* prime minister under George III.
Stuart, Colonel John: superintendent of Indian affairs, Southern Department, based at Charleston.
Swammerdam, Jan (1637–1680): entomologist and author of a *General History of Insects,* published in Dutch (1669); one of the early microscopists.

Templeman, Peter (1711–1769): physician; secretary of the Royal Society.
Tennent, John (c. 1700–1742): Virginia physician; author of *Every Man His Own Doctor,* edited by Franklin (Philadelphia, 1741).
Tournefort, Joseph Pitton de (1656–1708): French botanist; author of *Elemens de botanique* (3 vols., Paris, 1694).
Tschiffely, Samuel: Swiss chemist and physician; representing the Helvetia Company (composed of Swiss citizens who wanted to emigrate), he petitioned for 20,000 acres for Swiss and German Protestants.

Vaillant, Sebastian: French botanist; critic of Tournefort; said to have introduced Linnaeus to the problem of sexuality in plants.
Vernon, William (d. 1762): naturalist; Cambridge Fellow; sent to Maryland by the Royal Society in 1698.

Weiser, Joseph Conrad (1699–1760): Indian interpreter; with Lewis Evans, accompanied John Bartram on trip to Onandaga.
Whitefield, George (1714–1770): Methodist minister; Oxford graduate; founded an orphanage and school in Georgia in 1738; purchased 5,000 acres in Pennsylvania for a school for blacks.
Williamson, John (d. 1780): nurseryman with garden in Kensington; one of Bartram's first and best customers.
Witt, Christopher (1675–1765): physician in Germantown, Pennsylvania; came to North America from Wiltshire, England, in 1704; his many interests included plants, clock making, and the occult.
Wragg, William (1714–1777?): Charleston, South Carolina, merchant; close friend of Alexander Garden.
Wrangel, Charles Magnus (d. 1786): Lutheran pastor of the Old Swedes Church

while in Philadelphia; in 1768 returned to Sweden, where he was court chaplain and later bishop.

Wyly, Samuel and William: Irish Quaker who settled along the Wateree River in South Carolina, near present-day Camden.

Young, William, Jr. (1742–1785): plant collector in Philadelphia; brought to London by Queen Charlotte in 1764 to study under John Hill.

BIBLIOGRAPHY

Manuscript Collections

Academy of Natural Sciences of Philadelphia, Library of: John Bartram (1699–1777) Papers, 1757–1941, Collection 15, Manuscript/Archives Unit.

American Philosophical Society Library: Miscellaneous Manuscripts Collection; West Collection; Bartram Association Deposit; Franklin Papers; Bartram-Collinson Papers; John Bartram Collection; Benjamin Franklin Papers; Edward E. Wildman transcript of Bartram Papers; Papers of Carlotta Herring-Brown.

Beinecke Rare Book and Manuscript Library, Yale University: Jared Eliot Collection.

Boston Public Library, Department of Rare Books and Manuscripts.

British Library, London: Sloane Manuscripts; Add. Ms. 21648; Add. Ms. 28727.

Chicago Historical Society, Archives and Manuscripts Department.

College of Physicians of Philadelphia: Historical Collections of the Library; University of Pennsylvania Manuscript Collections.

Friends Historical Library, Swarthmore College.

Gray Herbarium Library, Harvard University: Gray Herbaria Archives Historic Letters Collection.

Haverford College Library, Haverford, Pa.: Charles Roberts Autograph Letters Collection.

Historical Society of Pennsylvania Library: Bartram Papers; Logan Papers (James); Deborah Logan Papers; Autograph Collection of Physicians and Chemists; Autograph Collection of Simon Gratz; Maria Dickinson Collection; Gratz Collection of Notable Americans; Dreer Scientists Collection; Library Company of Philadelphia Deposit; Gratz Collection of European Physicians; Society Collection of Photostats.

Hunt Institute for Botanical Documentation, Carnegie-Mellon University.
Linnean Society of London Archives: James Collection, Mss. 298, 323; Collinson's Common Place Book; Linnean Correspondence I.
Muséum National d'Histoire Naturelle, Laboratoire de Phanérogamie, Paris.
Natural History Museum, Department of Library Services, London.
William Allan Neilson Library, Rare Book Room, Smith College.
New-York Historical Society: Bartram Folder.
New York Public Library: Emmet Collection and Miscellaneous Papers, both in the Rare Books and Manuscripts Division, Astor, Lenox, and Tilden Foundations.
Oxford University, Department of Botany: Sherardian Collection.
Royal Society for the Encouragement of Arts, Manufactures and Commerce, Library, London.
Royal Society of London Archives: Letters and Papers, Decades 1–4.
Royal Swedish Academy of Sciences Library, Stockholm.
Salford, City of, Arts and Leisure Department, Salford, England.
University of Uppsala Library, Uppsala, Sweden.

Bartram's Published Letters and Papers (Chronological)

"A Letter from John Bartram, M.D. to Peter Collinson, F.R.S. concerning a Cluster of small teeth observed by him at the Root of each Fang or Great tooth in the Head of a Rattle-Snake, upon dissecting it." *Philosophical Transactions of the Royal Society* 41 (1740):358–59.

"Indian Physick." Preface in *Poor Richard's Almanack*, by Benjamin Franklin [Richard Saunders]. Philadelphia, 1741.

"Extract of a Letter from Dr. John Bartram, to Mr. Peter Collinson, F.R.S. containing some Observations Concerning the Salt-Marsh Muscle, the Oyster Banks, and the Fresh-Water Muscle of Pennsylvania." *Philosophical Transactions of the Royal Society* 43 (1744):157–59.

"An Account of some very curious Wasps' Nests made of Clay in Pennsylvania, by Mr. John Bartram: Communicated by Mr. Peter Collinson, F.R.S." *Philosophical Transactions of the Royal Society* 43 (1745):363–65.

"A Description of the Great Black Wasp, from Pensylvania, as communicated from Mr. John Bartram, to Mr. Peter Collinson, F.R.S." *Philosophical Transactions of the Royal Society* 46 (1749):278–79.

"An Essay for the improvement of estates, by raising a durable timber for fencing, and other uses." In *Poor Richard Improved*, ed. Benjamin Franklin [Richard Saunders]. Philadelphia, 1749.

"May Flies." *Philosophical Transactions of the Royal Society* 43 (1750):400–402.

"Some Observations on the Dragon-Fly or Libella of Pensilvania, collected from Mr. John Bartram's Letters, communicated by Peter Collinson, F.R.S." *Philosophical Transactions of the Royal Society* 46 (1750):323–25.

Preface and Appendix to *Medicina Britannica*, by Thomas Short. 3d ed. Philadelphia, 1751. Reprint, 1765.

Observations on the Inhabitants, Climate, Soil, Rivers, Productions, Animals, and other matters Worthy of Notice made in travels from Pensilvania to Onondaga, Oswego and the Lake Ontario in Canada, with account of Niagara by Peter Kalm. London, 1751. Reprint (with additional map and plate), Rochester, 1895. Reprinted in John Bartram, Lewis Evans, and Conrad Weiser, *A Journey from Pennsylvania to Onondaga in 1743*. Introduction by Whitfield J. Bell, Jr. Barre, Mass., 1973.

"Of the Great Black Wasp of Pennsylvania, communicated to the Royal Society by Mr. P. Collinson, F.R.S., being an Extract of his Friend, Mr. John Bartram's Letter." *Gentleman's Magazine* 21 (February 1751):101.

"Some Remarks on Dr. Alston's Dissertation on the Sexes of Plants by two celebrated botanists of North America, both dated June 10, 1755." *Gentleman's Magazine* 25 (September 1755):407–8.

"A Letter from Mr. John Bartram of Pensylvania, to P. Collinson, Esq., F.R.S., in which there is a remarkable Conformity of Sentiments with the Author of some Physico-mechanical Conjectures on the Propagation of the shocks of Earthquakes (see p. 221) tho' it is impossible they could borrow one from another." *Gentleman's Magazine* 26 (October 1756):474–75.

"Extract of a Letter from Mr. John Bartram, of Philadelphia, to Benjamin Franklin, Ll.D. F.R.S. relating to a remarkable Aurora Borealis." *Philosophical Transactions of the Royal Society* 52 (1762):97.

"Observations made by Mr. John Bartram, at Pensilvania, on the Yellowish Wasp of that Country: In a Letter to Mr. Peter Collinson, F.R.S." *Philosophical Transactions of the Royal Society* 53 (1763):87–88.

With William Stork. *An Account of East Florida with a Journal kept by John Bartram of Philadelphia, Botanist to His Majesty for the Floridas: upon a Journey from St. Augustine up the River St. Johns.* London, 1766. 2d ed., 1767. 3d ed. (including plant list by John Ellis), 1769. 4th ed., 1774. Reprint of 1767 ed., 1881.

"Diary of a Journey Through the Carolinas, Georgia, and Florida from July 1, 1765, to April 10, 1766." Annotated by Francis Harper. *Transactions of the American Philosophical Society,* n.s. 33, pt. 1 (December 1942):1–120.

"An Extract of Mr. Wm. [sic] Bartram's Observations in a journey up the River Savannah in Georgia, with his son, on discoveries." *Gentleman's Magazine* 37 (April 1767):166–68.

"Additional Observations on the Cicada Septendecim. By the late Mr. John Bartram. From a MS in the possession of the editor." Edited by Benjamin S. Barton. *Philadelphia Medical and Physical Journal* 1, pt. 1 (1804):56–59.

"Memorandums concerning the Earthquakes of North America." Edited by Benjamin S. Barton. *Philadelphia Medical and Physical Journal* 1, pt. 1 (1804):65–67.

"Notices of the Epidemics of Pennsylvania and New-Jersey, in the Years 1746, 1747, 1748, and 1749." Edited by Benjamin S. Barton. *Philadelphia Medical and Physical Journal* 1, pt. 1(1804):3–5.

"Native American or Indian Dogs." Edited by Benjamin S. Barton. *Philadelphia Medical and Physical Journal* 1, pt. 2 (1805):18–19.

Books and Articles

Alston, Charles. "On the Sexes of Plants." *Gentleman's Magazine* 24 (1754):465–66.

American Philosophical Society. "Manuscript Minutes of its Meetings." *Proceedings of the American Philosophical Society* 22 (1884–85):1–711.

Anonymous. "The Disownment of John Bartram." *Bulletin of the Friends Historical Association* 17 (Spring 1928):16–22.

Barnhart, John Hendley. "Bartram Bibliography." *Bartonia,* supp. 12 (December 31, 1931):51–67.

Bartram, William. "Some Account of the Late Mr. John Bartram of Pennsylvania." *Medical and Physical Journal* 1, pt. 1 (1804):115–24.

———. *The Travels of William Bartram.* Naturalist's Edition. Edited by Francis Harper. New Haven, 1958.

Bell, Whitfield J., Jr. "A Box of Old Bones: A Note on the Identification of the Mastodon, 1766–1806." *Proceedings of the American Philosophical Society* 93 (May 1949):169–77.

———, and Ketcham, Ralph L. "A Tribute to John Bartram, with a Note on Jacob Engelbrecht." *Pennsylvania Magazine of History and Biography* 83 (October 1959):446–51.

Berkeley, Edmund, and Dorothy Smith Berkeley. *Dr. Alexander Garden of Charles Town.* Chapel Hill, 1969.

———. *Dr. John Mitchell: The Man Who Made the Map of North America.* Chapel Hill, 1974.

———. *John Clayton: Pioneer of American Botany.* Chapel Hill, 1963.

———. *The Life and Travels of John Bartram: From Lake Ontario to the River St. John.* Gainesville: University Presses of Florida, 1982. Paperback reprint, 1990.

Britten, James. *The Sloane Herbarium.* Edited by J. F. Dandy. London, 1958.

Byrd, William. *The Correspondence of the Three William Byrds of Westover, Virginia, 1684–1776.* Edited by Marion Tinling. 2 vols. Charlottesville, 1977.

Catesby, Mark. *The Natural History of Carolina, Florida and the Bahama Islands.* 2 vols. London, 1729–47. Revised by [George] Edwards, Royal College of Physicians, London, 1771.

Cheston, Emily Read. *John Bartram, 1699–1777: His Garden and His House.* 2d ed. Philadelphia, 1953.

Clayton, John, and John Frederick Gronovius. *Flora Virginica.* Leiden, 1762.

Clokie, Hermia Newman. *An Account of the Herbaria of the Department of Botany in the University of Oxford.* Oxford, 1964.

Colden, Cadwallader. *The Letters and Papers of Cadwallader Colden, 1730–1742.* 8 vols. New York, 1920.

Darlington, William, ed. *Memorials of John Bartram and Humphry Marshall.* Philadelphia, 1849. Facsimile of the 1849 edition, introduction by Joseph Ewan. New York, 1967.

Dillenius, Johann Jacob. *Historia Muscorum.* London, 1741.

Dillwyn, Lewis Weston. *Hortus Collinsonianus—An Account of the Plants Cultivated by the Late Peter Collinson, Esq., F.R.S.* Swansea, 1843.

Earnest, Ernest. *John and William Bartram, Botanists and Explorers.* Philadelphia, 1940.

Edwards, George. *Essays upon Natural History and Other Miscellaneous Subjects.* London, 1770.

———. *A Natural History of Uncommon Birds and Some Other Rare and Undescribed Animals.* 4 vols. London, 1743–51.

Ewan, Joseph. *William Bartram, Botanical and Zoological Drawings, 1756–1788.*

Eyles, W. A. "The Extent of Geological Knowledge in the Eighteenth Century and the Methods by Which It Was Diffused." In *Towards a History of Geology,* ed. Cecil J. Schneer. Cambridge, Mass., 1969.

Fothergill, John. *Some Account of the Late Peter Collinson.* London, 1770.

Franklin, Benjamin. *The Autobiography of Benjamin Franklin.* New York, 1955.

———. *The Papers of Benjamin Franklin.* 21 vols. New Haven, 1959–78.

———. [Richard Saunders], ed. *Poor Richard Improved.* Philadelphia, 1749.

———. [Richard Saunders]. *Poor Richard's Almanack.* Philadelphia, 1732–57.

———. *The Works of Benjamin Franklin.* Edited by Jared Sparks. 10 vols. Boston, 1856.

———. *The Writings of Benjamin Franklin.* Edited by Albert Henry Smyth. 10 vols. New York, 1907.

Frick, George Frederick, and Raymond Phineas Stearns. *Mark Catesby, the Colonial Audubon.* Urbana, Ill., 1961.

Gipson, Lawrence Henry. *Lewis Evans.* Philadelphia, 1939.

Gronovius, John Frederick. *Index Suppelactilis Lapidae quum collegit.* London, 1750.

———. "An Unpublished Letter by Gronovius." Edited by Helen A. Choate. *Torreya* 16:116–20.

———, ed. *Flora Virginica,* by John Clayton Leiden, 1739, 1743.

Harper, Francis. See Bartram, John, "Diary of a Journey" (under Bartram's Published Letters and Papers); and Bartram, William, *The Travels of William Bartram.*

Hildeburn, Charles R. "Sir John St. Clair. Baronet." *Pennsylvania Magazine of History and Biography* 9 (January 1885):1–14.

Hindle, Brooke. *The Pursuit of Science in Revolutionary America, 1735–1789.* Chapel Hill, 1956.

Kalm, Peter. *Kalm's Account of His Visit to England on His Way to America in 1748.* Edited by Joseph Lucas. London, 1792.

———. *Peter Kalm's Travels in North America.* Edited by Adolph B. Benson. 2 vols. New York, 1937.

Lambert, Arthur Bourke. "Notes Relating to Botany. Collected from the Manuscripts of the Late Peter Collinson." *Transactions of the Linnean Society* 10 (1811). London.

Leach, Frank Willing. "Old Philadelphia Families, no. 80: Bartram." (Philadelphia) *North American,* December 20, 1908.

Leighton, Ann. *American Gardens in the Eighteenth Century.* Boston, 1976.

Linnaeus, Carolus. *A Selection of the Correspondence of Linnaeus and Other Naturalists.* Edited by James Edward Smith. 2 vols. London, 1821.

Logan, Martha. "Letters of Martha Logan to John Bartram, 1760–63." Edited by Mary Barbot Prior. *South Carolina Historical Magazine* 59 (1958):38–48.

Marshall, Humphry. *Arbustum Americanum.* Philadelphia, 1785.

Meehan, Thomas. "John Bartram." *Meehan's Monthly* 1 (August 1891):31.

———. "John Bartram." *Meehan's Monthly* 3 (August 1893):126.

———. "John Bartram's Wood-shed." *Meehan's Monthly* 9 (June 1899):96.

Miller, Philip. *The Gardener's Dictionary Containing the Methods of Cultivating and Improving the Kitchen, Flower, Fruit and Pleasure Garden.* London, 1752.

Mitchell, John. "Dissertatio Brevis de Principiis botanicorum et zoologorum de que . . . Generum plantarum recens conditorum . . . ." *Acta Physico-Medica Academae Caesare . . . Ephemerides* 8 (1748):118–224.

Mowat, Charles L. "The Tribulations of Denys Rolle." *Florida Historical Quarterly* 23 (July 1944):1–74.

Pennant, Thomas. *Arctic Zoology.* 2 vols. London, 1784.

Pennsylvania Gazette, 1732–77.

Pinckney, Elise, ed. *Thomas and Elizabeth Lamboll: Early Charleston Gardeners.* Leaflet 28, Charleston Museum. Charleston, S.C., 1969.

Prince, Winifred Notman. "John Bartram and Thorndon Park." *Garden Journal* 7 (1957):141–43, 152, and 8 (1957):189–91.

———. "John Bartram in the Cedar Swamps." *Notes and Documents* 81 (January 1957):86–88.

Pyle, Howard. "Bartram and his garden." *Harper's New Monthly Magazine* 60 (February 1880):321–30.
Schneer, Cecil J., ed. *Toward a History of Geology*. Cambridge, Mass., and London, 1969.
Simpson, George Gaylord. "The Beginnings of Vertebrate Paleontology in North America." *Proceedings of the American Philosophical Society* 86 (September 1942:130–88.
Smallwood, William Martin, and Mabel Sarah Coon Smallwood. *Natural History and the American Mind*. New York, 1941.
Sparks, Jared, ed. *The Works of Benjamin Franklin*. 10 vols. Boston, 1856.
Stearns, Raymond Phineas. *Science in the British Colonies of America*. Urbana, Ill., 1970.
Swem, E. G. *Brothers of the Spade: Correspondence of Peter Collinson of London, and of John Custis of Williamsburg, Virginia, 1734–1746*. Barre, Mass., 1957.
Tolles, Frederick B. *James Logan and the Culture of Provincial America*. Boston, 1957.
True, Rodney Howard. "John Bartram's Life and Botanical Explorations." *Bartonia*, supp., 12 (December 1931):7–19.
Van Doren, Carl. "The Beginnings of the American Philosophical Society." *Proceedings of the American Philosophical Society* 87(1943):277–89.
West, Francis D. "The Mystery of the Death of William Bartram, Father of John Bartram, the Botanist." *Pennsylvania Genealogical Magazine* 20 (1957):253.
White, George W. "Early American Geology." *Scientific Monthly* (March 1953):134–41.
Wynne, William. "Some Account of the Nursery Gardens and the State of Horticulture in the Neighborhood of Philadelphia. . . ." *Gardener's Magazine* 8 (June 1832):272–77. London.
Young, William, Jr. *Botanica Neglecta. William Young, Jr.* Edited by Samuel N. Rhodes. Philadelphia, 1916.
Zirkle, Conway. *The Beginnings of Plant Hybridization*. Philadelphia, 1935.
———. "Plant Hybridization and Plant Breeding in Eighteenth-Century American Agriculture." *Agricultural History* 43 (January 1969):25–39.

INDEX

Page numbers in italics refer to location of biographical information in the glossary of names.

Aiton, William, 711–12, 717, 725, *784*
Alexander, James, 342–43, 407, 410, 430, 441, 458, 463, 512, 513, 516, 521, 530, 534, 572, 583, 613, *784*
Allen, William, 717, *784*
Alston, Charles, 385, 385n.4, *784*
American Philosophical Society: Bartram suggests founding of, 66; Collinson questions requisites for, 93; organization and early meetings of, 237, 238; poor progress of, 251–52, 263; receives requests for information from abroad, 261, 280
American Revolution, 765, 768, 770–71, 791; Boston Tea Party, 764, 767
Animals, 558, 581, 582, 583, 585–86, 590, 592, 606, 679, 695, 702, 717; disappearance of, 748, 752; extinction of, 755, 760; migration of, 746–47, 748. *See also* under individual names
Argyll, Duke of. *See* Campbell, Archibald
Aurora borealis, 431, 710

Baltimore oriole, 209, 217
Bard, John, 282, 289, 612, 640, *784*

Bard, Samuel, 612, 640, *784*
Bartram, Ann Mendenhall (second wife), xi, 3, 9, 21, 23, 40, 105, 107, 215, 234, 425, 540, *784*; letter to son William, 535
Bartram, Archibald, 501
Bartram, Benjamin (son), xii, 517, 558, 565, 575
Bartram, Elizabeth (daughter), xii, 739, 742, 749
Bartram, George, 501, 652, *784*
Bartram, Isaac (son), xii, 405, 407n.1, 515, 532, 548, 690, *784*; letter to father, 652
Bartram, James (brother), xi–xii, 532, 738–39, 744
Bartram, James (son), xii
Bartram, John, botanist: agriculture and farming practices of, 211–12, 222, 294–97, 322–23, 336–37, 342, 402, 524–25, 585; and American Philosophical Society (*see* American Philosophical Society); on animal migration, 44–46; asks Billy's assistance, 651; birth and family background of, xi; books owned by, 34, 65, 70, 80, 89, 122, 129, 130, 132–33,

799

Bartram, John, botanist (continued)
148, 150, 160, 179, 181, 184–85, 187, 190, 192–93, 194, 195, 196, 197, 199, 200, 202, 205, 207, 210, 212, 224, 225, 236, 248, 249, 252, 275, 278, 283, 287, 289, 309, 317, 329; children of, xii; coat of arms of, 502; conservation concerns of, 760; cost of horse for, 654–55; drawings by, 150, 151n.3, 186, 191, 195, 196, 200, 207–8, 329, 464, 694, 704; education of, xii; and epidemics, 258, 281, 284, 290, 292–93, 437, 543, 544; on evolution, inorganic, 358–59, 383, 437, 716–17; experiments of, 120, 131–32, 135, 136, 208–9, 262, 272, 474; and fossils, 244, 268, 289, 356, 367, 383, 384, 388, 437, 562–63, 674, 689, 722; and Franklin (see Franklin, Benjamin); and Garden (see Garden, Alexander); garden of (drawing), 464; *Genus Bartramia,* 145–46, 280, 282, 435; greenhouse of, 486, 492, 510, 579, 636; and Gronovius (see Gronovius, John F.); and Indians (see Indians); introduced troublesome plants, 451–54; land owned by, xi–xii; maps made by, 70, 88, 114, 150, 154, 186, 200, 228; marriages of, xii; medical concerns and practices of, xii, 224, 258–59, 343, 780–83; on medicinal plants, 44, 91, 106, 133, 145, 147, 185, 196, 204–5, 207, 231, 232, 240, 249, 252, 258–59, 286, 289, 290–91, 430–31, 677, 780–83; on *Medicina Britannica,* 343, 346, 780–83; microscope studies by, 32, 61–63, 71, 120, 230, 234, 241, 272; on plant geography, 720–22; on plant succession, 92; publications of (see bibliography); religious views of, 222, 381, 442–51 passim, 552, 579, 772–75; on sex in plants, 120, 131–32, 136, 214, 226, 385–86, 420, 439, 488–89, 529, 533; and Society of Gentlemen, 737–38, 751, 753, 756; and smallpox, 412; specimens sent to king by, 666, 681, 682, 701, 708; subscriptions for, in England, 23, 26, 27, 28, 29, 49, 73, 193–94, 198, 219, 234, 240, 276, 291; subscriptions for, in the colonies, 153, 166, 173, 182, 188–89, 216, 217; tree descriptions by, 369, 374–75, 376, 379–80, 395, 407, 410, 777–79; on world water cycle, 719–20; writings suggested to, 246, 247, 708–9, 713–14, 777
—collecting trips of: to Carolina, 378, 485, 491–92, 529, 557, 573, 574, 585, 586, 589, 591, 635; to Catskills, 202, 204–5; to Congress of Picolata, 660; to Delaware Water Gap, 224, 313–14; to eastern shore of Maryland and Virginia, 80; to Florida, 651, 659, 660, 662–63n.1; to Minisinks, 134–40; to New Jersey, 201; to Onondaga (Oswego), 201–2, 211, 212, 219, 223, 228, 239, 240; to Pittsburgh, 525, 529, 530, 536–37, 553, 557–58, 559, 562, 567; to Shenandoah Valley of Virginia, 471–72; to Williamsburg, Virginia, 101–3
—honors received: elected member of Royal Academy of Sciences of Stockholm, 712; given gold medal by Society of Gentlemen of Edinburgh, 751; inadequacy of king's award, 656; named "King's Botanist" by George III, 644, 646; questions about title, 654, 679–80; questions about continuance of award, 714, 715, 735, 739, 740, 743, 744; received silver cup from Sloane, 225
—houses of, 68, 415–16, 464; picture of home, 69; drawing of house and garden, 464, 470
—on natural history of insects: bee, 175–76; cicada (locust), 46–47, 67, 68, 78, 88, 95, 303–4; dragonflies, 299–300; hornets, 177, 209; mayflies, 300–301; wasps, 75–76, 87, 175, 177, 255, 275
—letters to: Ann Bartram, 653; Archibald Bartram, 501; Moses Bartram, 574; William Bartram (brother), 542; William Bartram (son), 518, 524, 535, 536, 543, 574, 649, 651, 661, 663, 669, 738, 744, 749; Bayard, 155, 174, 188; Bouquet, 555; Byrd, 98, 120; Catcott, 193, 225; Catesby, 152, 174, 194, 210; Clayton, 244; Cadwallader Colden, 204, 205, 211, 213, 218, 221, 236, 237, 247, 248, 251, 258, 259, 264, 271, 281, 286; Jane Colden, 414; Colhoun, 122; Michael Collinson, 746, 752; Cressy, 130, 138, 142, 153, 173; Custis, 99; D'Alibard, 366; De Jussieu, 645; Dillenius, 96, 107, 128, 203, 226; Drotting, 639; Dudley, 105; Eliot, 320, 336, 342, 401, 415, 536, 576; Fothergill, 239, 267, 715, 723, 726, 732, 734, 740; Franklin, 147, 294, 425, 431, 708, 709, 726, 755, 739, 753; Garden, 388, 402, 550; Gronovius, 227, 247, 263, 265, 283, 313, 338, 339, 356, 377; Hope, 640; Linnaeus, 293, 345, 355, 356; James Logan, 61, 292; Marshall, 495;

Miller, 379, 410, 423, 435, 456; Mitchell, 238; Randolph, 119; Rush, 690; Sibthorp, 573; Sloane, 160, 175, 207, 224, 225, 268; Solander, 589; Templeman, 524; Wrangell, 741

Bartram, John, Jr. (son), xii, xiii, 784; acts for his father, 657, 659, 668; assists his father, 616, 630; corresponds with Bergius in Sweden, 713; inherits spirit of his father, 630; interest of, in insects and plants, 697; marriage of, 739, 742; receives requests for seeds and plants, 546, 698, 753, 762, 765; sends insects to Lewin, 700, 718, 732; takes over father's garden and business, 749

Bartram, Mary Maris (first wife), xii

Bartram, Mary (daughter), xii, 402, 742–43

Bartram, Moses (son), 784; as apothecary and drug salesman, 515, 532, 548; and Collinson, 328, 332, 335, 346, 406, 418, 423, 467, 630, 697, 700, 703; as merchant seaman, stranded in England, 326–27; portrait of, 326; as seaman and ship captain, 393, 425, 430, 461

Bartram, Richard (son), xii

Bartram, William (father), xi–xii, 784

Bartram, Col. William (half-brother), 485n.1, 655, 784; death of, 739n.1; letters to Bartram from, 490, 500, 514, 531, 537, 544, 561

Bartram, William (son), xii, 785; accompanies father on collecting trips, 357, 362; apprenticed to a merchant, 412, 414; attempts sales in Carolina, 501, 529, 538, 543, 545, 622; Collinson encourages early drawing by, 350; concerned about a career, 384, 394, 399, 405, 408; declines De Brahm's offer, 675; describes *Ixia*, 691–93; determined to be a planter, 661–62n.1, 663–65, 668; dissertation by, on Florida productions, 700; drawings and paintings of, praised in London, 378n.1, 378, 393, 418, 463, 476, 667, 680, 685, 697, 699, 700, 701, 703, 704; draws both plants and animals, 376, 377, 397, 478, 482, 723, 778; Edwards sends bird books to, 404, 496, 516; flees his creditors, 734, 743, 744; Fothergill's encouragement of, 707, 711, 728, 729, 750, 753, 758, 759, 762, 764, 765, 768; George Bartram pays debts of, 738; Laurens deplores his situation, 670–78; letters of, to father, 511, 515, 768; plans trip to Pensacola, 768; plants and drawing his "darling delight," 387, 403; portrait of, as a youth, 326; returns to Charlestown, 768; sends drawings to Bentinck, Eliot, Linnaeus, 415, 713, 734; studies French and Latin, 377, 381–82; travels to Florida with father, 655; trouble of, finding work, 694

Bartram, William (nephew), 490, 501, 531–32, 542–43, 785; death of, 739n.1

Bayard, Peter: Bartram's letters to, 155, 174, 188

Bears, 45, 206–7, 686

Bentinck, Margaret Cavendish, Duchess of Portland, 704, 725, 729, 731, 732, 734, 785

Bergius, Peter, 712, 713

Birds, 480, 717; description of butcher bird, 308; migration of, 413–14, 422; nests of, 184, 185, 208, 217, 226, 229, 235, 240; preservation of, 184

Bland, Elias, 218, 230, 231, 785; letters to Bartram from, 233, 237, 298

Bond, Phineas, 227, 230, 243, 266, 280, 785

Bond, Thomas, 94–95, 104, 261, 288, 423, 430, letter to Bartram from, 112

Bond, Dr. (unclear whether Phineas or Thomas), 261, 288, 423, 430

Borthwick, William, 785; letters to Bartram from, 595, 626

Boston Tea Party, 764, 767

Bouquet, Henry, 565, 571, 577, 581, 583, 589, 592, 604, 615, 649, 651, 785; death of, 658n.2; letters to Bartram from, 541, 547, 563; portraits of, 542, 605

Braddock, Edward: defeat of, 386–87

Breintnall, Joseph, 785; asks about tree size, 216; death of, 273; library rules of, 129; makes leaf impressions, xii–xiii; and rattlesnake, 35; receives books, goods, letters, and messages, 3, 9, 11, 22, 23, 27, 36, 49, 60, 63, 85, 90, 109, 190; snakeroot, impression of, 15

Buffalo, 114, 702

Buffon, Comte de. See Leclerc, Georges Louis

Bush, John, letter to Bartram from, 630

Bute, Earl of. See Stuart, John

Byrd, William, 785; Bartram sends regards to, 126; Bartram visits, 102; charming of rattlesnake by, 68; garden of, 98, 102, 121, 122; letter of introduction to, 84; library of, 162; letters to Bartram from, 100, 115; portrait of, 98; and Westover, 102, 621

801

Campbell, Archibald, Third Duke of Argyll, 785; Mitchell obtains plants and seeds for, 287, 288, 290, 291, 311, 312, 319, 320

Catcott, Alexander Stopford, 785; letters to Bartram from, 179, 187, 200, 245; sends Bartram catalogue of his garden, 237

Catesby, Mark, 785; asks Bartram to draw a plant, 150; Bartram sends birds' nests, skins, and turtle eggs to, 208, 209, 217, 218, 228–29; Bartram sends flowers, plants, and seeds to, 117, 118, 148, 163, 170, 235, 250, 269; books of, 192, 199, 224, 369; Collinson wants flowers for, 81, 108; Collinson shows Bartram's insects to, 192; drawings of, 91, 150, 357, 376, 391, 414, 492, 496, 600; has questions about birds, 185, 196; letters to Bartram from, 132, 151, 182, 273; overlooked in America, 95, 316, 318; owes Bartram a letter, 275; pleased by Bartram's letter, 156; presents to Bartram from, 202; report of death of, 310; resided only in Virginia and Carolina, 328

Chalmers, Lionel, 754n.1, 762, 763, 764, 770, 785; letters to Bartram from, 758, 765

Chancellor, William, 529, 785

Chelsea Physic Garden, 21–22, 179, 394, 420, 477, 700, 785

Chew, Samuel, xiii, 229, 251, 785

Clams, 254, 330

Clayton, John, xiv, 102, 114, 239, 345, 440, 486, 608, 785; and American Philosophical Society, 261; Bartram visits, 489, 491; corresponds with Bartram, 250, 341; exchanges plants and seeds, 510, 621; *Flora Virginica,* 130, 626n.2; garden of, 121, 492, 597, 634, 642, 649–50; and Gronovius, 343; letters to Bartram from, 489, 490, 491, 510, 587, 621, 634, 642, 649; on sex in plants, 394–95; and tipitiwichet, 621, 634

Colden, Alexander, 496, 520, 554, 563, 587, 602, 611, 785

Colden, Cadwallader, xv, 150–51, 156, 165, 181, 202, 216, 218, 241, 345, 354, 360, 387–88, 404, 406, 748, 785; letters to Bartram from, 219, 246, 262, 277, 284, 371; portrait of, 203

Colden, Jane, 360, 364n.2, 393, 414, 785

Coldenia, 280, 282

Colhoun, Alexander: letters to Bartram from, 123, 128

Collinson, Michael, 341, 459, 512, 513, 633, 682, 688, 709, 710–11, 714, 715, 717, 724–25, 726, 729, 734, 785; letters to Bartram from, 730, 736, 740, 745, 746, 748, 754, 756, 760, 763, 767

Collinson, Peter, 706, 785; and Alexander, 458, 465, 512, 513, 521, 530, 534, 572; and Bartram's tree descriptions, 335, 376, 377, 395, 399, 777; and Billy Bartram, 393, 394, 404, 418, 655, 665–66, 667, 680, 683, 685, 694, 697, 704; and John Bartram, Jr., 655, 657, 659, 667, 698, 699, 700; and Moses Bartram, 326, 335, 341, 344, 409, 410, 412, 418, 428, 461, 467, 476, 667, 680, 700; butterfly collecting by, 6–7, 76, 77; and Catesby, 91, 118, 150, 158, 190, 191, 202, 228, 229, 275; and Chew, xiii, 229, 251; and Colden, 156, 165, 218, 235, 371, 406; and Dillenius, 47, 48, 50, 148, 187, 192; and Dobbs, 285, 298, 301, 493, 531, 597, 633; and duchess of Portland, 704, 706; and Dudley, 30, 31, 37, 42, 65, 71, 151; and Edwards, 351, 398, 460, 480, 496; and Ehret, 398, 399, 667; and Eliot, 332, 389, 408, 467, 475; and Ellis, 646, 657, 683, 706; and Fothergill, 566, 580, 674, 683, 686, 687, 688, 706, 707, 730; and Franklin, 286, 332, 391, 398, 421, 460, 482, 498, 512, 545, 553, 565, 566, 581, 586, 600, 648, 689; and Garden, 395, 586; garden of, 601, 674; and Gordon, 277, 351, 375, 382, 409, 493, 520, 530, 552, 586, 593, 595, 596, 616, 629, 674; and Gronovius, 36, 90, 105, 130, 145, 146, 169, 181, 235, 268, 275, 313, 327, 343, 399, 561; and Indians, 408, 422–23, 482, 581, 615, 618, 623, 674; and "King's Botanist," 644, 646, 654, 656, 657, 659, 666, 680, 682, 684, 697, 701; and Library Company of Philadelphia, 9, 14, 23, 129, 134, 214, 492; and Linnaeus, 72, 90, 235, 600; and Logan, 34, 43, 71, 72, 73, 80, 89, 108, 111, 113, 121; and mammoths, 363, 566, 580, 581, 592, 632, 689; and Miller, 21, 22, 44, 56, 119, 138, 148, 270, 394, 395, 462, 674; and Mitchell, 155, 311, 317, 341, 371; and Lord Petre, eighth baron, 8, 12, 23, 26, 33, 41, 42, 74, 81, 86, 88, 109, 110, 111, 126, 130, 145, 148, 150, 167–68, 186, 198–99, 319; and Lord Petre, ninth baron, 602; and Pitt, 560, 588, 607, 616; and rattlesnakes, 35, 38–39; and duke of

Richmond, 319; and Royal Society of London, 68, 88, 300, 304, 305; and Sloane, 41, 166, 178–79, 180, 187, 191, 197, 202, 215, 235; and Solander, 546, 561, 582, 593, 600, 616, 629, 655, 658, 666, 667, 684, 685, 700, 702; on Stamp Act, 656; subscriptions for Bartram, 27, 29, 194, 198, 234, 249, 276; and tipitiwichet, 571, 580, 593, 595, 600, 631; wife's death, 347; and Witt, 14, 18, 20, 28, 31, 35, 57, 68, 86, 93, 94, 124, 126, 129, 132, 136, 137, 131, 145, 154, 215, 269, 463, 481, 482, 517, 529, 530, 538, 553, 561, 602, 648; and Young, 647, 666, 682, 706

Continental drift, 383

Crabs, 228, 240, 242, 253–54, 279, 280, 330

Cressy, J. Slingsby, 785; letters to Bartram from, 133, 166

Crocodiles, 496, 578, 586–87, 590

Croghan, George, 563, 566, 689, 785

Cullen, William, 786; letter to Bartram from, 717

Custis, John, 73, 84, 102, 114, 116, 122, 126, 150, 229, 235, 786; portrait of, 100

D'Alibard, Thomas F., 380, 786

Darlington, William, xiii–xv

De Brahm, William Gerard, 675, 786

De Crevecoeur, St. John, 646

Deer, 114, 135, 171, 183, 398, 574

De Jussieu, Antoine, 112

De Jussieu, Bernard, 329, 786

Delaware Water Gap, 313–15, 367; ill., 314

Denny, William, 406, 409, 413, 459, 463, 467, 786

De Ponthieu, Henry and John, 517, 530, 534, 552, 560–61, 571, 583, 593, 594, 786; letters to Bartram from, 466, 528, 598

Dillenius, Johann Jacob, 786; appreciates Bartram's mosses and seeds, 138, 163, 208, 235; Catcott corresponds with, 179; Collinson sends Bartram's seeds and requests to, 137; desires mosses, 109; identifies Bartram's plants, 48–58 passim, 283; interests Bartram in mosses, 152; letters to Bartram from, 47, 97, 144, 156, 192, 233; recommends burgundy trefoil, 108; sends Miller's *Dictionary* to Bartram, 65, 224; sends seeds to Bartram, 83, 90, 95, 202; sends Bartram his *Historia Muscorum,* 187,

196, 202, 224; sends papers to Bartram, 150, 157, 159, 190

Dobbs, Arthur, 786; Bartram advises Billy to visit, 519; and Collinson, 597; letters to Bartram from, 298, 301, 331, 499, 541; map of, 371; orders seeds from Bartram, 285; plants sent by Bartram to, 485n.1; promises seeds to Bartram, 493, 626; sends plants to Bartram, 531; and tipitiwichet, 633; visited by Billy, 529, 535

Douglass, William, 247, 408, 786

Drotting, Louisa Ulrika, 639, 786

Dublin Society, 331, 332n.1, 350, 371

Dudley, Paul, 30, 31, 42, 71, 151, 786

Edinburgh, 639, 640, 643, 676, 681, 699, 732, 753

Edwards, George, 351, 398, 404, 408, 413, 422, 460, 480, 496, 516, 567, 786

Ehret, Georg Dionysius, 398, 399, 667, 778, 786

Eliot, Jared, 332, 387, 408, 467, 475, 476, 551, 622, 786

Elk, 114, 183–84, 190

Ellis, John, 786; agent for East Florida, 646; Bartram sends colocasia nuts to, 735; and book of corallines, 408; eager for Florida plants and seeds, 657, 676–77, 683; Fothergill sends paper of, to Bartram, 731, 732n.1; on preserving seeds, 751, 752n.1; recommends Bartram to Governor Grant, 656; thinks Young's brochure poorly printed, 706

Ellis, William: Collinson sends book of husbandry by, to Bartram, 59, 61n.2, 65

Evans, Lewis, 262, 265, 272, 786; Collinson sends book on birds to, 230, 241; maps made by, 305, 584; journal of trip to Oswego, 223n.2

Fish: lack of, in the Ohio river, 563; natural history of, 253, 255n.2, 278–79; preservation of, 330

Fletcher, Andrew, 677, 681, 786

Flora Virginica, 130, 145, 147, 154, 183, 205, 227, 228n.1, 238, 246, 260, 263, 346, 395, 400, 420, 625; second edition, 580, 694

Florida: Bartram's journal of trip to, 709; Bartram's and Billy's travels there, 644, 651, 662–63n.1; Billy's description of *Ixia* from, 691–93; Billy's travels to, 700, 750, 764, 769; Bouquet invites Bartram to go with him to, 649; Collinson's

Florida *(continued)*
comments on, 666, 679–80, 704; Ellis appointed agent for, 646; Ellis writes to governor of Pensacola about Bartram's trip to, 656; history of, 592; honeybees in, 685; Laurens visits Billy in, 670

Fothergill, John, 250, 674, 686, 726, 786; Bartram sends plants to, 682, 683, 688; garden of, 751, 754; geological interests of, 260, 262, 384, 566; letters to Bartram from, 230, 256, 309, 687, 706, 710, 728, 731, 750, 753, 764; portrait of, 231; prescribes for Bartram, 678, 681

Foxes, 158, 184, 194

France: Bartram sends plants to, 106; expected to attack Philadelphia, 292; French botanists cut off by American Revolution, 771; interferes with Bartram's shipments, 266, 278, 385, 421; and Indians, 400, 412–13, 612, 614, 615, 622; letter to Sloane returned by, 261; peace with, 521, 579, 581, 588; Pitt's expedition against, 560, 607; seeds sent from Canada to, 477; ships taken by, 240, 329, 434, 439

Frogs, 346–47, 350, 376–77, 392, 417, 724, 729, 732, 750, 753–54, 765

Franklin, Benjamin, 106, 238, 247, 288, 332, 342, 345, 353, 366, 385, 402, 639, 640, 641–42, 711, 743, 786; advises Bartram about Billy, 404–5, assists Bartram with specimens, 708, 709; electrical experiments of, 287, 340, 341, 368; encloses letter from Flint, 727–28; letters to Bartram from, 433, 642, 713, 727, 744, 749, 751, 771; portrait of, 426; as postmaster, 289, 490n.1, 507, 611, 621, 635, 650; receives degree from Oxford, 504; stove of, 278, 340, 368, 394

Frederick, Prince of Wales, 787; Bute requests seeds for, 312; encourages establishment of Royal Botanic Gardens at Kew, 513n.1; reports of death of, 312, 320

Freeman, James, 787; asked to take charge of Bartram's affairs, 710–11, 715, 724, 726, 729, 731–32; Bartram asks Michael Collinson to pay, 752, 753; Bartram uneasy about no letter from, 734, 740; and Fothergill, 750, 753; Franklin refers inquiries to, 749; letters to Bartram from, 743, 756, 762, 763, 766, 768, 770

Gale, Benjamin, 551, 578, 787; letter to Bartram from, 695

Garden, Alexander, 395, 493–94, 575, 661, 662, 787; as botanist, 441, 493, 506, 517, 538, 586, 657; as busy doctor, 523; illness of, 614, 649; letters to Bartram from, 498, 507, 521, 548, 658

Gardenia ("Warner's Jessamin"), 674, 675n.1, 694, 742

Geography, 362, 363, 747

Geology: Bartram sends curiosities and fossils to Gronovius, 356; Bartram speculates on origin of soils, 358–59, 362–63; coastal soil formation, 338; composition of soils, 716; earthquakes, 405; fossils in mountain rocks, 383; origin of limestone and marble, 407, 471; production of iron from sand, 516, 551; sea mounts, 753; silver and lead mines, 584; use of magnet to test soils for iron, 577

George III, king of England: appoints Bartram King's Botanist, 644, 645; Bartram sends plants and seeds to, 638–39, 641, 677, 697, 709, 723

Germans (Palatines), 115–16, 395, 607, 710; acacia seeds for Germany, 600; complaints by, 631; medicinal plants of, 44; and Caspar Wistar, 98–99, 101

Ginseng: abundant near Onondaga, 221; Bartram discovers, 106; Bartram describes where found, 127, 271; Bartram thinks overrated, 122; Bond on, 112; Collinson on Chinese variety, 110, 113; Collinson wants plants and seeds of, 124, 128, 137, 158, 168, 186, 189, 196, 214, 235, 513, 596; Fothergill on, 710

Gooch, William, 102, 104n.6

Gordon, Lord Adam, 649n.1

Gordon, James, 382, 462, 480, 520, 534, 552, 590, 596, 611–12, 631, 633, 745, 787; letters to Bartram from, 316, 607

Gover, Robert, 84, 113

Grace, Robert, 43, 49, 64, 79

Grant, James, 652, 656, 680n.3, 787

Gray, Christopher, 307, 318, 325; letters to Bartram from, 352, 395

Green, Samuel, 538–39, 545, 787; letters to Bartram from, 513, 532, 539

Greer, Thomas: letter to Bartram from, 545

Gronovius, John F., 105, 343, 787; admires descriptions and drawings sent by Bartram, 399, 778; and Colden, 248, 277; fossils sent to, by Bartram, 289, 367; instructions sent to Bartram from, 259–60, 262; letters to Bartram from, 241, 253, 278, 310, 329, 366; names new genera *Bartramia* and *Coldenia,* 282,

284; portrait of, 227; returns Bartram's specimens mounted, 145; sends Bartram *Flora Virginica,* 130; sends Bartram *Index Lapidae* and *Caracters Plantarum,* 224, 226, 275; sends Bartram new edition of *Flora Virginica,* 561, 580; specimens sent to, 36, 165, 169–70, 181, 244, 268, 356

Gross: letter to Bartram from, 487

Groundhog (monac), 149, 159, 180, 183, 191, 196

Gully (Gulley), Anthony (son-in-law of Col. William Bartram), 500–501, 512, 515, 524, 532, 533, 535, 536, 745

Habersham, James, acting governor of Georgia, 653–54

Hill, John, 374, 406, 418, 641, 787; letter to Bartram from, 677

Hill, Dr. of London Town, Maryland, 43, 85

Historical Society of Pennsylvania, xiii–xv

Holladay, James, 43

Hope, John, 676, 681, 682, 683, 684, 689, 703, 751, 753, 787; letters to Bartram from, 612, 643, 737

Hopton, Sarah, 547, 548, 787; letter to Bartram from, 550

Hummingbirds, 61, 186, 199, 229

Indians: agitated by French, 579, 581, 614, 622; attacks by, 283, 378, 386–87, 400–401, 404, 412, 425, 431, 471, 491, 604, 649, 769; Bartram's hostility toward, 525, 609; catawbas, 665; cheating of, by whites, 615, 618, 622, 623; Cherokees, 482, 491, 541, 666, 769, 770; courtesy of, 221; Creeks, 491, 769, 770; Five Nations of, 201–2, 219, 221, 223, 226, 239; graves and curiosities of, 148, 178–79, 207, 242–43, 272–73, 277–78; medicines of, 206, 240, 267–68, 674, 782; practices of, 209–10, 217, 290, 316; Seminoles, 769–70; traditions of, 566, 568–69; treaties with, 422, 482, 541, 578, 581, 612, 613; treatment of, by traders, 432

Insects, natural history of. *See* Bartram, John

Ixia: description of, by William Bartram (son), 691–93

Jardin du Roi, 112, 394, 645–46

Johnson, William, 650, 651, 787

Jones, Thomas: letter to Bartram from, 714

Kalm, Peter, 293, 307, 324, 383, 787; article on Niagara Falls by, 331–32n.2; and Bartram, 346, 355, 380; catalogue of North American plants by, 340, 356; learns Indian remedy from Colonel Johnson, 782; letter to Bartram from, 304; publishes two volumes in Swedish, 396–97; and Wrangell, 713

Kearsley, John, 60, 67, 136, 214, 341, 787

Kenny, James, 541, 542n.2, 564, 787

Kew. *See* Royal Botanic Gardens

Kingsessing, xi–xii

Kinloch, Francis, 665, 665n.1, 676

Kuhn, Adam, 588, 689n.1, 742, 743n.1, 787

Lamboll, Thomas, 453, 496, 558, 561, 566, 636, 644, 653, 658, 662, 684, 686, 688, 694, 695, 787; letters to Bartram from, 504, 511, 549, 575, 614, 620, 634, 637, 638, 648; reported death of, 768; wife of, 559, 654, 656, 661, 664, 665, 669, 677, 695, 768

Lane, John: letter to Bartram from, 663

Laurens, Henry, 661–62, 663n.5, 664, 788; letter to Bartram from, 670; portrait of, 671

Law, lawyers, 220, 222, 271

Lawson, Isaac, 144, 150, 159, 163, 170, 192, 196

Leclerc, Georges Louis, Comte de Buffon, 384, 385n.1, 394, 787

Lennox, Charles. *See* Richmond, second duke of

Lewin, John William, 697, 732, 743, 787; letter to Bartram from, 718

Library Company of Philadelphia, 408, 492, 787; and Bartram, 9, 23, 129, 134, 146, 187, 189, 192, 198, 214; Darby plans similar library, 218

Linnaeus, Carolus, 90, 271, 289, 317, 343, 380, 396, 406, 414, 434, 435, 438, 457, 600, 684, 713, 742, 788; assists Gronovius in naming *Bartramia* and *Coldenia,* 280, 282; Bartram glad to oblige, 105; Bartram promises to send descriptions of American evergreens when published to, 778; books of, 31–32, 72, 212, 216, 224, 226, 228, 263, 280, 329–30; Colden corresponds with, 248; Collinson urges to name plant for Bartram, 235, 241; plants wanted by, 90; portrait of, 294

Lizards, 195, 244–45

Logan, James, 34, 71, 80, 84, 85, 111, 113,

Logan, James (continued)
121, 146, 147, 196, 788; Bartram takes Colden to visit, 266; Collinson advises Bartram to see, 72, 90, 105, 108; does not encourage American Philosophical Society, 238; gives books to Bartram, 224; letter to Bartram from, 31; opposes subscription for Bartram, 216; and Shippen, 43; portrait of, 32; wants sloe trees, 73, 89

Logan, Martha, 498, 508, 518n.1, 594, 788; Bartram's "fascinated widow," 559; letters to Bartram from, 500, 505, 519, 522, 547, 617, 636, 651; sends plants and seeds to Bartram, 559, 590, 614

Logan, William, 578, 674, 788

Mammoths (mastodon), 579–80, 581, 590–91, 696, 752; Croghan and Greenwood discovered skeletons of, 563; Indian traditions concerning, 568–69; picture of, 569; Siberian, 701; teeth of, 564, 566, 628–29, 632, 689

Manigault, Gabriel, 662, 663n.6

Marshall, Humphry, xiii

Martens, 159, 171

Miller, Philip, 50, 148, 241, 283, 382, 407, 408, 418, 432, 462, 473, 596, 674, 788; contributes to subscription for Bartram, 29, 194, 234, 276; gives Collinson seeds for Bartram, 21–22; letters to Bartram from, 396, 399, 433, 438, 468, 476; questions Bartram's account of pines, 270

Mineral springs, 232, 240, 287, 288, 291; bituminous, 264; hot, 384, 394, 407, 577, 584; salt, 221, 223; sulphurous, used by Indians, 262, 267–68, testing of, 256–57

Mitchell, John, 250, 317, 341, 351, 371, 372, 376, 384, 596, 788; and anatomy of the opossum, 155; poor health of, 266, 280; letters to Bartram from, 287, 288, 290, 311, 319; and map of North America, 397, 399n.1; and pines of Virginia, 265, 272; promises Bartram descriptions of Virginia plants, 247; sends specimens of Virginia plants to Collinson, 235; visits Bartram, 247–48

Mockingbirds, 704

Mohole Project, 404

Moles, 181, 197, 218, 685, 703, 705

Moneypenny, Al: letter to Bartram from, 499

Moose, 114, 159, 171, 183, 201, 324, 371, 416–17, 702

Morgan, John, 758

Morris, Lewis, 134, 162, 163, 171, 181, 190, 201, 788

Moultrie, John, Jr., 661, 662n.3

Muskrat, 154, 157, 197 (marsh mouse?), 217, 266, 268, 278

Mussels, 135, 148, 186; freshwater, 164–65, 172–73, 180, 182n.1, 183; sea, 160–61, 163–64, 279, 280

Norfolk, Duke of, 146, 170, 189, 208, 211, 219, 234–35; report of death of, 198–99; subscribes to assist Bartram, 194

Norris, Isaac, Jr., 14, 16, 788

Northumberland, First Duke of. See Percy, Hugh (Smithson)

Onondaga. See Oswego

Opossum, reproduction of, 114–15, 135, 154–55, 158, 375

Ord, Thomas, 610; letter to Bartram from, 609

Oswego, 221, 223

Oxford, 26, 43, 47, 48, 50, 51; botanical collections of, 554

Panthers, 70, 88–89, 417, 592, 606

Parsons, James, 623, 624–25 (letter to Collinson), 635, 788

Passenger pigeons, 45–46, 67, 88, 245, 398, 413

Pemberton, Israel, Jr., 17, 20, 21, 25, 26, 27, 49, 129, 788

Penn, Thomas, 64, 82, 108, 113, 115, 121, 216, 241, 289, 299, 302, 317, 378, 494, 788; asks Bartram to procure curiosities, 219; and Catesby, 95, 152; has mammoth's tooth, 566; and Penn, 146, 217

Pennant, Thomas, 788; letter to Bartram from, 717

Percy, Hugh (Smithson), First Duke of Northumberland, 285, 291, 299, 308, 312, 325, 409, 421, 789; and Michael Collinson, 725; urges Bartram to explore Florida, 649

Petiver, James, 224, 236, 789

Petre, Robert James, Eighth Baron, 6, 8, 9n.2, 12, 31, 33, 34, 80, 81, 95, 145, 146, 148, 169, 170, 190, 235, 319, 475, 493, 602, 789; admires American waterfowl, 25; Bartram sends mosses to, 143; Collinson gives hummingbird's nest and eggs to, 61; contributes handsomely to Bartram's subscription, 23, 26, 29, 194; desires cedar berries, 110, 111; desires live squirrels, terrapins, and turtles, 28, 42, 74, 86; plants 10,000 American shrubs and trees, 167–68; pleased by Bartram's journal and map, 41, 70, 88, 186; sends *Arbutus* seeds to Bartram, 109; sends books to Bartram, 126, 150, 160, 224; death of, 198, 199, 211, 212

Petre, Lord, Ninth Baron, 602, 611

Petre, Lady, wife of eighth baron, 125, 186, 611, 619; sends pear tree seed to Bartram, 117; thanks Bartram for musk, 138

Pheasant (grouse), 316, 318, 328, 579

Pitt, William, 616, 767, *789;* Bartram "melancholy" for his loss, 560, 588; peace of, 607

Plukenet, Leonard, 47, 96, 129, *789*

Poole, R.: letter to Bartram from, 310

Porcupines, 156, 171–72, 245

Portland, Duchess of. *See* Bentinck, Margaret Cavendish

Powell, Nathaniel, 323, 324, 372, 383, 384, 440, 513, 517, 521, 534, 552, *789;* letters to Bartram from, 352, 483

Powell, William, 512, 531, 534, 535, 536, 541, 633, *789;* letter to Bartram from, 509

Pringle, John, 639, *789*

Purver, Anthony, 710, 715, *789*

Randolph, Isham, 84, 99, 114, 150, *789;* Bartram visits, 102, 103; desires correspondence with Bartram, 105; letter to Bartram from, 119; report of death of, 228

Rats, 118, 125, 137, 679

Read, Charles, 42, 107, 157, 158

Reindeer, 702

Richmond, Second Duke of (Charles Lennox), 34, 146, 190, 199, 208, 235, 249, 276, 283, 285, 292, *789;* contributes to subscription for Bartram, 29, 31, 194, 219, 234; death of, 319

Richmond, Third Duke of, 702

Rolle, Lord Denys, 480, 504, 637, 665n.2, *789*

Royal Academy of Sciences of Stockholm: Bartram elected, 712–13, 719, 742, 761

Royal Botanic Gardens (Kew), 513, 674, 685, 697–98, 711–12, 724

Royal Society of Arts. *See* Templeman, Peter

Royal Society of London, 3, 68, 88, 155

Rush, Benjamin, 712, *789;* portrait of, 690

Russell, Alexander, 657, *789*

Rutherford, John, 212, 213, 214, 258, *789*

St. Augustine, 666, 668, 669, 675, 676, 694, 704, 749, 769

St. Clair, John: letters to Bartram from, 503, 508, 510, 540, *789*

St. Johns River, 664–65, 668, 670, 674, 675, 679, 691–93, 723, 765, 769, 770

Salisbury, Francis, 155, 172, 174, 200

Sea mounts, 340, 368, 403

Shelburne, William Petty Fitzmaurice, 689, *790*

Shells, 31, 84, 114, 121, 178, 180, 217, 242, 265, 271, 328, 330, 334, 644, 704, 706, 731, 757, 763

Shippen, Edward, 32, 43

Shippen, William, 562, 572, 578, 586, 628, 631, 638, *789*

Shirley, William, 308, 324; letter to Bartram from, 305

Shoemaker, Samuel, 247, 280

Short, Thomas, 780, *789*

Sibthorp, Humphrey, *790;* letter to Bartram from, 554

Silk production, 219–20, 222, 739, 744

Slaves, 661–62, 663–64, 665, 672

Sloane, Hans, 8, 41, 155, 156, 162, 166, 170, 180, 191, 194, 202, 208, 217, 223, 235, 241, 243, 250, 274, 281, *790;* Bartram sends curiosities to, 283; Bartram sends marsh mole and blackbird to, 218; Bartram asks for silver cup from, 215, 225; letters to Bartram from, 178, 236, 261; sends books to Bartram, 181, 184–85, 187, 248, 249

Smithson, Hugh. *See* Percy, Hugh (Smithson)

Snails, 121, 330, 370, 644–45

Snakes, 95, 228, 290, 333, 358, 723; rattlesnakes, 3, 11, 18, 35, 38, 40, 67–68, 80, 91, 206, 357, 361, 752, 755, 782; snake stones, 696n.1

Snowbirds, 413

Solander, Daniel, 616, 657, 666, 667, 685, 688, 700, 702, *790;* admires Billy's drawings, 703; Bartram sends roots to, 572; circumnavigates globe with Sir Joseph Banks, 761; Collinson on, 655, 684; letters to Bartram from, 601, 625; names Bartram's specimens, 546, 561, 567, 600, 629, 635, 658; thinks many of Bartram's specimens are new genera, 393

Spencer, Archibald, 238, *790*

Squirrels, 42, 75
Stork, William, 679, 680n.2
Stuart, John, Earl of Bute, 287, 312, 615, 649, 677, 709, 724–25, *790*
Stuart, John, 652, 759, *790*
Swallows, 226–27, 235, 460; barn, 437; chimney, 184, 185, 208–9, 217, 437
Swammerdam, Jan, 253, 254, 279, 280, *790*
Sweden, xi, 639, 712–13, 761–62
Swiss (Switzers), 115–16, 357, 529
Swinhoe, John, 376, 393, 395, 405, 413, 422; letter to Bartram from, 344

Templeman, Peter, *790*; illustration of Bartram's reply, 527; letter to Bartram from, 494
Tennent, John, 106, 129, 137, 147, 158, *790*
Terrapins and turtles, 9, 14, 28, 42, 74–75, 86, 104, 109, 118, 210, 226, 228–29, 236, 240, 274–75, 307, 318, 319, 333, 341, 343, 349, 370, 375, 381, 391–92, 397, 398–99, 460, 479, 482, 516, 530, 531, 563, 578, 590, 593, 600, 704–5, 707, 711, 715, 726, 729, 765
Tipitiwichet, 565, 570, 571, 580, 593, 595, 600, 616, 621, 626, 629, 631, 633, 634, 638, 691
Tschiffely, Samuel, 115, 116, 119, 120, 126, *790*

Weather, 372–73, 378–79, 388, 389–90, 401, 406, 426, 427, 558, 564, 567, 579, 589, 621–22, 628, 634, 653, 675, 722, 727, 739, 753

Weiksell, John: letter to Bartram from, 761
Weiser, Conrad, 202–3, 219, 248, *790*
Whippoorwill, 184, 190, 194–95, 210
White, John, 13, 17, 72, 81, 82, 83
Whitefield, George, 139–40, 150, 161–62, 182, *790*; portrait of, 161
Wildman, Edward E., xiv, xv
Williamson, John, and Co., 285, 291, 323, 324, 325, 332, 343–44, 372, 405, 410, 418, 422, 483, 521, 534, *790*
Willing, Thomas (Byrd's brother-in-law), 588, 621
Wistar, Caspar, 98–99, 101
Witt, Christopher, 14, 18, 20, 28, 31, 57, 68, 86, 93, 108, 124, 126, 132, 136, 137, 138, 168, 191, 214, 236, 241, 388, 391, 481–82, 516, 517, 529, 530, 561, 586, 632, *791*; Bartram's account of, 611; death of, 553, 648; easily imposed upon, 129, 154; loses sight, 463; rarities of, 145; and rattlesnakes, 35; on sassafras oil, 267; and snakestones, 215; and spirit of divination, 269
Wolley, Edmond, 63, 68, 121, 127, 163, 170, 192
Wragg, Mrs. William, 519, 522, *790*
Wrangell, Charles Magnus, 635, 654, 713, *790*; letter to Bartram from, 712
Wright, James, 581; letter to Bartram from, 568
Wyly, Samuel, 574, 620, 635, 636, 648, *791*

Young, William, Jr., 638, 641, 647, 666, 677, 682, 706, 735, 739, 740, 744, 750, *791*

About the Editors

Edmund Berkeley and Dorothy Smith Berkeley have published numerous biographies of notable figures in natural history, including John Clayton, Alexander Garden, John Mitchell, Moses Ashley Curtis, and George William Featherstonhaugh. Before his retirement, Edmund Berkeley taught at Washington and Lee University, the University of the South, and the University of North Carolina.